The Leadership Experience

SEVENTH EDITION

RICHARD L. DAFT
Owen Graduate School of Management
Vanderbilt University

With the assistance of
Patricia G. Lane

CENGAGE Learning®

Australia • Brazil • Mexico • Singapore • United Kingdom • United States

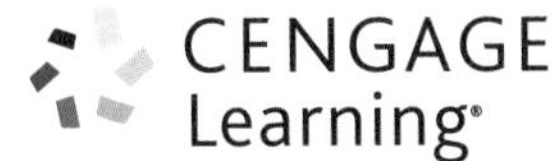

The Leadership Experience
Seventh Edition
Richard L. Daft
With the assistance of Patricia G. Lane

Vice President, General Manager, Social Science & Qualitative Business: Erin Joyner

Product Director: Jason Fremder

Product Manager: Mike Roche

Content Developer: Jamie Mack

Product Assistant: Allie Janneck

Marketing Director: Kristen Hurd

Marketing Manager: Emily Horowitz

Marketing Coordinator: Casey Binder

Art and Cover Direction, Production Management, and Composition: Cenveo Publisher Services

Intellectual Property

Analyst: Diane Garrity

Project Manager: Sarah Shainwald

Manufacturing Planner: Ron Montgomery

Cover Image(s): Moment/Getty Images; blackzheep/Shutterstock.com

Interior design credits: Design Pics/The Irish Image Collection/Getty Images; Steve Weinrebe/Photographer's Choice RF/Getty Images; Bastar/Vetta/Getty Images; Vinimay Kaul/EyeEm/Getty Images; Matic Stojs/ShutterStock.com

Library of Congress Control Number: 2016940679

ISBN-13: 978-1-337-10227-8

Cengage Learning
20 Channel Center Street
Boston, MA 02210
USA

Cengage Learning is a leading provider of customized learning solutions with employees residing in nearly 40 different countries and sales in more than 125 countries around the world. Find your local representative at **www.cengage.com**.

Cengage Learning products are represented in Canada by Nelson Education, Ltd.

To learn more about Cengage Learning Solutions, visit **www.cengage.com**

Purchase any of our products at your local college store or at our preferred online store **www.cengagebrain.com**

Printed in Canada
Print Number: 01 Print Year: 2016

To the spiritual leaders who shaped my growth and development as a leader and as a human being.

BRIEF CONTENTS

PART 1: INTRODUCTION TO LEADERSHIP 1

1. What Does It Mean to Be a Leader? 2

PART 2: RESEARCH PERSPECTIVES ON LEADERSHIP 33

2. Traits, Behaviors, and Relationships 34
3. Contingency Approaches to Leadership 64

PART 3: THE PERSONAL SIDE OF LEADERSHIP 97

4. The Leader as an Individual 98
5. Leadership Mind and Emotion 134
6. Courage and Moral Leadership 166
7. Followership 196

PART 4: THE LEADER AS A RELATIONSHIP BUILDER 225

8. Motivation and Empowerment 226
9. Leadership Communication 260
10. Leading Teams 292
11. Developing Leadership Diversity 326
12. Leadership Power and Influence 360

PART 5: THE LEADER AS SOCIAL ARCHITECT 393

13. Creating Vision and Strategic Direction 394
14. Shaping Culture and Values 428
15. Leading Change 462

Name Index 494

Index of Organizations 498

Subject Index 502

CONTENTS

PART 1: INTRODUCTION TO LEADERSHIP 1

Chapter 1: What Does It Mean to Be a Leader? 2

1.1 Why We Need Leadership 4

1.1a Defining Leadership 5

1.1b Everyday Leadership 6

Leader's Bookshelf 7

1.2 The New Reality for Leaders 8

1.2a From Stabilizer to Change Manager 9

1.2b From Controller to Facilitator 9

1.2c From Competitor to Collaborator 10

Leader's Self-Insight 1.1 11

1.2d From Diversity Avoider to Diversity Promoter 11

Consider This! 12

1.2e From Hero to Humble 12

In the Lead 13

1.3 How Leadership Differs from Management 14

1.3a Providing Direction 14

1.3b Aligning Followers 15

1.3c Building Relationships 16

1.3d Developing Personal Leadership Qualities 16

1.3e Creating Outcomes 16

Leader's Self-Insight 1.2 17

1.4 Evolving Theories of Leadership 17

1.4a Historical Overview of Major Approaches 18

1.4b A Model of Leadership Evolution 19

1.5 Leadership Can Be Learned 21

1.5a Leader Fatal Flaws 21

Leader's Self-Insight 1.3 22

1.5b Leader Good Behaviors 23

In the Lead 23

1.6 Mastering the Art and Science of Leadership 24

1.7 Organization of This Book 24

Leadership Essentials 26

Discussion Questions 27

Leadership at Work 27

Leadership Right–Wrong 27

Leadership Development: Cases for analysis 29

Sales Engineering Division 29

The Marshall Plan 29

References 30

PART 2: RESEARCH PERSPECTIVES ON LEADERSHIP 33

Chapter 2: Traits, Behaviors, and Relationships 34

2.1 The Trait Approach 36

2.1a Optimism and Self-Confidence 37

Leader's Bookshelf 38

2.1b Honesty and Integrity 38

Leader's Self-Insight 2.1 40

2.1c Drive 40

In the Lead 40

2.2 Know Your Strengths 41

2.2a What Are Strengths? 41

2.2b Matching Strengths with Roles 42

2.3 Behavior Approaches 43

2.3a Autocratic versus Democratic Behaviors 43
Consider This! 44
In the Lead 45
2.3b Ohio State Studies 46
Leader's Self-Insight 2.2 47
In the Lead 47
2.3c University of Michigan Studies 48
2.3d The Leadership Grid 49
In the Lead 50
2.3e Theories of a "High-High" Leader 50
2.4 Individualized Leadership 52
2.4a Vertical Dyad Linkage Model 53
2.4b Leader–Member Exchange 54
2.4c Partnership Building 54
Leader's Self-Insight 2.3 55
2.5 Entrepreneurial Traits and Behaviors 55
Leadership Essentials 56
Discussion Questions 57
Leadership at Work 58
Your Ideal Leader Traits 58
Leadership Development: Cases for Analysis 58
Consolidated Products 58
Transition to Leadership 60
References 61

Chapter 3: Contingency Approaches to Leadership 64
3.1 The Contingency Approach 66
Leader's Bookshelf 67
Leader's Self-Insight 3.1 69
3.2 Hersey and Blanchard's Situational Theory 69
3.2a Leader Style 70
3.2b Follower Readiness 71
In the Lead 72
Leader's Self-Insight 3.2 73
3.3 Fiedler's Contingency Model 73
3.3a Leadership Style 73
3.3b Situation 74
3.3c Contingency Theory 75
In the Lead 75
3.4 Path–Goal Theory 77
3.4a Leader Behavior 77
In the Lead 79
3.4b Situational Contingencies 79
Consider This! 80
3.4c Use of Rewards 80
3.5 The Vroom–Jago Contingency Model 81
3.5a Leader Participation Styles 82
3.5b Diagnostic Questions 83
3.5c Selecting a Decision Style 83
In the Lead 87
3.6 Substitutes for Leadership 88
In the Lead 89
Leader's Self-Insight 3.3 90
Leadership Essentials 91
Discussion Questions 92
Leadership at Work 92
Task versus Relationship Role Play 92
Leadership Development: Cases for Analysis 93
Alvis Corporation 93
An Impossible Dream? 94
References 95

PART 3: THE PERSONAL SIDE OF LEADERSHIP 97

Chapter 4: The Leader as an Individual 98
4.1 The Secret Ingredient for Leadership Success 100
4.1a The Importance of Self-Awareness 100
4.1b Leader Blind Spots 101
4.2 Personality and Leadership 102
In the Lead 102
4.2a A Model of Personality 102
Leader's Self-Insight 4.1 103
Leader's Bookshelf 106
4.2b Personality Traits and Leader Behavior 106
In the Lead 107
Leader's Self-Insight 4.2 108
4.3 Values and Attitudes 109
4.3a Instrumental and End Values 109
Leader's Self-Insight 4.3 110
In the Lead 111
4.3b How Attitudes Affect Leadership 112

Consider This! 112
4.4 Social Perception and Attributions 114
4.4a Perceptual Distortions 114
4.4b Attributions 115
In the Lead 116
4.5 Cognitive Differences 116
4.5a Patterns of Thinking and Brain Dominance 117
Leader's Self-Insight 4.4 118
In the Lead 119
4.5b Problem-Solving Styles: Jungian Types 120
4.6 Working with Different Personality Types 122
Leader's Self-Insight 4.5 123
Leadership Essentials 126
Discussion Questions 127
Leadership at Work 127
Past and Future 127
Leadership Development: Cases for Analysis 128
A Nice Manager 128
Environmental Designs International 130
References 131

Chapter 5: Leadership Mind and Emotion 134
5.1 Leading with Head and Heart 136
5.2 Mental Models 136
5.2a Assumptions 138
5.2b Changing or Expanding Mental Models 138
In the Lead 139
5.3 Developing a Leader's Mind 140
5.3a Independent Thinking 140
Leader's Bookshelf 141
5.3b Open-Mindedness 142
Leader's Self-Insight 5.1 143
5.3c Systems Thinking 144
5.3d Personal Mastery 145
5.4 Emotional Intelligence 146
5.4a What Are Emotions? 146
5.4b Why Are Emotions Important? 147
5.4c The Components of Emotional Intelligence 149
In the Lead 152
Leader's Self-Insight 5.2 153
5.5 Leading with Love versus Leading with Fear 153
Leader's Self-Insight 5.3 154
5.5a Fear in Organizations 155
In the Lead 155
5.5b Bringing Love to Work 156
Consider This! 157
5.5c Why Followers Respond to Love 158
Leadership Essentials 158
Discussion Questions 159
Leadership at Work 160
Mentors 160
Leadership Development: Cases for Analysis 160
The New Boss 160
The USS Florida 162
References 163

Chapter 6: Courage and Moral Leadership 166
6.1 Moral Leadership Today 168
6.1a The Ethical Climate in Business 168
Leader's Bookshelf 169
6.1b Leaders Set the Ethical Tone 169
In the Lead 170
Leader's Self-Insight 6.1 172
6.2 Acting Like a Moral Leader 173
6.3 Becoming a Moral Leader 174
6.4 Servant Leadership 176
6.4a Authoritarian Management 176
6.4b Participative Management 177
6.4c Stewardship 177
6.4d The Servant Leader 178
In the Lead 179
Leader's Self-Insight 6.2 180
6.5 Leading with Courage 180
6.5a What Is Courage? 181
Consider This! 181
In the Lead 182
Leader's Self-Insight 6.3 184
6.5b How Does Courage Apply to Moral Leadership? 184
6.5c Finding Personal Courage 185
In the Lead 186
Leadership Essentials 187

Discussion Questions 188
Leadership at Work 189
Scary Person 189
Leadership Development: Cases for Analysis 189
"What Should I Say?" 189
The Boy, the Girl, the Ferryboat Captain, and the Hermits 191
References 192

Chapter 7: Followership 196
7.1 The Art of Followership 198
7.1a Learn to Manage Up as Well as Down 199
7.1b Managing Up Presents Unique Challenges 199
In the Lead 199
7.2 What Your Leader Wants from You 200
7.3 Styles of Followership 201
Leader's Self-Insight 7.1 203
In the Lead 204
Consider This! 205
7.4 Strategies for Managing Up 205
7.4a Understand the Leader 205
7.4b Tactics for Managing Up 206
Leader's Self-Insight 7.2 207
Leader's Bookshelf 209
In the Lead 209
7.5 The Power and Courage to Manage Up 210
7.5a Sources of Power for Managing Up 210
7.5b Necessary Courage to Manage Up 211
In the Lead 213
7.6 What Followers Want from Leaders 213
7.6a Clarity of Direction 214
7.6b Opportunities for Growth 214
7.6c Frequent, Specific, and Immediate Feedback 216
Leader's Self-Insight 7.3 217
7.6d Protection from Organizational Intrusions 217
Leadership Essentials 218
Discussion Questions 218
Leadership at Work 219
Follower Role Play 219
Leadership Development: Cases for Analysis 220
Waiting for Clearance 220
Jake's Pet Land 221
References 222

PART 4: THE LEADER AS A RELATIONSHIP BUILDER 225

Chapter 8: Motivation and Empowerment 226
8.1 Leadership and Motivation 228
8.1a Intrinsic and Extrinsic Rewards 229
8.1b Positive and Negative Motives 230
Leader's Bookshelf 232
8.2 Needs-Based Theories of Motivation 232
8.2a Hierarchy of Needs Theory 233
8.2b Two-Factor Theory 234
In the Lead 235
8.2c Acquired Needs Theory 236
Leader's Self-Insight 8.1 237
8.3 Other Motivation Theories 237
Consider This! 238
8.3a Reinforcement Perspective on Motivation 238
8.3b Expectancy Theory 240
8.3c Equity Theory 241
Leader's Self-Insight 8.2 242
8.4 Empowering People to Meet Higher Needs 243
8.4a The Psychological Model of Empowerment 244
8.4b Job Design for Empowerment 244
8.4c Empowerment Applications 246
In the Lead 246
Leader's Self-Insight 8.3 248
8.5 Giving Meaning to Work through Engagement 248
In the Lead 249
8.6 New Ideas for Motivation 250
8.6a The Making Progress Principle 250
8.6b Building a Thriving Workforce 250
Leadership Essentials 251
Discussion Questions 252
Leadership at Work 252
Should, Need, Like, Love 252
Leadership Development: Cases for Analysis 254
Commissions for Charlotte 254

Sun Spots 255
References 256

Chapter 9: Leadership Communication 260
9.1 How Leaders Communicate 262
9.1a Management Communication 263
Leader's Self-Insight 9.1 264
9.1b The Leader as Communication Champion 264
Consider This! 265
9.2 Leading Strategic Conversations 266
In the Lead 266
9.2a Creating an Open Communication Climate 267
9.2b Asking Questions 267
9.2c Listening 268
Leader's Self-Insight 9.2 270
9.2d Dialogue 270
9.2e Communicating with Candor 272
Leader's Self-Insight 9.3 273
In the Lead 273
9.2f The Power of Stories 274
Leader's Bookshelf 275
9.3 Communicating to Persuade and Influence 275
9.4 Selecting the Correct Communication Channel 276
9.4a The Continuum of Channel Richness 277
In the Lead 278
9.4b Effectively Using Electronic Communication Channels 279
9.5 Nonverbal Communication 281
9.6 Current Communication Challenges 281
9.6a Leadership via Social Media 281
9.6b Being Crisis-Ready 282
In the Lead 283
Leadership Essentials 283
Discussion Questions 284
Leadership at Work 285
Listen Like a Professional 285
Leadership Development: Cases for Analysis 286
The Superintendent's Directive 286
Hunter-Worth 287
References 288

Chapter 10: Leading Teams 292
10.1 The Value of Teams 294
10.1a What Is a Team? 294
Consider This! 295
10.1b Types of Teams 295
In the Lead 297
10.2 The Dilemma for Team Members 298
Leader's Self-Insight 10.1 299
10.3 Leading a Team to High Performance 300
Leader's Bookshelf 301
10.4 Team Processes 301
10.4a How Teams Develop 302
10.4b Team Cohesiveness 303
In the Lead 304
10.4c Team Norms 305
10.5 What Team Members Must Contribute 306
10.5a Essential Team Competencies 306
Leader's Self-Insight 10.2 307
10.5b Team Member Roles 307
10.6 Leading a Virtual Team 308
In the Lead 309
10.6a Uses of Virtual Teams 309
10.6b Challenges of Virtual Teams 310
10.7 Handling Team Conflict 311
10.7a Types of Conflict 312
10.7b Balancing Conflict and Cooperation 312
10.7c Causes of Conflict 313
10.7d Styles to Handle Conflict 313
Leader's Self-Insight 10.3 315
10.7e Negotiation 316
Leadership Essentials 317
Discussion Questions 317
Leadership at Work 318
Team Feedback 318
Leadership Development: Cases for Analysis 319
Decision Time 319
Devereaux-Dering Group 320
References 322

Chapter 11: Developing Leadership Diversity 326
11.1 Leading People Who Aren't Like You 328
Leader's Self-Insight 11.1 329

11.2 Diversity Today 329
11.2a Definition of Diversity 329
11.2b Changing Attitudes toward Diversity 330
In the Lead 331
11.2c The Value of Organizational Diversity 331
11.3 Challenges Minorities Face 332
11.3a Prejudice, Stereotypes, and Discrimination 332
Leader's Self-Insight 11.2 333
11.3b The Glass Ceiling 334
Leader's Bookshelf 336
In the Lead 337
11.4 Ways Women Lead 337
Consider This! 338
11.4a Women as Leaders 339
11.4b Is Leader Style Gender-Driven? 340
In the Lead 340
11.5 Global Diversity 341
11.5a The Sociocultural Environment 341
Leader's Self-Insight 11.3 342
11.5b Social Value Systems 343
11.5c Developing Cultural Intelligence 344
11.5d Leadership Implications 345
11.6 Becoming an Inclusive Leader 346
In the Lead 347
11.7 Ways to Encourage the Advancement of Women and Minorities 349
11.7a Employee Affinity Groups 349
11.7b Minority Sponsorship 350
Leadership Essentials 351
Discussion Questions 352
Leadership at Work 352
Personal Diversity 352
Leadership Development: Cases for Analysis 353
True to Myself 353
The Trouble with Bangles 355
References 356

Chapter 12: Leadership Power and Influence 360
12.1 Four Kinds of Influential Leadership 362
12.1a Transformational Leadership 362
12.1b Charismatic Leadership 363
Leader's Self-Insight 12.1 364
12.1c Coalitional Leadership 365
In the Lead 366
12.1d Machiavellian-Style Leadership 368
Leader's Bookshelf 369
Leader's Self-Insight 12.2 370
In the Lead 371
12.2 Using Hard versus Soft Power 371
12.2a Specific Types of Power 372
In the Lead 374
12.2b Follower Responses to the Use of Power 375
Consider This! 376
12.3 Increasing Power through Political Activity 376
12.3a Leader Frames of Reference 377
12.3b Political Tactics for Asserting Leader Influence 378
Leader's Self-Insight 12.3 379
In the Lead 382
12.4 Don't Take Power Personally 382
Leadership Essentials 384
Discussion Questions 385
Leadership at Work 386
Circle of Influence 386
Leadership Development: Cases for Analysis 387
The Suarez Effect 387
Waite Pharmaceuticals 388
References 390

PART 5: THE LEADER AS SOCIAL ARCHITECT 393

Chapter 13: Creating Vision and Strategic Direction 394
13.1 The Leader's Job: Looking Forward 396
13.1a Stimulating Vision and Action 396
Consider This! 397
13.1b Strategic Leadership 398
In the Lead 399

13.2 Leadership Vision 400

Leader's Self-Insight 13.1 402

13.2a What Vision Does 402

Leader's Self-Insight 13.2 404

13.2b Common Themes of Vision 404

In the Lead 406

13.2c Leader Steps to Creating a Vision 406

13.3 Mission 407

13.3a What Mission Does 407

Leader's Bookshelf 408

13.3b A Framework for Noble Purpose 410

In the Lead 412

13.4 The Leader as Strategist-in-Chief 413

13.4a How to Achieve the Vision 413

13.4b How to Execute 415

In the Lead 415

Leader's Self-Insight 13.3 416

Leadership Essentials 419

Discussion Questions 420

Leadership at Work 420

Future Thinking 420

Leadership Development: Cases for Analysis 422

The New Museum 422

The Visionary Leader 423

References 425

Chapter 14: Shaping Culture and Values 428

14.1 Organizational Culture 430

14.1a What Is Culture? 430

Leader's Bookshelf 431

14.1b Importance of Culture 432

In the Lead 433

Consider This! 434

14.2 Culture Strength, Responsiveness, and Performance 435

14.2a Responsive Cultures 435

Leader's Self-Insight 14.1 436

14.2b The High-Performance Culture 437

In the Lead 439

14.3 Cultural Leadership 440

14.3a Ceremonies 441

14.3b Stories 441

14.3c Symbols 441

14.3d Specialized Language 442

14.3e Selection and Socialization 442

14.3f Daily Actions 443

14.4 The Competing Values Approach to Shaping Culture 443

Leader's Self-Insight 14.2 445

14.4a Adaptability Culture 446

In the Lead 446

14.4b Achievement Culture 446

14.4c Involvement Culture 447

14.4d Consistency Culture 447

14.5 Ethical Values in Organizations 448

In the Lead 448

14.6 Values-Based Leadership 449

14.6a Personal Values 449

In the Lead 449

14.6b Spiritual Values 450

Leader's Self-Insight 14.3 451

Leadership Essentials 453

Discussion Questions 454

Leadership at Work 454

Walk the Talk 454

Leadership Development: Cases for Analysis 456

Culture Clash 456

5 Star and Amtech 457

References 458

Chapter 15: Leading Change 462

15.1 Leadership Means Leading Change 464

15.1a Resistance Is Real 464

15.1b The Leader as Change Agent 465

Leader's Self-Insight 15.1 466

In the Lead 466

15.2 A Framework for Change 467

15.3 Using Appreciative Inquiry 469

15.3a Applying Appreciative Inquiry on a Large Scale 469

Leader's Self-Insight 15.2 470

In the Lead 472

15.3b Applying Appreciative Inquiry Every Day 472

Leader's Bookshelf 473

15.4 Leading Creativity for Change 473

15.4a Instilling Creative Values 474
15.4b Leading Creative People 475
Leader's Self-Insight 15.3 477
15.5 Implementing Change 481
Consider This! 481
15.5a Helping People Change 482
15.5b The Keys That Help People Change 483
In the Lead 484
Leadership Essentials 486
Discussion Questions 486
Leadership at Work 487
Organizational Change Role Play 487
Leadership Development: Cases for Analysis 488
"From This Point On. . ." 488
Riverside Pediatric Associates 489
References 491

Name Index 494
Index of Organizations 498
Subject Index 502

ABOUT THE AUTHOR

Richard L. Daft, Ph.D., is the Brownlee O. Currey, Jr., Professor of Management and Principal Senior Lecturer in the Owen Graduate School of Management at Vanderbilt University. Professor Daft specializes in the study of leadership and organization theory. Dr. Daft is a Fellow of the Academy of Management and has served on the editorial boards of *Academy of Management Journal*, *Administrative Science Quarterly*, and *Journal of Management Education*. He also served as the associate dean at the Owen School, was the associate editor-in-chief of *Organization Science*, and served for three years as associate editor of *Administrative Science Quarterly*.

Professor Daft has authored or coauthored 14 books. His latest books include *The Executive and the Elephant: A Leader's Guide to Building Inner Excellence* (Jossey-Bass, 2010) and *Building Management Skills: An Action First Approach* (with Dorothy Marcic, Cengage/Southwest, 2014). He is also the author of *Organization Theory and Design* (Cengage/Southwest, 2016), *Management* (Cengage/Southwest, 2018), *and Fusion Leadership: Unlocking the Subtle Forces That Change People and Organizations* (with Robert Lengel, Berrett-Koehler, 2000). He has also authored dozens of scholarly articles, papers, and chapters. His work has been published in *Organizational Dynamics*, *Administrative Science Quarterly*, *Academy of Management Journal*, *Academy of Management Review*, *Strategic Management Journal*, *Journal of Management*, *Accounting Organizations and Society*, *Management Science*, *MIS Quarterly*, *California Management Review*, *Leadership Excellence*, *Leader to Leader*, and *Organizational Behavior Teaching Review*.

Dr. Daft also is an active teacher and consultant. He has taught leadership, leading change, management, organizational theory, and organizational behavior. He has also produced for-profit theatrical productions and helped manage a start-up enterprise. He has been involved in management development and consulting for many companies and government organizations, including the National Academy of Science, Oak Ridge National Laboratory, American Banking Association, AutoZone, Aegis Technology, Bell Canada, Aluminum Bahrain (Alba), Bridgestone, TVA, Cardinal Healthcare, Pratt & Whitney, Allstate Insurance, State Farm Insurance, the United States Air Force, the U.S. Army, Central Parking System, USAA, Bristol-Myers Squibb, Eli Lilly, Vulcan Materials, and the Vanderbilt University Medical Center.

PREFACE

Many leaders have recently had their assumptions challenged about how organizations succeed. Leaders are struggling to make sense of the shifting environment and to learn how to lead the people in their companies effectively and successfully in the midst of turmoil. The crisis in the housing, mortgage, and finance industries and resulting recession; volatile oil prices; ethical scandals; political turmoil; and other events have dramatically shifted the organizational and economic landscape. This edition of *The Leadership Experience* addresses themes and issues that are directly relevant to the current turbulent environment. My vision for the seventh edition is to give students an exciting, applied, and comprehensive view of what leadership is like in today's world. *The Leadership Experience* integrates recent ideas and applications with established scholarly research in a way that makes the topic of leadership come alive. Organizations are undergoing major changes, and this textbook addresses the qualities and skills leaders need in this rapidly evolving world.

Recent chaotic events, combined with factors such as a growing need for creativity and innovation in organizations, the rise of social media, the growth of e-business and mobile commerce, the use of virtual teams and telecommuting, globalization, the growing problem of cybercrime, and other ongoing transformations place new demands on leaders that go far beyond the topics traditionally taught in courses on management or organizational behavior. My experiences teaching leadership to students and managers, and working with leaders to change their organizations, have affirmed for me the value of traditional leadership concepts while highlighting the importance of including new ideas and applications.

The Leadership Experience thoroughly covers the history of leadership studies and the traditional theories but goes beyond that to incorporate valuable ideas such as leadership vision, shaping culture and values, leadership courage, and the importance of moral leadership. The book expands the treatment of leadership to capture the excitement of the subject in a way that motivates students and challenges them to develop their leadership potential.

NEW TO THE SEVENTH EDITION

A primary focus for revising *The Leadership Experience*, seventh edition, has been to relate leadership concepts and theories to real events in today's turbulent environment. Each chapter has been revised and updated to bring in current issues and events that leaders are facing.

Topics and application examples that have been added or expanded in the seventh edition include:

- *developing a global mindset*
- *leading with humility*
- *leadership courage as a skill*
- *the influence of emotions on performance*
- *the importance of self-awareness for leadership*
- *entrepreneurial leadership*
- *overcoming bias in the workplace*
- *candid communication*
- *how leaders use social media*
- *leadership coaching*
- *balancing conflict and cooperation*
- *agile leadership*
- *fostering a thriving workforce*
- *team competencies*
- *how to confront others during conflict*
- *diversity of thought*
- *co-creating a vision*
- *building a high-performance culture through values and results*
- *the mental transition required for people to change behavior*
- *using a positive emotional attractor*

Some of the new examples of leaders and leadership within organizations that show practical applications of key concepts include:

- Pope Francis
- Mickey Drexler, J. Crew
- Warren Buffett, Berkshire Hathaway
- Satya Nadella, Microsoft
- Laura Smith, Yola
- Nancy Dubec, A&E Networks
- Angela Ahrendts, Apple
- Coach Ron Rivera, Carolina Panthers
- Chade-Meng Tan, Google
- Kip Tindell, Container Store
- Gen. Stanley McChrystal, U. S. Army
- Rich Gee, Rich Gee Group
- Dan Price, Gravity Payments
- Grant Reid, Mars Inc
- Zingerman's
- Honda Engine Plant
- Seattle Seahawks
- Earl's Restaurants
- Mattel Toys
- Chris Rufer, Morning Star
- Golden State Warriors
- Vivek Gupta, Zensar Technologies
- Inga Beale, Lloyd's of London
- Intel
- HealthFitness
- Norman Seabrook, Riker's Island
- Dick Costolo, Twitter
- BNSF Railway
- Rui Sousa, Ronnie McKnight,Tom Camp, UPS
- Natarajan Chandrasekaran, Tata Consultancy
- Marvin Ellison, J. C. Penney
- Jon Fairest, Sanofi Canada

The Leadership Experience continues to offer students great opportunities for self-assessment and leadership development. An important aspect of learning to be a leader involves looking inward for greater self-understanding, and the seventh edition provides many opportunities for this type of reflection. Each chapter includes multiple questionnaires or exercises that enable students to learn about their own leadership beliefs, values, competencies, and skills. These exercises help students gauge their current standing and connect the chapter concepts and examples to ideas for expanding their own leadership abilities. A few of the self-assessment topics involve engagement, networking, ethical maturity, personality traits, leading diverse people, developing a personal vision, spiritual leadership, candor, leadership courage, optimism, and leading with love versus leading with fear. Self-assessments related to basic leadership abilities such as listening skills, emotional intelligence, motivating others, and using power and influence are also included. Additional self-assessments are available within MindTap.

ORGANIZATION

The organization of the book is based on first understanding basic ways in which leaders differ from managers, and the ways leaders set direction, seek alignment between organizations and followers, build relationships, and create change. Thus, the organization of this book is in five parts:

1. Introduction to Leadership
2. Research Perspectives on Leadership
3. The Personal Side of Leadership
4. The Leader as a Relationship Builder
5. The Leader as Social Architect

The book integrates materials from both micro and macro approaches to leadership, from both academia and the real world, and from traditional ideas and recent thinking.

DISTINGUISHING FEATURES

This book has a number of special features that are designed to make the material accessible and valuable to students.

In the Lead *The Leadership Experience* is loaded with new examples of leaders in both traditional and contemporary organizations. Each chapter opens with a real-life example that relates to the chapter content, and several additional examples are highlighted within each chapter. These examples are drawn from a wide variety of organizations including education, the military, government agencies, businesses, and nonprofit organizations.

Consider This! Each chapter contains a *Consider This* box that is personal, compelling, and inspiring. This box may be a saying from a famous leader, or wisdom from the ages. These *Consider This* boxes provide novel and interesting material to expand the reader's thinking about the leadership experience.

Leader's Bookshelf In this edition, six of the 15 chapters have new Leader's Bookshelf reviews. A unique feature of *The Leadership Experience* is that each chapter includes a review of a recent book relevant to the chapter's content. The Leader's Bookshelf connects students to issues and topics being read and discussed in the worlds of academia, business, military, education, and nonprofit organizations.

New Leader Action Memo This feature helps students apply the chapter concepts in their own lives and leadership activities and directs them to self-assessments related to various chapter topics.

Leader's Self-Insight These boxes provide self-assessments for learners and an opportunity to experience leadership issues in a personal way. These exercises take the form of questionnaires, scenarios, and activities.

Student Development Each chapter ends with discussion questions and then two activities for student development. The first, **Leadership at Work**, is a practical, skill-building activity that engages the student in applying chapter concepts to real-life leadership. These exercises are designed so students can complete them on their own outside of class or in class as part of a group activity. Instructor tips are given for maximizing in-class learning with the Leadership at Work exercises. **Leadership Development: Cases for Analysis**, the second end-of-chapter activity, provides two short, problem-oriented cases for analysis. These cases test the student's ability to apply concepts when dealing with real-life leadership issues. The cases challenge the student's cognitive understanding of leadership ideas while the Leadership at Work exercises and the feedback questionnaires assess the student's progress as a leader.

Business Insights: Essentials' intuitive user interface makes it easy for students and instructors to search and find in-depth information on businesses, industries, and products. Features and benefits include the ability to search across multiple data types from a single search box with targeted search options by category. This includes company information, articles, industry data, SWOT Reports, Thomson Reuters Company Financials and Investment Reports, Market Share Reports, and Industry Essays. We have created assignments based on articles that connect directly with the content covered in your text, including assessment questions to test students on their knowledge of the content and emphasizing real-world examples.

MindTap® Management for Daft's *The Leadership Experience, 7th Edition,* is the digital learning solution that helps instructors to engage and transform today's students into critical thinkers. Through paths of dynamic assignments and applications that you can personalize, real-time course analytics, and an accessible reader, MindTap helps you turn cookie-cutter into cutting-edge, apathy into engagement, and memorizers into higher-level thinkers.

As an instructor using MindTap, you have at your fingertips the right content and a unique set of tools curated specifically for your course, all in an interface designed to improve workflow and save time when planning lessons and course structure. The control over building and personalizing your course is all yours, so you can focus on the most relevant material while also lowering costs for your students. Stay connected and informed in your course through real-time student tracking that provides the opportunity to adjust the course as needed based on analytics of interactivity in the course.

The MindTap Assignments are fully integrated with the text, providing calculated combinations of lower- and higher-order thinking skills exercises. Students can work together in the **experiential exercises** to create videos, write papers, deliver presentations, and more. Interactive Self-Assessments engage students by helping them make personal connections to the content presented in each chapter. A flexible grading system offers grade analytics and grade book export tools to work with any learning management system.

ANCILLARIES

This edition offers a wide range of instructor ancillaries to fully enable instructors to bring the leadership experience into the classroom. These ancillaries include:

Instructor's Manual

A comprehensive Instructor's Manual is available to assist in lecture preparation. Included in the Instructor's Manual are the chapter outlines, suggested answers to end-of-chapter materials, suggestions for further study, and a quick-glance overview for each chapter of the available MindTap resources to assist instructors in their planning.

Test Bank

Cengage Learning Testing Powered by Cognero is a flexible, online system that allows you to author, edit, and manage test bank content from multiple Cengage Learning solutions; create multiple test versions in an instant; and deliver tests from your LMS, your classroom, or wherever you want. The test bank for *The Leadership Experience*, seventh edition, includes approximately 60 questions per chapter to help you in writing examinations. Types of questions include true/false, multiple choice, completion, short-answer, and essay, with all questions tagged to relevant national competencies. To ensure consistency across our entire package, the content of the test bank has been fully reviewed and updated by the same authors who have crafted our new digital resources.

PowerPoint Lecture Presentations

An asset to any instructor, the PowerPoint lecture presentations include outlines for every chapter, illustrations from the text, and additional examples to provide learning opportunities for students.

Videos

Videos compiled specifically to accompany *The Leadership Experience*, seventh edition, allow students to engage with the textual material by applying theories and concepts to real-world situations.

ACKNOWLEDGMENTS

Textbook writing is a team enterprise. This book has integrated ideas and support from many people whom I want to acknowledge. I want to extend special thanks to my editorial associate, Pat Lane. I could not have undertaken this revision without Pat's help. She skillfully drafted materials for the chapters, found original sources, and did an outstanding job with last-minute changes, the copyedited manuscript, art, and galley proofs. Pat's talent and personal enthusiasm for this text added greatly to its excellence.

Here at Vanderbilt I want to thank my assistant, Linda Roberts, for the tremendous volume and quality of work she accomplished on my behalf that gave me time to write. Eric Johnson, the dean at Owen, and Sal March, associate dean, have maintained a positive scholarly atmosphere and supported me with the time and resources to complete the revision of this book. I also appreciate the intellectual stimulation and support from friends and colleagues at the Owen School—Bruce Barry, Ray Friedman, Jessica Kennedy, Rich Oliver, David Owens, Ty Park, Ranga Ramanujam, Bart Victor, and Tim Vogus.

I want to acknowledge the reviewers who provided feedback. Their ideas helped me improve the book in many areas:

Thomas H. Arcy
University of Houston—Central Campus

Janey Ayres
Purdue University

Kristin Backhaus
SUNY New Paltz

Bill Bommer
Georgia State University

William Russell Brown
Navarro College

Jared Caughron
University of Oklahoma

Meredith Rentz Cook
North Central Texas College

Glenn K. Cunningham
Duquesne University

Jeffrey Fisher
Embry Riddle Aeronautical University

Ron Franzen
Saint Luke's Hospital

Adrian Guardia
Texas A&M University—San Antonio

Delia J. Haak
John Brown University

Nell Hartley
Robert Morris College

Ann Horn-Jeddy
Medaille College

Ellen Jordan
Mount Olive College

Alyson Livingston
North Central Texas College

Gregory Manora
Auburn University–Montgomery

Joseph Martelli
The University of Findlay

Richard T. Martin
Washburn University

Jalane Meloun
Barry University

Mark Nagel
Normandale Community College

Ranjna Patel
Bethune Cookman College

Chad Peterson
Baylor University

Gordon Riggles
University of Colorado

Miriam Rothman
University of San Diego

Bill Service
Samford University

Dan Sherman
University of Alabama at Huntsville

Bret Simmons
North Dakota State University

Shane Spiller
University of Montevallo

Shand H. Stringham
Duquesne University

Ahmad Tootonchi
Frostburg State University

Mary L. Tucker
Ohio University

Joseph W. Weiss
Bentley University

Donald D. White
University of Arkansas

Xavier Whitaker
Baylor University

Jean Wilson
The College of William and Mary

George A. Wynn
University of Tampa

The developers at Cengage Learning also deserve special mention. Senior Product Manager Mike Roche supported the concept for this book and obtained the resources necessary for its completion. Associate Content Developer Jamie Mack provided terrific support for the book's writing, reviews, and production.

I also thank Bob Lengel at the University of Texas at San Antonio. Bob's enthusiasm for leadership many years ago stimulated me to begin reading, teaching, and training in the area of leadership development. His enthusiasm also led to our collaboration on the book *Fusion Leadership: Unlocking the Subtle Forces That Change People and Organizations*. I thank Bob for keeping the leadership dream alive, which in time enabled me to pursue my dream of writing this leadership textbook.

Finally, I want to acknowledge my loving daughters Danielle, Amy, Roxanne, Solange, and Elizabeth. Although everyone is now pursuing their own lives and careers, I appreciate the good feelings and connections with my children and grandchildren. On occasion, we have been able to travel, vacation, watch a play, or just be together—all of which reconnect me to the things that really count.

Richard L. Daft
Nashville, Tennessee

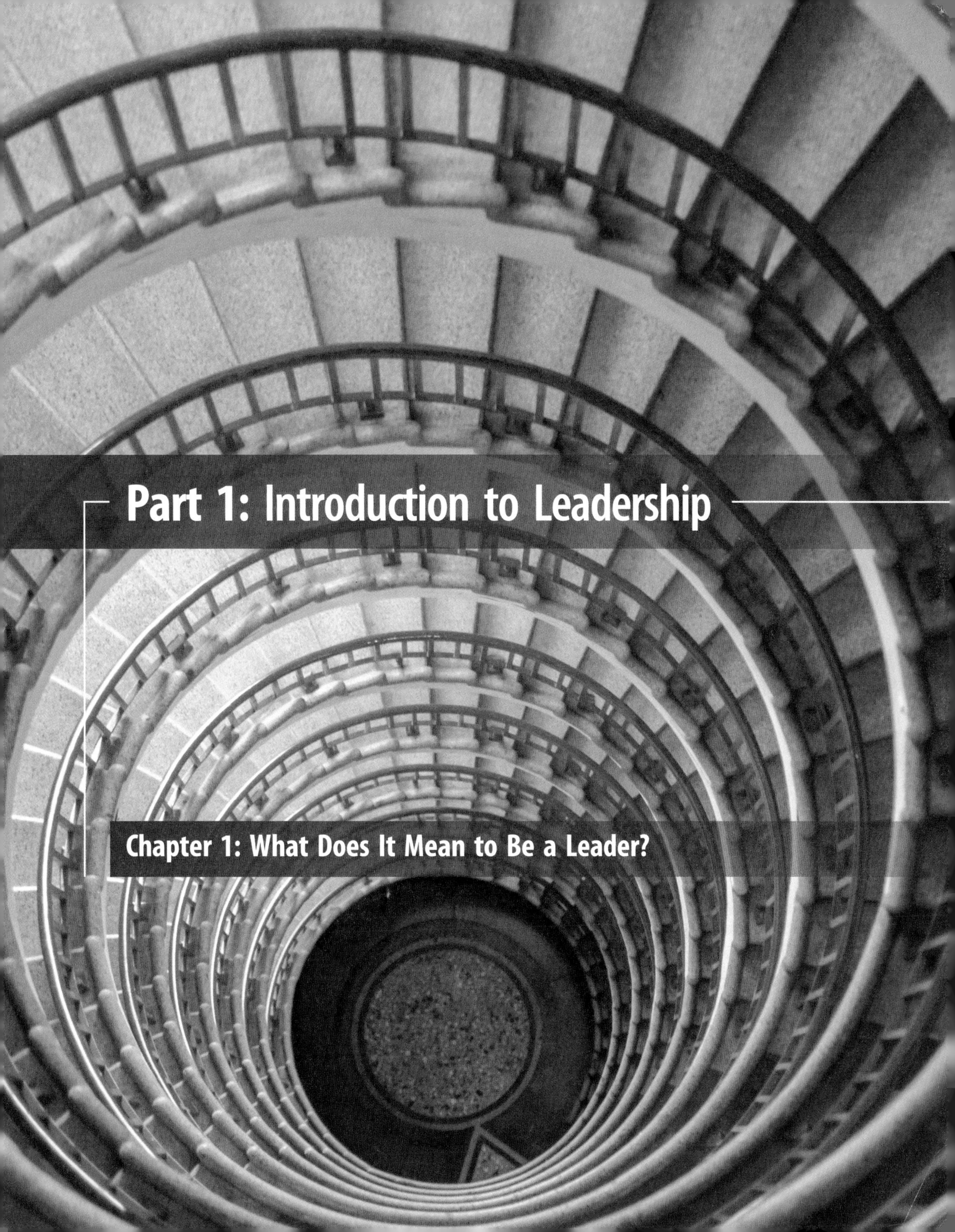

Part 1: Introduction to Leadership

Chapter 1: What Does It Mean to Be a Leader?

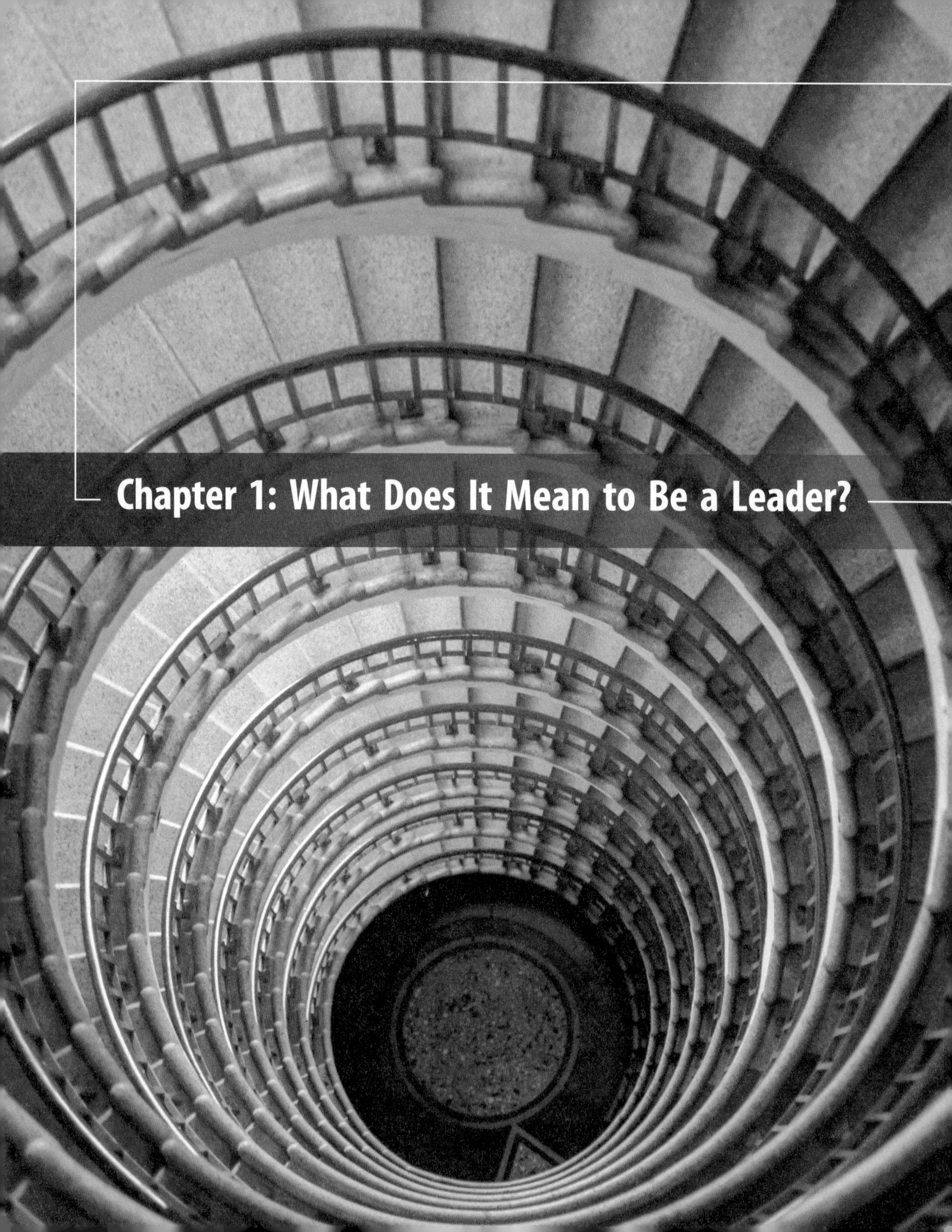

Chapter 1: What Does It Mean to Be a Leader?

YOUR **LEADERSHIP** CHALLENGE

After reading this chapter, you should be able to:

- Understand the full meaning of leadership and see the leadership potential in yourself and others.
- Recognize and facilitate the six fundamental transformations in today's organizations and leaders.
- Identify the primary reasons for leadership derailment and the new paradigm skills that can help you avoid it.
- Recognize the traditional functions of management and the fundamental differences between leadership and management.
- Appreciate the crucial importance of providing direction, alignment, relationships, personal qualities, and outcomes.
- Explain how leadership has evolved and how historical approaches apply to the practice of leadership today.

CHAPTER **OUTLINE**

4 Why We Need Leadership
8 The New Reality for Leaders
14 How Leadership Differs from Management
17 Evolving Theories of Leadership
21 Leadership Can Be Learned
24 Mastering the Art and Science of Leadership
24 Organization of This Book

In the Lead

13 Pope Francis, Roman Catholic Church
23 Google

Leader's Self-Insight

11 Your Learning Style: Using Multiple Intelligences
17 Your Leadership Potential
22 Are You on a Fast Track to Nowhere?

Leader's Bookshelf

7 My Life in Leadership: The Journey and Lessons Learned Along the Way

Leadership at Work

27 Leadership Right–Wrong

Leadership Development: Cases for Analysis

29 Sales Engineering Division
29 The Marshall Plan

Abraham Lincoln had less leadership experience than any previous president, but when historians rank the "greatest presidents," Lincoln frequently tops the list. Interest in Lincoln's leadership swelled with the release of Steven Spielberg's historical film *Lincoln*, which was a huge critical and commercial success, grossing more than $250 million at the box office and garnering 12 Academy Award nominations. "Lincoln's presidency is a big, well-lit classroom for business leaders seeking to build successful, enduring organizations," said Howard Schultz, CEO of Starbucks. In this era of disconnected and often morally bankrupt leaders, it is no wonder the skills, strengths, and character of Lincoln have struck a chord. Lincoln once provoked an opponent to tears by using his expert communication skills to mimic and ridicule his rival. Soon afterward, the man who would later become the 16th president of the United States felt disappointed and ashamed of his own behavior and sought out his opponent to offer an apology. Lincoln took this as a valuable lesson about channeling his emotions, practicing empathy, and using his abilities to promote good. From then on, Lincoln applied his superb leadership and communication skills to serve the higher interests of the American people rather than his own goals and ego. His ability to control his emotions and stay committed to a vision even under intense hardship, his commitment to go into the field and establish connections with soldiers and the general public, and his willingness to listen to different points of view and to share credit for successes and take blame for failures all tap into a deep longing within people for genuine leadership.[1]

The public trust in leaders may be at an all-time low. Referring to the dire economic situation that followed the ethical and financial problems in the mortgage and finance industries, David Rothkopf wrote in the *Washington Post*, "This is not just a global economic crisis. It is a global leadership crisis."[2]

1-1 WHY WE NEED LEADERSHIP

Many of us think of leadership in a way similar to what U.S. Supreme Court Justice Potter Stewart said about obscenity in reviewing a 1964 pornography case: we may not be able to define it but "we know it when we see it."[3] People can clearly see leadership in Abraham Lincoln, but many are having a hard time seeing it in current political, business, military, and even religious leaders. General David Petraeus, one of the most decorated military leaders of his generation, stepped down as director of the Central Intelligence Agency after the FBI inadvertently discovered he had an extramarital affair with his biographer and began investigating for potential leaks of classified information. The British Broadcasting Corporation (BBC) was tarnished by allegations that managers covered up years of sexual abuse by a well-known reporter.[4] Senator Chuck Grassley recently probed the financial records of six well-known televangelists, including Creflo Dollar and Kenneth Copeland, after reports that tax-exempt donations were financing lavish lifestyles for the religious leaders, including mansions, Rolls Royce cars, and private jets.[5] Nearly every month brings a new report of a business leader somewhere lying to, misleading, or cheating employees, customers, or the government. No wonder survey after survey shows that confidence in leaders is sinking and suspicion and distrust are rising.[6]

Yet there are good leaders working in every organization, large and small. In fact, quality leadership is all around us every day, in all facets of our lives—our families, schools, communities, social clubs, and volunteer organizations, as well as in the world of business, sports, religion, government, and the military. Without good leadership, our institutions and society would fall apart.

Before we can examine what makes an effective leader, we need to know what leadership means. Scholars and other writers have offered hundreds of definitions of the term *leadership*, prompting James McGregor Burns to conclude that leadership "is one of the most observed and least understood phenomena on earth."[7] Defining leadership has been a complex and elusive problem largely because the nature of leadership itself is complex. Some have even suggested that leadership is nothing more than a romantic myth, perhaps based on the false hope that someone will come along and solve our problems by sheer force of will.[8]

There is some evidence that people do pin their hopes on leaders in ways that are not always realistic. Think about how some struggling companies recruit well-known, charismatic CEOs and invest tremendous hopes in them, only to find that their problems actually get worse.[9] For example, Yahoo hired former Autodesk CEO Carol Bartz in 2009 with high hopes that the star leader could turn the struggling company around, only to ask her to leave a couple of years later as Yahoo's fortunes continued to slide. In mid-2012, Yahoo hired former Google executive Marissa Mayer as the fifth CEO in five years.

Particularly when times are tough, people often look to a grand, charismatic type of leader to alleviate fear and uncertainty. Think of how Barack Obama sailed to the U.S. presidency in 2008 based largely on his charisma and the ability to make people feel hopeful in a time of uncertainty. In recent years, the romantic or heroic view of leadership has been challenged.[10] Much progress has been made in understanding the essential nature of leadership as a real and powerful influence in organizations and societies.

1-1a Defining Leadership

Leadership studies are an evolving discipline, and the concept of leadership will continue to develop. For the purpose of this book, we will focus on a single definition that delineates the essential elements of the leadership process: **Leadership** is an influence relationship among leaders and followers who intend real changes and outcomes that reflect their shared purposes.[11]

Exhibit 1.1 summarizes the key elements in this definition. Leadership involves influence; it occurs among people; those people intentionally desire significant changes; and the changes reflect purposes shared by leaders and followers. *Influence* means that the relationship among people is not passive; however, also inherent in this definition is the concept that influence is multidirectional and noncoercive. The basic cultural values in North America make it easiest to think of leadership as something a leader does to a follower.[12] However, leadership is reciprocal. In most organizations, superiors influence subordinates, but subordinates also influence superiors. The people involved in the relationship want substantive *changes*—leadership involves creating change, not maintaining the status quo. In addition, the changes sought are not dictated by leaders but reflect *purposes* that leaders and followers share. Moreover, change is toward an outcome that both the leader and the followers want, a desired future or shared purpose that motivates them toward this more preferable outcome. An important aspect of leadership is influencing others to come together around a common vision. Thus, leadership involves the influence of people to bring about change toward a desirable future.

Leadership
an influence relationship among leaders and followers who intend real changes and outcomes that reflect their shared purposes

EXHIBIT 1.1 What Leadership Involves

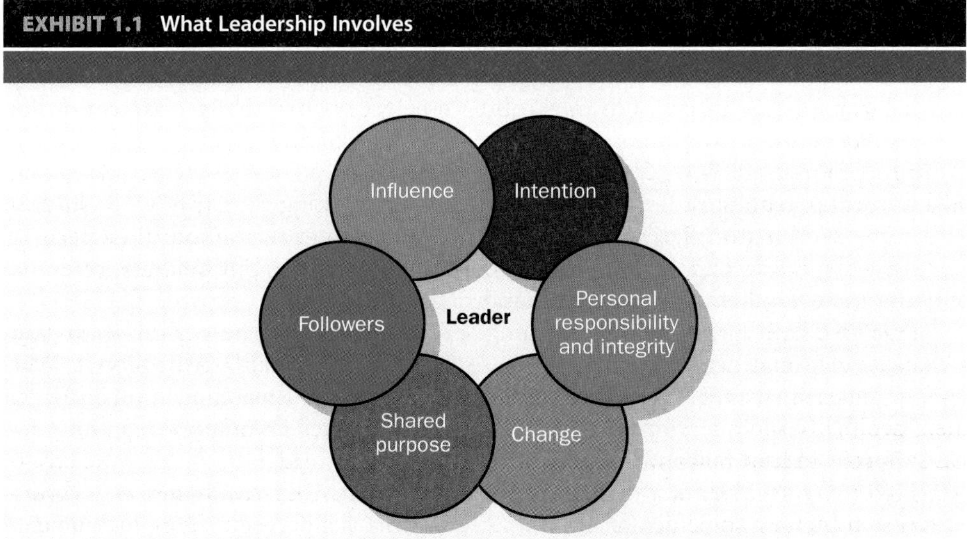

Also, leadership is a *people* activity and is distinct from administrative paperwork or planning activities. Leadership occurs *among* people; it is not something done *to* people. Since leadership involves people, there must be *followers*. An individual performer who achieves excellence as a scientist, musician, athlete, or woodcarver may be a leader in her field of expertise but is not a leader as defined in this book unless followers are involved. Followers are an important part of the leadership process, and all leaders are sometimes followers as well. Good leaders know how to follow, and they set an example for others. The issue of *intention* or will means that people—leader and followers—are actively involved in the pursuit of change. Each person takes personal responsibility to achieve the desired future.

One stereotype is that leaders are somehow different, that they are above others; however, in reality, the qualities needed for effective leadership are the same as those needed to be an effective follower.[13] Effective followers think for themselves and carry out assignments with energy and enthusiasm. They are committed to something outside their own self-interest, and they have the courage to stand up for what they believe. Good followers are not "yes people" who blindly follow a leader. Effective leaders and effective followers may sometimes be the same people, playing different roles at different times. At its best, leadership is shared among leaders and followers, with everyone fully engaged and accepting higher levels of responsibility.

1-1b Everyday Leadership

Using this definition of leadership makes clear that leadership can come from anyone. When we stop equating leadership with greatness and public visibility, it becomes easier to see our own opportunities for leadership and recognize the leadership of people we interact with every day. Leaders come in all shapes and sizes, and many true leaders are working behind the scenes. Leadership that has big outcomes often starts small.

- Wendy Kopp was a senior at Princeton University when she first came up with the idea of a sort of "Peace Corps for teachers," a national organization that would recruit recent college graduates to commit to teach for two years at some of America's toughest public schools. One of her Princeton professors admits he called her "deranged" when she proposed the idea to him. Yet Teach for America, the organization Kopp started, became one of the most respected educational initiatives in the United States. As the organization has grown larger, it has come under attack, but most observers agree it has changed education for the better and it continues to harness the idealism of young college graduates as a force for good.[14]
- Clinical psychologist Barbara Van Dahlen was working primarily with children in the Washington, D.C., area when she became concerned about the effects of the wars in Iraq and Afghanistan on the mental health of U.S. soldiers, veterans, and their families. Van Dahlen founded Give an Hour to provide free services that give help and hope to returning service members. The organization now has a national network of more than 6,100 mental health professionals who volunteer their time. Give an Hour also works with other organizations, such as Bare the Burden, a nonprofit organization that creates an online community for veterans to heal by connecting with others.[15]
- During his five years working as a car salesman, Robert Chambers was disgusted by how some dealers and finance institutions preyed on low-income customers. After he retired from a varied career, the 62-year-old electrical engineer

LEADER'S BOOKSHELF

My Life in Leadership: The Journey and Lessons Learned Along the Way

by Frances Hesselbein

What college dropout transformed one of the world's largest volunteer organizations, was named *Fortune* magazine's "Best Nonprofit Manager in America," and received America's highest civilian honor, the Presidential Medal of Freedom? The answer: Frances Hesselbein, who began her amazing leadership journey as a somewhat reluctant volunteer leader of Girl Scout Troup 17 in Johnstown, Pennsylvania, when she was in her early twenties. In her autobiography, *My Life in Leadership*, Hesselbein, now in her late 90s, shares what she has learned about leadership throughout her long career.

"LEADERSHIP IS A MATTER OF HOW TO BE, NOT HOW TO DO"

Hesselbein argues that "it is the quality and character of the leader that determines performance." For her, leadership is about serving others. From her beginning as a volunteer Scout leader, she eventually became CEO of the Girl Scouts of the USA, and later was founding president of famed management scholar Peter Drucker's Leader to Leader Institute (she still serves as CEO of the organization, recently renamed the Frances Hesselbein Leadership Institute). Here are a few of the key lessons Hesselbein has learned along the way:

- ***Have a Clear Mission That Everyone Can Support.*** As soon as she became CEO of the national Girl Scouts, Hesselbein took a close look at the mission of the organization and began asking leaders at all levels, as well as girls themselves, what they really valued, wanted, and needed. "Because we included everyone, it became theirs, not ours," she says. Hesselbein calls the mission, vision, and values "the soul of the organization," which should be central "even as we abandon the vestiges of the past that spell irrelevance in the future."
- ***Be Inclusive.*** Hesselbein also ditched the hierarchy, sharing information and power with leaders at all levels from the beginning. A concept she called "circular management," put the leader in the middle of the organizational chart rather than at the top of a hierarchy. Everyone was a member of a team, and there were no superiors and subordinates. Being inclusive develops leaders at every level and increases the energy and creativity of the entire organization.
- ***Make Learning a Top Priority.*** Organizations have to keep changing and adapting when it's necessary. "The first item in your budget should be learning, education, and development of your people," she says.

THE GREAT ADVENTURE

Hesselbein tells her story in *Learning to Lead* as a great adventure that she enjoyed every step of the way. It is a story told in a very personal way, but one that is packed with observations and reflections that are as relevant to today's leaders as when Hesselbein first began her long leadership journey as a volunteer Girl Scout leader.

Source: *Learning to Lead*, by Frances Hesselbein, is published by Jossey-Bass.

decided to do something about it. He founded More Than Wheels, which helps low-income people buy new, base-model cars at low prices and on good loan terms. With branches in New Hampshire, Vermont, and Maine, More Than Wheels has negotiated price and extended warranty deals with a dozen or so auto dealers and worked with banks to provide low interest rates. More Than Wheels guarantees the loan and then works with clients to help them manage their finances, improve their credit scores, and improve their future.[16]

There are opportunities for leadership all around us that involve influence and change toward a desired goal or outcome. As further illustrated in the Leader's Bookshelf, widely known and highly respected leaders often begin their leadership journeys in small ways. The leaders of tomorrow's organizations will come from anywhere and everywhere, just as they always have. Do you have the capacity and commitment required for taking a leadership role in your school, community, or workplace? You can start now, wherever you are, to practice leadership in your own life. Leadership is an everyday way of acting and thinking that has little to do with a title or formal position in an organization. As we will discuss in the following section, business leaders need to understand this tenet more than ever in the world of the twenty-first century.

NEW LEADER
ACTION MEMO

As a leader, you can recognize opportunities for leadership and act to influence others and bring about changes for a better future.

1-2 THE NEW REALITY FOR LEADERS

Social media. Globalization. Mobile commerce. Geopolitical wars. Renewable technologies and smart machines. Outsourcing. Climate change and resource scarcity. Telecommuting and virtual teams. Cybercrime. Redistribution of economic power. Massive changes in the world mean today's leaders are facing challenges they couldn't even imagine just a few years ago.[17] In a survey by the Center for Creative Leadership, 84 percent of leaders surveyed say the definition of effective leadership changed significantly within the first few years of the twenty-first century.[18] And that was even *before* social and mobile technologies began reshaping everyday life and work. Social connectedness and mobility are becoming central aspects of every leader's job.

Some historians and other scholars believe our world is undergoing a transformation more profound and far-reaching than any experienced since the dawn of the modern age and the Industrial Revolution more than 500 years ago. Today's leaders operate in a world where little is certain, the pace is relentless, and everything is more complex. This transformation requires a transition from a traditional to a new leadership paradigm, as outlined in Exhibit 1.2.[19] A **paradigm** is a shared mindset that represents a fundamental way of thinking about, perceiving, and understanding the world.

Paradigm
a shared mindset that represents a fundamental way of thinking about, perceiving, and understanding the world

Although many leaders are still operating from an old-paradigm mindset, as outlined in the first column of Exhibit 1.2, they are increasingly ineffective. Successful leaders will respond to the new reality outlined in the second column of the exhibit.

EXHIBIT 1.2 The New Reality for Leaders

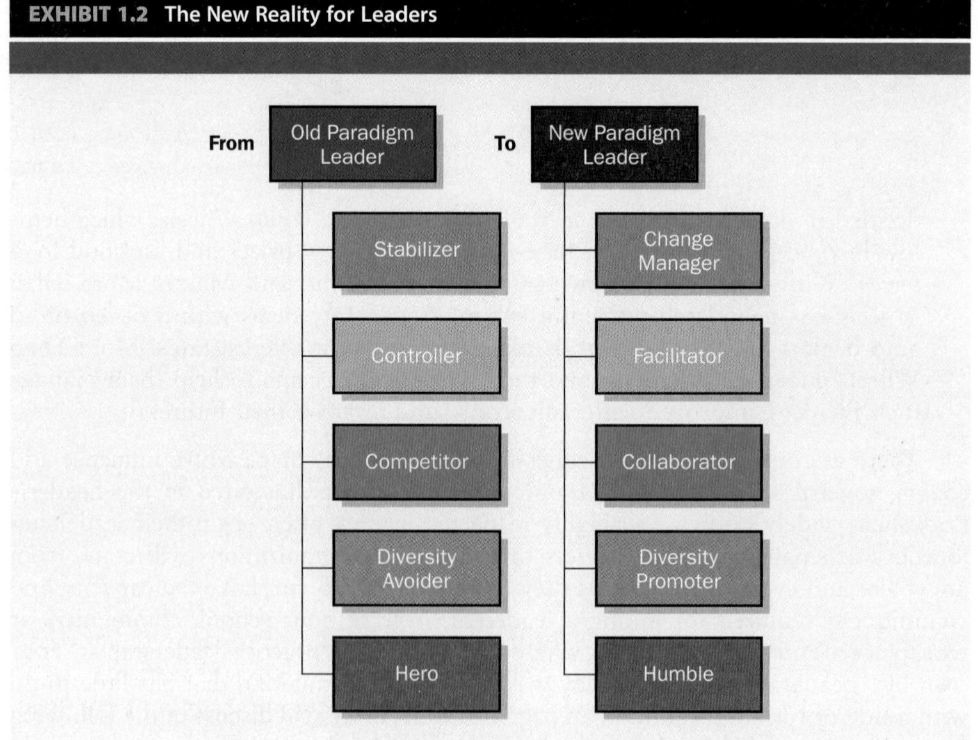

1-2a From Stabilizer to Change Manager

In the past, many leaders assumed that if they could just keep things running on a steady, even keel, the organization would be successful. Yet today's world is in constant motion, and nothing seems certain anymore. If leaders still had an illusion of stability at the dawn of the twenty-first century, it is surely shattered by now. Consider the following recent events:

- A powerful earthquake in Japan triggered massive tsunami waves that damaged the nuclear reactors at the Fukushima Daiichi power plant and led to the shutdown of numerous companies, creating supply chain disruptions for manufacturers around the world. In the wake of the disaster, managers at Tokyo Electric Power Company (Tepco) were criticized for failing to act quickly enough to cool the reactors at Fukushima. Trying to protect their investment, they hesitated to use seawater, which they knew could damage the reactors, leading to the second-largest nuclear disaster in history.[20]
- In 2015, the Volkswagen Group, one of the largest car manufacturers in the world and known as maker of "the people's car," was discovered to have used software designed to cheat U.S. emissions tests, affecting 11 million vehicles worldwide. Actual exhaust emissions turned out to be up to 40 times higher than the emission tests revealed. VW's emissions scandal cast doubt on the reputations and emissions validity of other auto manufacturers such as Mercedes and BMW. Germany's national economy and auto suppliers worldwide will likely be hurt as VW sales decline.[21]
- Greece was in a deep recession in 2015 due to huge debts to the European Union (EU). Sharp cutbacks in government spending had decimated personal incomes and businesses in the region. Ireland and Spain faced similar debt problems previously, causing talk of a possible breakup of the euro system (the single currency adopted by EU countries), which would deal a severe blow to the global financial system. Leaders of multinational firms have to take steps to protect themselves, as well as consider what they will do in the event that a return to national currencies requires a rethinking of everything from how to expand operations to how to pick suppliers or pay employees.[22]

Most leaders, whether in business, politics, the military, education, social services, the arts, or the world of sports, recognize that trying to maintain stability in a world of such unexpected and far-reaching change is a losing battle. "You have to be able to react very quickly," said Ellen Kullman, recently retired CEO of DuPont, referring to the impact of events such as the Japanese tsunami and the EU financial crisis. "And the world is so connected that the feedback loops are more intense."[23]

Today's best leaders accept the inevitability of change and crisis and tap into them as potential sources of energy and self-renewal. Adaptability is the watchword of the day.

1-2b From Controller to Facilitator

Leaders in powerful positions once believed strict control was needed for the organization to function efficiently and effectively. Rigid organizational hierarchies, structured jobs and work processes, and detailed, inviolate procedures let everyone know that those at the top had power and those at the bottom had none.

Today, the old assumptions about the distribution of power are no longer valid. An emphasis on control and rigidity serves to squelch motivation, innovation, and morale rather than produce desired results. Effective leaders share power rather than hoard it and find ways to increase an organization's brainpower by getting everyone in the organization involved and committed. Rather than being a controller, the leader is a facilitator who helps people do and be their best by removing obstacles to performance, getting people what they need, providing learning opportunities, and offering support and feedback.

One reason for this is that the financial basis of today's economy is becoming *information* rather than the tangible assets of land, buildings, and machines. This means human capital is becoming more important than financial capital, which increases the power of employees. "Ideas are now more important than materials," as former Israeli president Shimon Peres once put it.[24] When all the organization needed was workers to run machines eight hours a day, traditional command-and-control systems generally worked quite well, but success today depends on the intellectual capacity of all employees. One of the leader's most challenging jobs is to enable people to embrace and use their power effectively.[25]

When he took over as CEO of India's struggling HCL Technologies in 2005, Vineet Nayar took a huge risk that proved to be a highly effective route to true employee empowerment and increasing revenues. His revolutionary move was to organize the company around the principle of "employees first, customers second." Nayar created an open online forum where people could post questions and leaders would answer. Employees were overjoyed that leaders were willing to acknowledge the problems in the company, and they began proposing solutions. This began the transfer of power and responsibility for solving problems from top executives to employees. In the new HCL, the job of leaders is to serve employees.[26] Nayar, who served as CEO until 2013, wrote a book titled *Employees First, Customers Second: Turning Conventional Management Upside Down* to explain how leaders can tap into the power of this unconventional approach.[27]

1-2c From Competitor to Collaborator

Social media has "put connectivity on steroids," blurring and sometimes obliterating boundaries within and between organizations.[28] In a hyperconnected, networked age, collaboration becomes more important than competition. Successful leaders harness and make the most of ideas, talent, and resources from across boundaries of all kinds. Although some companies still encourage internal competition and aggressiveness, most successful leaders stress teamwork, compromise, and cooperation. Self-directed teams and other forms of horizontal collaboration spread knowledge and information throughout the organization.

Effective leaders also work collaboratively with suppliers, customers, governments, universities, and other organizations. There is a growing trend within companies to think of themselves as teams that create value jointly rather than as autonomous entities in competition with all others.

Collaboration presents greater leadership challenges than did the old concept of competition. Leaders first have to develop their own collaborative mindset and then create an environment of teamwork and community that fosters collaboration and mutual support. They learn to keep the lines of communication open and use influence rather than wielding their authority to quell harmful politicking, get buy-in on important matters, and move things forward.[29]

NEW LEADER
ACTION MEMO

Go to Leader's Self-Insight 1.1 to learn about your own "intelligence" for dealing with collaboration and with the other new realities facing leaders.

LEADER'S SELF-INSIGHT 1.1

Your Learning Style: Using Multiple Intelligences

Instructions: Multiple-intelligence theory suggests that there are several different ways of learning about things in a topsy-turvy world; hence there are multiple "intelligences," of which five are interpersonal (learn via interactions with others), intrapersonal (own inner states), logical–mathematical (rationality and logic), verbal–linguistic (words and language), and musical (sounds, tonal patterns, and rhythms). Most people prefer one or two of the intelligences as a way of learning, yet each person has the potential to develop skills in each of the intelligences.

The following items will help you identify the forms of intelligence that you tend to use or enjoy most, as well as the forms that you use less. Please check each item below as Mostly False or Mostly True for you.

	Mostly False	Mostly True
1. I like to work with and solve complex problems.	_____	_____
2. I recently wrote something that I am especially proud of.	_____	_____
3. I have three or more friends.	_____	_____
4. I like to learn about myself through personality tests.	_____	_____
5. I frequently listen to music on the radio or iPod-type player.	_____	_____
6. Math and science were among my favorite subjects.	_____	_____
7. Language and social studies were among my favorite subjects.	_____	_____
8. I am frequently involved in social activities.	_____	_____
9. I have or would like to attend personal growth seminars.	_____	_____
10. I notice if a melody is out of tune or off key.	_____	_____
11. I am good at problem solving that requires logical thinking.	_____	_____
12. My conversations frequently include things I've read or heard about.	_____	_____
13. When among strangers, I easily find someone to talk to.	_____	_____
14. I spend time alone meditating, reflecting, or thinking.	_____	_____
15. After hearing a tune once or twice, I am able to sing it back with some accuracy.	_____	_____

Scoring and Interpretation

Count the number of items checked Mostly True that represent each of the five intelligences as indicated below.

Questions 1, 6, 11: Logical–mathematical intelligence.
Mostly True = ________.
Questions 2, 7, 12: Verbal–linguistic intelligence.
Mostly True = ________.
Questions 3, 8, 13: Interpersonal intelligence.
Mostly True = ________.
Questions 4, 9, 14: Intrapersonal intelligence.
Mostly True = ________.
Questions 5, 10, 15: Musical intelligence.
Mostly True = ________.

Educational institutions tend to stress the logical–mathematical and verbal–linguistic forms of learning. How do your intelligences align with the changes taking place in the world? Would you rather rely on using one intelligence in depth or develop multiple intelligences? Any intelligence above for which you received a score of 3 is a major source of learning for you, and a score of zero means you may not use it at all. How do your intelligences fit your career plans and your aspirations for the type of leader you want to be?

Sources: Based on Kirsi Tirri, Petri Nokelainen, and Martin Ubani, "Conceptual Definition and Empirical Validation of the Spiritual Sensitivity Scale," *Journal of Empirical Theology* 19 (2006), pp. 37–62; and David Lazear, "Seven Ways of Knowing: Teaching for Multiple Intelligences," (Palatine, IL: IRI/Skylight Publishing, 1991).

1-2d From Diversity Avoider to Diversity Promoter

Many of today's organizations were built on assumptions of uniformity, separation, and specialization. People who think alike, act alike, and have similar job skills are grouped into a department, such as accounting or manufacturing, separate from other departments. Homogenous groups find it easy to get along, communicate, and understand one another. The uniform thinking that arises, however, can be a disaster in a world becoming more multinational and diverse.

Bringing diversity into the organization is the way to attract the best human talent and develop an organizational mindset broad enough to thrive in a multinational world. Carlos Ghosn, CEO of Nissan, says one reason his company has been able to cope with change and crises better than some of its competitors is its highly diverse culture and workforce.[30] Two business school graduates in their twenties discovered the importance of diversity when they started a specialized advertising firm. They worked hard, and as the firm grew, they hired more people just like themselves—bright, young, intense college graduates who were committed and hard working. The firm grew to about 20 employees over two and a half years, but the expected profits never materialized. The two entrepreneurs could never get a handle on what was wrong, and the firm slid into bankruptcy. Convinced the idea was still valid, they started over, but with a new philosophy. They sought employees with different ages, values, ethnic backgrounds, and work experience. People had different styles, yet the organization seemed to work better. People played different roles, and the diverse experiences of the group enabled the firm to respond to unique situations and handle a variety of organizational and personal needs. The advertising firm is growing again, and this time it is also making a profit.

Consider **This!**

Should Leaders Live by the Cowboy Code?

1. A cowboy never takes unfair advantage—even of an enemy.
2. A cowboy never goes back on his word or betrays a trust.
3. A cowboy always tells the truth.
4. A cowboy is kind and gentle with children, the elderly, and animals.
5. A cowboy is free from racial or religious prejudice.
6. A cowboy is always helpful and lends a hand when anyone is in trouble.
7. A cowboy is a good worker.
8. A cowboy stays clean in thought, speech, action, and personal habits.
9. A cowboy respects womanhood, parents, and the laws of his nation.
10. A cowboy is a patriot to his country.

Source: Gene Autry's Cowboy Commandments are reported, with some variations in wording, in multiple sources.

1-2e From Hero to Humble

Another shift is the move from celebrating the "leader-as-hero" to recognizing the hard-working behind-the-scenes leader who quietly builds a strong, enduring company by supporting and developing others rather than touting his or her own abilities and successes.[31] Recall from this chapter's opening example how Abraham Lincoln made an intentional choice early in his political career to use his abilities to serve the interests of the American people rather than to feed his own ego. This chapter's *Consider This* box presents 10 commandments based on 1950s western film star Gene Autry's Cowboy Code that can be regarded as applicable to new-paradigm leaders even today.

One reason for the shift from hero to humble is that it is less and less realistic for an individual leader to meet all the challenges a team or organization faces in a complex and rapidly changing world. Another is that ambitious, highly self-confident, charismatic leaders have been at the forefront of some of the ethical scandals and business failures of recent years. The hero leader may make more risky and daring decisions, often without considering the greater good, whereas a humble leader will seek advice and take time to think through the possible consequences of his or her actions.[32] A recent study from the W.P. Carey School of Business at Arizona State University found that the most effective CEOs, for example, were those who led with humility by empowering and appreciating their employees, being open to feedback, and putting the greater good above their own self-interest.[33]

Jim Collins, author of *Good to Great* and *Great by Choice*, calls this new breed "Level 5 leaders."[34] In contrast to the view of great leaders as larger-than-life personalities with strong egos and big ambitions, Level 5 leaders often seem shy and unpretentious and have no need to be in the limelight. They are more concerned with the success of the team or company than with their own success.

These leaders are characterized by an almost complete lack of ego, coupled with a fierce resolve to do what is best for the organization. They accept full responsibility for mistakes, poor results, or failures, but they typically give credit for successes to other people. One corporate example is Sir Terry Leahy, who recently retired after more than a decade leading Britain's Tesco. That is a long and successful tenure for a leader whom most people know little about. Leahy didn't court personal publicity, much to the chagrin of journalists, and he put his energies into promoting Tesco and its employees rather than himself.[35] Although most research regarding the new type of leader has been on corporate CEOs like Sir Terry Leahy, it is important to remember that new-paradigm or Level 5 leaders are in all positions in all types of organizations. Perhaps not surprisingly, Pope Francis is an excellent example of a humble leader. He chose to be named after St. Francis of Assisi to illustrate that humility and service come first. But the popular pope also illustrates many other qualities of the new-paradigm leader.

> *"Humility is not weakness. Humility has its effect across levels of an organization in an empowered uplifting way. You can't browbeat people into performance."*
>
> Angelo Kinicki, Management Professor, Author, and Consultant

IN THE LEAD

Pope Francis, Roman Catholic Church

He was chosen as *Time* magazine's 2013 "Person of the Year," is a leader in Google searches, has tripled attendance at papal events with his humility, empathy, and commitment to the disenfranchised, and created a huge stir when he visited the United States for the first time in September 2015. The leader considered "everyone's pope" has become a celebrity among managers, leadership coaches, entrepreneurs, and CEOs, too.

In a short period of time, Francis has brought about tremendous change and revival in a huge, global organization that has suffered devastating scandals in recent years and, not so long ago, seemed on the verge of becoming irrelevant. He did it by using not only his personal charisma and character but also leadership skills that anyone can apply. For example, Francis doesn't fear change and is willing to take risks. He has reached out to atheists and agnostics, proclaimed a year of jubilee for women who have had abortions but have since chosen to reflect on the Church's teachings on the subject, and declared that God has redeemed all of us, not just Catholics. Francis has also demonstrated the importance of empowering rather than controlling subordinates. He transformed the Synod of Bishops into a decision-making group rather than a ceremonial one. He created a global Council of Cardinal Advisers made up of members who reflect diverse views. He is always willing to listen to advice from anyone and uses social media. He has washed the feet of prisoners, women, and Muslims, rather than performing the traditional ritual only on priests, as a way to show the value of every person and what each person can contribute. He makes personal telephone calls to unsuspecting people, such as the 14-year-old brother of a gas station attendant killed in an armed robbery and a Vatican critic who was ill in the hospital.

Francis is willing to listen, to collaborate, and to take advice, but he also isn't afraid to move forward with his own ideas when he believes this serves the greater good and is in the best interest of the organization.[36]

NEW LEADER
ACTION MEMO

As a leader, you can respond to the reality of change and crisis, the need for empowerment, collaboration, and diversity, and the importance of a higher purpose. You can channel your ambition toward achieving larger organizational goals rather than feeding your own ego.

Once a relatively obscure Jesuit cardinal, Pope Francis has become one of the most recognized—and some believe most effective—leaders in the world. Within two years, he has brought significant positive changes, including economic reforms at the Vatican and evolving discussions about social issues. He shows that, rather than playing it safe or being blinded by fear of failure, leaders can bring fresh perspectives to problems and apply their skills to achieve a higher purpose.

1-3 HOW LEADERSHIP DIFFERS FROM MANAGEMENT

Management can be defined as the attainment of organizational goals in an effective and efficient manner through planning, organizing, staffing, directing, and controlling organizational resources. So, what is it that distinguishes the process of leadership from that of management? Managers and leaders are not inherently different types of people. There are managers at all hierarchical levels who are also good leaders, and many people can develop the qualities needed for effective leadership and management. Both are essential in organizations and must be integrated effectively to lead to high performance.[37] That is, leadership cannot replace management; the two have to go hand-in-hand.

NEW LEADER
ACTION MEMO

You can evaluate your own leadership potential by completing the quiz in Leader's Self-Insight 1.2.

Exhibit 1.3 compares management to leadership in five areas crucial to organizational performance—providing direction, aligning followers, building relationships, developing personal qualities, and creating leader outcomes.[38]

1-3a Providing Direction

Both leadership and management are concerned with providing direction for the organization, but there are differences. Management focuses on establishing detailed plans and schedules for achieving specific results, then allocating resources to accomplish the plan. Leadership calls for creating a compelling vision of the future, setting the context within which to view challenges and opportunities, and developing farsighted strategies for producing the changes needed to achieve the vision. Whereas management calls for keeping an eye on the bottom line and short-term results, leadership means keeping an eye on the horizon and the long-term future.

Management
the attainment of organizational goals in an effective and efficient manner through planning, organizing, staffing, directing, and controlling organizational resources

Vision
a picture of an ambitious, desirable future for the organization or team

A **vision** is a picture of an ambitious, desirable future for the organization or team. It can be as lofty as Motorola's aim to "become the premier company in the

EXHIBIT 1.3 Comparing Management and Leadership

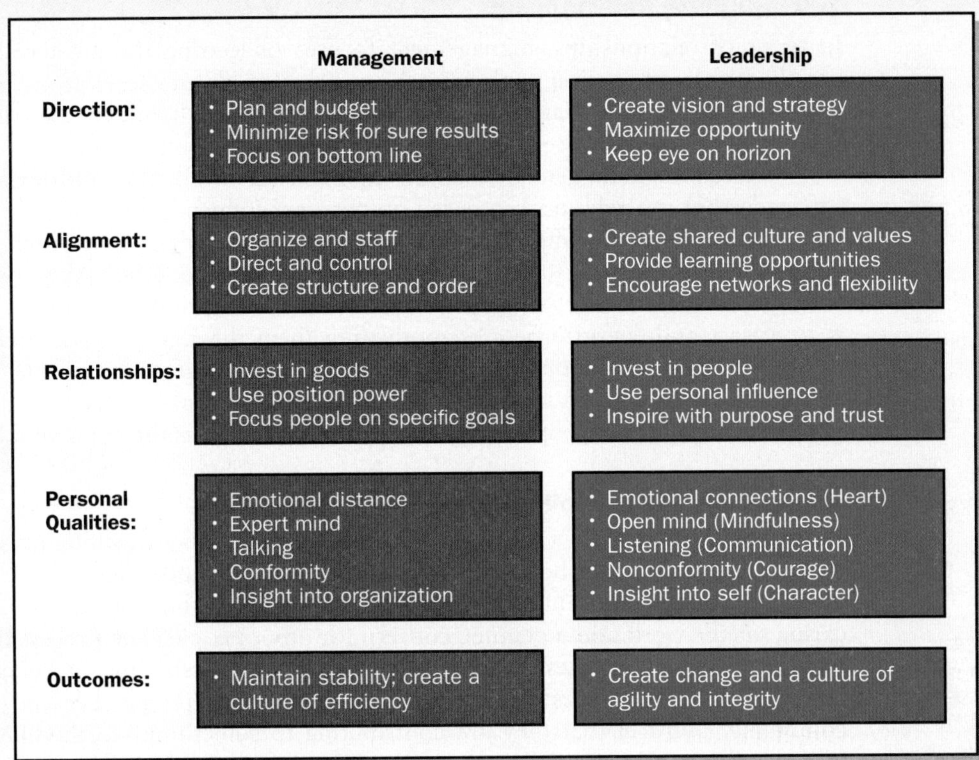

Sources: Based on John P. Kotter, *A Force for Change: How Leadership Differs from Management* (New York: The Free Press, 1990) and ideas in Kevin Cashman, "Lead with Energy," *Leadership Excellence* (December 2010), p. 7; Henry Mintzberg, *Managing* (San Francisco: Berrett-Koehler, 2009); and Mike Maddock, "The One Talent That Makes Good Leaders Great," *Forbes* (September 26, 2012), www.forbes.com/sites/mikemaddock/2012/09/26/the-one-talent-that-makes-good-leaders-great/ (accessed March 7, 2013).

world" or as down-to-earth as the Swedish company IKEA's simple vision "to provide affordable furniture for people with limited budgets."

1-3b Aligning Followers

Management entails organizing a structure to accomplish the plan; staffing the structure with employees; and developing policies, procedures, and systems to direct employees and monitor implementation of the plan. Leadership is concerned instead with communicating the vision and developing a shared culture and set of core values that can lead to the desired future state. Whereas the vision describes the destination, the culture and values help define the journey toward it so that everyone is lined up in the same direction.

Leadership provides learning opportunities so people can expand their minds and abilities and assume responsibility for their own actions. Think about classes you have taken at your college or university. In some classes, the professor tells students exactly what to do and how to do it, and many students expect this kind of direction and control. Have you ever had a class where the instructor instead inspired and encouraged you and your classmates to find innovative ways to meet goals? The difference reflects a rational management versus a leadership approach.

1-3c Building Relationships

In terms of relationships, management focuses on getting the most results out of people so that production goals are achieved and goods and services are provided to customers in a timely manner. Leadership, on the other hand, focuses on investing more in people so they are energized and inspired to accomplish goals.

Whereas the management relationship is based on position and formal authority, leadership is a relationship based on personal influence and trust. For example, in an authority relationship, both people accept that a manager can tell a subordinate to be at work at 7:30 A.M. or her pay will be docked. Leadership, on the other hand, relies on influence, which is less likely to use coercion. The role of leadership is to attract and energize people, motivating them through purpose and challenge rather than rewards or punishments.[39] The differing source of power is one of the key distinctions between management and leadership. Take away a manager's formal position, and will people choose to follow her? That is the mark of a leader.

1-3d Developing Personal Leadership Qualities

NEW LEADER
ACTION MEMO

As a leader, you can awaken your leadership qualities of enthusiasm, integrity, courage, and moral commitment. You can make emotional connections with followers to increase your leadership effectiveness.

Leadership is more than a set of skills; it relies on a number of subtle personal qualities that are hard to see but are very powerful. These include things like enthusiasm, integrity, courage, and humility. First of all, good leadership springs from a genuine caring for the work and a genuine concern for other people. The process of management generally encourages emotional distance, but leadership means being emotionally connected to others. Where there is leadership, people become part of a community and feel that they are contributing to something worthwhile. Whereas management means providing answers and solving problems, leadership requires the courage to admit mistakes and doubts, to listen, and to trust and learn from others.

Developing leadership qualities takes work. For leadership to happen, leaders may have to undergo a journey of self-discovery and personal understanding.[40] Leadership experts agree that a top characteristic of effective leaders is that they know who they are and what they stand for. In addition, leaders have the courage to act on their beliefs.

True leaders tend to have open minds that welcome new ideas rather than closed minds that criticize new ideas. Leaders listen and discern what people want and need more than they talk to give advice and orders. Leaders are willing to be nonconformists, to disagree and say no when it serves the larger good, and to accept nonconformity from others rather than try to squeeze everyone into the same mindset.

1-3e Creating Outcomes

The differences between management and leadership create two differing outcomes, as illustrated at the bottom of Exhibit 1.3. Management maintains a degree of stability, predictability, and order through a *culture of efficiency*. Leadership, on the other hand, creates change, often radical change, within a *culture of agility and integrity* that helps the organization thrive over the long haul by promoting openness and honesty, positive relationships, and long-term innovation. Leadership facilitates the courage needed to make difficult and unconventional decisions that may sometimes hurt short-term results.

LEADER'S SELF-INSIGHT 1.2

Your Leadership Potential

Instructions: Questions 1–6 below are about you right now. Questions 7–14 are about how you would like to be if you were the head of a major department at a corporation. Answer Mostly False or Mostly True to indicate whether the item describes you accurately or whether you would strive to perform each activity as a department head.

Now	**Mostly False**	**Mostly True**
1. When I have a number of tasks or homework assignments to do, I set priorities and organize the work to meet the deadlines.	_____	_____
2. When I am involved in a serious disagreement, I hang in there and talk it out until it is completely resolved.	_____	_____
3. I would rather sit in front of my computer than spend a lot of time with people.	_____	_____
4. I reach out to include other people in activities or when there are discussions.	_____	_____
5. I know my long-term vision for career, family, and other activities.	_____	_____
6. When solving problems, I prefer analyzing things myself to working through them with a group of people.	_____	_____

Head of Major Department	**Mostly False**	**Mostly True**
7. I would help subordinates clarify goals and how to reach them.	_____	_____
8. I would give people a sense of long-term mission and higher purpose.	_____	_____
9. I would make sure jobs get out on time.	_____	_____
10. I would scout for new product or service opportunities.	_____	_____
11. I would give credit to people who do their jobs well.	_____	_____
12. I would promote unconventional beliefs and values.	_____	_____
13. I would establish procedures to help the department operate smoothly.	_____	_____
14. I would verbalize the higher values that I and the organization stand for.	_____	_____

Scoring and Interpretation

Count the number of Mostly True answers to even-numbered questions: _____. Count the number of Mostly True answers to odd-numbered questions: _____. Compare the two scores.

The even-numbered items represent behaviors and activities typical of leadership. Leaders are personally involved in shaping ideas, values, vision, and change. They often use an intuitive approach to develop fresh ideas and seek new directions for the department or organization. The odd-numbered items are considered more traditional management activities. Managers respond to organizational problems in an impersonal way, make rational decisions, and work for stability and efficiency.

If you answered yes to more even-numbered than odd-numbered items, you may have potential leadership qualities. If you answered yes to more odd-numbered items, you may have management qualities. Management qualities are an important foundation for new leaders because the organization first has to operate efficiently. Then leadership qualities can enhance performance. Both sets of qualities can be developed or improved with awareness and experience.

Sources: Based on John P. Kotter, *Leading Change* (Boston, MA: Harvard Business School Press, 1996), p. 26; Joseph C. Rost, *Leadership for the Twenty-first Century* (Westport, CT: Praeger, 1993), p. 149; and Brian Dumaine, "The New Non-Manager Managers," *Fortune* (February 22, 1993), pp. 80–84.

1-4 EVOLVING THEORIES OF LEADERSHIP

To understand leadership as it is viewed and practiced today, it is important to recognize that the concept of leadership has changed over time. Leadership typically reflects the larger society, and theories have evolved as norms, attitudes, and understandings in the larger world have changed.[41]

1-4a Historical Overview of Major Approaches

The various leadership theories can be categorized into six basic approaches, each of which is briefly described in this section. Many of these ideas are still applicable to leadership studies today and are discussed in various chapters of this text.

Great Man Theories This is the granddaddy of leadership concepts. The earliest studies of leadership adopted the belief that leaders (who were always thought of as male) were born with certain heroic leadership traits and natural abilities of power and influence. In organizations, social movements, religions, governments, and the military, leadership was conceptualized as a single "Great Man" who put everything together and influenced others to follow along based on the strength of inherited traits, qualities, and abilities.

Trait Theories Studies of these larger-than-life leaders spurred research into the various traits that defined a leader. Beginning in the 1920s, researchers looked to see if leaders had particular traits or characteristics, such as intelligence or energy, that distinguished them from nonleaders and contributed to success. It was thought that if traits could be identified, leaders could be predicted, or perhaps even trained. Although research failed to produce a list of traits that would always guarantee leadership success, the interest in leadership characteristics has continued to the present day.

Behavior Theories The failure to identify a universal set of leadership traits led researchers in the early 1950s to begin looking at what a leader does rather than who he or she is. One line of research focused on what leaders actually do on the job, such as various management activities, roles, and responsibilities. These studies were soon expanded to try to determine how effective leaders differ in their behavior from ineffective ones. Researchers looked at how a leader behaved toward followers and how this correlated with leadership effectiveness or ineffectiveness. Chapter 2 discusses trait and behavior theories.

Contingency Theories Researchers next began to consider the contextual and situational variables that influence what leadership behaviors will be effective. The idea behind contingency theories is that leaders can analyze their situations and tailor their behavior to improve leadership effectiveness. Major situational variables are the characteristics of followers, characteristics of the work environment and follower tasks, and the external environment. Contingency theories, sometimes called *situational theories*, emphasize that leadership cannot be understood in a vacuum separate from various elements of the group or organizational situation. Chapter 3 covers contingency theories.

Influence Theories These theories examine influence processes between leaders and followers. One primary topic of study is *charismatic leadership* (Chapter 12), which refers to leadership influence based not on position or formal authority but, rather, on the qualities and charismatic personality of the leader. Related areas of study are *leadership vision* (Chapter 13) and *organizational culture* (Chapter 14). Leaders influence people to change by providing an inspiring vision of the future and shaping the culture and values needed to attain it. Several chapters of this text relate to the topic of influence because it is essential to understanding leadership.

Relational Theories Since the late 1970s, many ideas of leadership have focused on the relational aspect, that is, how leaders and followers interact and influence one another. Rather than being seen as something a leader does to a follower, leadership is viewed as a relational process that meaningfully engages all participants and enables each person to contribute to achieving the vision. Interpersonal relationships are seen as the most important facet of leadership effectiveness.[42] Two significant relational theories are *transformational leadership* (Chapter 12) and *servant leadership* (Chapter 6).

Other important relational topics covered in various chapters of the text include the personal qualities that leaders need to build effective relationships, such as emotional intelligence, a leader's mind, integrity and high moral standards, and personal courage. In addition, leaders build relationships through motivation and empowerment, leadership communication, team leadership, and embracing diversity.

1-4b A Model of Leadership Evolution

Exhibit 1.4 provides a framework for examining the evolution of leadership from the early Great Man theories to today's relational theories. Each cell in the model summarizes an era of leadership thinking that was dominant in its time but may be less appropriate for today's world.[43]

Leadership Era 1 This era may be conceptualized as pre-industrial and pre-bureaucratic. Most organizations were small and were run by a single individual who many times hired workers because they were friends or relatives, not necessarily

EXHIBIT 1.4 Leadership Evolution

Scope \ Environment	Stable	Turbulent
Organization	**Era 2** **Rational Management** • Behavior theories • Contingency theories Organization: • Vertical hierarchy, bureaucracy • Functional management	**Era 3** **Team or Lateral Leadership** • Influence theories Organization: • Horizontal organization • Cross-functional teams
Individual	**Era 1** **Great Person Leadership** • Great Man theories • Trait theories Organization: • Pre-bureaucratic organization • Administrative principles	**Era 4** **Agile Leadership** • Relational theories • Level 5 leadership Organization: • High-performance culture • Shared vision, alignment • Facilitate change and adaptation

because of their skills or qualifications. The size and simplicity of organizations and the stable nature of the environment made it easy for a single person to understand the big picture, coordinate and control all activities, and keep things on track. This is the era of Great Man leadership and the emphasis on personal traits of leaders. A leader was conceptualized as a single hero who saw the big picture and how everything fit into a whole.

Leadership Era 2 In Era 2, we see the emergence of hierarchy and bureaucracy. Although the world remains stable, organizations have begun to grow so large that they require rules and standard procedures to ensure that activities are performed efficiently and effectively. Hierarchies of authority provide a sensible mechanism for supervision and control of workers, and decisions once based on rules of thumb or tradition are replaced with precise procedures. This era sees the rise of the "rational manager" who directs and controls others using an impersonal approach. Employees aren't expected to think for themselves; they are expected to do as they're told, follow rules and procedures, and accomplish specific tasks. The focus is on details rather than the big picture.

The rational manager was well-suited to a stable environment. The behavior and contingency theories worked here because leaders could analyze their situation, develop careful plans, and control what happened. But rational management is no longer sufficient for leadership in today's world.

NEW LEADER
ACTION MEMO

As a leader, you can use the leadership skills that fit the correct era for your organization. You can use influence and relational aspects as appropriate for your organization.

Leadership Era 3 This era represented a tremendous shock to managers in North America and Europe. Suddenly, the world was no longer stable, and the prized techniques of rational management were no longer successful. Beginning with the OPEC oil embargo of 1972 to 1973 and continuing with the severe global competition of the 1980s and early 1990s, many managers saw that environmental conditions had become chaotic. The Japanese began to dominate world commerce with their ideas of team leadership and superb quality. This became an era of great confusion for leaders. They tried team-based approaches, downsizing, reengineering, quality programs, and empowerment as ways to improve performance and get more motivation and commitment from employees.

This is the era of the team leader and the change leader. Influence was important because of the need to change organizational structures and cultures. This era sees the emergence of knowledge work, an emphasis on horizontal collaboration, and a shift to influence theories. Rather than conceiving of leadership as one person always being firmly "in charge," leadership is often shared among team leaders and members, shifting to the person with the most knowledge or expertise in the matter at hand.[44]

Leadership Era 4 Enter the digital, mobile, social-media age. It seems that everything is changing, and changing fast. Era 4 represents **agile leadership**, which means giving up control in the traditional sense to ensure organizational flexibility and responsiveness to a changing world. Leaders influence others through relationships and networks and through shared vision and values rather than through hierarchical power and control. Agile leaders are constantly experimenting, learning, and changing, in both their personal and professional lives, and they encourage the development and growth of other people and the organization. Era 4 requires the full scope of leadership that goes far beyond rational management or even team leadership.

Agile leadership
giving up control in the traditional sense and encouraging the growth and development of others to ensure organizational flexibility and responsiveness

Implications The flow from Great Man leadership to rational management to team leadership to agile leadership illustrates trends in the larger world. The implication is that leadership reflects the era or context of the organization and society. Most of today's organizations and leaders are still struggling with the transition from a stable to a chaotic environment and the new skills and qualities needed in this circumstance. Thus, Era 3 issues of diversity, team leadership, empowerment, and horizontal relationships are increasingly relevant. In addition, many leaders are rapidly shifting into Era 4 leadership by focusing on change management and facilitating a vision and values to encourage high performance, agility, and continuous adaptation in a fast-shifting world. Agile leaders align themselves with new social technologies that can create networks of leaders throughout the organization. Era 3 and Era 4 leadership is what much of this book is about.

1-5 LEADERSHIP CAN BE LEARNED

Many leaders are caught in the transition between the practices and principles that defined the industrial era and the new reality of the twenty-first century. Attempts to achieve collaboration, empowerment, and diversity in organizations may fail because the beliefs and thought processes of leaders as well as employees are stuck in an old paradigm that values control, stability, and homogeneity. It is difficult for many leaders to let go of methods and practices that have made them and their organizations successful in the past. Yet leaders can make the leap to a new paradigm by intentionally practicing and applying new paradigm principles.

NEW LEADER
ACTION MEMO

Leader's Self-Insight 1.3 gives you a chance to test your people skills and see if there are areas you need to work on.

1-5a Leader Fatal Flaws

One of the most important aspects of shifting to the new paradigm of leadership is intentionally using soft, interpersonal skills to build a culture of performance, trust, and collaboration. A few clues about the importance of acquiring new leadership skills are brought to light by studies that look at what causes managers to "derail" in their careers. **Derailment** refers to a phenomenon in organizations in which a manager with an impressive track record reaches a certain level but goes off track and can't advance because of a mismatch between job needs and the manager's personal skills and qualities.[45] Studies conducted in numerous organizations in different countries indicate that managers fail more frequently because they are deficient with soft, human skills rather than a lack of hard work or technical skills.[46] Derailed managers are successful people who excelled in a functional area and were expected to go far, but they reached a plateau, were fired, or were forced to retire early.

Researchers at the Center for Creative Leadership in Greensboro, North Carolina, have been looking at what causes manager derailment for two decades.[47] They conclude that there are five top flaws that cause managers to derail, as shown in Exhibit 1.5. Note that many of these flaws relate to the lack of human skills. Unsuccessful managers fail to meet business objectives because they spend too much time promoting themselves rather than working. They are overly ambitious and selfish and may not follow through on promises. They are often insensitive and critical, not trustworthy, do not learn from feedback and mistakes, can't build and develop the right teams, and are unable to see the big picture when promoted into a general management position. Additional studies confirm that the biggest leader mistakes are people mistakes rather than technical ones.[48]

Derailment
a phenomenon in which a manager with an impressive track record reaches a certain level but goes off track and can't advance because of a mismatch between job needs and personal skills and qualities

LEADER'S SELF-INSIGHT 1.3

Are You on a Fast Track to Nowhere?

Instructions: Many people on the fast track toward positions of leadership find themselves suddenly derailed and don't know why. Many times, a lack of people skills is to blame. To help you determine whether you need to work on your people skills, take the following quiz, answering each item as Mostly False or Mostly True. Think about a job or volunteer position you have now or have held in the past as you answer the following items.

People Skills	Mostly False	Mostly True
1. Other people describe me as very good with people.	______	______
2. I often smile and laugh with teammates or classmates.	______	______
3. I often reach out to engage people, even strangers.	______	______
4. I often express appreciation to other people.	______	______

Dealing with Authority	Mostly False	Mostly True
1. I quickly speak out in meetings when leaders ask for comments or ideas.	______	______
2. If I see a leader making a decision that seems harmful, I speak up.	______	______
3. I experience no tension when interacting with senior managers, either inside or outside the organization.	______	______
4. I have an easy time asserting myself toward people in authority.	______	______

Networking	Mostly False	Mostly True
1. I spend part of each week networking with colleagues in other departments.	______	______
2. I have joined multiple organizations for the purpose of making professional contacts.	______	______
3. I often use lunches to meet and network with new people.	______	______
4. I actively maintain contact with peers from previous organizations.	______	______

Scoring and Interpretation

Tally the number of "Mostly Trues" checked for each set of questions.

People Skills: ______ Dealing with Authority: ______ Networking: ______

If you scored 4 in an area, you're right on track. Continue to act in the same way.

If your score is 2 – 3, you can fine-tune your skills in that area. Review the questions where you said Mostly False and work to add those abilities to your leadership skill set.

A score of 0 – 1 indicates that you may end up dangerously close to derailment. You should take the time to do an in-depth self-assessment and find ways to expand your interpersonal skills.

EXHIBIT 1.5 Five Fatal Flaws That Cause Derailment

1. Performance Problems	2. Problems with Relationships	3. Difficulty Changing	4. Difficulty Building and Leading a Team	5. Too Narrow Management Experience
Failing to meet business objectives because of too much time promoting themselves and playing politics, a failure to fulfill promises, or a lack of attention to priorities.	*Being insensitive, manipulative, critical, and not trustworthy in relationships with peers, direct reports, customers, and others.*	*Not learning from feedback and mistakes to change old behaviors; defensive, unable to handle pressure, unable to change management style to meet new demands.*	*Poor management of direct reports; inability to get work done through others; not identifying and hiring the right people.*	*Inability to work effectively or collaborate outside their current function; failing to see big picture when moved into general management position over several functions.*

Source: Based on Yi Zhang, Jean Brittain Leslie, and Kelly M. Hannum, "Trouble Ahead: Derailment Is Alive and Well," *Thunderbird International Business Review* 55, no. 1 (January–February 2013), pp. 95–102.

1-5b Leader Good Behaviors

The best leaders, at all levels, are those who are genuinely interested in other people and find ways to bring out the best in them.[49] Successful organizations, such as Google, pay attention to developing leaders in the soft skills needed to effectively lead technical people in a changing environment.

IN THE LEAD

Google

In 2015, Google was named the best company to work for by *Fortune* magazine for the sixth year in a row. Being a great place to work didn't happen by accident. Google's human resources department, called People Operations—or POPS for short—monitors employees' happiness and well-being to an incredible degree, using data to track everything and learn where improvements are needed.

One thing it discovered is that good leaders make a tremendous difference. Google looked at what successful leaders—those who have lower attrition rates and get better performance from their teams—do that makes them different from less successful ones. Analyzing performance reviews and feedback surveys, Google executives used the findings to help make bad leaders better. Even in a company that depends on technical expertise, Google found that soft, human skills are essential. Technical expertise ranked dead last among eight desirable leader qualities, as shown in "Google's Eight Rules for Good Leader Behavior."

Google discovered that employees want leaders who listen to them, build positive and productive relationships, and show an interest in their lives and careers. Google incorporates these eight desirable leader behaviors into leadership performance and evaluation systems as well as into feedback and training programs. When the company targeted unsuccessful leaders and coached them to develop soft skills and display these eight behaviors, the managerial ranks improved, with collective feedback scores going up every year since 2009.[50]

Google's Eight Rules for Good Leader Behavior

1. Be a good coach.
2. Empower your team and don't micromanage.
3. Express interest in team members' success and personal well-being.
4. Don't be a sissy. Be productive and results-oriented.
5. Be a good communicator and listen to your team.
6. Help your employees with career development.
7. Have a clear vision and strategy for the team.
8. Have key technical skills so you can help advise the team.[51]

NEW LEADER
ACTION MEMO

As a leader, you can cultivate your people skills to avoid executive derailment. You can treat others with kindness, interest, and respect and avoid overmanaging by selecting good followers and delegating effectively.

The skills on Google's list of desirable behaviors can help leaders avoid the fatal flaws that derail careers. In addition, today's successful leaders intentionally value change over stability, empowerment over control, collaboration over competition, diversity over uniformity, and integrity over self-interest, as discussed earlier. The industry of *executive coaching* emerged partly to help people through the transition to a new paradigm of leadership. Executive coaches encourage leaders to confront their own flaws and hang-ups that inhibit effective leadership, and then help them develop stronger emotional and interpersonal skills.

1-6 MASTERING THE ART AND SCIENCE OF LEADERSHIP

There's an age-old question: Are leaders born or made? In one survey, 19 percent of top executives said leaders are born, 52 percent said they are made, and 29 percent said they are both born and made.[52] It may be true that some inborn qualities and personality characteristics can provide a foundation for being a good leader, but most people can learn to be good leaders no matter their innate characteristics. Interestingly, in the above-mentioned survey, both those who thought leaders are born and those who thought they are made mention learning from experience as a key to becoming a good leader.

Leadership can be learned, but it is important to remember that leadership is both an art and a science. It is an art because many leadership skills and qualities cannot be learned from a textbook. Leadership takes practice and hands-on experience, as well as intense personal exploration and development. However, leadership is also a science because a growing body of knowledge and objective facts describes the leadership process and how to use leadership skills to attain organizational goals. This is where a textbook or a course on leadership can help you to be a better leader.

Knowing about leadership research helps people analyze situations from a variety of perspectives and learn how to be more effective. By exploring leadership in both business and society, students gain an understanding of the importance of leadership to an organization's success, as well as the difficulties and challenges involved in being a leader. Studying leadership can also lead to the discovery of abilities you never knew you had. When students in a leadership seminar at Wharton were asked to pick one leader to represent the class, one woman was surprised when she outpolled all other students. Her leadership was drawn out not in the practice of leadership in student government, volunteer activities, or athletics but in a classroom setting.[53] Studying leadership gives you skills you can apply to the practice of leadership in your everyday life. Exhibit 1.6 gives some tips for how you can begin honing your leadership skills.

Many people have never tried to be leaders because they have no understanding of what leaders actually do. The chapters in this book are designed to help you gain a firm knowledge of what leadership means and some of the skills and qualities that make a good leader. You can build competence in both the art and the science of leadership by completing the Self-Insight exercises throughout the book, by working on the activities and cases at the end of each chapter, and by applying the concepts you learn in class, in your relationships with others, in student groups, at work, and in voluntary organizations. Although this book and your instructors can guide you in your development, only you can apply the concepts and principles of leadership in your daily life. Learning to be a leader starts now, with you. Are you up to the challenge?

1-7 ORGANIZATION OF THIS BOOK

The plan for this book reflects the shift to a new paradigm summarized in Exhibit 1.2 and the discussion of management versus leadership summarized in Exhibit 1.3. The framework in Exhibit 1.7 illustrates the organization of the book.

Part 1 introduces leadership, its importance, and the transition to a new leadership paradigm. Part 2 explores basic research perspectives that evolved during a more stable time when rational management approaches were effective. These basic

EXHIBIT 1.6 Learning to Be a Leader

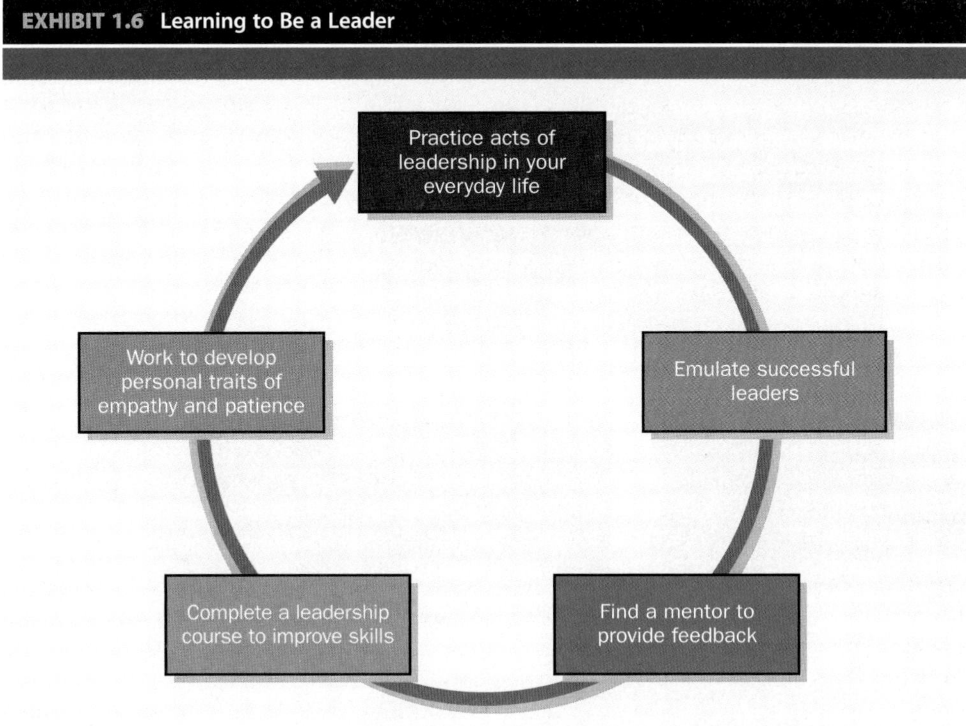

Source: Based on "Guidelines for the Apprentice Leader," in Robert J. Allio, "Masterclass: Leaders and Leadership—Many Theories, But What Advice Is Reliable?" *Strategy & Leadership* 41, no. 1 (2013), pp. 4–14.

perspectives, including the Great Man and trait theories, behavior theories, and contingency theories, are relevant to dealing with specific tasks and individuals and are based on a premise that leaders can predict and control various aspects of the environment to keep the organization running smoothly.

Parts 3, 4, and 5 focus on leadership perspectives that reflect the paradigm shift to the turbulent, unpredictable nature of the environment and the need for fresh leader approaches. Part 3 discusses the personal side of leadership and looks at some of the qualities and forces that are required to be effective in the new reality. These chapters emphasize the importance of self-awareness and self-understanding, the development of one's own leadership mind and heart, moral leadership and courage, and appreciating the role of followership. Part 4 is about building effective relationships, including motivating and empowering others, communicating as a leader, leading teams, embracing the diversity of today's world, and using power and influence.

Part 5 brings together all of these ideas to examine the leader as builder of a social architecture that can help an organization create a brighter future. These chapters deal with creating vision and strategic direction, aligning culture and values to achieve the vision, and leading change.

Taken together, the sections and chapters paint a complete portrait of the leadership experience as it has evolved to the present day and emphasize the new paradigm skills and qualities that are relevant from today and into the future. This book blends systematic research evidence with real-world experiences and impact.

EXHIBIT 1.7 Framework for the Book

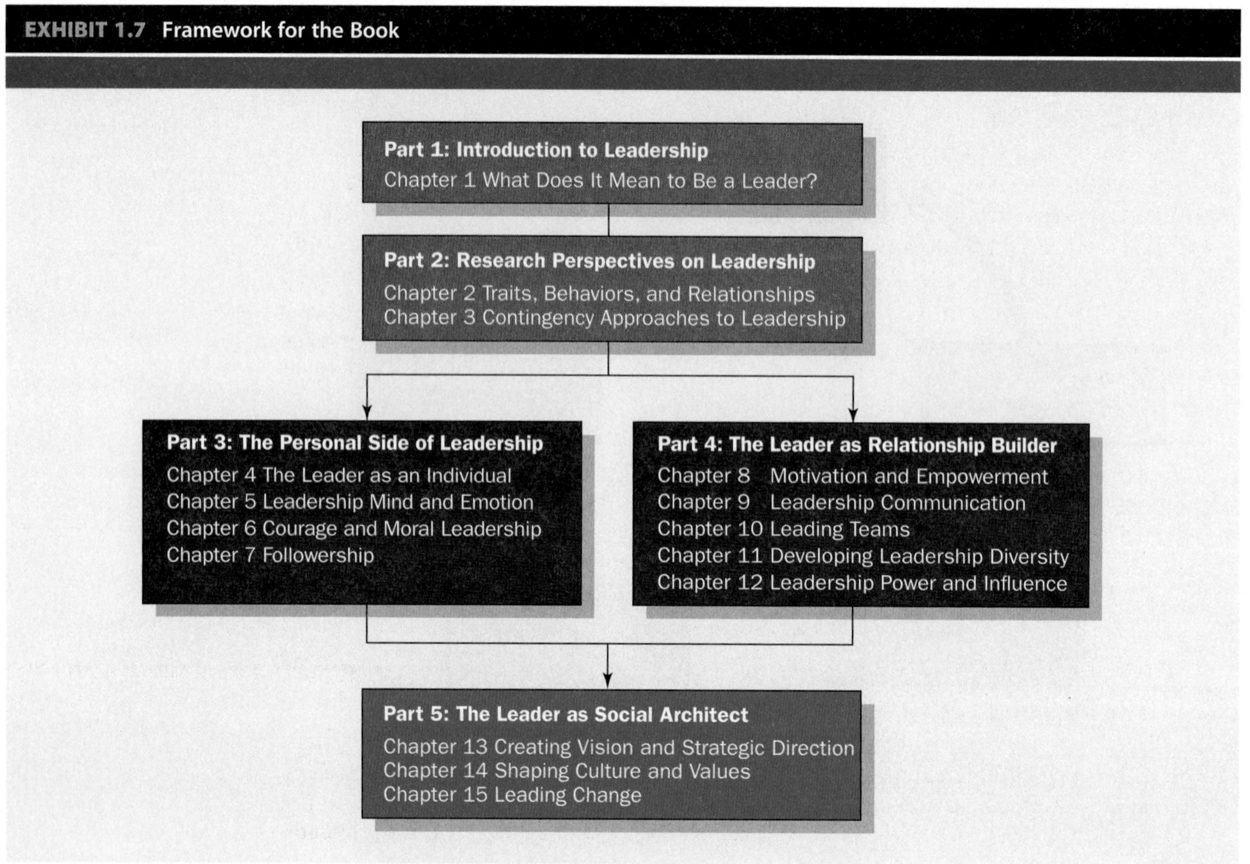

LEADERSHIP ESSENTIALS

- This chapter introduced the concept of leadership and explained how individuals can grow as leaders. Leadership is defined as an influence relationship among leaders and followers who intend real changes and outcomes that reflect their shared purposes. Thus leadership involves people in a relationship, influence, change, a shared purpose, and taking personal responsibility to make things happen. Most of us are aware of famous leaders, but most leadership that changes the world starts small and may begin with personal frustrations about events that prompt people to initiate change and inspire others to follow them. Your leadership may be expressed in the classroom, at work, or in your neighborhood, religious community, or volunteer organizations.
- Concepts of leadership have evolved over time. Major research approaches include Great Man theories, trait theories, behavior theories, contingency theories, influence theories, and relational theories. Elements of all these approaches are still applicable to the study of leadership.
- The biggest challenge facing leaders today is the changing world that wants a new paradigm of leadership. The new reality involves the shift from stability to change, from control to empowerment, from competition to collaboration, and from uniformity to diversity. In addition, the concept of leader as hero is giving way to that

of the humble leader who develops others and shares credit for accomplishments. These dramatic changes suggest that a philosophy based on control and personal ambition will probably fail in the new era. The challenge for leaders is to evolve to a new mindset that relies on human skills, integrity, and teamwork.

- The "soft" skills of leadership complement the "hard" skills of management, and both are needed to effectively guide organizations. Although leadership is often equated with good management, leadership and management are different processes. Management strives to maintain stability and improve efficiency. Leadership, on the other hand, is about creating a vision for the future, designing social architecture that shapes culture and values, inspiring and motivating followers, developing personal qualities, and creating change within a culture of integrity. Leadership can be integrated with management to achieve the greatest possible outcomes. Organizations need to be both managed and led, particularly in today's turbulent environment. Many managers already have the qualities needed to be effective leaders, but they may not have gone through the process needed to bring these qualities to life. Leadership is an intentional act. It is important to remember that most people are not born with natural leadership skills and qualities, but leadership can be learned and developed.

DISCUSSION QUESTIONS

1. Look through recent magazines and newspapers and identify one leader who seems to illustrate the "leader-as-hero" mindset and one who seems more typical of the humble Level 5 leader described in the text. Describe their differing characteristics. Which was easier to find?
2. What do you consider your own strengths and weaknesses for leadership? Discuss your answer with another student.
3. Of the elements in the leadership definition as illustrated in Exhibit 1.1, which is the easiest for you? Which is hardest? Explain.
4. How might the paradigm shift from competition to collaboration make the job of a leader more difficult? Could it also make the leader's job easier? Discuss.
5. Describe the best leader you have known. How did this leader acquire his or her capability?
6. Why do you think there are so few people who succeed at both management and leadership? Is it reasonable to believe someone can be good at both? Discuss.
7. Discuss some recent events and societal changes that might have contributed to a shift "from hero to humble." Do you agree or disagree that humility is important for good leadership?
8. "Leadership is more concerned with people than is management." Do you agree? Discuss.
9. What personal capacities should a person develop to be a good leader versus those developed to be a good manager?
10. Why is leadership considered both an art and a science?

LEADERSHIP AT WORK

Leadership Right–Wrong

Leader Wrong: Think of a specific situation in which you were working with someone who was in a leadership position over you and that person was doing something that was wrong for you. This person might have been a coach, teacher, team leader, employer, immediate boss, family member, or anyone who had a leadership position over you. "Wrong for you" means that person's behavior reduced your effectiveness, made you or your coworkers less productive, and was demotivating to you or your colleagues. *Write a few words below that describe what the leader was doing that was wrong for you.*

___

___

___

Think of a second situation in which someone in a leadership position did something wrong for you. *Write a few words below that describe what the leader was doing that was wrong for you.*

___

___

___

Leader Right: Think of a specific situation in which you were working with someone who was in a leadership position over you and that person was doing something that was *right* for you. This person might have been a coach, teacher, team leader, employer, immediate boss, family member, or anyone who had a leadership position over you. "Right for you" means that person's behavior made you or your coworkers more productive, highly motivated you or others, and removed barriers to make you more successful. *Write a few words below that describe what the leader was doing that was right for you.*

___

___

___

Think of a second situation in which someone in a leadership position did something right for you. *Write a few words below that describe what the leader was doing that was right for you.*

___

___

___

The previous answers are data points that can help you understand the impact of leader behaviors. Analyze your four incidents—what are the underlying qualities of leadership that enable you to be an effective performer? Discuss your answers with another student. What leadership themes are present in the eight combined incidents? What do these responses tell you about the qualities you want and don't want in your leaders?

In Class: An interesting way to use this exercise in class is to have students write (five words maximum) their leader "rights" on one board and their leader "wrongs" on another board. The instructor can ask small groups to identify underlying themes in the collective set of leader data points on the boards to specify what makes an effective leader. After students establish four or five key themes, they can be challenged to identify the one key theme that distinguishes leaders who are effective from those who are not.

Source: Based on Melvin R. McKnight, "Organizational Behavior as a Phenomenological, Free-Will Centered Science," Working Paper, College of Business Administration, Northern Arizona University, 1997.

LEADERSHIP DEVELOPMENT: CASES FOR ANALYSIS

Sales Engineering Division

When DGL International, a manufacturer of refinery equipment, brought in John Terrill to manage its Sales Engineering division, company executives informed him of the urgent situation. Sales Engineering, with 20 engineers, was the highest-paid, best-educated, and least-productive division in the company. The instructions to Terrill: Turn it around. Terrill called a meeting of the engineers. He showed great concern for their personal welfare and asked point blank: "What's the problem? Why can't we produce? Why does this division have such turnover?"

Without hesitation, employees launched a hail of complaints. "I was hired as an engineer, not a pencil pusher." "We spend over half of our time writing asinine reports in triplicate for top management, and no one reads the reports." "We have to account for every penny, which doesn't give us time to work with customers or new developments."

After a two-hour discussion, Terrill began to envision a future in which engineers were free to work with customers and join self-directed teams for product improvement. Terrill concluded he had to get top management off the engineers' backs. He promised the engineers, "My job is to stay out of your way so you can do your work, and I'll try to keep top management off your backs, too." He called for the day's reports and issued an order effective immediately that the originals be turned in daily to his office rather than mailed to headquarters. For three weeks, technical reports piled up on his desk. By month's end, the stack was nearly three feet high. During that time no one called for the reports. When other managers entered his office and saw the stack, they usually asked, "What's all this?" Terrill answered, "Technical reports." No one asked to read them.

Finally, at month's end, a secretary from finance called and asked for the monthly travel and expense report. Terrill responded, "Meet me in the president's office tomorrow morning."

The next morning the engineers cheered as Terrill walked through the department pushing a cart loaded with the enormous stack of reports. They knew the showdown had come.

Terrill entered the president's office and placed the stack of reports on his desk. The president and the other senior executives looked bewildered.

"This," Terrill announced, "is the reason for the lack of productivity in the Sales Engineering division. These are the reports your people require every month. The fact that they sat on my desk all month shows that no one reads this material. I suggest that the engineers' time could be used in a more productive manner, and that one brief monthly report from my office will satisfy the needs of the other departments."

QUESTIONS

1. Does John Terrill's leadership style fit the definition of leadership in Exhibit 1.1? Is it part of a leader's job to manage upward? Explain.
2. With respect to Exhibit 1.4, in what leadership era is Terrill? In what era is headquarters? Explain.
3. What approach would you have taken in this situation? What do you think the response of the senior executives will be to Terrill's action?

The Marshall Plan

Marshall Gordon was recognized by associates and competitors as *a man on a mission.* One of four members of the design team for a large chair manufacturing corporation, Marshall's obsession with the creation of comfortable seating dated to a childhood back injury and a lifetime of pain. He recognized, more than most in the industry, the importance of designing chairs that offered some relief to those suffering from debilitating back, hip, and neck pain as well as helping people of all ages to avoid problems with proper posture. In his early days with the company the staff jokingly called his approach the Marshall Plan, after America's 1947 initiative (named for Secretary of State George Marshall) to rebuild European economies after the war. Like someone fighting to save the world, Marshall Gordon brought passion and a creative intensity to design meetings as if each drawing, each design tweak would change civilization as we knew it.

Single and with no apparent family or friendship ties, Marshall was married to his work. He seemed to thrive on 70-hour work weeks, although as a salaried manager, he received no overtime pay. Even his "down time" at meals or on weekends was spent sketching, studying the latest in ergonomics, or reconnoitering each design adjustment by competitors.

"When you visit a furniture store, you fully expect to see Marshall, skulking about in trench coat and hat, checking to see what the competition is offering," says fellow team member John Craddock. "We all laugh about it. The guy brings—actually brings—chairs to meetings and tears them apart to show us some miniscule *discovery*."

This obsession with chairs, pain and gravity, and one-upping the competition has made Marshall a valuable employee and earned him a reputation in the industry for creative design. Not since Peter Opsvik's Gravity Balans ergonomic chair of the 1970s has anyone made such an impact on the industry. The effect of Marshall's work on company profits is undeniable. The fact that competitors are chomping at the bit to lure him away is also undeniable.

But the Marshall Plan comes at a price. Over the 15 years he has worked with the company, five as leader of the design group, there has been a constant turnover within the design group as frustrated workers leave the company to "get away from Marshall."

"Anything you could learn from this brilliant and dedicated man is destroyed by his cold, calculating attitude," Craddock complains. "I came to this company excited about the chance to work with him. But any knowledge he possesses is carefully guarded. His design ideas are perfect, while ours are picked apart. We all swear he has listening devices scattered around everywhere, because if the rest of the team huddles in some corner of the world to discuss a design idea, *voila*! He walks into the next meeting with *our* idea. Once when he was a few minutes late to a meeting, we thought we had beaten him and quickly presented our idea. Just then, he walks in, and announces, 'Ideas must be in the air. I have something very similar,' and throws his completed design on screen. Guess who won."

Marshall presents a continuing challenge to company management, having both incredible positive and negative influence on the culture. While his contributions to design and profits far exceed those of other employees, his negative effect on the culture and his team's creativity and morale results in the loss of talented people and a climate of suspicion and discontent. His threat, "I can take my talents elsewhere," hangs over top management like a sledge hammer.

Now, Craddock and Leslie Warren, other talented members of the design team, have approached management with their own ultimatum: *Do something about Marshall or we resign.*

QUESTIONS

1. If you were a top leader, how would you respond to the ultimatum? Be specific. Explain why.
2. What is Marshall missing with respect to his leadership abilities? How do you explain his poor leadership behavior?
3. If you were Marshall's manager, how might you increase Marshall's awareness of the negative impact he is having on his team? How would you guide him toward better team leadership, sharing his knowledge with others, and mentoring his team members?

REFERENCES

1. Nancy F. Koehn, "Lincoln's School of Management," *The New York Times* (January 26, 2013); Catherine L. Moreton, "10 Qualities That Make Abraham Lincoln a Great Leader," *HR and Employment Law White Papers, Business and Legal Resources* (June 25, 2008), https://hr.blr.com/whitepapers/Staffing-Training/Leadership/10-Qualities-that-Made-Abraham-Lincoln-a-Great-Lea (accessed March 4, 2013); Hitendra Wadhwa, "Lessons in Leadership: How Lincoln Became America's Greatest President," *Inc.com* (February 12, 2012), http://www.inc.com/hitendra-wadhwa/lessons-in-leadership-how-abraham-lincoln-became-americas-greatest-president.html (accessed March 4, 2013); and Richard Brookhiser, "What Would Lincoln Do" Modern-Day Leaders Could Learn a Lot from Our 16th President (February 14, 2014),

http://online.wsj.com/news/articles/SB10001424052702303704304579382882084406374?mod=WSJ_hppMIDDLENexttoWhatsNewsSecond (accessed October 5, 2015). The Howard Schultz quote is from Koehn.
2. David Rothkopf, "Somebody Take Control. (Anybody. Really. Please.): Where Are All the Leaders?" *The Washington Post* (March 29, 2009), p. B1.
3. Thanks to Doug Moran, "Great Leadership," *Leadership Excellence* (September 2011), p. 18, for this analogy.
4. John F. Burns and Stephen Castle, "BBC's Leaders Faulted as Lax in Handling Sex Abuse Crisis," *The New York Times* (December 19, 2012), http://www.nytimes.com/2012/12/20/world/europe/pollard-report-bbc-jimmy-savile-sexual-abuse-inquiry.html?pagewanted=all&_r=0 (accessed March 4, 2013).
5. "Sen. Grassley Probes Televangelists' Finances," *USA TODAY* (November 7, 2007), http://usatoday30.usatoday.com/news/washington/2007-11-07-televangelist-probe_N.htm (accessed March 4, 2013).
6. See various surveys and studies reported in Paul Harris, "Leadership Role Models Earn Trust and Profits," *T+D* 64, no. 3 (2010), pp. 47–50.
7. Gary Cohen, "Defining Leadership," *Leadership Excellence* (August 2009), pp. 16–17; Warren Bennis and Burt Nanus, *Leaders: The Strategies for Taking Charge* (New York: Harper & Row, 1985), p. 4; and James MacGregor Burns, *Leadership* (New York: Harper & Row, 1978), p. 2.
8. J. Meindl, S. Ehrlich, and J. Dukerich, "The Romance of Leadership," *Administrative Science Quarterly* 30 (1985), pp. 78–102; and Mitchell C. Bligh, Jeffrey C. Kohles, and Rajnandini Pillai, "Romancing Leadership: Past, Present, Future," *The Leadership Quarterly* 22 (2011), pp. 1058–1077.
9. Rakesh Khurana, "The Curse of the Superstar CEO," *Harvard Business Review* (September 2002), pp. 60–66.
10. Khurana, "The Curse of the Superstar CEO"; Mitch McCrimmon, "The Ideal Leader," *Ivey Business Journal* (January–February 2011); Joseph A. Raelin, "The Myth of Charismatic Leaders," *Training and Development* (March 2003), p. 46; and Betsy Morris, "The New Rules," *Fortune* (July 24, 2006), pp. 70–87.
11. Joseph C. Rost, *Leadership for the Twenty-First Century* (Westport, CT: Praeger, 1993), p. 102; and Joseph C. Rost and Richard A. Barker, "Leadership Education in Colleges: Toward a 21st Century Paradigm," *The Journal of Leadership Studies* 7, no. 1 (2000), pp. 3–12.
12. Peter B. Smith and Mark F. Peterson, *Leadership, Organizations, and Culture: An Event Management Model* (London: Sage Publications, 1988), p. 14.
13. Robert E. Kelley, "In Praise of Followers," *Harvard Business Review* (November–December 1988), pp. 142–148.
14. Bill George, "Truly Authentic Leadership" (Special Report: America's Best Leaders), *U.S. News & World Report* (October 30, 2006), pp. 52–53; Victoria Strauss, "It's Time for Teach for America to Fold: Former TFAer," (The Answer Sheet blog), *The Washington Post* (February 28, 2013), http://www.washingtonpost.com/blogs/answer-sheet/wp/2013/02/28/its-time-for-teach-for-america-to-fold-former-tfaer/ (accessed March 5, 2013); and "Is Teach for America Working?" (Room for Debate Opinion Page), *The New York Times* (August 30, 2012), http://www.nytimes.com/roomfordebate/2012/08/30/is-teach-for-america-working/ (accessed March 5, 2013).
15. "Barbara Van Dahlen" segment in "The World's 100 Most Influential People 2012," *Time* http://www.time.com/time/specials/packages/article/0,28804,2111975_2111976,00.html (accessed March 4, 2013); and Barbara Van Dahlen, "Recognizing Options for Healing This Veterans Day," *Huffington Post* (November 13, 2012), http://www.huffingtonpost.com/barbara-van-dahlen-phd/veterans-health-care_b_2092411.html (accessed March 4, 2013).
16. Scott R. Schmedel, "Making a Difference," *The Wall Street Journal* (August 21, 2006), pp. R5, R12; and "More Than Wheels: About," http://www.morethanwheels.org/about (accessed March 5, 2012).
17. These changes and challenges are based in part on Thomas W. Malnight and Tracey S. Keys, "The Great Power Shift: 10 Trends Business Leaders Need to Watch in 2013," as reported in "The World in 2013: Global Trends for 2013; A Top Ten for Business Leaders," Cassandra blog, *The Economist* (November 26, 2012), http://www.economist.com/blogs/theworldin2013/2012/11/global-trends-2013 (accessed March 5, 2013). The complete Global Trends 2013 report is available for purchase at http://www.globaltrends.com/reports/gt-2013
18. Center for Creative Leadership survey reported in Andre Martin, "What Is Effective Leadership Today? A New Study Finds Collaboration Prized over Heroics," *Chief Executive* (July–August 2006), p. 24.
19. This discussion is based on Dominic Barton, Andrew Grant, and Michelle Horn, "Leading in the 21st Century," *McKinsey Quarterly*, no. 3 (2012), pp. 30–47; Olivia Parr Rud, "Book Highlight—Adaptability: A Key to Business Intelligence Success," *Global Business and Organizational Excellence* (January–February 2010), pp. 76–85; Ken Shelton, "Reinventing Leadership," *Leadership Excellence* (July 2012), p. 9; Fahri Karakas, "The Twenty-First Century Leader: Social Artist, Spiritual Visionary, and Cultural Innovator," *Global Business and Organizational Excellence* (March/April 2007), pp. 44–50; Daniel C. Kielson, "Leadership: Creating a New Reality," *The Journal of Leadership Studies* 3, no. 4 (1996), pp. 104–116; and Mark A. Abramson, "Leadership for the Future: New Behaviors, New Roles, and New Attitudes," *The Public Manager* (Spring 1997).
20. Norihiko Shirouzu, Phred Dvorak, Yuka Hayashi, and Andrew Morse, "Bid to 'Protect Assets' Slowed Reactor Fight," *The Wall Street Journal* (March 19, 2011), http://online.wsj.com/article/SB10001424052748704608504576207912642629904.html (accessed August 6, 20120); and Peter Valdes-Dapena, "Japan Earthquake Impact Hits U.S. Auto Plants," *CNNMoney* (March 30, 2011), http://money.cnn.com/2011/03/28/autos/japan_earthquake_autos_outlook/index.htm# (accessed June 13, 2012).
21. William Boston and Sarah Sloat, "Volkswagen Emissions Scandal Relates to 11 Million Cars," *The Wall Street Journal* (September 22, 2015), http://www.wsj.com/articles/volkswagen-emissions-scandal-relates-to-11-million-cars-1442916906 (accessed October 5, 2015), and Jack Ewing, "Diesel Scandal at VW Spreads to Core Market," *The New York Times* (September 23, 2015), p. A1.
22. Vanessa Fuhrmans, and Dana Cimilluca, "Business Braces for Europe's Worst—Multinationals Scramble to Protect Cash, Revise Contracts, Tighten Payment Terms," *The Wall Street Journal* (June 1, 2012), p. B1.
23. Quoted in Barton et al., "Leading in the 21st Century."
24. Quoted in Barton et al., "Leading in the 21st Century."
25. Charles Handy, *The Age of Paradox* (Boston: Harvard Business School Press, 1994), pp. 146–147; and Geoff Colvin, "Leader Machines," *Fortune* (October 1, 2007), pp. 98–106.
26. J. P. Donlon, "What, Put Your Customers Second? Are You Kidding?" (CEO Chronicles), *Chief Executive* (November–December 2010), pp. 14–16; "HCL Technologies CEO, Vineet Nayar, Gets 'Leader in the Digital Age' Award at CeBIT 2011," *Entertainment Close-Up* (March 11, 2011); and Stephen Denning, "Masterclass: The Reinvention of Management," *Strategy & Leadership* 39, no. 2 (2011), pp. 9–17.
27. Vineet Nayar, *Employees First, Customers Second: Turning Conventional Management Upside Down* (Boston: Harvard Business Review Press, 2010).
28. Herminia Ibarra and Morten T. Hansen, "Are You a Collaborative Leader?" *Harvard Business Review* (July–August 2011), pp. 69–74.
29. Ibarra and Hansen, "Are You a Collaborative Leader?"; and Sally Helgesen, "Leading in 24/7: What Is Required?" *Leader to Leader* (Summer 2012), pp. 38–43.
30. Barton et al., "Leading in the 21st Century."
31. See James Collins, *Good to Great: Why Some Companies Make the Leap . . . and Others Don't* (New York: HarperCollins, 2001); Charles A. O'Reilly III and Jeffrey Pfeffer, *Hidden Value: How Great Companies Achieve Extraordinary Results with Ordinary People* (Boston:

Harvard Business School Press, 2000); Rakesh Khurana, *Searching for a Corporate Savior: The Irrational Quest for Charismatic CEOs* (Princeton, NJ: Princeton University Press, 2002); Joseph Badaracco, *Leading Quietly* (Boston: Harvard Business School Press, 2002); Jason Jennings, *Think Big, Act Small: How America's Best Performing Companies Keep the Startup Spirit Alive* (New York: Portfolio/Penguin, 2005); Ryan Underwood, "The CEO Next Door," *Fast Company* (September 2005), pp. 64–66; and Linda Tischler, "The CEO's New Clothes," *Fast Company* (September 2005), pp. 27–28.

32. David Brooks, "The Humble Hound," *The New York Times* (April 10, 2010), p. A27; Charalambos A. Vlachoutsicos, "How to Cultivate Engaged Employees," *Harvard Business Review* (September 2011), pp. 123–126; and Rob Nielsen, Jennifer A. Marrone, and Holly S. Slay, "A New Look at Humility: Exploring the Humility Concept and Its Role in Socialized Charismatic Leadership," *Journal of Leadership and Organizational Science* 17, no. 1 (2010), pp. 33–43.
33. Amy Y. Ou, Anne S. Tsui, Angelo J. Kinicki, David A. Waldman, Zhixing Xiao, and Lynda Jiwen Song, "Humble Chief Executive Officers' Connections to Top Management Team Integration and Middle Managers' Responses," *Administrative Science Quarterly* 59, no. 1 (March 2014): 34–72; and Laurie Merrill, "Study Finds Humble Bosses Are Best," *USA Today* (July 30, 2014), http://www.usatoday.com/story/money/business/2014/07/30/asu-study-humble-bosses-b-est/13352105/ (accessed October 5, 2015).
34. Jim Collins, "Level 5 Leadership: The Triumph of Humility and Fierce Resolve," *Harvard Business Review* (January 2001), pp. 67–76; Collins, "Good to Great," *Fast Company* (October 2001), pp. 90–104; Edward Prewitt, "The Utility of Humility," *CIO* (December 1, 2002), pp. 104–110; A. J. Vogl, "Onward and Upward" (an interview with Jim Collins), *Across the Board* (September–October 2001), pp. 29–34; and Stefan Stern, "A New Leadership Blueprint," *Management Today* (October 1, 2010), http://www.managementtoday.co.uk/features/1032244/a-new-blueprint-leaders/ (accessed March 13, 2013).
35. As described in Stefan Stern, "A New Leadership Blueprint," *Management Today* (October 1, 2010), p. 38.
36. Noah Rayman, "5 Leadership Lessons You Can Learn from Pope Francis," *Time* (March 10, 2015), http://time.com/3737887/pope-francis-leadership-lessons/ (accessed October 6, 2015); William Vanderbloemen, "5 Leadership Lessons from Pope Francis," *Fast Company* (September 25, 2015), http://www.fastcompany.com/3051514/know-it-all/5-lessons-every-leader-can-learn-from-pope-francis (accessed October 6, 2015); Minda Zetlin, "Why Pope Francis Is So Effective: 8 Lessons for Every Leader," *Inc.* (August 1, 2014), http://www.inc.com/minda-zetlin/why-pope-francis-is-so-effective-8-lessons-for-every-leader.html (accessed October 6, 2015); Ben Brumfield, "Pope Francis Surprised by Warmth of Americans and Devoutness of the Faithful," *CNN* (September 28, 2015), http://www.cnn.com/2015/09/28/us/pope-trip-wrap-vatican/ (accessed October 6, 2015); and Susan Cramm, "Leadership Gone Viral," *Strategy + Business* (January 17, 2014), http://www.strategy-business.com/blog/Leadership-Gone-Viral?gko=96623 (accessed October 6, 2015).
37. Gary Yukl and Richard Lepsinger, "Why Integrating the Leading and Managing Roles Is Essential for Organizational Effectiveness," *Organizational Dynamics* 34, no. 4 (2005), pp. 361–375; Henry Mintzberg, *Managing* (San Francisco: Berrett-Koehler, 2009); Andrew Saunders, "Rebuilding Management's Good Name," *Management Today* (May 2011), pp. 44–46; John Kotter, "Change Leadership: How Can You Accelerate Results?" *Leadership Excellence* (January 2013), pp. 6–7; and Alan Murray, "What Is the Difference Between Management and Leadership?" *The Wall Street Journal* (2009), http://guides.wsj.com/management/developing-a-leadership-style/what-is-the-difference-between-management-and-leadership/ (accessed June 28, 2009).
38. This section is based on John P. Kotter, *A Force for Change: How Leadership Differs from Management* (New York: The Free Press, 1990), pp. 3–18; John P. Kotter, "What Leaders Really Do," *Harvard Business Review* (December 2001), pp. 85–96; and ideas in Kevin Cashman, "Lead with Energy: Apply the Resilience Principle," *Leadership Excellence* (December 2010), p. 7; Henry Mintzberg, *Managing* (San Francisco: Berrett-Koehler, 2009); and Mike Maddock, "The One Talent That Makes Good Leaders Great," *Forbes* (September 26, 2012), http://www.forbes.com/sites/mikemaddock/2012/09/26/the-one-talent-that-makes-good-leaders-great/ (accessed March 7, 2013).
39. Warren Bennis, *Why Leaders Can't Lead* (San Francisco: Jossey Bass, 1989).
40. Abraham Zaleznik, "Managers and Leaders: Are They Different?" *Harvard Business Review* (March–April 1992), pp. 126–135; David Rooke and William R. Torbert, "7 Transformations of Leadership," *Harvard Business Review* (April 2005), pp. 67–76; and Rooke and Torbert, *Action Inquiry: The Secret of Timely and Transforming Leadership* (San Francisco: Berrett-Koehler, 2004).
41. Jim Boneau and Gregg Thompson, "Leadership 4.0: It's a Brave New Approach," *Leadership Excellence* (January 2013), p. 6.
42. Based on Susan R. Komives, Nance Lucas, and Timothy R. McMahon, *Exploring Leadership: For College Students Who Want to Make a Difference* (San Francisco: Jossey-Bass Publishers, 1998); and Shann R. Ferch and Matthew M. Mitchell, "Intentional Forgiveness in Relational Leadership: A Technique for Enhancing Effective Leadership," *The Journal of Leadership Studies* 7, no. 4 (2001), pp. 70–83.
43. This discussion draws ideas from Boneau and Thompson, "Leadership 4.0: It's a Brave New Approach."
44. Craig L. Pearce, "The Future of Leadership: Combining Vertical and Shared Leadership to Transform Knowledge Work," *Academy of Management Executive* 18, no. 1 (2004), pp. 47–57.
45. Yi Zhang, Jean Brittain Leslie, and Kelly M. Hannum, "Trouble Ahead: Derailment Is Alive and Well," *Thunderbird International Business Review* 55, no. 1 (January–February 2013), pp. 95–102.
46. See studies reported in Joyce Hogan, Robert Hogan, and Robert B. Kaiser, "Management Derailment: Personality Assessment and Mitigation," *Hogan Assessment Systems*, http://www.hoganassessments.com/_hoganweb/documents/Management_Derailment.pdf.
47. Yi Zhang et al., "Trouble Ahead: Derailment Is Alive and Well"; and Morgan W. McCall Jr. and Michael M. Lombardo, "Off the Track: Why and How Successful Executives Get Derailed" (Technical Report No. 21), (Greensboro, NC: Center for Creative Leadership, January 1983).
48. Hogan et al., "Management Derailment: Personality Assessment and Mitigation"; George Kohlrieser, "People Mistakes: These 10 Are Very Dangerous," *Leadership Excellence* (October 2012), p. 16; Clinton O. Longenecker and Laurence S. Fink, "Fixing Management's Fatal Flaws," *Industrial Management* (July–August 2012), pp. 12–17; E. Van Velsor and J. B. Leslie, "Why Executives Derail: Perspectives Across Time and Cultures," *Academy of Management Executive* 9, no. 4 (1995), pp. 62–72; and Morgan W. McCall Jr. and Michael M. Lombardo, "Off the Track: Why and How Successful Executives Get Derailed" (Technical Report No. 21), (Greensboro, NC: Center for Creative Leadership, January 1983).
49. Ram Charan and Geoffrey Colvin, "Why CEOs Fail," *Fortune* (June 21, 1999), pp. 68–78.
50. This example is based on Farhad Manjoo, "The Happiness Machine: How Google Became Such a Great Place to Work," *Slate Magazine*, http://www.slate.com/articles/technology/technology/2013/01/google_people_operations_the_secrets_of_the_world_s_most_scientific_human.html (accessed March 8, 2013); and David A. Garvin, "How Google Sold Its Engineers on Management," *Harvard Business Review* (December 2013), pp. 74–82.
51. List of Google's Rules from Adam Bryant, "Google's Quest to Build a Better Boss," *The New York Times* (March 12, 2011).
52. Survey by the Center for Creative Leadership, reported in Phaedra Brotherton, "Leadership: Nature or Nurture?" *T+D* (February 2013), p. 25.
53. Russell Palmer, "Can Leadership Be Learned?" *Business Today* (Fall 1989), pp. 100–102.

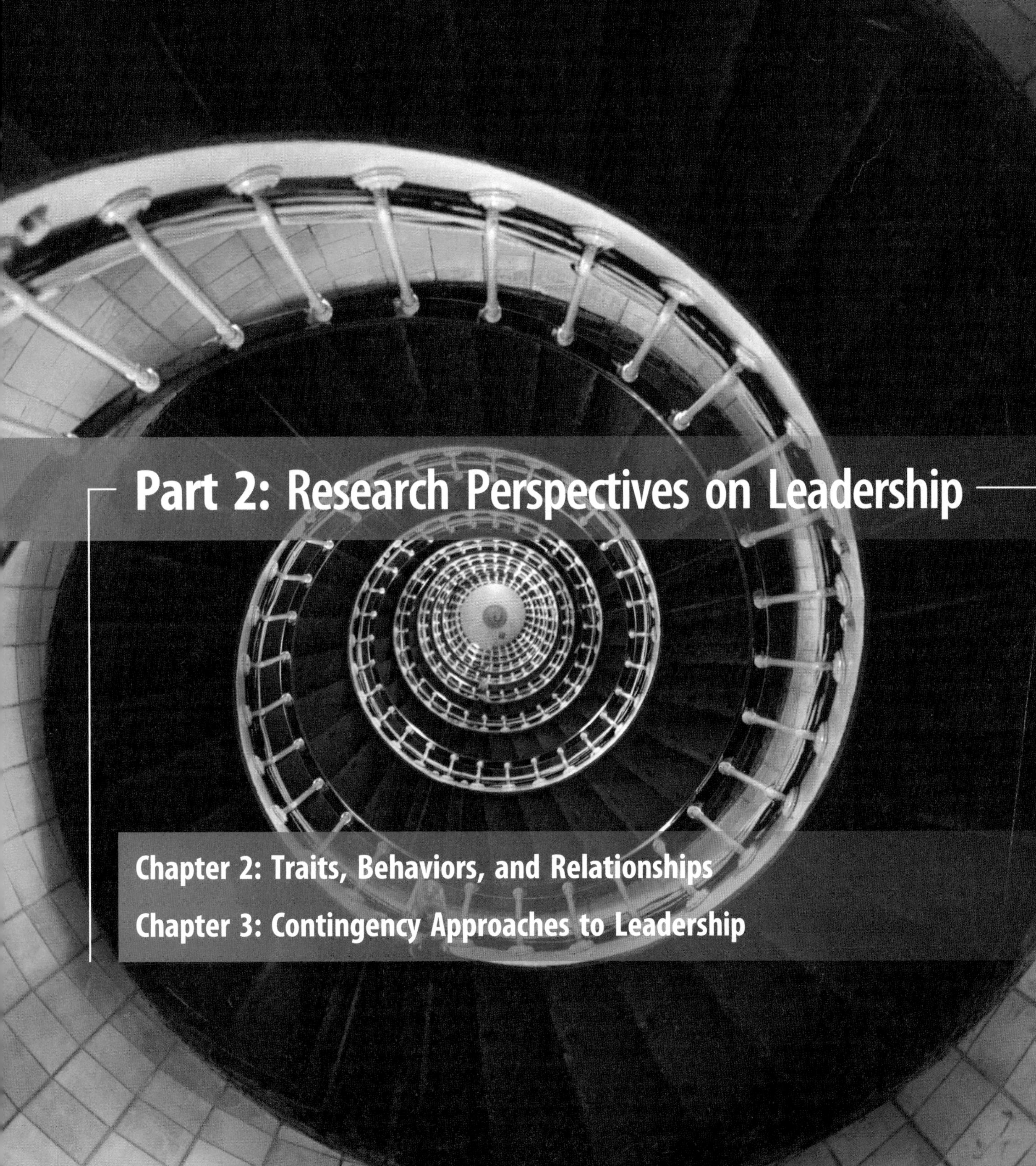

Part 2: Research Perspectives on Leadership

Chapter 2: Traits, Behaviors, and Relationships

Chapter 3: Contingency Approaches to Leadership

Chapter 2: Traits, Behaviors, and Relationships

YOUR **LEADERSHIP** CHALLENGE

After reading this chapter, you should be able to:

- Outline some personal traits and characteristics that are associated with effective leaders.
- Identify your own traits that you can transform into strengths and bring to a leadership role.
- Distinguish among various roles leaders play in organizations, including operations roles, collaborative roles, and advisory roles, and where your strengths might best fit.
- Recognize autocratic versus democratic leadership behavior and the impact of each.
- Know the distinction between people-oriented and task-oriented leadership behavior and when each should be used.
- Understand how the theory of individualized leadership has broadened the understanding of relationships between leaders and followers.
- Describe some key characteristics of entrepreneurial leaders.

CHAPTER **OUTLINE**

36 **The Trait Approach**

41 **Know Your Strengths**

43 **Behavior Approaches**

52 **Individualized Leadership**

55 **Entrepreneurial Traits and Behaviors**

In the Lead

40 **Marissa Mayer, Yahoo**

45 **Warren Buffett, Berkshire Hathaway**

47 **Col. Joe D. Dowdy and Maj. Gen. James Mattis, U.S. Marine Corps**

50 **Denise Morrison, Campbell Soup Company, and Michael Arrington, TechCrunch**

Leader's Self-Insight

40 **Rate Your Optimism**

47 **What's Your Leadership Orientation?**

55 **Your "LMX" Relationship**

Leader's Bookshelf

38 **Give and Take: A Revolutionary Approach to Success**

Leadership at Work

58 **Your Ideal Leader Traits**

Leadership Development: Cases for Analysis

58 **Consolidated Products**

60 **Transition to Leadership**

Soon after her husband was elected the first African American president in the United States, Michelle Obama appeared on "The Tonight Show" wearing a stylish outfit consisting of a pencil skirt, a yellow and brown tank top, and a mustard yellow cardigan. When then-host Jay Leno asked about her wardrobe, saying "I'm guessing about 60 grand? Sixty, 70 thousand for that outfit?" she replied, "Actually, this is a J. Crew ensemble." The audience roared. Obama also incorporated J. Crew items into her inauguration look. The man behind J. Crew, Millard S. (Mickey) Drexler, is a retail legend, known as both a visionary and something of a control freak. He turned Gap into a global fashion powerhouse in the 1990s, started Old Navy a decade or so later, and transformed J. Crew into a cult brand in the early years of the twenty-first century. When he took over as CEO, J. Crew was deeply in debt and struggling to survive. At the age of 70, Drexler is still going strong, but his leadership style and tendency to micromanage and focus on every detail, from vetting every new employee to deciding on the size of pockets or the look of a label, has recently come under scrutiny. By late 2015, even though J. Crew was still popular, sales were falling and the magic was fading. Yet owners continued to support Drexler and give him free rein as CEO. "Call it 'the great man' problem," one *New York Times* reporter phrased it, questioning whether any company should be so closely tied to the characteristics, style, and actions of one individual.[1]

We introduced the idea of "Great Man" leadership in Chapter 1, and the Mickey Drexler example shows that the concept hasn't completely died. The earliest leadership studies proposed that certain people had natural traits and abilities of power and influence that enabled them to put everything together and influence others in a way that other people could not. Although few today would argue that leadership is based on inborn traits, interest in the characteristics that define a good leader continues. As this example illustrates, current thinking on leadership incorporates a variety of ideas and concepts from the past.

Personal traits captured the imagination of the earliest leadership researchers, but if we look at any two successful and effective leaders they will likely share some traits but have others that are quite dissimilar. Each individual has a unique set of qualities, characteristics, and strengths to bring to a leadership role. In addition, leaders can learn to overcome some potentially limiting traits, such as a lack of self-confidence or a quick temper. Consequently, many researchers have examined the behavior of leaders to determine what behavioral features comprise leadership style and how particular behaviors relate to effective leadership.

This chapter first examines the evolution of the trait approach and the importance of leaders understanding and applying their own unique leadership strengths. Then we provide an overview of the behavior approach and introduce the theory of individualized leadership, which looks at behavior between a leader and each individual follower, differentiating one-on-one behavior from leader-to-group behavior. The path illuminated by the research into leader traits and behaviors is a foundation for the field of leadership studies and still enjoys remarkable dynamism for explaining leader success or failure.

2-1 THE TRAIT APPROACH

Traits are the distinguishing personal characteristics of a leader, such as intelligence, honesty, self-confidence, and appearance. Research early in the twentieth century examined leaders who had achieved a level of greatness and hence became known as the Great Man approach. Fundamental to this theory was the idea that some people are born with traits that make them natural leaders. The **Great Man approach** sought to identify the traits leaders possessed that distinguished them from people who were not leaders. Generally, research found only a weak relationship between personal traits and leader success.[2] Indeed, the diversity of traits that effective leaders possess indicates that leadership ability is not a genetic endowment.

Nevertheless, with the advancement of the field of psychology during the 1940s and 1950s, trait approach researchers expanded their examination of personal attributes by using aptitude and psychological tests. These early studies looked at personality traits such as creativity and self-confidence, physical traits such as age and energy level, abilities such as knowledge and fluency of speech, social characteristics such as popularity and sociability, and work-related characteristics such as the desire to excel and persistence against obstacles.[3]

In a 1948 literature review,[4] Stogdill examined more than 100 studies based on the trait approach. He uncovered several traits that appeared consistent with effective leadership, including general intelligence, initiative, interpersonal skills, self-confidence, drive for responsibility, and personal integrity. Stogdill's findings also

Traits
the distinguishing personal characteristics of a leader, such as intelligence, honesty, self-confidence, and appearance

Great Man approach
a leadership perspective that sought to identify the inherited traits leaders possessed that distinguished them from people who were not leaders

indicated, however, that the importance of a particular trait was often relative to the situation. Initiative, for example, may contribute to the success of a leader in an entrepreneurial situation, but it may be irrelevant to a leader in a stable bureaucracy. Thus, possessing certain personal characteristics is no guarantee of success.

Many researchers discontinued their efforts to identify leadership traits in light of Stogdill's 1948 findings and turned their attention to examining leader behavior and leadership situations. However, others continued with expanded trait lists and research projects. Stogdill's subsequent review of 163 trait studies conducted between 1948 and 1970 concluded that some personal traits do indeed seem to contribute to effective leadership.[5] The study identified many of the same traits found in the 1948 survey, along with several additional characteristics, including aggressiveness, independence, and tolerance for stress. However, Stogdill again cautioned that the value of a particular trait or set of traits varies with the organizational situation.

In recent years, there has been a resurgence of interest in examining leadership traits. A review by Kirkpatrick and Locke identified a number of personal traits that distinguish leaders from nonleaders, including some pinpointed by Stogdill.[6] Other studies have focused on followers' perceptions and indicate that certain traits are associated with people's perceptions of who is a leader. For example, one study found that the traits of intelligence, masculinity, and dominance were strongly related to how individuals perceived leaders.[7] Others have found that charismatic CEOs are perceived to be more effective than other leaders, even though there is no evidence showing they actually are.[8]

In summary, trait research has been an important part of leadership studies throughout the twentieth century and continues into the twenty-first, as illustrated by this chapter's Leader's Bookshelf, which suggests that a trait of *selflessness* is the secret to genuine and lasting leadership success. Several other traits, including optimism and a cheerful attitude, have recently gained attention as important for successful leaders. Britain's Royal Navy takes cheerfulness so seriously that it tracks how leader cheerfulness affects morale and effectiveness.[9] As discussed in Chapter 1, humility, including a willingness to admit mistakes and make oneself vulnerable, has emerged as an important trait in today's collaborative world.[10]

"What I've really learned over time is that optimism is a very, very important part of leadership. . . . People don't like to follow pessimists."

Robert Iger,
Chairman and CEO of The Walt Disney Company

Exhibit 2.1 presents some of the traits and their respective categories that have been identified through trait research over the years. Many researchers still contend that some traits are essential to effective leadership, but only in combination with other factors.[11] A few traits typically considered highly important for leadership are optimism, self-confidence, honesty and integrity, and drive.

2-1a Optimism and Self-Confidence

Recent research points to a positive outlook and a cheerful attitude as keys to effective leadership.[12] **Optimism** refers to a tendency to see the positive side of things and expect that things will turn out well. Numerous surveys indicate that optimism is the single characteristic most common to top executives. People rise to the top because they can see opportunities where others see problems and can instill in others a sense of hope for the future. Leaders at all levels need some degree of optimism to see possibilities even through the thickest fog and rally people around a vision for a better tomorrow. Although hundreds of experiments support the notion that people possess ingrained tendencies toward either optimism or pessimism, leaders can train themselves to deliberately focus on the positive rather than the negative and interpret situations in more positive, optimistic ways.[13]

NEW LEADER
ACTION MEMO

People generally prefer to follow leaders who are optimistic rather than pessimistic about the future. Complete the questionnaire in Leader's Self-Insight 2.1 to assess your level of optimism.

Optimism
a tendency to see the positive side of things and expect that things will turn out well

Self-confidence
assurance in one's own judgments, decision making, ideas, and capabilities

A related characteristic is having a positive attitude about oneself. Leaders who know themselves develop **self-confidence**, which is general assurance in one's own

LEADER'S BOOKSHELF

Give and Take: A Revolutionary Approach to Success

by Adam Grant

Contrary to popular belief, good guys don't always finish last. In fact, in the book *Give and Take: A Revolutionary Approach to Success*, Adam Grant asserts that a trait of selflessness can help leaders be more effective and more successful. Grant, the youngest tenured professor ever at the Wharton School at the University of Pennsylvania, suggests that good leaders are those who give the most and view their success as "individual achievements that have a positive impact on others."

ARE YOU A GIVER, A TAKER, OR A MATCHER?

Grant proposes that we all assume one of three basic approaches toward others—that of a *giver*, a *taker*, or a *matcher*.

- ***Givers focus on what others need and give selflessly.*** They give time and energy, or anything else that is asked of them, without expecting anything in return. Grant uses the example of billionaire Jon Huntsman Sr., founder of Huntsman Chemical, who once left $200 million on the table when negotiating with a man whose wife had just died, simply because he thought it was the right thing to do. As leaders, givers more easily delegate and collaborate with others, listen to others, give credit to others, and share power and responsibility.
- ***Takers put their own interests first.*** Takers are selfish people who want to win, no matter who else loses. As leaders, they typically try to influence others by gaining dominance and control over them. They collaborate only when it benefits them personally and rarely share credit for successes. Takers often win in the short run but they are much less likely to build success over the long term.
- ***Matchers strive for a balance of giving and taking.*** Matchers try to achieve an equal balance between what they give and what they get in return. As leaders, they network and collaborate strategically, expecting something in return that will be of benefit to them. They play a juggling act in an effort to serve their individual interests while still being fair to others.

DOES IT PAY TO BE NICE?

Grant applies scientific research and weaves in numerous real-life stories to support his premise that givers end up being the most successful among the three groups. His advice is to "focus attention and energy on making a difference in the lives of others, and success might follow as a by-product." Leaders who are givers help a wide range of people in the organization, develop everyone's skills to support the greater good, and strive to bring out the best in everyone. By investing in the success of their followers, leaders who are givers build their own success and a legacy of enduring greatness.

Source: *Give and Take*, by Adam Grant, is published by Viking.

judgments, decision making, ideas, and capabilities. Self-confidence doesn't mean being arrogant and prideful but rather knowing and trusting in oneself. Self-confidence is related to *self-efficacy*, which refers to a person's strong belief that he or she can successfully accomplish a specific task or outcome.[14] A leader who has a positive self-image and displays certainty about his or her own ability to achieve an outcome fosters confidence among followers, gains respect and admiration, and creates motivation and commitment among followers for the mission at hand.

NEW LEADER
ACTION MEMO

As a leader, you can develop the personal traits of self-confidence, integrity, and drive, which are important for successful leadership in every organization and situation. You can work to keep an optimistic attitude and be ethical in your decisions and actions.

Active leaders need self-confidence and optimism. How many of us willingly follow someone who is jaded and pessimistic, or someone who obviously doesn't believe in himself or herself? Leaders initiate change, and they often must make decisions without adequate information. Without the confidence to move forward and believe things will be okay, even if an occasional decision is wrong, leaders could be paralyzed into inaction. Setbacks have to be overcome. Risks have to be taken. Competing points of view have to be managed, with some people left unsatisfied. The characteristics of optimism and self-confidence enable a leader to face all these challenges.[15]

2-1b Honesty and Integrity

Positive attitudes have to be tempered by strong ethics or leaders can get into trouble. Consider Bernard Madoff, who masterminded the largest financial fraud in history and was sent to jail on 11 criminal charges, including securities fraud and perjury. As a leader, Madoff displayed strong self-confidence and optimism, which is

EXHIBIT 2.1 Some Leader Characteristics

Personal Characteristics	**Social Characteristics**
Energy	Sociability, interpersonal skills
Passion	Cooperativeness
Humility	Ability to enlist cooperation
Physical stamina	Tact, diplomacy
Intelligence and Ability	**Work-Related Characteristics**
Intelligence, cognitive ability	Drive, desire to excel
Knowledge	Dependability
Judgment, decisiveness	Fair-mindedness
Personality	Perseverance, tenacity
Optimism	**Social Background**
Cheerfulness	Education
Self-confidence	Mobility
Honesty and integrity	
Charisma	
Desire to lead	
Independence	

Sources: *Bass and Stogdill's Handbook of Leadership: Theory, Research, and Management Applications*, 3rd ed. (New York : The Free Press, 1990), pp. 80–81; S. A. Kirkpatrick and E. A. Locke, "Leadership: Do Traits Matter?" *Academy of Management Executive* 5, no. 2 (1991), pp. 48–60; and James M. Kouzes and Barry Z. Posner, *The Leadership Challenge: How to Get Extraordinary Things Done in Organizations* (San Francisco: Jossey-Bass, 1990).

one reason he was able to attract so many investors. The problem was that he didn't have a strong ethical grounding to match. Due to Madoff's scam, thousands of people were swindled out of their life's savings, charities and foundations were ruined, and pension funds were wiped out, while Madoff and his wife lived in luxury.[16]

Effective leaders are ethical leaders. One aspect of being an ethical leader is being honest with followers, customers, shareholders, and the public, and maintaining one's integrity. **Honesty** refers to truthfulness and nondeception. It implies an openness that followers welcome. **Integrity** means that a leader's character is whole, integrated, and grounded in solid ethical principles, and he or she acts in keeping with those principles. Leaders who model their ethical convictions through their daily actions command admiration, respect, and loyalty. Honesty and integrity are the foundation of trust between leaders and followers.

Sadly, trust is sorely lacking in many organizations following years of corporate scandals and rampant greed. Leaders need the traits of honesty and integrity to rebuild trusting and productive relationships. People today are wary of authority and the deceptive use of power, and they are hungry for leaders who hold high moral standards. Successful leaders have also been found to be highly consistent, doing exactly what they say they will do when they say they will do it. Successful leaders prove themselves trustworthy. They adhere to basic ethical principles and consistently apply them in their leadership. One survey of 1,500 managers asked the values most desired in leaders. Honesty and integrity topped the list. The authors concluded:

> *Honesty is absolutely essential to leadership. After all, if we are willing to follow someone, whether it be into battle or into the boardroom, we first want to assure ourselves that the person is worthy of our trust. We want to know that he or she is being truthful, ethical, and principled. We want to be fully confident in the integrity of our leaders.*[17]

Honesty
truthfulness and nondeception

Integrity
the quality of being whole and integrated and acting in accordance with solid ethical principles

LEADER'S SELF-INSIGHT 2.1

Rate Your Optimism

Instructions: This questionnaire is designed to assess your level of optimism as reflected in your hopefulness about the future. There are no right or wrong answers. Please indicate your personal feelings about whether each statement is Mostly False or Mostly True by checking the answer that best describes your attitude or feeling.

	Mostly False	Mostly True
1. I nearly always expect a lot from life.	_____	_____
2. I try to anticipate when things will go wrong.	_____	_____
3. I always see the positive side of things.	_____	_____
4. I often start out expecting the worst, although things usually work out okay.	_____	_____
5. I expect more good things to happen to me than bad.	_____	_____
6. I often feel concern about how things will turn out for me.	_____	_____
7. If something can go wrong for me, it usually does.	_____	_____
8. Even in difficult times, I usually expect the best.	_____	_____
9. I am cheerful and positive most of the time.	_____	_____
10. I consider myself an optimistic person.	_____	_____

Scoring and Interpretation

Give yourself one point for checking Mostly True for items 1, 3, 5, 8, 9, 10. Also give yourself one point for checking Mostly False for items 2, 4, 6, 7. Enter your score here: _____ If your score is 8 or higher, it may mean that you are high on optimism. If your score is 3 or less, your view about the future may be pessimistic. For the most part, people like to follow a leader who is optimistic rather than negative about the future. However, too much optimism may exaggerate positive expectations that are never fulfilled. If your score is low, what can you do to view the world through a more optimistic lens?

Source: These questions were created based on several sources.

2-1c Drive

Another characteristic considered essential for effective leadership is drive. Leaders often are responsible for initiating new projects as well as guiding projects to successful completion. **Drive** refers to high motivation that creates a high effort level by a leader. Leaders with drive seek achievement, have energy and tenacity, and are often perceived as ambitious. If people don't strive to achieve something, they rarely do. Ambition can enable leaders to set challenging goals and take initiative to reach them.[18]

Drive
high motivation that creates a high effort level by a leader

A strong drive is also associated with high energy. Leaders work long hours over many years. They have stamina and are vigorous and full of life in order to handle the pace, the demands, and the challenges of leadership. During her first two years at Google, Marissa Mayer says she worked 100 hours a week. That pace likely didn't slow in her job at Yahoo.

IN THE LEAD

Marissa Mayer, Yahoo

Marissa Mayer set herself some tough goals as the new president and CEO of Yahoo, but being tough is part of Mayer's DNA. Mayer is known for being incredibly energetic and ambitious. She loves hard work and challenge. "She doesn't need any sleep," said Craig Silverstein, who worked with her at Google and now develops software for Kahn Academy.

That's clearly an overstatement, but Mayer has demonstrated that she has almost superhuman stamina and a strong drive to succeed. In the early years at Google, she routinely worked 100-hour weeks and occasionally pulled all-nighters. Soon after joining Yahoo as CEO, Mayer had her first baby and returned to work two weeks after the delivery.

Even in high school, Mayer was known as an overachiever who refused to settle for less than the best from herself or others. As captain of the pom-pom squad, she scheduled practices that lasted for hours to make sure everyone was synchronized. It was during her first management job at Google that she incorporated the idea of pushing beyond her comfort zone into her career philosophy. She isn't afraid to take risks in the interest of helping the team and organization succeed. Mayer created a firestorm of criticism when she issued a policy early in her tenure at Yahoo that employees can no longer work from home, but she stuck by her decision without regrets or apologies. She believes Yahoo is in a crisis situation and to succeed needs the creative energy that comes from people working face to face and side by side. Some people believe she will eventually relax the tough "all hands in the office" policy, since flexibility is another of her characteristics. However, she won't relax her high standards or the requirement that employees be as dedicated to Yahoo's success as she is.[19]

Working 100-hour weeks certainly isn't necessary for effective leadership, but all leaders have to display drive and energy to be successful. Clearly, various traits such as drive, self-confidence, optimism, and honesty have great value for leaders. One study of 600 executives by Hay Group, a global organizational and human resources consulting firm, found that 75 percent of the successful executives studied possessed the characteristics of self-confidence and drive.[20]

In Chapter 4, we will further consider individual characteristics and qualities that play a role in leadership effectiveness. However, good leaders know it isn't about identifying specific individual traits but rather understanding one's own unique set of strengths and capabilities and learning how to make the most of them.[21]

2-2 KNOW YOUR STRENGTHS

Some people tend to think a leader should have a complete set of skills, characteristics, and abilities to handle any problem, challenge, or opportunity that comes along. This myth of the "complete leader" can cause stress and frustration for leaders and followers, as well as damage to the organization.[22] *Interdependence* is the key to effective leadership. Sixty percent of leaders in one survey acknowledge that leaders face challenges that go beyond any individual's capabilities.[23] Therefore, the best leaders recognize and hone their strengths while trusting and collaborating with others to make up for their weak points.

Everyone has strengths, but many leaders fail to recognize and apply them, often because they are hampered by the idea that they should be good at everything. Benjamin Franklin referred to wasted strengths as "sundials in the shade."[24] Only when leaders understand their strengths can they use these abilities effectively to make their best contribution.

2-2a What Are Strengths?

A **strength** arises from a natural talent that has been supported and reinforced with knowledge and skills.[25] Talents can be thought of as innate traits and naturally

Strength
a natural talent or ability that has been supported and reinforced with learned knowledge and skills

recurring patterns of thought, feeling, and behavior. One person might be naturally outgoing and curious, for example; another might have a natural talent for being organized. Once recognized, talents can be turned into strengths by consciously developing and enhancing them with learning and practice. Unless they are honed and strengthened and put to use, talents are merely aspects of one's potential.

One neat thing about understanding your strengths is the philosophy "concentrate on your strengths, not your weaknesses." You excel in life by maximizing your strengths, not by fixing your weaknesses. When you live and work from your strengths, you are more motivated, competent, and satisfied. Strengths are important because you can focus your life around them, and your energy, enthusiasm, and effectiveness can be the basis of your leadership. Why devote your energy to trying to fix your weaknesses or expend much thought and effort performing tasks that don't match your strengths? When people use their talents and strengths, they feel good and enjoy their work without extra effort; hence they are effective and make a positive contribution.

How does a leader know which traits or behavior patterns can be turned into strengths? Warren Buffett recommends that people do what fits their natural interests and abilities, which is reflected in the work they like to do. Buffett says he finds investing so much fun that he would do it for free. Buffett tried other work early in his career but found it so unsatisfying that he knew he wouldn't want to do it for any amount of money. The legendary self-made billionaire and chairman of Berkshire Hathaway was the third richest person in the world in 2015. Yet it isn't the money that drives him, but the love of the work. His career advice is to find work or a career that you really enjoy, and it will fit the natural strengths of your mental wiring.[26]

2-2b Matching Strengths with Roles

Recent research suggests that different leader strengths might be better suited to different types of leadership roles.[27] Exhibit 2.2 illustrates three types of leadership roles identified in today's organizations by a team of experts at Hay Group. The researchers found that, although there is a core set of competencies that all leaders need, there is significant variation in the personal characteristics, behaviors, and skills that correlate with success in the different roles.

Operational role
a vertically oriented leadership role in which an executive has direct control over people and resources and the position power to accomplish results

The **operational role** is the closest to a traditional, vertically oriented management role, where an executive has direct control over people and resources to

EXHIBIT 2.2 Three Types of Leadership Roles

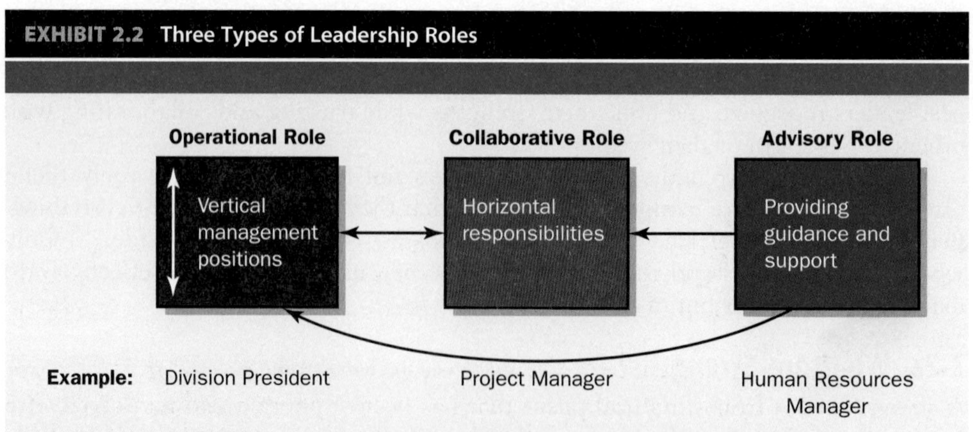

accomplish results. Operational leaders fill traditional line and general management positions in a business, for example. They set goals, establish plans, and get things done primarily through the vertical hierarchy and the use of position power. Operational leaders are doggedly focused on delivering results. They need high self-confidence and tend to be assertive, always pushing forward and raising the bar. Successful operational leaders are typically analytical and knowledgeable, yet they also have the ability to translate their knowledge into a vision that others can become passionate about.

The **collaborative role** is a horizontal role and includes people such as project managers, matrix managers, and team leaders in today's more horizontally organized companies. This role, which has grown tremendously in importance in recent years, is quite challenging. Leaders in collaborative roles typically don't have the strong position power of the operational role. They often work behind the scenes, using their personal power to influence others and get things done. Collaborative leaders need excellent people skills in order to network, build relationships, and obtain agreement through personal influence. They also are highly proactive and tenacious, and they exhibit extreme flexibility to cope with the ambiguity and uncertainty associated with the collaborative role.

Leaders in an **advisory role** provide guidance and support to other people and departments in the organization. Advisory leadership roles are found, for example, in departments such as legal, finance, and human resources. These leaders are responsible for developing broad organizational capabilities rather than accomplishing specific business results. Advisory leaders need great people skills and the ability to influence others through communication, knowledge, and personal persuasion. In addition, leaders in advisory roles need exceptionally high levels of honesty and integrity to build trust and keep the organization on solid ethical ground.

The Hay Group research findings shed new light on the types of roles leaders fill in today's organizations and emphasize that an individual's strengths can influence how effective a leader might be in a particular role. Leadership success partly depends on matching leaders with roles where their strengths can be most effective.

NEW LEADER
ACTION MEMO

As a leader, you can understand the type of leadership role in which your strengths would be most effective and satisfying. You can pursue an operational, collaborative, or advisory leadership role depending on your natural tendencies.

Collaborative role
a horizontal leadership role (such as team leader) in which the leader often works behind the scenes and uses personal power to influence others and get things done.

Advisory role
a leadership role that provides advice, guidance, and support to other people and departments in the organization

2-3 BEHAVIOR APPROACHES

As suggested in the previous discussion, strengths are not just personal traits but also patterns of behavior. Rather than looking at an individual's personal traits, diverse research programs on leadership behavior have sought to uncover the behaviors that effective leaders engage in. Behaviors can be learned more readily than traits, enabling leadership to be accessible to all.

2-3a Autocratic versus Democratic Behaviors

One study that served as a precursor to the behavior approach recognized autocratic and democratic leadership styles. An **autocratic** leader is one who tends to centralize authority and derive power from position, control of rewards, and coercion. A **democratic** leader delegates authority to others, encourages participation, relies on subordinates' knowledge for completion of tasks, and depends on subordinate respect for influence.

The first studies on these leadership behaviors were conducted at the University of Iowa by Kurt Lewin and his associates.[28] The research included groups of children, each with its own designated adult leader who was instructed to act in either

Autocratic
a leader who tends to centralize authority and derive power from position, control of rewards, and coercion

Democratic
a leader who delegates authority to others, encourages participation, relies on subordinates' knowledge for completion of tasks, and depends on subordinate respect for influence

an autocratic or a democratic style. These experiments produced some interesting findings. The groups with autocratic leaders performed highly so long as the leader was present to supervise them. However, group members were displeased with the close, autocratic style of leadership, and feelings of hostility frequently arose. The performance of groups who were assigned democratic leaders was almost as good, and these groups were characterized by positive feelings rather than hostility. In addition, under the democratic style of leadership, group members performed well even when the leader was absent. The participative techniques and majority-rule decision making used by the democratic leader trained and involved the group members so that they performed well with or without the leader present. These characteristics of democratic leadership may partly explain why the empowerment of employees is a popular trend in companies today. This chapter's Consider This box presents the notion that democratic leaders may get better results because they allow followers to feel their own power and worth.

Consider **This!**

Minimal Leadership

When the Master governs, the people are hardly aware that he [she] exists.
Next best is a leader who is loved.
Next, one who is feared.
The worst is one who is despised.
If you don't trust the people, you make them untrustworthy.
The Master doesn't talk, he [she] acts.
When his [her] work is done, the people say, "Amazing: we did it all by ourselves."

Source: From *Tao Te Ching*, translated by S. Mitchell, (New York: Harper Perennial, 1988), p. 17.

This early work implied that leaders were either autocratic or democratic in their approach. However, further work by Tannenbaum and Schmidt indicated that leadership behavior could exist on a continuum reflecting different amounts of employee participation.[29] Thus, one leader might be autocratic (boss-centered), another democratic (subordinate-centered), and a third a mix of the two styles. Exhibit 2.3 illustrates the leadership continuum.

NEW LEADER **ACTION MEMO**

As a leader, you can use a democratic leadership style to help followers develop decision-making skills and perform well without close supervision. An autocratic style might be appropriate when there is time pressure or followers have low skill levels.

Tannenbaum and Schmidt also suggested that the extent to which leaders should be boss-centered or subordinate-centered depended on organizational circumstances and that leaders might adjust their behaviors to fit the circumstances. For example, if there is time pressure on a leader, or if it takes too long for subordinates to learn how to make decisions, the leader will tend to use an autocratic style. When subordinates are able to learn decision-making skills readily, a democratic style can be used. Also, the greater the skill difference, the more autocratic the leader approach because it is difficult to bring subordinates up to the leader's expertise level.[30]

EXHIBIT 2.3 Leadership Continuum

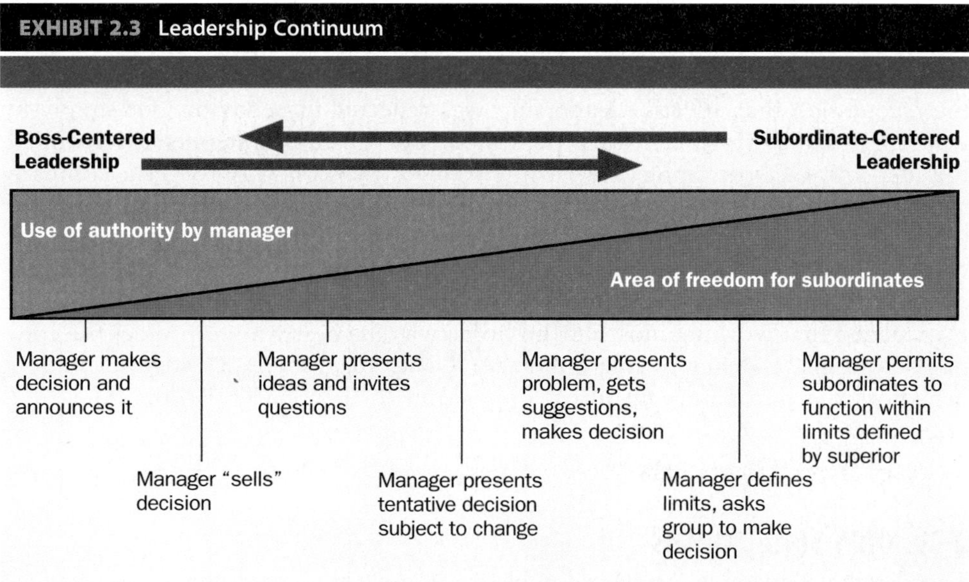

Source: *Harvard Business Review.* An exhibit from Robert Tannenbaum and Warren Schmidt, "How to Choose a Leadership Pattern" (May–June 1973). Copyright 1973 by the president and Fellows of Harvard College.

Jack Hartnett, former president of D. L. Rogers Corporation and franchise owner of 54 Sonic drive-in restaurants, provides an example of the autocratic leadership style. He tells workers to "do it the way we tell you to do it," rather than asking for their input or suggestions.[31] The style works well in the fast-food restaurant business where turnover is typically high and many employees are young and low skilled. In contrast, Warren Buffett, introduced earlier, is an excellent example of a democratic leader.

IN THE LEAD

Warren Buffett, Berkshire Hathaway

He is one of the richest people in the world, but Warren Buffett is also considered one of the warmest, most humble, and most approachable. Each year, Buffett hosts in his hometown of Omaha, Nebraska, about 160 business students from universities around the world, answering questions and listening to their ideas.

Within the numerous companies under his leadership, Buffett also emphasizes communication, mutual trust, respect, and a nurturing work environment. He places a high value on interacting and collaborating with employees at all levels. He lets the managers of the various companies run their own show, believing they are the ones who best know how to do it. Buffett's democratic leadership style is reflected in an excerpt from a memo he sent to top managers: "Talk to me about what is going on as little or as much as you wish. Each of you does a first-class job of running your operation with your own individual style and you don't need me to help."[32]

The findings about autocratic and democratic leadership in the original University of Iowa studies indicated that leadership behavior had a definite effect on outcomes such as follower performance and satisfaction. Equally important was the recognition that effective leadership was reflected in behavior, not simply by what personality traits a leader possessed. For example, Stephen McDonnell, founder and CEO of Applegate Farms, believes the best way to get a company running smoothly is to give everyone access to relevant information, empower them with the freedom and responsibility to act on it, and then stay out of the way. McDonnell doesn't even go into the office most days, although he is a self-confessed control-freak boss, full of anxiety and obsessed with meeting goals. He realized that working mostly from home was the best way to protect the company from his tendency to micromanage.[33] This suggests that leaders can adopt behaviors that are almost in direct opposition to their natural traits when it is necessary.

2-3b Ohio State Studies

NEW LEADER
ACTION MEMO

Discover your leadership orientation related to consideration and initiating structure by completing the self-assessment exercise in Leader's Self-Insight 2.2.

The idea that leadership is reflected in behavior and not just personal traits provided a focus for subsequent research. One early series of studies on leadership behavior was conducted at The Ohio State University. Researchers conducted surveys to identify specific dimensions of leader behavior. Narrowing a list of nearly 2,000 leader behaviors into a questionnaire containing 150 examples of definitive leader behaviors, they developed the Leader Behavior Description Questionnaire (LBDQ) and administered it to employees.[34] Hundreds of employees responded to various examples according to the degree to which their leaders engaged in the behaviors. The analysis of ratings resulted in two wide-ranging categories of leader behavior, later called *consideration* and *initiating structure*.

Consideration describes the extent to which a leader cares about subordinates, respects their ideas and feelings, and establishes mutual trust. Showing appreciation, listening carefully to problems, and seeking input from subordinates regarding important decisions are all examples of consideration behaviors.

Initiating structure describes the extent to which a leader is task oriented and directs subordinates' work activities toward goal achievement. This type of leader behavior includes directing tasks, getting people to work hard, planning, providing explicit schedules for work activities, and ruling with an iron hand.

Although many leaders fall along a continuum that includes both consideration and initiating structure behaviors, these behavior categories are independent of one another. In other words, a leader can display a high degree of both behavior types or a low degree of both behavior types. Additionally, a leader might demonstrate high consideration and low initiating structure, or low consideration and high initiating structure behavior. Research indicates that all four of these leader style combinations can be effective.[35] The following examples describe two U.S. Marine leaders who display different types of leadership behavior that correlate to the *consideration* and *initiating structure* styles. Sometimes these styles clash.

Consideration
the extent to which a leader is sensitive to subordinates, respects their ideas and feelings, and establishes mutual trust

Initiating structure
the extent to which a leader is task oriented and directs subordinates' work activities toward goal achievement

LEADER'S SELF-INSIGHT 2.2

What's Your Leadership Orientation?

Instructions: The following questions ask about your personal leadership orientation. Each item describes a specific kind of behavior but does not ask you to judge whether the behavior is desirable or undesirable.

Read each item carefully. Think about how often you engage in the behavior described by the item in a work or school group. Please indicate whether each statement is Mostly False or Mostly True by checking the answer that best describes your behavior.

		Mostly False	Mostly True
1.	I put into operation suggestions agreed to by the group.		
2.	I treat everyone in the group with respect as my equal.		
3.	I back up what other people in the group do.		
4.	I help others with their personal problems.		
5.	I bring up how much work should be accomplished.		
6.	I help assign people to specific tasks.		
7.	I frequently suggest ways to fix problems.		
8.	I emphasize deadlines and how to meet them.		

Scoring and Interpretation

Consideration behavior score—count the number of checks for Mostly True for items 1–4. Enter your consideration score here: ______.

A higher score (3 or 4) suggests a relatively strong orientation toward consideration behavior by you as a leader. A low score (2 or less) suggests a relatively weak consideration orientation.

Initiating structure behavior score—count the number of checks for Mostly True for items 5–8. Enter your initiating structure score here: ______.

A higher score (3 or 4) suggests a relatively strong orientation toward initiating structure behavior by you as a leader. A low score (2 or less) suggests a relatively weak orientation toward initiating structure behavior.

Source: Sample items adapted from: Edwin A Fleishman 's *Leadership Opinion Questionnaire*. (Copyright 1960, Science Research Associates, Inc., Chicago, IL). This version is based on Jon L. Pierce and John W. Newstrom, *Leaders and the Leadership Process: Readings, Self-Assessments & Applications*, 2nd ed. (Boston: Irwin McGraw-Hill, 2000).

IN THE LEAD

Col. Joe D. Dowdy and Maj. Gen. James Mattis, U.S. Marine Corps

Only a few weeks into the war in Iraq, Marine Col. Joe D. Dowdy had both accomplished a grueling military mission and been removed from his command by Maj. Gen. James Mattis. The complicated and conflicting tales of why Col. Dowdy was dismissed are beyond the scope of this text, but one issue that came under examination was the differing styles of Col. Dowdy and Gen. Mattis, as well as the difficult, age-old wartime tension of "men versus mission."

Gen. Mattis has been referred to as a "warrior monk," consumed with the study of battle tactics and a leader whose own battle plans in Iraq were considered brilliant. Gen. Mattis saw speed as integral to success in the early days of the Iraqi war, pushing for regiments to move quickly to accomplish a mission despite significant risks. For Col. Dowdy, some risks seemed too high, and he made decisions that delayed his mission but better protected his marines. Col. Dowdy was beloved by his followers because he was deeply concerned about their welfare, paid attention to them as individuals, and treated them as equals, going so far as to decline certain privileges that were available only to officers.

Despite their different styles, both leaders were highly respected by followers. When asked about Gen. Mattis, Gunnery Sgt. Robert Kane, who has served under both leaders, says he would certainly "follow him again." However, when he learned that Col. Dowdy had been dismissed, Sgt. Kane says he "wanted to go with him. If [he] had said 'Get your gear, you're coming with me,' I would've gone, even if it meant the end of my career."[36]

Gen. Mattis might be considered highly task oriented, reflecting an initiating structure approach, while Col. Dowdy seems more people oriented, reflecting a consideration behavioral style. Whereas Gen. Mattis typically put the mission first, combined with a concern for the marines under his command, Col. Dowdy typically put marines first, even though he also gave his all to accomplish the mission.

Additional studies that correlated these two leader behavior types and impact on subordinates initially demonstrated that "considerate" supervisors had a more positive impact on subordinate satisfaction than did "structuring" supervisors.[37] For example, when leader effectiveness was defined by voluntary turnover or amount of grievances filed by subordinates, considerate leaders generated less turnover and fewer grievances. But research that utilized performance criteria, such as group output and productivity, showed initiating structure behavior was rated more effective. Other studies involving aircraft commanders and university department heads revealed that leaders rated effective by subordinates exhibited a high level of both consideration and initiating structure behaviors, whereas leaders rated less effective displayed low levels of both behavior styles.[38]

2-3c University of Michigan Studies

Studies at the University of Michigan took a different approach by directly comparing the behavior of effective and ineffective supervisors.[39] The effectiveness of leaders was determined by productivity of the subordinate group. Initial field studies and interviews at various job sites gave way to a questionnaire not unlike the LBDQ, called the Survey of Organizations.[40]

Over time, the Michigan researchers established two types of leadership behavior, each type consisting of two dimensions.[41] First, **employee-centered** leaders display a focus on the human needs of their subordinates. Leader support and interaction facilitation are the two underlying dimensions of employee-centered behavior. This means that in addition to demonstrating support for their subordinates, employee-centered leaders facilitate positive interaction among followers and seek to minimize conflict. The employee-centered style of leadership roughly corresponds to the Ohio State concept of consideration.

In contrast to the employee-centered leader, the **job-centered** leader directs activities toward scheduling, accomplishing tasks, and achieving efficiency. Goal emphasis and work facilitation are dimensions of this leadership behavior. By focusing on reaching task goals and facilitating the structure of tasks, job-centered behavior approximates that of initiating structure.

However, unlike the consideration and initiating structure styles defined by the Ohio State studies, Michigan researchers considered employee-centered leadership and job-centered leadership to be distinct styles in opposition to one another. A leader is identifiable by behavior characteristic of one or the other style but not both. Another hallmark of later Michigan studies is the acknowledgment that often the behaviors of goal emphasis, work facilitation, support, and interaction facilitation can be meaningfully performed by a subordinate's peers rather than only by the designated leader. Other people in the group could supply these behaviors, which enhanced performance.[42]

In addition, while leadership behavior was demonstrated to affect the performance and satisfaction of subordinates, performance was also influenced by other factors related to the situation within which leaders and subordinates worked. The importance of situation will be explored in the next chapter.

Employee-centered
a leadership behavior that displays a focus on the human needs of subordinates

Job-centered
leadership behavior in which leaders direct activities toward efficiency, cost-cutting, and scheduling, with an emphasis on goals and work facilitation

2-3d The Leadership Grid

Blake and Mouton of the University of Texas proposed a two-dimensional leadership theory called the **Leadership Grid** that builds on the work of the Ohio State and Michigan studies.[43] Based on a week-long seminar, researchers rated leaders on a scale of one to nine according to two criteria: the concern for people and the concern for production. The scores for these criteria are plotted on a grid with an axis corresponding to each concern. Exhibit 2.4 depicts the two-dimensional model and five of the seven major leadership styles.

Team management (9,9) is often considered the most effective style and is recommended because organization members work together to accomplish tasks. *Country club management* (1,9) occurs when primary emphasis is given to people rather than to work outputs. *Authority-compliance management* (9,1) occurs when efficiency in operations is the dominant orientation. *Middle-of-the-road management* (5,5) reflects a moderate amount of concern for both people and production. *Impoverished management* (1,1) means the absence of a leadership philosophy; leaders exert little effort toward interpersonal relationships or work accomplishment. Consider these examples:

The Leadership Grid a two-dimensional leadership model that describes major leadership styles based on measuring both concern for people and concern for production

EXHIBIT 2.4 The Leadership Grid® Figure

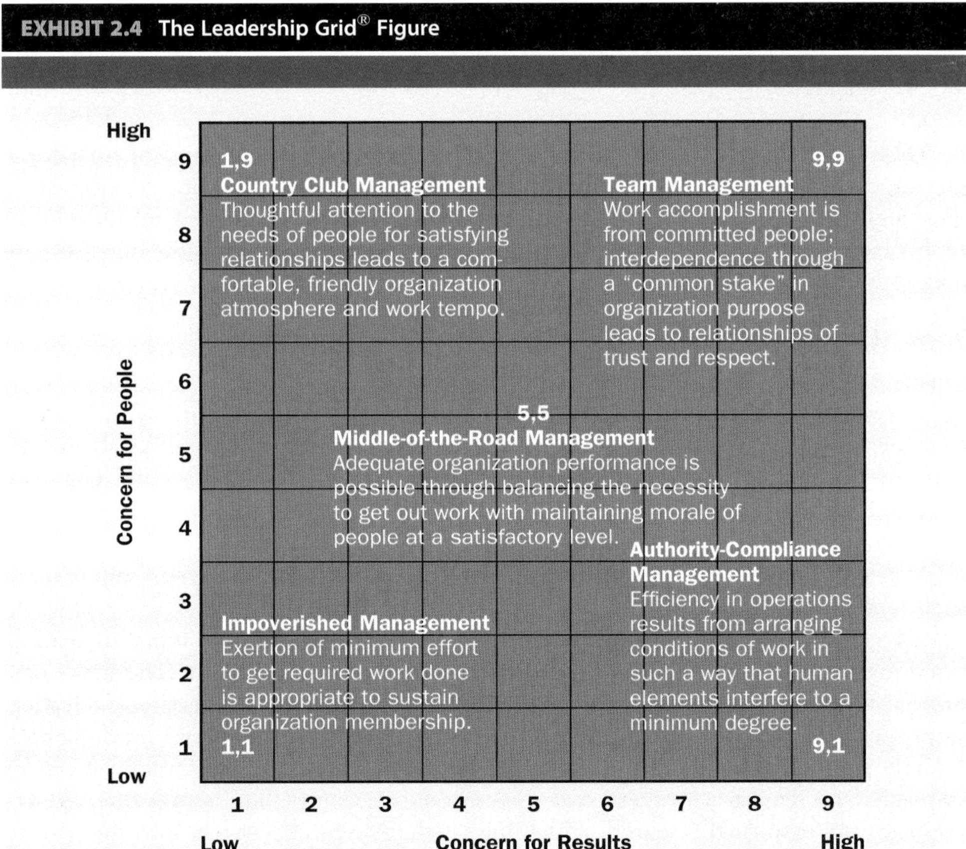

Source: The Leadership Grid figure from *Leadership Dilemma—Grid Solutions* by Robert R. Blake and Anne Adams McCanse (formerly the Managerial Grid by Robert R. Blake and Jane S. Mouton). Houston: Gulf Publishing Company, p. 29. Copyright 1991 by Scientific Methods, Inc. Reproduced by permission of the owners.

IN THE LEAD

Denise Morrison, Campbell Soup Company, and Michael Arrington, TechCrunch

Douglas Conant, former CEO of Campbell Soup Company, met Denise Morrison in 1995 when he was CEO of Nabisco and she cold-called him looking for a job. He found in Morrison a kindred spirit in terms of leadership style and hired her; she later followed him to Campbell in 2003—and into the company's top executive seat eight years later. Like Conant, Morrison is a strong proponent of empowerment and employee engagement. She has been referred to as "tough on the issues but tender on people." Morrison is known to be patient and supportive, even though she can make difficult operational decisions without letting her emotions cloud her judgment.

Compare Morrison's approach to that of Michael Arrington, founder of TechCrunch, the company that publishes the influential blog of the same name. Arrington started the blog because he enjoys the research and writing, and he admits he isn't very good at the "people management" part of his job. "It's hard to be a coach and a player at the same time," Arrington says. "Plus, I'm moody." Arrington says his style is to bust down doors and clean up the mess later. Recognizing his weak point in being a manager of people, Arrington hired Heather Harde as CEO of the company, which enabled TechCrunch to grow and allowed Arrington to focus on what he was best at doing. Both Arrington and Harde have since left the company after public clashes with Arianna Huffington of *The Huffington Post*.[44]

The leadership of Denise Morrison is characterized by high concern for people and moderate concern for tasks and production. Michael Arrington, in contrast, is very high on concern for production and relatively low on concern for people. In each case, both concerns shown in The Leadership Grid are present, but they are integrated in different amounts.

2-3e Theories of a "High-High" Leader

The leadership styles described by the researchers at Ohio State, University of Michigan, and University of Texas pertain to variables that roughly correspond to one another: consideration and initiating structure; employee-centered and job-centered; concern for people and concern for production. The research into the behavior approach culminated in two predominate types of leadership behaviors—people-oriented and task-oriented. Exhibit 2.5 illustrates how the various studies fall within these two behavior categories and lists some behaviors that are representative of each type of leadership.

The findings about two underlying dimensions and the possibility of leaders rated high on both dimensions raise three questions to think about. The first question is whether these two dimensions are the most important behaviors of leadership. Certainly, these two behaviors are important. They capture fundamental, underlying aspects of human behavior that must be considered for organizations to succeed. One reason why these two dimensions are compelling is that the findings are based on empirical research, which means that researchers went into the field to study real leaders across a variety of settings. When independent streams of field research reach similar conclusions, they probably represent a fundamental theme in leadership behavior. A review of 50 years of leadership research, for example, identified task-oriented behavior and people-oriented behavior as primary categories

EXHIBIT 2.5 Themes of Leader Behavior Research

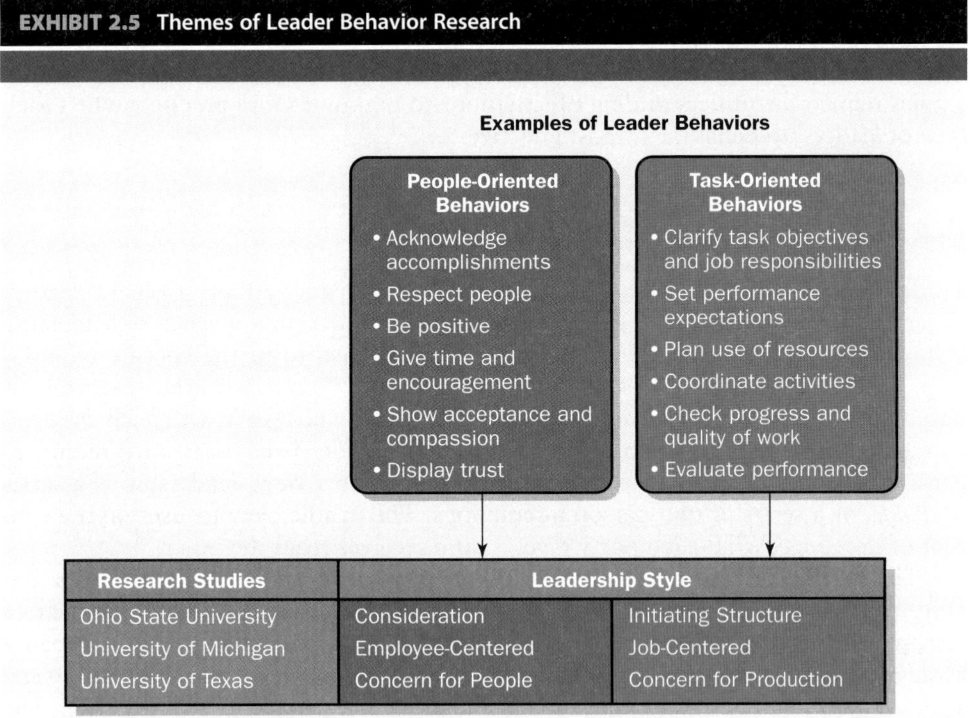

Sources: Based on Marilyn R. Zuckerman and Lewis J. Hatala, *Incredibly American: Releasing the Heart of Quality* (Milwaukee, WI: American Society for Quality, 1992), pp. 141–142; and Mark O'Connell, Gary Yukl, and Thomas Taber, "Leader Behavior and LMX: A Constructive Replication," *Journal of Managerial Psychology* 27, no. 2 (2012), pp. 143–154.

related to effective leadership in numerous studies.[45] Concern for tasks and concern for people must be shown toward followers at some reasonable level, either by the leader or by other people in the system. Although these are not the only important behaviors, as we will see throughout this book, they certainly require attention.

> NEW LEADER **ACTION MEMO**
>
> As a leader, you can succeed in a variety of situations by showing concern for both tasks and people. People-oriented behavior is related to higher follower satisfaction, and task-oriented behavior is typically associated with higher productivity.

The second question is whether people orientation and task orientation exist together in the same leader, and how. The grid theory argues that yes, both are present when people work with or through others to accomplish an activity. Although leaders may be high on either style, there is considerable belief that the best leaders are high on both behaviors. Eddy Cue, senior vice president of Internet Software and Services at Apple and one of CEO Tim Cook's trusted advisers, provides an example of a leader who succeeds on both dimensions. Cue is known as a master strategist and tactician who focuses people on key goals for new product launches, establishes plans to reach targets, and may even step in to handle tasks himself to get things done on time. Yet employees also appreciate his softer, people-oriented side. When the development of the iCloud service wasn't going well, Cue stayed calm and told employees he had confidence in them. He's respected for being easygoing and friendly and for being willing to make himself vulnerable with employees by openly admitting mistakes.[46]

The third question concerns whether people can actually change themselves into leaders high on people or task orientation. In the 1950s and 1960s, when the Ohio State and Michigan studies were underway, the assumption of researchers was that the behaviors of effective leaders could be emulated by anyone wishing to become an effective leader. In general it seems that people can indeed learn new leader behaviors. Although "high-high" leadership is not the only effective style, researchers have looked to this kind of leader as a candidate for success in a wide variety of situations. However, as we will see in Chapter 3, the next generation of leadership studies refined the understanding of situations to pinpoint more precisely when each type of leadership behavior is most effective.

2-4 INDIVIDUALIZED LEADERSHIP

Traditional trait and behavior theories assume that a leader adopts a general leadership style that is used with all group members. A more recent approach to leadership behavior research, *individualized leadership*, looks instead at the specific relationship between a leader and each individual follower.[47] **Individualized leadership** is based on the notion that a leader develops a unique relationship with each subordinate or group member, which determines how the leader behaves toward the member and how the member responds to the leader. In this view, leadership is a series of *dyads*, or a series of two-person interactions. The dyadic view focuses on the concept of *exchange*, what each party gives to and receives from the other.[48]

Individualized leadership
a theory based on the notion that a leader develops a unique relationship with each subordinate or group member, which determines how the leader behaves toward the member and how the member responds to the leader

The first individualized leadership theory was introduced nearly 40 years ago and has been steadily revised ever since. Exhibit 2.6 illustrates the development of research in this area. The first stage was the awareness of a relationship between a leader and each individual rather than between a leader and a group of followers. The second stage examined specific attributes of the exchange relationship. The

EXHIBIT 2.6 Stages of Development of Individualized Leadership

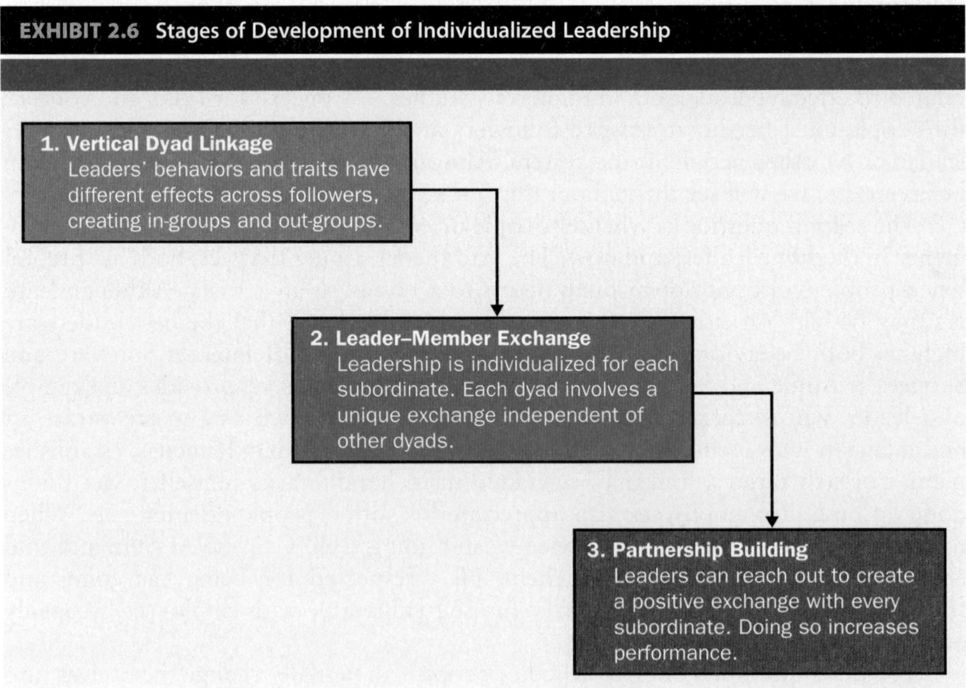

Sources: Based on Fred Danereau, "A Dyadic Approach to Leadership: Creating and Nurturing This Approach Under Fire," *Leadership Quarterly* 6, no. 4 (1995), pp. 479–490, and George B. Graen and Mary Uhl-Bien, "Relationship-Based Approach to Leadership: Development of Leader–Member Exchange (LMX) Theory of Leadership over 25 Years: Applying a Multi-Level, Multi-Domain Approach," *Leadership Quarterly* 6, no. 2 (1995), pp. 219–247.

third stage explored whether leaders could intentionally develop partnerships with each group member.

2-4a Vertical Dyad Linkage Model

The **vertical dyad linkage (VDL) model** argues for the importance of the dyad formed by a leader with each member of the group. Initial findings indicated that followers provided very different descriptions of the same leader. For example, some reported a leader, and their relationship with the leader, as having a high degree of mutual trust, respect, and obligation. These high-quality relationships might be characterized as high on both people and task orientation. Other followers reported a low-quality relationship with the same leader, such as having a low degree of trust, respect, and obligation. These followers perceived the leader as being low on important leadership behaviors.

Based on these two extreme behavior patterns, subordinates were found to exist in either an in-group or an out-group in relation to the leader. Exhibit 2.7 delineates the differences in leader behavior toward in-group versus out-group members. A recent survey of 17,000 federal employees found that 28 percent believed their own supervisor had granted advantages to someone based on personal feelings or relationships, and 53 percent believed such favoritism had influenced the decisions or actions of other supervisors in their organization.[49] Most of us who have had experience with any kind of group, whether it be a college class, an athletic team, or a work group, recognize that some leaders may spend a disproportionate amount of time with certain people and that these "insiders" are often highly trusted and may obtain special privileges. In the terminology of the VDL model, these people would be considered to participate in an *in-group relationship* with the leader, whereas other members of the group who did not experience a sense of trust and extra consideration would participate in an *out-group relationship*. In-group members, those who rated the leader highly, had developed close relationships with the leader and often became assistants who played key roles in the functioning of the work unit. Out-group members were not key players in the work unit.

Vertical dyad linkage (VDL) model
a model of individualized leadership that argues for the importance of the dyad formed by a leader with each member of the group

EXHIBIT 2.7 Leader Behavior toward In-Group versus Out-Group Members

In-Group Subordinates	Out-Group Subordinates
• Provides support and encouragement when employee faces a difficult, stressful task • Discusses objectives; trusts employee to use his or her own approach in solving problems and reaching goals • Listens to employee's suggestions and ideas about how work is done • Treats mistakes as opportunities for coaching and developing employee • Gives employee interesting assignments; may allow employee to choose assignment • Sometimes defers to subordinate's opinion • Praises accomplishments and performance improvements	• Shows little consideration if employee is having difficulty with a task • Gives the employee specific directives for how to accomplish tasks and attain goals • Shows little interest in employee's comments and suggestions • Criticizes or punishes mistakes • Assigns primarily routine jobs and monitors employee closely • Usually imposes own views • Focuses on areas of poor performance

Sources: Based on Jean François Manzoni and Jean-Louis Barsoux, "The Set-Up-to-Fail Syndrome," *Harvard Business Review* (March–April 1988), pp. 110–113; and Mark O'Donnell, Gary Yukl, and Thomas Taber, "Leader Behavior and LMX: A Constructive Replication," *Journal of Management Psychology* 27, no. 2 (2012), pp. 143–154.

NEW LEADER
ACTION MEMO

Answer the questions in Leader's Self-Insight 2.3 to understand how LMX theory applies to your own work experience.

Thus, by focusing on the relationship between a leader and each individual, the VDL research found great variance of leader style and impact within a group of followers.

2-4b Leader–Member Exchange

Stage two in the development of the individualized leadership theory explored the **leader–member exchange (LMX)** in more detail, discovering that the impact on outcomes depends on how the LMX process develops over time. Studies evaluating characteristics of the LMX relationship explored such things as communication frequency, value agreement, characteristics of followers, job satisfaction, performance, job climate, and commitment. Leaders typically tend to establish in-group exchange relationships with individuals who have characteristics similar to those of the leader, such as similarity in background, interests, and values, and with those who demonstrate a high level of competence and interest in the job. Overall, studies have found that the quality of the LMX relationship is substantially higher for in-group members. LMX theory proposes that this higher-quality relationship will lead to higher performance and greater job satisfaction for in-group members, and research in general supports this idea.[50] High-quality LMX relationships have been found to lead to very positive outcomes for leaders, followers, work units, and the organization. For followers, a high-quality exchange relationship may mean more interesting assignments, greater responsibility and authority, and tangible rewards such as pay increases and promotions. Leaders and organizations clearly benefit from the increased effort and initiative of in-group participants to carry out assignments and tasks successfully.

2-4c Partnership Building

NEW LEADER
ACTION MEMO

As a leader, you can build a positive, individualized relationship with each follower to create an equitable work environment and provide greater benefits to yourself, followers, and the organization.

In this third phase of research, the focus was on whether leaders could develop positive relationships with a large number of subordinates. Critics of early LMX theory pointed out the dangers of leaders establishing sharply differentiated in-group and out-group relationships, in that this may lead to feelings of resentment or even hostility among out-group participants.[51] If leaders are perceived to be granting excessive benefits and advantages to in-group members, members of the out-group may rebel, which can damage the entire organization. Moreover, some studies have found that leaders tend to categorize employees into in-groups and out-groups as early as five days into their relationship.[52]

Thus, the third phase of research in this area focused on whether leaders could develop positive relationships with *all* followers. In this approach, the leader views each person independently and may treat each one in a different but positive way. That is, leaders strive to develop a positive relationship with each subordinate, but the positive relationship will have a different form for each person. For example, one person might be treated with "consideration" and another with "initiating structure," depending on what followers need to feel involved and to succeed.

Leader–member exchange (LMX) individualized leadership model that explores how leader–member relationships develop over time and how the quality of exchange relationships affects outcomes

In the LMX research study, leaders were trained to offer the opportunity for a high-quality relationship to all group members, and the followers who responded to the offer dramatically improved their performance. As these relationships matured, the entire work group became more productive, and the payoffs were tremendous. Leaders could count on followers to provide the assistance needed for high performance, and followers participated in and influenced decisions. The implications of this finding are that true performance and productivity gains can be achieved by having the leader develop positive relationships one on one with each subordinate.

LEADER'S SELF-INSIGHT 2.3

Your "LMX" Relationship

Instructions: What was the quality of your leader's relationship with you? Think back to a job you held and recall your feelings toward your leader, or if currently employed use your supervisor. Please answer whether each of the following items was Mostly False or Mostly True for you.

	Mostly False	Mostly True
1. I very much liked my supervisor as a person.	_____	_____
2. My supervisor defended my work to people above him if I made a mistake.	_____	_____
3. The work I did for my supervisor went well beyond what was required.	_____	_____
4. I admired my supervisor's professional knowledge and ability.	_____	_____
5. My supervisor was enjoyable to work with.	_____	_____
6. I applied extra effort to further the interests of my work group.	_____	_____
7. My supervisor championed my case to others in the organization.	_____	_____
8. I respected my supervisor's management competence.	_____	_____

Scoring and Interpretation

LMX theory is about the quality of a leader's relationship with subordinates. If you scored 6 or more Mostly True, your supervisor clearly had an excellent relationship with you, which is stage two in Exhibit 2.6. You had a successful dyad. If your supervisor had an equally good relationship with every subordinate, that is a stage-three level of development (partnership building). If you scored 3 or fewer Mostly True, then your supervisor was probably at level one, perhaps with different relationships with subordinates, some or all of which were unsuccessful. What do you think accounted for the quality of your and other subordinates' relationships (positive or negative) with your supervisor? Discuss with other students to learn why some supervisors have good LMX relationships.

Source: Based on Robert C. Liden and John M. Maslyn, "Multidimensionality of Leader–Member Exchange: An Empirical Assessment through Scale Development," *Journal of Management* 24 (1998), pp. 43–72.

2-5 ENTREPRENEURIAL TRAITS AND BEHAVIORS

Another topic of special concern in today's fast-changing world is what traits encourage entrepreneurship. *Entrepreneurship* refers to initiating a business venture, organizing the necessary resources, and assuming the associated risks and rewards.[53] An entrepreneur recognizes a viable idea for a business product or service and carries it out by finding and assembling the necessary resources—money, people, machinery, location—to undertake the business venture.

Entrepreneurial leaders display many of the same characteristics as other leaders, but some traits are particularly important for entrepreneurs. Four characteristics considered highly important to entrepreneurial leaders are the following:[54]

- **Vision and dissatisfaction with the present.** To start something new requires that the entrepreneur be dissatisfied with the way things are now and have a clear vision for how things should be. For example, in the 1970s Bill Gates had what at the time was a radical vision that software itself was a business, and he clearly stated his dissatisfaction that it wasn't. Gates pursued his vision, encapsulated in the idea of a computer in every home and on every desk running Microsoftware. Entrepreneurs are more concerned with innovation, creativity, and creating new processes than with maintaining the status quo.
- **Ability to get people on board.** Entrepreneurial leaders have to continually recruit others to join in, support, and add to the vision. Gates made his vision

for a software business widely known and actively engaged with hardware makers like IBM to put the vision into action.

- **Flexibility, openness to feedback, and ability to learn and adapt.** No one has all the answers, and entrepreneurial leaders must be willing to listen, learn, and adapt. Clara Shih, who started Hearsay Social, a platform that helps large companies manage their employees' presence on social media sites, worked hard not only to raise millions in financing but to gain the support of Facebook COO Sheryl Sandberg as a mentor to help her learn and adapt to changes in the industry.[55]
- **Persistence and execution.** Entrepreneurial leaders are tenacious in pursuit of the vision and take active steps in the here and now to bring the future to life. If one thing doesn't work out, they try another. They are typically highly self-motivated and are willing to stretch themselves and take risks to achieve the vision.

For some leaders, entrepreneurial traits come naturally, but many people can develop these characteristics, as with other leadership qualities. Entrepreneurial leaders start new companies, as Bill Gates did with Microsoft and Clara Shih did with Hearsay Social, but they also exist within established organizations. These leaders take risks to create novel solutions to competitive challenges confronting a business, especially the development or enhancement of products and services. Entrepreneurial leadership is a source of innovation and change for established companies.

LEADERSHIP ESSENTIALS

- The point of this chapter is to understand the importance of traits and behaviors in the development of leadership theory and research. Some traits associated with effective leadership include optimism, self-confidence, honesty, and drive. A large number of personal traits and abilities have been associated with successful leaders, but traits themselves are not sufficient to guarantee effective leadership.
- Natural traits and behavior patterns can be developed into strengths. It is important for leaders to recognize their strengths and acknowledge the interdependence that is a key to effective leadership.
- Research suggests that different leader strengths might be better suited to different types of leadership roles. The chapter describes three types of roles: operational roles, collaborative roles, and advisory roles. Leaders can be more effective when they are in positions that best match their natural tendencies.
- The behavior approach explored autocratic versus democratic leadership, consideration versus initiating structure, employee-centered versus job-centered leadership, and concern for people versus concern for production. The theme of people versus tasks runs through this research, suggesting these are fundamental behaviors through which leaders meet followers' needs. There has been some disagreement in the research about whether a specific leader is either people- or task oriented or whether one can be both. Today, the consensus is that leaders can achieve a "high-high" leadership style.
- Another approach is the dyad between a leader and each follower. Followers have different relationships with the leader, and the ability of the leader to

develop a positive relationship with each follower contributes to team performance. The LMX theory says that high-quality relationships have a positive outcome for leaders, followers, work units, and the organization. Leaders can attempt to build individualized relationships with each person as a way to meet needs for both consideration and structure.

- The historical development of leadership theory presented in this chapter introduces some important ideas about leadership. Although certain personal traits and abilities indicate a greater likelihood for success in a leadership role, they are not in themselves sufficient to guarantee effective leadership. Behaviors are equally significant. Therefore, the style of leadership demonstrated by an individual greatly determines the outcome of the leadership endeavor. Often, a combination of behavioral styles is most effective. To understand the effects of leadership on outcomes, the specific relationship behavior between a leader and each follower is also an important consideration.
- Entrepreneurial leadership is of great concern in today's turbulent environment because entrepreneurial leadership is an important source of innovation and change. Entrepreneurial leaders take risks to bring new organizations into being or create novel solutions to competitive challenges confronting existing organizations.

DISCUSSION QUESTIONS

1. Why is it important for leaders to know their strengths? Do you think leaders should spend equal time learning about their weak points?
2. Suggest some personal traits of leaders you have known. What traits do you believe are most valuable? Why?
3. The chapter suggests that optimism is an important trait for a leader, yet some employees complain that optimistic leaders create significant stress because they don't anticipate problems and expect their subordinates to meet unreasonable goals. Do you agree? Why?
4. What is the difference between trait theories and behavioral theories of leadership?
5. Would you feel most comfortable using a "consideration" or an "initiating-structure" leadership style? Discuss the reasons for your answer.
6. The vertical dyad linkage model suggests that followers respond individually to the leader. If this is so, what advice would you give leaders about displaying people-oriented versus task-oriented behavior?
7. Does it make sense to you that a leader should develop an individualized relationship with each follower? Explain advantages and disadvantages to this approach.
8. Why would subordinates under a democratic leader perform better in the leader's absence than would subordinates under an autocratic leader?
9. Why is an entrepreneurial leader important to an organization? How is this role different from other leader roles?
10. Pick three traits from the list in Exhibit 2.1 that you think would be most valuable for a leader in an operational role. Pick three that you think would be most valuable for a leader in a collaborative role. Explain your choices.

LEADERSHIP AT WORK

Your Ideal Leader Traits

Spend some time thinking about someone you believe is an ideal leader. For the first part of the exercise, select an ideal leader you have heard about whom you don't personally know. It could be someone like Mother Teresa, Martin Luther King, Abraham Lincoln, or any national or international figure that you admire. Write the person's name here: ___________. Now, in the space below, write down three things you admire about the person, such as what he or she did or the qualities that person possesses.

____

____

____

For the second part of the exercise, select an ideal leader whom you know personally. This can be anyone from your life experiences. Write the person's name here: ___________. Now, in the space below, write down three things you admire about the person, such as what he or she did or the qualities that person possesses.

____

____

____

The first leader you chose represents something of a projective test based on what you've heard or read. You imagine the leader has the qualities you listed. The deeds and qualities you listed say more about what you admire than about the actual traits of the leader you chose. This is something like an inkblot test, and it is important because the traits you assign to the leader are traits you are aware of, have the potential to develop, and indeed can develop as a leader. The qualities or achievements you listed are an indicator of the traits you likely will express as you develop into the leader you want to become.

The second leader you chose is someone you know, so it is less of a projective test and represents traits you have had direct experience with. You know these traits work for you and likely will become the traits you develop and express as a leader.

What is similar about the traits you listed for the two leaders? Different? Interview another student in class about traits he or she admires. What do the traits tell you about the person you are interviewing? What are the common themes in your list and the other student's list of traits? To what extent do you display the same traits as the ones on your list? Will you develop those traits even more in the future?

____

____

____

LEADERSHIP DEVELOPMENT: CASES FOR ANALYSIS

Consolidated Products

Consolidated Products is a medium-sized manufacturer of consumer products with nonunionized production workers. Ben Samuels was a plant manager for Consolidated Products for

10 years, and he was very well liked by the employees there. They were grateful for the fitness center he built for employees, and they enjoyed the social activities sponsored by the plant several times a year, including company picnics and holiday parties. He knew most of the workers by name, and he spent part of each day walking around the plant to visit with them and ask about their families or hobbies.

Ben believed that it was important to treat employees properly so they would have a sense of loyalty to the company. He tried to avoid any layoffs when production demand was slack, figuring that the company could not afford to lose skilled workers that are so difficult to replace. The workers knew that if they had a special problem, Ben would try to help them. For example, when someone was injured but wanted to continue working, Ben found another job in the plant that the person could do despite having a disability. Ben believed that if you treat people right, they would do a good job for you without close supervision or prodding. Ben applied the same principle to his supervisors, and he mostly left them alone to run their departments as they saw fit. He did not set objectives and standards for the plant, and he never asked the supervisors to develop plans for improving productivity and product quality.

Under Ben, the plant had the lowest turnover among the company's five plants, but the second worst record for costs and production levels. When the company was acquired by another firm, Ben was asked to take early retirement, and Phil Jones was brought in to replace him.

Phil had a growing reputation as a manager who could get things done, and he quickly began making changes. Costs were cut by trimming a number of activities such as the fitness center at the plant, company picnics and parties, and the human relations training programs for supervisors. Phil believed that human relations training was a waste of time; if employees don't want to do the work, get rid of them and find somebody else who does.

Supervisors were instructed to establish high performance standards for their departments and insist that people achieve them. A computer monitoring system was introduced so that the output of each worker could be checked closely against the standards. Phil told his supervisors to give any worker who had substandard performance one warning, and then if performance did not improve within two weeks to fire the person. Phil believed that workers don't respect a supervisor who is weak and passive. When Phil observed a worker wasting time or making a mistake, he would reprimand the person right on the spot to set an example. Phil also checked closely on the performance of his supervisors. Demanding objectives were set for each department, and weekly meetings were held with each supervisor to review department performance. Finally, Phil insisted that supervisors check with him first before taking any significant actions that deviated from established plans and policies.

As another cost-cutting move, Phil reduced the frequency of equipment maintenance, which required machines to be idled when they could be productive. Since the machines had a good record of reliable operation, Phil believed that the current maintenance schedule was excessive and was cutting into production. Finally, when business was slow for one of the product lines, Phil laid off workers rather than finding something else for them to do.

By the end of Phil's first year as plant manager, production costs were reduced by 20 percent and production output was up by 10 percent. However, three of his seven supervisors left to take other jobs, and turnover was also high among the machine operators. Some of the turnover was due to workers who were fired, but competent machine operators were also quitting, and it was becoming increasingly difficult to find any replacements for them. Finally, there was increasing talk of unionizing among the workers.[56]

QUESTIONS

1. Compare the leadership traits and behaviors of Ben Samuels and Phil Jones.
2. Which leader do you think is more effective? Why? Which leader would you prefer to work for?
3. If you were Phil Jones's boss, what would you do now?

Transition to Leadership

My name is Michael Collins. When I was named Southwest Regional Manager of Creighton Auto Parts, a major parts sales and service corporation, I saw the transition period before and immediately following my appointment as an exciting new opportunity. With a degree in automotive engineering and several years' experience in parts manufacturing (design and plant management), I came to the new position with strong industry connections and a keen eye for trends and product innovation.

During the initial stages of the transition, I met with the outgoing regional manager, receiving his input about ongoing business issues, how current services tallied with the corporation's short- and long-term goals, and what he saw as the strengths and weaknesses of the various stores and personnel within the region. While some of these meetings took place at his office, I wanted to avoid the appearance of depending on "the old man" for guidance, so I scheduled most of our meetings off-site to provide more opportunities for frank discussion covering procedures, products and services, and individual stakeholders from employees and board members to suppliers and customers.

In addition, I spent a great deal of time making my own assessments. I knew my company honeymoon period would be limited. My vision and my implementation program had to be clear with well-defined strategies. As a first step, I sent a lengthy e-mail message to all key players on my new leadership team both as introduction and as a prelude to establishing my vision and transition program.

I traveled around the region meeting with the store managers on my regional team, as well as holding informal meetings with front-line employees. In so doing, I was surprised to tap into the rumor mill and find individuals who were eager to talk openly about their goals, ideas, opinions, and complaints. My questions to front-line workers, in particular, had both positive and negative aspects. I questioned them about their length of service, what they liked most about the company, what areas they thought could be improved, how they rated the culture—things like that. I discovered that for most of them, this was more than just a job. Many had worked for the company for a number of years and had a great deal of pride in the company, as well as a deep sense of responsibility toward their customers.

However, I found this portion of my on-site visits the most intrusive on my time, and in many cases I regretted the amount of time I spent listening to workers. I wondered if the advance warning of my visit allowed too much time for people to prepare their answers. I wondered how many were genuine in their responses and how many were just trying to hold on to their jobs. Worse, I found myself hostage to those who wanted to rant on and on about workplace issues, their training, their bosses, even their customers. I talked to a few customers and didn't get much from that either. As I proceeded through the on-site visits, I found myself growing impatient, increasingly checking my watch to see how soon I should leave for the next appointment on a packed schedule. I admit I expected more from this portion of the transition than I received. However, once I committed to this, I felt obligated to see it through.

More rewarding was the time spent with the marketing staff exploring customer satisfaction levels. In focusing on customers, I zeroed in on three research areas: customer complaints, area demographics, and the compounding customer—those return customers who generate additional sales among their friends and family. Why do customers come? What makes them return? What are their personal "hot buttons"—needs or breaking points in dealing with service industries? Our market research showed large segments of our population in four areas: under 30, over 60, Hispanics, and women. We also saw an increasing number of unemployed and under-employed do-it-yourself customers trying to keep the family vehicle going just a little longer. I personally love analyzing market data.

My question for regional service, sales, and marketing was "how are we reaching and retaining these segments of the population?" Do advertising, Web sites, direct mailing, coupon campaigns, and other marketing strategies match these demographics? For example, are we providing and training Spanish-language sales and service experts and consumer information? With large segments of young people, senior citizens, the unemployed, and single moms, wouldn't these large segments of the population offer fabulous compounding opportunities with focused marketing and price breaks?

As I take the reins, I am excited about the marketing challenges and opportunities ahead. I am an idea guy, a hands-on manager whose ideal is the Renaissance man capable of doing many things very well. I like to surround myself with similar kinds of people. I generate ideas and expect follow-up and accountability. The leadership model I embrace sets the bar high for me and for everyone who works for me. I look forward to injecting a new vision and new standards of service throughout the region.

QUESTIONS

1. What do you see as Michael Collins's leadership traits? Which of these traits do you consider a strength? A weakness? Explain.
2. What do you think of Michael Collins's approach to leading the region? How would you characterize his people-oriented versus task-oriented style? Why?
3. How might an understanding of individualized leadership be useful to Collins with respect to his relationship with marketing versus store personnel?

REFERENCES

1. Steven Davidoff Solomon, "J. Crew Struggles with Its 'Great Man' Dilemma," *The New York Times* (June 10, 2015), p. B4; Stephanie Clifford, "J. Crew Benefits As Mrs. Obama Wears the Brand," *The New York Times* (November 17, 2008), http://www.nytimes.com/2008/11/17/business/media/17crew.html?_r=0 (accessed October 8, 2015); and Keith Bedford, "Mickey Drexler Leads J. Crew by Doing the Things Managers Aren't Supposed To," *Quartz* http://qz.com/181569/j-crew-mickey-drexler-leads-by-doing-everything-managers-arent-supposed-to/ (accessed October 8, 2015).
2. G. A. Yukl, *Leadership in Organizations* (Upper Saddle River, NJ: Prentice Hall, 1981); and S. C. Kohs and K. W. Irle, "Prophesying Army Promotion," *Journal of Applied Psychology* 4 (1920), pp. 73–87.
3. Yukl, *Leadership in Organizations*, p. 254.
4. R. M. Stogdill, "Personal Factors Associated with Leadership: A Survey of the Literature," *Journal of Psychology* 25 (1948), pp. 35–71.
5. R. M. Stogdill, Handbook of Leadership: A Survey of the Literature (New York: The Free Press, 1974) ; and Bernard M. Bass, Bass & Stogdill's Handbook of Leadership: Theory, Research, and Managerial Applications, 3rd ed. (New York: The Free Press, 1990).
6. S. A. Kirkpatrick and E. A. Locke, "Leadership: Do Traits Matter?" *The Academy of Management Executive* 5, no. 2 (1991), pp. 48–60.
7. R. G. Lord, C. L. DeVader, and G. M. Alliger, "A Meta-Analysis of the Relation between Personality Traits and Leadership Perceptions: An Application of Validity Generalization Procedures," *Journal of Applied Psychology* 71 (1986), pp. 402–410.
8. Study reported in "From the Front Lines: How Does Leadership Personality Affect Performance?" *Leader to Leader* (Winter 2007), pp. 56–57; and Bradley R. Agle, Nandu J. Nagarajan, Jeffrey A. Sonnenfeld, and Dhinu Srinivasan, "Does CEO Charisma Matter? An Empirical Analysis of the Relationships among Organizational Performance, Environmental Uncertainty, and Top Management Team Perceptions of CEO Charisma," *Academy of Management Journal* 49, no. 1 (2006), pp. 161–174.
9. Andrew St. George, "Leadership Lessons from the Royal Navy," *McKinsey Quarterly* (January 2013), http://www.mckinseyquarterly.com/Leadership_lessons_from_the_Royal_Navy_3053 (accessed February 7, 2013).
10. Patrick Lencioni, "The Most Important Leadership Trait You Shun," *The Wall Street Journal* (June 21, 2010), http://online.wsj.com/article/SB10001424052748704895204575321380627619388.html (accessed March 11, 2013).
11. Edwin Locke and Associates, *The Essence of Leadership* (New York: Lexington Books, 1991).
12. A summary of various studies and surveys is reported in Del Jones, "Optimism Puts Rose-Colored Tint in Glasses of Top Execs," *USA Today* (December 15, 2005).
13. See Elaine Fox, "The Essence of Optimism," *Scientific American Mind* (January–February 2013), pp. 22–27.
14. Arthur Bandura, "Self-efficacy," in V. S. Ramachaudran, ed., *Encyclopedia of Human Behavior*, vol. 4 (New York: Academic Press, 1994), pp. 71–81; and Elizabeth A. McDaniel and Holly DiBella-McCarthy, "Reflective Leaders Become Causal Agents of Change," *Journal of Management Development* 31, no. 7 (2012), pp. 663–671.
15. Shelley A. Kirkpatrick and Edwin A. Locke, "Leadership: Do Traits Matter?" *Academy of Management Executive* 5, no. 2 (1991), pp. 48–60.
16. Larry Neumeister and Tom Hays, "Madoff Sent to Jail as Furious Victims Applaud," *The Huffington Post* (March 12, 2009), http://www.huffingtonpost.com/2009/03/12/madoff-arrives-in-court-f_n_174194.html (accessed May 30, 2013); and Julie Creswell and Landon Thomas Jr., "The Talented Mr. Madoff," *The New York Times* (January 25, 2009), p. BU1.
17. James M. Kouzes and Barry Z. Posner, *Credibility: How Leaders Gain and Lose It, Why People Demand It* (San Francisco: Jossey-Bass, 1993), p. 14.
18. Kirkpatrick and Locke, "Leadership: Do Traits Matter? "
19. Patricia Sellers, "Marissa Mayer: Ready to Rumble at Yahoo," *Fortune* (October 29, 2012), pp. 118–128; and Julianne Pepitone, "Marissa Mayer: Yahoos Can No Longer Work from Home," *CNN Money* (February 25, 2013), http://money.cnn.com/2013/02/25/technology/yahoo-work-from-home/index.html (accessed March 11, 2013).
20. "Towards a More Perfect Match: Building Successful Leaders by Effectively Aligning People and Roles," Hay Group Working Paper (2004); and "Making Sure the Suit Fits," *Hay Group Research Brief* (2004). Both available from 116 Huntington Avenue, Boston, MA 02116: Hay Group, The McClelland Center,, or at http://www.haygroup.com.
21. The following is based on Marcus Buckingham and Donald O. Clifton, *Now, Discover Your Strengths* (New York: The Free Press, 2001); and

Chuck Martin with Peg Dawson and Richard Guare, *Smarts: Are We Hardwired for Success?* (New York: AMACOM, 2007).

22. Deborah Ancona, Thomas W. Malone, Wanda J. Orlikowski, and Peter M. Senge, "In Praise of the Incomplete Leader," *Harvard Business Review* (February 2007), pp. 92–100.
23. Center for Creative Leadership survey results, reported in "The Demise of the Heroic Leader," *Leader to Leader* (Fall 2006), pp. 55–56.
24. Buckingham and Clifton, *Now, Discover Your Strengths*, p. 12.
25. Ibid.
26. Bill George, "The Master Gives It Back," segment in "Special Report: America's Best Leaders," *U.S. News and World Report* (October 30, 2006), pp. 50–87; and Richard L. Daft, *The Executive and the Elephant: A Leader's Guide to Building Inner Excellence* (San Francisco: Jossey-Bass, 2010), p. 149.
27. This discussion is based on Ron Garonzik, Geoff Nethersell, and Scott Spreier, "Navigating through the New Leadership Landscape," *Leader to Leader* (Winter 2006), pp. 30–39; "Towards a More Perfect Match: Building Successful Leaders by Effectively Aligning People and Roles," Hay Group Working Paper (2004); and "Making Sure the 'Suit' Fits," Hay Group Research Brief (2004). Available from 116 Huntington Avenue, Boston, MA, 02116: Hay Group, The McClelland Center, or at http://www.haygroup.com.
28. K. Lewin, "Field Theory and Experiment in Social Psychology: Concepts and Methods," *American Journal of Sociology* 44 (1939), pp. 868–896; K. Lewin and R. Lippett, "An Experimental Approach to the Study of Autocracy and Democracy: A Preliminary Note," *Sociometry* 1 (1938), pp. 292–300; and K. Lewin, R. Lippett, and R. K. White, "Patterns of Aggressive Behavior in Experimentally Created Social Climates," *Journal of Social Psychology* 10 (1939), pp. 271–301.
29. R. Tannenbaum and W. H. Schmidt, "How to Choose a Leadership Pattern," *Harvard Business Review* 36 (1958), pp. 95–101.
30. F. A. Heller and G. A. Yukl, "Participation, Managerial Decision-Making and Situational Variables," *Organizational Behavior and Human Performance* 4 (1969), pp. 227–241.
31. "Jack's Recipe (Management Principles Used by Jack Hartnett, President of D. L. Rogers Corp.)," sidebar in Marc Ballon, "Extreme Managing: Equal Parts Old-Fashioned Dictator and New Age Father Figure, Jack Hartnett Breaks Nearly Every Rule of the Enlightened Manager's Code," *Inc.* (July 1998), p. 60.
32. Eileen Newman Rubin, "Assessing Your Leadership Style to Achieve Organizational Objectives," *Global Business and Organizational Excellence* (September–October 2013), pp. 55–66; Bill George, "The Master Gives It Back," segment in "Special Report: America's Best Leaders," *U.S. News and World Report* (October 30, 2006), pp. 50–87; and Richard L. Daft, *The Executive and the Elephant: A Leader's Guide to Building Inner Excellence* (San Francisco: Jossey-Bass, 2010), p. 149.
33. Donna Fenn, "The Remote Control CEO," *Inc.* (October 2005), pp. 96–101, 144–146.
34. J. K. Hemphill and A. E. Coons, "Development of the Leader Behavior Description Questionnaire," in R. M. Stogdill and A. E. Coons, eds., *Leader Behavior: Its Description and Measurement* (Columbus: Ohio State University, Bureau of Business Research, 1957).
35. P. C. Nystrom, "Managers and the High-High Leader Myth," *Academy of Management Journal* 21 (1978), pp. 325–331; and L. L. Larson, J. G. Hunt, and Richard N. Osborn, "The Great High-High Leader Behavior Myth: A Lesson from Occam's Razor," *Academy of Management Journal* 19 (1976), pp. 628–641.
36. Christopher Cooper, "Speed Trap: How a Marine Lost His Command in Race to Baghdad," *The Wall Street Journal* (April 5, 2004), pp. A1, A15.
37. E. W. Skinner, "Relationships between Leadership Behavior Patterns and Organizational-Situational Variables," *Personnel Psychology* 22 (1969), pp. 489–494; E. A. Fleishman and E. F. Harris, "Patterns of Leadership Behavior Related to Employee Grievances and Turnover," *Personnel Psychology* 15 (1962), pp. 43–56; and Ronald F. Piccolo, Joyce E. Bono, Kathrin Heinitz, Jens Rowold, Emily Duehr, and Timothy A. Judge, "The Relative Impact of Complementary Leader Behaviors: Which Matter Most?" *The Leadership Quaterly* 23 (2012), pp. 567–581.
38. A. W. Halpin and B. J. Winer, "A Factorial Study of the Leader Behavior Descriptions," in R. M. Stogdill and A. E. Coons, eds., *Leader Behavior: Its Descriptions and Measurement* (Columbus: Ohio State University, Bureau of Business Research, 1957); and J. K. Hemphill, "Leadership Behavior Associated with the Administrative Reputations of College Departments," *Journal of Educational Psychology* 46 (1955), pp. 385–401.
39. R. Likert, "From Production- and Employee-Centeredness to Systems 1–4," *Journal of Management* 5 (1979), pp. 147–156.
40. J. Taylor and D. Bowers, *The Survey of Organizations: A Machine Scored Standardized Questionnaire Instrument* (Ann Arbor: Institute for Social Research, University of Michigan, 1972).
41. D. G. Bowers and S. E. Seashore, "Predicting Organizational Effectiveness with a Four-Factor Theory of Leadership," *Administrative Science Quarterly* 11 (1966), pp. 238–263.
42. Ibid.
43. Robert Blake and Jane S. Mouton, *The Managerial Grid III* (Houston: Gulf Publishing Company, 1985).
44. Diane Brady and Matthew Boyle, "Campbell's Recipe for a CEO Yields Denise Morrison," *Business Week* (June 23, 2011), http://www.businessweek.com/magazine/content/11_27/b4235060614059.htm (accessed March 12, 2013); Michael Arrington, "The Way I Work: My Style Is to Bust the Door Down and Clean the Mess Up Later," *Inc.* (October 2010), pp. 124–128; and Jeff Bercovici, "TechCrunch CEO Reported Out after Clashing with HuffPost-ers," *Forbes* (November 17, 2011), http://www.forbes.com/sites/jeffbercovici/2011/11/17/techcrunch-ceo-reported-out-after-clashing-with-huffpost-ers/ (accessed March 13, 2013).
45. Gary Yukl, "Effective Leadership Behavior: What We Know and What Questions Need More Attention," *Academy of Management Perspectives* 26 (November 2012), pp. 66–80; and Gary Yukl, Angela Gordon, and Tom Taber, "A Hierarchical Taxonomy of Leadership Behavior: Integrating a Half Century of Behavior Research," *Journal of Leadership and Organizational Studies* 9, no. 1 (2002), pp. 15–32.
46. Jessica E. Lessin, "Eddy Cue: Apple's Rising Mr. Fix-It," *The Wall Street Journal* (November 28, 2012), p. B1.
47. Francis J. Yammarino and Fred Dansereau, "Individualized Leadership," *Journal of Leadership and Organizational Studies* 9, no. 1 (2002), pp. 90–99; Gary Yukl, Mark O'Donnell, and Thomas Taber, "Influence of Leader Behaviors on the Leader-Member Exchange Relationship," *Journal of Managerial Psychology* 24, no. 4 (2009), pp. 289–299; and M. O'Donnell, G. Yukl, and T. Taber, "Leader Behavior and LMX: A Constructive Replication," *Journal of Management Psychology* 27, no. 2 (2012), pp. 143–154.
48. This discussion is based on Fred Dansereau, "A Dyadic Approach to Leadership: Creating and Nurturing This Approach under Fire," *Leadership Quarterly* 6, no. 4 (1995), pp. 479–490; and George B. Graen and Mary Uhl-Bien, "Relationship-Based Approach to Leadership: Development of Leader–Member Exchange (LMX) Theory of Leadership over 25 Years: Applying a Multi-Level Multi-Domain Approach," *Leadership Quarterly* 6, no. 2 (1995), pp. 219–247.
49. Tom Fox, "Do Your Employees Think You Play Favorites? Three Ways to Tell," *The Washington Post* (January 30, 2014), https://www.washingtonpost.com/news/on-leadership/wp/2014/01/30/do-your-employees-think-you-play-favorites-three-ways-to-tell/ (accessed October 9, 2015).
50. See A. J. Kinicki and R. P. Vecchio, "Influences on the Quality of Supervisor-Subordinate Relations: The Role of Time Pressure, Organizational Commitment, and Locus of Control," *Journal of Organizational Behavior* (January 1994), pp. 75–82; R. C. Liden, S. J. Wayne, and D. Stilwell, "A Longitudinal Study on the Early Development of Leader–Member Exchanges," *Journal of Applied Psychology* (August 1993), pp. 662–674; Yammarino and Dansereau, "Individualized Leadership"; Jean-François Manzoni and Jean-Louis Barsoux, "The

Set-Up-to-Fail Syndrome," *Harvard Business Review* 76 (March–April 1998), pp. 101–113; Yukl et al., "Influence of Leader Behaviors on the Leader-Member Exchange Relationship"; and O'Donnell et al., "Leader Behavior and LMX: A Constructive Replication."

51. W. E. McClane, "Implications of Member Role Differentiation: Analysis of a Key Concept in the LMX Model of Leadership," *Group and Organization Studies* 16 (1991), pp. 102–113; and Gary Yukl, *Leadership in Organizations*, 2nd ed. (Upper Saddle River, NJ: Prentice Hall, 1989).
52. Manzoni and Barsoux, "The Set-Up-to-Fail Syndrome."
53. Donald F. Kuratko and Richard M. Hodgetts, *Entrepreneurship: A Contemporary Approach*, 4th ed. (Fort Worth, TX: Dryden Press, 1998), p. 30.
54. These are based on Todd Warner, "5 Essential Qualities for Entrepreneurial Leadership," *Forbes* (June 8, 2012), http://www.forbes.com/sites/startupviews/2012/06/08/5-essential-qualities-for-entrepreneurial-leadership/ (accessed October 9, 2015); Kristina L. Guo, "Core Competencies of the Entrepreneurial Leader in Health Care Organizations," *Health Care Manager* 28 (January–March 2009), pp. 19–29; and Gary A. Knight, "Cross-Cultural Reliability and Validity of a Scale to Measure Firm Entrepreneurial Orientation," *Journal of Business Venturing* 12 (1997), pp. 213–225.
55. Colleen Leahey, "Doing It for Themselves," *Fortune* (October 17, 2011), pp. 144–148.
56. Reprinted with permission from Gary Yukl, *Leadership in Organizations*, 4th ed. (Upper Saddle River, NJ: Prentice Hall, 1998), p. 66.

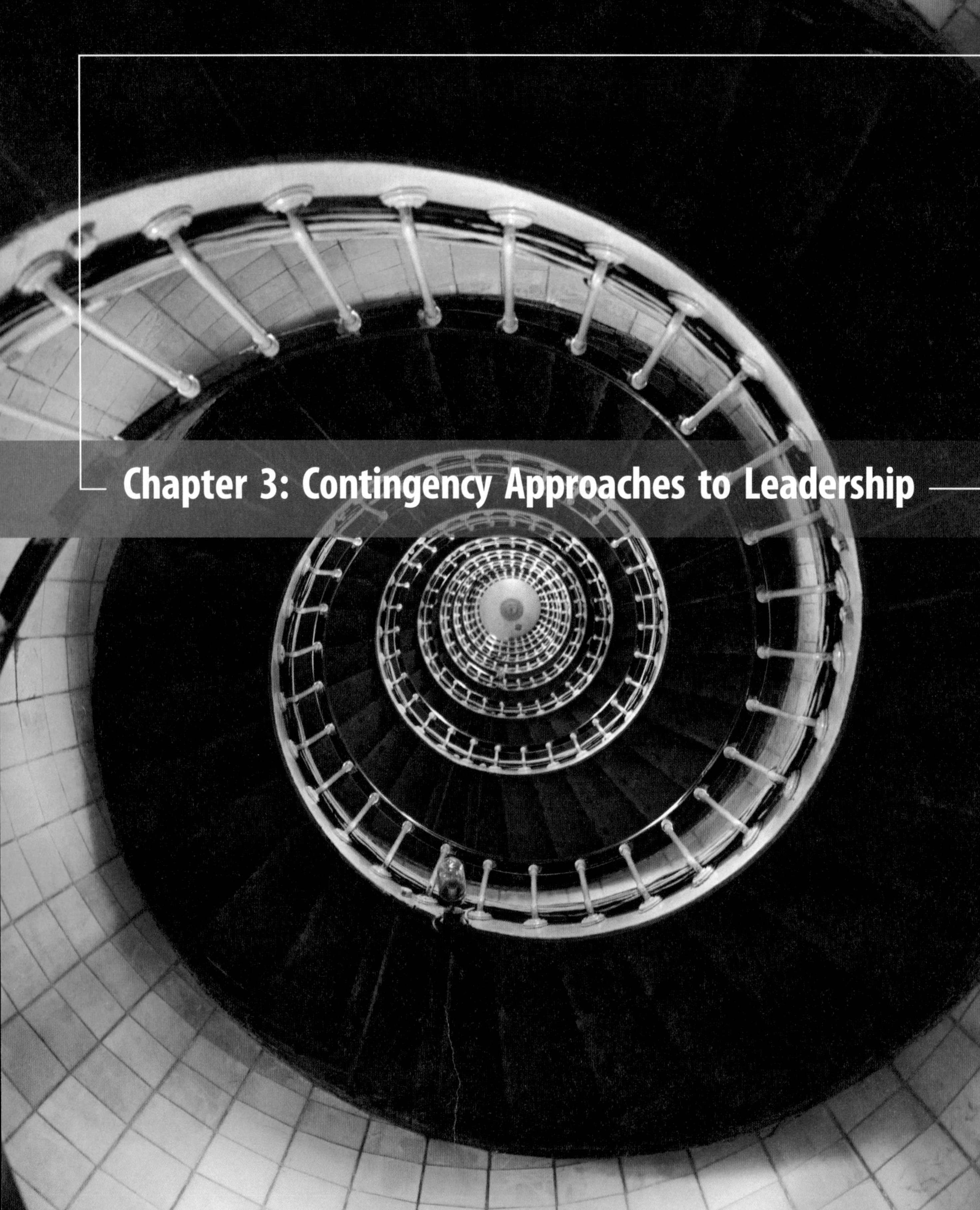

Chapter 3: Contingency Approaches to Leadership

YOUR **LEADERSHIP** CHALLENGE

After reading this chapter, you should be able to:

- Understand how leadership is often contingent on people and situations.
- Apply Hersey and Blanchard's situational theory of leader style to the level of follower readiness.
- Apply Fiedler's contingency model to key relationships among leader style, situational favorability, and group task performance.
- Explain the path–goal theory of leadership.
- Use the Vroom–Jago model to identify the correct amount of follower participation in specific decision situations.
- Know how to use the power of situational variables to substitute for or neutralize the need for leadership.

CHAPTER **OUTLINE**

66 **The Contingency Approach**

69 **Hersey and Blanchard's Situational Theory**

73 **Fiedler's Contingency Model**

77 **Path–Goal Theory**

81 **The Vroom–Jago Contingency Model**

88 **Substitutes for Leadership**

In The Lead

72 **Laura Smith, Yola**

75 **Sergio Marchionne, Fiat Chrysler Automobiles**

79 **Alan Robbins, Plastic Lumber Company**

87 **Art Weinstein, Whitlock Manufacturing**

88 **Daniel Snyder, Washington Redskins**

Leader's Self-Insight

69 **T–P Leadership Questionnaire: An Assessment of Style**

73 **Are You Ready?**

90 **Measuring Substitutes for Leadership**

Leader's Bookshelf

67 **Shackleton's Way: Leadership Lessons from the Great Antarctic Explorer**

Leadership at Work

92 **Task versus Relationship Role Play**

Leadership Development: Cases for Analysis

93 **Alvis Corporation**

94 **An Impossible Dream?**

A few hours after being named only the third CEO in Microsoft's history, Satya Nadella held a short impromptu town hall Webcast, near the end of which he said, "If you have to get back to [something] because it's more interesting or important, please . . ." The gesture reflects the style of Nadella, who previously led the company's cloud and enterprise businesses, as a quiet, humble leader who emphasizes listening, helpfulness, and collaboration. Previous CEO Steve Ballmer, in contrast, had a forceful, driven approach to leadership and was known for his competitiveness and exuberant displays of emotion.[1] Yet both leaders have been successful within the same organization.

This example points to what researchers of leader traits and behaviors eventually discovered: Many different leadership styles can be effective. What, then, determines the success of a leadership style?

One factor that affects what leadership approach will be most effective is the situation in which leadership activities occur. Over the years, researchers have observed that leaders frequently behave situationally—that is, they adjust their leadership style depending on a variety of factors in the situations they face. In this chapter, we discuss the elements of leader, followers, and the situation, and the impact each has upon the others. We examine several theories that define how leadership styles, follower attributes, and organizational characteristics fit together to enable successful leadership. The important point of this chapter is that the most effective leadership approach depends on many factors. Understanding the contingency approaches can help a leader adapt his or her approach, although it is important to recognize that leaders also develop their ability to adapt through experience and practice.

3-1 THE CONTINGENCY APPROACH

The failure to find universal leader traits or behaviors that would always determine effective leadership led researchers in a new direction. Although leader behavior was still examined, the central focus of the new research was the situation in which leadership occurred. The basic tenet of this focus was that behavior effective in some circumstances might be ineffective under different conditions. Thus, the effectiveness of leader behavior is *contingent* upon organizational situations. Aptly called *contingency approaches*, these theories explain the relationship between leadership styles and effectiveness in specific situations.

In Exhibit 3.1, the universalistic approach as described in Chapter 2 is compared to the contingency approach described in this chapter. In Chapter 2, researchers were investigating traits or behaviors that could improve performance and satisfaction in any or all situations. They sought universal leadership traits and behaviors. **Contingency** means that one thing depends on other things, and for a leader to be effective there must be an appropriate fit between the leader's behavior

Contingency
a theory meaning one thing depends on other things

EXHIBIT 3.1 Comparing the Universalistic and Contingency Approaches to Leadership

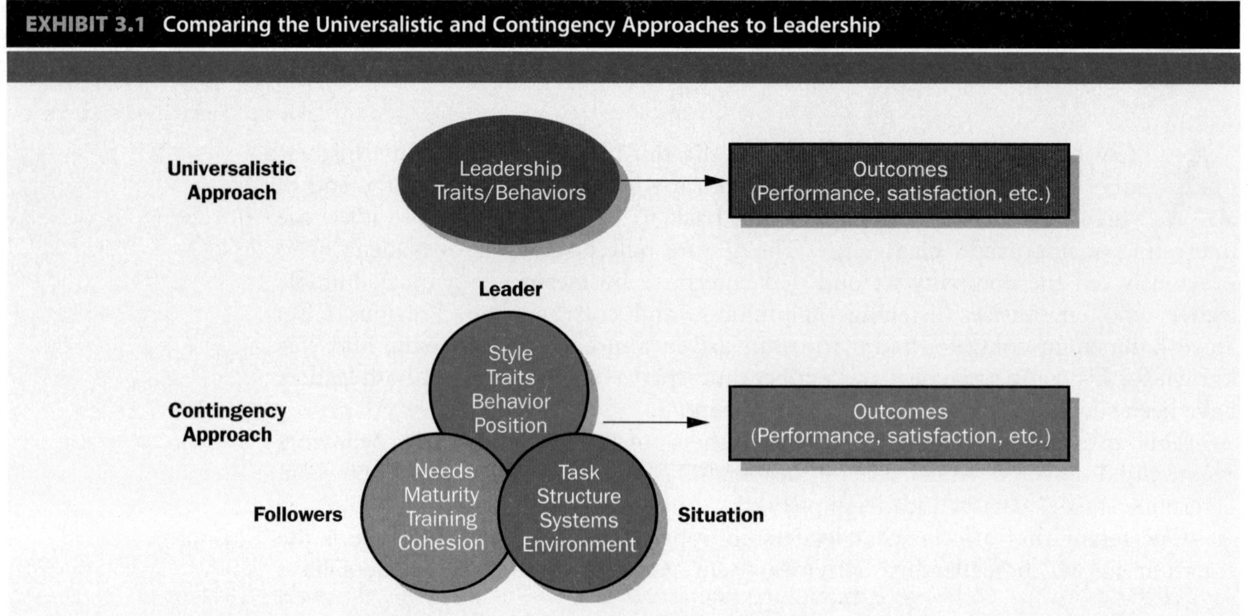

LEADER'S BOOKSHELF

Shackleton's Way: Leadership Lessons from the Great Antarctic Explorer

by Margot Morrell and Stephanie Capparell

"Men wanted for hazardous journey. Small wages. Bitter cold. Long months of complete darkness. Constant danger. Safe return doubtful. Honour and recognition in case of success."

Would you sign up for this job? When Sir Ernest Shackleton set out with a crew of 27 in 1914 with the goal of crossing the continent of Antarctica on foot, he probably didn't understand how utterly true the wording of his ad would turn out to be. His boat, the *Endurance*, never even touched land but became stuck in ice in the Weddell Sea for months and eventually sank. The men were left drifting on ice floes 1,200 miles from civilization, in dangerous cold, with only three lifeboats and limited provisions. They must have been terrified, and things didn't get much better for almost two long, brutal years. But, amazingly, every member of Shackleton's crew survived.

Margot Morrell and Stephanie Capparell analyzed the diaries of Shackleton and crew members to understand what brand of leadership enabled their survival through severe cold, isolation, near starvation, life-threatening storms, and all manner of other hardships. Their book tells a fascinating and inspiring adventure story but also offers lessons for today's leaders about how to lead in a situation of great stress and hardship.

LESSONS FOR LEADING IN TOUGH TIMES

Shackleton's team eventually made it to a small island and waited while Shackleton and a few members took a small boat 800 miles over treacherous seas to a whaling station, and then Shackleton took a ship back to rescue the others. Here are some tips from Shackleton's handling of the crew that apply to leading through any tough situation.

- ***Step up immediately***. After they abandoned the sinking ship, Shackleton encouraged people with a simple speech that acknowledged the dangers but expressed optimism and made clear that he was in charge and he would lead them through this. "Optimism is true moral courage," Shackleton is quoted as saying. By expressing optimism, Shackleton reminded crew members of the faith he had in each of them.
- ***Keep fairness in mind always***. Shackleton placed great value on every member of the crew, and he gained their admiration and respect by his fair, consistent, and egalitarian treatment of them. Each member was expected to do any job on the ship. One high-ranking crew member wrote: "[S]crubbing the floors . . . humbles one and knocks out of one any last remnants of false pride that one may have left in one and for this reason I do it voluntarily."
- ***Let everyone contribute to success***. When disaster struck, Shackleton knew the various tasks that had to be performed if the group were to survive, and he made sure everyone had assignments that let them contribute to the solution to their dire predicament. To keep spirits high, he used humor and other diversions (one of the few items he rescued from the sinking ship was a banjo). He took the most difficult people into his own tent to win their support and prevent them from infecting the rest of the crew with discouragement.

ADAPTABILITY MAKES IT POSSIBLE

Shackleton always looked ahead and kept his eye on the big picture, which enabled him to quickly change course in the face of the unexpected. Communication, especially by *listening*, helped him see when a new course of action might be needed. Just before the *Endurance* sailed, he fired the cook and three crew members because he learned through listening and observation that they could damage the morale and effectiveness of the crew. "Shackleton's optimism was never foolhardy," the book points out. He had confidence in his own abilities and in the abilities of his crew, and he was able to stay flexible enough to abandon what wasn't working and try something new. It's a big part of the reason the group survived—and why eight of the crew members came forward to join Shackleton on his final expedition some years later.

Source: *Shackleton's Way*, by Margot Morrell and Stephanie Capparell, is published by Viking Penguin.

and style and the conditions in the situation. A leadership style that works in one situation might not work in another situation. There is no one best way of leadership. Contingency means "it depends." Many leaders today look to an early twentieth-century explorer for inspiration on how to lead through an extreme situation, as described in this chapter's Leader's Bookshelf.

The contingencies most important to leadership as shown in Exhibit 3.1 are the situation and followers. Research implies that situational variables such as task, structure, context, and environment are important to leadership style. The nature of followers

EXHIBIT 3.2 Meta-Categories of Leader Behavior and Four Leader Styles

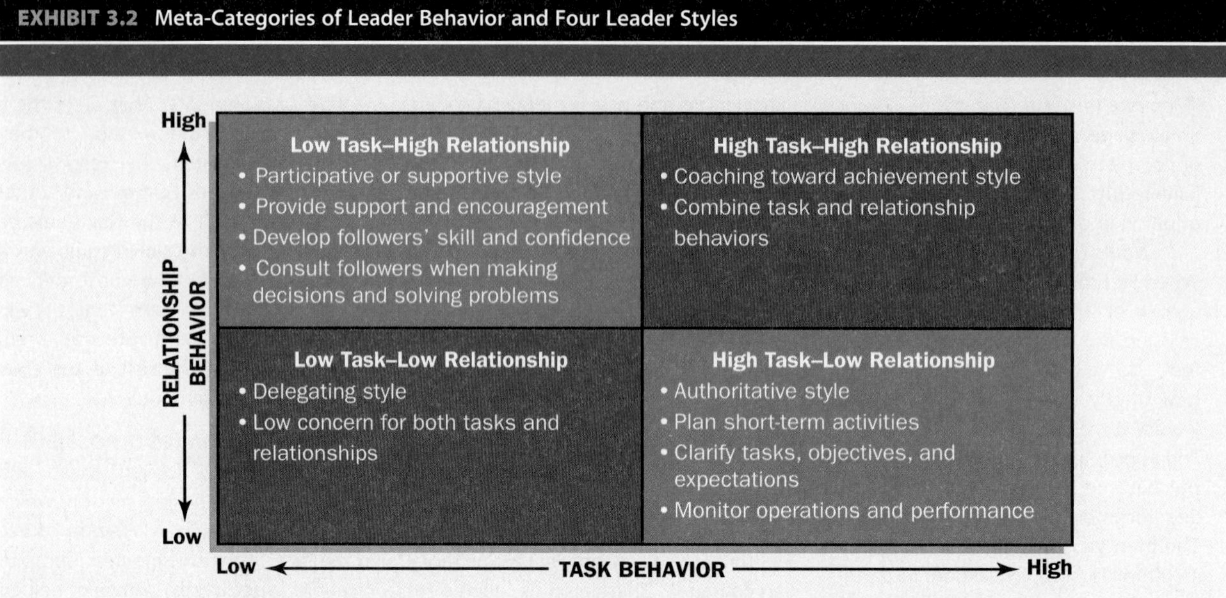

Sources: Based on Gary Yukl, Angela Gordon, and Tom Taber, "A Hierarchical Taxonomy of Leadership Behavior: Integrating a Half Century of Behavior Research," *Journal of Leadership and Organization Studies* 9, no. 1 (2002), pp. 15–32 and Gary Yukl, "Effective Leadership Behavior: What We Know and What Questions Need More Attention," *Academy of Management Perspectives* (November 2012), pp. 66–81.

has also been identified as a key contingency. Thus, the needs, maturity, and cohesiveness of followers make a significant difference to the best style of leadership.

Several models of situational leadership have been developed. The situational theory of Hersey and Blanchard, the contingency model developed by Fiedler and his associates, path–goal theory, the Vroom–Jago model of decision participation, and the substitutes-for-leadership concept will all be described in this chapter. These **contingency approaches** seek to delineate the characteristics of situations and followers and examine the leadership styles that can be used effectively. Assuming that a leader can properly diagnose a situation and muster the flexibility to behave according to the appropriate style, successful outcomes are highly likely.

NEW LEADER **ACTION MEMO**

Complete the questionnaire in Leader's Self-Insight 3.1 to assess your relative emphasis on two important categories of leadership behavior.

Two basic leadership behaviors that can be adjusted to address various contingencies are *task behavior* and *relationship behavior*, introduced in Chapter 2. Research has identified these two *meta-categories*, or broadly defined behavior categories, as applicable to leadership in a variety of situations and time periods.[2] A leader can adapt his or her style to be high or low on both task and relationship behavior. Exhibit 3.2 illustrates the four possible behavior approaches—low task–high relationship, high task–high relationship, high task–low relationship, and low task–low relationship. The exhibit describes typical task and relationship behaviors. High task behaviors include planning short-term activities, clarifying tasks, objectives, and role expectations, and monitoring operations and performance. High relationship behaviors include providing support and recognition, developing followers' skills and confidence, and consulting and empowering followers when making decisions and solving problems. Most leaders typically lean toward being stronger in either task-oriented or relationship-oriented behavior, but most experts suggest that a balance of concern for tasks and concern for people is crucial for leadership success over the long term.[3]

Contingency approaches
approaches that seek to delineate the characteristics of situations and followers and examine the leadership styles that can be used effectively

LEADER'S SELF-INSIGHT 3.1

T–P Leadership Questionnaire: An Assessment of Style

Instructions: The following items describe aspects of leadership behavior. *Assume you are the appointed leader of a student group and feel the pressure for performance improvements to succeed. Respond to each item according to the way you would most likely act in this pressure situation.* Indicate whether each item below is Mostly False or Mostly True for you as a work-group leader.

	Mostly False	Mostly True
1. I would hold members personally accountable for their performance.	_____	_____
2. I would assign members to specific roles and tasks.	_____	_____
3. I would ask the members to work harder.	_____	_____
4. I would check on people to know how they are doing.	_____	_____
5. I would focus more on execution than on being pleasant with members.	_____	_____
6. I would try to make members' work more pleasant.	_____	_____
7. I would focus on maintaining a pleasant atmosphere on the team.	_____	_____
8. I would let members do their work the way they think best.	_____	_____
9. I would be concerned with people's personal feelings and welfare.	_____	_____
10. I would go out of my way to be helpful to members.	_____	_____

Scoring and Interpretation

The T–P Leadership Questionnaire is scored as follows: Your T score represents task orientation and is the number of Mostly True answers for questions 1–5. Your P score represents your people or relationship orientation and is the number of Mostly True answers for questions 6–10. A score of 4 or 5 would be considered high for either T or P. A score of 0 or 1 would be considered low. T = _ _ _. P = _ _ _.

Some leaders focus on people needs, leaving task concerns to followers. Other leaders focus on task details with the expectation that followers will carry out instructions. Depending on the situation, both approaches may be effective. The important issue is the ability to identify relevant dimensions of the situation and behave accordingly. Through this questionnaire, you can identify your relative emphasis on the two dimensions of task orientation (T) and people orientation (P). These are not opposite approaches, and an individual can rate high or low on either or both.

What is your leadership orientation? Compare your results from this assignment to your result from the quiz in Leader's Self-Insight 2.2 in Chapter 2. What would you consider an ideal leader situation for your style?

Source: Based on the T–P Leadership Questionnaire as published in "Toward a Particularistic Approach to Leadership Style: Some Findings," by T. J. Sergiovanni, R. Metzcus, and L. Burden, *American Educational Research Journal* 6, no. 1 (1969), pp. 62–79.

Both Hersey and Blanchard's situational theory and Fiedler's contingency model, discussed in the following sections, use these meta-categories of leadership behavior but apply them based on different sets of contingencies.

3-2 HERSEY AND BLANCHARD'S SITUATIONAL THEORY

The **situational theory** developed by Hersey and Blanchard is an interesting extension of the Leadership Grid outlined in Chapter 2. This approach focuses on the characteristics of followers as the most important element of the situation and consequently of determining effective leader behavior. The point of Hersey and Blanchard's theory is that subordinates vary in readiness level. People low in task readiness, because of little ability or training, or insecurity, need a different leadership style than those who are high in readiness and have good ability, skills, confidence, and willingness to work.[4]

Situational theory
Hersey and Blanchard's extension of the Leadership Grid focusing on the characteristics of followers as the important element of the situation, and consequently, of determining effective leader behavior

3-2a Leader Style

According to the situational theory, a leader can adopt one of four leadership styles, based on a combination of relationship (concern for people) and task (concern for production) behavior. The appropriate style depends on the readiness level of followers.

Exhibit 3.3 summarizes the relationship between leader style and follower readiness. The upper part of the exhibit indicates the style of the leader, which is based on a combination of concern for people and concern for production tasks. The bell-shaped curve is called a prescriptive curve because it indicates when each style should be used. The four styles are telling, selling, participating, and delegating. The *telling style (S1)* is a very directive approach that reflects a high concern for tasks and a low concern for people and relationships, as shown in the exhibit. The leader provides detailed objectives and explicit instructions about how tasks should be accomplished. The *selling style (S2)* is based on a high concern for both relationships and tasks. With this approach, the leader provides task instruction and personal support, explains

EXHIBIT 3.3 The Situational Model of Leadership

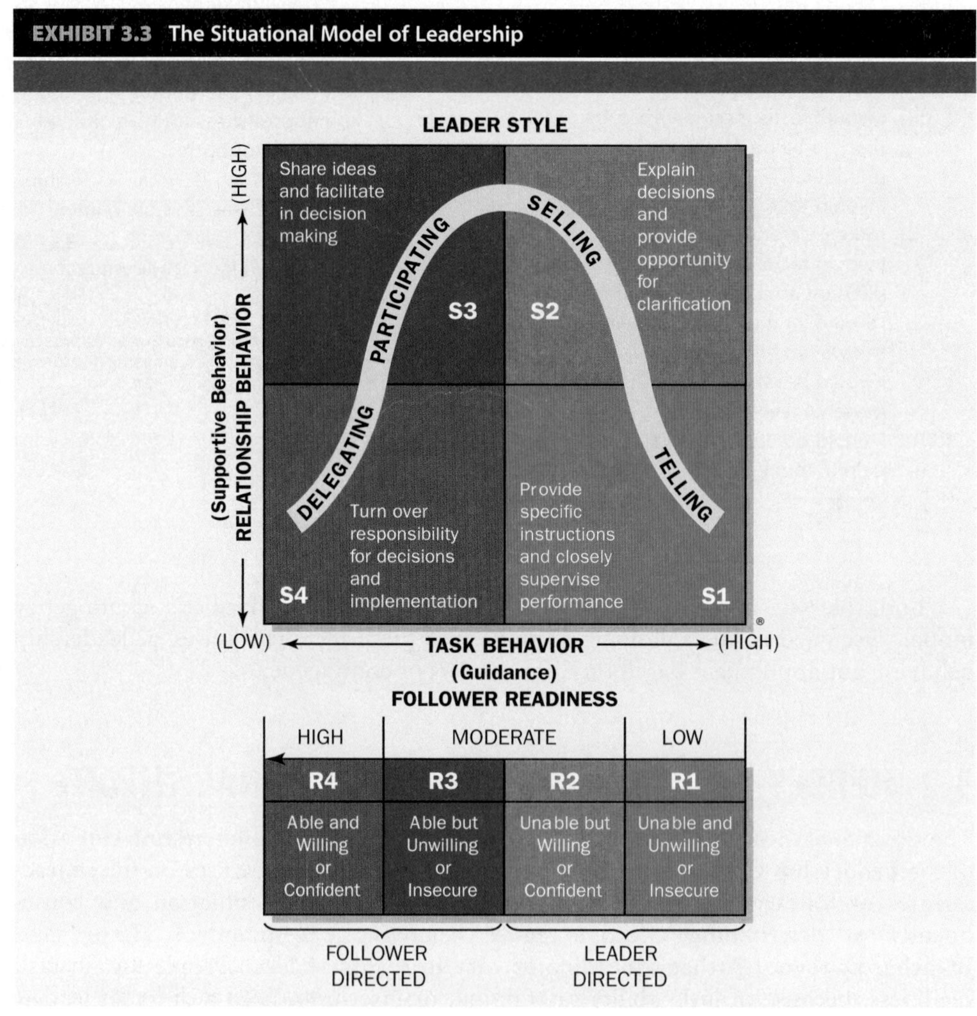

Source: Adapted from The Hersey and Blanchard Situational Leadership Model / The Center for Leadership Studies, Inc.

decisions, and gives followers a chance to ask questions and gain clarity about work tasks. The *participating style (S3)* is characterized by high relationship and low task behavior. The leader encourages participation, consults with followers, and facilitates decision making. The fourth style, the *delegating style (S4)*, reflects a low concern for both tasks and relationships. This leader provides little direction or support because complete responsibility for decisions and their implementation is turned over to followers.

3-2b Follower Readiness

The appropriate style depends on the readiness level of followers, indicated in the lower part of Exhibit 3.3. R1 represents low readiness and R4 represents high follower readiness. The essence of Hersey and Blanchard's situational theory is for the leader to diagnose a follower's readiness and select a style that is appropriate for the readiness level, such as the follower's degree of education and skills, experience, self-confidence, and work attitudes.

R1 Low Readiness When one or more followers exhibit very low levels of readiness, the leader has to use a telling style, telling followers exactly what to do, directing them in how to do it, and specifying timelines. For example, Phil Hagans owns two McDonald's franchises in northeast Houston and gives many young workers their first job. He uses a telling style regarding everything from how to dress to the correct way to clean the grill, giving young workers the strong direction they need to develop to higher levels of skill and self-confidence.[5]

R2 Moderate Readiness A selling leadership style works well when followers lack some skills or experience for the job but demonstrate confidence, ability, and willingness to learn. With a selling style, the leader gives some direction but also explains decisions and clarifies tasks for followers rather than merely instructing how tasks should be performed. Sheryl Sandberg uses a selling style as chief operating officer at Facebook. Many Facebook employees are fresh out of college with little experience, but they are energetic, enthusiastic, and committed. Sandberg's style combines decisive leadership with persuasion and consensus building. She uses logic and data to explain her decisions, but she also seeks input and feedback from employees. She describes herself as a leader who tends to "mentor and demand at the same time."[6]

NEW LEADER
ACTION MEMO

As a leader, you can tell followers how to perform their tasks if they have few skills, little experience, or low self-confidence. If followers have a moderate degree of skill and show enthusiasm and willingness to learn, provide direction but seek followers' input and explain your decisions.

R3 High Readiness A participating style can be effective when followers have the necessary education, skills, and experience but might be insecure in their abilities and need some encouragement from the leader. The leader can guide followers' development and act as a resource for advice and assistance. An example of the participating style is Eric Brevig, a visual-effects supervisor with Industrial Light and Magic, who maximizes the creativity of artists and animators by encouraging participation. Rather than telling people how to do their jobs, Brevig presents them with a challenge and works with them to figure out the best way to meet it.[7]

R4 Very High Readiness The delegating style of leadership can be effectively used when followers have very high levels of ability, experience, confidence, and willingness to accept responsibility for their own task behavior. The leader provides a general goal and sufficient authority to do the tasks as followers see fit. Highly educated professionals such as lawyers, college professors, and social workers would typically fall into this category. There are followers in almost every organization who demonstrate very high readiness.

NEW LEADER
ACTION MEMO

As a leader, you can act as a resource to provide advice and guidance when followers have a high level of skill, experience, and responsibility. Delegate responsibility for decisions and their implementation to followers who have very high levels of skill and positive attitudes.

In summary, the telling style (S1) works best for followers who demonstrate very low levels of readiness to take responsibility for their own task behavior, the selling style (S2) is effective for followers with moderate readiness, the participating style (S3) works well for followers with high readiness, and the delegating style (S4) is appropriate for followers with very high readiness. In today's multigenerational workplace, with people of widely different ages and readiness levels working side by side, many leaders find that they have to use multiple styles. Aaron Brown supervises a team at IBM that includes employees who span four decades in age, have work experience of between 3 and 30 years, and have varied attitudes, expectations, and ways of working.[8] For Brown, getting the best performance out of employees who differ so widely is as challenging—and as energizing—as coping with today's faster, more competitive business landscape.

Hersey and Blanchard's contingency model focuses only on the characteristics of followers, not those of the larger situation. The leader should evaluate subordinates and adopt whichever style is needed. Using an inappropriate style can hurt morale and performance, as illustrated by the following example.

IN THE LEAD

Laura Smith, Yola

When 26-year-old Laura Smith opened a yogurt and coffee shop in Washington, D.C. in 2010, she thought she had a winning formula with D.C.'s only fresh yogurt bar. Less than two years later, Yola closed its doors and Smith was looking for a new career. There were several reasons Yola didn't make it, not least of all the very high rent cost. Yet Smith also acknowledges that an incorrect leadership style hurt the business.

Smith says that if she could have a "do-over," she would provide more structure, more rules, and more boundaries for her employees, something that is needed in a business where most employees are young and have little work experience. Smith wanted to run her business by allowing employees to have the freedom to express their personal creativity, and she hated the idea of "telling grown adults when they can take breaks, exactly how to slice a scone out of a baking sheet, and exactly how many minutes late they can be." However, she soon found that her business became characterized by an attitude of permissiveness, where many employees showed up late, performed sloppy work, or did as little as possible while they were on the clock. No one was happy with the work environment.

Smith realized that her employees needed and even wanted to be told what and how to do things. "It's the thing I wish I could go back and do over—not because it would have saved my business but because everyone, myself included, would have been so much happier," she says.[9]

Laura Smith tried to use a selling or participating style because these approaches fit with her idea of what a "good" leader should be. She failed to realize that many of her employees were at a low readiness level and needed a telling style, with the leader providing clear instructions and specific rules regarding activities and work behavior.

In the Hersey–Blanchard model, leaders can tailor their approach to individual subordinates, similar to the leader–member exchange theory described in Chapter 2.

LEADER'S SELF-INSIGHT 3.2

Are You Ready?

Instructions: A leader's style can be contingent upon the readiness level of followers. Think of yourself working in your current or former job. Answer the following questions based on how you are on that job. Please answer whether each item is Mostly False or Mostly True for you in that job.

	Mostly False	Mostly True
1. I typically do the exact work required of me, nothing more or less.	_____	_____
2. I am often bored and uninterested in the tasks I have to perform.	_____	_____
3. I take extended breaks whenever I can.	_____	_____
4. I have great interest and enthusiasm for the job.	_____	_____
5. I am recognized as an expert by colleagues and coworkers.	_____	_____
6. I have a need to perform to the best of my ability.	_____	_____
7. I have a great deal of relevant education and experience for this type of work.	_____	_____
8. I am involved in "extra-work" activities such as committees.	_____	_____
9. I prioritize my work and manage my time well.	_____	_____

Scoring and Interpretation

In the situational theory of leadership, the higher the follower's readiness, the more participative and delegating the leader can be. Give yourself one point for each Mostly False answer to items 1–3 and one point for each Mostly True answer to items 4–9. A score of 8–9 points would suggest a "very high" readiness level. A score of 7–8 points would indicate a "high" readiness level. A score of 4–6 points would suggest "moderate" readiness, and 0–3 points would indicate "low" readiness. What is the appropriate leadership style for your readiness level? What leadership style did your supervisor use with you? What do you think accounted for your supervisor's style? Discuss your results with other students to explore which leadership styles are actually used with subordinates who are at different readiness levels.

If one follower is at a low readiness level, the leader must be very specific, telling the employee exactly what to do, how to do it, and when. For a follower high in readiness, the leader provides a general goal and sufficient authority to do the task as the follower sees fit. Leaders can carefully diagnose the readiness level of followers and then apply the appropriate style.

NEW LEADER
ACTION MEMO

Answer the questions in Leader's Self-Insight 3.2 to determine your own readiness level and the style of leadership that would be most appropriate for you as a follower.

3-3 FIEDLER'S CONTINGENCY MODEL

Fiedler and his associates developed a model that takes not only followers but other elements of the situation into consideration.[10] Although the model is somewhat complicated, the basic idea is simple: Match the leader's style with the situation most favorable for his or her success. **Fiedler's contingency model** was designed to enable leaders to diagnose both leadership style and organizational situation.

Fiedler's contingency model
a model designed to diagnose whether a leader is task-oriented or relationship-oriented and match leader style to the situation

3-3a Leadership Style

The cornerstone of Fiedler's theory is the extent to which the leader's style is relationship-oriented or task-oriented. A *relationship-oriented leader* is concerned with people. As with the consideration style described in Chapter 2, a relationship-oriented leader establishes mutual trust and respect and listens to employees' needs.

A *task-oriented leader* is primarily motivated by task accomplishment. Similar to the initiating structure style described in Chapter 2, a task-oriented leader provides clear directions and sets performance standards.

Leadership style was measured with a questionnaire known as the least preferred coworker (LPC) scale. The LPC scale has a set of 16 bipolar adjectives along an eight-point scale. Examples of the bipolar adjectives used by Fiedler on the LPC scale follow:

open	guarded
quarrelsome	harmonious
efficient	inefficient
self-assured	hesitant
gloomy	cheerful

If the leader describes the least preferred coworker using positive concepts, he or she is considered relationship-oriented, that is, a leader who cares about and is sensitive to other people's feelings. Conversely, if a leader uses negative concepts to describe the least preferred coworker, he or she is considered task-oriented, that is, a leader who sees other people in negative terms and places greater value on task activities than on people.

3-3b Situation

Fiedler's model presents the leadership situation in terms of three key elements that can be either favorable or unfavorable to a leader: the quality of leader–member relations, task structure, and position power.

Leader–member relations refers to group atmosphere and members' attitudes toward and acceptance of the leader. When subordinates trust, respect, and have confidence in the leader, leader–member relations are considered good. When subordinates distrust, do not respect, and have little confidence in the leader, leader–member relations are poor.

Task structure refers to the extent to which tasks performed by the group are defined, involve specific procedures, and have clear, explicit goals. Routine, well-defined tasks, such as those of assembly-line workers, have a high degree of structure. Creative, ill-defined tasks, such as research and development or strategic planning, have a low degree of task structure. When task structure is high, the situation is considered favorable to the leader; when low, the situation is less favorable.

Position power is the extent to which the leader has formal authority over subordinates. Position power is high when the leader has the power to plan and direct the work of subordinates, evaluate it, and reward or punish them. Position power is low when the leader has little authority over subordinates and cannot evaluate their work or reward them. When position power is high, the situation is considered favorable for the leader; when low, the situation is unfavorable.

When leader–member relations are good, task structure is high, and position power is strong, the situation is considered highly favorable to the leader. When leader–member relations are poor, task structure is low, and leader position power is weak, the situation is considered highly unfavorable to the leader. The situation

EXHIBIT 3.4 Fiedler's Classification: How Leader Style Fits the Situation

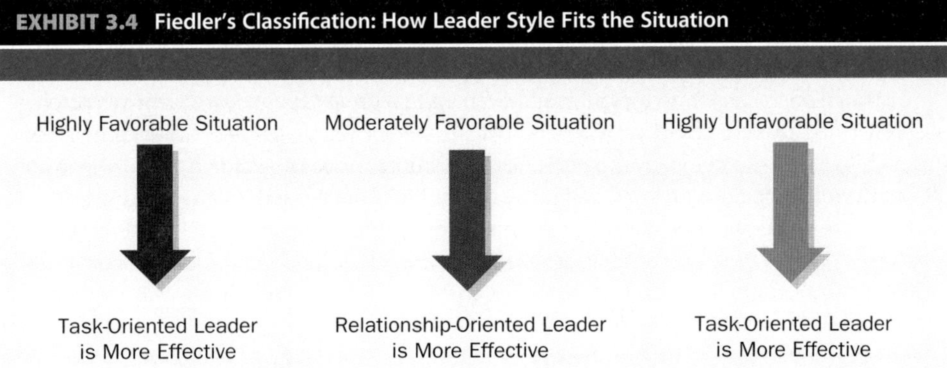

Source: Based on Fred E. Fiedler, "The Effects of Leadership Training and Experience: A Contingency Model Interpretation," *Administrative Science Quarterly* 17 (1972), p. 455.

would be considered moderately favorable when some of the three elements are high and others low. That is, a leader might have strong position power but tasks are unstructured and leader–member relations are poor. Or, leader–member relations might be good, but position power is weak and tasks are unstructured. There can be various levels of moderate favorability based on various combinations of the three key elements.

3-3c Contingency Theory

When Fiedler examined the relationships among leadership style, situational favorability, and group task performance, he found the pattern shown in Exhibit 3.4. Task-oriented leaders are more effective when the situation is either highly favorable or highly unfavorable. Relationship-oriented leaders are more effective in situations of moderate favorability.

The task-oriented leader excels in the highly favorable situation because everyone gets along, the task is clear, and the leader has power; all that is needed is for someone to take charge and provide direction. Similarly, if the situation is highly unfavorable to the leader, a great deal of structure and task direction are needed. A strong leader defines task structure and can establish authority over subordinates. Because leader–member relations are poor anyway, a strong task orientation will make no difference to the leader's popularity. Consider how Sergio Marchionne's task-oriented leadership style fit the situation he found at Chrysler.

IN THE LEAD

Sergio Marchionne, Fiat Chrysler Automobiles

The fate of the smallest of the Big Three U.S. automakers rests in the hands of Italian-born Sergio Marchionne, who rescued Fiat from the brink of collapse a few years ago with his close attention to detail. Marchionne is a strong task-oriented leader. Rather than settling into the top-floor executive suite at Chrysler's Auburn Hills, Michigan, headquarters, Marchionne chose an office in the fourth-floor engineering center. He carries six smartphones and keeps tabs on the smallest details, down to a faulty door handle on the new Dodge Charger. "If you really want to run the business," he says, "you need to get involved at this level."

Marchionne came into a highly unfavorable situation at Chrysler. Like General Motors, Chrysler had to be rescued by a federal bailout several years ago, and Marchionne took charge just after the company emerged from bankruptcy and Fiat assumed part ownership. Sales were slumping, Chrysler's image was tarnished, morale and motivation were low, costs were high, and operational problems plagued the company. Marchionne became known at Fiat for working long hours, seven days a week, and he told his top executives at Chrysler to plan on doing the same for the foreseeable future. He meets with managers regularly and gives them specific orders for what he wants to see accomplished. Managers who were committed to staying stuck in the old way of doing things were fired.

Chrysler has been slower to bounce back than GM, but Marchionne's task-oriented leadership is having a positive effect. Sales are improving, and operational problems have been brought under control. In addition, Marchionne's hard-hitting approach has brought a refreshing energy into the organization, giving employees a greater sense of hope and motivation.[11]

Sergio Marchionne's task-oriented style is appropriate for the difficult situation he found at Chrysler. Researchers at the University of Chicago looked at CEOs of companies in turnaround situations—where companies typically have high debt loads and a need to improve results in a hurry—and found that tough-minded, task-focused characteristics such as analytical skills, a focus on efficiency, and setting high standards were more valuable leader qualities than were relationship skills such as good communication, listening, and teamwork.[12]

NEW LEADER
ACTION MEMO

As a leader, you can effectively use a task-oriented style when the organizational situation is either highly unfavorable or highly favorable to you as a leader. Use a relationship-oriented style in situations of moderate favorability because human relations skills can create a positive atmosphere.

The relationship-oriented leader performs better in situations of moderate favorability because human relations skills are important in achieving high group performance. In these situations, the leader may be moderately well liked, have some power, and supervise jobs that contain some ambiguity. A leader with good interpersonal skills can create a positive group atmosphere that will improve relationships, clarify task structure, and establish position power.

A leader, then, needs to know two things in order to use Fiedler's contingency theory. First, the leader should know whether he or she has a relationship- or task-oriented style. Second, the leader should diagnose the situation and determine whether leader–member relations, task structure, and position power are favorable or unfavorable.

An important contribution of Fiedler's research is that it goes beyond the notion of leadership styles to try to show how styles fit the situation. Many studies have been conducted to test Fiedler's model, and the research in general provides some support for the model.[13] However, Fiedler's model has also been criticized.[14] Using the LPC score as a measure of relationship- or task-oriented behavior seems simplistic to some researchers, and the weights used to determine situation favorability seem to have been determined in an arbitrary manner. In addition, some observers argue that the empirical support for the model is weak because it is based on correlational results that fail to achieve statistical significance in the majority of cases. The model also isn't clear about how the model works over time. For instance, if a task-oriented leader such as Sergio Marchionne is matched with an unfavorable situation and is successful, the organizational situation is likely to improve, thus becoming a situation more appropriate for a relationship-oriented leader.

Will Marchionne's task-oriented style continue to be effective under more favorable circumstances at Chrysler? Can or should he try to shift to a more relationship-oriented leader style? Fiedler's model doesn't address this issue.

Finally, Fiedler's model and much of the subsequent research fail to consider *medium* LPC leaders, who some studies indicate are more effective than either high or low LPC leaders in a majority of situations.[15] Leaders who score in the mid-range on the LPC scale presumably balance the concern for relationships with a concern for task achievement more effectively than high or low LPC leaders, making them more adaptable to a variety of situations.

New research has continued to improve Fiedler's model,[16] and it is still considered an important contribution to leadership studies. However, its major impact may have been to stir other researchers to consider situational factors more seriously. A number of other situational theories have been developed in the years since Fiedler's original research.

3-4 PATH–GOAL THEORY

According to the **path–goal theory**, the leader's responsibility is to increase subordinates' motivation to attain personal and organizational goals.[17] As illustrated in Exhibit 3.5, the leader increases follower motivation by either (1) clarifying the follower's path to the rewards that are available or (2) increasing the rewards that the follower values and desires. Path clarification means that the leader works with subordinates to help them identify and learn the behaviors that will lead to successful task accomplishment and organizational rewards. Increasing rewards means that the leader talks with subordinates to learn which rewards are important to them—that is, whether they desire intrinsic rewards from the work itself or extrinsic rewards such as raises or promotions. The leader's job is to increase personal payoffs to subordinates for goal attainment and to make the paths to these payoffs clear and easy to travel.[18]

This model is called a contingency theory because it consists of three sets of contingencies—leader style, followers and situation, and the rewards to meet followers' needs.[19] Whereas the Fiedler theory made the assumption that new leaders could take over as situations change, in the path–goal theory, leaders change their behaviors to match the situation.

NEW LEADER
ACTION MEMO

As a leader, you can increase follower motivation, satisfaction, and performance by adopting a leadership behavior that will clarify the follower's path to receiving available rewards or increase the availability of rewards the follower desires.

3-4a Leader Behavior

The path–goal theory suggests a fourfold classification of leader behaviors.[20] These classifications are the types of behavior the leader can adopt and include supportive, directive, achievement-oriented, and participative styles.

Supportive leadership shows concern for subordinates' well-being and personal needs. Leadership behavior is open, friendly, and approachable, and the leader creates a team climate and treats subordinates as equals. Supportive leadership is similar to the consideration or people-oriented leadership described earlier. An example is Jay Goltz, an entrepreneur who owns five small businesses in Chicago, who has always used supportive leadership. He has loaned money to employees, guaranteed car loans, helped several employees buy houses, and even bailed a couple of employees out of jail.[21]

Path–goal theory
a contingency approach to leadership in which the leader's responsibility is to increase subordinates' motivation by clarifying the behaviors necessary for task accomplishment and rewards

EXHIBIT 3.5 Leader Roles in the Path–Goal Model

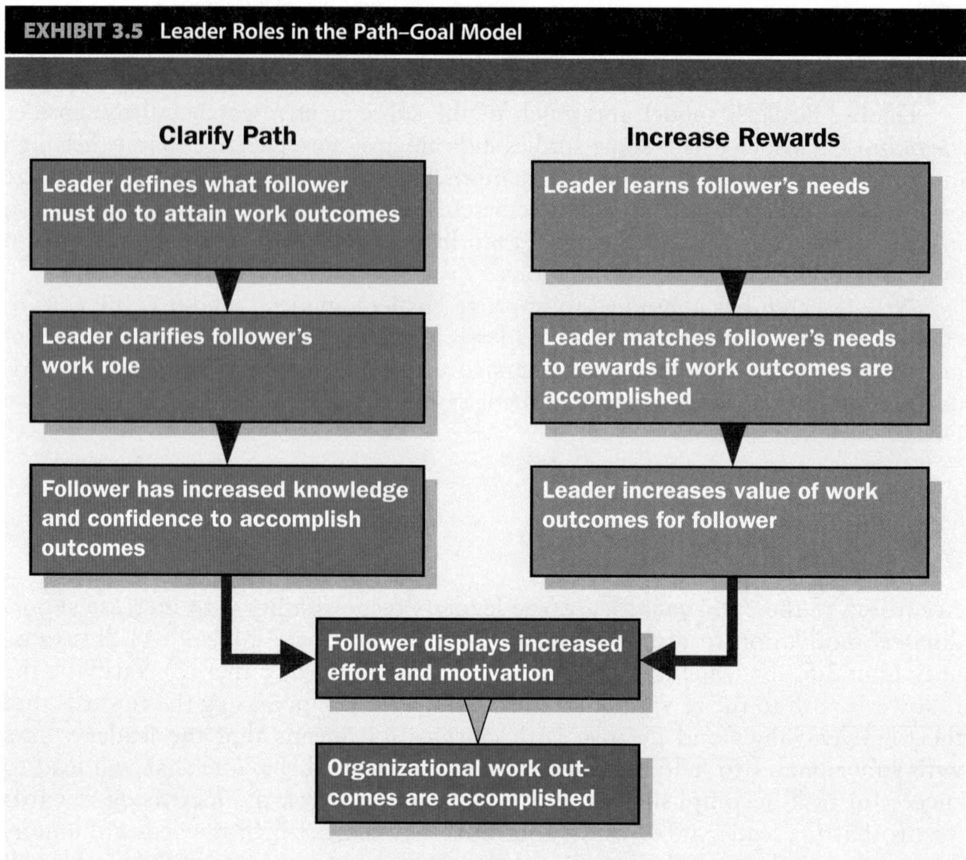

Source: Reprinted from *Organizational Dynamics*, 13 (Winter 1985), Bernard M. Bass, "Leadership: Good, Better, Best," pp. 26–40, Copyright 1985, with permission from Elsevier.

> *"The boss drives people; the leader coaches them. The boss depends on authority; the leader on good will. The boss inspires fear; the leader inspires enthusiasm."*
>
> H. Gordon Selfridge (1864–1947), founder of British retailer Selfridges.

Directive leadership tells subordinates exactly what they are supposed to do. Leader behavior includes planning, making schedules, setting performance goals and behavior standards, and stressing adherence to rules and regulations. Directive leadership behavior is similar to the initiating structure or task-oriented leadership style described earlier.

Participative leadership consults with subordinates about decisions. Leader behavior includes asking for opinions and suggestions, encouraging participation in decision making, and meeting with subordinates in their workplaces. The participative leader encourages group discussion and suggestions, similar to the coaching or supporting style in the Hersey and Blanchard model.

Achievement-oriented leadership sets clear and challenging goals for subordinates. Leader behavior stresses high-quality performance and improvement over current performance. Achievement-oriented leaders also show confidence in subordinates and assist them in learning how to achieve high goals.

The four types of leader behavior are not considered ingrained personality traits as in the earlier trait theories; rather, they reflect types of behavior that every leader is able to adopt, depending on the situation. Here's how Alan Robbins, founder of

Plastic Lumber Company, shifted from a participative to a directive style and got better results from his employees.

IN THE LEAD

Alan Robbins, Plastic Lumber Company

Alan Robbins started Plastic Lumber Company because he saw a way to both help the planet and make money by converting plastic milk and soda bottles into fake lumber. He also had definite ideas about how to run a company. Robbins wanted to be both a boss and a friend to his employees. His leadership style stressed teamwork and participation, and Robbins spent a lot of time running ideas by workers on the factory floor. However, he soon learned that most of his low-skilled workers didn't really want a chance to participate; they just wanted clear direction and consistent standards so that people knew what was expected of them.

The degree of freedom Robbins allowed with his participative style actually led to some serious problems. Some workers were frequently absent or late without calling, showed up under the influence of alcohol or drugs, and started fights on the factory floor. Letting employees participate in decision making weakened Robbins's authority in many employees' eyes. Those who genuinely wanted to do a good job were frustrated by the lack of order and the fact that some employees seemed to get away with anything.

Even though Robbins had a natural tendency to be a participative leader, he shifted to a directive leadership style to try to restore some order. With a comprehensive rules and policy manual, drug testing for all workers, and clear standards of behavior, the work environment and employee performance at Plastic Lumber improved significantly.[22]

Alan Robbins had believed his participative style would be appreciated by employees. However, employee satisfaction increased when he began using a directive style and specifying what was expected and what behaviors would not be tolerated. The directive style enabled people to focus on meeting performance standards by following clear procedures and guidelines. Thus, although Robbins would prefer to be participative, he realized it was not the best approach for the situation. The *Consider This* box provides an interesting perspective on the disadvantages of persisting in a behavior style despite the processes of change.

3-4b Situational Contingencies

The two important situational contingencies in the path–goal theory are (1) the personal characteristics of group members and (2) the work environment. Personal characteristics of followers are similar to Hersey and Blanchard's readiness level and include such factors as ability, skills, needs, and motivations. For example, if an employee has a low level of ability or skill, the leader may need to provide additional training or coaching in order for the worker to improve performance. If a subordinate is self-centered, the leader may use monetary rewards to motivate him or her. Subordinates who want or need clear direction and authority require a directive leader to tell them exactly what to do. Craft workers and professionals, however, may want more freedom and autonomy and work best under a participative leadership style.

Consider This!

The phrase "too much of a good thing" is relevant in leadership. Behavior that becomes overbearing can be a disadvantage by ultimately resulting in the opposite of what the individual is hoping to achieve.

Polarities

All behavior consists of opposites or polarities. If I do anything more and more, over and over, its polarity will appear. For example, striving to be beautiful makes a person ugly, and trying too hard to be kind is a form of selfishness.

Any overdetermined behavior produces its opposite:

- An obsession with living suggests worry about dying.
- True simplicity is not easy.
- Is it a long time or a short time since we last met?
- The braggart probably feels small and insecure.
- Who would be first ends up last.

Knowing how polarities work, the wise leader does not push to make things happen but allows a process to unfold on its own.

Source: John Heider, *The Tao of Leadership: Leadership Strategies for a New Age* (New York: Bantam Books, 1986), p. 3. Copyright 1985 Humanic Ltd., Atlanta, GA. Used with permission.

The work environment contingencies include the degree of task structure, the nature of the formal authority system, and the work group itself. The task structure is similar to the same concept described in Fiedler's contingency theory; it includes the extent to which tasks are defined and have explicit job descriptions and work procedures. The formal authority system includes the amount of legitimate power used by leaders and the extent to which policies and rules constrain employees' behavior. Work-group characteristics consist of the educational level of subordinates and the quality of relationships among them.

3-4c Use of Rewards

Recall that the leader's responsibility is to clarify *the path to rewards* for followers or to increase *the amount or type of rewards* to enhance satisfaction and job performance. In some situations, the leader works with subordinates to help them acquire the skills and confidence needed to perform tasks and achieve rewards already available. In others, the leader may develop new rewards to meet the specific needs of subordinates.

Exhibit 3.6 illustrates four examples of how leadership behavior is tailored to the situation. In the first situation, the subordinate lacks confidence; thus, the supportive leadership style provides the social support with which to encourage the subordinate to undertake the behavior needed to do the work and receive the rewards.

EXHIBIT 3.6 Path–Goal Situations and Preferred Leader Behaviors

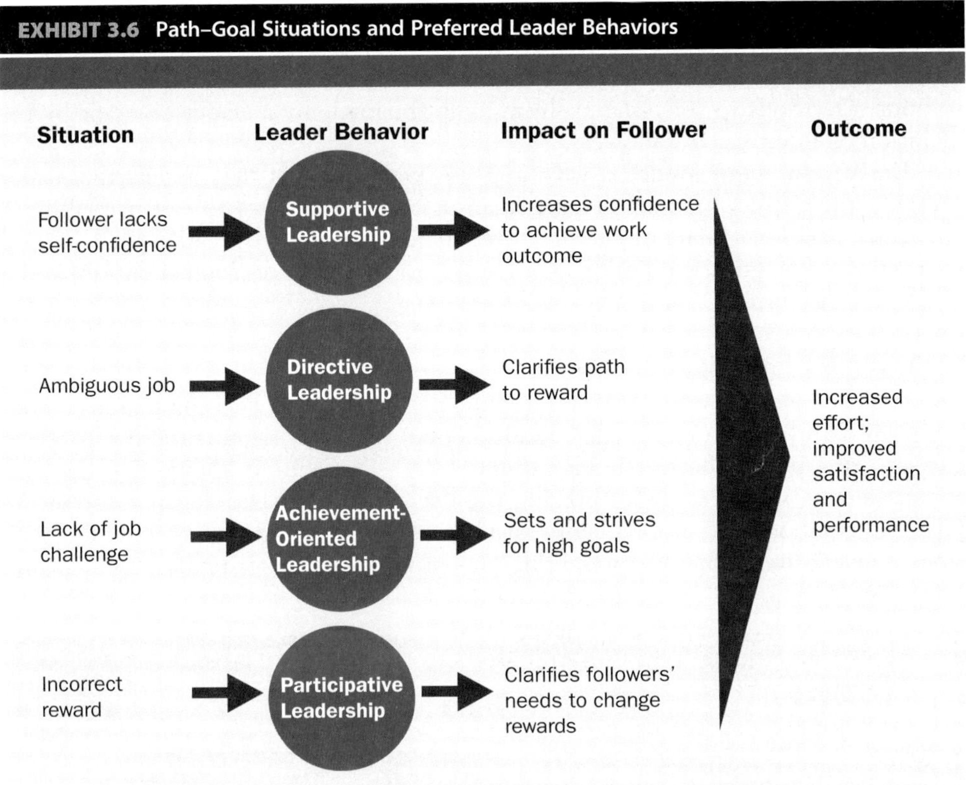

In the second situation, the job is ambiguous, and the employee is not performing effectively. Directive leadership behavior is used to give instructions and clarify the task so that the follower will know how to accomplish it and receive rewards. In the third situation, the subordinate is unchallenged by the task; thus, an achievement-oriented behavior is used to set higher goals. This clarifies the path to rewards for the employee. In the fourth situation, an incorrect reward is given to a subordinate, and the participative leadership style is used to change this. By discussing the subordinate's needs, the leader is able to identify the correct reward for task accomplishment. In all four cases, the outcome of fitting the leadership behavior to the situation produces greater employee effort by either clarifying how subordinates can receive rewards or changing the rewards to fit their needs.

Path–goal theorizing can be complex, but much of the research on it has been encouraging.[23] Using the model to specify precise relationships and make exact predictions about employee outcomes may be difficult, but the four types of leader behavior and the ideas for fitting them to situational contingencies provide a useful way for leaders to think about motivating subordinates.

3-5 THE VROOM–JAGO CONTINGENCY MODEL

Vroom–Jago contingency model
a contingency model that focuses on varying degrees of participative leadership and how each level of participation influences the quality and accountability of decisions

The **Vroom–Jago contingency model** shares some basic principles with the previous models, yet it differs in significant ways as well. This model focuses specifically on varying degrees of participative leadership and how each level of participation influences the quality and accountability of decisions. A number of situational factors shape the likelihood that either a participative or autocratic approach will produce the best outcome.

This model starts with the idea that a leader faces a problem that requires a solution. Decisions to solve the problem might be made by a leader alone or by the inclusion of a number of followers.

The Vroom–Jago model is very applied, which means that it tells the leader precisely the correct amount of participation by subordinates to use in making a particular decision.[24] The model has three major components: leader participation styles, a set of diagnostic questions with which to analyze a decision situation, and a series of decision rules.

3-5a Leader Participation Styles

The model employs five levels of subordinate participation in decision making, ranging from highly autocratic (leader decides alone) to highly democratic (leader delegates to group), as illustrated in Exhibit 3.7.[25] The exhibit shows five decision styles, starting with the leader making the decision alone (Decide); presenting the problem to subordinates individually for their suggestions and then making the decision (Consult Individually); presenting the problem to subordinates as a group,

EXHIBIT 3.7 Five Leader Decision Styles

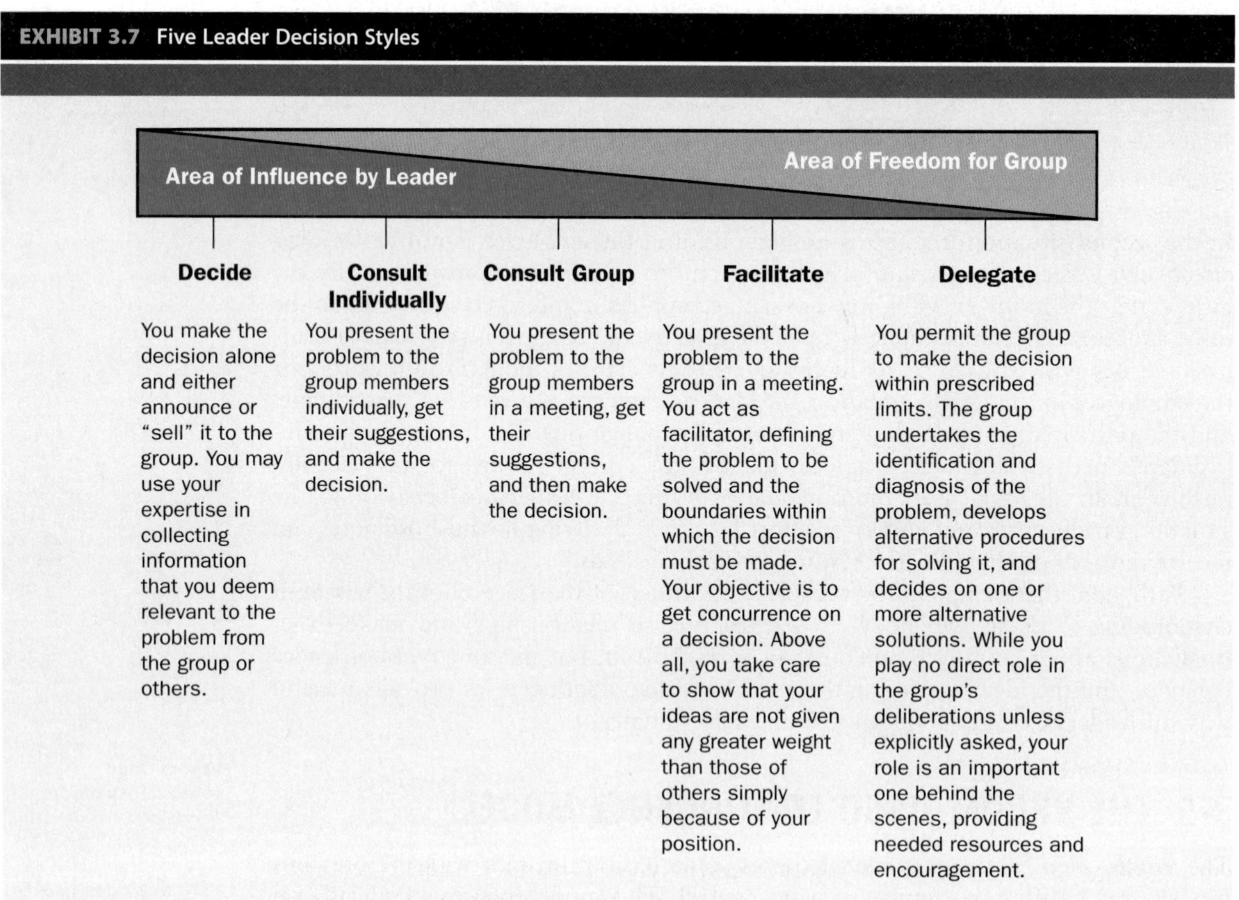

Source: Reprinted from *Organizational Dynamics*, 28, no. 4, Victor H. Vroom, "Leadership and the Decision-Making Process," pp. 82–94, Copyright 2000, with permission from Elsevier.

collectively obtaining their ideas and suggestions, then making the decision (Consult Group); sharing the problem with subordinates as a group and acting as a facilitator to help the group arrive at a decision (Facilitate); or delegating the problem and permitting the group to make the decision within prescribed limits (Delegate). The five styles fall along a continuum, and the leader should select one depending on the situation.

3-5b Diagnostic Questions

How does a leader decide which of the five decision styles to use? The appropriate degree of decision participation depends on a number of situational factors, such as the required level of decision quality, the level of leader or subordinate expertise, and the importance of having subordinates commit to the decision. Leaders can analyze the appropriate degree of participation by answering seven diagnostic questions.

1. **Decision significance:** *How significant is this decision for the project or organization?* If the decision is highly important and a high-quality decision is needed for the success of the project or organization, the leader has to be actively involved.
2. **Importance of commitment:** *How important is subordinate commitment to carrying out the decision?* If implementation requires a high level of commitment to the decision, leaders should involve subordinates in the decision process.
3. **Leader expertise:** *What is the level of the leader's expertise in relation to the problem?* If the leader does not have a high amount of information, knowledge, or expertise, the leader should involve subordinates to obtain it.
4. **Likelihood of commitment:** *If the leader were to make the decision alone, would subordinates have high or low commitment to the decision?* If subordinates typically go along with whatever the leader decides, their involvement in the decision-making process will be less important.
5. **Group support for goals:** *What is the degree of subordinate support for the team's or organization's objectives at stake in this decision?* If subordinates have low support for the goals of the organization, the leader should not allow the group to make the decision alone.
6. **Goal expertise:** *What is the level of group members' knowledge and expertise in relation to the problem?* If subordinates have a high level of expertise in relation to the problem, more responsibility for the decision can be delegated to them.
7. **Team competence:** *How skilled and committed are group members to working together as a team to solve problems?* When subordinates have high skills and high desire to work together cooperatively to solve problems, more responsibility for the decision making can be delegated to them.

These questions seem detailed, but considering these seven situational factors can quickly narrow the options and point to the appropriate level of group participation in decision making.

3-5c Selecting a Decision Style

Further development of the Vroom–Jago model added concern for time constraints and concern for follower development as explicit criteria for determining the level of participation. That is, a leader considers the relative importance of time versus follower development in selecting a decision style. This led to the development of two

NEW LEADER
ACTION MEMO

As a leader, you can use the Vroom–Jago model to determine the appropriate amount of follower participation to use in making a decision. You can follow the time-based guidelines when time is of the essence but use development-based guidelines when cultivating followers' decision-making skills is also important.

decision matrixes, a *time-based model* to be used if time is critical, for example if the organization is facing a crisis and a decision must be made immediately, and a *development-based model* to be used if time and efficiency are less important criteria than the opportunity to develop the thinking and decision-making skills of followers.

Consider the example of a small auto parts manufacturer, which owns only one machine for performing welds on mufflers. If the machine has broken down and production has come to a standstill, a decision concerning the purchase of a new machine is critical and has to be made immediately to get the production line moving again. In this case, a leader would follow the time-based model for selecting the decision style. However, if the machine is scheduled for routine replacement in three months, time is not a critical factor. The leader is then free to consider the importance of involving production workers in the decision making to develop their skills. Thus, the leader may follow the development-based model because time is not a critical concern.

Exhibit 3.8 and 3.9 illustrate the two decision matrixes—a timesaving-based model and an employee development–based model—that enable leaders to adopt a participation style by answering the diagnostic questions in sequence. Returning to the example of the welding machine, if the machine has broken down and must be replaced immediately, the leader would follow the timesaving-based model in Exhibit 3.8. The leader enters the matrix at the left side, at Problem Statement. The matrix acts as a funnel as you move left to right, responding to the situational questions across the top, answering high (H) or low (L) to each one, and avoiding crossing any horizontal lines.

The first question (decision significance) would be: *How significant is this decision for the project or organization*? If the answer is High, the leader proceeds to importance of commitment: *How important is subordinate commitment to carrying out the decision*? If the answer is High, the next question pertains to leader expertise: *What is the level of the leader's expertise in relation to the problem*? If the leader's knowledge and expertise are High, the leader next considers likelihood of commitment: *If the leader were to make the decision alone, how likely is it that subordinates would be committed to the decision*? If there is a high likelihood that subordinates would be committed, the decision matrix leads directly to the Decide style of decision making, in which the leader makes the decision alone and presents it to the group.

As noted earlier, this matrix assumes that time and efficiency are the most important criteria. However, consider how the selection of a decision style would differ if the leader had several months to replace the welding machine and considered follower development of high importance and time of little concern. In this case, the leader would follow the employee development–driven decision matrix in Exhibit 3.9. Beginning again at the left side of the matrix: *How significant is this decision for the project or organization*? If the answer is High, proceed to importance of commitment: *How important is subordinate commitment*? If high, the next question concerns likelihood of commitment (leader expertise is not considered because the development model is focused on involving subordinates, even if the leader has knowledge and expertise): *If the leader were to make the decision alone, how likely is it that subordinates would be committed to the decision*? If there is a high likelihood, the leader next considers group support: *What is the degree of subordinate support for the team's or organization's objectives at stake in this decision*? If the degree of support for goals is low, the leader proceeds directly to the Group

EXHIBIT 3.8 Timesaving-Based Model for Determining an Appropriate Decision-Making Style—Group Problems

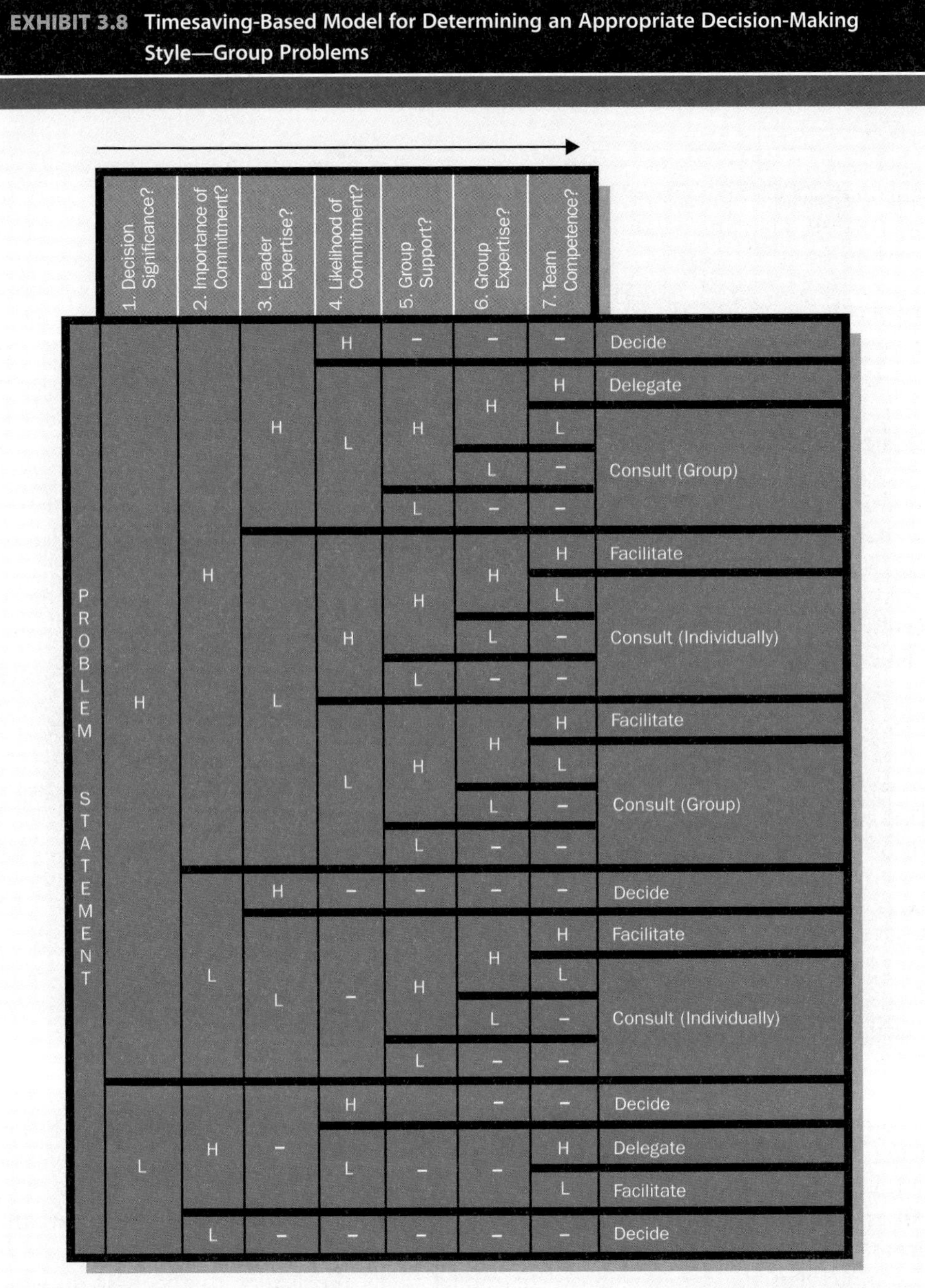

Source: Reprinted from *Organizational Dynamics*, 28, no. 4, Victor H. Vroom, "Leadership and the Decision-Making Process," pp. 82–94, Copyright 2000, with permission from Elsevier.

Consult decision style. However, if the degree of support for goals is high, the leader then asks: *What is the level of group members' knowledge and expertise in relation to the problem*? An answer of High would take the leader to the question: *How skilled and committed are group members to working together as a team to solve problems*?

EXHIBIT 3.9 Employee Development–Based Model for Determining an Appropriate Decision-Making Style—Group Problems

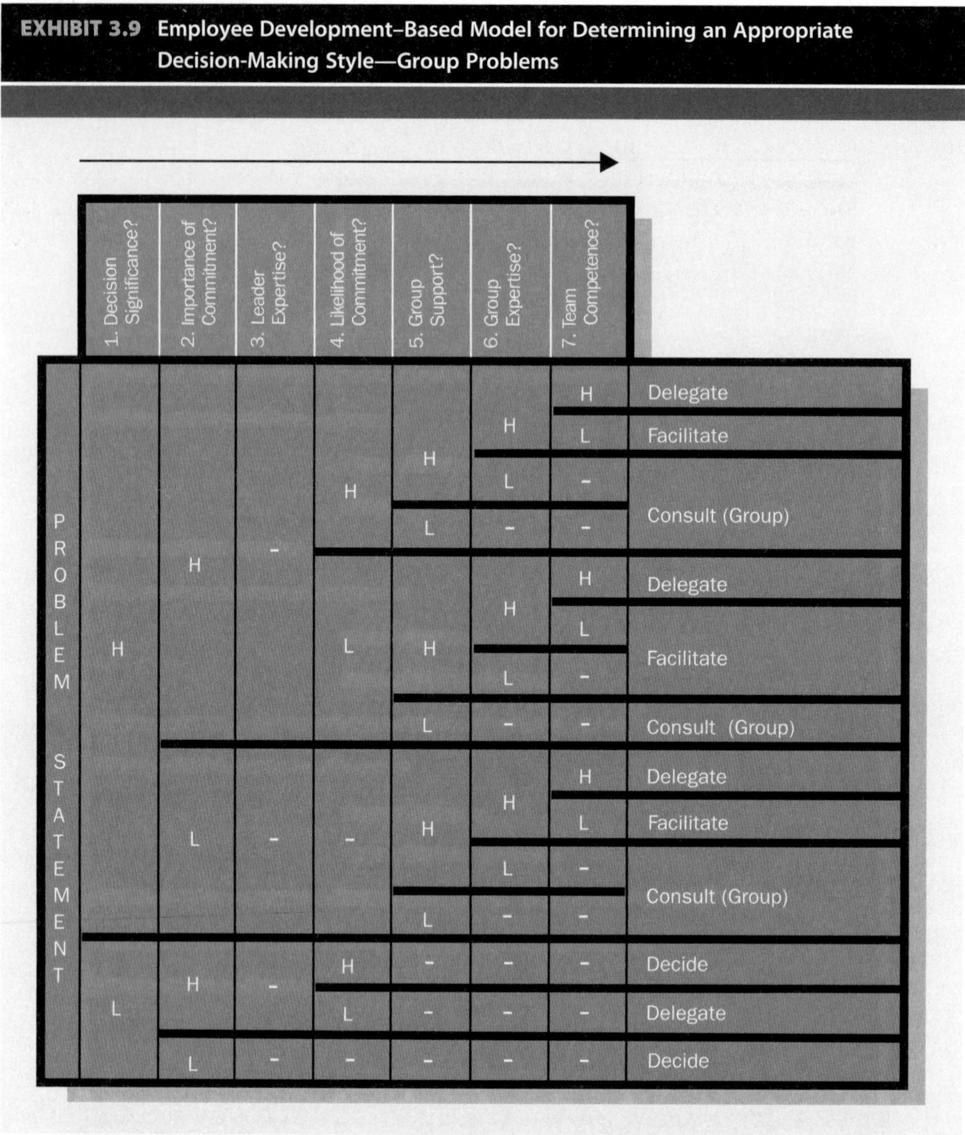

Source: Victor H. Vroom, "Leadership and the Decision-Making Process," *Organizational Dynamics* 28, no. 4 (Spring 2000), pp. 82–94. This is Vroom's adaptation of Tannenbaum and Schmidt's Taxonomy.

An answer of High would lead to the Delegate style, in which the leader allows the group to make the decision within certain limits.

Note that the timesaving-driven model takes the leader to the first decision style that preserves decision quality and follower acceptance, whereas the employee development–driven model takes other considerations into account. It takes less time to make an autocratic decision (Decide) than to involve subordinates by using a Facilitate or Delegate style. However, in many cases, time and efficiency are less important than the opportunity to foster subordinate development. In many of today's organizations, where knowledge sharing and widespread participation are considered critical to organizational success, leaders are placing greater emphasis on follower development when time is not a critical issue.

Leaders can quickly learn to use the model to adapt their styles to fit the situation. However, researchers have also developed a computer-based program that allows for greater complexity and precision in the Vroom–Jago model and incorporates the value of time and value of follower development as situational factors rather than portraying them in separate decision matrixes.

The Vroom–Jago model has been criticized as being less than perfect,[26] but it is useful to decision makers, and the model is supported by research.[27] Leaders can learn to use the model to make timely, high-quality decisions. Let's try applying the model to the following problem.

IN THE LEAD

Art Weinstein, Whitlock Manufacturing

When Whitlock Manufacturing won a contract from a large auto manufacturer to produce an engine to power its flagship sports car, Art Weinstein was thrilled to be selected as project manager. The engine, of Japanese design and extremely complex, has gotten rave reviews in the automotive press. This project has dramatically enhanced the reputation of Whitlock Manufacturing, which was previously known primarily as a producer of outboard engines for marine use.

Weinstein and his team of engineers have taken great pride in their work on the project, but their excitement was dashed by a recent report of serious engine problems in cars delivered to customers. Fourteen owners of cars produced during the first month had experienced engine seizures. Taking quick action, the auto manufacturer suspended sales of the sports car, halted current production, and notified owners of the current model not to drive the car. Everyone involved knows this is a disaster. Unless the engine problem is solved quickly, Whitlock Manufacturing could be exposed to extended litigation. In addition, Whitlock's valued relationship with one of the world's largest auto manufacturers would probably be lost forever.

As the person most knowledgeable about the engine, Weinstein has spent two weeks in the field inspecting the seized engines and the auto plant where they were installed. In addition, he has carefully examined the operations and practices in Whitlock's plant where the engine is manufactured. Based on this extensive research, Weinstein is convinced that he knows what the problem is and the best way to solve it. However, his natural inclination is to involve other team members as much as possible in making decisions and solving problems. He not only values their input, but he also thinks that by encouraging greater participation he strengthens the thinking skills of team members, helping them grow and contribute more to the team and the organization. Therefore, Weinstein chooses to consult with his team before making his final decision.

The group meets for several hours that afternoon, discussing the problem in detail and sharing their varied perspectives, including the information Weinstein has gathered during his research. Following the group session, Weinstein makes his decision. He will present the decision at the team meeting the following morning, after which testing and correction of the engine problem will begin.[28]

In the Whitlock Manufacturing case, either a timesaving-based or an employee development–based model can be used to select a decision style. Although timeliness is important, the leader's desire to involve subordinates can be considered equally important. Do you think Weinstein used the correct leader decision style? Let's examine the problem using the employee development–based decision tree since Weinstein is concerned about involving other team members. Moving from left to right in Exhibit 3.9, the questions and answers are as follows: *How significant is this decision for the organization?* Definitely High. Quality of the decision is of critical importance. The company's future may be at stake. *How important is subordinate commitment to carrying out the decision?* Also High. The team members must support and implement Weinstein's solution. Question 3 (leader expertise) is not considered in the employee development–driven model, as shown in Exhibit 3.9. The next question would be *If Weinstein makes the decision on his own, will team members have high or low commitment to it?* The answer to this question is probably also High. Team members respect Weinstein, and they are likely to accept his analysis of the problem. This leads to the question *What is the degree of subordinate support for the team's or organization's objectives at stake in this decision?* The answer, definitely High, leads to the question *What is the level of group members' knowledge and expertise in relation to the problem?* The answer to this question is probably Low, which leads to the Consult Group decision style. Thus, Weinstein used the style that would be recommended by the Vroom–Jago model.

Now, assume that Weinstein chose to place more emphasis on efficient use of time than on employee involvement and development. Using the timesaving-based decision matrix in Exhibit 3.8, answer the questions across the top of the matrix based on the information just provided (rate Weinstein's level of expertise in question 3 as high). Remember to avoid crossing any horizontal lines. What decision style is recommended? Is it the same as or different from that recommended by the employee development–based tree?

3-6 SUBSTITUTES FOR LEADERSHIP

The contingency leadership approaches considered so far have focused on the leader's style, the followers' nature, and the situation's characteristics. The final contingency approach suggests that situational variables can be so powerful that they actually substitute for or neutralize the need for leadership.[29] This approach outlines those organizational settings in which task-oriented and people-oriented leadership styles are unimportant or unnecessary.

Substitute
a situational variable that makes leadership unnecessary or redundant

Exhibit 3.10 shows the situational variables that tend to substitute for or neutralize leadership characteristics. A **substitute** for leadership makes the leadership

EXHIBIT 3.10 Substitutes and Neutralizers for Leadership

Variable		Task-Oriented Leadership	People-Oriented Leadership
Organizational variables	Group cohesiveness	Substitutes for	Substitutes for
	Formalization	Substitutes for	No effect on
	Inflexibility	Neutralizes	No effect on
	Low position power	Neutralizes	Neutralizes
Task characteristics	Highly structured task	Substitutes for	No effect on
	Automatic feedback	Substitutes for	No effect on
	Intrinsic satisfaction	No effect on	Substitutes for
Follower characteristics	Professionalism	Substitutes for	Substitutes for
	Training/experience	Substitutes for	No effect on
	Low value of rewards	Neutralizes	Neutralizes

style unnecessary or redundant. For example, highly educated, professional subordinates who know how to do their tasks do not need a leader who initiates structure for them and tells them what to do. In addition, long-term education often develops autonomous, self-motivated individuals. Thus, task-oriented and people-oriented leadership is substituted by professional education and socialization.[30]

Daniel Snyder, owner of the Washington Redskins football team, discovered that his strong task-oriented approach with his professional, talented coaches was counterproductive.

IN THE LEAD

Daniel Snyder, Washington Redskins

For many of Daniel Snyder's 15 or so years as owner of the Washington Redskins, he had a reputation as a meddlesome, overbearing boss who got in the way of people doing their jobs. He got involved in every detail of the team, even making big decisions on player acquisition himself.

But Snyder has proven that leaders can change. "He's stepped back from it," one insider says. "And he's having more fun because of it." Some associates say Snyder finally was able to step back because he got tired of all the losses the team racked up—and the criticism he got from fans and the media because of them.

When Snyder started staying in the background, the team seemed to get better. In 2012, the Redskins won their first NFC East division title since 1999, Snyder's first season as owner. "I think he deserves a lot of credit," said former general manager Charley Casserly, whom Snyder fired in 1999. "He's allowed them to do their jobs. They've turned the franchise around and made it a winner again."[31]

At the Washington Redskins, the skills, training, experience, and professionalism of coaches substituted for a task-oriented leadership style of the owner and also made a people-oriented style less important. Daniel Snyder decided to stay on the sidelines and let his coaches and players make the decisions on the field.

NEW LEADER
ACTION MEMO

As a leader, you can avoid leadership overkill. Adopt a style that is complementary to the organizational situation to ensure that both task needs and people needs are met.

Unlike a substitute, a **neutralizer** counteracts the leadership style and prevents the leader from displaying certain behaviors. For example, if a leader is physically removed from subordinates, the leader's ability to give directions to subordinates is greatly reduced. FedEx Office (formerly Kinko's) provides an example. With numerous locations widely scattered across regions, regional managers have very limited personal interaction with store managers and employees. Thus, their ability to both support and direct is neutralized.

Situational variables in Exhibit 3.10 include characteristics of the followers, the task, and the organization itself. For example, when subordinates are highly professional, such as research scientists in companies like Merck or Monsanto, both leadership styles are less important. The employees do not need either direction or support. With respect to task characteristics, highly structured tasks substitute for a task-oriented style, and a satisfying task substitutes for a people-oriented style.

Neutralizer
a situational characteristic that counteracts the leadership style and prevents the leader from displaying certain behaviors

When a task is highly structured and routine, like auditing cash, the leader should provide personal consideration and support that is not provided by the task. Satisfied people don't need as much consideration. Likewise, with respect to the organization itself, group cohesiveness substitutes for both leader styles. For example,

LEADER'S SELF-INSIGHT 3.3

Measuring Substitutes for Leadership

Instructions: Think about your current job or a job you have held in the past. Please answer whether each of the following items is Mostly False or Mostly True for you in that job.

	Mostly False	Mostly True
1. Because of the nature of the tasks I perform, there is little doubt about the best way to do them.	_____	_____
2. My job duties are so simple that almost anyone could perform them well after a little instruction.	_____	_____
3. It is difficult to figure out the best way to do many of my tasks and activities.	_____	_____
4. There is really only one correct way to perform most of the tasks I do.	_____	_____
5. After I've completed a task, I can tell right away from the results I get whether I have performed it correctly.	_____	_____
6. My job is the kind where you can finish a task and not know if you've made a mistake or error.	_____	_____
7. Because of the nature of the tasks I do, it is easy for me to see when I have done something exceptionally well.	_____	_____
8. I get lots of satisfaction from the work I do.	_____	_____
9. It is hard to imagine that anyone could enjoy performing the tasks I have performed on my job.	_____	_____
10. My job satisfaction depends primarily on the nature of the tasks and activities I perform.	_____	_____

Scoring and Interpretation

For your task structure score, give yourself one point for Mostly True answers to items 1, 2, and 4, and for a Mostly False answer to item 3. This is your score for Task Structure: _____

For your task feedback score, give yourself one point for Mostly True answers to items 5 and 7, and for a Mostly False answer to item 6. This is your score for Task Feedback: _____

For your intrinsic satisfaction score, score one point for Mostly True answers to items 8 and 10, and for a Mostly False answer to item 9. This is your score for Intrinsic Satisfaction: _____

A high score (3 or 4) for Task Structure or Task Feedback indicates a high potential for those elements to act as a substitute for *task-oriented leadership*. A high score (3) for Intrinsic Satisfaction indicates the potential to be a substitute for *people-oriented leadership*. Does your leader adopt a style that is complementary to the task situation, or is the leader guilty of *leadership overkill*? How can you apply this understanding to your own actions as a leader?

Source: Based on "Questionnaire Items for the Measurement of Substitutes for Leadership," Table 2 in Steven Kerr and John M. Jermier, "Substitutes for Leadership: Their Meaning and Measurement," *Organizational Behavior and Human Performance* 22 (1978), pp. 375–403.

the relationship that develops among air traffic controllers and jet fighter pilots is characterized by high-stress interactions and continuous peer training. This cohesiveness provides support and direction that substitute for formal leadership.[32] Formalized rules and procedures substitute for leader task orientation because the rules tell people what to do. Physical separation of leader and subordinate neutralizes both leadership styles.

NEW LEADER
ACTION MEMO

Measure how the task characteristics of your job or a job you've held in the past might act as substitutes for leadership by answering the questions in Leader's Self-Insight 3.3.

The value of the situations described in Exhibit 3.10 is that they help leaders avoid leadership overkill. Leaders should adopt a style with which to complement the organizational situation. For example, the work situation for bank tellers provides a high level of formalization, little flexibility, and a highly structured task. The head teller should not adopt a task-oriented style because the organization already provides structure and direction. The head teller should concentrate on a people-oriented style. In other organizations, if group cohesiveness or previous training meets employee social needs, the leader is free to concentrate on task-oriented behaviors. The leader can adopt a style complementary to the organizational situation to ensure that both task needs and people needs of followers are met.

Studies have examined how substitutes (the situation) can be designed to have more impact than leader behaviors on outcomes such as subordinate satisfaction.[33] The impetus behind this research is the idea that substitutes for leadership can be designed into organizations in ways to complement existing leadership, act in the absence of leadership, and otherwise provide more comprehensive leadership alternatives. For example, Paul Reeves, a foreman at Harmon Auto Parts, shared half-days with his subordinates during which they helped him perform his leader tasks. After Reeves's promotion to middle management, his group no longer required a foreman. Followers were trained to act on their own.[34] Thus, a situation in which follower ability and training were highly developed created a substitute for leadership.

The ability to use substitutes to fill leadership "gaps" is often advantageous to organizations. Indeed, the fundamental assumption of substitutes-for-leadership researchers is that effective leadership is the ability to recognize and provide the support and direction not already provided by task, group, and organization.

NEW LEADER
ACTION MEMO

As a leader, you can use a people-oriented style when tasks are highly structured and followers are bound by formal rules and procedures. You can adopt a task-oriented style if group cohesiveness and followers' intrinsic job satisfaction meet their social and emotional needs.

LEADERSHIP ESSENTIALS

- The most important point in this chapter is that situational variables affect leadership outcomes. The contingency approaches were developed to systematically address the relationship between a leader and the organization. The contingency approaches focus on how the components of leadership style, subordinate characteristics, and situational elements affect one another. Hersey and Blanchard's situational theory, Fiedler's contingency model, the path–goal theory, the Vroom–Jago model, and the substitutes-for-leadership concept each examine how different situations call for different styles of leadership behavior.
- Hersey and Blanchard contend that leaders can adjust their task or relationship style to accommodate the readiness level of their subordinates. According to Fiedler, leaders can determine whether their leadership style is suitable for the situation. Task-oriented leaders tend to do better in very favorable or very unfavorable situations, whereas relationship-oriented leaders do best in situations of intermediate favorability. The path–goal theory states that leaders can use a style that appropriately clarifies the path to desired rewards. The Vroom–Jago model indicates that leaders can choose a participative decision style based on contingencies such as quality requirement, commitment requirement, or the leader's knowledge and expertise. In addition, concern for time (the need for a fast decision) versus concern for follower development is taken into account. Finally, the substitutes-for-leadership concept recommends that leaders adjust their style to provide resources not otherwise provided in the organizational situation.
- By discerning the characteristics of tasks, subordinates, and organizations, leaders can determine the style that increases the likelihood of successful leadership outcomes. Therefore, effective leadership depends partly on developing diagnostic skills and being flexible in your leadership behavior.

NEW LEADER
ACTION MEMO

As a leader, you can provide minimal task direction and personal support to highly trained employees; followers' professionalism and intrinsic satisfaction substitute for both task- and people-oriented leadership.

DISCUSSION QUESTIONS

1. Consider Fiedler's theory as illustrated in Exhibit 3.4. How often do you think very favorable, intermediate, or very unfavorable situations occur to leaders in real life? Discuss.
2. Do you think leadership style is fixed and unchangeable, or can leaders be flexible and adaptable with respect to style? Why?
3. Consider the leadership position of the managing partner in a law firm. What task, subordinate, and organizational factors might serve as substitutes for leadership in this situation?
4. Compare Fiedler's contingency model with the path–goal theory. What are the similarities and differences? Which do you prefer?
5. If you were a first-level supervisor of a team of telemarketers, how would you go about assessing the readiness level of your subordinates? Do you think most leaders can easily shift their leadership style to suit the readiness level of followers?
6. Think back to teachers you have had, and identify one each who fits a supportive style, directive style, participative style, and achievement-oriented style according to the path–goal theory. Which style did you find most effective? Why?
7. Do you think leaders should decide on a participative style based on the most efficient way to reach the decision? Should leaders sometimes let people participate for other reasons?
8. Consider the situational characteristics of group cohesiveness, organizational formalization, and physical separation. How might each of these substitute for or neutralize task-oriented or people-oriented leadership? Explain.

LEADERSHIP AT WORK

Task versus Relationship Role Play

You are the new distribution manager for French Grains Bakery. Five drivers who deliver French Grains baked goods to grocery stores in the metropolitan area report to you. The drivers are expected to complete the delivery report to keep track of actual deliveries and any changes that occur. The delivery report is a key element in inventory control and provides the data for French Grains invoicing of grocery stores. Errors become excessive when drivers fail to complete the report each day, especially when store managers request different inventory when the driver arrives. As a result, French Grains may not be paid for several loaves of bread a day for each mistake in the delivery report. The result is lost revenue and poor inventory control.

One of the drivers accounts for about 60 percent of the errors in the delivery reports. This driver is a nice person and generally reliable, although he is occasionally late for work. His major problem is that he falls behind in his paperwork. A second driver accounts for about 30 percent of the errors, and a third driver for about 10 percent of the errors. The other two drivers turn in virtually error-free delivery reports.

You are a high task-oriented (and low relationship-oriented) leader and have decided to talk to the drivers about doing a more complete and accurate job with the delivery reports. Write below exactly how you will go about correcting this problem as a task-oriented leader. Will you meet with drivers individually or in a group? When and where will you meet with them? Exactly what will you say, and how will you get them to listen?

____

____

____

Now adopt the role of a high relationship-oriented (and low task-oriented) leader. Write below exactly what you will do and say as a relationship-oriented distribution manager. Will you meet with the drivers individually or in a group? What will you say, and how will you get them to listen?

____

____

____

In Class: The instructor can ask students to volunteer to play the roles of the distribution manager and the drivers. A few students can take turns role-playing the distribution manager in front of the class to show how they would handle the drivers as task- and relationship-oriented leaders. The instructor can ask other students for feedback on the leader's effectiveness and on which approach seems more effective for this situation and why.

Source: Based on K. J. Keleman, J. E. Garcia, and K. J. Lovelace, *Management Incidents: Role Plays for Management Development* (Dubuque, IA: Kendall Hunt Publishing Company, 1990), pp. 69–72.

LEADERSHIP DEVELOPMENT: CASES FOR ANALYSIS

Alvis Corporation

Kevin McCarthy is the manager of a production department in Alvis Corporation, a firm that manufactures office equipment. After reading an article that stressed the benefits of participative management, Kevin believes that these benefits could be realized in his department if the workers are allowed to participate in making some decisions that affect them. The workers are not unionized. Kevin selected two decisions for his experiment in participative management.

The first decision involved vacation schedules. Each summer the workers are given two weeks' vacation, but no more than two workers can go on vacation at the same time. In prior years, Kevin made this decision himself. He would first ask the workers to indicate their preferred dates, and he considered how the work would be affected if different people were out at the same time. It was important to plan a vacation schedule that would ensure adequate staffing for all of the essential operations performed by the department. When more than two workers wanted the same time period and they had similar skills, he usually gave preference to the workers with the highest productivity.

The second decision involved production standards. Sales had been increasing steadily over the past few years, and the company recently installed some new equipment to increase productivity. The new equipment would allow Kevin's department to produce more with the same number of workers. The company had a pay incentive system in which workers received a piece rate for each unit produced above a standard amount. Separate standards existed for each type of product, based on an industrial engineering study conducted a few years earlier. Top management wanted to readjust the production standards to reflect the fact that the new equipment made it possible for the workers to earn more without working any harder. The savings from higher productivity were needed to help pay for the new equipment.

Kevin called a meeting of his 15 workers an hour before the end of the workday. He explained that he wanted them to discuss the two issues and make recommendations. Kevin figured that the workers might be inhibited about participating in the discussion if he were present, so he left them alone to discuss the issues. Besides, Kevin had an appointment to meet with the quality control manager. Quality problems had increased after the new equipment was installed, and the industrial engineers were studying the problem in an attempt to determine why quality had gotten worse rather than better.

When Kevin returned to his department just at quitting time, he was surprised to learn that the workers recommended keeping the standards the same. He had assumed they knew the pay incentives were no longer fair and would set a higher standard. The spokesman for the group explained that their base pay had not kept up with inflation and the higher incentive pay restored their real income to its prior level.

On the vacation issue, the group was deadlocked. Several of the workers wanted to take their vacations during the same two-week period and could not agree on who should go. Some workers argued that they should have priority because they had more seniority, whereas others argued that priority should be based on productivity, as in the past. Since it was quitting time, the group concluded that Kevin would have to resolve the dispute himself. After all, wasn't that what he was being paid for?[35]

QUESTIONS

1. Analyze this situation using the Hersey–Blanchard model and the Vroom–Jago model. What do these models suggest as the appropriate leadership or decision style? Explain.
2. Evaluate Kevin McCarthy's leadership style before and during his experiment in participative management.
3. If you were Kevin McCarthy, what would you do now? Why?

An Impossible Dream?

What's wrong with the team? What's wrong with the team? Zequine Mansell's words repeated over and over in Allen Block's head as he boarded the plane from Los Angeles to Chicago.

Block was responsible for the technical implementation of the new customer relationship management (CRM) software being installed for western and eastern sales offices in both cities. The software was badly needed to improve follow-up sales for his company, Exert Systems. Exert sold exercise equipment to high schools and colleges, as well as to small and midsized businesses for recreation centers, through a national force of 310 salespeople. The company's low prices won a lot of sales; however, follow-up service was uneven, and the new CRM system promised to resolve those problems with historical data, inquiries, reminders, and updates going to sales reps daily. The CEO of Exert ordered the CRM system installed with all possible haste.

Block pulled a yellow pad and pen from the side pocket of his carry-on bag and tossed it in the seat beside the window, stashed the bag in the overhead compartment, and sat down as other passengers filed past. In an effort to shut out his thoughts, he closed his eyes and concentrated on the muffled voices and low whooshing sound of the air vents. An image appeared in his mind of his promotion to Mansell's job when she retired in two years. He blocked that thought and started doodling on the pad as a way of focusing his thoughts.

He wrote *what's wrong with the team* three times and began drawing arrows to circles bearing the names of his team members: Barry Livingston and Max Wojohowski in Los Angeles and Bob Finley, Lynne Johnston, and Sally Phillips in Chicago. He marked through Sally's name. She had jumped ship recently, taking her less-than-stellar but much-needed talents with her to another company. It was on a previous LA–Chicago flight that Sally had pumped him for feedback on her future with Exert. She had informed him that she had another job offer. She admitted it was less money, but she was feeling under pressure as a member of the team and she wanted more "quality of life." Block told Sally bluntly that her technical expertise, on which he placed top importance, was slightly below that of her peers, so future promotion was less likely despite her impressive people and team skills.

He wrote "quality of life," circled it, and then crossed it out and wrote "what the hell?" *Why should she get quality of life?* he mused. *I've barely seen my wife and kids since this project started*. Block's team was under a great deal of pressure, and he had needed Sally to stick it out. He told her so, but the plane had barely touched down when she went directly to the office and quit, leaving the team short-handed and too close to deadline to add another body.

What's wrong with the team? Block furiously scribbled as his thoughts raced: *(1) The deadline is ridiculously short*. Mansell had scheduled a 10-week completion deadline for the new CRM software, including installation and training for both cities.

He was interrupted by the stewardess. "Would you care for a drink, sir?"

"Yes. Just water."

Block took a sip and continued to write. *(2) Thank God for LA*. From the outset, Barry and Max had worked feverishly while avoiding the whining and complaining that seemed to overwhelm members of the Chicago team. The atmosphere was different. Although the project moved forward, meeting deadlines, there appeared to be less stress. The LA guys focused tirelessly on work, with no families to consider, alternating intense work with joking around. "Those are my kind of people," he thought. *(3) But there is Chicago*, he wrote. Earlier in the day Sam Matheny from sales had e-mailed, then called Block to tell him the two remaining members of the Chicago team appeared to be alternating between bickering and avoiding one another. Apparently this had been going on for some time. *What's with that*? Block wondered. *And why did Sam know and I didn't*? So that morning, before his flight, Block had to make time to call and text both Finley and Johnston. Finley admitted he had overreacted to Johnston.

"Look, man. I'm tired and stressed out. We've been working non-stop. My wife is not happy."

"Just get along until this project is completed," Block ordered.

"When will *that* be?" Finley asked before hanging up.

Block thought about Mansell's persistent complaints to him that the team appeared to have a lack of passion, and she admonished him to "get your people to understand the urgency of this project." Her complaints only added to his own stress level. He had long considered himself the frontrunner for Mansell's job when she retired in two years. But had his team ruined that dream? The sense of urgency could be measured now in the level of stress and the long hours they had all endured. He admitted his team members were unenthusiastic, but they seemed committed.

Is it too late to turn around and restore the level of teamwork? He tore off the sheet from the pad, crumpled it in his hand, and stared out the window.

QUESTIONS

1. How would you characterize Block's leadership approach (task versus people)? What approach do you think is correct for this situation? Why?
2. What would you do now if you were Block? How might you awaken more enthusiasm in your team for completing this project on time? Specify the steps you would take.
3. How would you suggest that Block modify his leadership style if he wants to succeed Mansell in two years? Be specific.

REFERENCES

1. Ryan Nakashima, "New Microsoft CEO's Collegial Style Sparks Hope," *USA Today* (February 9, 2014) http://www.usatoday.com/story/tech/2014/02/09/new-microsoft-ceo-hope/5340519/ (accessed October 12, 2015).
2. Gary Yukl, Angela Gordon, and Tom Taber, "A Hierarchical Taxonomy of Leadership Behavior: Integrating a Half Century of Behavior Research," *Journal of Leadership and Organization Studies* 9, no. 1 (2002), pp. 15–32; and Gary Yukl, "Effective Leadership Behavior: What We Know and What Questions Need More Attention," *Academy of Management Perspectives* (November 2012), pp. 66–81.
3. See Yukl, "Effective Leadership Behavior"; Lee Ellis, "Results/Relationships: Finding the Right Balance," *Leadership Excellence* (October 2012), p. 10; and Kate Ward, "Personality Style: Key to Effective Leadership," *Leadership Excellence* (August 2012), p. 14.
4. Paul Hersey and Kenneth H. Blanchard, *Management of Organizational Behavior: Utilizing Human Resources*, 4th ed. (Upper Saddle River, NJ: Prentice Hall, 1982).
5. Jonathan Kaufman, "A McDonald's Owner Becomes a Role Model for Black Teenagers," *The Wall Street Journal* (August 23, 1995), pp. A1, A6.
6. Carol Hymowitz, "New Face at Facebook Hopes to Map Out a Road to Growth," *The Wall Street Journal* (April 14, 2008), p. B1.
7. Cheryl Dahle, "Xtreme Teams," *Fast Company* (November 1999), pp. 310–326.
8. Carol Hymowitz, "Managers Find Ways to Get Generations to Close Culture Gap," (In the Lead column), *The Wall Street Journal* (July 9, 2007), p. B1.

9. Laura Smith, "Why I Regret Being a Nice Boss," *Slate.com* (October 2, 2014), http://www.slate.com/articles/business/building_a_better_workplace/2014/10/why_i_regret_being_a_nice_boss_setting_boundaries_with_employees.html (accessed October 12, 2015); and Jessica Sigman, "Closing Time: On Its Last Day, Yola Opens Up About Shutting Down," *Washington City Paper* (October 3, 2012), http://www.washingtoncitypaper.com/blogs/youngandhungry/2012/10/03/closing-time-on-its-last-day-yola-opens-up-about-shutting-down/ (accessed October 12, 2015).
10. Fred E. Fiedler, "Assumed Similarity Measures as Predictors of Team Effectiveness," *Journal of Abnormal and Social Psychology* 49 (1954), pp. 381–388; F. E. Fiedler, *Leader Attitudes and Group Effectiveness* (Urbana, IL: University of Illinois Press, 1958); and F. E. Fiedler, *A Theory of Leadership Effectiveness* (New York: McGraw-Hill, 1967).
11. Neal E. Boudette, "Fiat CEO Sets New Tone at Chrysler," *The Wall Street Journal* (June 21, 2009), http://online.wsj.com/article/SB124537403628329989.html (accessed September 14, 2012); and Jeff Bennett and Neal E. Boudette, "Boss Sweats Details of Chrysler Revival," *The Wall Street Journal* (January 31, 2011), p. A1; and Kate Linebaugh and Jeff Bennett, "Marchionne Upends Chrysler's Ways," *The Wall Street Journal* (January 12, 2010), http://online.wsj.com/article/SB10001424052748703652104574652364158366106.html (accessed September 14, 2012).
12. Reported in George Anders, "Theory & Practice: Tough CEOs Often Most Successful, a Study Finds," *The Wall Street Journal* (November 19, 2007), p. B3.
13. M. J. Strube and J. E. Garcia, "A Meta-Analytic Investigation of Fiedler's Contingency Model of Leadership Effectiveness," *Psychological Bulletin* 90 (1981), pp. 307–321; and L. H. Peters, D. D. Hartke, and J. T. Pohlmann, "Fiedler's Contingency Theory of Leadership: An Application of the Meta-Analysis Procedures of Schmidt and Hunter," *Psychological Bulletin* 97 (1985), pp. 274–285.
14. R. Singh, "Leadership Style and Reward Allocation: Does Least Preferred Coworker Scale Measure Tasks and Relation Orientation?" *Organizational Behavior and Human Performance* 27 (1983), pp. 178–197; D. Hosking, "A Critical Evaluation of Fiedler's Contingency Hypotheses," *Progress in Applied Psychology* 1 (1981), pp. 103–154; Gary Yukl, "Leader LPC Scores: Attitude Dimensions and Behavioral Correlates," *Journal of Social Psychology* 80 (1970), pp. 207–212; G. Graen, K. M. Alvares, J. B. Orris, and J. A. Martella, "Contingency Model of Leadership Effectiveness: Antecedent and Evidential Results," *Psychological Bulletin* 74 (1970), pp. 285–296; and R. P. Vecchio, "Assessing the Validity of Fiedler's Contingency Model of Leadership Effectiveness: A Closer Look at Strube and Garcia," *Psychological Bulletin* 93 (1983), pp. 404–408.
15. J. K. Kennedy, Jr., "Middle LPC Leaders and the Contingency Model of Leadership Effectiveness," *Organizational Behavior and Human Performance* 30 (1982), pp. 1–14; and S. C. Shiflett, "The Contingency Model of Leadership Effectiveness: Some Implications of Its Statistical and Methodological Properties," *Behavioral Science* 18, no. 6 (1973), pp. 429–440.
16. Roya Ayman, M. M. Chemers, and F. Fiedler, "The Contingency Model of Leadership Effectiveness: Its Levels of Analysis," *Leadership Quarterly* 6, no. 2 (1995), pp. 147–167.
17. Robert J. House, "A Path–Goal Theory of Leadership Effectiveness," *Administrative Science Quarterly* 16 (1971), pp. 321–338.
18. Ibid.
19. M. G. Evans, "Leadership," in S. Kerr, ed., *Organizational Behavior* (Columbus, OH: Grid, 1974), pp. 230–233.
20. Robert J. House and Terrence R. Mitchell, "Path–Goal Theory of Leadership," *Journal of Contemporary Business* (Autumn 1974), pp. 81–97.
21. Jay Goltz, "Are You a Kind Boss? Or Kind of a Boss?" (You're the Boss column), *The New York Times* (June 13, 2011), http://boss.blogs.nytimes.com/2011/06/13/are-you-a-kind-boss-or-kind-of-a-boss/ (accessed March 15, 2013); and Jay Goltz, "Rethinking the Relationship Between Bosses and Employees," *The New York Times* (December 22, 2014), http://boss.blogs.nytimes.com/2014/12/22/rethinking-the-relationship-between-bosses-and-employees/?_r=0 (accessed October 12, 2015).
22. Timothy Aeppel, "Personnel Disorders Sap a Factory Owner of His Early Idealism," *The Wall Street Journal* (January 14, 1998), pp. A1–A14.
23. Charles Greene, "Questions of Causation in the Path–Goal Theory of Leadership," *Academy of Management Journal* 22 (March 1979), pp. 22–41; and C. A. Schriesheim and Mary Ann von Glinow, "The Path–Goal Theory of Leadership: A Theoretical and Empirical Analysis," *Academy of Management Journal* 20 (1977), pp. 398–405.
24. V. H. Vroom and Arthur G. Jago, *The New Leadership: Managing Participation in Organizations* (Upper Saddle River, NJ: Prentice Hall, 1988).
25. The following discussion is based heavily on Victor H. Vroom, "Leadership and the Decision-Making Process," *Organizational Dynamics* 28, no. 4 (Spring 2000), pp. 82–94.
26. R. H. G. Field, "A Test of the Vroom–Yetton Normative Model of Leadership," *Journal of Applied Psychology* (October 1982), pp. 523–532; and R. H. G. Field, "A Critique of the Vroom–Yetton Contingency Model of Leadership Behavior," *Academy of Management Review* 4 (1979), pp. 249–251.
27. Vroom, "Leadership and the Decision-Making Process"; Jennifer T. Ettling and Arthur G. Jago, "Participation Under Conditions of Conflict: More on the Validity of the Vroom–Yetton Model," *Journal of Management Studies* 25 (1988), pp. 73–83; Madeline E. Heilman, Harvey A. Hornstein, Jack H. Cage, and Judith K. Herschlag, "Reactions to Prescribed Leader Behavior as a Function of Role Perspective: The Case of the Vroom–Yetton Model," *Journal of Applied Psychology* (February 1984), pp. 50–60; and Arthur G. Jago and Victor H. Vroom, "Some Differences in the Incidence and Evaluation of Participative Leader Behavior," *Journal of Applied Psychology* (December 1982), pp. 776–783.
28. Based on a decision problem presented in Victor H. Vroom, "Leadership and the Decision-Making Process," *Organizational Dynamics* 28, no. 4 (Spring, 2000), pp. 82–94.
29. S. Kerr and J. M. Jermier, "Substitutes for Leadership: Their Meaning and Measurement," *Organizational Behavior and Human Performance* 22 (1978), pp. 375–403; and Jon P. Howell and Peter W. Dorfman, "Leadership and Substitutes for Leadership among Professional and Nonprofessional Workers," *Journal of Applied Behavioral Science* 22 (1986), pp. 29–46.
30. J. P. Howell, D. E. Bowen, P. W. Doreman, S. Kerr, and P. M. Podsakoff, "Substitutes for Leadership: Effective Alternatives to Ineffective Leadership," *Organizational Dynamics* (Summer 1990), pp. 21–38.
31. Mark Maske, "Daniel Snyder, Washington Redskins Owner, Adopts Hands-Off Role—and Team Wins," *The Washington Post* (January 4, 2013), http://articles.washingtonpost.com/2013-01-04/sports/36209112_1_daniel-snyder-washington-redskins-redskins-park (accessed March 15, 2013).
32. Howell et al., "Substitutes for Leadership: Effective Alternatives."
33. P. M. Podsakoff, S. B. MacKenzie, and W. H. Bommer, "Transformational Leader Behaviors and Substitutes for Leadership as Determinants of Employee Satisfaction, Commitment, Trust, and Organizational Behaviors," *Journal of Management* 22, no. 2 (1996), pp. 259–298.
34. Howell et al., "Substitutes for Leadership."
35. Reprinted with permission from Gary Yukl, *Leadership in Organizations*, 7th ed. (Upper Saddle River, NJ: Prentice Hall, 2010), pp. 119–120.

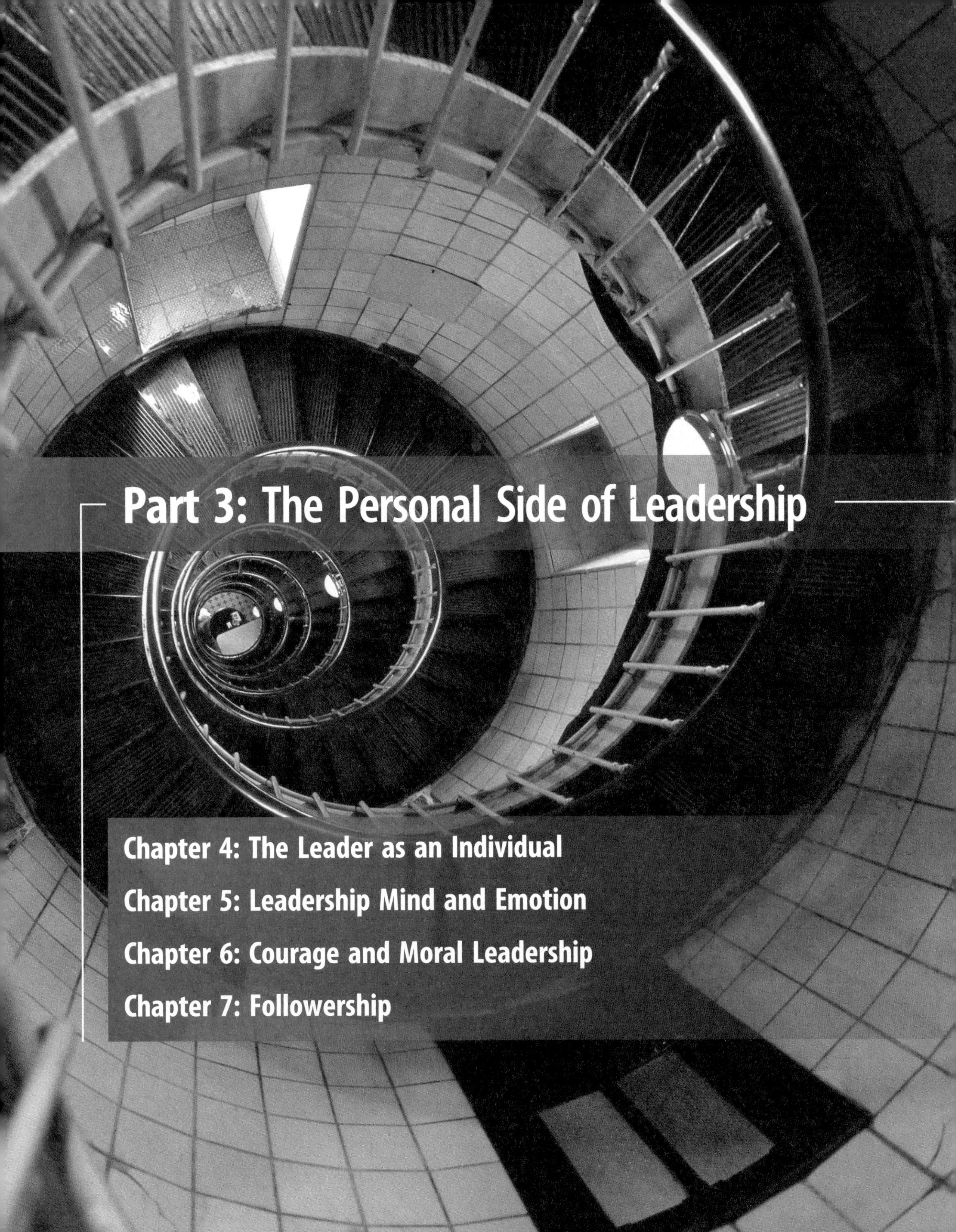

Part 3: The Personal Side of Leadership

Chapter 4: The Leader as an Individual

Chapter 5: Leadership Mind and Emotion

Chapter 6: Courage and Moral Leadership

Chapter 7: Followership

Chapter 4: The Leader as an Individual

YOUR **LEADERSHIP** CHALLENGE

After reading this chapter, you should be able to:

- Understand the importance of self-awareness and how to recognize your blind spots.
- Identify major personality dimensions and understand how personality influences leadership and relationships within organizations.
- Clarify your instrumental and end values and recognize how values guide thoughts and behavior.
- Define *attitudes* and explain their relationship to leader behavior.
- Explain attributions and recognize how perception affects the leader–follower relationship.
- Recognize individual differences in cognitive style and broaden your own thinking style to expand leadership potential.
- Understand how to lead and work with people with varied personality traits.

CHAPTER **OUTLINE**

100 **The Secret Ingredient for Leadership Success**

102 **Personality and Leadership**

109 **Values and Attitudes**

114 **Social Perception and Attributions**

116 **Cognitive Differences**

122 **Working with Different Personality Types**

In the Lead

102 **Lois Braverman, Ackerman Institute for the Family**

107 **Chris Hughes, Facebook and MyBarackObama.com**

112 **Admiral Vernon E. Clark, U.S. Chief of Naval Operations, 2000–2005**

116 **Kevin Kelly, Emerald Packaging**

120 **Angela Ahrendts, Apple**

Leader's Self-Insight

103 **The Big Five Personality Dimensions**

108 **Measuring Locus of Control**

110 **Instrumental and End Values**

118 **What's Your Thinking Style?**

123 **Personality Assessment: Jung's Typology**

Leader's Bookshelf

106 **Quiet: The Power of Introverts in a World That Can't Stop Talking**

Leadership at Work

127 **Past and Future**

Leadership Development: Cases for Analysis

128 **A *Nice* Manager**

130 **Environmental Designs International**

Nancy Dubec's first formal leadership job was as head of development at cable network A&E. Now that she's CEO of A&E Networks, which encompasses A&E, Lifetime, HISTORY, FYI and H2, as well as a number of other divisions, she still applies some of the lessons she learned in that job. "I suddenly had eight people reporting to me, and I had to let some of them go," Dubec says. Dubec realized she had a natural competitive streak and an instinctive drive to win and create. She also realized that some people thrive in that type of environment and some don't. The ability to look at each person as an individual with different needs, interests, personalities, skills, and styles helped Dubec rise to the top and have a big impact at A&E. She thinks building the best team requires a mix of styles and skills. "I'm a big believer in the idea that people tend to fall into one of three groups—you're either a thinker, a doer, or a feeler," she says, pointing out that the right balance of the three is essential for high team performance. Dubec says she is more of a *doer* so she is careful to make sure she has thinkers and feelers on her team and respects their approaches. "When you put the different kinds of people together in the right way, that can be very powerful," she says. "You never want that out of balance."[1]

Leaders' ability to understand their own personalities and attitudes, as well as their ability to understand individual differences among employees, can profoundly affect leadership effectiveness. Many of today's organizations use personality and other psychometric tests as a way to help people better understand themselves and relate to one another. In Chapter 2, we examined some traits, individual qualities, and behaviors that are thought to be consistent with effective leadership. Chapter 3 examined contingency theories of leadership, which consider the relationship between leader activities and the situations in which they occur, including followers and the environment. Clearly, organizational leadership is both an individual and an organizational phenomenon. In this chapter, we explore individual differences in more depth and examine how variations in personality, attitudes, values, and so forth influence the leader–follower relationship.

We begin by considering the importance of leaders knowing themselves, and we look at some potential blind spots leaders may have that limit their understanding and effectiveness. Next, we examine personality and some leader-related personality dimensions. Then the chapter considers how values affect leadership and the ways in which a leader's attitudes influence behavior. We also explore the role of perception, discuss attributions, and look at cognitive differences, including a discussion of thinking and decision-making styles and the concept of brain dominance. Finally, the chapter considers a few techniques for working with different personality types.

4-1 THE SECRET INGREDIENT FOR LEADERSHIP SUCCESS

A survey of 75 members of the Stanford Graduate School of Business's Advisory Council revealed the nearly unanimous answer to a question about the most important capability for leaders to develop: self-awareness.[2] **Self-awareness** means being aware of the internal aspects of one's nature, such as personality traits, emotions, values, attitudes, and perceptions, and appreciating how your patterns affect other people.

4-1a The Importance of Self-Awareness

Most leadership experts agree that a primary characteristic of effective leaders is that they know who they are and what they stand for.[3] When leaders deeply understand themselves, they remain grounded and constant, so that people know what to expect from them.

Yet being self-aware is easier said than done. When Charlotte Beers, former chairwoman and CEO of Ogilvy & Mather Worldwide, first became a management supervisor, she considered herself to be a friendly, approachable, easy-going leader. She was shocked when a friend told her that one of her colleagues described her management style as "menacing." That comment was devastating to Beers because it was the exact opposite of the way she thought of herself.[4] Many of us, like Charlotte Beers, have blind spots that hinder us from seeing who we really are and the

Self-awareness
being conscious of the internal aspects of one's nature, such as personality traits, emotions, values, attitudes, and perceptions, and appreciating how your patterns affect other people

effect our patterns of thought and behavior have on others. Beers now conducts seminars for women leaders, and one thing she tells them is the importance of clearly understanding themselves. The authors of a recent book profiling high achievers found that they all shared a similar characteristic: When faced with obstacles and failures, they underwent a ruthless self-examination to challenge their beliefs, biases, and assumptions.[5] A careful self-reflection is essential for most people to recognize their blind spots.

4-1b Leader Blind Spots

Doug Rauch, retired president of Trader Joe's, almost strangled the life out of his company as it grew because of his tendency to, as he puts it, "happily micromanage." Rauch recognized his zeal to control everything was hurting the company only when a brave senior buyer pulled him aside and said, "You're driving us crazy. You've got to back off." Rauch was surprised, but the comment helped him see his blind spot. He went to the team and admitted his problem, told them he was a "recovering controlaholic," and asked people to give him regular feedback so he didn't fall off the wagon.[6]

NEW LEADER
ACTION MEMO

As a leader, strive for self-awareness so that you know who you are and what you stand for. Undergo ruthless self-examination and seek feedback from others to avoid being derailed by blind spots.

Many leaders have **blind spots**—things they are not aware of or don't recognize as problems—that limit their effectiveness and hinder their career success.[7] One particularly damaging blind spot is displaying an aggressive, confrontational style, otherwise known as *being a jerk*. Lars Dalgaard, founder and former CEO of software company SuccessFactors (now part of SAP), says he never realized he acted like a jerk until a leadership coach helped him see that he ran roughshod over people's feelings. The coach helped Dalgaard make a conscious effort to build good relationships with employees and help others be more emotionally aware as well. SuccessFactors, which has an official "no jerks rule," has twice been voted one of the best places to work in the San Francisco Bay area.[8]

Stanford professor Robert Sutton argues that jerks not only hurt the people they work with but also damage organizational performance. Sutton distinguishes between people who are perpetual jerks and those who only occasionally act that way. Perpetual jerks are those leaders who bully, humiliate, and emotionally abuse others, particularly people in less powerful positions.[9] Even people who aren't perpetual jerks can suffer this blind spot. As leaders move up the hierarchy, people skills become more and more important, and leaders who have succeeded at lower levels often don't see that their approach is less effective as they advance in their careers. Jack Welch, the long-time former CEO of General Electric (GE), had to learn this lesson. When he was vying for the CEO position, his brashness and blunt approach almost cost him the job. GE's board knew Welch could generate profits, but they needed him to show them that he could act like a CEO, which meant recognizing and toning down his jerk qualities.[10]

"The challenge for leadership is to be strong, but not rude; be kind, but not weak; be bold, but not bully; be thoughtful, but not lazy; be humble, but not timid; be proud, but not arrogant; have humor, but without folly."

Jim Rohn (1930–2009), entrepreneur, author, and motivational speaker

Another blind spot some leaders have is being *too nice*. Leaders who are constantly trying to please everyone can't lead. They often make poor decisions because they can't tolerate even a mild degree of conflict.[11] When asked about her greatest weakness, Sue Murray, former executive director of the George Foundation, said, "I can be too nice when tough decisions need to be made, which is not helpful to anyone. It just prolongs the inevitable."[12] Unlike Murray, many "people pleasers" have a blind spot that prevents them from seeing that they are damaging their relationships and careers by being overly concerned with what others think of them.

Blind spots
characteristics or habits that people are not aware of or don't recognize as problems but which limit their effectiveness and hinder their career success

4-2 PERSONALITY AND LEADERSHIP

When a leader understands himself or herself and overcomes blind spots, it becomes easier to understand and interact effectively with others. Understanding personality differences is one aspect of knowing how to maximize your own effectiveness and that of the people you lead. **Personality** is the set of unseen characteristics and processes that underlie a relatively stable pattern of behavior in response to ideas, objects, or people in the environment. Lois Braverman, CEO of the Ackerman Institute for the Family, believes understanding and accepting individual personalities is essential for effective leadership.

IN THE LEAD

Lois Braverman, Ackerman Institute for the Family

If Lois Braverman could ask only a couple of questions to decide whether to hire a job candidate, one of them would be, "In terms of your personality and temperament, what will you bring that will be helpful to [this organization]?" Braverman's background as a psychotherapist makes her aware of how people's personality characteristics, as well as other individual differences, influence the workplace. She says she learned early on as a leader that her judgment in hiring could be skewed by "a great conversation." Someone who is likable and charming might be fun to interview, but it doesn't necessarily mean they are responsible and trustworthy, or that they have the personality traits and qualities needed for the job, she points out.

Another leadership benefit Braverman credits to her therapy background is an understanding that "reality is all about perception." Conflicts can arise in any organization, she says, because people genuinely perceive some aspect of the world differently. As a leader, Braverman helps people "make room for the differences" so that conflicts don't escalate and damage morale and performance. She also applies the rule to herself. "There's an administrative reality and there's a front line reality," she says, "and those realities are rarely the same." Making sure everyone feels that "their perception of reality at least has a chance to be heard" is one of the primary jobs of a leader.[13]

The following sections discuss personality in more detail. Later in the chapter, we take a closer look at the topic of perception in connection with leadership.

4-2a A Model of Personality

Personality
the set of unseen characteristics and processes that underlie a relatively stable pattern of behavior in response to ideas, objects, and people in the environment

Big Five personality dimensions
five general dimensions that describe personality: extroversion, agreeableness, conscientiousness, emotional stability, and openness to experience

Most people think of personality in terms of traits. As we discussed in Chapter 2, researchers have investigated whether any traits stand up to scientific scrutiny, and we looked at some traits associated with effective leadership. Although investigators have examined thousands of traits over the years, their findings have been distilled into five general dimensions that describe personality. These often are called the **Big Five personality dimensions**, which describe an individual's extroversion, agreeableness, conscientiousness, emotional stability, and openness to experience.[14] Each dimension contains a wide range of specific traits—for example, all of the personality traits that you would use to describe a teacher, friend, or boss could be categorized into one of the Big Five dimensions. These factors represent a continuum, in that a person may have a low, moderate, or high degree of each of the dimensions.

LEADER'S SELF-INSIGHT 4.1

The Big Five Personality Dimensions

Instructions: Each individual's collection of personality traits is different; it is what makes us unique. But, although each *collection* of traits varies, we all share many common traits. The following phrases describe various traits and behaviors. Rate how accurately each statement describes you, based on a scale of 1 to 5, with 1 being very inaccurate and 5 very accurate. Describe yourself as you are now, not as you wish to be. There are no right or wrong answers.

1	2	3	4	5
Very Inaccurate				Very Accurate

Extroversion					
I love large parties.	1	2	3	4	5
I feel comfortable around people.	1	2	3	4	5
I talk to a lot of different people at social gatherings.	1	2	3	4	5
I like being the center of attention.	1	2	3	4	5

Neuroticism (Low Emotional Stability)					
I often feel critical of myself.	1	2	3	4	5
I often envy others.	1	2	3	4	5
I am temperamental.	1	2	3	4	5
I am easily bothered by things.	1	2	3	4	5

Agreeableness					
I am kind and sympathetic.	1	2	3	4	5
I have a good word for everyone.	1	2	3	4	5
I never insult people.	1	2	3	4	5
I put others first.	1	2	3	4	5

Openness to New Experiences					
I am imaginative.	1	2	3	4	5
I see beauty in many things.	1	2	3	4	5
I really like art.	1	2	3	4	5
I love to learn new things.	1	2	3	4	5

Conscientiousness					
I am systematic and efficient.	1	2	3	4	5
I pay attention to details.	1	2	3	4	5
I am always prepared for class.	1	2	3	4	5
I put things back where they belong.	1	2	3	4	5

Which are your most prominent traits? For fun and discussion, compare your responses with those of classmates.

Source: These questions were adapted from a variety of sources.

Extroversion is made up of traits and characteristics that influence behavior in group settings. Extroversion refers to the degree to which a person is outgoing, sociable, talkative, and comfortable meeting and talking to new people. Someone low on extroversion may come across as quiet, withdrawn, and socially unassertive. This dimension also includes the characteristic of *dominance*. A person with a high degree of dominance likes to be in control and have influence over others. These people often are quite self-confident, seek out positions of authority, and are competitive and assertive. They like to be in charge of others or have responsibility for others. It is obvious that both dominance and extroversion could be valuable for a leader. However, not all effective leaders necessarily have a high degree of these characteristics.

For example, many successful top leaders, including Larry Page of Google; Warren Buffett of Berkshire Hathaway; Brenda Barnes, former CEO of Sara Lee; and Tim Cook, CEO of Apple, are introverts, people who become drained by social encounters and need time alone to reflect and recharge their batteries. One study found that 4 in 10 top executives test out to be introverts.[15] Thus, the quality of extroversion is not as significant as is often presumed. In addition, a high degree of

NEW LEADER
ACTION MEMO

See where you fall on the Big Five scale for extroversion, agreeableness, conscientiousness, emotional stability, and openness to experience by answering the questions in Leader's Self-Insight 4.1.

Extroversion
the degree to which a person is outgoing, sociable, talkative, and comfortable meeting and talking to new people

dominance could even be detrimental to effective leadership if not tempered by other qualities, such as agreeableness or emotional stability.

Agreeableness refers to the degree to which a person is able to get along with others by being good-natured, cooperative, forgiving, compassionate, understanding, and trusting. A leader who scores high on agreeableness seems warm and approachable, whereas one who is low on this dimension may seem cold, distant, and insensitive. Studies show that people who score high on agreeableness are more likely to get jobs and keep them than are less agreeable people.[16] Although there is also some evidence that people who are *overly* agreeable tend to be promoted less often and earn less money, the days are over when leaders can expect to succeed by running roughshod over others and looking out only for themselves.

Today's successful leaders are not the tough guys of the past but those men and women who know how to get people to like and trust them.[17] Leaders are making a concerted effort to present a friendlier face to employees, the public, and shareholders after years of headlines exposing white-collar crime, CEO arrogance, and complaints over exorbitant pay. Lee Raymond, the former CEO of ExxonMobil, made plenty of money for investors but was described by some shareholders as "stubborn, self-important, [and] rude." In contrast, Raymond's successor, Rex Tillerson, was publicly thanked at one annual meeting for his "friendliness, humor, and candor."[18]

The next personality dimension, **conscientiousness**, refers to the degree to which a person is responsible, dependable, persistent, and achievement oriented. A conscientious person is focused on a few goals, which he or she pursues in a purposeful way, whereas a less conscientious person tends to be easily distracted and impulsive. Recent research suggests that traits of conscientiousness are also more important than those of extroversion for effective leadership. A study at the Stanford Graduate School of Business found a link between how guilty people feel when they make serious mistakes and how well they perform as leaders.[19] Guilt can be a positive emotion for a leader because it is associated with a heightened sense of responsibility to others.

Consider former International Monetary Fund leader Dominique Strauss-Kahn, who was likely on his way to the French presidency before he was arrested in New York and charged with the sexual assault of a hotel housekeeper, with further allegations from other women later coming to light.[20] Strauss-Kahn displays a low level of conscientiousness, whereas a leader like Anne Mulcahy, former CEO of Xerox, reflects a high degree of this characteristic. Mulcahy felt a strong sense of responsibility to employees and shareholders when she was named CEO of Xerox in 2001.The company was in a free fall, with the stock price plummeting and its credit rating downgraded. Advisers urged Mulcahy to declare bankruptcy, but she chose instead to focus on a vision of restoring Xerox to greatness. Although she had tough decisions to make, she always kept the best interests of employees and shareholders in mind.[21]

The dimension of **emotional stability** refers to the degree to which a person is well adjusted, calm, and secure. A leader who is emotionally stable handles stress well, is able to handle criticism, and generally doesn't take mistakes or failures personally. Leaders with emotional stability typically develop positive relationships and can also improve relationships among others. Marillyn A. Hewson's high degree of emotional stability is part of the reason she was promoted to be the first female CEO of defense contractor Lockheed Martin, after the man originally

Agreeableness
the degree to which a person is able to get along with others by being good-natured, cooperative, forgiving, compassionate, understanding, and trusting

Conscientiousness
the degree to which a person is responsible, dependable, persistent, and achievement oriented

Emotional stability
the degree to which a person is well adjusted, calm, and secure

picked for the top job was fired following discovery of an ethical violation. It's a challenging time for Lockheed, but Hewson has shown that she can handle crises without becoming unhinged. Over her 30-year career at the company, her calm, steady hand has earned her a reputation for being able to combine toughness with graciousness. "Marillyn will be exactly what Lockheed Martin needs in terms of patching up its relationships . . ." said defense industry consultant Loren Thompson.[22]

Leaders who have a low degree of emotional stability are likely to become tense, anxious, or depressed. They generally have lower self-confidence and may explode in emotional outbursts when stressed or criticized. The related topic of *emotional intelligence* will be discussed in detail in the next chapter.

The final Big Five dimension, **openness to experience**, is the degree to which a person has a broad range of interests and is imaginative, creative, and willing to consider new ideas. These people are intellectually curious and often seek out new experiences through travel, the arts, movies, reading widely, or other activities. People lower in this dimension tend to have narrower interests and stick to the tried-and-true ways of doing things. Open-mindedness is important to leaders because, as we learned in Chapter 1, leadership is about change rather than stability. In an interesting study of three nineteenth-century leaders—John Quincy Adams, Frederick Douglass, and Jane Addams—one researcher found that early travel experiences and exposure to different ideas and cultures were critical elements in developing open-minded qualities in these leaders.[23] Travel during the formative years helped these leaders to develop a greater degree of openness to experience because it put them in situations that required adaptability.

NEW LEADER
ACTION MEMO

As a leader, you can learn about your own basic personality dimensions and how to emphasize the positive aspects of your personality in dealing with followers.

Few studies have carefully examined the connection between the Big Five and leadership success. One summary of more than 70 years of personality and leadership research did find evidence that four of the five dimensions were consistently related to successful leadership.[24] The researchers found considerable evidence that people who score high on the dimensions of extroversion, agreeableness, conscientiousness, and emotional stability are more successful leaders. Results for openness to experience were less consistent; that is, in some cases, higher scores on this dimension related to better performance, but they did not seem to make a difference in other cases. Yet, in a study by a team of psychologists of the personality traits of the greatest U.S. presidents (as determined by historians), openness to experience produced the highest correlation with historians' ratings of greatness. The study noted that presidents such as Abraham Lincoln and Thomas Jefferson were high on this personality dimension. Other personality dimensions the team found to be associated with great presidents were extroversion and conscientiousness, including traits such as assertiveness, setting ambitious goals, and striving for achievement. Although agreeableness did not correlate with greatness, the ability to empathize with others and being concerned for others, which could be considered elements of emotional stability, did.[25]

The value of the Big Five for leaders is primarily to help them understand their own basic personality dimensions and then learn to emphasize the positive and mitigate the negative aspects of their own natural styles. For example, people who are introverts often stagnate, especially in large organizations, because they have a difficult time getting noticed and are therefore less likely to be rewarded for their hard work.[26] Four out of five introverts surveyed said they believe extroverts are more likely to get ahead at their place of employment.[27] One experiment found that people who spoke up more often were rated as better leaders, even if they were less

Openness to experience
the degree to which a person has a broad range of interests and is imaginative, creative, and willing to consider new ideas

LEADER'S BOOKSHELF

Quiet: The Power of Introverts in a World That Can't Stop Talking

by Susan Cain

From kindergarten on in the United States, students are pressured to be more outgoing and speak up more in class. In college, grades are sometimes based on class participation, and students who don't forcefully push their ideas get sidelined. No wonder by the time we get to the workplace, we know that talk and social interaction are prized above quietness and thoughtfulness. In her book *Quiet*, Susan Cain argues that by succumbing to the charms of the extrovert, organizations are missing out on the creativity, insights, and ideas of the one-third to one-half of Americans who are introverts.

MISCONCEPTIONS ABOUT INTROVERTS

Cain's thoughtful examination, using research studies, historical examples, and individual stories, explodes some of the myths about introversion.

- ***Introverts are shy and antisocial.*** Some introverts are shy, but many are not. They simply interact in a different way. Whereas the extrovert will "work the room" at a party, the introvert prefers to carry on deeper conversations with one or a few people. Introverts need time alone to reflect and recharge, but that doesn't mean they don't also enjoy the company of other people.
- ***Introverts have a personality flaw.*** In a culture that prizes extroversion, the tendency of introverts toward solitary activity and quiet reflection marks them as having "a second-class personality trait, somewhere between a disappointment and a pathology." Cain points out many advantages to the introverted personality: introverts tend to think more deeply, make decisions more carefully, and stay on task longer. Introversion is uniquely conducive to creativity and innovation. Extrovert Steve Jobs was the pizzazz of Apple, but the company would never have existed if introverted cofounder Steven Wozniak had not spent long hours alone creating the first personal computer.
- ***Introverts don't make good leaders.*** This is perhaps the biggest misconception of all. Introverts such as Bill Gates and Warren Buffett succeed at the top of big corporations, but introverts also make excellent lower-level supervisors and managers because of their greater ability to listen. Cain cites research showing that introverts do very well leading teams, even those made up primarily of extroverts, because they can stand aside and let the good ideas flow rather than pushing their own thoughts and opinions.

CAN'T WE ALL JUST GET ALONG?

No one is totally an introvert or an extrovert. Each of us falls somewhere along a continuum on the scale of introversion–extroversion. The problem, Cain says, is the tendency in the United States and other Western cultures to revere extroverts and try to push everyone to that end of the scale. Cain challenges leaders to show respect and truly listen to their introverted colleagues and subordinates, not just be swayed by the loudest voices. "You need to do this as a manager," she says, "because you . . . want the best out of people's brains."

Source: *Quiet: The Power of Introverts in a World That Can't Stop Talking*, by Susan Cain, is published by Crown Publishers.

competent than their quieter colleagues.[28] Introverts can learn to behave in more extroverted ways when they need to in order to be more successful. For example, Richard Branson dresses up in silly costumes to publicize the Virgin Group, but he says that flamboyant public persona bears little resemblance to his innate personality. "I was a shy and retiring individual who couldn't make speeches and get out there," Branson says of himself prior to founding Virgin. "I had to train myself into becoming more of an extrovert" in order to promote the new company.[29]

In recent years, there has been a growing awareness that introverted people have some qualities that might actually make them better leaders, as described further in the Leader's Bookshelf.[30] Introversion or extroversion is simply one aspect of an individual's personality, and each style has both strengths and weaknesses. Exhibit 4.1 gives some tips for both introverts and extroverts to help them be more effective and successful.

4-2b Personality Traits and Leader Behavior

Two specific personality attributes that have a significant impact on behavior and are thus of particular interest for leadership studies are locus of control and authoritarianism.

Locus of Control Some people believe that their actions can strongly affect what happens to them. In other words, they believe they are "masters of their own fate." Others feel that whatever happens to them in life is a result of luck, chance, or outside people and events; they believe they have little control over their fate. A person's **locus of control** defines whether he or she places the primary responsibility within the self or on outside forces.[31] People who believe their actions determine what happens to them have a high *internal* locus of control (internals), whereas those who believe outside forces determine what happens to them have a high *external* locus of control (externals). One leader who reflects a strong internal locus of control is Chris Hughes, cofounder of Facebook.

NEW LEADER
ACTION MEMO

Do you believe luck, chance, or the actions of other people play a major role in your life, or do you feel in control of your own fate? Learn more about your locus of control by completing the questionnaire in Leader's Self-Insight 4.2.

Locus of control defines whether a person places the primary responsibility for what happens to him or her within himself/herself or on outside forces

EXHIBIT 4.1 Maximizing Leadership Effectiveness

Tips for Extroverts	Tips for Introverts
• *Don't bask in the glow of your own personality.* Learn to hold back and let others sometimes have the limelight. • *Try to underwhelm.* Your natural exuberance can cause you to miss important facts and ideas. • *Talk less; listen more.* Develop the discipline to let others speak first on an issue to avoid the appearance of arrogance. • *Don't be Mr. or Ms. Personality.* Extroverts sometimes fail to recognize others' needs and can easily wear people out rather than invigorate them.	• *Mix with people, speak up, and get out there.* Push yourself to get out there and connect with people both within and outside the organization. • *Practice being friendly and outgoing in settings outside of work.* Take your new skills to the office. • *Have a game plan.* Prepare well for meetings and presentations. Anticipate questions and rehearse a few talking points. • *Smile.* A frown or a soberly introspective expression can be misinterpreted. A bright countenance reflects confidence that you know where you're going and want others to follow.

Sources: Based on Patricia Wallington, "The Ins and Outs of Personality," *CIO* (January 15, 2003), pp. 42, 44; "From the Front Lines: Leadership Strategies for Introverts," *Leader to Leader* (Fall 2009), pp. 59–60; Joann S. Lublin, "Introverted Execs Find Ways to Shine," *The Wall Street Journal Asia* (April 18, 2011), p. 31; and Ginka Toegel and Jean-Louis Barsoux, "How to Become a Better Leader," *MIT Sloan Management Review* (Spring 2012), pp. 51–60.

IN THE LEAD

Chris Hughes, Facebook and MyBarackObama.com

Chris Hughes grew up in Hickory, North Carolina, as the only child of older parents. His father was a paper salesman and his mother a former public school teacher. When Hughes entered high school, he decided he wanted something different than graduating from the local school and getting a job in town. In fact, what he wanted was to attend a prestigious prep school and go on to an Ivy League university.

With his family's background and modest means, it was definitely an ambitious goal, but Hughes believed his fate was in his own hands. Without telling his parents, he began researching and applying to various boarding schools. Eventually he was offered a generous financial aid package from Phillips Academy in Andover, Massachusetts. A few years later, he left there with a scholarship to Harvard.

Hughes met Mark Zuckerberg and Dustin Moskovitz during his freshman year at Harvard and the three founded Facebook. Then, during the 2008 presidential campaign, Hughes became attracted to the idea of using new media to get Barack Obama elected. Volunteers flooded the site he built, MyBarackObama.com, from the day it launched. Hughes was later featured on the cover of *Fast Company* magazine as "The Kid Who Made Obama President."[32]

LEADER'S SELF-INSIGHT 4.2

Measuring Locus of Control

Instructions: For each of these 10 questions, indicate the extent to which you agree or disagree using the following scale:

1 = Strongly disagree
2 = Disagree
3 = Slightly disagree
4 = Neither agree nor disagree
5 = Slightly agree
6 = Agree
7 = Strongly agree

		Strongly Disagree — Strongly Agree
1.	When I get what I want, it's usually because I worked hard for it.	1 2 3 4 5 6 7
2.	When I make plans, I am almost certain to make them work.	1 2 3 4 5 6 7
3.	I prefer games involving some luck over games requiring pure skill.	1 2 3 4 5 6 7
4.	I can learn almost anything if I set my mind to it.	1 2 3 4 5 6 7
5.	My major accomplishments are entirely due to my hard work and ability.	1 2 3 4 5 6 7
6.	I usually don't set goals, because I have a hard time following through on them.	1 2 3 4 5 6 7
7.	Competition discourages excellence.	1 2 3 4 5 6 7
8.	Often people get ahead just by being lucky.	1 2 3 4 5 6 7
9.	On any sort of exam or competition, I like to know how well I do relative to everyone else.	1 2 3 4 5 6 7
10.	It's pointless to keep working on something that's too difficult for me.	1 2 3 4 5 6 7

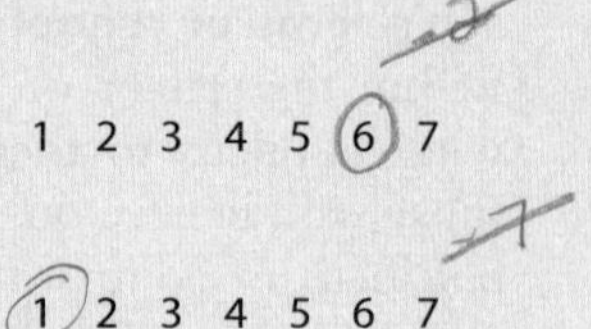

Scoring and Interpretation

To determine your score, reverse the values you selected for questions 3, 6, 7, 8, and 10 (1 = 7, 2 = 6, 3 = 5, 4 = 4, 5 = 3, 6 = 2, 7 = 1). For example, if you strongly disagreed with the statement in question 3, you would have given it a value of 1. Change this value to a 7. Reverse the scores in a similar manner for questions 6, 7, 8, and 10. Now add the point values from all 10 questions together.

Your score: ______

This questionnaire is designed to measure locus of control beliefs. Researchers using this questionnaire in a study of college students found a mean of 51.8 for men and 52.2 for women, with a standard deviation of 6 for each. The higher your score on this questionnaire, the more you tend to believe that you are generally responsible for what happens to you; in other words, high scores are associated with internal locus of control. Low scores are associated with external locus of control. Scoring low indicates that you tend to believe that forces beyond your control, such as powerful other people, fate, or chance, are responsible for what happens to you.

Source: Adapted from J. M. Burger, *Personality: Theory and Research* (Belmont, CA: Wadsworth, 1986), pp. 400–401. Original source for Burger's questionnaire is D. L. Paulhus, "Sphere-Specific Measures of Perceived Control," *Journal of Personality and Social Psychology* 44 (1983), pp. 1253–1265.

Chris Hughes exhibits many characteristics associated with internal locus of control. Research has shown real differences in behavior between internals and externals across a wide range of settings.[33] Internals in general are more self-motivated, are in better control of their own behavior, participate more in social and political activities, and more actively seek information. There is also evidence that internals are better able to handle complex information and problem solving, and that they are more achievement oriented than externals. In addition, people with a high internal locus of control are more likely than externals to try to influence others and thus more likely to assume or seek leadership opportunities. Moreover, people with a high internal locus of control will take responsibility for outcomes and changes, which is essential for leadership.[34]

People with a high external locus of control typically prefer to have structured, directed work situations. They are better able than internals to handle work that requires compliance and conformity, but they are generally not as effective in situations that require initiative, creativity, and independent action. Therefore, since externals do best in situations where success depends on complying with the direction or guidance of others, they are less likely to enjoy or succeed in leadership positions.

Authoritarianism The belief that power and status differences *should* exist in an organization is called **authoritarianism**.[35] Individuals who have a high degree of this personality trait tend to adhere to conventional rules and values, obey established authority, respect power and toughness, judge others critically, and disapprove of the expression of personal feelings. A leader's degree of authoritarianism will affect how the leader wields and shares power. A highly authoritarian leader is likely to rely heavily on formal authority and unlikely to want to share power with subordinates. High authoritarianism is associated with the traditional, rational approach to management described in Chapter 1 and the autocratic style of leadership described in Chapter 2. The new leadership paradigm requires that leaders be less authoritarian, although people who rate high on this personality trait can be effective leaders as well. Leaders should also understand that the degree to which followers possess authoritarianism influences how they react to the leader's use of power and authority. When leaders and followers differ in their degree of authoritarianism, effective leadership may be more difficult to achieve.

Understanding how personality traits and dimensions affect behavior can be an advantage for leaders, giving them valuable insights into their own behavior as well as that of followers. Another important area for understanding individual differences is values and attitudes.

NEW LEADER
ACTION MEMO

As a leader, you can improve your effectiveness by recognizing how traits such as authoritarianism and locus of control affect your relationships with followers. You can tone down a strong authoritarian personality to motivate others.

4-3 VALUES AND ATTITUDES

Individuals may differ significantly in the values and attitudes they hold. These differences affect the behavior of leaders and followers.

4-3a Instrumental and End Values

Values are fundamental beliefs that an individual considers to be important, that are relatively stable over time, and that have an impact on attitudes, perception, and behavior.[36] Values are what cause a person to prefer that things be done one way rather than another way. Whether we recognize it or not, we are constantly valuing things, people, or ideas as good or bad, pleasant or unpleasant, ethical or unethical, and so forth.[37]

One way to think about values is in terms of instrumental and end values.[38] Social scientist Milton Rokeach developed a list of 18 instrumental values and 18 end values that have been found to be more or less universal across cultures. The full list of Rokeach's values is shown in Leader's Self-Insight 4.3. **End values**, sometimes called *terminal values*, are beliefs about the kinds of goals or outcomes that are worth trying to pursue. For example, some people value security, a comfortable life, and good health above everything else as the important goals to strive for in life. Others may place greater value on social recognition, pleasure, and an exciting life. **Instrumental values** are beliefs about the types of behavior that are appropriate for reaching goals. Instrumental values include such things as being helpful to others, being honest, or exhibiting courage.

Authoritarianism
the belief that power and status differences should exist in an organization

Values
fundamental beliefs that an individual considers to be important, that are relatively stable over time, and that have an impact on attitudes and behavior

End values
sometimes called terminal values, these are beliefs about the kinds of goals or outcomes that are worth trying to pursue

Instrumental values
beliefs about the types of behavior that are appropriate for reaching goals

LEADER'S SELF-INSIGHT 4.3

Instrumental and End Values

Instructions: In each column below, place a check mark by the five values that are most important to you. After you have checked five values in each column, rank-order the checked values in each column from 1 to 5, with 1 = most important and 5 = least important.

Rokeach's Instrumental and End Values

End Values		Instrumental Values	
A comfortable life	_____	Ambition	_____
Equality	_____	Broad-mindedness	_____
An exciting life	_____	Capability	_____
Family security	_____	Cheerfulness	_____
Freedom	_____	Cleanliness	_____
Health	_____	Courage	_____
Inner harmony	_____	Forgiveness	_____
Mature love	_____	Helpfulness	_____
National security	_____	Honesty	_____
Pleasure	_____	Imagination	_____
Salvation	_____	Intellectualism	_____
Self-respect	_____	Logic	_____
A sense of accomplishment	_____	Ability to love	_____
Social recognition	_____	Loyalty	_____
True friendship	_____	Obedience	_____
Wisdom	_____	Politeness	_____
A world at peace	_____	Responsibility	_____
A world of beauty	_____	Self-control	_____

NOTE: The values are listed in alphabetical order, and there is no one-to-one relationship between the end and instrumental values.

Scoring and Interpretation

End values, according to Rokeach, tend to fall into two categories—personal and social. For example, mature love is a personal end value and equality is a social end value. Analyze the five end values you selected and their rank order, and determine whether your primary end values tend to be personal or social. What do your five selections together mean to you? What do they mean for how you make life decisions? Compare your end value selections with those of another person, with each of you explaining what you learned about your end values from this exercise.

Instrumental values also tend to fall into two categories—morality and competence. The means people use to achieve their goals might violate moral values (e.g., be dishonest) or violate one's personal sense of competence and capability (e.g., be illogical). Analyze the five instrumental values you selected and their rank order, and determine whether your primary instrumental values tend to focus on morality or competence. What do the five selected values together mean to you? What do they mean for how you will pursue your life goals? Compare your instrumental value selections with those of another person and describe what you learned from this exercise.

Warning: The two columns shown to the left do *not* represent the full range of instrumental and end values. Your findings would change if a different list of values were provided. This exercise is for discussion and learning purposes only and is not intended to be an accurate assessment of your actual end and instrumental values.

Sources: Robert C. Benfari, *Understanding and Changing Your Management Style* (San Francisco: Jossey-Bass, 1999), pp. 178–183; and M. Rokeach, *Understanding Human Values* (New York: The Free Press, 1979).

Although everyone has both instrumental and end values, individuals differ in how they order the values into priorities, which accounts for tremendous variation among people. Understanding one's own values clarifies what is important, which is essential for effective leadership. Exhibit 4.2 shows some interesting differences in how groups of managers and non-managers prioritized values in one study. The exhibit lists end values and instrumental values that were ranked significantly higher by each group, showing only those rankings that were statistically significant.[39] Leaders can identify and understand value differences to improve communication and effectiveness.

NEW LEADER
ACTION MEMO

Complete the exercise in Leader's Self-Insight 4.3 to see what you can learn about your own values and how they affect your decisions and actions. Were you surprised by any of your instrumental or end values?

National culture, generational differences, and family background can influence how people rank values. For example, in the United States, independence is highly valued and is reinforced by many institutions, including schools, religious organizations, and businesses. Other cultures place less value on independence and more value on being part of a tightly knit community. Younger people typically rank family security lower than do older people.[40] Some leaders cite their parents as a primary source of

EXHIBIT 4.2 Differences in Leaders' and Nonleaders' Value Rankings

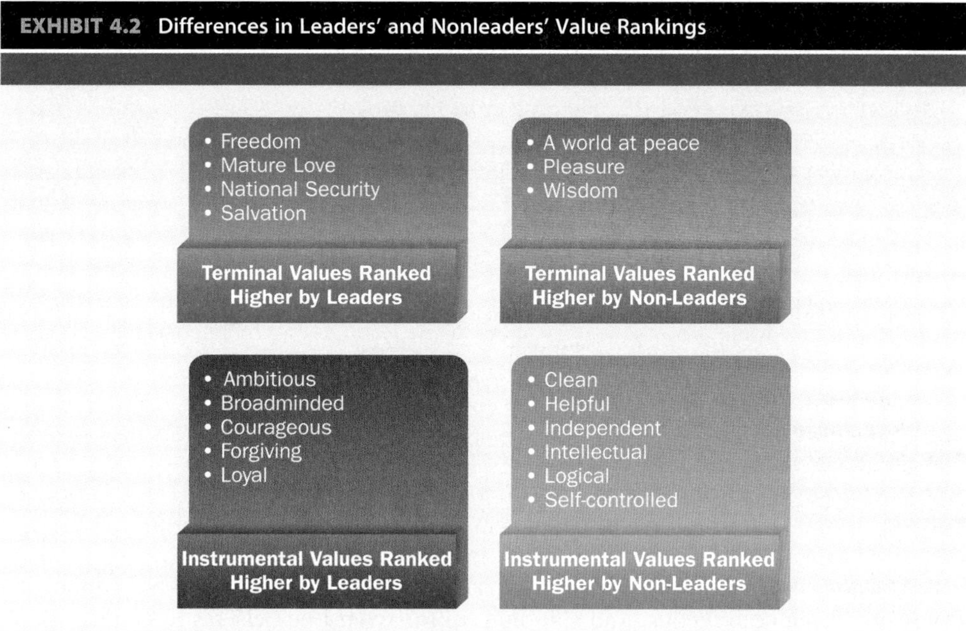

Source: Based on Table 2, Differences in Managers' versus Non-Managers' Terminal and Instrumental Value Ranking, in Edward F. Murphy Jr., Jane Whitney Gibson, and Regina A. Greenwood, "Analyzing Generational Values among Managers and Non-Managers for Sustainable Organizational Effectiveness," *SAM Advanced Management Journal* (Winter 2010), pp. 33–55.

their deeply held values. Bill Farmer, who retired from Time Warner Cable and is now president and CEO of United Way of the Bluegrass in Lexington, Kentucky, says his mother instilled in him the importance of giving back to the community. Farmer moved eight times in 28 years while with Time Warner and in each new city he volunteered with numerous nonprofit organizations and became actively involved in local initiatives designed to create a positive community environment.[41]

Our values are generally fairly well established by early adulthood, but a person's values can also change throughout life. This chapter's *Consider This* reflects on how the values that shape a leader's actions in a moment of crisis have been developed over time. Values may affect leaders and leadership in a number of ways.[42] For one thing, values influence how leaders relate to others. A leader who values obedience, conformity, and politeness may have a difficult time understanding and appreciating a follower who is self-reliant, independent, creative, and a bit rebellious. Personal values influence how leaders perceive opportunities, situations, and problems, as well as the decisions they make in response to them. Consider the decisions Vern Clark made as U.S. Chief of Naval Operations (CNO) from 2000 until his retirement in 2005.

IN THE LEAD

Admiral Vernon E. Clark, U.S. Chief of Naval Operations, 2000–2005

Admiral Vernon E. Clark, who retired in July 2005 after a 37-year career in the U.S. Navy, was the second-longest serving U.S. CNO. The job of the CNO is to advise the president on the conduct of war.

When Clark was named CNO in July 2000, the Navy was losing too many good sailors who didn't want to re-enlist. For Clark, getting and keeping good sailors who could protect the national security was a top priority, and all his decisions were based on valuing the people on the front lines. When Navy officials proposed budget cuts in training and development, Clark rebelled. Instead he *increased* the training budget, strongly supported an increase in pay for sailors, and established the *Naval Education and Training Command*, with 12 Centers of Excellence. Clark also revised the performance appraisal system to provide constructive feedback for people at all levels. Clark made it a priority to blur the lines between enlisted sailors and officers and revised the job assignment process so people didn't get forced into jobs and locations they didn't want. Always more concerned about doing things right than *being* right, Clark encouraged everyone to challenge assumptions, ask questions, and express conflicting views.

Thanks to Admiral Clark's emphasis on treating sailors right, first term re-enlistment soared from 38 percent to 56.7 percent within his first 18 months as CNO. Moreover, as the Navy retained more sailors, its ability to respond more quickly to protect the nation increased.[43]

A leader like Admiral Vernon Clark who places high value on supporting followers, being courageous, and standing up for what one believes in is much more likely to make decisions that may not always be popular but that he believes are right. Leaders can be more effective when they clarify their own values and understand how values guide their actions and affect their organizations. In addition, for many organizations today, clarifying and stating their corporate values, including ethical values, has become an important part of defining how the organization operates.

4-3b How Attitudes Affect Leadership

Attitude
an evaluation (either positive or negative) about people, events, or things

Values help determine the attitudes leaders have about themselves and about their followers. An **attitude** is an evaluation—either positive or negative—about people, events, or things. As we discussed in Chapter 2, an optimistic attitude or positive outlook on life is often considered a key to successful and effective leadership.

"The character that takes command in moments of critical choices has already been determined. It has been determined by a thousand other choices made earlier in seemingly unimportant moments. It has been determined by all those 'little' choices of years past—by all those times when the voice of conscience was at war with the voice of temptation—whispering a lie that 'it doesn't really matter.' It has been determined by all the day-to-day decisions made when life seemed easy and crises seemed far away, the decisions that piece by piece, bit by bit, developed habits of discipline or of laziness; habits of self-sacrifice or self-indulgence; habits of duty and honor and integrity—or dishonor and shame."

Source: President Ronald Reagan, quoted in Norman R. Augustine, "Seven Fundamentals of Effective Leadership," an original essay written for the Center for the Study of American Business, Washington University in St. Louis, *CEO Series*, no. 27 (October 1998).

A leader's attitudes toward followers influence how he or she relates to people.[44] Every leader's style is based to some extent on attitudes about human nature in general—ideas and feelings about what motivates people, whether people are basically honest and trustworthy, and the extent to which people can grow and change. One theory to explain differences in style was developed by Douglas McGregor, based on his experiences as a manager and consultant and his training as a psychologist.[45] McGregor identified two sets of assumptions about human nature, called **Theory X** and **Theory Y**, which represent two very different sets of attitudes about how to interact with and influence subordinates. Exhibit 4.3 explains the fundamental assumptions of Theory X and Theory Y.

In general, Theory X reflects the assumption that people are basically lazy and not motivated to work and that they have a natural tendency to avoid responsibility. Thus, a supervisor who subscribes to the assumptions of Theory X has the attitude that people must be coerced, controlled, directed, or threatened to get them to put forth their best effort. Referring back to Chapter 2, the Theory X leader would likely be task oriented and highly concerned with production rather than people. Theory Y, on the other hand, is based on assumptions that people do not inherently dislike work and will commit themselves willingly to work that they care about. Theory Y also assumes that, under the right conditions, people will seek out greater responsibility and will exercise imagination and creativity in the pursuit of solutions to organizational problems. A leader who subscribes to the assumptions of Theory Y does not believe people have to be coerced and controlled in order to perform effectively. These leaders are more often people oriented and concerned with relationships, although some Theory Y leaders can also be task- or production oriented. McGregor believed Theory Y to be a more realistic and productive approach for viewing subordinates and shaping leaders' attitudes. Studies exploring the relationship between leader attitudes and leadership success in general support his idea, although this relationship has not been carefully explored.[46]

Theory X
the assumption that people are basically lazy and not motivated to work and that they have a natural tendency to avoid responsibility

Theory Y
the assumption that people do not inherently dislike work and will commit themselves willingly to work that they care about

EXHIBIT 4.3 Attitudes and Assumptions of Theory X and Theory Y

Assumptions of Theory X	Assumptions of Theory Y
• The average human being has an inherent dislike of work and will avoid it if possible. • Because of the human characteristic of dislike for work, most people must be coerced, controlled, directed, or threatened with punishment to get them to put forth adequate effort toward the achievement of organizational objectives. • The average human being prefers to be directed, wishes to avoid responsibility, has relatively little ambition, and wants security above all.	• The expenditure of physical and mental effort in work is as natural as play or rest. The average human being does not inherently dislike work. • External control and the threat of punishment are not the only means for bringing about effort toward organizational objectives. A person will exercise self-direction and self-control in the service of objectives to which he or she is committed. • The average human being learns, under proper conditions, not only to accept but also to seek responsibility. • The capacity to exercise a relatively high degree of imagination, ingenuity, and creativity in the solution of organizational problems is widely, not narrowly, distributed in the population. • Under the conditions of modern industrial life, the intellectual potentialities of the average human being are only partially utilized.

Source: Based on Douglas McGregor, *The Human Side of Enterprise* (New York: McGraw-Hill, 1960), pp. 33–48.

4-4 SOCIAL PERCEPTION AND ATTRIBUTIONS

By **perception**, we mean the process people use to make sense out of their surroundings by selecting, organizing, and interpreting information. Values and attitudes affect perceptions, and vice versa. For example, a person might have developed the attitude that leaders are insensitive and arrogant, based on a pattern of perceiving arrogant and insensitive behavior from supervisors over a period of time. If the person moves to a new job, this attitude will continue to affect the way he or she perceives superiors in the new environment, even though his superiors in the new workplace might take great pains to understand and respond to employees' needs. As another example, a leader who greatly values ambition and career success may perceive a problem or a subordinate's mistake as an impediment to her own success, whereas a leader who values helpfulness and obedience might see it as a chance to help a subordinate improve or grow.

Because of individual differences in attitudes, personality, values, interests, and experiences, people often "see" the same thing in different ways. Consider that one survey of nearly 2,000 workers in the United States found that 92 percent of managers think they are doing an "excellent" or "good" job managing employees, but only 67 percent of workers agree. As another example, in a survey of finance professionals, 40 percent of women said they perceive that women face a "glass ceiling" that keeps them from reaching top management levels, whereas only 10 percent of men share that perception.[47]

4-4a Perceptual Distortions

Of particular concern for leaders are **perceptual distortions**, errors in perceptual judgment that arise from inaccuracies in perception. Some types of errors are so common that leaders should become familiar with them. These include stereotyping, the halo effect, projection, and perceptual defense. Leaders who recognize these perceptual distortions can better adjust their perceptions to more closely match objective reality.

Stereotyping is the tendency to assign an individual to a group or broad category (e.g., female, black, elderly or male, white, disabled) and then to attribute widely held generalizations about the group to the individual. Thus, someone meets a new colleague, sees he is in a wheelchair, assigns him to the category "physically disabled," and attributes to this colleague generalizations she believes about people with disabilities, which may include a belief that he is less able than other coworkers. However, the person's inability to walk should not be seen as indicative of lesser abilities in other areas. Indeed, the assumption of limitations may not only offend him, but it also prevents the person making the stereotypical judgment from benefiting from the many ways in which this person can contribute. Stereotyping prevents people from truly knowing those they classify in this way. In addition, negative stereotypes prevent talented people from advancing in an organization and fully contributing their talents to the organization's success.

The **halo effect** occurs when the perceiver develops an overall impression of a person or situation based on one characteristic, either favorable or unfavorable. In other words, a halo blinds the perceiver to other characteristics that should be used in generating a more complete assessment. The halo effect can play a significant role in performance appraisal. For example, a person with an outstanding attendance record may be assessed as responsible, industrious, and highly productive; another person with less-than-average attendance may be assessed as a poor performer.

Perception
the process people use to make sense out of the environment by selecting, organizing, and interpreting information

Perceptual distortions
errors in judgment that arise from inaccuracies in the perceptual process

Stereotyping
the tendency to assign an individual to a broad category and then attribute generalizations about the group to the individual

Halo effect
an overall impression of a person or situation based on one characteristic, either favorable or unfavorable

Either assessment may be true, but it is the leader's job to be sure the assessment is based on complete information about all job-related characteristics and not just his or her preferences for good attendance.

Projection is the tendency of perceivers to see their own personal traits in other people; that is, they project their own needs, feelings, values, and attitudes into their judgment of others. A leader who is achievement oriented might assume that subordinates are as well. This might cause the manager to restructure jobs to be less routine and more challenging without regard for employees' actual satisfaction. The best safeguards against errors based on projection are self-awareness and empathy.

Perceptual defense is the tendency of perceivers to protect themselves against ideas, objects, or people that are threatening. People perceive things that are satisfying and pleasant but tend to disregard things that are disturbing and unpleasant. In essence, people develop blind spots in the perceptual process so that negative sensory data do not hurt them. For example, the director of a nonprofit educational organization in Tennessee hated dealing with conflict because he had grown up with parents who constantly argued and often put him in the middle of their arguments. The director consistently overlooked discord among staff members until things would reach a boiling point. When the blow-up occurred, the director would be shocked and dismayed because he had truly perceived that everything was going smoothly among the staff. Recognizing perceptual blind spots can help people develop a clearer picture of reality.

4-4b Attributions

As people organize what they perceive, they often draw conclusions based on their perception.[48] **Attributions** are judgments about what caused an event or behavior—(a) something about the person or (b) something about the situation. For example, many people attribute the success or failure of an organization to the top leader, when in reality there may be many factors that contribute to organizational performance. People also make attributions or judgments as a way to understand what caused their own or another person's behavior:

- An *internal attribution* says characteristics of the person led to the behavior ("My subordinate missed the deadline because he's lazy and incompetent").
- An *external attribution* says something about the situation caused the person's behavior ("My subordinate missed the deadline because he didn't have the team support and resources he needed").

Attributions are important because they help people decide how to handle a situation. In the case of a subordinate missing a deadline, a leader who blames the mistake on the employee's personal characteristics might reprimand the person or, more effectively, provide additional training and direction. A leader who blames the mistake on external factors will try to help prevent such situations in the future, such as making sure team members have the resources they need, providing support to remove obstacles, and insuring that deadlines are realistic.

The Fundamental Attribution Error People tend to have biases that they apply when making attributions. When evaluating others, many people underestimate the influence of external factors and overestimate the influence of internal factors. This tendency is called the **fundamental attribution error**. Consider the case of someone being promoted to CEO. Employees, outsiders, and the media generally focus on the characteristics of the person that allowed him or her to achieve the promotion.

Projection
the tendency to see one's own personal traits in other people

Perceptual defense
the tendency to protect oneself by disregarding ideas, situations, or people that are unpleasant

Attributions
judgments about what caused a person's behavior—either characteristics of the person or of the situation

Fundamental attribution error
the tendency to underestimate the influence of external factors on another's behavior and overestimate the influence of internal factors

In reality, however, the selection of that person might have been heavily influenced by external factors, such as business conditions creating a need for someone with a strong financial or marketing background at that particular time.

The Self-Serving Bias Another bias that distorts attributions involves attributions we make about our own behavior. People tend to overestimate the contribution of internal factors to their successes and overestimate the contribution of external factors to their failures. This tendency, called the **self-serving bias**, means people give themselves too much credit for what they do well and give external forces too much blame when they fail. Thus, if a leader's subordinates say she doesn't listen well enough, and the leader thinks subordinates don't communicate well enough, the truth may actually lie somewhere in between. At Emerald Packaging, Kevin Kelly examined his attributions and improved his leadership effectiveness by overcoming the self-serving bias, as described in the following example.

IN THE LEAD

Kevin Kelly, Emerald Packaging

As the top leader of his family's California company, Emerald Packaging—a maker of plastic bags for the food industry—Kevin Kelly thought of himself as indispensable. He considered himself to be chief architect of the company's growing sales and profits. When Emerald began to falter, Kelly blamed it on his managers' resistance to new ideas that could keep the business thriving. He thought everyone needed to change except him.

For some time, Kelly's leadership approach was to reprimand and complain. Then, he decided to look at things in a different way. Was it really all his managers' fault? Realizing that everyone was under stress from several years of rapid growth, Kelly hired a pack of new managers to reinforce his exhausted troops. Surprisingly, though, things just seemed to get worse. Kelly had to face a hard truth: Rather than being the one person in the organization who didn't need to change, as Kelly had previously thought, he realized he was a big part of the problem.

Kelly sought consultants and classes to help boost his people skills. He began meeting regularly with veteran managers and new hires and implemented changes that successfully united the two groups into a cohesive team. Then, Kelly did something radical (at least for him). He took a real 10-day vacation, the first time he hadn't been in routine contact with Emerald since he took over the company. Visions of disaster filled his head as he wondered how they could get along without him. As it turned out, people got along just fine. Crises got solved, production continued, and customers didn't even seem to notice he was gone.

By examining his attributions and shifting his perception of himself, the organizational situation, and his managers' abilities, Kelly made changes that allowed his managers to flourish and his company to grow even more successful.[49]

Self-serving bias the tendency to overestimate the influence of internal factors on one's successes and the influence of external factors on one's failures

Cognitive style how a person perceives, processes, interprets, and uses information

4-5 COGNITIVE DIFFERENCES

The final area of individual differences we will explore is cognitive style. **Cognitive style** refers to how a person perceives, processes, interprets, and uses information. Thus, when we talk about cognitive differences, we are referring to varying approaches to perceiving and assimilating data, making decisions, solving problems, and relating to others.[50] Cognitive approaches are *preferences* that are not necessarily rigid, but most people tend to have only a few preferred habits of thought. One of the most widely recognized cognitive differences is between what we call left-brained and right-brained thinking patterns.

4-5a Patterns of Thinking and Brain Dominance

Neurologists and psychologists have long known that the brain has two distinct hemispheres. Furthermore, science has shown that the left hemisphere controls movement on the body's right side and the right hemisphere controls movement on the left. In the 1960s and 1970s, scientists also discovered that the distinct hemispheres influence thinking, which led to an interest in what has been called left-brained versus right-brained thinking patterns. The left hemisphere is associated with logical, analytical thinking and a linear approach to problem solving, whereas the right hemisphere is associated with creative, intuitive, values-based thought processes.[51] A program sponsored by the New York City Economic Development Corporation illustrates the difference. Artists and other creative people are crucial to the vibrancy of the city, but most artists (right-brain thinking) don't know how to plan and run a business (left-brain skills) so they have a hard time supporting themselves. The city has invested $ 50,000 in a program to teach right-brain creative people the left-brain skills they need to turn their creative works into money.[52] As another simplified example, people who are very good at verbal and written language (which involves a linear thinking process) are using the left brain, whereas those who prefer to interpret information through visual images are more right-brained.

Although the concept of left-brained versus right-brained thinking is not entirely accurate physiologically (not all processes associated with left-brained thinking are located in the left hemisphere and vice versa), this concept provides a powerful metaphor for two very different ways of thinking and decision making. It is also important to remember that everyone uses both left-brained and right-brained thinking, but to varying degrees.

More recently, these ideas have been broadened to what is called the **whole brain concept**.[53] Ned Herrmann began developing his concept of whole brain thinking while he was a manager at GE in the late 1970s and has expanded it through many years of research with thousands of individuals and organizations. The whole brain approach considers not only a person's preference for right-brained versus left-brained thinking but also for conceptual versus experiential thinking. Herrmann's whole brain model thus identifies four quadrants of the brain that are related to different thinking styles. Again, while not entirely accurate physiologically, the whole brain model is an excellent metaphor for understanding differences in thinking patterns. Some people strongly lean toward using one quadrant in most situations, whereas others rely on two, three, or even all four styles of thinking. An individual's preference for each of the four styles is determined through a survey called the *Herrmann Brain Dominance Instrument (HBDI)*, which has been administered to hundreds of thousands of individuals.

The whole brain model provides a useful overview of an individual's mental preferences, which in turn affect patterns of communication, behavior, and leadership.

Quadrant A is associated with logical thinking, analysis of facts, and processing numbers. A person who has a quadrant-A dominance is rational and realistic, thinks

NEW LEADER
ACTION MEMO

A simplified exercise to help you think about your own preferences appears in Leader's Self-Insight 4.4. Before reading further, follow the instructions and complete the exercise to get an idea about your dominant thinking style according to Herrmann's whole brain model. Then read the following descriptions of each quadrant.

Whole brain concept
an approach that considers not only a person's preference for right-brained versus left-brained thinking, but also conceptual versus experiential thinking; identifies four quadrants of the brain related to different thinking styles

Quadrant A
the part of the brain associated in the whole brain model with logical thinking, analysis of facts, and processing numbers

LEADER'S SELF-INSIGHT 4.4

What's Your Thinking Style?

Instructions: The following characteristics are associated with the four quadrants identified by Herrmann's whole brain model. Think for a moment about how you approach problems and make decisions. In addition, consider how you typically approach your work or class assignments and how you interact with others. Circle 10 of the terms below that you believe best describe your own cognitive style. Try to be honest and select terms that apply to you as you are, not how you might like to be. There are no right or wrong answers.

A	B	C	D
Analytical	Organized	Friendly	Holistic
Factual	Planned	Receptive	Imaginative
Directive	Controlled	Enthusiastic	Intuitive
Rigorous	Detailed	Understanding	Synthesizing
Realistic	Conservative	Expressive	Curious
Intellectual	Disciplined	Empathetic	Spontaneous
Objective	Practical	Trusting	Flexible
Knowledgeable	Industrious	Sensitive	Open-Minded
Bright	Persistent	Passionate	Conceptual
Clear	Implementer	Humanistic	Adventurous

The terms in column A are associated with logical, analytical thinking (quadrant A); those in column B with organized, detail-oriented thinking (quadrant B); those in column C with empathetic and emotionally based thinking (quadrant C); and those in column D with integrative and imaginative thinking (quadrant D). Do your preferences fall primarily in one of the four columns, or do you have a more balanced set of preferences across all four? If you have a strong preference in one particular quadrant, were you surprised by which one?

critically, and likes to deal with numbers and technical matters. Quadrant-A thinking might be thought of as the "scientist" part of the brain.[54] These people like to know how things work and to follow logical procedures. When a leader has a predominantly A-quadrant thinking style, he or she tends to be directive and authoritative. This leader focuses on tasks and activities and likes to deal with concrete information and facts. Opinions and feelings are generally not considered as important as facts.

Quadrant B deals with planning, organization of facts, and careful detailed review. A person who relies heavily on quadrant-B thinking is well-organized, reliable, and neat. This is the "manager" part of the brain.[55] These people like to establish plans and procedures and get things done on time. Leaders with a predominantly quadrant-B thinking style are typically conservative and highly traditional. They tend to avoid risks and strive for stability. Thus, they may insist on following rules and procedures, no matter what the circumstances are.

Quadrant B
the part of the brain associated in the whole brain model with planning, organizing facts, and careful, detailed review

Quadrant C is associated with interpersonal relationships and affects intuitive and emotional thought processes. C-quadrant individuals are sensitive to others and enjoy interacting with and teaching others; hence this might be considered the "teacher" part of the brain.[56] These people are typically emotional and expressive, outgoing, and supportive of others. Leaders with a predominantly quadrant-C style are friendly, trusting, and empathetic. They are concerned with people's feelings more than with tasks and procedures and may put emphasis on employee development and training.

Quadrant C
the part of the brain associated in the whole brain model with interpersonal relationships and intuitive and emotional thought processes

EXHIBIT 4.4 Herrmann's Whole Brain Model

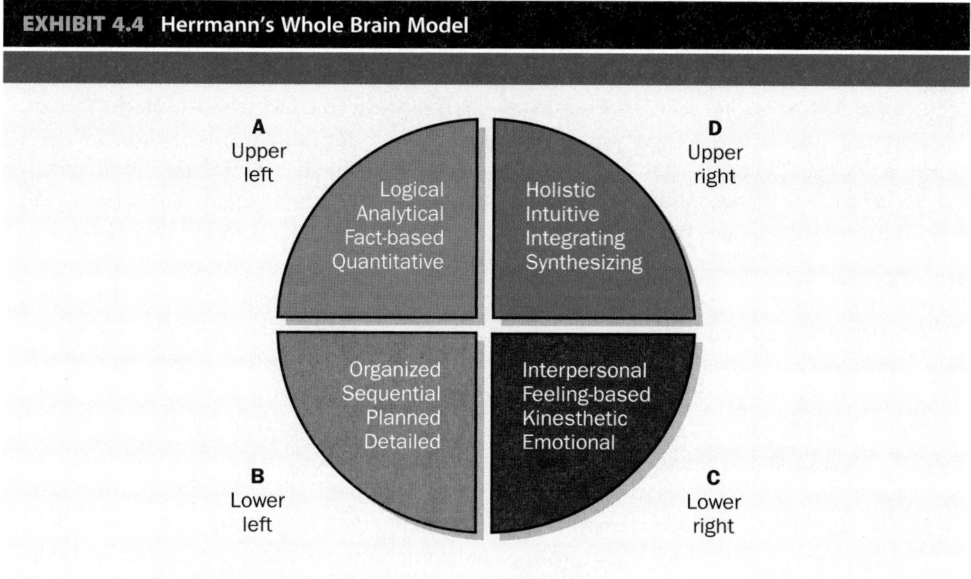

Source: Ned Herrmann, *The Whole Brain Business Book* (New York: McGraw-Hill, 1996) p. 15.

Quadrant D is associated with conceptualizing, synthesizing, and integrating facts and patterns, with seeing the big picture rather than the details. This is the "artist" part of the brain.[57] A person with a quadrant-D preference is visionary and imaginative, likes to speculate and break the rules, takes risks, and may be impulsive. These people are curious and enjoy experimentation and playfulness. The D-quadrant leader is holistic, imaginative, and entrepreneurial. This leader enjoys change, experimentation, and risk-taking and generally allows followers a great deal of freedom and flexibility.

Quadrant D
the part of the brain associated in the whole brain model with conceptualizing, synthesizing, and integrating facts and patterns

Exhibit 4.4 illustrates the model with its four quadrants and some of the mental processes associated with each. There is no style that is necessarily better or worse, though any of the styles carried to an extreme can be detrimental. Each style can have both positive and negative results for leaders and followers. It is important to remember that every individual, even those with a strong preference in one quadrant, actually has a coalition of preferences from each of the four quadrants.[58] Each of us has at least a few qualities of the scientist, manager, teacher, and artist.

In addition, Herrmann believes people can learn to use their "whole brain" rather than relying only on one or two quadrants. His research indicates that very few, if any, individuals can be wholly balanced among the four quadrants, but people can be aware of their preferences and engage in activities and experiences that help develop the other quadrants. Leaders who reach the top of organizations often have well-balanced brains, according to Herrmann's research. For example, Angela Ahrendts, who joined Apple as senior vice president for retail and online operations in 2014 after serving eight years as CEO of Burberry, uses a variety of thinking styles.

IN THE LEAD

Angela Ahrendts, Apple

It wasn't easy for Apple CEO Tim Cook to convince Angela Ahrendts to leave London and her top job at Burberry to come to work at Apple. But Cook knew her leadership was exactly what he needed to revitalize the retail division, integrate the retail and online operations, and expand the role of Apple stores to play a key social role in the communities they serve. "I visited Burberry stores and spent some time online. And you could tell that she got it at a deep level," Cook says. He convinced Ahrendts to bring that ability to think broadly and deeply to Apple, where 60 percent of employees now work in the retail division.

As CEO of British company Burberry, Ahrendts led a stunning turnaround by using creative, holistic thinking (Quadrant D) to transform it from an outdated brand into a "technologically savvy international fashion powerhouse." Another right-brain characteristic was her emphasis on building positive interpersonal relationships (Quadrant C). Yet Ahrendts also demonstrated left-brain thinking in her careful control of the company's finances (Quadrant B) and her ability to be realistic, analytical, and rational when it came to making difficult decisions (Quadrant A). When the recession hit in 2008, Ahrendts quickly took charge, putting on hold plans for new stores, cutting $78 million in expenses, freezing salaries, and changing company procedures to be more cost-effective.

At Apple, Ahrendts started her new job by focusing on rebuilding morale and trust in a division that hadn't had a leader for more than a year after the previous manager had left after only five months. Morale and trust had suffered from both the turnover and some of the decisions that manager had made, such as cutting work hours and benefits. Ahrendts put her right-brain skills to work on a listening tour, visiting the stores, call, centers, and back offices to answer questions, hear complaints, and reignite motivation and energy. As she did at Burberry, she is also using left-brain thinking to come up with ways to control finances that don't damage trust and morale.[59]

Ahrendts, who was listed as No. 16 on *Fortune* magazine's 2015 list of "Most Powerful Women," reflects the broad, balanced thinking style of a top leader. The typical CEO is a balanced thinker with at least two, usually three, and often four strong preferences and thus has a wide range of thinking options available to choose from. A broad range of thinking styles is particularly important at higher levels of organizations because leaders deal with a greater variety and complexity of people and issues.[60]

Understanding that individuals have different thinking styles can also help leaders be more effective in interacting with followers. Some leaders act as if everyone responds to the same material and behavior in the same way, but this isn't true. Some people prefer facts and figures, whereas others want to know about relationships and patterns. Some followers prefer freedom and flexibility, whereas others crave structure and order. Leaders can shift their styles and behaviors to more effectively communicate with followers and help them perform up to their full potential. Leaders can also recruit people with varied cognitive styles to help achieve important goals.

NEW LEADER
ACTION MEMO

As a leader, you can strive for "whole brain" thinking to deal effectively with a wide variety of people and complex issues. You can be aware of your natural thinking patterns and include other perspectives that help you develop a broader understanding.

4-5b Problem-Solving Styles: Jungian Types

Myers–Briggs Type Indicator (MBTI)™ test that measures how individuals differ in gathering and evaluating information for solving problems and making decisions

Another approach to cognitive differences grew out of the work of psychologist Carl Jung. Jung believed that differences in individual behavior resulted from preferences in how we go about gathering and evaluating information for solving problems and making decisions.[61] One of the most widely used tests in the United States, the **Myers–Briggs Type Indicator (MBTI)™** assessment, is one way of measuring how individuals differ in these areas.[62] The MBTI™ assessment has been taken by millions of people around the world and can help individuals better understand themselves and others.

The MBTI™ instrument uses four different pairs of attributes to classify people in one of 16 different personality types:

1. **Introversion versus extroversion:** This dimension focuses on where people gain interpersonal strength and mental energy. Extroverts (E) gain energy from being around others and interacting with others, whereas introverts (I) gain energy by focusing on personal thoughts and feelings.
2. **Sensing versus intuition:** This identifies how a person absorbs information. Those with a sensing preference (S) gather and absorb information through the five senses, whereas intuitive people (N) rely on less direct perceptions. Intuitives, for example, focus more on patterns, relationships, and hunches than on direct perception of facts and details.
3. **Thinking versus feeling:** This dimension relates to how much consideration a person gives to emotions in making a decision. Feeling types (F) tend to rely more on their values and sense of what is right and wrong, and they consider how a decision will affect other people's feelings. Thinking types (T) tend to rely more on logic and be very objective in decision making.
4. **Judging versus perceiving:** The judging versus perceiving dimension concerns an individual's attitudes toward ambiguity and how quickly a person makes a decision. People with a judging preference like certainty and closure. They enjoy having goals and deadlines and tend to make decisions quickly based on available data. Perceiving people, on the other hand, enjoy ambiguity, dislike deadlines, and may change their minds several times before making a final decision. Perceiving types like to gather a large amount of data and information before making a decision.

The various combinations of these preferences result in 16 unique types. There are a number of exercises available in print and on the Internet that can help people determine their preferences according to the MBTI™ assessment. Individuals develop unique strengths and weaknesses as a result of their preferences for introversion versus extroversion, sensing versus intuition, thinking versus feeling, and judging versus perceiving. As with the whole brain approach, MBTI™ types should not be considered ingrained or unalterable. People's awareness of their preferences, training, and life experiences can cause them to change their preferences over time.

Nearly 200 agencies of the U.S. government, including the Environmental Protection Agency (EPA), the Central Intelligence Agency (CIA), and the Department of Veterans Affairs, have been reported to use the MBTI™ instrument as part of their training programs. Brian Twillman of the EPA says at least a quarter of the agency's 17,000 federal employees have taken the test, and that without it "there would be a lot of blind spots within the agency."[63] A primary value of the MBTI™ assessment is that it starts an important dialogue about how people interact with others.

At Hallmark Cards, top executives wanted to develop leaders who could see things from different perspectives, work together for everyone's success, and fully engage and inspire both employees and customers. One approach to creating that new culture was using the MBTI™ to give managers greater self-awareness and insight into how their patterns of thought and behavior affected others. "We tend to place people into 'files' according to our perceptions of them, which are often skewed," said Mary Beth Ebmeyer, HR manager for corporate development.[64] By understanding different MBTI™ types, Hallmark leaders can flex their

NEW LEADER
ACTION MEMO

Go to Leader's Self-Insight 4.5 to complete an exercise that will identify your preferences for the four pairs of attributes identified by the MBTI™ assessment.

communication style as needed and connect more meaningfully with employees. In addition, being aware of their own MBTI™ type enables leaders to maximize their strengths and minimize their weaknesses. Leaders should remember that each type can have positive and negative consequences for behavior.

There has been an increasing application of the MBTI™ assessment in leadership studies.[65] These studies confirm that there is no "leader type," and all 16 of the MBTI™ types can function effectively as leaders. As with the four quadrants of the whole brain model, leaders can learn to use their preferences and balance their approaches to best suit followers and the situation. However, research reveals some interesting, although tentative, findings. For example, although extroversion is often considered an important trait for a leader, leaders in the real world are about equally divided between extroverts and introverts. In regard to the sensing versus intuition dimension, data reveal that sensing types are in the majority in fields where the focus is on the immediate and tangible (e.g., construction, banking, manufacturing). However, in areas that involve breaking new ground or long-range planning, intuitive leaders are in the majority. Thinking (as opposed to feeling) types are more common among leaders in business and industry as well as in the realm of science. In addition, thinking types appear to be chosen more often as managers even in organizations that value "feeling," such as counseling centers. Finally, one of the most consistent findings is that judging types are in the majority among the leaders studied.

Thus, based on the limited research, the two preferences that seem to be most strongly associated with successful leadership are thinking and judging. However, this doesn't mean that people with other preferences cannot be effective leaders. Much more research needs to be done before any conclusions can be reached about the relationship between MBTI™ types and leadership.

4-6 WORKING WITH DIFFERENT PERSONALITY TYPES

As this chapter has shown, leaders have to work with individuals who differ in many ways. Personality differences, in particular, can make the life of a leader interesting and sometimes exasperating. These differences can create an innovative environment but also lead to stress, conflict, and negative feelings.

Leaders can learn to work more effectively with different personality types by following some simple guidelines.[66]

- *Understand your own personality and how you react to others.* Avoid judging people based on limited knowledge, and realize that everyone has different facets to their personality. Learn to control your frustration to help you keep different personality types focused on the goal and the tasks needed to reach it.
- *Treat everyone with respect.* People like to be accepted and appreciated for who they are. Even if you find someone's personality grating, remain professional and keep your irritation to yourself. Don't gossip or joke about others.
- *Acknowledge each person's strengths.* Everyone wants to be recognized for their unique talents, so be sure to acknowledge and make use of people's useful personality characteristics. For instance, a pessimistic person can be difficult to be around, but these gloomy folks can sometimes be helpful by calling attention to legitimate problems with an idea or plan.
- *Strive for understanding.* A good approach to take with a personality type widely different from yours is to clarify questions every time there's a potential for miscommunication. Follow up each question or request with a statement explaining why you asked and how it will benefit the organization as well as the individual.

LEADER'S SELF-INSIGHT 4.5

Personality Assessment: Jung's Typology

Instructions: For each item below, circle either "a" or "b." In some cases, both "a" and "b" may apply to you. You should decide which is *more* like you, even if it is only slightly more true.

1. I would rather
   a. Solve a new and complicated problem
   b. Work on something that I have done before
2. I like to
   a. Work alone in a quiet place
   b. Be where "the action" is
3. I want a boss who
   a. Establishes and applies criteria in decisions
   b. Considers individual needs and makes exceptions
4. When I work on a project, I
   a. Like to finish it and get some closure
   b. Often leave it open for possible change
5. When making a decision, the most important considerations are
   a. Rational thoughts, ideas, and data
   b. People's feelings and values
6. On a project, I tend to
   a. Think it over and over before deciding how to proceed
   b. Start working on it right away, thinking about it as I go along
7. When working on a project, I prefer to
   a. Maintain as much control as possible
   b. Explore various options
8. In my work, I prefer to
   a. Work on several projects at a time, and learn as much as possible about each one
   b. Have one project that is challenging and keeps me busy
9. I often
   a. Make lists and plans whenever I start something and may hate to seriously alter my plans
   b. Avoid plans and just let things progress as I work on them
10. When discussing a problem with colleagues, it is easy for me
    a. To see "the big picture"
    b. To grasp the specifics of the situation
11. When the phone rings in my office or at home, I usually
    a. Consider it an interruption
    b. Don't mind answering it
12. The word that describes me better is
    a. Analytical
    b. Empathetic
13. When I am working on an assignment, I tend to
    a. Work steadily and consistently
    b. Work in bursts of energy with "down time" in between
14. When I listen to someone talk on a subject, I usually try to
    a. Relate it to my own experience and see if it fits
    b. Assess and analyze the message
15. When I come up with new ideas, I generally
    a. "Go for it"
    b. Like to contemplate the ideas some more
16. When working on a project, I prefer to
    a. Narrow the scope so it is clearly defined
    b. Broaden the scope to include related aspects
17. When I read something, I usually
    a. Confine my thoughts to what is written there
    b. Read between the lines and relate the words to other ideas
18. When I have to make a decision in a hurry, I often
    a. Feel uncomfortable and wish I had more information
    b. Am able to do so with available data
19. In a meeting, I tend to
    a. Continue formulating my ideas as I talk about them
    b. Only speak out after I have carefully thought the issue through
20. In work, I prefer spending a great deal of time on issues of
    a. Ideas
    b. People
21. In meetings, I am most often annoyed with people who
    a. Come up with many sketchy ideas
    b. Lengthen the meeting with many practical details
22. I tend to be
    a. A morning person
    b. A night owl
23. My style in preparing for a meeting is
    a. To be willing to go in and be responsive
    b. To be fully prepared and sketch out an outline of the meeting
24. In meetings, I would prefer for people to
    a. Display a fuller range of emotions
    b. Be more task oriented
25. I would rather work for an organization where
    a. My job was intellectually stimulating
    b. I was committed to its goals and mission

(continued)

Personality Assessment: Jung's Typology (*Continued*)

26. On weekends, I tend to
    a. Plan what I will do
    b. Just see what happens and decide as I go along
27. I am more
    a. Outgoing
    b. Contemplative
28. I would rather work for a boss who is
    a. Full of new ideas
    b. Practical

In the following, choose the word in each pair that appeals to you more:

29. a. Social
    b. Theoretical
30. a. Ingenuity
    b. Practicality
31. a. Organized
    b. Adaptable
32. a. Activity
    b. Concentration

Scoring

Count one point for each item listed below that you circled in the inventory.

	Score for I (Introversion)	**Score for E** (Extroversion)	**Score for S** (Sensing)	**Score for N** (Intuition)
	2a	2b	1b	1a
	6a	6b	10b	10a
	11a	11b	13a	13b
	15b	15a	16a	16b
	19b	19a	17a	17b
	22a	22b	21a	21b
	27b	27a	28b	28a
	32b	32a	30b	30a
Totals	______	______	______	______

Circle the one with more points: I or E

(If tied on I/E, don't count #11)

Circle the one with more points: S or N

(If tied on S/N, don't count #16)

	Score for T (Thinking)	**Score for F** (Feeling)	**Score for J** (Judging)	**Score for P** (Perceiving)
	3a	3b	4a	4b
	5a	5b	7a	7b
	12a	12b	8b	8a
	14b	14a	9a	9b
	20a	20b	18b	18a
	24b	24a	23b	23a
	25a	25b	26a	26b
	29b	29a	31a	31b
Totals	______	______	______	______

Circle the one with more points: T or F

(If tied on T/F, don't count #24)

Circle the one with more points: J or P

(If tied on J/P, don't count #23)

Your Score Is: I or E ______ S or N ______ T or F ______ J or P ______

Your type is: ______ (example: INTJ, ESFP, etc.)

(continued)

Personality Assessment: Jung's Typology (*Continued*)

Scoring and Interpretation

The scores above measure variables similar to the MBTI™ assessment based on the work of psychologist Carl Jung. The MBTI™ assessment, which was described in this chapter, identifies four dimensions and 16 different "types." The dominant characteristics associated with each dimension and each type are shown below. Remember that no one is a pure type; however, each person has preferences for introversion versus extroversion, sensing versus intuition, thinking versus feeling, and judging versus perceiving. Based on your scores on the survey, read the description of your dimension and type in the chart. Do you believe the description fits your personality?

Characteristics Associated with Each Dimension

Extroversion: Energized by outer world of people and objects, broad interests, thinks while speaking.	**Introversion**: Energized by inner world of thoughts and ideas, deep interests, thinks before speaking.
Sensing: Likes facts, details, and practical solutions.	**Intuition**: Likes meanings, theory, associations among data, and possibilities.
Thinking: Makes decisions by analysis, logic, and impersonal criteria.	**Feeling**: Makes decisions based on values, beliefs, and concern for others.
Judging: Lives life organized, stable, systematic, and under control.	**Perceiving**: Lets life happen, spontaneous, open-ended, last minute.

Characteristics Associated with Each Type

ISTJ: Organizer, trustworthy, responsible, good trustee or inspector.	**ISFJ**: Quiet, conscientious, devoted, handles detail, good conservator.	**INFJ**: Perseveres, inspirational, quiet caring for others, good counselor.	**INTJ**: Independent thinker, skeptical, theory, competence, good scientist.
ISTP: Cool, observant, easy-going, good craftsperson.	**ISFP**: Warm, sensitive, team player, avoids conflict, good artist.	**INFP**: Idealistic, strong values, likes learning, good at noble service.	**INTP**: Designer, logical, conceptual, likes challenges, good architect.
ESTP: Spontaneous, gregarious, good at problem solving and promoting.	**ESFP**: Sociable, generous, makes things fun, good as entertainer.	**ENFP**: Imaginative, enthusiastic, starts projects, good champion.	**ENTP**: Resourceful, stimulating, dislikes routine, tests limits, good inventor.
ESTJ: Order, structure, practical, good administrator or supervisor.	**ESFJ**: People skills, harmonizer, popular, does things for people, good host.	**ENFJ**: Charismatic, persuasive, fluent presenter, sociable, active, good teacher.	**ENTJ**: Visionary planner, takes charge, hearty speaker, natural leader.

- *Remember that everyone wants to fit in.* No matter their personalities, people typically take on behavior patterns that are the norm for their environment. Leaders can create norms that keep everyone focused on positive interactions and high performance.

Occasional personality conflicts are probably inevitable in any group or organization, but by using these techniques, leaders can generally keep the work environment positive and productive.

LEADERSHIP ESSENTIALS

- This chapter explored the importance of self-awareness and some of the individual differences that affect leaders and the leadership process. Individuals differ in many ways, including personality, values and attitudes, and styles of thinking and decision making.
- One model of personality, the Big Five personality dimensions, examines whether individuals score high or low on the dimensions of extroversion, agreeableness, conscientiousness, emotional stability, and openness to experience. Although there is some indication that a high degree of each of the personality dimensions is associated with successful leadership, individuals who score low on various dimensions may also be effective leaders. Two specific personality traits that have a significant impact on leader behavior are locus of control and authoritarianism.
- Values are fundamental beliefs that cause a person to prefer that things be done one way rather than another. One way to think about values is in terms of instrumental and end values. End values are beliefs about the kinds of goals that are worth pursuing, whereas instrumental values are beliefs about the types of behavior that are appropriate for reaching goals. Values also affect an individual's attitudes. A leader's attitudes about self and others influence how the leader behaves toward and interacts with followers. Two sets of assumptions called Theory X and Theory Y represent two very different sets of attitudes leaders may hold about people in general.
- Differences in personality, values, and attitudes influence perception, which is the process people use to select, organize, and interpret information. Perceptual distortions include stereotyping, the halo effect, projection, and perceptual defense. Attributions refer to how people explain the causes of events or behaviors. Based on their perception, people may make either internal or external attributions.
- Another area of individual differences is cognitive style. The whole brain concept explores a person's preferences for right-brained versus left-brained thinking and for conceptual versus experiential thinking. The model provides a powerful metaphor for understanding differences in thinking styles. Individuals can learn to use their "whole brain" rather than relying on one thinking style. Another way of looking at cognitive differences is the MBTI™, which measures an individual's preferences for introversion versus extroversion, sensing versus intuition, thinking versus feeling, and judging versus perceiving.
- Finally, the chapter offered some tips for how leaders can work more effectively with varied personality types. By understanding their own personalities, treating everyone with respect, recognizing people's unique abilities, circumventing

communication breakdowns, and creating a positive environment, leaders can better keep diverse people productive and focused on goals instead of personality differences.

DISCUSSION QUESTIONS

1. Do you agree that self-awareness is essential for being a good leader? Can you think of some specific negative consequences that might result from a leader not having self-awareness?
2. Extroversion is often considered a "good" quality for a leader to have. Why might introversion be considered an equally positive quality?
3. A survey found that 79 percent of CEOs surveyed fall into the category of being "highly optimistic," whereas a much lower percentage of chief financial officers were rated as highly optimistic. Do you think these differences reflect personality characteristics or the different requirements of the two jobs? Discuss.
4. The chapter suggests that one way to work effectively with different personalities is to treat everyone with respect. How might a leader deal with a subordinate who is perpetually rude, insensitive, and disrespectful to others?
5. What might be some reasons the dimension of "openness to experience" correlates so strongly with historians' ratings of the greatest U.S. presidents but has been less strongly associated with business leader success? Do you think this personality dimension might be more important for business leaders of today than it was in the past? Discuss.
6. Leaders in many of today's organizations use the results of personality testing to make hiring and promotion decisions. Discuss some of the pros and cons of this approach.
7. From Leader's Self-Insight 4.3, identify four or five values (instrumental or end values) that could be a source of conflict between leaders and followers. Explain.
8. Do you believe understanding your preferences according to the whole brain model can help you be a better leader? Discuss.
9. How can a leader use an understanding of brain dominance to improve the functioning of the organization?
10. Hallmark Cards discovered that its mid- and upper-level managers were primarily *thinking* types, but top executives displayed primarily *feeling* preferences. Why do you think this might be?

LEADERSHIP AT WORK

Past and Future

Draw a life line below that marks high and low experiences during your life. Think of key decisions, defining moments, peak experiences, and major disappointments that shaped who you are today. Draw the line from left to right, and identify each high and low point with a word or two.

Birth Year: Today's Date:

What made these valued experiences? How did they shape who you are today?

____

____

Now take the long view of your life. In 10-year increments, write below the leader experiences you want to have. Provide a brief past-tense description of each decade (e.g., next 10 years—big starting salary, bored in first job, promoted to middle management).

Next 10 years: ______________________________

____

Following 10 years: ______________________________

____

Following 10 years: ______________________________

____

Following 10 years: ______________________________

____

What personal skills and strengths will you use to achieve the future?

____

____

What is your core life purpose or theme as expressed in the life line and answers above?

____

____

What would your desired future self say to your present self?

____

____

How do your answers above relate to your scores on the Leader Self-Insight questionnaires you completed in this chapter?

____

____

LEADERSHIP DEVELOPMENT: CASES FOR ANALYSIS

A *Nice* Manager

Chisum Industries' management promotion process was a benchmark for providing lateral moves as well as promotion to the next level within the company. With offices, plants, and warehouses located in seven Texas cities, opportunities for the best and brightest were extensive for middle management employees. The process invited candidates to explore goals, strengths, and weaknesses and to recount real-life scenarios and accomplishments. The selection team also visited the worksites of candidates for on-the-job observations and talks with fellow workers before bringing the final candidates to Dallas for interviews. The process offered personal insight and growth opportunities to all candidates for promotion.

In March 2015, top management, including Marcus Chisum, Karl Jacobson, Mitch Ivey, Wayne Hughes, and Barbara Kennedy, were midway through a meeting to consider which of four middle management candidates to promote to the top position in the San Antonio office.

Marcus: "Who do we have next?"

Barbara: "Harry Creighton." Scanning the group, Marcus sees a few nods and a shrug.

Marcus: "Feedback?"

Karl and Wayne, simultaneously: "Great guy."

Karl: "We all know that Harry came into a situation in which that particular location was suffering a drop in performance. Morale was low and there were rumors of layoffs. He came in and calmed employee fears and has done a good job of raising performance levels."

Wayne: "He has a great relationship with employees. As we went around and talked to people, it was obvious that he has developed a level of trust and a vision that workers buy into."

Barbara: "The word that kept coming up among the workers was 'nice.'" As was his habit during meetings, Mitch leaned back in his chair, tapping his pencil on the table. Initially annoyed by the habit, over time the team had gotten used to the sound.

Marcus: "Mitch, your initial reaction to his name was a shrug. What are you thinking?"

Mitch: "Just wondering if *nice* is what we're looking for here?" The remark was met with laughter. "Tell me, how does a manager achieve an across-the-board reputation as a *nice* guy? I've worked for and with a number of managers during my life. I respected them, thought many of them were fair and up-front in their treatment of us; thought some were jerks who should be canned . . ."

Marcus: "I hope I don't fall into that last category." (Laughter)

Mitch: "I don't recall any consensus about a manager being *nice*."

Karl: "Several people mentioned that Harry always has their back."

Barbara: "I got the impression that Harry covers for them."

Marcus: "Meaning what?"

Wayne: "Meaning, giving them some slack when it comes to things like overlooking their weaknesses, a little sloppiness with deadlines or taking time off."

Barbara: "Several mentioned that he's always willing to . . . let me look at my notes . . . '*Always willing to step in and help out.*' The phrase came up more than a few times and when I pressed them, they didn't elaborate. But I wondered . . ."

Karl: " . . . Is he managing or taking on some of their responsibilities?"

Barbara: "Exactly."

Mitch: "It's bothering me that he comes across as the parent who does his kid's project for the science fair."

Wayne: "I don't think it's that bad, but when you look at him in comparison with the other candidates, it makes me question whether he can take on the tough part of top management. There is nothing distinctive about him or his style."

Karl: "There's no *edge* here. No sense of boundaries. Does he want to manage employees or be popular with them? Can he say 'No' and mean it?"

Barbara: "Does Harry have the capability to walk that fine line that separates leaders; that distinguishes respect versus popularity or encouragement and support over *stepping in and helping out?*"

Marcus: "So, we see some good things about Harry. He has a lot of potential. But we also see that he has not yet reached a level where we can entrust him with this top management position. Our task here, then, is to move on with the selection process, but over the next weeks I would like for us to consider ways to help Harry reach that potential for future opportunities."

QUESTIONS

1. What does *nice* mean to you? Do you think nice is a good trait for leaders or the kiss of death?
2. Is *nice* related to any concepts in the chapter, such as one of the big five personality dimensions, Myers–Briggs components, or left–right brain dominance? Discuss.
3. If Harry is passed over for promotion, what feedback and advice would you give him about how to improve his leadership skills for possible future promotion?

Environmental Designs International

When Lee Keiko returned from a quick lunch, she scanned her e-mail inbox for the message she had been dreading. She found it, labeled "high priority," among a dozen other e-mails and sank back in her chair as she mentally prepared to open it. Keiko felt a tightening in her stomach as she clicked on the message and braced herself for the assault she had grown to expect from Barry Carver, her boss at Environmental Designs International (EDI), a rapidly growing "green" company that specializes in retrofitting commercial buildings to improve their energy efficiency.

The primary clients of EDI are owners of skyscrapers who renovate their buildings to reduce energy use and cut down on greenhouse gas emissions, a contributor to global warming. Within these towering skyscrapers, the largest energy guzzlers are lighting, cooling, and heating. Owners of New York City's Empire State Building expect to reduce the skyscraper's energy use by 38 percent within five years at an annual savings of $ 4.4 million after this 78-year-old building is retrofitted.

Keiko had expected Carver's scathing e-mail and knew he would lambaste her and her team for missing last Friday's deadline for submitting a proposal to retrofit a 60-story Chicago skyscraper to meet new federal green standards. Keiko had warned Carver of the possible delay in completing the proposal due to changing federal regulations for energy efficiency. It was truly out of her hands. She had even consulted with the client to alert them of the delay, and they had agreed to an extended deadline.

Nevertheless, Carver was angry about the delay and fired off an e-mail that was brusque and insensitive. "I depend on you to meet deadlines and work effectively with regulatory agencies. Your ineptness may cost us this important project," he exclaimed in his e-mail to Keiko. "Why aren't you as committed to this project as I am? I can't do this alone," he stated. This was one more example of how Carver often made life miserable for his subordinates, verbally attacking them to get results. Carver had also started alienating his peers. During a recent meeting to discuss the replacement of thousands of windows in the Chicago skyscraper, Carver embarrassed a colleague by accusing him of selecting a vendor without doing a price comparison among vendors. "How can I value your recommendation, Troy, if you fail to do your homework? I need new prices by Friday!" shouted Carver.

Carver was a highly skilled architect and responsible for managing a team of designers in EDI's Chicago office. Although his abrupt personality had helped him climb the corporate ladder, his intimidating communication style was beginning to create problems and hamper his ability to get results. Carver learned in his performance review that his work relationships were suffering and the complaints about him were increasing. Even his long-time peers were avoiding him as much as possible and finding ways to work around him.

Sensitive to the growing animosity toward him, Carver began to reconsider how he interacted with his staff and peers. He felt motivated to begin using some of the tools he had recently learned in the executive education course he had just completed. During one of the skills-assessment activities, Carver learned that he could get better results by communicating more gently, building consensus, and working in a more team-oriented manner. Further, he realized he had to find ways to handle his anger and frustration when dealing with federal regulatory agencies and the inevitable delays that hampered progress on big construction projects. As he thought about the skills assessment, Carver wondered if he could soften his image and perhaps even be considered for a senior management position he was eyeing in EDI's Los Angeles office.

Sources: Based on information in Gerry Yemen, Erika H. James, and James G. Clawson, "Nicholas Gray: The More Things Change . . .," (Darden Business Publishing, University of Virginia, Copyright 2003; and Mireya Navarro, "The Empire State Building Plans a Growth Spurt, Environmentally," *The New York Times* (April 7, 2009), p. A25.

QUESTIONS

1. "At the senior management level, you get hired for competence. You get fired for personality." In your opinion, is this statement true or false? How does it relate to Barry Carver and his current leadership style?
2. Identify the behaviors described in this case that were damaging to Barry Carver's work relationships. Why would a manager behave this way? What negative consequences did these behaviors have on his peers and subordinates?
3. How realistic is it that Carver (or anyone) can change his own leadership skills? What kind of help might he need?

REFERENCES

1. Adam Bryant, "Nancy Dubec of A&E: Mixing Doers, Thinkers and Feelers" (Corner Office column), *The New York Times* (March 19, 2015), http://www.nytimes.com/2015/03/22/business/nancy-dubuc-of-ae-mixing-doers-thinkers-and-feelers.html?_r=0 (accessed October 13, 2015).
2. Reported in William W. George, Peter Sims, Andrew N. MacLean, David Mayer, and Diana Mayer, "Discovering Your Authentic Leadership," *Harvard Business Review* (February 2007), pp. 129–138.
3. Bill George, "Leadership Skills: It Starts with Self-Awareness," *Leadership Excellence* (June 2011), p. 13; Tricia Bisoux, "What Makes Leaders Great" (interviews with leadership experts), *BizEd* (September–October 2005), pp. 40–45; Warren Bennis, *Why Leaders Can't Lead* (San Francisco: Jossey-Bass, 1989); Daniel Goleman, "What Makes a Leader?" *Harvard Business Review* (November–December 1998), p. 93ff; and Richard E. Boyatzis, *The Competent Manager: A Model for Effective Performance* (New York: Wiley, 1982).
4. Charlotte Beers, interviewed by Adam Bryant, "The Best Scorecard Is the One You Keep for Yourself," *The New York Times* (March 31, 2012), http://www.nytimes.com/2012/04/01/business/charlotte-beers-on-the-importance-of-self-assessment.html?pagewanted=all (accessed April 1, 2012).
5. Camille Sweeney and Josh Gosfield, *The Art of Doing: How Superachievers Do What They Do and How They Do It So Well* (New York: Plume/Penguin, 2013), as reported in Sweeney and Gosfield, "Secret Ingredient for Success," *The New York Times* (January 20, 2013), p. SR4.
6. Doug Rauch, "Failure Chronicles: 'You're Driving Us Crazy. You've Got to Back Off,'" *Harvard Business Review* (April 2011), p. 56.
7. Steven Snyder, "Leadership Struggle: It's an Art to Be Mastered," *Leadership Excellence* (January 2013), p. 11; and Ira Chaleff, "Avoid Fatal Crashes: Leaders and Their Blind Spots," *Leadership Excellence* (May 2012), p. 13.
8. Sue Shellenbarger, "To Combat an Office Tyrant, Look at the Roots," *The Wall Street Journal* (April 28, 2010); and Ed Frauenheim, "Pulling No Punches," *Workforce Management* (October 6, 2008), p. 1.
9. Robert I. Sutton, *The No Asshole Rule: Building a Civilized Workplace and Surviving One That Isn't* (New York: Warner Business Books, 2007).
10. Marshall Goldsmith, "People Skills: These Matter Most at the Top Level," *Leadership Excellences* (June 2007), p. 9.
11. Alex Lickerman, "The Good Guy Contract," *Psychology Today* (March–April 2010), pp. 42–43.
12. Quoted in L. Mitchell, "Ten Things I Don't Put on My C.V.: Sue Murray," *Age* (October 25, 2008), p. 3.
13. Adam Bryant, "Making Room for Differences," (Corner Office column), *The New York Times* (February 7, 2015), http://www.nytimes.com/2015/02/08/business/corner-office-making-room-for-differences.html?_r=0 (accessed October 13, 2015).
14. J. M. Digman, "Personality Structure: Emergence of the Five-Factor Model," *Annual Review of Psychology* 41 (1990), pp. 417–440; M. R. Barrick and M. K. Mount, "Autonomy as a Moderator of the Relationships between the Big Five Personality Dimensions and Job Performance," *Journal of Applied Psychology* (February 1993), pp. 111–118; J. S. Wiggins and A. L. Pincus, "Personality: Structure and Assessment," *Annual Review of Psychology* 43 (1992), pp. 473–504; and Carl Zimmer, "Looking for Personality in Animals, of All People," *The New York Times* (March 1, 2005), p. F1.
15. Del Jones, "Not All Successful CEOs Are Extroverts," *USA Today* (June 6, 2006), p. B1; and Bryan Walsh, "The Upside of Being an Introvert (and Why Extroverts Are Overrated)," *Time* (February 6, 2012), pp. 40–45.
16. Reported in Daisy Grewal, "When Nice Guys Finish First," *Scientific American Mind* (July–August 2012), pp. 62–65.
17. Anthony J. Mayo and Nitin Nohria, "Double-Edged Sword," *People Management* (October 27, 2005), pp. 36–38; Carol Hymowitz,

"Rewarding Competitors over Collaborators No Longer Makes Sense" (In the Lead column), *The Wall Street Journal* (February 13, 2006), p. B1; and Joseph Nocera, "In Business, Tough Guys Finish Last," *The New York Times* (June 18, 2005), p. C1.

18. Diane Brady, "Charm Offensive," *BusinessWeek* (June 26, 2006), pp. 76–80.
19. Research reported in J. J. McCorvey, "Research Corner: Feeling Guilty? Good. Why Guilt Makes You a Better Leader," *Inc.* (July–August 2012), p. 26; and Rachel Emma Silverman, "Plagued by Guilt? You May Be Management Material," *The Wall Street Journal* (May 29, 2012), http://blogs.wsj.com/atwork/2012/05/29/plagued-by-guilt-you-may-be-management-material/ (accessed June 3, 2012).
20. Anne-Elisabeth Moutet, "Dominique Strauss-Kahn: A Frenchman Sunk by a Sex Scandal?" *The Telegraph* (May 16, 2011), http://www.telegraph.co.uk/news/worldnews/europe/france/8515714/Dominique-Strauss-Kahn-A-Frenchman-sunk-by-a-sex-scandal.html (accessed August 26, 2012).
21. Bill George, "The Courage to Say 'No' to Wall Street" (segment in "America's Best Leaders"), *U.S. News & World Report* (December 1–December 8, 2008), pp. 34–51; Andrew Davidson, "Xerox Saviour in the Spotlight," *Sunday Times* (June 1, 2008), p. 6; and David K. Williams, "Top 10 List: The Greatest Living Business Leaders Today," *Forbes* (July 24, 2012), www.forbes.com/sites/davidkwilliams/2012/07/24/top-10-list-the-greatest-living-business-leaders-today/ (accessed March 4, 2013).
22. Marjorie Censer, "After Nearly 30 Years with Lockheed, Hewson Is Named Chief Executive," *The Washington Post* (November 13, 2012), http://www.washingtonpost.com/business/capitalbusiness/after-nearly-30-years-with-lockheed-hewson-is-named-chief-executive/2012/11/13/173cc04a-2cdc-11e2-a99d-5c4203af7b7a_story.html?wprss=rss_business (accessed November 14, 2012); and Doug Cameron and Joann S. Lublin, "Vaulted to Top at Lockheed, and Ready to Navigate Cliff," *The Wall Street Journal Online* (November 11, 2012), http://online.wsj.com/article/SB10001424127887324439804578113250113672078.html (accessed March 19, 2013).
23. James B. Hunt, "Travel Experience in the Formation of Leadership: John Quincy Adams, Frederick Douglass, and Jane Addams," *The Journal of Leadership Studies* 7, no. 1 (2000), pp. 92–106.
24. R. T. Hogan, G. J. Curphy, and J. Hogan, "What We Know about Leadership: Effectiveness and Personality," *American Psychologist* 49, no. 6 (1994), pp. 493–504.
25. Randolph E. Schmid, "Psychologists Rate What Helps Make a President Great," *Johnson City Press* (August 6, 2000), p. 10; and "Personality and the Presidency" segment on *NBC News* with John Siegenthaler Jr. (August 5, 2000).
26. Jack and Suzy Welch, "Release Your Inner Extrovert," *BusinessWeek* (December 8, 2008), p. 92; and Nancy Ancowitz, "Success Isn't Only for the Extroverts," *The New York Times* (November 1, 2009), p. BU8.
27. Reported in "From the Front Lines: Leadership Strategies for Introverts," *Leader to Leader* (Fall 2009), pp. 59–60.
28. Reported in Jeffrey Kluger, "Why Bosses Tend to Be Blowhards," *Time* (March 2, 2009), p. 48.
29. Ginka Toegel and Jean-Louis Barsoux, "How to Become a Better Leader," *MIT Sloan Management Review* (Spring 2012), pp. 51–60.
30. Susan Cain, "Hire Introverts," *The Atlantic* (July–August 2012), p. 68; Adam M. Grant, Francesca Gino, and David A. Hofmann, "The Hidden Advantages of Quiet Bosses," *Harvard Business Review* (December 2010), p. 28; Susan Cain, "Must Great Leaders Be Gregarious?" *The New York Times* (September 16, 2012), p. SR–8; and Walsh, "The Upside of Being an Introvert."
31. "Theories of Emeritus Professor Julian Rotter Still Relevant to Field of Clinical Psychology" *U.S. Fed News Service, Including US State News* (August 12, 2012) (retrieved from http://search.proquest.com.proxy.library.vanderbilt.edu/docview/1032581459?accountid=14816); P. E. Spector, "Behavior in Organizations as a Function of Employee's Locus of Control," *Psychological Bulletin* (May 1982), pp. 482–497; and H. M. Lefcourt, "Durability and Impact of the Locus of Control Construct," *Psychological Bulletin* 112 (1992), pp. 411–414.
32. Ellen McGirt, "Boy Wonder," *Fast Company* (April 2009), pp. 58–65, 96–97.
33. Spector, "Behavior in Organizations as a Function of Employee's Locus of Control"; Lefcourt, "Durability and Impact of the Locus of Control Construct"; and J. B. Miner, *Industrial-Organizational Psychology* (New York: McGraw-Hill, 1992), p. 151.
34. Elizabeth A. McDaniel and Holly DiBella-McCarthy, "Reflective Leaders Become Causal Agents of Change," *Journal of Management Development* 31, no. 7 (2012), pp. 663–671.
35. T. W. Adorno, E. Frenkel-Brunswick, D. J. Levinson, and R. N. Sanford, *The Authoritarian Personality* (New York: Harper & Row, 1950).
36. E. C. Ravlin and B. M. Meglino, "Effects of Values on Perception and Decision Making: A Study of Alternative Work Value Measures," *Journal of Applied Psychology* 72 (1987), pp. 666–673.
37. Robert C. Benfari, *Understanding and Changing Your Management Style* (San Francisco: Jossey-Bass, 1999), p. 172.
38. Milton Rokeach, *The Nature of Human Values* (New York: The Free Press, 1973); and M. Rokeach, *Understanding Human Values* (New York: The Free Press, 1979).
39. Edward F. Murphy Jr., Jane Whitney Gibson, and Regina A. Greenwood, "Analyzing Generational Values among Managers and Non-Managers for Sustainable Organizational Effectiveness," *SAM Advanced Management Journal* (Winter 2010), pp. 33–55.
40. Murphy et al., "Analyzing Generational Values among Managers and Non-Managers."
41. Lynne Jeter, "Early Lessons Helped Form Leadership Skills," *The Mississippi Business Journal* (March 13, 2006), p. 23; and "2011 Harvey E. Beech Outstanding Alumni Award; BAR Awards Profile—William W. Farmer," University of North Carolina General Alumni Association, https://alumni.unc.edu/awards-profile-william-w-farmer/ (accessed October 14, 2015).
42. Based on G. W. England and R. Lee, "The Relationship between Managerial Values and Managerial Success in the United States, Japan, India, and Australia," *Journal of Applied Psychology* 59 (1974), pp. 411–419.
43. Example from Michael Lee Stallard, "Great Leaders Connect: Using Their Vision, Values, and Voice," *Leadership Excellence* (August 2012), p. 19.
44. Based on Richard L. Hughes, Robert C. Ginnett, and Gordon J. Curphy, *Leadership: Enhancing the Lessons of Experience* (Boston: Irwin McGraw-Hill, 1999), pp. 182–184.
45. Douglas McGregor, *The Human Side of Enterprise* (New York: McGraw-Hill, 1960).
46. J. Hall and S. M. Donnell, "Managerial Achievement: The Personal Side of Behavioral Theory," *Human Relations* 32 (1979), pp. 77–101.
47. Andrea Coombes, "Managers Rate Themselves High but Workers Prove Tough Critics," *The Wall Street Journal* (September 26, 2006), p. B8; and Jaclyne Badal, "Surveying the Field: Cracking the Glass Ceiling" (sidebar in Theory & Practice column), *The Wall Street Journal* (June 19, 2006), p. B3.
48. This is a very brief introduction to the subject of attributions and their role in organizations. For a recent overview of the research on attributional theory and a special issue devoted to the topic, see Marie Dasborough, Paul Harvey, and Mark J. Martinko, "An Introduction to Attributional Influences in Organizations," *Group & Organization Management* 36, no. 4 (2011), pp. 419–426.
49. Kevin Kelly, "Branching Out," *Fortune Small Business* (December 2005–January 2006), p. 39; and Kevin Kelly, "Take a Real Vacation," *Fortune Small Business* (July–August 2006), p. 28.
50. Dorothy Leonard and Susaan Straus, "Putting Your Company's Whole Brain to Work," *Harvard Business Review* (July–August 1997), pp. 111–121.

51. Henry Mintzberg, "Planning on the Left Side and Managing on the Right," *Harvard Business Review* (July–August 1976), pp. 49–57; Richard Restak, "The Hemispheres of the Brain Have Minds of Their Own," *The New York Times* (January 25, 1976); and Robert Ornstein, *The Psychology of Consciousness* (San Francisco: W. H. Freeman, 1975).
52. Kate Taylor, "Creative Types, Learning to Be Business-Minded," *The New York Times* (June 19, 2010), p. C1.
53. This discussion is based on Ned Herrmann, *The Whole Brain Business Book* (New York: McGraw-Hill, 1996).
54. This analogy is based on Peter Gloor, "To Become a Better Manager Stop Being a Manager," *Ivey Business Journal* (March–April 2011), http://www.iveybusinessjournal.com/topics/the-organization/to-become-a-better-manager-stop-being-a-manager (accessed March 20, 2013).
55. Ibid.
56. Ibid.
57. Ibid.
58. Herrmann, *The Whole Brain Business Book*, p. 103.
59. Based on Nancy Hass, "Earning Her Stripes," *The Wall Street Journal Magazine* (September 9, 2010), http://magazine.wsj.com/features/the-big-interview/earning-her-strips/ (accessed March 20, 2013); and Jennifer Reingold, "What the Heck Is Angela Ahrendts Doing at Apple?" *Fortune* (September 15, 2015), pp. 100–108.
60. Herrmann, *The Whole Brain Business Book*, p. 179.
61. Carl Jung, *Psychological Types* (London: Routledge and Kegan Paul, 1923).
62. Otto Kroeger and Janet M. Thuesen, *Type Talk* (New York: Delacorte Press, 1988); Kroeger and Thuesen, *Type Talk at Work* (New York: Dell, 1992); "Conference Proceedings," *The Myers–Briggs Type Indicator and Leadership: An International Research Conference* (January 12–14, 1994); and S. K. Hirsch, *MBTI™ Team Member's Guide* (Palo Alto, CA: Consulting Psychologists Press, 1992).
63. Reported in Lillian Cunningham, "Does It Pay to Know Your Type?" *The Washington Post* (December 14, 2012), http://articles.washingtonpost.com/2012-12-14/national/35847528_1_personality-types-myers-briggs-type-indicator-financial-success (accessed March 20, 2013).
64. Example in Jennifer Overbo, "Using Myers–Briggs Personality Type to Create a Culture Adapted to the New Century," *T + D* (February 2010), pp. 70–72.
65. Based on Mary H. McCaulley, "Research on the MBTI™ and Leadership: Taking the Critical First Step," *Keynote Address, The Myers–Briggs Type Indicator and Leadership: An International Research Conference* (January 12–14, 1994).
66. These techniques are based on Jamie Walters and Sarah Fenson, "Building Rapport with Different Personalities," Inc.com (March 2000), http://www.inc.com/articles/2000/03/17713.html; Tim Millett, "Learning to Work with Different Personality Types," http://ezinearticles.com/?Learning-To-Work-With-Different-Personality-Types&id=725606; and Carol Ritberter, "Understanding Personality: The Secret to Managing People," http://www.dreammanifesto.com/understanding-personality-the-secret-of-managing-people.html (accessed April 17, 2008).

Chapter 5: Leadership Mind and Emotion

YOUR **LEADERSHIP** CHALLENGE

After reading this chapter, you should be able to:

- Recognize how mental models guide your behavior and relationships.
- Engage in independent thinking by staying mentally alert, thinking critically, and being mindful rather than mindless.
- Break out of categorized thinking patterns and open your mind to new ideas and multiple perspectives.
- Begin to apply systems thinking and personal mastery to your activities at school or work.
- Exercise emotional intelligence, including being self-aware, managing your emotions, motivating yourself, displaying empathy, and managing relationships.
- Apply the difference between motivating others based on fear and motivating others based on love.

CHAPTER **OUTLINE**

136 **Leading with Head and Heart**

136 **Mental Models**

140 **Developing a Leader's Mind**

146 **Emotional Intelligence**

153 **Leading with Love versus Leading with Fear**

In the Lead

139 **Ron Rivera, Carolina Panthers**

152 **Chade-Meng Tan, Google**

155 **Akshay Kothari and Ankit Gupta, Pulse News**

Leader's Self-Insight

143 **Mindfulness**

153 **Emotional Intelligence**

154 **Love or Fear?**

Leader's Bookshelf

141 **What Got You Here Won't Get You There**

Leadership at Work

160 **Mentors**

Leadership Development: Cases for Analysis

160 **The New Boss**

162 **The USS *Florida***

As Lieutenant Colonel Howard Olson surveys the crowd before him, he knows that most of the people in the room outrank him. Still, Olson opens his talk with the following statement: "Each and every one of you has something that makes you a jerk.... Some of you have more than one. I know. I've talked to you."

The lecture is part of what the U.S. Army informally calls "charm school," a week-long course held annually for the select few who are promoted to brigadier general. Everyone knows about the Army's skill at getting new recruits in boot camp to think and act in a new way, but few people have seen firsthand the training it uses to get high-ranking officers to make a mental and emotional leap. At charm school, new generals are advised to get in touch with their inner jerk and work on overcoming that aspect of their personality. Charm school is designed as a reminder that the great officers are those who genuinely care about their soldiers. Other recurring themes during the training include avoiding even the appearance of ethical violations, leading with moral courage, and overcoming arrogance, the "first deadly sin of the general officer."[1]

There's no equivalent training in corporate America, but the lessons taught at the Army's charm school are also being taken to heart at many of today's business organizations, where leaders are learning to build work relationships based on trust, humility, caring, and respect.

This chapter and the next examine current thinking about the importance of leaders becoming fully integrated people by exploring the full capacities of their minds, emotions, and spirits. Noted leadership author and scholar Warren Bennis has said that "there's no difference between being a really effective leader and becoming a fully integrated person."[2] This chapter first examines the importance of leading with both head and heart (mind and emotion). Then we expand on some of the ideas introduced in the previous chapter to consider how the ability to shift our thinking and feeling can help leaders alter their behavior, influence others, and be more effective. We discuss the concept of mental models and look at how qualities such as independent thinking, an open mind, and systems thinking are important for leaders. Then we take a closer look at human emotions, the concept of emotional intelligence, and the emotions of love versus fear in leader–follower relationships. The next chapter will turn to spirit as reflected in moral leadership and courage.

5-1 LEADING WITH HEAD AND HEART

As most of us know from personal experience, working effectively with other people requires that we draw on subtle aspects of ourselves—our thoughts, beliefs, and feelings—and appeal to those aspects in others. Anyone who has participated on an athletic team knows how powerfully thoughts and emotions can affect performance. Interestingly, though, many people in leadership roles tend to forget the emotional aspect of leading.

To succeed in today's environment requires *whole leaders* who use both head and heart.[3] Leaders have to use their heads to tend to organizational issues such as goals and strategies, production schedules, structure, finances, operational issues, and so forth. They also have to use their hearts to tend to human issues, such as understanding, supporting, and developing others. Using heart in leadership is particularly important in times of uncertainty and rapid change. Current issues that require leaders to use both head and heart include how to give people a sense of meaning and purpose when major changes occur almost daily; how to make employees feel valued and respected in an age of massive layoffs and job uncertainty; and how to keep morale and motivation high in the face of corporate bankruptcies and dissolutions, ethical scandals, and economic crises.

NEW LEADER
ACTION MEMO

As a leader, you can lead with both head and heart. You can expand the capacity of your mind, emotions, and spirit by consciously engaging in activities that use aspects of the whole self.

A broad literature has emphasized that being a whole person means operating from mind, heart, spirit, and body.[4] In Chapter 4, we introduced some ideas about how individuals think, make decisions, and solve problems based on values, attitudes, and patterns of thinking. This chapter builds on some of those ideas to provide a broader view of leadership mind and emotions.

5-2 MENTAL MODELS

A mental model can be thought of as an internal picture that affects a leader's thoughts, actions, and relationships with others. **Mental models** are theories people hold about specific systems in the world and their expected behavior.[5] A system means any set of elements that interact to form a whole and produce a specified outcome. To understand what is meant by a mental model, consider an electrical circuit as a system. Exhibit 5.1 shows the elements of an electrical circuit system.

Mental models
theories people hold about specific systems in the world and their expected behavior

EXHIBIT 5.1 Elements of a System

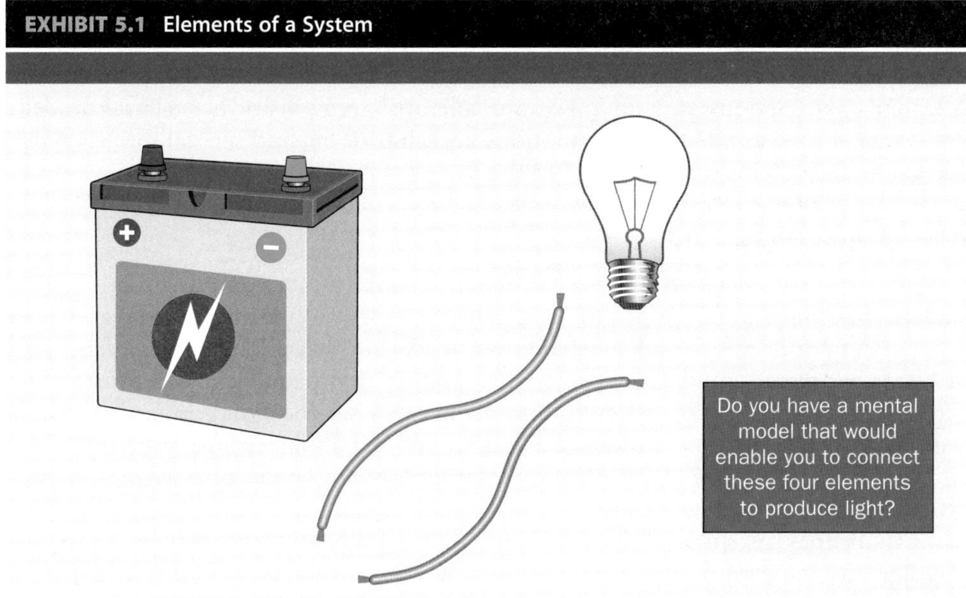

A mental model would give you a picture in your mind of how these four elements fit together to produce the outcome of light. Just as an electric circuit is a system, an organization is a system, as is a football team, a sorority pledge drive, or the registration system at a university. An accurate mental model helps a leader understand how to arrange the key elements in these systems to get the desired outcome.

Leaders have many mental models that tend to govern how they interpret experiences and how they act in response to people and situations. Consider the two different mental models in the following quote from Robert Townsend, former CEO of Avis Rent-a-Car. To have a successful organization, he advised leaders, "you'll have to give up being an administrator who loves to run others and become a manager who carries water for his people so they can get on with the job."[6] The first part of the phrase reflects a mental model that it is the leader's job to control people, whereas the second part reflects a mental model that the leader is a servant who helps people do their best. Exhibit 5.2 shows the mental model that Google's top leaders use to keep the company on the cutting edge as its core business of search matures. At Google, leaders believe that risk-taking, a little craziness, and making mistakes are important for the sake of innovation. Too much structure and control is considered death to the company.[7]

NEW LEADER
ACTION MEMO

As a leader, you can become aware of your mental models and how they affect your thinking and behavior. You can learn to regard your assumptions as temporary ideas and strive to expand your mindset.

EXHIBIT 5.2 Google Leaders' Mental Model

- Stay uncomfortable
- Let failure coexist with triumph
- Use a little less "management" than you need
- Defy convention
- Move fast and figure things out as you go

Source: Based on Adam Lashinsky, "Chaos by Design," *Fortune* (October 2, 2006), pp. 86–98.

Leaders at Google, as well as other organizations, strive to create mental models that are aligned with organizational needs, goals, and values. However, personal values, attitudes, beliefs, biases, and prejudices can all affect one's mental model. A leader's assumptions play an important role in shaping his or her mental models, but leaders can examine their assumptions and shift or expand mental models when needed to keep their organizations healthy.[8]

5-2a Assumptions

In Chapter 4, we discussed two very different sets of attitudes and assumptions that leaders may have about subordinates, called Theory X and Theory Y, and how these assumptions affect leader behavior. A leader's assumptions naturally are part of his or her mental model. Someone who assumes that people can't be trusted will act very differently in a situation than someone who has the assumption that people are basically trustworthy. Leaders have assumptions about events, situations, and circumstances as well as about people. Assumptions can be dangerous because people tend to accept them as "truth."

J.C. Penney provides a good example. Ron Johnson, who helped create the popular and successful Apple retail stores, was hired to save J.C. Penney from a slow death, but he was fired just 17 months into the job. Johnson's assumptions about the transformation, which included making stores and merchandise more upscale, were based on his experience with what worked at Apple. He created in-store "boutiques" with expensive shelving and signage and pushed stores to stock youthful, slim-fitting clothing and European designs, reflecting a shift away from the retailer's core customers. The problem is that J.C. Penney isn't Apple. Customers flock to Apple stores for cutting-edge, status-symbol products, but J.C. Penney's customers want basic clothing and home goods at low prices. Johnson's remake assumed the only department store customer that mattered was the one "who shops at Target or Macy's or Nordstrom's," said Margaret Bogenrief of ACM Partners.[9] In 2015, Marvin Ellison took over as the third CEO at Penney in four years. One of Ellison's biggest jobs will be working with other top Penney's leaders to bring more realistic assumptions to the challenge of reinventing an iconic brand for a new era.

As this example illustrates, it is important for leaders to regard their assumptions as temporary ideas rather than fixed truths. The more aware a leader is of his or her assumptions, the more the leader understands how assumptions guide behavior and decisions. In addition, the leader can question whether long-held assumptions fit the reality of the current situation. Questioning assumptions can help leaders understand and shift their mental models.

5-2b Changing or Expanding Mental Models

The mindset of top leaders has always played a key role in organizational success. A Harvard University study ranking the top 100 business leaders of the twentieth century found that they all shared what the researchers refer to as "contextual intelligence," the ability to sense the social, political, technological, and economic context of the times and adopt a mental model that helped their organizations best respond.[10] In a world of rapid and discontinuous change, the greatest factor determining the success of leaders and organizations may be the ability to change or expand one's mental model.[11] Consider how Ron Rivera, head coach of the Carolina Panthers, expanded his mental model of how to lead a football team.

IN THE LEAD

Ron Rivera, Carolina Panthers

Most NFL coaches keep the time they spend in the locker room to a minimum. Ron Rivera, head coach of the Carolina Panthers, used to do that too, but after asking for advice from fighter pilots about how to promote honesty and trust, Rivera shifted his mental model from one of maintaining distance from players to one of getting to know and understand players at a deep personal level. Now he's in the locker room interacting with players all the time. "Unless you are exposed to them [in the locker room], when they let their hair down, you won't get to know them," he says.

After being advised to "remove rank" when talking to subordinates, Rivera took a bunch of players to dinner and asked them to give honest feedback. He was amazed at some of the things he heard. "I'm blown away," he said. "You guys should have told me!" That's when he embarked on a crusade to create a culture of total honesty, where players felt they could ask him or tell him anything. Rivera set up a second office closer to the locker room and he regularly visits the training room and cafeteria, as well as the locker room, to interact informally with players. "I have answered questions in the locker room about whether a player should get puppies," Rivera said. "I told them having a puppy is just like having a baby, there's a lot of responsibility."[12]

Having closer personal relationships with his players helps Rivera monitor morale and smooth problems that might interfere with high performance. Leaders have to keep open minds and be willing to question assumptions and shift their mental models when new approaches are needed.

Organizations are vulnerable when leaders stick with obsolete mental models in the face of new realities. For example, market share for the BlackBerry smartphone has plummeted in recent years because leaders at Research in Motion stayed with what worked in the past and had a hard time shifting their mental model to keep the company competitive in an environment that changed quickly with the introduction of Apple and Samsung smartphones. On the other hand, leaders at Apple, particularly the late Steve Jobs, have been masters at shifting or expanding their mental models over the years. One researcher who interviewed Steve Jobs said he could "sometimes throw you off balance by suddenly adopting your position as his own, without ever acknowledging that he ever thought differently." One reason Apple is so successful today, this researcher asserts, is that Steve Jobs was a genius at reframing issues and shifting mental models—his own, his employees', his partners', and his customers'. Before the iPhone, no one had ever thought of something like the App Store or the possibility of demanding a share of the revenue from wireless carriers, for instance.[13]

Unfortunately, many leaders become prisoners of their own assumptions and mindsets because these led to success in the past. They find themselves simply going along with the traditional way of doing things—whether it be running a business such as Research in Motion, managing a foundation, handling insurance claims, selling cosmetics, or coaching a basketball team—without even realizing they are making decisions and acting within the limited frame of their own mental model.[14]

One specific challenge for the mental models of leaders is to navigate through ambiguities and complexities on a global scale that far exceed anything they encounter within their traditional management responsibilities.[15] A **global mindset** can be defined as the ability of managers to appreciate and influence individuals, groups, organizations, and systems that represent different social, cultural, political, institutional, intellectual, or psychological characteristics.[16] A manager with a global mindset can perceive and respond to many different perspectives at the same time rather than being stuck in a domestic mental model that sees everything from one's own limited personal or cultural perspective. One of the best ways managers develop a global mindset is by engaging with people from different cultures. Ken Powell, CEO of General Mills, says being given international positions early in his career convinced him that getting people out of their comfort zone was the best way to develop leaders.[17]

Despite the mental discomfort and sense of disorientation it might cause, leaders must allow their mental models to be challenged and even demolished.[18] Becoming aware of assumptions and understanding how they influence emotions and actions is the first step toward being able to shift mental models and see the world in a new way. Effective leaders learn to continually question their own beliefs, assumptions, and perceptions in order to see things in unconventional ways and meet the challenge of the future head on.[19] Leaders who are unable to see and change their own ineffective mental models often need outside help, as described in this chapter's Leader's Bookshelf.

5-3 DEVELOPING A LEADER'S MIND

How do leaders expand their mental models? The leader's mind can be developed beyond the nonleader's in four critical areas: independent thinking, open-mindedness, systems thinking, and personal mastery. Taken together, these four disciplines provide a foundation that can help leaders examine their mental models and overcome blind spots that may limit their leadership effectiveness and the success of their organizations.

Global mindset
the ability of managers to appreciate and influence individuals, groups, organizations, and systems that represent different social, cultural, political, institutional, intellectual, or psychological characteristics

Independent thinking
questioning assumptions and interpreting data and events according to one's own beliefs, ideas, and thinking, rather than preestablished rules or categories defined by others

Mindfulness
a state of focused attention on the present moment and a readiness to create new mental categories in the face of evolving information and shifting circumstances

5-3a Independent Thinking

Independent thinking means questioning assumptions and interpreting data and events according to one's own beliefs, ideas, and thinking, not according to preestablished rules, routines, or categories defined by others. People who think independently are willing to stand apart, to have opinions, to say what they think, and to determine a course of action based on what they personally believe rather than on what other people think or say. Consider the female manager who left Ralston Purina for a marketing job at Eveready in the mid-1980s. Eveready had become a household name because of its sales of inexpensive red plastic and metal flashlights, but the flashlight business was in decline. This manager questioned why flashlights couldn't be made in colors like pink, baby blue, and lime green that would appeal to women—and why weren't they sold in grocery stores? It wasn't a popular decision, but once top executives agreed to go along with the new ideas, the flashlight business rebounded.[20] Good leadership isn't about following the rules of others but standing up for what you believe is best for the organization.

To think independently means staying mentally alert and thinking critically. Independent thinking is one part of what is called leader mindfulness.[21] **Mindfulness** can be defined as a state of focused attention on the present moment and a readiness to create new mental categories in the face of evolving

LEADER'S BOOKSHELF

What Got You Here Won't Get You There

by Marshall Goldsmith and Mark Reiter

Success, says executive coach Marshall Goldsmith, makes many people believe they must be doing everything right. Therefore, as leaders move up the hierarchy they often continue to rely on mental models about interpersonal relationships that seemed to work when they were in lower-level positions. Consequently, they may sabotage their effectiveness and career advancement. "All other things being equal, your people skills (or lack of them) become more pronounced the higher up you go," Goldsmith writes in *What Got You Here Won't Get You There*. Goldsmith and his collaborator, Mark Reiter, identify 20 mental habits that damage leader relationships at higher levels.

NOBODY'S PERFECT

Every leader has some habits or negative behaviors that can limit his or her effectiveness. Following are a few of the behavioral flaws Goldsmith and Reiter describe. Do you recognize any of these in your own behaviors?

- ***The Need to Win at All Costs and in All Situations.*** We all know them—those people who feel like they have to win every argument and always be right. They want to win the big points, the small points, and everything in between. If they go along with another's idea that doesn't work out, they adopt an "I told you so" attitude. In the workplace, a top leader's need to be right and to point out that he or she is right damages relationships and destroys teamwork.
- ***Clinging to the Past.*** There's nothing wrong with looking at and understanding the past as a way to come to terms with it or learn from it. Too often, though, people cling to the past as a way to blame others for things that have gone wrong in their lives, using the past as a weapon to control others or punish them for not doing exactly what the leader wants.
- ***Never Being Able to Say You're Sorry.*** It's not true that "love means never having to say you're sorry." Apologizing is love in action. Refusing to apologize probably causes more ill will—whether in a romance, a family, or a work relationship—than any other interpersonal flaw. "People who can't apologize at work may as well be wearing a T-shirt that says: 'I don't care about you,'" Goldsmith writes.

CHANGE IS POSSIBLE

As an executive coach, Goldsmith has spent his career helping leaders find and fix the mental models that hold them back. His prescription for success can benefit any leader who genuinely wants to improve his or her interpersonal relationships. The first step is to gather feedback that helps you identify the specific behaviors you need to change. Next, focus your mind on fixing the problem by apologizing for your behavioral flaws, advertising your efforts to change, listening to ideas from others, showing gratitude for others' contributions to your change process, and following up on your progress. When you are mindful of your dependence on others, Goldsmith points out, other people typically not only agree to help you be a better person, they also try to become better people themselves.

Source: *What Got You Here Won't Get You There* by Marshall Goldsmith and Mark Reiter, is published by Hyperion Books.

information and shifting circumstances.[22] Mindfulness involves independent thinking, and it requires leader curiosity and learning. Mindful leaders are open-minded and stimulate the thinking of others through their curiosity and questions. Mindfulness is the opposite of *mindlessness*, which means blindly accepting rules and labels created by others. Mindless people let others do the thinking for them, but mindful leaders are always open to new ideas and approaches.

Being mindful and thinking independently is important for leaders because they can easily become overwhelmed with the amount and variety of tasks that confront them. The deluge of e-mail, text messages, Web conferences, blogs, and so forth has intensified the problem. It is easy to begin doing things on autopilot.[23] But in the world of organizations, circumstances are constantly changing. What worked in one situation may not work the next time. In these conditions, mental laziness, operating on autopilot, and accepting others' answers can hurt the organization and all its members. Consider what happened to entrepreneur Kord Campbell, who failed for 12 days to notice an e-mail from a large company interested in buying his small Internet startup. Why? With the hectic pace of his life, Campbell had been operating on autopilot. "It seems he can no longer be fully in the moment," says his wife.[24]

Good leaders apply critical thinking to explore a situation, problem, or question from multiple perspectives and integrate all the available information into a possible solution. When leaders think critically, they question all assumptions, vigorously seek divergent opinions, and try to give balanced consideration to all alternatives.[25]

NEW LEADER
ACTION MEMO

Evaluate your skill in three dimensions of mindfulness, including intellectual stimulation, by completing the exercise in Leader's Self-Insight 5.1.

Thinking independently and critically is hard work, and most of us can easily relax into temporary mindlessness, accepting black-and-white answers and relying on standard ways of doing things. Leaders at BP have been faulted for deciding to finish work sealing the well at the Deepwater Horizon oil rig in the Gulf of Mexico despite some key pressure test discrepancies. They followed procedures that had worked fine in the past, but this proved to be a fatal decision at Deepwater Horizon. The rig exploded within hours, killing 11 workers and leaving oil on beaches from Louisiana to Florida.[26]

Good leaders also encourage followers to be mindful rather than mindless.[27] Bernard Bass, who has studied charismatic and transformational leadership, talks about the value of *intellectual stimulation*—arousing followers' thoughts and imaginations as well as stimulating their ability to identify and solve problems creatively.[28] People admire leaders who awaken their curiosity, challenge them to think and learn, and encourage openness to new, inspiring ideas and alternatives.

5-3b Open-Mindedness

The power of the conditioning that limits our thinking and behavior is illustrated by what has been called the *Pike Syndrome.* In an experiment, a northern pike is placed in one half of a large glass-divided aquarium, with numerous minnows placed in the other half. The hungry pike makes repeated attempts to get the minnows but succeeds only in battering itself against the glass, finally learning that trying to reach the minnows is futile. The glass divider is then removed, but the pike makes no attempt to attack the minnows because it has been conditioned to believe that reaching them is impossible. When people assume they have complete knowledge of a situation because of past experiences, they exhibit the Pike Syndrome, a trained incapacity that comes from rigid commitment to what was true in the past and an inability to consider alternatives and different perspectives.[29]

Leaders have to forget many of their conditioned ideas to be open to new ones. This openness—putting aside preconceptions and suspending beliefs and opinions—can be referred to as "beginner's mind." When someone becomes an expert in a particular subject, their mind often becomes closed to the perspectives of other people. Psychologist Elizabeth Newton conducted an experiment in which she gave one set of people, called "tappers," a list of well-known songs and asked them to rap their knuckles on a tabletop to the rhythm of the tunes. Another set of people, called "listeners," were asked to name the songs. The tappers said they thought listeners would get the songs right about half the time. In reality, the listeners guessed only 3 out of 120 songs that were tapped. The tappers might be considered to have "expert minds" in this situation. The song was so clear in their minds that they couldn't understand how the listeners could not hear it.[30]

The expert mind becomes a danger in organizations because it rejects new ideas based on past experience and knowledge. This danger of the expert mind's conclusions becomes frighteningly clear when it comes to the field of medicine. Doctors get their diagnoses wrong 15 to 20 percent of the time because they rely on standard ways of thinking and past experience. Many of these errors in judgment result in

LEADER'S SELF-INSIGHT 5.1

Mindfulness

Instructions: Think back to how you behaved toward others at work or in a group when you were in a formal or informal leadership position. Please respond to the following items based on how often you exhibited each behavior. Indicate whether each item is Mostly False or Mostly True for you.

	Mostly False	Mostly True
1. Enjoyed hearing new ideas.		✓
2. Challenged someone to think about an old problem in a new way.		✓
3. Tried to integrate conversation points at a higher level.		✓
4. Felt appreciation for the viewpoints of others.		✓
5. Would ask someone about the assumptions underlying his or her suggestions.		✓
6. Came to my own conclusion despite what others thought.		✓
7. Was open about myself to others.		✓
8. Encouraged others to express opposing ideas and arguments.		✓
9. Fought for my own ideas.		✓
10. Asked "dumb" questions.	✓	
11. Offered insightful comments on the meaning of data or issues.	✓	
12. Asked questions to prompt others to think more about an issue.	✓	
13. Expressed a controversial opinion.		✓
14. Encouraged opposite points of view.		✓
15. Suggested ways of improving my and others' ways of doing things.		✓

Scoring and Interpretation

Give yourself one point for each Mostly True checked for items 1–8 and 10–15. Give yourself one point for checking Mostly False for item 9. A total score of 12 or higher would be considered a high level of overall mindfulness. There are three subscale scores that represent three dimensions of leader mindfulness. For the dimension of open or beginner's mind, sum your responses to questions 1, 4, 7, 9, and 14. For the dimension of independent thinking, sum your scores for questions 3, 6, 11, 13, and 15. For the dimension of intellectual stimulation, sum your scores for questions 2, 5, 8, 10, and 12.

My scores are:
Open or Beginner's Mind: 5
Independent Thinking: 4
Intellectual Stimulation: 3

These scores represent three aspects of leader mindfulness—what is called open mind or beginner's mind, independent thinking, and intellectual stimulation.

A score of 4 or higher on any of these dimensions is considered high because many people do not practice mindfulness in their leadership or group work. A score of 3 is about average, and 2 or less would be below average. Compare your three subscale scores to understand the way you use mindfulness. Analyze the specific questions for which you did not get credit to see more deeply into your pattern of mindfulness strengths or weaknesses. An open mind, independent thinking, and intellectual stimulation are valuable qualities to develop for effective leadership.

Sources: The questions above are based on ideas from R. L. Daft and R. M. Lengel, *Fusion Leadership*, Chapter 4 (Oakland, CA: Berrett-Koehler, 2000); B. Bass and B. Avolio, *Multifactor Leadership Questionnaire*, 2nd ed. (Menlo Park, CA: Mind Garden, Inc.); and P. M. Podaskoff, S. B. MacKenzie, R. H. Moorman, and R. Fetter, "Transformational Leader Behaviors and Their Effects on Followers' Trust in Leader, Satisfaction, and Organizational Citizenship Behaviors," *Leadership Quarterly* 1, no. 2 (1990), pp. 107–142.

serious harm or death. Dr. Jerome Groopman, author of *How Doctors Think*, now teaches students at Harvard Medical School to avoid common traps such as the one he fell into early in his career. As a young doctor, he listened to the complaints of an elderly patient and quickly concluded that she had indigestion. The medication he gave her provided little relief, but his mind was fixed on his initial diagnosis. As it turned out, the patient had a tear in her aorta and died in the emergency room several weeks later. It's a lesson Groopman never forgot.[31]

In contrast to the expert mind, the beginner's mind reflects the openness and innocence of a young child just learning about the world. Effective leaders strive to

NEW LEADER
ACTION MEMO

As a leader, you can train yourself to think independently. You can be curious, keep an open mind, and look at a problem or situation from multiple perspectives before reaching your conclusions.

keep open minds and cultivate an organizational environment that encourages curiosity and learning. They understand the limitations of past experience and reach out for diverse perspectives. Rather than seeing any questioning of their ideas as a threat, these leaders encourage everyone to openly debate assumptions, confront paradoxes, question perceptions, and express feelings.[32]

5-3c Systems Thinking

Systems thinking is the ability to see the synergy of the whole rather than just the separate elements of a system and to learn to reinforce or change whole system patterns.[33] With systems thinking, a leader sees the big picture and connects the dots rather than just looking at the dots in isolation. Many people have been trained to solve problems by breaking a complex system, such as an organization, into discrete parts and working to make each part perform as well as possible. However, the success of each piece does not add up to the success of the whole. In fact, sometimes changing one part to make it better actually makes the whole system function less effectively. For example, a small city embarked on a road-building program to solve traffic congestion without whole-systems thinking. With new roads available, more people began moving to the suburbs. The solution actually increased traffic congestion, delays, and pollution by enabling suburban sprawl.[34]

It is the *relationship* among the parts that form a whole system—whether it be a community, an automobile, a nonprofit agency, a human being, or a business organization—that matters. Systems thinking enables leaders to look for patterns of movement over time and focus on the qualities of rhythm, flow, direction, shape, and networks of relationships that accomplish the performance of the whole. Systems thinking is a mental discipline and framework for seeing patterns and interrelationships.

It is important to see an organizational system as a whole because of its complexity. Complexity can overwhelm leaders, undermining confidence. When leaders can see the structures that underlie complex situations, they can facilitate improvement. But it requires a focus on the big picture. Leaders can develop what David McCamus, former chairman and CEO of Xerox Canada, calls "peripheral vision"—the ability to view the organization through a wide-angle lens rather than a telephoto lens—so that they perceive how their decisions and actions affect the whole.[35]

NEW LEADER
ACTION MEMO

As a leader, you can cultivate an ability to analyze and understand the relationships among parts of a team, organization, or other system to avoid making changes that have unintended negative consequences.

An important element of systems thinking is to discern circles of causality. Peter Senge, author of *The Fifth Discipline*, argues that reality is made up of circles rather than straight lines. For example, Exhibit 5.3 shows circles of influence for increasing a retailer's profits. The events in the circle on the left are caused by the decision to increase the advertising budget to aggressively promote products. The advertising promotions increase sales, which increases profits, which provides money to further increase the advertising budget.

But another circle of causality is being influenced as well. The decision by leaders in marketing has consequences for the operations department. As sales and profits increase, the operations department is forced to stock up with greater inventory. Additional inventory creates a need for more warehouse space. Building a new warehouse causes a delay in stocking up. After the warehouse is built, new people have to be hired. All of this increases company costs, which has a negative impact on profits. Thus, understanding the consequences of their decisions via

Systems thinking
the ability to see the synergy of the whole rather than just the separate elements of a system and to learn to reinforce or change whole system patterns

EXHIBIT 5.3 Systems Thinking and Circles of Causality

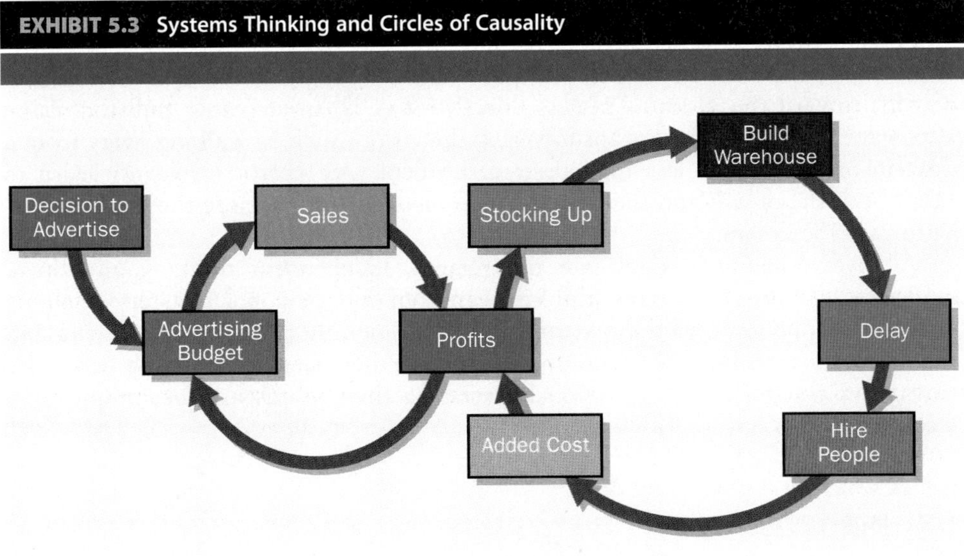

Source: Based on concepts presented in Peter M. Senge, *The Fifth Discipline: The Art and Practice of the Learning Organization* (New York: Doubleday/Currency, 1990).

circles of causality enables leaders to plan and allocate resources to warehousing as well as to advertising to ensure stable increases in sales and profits. Without understanding the system, top leaders would fail to understand why increasing the advertising budget could actually create inventory delays and temporarily reduce profits.

5-3d Personal Mastery

Another concept introduced by Senge is personal mastery. **Personal mastery** means mastering yourself in a way that facilitates your leadership and achieves desired results.[36] Mastering yourself embodies three qualities—clarity of mind, clarity of objectives, and organizing to achieve objectives.

First, *clarity of mind* means a commitment to the truth of current reality. Leaders are relentless in uncovering the mental models that limit and deceive them and are willing to challenge assumptions and standard ways of doing things. These leaders will break through denial of reality in themselves and others. Their quest for truth leads to a deeper awareness of themselves and of the larger systems and events within which they operate. Clarity of mind enables them to deal with reality, which increases the opportunity to achieve desired results.

Second, leaders engaged in personal mastery know what is important to them so that their objectives are clear. *Clarity of objectives* helps leaders focus on the end result, the vision or dream that motivates them and their team or organization. They have a clear vision of a desired future, and their purpose is to achieve that future. One element of personal mastery, then, is the discipline of continually focusing and defining what one wants as the desired future.

Third, often there is a large gap between one's vision and the current situation. The gap between the desired future and today's reality, say between the dream of starting a business and the reality of having no capital, can be discouraging. But the

> *"Self-discipline is a form of freedom. Freedom from laziness and lethargy, freedom from the expectations and demands of others, freedom from weakness and fear—and doubt. Self-discipline allows a [person] to feel his individuality, his inner strength, his talent. He is master of, rather than a slave to, his thoughts and emotions."*
>
> H. A. Dorfman, author of *The Mental Game of Baseball*

Personal mastery
the discipline of mastering yourself; it embodies clarity of mind, clarity of objectives, and organizing to achieve objectives

gap is the source of creative energy. *Organizing to achieve objectives* is a way to bridge the disparity between current reality and the vision of a better future. The effective leader lets the vision pull reality toward it by reorganizing current activities to work toward the vision. The less effective way is to let reality pull the vision downward toward it. This means lowering the vision, such as walking away from a problem or settling for less than desired. Leaders with personal mastery learn to accept both the dream and the reality simultaneously and to close the gap by moving toward the dream.

All five elements of mind are interrelated. Independent thinking and open-mindedness improve systems thinking and enable personal mastery, helping leaders shift and expand their mental models. Since they are all interdependent, leaders working to improve even one element of their mental approach can move forward in a significant way toward mastering their minds and becoming more effective.

5-4 EMOTIONAL INTELLIGENCE

Psychologists and other researchers, as well as people in all walks of life, have long recognized the importance of cognitive intelligence, or IQ, in determining a person's success and effectiveness. In general, research shows that leaders score higher than most people on tests of cognitive ability, such as IQ tests, and that cognitive ability is positively associated with effective leadership.[37] Increasingly, leaders and researchers are recognizing the critical importance of emotional intelligence, or EQ, as well. Some have suggested that emotion, more than cognitive ability, drives our thinking and decision making, as well as our interpersonal relationships.[38] In a study of leaders, two-thirds of the difference between average and top-performing leaders was found to be due to emotional competence, with only one-third due to technical skills.[39]

Emotional intelligence refers to a person's abilities to perceive, identify, understand, and successfully manage emotions in self and others. Being emotionally intelligent means being able to effectively manage ourselves and our relationships.[40] The U.S. Air Force started using EQ to select recruiters after learning that the best recruiters scored higher in EQ competencies. Leaders who score high in EQ are typically more effective and rated as more effective by peers and subordinates.[41]

5-4a What Are Emotions?

There are hundreds of emotions and more subtleties of emotion than there are words to explain them. An important ability for leaders is to understand the range of emotions people have and how these emotions may manifest themselves. One model that is useful for leaders distinguishes the major positive and negative emotions, as illustrated in Exhibit 5.4.[42] These primary emotions and some of their variations are as follows:

- *Anger*: fury, outrage, frustration, exasperation, indignation, animosity, annoyance, irritability, hostility
- *Sadness*: grief, sorrow, gloom, melancholy, self-pity, loneliness, dejection, despair, discouragement
- *Relief*: release, reassurance, ease, contentment

Emotional intelligence
a person's abilities to perceive, identify, understand, and successfully manage emotions in self and others

EXHIBIT 5.4 Positive and Negative Emotions

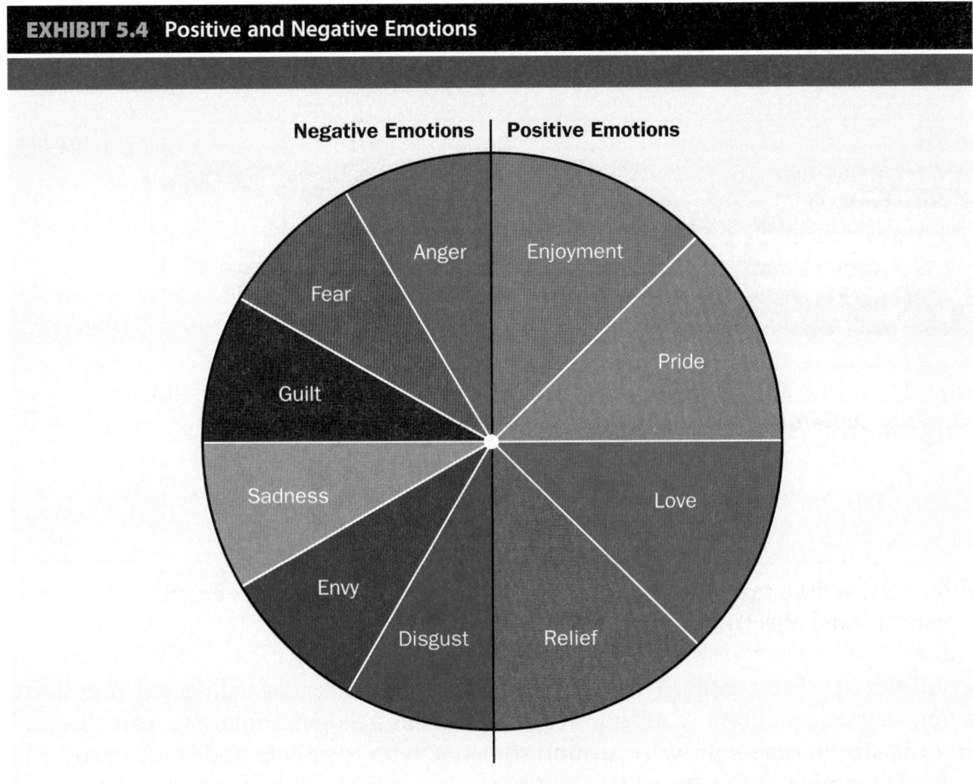

- *Fear*: anxiety, apprehension, nervousness, concern, consternation, wariness, edginess, dread, fright, terror, panic
- *Enjoyment*: happiness, joy, delight, amusement, sensual pleasure, thrill, rapture, euphoria
- *Love*: affection, acceptance, respect, friendliness, trust, kindness, affinity, devotion, adoration, infatuation
- *Envy*: jealousy, resentment, suspicion, spite
- *Disgust*: contempt, disdain, scorn, abhorrence, aversion, distaste, revulsion
- *Pride*: satisfaction, dignity, self-esteem, fulfillment
- *Guilt*: shame, embarrassment, chagrin, remorse, humiliation, regret, mortification, contrition

Some leaders act as if people leave their emotions at home when they come to work, but we all know this isn't true. Indeed, a key component of leadership is being emotionally connected to others and understanding how emotions affect working relationships and performance.

5-4b Why Are Emotions Important?

In a study of entrepreneurs, researchers at Rensselaer Polytechnic Institute found that those who are more expressive of their own emotions and more in tune with the emotions of others make more money, as illustrated in Exhibit 5.5.[43] One reason for this is that leaders who harness and direct the power of emotions to improve

EXHIBIT 5.5 Emotional Intelligence and Earning Power

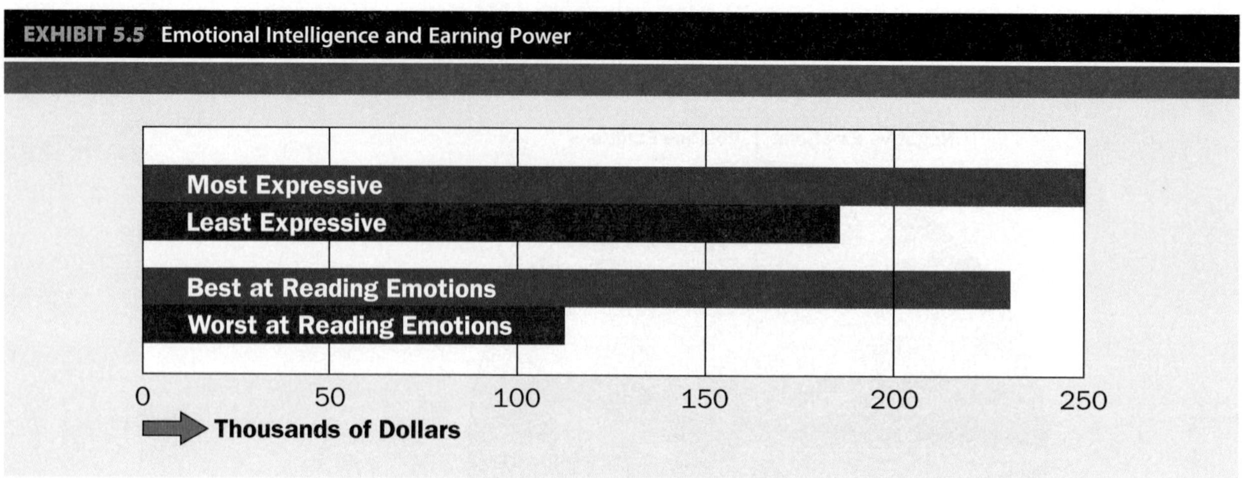

Source: Rensselaer Polytechnic Institute, Lally School of Management and Technology, as reported in *BusinessWeek Frontier* (February 5, 2001), p. F4.

followers' satisfaction, morale, and motivation get better results and enhance overall organizational effectiveness.

Emotions Are Contagious The emotional state of the leader influences the entire team, department, or organization.[44] Most of us recognize that we can "catch" emotions from others. If we're around someone who is smiling and enthusiastic, the positive emotions rub off on us. Conversely, someone in a bad mood can bring us down. At Mesa Airlines, CEO Jonathan Ornstein's former administrative assistant says she was in charge of tracking the unpredictable and frequently short-tempered leader's moods and warning other executives when they needed to stay away. "Sometimes he would come into the office in a bad mood . . . and it would set the tone for the whole office," she says.[45] This *emotional contagion* means that leaders who are able to maintain balance and keep themselves motivated can serve as positive role models to help motivate and inspire those around them. The energy level of the entire organization increases when leaders are optimistic and hopeful rather than angry or depressed. Interesting new research by organization behavior scientists suggests that negative emotions might spread more easily than positive ones because people's positive emotions are generally less influenced by other people. Psychologists have also found that negative people and events have a disproportionately large effect on our emotions and moods.[46]

Therefore, leaders recognize the importance not only of keeping their own emotions in balance but also of helping others manage negative emotions so they don't infect the entire team or organization. Leaders "tune in" to the emotional state of others, bring unhealthy or negative emotions to the surface, and encourage people to explore and use positive emotion in their everyday work.[47] One study found that untrained teams made up of members with high emotional intelligence performed as well as trained teams made up of members who rated low on emotional intelligence.[48]

Emotions Influence Performance As suggested by the team study just mentioned, emotions have a strong influence on performance. Much evidence points to a clear connection between people's moods and various aspects of their performance, such

EXHIBIT 5.6 Positive Leadership and Performance

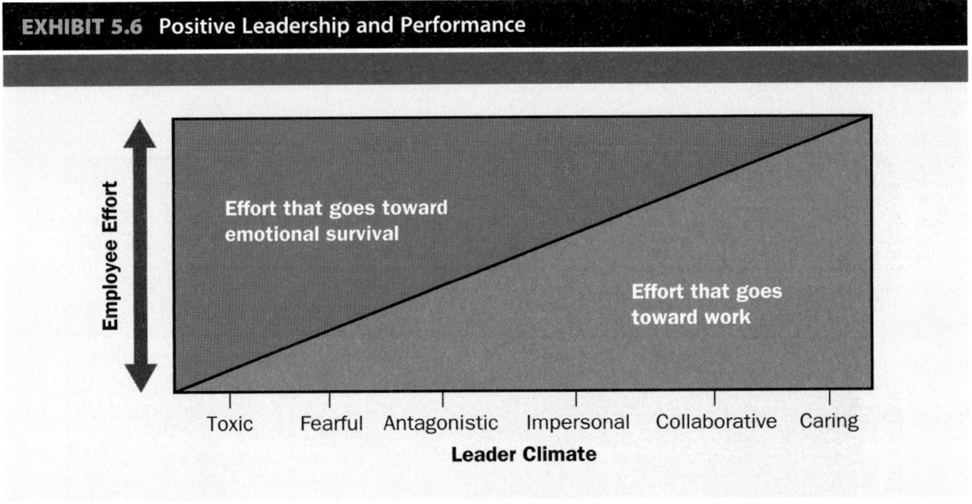

Source: Based on "Success & the Team Climate," Team Leadership Toolkit, Lindsay-Sherwin Company Web site, http://www.lindsay-sherwin.co.uk/guide_team_leadership/html_team_development/1_success_and_team_climate.htm (accessed May 13, 2011).

as teamwork, creativity, decision making, and task performance.[49] Negative moods drain energy and prevent people from doing their best.

An entire organization in a bad mood can't succeed because people have no energy and feel anxious, disillusioned, or hopeless. In this kind of toxic work environment, most of an individual's effort is used for emotional survival, as illustrated in Exhibit 5.6. In a positive environment, on the other hand, most of a person's effort is available for work. When a leader is able to unlock positive emotions of joyfulness, appreciation, or love, people's energy, creativity, and intellectual commitment expand. Employees are able to grasp more data, be more creative and resourceful in their solutions, and produce superior results. Positive emotions mean the decline of negative emotions such as sadness, anger, anxiety, and fear. Positive instead of negative emotions enable individuals to perform to the best of their abilities.[50]

A *Gallup Management Journal* survey emphasizes that leaders, especially frontline supervisors, have a lot to do with whether employees have positive or negative feelings about their work lives.[51] Research into the factors affecting mood in the workplace is growing. One thing seems clear: almost everything that influences people's moods in the workplace is under the control of leaders.[52] That is why leaders need a high degree of emotional intelligence. They have to regulate their own emotions to remain positive and hopeful and then pull others up with them.

5-4c The Components of Emotional Intelligence

In discussing Abraham Lincoln's leadership, noted historian Doris Kearns Goodwin attributes the sixteenth U.S. president's almost magical touch not to charisma or political astuteness but to emotional intelligence.[53] The competencies and abilities of emotional intelligence are grouped into four fundamental categories, as illustrated in Exhibit 5.7.[54] It is important to remember that emotional intelligence can be learned and developed. Anyone can strengthen his or her abilities in these four categories.

EXHIBIT 5.7 The Components of Emotional Intelligence

	SELF	OTHERS
AWARENESS	**Self-Awareness** • Emotional self-awareness • Accurate self-assessment • Self-confidence	**Social Awareness** • Empathy • Organizational awareness • Service orientation
BEHAVIOR	**Self-Management** • Emotional self-control • Trustworthiness • Conscientiousness • Adaptability • Optimism • Achievement-orientation • Initiative	**Relationship Management** • Development of others • Inspirational leadership • Influence • Communication • Change catalyst • Conflict management • Bond building • Teamwork and collaboration

Source: Adapted from Richard E. Boyatzis and Daniel Goleman, *The Emotional Competence Inventory—University Edition* (Boston, MA: The Hay Group, 2001).

Self-Awareness Self-awareness includes the ability to recognize and understand your own emotions and how they affect your life and work. It is the basis of all the other competencies. People who are in touch with their emotions are better able to guide their own lives. Leaders with a high level of self-awareness learn to trust their "gut feelings" and realize that these feelings can provide useful information about difficult decisions. Answers are not always clear as to whether to propose a major deal, let an employee go, reorganize a business, or revise job responsibilities. When the answers are not available from external sources, leaders have to rely on their own feelings. This component also includes the ability to accurately assess your own strengths and limitations, along with a healthy sense of self-confidence.

Self-Management The second key component, self-management, includes the ability to control disruptive, unproductive, or harmful emotions and desires. An interesting experiment from the 1960s sheds some light on the power of self-management. A group of four-year-olds and five-year-olds were offered a marshmallow, which the researcher placed in front of each child on the desk. Then, the children were told that if they could wait a few minutes while the researcher ran an errand, they would be given two marshmallows. Some children were unable to resist the temptation of a marshmallow "right now" and ate theirs immediately. Others employed all sorts of techniques, from singing or talking to themselves to hiding under the desk, to resist their impulses and earn the reward of two marshmallows instead of one. Researchers then followed the children over a period of 20 years and found some interesting results. As young men and women, the ones who had resisted the desire to eat the marshmallow revealed a much higher ability to handle stress and embrace difficult challenges. They also were more self-confident, trustworthy, dependable, and tenacious in pursuing goals.[55] The children who developed techniques for self-management early in life carried these with them into adulthood.

It is never too late for people to learn how to manage their emotions and impulses. Some leaders look to expert customer service representatives (CSRs) as role models. Research shows that 70 percent of customers who have a problem with a product or service are in a rage by the time they talk with a CSR. The best CSRs, such as Beverly Smith, who takes outpatient calls at a San Francisco medical center, and Zane Bond, who is the "go-to guy for angry callers" at a software company, have learned to control their own emotions, remain calm, and listen with warmth and empathy. When the customer calms down, the problem can usually be fixed.[56]

NEW LEADER
ACTION MEMO

As a leader, you can recognize and manage your own emotions so that negative feelings don't cloud your mind, distort your judgment, or cripple your ability to lead.

Other characteristics in this category include *trustworthiness*, which means consistently displaying honesty and integrity; *conscientiousness*, which means managing and honoring your responsibilities; and *adaptability*, which refers to the ability to adjust to changing situations and overcome obstacles. Showing initiative to seize opportunities and achieve high internal standards is also a part of self-management. Leaders skilled at self-management remain hopeful and optimistic despite obstacles, setbacks, or even outright failures. Martin Seligman, a professor of psychology at the University of Pennsylvania, once advised the MetLife insurance company to hire a special group of job applicants who tested high on optimism but failed the normal sales aptitude test. Compared to salespeople who passed the regular aptitude test but scored high on pessimism, the "optimistic" group made 21 percent more sales in their first year and 57 percent more in the second.[57]

Social Awareness The component of social awareness relates to one's ability to understand others. Socially aware leaders practice **empathy**, which means being able to put yourself in other people's shoes, sense their emotions, and understand their perspective. These leaders understand that effective leadership sometimes means pushing people beyond their comfort zone, and they are sensitive to the fear or frustration this can engender in followers. They learn to engage in "professional intimacy," which means they can display compassion and concern for others without becoming so wrapped up in others' emotions that it clouds their judgment.[58] Socially aware leaders are also capable of understanding divergent points of view and interacting effectively with many different types of people and emotions. The related characteristic of *organizational awareness* refers to the ability to navigate the currents of organizational life, build networks, and effectively use political behavior to accomplish positive results. This component also includes a *service orientation*, which refers to the ability to recognize and serve the needs of employees, customers, or clients.

Relationship Management Relationship management refers to the ability to connect with others and build positive relationships. Leaders with high emotional intelligence are aware of the impact their behaviors have on others, and they treat people with compassion, sensitivity, and kindness.[59] This aspect of EQ encompasses developing others, inspiring others with a powerful vision, learning to listen and communicate clearly and convincingly, and using emotional understanding to influence others in positive ways. Leaders use their understanding of emotions to inspire change and lead people toward something better, to build teamwork and collaboration, and to resolve conflicts that inevitably arise. These leaders cultivate and maintain a web of relationships both within and outside the organization.

Poor relationship management is one reason Jack Griffin was forced out as CEO of Time Inc. after less than six months on the job. His brusque style and inability to connect with managers doomed his job with Time. Senior executives said they

Empathy
being able to put yourself in someone else's shoes

NEW LEADER
ACTION MEMO

As a leader, you can empathize with others, treat people with compassion and sensitivity, build teamwork, and learn to listen, interpret emotions, and resolve interpersonal conflicts.

feared that top managers who had to work directly with him would begin leaving the company if Griffin stayed on much longer.[60]

Taken together, the four components shown in Exhibit 5.7 build a strong base of emotional intelligence that leaders can use to more effectively guide teams and organizations. When Google engineer Chade-Meng Tan started feeling like he was becoming a "cog in the great machine," he decided to develop a program that would help him as well as other Googlers strengthen their emotional intelligence.

IN THE LEAD

Chade-Meng Tan, Google

Chade-Meng Tan's title at Google is Jolly Good Fellow, and the position requires him to "enlighten minds, open hearts, create world peace." Tan got the appointment to Jolly Good Fellow because of an influential course he developed called "Search Inside Yourself." Tan worked with a team that included outside consultants, a Stanford scientist, and Marc Lesser, a Zen teacher with an MBA and experience as an entrepreneur. Lesser explains that the course is based on the components of emotional intelligence, "or, as we call them, leadership skills."

Everyone at Google has to be a leader, and at Google leadership is equated with mindfulness and emotional intelligence. In 2015, approximately 1,500 Googlers went through the training and thousands were on a waiting list for future open seats. The goal of the program is to help people become more aware of their emotions, develop greater empathy and compassion toward others, and be more able to build enduring relationships. Greater emotional intelligence, Lesser says, also improves communication and collaboration by enabling people to think calmly and clearly, listen more closely to others, and be more mindful.[61]

The first Search Inside Yourself course was offered in 2007, and five years later Tan and his team made the course available to organizations outside of Google. Today, Lesser serves as CEO of the nonprofit Search Inside Yourself Leadership Institute (SIYLI) and Tan's book, also called *Search Inside Yourself*, has been endorsed by the Dalai Lama and former U.S. President Jimmy Carter. One research project suggests that all effective leadership styles arise from different components of emotional intelligence.[62]

NEW LEADER
ACTION MEMO

Evaluate your level of emotional intelligence by completing the questionnaire in Leader's Self-Insight 5.2.

Emotional intelligence is crucial for building a work environment that many of today's organizations want—one in which leaders are more interactive than "command-and-control," where leadership is spread across all levels, and where individual goals are met through teamwork, connection, and collaboration. In an environment where relationships with employees and customers are becoming more important than technology and material resources, interest in developing leaders' emotional intelligence continues to grow. Moreover, there is growing evidence that emotional intelligence has a positive influence on many aspects of leader performance.[63]

A high level of self-awareness and an ability to manage one's own emotions enable a leader to display self-confidence, earn respect and trust, and consider the needs of others. Emotionally competent leaders are more resilient, more adaptable to ever-changing circumstances, more willing to step outside their comfort zone, and more open to the opinions and ideas of others.[64]

LEADER'S SELF-INSIGHT 5.2

Emotional Intelligence

Instructions: For each of the following items, rate how well you display the behavior described. Before responding, try to think of actual situations in which you have had the opportunity to use the behavior. Indicate whether each item is Mostly False or Mostly True for you.

	Mostly False	Mostly True
1. Associate different internal physiological cues with different emotions.		
2. Relax when under pressure in situations.		
3. Know the impact that your behavior has on others.		
4. Initiate successful resolution of conflict with others.		
5. Know when you are becoming angry.		
6. Recognize when others are distressed.		
7. Build consensus with others.		
8. Produce motivation when doing uninteresting work.		
9. Help others manage their emotions.		
10. Make others feel good.		
11. Identify when you experience mood shifts.		
12. Stay calm when you are the target of anger from others.		
13. Know when you become defensive.		
14. Follow your words with actions.		
15. Engage in intimate conversations with others.		
16. Accurately reflect people's feelings back to them.		

Scoring and Interpretation

Sum your Mostly True responses to the 16 questions to obtain your overall emotional intelligence score. Your score for self-awareness is the total of questions 1, 5, 11, and 13. Your score for self-management is the total of questions 2, 8, 12, and 14. Your score for social awareness is the sum of questions 3, 6, 9, and 15. Your score for relationship management is the sum of questions 4, 7, 10, and 16. This questionnaire provides some indication of your emotional intelligence. If you received a total score of 14 or more, you are certainly considered a person with high emotional intelligence. A score from 10 to 13 means you have a good platform of emotional intelligence from which to develop your leadership capability. A score of 7 to 9 would be moderate emotional intelligence. A score below 7 indicates that you realize that you are probably below average in emotional intelligence.

For each of the four components of emotional intelligence—self-awareness, self-management, social awareness, and relationship management—a score of 4 is considered high, whereas a score of 2 or fewer would be considered low. Review the discussion in this chapter about the four components of emotional intelligence and think about what you might do to develop those areas where you scored low. Compare your scores to those of other students. What can you do to improve your scores?

Source: Adapted from Hendrie Weisinger, *Emotional Intelligence at Work* (San Francisco: Jossey-Bass, 1998), pp. 214–215.

Perhaps most importantly, emotional intelligence enables leaders to recognize and respect followers as whole human beings with feelings, opinions, and ideas of their own. They can use their emotional intelligence to help followers grow and develop, see and enhance their self-image and feelings of self-worth, and help meet their needs and achieve personal and organizational goals.

NEW LEADER
ACTION MEMO

As a leader, you can develop emotional intelligence and act as a positive role model by being optimistic and enthusiastic.

5-5 LEADING WITH LOVE VERSUS LEADING WITH FEAR

Traditionally, leadership has been based on inspiring fear in employees. An unspoken notion among many senior-level executives is that fear is a good thing and benefits the organization.[65] Indeed, fear can be a powerful motivator, but many of today's leaders are learning that an environment that reflects care and respect for

LEADER'S SELF-INSIGHT 5.3

Love or Fear?

Instructions: The following items describe reasons why you work. *Answer the questions twice*, the first time for doing work (or homework) that is not your favorite and the second time for doing a hobby or sports activity that you enjoy. *Consider each item thoughtfully and respond according to your inner motivation and experience.* Indicate whether each item is Mostly False or Mostly True for you.

	Mostly False	Mostly True
1. I feel it is important to perform well so I don't look bad.	______	✓
2. I have to force myself to complete the task.	______	✓
3. I don't want to have a poor outcome or get a poor grade.	______	✓
4. I don't want to embarrass myself or do less well than others.	______	✓
5. The experience leaves me feeling relieved that it is over.	______	✓
6. My attention is absorbed entirely in what I am doing.	______	✓
7. I really enjoy the experience.	______	✓
8. Time seems to pass more quickly than normal.	______	✓
9. I am completely focused on the task at hand.	______	✓
10. The experience leaves me feeling great.	______	✓

Scoring and Interpretation

These items reflect motivation shaped by either love or fear. Your "fear of failure" score is the number of Mostly True answers for questions 1–5. Your "love of task" score is the number of Mostly True answers for questions 6–10. A score of 4 or 5 would be considered high for either love or fear, and a score of 0–2 would be considered low. You would probably score more points for "love of task" for your hobby or sports activity than for homework.

Some people are motivated by high internal standards and fear of not meeting those standards. This may be called fear of failure, which often spurs people to great accomplishment. Love of task provides a great intrinsic pleasure but won't always lead to high achievement. Love of task is related to the idea of "flow" wherein people become fully engaged and derive great satisfaction from their activity. Would love or fear influence your choice to become a leader or how you try to motivate others? Discuss with other students the relative importance of love or fear motivation in your lives.

Love in the workplace means genuinely caring for others and sharing one's knowledge, understanding, and compassion to enable others to grow and succeed.

people is much more effective than one in which people are fearful. When organizational success depended primarily on people mindlessly following orders, leading with fear often met the organization's needs. Today, though, success in most organizations depends on the knowledge, mindpower, commitment, creativity, and enthusiasm of everyone in the organization. A fear-based organization loses its best people, and the knowledge they take with them, to other firms. In addition, even if people stay with the organization, they typically don't perform up to their real capabilities. As discussed earlier, there is evidence that people who experience positive emotions at work perform better.[66]

NEW LEADER
ACTION MEMO

To learn about your own motivations concerning love versus fear, complete the exercise in Leader's Self-Insight 5.3.

Showing respect and trust also allows people to feel emotionally connected with their work so that their lives are richer and more balanced. Leaders can rely on negative emotions such as fear to fuel productive work, but by doing so they may slowly destroy people's spirits, which ultimately is bad for employees and the organization.[67] Consider, for example, that two-thirds of employees surveyed said their performance declined after being the victim of rudeness or hostility at work. Four out of five said they lost work time fretting about the unpleasant incident, three-quarters said their commitment to their employer declined, and 12 percent even quit their jobs.[68]

5-5a Fear in Organizations

The workplace can hold many kinds of fear, including fear of failure, fear of change, fear of personal loss, fear of being judged, and fear of the boss. All of these fears can prevent people from doing their best, from taking risks, and from challenging and changing the status quo. Consider how Akshay Kothari and Ankit Gupta had to overcome their fears to create one of the 50 original apps in Apple's App Store Hall of Fame.

IN THE LEAD

Akshay Kothari and Ankit Gupta, Pulse News

Akshay Kothari and Ankit Gupta were graduate students at Stanford University's acclaimed d.school (formally known as the Hasso Plattner Institute of Design) when they took a class designed to get people out of their comfort zones so they could confront and overcome the fears that stand in the way of creativity and goal achievement.

Both were self-described "geeks." Although they were technically brilliant, shyness often prevented them from pursuing goals that involved too much interaction with people. To fight the fear, they decided to work on their class project—a news reader for the then newly released iPad—at a café off campus. Approaching strangers and asking for feedback on their ideas and prototype was definitely a stretch for the two, and the negative feedback often hurt.

But, over time, Akshay says, they went "from people saying 'This is crap,' to 'Is this app preloaded on every iPad?'" The result of their project, Pulse News, was praised by Steve Jobs at a worldwide developer's conference, won the prestigious Apple Design award, and has been downloaded by more than 20 million people.[69]

Overcoming their fears not only enabled Akshay Kothari and Ankit Gupta to complete a successful class project, it gave them the confidence to found a company that revolutionized the mobile news reading experience. Pulse is expanding into social media with the addition of Pulse Highlights, which allows users to see when their friends have shared the story they are reading. That means people can go to Pulse not only to read content from sites they trust but also to discover new sources and stories.[70]

NEW LEADER
ACTION MEMO

As a leader, you can choose to lead with love, not with fear. You can show respect and trust toward followers and help people to learn, grow, and contribute their best to achieve the organization's vision.

Consequences of Fear Fear gets in the way of people feeling good about their work, themselves, and the organization. It creates an atmosphere in which people feel powerless, so that their confidence, commitment, enthusiasm, imagination, and motivation are diminished.[71] One major drawback of leading with fear is that it creates avoidance behavior because no one wants to make a mistake. Fear in the workplace weakens trust and communication. Employees feel threatened by repercussions if they speak up about work-related concerns. A survey of employees in 22 organizations found that 70 percent of them "bit their tongues" at work because they feared repercussions. Twenty-seven percent reported that they feared losing their credibility or reputation if they spoke up. Other fears reported were lack of career advancement, possible damage to the relationship with their supervisor, demotion or losing their job, and being embarrassed or humiliated in front of others.[72] When people are afraid to speak up, important issues are suppressed and problems hidden. Employees are afraid to talk about a wide range of issues, but by far the largest category of "undiscussables" is the behavior of executives,

EXHIBIT 5.8 Indicators of Love versus Fear in Organizations

Fear-Driven Indicators	Love-Driven Indicators
Caution and secrecy	Openness and authenticity, even when it's difficult
Blaming and attacking	Understanding diverse viewpoints
Excessive control	Expecting others to do great things
Sideline criticalness	Involvement and discernment
Coming unglued	Keeping perspective
Aloofness and distance	Interpersonal connection
Resistance hidden	Resistance out in open, explored

Source: Daniel Holden, "Team Development: A Search for Elegance," *Industrial Management* (September–October 2007), pp. 20–25. Copyright © by Institute of Industrial Engineers.

particularly their interpersonal and relationship skills. When leaders inspire fear, they destroy the opportunity for feedback, blinding them to reality and denying them the chance to correct damaging decisions and behaviors.

Relationship with Leaders Leaders control the fear level in the organization. Exhibit 5.8 outlines some indicators of love-based versus fear-based leadership in organizations.[73] Organizations driven by love are marked by openness and authenticity, a respect for diverse viewpoints, and emphasis on positive interpersonal relationships. Organizations driven by fear, on the other hand, are characterized by cautiousness and secrecy, blaming others, excessive control, and emotional distance among people. The relationship between an employee and his or her direct supervisor is the primary factor determining the level of fear experienced at work. Unfortunately, the legacy of fear and mistrust associated with traditional hierarchies in which bosses gave orders and employees jumped to obey "or else" still colors life in many organizations. Leaders can create a new environment that enables people to feel safe speaking their minds. Leaders can act from love rather than fear to free employees and the organization from the chains of the past.

5-5b Bringing Love to Work

Leaders can learn to bind people together for a shared purpose through positive forces such as caring and compassion, listening, and connecting to others on a personal level. The emotion that attracts people to take risks, learn, grow, and move the organization forward comes from love, not fear. Leaders should also remember that love is more than a feeling; to be a real force, it is translated into behavior. Stephen Covey points out that in all the great literature, love is a verb rather than a noun.[74] Love is something you do, the sacrifices you make, and the giving of yourself to others, as illustrated by the poignant story in this chapter's *Consider This*.

Organizations have traditionally rewarded people for strong qualities such as rational thinking, ambition, and competitiveness. These qualities are important, but their overemphasis has left many organizational leaders out of touch with their softer, caring, creative capabilities, unable to make emotional connections with others and afraid to risk showing any sign of weakness or emotion. What does it mean to lead with love? In all groups and organizations feelings of compassion, respect, and loyalty are translated into action, such as acts of friendliness, teamwork, cooperation, listening, understanding, and serving others above oneself. Sentiments emerge as action. Exhibit 5.9 shows results of an exercise in which people

Consider **This!**

The Greatest Is Love

Army Staff Sgt. Ian Newland saw the enemy grenade land in his Humvee. In the next instant, his friend Ross McGinnis threw himself onto that grenade. "I try not to live my life in vain for what he's done," said Newland. When asked why McGinnis did it, Newland simply said, "He loved us."

During the Iraq war, at least five U.S. soldiers died because they used their own bodies to shield their comrades from grenades. "What a decision that is," said Temple University psychologist Frank Farley. "I can't think of anything more profound in human nature." A Navy lieutenant said of a comrade who sacrificed his life by blocking a grenade thrown onto a rooftop near his team, "You think about him every day. And everything pretty much revolves around what he did."

Source: Based on Gregg Zoroya, "Coping After a Hero Dies Saving You in Iraq," *USA Today* (September 20, 2007).

EXHIBIT 5.9 The Practical Aspects and Outcomes of Caring About Others

What do you do when you care for someone?*	What does it feel like to be cared about?*
1. reach out	1. valuable
2. embrace, hug	2. alive
3. be there with them	3. responsive
4. compassion	4. positive outlook
5. acceptance	5. exhilarated
6. share dreams	6. respect
7. acknowledge accomplishments	7. free
8. trust	8. important
9. encourage	9. good
10. be a cheerleader	10. safe
11. tell you care	11. more open to express yourself
12. relate feelings	12. elevates self-esteem
13. respect them	13. boosts morale
14. be positive	14. proud
15. give them a smile	15. loved
16. give them time	16. worthy
17. give them recognition	17. blessed
18. protect	18. you make a difference
19. reassure	19. fulfilled
20. celebrate with	20. happy

*These are the actual, unedited words called out by participants and written on a whiteboard during a seminar at which people were asked these two questions.

Source: Marilyn R. Zuckerman and Lewis J. Hatala, *Incredibly American: Releasing the Heart of Quality.* © 1992. American Society for Quality. Reprinted with permission from the authors.

reported what they do to show others they care and what it feels like to be cared about. Leaders who fail often do so because they are blind to the importance of the attributes in Exhibit 5.9. Sometimes leaders act from their own fear, which creates fear in others. A leader's fear can manifest itself in arrogance, selfishness, deception, unfairness, and disrespect for others.[75]

5-5c Why Followers Respond to Love

Most people yearn for more than a paycheck from their jobs. Leaders who lead with love have extraordinary influence because they meet five unspoken employee needs:

Hear and understand me.
Even if you disagree with me, please don't make me wrong.
Acknowledge the greatness within me.
Remember to look for my loving intentions.
Tell me the truth with compassion.[76]

When leaders address these subtle emotional needs directly, people typically respond by loving their work and becoming emotionally engaged in solving problems and serving customers. Enthusiasm for work and the organization increases. People want to believe that their leaders genuinely care. From the followers' point of view, love versus fear has different motivational potential.

- **Fear-based motivation**: I need a job to pay for my basic needs (fulfilling lower needs of the body). You give me a job and I will give you just enough to keep my job.
- **Love-based motivation**: If the job and the leader make me feel valued as a person and provide a sense of meaning and contribution to the community at large (fulfilling higher needs of heart, mind, and body), then I will give you all I have to offer.[77]

Many examples throughout this book illustrate what happens when positive emotion is used. One management consultant went so far as to advise that finding creative ways to love could solve every imaginable leadership problem.[78] Rational thinking and technical skills are important, but leading with love builds trust, stimulates creativity, inspires commitment, and unleashes boundless energy.

Leaders can develop their capacity for the positive emotions of love and caring. When Walt Bettinger, president and CEO of Charles Schwab, was in college, he learned a lesson he tries to apply every day. The professor handed each student a blank sheet of paper and gave them one final exam question: *What's the name of the lady who cleans this building?* The students had spent four hours a night twice a week in the building for 10 weeks, encountering the cleaning lady several times a night as they went to get a soft drink or use the restroom. Bettinger says, "I didn't know Dottie's name—her name was Dottie—but I've tried to know every Dottie since."[79]

Fear-based motivation motivation based on fear of losing a job

Love-based motivation motivation based on feeling valued in the job

LEADERSHIP ESSENTIALS

- Leaders use emotional as well as intellectual capabilities and understandings to guide organizations through a turbulent environment and help people feel energized, motivated, and cared for in the face of rapid change, uncertainty, and job insecurity. People can learn to be *whole leaders* who lead with both the head and the heart.

- Leaders should be aware of how their mental models affect their thinking and may cause "blind spots" that limit understanding. Becoming aware of assumptions is a first step toward shifting or expanding one's mental model and being able to see the world in new and different ways. One challenge for today's leaders is developing a global mindset.
- Four key issues important to expanding and developing a leader's mind are independent thinking, open-mindedness, systems thinking, and personal mastery. Personal mastery involves clarity of mind, clarity of objectives, and an organized system for achieving objectives.
- Leaders should also understand the importance of emotions and emotional intelligence. Understanding emotions is imperative because emotions are contagious and emotions influence individuals' performance.
- Four basic components of emotional intelligence are self-awareness, self-management, social awareness, and relationship management. Emotionally intelligent leaders can have a positive impact on organizations by helping employees grow, learn, and develop; creating a sense of purpose and meaning; instilling unity and team spirit; and basing relationships on trust and respect, which allows employees to take risks and fully contribute to the organization.
- Traditional organizations have relied on fear as a motivator. Although fear does motivate people, it prevents people from feeling good about their work and often causes avoidance behavior. Fear can reduce trust and communication so that important problems and issues are hidden or suppressed. Leaders can choose to lead with love instead of fear. Love can be thought of as a motivational force that enables people to feel alive, connected, and energized. People respond to love because it meets unspoken needs for respect and affirmation. Rational thinking is important to leadership, but it takes love to build trust, creativity, and enthusiasm.

DISCUSSION QUESTIONS

1. How do you feel about developing the emotional qualities of yourself and other people in the organization as a way to be an effective leader? Discuss.
2. What does it mean to be a *whole leader* as described in the chapter? Can you give an example from your experience? Discuss.
3. Why is it so hard for people to change their assumptions? What are some specific reasons why leaders need to be aware of their mental models?
4. Discuss the similarities and differences between mental models and open-mindedness.
5. What is the concept of personal mastery? How important is it to a leader?
6. Which of the four elements of emotional intelligence do you consider most essential to an effective leader? Why?
7. Consider fear and love as potential motivators. Which is the best source of motivation for college students? For members of a new product development team? For top executives at a media conglomerate? Why?
8. Have you ever experienced love and/or fear from leaders at work? How did you respond? Is it possible that leaders might carry love too far and create negative rather than positive results? Discuss.

9. Do you think it is appropriate for a leader to spend time developing people's emotional intelligence? Why or why not?
10. Think about the class for which you are reading this text as a system. How might making changes without whole-systems thinking cause problems for students?

LEADERSHIP AT WORK

Mentors

Think of a time when someone reached out to you as a mentor or coach. This might have been a time when you were having some difficulty and the person who reached out would have done so out of concern for you rather than for their own self-interest.

Below, briefly describe the situation, who the mentor was, and what the mentor did for you.

____

____

____

Mentoring comes from the heart, is a generous act, and is usually deeply appreciated by the recipient. How does it feel to recall the situation in which a mentor assisted you?

____

____

____

Share your experience with one or more students. What are the common characteristics that mentors possess based on your combined experiences?

____

____

____

In Class: A discussion of experiences with mentors is excellent for small groups. The instructor can ask each group to identify the common characteristics that their mentors displayed and each group's conclusions can be written on the board. From these lists of mentor characteristics, common themes associated with mentors can be defined. The instructor can ask the class the following questions: What are the key characteristics of mentors? Based on the key mentor characteristics, is effective mentoring based more on a person's heart or mind? Will you (the student) reach out as a mentor to others in life, and how will you do it? What factors might prevent you from doing so?

LEADERSHIP DEVELOPMENT: CASES FOR ANALYSIS

The New Boss

Sam Nolan clicked the mouse for one more round of solitaire on the computer in his den. He'd been at it for more than an hour, and his wife had long ago given up trying to persuade him to join her for a movie or a rare Saturday night on the town. The mind-numbing game seemed to be all that calmed Sam down enough to stop agonizing about work and how his job seemed to get worse every day.

Nolan was chief information officer at Century Medical, a large medical products company based in Connecticut. He had joined the company four years ago, and since that time Century had made great progress integrating technology into its systems and processes. Nolan had already led projects to design and build two highly successful systems for Century. One was a benefits-administration system for the company's human resources department. The other was a complex Web-based purchasing system that streamlined the process of purchasing supplies and capital goods. Although the system had been up and running for only a few months, modest projections were that it would save Century nearly $2 million annually. The new Web-based system dramatically cut the time needed for processing requests and placing orders. Purchasing managers now had more time to work collaboratively with key stakeholders to identify and select the best suppliers and negotiate better deals.

Nolan thought wearily of all the hours he had put in developing trust with people throughout the company and showing them how technology could not only save time and money but also support team-based work, encourage open information sharing, and give people more control over their own jobs. He smiled briefly as he recalled one long-term HR employee, 61-year-old Ethel Moore. She had been terrified when Nolan first began showing her the company's intranet, but she was now one of his biggest supporters. In fact, it had been Ethel who had first approached him with an idea about a Web-based job posting system. The two had pulled together a team and developed an idea for linking Century managers, internal recruiters, and job applicants using artificial intelligence software on top of an integrated Web-based system. When Nolan had presented the idea to his boss, executive vice president Sandra Ivey, she had enthusiastically endorsed it. Within a few weeks the team had authorization to proceed with the project.

But everything began to change when Ivey resigned her position six months later to take a plum job in New York. Ivey's successor, Tom Carr, seemed to have little interest in the project. During their first meeting, Carr had openly referred to the project as a waste of time and money. He immediately disapproved several new features suggested by the company's internal recruiters, even though the project team argued that the features could double internal hiring and save millions in training costs. "Just stick to the original plan and get it done. All this stuff needs to be handled on a personal basis anyway," Carr countered. "You can't learn more from a computer than you can talking to real people—and as for internal recruiting, it shouldn't be so hard to talk to people if they're already working right here in the company." Carr seemed to have no understanding of how and why technology was being used. He became irritated when Ethel Moore referred to the system as "Web-based." He boasted that he had never visited Century's intranet site and suggested that "this Internet obsession" would blow over in a few years anyway. Even Ethel's enthusiasm couldn't get through to him. "Technology is for those people in the IS department. My job is people, and yours should be, too," Carr shouted. Near the end of the meeting, Carr even jokingly suggested that the project team should just buy a couple of good filing cabinets and save everyone some time and money.

Nolan sighed and leaned back in his chair. The whole project had begun to feel like a joke. The vibrant and innovative human resources department his team had imagined now seemed like nothing more than a pipe dream. But despite his frustration, a new thought entered Nolan's mind: "Is Carr just stubborn and narrow-minded or does he have a point that HR is a people business that doesn't need a high-tech job posting system?"

QUESTIONS

1. Describe the two different mental models represented in this story.
2. What are some of the assumptions that shape the mindset of Sam Nolan? Of Tom Carr?
3. Do you think it is possible for Carr to shift to a new mental model? If you were Sam Nolan, what would you do?

Sources: Based on Carol Hildebrand, "New Boss Blues," *CIO Enterprise*, Section 2 (November 15, 1998), pp. 53–58; and Megan Santosus, "Advanced Micro Devices' Web-Based Purchasing System," *CIO*, Section 1 (May 15, 1998), p. 84. A version of this case originally appeared in Richard L. Daft, *Organization Theory and Design*, 7th ed. (Cincinnati, OH: South-Western, 2001), pp. 270–271.

The USS *Florida*

The atmosphere in a Trident nuclear submarine is generally calm and quiet. Even pipe joints are cushioned to prevent noise that might tip off a pursuer. The Trident ranks among the world's most dangerous weapons—swift, silent, and armed with 24 long-range missiles carrying 192 nuclear warheads. Trident crews are the cream of the Navy crop, and even the sailors who fix the plumbing exhibit a white-collar decorum. The culture aboard ship is a low-key, collegial one in which sailors learn to speak softly and share close quarters with an ever-changing roster of shipmates. Being subject to strict security restrictions enhances a sense of elitism and pride. To move up and take charge of a Trident submarine is an extraordinary feat in the Navy—fewer than half the officers qualified for such commands ever get them. When Michael Alfonso took charge of the USS *Florida*, the crew welcomed his arrival. They knew he was one of them—a career Navy man who joined up as a teenager and moved up through the ranks. Past shipmates remembered him as basically a loner, who could be brusque but generally pleasant enough. Neighbors on shore found Alfonso to be an unfailingly polite man who kept mostly to himself.

The crew's delight in their new captain was short-lived. Commander Alfonso moved swiftly to assume command, admonishing his sailors that he would push them hard. He wasn't joking—soon after the *Florida* slipped into deep waters to begin a postoverhaul shakedown cruise, the new captain loudly and publicly reprimanded those whose performance he considered lacking. Chief Petty Officer Donald MacArthur, chief of the navigation division, was only one of those who suffered Alfonso's anger personally. During training exercises, MacArthur was having trouble keeping the boat at periscope depth because of rough seas. Alfonso announced loudly, "You're disqualified." He then precipitously relieved him of his diving duty until he could be recertified by extra practice. Word of the incident spread quickly. Crew members, accustomed to the Navy's adage of "praise in public, penalize in private," were shocked. It didn't take long for this type of behavior to have an impact on the crew, according to Petty Officer Aaron Carmody: "People didn't tell him when something was wrong. You're not supposed to be afraid of your captain, to tell him stuff. But nobody wanted to."

The captain's outbursts weren't always connected with job performance. He bawled out the supply officer, the executive officer, and the chief of the boat because the soda dispenser he used to pour himself a glass of Coke one day contained Mr. Pibb instead. He exploded when he arrived unexpectedly at a late-night meal and found the fork at his place setting missing. Soon, a newsletter titled *The Underground* was being circulated by the boat's plumbers, who used sophomoric humor to spread the word about the captain's outbursts over such petty matters. By the time the sub reached Hawaii for its "Tactical Readiness Evaluation," an intense week-long series of inspections by staff officers, the crew was almost completely alienated. Although the ship tested well, inspectors sent word to Rear Admiral Paul Sullivan that something seemed to be wrong on board, with severely strained relations between captain and crew. On the Trident's last evening of patrol, much of the crew celebrated with a film night—they chose *The Caine Mutiny* and *Crimson Tide*, both movies about Navy skippers who face mutinies and are relieved of command at sea. When Humphrey Bogart, playing the captain of the fictional USS *Caine*, exploded over a missing quart of strawberries, someone shouted, "Hey, sound familiar?"

When they reached home port, the sailors slumped ashore. "Physically and mentally, we were just beat into the ground," recalls one. Concerned about reports that the crew seemed "despondent," Admiral Sullivan launched an informal inquiry that eventually led him to relieve Alfonso of his command. It was the first-ever firing of a Trident submarine commander. "He had the chance of a lifetime to experience the magic of command, and he squandered it," Sullivan said. "Fear and intimidation lead to certain ruin." Alfonso himself seemed dumbfounded by Admiral Sullivan's actions, pointing out that the USS *Florida* under his command posted "the best-ever grades assigned for certifications and inspections for a postoverhaul Trident submarine."

QUESTIONS

1. Analyze Alfonso's impact on the crew in terms of love versus fear. What might account for the fact that he behaved so strongly as captain of the USS *Florida*?
2. Which do you think a leader should be more concerned about aboard a nuclear submarine—high certification grades or high-quality interpersonal relationships? Do you agree with Admiral Sullivan's decision to fire Alfonso? Discuss.
3. Discuss Commander Alfonso's level of emotional intelligence in terms of the four components listed in the chapter. What advice would you give him?

Source: Based on Thomas E. Ricks, "A Skipper's Chance to Run a Trident Sub Hits Stormy Waters," *The Wall Street Journal* (November 20, 1997), pp. A1, A6.

REFERENCES

1. Thomas E. Ricks, "Charmed Forces: Army's 'Baby Generals' Take a Crash Course in Sensitivity Training," *The Wall Street Journal* (January 19, 1998), p. A1.
2. Warren Bennis, quoted in Tricia Bisoux, "What Makes Great Leaders," *BizEd* (September–October 2005), pp. 40–45.
3. Stacey Philpot, "Whole Leadership," *Leadership Excellence* (July 2010), p. 6.
4. This basic idea is found in a number of sources, among them Jack Hawley, *Reawakening the Spirit in Work* (San Francisco: Berrett-Koehler, 1993); Aristotle, *The Nicomachean Ethics*, trans. by the Brothers of the English Dominican Province, rev. by Daniel J. Sullivan (Chicago: Encyclopedia Britannica, 1952); Alasdair MacIntyre, *After Virtue: A Study in Moral Theory* (Notre Dame, IN: University of Notre Dame Press, 1984); and Stephen Covey, *The Seven Habits of Highly Effective People: Powerful Lessons in Personal Change* (New York: Fireside Books/Simon & Schuster, 1990).
5. W. B. Rouse and N. M. Morris, "On Looking Into the Black Box: Prospects and Limits in the Search for Mental Models," *Psychological Bulletin* 100 (1986), pp. 349–363; Beng-Chong Lim and Katherine J. Klein, "Team Mental Models and Team Performance: A Field Study of the Effects of Team Mental Model Similarity and Accuracy," *Journal of Organizational Behavior* 27 (2006), pp. 403–418; Vanessa Urch Druskat and Anthony T. Pescosolido, "The Content of Effective Teamwork Mental Models in Self-Managing Teams: Ownership, Learning, and Heedful Interrelating," *Human Relations* 55, no. 3 (2002), pp. 283–314; and Peter M. Senge, *The Fifth Discipline: The Art and Practice of the Learning Organization* (New York: Doubleday, 1990).
6. From Robert Townsend, *Up the Organization*, quoted in "Everything You Wanted to Know about Leadership, from the Man Who Broke All the Rules," *The Conference Board Review* (September–October 2007), pp. 37–41.
7. Adam Lashinsky, "Chaos by Design," *Fortune* (October 2, 2006), pp. 86–98.
8. The following discussion is based partly on Robert C. Benfari, *Understanding and Changing Your Management Style* (San Francisco: Jossey-Bass, 1999), pp. 66–93.
9. Stephanie Clifford, "Chief's Silicon Valley Stardom Quickly Clashed at J.C. Penney," *The New York Times* (April 9, 2013), http://www.nytimes.com/2013/04/10/business/how-an-apple-star-lost-his-luster-at-penneys.html?emc=eta1&_r=0 (accessed April 24, 2013); Stephanie Clifford, "J.C. Penney Ousts Chief of 17 Months," *The New York Times*, April 8, 2013, http://www.nytimes.com/2013/04/09/business/ron-johnson-out-as-jc-penney-chief.html?pagewanted=all&_r=0 (accessed April 24, 2013); and Andrew Ross Sorkin, "A Dose of Realism for the Chief of J.C. Penney," *The New York Times*, November 12, 2011, http://dealbook.nytimes.com/2012/11/12/a-dose-of-realism-for-the-chief-of-j-c-penney/ (accessed March 26, 2013).
10. Anthony J. Mayo and Nitin Nohria, *In Their Time: The Greatest Business Leaders of the 20th Century* (Boston: Harvard Business School Press, 2005).
11. Prasad Kajpa, "Steve Jobs and the Art of Mental Model Innovation," *Ivey Business Journal* (May–June 2012), http://www.iveybusinessjournal.com/topics/leadership/steve-jobs-and-the-art-of-mental-model-innovation (accessed March 26, 2013); David J. Glew, Stephen C. Harper, and Jonathan D. Rowe, "Is Your Organization a Target?" *Industrial Management* (November–December 2010), pp. 15–20; Geoffrey Colvin, "The Most Valuable Quality in a Manager," *Fortune* (December 29, 1997), pp. 279–280; and Marlene Piturro, "Mindshift," *Management Review* (May 1999), pp. 46–51.
12. Based on Kevin Clark, "The Coach Who Won't Leave the Locker Room," *The Wall Street Journal* (October 13, 2015), http://www.wsj.com/articles/the-coach-who-wont-leave-the-locker-room-1444755991 (accessed October 15, 2015).
13. Kajpa, "Steve Jobs and the Art of Mental Model Innovation."
14. Glew et al., "Is Your Organization a Target?"; Gary Hamel, "Why . . . It's Better to Question Answers Than to Answer Questions," *Across the Board* (November–December 2000), pp. 42–46; and Jane C. Linder and Susan Cantrell, "It's All in the Mind (set)," *Across the Board* (May–June 2002), pp. 39–42.
15. This section is based on Schon Beechler and Dennis Baltzley, "Creating a Global Mindset," *Chief Learning Officer* (May 29, 2008), http://clomedia.com/articles/view/creating_a_global_mindset/1 (accessed June 26, 2012); Mansour Javidan and Jennie L. Walker, "A Whole New Global Mindset for Leadership," *People & Strategy* 35, no. 2 (2012), pp. 36–41; and Stephen L. Cohen, "Effective Global Leadership Requires a Global Mindset," *Industrial and Commercial Training* 42, no. 1 (2010), pp. 3–10.
16. Definition based on Mansour Javidan and Mary B. Teagarden, "Conceptualizing and Measuring Global Mindset," *Advanced in Global Leadership* 6 (2011), pp. 13–39; and Beechler and Baltzley, "Creating a Global Mindset."
17. Ken Powell, interviewed by Beth Kowitt, "Move Beyond Your Comfort Zone," *Fortune* (May 4, 2009), p. 48.
18. Anil K. Gupta and Vijay Govindarajan, "Cultivating a Global Mindset," *Academy of Management Executive* 16, no. 1 (2002), pp. 116–126.
19. Hamel, "Why . . . It's Better to Question Answers Than to Answer Questions"; Geoffrey Colvin, "Managing in Chaos," *Fortune* (October 2, 2006), pp. 76–82.
20. Example cited in Janet Rae-Dupree, "Innovative Minds Don't Think Alike," *The New York Times* (December 30, 2007), http://www.nytimes.com/2007/12/30/business/30know.html?pagewanted=all&_r=0 (accessed December 30, 2007).

21. Daniel Levinthal and Claus Rerup, "Crossing an Apparent Chasm: Bridging Mindful and Less-Mindful Perspectives on Organizational Learning," *Organization Science* 17, no. 4 (August 2006), pp. 502–513; and Ellen Langer and John Sviokla, "An Evaluation of Charisma from the Mindfulness Perspective," unpublished manuscript, Harvard University. Part of this discussion is also drawn from Richard L. Daft and Robert H. Lengel, *Fusion Leadership: Unlocking the Subtle Forces That Change People and Organizations* (San Francisco: Berrett-Koehler, 1998).
22. Based on Michael Chaskalson, *The Mindful Workplace* (Chichester, West Sussex: Wiley-Blackwell, 2011); Ellen J. Langer, "Minding Matters: The Consequences of Mindlessness-Mindfulness," in *Advances in Experimental Social Psychology*, vol. 22, L. Berkowitz, ed. (San Diego: Academic Press, 1989), pp. 137–173; and Levinthal and Rerup, "Crossing an Apparent Chasm."
23. Bauback Yeganeh, "Mindful Leader," *Leadership Excellence* (March 2012), p. 7.
24. Matt Richtel, "Hooked on Gadgets, and Paying a Mental Price," *The New York Times* (June 6, 2010), http://www.nytimes.com/2010/06/07/technology/07brain.html?pagewanted=all&_r=0 (accessed June 7, 2010).
25. T. K. Das, "Educating Tomorrow's Managers: The Role of Critical Thinking," *The International Journal of Organizational Analysis* 2, no. 4 (October 1994), pp. 333–360.
26. Russell Gold and Neil King Jr. "The Gulf Oil Spill: Red Flags Were Ignored Aboard Doomed Rig," *The Wall Street Journal* (May 13, 2010), p. A6.
27. See Theresa M. Glomb, Michelle K. Duffy, Joyce E. Bono, and Tao Yang, "Mindfulness at Work," *Research in Personnel and Human Resources Management* 30 (2011), pp. 115–157, for a discussion of the value of mindfulness at work.
28. Bernard M. Bass, *Leadership and Performance Beyond Expectations* (New York: The Free Press, 1985); and B. M. Bass, *New Paradigm Leadership: An Inquiry into Transformational Leadership* (Alexandria, VA: U.S. Army Research Institute for the Behavioral and Social Sciences, 1996).
29. The Pike Syndrome has been discussed in multiple sources.
30. Janet Rae-Dupree, "Innovative Minds Don't Think Alike" (December 30, 2007), p. 3.3.
31. Jerome Groopman, "Mental Malpractice" (Op-Ed column), *The New York Times* (July 7, 2007), p. A13.
32. Chris Argyris, *Flawed Advice and the Management Trap* (New York: Oxford University Press, 2000); and Eileen C. Shapiro, "Managing in the Cappuccino Economy" (review of *Flawed Advice*), *Harvard Business Review* (March–April 2000), pp. 177–183.
33. This section is based on Peter M. Senge, *The Fifth Discipline: The Art and Practice of the Learning Organization* (New York: Doubleday, 1990); John D. Sterman, "Systems Dynamics Modeling: Tools for Learning in a Complex World," *California Management Review* 43, no. 4 (Summer, 2001), pp. 8–25; Andrea Gabor, "Seeing Your Company as a System," *Strategy Business* (Summer 2010), http://www.strategy-business.com/article/10210?gko=20cca (accessed June 20, 2012); and Ron Zemke, "Systems Thinking," *Training* (February 2001), pp. 40–46.
34. This example is cited in Sterman, "Systems Dynamics Modeling."
35. Peter M. Senge, Charlotte Roberts, Richard B. Ross, Bryan J. Smith, and Art Kleiner, *The Fifth Discipline Fieldbook* (New York: Currency/Doubleday, 1994), p. 87.
36. Peter Senge, *The Fifth Discipline*; and David Allen, *Getting Things Done: The Art of Stress-Free Productivity* (New York: Viking Penguin, 2001).
37. Timothy A. Judge, Amy E. Colbert, and Remus Ilies, "Intelligence and Leadership: A Quantitative Review and Test of Theoretical Propositions," *Journal of Applied Psychology* (June 2004), pp. 542–552.
38. Sigal G. Barsade and Donald E. Gibson, "Why Does Affect Matter in Organizations?" *Academy of Management Perspectives* 21, no. 1 (February 2007), pp. 36–59; Daniel Goleman, *Emotional Intelligence: Why It Can Matter More Than IQ* (New York: Bantam Books, 1995); John D. Mayer and David Caruso, "The Effective Leader: Understanding and Applying Emotional Intelligence," *Ivey Business Journal* (November–December 2002); Pamela Kruger, "A Leader's Journey," *Fast Company* (June 1999), pp. 116–129; and Hendrie Weisinger, *Emotional Intelligence at Work* (San Francisco: Jossey-Bass, 1998).
39. Study by Daniel Goleman, co-chairman of the Consortium for Research on Emotional Intelligence in Organizations, reported in Diann Daniel, "Soft Skills for CIOs and Aspiring CIOs: Four Ways to Boost Your Emotional Intelligence," *CIO* (June 25, 2007), http://www.cio.com (accessed October 18, 2007).
40. Based on Goleman, *Emotional Intelligence*; Goleman, "Leadership That Gets Results," *Harvard Business Review* (March–April 2000), pp. 79–90; J. D. Mayer, D. R. Caruso, and P. Salovey, "Emotional Intelligence Meets Traditional Standards for an Intelligence," *Intelligence* 27, no. 4 (1999), pp. 266–298; Neal M. Ashkanasy and Catherine S. Daus, "Emotion in the Workplace: The New Challenge for Managers," *Academy of Management Executive* 16, no. 1 (2002), pp. 76–86; and Weisinger, *Emotional Intelligence at Work*.
41. Studies reported in Stephen Xavier, "Are You at the Top of Your Game? Checklist for Effective Leaders," *Journal of Business Strategy* 26, no. 3 (2005), pp. 35–42; and Joyce E. Bono and Remus Ilies, "Charisma, Positive Emotions, and Mood Contagion," *The Leadership Quarterly* 17 (2006), pp. 317–334.
42. This section is based largely on Goleman, *Emotional Intelligence: Why It Can Matter More Than IQ*, pp. 289–290.
43. Rensselaer Polytechnic Institute, Lally School of Management and Technology, as reported in *BusinessWeek Frontier* (February 5, 2001), p. F4.
44. This discussion is based on V. Vijayalakshmi and Sanghamitra Bhattacharyya, "Emotional Contagion and Its Relevance to Individual Behavior and Organizational Processes: A Position Paper," *Journal of Business Psychology* 27 (2012), pp. 363–374; E. Hatfield, J. T. Cacioppo, and R. L. Rapson, *Emotional Contagion* (New York: Cambridge University Press, 1994); Barsade and Gibson, "Why Does Affect Matter in Organizations?"; and Bono and Ilies, "Charisma, Positive Emotions, and Mood Contagion."
45. Jeff Bailey, "Outsize Personality Tries to Create a Regional Airline to Match," *The New York Times* (January 19, 2007), p. C1.
46. Research by Noah Eisenkraft and Hillary Anger Elfenbein reported in Nicole Branan, "The 'Me' Effect," *Scientific American Mind* (November–December 2010), pp. 14–15; Noah Eisenkraft and Hillary Anger Elfenbein, "The Way You Make Me Feel," *Psychological Science* 21 (April 2010), pp. 505–510; Robert I. Sutton, "How Bad Apples Infect the Tree," *The New York Times* (November 28, 2010), p. BU.8; and Roy Baumeister et al., "Bad Is Stronger Than Good," *Review of General Psychology* 5, no. 4 (2001), pp. 323–370.
47. Daniel Goleman, Richard Boyatzis, and Annie McKee, "The Emotional Reality of Teams," *Journal of Organizational Excellence* (Spring 2002), pp. 55–65.
48. P. J. Jordan, N. M. Ashkanasy, C. E. J. Härtel, and G. S. Hooper, "Workgroup Emotional Intelligence: Scale Development and Relationship to Team Process Effectiveness and Goal Focus," *Human Resource Management Review* 12, no. 2 (Summer 2002), pp. 195–214.
49. See studies reported in Barsade and Gibson, "Why Does Affect Matter in Organizations?"; Bono and Ilies, "Charisma, Positive Emotions, and Mood Contagion; and David Bolchover, "Why Mood Matters," *Management Today* (November 1, 2008), p. 46.
50. Barbara L. Fredrickson, "What Good Are Positive Emotions?" *Review of General Psychology* 2, no. 3 (1998), pp. 300–319; Barsade and Gibson, "Why Does Affect Matter"; and Bolchover, "Why Mood Matters."
51. Jerry Krueger and Emily Killham, "At Work, Feeling Good Matters," *Gallup Management Journal* (December 8, 2005).
52. Bolchover, "Why Mood Matters."

53. Diane Coutu, "Leadership Lessons from Abraham Lincoln," *Harvard Business Review* (April 2009), pp. 43–47.
54. Daniel Goleman, "Emotional Mastery: Seek to Excel in Four Dimensions," *Leadership Excellence* (June 2011), pp. 12–13; Goleman, "Leadership That Gets Results"; and Daniel Goleman, "How to Be Emotionally Intelligent," *The New York Times* (April 7, 2015), http://www.nytimes.com/2015/04/12/education/edlife/how-to-be-emotionally-intelligent.html?_r=0 (accessed October 28, 2015).
55. Dave Marcum, Steve Smith, and Mahan Khalsa, "The Marshmallow Conundrum," *Across the Board* (March–April 2004), pp. 26–30.
56. Sue Shellenbarger, "Health & Fitness: How to Keep Your Cool in Angry Times," *The Wall Street Journal Asia* (September 27, 2010), p. 11.
57. Alan Farnham, "Are You Smart Enough to Keep Your Job?" *Fortune* (January 15, 1996), pp. 34–47.
58. Peter J. Frost, "Handling the Hurt: A Critical Skill for Leaders," *Ivey Management Journal* (January–February 2004).
59. Rolf W. Habbel, "The Human[e] Factor: Nurturing a Leadership Culture," *Strategy & Business* 26 (First Quarter 2002), pp. 83–89; and Melvin Smith and Diana Bilimoria, "Heart of Leadership: Engage with Emotional Intelligence," *Leadership Excellence* (March 2012), p. 5.
60. Jeremy W. Peters, "Time Inc. Chief Executive Jack Griffin Out," *The New York Times* (February 17, 2011), http://mediadecoder.blogs.nytimes.com/2011/02/17/time-inc-chief-executive-jack-griffin-out/ (accessed April 1, 2013).
61. Based on Vivian Giang, "Inside Google's Insanely Popular Emotional-Intelligence Course," *Fast Company* (March 25, 2015), http://www.fastcompany.com/3044157/the-future-of-work/inside-googles-insanely-popular-emotional-intelligence-course (accessed October 19, 2015).
62. Research study results reported in Goleman, "Leadership That Gets Results."
63. Barsade and Gibson, "Why Does Affect Matter in Organizations?"; Frank Walter, Michael S. Cole, and Ronald H. Humphrey, "Emotional Intelligence: Sine Qua Non of Leadership or Folderol?" *Academy of Management Perspectives* (February 2011), pp. 45–58; and Kenneth M. Nowack, "Emotional Intelligence: Defining and Understanding the Fad," *T D* (August 2012), pp. 60–63.
64. Xavier, "Are You at the Top of Your Game?"
65. This discussion is based in part on Kathleen D. Ryan and Daniel K. Oestreich, *Driving Fear Out of the Workplace: How to Overcome the Invisible Barriers to Quality, Productivity, and Innovation* (San Francisco: Jossey-Bass, 1991); and Scott A. Snook, "Love and Fear and the Modern Boss," *Harvard Business Review* (January 2008), pp. 16–17.
66. S. Lyubomirsky, L. King, and E. Diener, "The Benefits of Frequent Positive Affect: Does Happiness Lead to Success?" *Psychological Bulletin* 131, no. 6 (2005), pp. 803–855; R. Cropanzano and T. A. Wright, "When a 'Happy' Worker Is Really a 'Productive' Worker: A Review and Further Refinement of the Happy-Productive Worker Theory," *Consulting Psychology Journal: Practice and Research* 53, no. 3 (2001), pp. 182–199; and Barsade and Gibson, "Why Does Affect Matter in Organizations?"
67. David E. Dorsey, "Escape from the Red Zone," *Fast Company* (April/May 1997), pp. 116–127.
68. Susan G. Hauser, "The Degeneration of Decorum," *Workforce Management* (January 11, 2011), pp. 16–18, 20–21.
69. Tom Kelley and David Kelley, "Reclaim Your Creative Confidence," *Harvard Business Review* (December 2012), pp. 115–117; and Frederic Lardinois, "Pulse News Reader Dips Its Toes into Social with New 'Highlights' Feature," *TechCrunch* (February 12, 2013), http://techcrunch.com/2013/02/12/pulse-news-reader-dips-its-toes-into-social/ (accessed April 1, 2013).
70. *Ibid.* Frederic Lardinois, "Pulse News Reader Dips Its Toes into Social with New 'Highlights' Feature," *TechCrunch* (February 12, 2013), http://techcrunch.com/2013/02/12/pulse-news-reader-dips-its-toes-into-social/ (accessed April 1, 2013).
71. This section is based on Ryan and Oestreich, *Driving Fear Out of the Workplace*; and Therese R. Welter, "Reducing Employee Fear: Get Workers and Managers to Speak Their Minds," *Small Business Report* (April 1991), pp. 15–18.
72. Ryan and Oestreich, *Driving Fear Out of the Workplace*, p. 43.
73. Daniel Holden, "Team Development: A Search for Elegance," *Industrial Management* (September–October 2007), pp. 20–25.
74. Covey, *The Seven Habits of Highly Effective People*, p. 80.
75. Donald G. Zauderer, "Integrity: An Essential Executive Quality," *Business Forum* (Fall 1992), pp. 12–16.
76. Hyler Bracey, Jack Rosenblum, Aubrey Sanford, and Roy Trueblood, *Managing from the Heart* (New York: Dell Publishing, 1993), p. 192.
77. Madan Birla with Cecilia Miller Marshall, *Balanced Life and Leadership Excellence* (Memphis, TN: The Balance Group, 1997), pp. 76–77.
78. Rodney Ferris, "How Organizational Love Can Improve Leadership," *Organizational Dynamics* 16, no. 4 (Spring 1988), pp. 40–52.
79. Kristy J. O'Hara, "Role Player," *Smart Business Akron/Canton* (March 2009), p. 14.

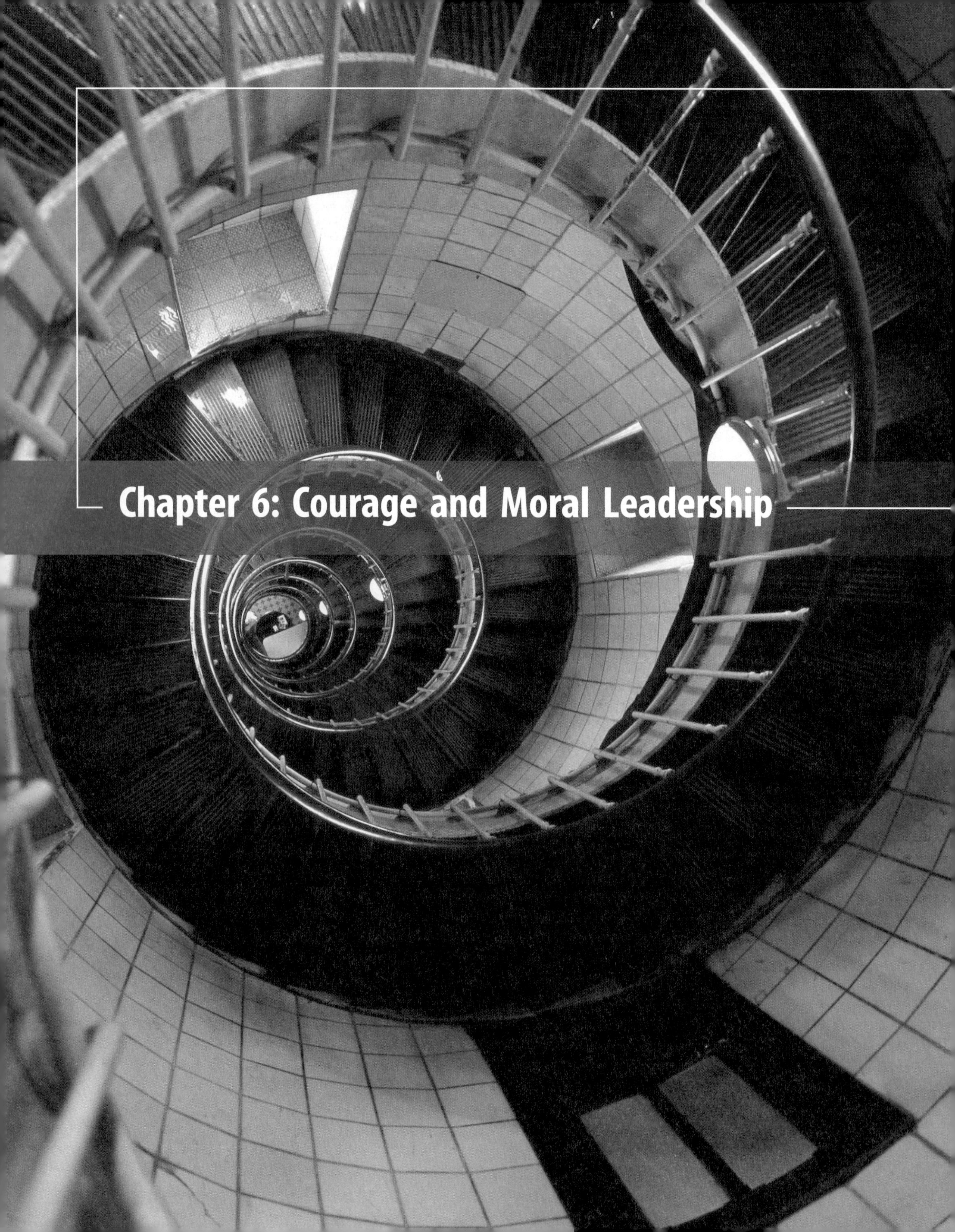

Chapter 6: Courage and Moral Leadership

YOUR **LEADERSHIP** CHALLENGE

After reading this chapter, you should be able to:

- Combine a rational approach to leadership with a concern for people and ethics.
- Understand how leaders set the ethical tone in organizations and recognize the distinction between ethical and unethical leadership.
- Recognize your own stage of moral development and ways to accelerate your moral maturation.
- Know and use mechanisms that enhance an ethical organizational culture.
- Apply the principles of stewardship and servant leadership.
- Recognize courage in others and unlock your own potential to live and act courageously.

CHAPTER **OUTLINE**

168 **Moral Leadership Today**

173 **Acting Like a Moral Leader**

174 **Becoming a Moral Leader**

176 **Servant Leadership**

180 **Leading with Courage**

In the Lead

170 **Kip Tindell, Container Store**

179 **Adam Grant, Wharton School of the University of Pennsylvania**

182 **Paula Reid, U.S. Secret Service**

186 **General Stanley A. McChrystal, United States Army**

Leader's Self-Insight

172 **Ethical Maturity**

180 **Your Servant Leadership Orientation**

184 **Assess Your Moral Courage**

Leader's Bookshelf

169 **Discover Your True North**

Leadership at Work

189 **Scary Person**

Leadership Development: Cases for Analysis

189 **What Should I Say?**

191 **The Boy, the Girl, the Ferryboat Captain, and the Hermits**

By the time she was shot in the head in an assassination attempt by Taliban gunmen in October 2012, 14-year-old Malala Yousafzai had been a leader in the fight for girls' education in Pakistan for more than three years. Yousafzai began writing a blog under a pseudonym for the BBC at the age of 11, detailing her life under Taliban rule, their control of the Swat Valley, and her advocacy of education for girls. After the Pakistan military ousted the militants from her region, Yousafzai began speaking publicly. A *New York Times* documentary and interviews by both print and television media raised her profile further and put her in the direct aim of the Taliban. After life-saving surgeries in Pakistan following the shooting, Yousafzai was flown to Birmingham, England, where she underwent many more surgeries—and where, within six months, she returned to school. In 2014, Yousafzai was honored as one of the recipients of the Nobel Peace Prize, and she continues to speak passionately for her cause despite continuing death threats.[1]

Malala Yousafzai knew very early in life that being an influential leader means learning who you are and what you stand for, and then having the courage to act. Leaders demonstrate confidence and commitment in what they believe and what they do. A deep devotion to a cause or a purpose larger than oneself sparks the courage to act, as it does for Malala Yousafzai, who said upon her return to school, "I want all girls in the world to have this basic opportunity."[2]

In addition, Malala Yousafzai's story illustrates that real leadership has less to do with making use of other people than with serving other people. Placing others ahead of oneself is a key to successful leadership, whether in social activism, politics, war, education, sports, social services, or business.

This chapter explores ideas related to courage and moral leadership. In the previous chapter, we discussed mind and emotion, two of the three elements that come together for successful leadership. This chapter focuses on the third element, spirit—on the ability to look within, to contemplate the human condition, to think about what is right and wrong, to see what really matters in the world, and to have the courage to stand up for what is worthy and right. We begin by looking at the situation in which most organizations currently operate, the dilemma leaders face in the modern world, and the importance of leaders setting an ethical tone within the organization. Next we explore how leaders can act in a moral way, examine a model of personal moral development, and look at the importance of stewardship and servant leadership. The final sections of the chapter explore what courage means and how leaders develop the courage for moral leadership to flourish.

6-1 MORAL LEADERSHIP TODAY

The names of once-revered corporations such as AIG, Lehman Brothers, Bear Stearns, and Countrywide have become synonymous with greed, deceit, arrogance, or lack of moral conscience. Although the high-profile stories of ethical misconduct in organizations have slowed a bit, there are plenty of leaders still on the hot seat because of immoral or unethical behavior: Brian Dunn of Best Buy and Mark Hurd of Hewlett-Packard both resigned under pressure due to inappropriate relationships with female employees. Scott Thompson resigned as CEO of Yahoo after only four months on the job because reports revealed he had inaccurately claimed on his resume that he had a degree in computer science.[3] And at the nonprofit Wyckoff Heights Medical Center in one of the poorest neighborhoods in Brooklyn, an investigation revealed a pattern of insider dealing that lavishly benefited top managers, board members, and local politicians while damaging the organization to the point that it might be closed, further limiting health-care options for the poor.[4]

6-1a The Ethical Climate in Business

Leaders face many pressures that challenge their ability to do the right thing. The most dangerous obstacles for leaders are personal weakness and self-interest rather than full-scale corruption.[5] Pressures to cut costs, increase profits, meet the demands of vendors or business partners, and look successful can all contribute to ethical lapses. For example, leading up to and during the 2008 housing and financial crisis, leaders at Standard & Poor's, the ratings agency, were reported to have ignored ethical danger signals and chosen to put short-term interests ahead of truthful ratings in order to produce ratings that were desired by banks putting together mortgage deals. A civil suit filed by the U.S. Justice Department alleged that S&P leaders knowingly issued unwarranted high ratings to maintain business.[6] Their actions and those of leaders in many other companies contributed to the collapse of the housing market and a worldwide financial crisis.

NEW LEADER
ACTION MEMO

As a leader, you can put ethical values into action and set the example you want followers to live by. You can resist pressures to act unethically just to avoid criticism or achieve short-term gains.

Another challenge in today's business environment is an overemphasis on pleasing shareholders, which may cause some managers to behave unethically toward

LEADER'S BOOKSHELF

Discover Your True North

by Bill George with Peter Sims

Authentic, ethical leadership has become a popular topic in today's world of organizational scandals. According to Bill George, former CEO of Medtronic and a Harvard Business School professor, authentic leaders are people who are guided by their "true north," which refers to their most sacred, deeply held values. *Discover Your True North,* written by George with Peter Sims, describes the journey people take to become authentic leaders who know and understand themselves, act consistent with their ethical values despite the pressures of the real world, and empower and inspire others with a higher purpose.

HOW TO BE AN AUTHENTIC, ETHICAL LEADER

"You cannot fake it to make it, because people sense intuitively whether you are genuine," George and Sims say. They describe what it means to be an authentic leader and use numerous stories and anecdotes to illustrate their points. Here are three facets of their leadership plan for becoming an authentic ethical leader:

- ***Know Yourself.*** Self-awareness is crucial because leadership is an outward manifestation of who you are as a person. Leaders first have to know who they are, understand how their life experiences have shaped them, and recognize their strengths and weaknesses. To be come more self-aware, David Pottruck, former CEO of Charles Schwab, forced himself to ask for regular feedback from everyone around him after he learned that colleagues viewed his aggressive style as self-serving.
- ***Honor Your Values.*** Authentic leaders know what matters to them, the ethical values that they hold most dear, and the principles that guide their lives and leadership. Moreover, they stand by these deeply held values despite outside pressures and seductions. The authors tell the disheartening story of Lance Armstrong, who allowed a "ruthless quest for glory" to override his personal values.
- ***Find Your Career Sweet Spot.*** Leaders also must know what drives them and how they can make their best contribution. They do so by balancing external motivations such as power or money with internal motivations such as helping others or making a difference in the world. Warren Buffett found his sweet spot with his realization that "I don't want to live like a king. I just want to invest."

FIND YOUR OWN TRUE NORTH

"Discovering your True North is hard work," George notes at the beginning of this book. "It may take you many years to find it, as was the case for me." However, as the interviews with hundreds of leaders reveal, leadership is an exciting journey. The leadership insights and lessons in this book can serve as a compass to keep you on the right path to being an authentic leader who can make a positive, lasting difference.

Source: *Discover Your True North*, by Bill George with Peter Sims, is published by Jossey-Bass.

customers, employees, and the broader society.[7] Managers are under enormous pressure to meet short-term earnings goals, and some even use accounting gimmicks or other techniques to show returns that meet market expectations rather than ones that reflect true performance.[8] All leaders want their organizations to appear successful, and they can sometimes do the wrong thing just so they will look good to others. The question for leaders is whether they can summon the fortitude to do the right thing despite outside pressures. "Life is lived on a slippery slope," says Harvard Business School's Richard Tedlow. "It takes a person of character to know what lines you don't cross."[9]

Sticking to one's core values in the face of pressure is one key part of leading authentically and ethically. Jon Huntsman, who served in the administration of President Richard Nixon and experienced the Watergate scandal of the 1970s, says "an amoral atmosphere permeated the White House" at that time. Huntsman left his position after being pressured to entrap a rival politician. Huntsman is one of the leaders represented in the book *Discover Your True North*, which is described further in the Leader's Bookshelf.

6-1b Leaders Set the Ethical Tone

Top leaders in particular are facing closer scrutiny because what goes on at the top sets the standard for the rest of the organization. In a study of *Fortune*

100 companies, fully 40 percent were found to have been engaged in activities that could be considered unethical.[10] Moreover, researchers concluded that the misdeeds in many cases could be traced to the failure of top executives to enforce and live up to high ethical standards.

Leaders carry a tremendous responsibility for setting the ethical climate and acting as positive role models for others.[11] Leaders signal what matters through their behavior, and when leaders operate from principles of selfishness and greed, many employees come to see that type of behavior as okay. At the now-defunct Bear Stearns, for example, senior executives were openly arrogant and ambitious for personal successes, and they built a "sharp-elbowed, opportunistic culture" in which rules and basic standards of fairness, honesty, and honor could be bent for the sake of achieving personal gain.[12] Contrast the Bear Stearns approach to the culture Kip Tindell has built at the Container Store.

IN THE LEAD

Kip Tindell, Container Store

At the Container Store, CEO Kip Tindell renamed Valentine's Day "We Love Our Employees Day." Managers bring gifts and chocolates and make a point of telling employees they love them. It's just one symbol of the importance Container Store puts on treating people and relationships with love and respect.

When Tindell cofounded the Container Store in 1978, he knew he wanted to build a different kind of company, one where employees were treated well and paid well and business was conducted with ethical values in mind. Tindell's approach, which he calls the Foundation Principles, is a key part of the corporate culture at Container Store and aligns with a philosophy that has been called *conscious capitalism*. It means having a higher purpose besides just making money by focusing on employees, customers, suppliers, and the community as well as on shareholders; seeking to bring out the best in people; and fostering trust and respect. It's a model "for conducting business without any trade-offs." Managers make clear what the company stands for and everyone is expected to honor the values 100 percent of the time.

In addition to the We Love Our Employees Day, Container Store has an annual chili cook-off and other special events. Whenever there's news to celebrate, people are gathered together for games and snacks and lots of confetti. Tindell believes it is important to recognize employees' efforts not only because it makes them happier and more fulfilled but also because that trickles down and makes better, stronger families and communities. "I enjoy making money for myself and the people around me," Tindell says. "I'm not saying this is the only way to make money. I'm saying this is the best way."[13]

Kip Tindell has built a culture of integrity and ethical leadership at the Container Store by putting people and relationships above just making money. Exhibit 6.1 compares ethical and unethical leadership. The behaviors listed in column 1 contribute to an organizational climate of trust, fairness, and doing the right thing, such as the one at Container Store. Column 2 lists the opposite

EXHIBIT 6.1 Comparing Ethical versus Unethical Leadership

The Ethical Leader	The Unethical Leader
Possesses humility	Is arrogant and self-serving
Maintains concern for the greater good	Excessively promotes self-interest
Is honest and straightforward	Practices deception
Fulfills commitments	Breaches agreements
Strives for fairness	Deals unfairly
Takes responsibility	Shifts blame to others
Shows respect for each individual	Diminishes others' dignity
Encourages and develops others	Neglects follower development
Serves others	Withholds help and support
Shows courage to stand up for what is right	Lacks courage to confront unjust acts

Source: Based on Donald G. Zauderer, "Integrity: An Essential Executive Quality," *Business Forum* (Fall 1992), pp. 12–16.

behaviors, which contribute to a climate ripe for ethical and legal abuses, such as at Bear Stearns.[14]

NEW LEADER
ACTION MEMO

Go to Leader's Self-Insight 6.1 and complete the questions to learn whether your behavior and decisions suggest that you will be an ethical leader.

Ethical leaders aren't preoccupied with their own importance. They keep the focus on employees, customers, and the greater good rather than taking every opportunity to satisfy their self-interest, feed their greed, or nourish their egos. Unethical leaders typically pay more attention to gaining benefits for themselves than to the company or the larger society. For example, an investigation of New York State's pension fund for public workers found that former New York Comptroller Alan Hevesi and other political leaders and advisors accepted millions in sham consulting fees, travel expenses, campaign contributions, and other favors in exchange for giving specified investment firms parts of the fund to manage, enabling the firms to earn hefty management fees. Hevesi and advisor Hank Morris both pleaded guilty to felony corruption charges. Hevesi was paroled in February 2013 after serving 20 months in prison.[15]

Also shown in Exhibit 6.1, ethical leaders are honest with employees, partners, customers, vendors, and shareholders. They strive for fairness and take care to honor their agreements or commitments to others. Unethical leaders, on the other hand, often practice deception. In a *USA Today* survey some years ago, 82 percent of CEOs said they lied about their golf scores. Sure, it's a small thing, but little by little, dishonesty can become a way of life and business.[16]

Ethical leaders tend to share the credit for successes and accept the blame when things go wrong, whereas unethical leaders often take credit for followers' accomplishments and diminish the dignity of others by treating people with discourtesy and disrespect. Ethical leaders help followers develop their potential and have a role in decision making, whereas unethical leaders often see followers as a means to an end.

Finally, one of the primary ways leaders contribute to an ethical organization is by speaking up against acts they believe are wrong. If a leader knows someone is being treated unfairly by a colleague and does nothing, the leader is setting a precedent for others to behave unfairly as well. Peers and subordinates with lax ethical standards feel free to act as they choose. Consider what happened at Pennsylvania State University. In 2001, Mike McQueary, at the time a graduate assistant in the football program, reported to the head football coach Joe Paterno that he saw defensive coordinator Jerry Sandusky possibly sexually abusing a young

LEADER'S SELF-INSIGHT 6.1

Ethical Maturity

Instructions: Think about how you typically behave and make decisions and respond honestly to the following statements. Answer as you actually behave, not as you would want to behave.

	Mostly False	Mostly True
1. I can clearly state the principles and values that guide my actions.		✓
2. I promptly own up to my own mistakes and failures.		✓
3. I am able to quickly "forgive and forget" when someone has made a serious mistake that affects me.	✓	
4. When making a difficult decision, I take the time to assess my principles and values.		✓
5. I have a reputation among my friends and coworkers for keeping my word.		✓
6. I intentionally reflect on my mistakes to improve my performance.		✓
7. When someone asks me to keep a confidence, I always do so completely.		✓
8. When things go wrong, I seldom blame others or circumstances.		✓
9. I am able to forgive myself soon after a serious mistake.	✓	
10. My coworkers would say that my behavior is very consistent with my values.		✓

Scoring and Interpretation

Give yourself 1 point for each Mostly True answer you checked above. Total Score __8__. Your score for the ethical maturity scale suggests whether you are on track to become an ethical leader as described in Exhibit 6.1. A high score of 8–10 is suggestive of someone who is more concerned with values and other people than with self-interest. A score of 0–3 would be considered low, and a score of 4–7 is the middle ground. Your score also provides a clue about your level of moral development shown in Exhibit 6.4. The postconventional level of development means that you consider principles and values, take personal responsibility, and do not blame others. A high score suggests that you have a highly developed moral sense. A lower score suggests you may be at the conventional or even preconventional level. Reflect on what your score means to you.

Source: Based on and adapted from Doug Lennick and Fred Kiel, *Moral Intelligence: Enhancing Business Performance and Leadership Success* (Upper Saddle River, NJ: Cordon School Publications, 2005), pp. 251–263.

boy in the locker room. Athletic director Tim Curley and at least two top administrators also soon learned of the incident. But no one took the steps necessary to stop the behavior, and Sandusky went on to molest more boys before one of his victims brought the abuse to light. More than 10 years after McQueary's initial report, Sandusky was convicted on 45 counts of child sexual abuse. The courts and the public were astonished to learn how many people apparently knew about Sandusky's behavior and did nothing beyond talking with Sandusky and urging him to get professional help.[17]

How can leaders turn a blind eye to such behavior? *The fact is that most managers have a natural inclination to protect their organizations*. In addition, leaders have to fight against a tendency for people "to see what we want to see, not see what we don't want to see, and to hope a problem will go away on its own," a tendency that causes leaders such as those at Penn State to make decisions "that later come to be seen by others as ethically indefensible."[18] Penn State leaders aren't alone in this tendency to protect the organization even at the risk of allowing unethical or illegal behavior to continue. For many reasons, it is often hard to stand up for what is right, but this is a primary way in which leaders create an environment of integrity.

6-2 ACTING LIKE A MORAL LEADER

At Penn State, numerous leaders were accused of putting winning football games and protecting the school's reputation ahead of morality. At other organizations, leaders may put meeting economic goals ahead of doing the right thing. Companies that get into ethical trouble typically have top leaders who make quarterly earnings and the share price their primary purpose of business and the most important measure of individual and organizational success.[19] When leaders forget that business is about *values* and not just economic performance, organizations and the broader society are hurt in the process.

Moral leadership doesn't mean ignoring profit and loss, share price, production costs, and other hard, measurable facts, but it does require recognizing and adhering to ethical values and acknowledging the importance of human meaning, quality, and higher purpose.[20] Henry Ford's century-old comment seems tailor-made for today's poor ethical climate: "For a long time people believed that the only purpose of industry was to make a profit. They are wrong. Its purpose is to serve the general welfare."[21]

NEW LEADER
ACTION MEMO

As a leader, you can drive fear out of the organization so that followers feel comfortable reporting problems or ethical abuses. You can establish clear ethics policies, reward ethical conduct, and show zero tolerance for violations.

Despite the corporate realities of greed, competition, and the drive to achieve goals and profits, leaders can act based on moral values and encourage others to develop and use moral values and adhere to ethical standards of conduct in the workplace. *The single most important factor in ethical decision making in organizations is whether leaders show a commitment to ethics in their talk and especially their behavior.*[22] Employees learn about the values that are important in the organization by watching leaders.

Exhibit 6.2 lists some specific ways leaders act to build an environment that allows and encourages people to behave ethically. Leaders create organizational systems and policies that support ethical behavior, such as creating open-door policies that encourage people to talk about anything without fear, establishing clear ethics codes, rewarding ethical conduct, and showing zero tolerance for violations. Many companies have hired high-level chief compliance officers to police managers and employees.[23] Most companies have established codes of ethics to guide employee behavior or lists of core values that employees are expected to honor. Exhibit 6.3 lists the core values for More Than Wheels, which has a mission "To help struggling individuals & families break the cycle of poor financial decision making by using

EXHIBIT 6.2 How to Act Like a Moral Leader

1. Articulate and uphold high moral principles.
2. Focus on what is right for the organization as well as all the people involved.
3. Set the example you want others to live by.
4. Be honest with yourself and others.
5. Drive out fear and eliminate undiscussables.
6. Establish and communicate ethics policies.
7. Develop a backbone—show zero tolerance for ethical violations.
8. Reward ethical conduct.
9. Treat everyone with fairness, dignity, and respect, from the lowest to the highest level of the organization.
10. Do the right thing in both your private and professional life—even if no one is looking.

Source: Based on Linda Klebe Treviño, Laura Pincus Hartman, and Michael Brown, "Moral Person and Moral Manager: How Executives Develop a Reputation for Ethical Leadership," *California Management Review* 42, no. 4 (Summer 2000), pp. 128–142; Christopher Hoenig, "Brave Hearts," *CIO* (November 1, 2000), pp. 72–74; and Patricia Wallington, "Honestly?!" *CIO* (March 15, 2003), pp. 41–42.

EXHIBIT 6.3 More Than Wheels Core Values

At More Than Wheels our Core Values guide us in achieving our mission by working with clients and partners towards the goal of building lasting financial outcomes for our clients.

Trust
We respect and believe in one another and in our customers.
We speak the truth to each other, even when it's hard.
We value one another's opinions.

Nonjudgmental
We deal with current reality, without judgment.
We are pragmatic and forward-looking.

Accountability
We live up to our agreements.
We are relentless about reaching our goals and creatively solving problems.
We do the very best we can for our clients.

Teamwork
We value collaboration.
Our success relies on teamwork.

Learning
We learn from one another and from our successes and failures.
We strive for continual and meaningful improvement in our work.

Source: More Than Wheels Mission and Core Values, http://www.morethanwheels.org/mission (Retrieved May 18, 2013).

the car buying process to catalyze lasting change, financial stability and control."[24] Most importantly, leaders articulate and uphold high ethical standards, and they behave morally even if they think no one is looking. If leaders cut corners or bend the rules when they think they won't get caught, they and their organizations will ultimately suffer the consequences.

There is some evidence that doing right by employees, customers, and the community, as well as by shareholders, is good business. For example, a recent study of the top 100 global companies that have made a commitment to environmental sustainability found they had significantly higher sales growth, return on assets, profits, and cash flow from operations in at least some areas of business.[25] Another review of the financial performance of large U.S. corporations considered "best corporate citizens" found that they enjoy both superior reputations and superior financial performance.[26] Similarly, Governance Metrics International, an independent corporate governance ratings agency in New York, reports that the stocks of companies run on more selfless principles perform better than those run in a self-serving manner.[27]

6-3 BECOMING A MORAL LEADER

Leadership is not merely a set of practices with no association with right or wrong. All leadership practices can be used for good or evil and thus have a moral dimension. Leaders choose whether to act from selfishness and greed to diminish others or to behave in ways that serve others and motivate people to expand their potential as employees and as human beings.[28] **Moral leadership** is about distinguishing right from wrong and doing right, seeking the just, the honest, the good, and the right conduct in achieving goals and fulfilling purpose. Leaders have great

Moral leadership distinguishing right from wrong and doing right; seeking the just, honest, and good in the practice of leadership

influence over others, and moral leadership uplifts people and enhances the lives of others. Immoral leadership takes away from others in order to enhance oneself.[29]

Leaders most often know what is right; the question becomes how they choose to act on it and what internal strengths and external policies and processes are in place to enable them to follow through on doing the right thing.[30] One internal characteristic that influences a leader's capacity to make moral choices is the individual's level of moral development.[31] Exhibit 6.4 shows a simplified illustration of one model of personal moral development.

At the **preconventional level**, individuals are egocentric and concerned with receiving external rewards and avoiding punishments. They obey authority and follow rules to avoid detrimental personal consequences or satisfy immediate self-interests. The basic orientation toward the world is one of taking what one can get. Someone with this orientation in a leadership position would tend to be autocratic toward others and to use the position for personal advancement.

At level two, the **conventional level**, people learn to conform to the expectations of good behavior as defined by colleagues, family, friends, and society. People at this level follow the rules, norms, and values in the corporate culture. If the rules are to not steal, cheat, make false promises, or violate regulatory laws, a person at this level will attempt to obey. People at the conventional level adhere to the norms of the larger social system. If the social system says it is okay to inflate bills to the government or make achieving the bottom line more important than honesty and integrity, they will usually go along with that norm also. Consider the cheating scandals that have rocked several respected schools, including the Air Force Academy, Stuyvesant High School in Manhattan, and Harvard University. Interviews with students and former students at Stuyvesant indicate that many of them were simply going along with the system, a culture in which students band together and cheat in a common understanding that it is a "necessary evil" to reach their goals. Many classes have private Facebook groups, for instance, where students can post full sets of answers to tests—one student said it is expected that people will help each other out.[32] Howard Gardner, a professor at the Graduate School of Education, says

Preconventional level the level of personal moral development in which individuals are egocentric and concerned with receiving external rewards and avoiding punishments

Conventional level the level of personal moral development in which people learn to conform to the expectations of good behavior as defined by colleagues, family, friends, and society

EXHIBIT 6.4 Three Levels of Personal Moral Development

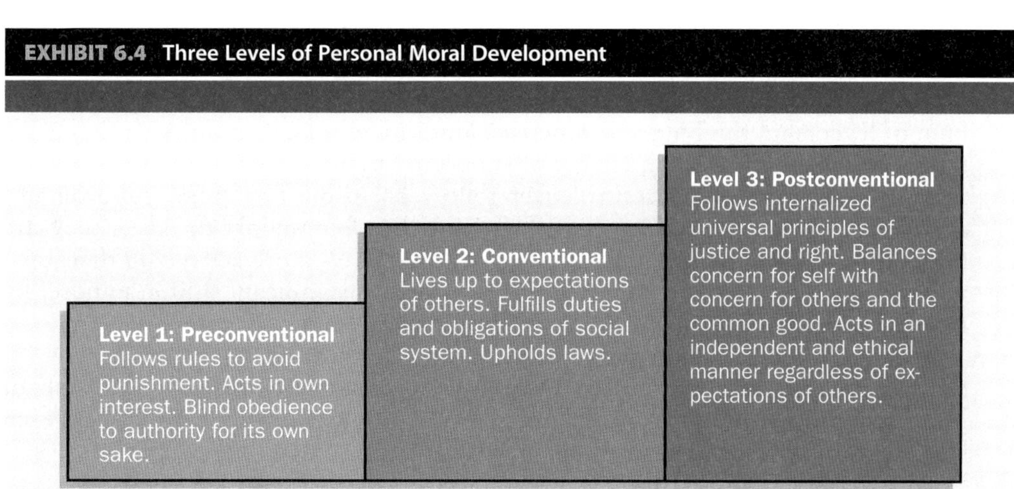

Sources: Based on Lawrence Kohlberg, "Moral Stages and Moralization: The Cognitive-Developmental Approach," in *Moral Development and Behavior: Theory, Research, and Social Issues*, ed. Thomas Likona (Austin, TX: Holt, Rinehart and Winston, 1976), pp. 31–53; and Jill W. Graham, "Leadership, Moral Development, and Citizenship Behavior," *Business Ethics Quarterly* 5, no. 1 (January 1995), pp. 43–54.

"the ethical muscles [of students] have atrophied" because of a broader societal culture that exalts success at any cost—going along with the system.[33]

At the **postconventional level**, sometimes called the *principled level*, leaders are guided by an internalized set of principles universally recognized as just and right. People at this level may even disobey rules or laws that violate these principles. These internalized values become more important than the expectations of other people in the organization or community. Would students at a postconventional level of moral development cheat on tests as those mentioned above did, since others were cheating to get ahead? A recent study suggests they would not. In a stock trading simulation, researchers gave randomly selected business school students "insider information" on actual stock earnings, allowing them to accept or reject the information. Those students who rejected the insider information scored higher on moral development, in the postconventional range, whereas those who accepted the information scored at lower levels.[34]

Most adults operate at level two of moral development, and some have not advanced beyond level one. Only about 20 percent of American adults reach the third, postconventional level of moral development, although most of us have the capacity to do so.[35] A leader at this level is visionary, empowering, and committed to serving others and a higher cause. These leaders can impartially apply universal standards to resolve moral conflicts and balance self-interest with a concern for others and for the common good. Research has consistently found a direct relationship between higher levels of moral development and more ethical behavior on the job, including less cheating, a tendency toward helpfulness to others, and the reporting of unethical or illegal acts, known as whistleblowing.[36]

6-4 SERVANT LEADERSHIP

What is a leader's moral responsibility toward followers? Is it to limit and control them to meet the needs of the organization? Is it to pay them a fair wage? Or is it to enable them to grow and create and expand themselves as human beings?

Much of the thinking about leadership today implies that moral leadership involves turning followers into leaders, thereby developing their potential rather than using a leadership position to control or limit people. The ultimate expression of this leadership approach is called *servant leadership*, which can best be understood by comparing it to other approaches. Exhibit 6.5 illustrates a continuum of leadership thinking and practice. Traditional organizations were based on the idea that the leader is in charge of subordinates and the success of the organization depends on leader control over followers. In the first stage, subordinates are passive—not expected to think for themselves but simply to do as they are told. Stage two in the continuum involves subordinates more actively in their own work. Stage three is stewardship, which represents a significant shift in mindset by moving responsibility and authority from leaders to followers.

Servant leadership represents a stage beyond stewardship, where leaders give up control and make a choice to serve employees. Along the continuum, the focus of leadership shifts from leader to followers. In the following sections, we discuss each stage of this leadership continuum in more detail.

Postconventional level the level of personal moral development in which leaders are guided by an internalized set of principles universally recognized as right

6-4a Authoritarian Management

The traditional understanding of leadership is that leaders are good managers who direct and control their people. Followers are obedient subordinates who follow orders.

EXHIBIT 6.5 Changing Leader Focus from Self to Others

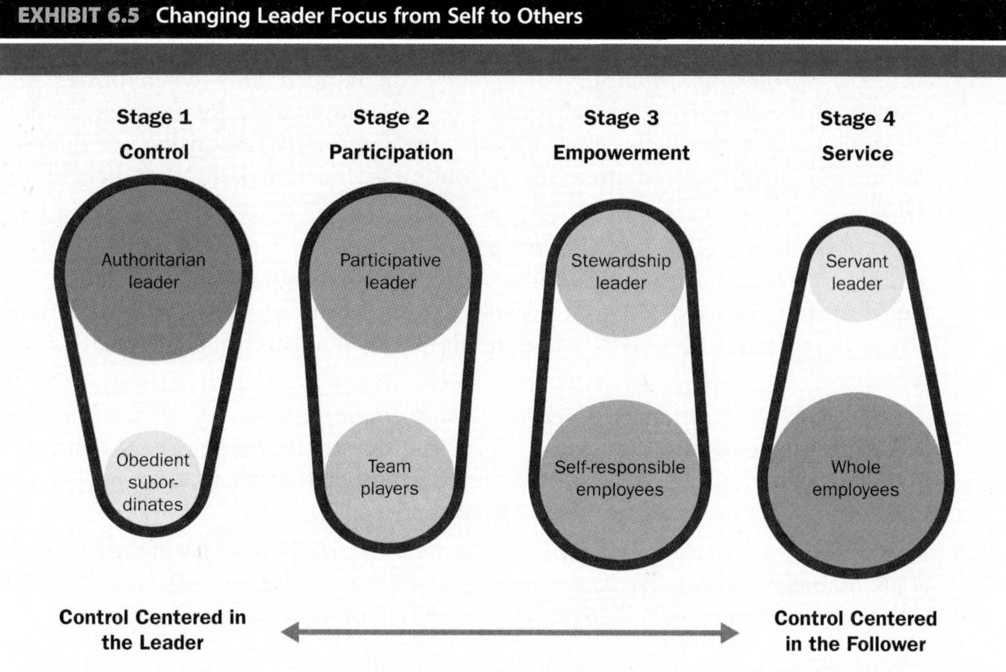

In Chapter 2, we discussed the autocratic leader, who makes the decisions and announces them to subordinates. Power, purpose, and privilege reside with those at the top of the organization. At this stage, leaders set the strategy and goals, as well as the methods and rewards for attaining them. Organizational stability and efficiency are paramount, and followers are routinized and controlled along with machines and raw materials. Subordinates are given no voice in creating meaning and purpose for their work and no discretion as to how they perform their jobs. This leadership mindset emphasizes tight top-down control, employee standardization and specialization, and management by impersonal measurement and analysis.

6-4b Participative Management

Since the 1980s, many organizations have made efforts to actively involve employees. Leaders have increased employee participation through employee suggestion programs, participation groups, and quality circles. Teamwork has become an important part of how work is done in most organizations. Studies indicate that around 70 percent of the largest U.S. corporations have adopted some kind of employee participation program or shifted to a team design. However, many of these programs do not redistribute power and authority to lower-level workers.[37] The mindset is still paternalistic in that leaders determine purpose and goals, make final decisions, and decide rewards. Employees are expected to make suggestions for quality improvements, act as team players, and take greater responsibility for their own jobs, but they are not allowed to be true partners in the enterprise.[38]

Stewardship
a belief that leaders are deeply accountable to others as well as to the organization, without trying to control others, define meaning and purpose for others, or take care of others

6-4c Stewardship

Stewardship is a pivotal shift in leadership thinking. **Stewardship** means that leaders are guardians and curators of organizational resources and values and they place the long-term interests of the organization first.[39] As stewards, leaders empower followers to make decisions and have control over how they do their own jobs. Four principles provide the framework for stewardship.

1. *Adopt a partnership mindset.* Partnership can happen only when power and control shift away from formal leaders to core employees. As partners, leaders and followers are totally honest with one another, jointly responsible for defining vision and purpose, and mutually accountable for outcomes that benefit the whole.
2. *Give decision-making power and the authority to act to those closest to the work and the customer.* This means reintegrating the "managing" and the "doing" of work, so that everyone becomes a leader and is also doing some of the core work of the organization. Nobody gets paid simply to plan and manage the work of others.
3. *Tie rewards to contributions rather than formal positions.* With stewardship, everyone's fortunes are connected to the success of the enterprise. Stewardship involves redistributing wealth by designing compensation so that people can make significant gains when they make exceptional contributions.
4. *Expect core work teams to build the organization.* Teams of employees define goals, maintain controls, create a nurturing environment, and organize and reorganize themselves to respond to a changing environment and marketplace.

NEW LEADER
ACTION MEMO

As a leader, you can apply the principles of stewardship and treat followers as true partners by sharing power and authority for setting goals, making decisions, and maintaining control over their own work and performance.

Stewardship leaders guide the organization without dominating it and facilitate followers without controlling them. At Julia's House, a children's hospice in Dorset (United Kingdom) that has won numerous awards including *The Sunday Times* Best Companies award, the CEO and all department heads sit in an open-plan office with other staff to signal a partnership approach. The organization chart was redesigned to read left to right rather than the usual vertical hierarchy.[40] Stewardship allows for a relationship between leaders and followers in which each makes significant, self-responsible contributions to organizational success. In addition, it gives followers a chance to use their minds, bodies, and spirits on the job, thereby allowing them to be whole human beings.

6-4d The Servant Leader

Servant leadership takes stewardship assumptions about leaders and followers one step further. Robert Wood Johnson, who built Johnson & Johnson from a small private company into one of the world's greatest corporations, summarized his ideas about management in the expression "to serve." In a statement called "Our Management Philosophy," Johnson went on to say, "It is the duty of the leader to be a servant to those responsible to him." [41] Johnson died decades ago, but his beliefs about the moral responsibility of a leader are as fresh and compelling (and perhaps as controversial) today as they were when he wrote them.

Servant leadership is leadership upside down. Servant leaders transcend self-interest to serve the needs of others, help others grow and develop, and provide opportunity for others to gain materially and emotionally. Fred Keller has built a $250 million plastics manufacturing company, Cascade Engineering, by continuously asking one question: *What good can we do?* Keller started the business 40 years ago with six employees. Today, it has 1,000 employees in 15 business divisions. Keller has made serving others a cornerstone of the business. The company offers jobs to welfare recipients, and Keller donates large amounts to various philanthropic causes, both as an individual and through Cascade.[42]

Servant leadership leadership in which the leader transcends self-interest to serve the needs of others, help others grow, and provide opportunities for others to gain materially and emotionally

There has been an explosion of interest in the concept of leader as servant in recent years.[43] Servant leadership was first described by Robert Greenleaf in his book, *Servant Leadership*.[44] There are four basic precepts in Greenleaf's model:[45]

1. *Put service before self-interest.* In this view, the organization exists as much to provide meaningful work to the person as the person exists to perform work for the organization.
2. *Listen first to affirm others.* One of the servant leader's greatest gifts to others is listening authentically.
3. *Inspire trust by being trustworthy.* Servant leaders build trust by doing what they say they will do, being honest with others, and focusing on the well-being of others.
4. *Nourish others and help them become whole.* Servant leaders care about followers and believe in the unique potential of each person to have a positive impact on the world.

The servant leader's top priority is service to employees, customers, shareholders, and the general public. Leadership flows out of the act of service because it enables other people to grow and become all they are capable of being.[46] For organizational psychologist Adam Grant, serving others provides powerful motivation and creative energy, as described in the following example.

IN THE LEAD

Adam Grant, Wharton School of the University of Pennsylvania

Adam Grant has been studying the power of service to others since he was an undergraduate student at Harvard. He took a job selling advertisements for a travel guide series but didn't do so well. Only when he met another student and learned that her job at the same company was essential for paying her way through college did he find purpose and meaning in his work. He eventually sold the largest advertising package in company history. "When I was representing the interests of students, I was willing to fight to protect them," he says.

Grant went on to earn a graduate degree in organizational psychology and now teaches at the Wharton School, where he is the youngest-tenured and highest-rated professor. Grant goes far beyond the typical professor in helping students. He writes lengthy letters of recommendation for students or former students approximately 100 times a year. He provides introductions for students to influential people he knows. He answers hundreds of e-mail messages a day from students, colleagues, and even people he doesn't know, providing information or assistance. Helpfulness is the watchword Grant lives by. Moreover, he argues that the greatest untapped source of motivation and productivity in organizations is service to others.

Grant has hard data from several experiments to back up his claim that focusing on the contributions we make to improve other people's lives makes us more motivated and productive. For example, call center workers seeking donations to fund college scholarships increased their effort and brought in 171 percent more revenue after hearing a student talk about how his life had been changed by a scholarship—even though the workers themselves didn't think they had been influenced by the student's brief talk.[47]

LEADER'S SELF-INSIGHT 6.2

Your Servant Leadership Orientation

Instructions: Think about situations in which you were in a formal or informal leadership role in a group or organization. Imagine using your personal approach as a leader. To what extent does each of the following statements characterize your leadership? Please answer whether each item is Mostly False or Mostly True for you.

	Mostly False	Mostly True
1. My actions meet the needs of others before my own.	____	____
2. I explicitly enable others to feel ownership for their work.	____	____
3. I like to consult with people when making a decision.	____	____
4. I'm a perfectionist.	____	____
5. I like to be of service to others.	____	____
6. I try to learn the needs and perspectives of others.	____	____
7. I consciously utilize the skills and talents of others.	____	____
8. I am assertive about the right way to do things.	____	____
9. I give away credit and recognition to others.	____	____
10. I believe that others have good intentions.	____	____
11. I quickly inform others of developments that affect their work.	____	____
12. I tend to automatically take charge.	____	____
13. I encourage the growth of others, expecting nothing in return.	____	____
14. I value cooperation over competition as a way to energize people.	____	____
15. I involve others in planning and goal setting.	____	____
16. I put people under pressure when needed.	____	____

Scoring and Interpretation

There are four subscale scores that represent four dimensions of leadership—authoritarian, participative, stewardship, and servant. For each dimension below, give yourself one point for each Mostly True response to the items indicated.

My leadership scores are:

Authoritarian, items 4, 8, 12, 16: ____
Participative, items 2, 6, 10, 14: ____
Stewardship, items 3, 7, 11, 15: ____
Servant, items 1, 5, 9, 13: ____

These scores represent the four aspects of leadership called authoritarian, participative, stewardship, and servant as described in the text and illustrated in Exhibit 6.5. A score of 3–4 on any of these dimensions would be considered above average, and a score of 0–1 is below average.

Compare your four scores to each other to understand your approach to stewardship and servant leadership. On which of the four dimensions would you like to have the highest score? The lowest? Study the specific questions on which you scored Mostly True or Mostly False to analyze your pattern of strengths and weaknesses. It is not possible to display all four dimensions of leadership simultaneously, so you should think about the dimension you want to emphasize to reflect your leader ideal.

NEW LEADER
ACTION MEMO

As a leader, you can put the needs, interests, and goals of others above your own and use your personal gifts to help others achieve their potential. Complete the questionnaire in Leader's Self-Insight 6.2 to evaluate your leadership approach along the dimensions of authoritarian leadership, participative leadership, stewardship, and servant leadership.

Grant's recent book about the power of giving versus taking was described in the Leader's Bookshelf in Chapter 2. Grant's insights suggest that servant leadership can mean something as simple as encouraging others in their personal development and helping them understand the larger purpose in their work. ServiceMaster, which cleans and maintains hospitals, schools, and other buildings, provides a good example. Leaders care how employees feel about themselves, about their work, and about the people they interact with. They instill a sense of dignity, responsibility, and meaningfulness in menial tasks like scrubbing floors and cleaning toilets. One employee who works in a hospital, for example, says she sees herself as part of a team that helps sick people get well.[48]

6-5 LEADING WITH COURAGE

Leaders sometimes have to reach deep within themselves to find the courage and strength of character to serve others, resist temptation, behave morally, or stand up for ethical principles when others may ridicule them or when they may suffer financially or emotionally for their actions.

Some would say that without courage, leadership cannot exist.[49] However, for many leaders, particularly those working in large organizations, the importance of courage is easily obscured—the main thing is to get along, fit in, and do whatever brings promotions and pay raises. In a world of stability and abundance, leaders can often forget even the *meaning* of courage, so how can they know where to find it when they need it? In the following sections, we examine the nature of leadership courage and discuss some ways courage is expressed in organizations. The final section of the chapter explores the sources of leadership courage.

"Leadership must start from within—from within the leader's heart—where real courage resides."

Peter Voyer, senior artillery officer in the Canadian Army

6-5a What Is Courage?

Many people know intuitively that courage can carry you through deprivation, ridicule, and rejection and enable you to achieve something about which you care deeply. Courage is both a moral and a practical matter for leaders. A lack of courage is what allows greed and self-interest to overcome concern for the common good.[50] **Courage** is the mental and moral strength to engage in, persevere through, and withstand danger, difficulty, or fear. Courage doesn't mean the absence of doubt, confusion, or fear, but the ability to act in spite of them when it is necessary for the greater good. In fact, if there were no fear or doubt, courage would not be needed.

The courage to take risks has always been important for living a full, rewarding life, as discussed in the *Consider This* box. Yet the courage to resist jumping on the bandwagon and taking unnecessary or unethical risks is equally important. For today's organizations, things are constantly changing, and leaders thrive by solving problems through trial and error. They create the future by moving forward in the face of uncertainty, by taking chances, by acting with courage.[51]

Courage
the mental and moral strength to engage in, persevere through, and withstand danger, difficulty, or fear

To *laugh* ... is to risk appearing the fool.
To *weep* ... is to risk appearing sentimental.
To *reach out* ... is to risk involvement.
To *expose feelings* ... is to risk exposing your true self.
To *place your ideas and dreams before a crowd* ... is to risk rejection.
To *love* ... is to risk not being loved in return.
To *live* ... is to risk dying.
To *hope* ... is to risk despair.
To *try* ... is to risk failure.
But risks must be taken, because the greatest hazard in life is to risk nothing. Those who risk nothing do nothing and have nothing.
They may avoid suffering and sorrow, but they cannot learn, feel, change, grow, or love.
Chained by their certitude, they are slaves; they have forfeited their freedom.
Only one who risks is free.

People experience all kinds of fears, including fear of death, mistakes, failure, embarrassment, change, loss of control, loneliness, pain, uncertainty, abuse, rejection, success, and public speaking. It is natural and right for people to feel fear when real risk is involved, whether the risk is losing your life, losing your job, losing a loved one, or losing your reputation.

However, many times it isn't fear as an actual threat that holds people back, but rather F.E.A.R., which stands for *False Evidence Appearing Real*. This kind of "fear" arises not from a true threat but from our own thoughts. This type of fear might be better termed *anxiety*, and this is what writer Seth Godin had to say about it: "Anxiety is nothing but repeatedly re-experiencing failure in advance. What a waste."[52] This reflects that many fears are learned and prevent people from doing what they want. Adam Grant, the Wharton professor profiled earlier in this chapter, for example, had a phobia about speaking in public, so he forced himself as a graduate student to lecture as much as possible and take advantage of every opportunity to speak publicly so he could learn to step through the fear (really F.E.A.R.) that was holding him back from achieving his goals.[53] True leaders step through these learned fears to accept responsibility, take risks, make changes, speak their minds, and fight for what they believe.

Courage Means Accepting Responsibility Leaders make a real difference in the world when they are willing to step up and take personal responsibility. Some people just let life happen to them; leaders make things happen. Courageous leaders create opportunities to make a difference in their organizations and communities. One example is Malala Yousafzai, the young girl shot by the Taliban who was described in the chapter-opening example. A business example is John W. Rowe, former chairman and CEO of Aetna. When Rowe, a gerontologist and professor of medicine, was hired in 2000, Aetna was in shambles. The investment community viewed Rowe's appointment with skepticism. One analyst even told Rowe he expected the company's performance to decline with him in charge. Rowe didn't let that bother him; he simply accepted responsibility for fixing what was wrong and redefined the mission and core values to focus on quality care, which he made the guiding principle for all company decisions. By the time Rowe retired in 2006, Aetna had gone from last place to first in trustworthiness and went from losing $1 million to making $5 million a day.[54]

NEW LEADER
ACTION MEMO

As a leader, you can develop the backbone to accept personal responsibility for achieving desired outcomes, going against the status quo, and standing up for what you believe. You can learn to push beyond your comfort zone and break through the fear that limits you.

Courage Often Means Nonconformity Leadership courage means going against the grain, breaking traditions, reducing boundaries, and initiating change. Leaders are willing to take risks for a larger, ethical purpose, and they encourage others to do so.

Going against the status quo can be difficult. Consider the case of Paula Reid, who went against the "boys will be boys" status quo at the U.S. Secret Service in breaking open the Cartagena prostitution scandal.

IN THE LEAD

Paula Reid, U.S. Secret Service

Prostitution is legal in Cartagena, Colombia, but when a U.S. Secret Service agent allegedly refused to pay, it set off a scandal that got several agents fired and tarnished the agency's reputation. Paula Reid, the new supervising manager for the Miami office of the U.S. Secret Service, a prestigious division that oversees the South American region, acted swiftly when she received a report of a disturbance at the hotel where agents preparing for President Barack Obama's visit to Cartagena were staying. Reid didn't particularly care whether prostitution was legal or illegal. The bottom line for her was that visits to strip clubs, heavy drinking, and hiring prostitutes are not acceptable ethical behaviors for Secret Service agents charged with protecting the president of the United States.

Based on information from the hotel manager, Reid swiftly rounded up a dozen agents, ordered them out of the country, and notified her superiors that she had found evidence of "egregious misconduct." The resulting scandal threw the Secret Service into turmoil and put Director Mark Sullivan and other top leaders on the hot seat. Yet, for Reid, the "boys will be boys" mentality is not acceptable in today's world. "If every boss was Paula Reid," said a former agent, "the Secret Service would never have a problem. It would be a lot more boring, but never a problem."[55]

The U.S. Secret Service has apparently tolerated moral lapses in the behavior of agents over the years, but Paula Reid believed that had to change. She acted in spite of a potential internal backlash because she believed the actions of the agents both hurt the agency's reputation and damaged its ability to fulfill its protective and investigative missions.

Most leaders initiating change find some cooperation and support, but they also encounter resistance, rejection, loneliness, and even ridicule. It's often easier to stay with what is familiar, even if it will lead to certain failure, than to initiate bold change.

Courage Means Pushing beyond the Comfort Zone To take a chance and improve things means leaders have to push beyond their comfort zones. When people go beyond the comfort zone, they encounter an internal "wall of fear." A social experiment from 30 years ago illustrates the wall of fear that rises when people push beyond their comfort zones. To explore the web of unwritten rules that govern people's behavior on New York City subways, Dr. Stanley Milgram asked his first-year graduate students to board a crowded train and ask someone for a seat. Milgram's focus of interest soon shifted to the students themselves, as the seemingly simple assignment proved to be extremely difficult, even traumatic. Most students found it decidedly uncomfortable to bluntly ask someone for a seat. One now says of the experiment: "I was afraid I was going to throw up."[56] People may encounter the internal wall of fear when about to ask someone for a date, confront the boss, break off a relationship, launch an expensive project, or change careers. Facing the internal wall of fear is when courage is needed most.

Courage Means Asking for What You Want and Saying What You Think Leaders have to speak out to influence others. However, the desire to please others—especially the boss—can sometimes block the truth. Everyone wants approval, so it is difficult to say things when you think others will disagree or disapprove. Author and scholar Jerry Harvey tells a story of how members of his extended family in Texas decided to drive 40 miles to Abilene for dinner on a hot day when the car air conditioning did not work. They were all miserable. Talking about it afterward, each person admitted they had not wanted to go but went along to please the others. The **Abilene Paradox** is the name Harvey uses to describe the tendency of people to not voice

Abilene Paradox
the tendency of people to resist voicing their true thoughts or feelings in order to please others and avoid conflict

LEADER'S SELF-INSIGHT 6.3

Assess Your Moral Courage

Instructions: Think about situations in which you either assumed or were given a leadership role in a group or organization. Imagine using your own courage as a leader. To what extent does each of the following statements characterize your leadership? Please answer whether each item is Mostly False or Mostly True for you.

	Mostly False	**Mostly True**
1. I risk substantial personal loss to achieve the vision.		✓
2. I take personal risks to defend my beliefs.		✓
3. I say no even if I have a lot to lose.		✓
4. I consciously link my actions to higher values.		✓
5. I don't hesitate to act against the opinions and approval of others.		✓
6. I quickly tell people the truth, even when it is negative.		✓
7. I feel relaxed most of the time.	✓	
8. I speak out against organizational injustice.	✓	
9. I stand up to people if they make offensive remarks.		✓
10. I act according to my conscience even if it means I lose status and approval.		✓

Scoring and Interpretation

Each of the preceding questions pertains to some aspect of displaying courage in a leadership situation. Add up your points for Mostly True answers: 8. If you received a score of 7 or higher, you have real potential to act as a courageous leader. A score below 3 indicates that you avoid difficult issues or have not been in situations that challenge your moral leadership. Is your score consistent with your understanding of your own courage? Look at the individual questions for which you scored Mostly False or Mostly True and think about your specific strengths and weaknesses. Compare your score to that of other students. How might you increase your courage as a leader? Do you want to?

NEW LEADER
ACTION MEMO

Assess your level of leadership courage by completing the exercise in Leader's Self-Insight 6.3.

their true thoughts because they want to please others.[57] Courage means speaking your mind even when you know others may disagree with you and may even deride you. Courage also means asking for what you want and setting boundaries. It is the ability to say no to unreasonable demands from others, as well as the ability to ask for what you want to help achieve the vision.

Courage Means Fighting for What You Believe Courage means fighting for valued outcomes that benefit the whole. Leaders take risks, but they do so for a higher purpose. For example, Ashok Khemka has been a government worker in India for 21 years, and during that time period he has been demoted or transferred to another department 43 times. Why? Because Khemka is a tireless fighter against corruption, and sometimes he ruffles the wrong feathers. Some people—especially bosses who are bending the rules—see him as a troublemaker, but India's anti-corruption activists and many people in the community fully support him. "There are two kinds of government officers—officers who work only to please their political masters, and other officers [like Khemka] who work to uphold the law, who work for justice and the poor," said advocate Kuldip Tiwari.[58]

6-5b How Does Courage Apply to Moral Leadership?

There are many people working in organizations who have the courage to be unconventional, to step up and take responsibility, and to do what they believe is right. Balancing profit with people, self-interest with service, and control with stewardship requires individual moral courage.

Acting Like a Moral Leader Requires Personal Courage To practice moral leadership, leaders have to know themselves, understand their strengths and weaknesses, know what they stand for, and often be nonconformists. Honest self-analysis can be painful, and acknowledging one's limitations in order to recognize the superior abilities of others takes personal strength of character. In addition, moral leadership means building relationships, which requires listening, having significant personal experiences with others, and making yourself vulnerable—qualities that frighten many people. Yet, by getting close and doing what is best for others—sharing the good and the bad, the pain and anger as well as the success and the joy—leaders bring out the best qualities in others.[59]

An example of this in practice is when William Peace had to initiate a layoff as general manager of the Synthetic Fuels Division of Westinghouse. Peace had the courage to deliver the news about layoffs personally. He took some painful blows in the face-to-face meetings he held with the workers to be laid off, but he believed allowing people to vent their grief and anger at him and the situation was the moral thing to do. His action sent a message that leaders valued employees as human beings with feelings. Thus, employees rededicated themselves to helping save the division.[60] For Peace, the courage to practice moral leadership by personally facing employees gained respect, renewed commitment, and higher performance, even though he suffered personally in the short run.

Opposing Unethical Conduct Requires Courage **Whistleblowing** means employee disclosure of illegal, immoral, or unethical practices in the organization.[61] One recent example is Charles M. Smith, who was the senior civilian overseeing the U.S. Army's multibillion-dollar contract with KBR when he faced a test of courage. Smith couldn't find evidence justifying more than $1 billion in costs for food, housing, and other services from the contractor, but he was being asked to approve the payments anyway. He refused to sign off, despite pressures from both Army and civilian officials. Smith was removed from his job and transferred to another position. He retired soon afterward and went to the media with the story.[62]

Whistleblowing
employee disclosure of illegal, immoral, or unethical practices in the organization

As this example shows, it is highly risky for employees to blow the whistle because they may lose their jobs, be ostracized by coworkers, or be transferred to undesirable positions. Michael Woodford, former president and CEO of Olympus, described what it was like to be at the center of a major whistleblowing scandal. Woodford had been with Olympus for 30 years when he was named president and CEO in early 2011. He soon discovered that unauthorized payments had been made to third parties in an effort to hide significant losses. He went to the board, but they ignored his findings. After he went public, Woodford was voted out of a job. He describes what happened next: "I was petrified. You feel your career is slipping away." Woodford says as painful as the experience was, it was a huge education, and he has no regrets for doing the right thing. The entire board at Olympus eventually resigned, and three senior executives pleaded guilty to fraud.[63]

Most whistleblowers, like Charles Smith and Michael Woodford, realize they may suffer financially and emotionally, but they act courageously to do what they think is right. As Woodford says, "If you know something is wrong and you don't deal with it, you are complicit."[64]

6-5c Finding Personal Courage

How does a leader find the courage to step through fear and confusion, to act despite the risks involved? All of us have the potential to live and act courageously.

NEW LEADER
ACTION MEMO

As a leader, you can find your personal courage by committing to something you deeply believe in. You can welcome potential failure as a means of growth and development and build bonds of caring and mutual support with family, friends, and colleagues to reduce fear.

There are a number of ways leaders can unlock the courage within themselves, including committing to causes they believe in, connecting with others, harnessing anger, and developing their skills.

Believe in a Higher Purpose Courage comes easily when we fight for something we really believe in. Leaders who have a strong emotional commitment to a larger vision or purpose find the courage to step through fear. When Charles Smith, the leader who refused to pay KBR, was asked about his decision, he said, "Ultimately, the money that was going to KBR was money being taken away from the troops, and I wasn't going to do that."[65] For Smith, caring about the well-being of soldiers gave him the courage to refuse payments to a contractor that he believed were fraudulent. Noorjahan Akbar, the 21-year-old founder of Young Women for Change, says numerous activists fighting for women's rights in Afghanistan have been injured or killed, but it only strengthened their resolve to push for change. Akbar and others don't risk their lives just for the thrill of it. They do it for a cause they deeply believe in.[66] General Stanley McChrystal (U.S. Army Retired) explains how a higher purpose of serving followers can be a source of courage.

IN THE LEAD

General Stanley A. McChrystal, United States Army

General Stanley McChrystal, who retired from the U.S. Army as a four-star general after more than 34 years of service, is best known for leading the covert Joint Special Operations Command during the Persian Gulf Wars and commanding all American and coalition forces in Afghanistan.

McChrystal says his greatest fear has always been failing the organization and his followers. "It's not fear of getting shot at, or worrying that you're going to crash the airplane, or something like that . . .," he says. Leading people, particularly in warfare situations, means that you have a huge commitment to a lot of people. To overcome the fear, McChrystal focuses on the problem at hand and how to achieve the best possible outcome for his followers and the organization.

McChrystal bases much of his leadership philosophy on advice that came from his mentor, Lieutenant General John Vines, whom McChrystal describes as the perfect model of a servant leader. Courage comes from committing to and investing in followers, who are the ones doing the hard work on the front lines. "I think of the young private on a checkpoint in Baghdad . . . who has almost no control [over what happens] and lots of time on his hands to think," McChrystal says. "When I look at courage, I look at the 18-year-old kid . . . standing out there doing that. . . . That's pretty humbling."[67]

Draw Strength from Others Caring about others and having support from others is a potent source of courage in a topsy-turvy world. Support for this proposition comes from studies of the civil rights movement in the southern United States in the 1960s. In the Mississippi Freedom Summer Project, young volunteers were recruited to register black voters, run Freedom Schools, and raise civil rights awareness. Within days of the volunteers arriving in Mississippi, three were kidnapped and killed. Throughout the summer, dozens of churches were set on fire, safe houses were bombed, and volunteers were shot at, beaten, and arrested. A quarter of the volunteers in the program dropped out. Researchers have looked at what distinguished those who stayed from those who left. The volunteers who stayed were far more likely to have what is referred to as *strong ties*, close friends who were also in the program and people they were close to back home who were deeply interested in their lives and activities. Those who left the program were just as committed to the goals and purpose, but they typically didn't have the same social support.[68]

People who feel alone in the world take fewer risks because they have more to lose.[69] Interestingly, although social media such as Twitter and Facebook have made it easier for people to join with others to support social causes or push for change within organizations, there is some evidence that social media actually reduce strong ties (deep personal connections), making it harder for people to express courage when they need it.[70]

Harness Frustration and Anger If you have ever been really angry about something, you know that it can cause you to forget about fear of failure, fear of embarrassment, or fear that others won't like you. Peggy Payne, now in her mid-60s, has had a highly successful career as a journalist and author but says she still gets angry when she thinks about not being chosen to attend the prestigious Governor's School of North Carolina when she was 16 years old. The anger, she says, helped fuel a commitment to show everyone she could be successful.[71] Frustration and anger spurred Glenn McIntyre to found a company. After he was paralyzed in a motorcycle accident, McIntyre got angry every time he stayed at a hotel. His anger and frustration over how poorly hotels served disabled guests gave him the courage to stop feeling sorry for himself and start a new business, Access Designs. The firm helps hotels such as Quality Suites and Renaissance Ramada redesign their spaces to be more usable for disabled travelers.[72] Anger, in moderate amounts, is a healthy emotion that provides energy to move forward. The challenge is to harness anger and use it appropriately.[73]

Take Small Steps In most cases within organizations, finding courage is a deliberate act rather than an instantaneous response.[74] Courage can be thought of as a decision-making skill that is developed through conscious thought and practice. Courageous leaders are not reckless and foolhardy; they typically are people who have developed the skills and resources they need to take a difficult stand or pursue a tough course of action. In addition, courageous leaders can develop courageous followers by modeling courage in their own behavior and by helping people practice courage.

One leader who was promoted to CFO was being pressured to restate restructuring charges so it would look more favorable and help the stock price. Rather than simply refusing to do so, this leader developed an integrity campaign, reminding people of the firm's strong tradition of values-driven leadership. This provided support to other leaders who didn't want to go along with the unethical behavior but didn't have the courage to resist pressures from more senior executives.[75] Good leaders remind themselves that dealing with difficult ethical issues is a crucial part of their jobs.

LEADERSHIP ESSENTIALS

- This chapter explored a number of ideas concerning moral leadership and leadership courage. People want honest and trustworthy leaders. However, leaders face many pressures that challenge their ability to do the right thing—pressures to cut costs, increase profits, meet the demands of various stakeholders, and look successful. Creating an ethical organization requires that leaders act based on moral principles.

- Leaders are the symbols for the organization's ethical climate. When they excessively promote self-interest, practice deception and breach agreements, and lack the courage to confront unjust acts, they hurt the organization and everyone associated with it. Ethical leaders are humble, honest, and straightforward. They maintain a concern for the greater good, strive for fairness, and demonstrate the courage to stand up for what is right. Acting as a moral leader means demonstrating the importance of serving people and society as well as increasing profits or personal gain.
- One personal consideration for leaders is the level of moral development. Leaders use an understanding of the stages of moral development to enhance their own as well as followers' moral growth. Leaders who operate at higher stages of moral development focus on the needs of followers and universal moral principles.
- Ideas about control versus service between leaders and followers are changing and expanding, reflected in a continuum of leader–follower relationships. The continuum varies from authoritarian managers to participative managers to stewardship to servant leadership. Leaders who operate from the principles of stewardship and servant leadership can help build ethical organizations.
- The final sections of the chapter discussed leadership courage and how leaders can find their own courage. Courage means having the mental and moral strength to confront, persevere through, and withstand danger, difficulty, or fear. Courageous leaders accept responsibility, take risks and make changes, speak their minds, and fight for what they believe. Two expressions of courage in organizations are moral leadership and ethical whistleblowing. Sources of courage include belief in a higher purpose, connection with others, harnessing anger, and developing courage step by step.

DISCUSSION QUESTIONS

1. What are some pressures you face as a student that challenge your ability to do the right thing? Do you expect to face more or fewer pressures as a leader? Discuss what some of these pressures might be.
2. If most adults are at a conventional level of moral development, what does this mean for their potential for moral leadership?
3. How might understanding the difference between "fear" and "F.E.A.R.," as described in the chapter, make you a better leader? Can you name an example from your own life of "false evidence appearing real"?
4. One finding is that when leaders are under stress so that fear and risk increase, they tend to revert to an authoritarian, command-and-control style. As a leader, how might you find the courage to resist this tendency?
5. If you were in a position as a student similar to Mike McQueary at Pennsylvania State University, what do you think you would do? Why?
6. Should serving others be placed at a higher moral level than serving oneself? Discuss.
7. If it is immoral to prevent those around you from growing to their fullest potential, are you being moral?
8. Leaders at several organizations, including Hostess Brands (Twinkies), Sbarro, and Blockbuster, have gotten significant raises or bonuses shortly before the firms filed for

bankruptcy. The companies have argued that it was a necessary step to keep managers during a difficult time. Do you think this is a legitimate argument from an ethical standpoint? Discuss.

9. Do you agree that it is important for leaders to do the right thing even if no one will ever know about it? Why or why not?
10. A consultant recently argued that the emphasis on corporate governance and social responsibility has distracted leaders from key business issues such as serving customers and beating competitors. Do you agree? Should leaders put business issues first or ethical issues first?

LEADERSHIP AT WORK

Scary Person

Think of a person in your life right now who is something of a scary person for you. Scary people are those you don't really know but who are scary to you because you anticipate that you won't like them, perhaps because you don't like the way they act or look from a distance, and hence you avoid building relationships with them. A scary person might be a student at school, someone at work, a neighbor, or someone you are aware of in your social circle.

Scary people trigger a small amount of fear in us—that is why we avoid them and don't really get to know them. A test of courage is whether you can step through your fear. You will experience fear many times as a leader.

For this exercise, your assignment is to reach out to one or more scary persons in your life. Invite the person for lunch or just walk up and introduce yourself and start a conversation. Perhaps you can volunteer to work with the person on an assignment. The key thing is to step through your fear and get to know this person well enough to know what he or she is really like.

After you have completed your assignment, share what happened with another person. Were you able to reach out to the scary person? What did you discover about the scary person? What did you discover about yourself by doing this activity? If you found the exercise silly and refused to do it, you may have let F.E.A.R. get the better of you by rationalizing that the assignment has little value.

In Class: The instructor can give this assignment to be done prior to a specific class session. During class it is a good exercise for students to discuss their scary person experiences among themselves in small groups. The instructor can ask students to report to their groups about the scary person, revealing as many details as they are comfortable with, explaining how they summoned the courage to reach out, and the result. After the groups have finished their exchange, the instructor can ask a couple of student volunteers to report their experiences to the entire class. Then students can be asked questions such as: Looking back on this experience, what is courage? How was it expressed (or not) in this exercise? How will fear and courage be part of your organizational leadership?

LEADERSHIP DEVELOPMENT: CASES FOR ANALYSIS

"What Should I Say?"

The sudden heart attack of his predecessor, Bill Andrews, propelled Russell Hart into a temporary top management assignment for Kresk International in the company's new Middle East Division in Riyadh, Saudi Arabia. Kresk management had targeted Saudi as a must-have division and was enthusiastic about the expansion.

After six months of a one-year assignment in Riyadh with travel throughout the Middle East, Russell was making a brief trip to Dallas to report at the semiannual board meeting before returning to Saudi. He understood that in addition to his assessment of the company's situation in the region, a portion of the board meeting would focus on the improved health of Andrews and, based on that, a determination would be made as to whether he or Bill Andrews would have the permanent assignment at the end of the year. The two were close friends and had corresponded regularly over the past months, and Russell looked forward to Bill's full recovery and return to work. However, single and adventurous by nature, Russell enjoyed the company's top assignment and hoped to impress management at the meeting so that he would be named director of the Middle East Division.

"Here's where my personal ambitions and my personal ethics collide," Russell admitted to his assistant Christopher Dunn as the Kresk corporate jet left Riyadh. "I mean, look at all of this. It's a dream job. It's *my* dream job and I can do this. If anyone had told me back in high school in Nebraska that I would be on a corporate jet flying from Saudi Arabia, I'd have laughed them out of Sydney."

"Excuse me, Russell, would you and Christopher care for anything to drink?" the cabin attendant asked.

"Yes, a *Jameson*," Russell said.

"Same here," Christopher added.

As the attendant walked away, Russell leaned over, speaking quietly. "Corporate is *so* enthusiastic about this region. They are expecting nothing short of a glowing report that basically says, 'Wow, we really hit the jackpot with this move.' And that's what we've put together here over the past few weeks. It looks fantastic! But my little man in here," he said, pointing to his stomach, "keeps nagging me—do I give them, 'Wow, we hit the jackpot' and become the darling of the company, or do I give them the truth, that we have some potential serious problems with this division..."

"... And hand the job to Bill," Christopher said as the drinks arrived.

"Exactly. By the end of the year, their numbers may look great and they may meet our performance standards, but I have serious problems with the management here. I realize that we're working with a different culture and I can make allowances. I have no problem pacing my day around their prayer obligations. I know to avoid any business during Ramadan or around the two Eids. I've become comfortable meeting a sheikh or *sayyid** and I've even lost my sense of self-consciousness when a businessman holds my hand to lead me into a room. I can deal with all of these things. But there is a level here within the organization that bothers me and that I think would bother most managers at headquarters and *that's* what I struggle with in this report. Should I be honest?"

"Well, you know—honesty is the best..."

"Don't say it. This is my career we're talking about."

"OK, what do you want to add—or *not* add?"

"The major problem here is Youssef Said," Russell said.

"I know. But I think I would stay away from mentioning that. The company loves the guy. Bill Andrews has been his champion because of excellent results, at least in the short run."

"I don't agree. And I think they won't when they see him in action. I don't understand why Bill supports him."

"They've *seen* him in action," Christopher said.

"Oh, they've seen what he *wants* them to see. You and I have seen his interaction with staff and employees on a daily basis. His mistreatment of people is appalling. I see a total disregard for the opinions of others, and he seems to take considerable pleasure in humiliating people. He screams at them! A few have quit. I've questioned him about it a couple of times and all he says is, 'I know. Please understand ...' "

"It is the way it is done here," Christopher said, completing the phrase the two heard on a regular basis.

"I *don't* believe it is the way it's done here. It's not our culture, at least not in the U.S. and Europe. I think this has always been *his* way. I wonder about the effects on morale, and I think the people who work here will believe the company is in agreement with him and that this is our policy," Russell said. "Youssef has that little inner circle of family and friends that he trusts and really nothing beyond that. To me, it seems he's always working a deal, bending a rule. I know that Arabs love to trade and love to negotiate, but there are too many favors, too many unwritten agreements and payments, and I wonder if we should intervene. I wonder if international laws or the company's own ethics are being set aside. I have serious doubts that this guy is going to work with the Kresk culture and our company ethics. But do I need to include my concerns in this initial report . . ."

"Or will you just be busting the board's bubble, and raise doubts about Bill, or perhaps they will doubt you and risk your shot at the job you want?"

"On the other hand, if I am seeing what I consider severe long-term problems and say nothing now, in this report, and the problems show up later, will *I* be guilty of breaking a code of ethics?" Russell paused. "So, Christopher, what do I say tomorrow at the board meeting?"

QUESTIONS

1. What do you think Russell Hart should include in his report about Youssef Said? Why? What would you do in his position?
2. What amount or kind of courage will be required for Hart to disclose everything honestly? How would you advise Hart to acquire that courage?
3. At which stage of Kohlberg's moral development scale would you place Youssef Said, Russell Hart, and Bill Andrews? Why?

Notes: *Descendant of the Prophet Muhammad

The Boy, the Girl, the Ferryboat Captain, and the Hermits

There was an island, and on this island there lived a girl. A short distance away there was another island, and on this island there lived a boy. The boy and the girl were very much in love with each other.

The boy had to leave his island and go on a long journey, and he would be gone for a very long time. The girl felt that she must see the boy one more time before he went away. There was only one way to get from the island where the girl lived to the boy's island, and that was on a ferryboat that was run by a ferryboat captain. And so the girl went down to the dock and asked the ferryboat captain to take her to the island where the boy lived. The ferryboat captain agreed and asked her for the fare. The girl told the ferryboat captain that she did not have any money. The ferryboat captain told her that money was not necessary: "I will take you to the other island if you will stay with me tonight."

The girl did not know what to do, so she went up into the hills on her island until she came to a hut where a hermit lived. We will call him the first hermit. She related the whole story to the hermit and asked for his advice. The hermit listened carefully to her story, and then told her, "I cannot tell you what to do. You must weigh the alternatives and the sacrifices that are involved and come to a decision within your own heart."

And so the girl went back down to the dock and accepted the ferryboat captain's offer. The next day, when the girl arrived on the other island, the boy was waiting at the dock to greet her. They embraced, and then the boy asked her how she got over to his island, for he knew she did not have any money. The girl explained the ferryboat captain's offer and what she did. The boy pushed her away from him and said, "We're through. That's the end. Go away from me. I never want to see you again," and he left her.

The girl was desolate and confused. She went up into the hills of the boy's island to a hut where a second hermit lived. She told the whole story to the second hermit and asked him what she should do. The hermit told her that there was nothing she could do, that she was welcome to stay in his hut, to partake of his food, and to rest on his bed while he went down into the town and begged for enough money to pay the girl's fare back to her own island.

When the second hermit returned with the money for her, the girl asked him how she could repay him. The hermit answered, "You owe me nothing. We owe this to each other. I am only too happy to be of help." And so the girl went back down to the dock and returned to her own island.

QUESTIONS

1. List in order the characters in this story that you like, from most to least. What values governed your choices?
2. Rate the characters on their level of moral development. Explain.
3. Evaluate each character's level of courage. Discuss.

REFERENCES

1. Christine Roberts, "Malala Yousafzai Returns to School for First Time since She Was Shot by the Taliban," *Daily News* (March 19, 2013), http://www.thedailybeast.com/articles/2012/10/18/sisters-in-arms-young-afghan-activist-continues-malala-s-fight.html#body_text2 (accessed April 2, 2013); Alia E. Dastagir, "Pakistan Girl Shot by Taliban Seals Book Deal," *USA Today* (March 28, 2013), http://www.usatoday.com/story/news/world/2013/03/27/malala-pakistan-book-deal/2026697/ (accessed April 2, 2013); and "Young Journalist Inspires Fellow Students," *Institute for War and Peace Reporting* (December 5, 2009), http://iwpr.net/report-news/young-journalist-inspires-fellow-students-0 (accessed April 2, 2013).
2. Roberts, "Malala Yousafzai Returns to School."
3. Ben Worthen and Joann S. Lublin, "Mark Hurd Neglected to Follow H-P Code," *The Wall Street Journal* (August 9, 2010), p. B1; Miguel Bustillo, "Best Buy Chairman to Resign After Probe," *The Wall Street Journal* (May 15, 2012), http://online.wsj.com/article/SB10001424052702304192704577403922338506912.html (accessed April 3, 2013); and Amir Efrati and Joann S. Lublin, "Yahoo CEO's Downfall," *The Wall Street Journal Online* (May 15, 2012), http://online.wsj.com/article/SB10001424052702304192704577404530999458956.html (accessed July 2, 2012).
4. Anemona Hartocollis, "At Ailing Brooklyn Hospital, Insider Deals and Lavish Perks," *The New York Times* (March 26, 2012), p. A1.
5. Chuck Salter, paraphrasing Bill George, former CEO of Medtronic, in "Mr. Inside Speaks Out," *Fast Company* (September 2004), pp. 92–93.
6. Floyd Norris, "In Actions, S. & P. Risked Andersen's Fate," *The New York Times* (February 7, 2013), http://www.nytimes.com/2013/02/08/business/sp-may-have-tempted-arthur-andersens-fate.html?pagewanted=all&_r=0 (accessed February 8, 2013).
7. Margaret Wheatley, "Fearless Leaders: We Need Them Here and Now," *Leadership Excellence* (June 2010), pp. 5–6.
8. Roger Martin, "The CEO's Ethical Dilemma in the Era of Earnings Management," *Strategy & Leadership* 39, no. 6 (2011), pp. 43–47.
9. Quoted in David Wessel, "Venal Sins: Why the Bad Guys of the Boardroom Emerged en Masse," *The Wall Street Journal* (June 20, 2002), pp. A1, A6.
10. Ronald W. Clement, "Just How Unethical Is American Business?" *Business Horizons* 49 (2006), pp. 313–327.
11. Gary R. Weaver, Linda Klebe Treviño, and Bradley Agle, "'Somebody I Look Up To': Ethical Role Models in Organizations," *Organizational Dynamics* 34, no. 4 (2005), pp. 313–330; Joseph L. Badaracco Jr., and Allen P. Webb, "Business Ethics: A View from the Trenches," *California Management Review* 37, no. 2 (Winter 1995), pp. 8–28; and Arlen W. Langvardt, "Ethical Leadership and the Dual Roles of Examples," *Business Horizons* 55 (2012), pp. 373–384.
12. Michiko Kakutani, "The Tsunami That Buried a Wall Street Giant," *The New York Times* (March 10, 2009), p. C4.
13. Based on Susan Berfield, "Will Investors Put the Lid on the Container Store's Generous Wages?" *Bloomberg Business Week* (February 19, 2015), http://www.bloomberg.com/news/articles/2015-02-19/container-store-conscious-capitalism-and-the-perils-of-going-public (accessed October 20, 2015).
14. This section is based on Donald G. Zauderer, "Integrity: An Essential Executive Quality," *Business Forum* (Fall, 1992), pp. 12–16.
15. "New York's Pension Scandal," *The New York Times* (October 7, 2010), http://www.nytimes.com/2010/10/08/opinion/08fri2.html?_r=0 (accessed April 3, 2013); and "Review Shows NY Pension Fund Fixed Ethics," *The Wall Street Journal* (February 19, 2013), http://online.wsj.com/article/APa0f276305f884319a004f97a2de34b8a.html (accessed April 3, 2013).
16. Patricia Wallington, "Honestly?!" *CIO* (March 15, 2003), pp. 41–42.
17. Langvardt, "Ethical Leadership and the Dual Roles of Examples"; Jeremy Roebuck and Amy Worden, "McQueary Affirms Report to Officials: Says He Told of Seeing 'Severe Sexual Acts' in the Showers," *Philadelphia Inquirer* (December 17, 2011), p. A1; Jo Becker, "E-Mails Suggest Paterno Role in Silence on Sandusky," *The New York Times* (July 1, 2012), http://www.nytimes.com/2012/07/01/sports/ncaafootball/paterno-may-have-influenced-decision-not-to-report-sandusky-e-mails-indicate.html?_r=1&emc=eta1 (accessed July 9, 2012); Drew Sharp, "At Penn State, Football Bigger Than Principle," *Pittsburgh Post-Gazette* (June 25, 2012), p. A8; and Alina Tugend, "Doing the Ethical Thing May Be Right, But It Isn't Automatic," *The New York Times* (November 18, 2011).
18. Langvardt, "Ethical Leadership and the Dual Roles of Examples."
19. Carly Fiorina, "Corporate Leadership and the Crisis," *The Wall Street Journal* (December 12, 2008), p. A19.
20. Al Gini, "Moral Leadership and Business Ethics," *The Journal of Leadership Studies* 4, no. 4 (Fall 1997), pp. 64–81.
21. Henry Ford Sr., quoted by Thomas Donaldson, *Corporations and Morality* (Upper Saddle River, NJ: Prentice Hall, 1982), p. 57.
22. Michael E. Brown and Linda K. Treviño, "Ethical Leadership: A Review and Future Directions," *The Leadership Quarterly* 17 (2006), pp. 595–616; Darin W. White and Emily Lean, "The Impact of Perceived Leader Integrity on Subordinates in a Work Team Environment," *Journal of Business Ethics* 81 (2008), pp. 767–778; Weaver, Treviño, and Agle, "'Somebody I Look Up To'"; and Badaracco and Webb, "Business Ethics: A View from the Trenches."
23. Joseph Weber, "The New Ethics Enforcers," *BusinessWeek* (February 13, 2006), pp. 76–77.
24. More Than Wheels Mission and Core Values, http://www.morethanwheels.org/mission (accessed May 18, 2013).
25. Rashid Ameer and Radiah Othman, "Sustainability Practices and Corporate Financial Performance: A Study Based on the Top Global Corporations," *Journal of Business Ethics* 108, no. 1 (June 2012), pp. 61–79.
26. Curtis C. Verschoor and Elizabeth A. Murphy, "The Financial Performance of Large U.S. Firms and Those with Global Prominence: How Do the Best Corporate Citizens Rate?" *Business and Society Review* 107, no. 3 (Fall 2002), pp. 371–381.
27. Phred Dvorak, "Finding the Best Measure of 'Corporate Citizenship,'" *The Wall Street Journal* (July 2, 2007), p. B3.
28. Zauderer, "Integrity: An Essential Executive Quality."
29. James M. Kouzes and Barry Z. Posner, *Credibility: How Leaders Gain and Lose It, Why People Demand It* (San Francisco: Jossey-Bass, 1993), p. 255.
30. Mary C. Gentile, "Combating Ethical Cynicism and Voicing Values in the Workplace," *Ivey Business Journal* (May–June 2011), http://

www.iveybusinessjournal.com/topics/leadership/combating-ethical-cynicism-and-voicing-values-in-the-workplace (accessed April 3, 2013).

31. Lawrence Kohlberg, "Moral Stages and Moralization: The Cognitive Developmental Approach," in Thomas Likona, ed., *Moral Development and Behavior: Theory, Research, and Social Issues* (Austin, TX: Holt, Rinehart and Winston, 1976), pp. 31–53; Linda K. Treviño, Gary R. Weaver, and Scott J. Reynolds, "Behavioral Ethics in Organizations: A Review," *Journal of Management* 32, no. 6 (December 2006), pp. 951–990; Jill W. Graham, "Leadership, Moral Development, and Citizenship Behavior," *Business Ethics Quarterly* 5, no. 1 (January 1995), pp. 43–54; James Weber, "Exploring the Relationship between Personal Values and Moral Reasoning," *Human Relations* 46, no. 4 (April 1993), pp. 435–463; and Duane M. Covrig, "The Organizational Context of Moral Dilemmas: The Role of Moral Leadership in Administration in Making and Breaking Dilemmas," *The Journal of Leadership Studies* 7, no. 1 (2000), pp. 40–59.
32. Vivian Yee, "Stuyvesant Students Describe the How and the Why of Cheating," *The New York Times* (September 25, 2012), http://www.nytimes.com/2012/09/26/education/stuyvesant-high-school-students-describe-rationale-for-cheating.html?pagewanted=all (accessed April 3, 2013).
33. Quoted in Richard Pérez-Peña, "Studies Find More Students Cheating, with High Achievers No Exception," *The New York Times* (September 7, 2010), http://www.nytimes.com/2012/09/08/education/studies-show-more-students-cheat-even-high-achievers.html (accessed April 3, 2013).
34. Anthony F. Buono et al., "Acting Ethically: Moral Reasoning and Business School Student Behavior," *SAM Advanced Management Journal* (Summer 2012), pp. 18–26.
35. J. R. Rest, D. Narvaez, M. J. Bebeau, and S. J. Thoma, *Postconventional Moral Thinking: A Neo-Kohlbergian Approach* (Mahwah, NJ: Lawrence Erlbaum, 1999).
36. James Weber, "Exploring the Relationship between Personal Values and Moral Reasoning," *Human Relations* 46, no. 4 (April 1993), pp. 435–463.
37. White and Lean, "The Impact of Perceived Leader Integrity on Subordinates in a Work Team Environment"; Peter Block, "Reassigning Responsibility," *Sky* (February 1994), pp. 26–31; and David P. McCaffrey, Sue R. Faerman, and David W. Hart, "The Appeal and Difficulty of Participative Systems," *Organization Science* 6, no. 6 (November–December 1995), pp. 603–627.
38. Block, "Reassigning Responsibility."
39. This discussion of stewardship is based on Peter Block, *Stewardship: Choosing Service over Self-Interest* (San Francisco: Berrett-Koehler, 1993), pp. 29–31; Block, "Reassigning Responsibility"; Morela Hernandez, "Promoting Stewardship Behavior in Organizations: A Leadership Model," *Journal of Business Ethics* 80, no. 1 (June 2008), pp. 121–128; Morela Hernandez, "Toward an Understanding of the Psychology of Stewardship," *Academy of Management Review* 37, no. 2 (2012), pp. 172–193; and Gary Hamel, "Leaders as Stewards: What Matters Are Bedrock Values," *Leadership Excellence* (August 2012), p. 5.
40. Martin Edwards, "Workforce Engagement: Case Study of an Award-Winning Leadership Model," *Industrial and Commercial Training* 44, no. 3 (2012), pp. 132–138.
41. Lawrence G. Foster, *Robert Wood Johnson—The Gentleman Rebel* (Lemont, PA: Lillian Press, 1999); and John Cunniff, "Businessman's Honesty, Integrity Lesson for Today," *Johnson City Press* (May 28, 2000).
42. Adam Bluestein, "Start a Company. Change the World." *Inc.* (May 2011), pp. 71–80.
43. Sen Sendjaya and James C. Sarros, "Servant Leadership: Its Origin, Development, and Application in Organizations," *Journal of Leadership and Organizational Studies* 9, no. 2 (2002), pp. 57–64. Examples include B. M. Bass, "The Future of Leadership in Learning Organizations," *The Journal of Leadership Studies* 7, no. 3 (2000), pp. 18–40; I. H. Buchen, "Servant Leadership: A Model for Future Faculty and Future Institutions," *The Journal of Leadership Studies* 5, no. 1 (1998), pp. 125–134; Y. Choi and R. R. Mai-Dalton, "On the Leadership Function of Self-Sacrifice," *Leadership Quarterly* 9, no. 4 (1998), pp. 475–501; and R. F. Russell, "The Role of Values in Servant Leadership," *Leadership and Organizational Development Journal* 22, no. 2 (2001), pp. 76–83.
44. Robert K. Greenleaf, *Servant Leadership: A Journey into the Nature of Legitimate Power and Greatness* (Mahwah, NJ: Paulist Press, 1977).
45. The following is based on Greenleaf, *Servant Leadership*; Walter Kiechel III, "The Leader as Servant," *Fortune* (May 4, 1992), pp. 121–122; and Mary Sue Polleys, "One University's Response to the Anti-Leadership Vaccine: Developing Servant Leaders," *The Journal of Leadership Studies* 8, no. 3 (2002), pp. 117–130.
46. Sendjaya and Sarros, "Servant Leadership: Its Origin, Development, and Application in Organizations."
47. Susan Dominus, "Is Giving the Secret to Getting Ahead?" *The New York Times Magazine* (March 27, 2013). http://www.nytimes.com/2013/03/31/magazine/is-giving-the-secret-to-getting-ahead.html?pagewanted=all&_r=0 (accessed April 4, 2013).
48. C. William Pollard, "The Leader Who Serves," in Frances Hesselbein, Marshall Goldsmith, and Richard Beckhard, eds., *The Leader of the Future* (San Francisco: Jossey-Bass, 1996), pp. 241–248; and C. W. Pollard, "The Leader Who Serves," *Strategy and Leadership* (September–October 1997), pp. 49–51.
49. Peter Voyer, "Courage in Leadership: From the Battlefield to the Boardroom," *Ivey Business Journal* (November–December 2011), http://www.iveybusinessjournal.com/topics/leadership/courage-in-leadership-from-the-battlefield-to-the-boardroom (accessed November 24, 2011).
50. John McCain, "In Search of Courage," *Fast Company* (September 2004), pp. 53–56.
51. Richard L. Daft and Robert H. Lengel, *Fusion Leadership: Unlocking the Subtle Forces That Change People and Organizations* (San Francisco: Berrett-Koehler, 1998).
52. The F.E.A.R. acronym and the quote are from Brian Clark, "Is F.E.A. R. Holding You Back?" *Copyblogger.com* (May 28, 2010), http://www.copyblogger.com/f-e-a-r/ (accessed May 19, 2011).
53. Dominus, "Is Giving the Secret to Getting Ahead?"
54. Brian Moriarty and R. Edward Freeman, "Case in Point: To Go from Worst to First, Alter the Business Model," *The Washington Post* (December 10, 2011), http://articles.washingtonpost.com/2011-12-10/business/35286296_1_aetna-employees-john-w-rowe-business-model (accessed December 11, 2011).
55. Carol D. Leonnig and David Nakamura, "Official Quickly Corralled Agents," *The Washington Post* (April 22, 2012), p. A1; David Nakamura, "Out of Public Eye, a Disgusted Secret Service Director," *The Washington Post* (April 26, 2012), p. A1; Carol D. Leonnig and David Nakamura, "Four in Secret Service Fight Back," *The Washington Post* (May 23, 2012), p. A1; and William Neuman, "Prostitutes Perplexed as Glare Falls on City's Brothels," *The New York Times* (April 25, 2012), http://www.nytimes.com/2012/04/26/world/americas/cartagenas-prostitutes-perplexed-by-global-glare.html?_r=0 (accessed April 6, 2013).
56. Michael Luo, "Revisiting a Social Experiment, and the Fear That Goes with It," *The New York Times* (September 14, 2004), Section B, p. 1.
57. Jerry B. Harvey, *The Abilene Paradox and Other Meditations on Management* (Lexington, MA: Lexington Books, 1988), pp. 13–15.
58. Simon Denyer, "Incorruptible Indian Bureaucrat Hounded Out of Office for Fighting Graft—43 Times," *The Washington Post* (October 22, 2012), http://articles.washingtonpost.com/2012-10-22/world/35500968_1_ashok-khemka-vadra-case-robert-vadra (accessed October 23, 2012).
59. A. J. Vogl, "Risky Work" (an interview with Max DuPree), *Across the Board* (July/August 1993), pp. 27–31.
60. William H. Peace, "The Hard Work of Being a Soft Manager," *Harvard Business Review* (November–December 1991), pp. 40–47.
61. Janet P. Near and Marcia P. Miceli, "Effective Whistle-Blowing," *Academy of Management Review* 20, no. 3 (1995), pp. 679–708.

62. James Risen, "Army Overseer Tells of Ouster over KBR Stir," *The New York Times* (June 17, 2008), http://www.nytimes.com/2008/06/17/washington/17contractor.html?pagewanted=all&_r=0 (accessed April 8, 2013); and John Baldoni, "Putting Courage into Action for Others and Yourself," *Leader to Leader* (Winter 2011), pp. 24–26.
63. Robert Jeffery, "Whistleblowers: 'Suddenly I Was the Lead in a John Grisham Novel': How Michael Woodford, The CEO Who Exposed the Olympus Fraud, Gambled His Career on Doing the Right Thing," *People Management* (November 2012), pp. 28–29.
64. Ibid.
65. Risen, "Army Overseer Tells of Ouster."
66. Alyse Walsh, "Sisters in Arms: Young Afghan Activist Continues Malala's Fight," *The Daily Beast* (October 18, 2012), http://www.thedailybeast.com/articles/2012/10/18/sisters-in-arms-young-afghan-activist-continues-malala-s-fight.html (accessed April 8, 2013).
67. General Stanley McChrystal, as told to Kris Frieswick, "How I Deal With My Biggest Fear," *Inc.* (July-August 2015), pp. 90–91; and Dan Schawbel, "Stanley McChrystal: What the Army Can Teach You About Leadership," *Forbes* (July 13, 2015), http://www.forbes.com/sites/danschawbel/2015/07/13/stanley-mcchrystal-what-the-army-can-teach-you-about-leadership/ (accessed October 20, 2015).
68. Discussed in Malcolm Gladwell, "Small Change: Why the Revolution Will Not Be Tweeted," *The New Yorker* (October 4, 2010), http://www.newyorker.com/reporting/2010/10/04/101004fa_fact_gladwell (accessed April 8, 2013).
69. James M. Kouzes and Barry Z. Posner, *The Leadership Challenge: How to Get Extraordinary Things Done in Organizations* (San Francisco: Jossey-Bass, 1988).
70. Gladwell, "Small Change: Why the Revolution Will Not Be Tweeted"; and Wheatley, "Fearless Leaders."
71. Peggy Payne, "How Insults Spur Success," *The New York Times* (October 15, 2011), http://www.nytimes.com/2011/10/16/jobs/16pre.html?_r=0 (accessed April 8, 2013).
72. Michael Warshaw, ed., "Great Comebacks," *Success* (July/August 1995), pp. 33–46.
73. Ira Chaleff, *The Courageous Follower: Standing Up to and for Our Leaders* (San Francisco: Berrett-Koehler, 1995).
74. This section is based on Kathleen K. Reardon, "Courage as a Skill," *Harvard Business Review* (January 2007), pp. 58–64; Mary C. Gentile, "Managing Yourself: Keeping Your Colleagues Honest," *Harvard Business Review* (March 2010), pp. 114–117; and Wheatley, "Fearless Leaders."
75. Based on Wheatley, "Fearless Leaders"; and Gentile, "Managing Yourself: Keeping Your Colleagues Honest" (example reported in Gentile).

Chapter 7: Followership

YOUR **LEADERSHIP** CHALLENGE

After reading this chapter, you should be able to:

- Effectively manage both up and down the hierarchy.
- Recognize your followership style and take steps to become a more effective follower.
- Understand the leader's role in developing effective followers.
- Apply the principles of effective followership, including responsibility, service, challenging authority, participating in change, and knowing when to leave.
- Implement the strategies for effective followership at school or work.
- Know what followers want from leaders and what leaders expect from followers.
- Use feedback and leadership coaching to help followers grow and achieve their potential.

CHAPTER **OUTLINE**

198 **The Art of Followership**

200 **What Your Leader Wants from You**

201 **Styles of Followership**

205 **Strategies for Managing Up**

210 **The Power and Courage to Manage Up**

213 **What Followers Want from Leaders**

In the Lead

199 **Irvin D. Yalom and Marcia Reynolds**

204 **Dawn Marshall, Pathmark**

209 **John Stroup, Belden Inc.**

213 **Laura Stein, Clorox Company**

Leader's Self-Insight

203 **The Power of Followership**

207 **Are You an Annoying Follower?**

217 **Ready for Coaching**

Leader's Bookshelf

209 **Leadership Is Half the Story: Rethinking Followership, Leadership, and Collaboration**

Leadership at Work

219 **Follower Role Play**

Leadership Development: Cases for Analysis

220 **Waiting for Clearance**

221 **Jake's Pet Land**

Rich Gee founded his own executive coaching firm more than 10 years ago and the Rich Gee Group motto, "No Excuses. Make It Happen," encapsulates his belief that people can shape the life and career they want.[1] He knows what he's talking about. Working for 20 years in the corporate world, Gee once had a boss who called him into the office and criticized him for leaving work at 5:00 p.m. When questioned, the boss acknowledged that Gee was doing good work and meeting deadlines. Gee reminded him that he arrived at the office at 6:30 a.m., two hours earlier than his colleagues. He also told the boss that he could be reached by cell phone at any time and pointed out that he always responded quickly to emergency requests. Gee began keeping his boss up-to-date on his projects and checking in with him every day before he left. Gee says the boss soon "saw that it wasn't hours that mattered—it was how hard I worked." By opening better communication lines with his boss, Gee improved their relationship and continued to be able to work hours that took advantage of his best work time and enabled him to meet personal commitments as well as goals for the organization.[2]

Rich Gee was doing what good followers do. He made sure he understood his leader's concerns and worked to build a positive relationship that enabled him to do his best job as a follower and also let the leader feel comfortable that Gee would help the leader meet his goals for the organization.

In this chapter, we examine the important role of followership, including the nature of the follower's role, what leaders want from followers, and the different styles of followership that individuals express. The chapter explores how effective followers behave, discusses strategies for managing up, and looks at the sources of power and courage for managing up. Finally, we look at what followers want from leaders and examine the leader's role in developing and supporting followers.

7-1 THE ART OF FOLLOWERSHIP

Leadership and followership are closely intertwined. Considering leadership the sole basis for the success of the organization is a flawed assumption, and it limits the opportunity for people throughout the organization to accept responsibility and make active, valuable contributions.[3] For any group or organization to succeed, there must be people who willingly and effectively follow just as there must be those who willingly and effectively lead. Followership is the testing ground, a place to learn skills valuable for leadership. Moreover, leadership and followership are fundamental roles that individuals shift into and out of under various conditions. Everyone—leaders included—is a follower at one time or another. Indeed, despite the focus on leadership, most of us are more often followers than leaders.[4] Therefore, it is important for people to learn to manage both up and down the hierarchy, as illustrated in Exhibit 7.1

EXHIBIT 7.1 Good Leaders Manage Both Up and Down the Hierarchy

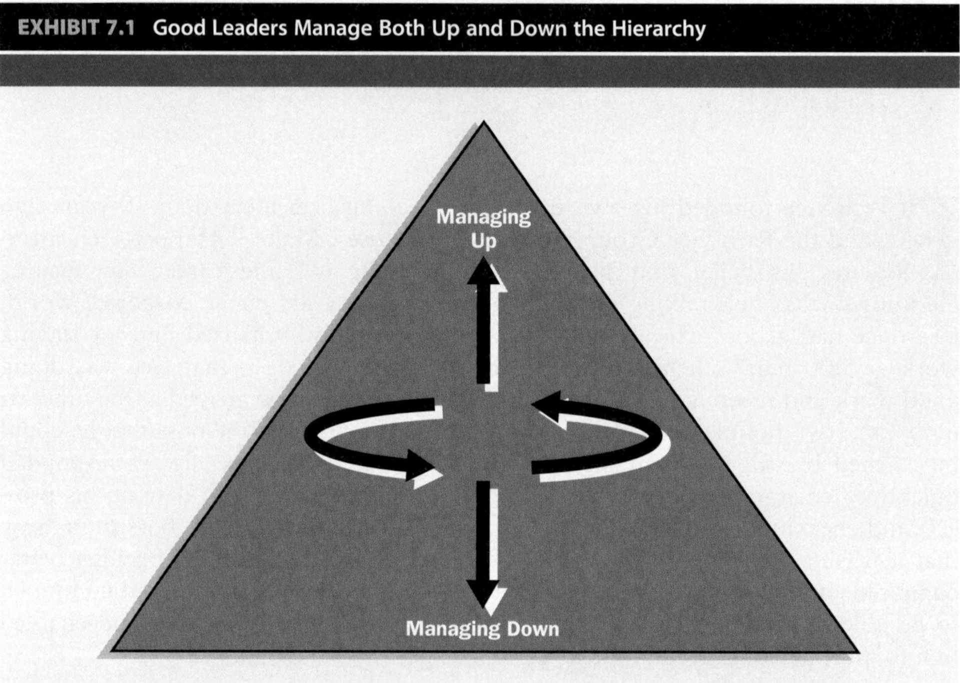

Source: Based on Mark Hurwitz and Samantha Hurwitz, "The Romance of the Follower: Part 2," *Industrial and Commercial Training* 41, no. 4 (2009), pp. 199–206.

7-1a Learn to Manage Up as Well as Down

Managing up means consciously and deliberately developing a meaningful, task-related, mutually respectful relationship with your direct superiors; offering insight, information, guidance, and initiative; and challenging your superiors when necessary in order to enable all members to do their best work for the organization.[5] People who effectively manage both up and down the hierarchy are more successful. Leaders at higher organizational levels depend on their subordinates for information, support, and assistance in accomplishing the organization's goals, so your boss needs you to manage up. In addition, your subordinates depend on you to help them get the information, resources, support, and recognition they need and deserve from higher levels. People like working for leaders who have influence with their superiors because it enhances their own status in the organization and helps them get what they need to do their jobs well.[6] You can't be a really good leader unless you manage the boss as skillfully as you manage employees.

7-1b Managing Up Presents Unique Challenges

Many new leaders are uncomfortable with the idea of managing their boss. Their overriding concern is pleasing the boss and keeping him or her happy. Therefore, they hesitate to pass along any information that might not be welcome, and they avoid questioning any of their superior's assumptions, ideas, or decisions.[7] In the long run, these self-protective strategies hurt the employee, the boss, and the organization.

One reason we may have difficulty managing upward is that we're not "in control" in this relationship as we are in our relationships with subordinates. It is natural that we try to protect ourselves in a relationship where we feel we have little control and little power.[8] Yet in reality we have more power than we know. Bosses need our support—our talent, information, ideas, and honesty—in order to do their jobs well, just as we need their support to do our best work. Everyone benefits when leaders learn to effectively manage relationships with superiors as well as subordinates. Consider the following examples.

Managing up
consciously and deliberately developing a meaningful, task-related, mutually respectful relationship with your direct superiors

IN THE LEAD

Irvin D. Yalom and Marcia Reynolds

Irvin D. Yalom, emeritus professor of psychiatry at Stanford University, has some interesting stories from his counseling experience with clients in individual and group therapy. One woman ranted at length in a group therapy session about her boss, who never listened and refused to pay her any respect. There's nothing funny about a bad boss, but the interesting thing about this client was that as her work with Yalom continued, her complaints about her terrible boss persisted through three different jobs with three different supervisors. It is likely that not only she but also her supervisors, colleagues, and the companies where she worked suffered due to her unproductive relationships with her superiors.

Contrast this woman's attitude and approach to that of Marcia Reynolds, who once worked for a micromanaging boss who was always criticizing and correcting her work. Reynolds decided to stop resenting his micromanaging and instead "act as though he were the world's best boss with the world's best employee." Instead of complaining and pushing back when her boss micromanaged, Reynolds was cheerful and helpful. She says an interesting thing happened: "When I stopped resisting, he started trusting me. When there was no longer any resistance, he quit fighting. Doing that really empowered me." As her boss increasingly trusted Reynolds, his micromanaging continued to abate, their relationship continued to improve, and both were happier and more productive. Reynolds was able to do her job better and get her subordinates what they needed by learning to manage up.[9]

Marcia Reynolds improved her relationship with her boss by understanding that being supportive and helpful was more productive than being resentful. To effectively manage up requires understanding what leaders want and need.

7-2 WHAT YOUR LEADER WANTS FROM YOU

Leaders and organizational situations vary, but there are some qualities and behaviors that every good leader wants from his or her followers. The following are ones that have been shown to contribute to productive and rewarding leader–follower relationships.[10]

1. ***A Make-It-Happen Attitude.*** Leaders don't want excuses. They want results. A leader's job becomes smoother when he or she has followers who are positive and self-motivated, who can get things done, who accept responsibility, and who excel at required tasks. Leaders value those people who propose ideas, show initiative, and take responsibility when they see something that needs to be done or a problem that needs to be solved. For example, when the night janitor at FAVI, a French copper-alloy foundry, was cleaning one night, the phone rang and she answered it to discover that an important visitor to the company had been delayed and was now waiting at the airport without the promised ride to his hotel. (FAVI's CEO had left the airport when the visitor didn't arrive as expected.) The janitor took the keys to one of the company cars, drove 90 minutes to pick up the visitor and deliver him to his hotel, then went back to finish the cleaning she had interrupted three hours earlier. Although this was nowhere close to being within her official job duties, the employee knew that leaders in the company valued and rewarded people who had the gumption to take responsibility for getting things done.[11]
2. ***A Willingness to Collaborate.*** Leaders are responsible for much more in the organization than any individual follower's concerns, feelings, and performance. Each follower is a part of the leader's larger system and should realize that his or her actions affect the whole. Larry Bossidy, former chairman and CEO of AlliedSignal and of Honeywell, tells about a conflict between the heads of manufacturing and marketing at one organization. The two managers didn't communicate with one another, so inventories were always out of whack. The CEO finally had to fire them both because their refusal to cooperate was hurting the organization. They got their jobs back when they jointly called and said they got the point and would change their behavior.[12]
3. ***The Motivation to Stay Up-to-Date.*** Bosses want followers to know what is happening in the organization's industry or field of endeavor. In addition, they want people to understand their customers, their competition, and how changes in technology or world events might affect the organization. Most people try to

learn all they can in order to get a job, but they sometimes grow complacent and fail to stay current with what's going on outside the narrow confines of their day-to-day work.

4. ***The Passion to Drive Your Own Growth.*** Similarly, leaders want followers who seek to enhance their own growth and development rather than depending solely on the leader to do it. Anything that exposes an individual to new people and ideas can enhance personal and professional development. One example is when followers actively network with others inside and outside the organization. Another is when followers take on difficult assignments, which demonstrates a willingness to face challenges, stretch their limits, and learn.

7-3 STYLES OF FOLLOWERSHIP

Despite the importance of followership and the crucial role that followers play in the success of any endeavor, research on the topic is limited. One theory of followership was proposed by Robert E. Kelley, who conducted extensive interviews with leaders and followers and came up with five styles of followership.[13] These followership styles are categorized according to two dimensions. The first dimension is the quality of independent, **critical thinking** versus dependent, **uncritical thinking**. Critical thinking means approaching subjects, situations, and problems with thoughtful questions and in an unbiased way, gathering and assessing ideas and information objectively, and mentally penetrating into underlying implications of various alternatives. This recalls our discussion of mindfulness in Chapter 5; independent critical thinkers are mindful of the effects of their and other people's behavior on achieving organizational goals. They are aware of the significance of their own actions and the actions of others. They can weigh the impact of decisions on the vision set forth by a leader and offer constructive criticism, creativity, and innovation. Conversely, a dependent, uncritical thinker does not consider possibilities beyond what he or she is told, does not contribute to the cultivation of the organization, and accepts the leader's ideas without assessing or evaluating them.

According to Kelley, the second dimension of followership style is *active versus passive behavior*. An active individual participates fully in the organization, engages in behavior that is beyond the limits of the job, demonstrates a sense of ownership, and initiates problem solving and decision making. A passive individual is characterized by a need for constant supervision and prodding by superiors. Passivity is often regarded as laziness; a passive person does nothing that is not required and avoids added responsibility.

The extent to which one is active or passive and is a critical, independent thinker or a dependent, uncritical thinker determines whether he or she is an alienated follower, a passive follower, a conformist, a pragmatic survivor, or an effective follower, as shown in Exhibit 7.2.

The **alienated follower** is an independent, critical thinker but is passive in the organization. Alienated followers are often effective followers who have experienced setbacks and obstacles, perhaps promises broken by superiors. Thus, they are capable, but they focus exclusively on the shortcomings of the organization and other people. Often cynical, alienated followers are able to think independently, but they do not participate in developing solutions to the problems or deficiencies they see. For example, Barry Paris spent more than 10 years writing on and off for the *Pittsburgh Post-Gazette*, where he was known for his bad attitude and lack of

Critical thinking
thinking independently and being mindful of the effects of one's own and other people's behavior on achieving the organization's vision

Uncritical thinking
failing to consider possibilities beyond what one is told; accepting the leader's ideas without thinking

Alienated follower
a person who is an independent, critical thinker but is passive in the organization

EXHIBIT 7.2 Followership Styles

Follower Type	Thinking Style	Level of Engagement
Alienated Follower	Independent, critical thinker	Passive in the organization
Conformist	Dependent, uncritical thinker	Active in the organization
Pragmatic Survivor	Both as needed	Both as needed
Passive Follower	Dependent, uncritical thinker	Passive in the organization
Effective Follower	Independent, critical thinker	Active in the organization

Source: Based on information in Robert E. Kelley, *The Power of Followership* (New York: Doubleday, 1992)

NEW LEADER
ACTION MEMO

Complete the questionnaire in Leader's Self-Insight 7.1 to evaluate how well you carry out a followership role.

enthusiasm and teamwork. Eventually Paris realized that he wasted that time ruminating over what he perceived as the hypocrisy of journalistic objectivity. "I could never resign myself to it," says Paris. Thus, rather than doing his best and trying to help others maintain standards of integrity and objectivity, he allowed hostility and cynicism to permeate his work.[14]

The **conformist** participates actively in the organization but does not use critical thinking skills in his or her task behavior. In other words, a conformist typically carries out any and all orders regardless of the nature of those tasks. The conformist participates willingly but without considering the consequences of what he or she is being asked to do—even at the risk of contributing to a harmful endeavor. For example, the thousands of people who have lost their homes to foreclosure can blame not only top executives in firms like Countrywide, Fannie Mae, and IndyMac Bank who embraced the rampant sale of subprime mortgages (sometimes called *liars' loans*) but also many conformist managers and employees who blindly went along with the strategy. In his book *The Foreclosure of America*, former Countrywide executive Adam Michaelson writes of the groupthink and blind conformity that squelched resistance and led people to go along with company actions even if they thought they were wrong.[15] A conformist is concerned only with avoiding conflict. This style often results from rigid rules and authoritarian environments in which leaders perceive subordinate recommendations as a challenge or threat.[16]

The **pragmatic survivor** has qualities of all four extremes—depending on which style fits with the prevalent situation. This type of follower uses whatever style best benefits his or her own position and minimizes risk. Within any given company, some 25 to 35 percent of followers tend to be pragmatic survivors, avoiding risks and fostering the status quo, often for political reasons. Government appointees often demonstrate this followership style because they have their own agendas and a short period of time in which to implement them. They may appeal to the necessary individuals, who themselves have a limited time to accomplish goals and are therefore willing to do whatever is necessary to survive in the short run. Pragmatic survivors also may emerge when an organization is going through desperate times, and followers find themselves doing whatever is needed to get themselves through the difficulty.[17]

The **passive follower** exhibits neither critical, independent thinking nor active participation. Being passive and uncritical, these followers display neither initiative nor a sense of responsibility. Their activity is limited to what they are told to do, and they accomplish things only with a great deal of supervision. The assistant manager at one large hotel found herself having to supervise her boss's daughter, who failed to follow procedures, had to be told over and over when and how to perform

Conformist
a follower who participates actively in the organization but does not use critical thinking skills in his or her task behavior

Pragmatic survivor
a follower who has qualities of all four extremes (alienated, effective, passive, conformist), depending on which style fits with the prevalent situation

Passive follower
a person in an organization who exhibits neither critical, independent thinking nor active participation

LEADER'S SELF-INSIGHT 7.1

The Power of Followership

Instructions: For each of the following statements, think of a specific situation in which you worked for a boss in an organization. Then answer whether each item is Mostly False or Mostly True for you in that follower situation.

	Mostly False	Mostly True
1. I often commented to my manager on the broader importance of data or events.		✓
2. I thought carefully and then expressed my opinion about critical issues.		✓
3. I frequently suggested ways of improving my and others' ways of doing things.		✓
4. I challenged my manager to think about an old problem in a new way.	✓	
5. Rather than wait to be told, I would figure out the critical activities for achieving my unit's goals.		✓
6. I independently thought up and championed new ideas to my boss.		✓
7. I tried to solve the tough problems rather than expect my leader to do it.		✓
8. I played devil's advocate if needed to demonstrate the upside and downside of initiatives.		✓
9. My work fulfilled a higher personal goal for me.		✓
10. I was enthusiastic about my job.		✓
11. I understood my leader's goals and worked hard to meet them.		✓
12. The work I did was significant to me.		✓
13. I felt emotionally engaged throughout a typical day.		✓
14. I had the opportunity to do what I do best each day.		✓
15. I understood how my role contributed to the company's success.		✓
16. I was willing to put in a great deal of effort beyond what was normally expected.		✓

Scoring and Interpretation

Questions 1–8 measure independent thinking. Sum the number of Mostly True answers checked and write your score below.

Questions 9–16 measure active engagement. Sum the number of Mostly True answers checked and write your score below.

Independent Thinking Total Score 7/8

Active Engagement Total Score 8/8

These two scores indicate how you carried out your followership role. A score of 2 or below is considered low. A score of 6 or higher is considered high. A score of 3–5 is in the middle. Based on whether your score is high, middle, or low, assess your followership style below.

Followership Style	Independent Thinking Score	Active Engagement Score
Effective	High	High
Alienated	High	Low
Conformist	Low	High
Pragmatist	Middle	Middle
Passive	Low	Low

How do you feel about your followership style? Compare your style with that of others in your class. What might you do to be more effective as a follower?

Sources: Based on Douglas R. May, Richard L. Gilson, and Lynn M. Harter, "The Psychological Conditions of Meaningfulness, Safety, and Availability and the Engagement of the Human Spirit at Work," *Journal of Occupational and Organizational Psychology* 77 (March 2004), pp. 11–38; Robert E. Kelley, *The Power of Followership: How to Create Leaders People Want to Follow and Followers Who Lead Themselves* (New York: Doubleday, 1992); and Towers Perrin HR Services, "Working Today: Understanding What Drives Employee Engagement," (2003), www.towersperrin.com

tasks, and showed little interest in the job, reflecting the characteristics of a passive follower.[18] Passive followers leave the thinking to their leaders. Sometimes, however, this style is the result of a leader who expects and encourages passive behavior. Followers learn that to show initiative, accept responsibility, or think creatively is not rewarded and may even be punished by the leader, so they grow increasingly passive.

Passive followers are often the result of leaders who are overcontrolling of others and who punish mistakes.[19]

The **effective follower** is both a critical, independent thinker and active in the organization. Effective followers behave the same toward everyone regardless of their position in the organization. They do not try to avoid risk or conflict. Rather, effective followers have the courage to initiate change and put themselves at risk or in conflict with others, even their leaders, to serve the best interests of the organization.

Characterized by both mindfulness and a willingness to act, effective followers are essential for an organization to be effective. They are capable of self-management, discern strengths and weaknesses in themselves and in the organization, are committed to something bigger than themselves, and work toward competency, solutions, and a positive impact. Dawn Marshall, a cashier at Pathmark, illustrates the characteristics of the effective follower.

Effective follower
a critical, independent thinker who actively participates in the organization

IN THE LEAD

Dawn Marshall, Pathmark

Five hours into her shift, four harried customers line up at Dawn Marshall's cash register at the Pathmark supermarket in Upper Derby, Pennsylvania. Eight minutes and 27 bags later, they're all out the door with smiles on their faces. Few people would think Marshall has a glamorous or influential job—but she treats it like the most significant job in the world.

Marshall specializes in giving people a little bit of luxury in the mundane chore of grocery shopping. She's a good cashier, but her forte is bagging. Marshall knows how to pack the flimsy plastic bags so that eggs don't get broken, bread doesn't get squashed, and ground beef doesn't leak all over the cereal boxes. She even won a National Grocers Association contest as the best bagger in America, based on speed, bag-building technique, style, and attitude. "I believe it's an art that should be taken seriously," Marshall says of her work. Many Pathmark customers agree. They're tired of cashiers and baggers who simply throw the stuff in bags without giving a care for the customer's convenience or needs. One customer admits that she shops at Pathmark rather than a store closer to her home because of Marshall. "I like her attitude," says the customer. "Clone her."

Even though Marshall works on her feet all day and often has to put up with rude or insensitive customers, she handles whatever comes her way with a positive attitude. For Marshall, her job is not bagging groceries but making people's lives easier. Thus, she approaches her work with energy and enthusiasm, striving to do her best in every encounter. She doesn't need close supervision or someone pushing her to work harder. The busier it is, the better she likes it.[20]

NEW LEADER
ACTION MEMO

As a leader, you can also be an effective follower. You can think independently and critically instead of blindly accepting what your superiors tell you. Rather than dwelling on the shortcomings of others, you can look for solutions.

Dawn Marshall has taken what some would consider a boring, low-paying job and imbued it with meaning and value. She accepts responsibility for her own personal fulfillment and finds ways to expand her potential and use her capacities to serve the needs of others and the organization. Effective followers like Dawn Marshall also act as leaders by setting an example and using a positive attitude to inspire and uplift other people.

Effective followers are far from powerless—and they know it. Therefore, they do not despair in their positions, nor do they resent or manipulate others. This chapter's *Consider This* describes one writer's meaning of effective followership.

Consider**This!**

Our Deepest Fear

Our deepest fear is not that we are inadequate, Our deepest fear is that we are powerful beyond measure.

It is our light, not our darkness, that most frightens us.
We ask ourselves, who am I to be brilliant, gorgeous, talented and fabulous?
Actually, who are you NOT to be? You are a child of God.
Your playing small doesn't serve the world.
There's nothing enlightened about shrinking so that other people won't feel insecure around you.
We were born to make manifest the glory . . . that is within us.
It's not just in some of us; it's in everyone.
And as we let our own light shine, we unconsciously give other people permission to do the same.
As we are liberated from our own fear, our presence automatically liberates others.

Source: From *A Return to Love: Reflections on the Principles of a Course in Miracles*, by Marianne Williamson, published by HarperCollins.

7-4 STRATEGIES FOR MANAGING UP

There is growing recognition that how followers manage their leaders is just as important as how their leaders manage them.[21] Two aspects of managing up are understanding the leader and using specific tactics to improve the leader–follower relationship.

7-4a Understand the Leader

We all spend time and energy trying to understand people who are important to us, so it only makes sense that you do the same with your boss if you want to have a productive working relationship. It is up to you to take the initiative to learn about your leader's goals, needs, strengths and weaknesses, and organizational constraints.

In addition, effective followers study their leader's preferred work style. No two individuals work alike or behave alike under the same circumstances. Effective followers learn their leader's preferences and adapt to them. Interviews with senior executives confirm that this strategy is both effective and appropriate for influencing the leader–follower relationship.[22] You can pay close attention to the leader's behavior in the following areas to know how to be a more effective follower:[23]

- Does the leader like to know all the details of your plans, projects, and problems, or does she just want the big picture?

- Is the leader controlling or empowering? Does he want to closely supervise and be in control of people's behavior or delegate freely and look for opportunities to help individuals grow and develop to their highest potential?
- Does the leader like to carefully analyze information and alternatives before making a decision, or is she more inclined to make quick decisions and take action?
- Is the leader a reader or a listener? Does he like to have materials presented in written form so he has time to study and analyze them by himself first, or does he prefer an oral presentation where he can ask questions on the spot?
- Is she a numbers person or a word person? Does she want statistics and figures to back up your report or request?
- Is the leader an extrovert or an introvert? Do interactions with large groups of people energize or tire him? Does he like to be involved with people all day or need time alone to think and recharge?

Effective followers seek out all the information they can about their leader from talking to the boss, talking to others, and paying attention to clues in the leader's behavior, so that they are sensitive to the leader's work style and needs. For example, people working with U.S. President Barack Obama learned that he is an introvert who likes to have time to reflect. He preferred to have decision memos, briefing materials, and other items in writing so he could carefully study them and think of questions he wanted to ask. Obama liked to consider a lot of information and a variety of opinions before acting. President George W. Bush, on the other hand, was an extrovert who preferred oral briefings and relatively quick decisions.[24]

7-4b Tactics for Managing Up

Most followers at some point complain about the leader's deficiencies, such as a failure to listen, to encourage, or to recognize followers' efforts.[25] Sometimes, though, we need to look in the mirror before blaming our leaders for an unsatisfying or unproductive relationship. The authors of a new book on leadership and followership report that poor followership is cited as one of the top three reasons people get fired, and often the primary one. This provides solid evidence that it is just as important to build up one's followership skills as to develop leadership abilities, as further described in the Leader's Bookshelf. To be effective, followers develop a meaningful, task-related relationship with their bosses that enables them to add value to the organization even when their ideas differ from those of the leader.[26]

> NEW LEADER
> **ACTION MEMO**
>
> Leader's Self-Insight 7.2 gives you a chance to see if you're guilty of being an annoying follower.

Followers should also be aware of behaviors that can annoy leaders and interfere with building a quality relationship. One business magazine interviewed powerful people about their pet peeves and identified more than two dozen misdemeanors that followers often commit without being aware of it.[27]

Most relationships between leaders and followers are characterized by some emotion and behavior based on authority and submission. Leaders are authority figures and may play a disproportionately large role in the mind of a follower.[28] Exhibit 7.3 illustrates four tactics that enable followers to overcome the authority-based relationship and develop an effective, respectful relationship with their leaders.

Be a Resource for the Leader Effective followers align themselves with the purpose and the vision of the organization. By understanding the vision and goals, followers can be a resource of strength and support for the leader. An effective follower can

LEADER'S SELF-INSIGHT 7.2

Are You an Annoying Follower?

1. If you think there might be a mistake in something you've done, what do you do?
   A. Fess up. It's better to share your concerns up front so your boss can see if there is a problem and get it corrected before it makes him look bad.
   B. Try to hide it for now. Maybe there isn't really a problem, so there's no use in making yourself look incompetent.
2. How do you handle a criticism from your boss?
   A. Poke your head in her door or corner her in the cafeteria multiple times to make sure everything is okay between the two of you.
   B. Take the constructive criticism, make sure you understand what the boss wants from you, and get on with your job.
3. You're in a crowded elevator with your boss after an important meeting where you've just landed a million-dollar deal. You:
   A. Celebrate the victory by talking to your boss about the accomplishment and the details of the meeting.
   B. Keep your mouth shut or talk about non-business-related matters.
4. Your boss has an open-door policy and wants people to feel free to drop by her office any time to talk about anything. You pop in just after lunch and find her on the phone. What do you do?
   A. Leave and come back later.
   B. Wait. You know most of her phone calls are quick, so she'll be free in a few minutes.
5. You've been called to the boss's office and have no idea what he wants to talk about.
   A. You show up on time, empty-handed, to concentrate on what the boss has to say.
   B. You show up on time with a pen, paper, and your calendar or mobile device.
6. You've been trying to get some face time with your boss for weeks and luckily catch him or her in the bathroom. You:
   A. Take care of personal business and get out of there.
   B. Grab your chance to schmooze with the boss. Ask a question or tell a joke. You might not get another chance any time soon.

Here are the appropriate follower behaviors.

1. **A.** Honest self-assessment and fessing up to the boss builds mutual confidence and respect. Nothing destroys trust faster than incompetence exposed after the fact.
2. **B.** David Snow, former president and COO of Empire Blue Cross and Blue Shield, refers to insecure, thin-skinned people who have to check in frequently after a criticism as *door swingers*. Door swingers are annoying in both our personal and work lives. Just get on with things.
3. **B.** You have no idea who else is in the elevator. Keep your mouth shut. You can crow about the new deal later in private.
4. **A.** There's nothing worse than having someone hovering while you're trying to carry on a phone conversation. Leave a note with your boss's assistant or come back later.
5. **B.** You can usually be safe in assuming your boss hasn't called you in for idle chitchat. Never show up without a pen and paper or tablet to make notes.
6. **A.** At best, to use the bathroom as a place to try to impress the boss makes you look desperate. It also shows a lack of tact and judgment.

Most of these seem obvious, but based on interviews with leaders, subordinates commit these mistakes over and over in the workplace. Keep these missteps in mind so you don't become an annoying follower.

Source: Based on William Speed Weed, Alex Lash, and Constance Loizos, "30 Ways to Annoy Your Boss," *MBA Jungle* (March–April 2003), pp. 51–55.

complement the leader's weaknesses with the follower's own strengths.[29] Similarly, effective followers indicate their personal goals and the resources they bring to the organization. Effective followers inform their leaders about their own ideas, beliefs, needs, and constraints. The more leaders and followers can know the day-to-day activities and problems of one another, the better resources they can be for each other. At one organization, a group of disabled employees took advantage of a board meeting to issue rented wheelchairs to the members, who then tried to move around the factory in them. Realizing what the workers faced, the board got the factory's ramps improved, and the employees became a better resource for the organization.[30]

EXHIBIT 7.3 Ways to Influence Your Leader

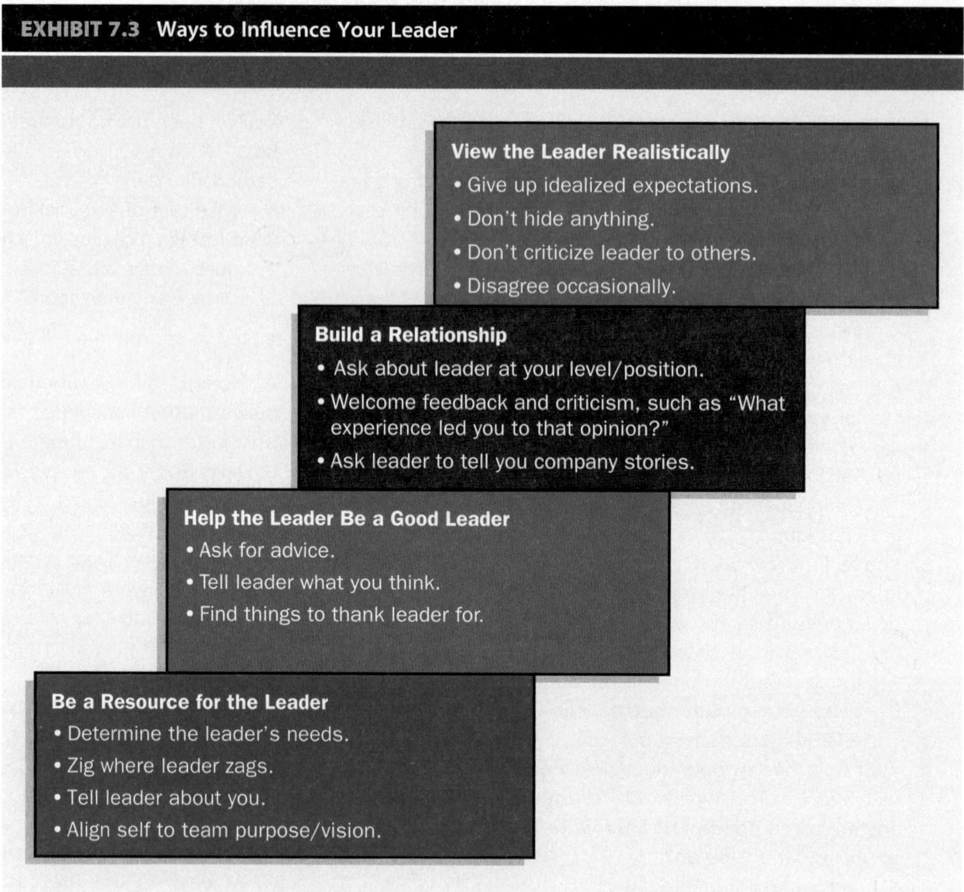

NEW LEADER
ACTION MEMO

As a leader, you can use strategies for managing up to create an equitable and respectful relationship with your superiors. You can help your supervisor be the best he or she can be by getting beyond submissive feelings and behaviors, recognizing that leaders are fallible, and being a resource for the leader.

Help the Leader Be a Good Leader Followers' influence upon a leader can enhance the leader or accentuate the leader's shortcomings.[31] Good followers seek the leader's counsel and look for ways the leader can help improve their skills, abilities, and value to the organization. They help their leaders to be good leaders by simply saying what they need in order to be good followers. If a leader believes a follower values his or her advice, the leader is more likely to give constructive guidance rather than unsympathetic criticism.

A leader can also become a better leader when followers compliment the leader for behavior that followers appreciate, such as listening, rewarding followers' contributions, and sharing credit for accomplishments.[32] In addition, a follower can provide enthusiastic support for a leader, but not to the extent that the follower fails to be candid with a leader who is unethical or threatens the values or objectives of the organization. It is in leaders' best interests when followers help them make needed changes or avoid ethical problems.[33]

Build a Relationship with the Leader Effective followers work toward an authentic relationship with their leaders, which includes developing trust and speaking honestly on the basis of that trust.[34] By building a relationship with the leader, a follower makes every interaction more meaningful to the organization. Furthermore, the relationship is imbued with mutual respect rather than authority and submission. John Stroup, CEO of Belden Inc., says he learned this in a previous job at Danaher Corporation.

LEADER'S BOOKSHELF

Leadership Is Half the Story: Rethinking Followership, Leadership, and Collaboration

by Marc and Samantha Hurwitz

You just got promoted to a high-level executive job. Thank goodness, no more worrying about all that "managing up" stuff, right? *Wrong*. "Followership . . . becomes more, not less, important as we move up the organizational ladder," Marc and Samantha Hurwitz say in their book *Leadership Is Half the Story*. The two have been studying followership for more than a decade and have found that "in any performance evaluation, about half is likely based on followership."

WHAT POOR FOLLOWERS DON'T DO

Unfortunately, most people know what it feels like to work for a bad boss. But, unless we've been in a leadership position, most of us don't realize how it feels to have a poor follower. Based on the Hurwitzes' research, here are a few of the mistakes poor followers make that can get them fired, along with some tips for how to avoid them:

- ***They Don't Practice "Offensive Communication."*** Poor followers wait for the supervisor to ask, but great followers take the offensive and provide a "dashboard" of key information to keep their leaders up to date on what they are doing. Remember that your leader is at least as busy as you are. Providing regular summaries of your projects and results makes the leader's job easier, as well as increasing your visibility in the organization. Good followers also make sure the communication style suits the leader. They don't provide a lengthy written report when the leader wants a two-minute verbal update.
- ***They Don't Tailor Their Innovative Thinking to the Leader's Needs.*** The Hurwitzes call this mistake "thinking outside the boss." Leaders want followers who take initiative and think innovatively, but many people fail to clarify what the leader wants and needs. Good followers let their creative juices flow, but they first seek to understand what kind of creativity the leader needs, what resources and constraints exist for doing new things, and how much risk the leader is comfortable with.
- ***They Don't Try to Understand a New Boss.*** Poor followers act like *boss-stritches*, putting their heads in the sand and going on as if nothing has changed except that they have to call a new person boss. Great followers, on the other hand, realize how important it is to learn about the new leader's priorities, preferences, strengths and weaknesses, and pet peeves. They adapt to the leader to make sure they are the best partners possible in the relationship with their new leader.

MAKE A FLIP

The Hurwitzes use the acronym FliP (Followership, leadership, innovation, and Partnership) as the foundation for talking about the important components of a strong organization, and they incorporate numerous FliPtips and FliPskills for both leaders and followers into the book. "Followership is the other side of the leadership equation," they write. "Everybody can't be leading all the time. And, when you aren't leading, you need to take on an active, engaged, thoughtful followership role."

Source: *Leadership Is Half the Story*, by Marc and Samantha Hurwitz, is published by the University of Toronto Press.

IN THE LEAD

John Stroup, Belden Inc.

John Stroup, CEO of Belden Inc., a maker of electrical cables, says he is much more likely to promote followers who disagree with and challenge him occasionally. However, the key is whether they have the savvy to do it the right way. In his previous job at Danaher Corporation, Stroup saw some newly recruited senior managers get fired or transferred because they pushed for changes or urged their bosses to adopt ideas before they had built credibility with their superiors.

Stroup took the lesson to heart and began building positive and respectful relationships with his immediate supervisor and other top executives. Eventually, he told them he wanted to make a change in his division by offering certain customers complete solutions for their specific needs. It was a departure from standard procedures, and it represented a risky strategic shift for the company. His supervisor disagreed with the decision, but after hearing Stroup's arguments, he eventually went along with it because "he recognized my strengths,"

Stroup says. "I felt comfortable enough to push my point of view," he adds, because the relationship was one based on trust and mutual respect.

The idea was a huge success, and Stroup was soon promoted to a group executive position.[35]

Other leaders have also learned that building a positive, respectful relationship with the boss is the best way to get important changes implemented. Followers can generate respect by asking questions about the leader's experiences in the follower's position, actively seeking feedback, and clarifying the basis for specific feedback and criticism from the leader. By doing so, followers are getting beyond submissive behavior by asking leaders to be accountable for their criticism, to have empathy for the followers' position, and to share history about something both parties have in common—the organization.

View the Leader Realistically Unrealistic follower expectations present one of the biggest barriers to effective leader–follower relationships.[36] Whereas it is reasonable to expect your superiors to be competent, it is naïve and unrealistic to expect them to be perfect. When we accept that leaders are fallible and will make many mistakes, we open the path to an equitable relationship. Followers should view leaders as they really are, not as followers think they should be.

"In many ways, great followership is harder than leadership. It has more dangers and fewer rewards."

Warren Bennis, leadership expert; author of *Still Surprised: A Memoir of a Life in Leadership*

Similarly, effective followers present realistic images of themselves. Followers do not try to hide their weaknesses or cover their mistakes, nor do they criticize their leaders to others. Hiding mistakes is symptomatic of conforming or passive followers, and followers who waste their time trashing their superiors or the company intensify estrangement and reinforce the mindset of an alienated follower. These kinds of alienated and passive behaviors can have negative—and sometimes disastrous—consequences for leaders, followers, and the organization. Instead of criticizing a leader to others, it is far more constructive to directly disagree with a leader on matters relevant to the department's or organization's work.

7-5 THE POWER AND COURAGE TO MANAGE UP

There are followers in almost every organization who remind us "how hollow the *label of leadership* sometimes is—and how heroic followership can be."[37] But standing up to the boss isn't easy. Finding the courage to effectively manage up comes easier when you realize how much leaders depend on followers.[38] It's a fact that our bosses typically have more power than we do. Yet subordinates have more power than many people realize.

7-5a Sources of Power for Managing Up

Exhibit 7.4 outlines several sources of power that can be used by followers to manage up.

Personal Sources One personal source of upward influence is the follower's knowledge and skills that are valuable to the organization. A subordinate with useful *knowledge* is of real benefit to the leader, and his or her departure would be a loss.

EXHIBIT 7.4 Sources of Power for Managing Up

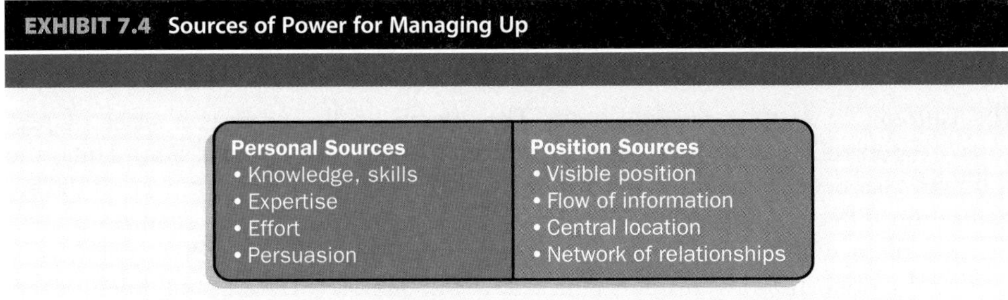

In addition, someone who has a demonstrated record of performance often develops *expertise* and in this way can influence the boss's decisions. A record of successes and a history of contributions can gain a follower expert status. When someone is recognized as an expert, that person often can influence activities because he or she becomes an indispensable resource to the leader. The power to influence is also associated with the *effort* followers put forth. By demonstrating a willingness to learn, to accept difficult or undesirable projects, and to initiate activities beyond the scope of expected effort, people can increase their power.[39]

Another way to influence up is with *persuasion*, which refers to the direct appeal to leaders for desired outcomes.[40] Rational persuasion—using facts and reason—is typically the most effective approach when trying to manage upward. By treating the issue in a businesslike manner, formulating a carefully crafted argument and supporting it with details, followers gain attention and respect.[41] However, followers can use a variety of influence tactics, depending on their own personalities and styles and the preferences and style of the leader.[42] Chapter 12 will discuss influence tactics in detail.

Position Sources A follower's formal position also provides sources of power. For example, certain jobs or physical locations can render the follower *visible* to numerous individuals. A position that is key to the *flow of information* can establish that position and the person in it as critical—thus, influential—to those who need the information. A *central location* provides influence because the follower becomes known to many people and contributes to the work of many. Access to people and information in an organization provides a means to establish relationships with a broad range of people both inside and outside the organization. With a *network of relationships*, followers have more clout with the leader and more opportunity to persuade and make significant contributions.

7-5b Necessary Courage to Manage Up

Some people tend to think, "Who am I to challenge the CEO (or director, or team leader)?" Yet leaders depend on followers who are willing to step up and challenge them when it is in the interest of the organization. Good followers are not *yes men* (or women). They are people who think for themselves and conduct their work lives with courage and integrity.[43] The discussion of courage and integrity in Chapter 6 applies to followers as well as leaders. To be effective, followers have to know what they stand for and be willing to express their own ideas and opinions to their leaders, even though this might mean risking their jobs, being demeaned, or feeling inadequate.[44] Effective followers have the courage to accept responsibility, challenge

NEW LEADER
ACTION MEMO

As a follower, you can assume responsibility for your own personal development, behavior, and work performance. You can look for opportunities to make a difference, seek to meet organizational needs, serve others, and work toward the common good.

NEW LEADER
ACTION MEMO

As a follower, you can support your leaders through difficult times, but have the courage to challenge your superiors when their behavior or decisions contradict the best interests of the organization.

authority, participate in change, serve the needs of the organization, and leave the organization when necessary.[45]

The Courage to Assume Responsibility The effective follower feels a sense of personal responsibility and ownership in the organization and its mission. Thus, the follower assumes responsibility for his or her own behavior and its impact on the organization. Effective followers do not presume that a leader or an organization will provide them with security, permission to act, or personal growth. Instead, they initiate the opportunities through which they can achieve personal fulfillment, exercise their potential, and provide the organization with the fullest extent of their capabilities.

The Courage to Challenge Effective followers do not sacrifice their personal integrity or the good of the organization in order to maintain harmony. If a leader's actions and decisions contradict the best interests of the organization, effective followers take a stand. Obedience is considered a high virtue in military organizations, for example, but the U.S. Army teaches soldiers that they have a duty to disobey illegal or immoral orders.[46] Good leaders want followers who are willing to challenge them for the good of the organization. At Tyco International, which was one of the few large corporations that got caught up in the accounting scandals of the early 2000s and managed to restore its reputation, "the only career-ending move [today] is to not bring bad news forward," says Laurie Siegel, senior vice president of human resources. It is a guiding principle at Tyco for leaders to surround themselves with people who will speak up and hold them accountable. Managers' leadership behaviors are assessed annually and include an evaluation of whether they are willing to challenge their superiors when necessary.[47]

The Courage to Participate in Transformation Effective followers view the struggle of corporate change and transformation as a mutual experience shared by all members of the organization. When an organization undergoes a difficult transformation, effective followers support the leader and the organization. They are not afraid to confront the changes and to work toward reshaping the organization. David Chislett of Imperial Oil's Dartmouth, Nova Scotia, refinery, was faced with this test of courage. The refinery was the least efficient in the industry and the board of directors gave management nine months to turn things around. Chislett's bosses asked him to give up his management position and return to the duties of a wage earner as part of an overall transformation strategy. He agreed to the request, thereby contributing to the success of the refinery's transformation.[48]

The Courage to Serve An effective follower discerns the needs of the organization and actively seeks to serve those needs. Just as leaders can serve others, as discussed in the previous chapter, so can followers. A follower can provide strength to the leader by supporting the leader and by contributing to the organization in areas that complement the leader's position. By displaying the will to serve others over themselves, followers act for the common mission of the organization with a passion that equals that of a leader. Laura Stein, general counsel of The Clorox Company, proved herself to be an exceptional follower after the company hired an outside CEO.

IN THE LEAD

Laura Stein, The Clorox Company

One expert estimates that managers have a 30 percent to 40 percent chance of being fired after a company hires an outside CEO. The best strategy? Make it your job to serve the new leader and help him or her succeed.

That's what Laura Stein, general counsel of Clorox, did. Before Donald Knauss (now retired) even took the CEO job, Stein did extensive research on him to help her know how to work with him most effectively. She learned, for example, that Knauss prefers one-page memos rather than reams of data and informal interactions rather than formal meetings. In addition, she began looking for how she could best serve Knauss and the organization as it embarked on a new path. Even if she disagreed with any strategic changes he wanted to make, Stein believed it was her job to support them.

Since Stein had previously worked in China, she volunteered to informally advise colleagues about revamping the company's strategy in that country. Knauss appreciated Stein's proactive, service-oriented approach. "She will help anyone who asks for help," he says. Within months of taking the CEO job, Knauss had broadened Stein's duties and power and she was eventually promoted to executive vice president–general counsel. Stein continues serving the company's current leader, Benno Dorrer, who was promoted to CEO in late 2014.[49]

The Courage to Leave Sometimes organizational or personal changes create a situation in which a follower must withdraw from a particular leader–follower relationship. People might know they need new challenges, for example, even though it is hard to leave a job where they have many friends and valued colleagues. If followers are faced with a leader or an organization unwilling to make necessary changes, it is time to take their support elsewhere. In addition, a follower and leader may have such strong differences of opinion that the follower can no longer support the leader's decisions and feels a moral obligation to leave. U.S. major general John Batiste turned down a promotion to three-star general and resigned because he felt he could no longer support civilian leaders' decisions regarding the war in Iraq. The role of military officers is to advise civilian leaders and then carry out orders even when they disagree. General Batiste spent weeks torn between his sense of duty and respect for the chain of command and a feeling that he owed it to his soldiers to speak out against leaders' decisions. Ultimately, believing he could no longer serve his leaders as he should, the general had the courage to leave the job, even though it meant the end of a lifelong career he highly valued.[50]

7-6 WHAT FOLLOWERS WANT FROM LEADERS

Throughout much of this chapter, we've talked about demands on followers and how followers can become more effective and powerful in the organization. However, the full responsibility doesn't fall on the follower. Good followers are created partly by leaders who understand their requirements and obligations for developing people.[51]

Research indicates that followers have expectations about what constitutes a desirable leader.[52] Exhibit 7.5 shows the top four choices in rank order based on surveys of followers about what they desire in leaders and colleagues.

EXHIBIT 7.5 Rank Order of Desirable Characteristics

Desirable Leaders Are	Desirable Colleagues (Followers) Are
Honest	Honest
Forward-thinking	Cooperative
Inspiring	Dependable
Competent	Competent

Source: Adapted from James M. Kouzes and Barry Z. Posner, *Credibility: How Leaders Gain and Lose It, Why People Demand It* (San Francisco, CA: Jossey-Bass Publishers, 1993), p. 255.

Followers want their leaders to be honest, forward-thinking, inspiring, and competent. A leader must be worthy of trust, envision the future of the organization, inspire others to contribute, and be capable and effective in matters that will affect the organization.

Followers want their fellow followers to be honest and competent but also dependable and cooperative. Thus, desired qualities of colleagues share two qualities with leaders—honesty and competence. However, followers themselves want other followers to be dependable and cooperative rather than forward-thinking and inspiring. The hallmark that distinguishes the role of leadership from the role of followership, then, is not authority, knowledge, power, or other conventional notions of what a follower is not. Rather, the distinction lies in the clearly defined leadership activities of fostering a vision and inspiring others to achieve that vision. Chapter 13 discusses vision in detail, and Chapter 14 describes how leaders shape cultural values that support achievement of the vision.

The results in Exhibit 7.5 also underscore the idea that behaviors of effective leaders and followers often overlap. Followers do not want to be subjected to leader behavior that denies them the opportunity to make valued contributions. Leaders have a responsibility to enable followers to fully contribute their ideas and abilities. Four specific ways leaders enhance the abilities and contributions of followers are by offering clarity of direction; providing opportunities for growth; giving honest, constructive feedback; and protecting followers from organizational roadblocks.

7-6a Clarity of Direction

It is the leader's job to clearly communicate where the group or organization is going and why.[53] Creating an inspiring vision is only one aspect of setting direction. Followers also need specific, unambiguous goals and objectives on both an individual and team level. Numerous studies have shown that clear, specific, challenging goals enhance people's motivation and performance.[54] Having clear goals helps people know where to focus their attention and energy, enables them to track their own progress, and lets them feel a sense of pride and accomplishment when goals are achieved.

Another aspect of clarifying direction is helping followers see how their own individual jobs fit in the larger context of the team, department, and total enterprise. This is one reason many leaders use open-book management. When people can see the bigger financial picture, they have a perspective on where the organization stands and how they can contribute.

Leadership coaching a method of directing or facilitating a follower with the aim of improving specific skills or achieving a specific development goal

7-6b Opportunities for Growth

Leaders can act as coaches to help followers upgrade their skills and enhance their career development. **Leadership coaching** is a method of directing or facilitating a follower with the aim of improving specific skills or achieving a specific development goal, such as developing time management skills, enhancing personal productivity, or preparing for new responsibilities. Coaching doesn't mean trying to change people and make them something other than what they are. Instead, it means helping followers realize their potential.[55]

To understand what it means to be a leadership coach, consider the difference in mindset and behavior required for managing versus coaching:

Managing	**Coaching**[56]
Telling	Empowering
Judging	Facilitating, removing obstacles
Controlling	Developing

Rather than telling followers what to do, directing and controlling their behavior, and judging their performance, which is a traditional management role, leadership coaching involves empowering followers to explore, helping them understand and learn, providing support, and removing obstacles that stand in the way of their ability to grow and excel.

Exhibit 7.6 shows benefits that followers get from leadership coaching, including gaining a new perspective, getting advice on handling specific organizational situations, dealing with organizational politics, and receiving encouragement and support. The biggest benefit that followers report, however, is getting clear, direct feedback on performance.[57]

EXHIBIT 7.6 Follower Benefits from Leadership Coaching

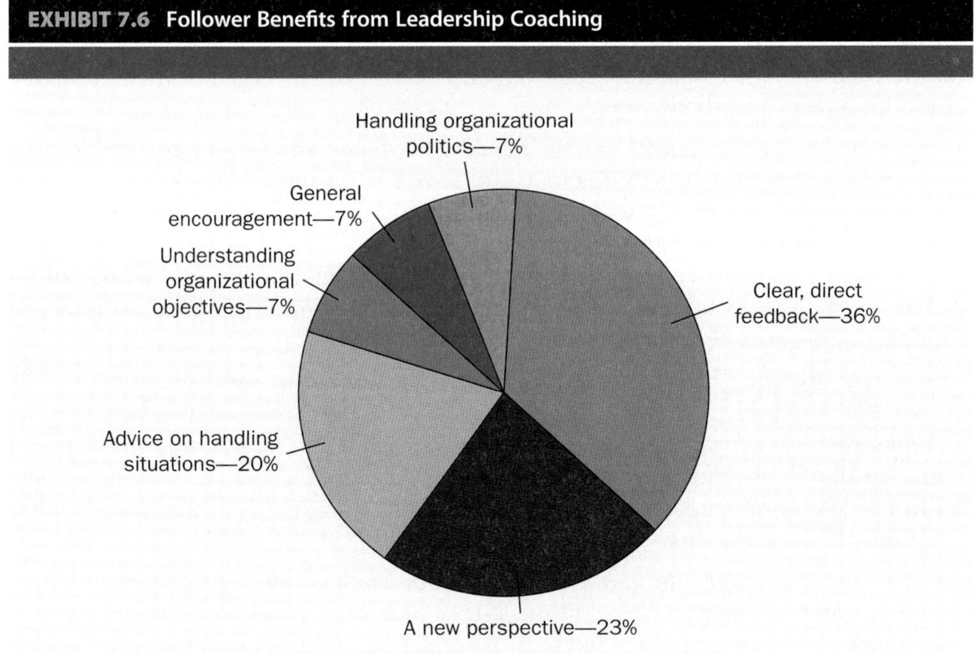

Source: "The Business Leader as Development Coach," *PDI Portfolio* (Winter 1996), p. 6; and Personnel Decisions International, http://www.personneldecisions.com.

NEW LEADER
ACTION MEMO

Answer the questions in Leader's Self-Insight 7.3 to learn if you have the correct mindset to benefit from leadership coaching.

7-6c Frequent, Specific, and Immediate Feedback

Candid feedback is one of the most important elements contributing to the growth and development of followers, but many leaders don't know how to give good feedback.[58] Effective leaders see feedback as a route to improvement and development, not as something to dread or fear. When a leader provides feedback, it signals that the leader cares about the follower's growth and career development and wants to help the person achieve his or her potential.[59]

Feedback occurs when a leader uses evaluation and communication to help individuals learn about themselves and improve.[60] Effective leaders provide both positive and negative constructive feedback on an ongoing basis. If someone handles a difficult task, for instance, the leader offers feedback on the spot rather than letting the person wonder how effective he or she was, perhaps imagining the worst. As former advertising account executive Ryan Broderick said, "hearing something is better than hearing nothing."[61]

Followers appreciate positive feedback, but they also want to know when they aren't doing what is expected of them, and they want the feedback to be specific enough to enable them to do better. Leaders who avoid giving any critical feedback "achieve kindness in the short term but heartlessness in the long run, dooming the problem employee to non-improvement."[62] Here are some ways leaders can provide feedback that benefits followers and takes less of an emotional toll on both leader and follower:[63]

1. *Make it timely*. People shouldn't have to wait for an annual review to know how they're doing or how they can improve. Leaders should give feedback as soon as possible after they observe a behavior or action they want to correct or reinforce. Often, this means immediately, such as when a leader says, "Great job on the presentation, Sal, and you used graphics very effectively. The only place I see it could have been better would be including some specifics like past sales figures. Do you know where to find that information, or would you like me to set up a meeting with our sales manager?" If leaders wait to offer feedback, it should be only long enough to gather necessary information or to marshal their thoughts and ideas.
2. *Focus on the performance, not the person*. Feedback should not be used simply to criticize a person or to point out faults. A person who feels like he or she is being attacked personally will not learn anything from the feedback. The focus should always be on how the follower can improve. Leaders have to point out work that is poorly done, but it is equally important to reinforce work that is done well. This helps people learn from what they do right and softens the impact of negative feedback.
3. *Make it specific*. Effective feedback describes the precise behavior and its consequences and explains why the leader either approves of the behavior or thinks there is a need for improvement. The leader might provide illustrations and examples to clarify what behavior is considered effective, and he or she always checks for understanding rather than assuming the follower knows what actions the leader wants.
4. *Focus on the desired future, not the past*. Good leaders don't drag up the failures and mistakes of the past. In addition, if it is clear that a follower's mistake was a one-time occurrence and not likely to be repeated, the leader will let it go rather than offering negative feedback. Effective feedback looks toward the future, minimizes fault-finding, and describes the desired behaviors and outcomes.

NEW LEADER
ACTION MEMO

As a leader, you can make feedback a regular habit and remember to include positive comments and praise as well as critical feedback. As a follower, you can view feedback as a chance to improve yourself. Reframe negative feedback in a way that helps you take positive action toward what you want out of your work and life.

Feedback
using evaluation and communication to help individuals and the organization learn and improve

LEADER'S SELF-INSIGHT 7.3

Ready for Coaching

Instructions: Think about your attitude toward personal growth and answer the following questions Mostly False or Mostly True.

	Mostly False	Mostly True
1. I have a strong desire to improve myself.		✓
2. I welcome suggestions for better ways of behaving.		✓
3. I am really honest with myself about my strengths and weaknesses.		✓
4. I welcome negative feedback.		✓
5. I follow through on commitments to change myself.		✓
6. I am very open with my peers about any mistakes I make.		✓
7. I draw my boss's attention to my successes.		✓
8. After making a mistake, I immediately let the affected people know about it and propose a solution.		✓

Scoring and Interpretation

Give yourself 1 point for each Mostly True answer. **Total Score** 8. Leadership coaching is one way leaders provide valuable feedback that helps people achieve their potential. The attitude of the follower is equally important to that of the leader for a successful coaching relationship. Your score for this questionnaire pertains to your readiness to receive coaching and feedback from another person. If your score is 6 or above, you probably have the correct mindset to benefit from leadership coaching. If your score is 3 or below you may not be receptive to coaching. If you are not open to receiving coaching for yourself, do you think you would be a good coach to others? Would you like to change your coaching mindset? What is the first step you might take?

Source: Based on Susan Battley, *Coached to Lead: How to Achieve Extraordinary Results with an Executive Coach* (San Francisco: Jossey-Bass, 2006), pp. 20–40.

7-6d Protection from Organizational Intrusions

Good followers want to do their jobs to the best of their abilities. They don't want to be continually interrupted by managers offering questions or suggestions, and they don't want to have to fight against organizational politics, leader uncertainties, or useless procedures. The best leaders "take pride in being human shields."[64] They stay out of the way so people can do their jobs, and they protect their followers from time wasters such as burdensome organizational practices (think routine reports that no one reads), pushy or critical higher executives, abusive or overly demanding customers or clients, and unnecessary meetings.

Good leaders take the heat so employees don't have to. One leader at Southwest Airlines interrupted a customer who was mistreating a gate agent, told him he wouldn't allow his employees to be treated that way, and accompanied the customer to another airline's counter to buy him a ticket. Will Wright, who was responsible for developing the computer games *The Sims* and *Spore*, charged his designers a dollar every time they called an unnecessary meeting that wasted artists' time.[65] Leaders invest time and effort into helping their subordinates be good followers. And when people can't or won't learn and change, good leaders get rid of the "bad apples" rather than letting them infect the entire team.

LEADERSHIP ESSENTIALS

- The important role of followership in organizations is increasingly recognized. Leaders and followers are interdependent, and people are followers more often than leaders.
- People who effectively manage both up and down the hierarchy are more successful, but managing up can be difficult for new leaders. Strategies for managing up include being a resource, helping the leader be a good leader, building a relationship with the leader, and viewing the leader realistically.
- Leaders want followers who are positive and self-motivated, who take action to get things done, who accept responsibility, and who excel at required tasks. An effective follower is both independent and active in the organization. Being an effective follower depends on not becoming alienated, conforming, passive, or a pragmatic survivor.
- Effective followership is not always easy. Effective followers display the courage to assume responsibility, to challenge their leaders, to participate in transformation, to serve others, and to leave the organization when necessary. Followers can recognize and rely on several personal and positional sources of power to gain the courage to manage up.
- Followers want both their leaders and their colleagues to be honest and competent. However, they want their leaders also to be forward-thinking and inspirational. The two latter traits distinguish the role of leader from follower. Followers want to be led, not controlled. They also want leaders to create an environment that enables people to contribute their best.
- Four specific ways leaders enhance the abilities and contributions of followers are by offering clarity of direction, providing opportunities for growth, giving honest, constructive feedback, and protecting followers from organizational intrusions.
- Followers want feedback that is timely and specific, focuses on performance rather than the person, and focuses on the future rather than dragging up mistakes of the past.

DISCUSSION QUESTIONS

1. Discuss the role of a follower. Why do you think so little emphasis is given to followership compared to leadership in organizations?
2. As a leader, what would you want most from followers? As a follower, what would you want most from your leader? How do these differ? Why?
3. Compare the alienated follower with the passive follower. Can you give an example of each? Have you ever been either one? How would you respond to each if you were a leader?
4. Why is managing up important in organizations? Describe the strategy for managing up that you most prefer. Explain.
5. The chapter describes five ways in which followers need to use courage. Which do you feel is most important? Least important? How might a follower derive the courage to behave in new ways to be more effective? Discuss.

6. Do you think you would respond better to feedback that is presented using a traditional scheduled performance review format or feedback that is presented as a routine part of everyday work activities? Discuss. How do you think leaders should frame negative feedback to achieve the best results?
7. Which type of follower courage is easiest for you to use? Hardest for you to use? Can you think of ways to expand your power for influencing up?
8. One organizational observer suggested that bosses who won't give negative feedback to followers who need it cause even more damage in the long run than those who fly off the handle when a follower makes a mistake. Do you agree? Discuss.
9. What does leadership coaching mean to you? How should leaders decide which followers they will provide with coaching?
10. What does it mean for a leader to act as a human shield? Do you believe this should be part of a leader's responsibility to followers?

LEADERSHIP AT WORK

Follower Role Play

You are a production supervisor at Hyperlink Systems. Your plant produces circuit boards that are used in Nokia cell phones and IBM computers. Hyperlink is caught in a competitive pricing squeeze, so senior management hired a consultant to study the production department. The plant manager, Sue Harris, asked that the consultant's recommendations be implemented immediately. She thought that total production would increase right away. Weekly production goals were set higher than ever. You don't think she took into account the time required to learn new procedures, and plant workers are under great pressure. A handful of workers have resisted the new work methods because they can produce more circuit boards using the old methods. Most workers have changed to the new methods, but their productivity has not increased. Even after a month, many workers think the old ways are more efficient, faster, and more productive.

You have a couple of other concerns with Harris. She asked you to attend an operations conference, and at the last minute sent another supervisor instead without any explanation. She has made other promises of supplies and equipment to your section and then has not followed through. You think she acts too quickly without adequate implementation and follow-up.

You report directly to Harris and are thinking about your responsibility as a follower. Write below specifically how you would handle this situation. Will you confront her with the knowledge you have? When and where will you meet with her? What will you say? How will you get her to hear you?

____

____

____

What style—effective, conformist, passive, alienated—best describes your response to this situation? Referring to Exhibit 7.3, which tactic would you like to use to assist Harris?

____

____

____

In Class: The instructor can ask students to volunteer to play the role of the plant manager and the production supervisor. A few students can take turns role-playing the production supervisor in front of the class to show different approaches to being a follower. Other students can be asked to provide feedback on each production supervisor's effectiveness and on which approach seems more effective for this situation.

Source: Based on K. J. Keleman, J. E. Garcia, and K. J. Lovelace, *Management Incidents: Role Plays for Management Development* (Dubuque, IA: Kendall Hunt Publishing Company, 1990), pp. 73–75, 83.

LEADERSHIP DEVELOPMENT: CASES FOR ANALYSIS

Waiting for Clearance

He wanted the help, but CEO Tony Bussard apparently wanted to relinquish none of the power when he agreed with board members of Alvon Biometrics to maintain control over the financial and administrative side of the company while naming a COO to oversee day-to-day operations.

Everyone agreed that the job was too big for one guy. After months of assessments, interviews, and discussion, Juan Carlos De la Vega was hired as COO for the company.

De la Vega came to Alvon from a smaller rival company and was initially excited about his new position and the future of Alvon. De la Vega trained in military security investigations and became interested in the measuring and statistical analysis of biological data that included fingerprints, eye retinas and irises, voice patterns, and facial patterns that could be used in security systems. He had worked his way up through rival Bi-Tech to a position in middle management and jumped at the opportunity to guide a major company in the field about which he was so passionate. "That is *so cool*," was a De la Vega trademark comment as he delighted in the giant leaps of each system's gadgetry.

But De la Vega's exciting new position came with its own set of frustrations as he tried to plunge into the rapidly changing technology while simultaneously fitting into the organization and tip-toeing around Tony Bussard's ego.

Bussard welcomed De la Vega with the gusto of an under-fire field officer who looks up to see reinforcements riding into the fray. He enthusiastically introduced the new COO to everyone and raved, almost to the point of embarrassment, about De la Vega's experience and level of expertise in the field of biometrics.

"You've made my job a whole lot easier," Bussard gushed. "We're all thrilled to have you."

Now, one year into the job, De la Vega was still wondering what was expected of him and where Bussard's duties ended and his duties began. Those things were never actually spelled out in an agreement, and the boundaries remained vague and confusing. Even during the initial job interviews, Bussard and board members showed great interest in De la Vega's background and talked endlessly about Bussard's vision for the future. But now, in retrospect, the COO realized that there was little or no discussion of *his* vision or any mention about how he would fit into the future being laid out for him.

With no clear agreement, De la Vega's earnest efforts to get guidance about his responsibilities seemed to be brushed aside by the CEO, who remained elusive and vague.

"If he tells me one more time, 'Yeah, yeah, we'll talk,' I think I will scream," De la Vega complained. "I want to feel like a COO, not a sidekick to the CEO. At the same time, I don't want to push so hard that Bussard and the board members become concerned that they made a mistake in selecting me."

The confusion about De la Vega's role also filtered down the ranks. Employees, expecting initiative from De la Vega, remained uncertain about his range of responsibilities. People looked almost exclusively to Bussard for direction, bypassing the new COO. Workers liked De la Vega and admired his industry experience. However, old habits die hard, and the habit of yielding to Bussard's leadership remained intact. Even one year later, employees were reluctant to take a chance on angering Bussard by shifting even a portion of their attention and allegiance to De la Vega.

For his part, De la Vega knew the time for clarity was now, but he hesitated, not knowing exactly how or when to approach the CEO from a position of strength.

QUESTIONS

1. If you were De la Vega, what would you do at this point? Do you think De la Vega has waited too long to make a substantial change in his relationship with Bussard? Why?
2. How would you characterize De la Vega's style as a follower? What tactics might help improve his relationship with Bussard? Explain.
3. If you were in De la Vega's position, what would you have done from the beginning? Be specific about your actions and timing.

Jake's Pet Land

Adam Gerrit glanced up from the cash register as his first customers of the day walked into Jake's Pet Land, a neighborhood pet store that is part of a small, regional chain. A young boy, obviously distraught, reluctantly placed a shoebox on the counter. "We have a problem," whispered the boy's dad, "and I would like to get a refund." Cautiously, Adam lifted the lid of the shoebox and found an ebony-colored chinchilla hunched in the corner of the box, huddled in wood chips and barely breathing. Normally inquisitive and active, the chinchilla was obviously sick. The boy's father, a loyal customer for several years, handed Adam a receipt. Adam knew the refund policy by heart: "The health of exotic animals is guaranteed for seven days after purchase. No refunds are granted after seven days." The chinchilla had been purchased 10 days ago, but Adam, as a long-time employee, knew his manager would agree to bend the rules in this case and grant this customer a full refund. Putting the policy manual out of his mind, Adam handed the customer a full refund of $125, saying to the distraught boy, "I'm sorry your little buddy didn't make it. Would you like to look for another pet?" Although he had clearly stretched the return policy rules, Adam felt confident that his store manager, Phillip Jordan, would support his decision.

Jordan did support Adam's decision to bend company rules if it meant retaining a loyal customer. Although the store's thick policy manual called for strict adherence to established procedures, Jordan encouraged employees to think independently when meeting the needs of customers. Jordan also felt strongly about building camaraderie among his small staff, even if it meant straying outside the edicts in the policy manual. For example, Jordan bought the entire staff pizza and soft drinks as a reward for their cheerful attitude when asked to stay late to clean out the stockroom after the store closed. While they restocked shelves and mopped the stockroom floor, his employees told stories, traded jokes, and enjoyed helping each other complete the job quickly. Jordan was proud of the productive yet friendly culture he had created, even if his district manager would frown on some of his decisions.

Without surprise, Jordan's store steadily increased revenue, up 5.4 percent from the previous year. Employees were motivated and enthusiastic. One factor contributing to the store's success was low employee turnover. Again setting company policy aside, Jordan retained his employees by offering slightly higher wages, granting small promotions with increased responsibilities, and rewarding "VIP" employees with free passes to a local theme park. Since all of the employees were pet owners, he also allowed employees to take home overstocked pet supplies and free samples of new pet foods. This loyalty to employees resulted in a successful store. But Jordan knew his district manager would abruptly end all of these practices if he knew about them, so Jordan learned to keep guarded secrets.

Trouble began when Jordan was transferred to another store, closer to his home, and a new manager with a completely different managerial style was brought in. Wedded to rules and procedures, Jan Whitall was driven by order and discipline. On Whitall's first day on the job, she set the tone for her tenure with this announcement: "The company's new compensation policy will be strictly followed in this store, and some of you will have your pay reduced to adhere to the new pay scales. This is uncomfortable for me, but it's the result of some questionable decisions by your previous manager." The morale of top performers, including Adam, plummeted. By the end of Whitall's first month, she had fired an employee for violating the store's return policy. The employee had granted a full refund for a ball python after the seven-day return period. Another employee was publicly reprimanded for giving a customer a sample of a new organic pet food to try before purchasing it. Stunned by these actions, employees became indignant and bristled under her tight authority. The friendly, warm culture had vanished. Adam Gerrit confided to his coworker, "I've applied for a position at the pet superstore down the road. Before I resign, I'm going to talk to Jan and see if she can lighten up on the rules."

Mustering his courage, Adam tapped on Whitall's office door and asked if he could talk with her. Putting down her reading glasses and pushing away the financial reports in front of her, Whitall motioned for him to sit down. "I'm worried about morale around here," Adam began. "Some of our best workers are leaving and I'm considering it, too. Under our previous manager, I loved coming to work and enjoyed the friendship of coworkers and customers. Now, everyone is in a sour mood and we've lost some customers." Taking a deep breath, he continued. "If you are willing to be more flexible with the company policies, I would be willing to stay." Unflustered, Whitall kept her firm stance. "Adam," she explained, "I'm responsible to the district manager, who long suspected that the previous manager wasn't adhering to company policies. It's my intention to do my job the way I've been instructed, and I'm sorry to hear you will be leaving."

As Adam left her office with his head down, Whitall mused to herself that the district manager would be proud of her ability to stand firm. In fact, he had recently complimented her on her approach. Neither realized that sales would take a surprising dip in the next quarter.

QUESTIONS

1. Which store manager—Phillip Jordan or Jan Whitall—would you prefer working for? How did each leader's style affect the culture of the pet store? Explain.
2. What kind of follower was Adam Gerrit? In general, what characteristics of followers do you admire? What characteristics would you want them to display when working for you?
3. If you were the district manager, which store manager would you prefer to have working for you? Why? In your opinion, which manager did a better job of managing up? Which manager did a better job of managing down?

REFERENCES

1. Rich Gee Group Website, http://richgee.com/about/ (accessed October 22, 2015).
2. Sue Shellenbarger, "When the Boss Works Long Hours, Must We All? How to Convey That You Are Working Hard Without Pulling All-Nighters," *The Wall Street Journal* (February 18, 2014), http://www.wsj.com/articles/SB10001424052702303491404579391103854539542 (accessed October 22, 2015); Ibid.
3. Robin Sronce and Lucy A. Arendt, "Demonstrating the Interplay of Leaders and Followers," *Journal of Management Education* 33, no. 6 (December 2009), pp. 699–724; Marc Hurwitz and Samantha Hurwitz, "The Romance of the Follower: Part 1," *Industrial and Commercial Training* 41, no. 2 (2009), pp. 80–86; and Marc Hurwitz and Samantha Hurwitz, "The Romance of the Follower: Part 2," *Industrial and Commercial Training* 41, no. 4 (2009), pp. 199–206.
4. Warren Bennis, "Art of Followership: Followers Engage in an Interdependent Dance," *Leadership Excellence* (January 2010), pp. 3–4; and Robert E. Kelley, "In Praise of Followers," *Harvard Business Review* (November/December 1988), pp. 142–148.
5. John G. Gabarro and John P. Kotter, "Managing Your Boss," Best of HBR 1980, *Harvard Business Review* (January 2005), http://hbr.org/2005/01/managing-your-boss/ar/1 (accessed April 18, 2011).
6. Rosabeth Moss Kanter, "Power Failure in Management Circuits," *Harvard Business Review* 57 (July–August, 1979), pp. 65–75.
7. Ronald J. DeLuga, "Kissing Up to the Boss: What It Is and What to Do about It," *Business Forum* 26 (2003), pp. 14–18; and Bennett Tepper, "Upward Maintenance Tactics in Supervisory Mentoring and Nonmentoring Relationships," *Academy of Management Journal* 38, no. 4 (1995), pp. 1191–1205.

8. Liz Simpson, "Why Managing Up Matters," *Harvard Management Update* (August 2002), pp. 3–5; and Stanley Bing, *Throwing the Elephant* (New York: HarperCollins, 2002).
9. Irvin D. Yalom, with Ben Yalom, "Mad about Me," *Inc.* (December 1998), pp. 37–38; and story told in Robert McGarvey, "And You Thought Your Boss Was Bad," *American Way* (May 1, 2006), pp. 69–74.
10. These are based on Larry Bossidy, "What Your Leader Expects of You and What You Should Expect," *Leadership Excellence* (February 2008), p. 6; Larry Bossidy, "What Your Leader Expects of You," *Harvard Business Review* (April 2007), pp. 58–65; and Peter F. Drucker, "Drucker on Management: Managing the Boss," *The Wall Street Journal* (August 1, 1986).
11. Vignette recounted in Isaac Getz, "Liberating Leadership: How the Initiative-Freeing Radical Organizational Form Has Been Successfully Adopted," *California Management Review* (Summer 2009), pp. 32–58.
12. Bossidy, "What Your Leader Expects of You."
13. Robert E. Kelley, *The Power of Followership* (New York: Doubleday, 1992).
14. Ibid.
15. Discussed in Michael G. Winston, "Say *No* to Yes Men," *Leadership Excellence* (November 2010), p. 15.
16. Kelley, *The Power of Followership*, pp. 111–112.
17. Ibid., pp. 111–112, pp. 117–118.
18. Based on an incident reported in "Ask Inc.," *Inc.* (March 2007), pp. 81–82.
19. Kelley, *The Power of Followership*, p. 123.
20. Melanie Trottman, "Baggers Get the Sack, but Dawn Marshall Still Excels as One," *The Wall Street Journal* (May 2, 2003), pp. A1, A6.
21. Bennis, "Art of Followership"; Sronce and Arendt, "Demonstrating the Interplay of Leaders and Followers"; Marshall Goldsmith, "Influencing Up: You Make a Difference," *Leadership Excellence* (January 2008), pp. 5–6; David K. Hurst, "How to Manage Your Boss," *Strategy + Business* no. 28 (Third Quarter 2002), pp. 99–103; Joseph L. Badaracco Jr., *Leading Quietly: An Unorthodox Guide to Doing the Right Thing* (Boston: Harvard Business School Press, 2002); and Michael Useem, *Leading Up: How to Lead Your Boss So You Both Win* (New York: Crown Business, 2001).
22. Hurwitz and Hurwitz, "The Romance of the Follower: Part 1."
23. Based on Jo Owen, "Manage Your Boss," *Industrial and Commercial Training* 39, no. 2 (2007), pp. 79–84.
24. Ryan Lizza, "The Political Scene: The Obama Memos," *The New Yorker* (January 30, 2012), pp. 36–49; Peter Baker, "How Obama's Afghanistan War Plan Came to Be," *International Herald Tribune* (December 7, 2009); and Ron Walters, "Afghanistan: The Big Decision," *The Washington Informer* (December 10–16, 2009).
25. Len Schlesinger, "It Doesn't Take a Wizard to Build a Better Boss," *Fast Company* (June/July 1996), pp. 102–107.
26. Ira Chaleff, "Courageous Followers: Should We Stand Up To or For Leaders?" *Leadership Excellence* (April 2011), p. 19; and Hurst, "How to Manage Your Boss."
27. William Speed Weed, Alex Lash, and Constance Loizos, "30 Ways to Annoy Your Boss," *MBA Jungle* (March–April 2003), pp. 51–55.
28. Judith Sills, "When You're Smarter Than Your Boss," *Psychology Today* (May–June 2006), pp. 58–59; Sarah Kershaw, "My Other Family Is the Office," *The New York Times* (December 4, 2008), p. E1; and Frank Pittman, "How to Manage Mom and Dad," *Psychology Today* (November/December 1994), pp. 44–74.
29. Ira Chaleff, *The Courageous Follower: Standing Up To and For Our Leaders* (San Francisco: Berrett-Koehler, 1995); and John J. Gabarro and John P. Kotter, "Managing Your Boss," *Harvard Business Review*, "Best of HBR" (January 2005), pp. 92–99.
30. Example from Christopher Hegarty, *How to Manage Your Boss* (New York: Ballantine, 1985), p. 147.
31. Chaleff, "Courageous Followers."
32. Ibid.
33. Ibid.
34. Chaleff, *The Courageous Follower: Standing Up To and For Our Leaders*.
35. Joann S. Lublin, "Arguing with the Boss: A Winning Career Strategy," *The Wall Street Journal* (August 9, 2012), http://online.wsj.com/article/SB10000872396390443991704577579201122821724.html (accessed April 9, 2013).
36. This is based on Goldsmith, "Influencing Up: You Make a Difference" and Hegarty, *How to Manage Your Boss*.
37. Warren Bennis, "Art of Followership: Followers Engage in an Interdependent Dance," *Leadership Excellence* (January 2010), pp. 3–4.
38. Gabarro and Kotter, "Managing Your Boss."
39. Peter Moroz and Brian H. Kleiner, "Playing Hardball in Business Organizations," *Industrial Management* (January/February 1994), pp. 9–11.
40. Warren Keith Schilit and Edwin A. Locke, "A Study of Upward Influence in Organizations," *Administrative Science Quarterly* 27 (1982), pp. 304–316.
41. Mary C. Gentile, "Keeping Your Colleagues Honest," *Harvard Business Review* (March 2010), pp. 114–117; and Goldsmith, "Influencing Up: You Make a Difference."
42. Deepti Bhatnagar, "Evaluation of Managerial Influence Tactics," *Journal of Managerial Psychology* 8, no. 1 (1993), pp. 3–9; and Daniel M. Cable and Timothy A. Judge, "Managers' Upward Influence Tactic Strategies: The Role of Manager Personality and Supervisor Leadership Style," *Journal of Organizational Behavior* 24 (2003), pp. 197–214.
43. Winston, "Say *No* to Yes Men."
44. David N. Berg, "Resurrecting the Muse: Followership in Organizations," presented at the 1996 International Society for the Psychoanalytic Study of Organizations (ISPSO) Symposium, New York, NY, June 14–16, 1996.
45. Chaleff, *The Courageous Follower: Standing Up To and For Our Leaders*.
46. Major (General Staff) Dr. Ulrich F. Zwygart, "How Much Obedience Does an Officer Need? Beck, Tresckow, and Stauffenberg—Examples of Integrity and Moral Courage for Today's Officer," Combat Studies Institute; U.S. Army Command and General Staff College, Fort Leavenworth, Kansas, http://www.cgsc.edu/CARL/download/csipubs/ObedienceOfficerNeed_Zwygart.pdf (accessed June 11, 2013).
47. "Ethics Lessons from Tyco for Today's Financial Crisis," a talk given by Eric Pillmore at Thunderbird School of Global Management, October 28, 2008, http://knowledgenetwork.thunderbird.edu/research/2008/10/30/takeaways-from-tyco-for-today%E2%80%99s-financial-crisis/ (accessed April 10, 2013); and Lublin, "Arguing with the Boss: A Winning Career Strategy."
48. Merle MacIsaac, "Born Again Basket Case," *Canadian Business* (May 1993), pp. 38–44.
49. Joann S. Lublin, "How to Prove You're Keeper to a New CEO," *The Wall Street Journal* (March 8, 2013), p. B8.
50. Greg Jaffe, "The Two-Star Rebel: For Gen. Batiste, a Tour in Iraq Turned a Loyal Soldier into Rumsfeld's Most Unexpected Critic," *The Wall Street Journal* (May 13, 2006), p. A1.
51. Berg, "Resurrecting the Muse."
52. James M. Kouzes and Barry Z. Posner, *Credibility: How Leaders Gain and Lose It, Why People Demand It* (San Francisco: Jossey-Bass, 1993).
53. This section is based largely on Bossidy, "What Your Leader Expects of You."
54. See Gary P. Latham and Edwin A. Locke, "Enhancing the Benefits and Overcoming the Pitfalls of Goal Setting," *Organizational Dynamics* 35, no. 4 (2006), pp. 332–338; Edwin A. Locke and Gary P. Latham, "Building a Practically Useful Theory of Goal Setting and Task Motivation: A 35-Year Odyssey," *The American Psychologist* 57, no. 9 (September 2002), p. 705ff.; Gary P. Latham and Edwin A. Locke, "Self-Regulation through Goal Setting," *Organizational Behavior and*

Human Decision Processes 50, no. 2 (1991), pp. 212–247; G. P. Latham and G. H. Seijts, "The Effects of Proximal and Distal Goals on Performance of a Moderately Complex Task," *Journal of Organizational Behavior* 20, no. 4 (1999), pp. 421–428; P. C. Early, T. Connolly, and G. Ekegren, "Goals, Strategy Development, and Task Performance: Some Limits on the Efficacy of Goal Setting," *Journal of Applied Psychology* 74 (1989), pp. 24–33; and E. A. Locke, "Toward a Theory of Task Motivation and Incentives," *Organizational Behavior and Human Performance* 3 (1968), pp. 157–189.

55. Patrick Sweeney, "Developing Leadership Potential through Coaching," *Chief Learning Officer* (March 2009), p. 22ff.
56. This table and the discussion are based on Andrea D. Ellinger and Robert P. Bostrom, "An Examination of Managers' Beliefs about Their Roles as Facilitators of Learning," *Management Learning* 33, no. 2 (2002), pp. 147–179.
57. "The Business Leader as Development Coach," *PDI Portfolio* (Winter 1996), p. 6; and Personnel Decisions International, http://www.personneldecisions.com (accessed May 3, 2009).
58. McKinsey & Company's *War for Talent 2000 Survey*, reported in E. Michaels, H. Handfield-Jones, and B. Axelrod, *The War for Talent* (Boston: Harvard Business School Press, 2001), p. 100; and Mark D. Cannon and Robert Witherspoon, "Actionable Feedback: Unlocking the Power of Learning and Performance Improvement," *Academy of Management Executive* 19, no. 2 (2005), pp. 120–134.
59. Jay M. Jackman and Myra H. Strober, "Fear of Feedback," *Harvard Business Review* (April 2003), pp. 101–108; and Bossidy, "What Your Leader Expects of You."
60. John C. Kunich and Richard I. Lester, "Leadership and the Art of Feedback: Feeding the Hands That Back Us," *The Journal of Leadership Studies* 3, no. 4 (1996), pp. 3–22.
61. Broderick quote is from Jared Sandberg, "Avoiding Conflicts, the Too-Nice Boss Makes Matters Worse," *The Wall Street Journal* (February 26, 2008), p. B1.
62. Sandberg, "Avoiding Conflicts."
63. Based on "Closing Gaps and Improving Performance: The Basics of Coaching," excerpt, originally published as Chapter 4 of *Performance Management: Measure and Improve the Effectiveness of Your Employees* (Boston, MA: Harvard Business School Press, 2006).
64. This section is based on Robert I. Sutton, "The Boss as a Human Shield," *Harvard Business Review* (September 2010), pp. 106–109.
65. These examples are from Sutton, "The Boss as Human Shield."

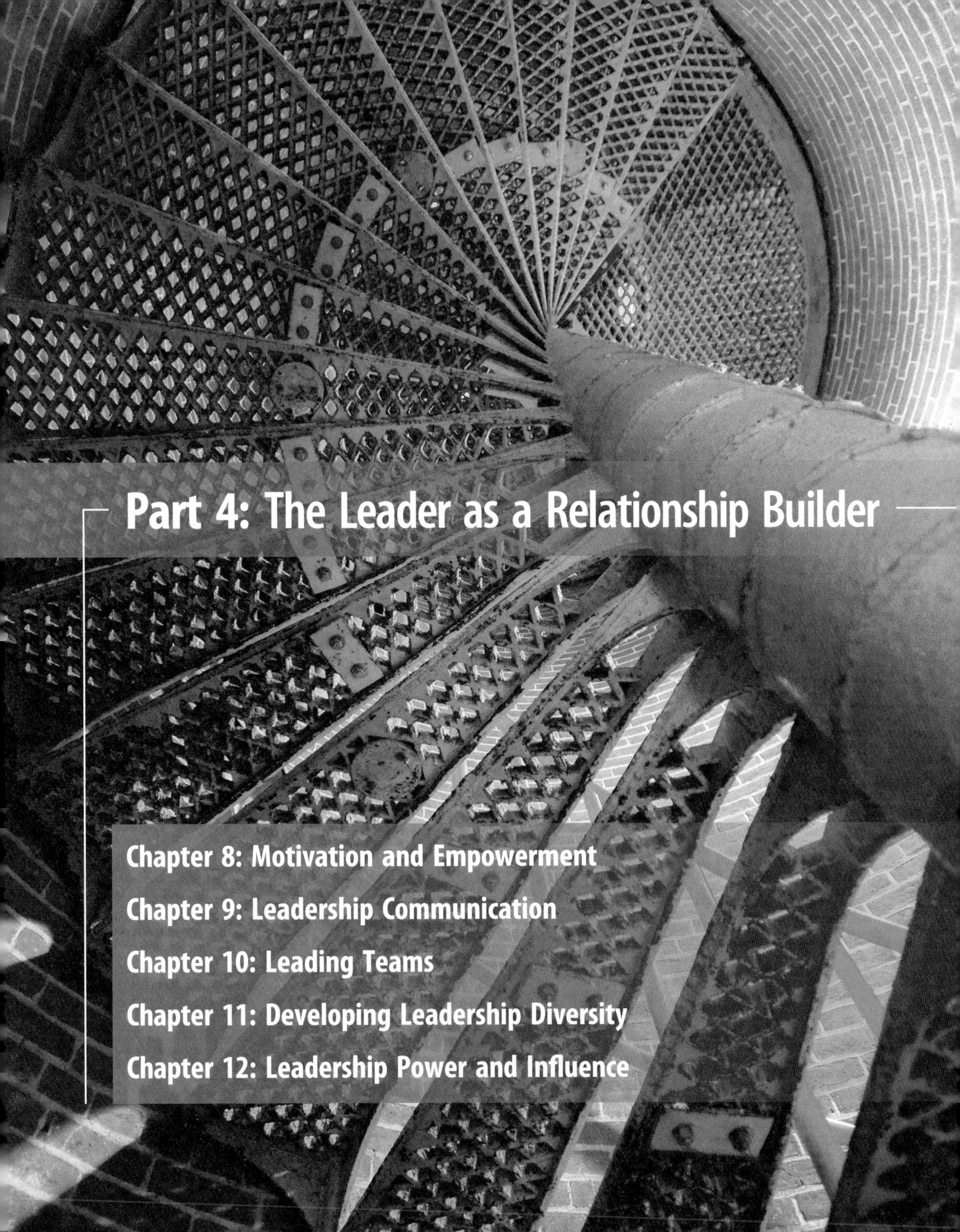

Part 4: The Leader as a Relationship Builder

Chapter 8: Motivation and Empowerment

Chapter 9: Leadership Communication

Chapter 10: Leading Teams

Chapter 11: Developing Leadership Diversity

Chapter 12: Leadership Power and Influence

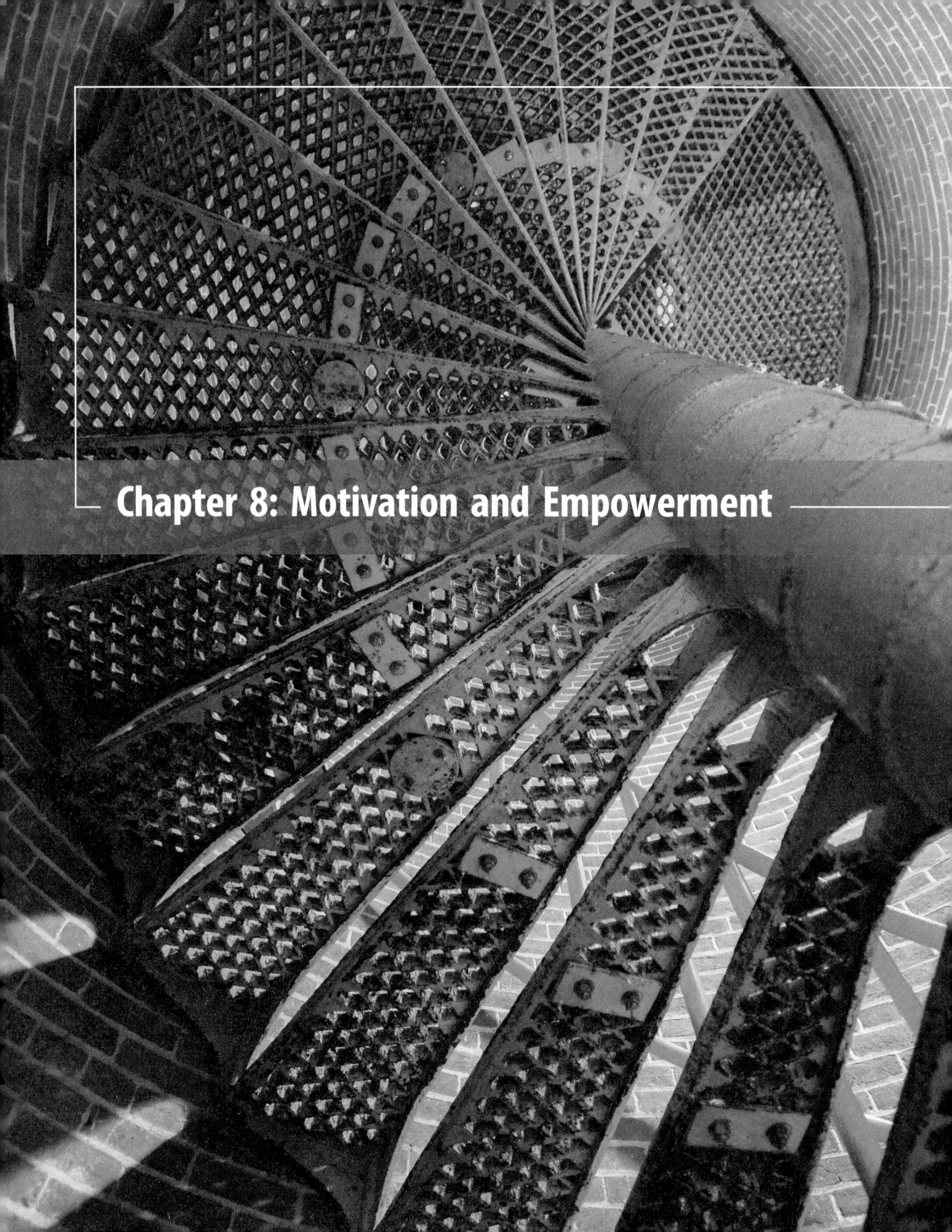

Chapter 8: Motivation and Empowerment

YOUR **LEADERSHIP** CHALLENGE

After reading this chapter, you should be able to:

- Recognize and apply the difference between intrinsic and extrinsic rewards.
- Appropriately tap into the motives that induce people to take action to accomplish important goals.
- Motivate others by meeting their higher-level needs.
- Apply needs-based theories of motivation and understand how the concept of equity applies to motivation.
- Describe the psychological and structural elements of empowerment and how empowerment contributes to motivation.
- Apply the job characteristics model to enrich jobs.
- Identify factors that play a role in employee engagement and use engagement to meet higher-level needs.
- Build a thriving workforce by giving people a sense of making progress toward meaningful goals.

CHAPTER **OUTLINE**

228 **Leadership and Motivation**

232 **Needs-Based Theories of Motivation**

237 **Other Motivation Theories**

243 **Empowering People to Meet Higher Needs**

248 **Giving Meaning to Work through Engagement**

250 **New Ideas for Motivation**

In the Lead

235 **Grant Reid, Mars Incorporated**

246 **Zingerman's Community of Businesses**

249 **Facebook**

Leader's Self-Insight

237 **Are Your Needs Met?**

242 **Your Approach to Motivating Others**

248 **Are You Engaged?**

Leader's Bookshelf

232 **Joy, Inc.: How We Built a Workplace People Love**

Leadership at Work

252 **Should, Need, Like, Love**

Leadership Development: Cases for Analysis

254 **Commissions for Charlotte**

255 **Sun Spots**

When Dan Price increased his company's minimum wage to $70,000 a year, he thought people would be happier and more motivated. At first, employees at Seattle-based Gravity Payments, a credit card processing company, celebrated. Then the problems started. The toughest one for Price was that he started losing some of his best people. A web developer quit, even though he had gotten a $9,000 raise. Why? He felt like he put 110 percent into his job and didn't like the fact that "people who were just clocking in and out were making the same as me." The financial manager also resigned, believing that the biggest raises were going to "the people with the least skills," rather than rewarding those who were making the greatest contribution. Even a couple of newly hired employees were unhappy, despite the fact that they were making a lot of money for an entry-level job. "Am I doing my job well enough to deserve this?" one asked. "I didn't earn it."[1]

Dan Price learned something that many good leaders know: Creating an organization with satisfied, motivated employees takes more than money. In fact, many people consider factors other than money to be more important to their motivation. In addition, motivation falters when people feel they aren't being treated fairly.

Some long-term experienced employees at Gravity Payments lost their motivation when they saw that newly hired people were earning the same as they were. Others believed they put in more effort and should be rewarded for it, rather than earning the same as people who simply "clocked in and out," as the unhappy web developer phrased it.

Paying people well is important, and Price has been praised for the goal of giving people more. However, motivation is a complex challenge that can't be handled simply by giving employees more money. For example, many leaders have found that creating an environment where people feel valued and respected is more important to high motivation than is boosting wages.

This chapter explores motivation in organizations and examines how leaders can bring out the best in followers. We look at the difference between intrinsic and extrinsic rewards, examine the needs that people bring to the workplace, and discuss how leaders tap into positive or negative motives that spur people to action. Individuals have both lower and higher needs, and there are different methods of motivation to meet those needs. The chapter presents several theories of motivation, with particular attention to the differences between leadership and conventional management methods for creating a motivated workforce. The final sections of the chapter explore empowerment, employee engagement, and how leaders create a thriving workforce by enabling people to feel a sense of progress in their work.

8-1 LEADERSHIP AND MOTIVATION

Most of us get up in the morning, go to school or work, and behave in ways that are predictably our own. We usually respond to our environment and the people in it with little thought as to why we work hard, invest extra time and energy in certain classes, or spend our leisure time pursuing specific recreational or volunteer activities. Yet all these behaviors are motivated by something. **Motivation** refers to the forces either internal or external to a person that arouse enthusiasm and persistence to pursue a certain course of action. Employee motivation affects productivity, so part of a leader's job is to channel followers' motivation toward the accomplishment of the organization's vision and goals.[2] The study of motivation helps leaders understand what prompts people to initiate action, what influences their choice of action, and why they persist in that action over time.

Motivation
the forces either internal or external to a person that arouse enthusiasm and persistence to pursue a certain course of action

Exhibit 8.1 illustrates a simple model of human motivation. People have basic needs, such as for friendship, recognition, or monetary gain, which translate into an

EXHIBIT 8.1 A Simple Model of Motivation

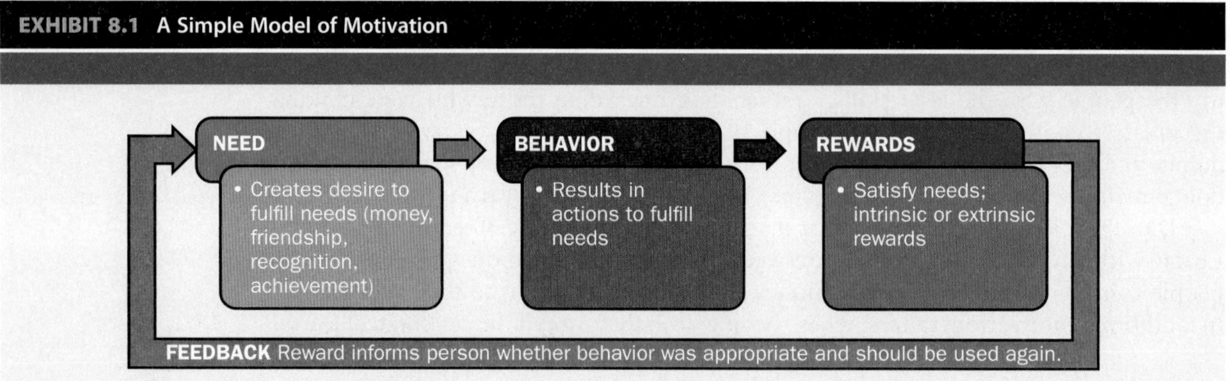

internal tension that motivates specific behaviors with which to fulfill the need. To the extent that the behavior is successful, the person is rewarded when the need is satisfied. The reward also informs the person that the behavior was appropriate and can be used again in the future.

The importance of motivation, as illustrated in Exhibit 8.1, is that it can lead to behaviors that reflect high performance within organizations. Studies have found that high employee motivation and high organizational performance and profits go hand in hand.[3] An extensive survey by the Gallup Organization, for example, found that when all of an organization's employees are highly motivated and performing at their peak, customers are 70 percent more loyal, turnover drops by 70 percent, and profits jump 40 percent.[4] Leaders can use motivation theory to help satisfy followers' needs and simultaneously encourage high work performance. When workers are not motivated to achieve organizational goals, the fault is often with the leader.

8-1a Intrinsic and Extrinsic Rewards

Rewards can be either intrinsic or extrinsic and meet both lower- and higher-level needs.[5] **Intrinsic rewards** come from the internal satisfaction and enjoyment a person receives in the process of performing a particular action. Solving a problem to benefit others may fulfill a personal mission, or the completion of a complex task may bestow a pleasant feeling of accomplishment. An intrinsic reward is internal and under the control of the individual, such as to engage in task behavior to satisfy a need for competency and self-determination.

Conversely, **extrinsic rewards** are given by another person, typically a supervisor, and include promotions and pay increases. Because they originate externally as a result of pleasing others, extrinsic rewards compel individuals to engage in a task behavior for an outside source that provides what they need, such as money to survive in modern society. Think about the difference in motivation for polishing a car if it belongs to you versus if you work at a car wash. Your good feelings from making your own car shine would be intrinsic. However, buffing a car that is but one of many in a day's work requires the extrinsic reward of a paycheck.[6]

NEW LEADER
ACTION MEMO

As a leader, you can provide extrinsic rewards, such as promotions, pay raises, and praise, but also help followers achieve intrinsic rewards and meet their higher-level needs for accomplishment, growth, and fulfillment.

Although extrinsic rewards are important, leaders work especially hard to help followers achieve intrinsic rewards. Intrinsic rewards appeal to the "higher" needs of individuals, such as for accomplishment, competence, fulfillment, and self-determination. Extrinsic rewards appeal to the "lower" needs of individuals, such as for material comfort and basic safety and security. Exhibit 8.2 outlines the distinction between conventional management and leadership approaches to motivation based on people's needs. Conventional management approaches often appeal to an individual's lower, basic needs and rely on extrinsic rewards and punishments to motivate people to behave in desired ways. These approaches are effective, but they are based on controlling the behavior of employees by manipulating their decisions about how to act. The higher needs of people may be unmet in favor of utilizing their labor in exchange for external rewards. Under conventional management, people perform adequately to receive rewards or avoid punishments because they will not necessarily derive intrinsic satisfaction from their work.

The leadership approach strives to motivate people by providing them with the opportunity to satisfy higher needs and become intrinsically rewarded. Employees in companies that are infused with a social mission, and that find ways to enrich the lives of others, are typically more highly motivated because of the intrinsic rewards they get from helping other people.[7] Leaders at any company can enable people to find meaning in their work. At Morrison Management Specialists, for example,

Intrinsic rewards
internal satisfactions a person receives in the process of performing a particular action

Extrinsic rewards
rewards given by another person, typically a supervisor, such as pay increases and promotions

EXHIBIT 8.2 Needs of People and Motivation Methods

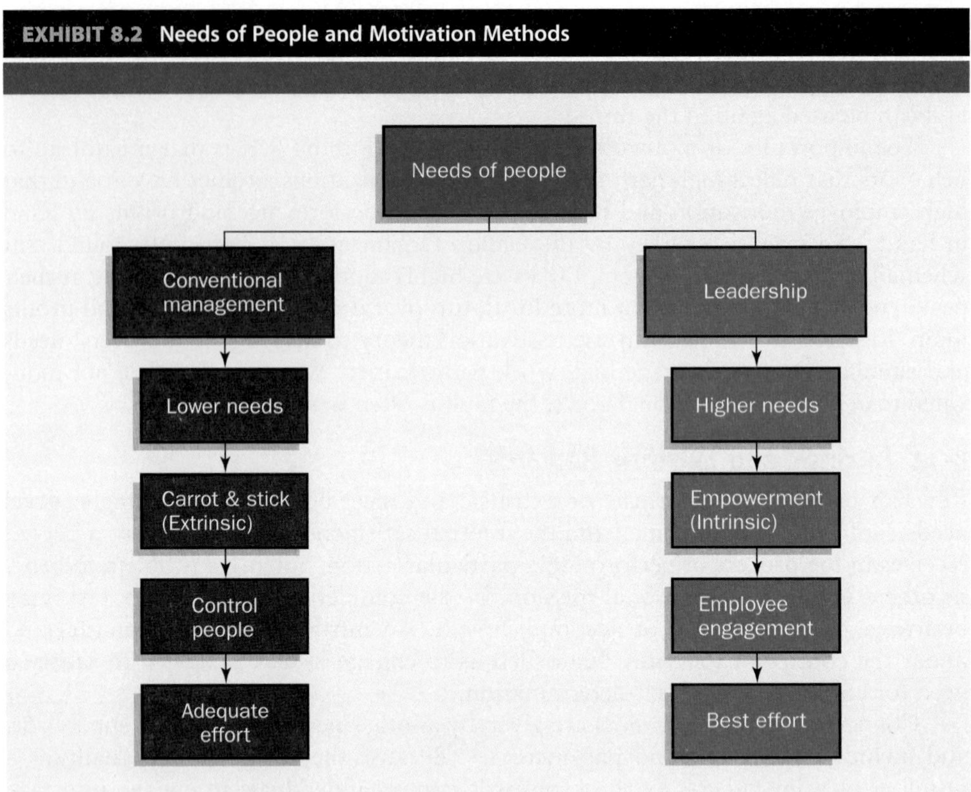

Source: Adapted from William D. Hitt, *The Leader-Manager: Guidelines for Action* (Columbus, OH: Battelle Press, 1988), p. 153.

which provides food, nutrition, and dining services to the health-care and senior living industries, leaders provide training sessions under the title of "Our Great Partnership" and strive to help people see how their jobs make a difference in the lives of elderly or ill people. A "People First" recognition program gives employees a chance to recognize one another for exceptional service.[8] Remember, however, that the source of an intrinsic reward is internal to the follower. Thus, what is intrinsically rewarding to one person may not be so to another. One way in which leaders try to enable all followers to achieve intrinsic rewards is by giving them more control over their own work and the power to affect outcomes. When leaders empower others, allowing them the freedom to determine their own actions, subordinates reward themselves intrinsically for good performance. They may become creative, innovative, and develop a greater commitment to their objectives. Thus motivated, they often achieve their best possible performance.

Ideally, work behaviors should satisfy both lower and higher needs while also serving the mission of the organization. Unfortunately, this is often not the case. The leader's motivational role, then, is to create a situation that integrates the needs of people—especially higher needs—and the fundamental objectives of the organization.

8-1b Positive and Negative Motives

People have both positive and negative motives that cause them to engage in specific behaviors or activities. For example, some people and corporations pay taxes to avoid the negative consequence of penalties or jail time. Others might pay taxes based on a positive motive of helping their communities and the larger society.

EXHIBIT 8.3 Four Categories of Motives

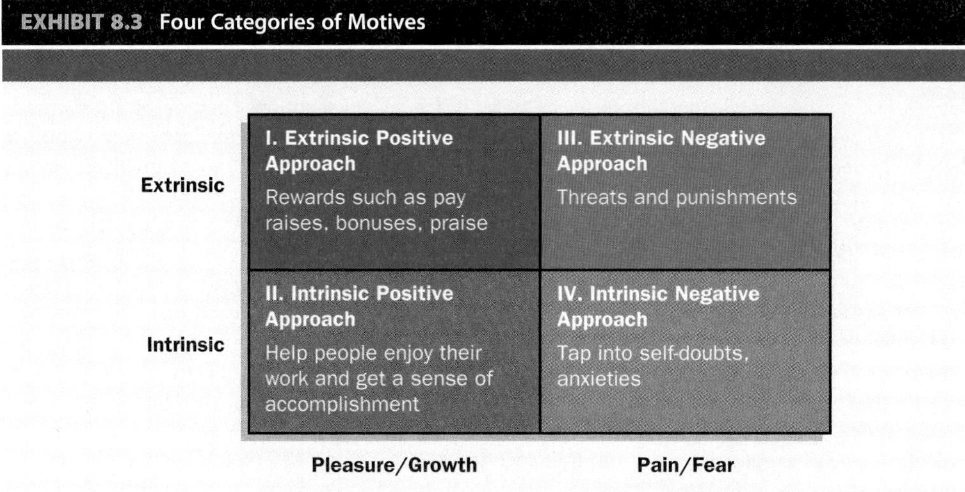

Source: Based on Bruce H. Jackson, "Influence Behavior: Become a Master Motivator," *Leadership Excellence* (April 2010), p. 14.

Exhibit 8.3 illustrates four categories of motives based on two criteria.[9] The horizontal dimension contrasts motives that are driven by fear or pain with those driven by growth or pleasure. The vertical dimension contrasts motives that come from within a person (intrinsic) against those triggered from without (extrinsic), such as by a leader's actions. The four quadrants represent four differing approaches leaders can use for motivating people. Quadrants I and II are both positive approaches to motivating. Quadrant I motivational methods attempt to influence behavior by using extrinsic rewards that create pleasure, such as giving an employee a pay raise, a bonus, or a gift. At Gogobot, a travel recommendation Web site, leaders offer employees $400 of credit that they can use for travel, food, or hotels as long as they write reviews for the site.[10] Many leaders are finding that small, unexpected rewards, such as gift cards, water bottles, or pizza vouchers, are highly effective extrinsic motivators. When people aren't expecting a reward, it can have a disproportionate psychological impact.[11] Extrinsic rewards are important, but good leaders don't rely on them as their primary motivational tool. Instead, they also strive to help people find meaning and joy in their work, using a Quadrant II motivational approach. Quadrant II techniques tap into deep-seated employee energy and commitment by helping people get deep personal satisfaction from their work. This chapter's Leader's Bookshelf describes how leaders at Menlo Innovations created a successful technology company with an explicit goal of helping people find joy in the workplace.

Good leaders rely on positive motives as much as they can. However, negative approaches also have value. In the real world, almost every leader sometimes has to impose some form of punishment or tap into negative motives to get desired actions and results. Quadrant III uses negative, extrinsic methods, such as threats or punishments, to get people to perform as desired. For example, some companies have found that penalizing employees for smoking or being overweight by charging extra for health insurance is an effective way to change behaviors and lower company healthcare costs. The practice is growing, with leaders citing behavioral science research showing that people typically respond more strongly to a potential loss (a penalty for not losing weight), referred to as *loss aversion*, than to an expected gain (a reward for losing weight). At Mohawk Industries, participation in the company's health-risk assessment program increased 97 percent after leaders began penalizing employees

LEADER'S BOOKSHELF

Joy, Inc.: How We Built a Workplace People Love

by Rich Sheridan

Rich Sheridan knows what it's like to work in a job where you're miserable. He was there in 1999, when he began exploring various business concepts and searching for ways to organize a workplace where people could be happy as well as productive. Two years later, Sheridan and two colleagues founded Menlo Innovations, a technology-services company, with the goal of creating an organization "with joyful people achieving joyful outcomes." At Menlo, employees willingly give their all because of the intrinsic satisfaction they get from their work.

THE BUSINESS VALUE OF JOY

Sheridan starts his book with a question: *Why joy?* He admits that talking about the business value of joy "sounds worse than squishy—it sounds ridiculous" to some people. Yet thousands of business people tour Menlo each year to learn what makes Menlo's work environment so effective. Joy is about more than having fun, Sheridan points out. Menlo is guided by the idea that "humans are wired to work on things bigger than themselves" and "to be in community with one another." Here are some of the ways Menlo leaders create joy:

- ***They keep people learning and collaborating***. All programmers work together in a big, noisy space where they can communicate across the room rather than by e-mail or phone. A radical idea at Menlo is that people work in pairs, with programmers sharing a single computer and passing the mouse and keyboard back and forth. Pairs are rotated on a weekly basis so people don't get stuck in one way of thinking. People also go out and spend time with clients, and clients frequently come into the office to work with Menlo teams.
- ***They pump fear out and safety in***. Working in pairs not only promotes learning but also "provides an emotional safety net." Leaders encourage continual experimentation and accept failure as a way to learn. Sheridan distinguishes between a culture where people "feel safe," meaning they will experiment, learn from mistakes, and don't need to ask permission, versus one where people are focused on "being safe," which means innovation and learning are stifled by fear of failure. Daily stand-up meetings at Menlo let people quickly describe what they're working on and where they might need help.
- ***They let employees make important decisions***. Employees have an exceptional degree of autonomy in how they manage their work. In addition, they're involved in all important decisions. Consider hiring. Applicants first participate in a group interview of about 30 people where they do simulated work in pairs, with each pair observed by a current staff member. The staff members, not the bosses, decide who gets to the next stage, which is working at the company for one day (paid). Then, a person gets hired on a three-week contract. Employees get a chance to really see if someone is a good fit with the Menlo culture before making a final decision.

CAN WE ALL BE JOYFUL AT WORK?

This is a fun-to-read story about a unique kind of workplace that might not be right for every company—financial information, including salaries, is transparent; internal e-mail is banned; and people can bring their dogs or babies to work. Yet it is also filled with ideas and suggestions for how leaders can bring a culture of joy, along with the energy and motivation it yields, to any organization.

Source: *Joy: How We Built a Workplace People Love*, by Rich Sheridan, is published by Portfolio/Penguin.

$100 if they didn't participate. Previously, the company offered rewards for participation, but enrollment rates remained low, which sparked the shift to penalties.[12]

The final category in Exhibit 8.3, Quadrant IV, reflects methods that attempt to motivate people by tapping into their self-doubts or anxieties, such as motivating people to work hard by emphasizing the weak economy and high unemployment rate. Fear can be a powerful motivator, but using fear to motivate people almost always has negative consequences for employee development and long-term performance. Effective leaders avoid the use of fear tactics.

8-2 NEEDS-BASED THEORIES OF MOTIVATION

Needs-based theories emphasize the needs that motivate people. As illustrated earlier in Exhibit 8.1, needs are the source of an internal drive that motivates behavior to fulfill the needs. An individual's needs are like a hidden catalog of the things he or she wants and will work to get. To the extent that leaders understand follower needs, they can design the reward system to direct energies and priorities toward attainment of shared goals.

8-2a Hierarchy of Needs Theory

Probably the most famous needs-based theory is the one developed by Abraham Maslow.[13] Maslow's **hierarchy of needs theory** proposes that humans are motivated by multiple needs and those needs exist in a hierarchical order, as illustrated in Exhibit 8.4, wherein the higher needs cannot be satisfied until the lower needs are met. Maslow identified five general levels of motivating needs.

- *Physiological*: The most basic human physiological needs include food, water, and oxygen. In the organizational setting, these are reflected in the needs for adequate heat, air, and base salary to ensure survival.
- *Safety*: Next is the need for a safe and secure physical and emotional environment and freedom from threats—that is, for freedom from violence and for an orderly society. In an organizational setting, safety needs reflect the needs for safe jobs, fringe benefits, and job security.
- *Belongingness*: People have a desire to be accepted by their peers, have friendships, be part of a group, and be loved. In the organization, these needs influence the desire for good relationships with coworkers, participation in a work team, and a positive relationship with supervisors.
- *Esteem*: The need for esteem relates to the desires for a positive self-image and for attention, recognition, and appreciation from others. Within organizations, esteem needs reflect a motivation for recognition, an increase in responsibility, high status, and credit for contributions to the organization.

Hierarchy of needs theory
Maslow's theory proposes that humans are motivated by multiple needs and those needs exist in a hierarchical order

EXHIBIT 8.4 Maslow's Hierarchy of Needs

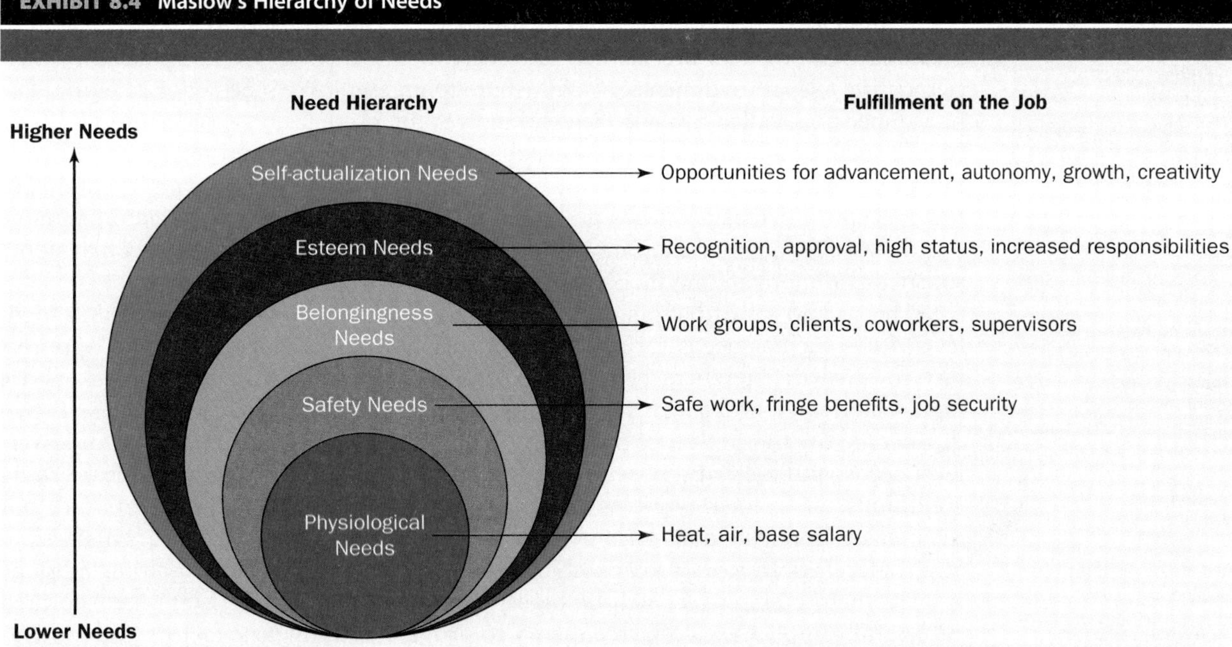

- *Self-actualization*: The highest need category, self-actualization, represents the need for self-fulfillment: developing one's full potential, increasing one's competence, and becoming a better person. Self-actualization needs can be met in the organization by providing people with opportunities to grow, be empowered and creative, and acquire training for challenging assignments and advancement.

According to Maslow's theory, physiology, safety, and belonging are deficiency needs. These lower-order needs take priority—they must be satisfied before higher-order, or growth, needs are activated. The needs are satisfied in sequence: Physiological needs are satisfied before safety needs, safety needs are satisfied before social needs, and so on. A person desiring physical safety will devote his or her efforts to securing a safer environment and will not be concerned with esteem or self-actualization. Once a need is satisfied, it declines in importance and the next higher need is activated. When a union wins good pay and working conditions for its members, for example, basic needs will be met and union members may then want to have social and esteem needs met in the workplace. In some Chinese factories, leaders have gone beyond financial incentives to try to meet belongingness and esteem needs of employees with work contests, American Idol–type singing contests, karaoke rooms, speed dating, dinners with managers, and more communications about the greater purpose of employees' contributions.[14]

8-2b Two-Factor Theory

Frederick Herzberg developed another popular needs-based theory of motivation called the *two-factor theory*.[15] Herzberg interviewed hundreds of workers about times when they were highly motivated to work and other times when they were dissatisfied and unmotivated to work. His findings suggested that the work characteristics associated with dissatisfaction were quite different from those pertaining to satisfaction, which prompted the notion that two factors influence work motivation.

Exhibit 8.5 illustrates the two-factor theory. The center of the scale is neutral, meaning that workers are neither satisfied nor dissatisfied. Herzberg believed that two entirely separate dimensions contribute to an employee's behavior at work. The first dimension, called **hygiene factors**, involves the presence or absence of job dissatisfiers, such as working conditions, pay, company policies, and interpersonal relationships. When hygiene factors are poor, work is dissatisfying. This is similar to the concept of deficiency needs described by Maslow. Good hygiene factors remove the dissatisfaction, but they do not in themselves cause people to become highly satisfied and motivated in their work.

The second set of factors does influence job satisfaction. **Motivators** fulfill high-level needs such as needs for achievement, recognition, responsibility, and opportunity for growth. Herzberg believed that when motivators are present, workers are highly motivated and satisfied. Thus, hygiene factors and motivators represent two distinct factors that influence motivation. Hygiene factors work in the area of lower-level needs, and their absence causes dissatisfaction. Inadequate pay, unsafe working conditions, or a noisy work environment will cause people to be dissatisfied, but their correction will not cause a high level of work enthusiasm and satisfaction. Higher-level motivators such as challenge, responsibility, and recognition must be in place before employees will be highly motivated. Leaders at Mars Incorporated successfully apply the two-factor theory to provide both hygiene factors and motivators, thus meeting employees' higher as well as lower needs.

NEW LEADER
ACTION MEMO

You can evaluate your current or a previous job according to Maslow's needs theory and Herzberg's two-factor theory by answering the questions in Leader's Self-Insight 8.1.

Hygiene factors
the first dimension of Herzberg's two-factor theory; involves working conditions, pay, company policies, and interpersonal relationships

Motivators
the second dimension of Herzberg's two-factor theory; involves job satisfaction and meeting higher-level needs such as achievement, recognition, and opportunity for growth

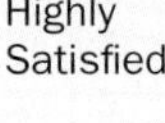

EXHIBIT 8.5 Herzberg's Two-Factor Theory

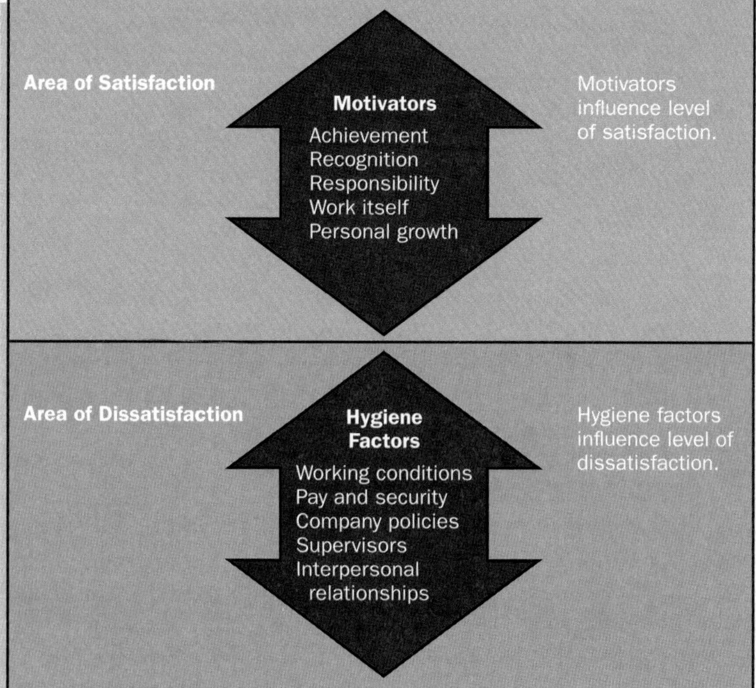

IN THE LEAD

Grant Reid, Mars Incorporated

President Grant Reid and other leaders at Mars, maker of candy such as M&Ms and Snickers and pet food such as Pedigree and Whiskas, seem to meet all the need categories in terms of both hygiene factors and motivators. Mars Incorporated, the third-largest private company in the United States, is intensely secretive, but an interview by *Fortune* after the company was named to its "The 100 Best Companies to Work For" list for the first time in 2013 revealed some interesting tidbits.

Once people get a job there, they rarely leave, reflecting that hygiene factors such as pay and benefits are good and working relationships are solid. Compensation is very good compared to similar companies. Many employees get bonuses from 10 percent to 100 percent of their salaries if their team performs well. Vending machines dispense free candy all day long, and employees in the pet food division can take their dogs to work. Employees have to punch a time clock, and their pay gets docked if they are late—but the policy applies to top executives just as it does to the lowest-level worker.

In addition to the egalitarian workplace, motivators include giving people the autonomy to experiment and propose new ideas and recognizing them for showing initiative. Employees have great opportunities for advancement, both within their division and in the larger corporation. When Reid took over as president in 2015, he had been with Mars for 26 years and served in several different business divisions and multiple functions during that time.

Leaders encourage employee growth and development. Jim Price began his career as a janitor at a Mars facility and is now quality and food-safety manager for Mars Chocolate North America. When Price started with the company, his supervisor urged him to attend community college at night, and Mars paid for his tuition and books. Many people at Mars get a mentor to learn a new skill. Executives often get paired with younger employees who introduce them to using social media. Development doesn't stop at the factory gates, either. People can take paid time off to volunteer for community activities such as cleaning parks, planting gardens, or assisting at medical clinics. A highly competitive program selects 80 or so people each year to spend up to six weeks working with Mars-related partners (such as growers of cocoa beans) in remote areas of other countries.[16]

The implication of the two-factor theory for leaders is clear. People have multiple needs, and the leader's role is to go beyond the removal of dissatisfiers to the use of motivators to meet higher-level needs and propel employees toward greater enthusiasm and satisfaction.

8-2c Acquired Needs Theory

Another needs-based theory was developed by David McClelland. The **acquired needs theory** proposes that certain types of needs are acquired during an individual's lifetime. In other words, people are not born with these needs but may learn them through their life experiences.[17] For example, the parents of Bill Strickland, who founded and runs Manchester Bidwell, a highly successful nonprofit organization that provides after-school and summer programs for at-risk young people, always encouraged him to follow his dreams. When he wanted to go south to work with the Freedom Riders in the 1960s, they supported him. His plans for tearing up the family basement and making a photography studio were met with equal enthusiasm. Strickland thus developed a *need for achievement* that enabled him to accomplish amazing results later in life.[18] Three needs most frequently studied are the need for achievement, need for affiliation, and need for power.

NEW LEADER
ACTION MEMO

As a leader, you can use good working conditions, satisfactory pay, and comfortable relationships to reduce job dissatisfaction. To spur greater follower satisfaction and enthusiasm, you can employ motivators—challenge, responsibility, and recognition.

- *Need for achievement*: the desire to accomplish something difficult, attain a high standard of success, master complex tasks, and surpass others
- *Need for affiliation*: the desire to form close personal relationships, avoid conflict, and establish warm friendships
- *Need for power*: the desire to influence or control others, be responsible for others, and have authority over others

For more than 20 years, McClelland studied human needs and their implications for management. People with a high need for achievement tend to enjoy work that is entrepreneurial and innovative. People who have a high need for affiliation are successful "integrators," whose job is to coordinate the work of people and departments.[19] Integrators include brand managers and project managers, positions that require excellent people skills. A high need for power is often associated with successful attainment of top levels in the organizational hierarchy. For example, McClelland studied managers at AT&T for 16 years and found that those with a high need for power were more likely to pursue a path of continued promotion over time.

Acquired needs theory
McClelland's theory that proposes that certain types of needs (achievement, affiliation, power) are acquired during an individual's lifetime

In summary, needs-based theories focus on underlying needs that motivate how people behave. The hierarchy of needs theory, the two-factor theory, and the

LEADER'S SELF-INSIGHT 8.1

Are Your Needs Met?

Instructions: Think of a specific job (current or previous) you have held. If you are a full-time student, think of your classes and study activities as your job. Please answer the following questions about those work activities. Indicate whether each item is Mostly False or Mostly True for you.

	Mostly False	Mostly True
1. I feel physically safe at work.	____	✓
2. I have good health benefits.	____	✓
3. I am satisfied with what I'm getting paid for my work.	____	✓
4. I feel that my job is secure as long as I want it.	____	✓
5. I have good friends at work.	____	✓
6. I have enough time away from my work to enjoy other things in life.	____	✓
7. I feel appreciated at work.	____	✓
8. People at my workplace respect me as a professional and expert in my field.	____	✓
9. I feel that my job allows me to realize my full potential.	____	✓
10. I feel that I am realizing my potential as an expert in my line of work.	____	✓
11. I feel I'm always learning new things that help me to do my work better.	____	✓
12. There is a lot of creativity involved in my work.	____	✓

Scoring and Interpretation

Compute the number of Mostly True responses for the questions that represent each level of Maslow's hierarchy, as indicated in the next column, and write your score where indicated:

Questions 1–2: Physiological and health needs.
Score = 2.
Questions 3–4: Economic and safety needs.
Score = 2.
Questions 5–6: Belonging and social needs.
Score = 2.
Questions 7–8: Esteem needs.
Score = 2.
Questions 9–12: Self-actualization needs.
Score = 4.

These five scores represent how you see your needs being met in the work situation. An average score for overall need satisfaction (all 12 questions) is typically 6, and the average for lower-level needs tends to be higher than for higher-level needs. Is that true for you? What do your five scores say about the need satisfaction in your job? Which needs are less filled for you? How would that affect your choice of a new job? In developed countries, lower needs are often taken for granted, and work motivation is based on the opportunity to meet higher needs. Compare your scores to those of another student. How does that person's array of five scores differ from yours? Ask questions about the student's job to help explain the difference in scores.

Reread the 12 questions. Which questions would you say are about the *motivators* in Herzberg's two-factor theory? Which questions are about *hygiene factors?* Calculate the average points for the motivator questions and the average points for the hygiene factor questions. What do you interpret from your scores on these two factors compared to the five levels of needs in Maslow's hierarchy?

Source: These questions are taken from *Social Indicators Research* 55 (2001), pp. 241–302, "A New Measure of Quality of Work Life (QWL) based on Need Satisfaction and Spillover Theories," M. Joseph Sirgy, David Efraty, Phillip Siegel and Dong-Jin Lee. Copyright © and reprinted with kind permission of Kluwer Academic Publishers.

acquired needs theory all identify the specific needs that motivate people. Leaders can work to meet followers' needs and hence elicit appropriate and successful work behaviors.

8-3 OTHER MOTIVATION THEORIES

Three additional motivation theories—the reinforcement perspective, expectancy theory, and equity theory—focus primarily on extrinsic rewards and punishments Relying on extrinsic rewards and punishments is sometimes referred to as the *carrot-and-stick approach*.[20] Behavior that produces a desired outcome is rewarded with a "carrot," such as a pay raise or promotion. Conversely, undesirable or unproductive behavior brings the "stick," such as a demotion or withholding a pay raise. Carrot-and-stick approaches tend to focus on lower needs, although higher needs can sometimes also be met. Read the story in this chapter's *Consider This* to gain some perspective on the use of carrots as motivators.

Consider **This!**

Does the Carrot Kill Satisfaction?

A shopkeeper got tired of the noise of a group of children who played outside his store every afternoon. One day, he asked them to leave and promised he'd give each of them $1 to come back and play there the next day. Of course, they showed up. Then the shopkeeper said he would give each one 50 cents to come back the following day. The next day he offered 25 cents for them to return. At that point, the children said they wouldn't be back the following day because it wasn't worth it for a quarter. The shopkeeper got what he wanted by shifting the children's motivation for playing there toward earning an extrinsic reward rather than for the intrinsic pleasure they originally received.

The moral of the story is that the motivation to seek an extrinsic reward, whether it's a bonus or professional approval, leads people to focus on the reward rather than on the intrinsic satisfaction they get from their activities. Extrinsic rewards are temporary. They typically address lower-level needs and focus people on immediate goals and deadlines rather than long-term success and happiness.

Sources: Several variations of this familiar story have been told in different sources, including Vincent F. Filak and Robert S. Pritchard, "Fulfilling Psychological vs. Financial Needs: The Effect of Extrinsic Rewards on Motivation and Attachment to Internships," presented in the Public Relations Division in the Association for Education in Journalism and Mass Communication Conference, August 2008, Chicago, http://citation.allacademic.com/meta/p_mla_apa_research_citation/2/7/2/3/1/pages272318/p272318-9.php (accessed April 20, 2013); Samuel S. Franklin, *The Psychology of Happiness: A Good Human Life* (New York: Cambridge University Press, 2010), pp. 61–62; and Alfie Kohn, *Punished by Rewards: The Trouble with Gold Stars, Incentive Plans, A's, Praise, and Other Bribes* (Boston: Houghton Mifflin, 1999).

Reinforcement theory
a motivational theory that looks at the relationship between behavior and its consequences by changing or modifying followers' on-the-job behavior through the appropriate use of immediate rewards or punishments

Behavior modification
the set of techniques by which reinforcement theory is used to modify behavior

Law of effect
states that positively reinforced behavior tends to be repeated and behavior that is not reinforced tends not to be repeated

Reinforcement
anything that causes a certain behavior to be repeated or inhibited

Positive reinforcement
the administration of a pleasant and rewarding consequence following a behavior

8-3a Reinforcement Perspective on Motivation

The reinforcement approach to employee motivation sidesteps the deeper issue of employee needs described in the needs-based theories. **Reinforcement theory** simply looks at the relationship between behavior and its consequences by changing or modifying followers' on-the-job behavior through the appropriate use of immediate rewards or punishments.

Behavior modification is the name given to the set of techniques by which reinforcement theory is used to modify behavior.[21] The basic assumption underlying behavior modification is the **law of effect**, which states that positively reinforced behavior tends to be repeated, and behavior that is not reinforced tends not to be repeated. **Reinforcement** is defined as anything that causes a certain behavior to be repeated or inhibited. Four ways in which leaders use reinforcement to modify or shape employee behavior are positive reinforcement, negative reinforcement, punishment, and extinction, as illustrated in Exhibit 8.6.

Positive reinforcement is the administration of a pleasant and rewarding consequence immediately following a desired behavior. A good example of positive

EXHIBIT 8.6 Shaping Behavior with Reinforcement

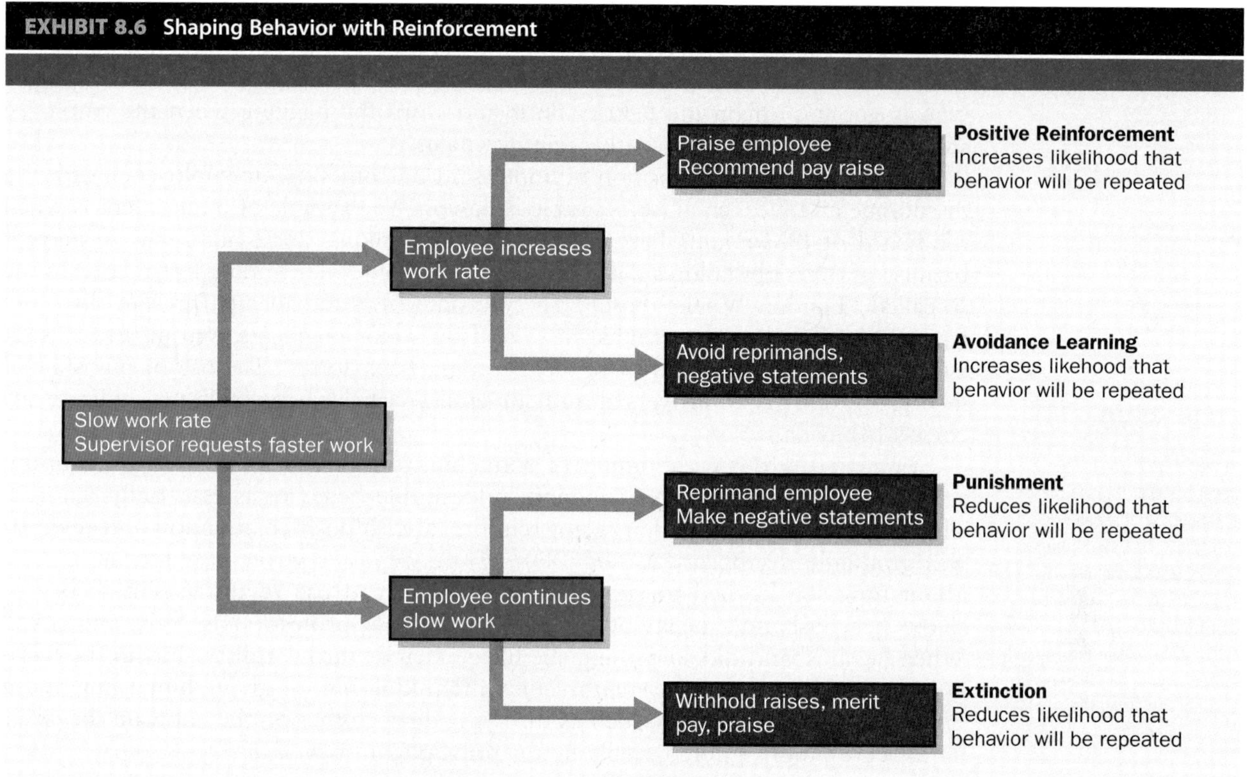

Source: Based on Richard L. Daft and Richard M. Steers, *Organizations: A Micro/Macro Approach* (Glenview, IL: Scott, Foresman, 1986) p. 109.

reinforcement is immediate praise for an employee who does a little extra in his or her work. Studies have shown that positive reinforcement does help to improve performance. In addition, nonfinancial reinforcements such as positive feedback, social recognition, and attention are just as effective as financial rewards.[22] A recent study of employees at a fine dining restaurant, for example, found that when leaders provided clear tasks and clear feedback on how well people were performing the tasks, motivation and performance improved. Cleaning and sanitizing of tables, chairs, floors, and restrooms increased by 63 percent and restocking of side stations increased by 48 percent.[23] Supervisor attention and feedback provide a psychological boost to motivation that has nothing to do with financial rewards.

> *"Nothing else can quite substitute for a few well-chosen, well-timed, sincere words of praise. They're absolutely free—and worth a fortune."*
>
> Sam Walton, founder of Walmart

In fact, many people consider factors other than money to be more important. In a McKinsey global survey on the motivational value of money, respondents rated "praise and commendation from their immediate supervisor" as being a more effective motivator than cash.[24] Unexpected praise or expressions of appreciation can give a tremendous motivational boost. Indra Nooyi, CEO of PepsiCo, sends thank-you notes not only to members of her team who do well but also to their spouses and parents.[25] In a recent Globoforce MoodTracker Survey, 82 percent of employees said being recognized for their efforts increased their motivation. "It made me work harder, want to come to work every day, and I was proud to work for my boss," said one respondent. However, only 65 percent of companies surveyed have employee recognition programs, and 41 percent of employees said they hadn't been recognized for a period of at least six months.[26]

Negative reinforcement the withdrawal of an unpleasant consequence once a behavior is improved

Negative reinforcement, sometimes referred to as *avoidance learning*, is the process of withdrawing an unpleasant consequence once a behavior is improved, thereby encouraging and strengthening the desired behavior. The idea is that people will change a specific behavior to avoid the undesired result that behavior provokes. As a simple example, a supervisor who constantly reminds or nags an employee who is goofing off on the factory floor and stops the nagging when the employee stops goofing off is using negative reinforcement.

Punishment is the imposition of unpleasant outcomes on an employee in order to discourage and weaken an undesirable behavior. An example of punishment is when the board of JPMorgan Chase cut CEO Jamie Dimon's 2012 bonus by 50 percent because of oversight failures that led to a multibillion-dollar trading loss related to the so-called "London Whale" fiasco. The punishment is intended to prevent the CEO from relying too heavily on what he is told by senior managers, and instead to seek evidence and corroboration of prudent trading behaviors.[27] The use of punishment in organizations is controversial and sometimes criticized for failing to indicate the correct behavior.

NEW LEADER
ACTION MEMO

As a leader, you can change follower behavior through the appropriate use of rewards and punishments. To establish new behaviors quickly, you can reinforce the desired behavior after each and every occurrence. To sustain the behaviors over a long time period, try reinforcing the behaviors intermittently.

Extinction is the withholding of something positive, such as leader attention, praise, or pay raises. With extinction, undesirable behavior is essentially ignored. The idea is that behavior that is not reinforced with positive attention and rewards will gradually disappear. A *New York Times* reporter wrote a humorous article about how she learned to stop nagging and instead use reinforcement theory to shape her husband's behavior after studying how professionals train animals.[28] When her husband did something she liked, such as throw a dirty shirt in the hamper, she would use *positive reinforcement*, thanking him or giving him a hug and a kiss. Undesirable behaviors, such as throwing dirty clothes on the floor, on the other hand, were simply ignored, applying the principle of *extinction*.

Leaders can apply reinforcement theory to influence the behavior of followers. They can reinforce behavior after each and every occurrence, which is referred to as *continuous reinforcement*, or they can choose to reinforce behavior intermittently, which is referred to as *partial reinforcement*. With partial reinforcement, the desired behavior is reinforced often enough to make the employee believe the behavior is worth repeating, even though it is not rewarded every time it is demonstrated. Continuous reinforcement can be very effective for establishing new behaviors, but research has found that partial reinforcement is more effective for maintaining behavior over extended time periods.[29]

8-3b Expectancy Theory

Expectancy theory suggests that motivation depends on individuals' mental expectations about their ability to perform tasks and receive desired rewards. Expectancy theory is associated with the work of Victor Vroom, although a number of scholars have made contributions in this area.[30] Expectancy theory is concerned not with understanding types of needs but with the thinking process that people use to achieve rewards.

Expectancy theory is based on the relationship among the person's effort, the possibility of high performance, and the desirability of outcomes following high performance. Exhibit 8.7 illustrates these elements and the relationships among them. The $E > P$ expectancy is the probability that putting effort into a task will lead to high performance. For this expectancy to be high, the individual must have the ability, previous experience, and necessary tools, information, and opportunity to perform. One interesting study of expectancy theory looked at patrol officer drug arrests in the midwestern United States. The research found that officers who made the most arrests were those who received specialized training to hone their skills

Punishment
the imposition of unpleasant outcomes on an employee following undesirable behavior

Extinction
the withdrawal of a positive reward, meaning that behavior is no longer reinforced and hence is less likely to occur in the future

Expectancy theory
a theory that suggests that motivation depends on individuals' mental expectations about their ability to perform tasks and receive desired rewards

EXHIBIT 8.7 Key Elements of Expectancy Theory

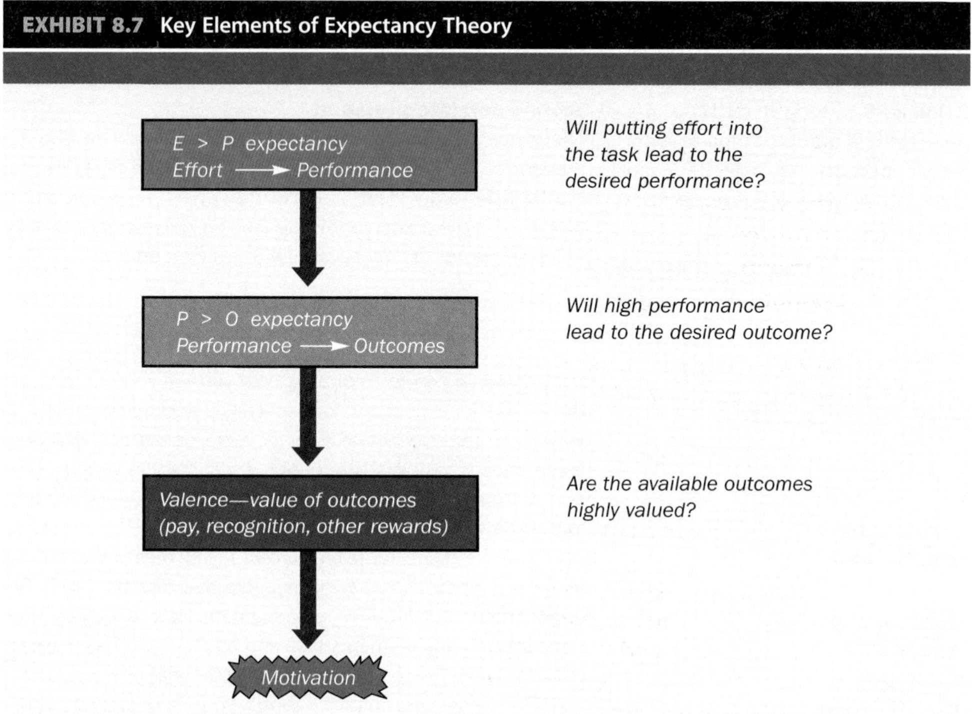

and who perceived that they had sufficient time and resources to properly investigate suspected drug activity.[31]

The $P > O$ expectancy involves whether successful performance will lead to the desired outcome. If this expectancy is high, the individual will be more highly motivated. *Valence* refers to the value of outcomes to the individual. If the outcomes that are available from high effort and good performance are not valued by an employee, motivation will be low. Likewise, if outcomes have a high value, motivation will be higher. A simple example to illustrate the relationships in Exhibit 8.7 is Alfredo Torres, a salesperson at Diamond Gift Shop. If Alfredo believes that increased selling effort will lead to higher personal sales, his $E > P$ expectancy is considered high. Moreover, if he also believes that higher personal sales will lead to a promotion or pay raise, the $P > O$ expectancy is also high. Finally, if Alfredo places a high value on the promotion or pay raise, valence is high and he will be highly motivated. For an employee to be highly motivated, all three factors in the expectancy model must be high.[32]

Like the path–goal theory of leadership described in Chapter 3, expectancy theory is personalized to subordinates' needs and goals. Every person is different, so leaders have to use a mix of incentives and rewards to motivate. A leader's responsibility is to understand each follower's "unique motivational profile" and then help followers meet their needs while attaining organizational goals.[33]

According to expectancy theory, leaders enhance motivation by increasing followers' expectancy—clarifying individual needs, providing the desired outcomes, and ensuring that people have the ability and support needed to perform well and attain their desired outcomes.

NEW LEADER
ACTION MEMO

Expectancy theory and reinforcement theory are widely used in all types of organizations and leadership situations. The questionnaire in Leader's Self-Insight 8.2 gives you the opportunity to see how effectively you apply these motivational ideas in your own leadership.

8-3c Equity Theory

Sometimes employees' motivation is affected not only by their expectancies and the rewards they receive but also by their perceptions of how fairly they are treated in

LEADER'S SELF-INSIGHT 8.2

Your Approach to Motivating Others

Instructions: Think about situations in which you were in a formal or informal leadership role in a group or organization. Imagine using your personal approach as a leader, and answer the following questions. Indicate whether each item is Mostly False or Mostly True for you.

	Mostly False	**Mostly True**
1. I ask the other person what rewards they value for high performance.	____	✓
2. I find out if the person has the ability to do what needs to be done.	____	✓
3. I explain exactly what needs to be done for the person I'm trying to motivate.	____	✓
4. Before giving somebody a reward, I find out what would appeal to that person.	____	✓
5. I negotiate what people will receive if they accomplish the goal.	____	✓
6. I make sure people have the ability to achieve performance targets.	____	✓
7. I give special recognition when others' work is very good.	____	✓
8. I only reward people if their performance is up to standard.	____	✓
9. I use a variety of rewards to reinforce exceptional performance.	____	✓
10. I generously praise people who perform well.	____	✓
11. I promptly commend others when they do a better-than-average job.	____	✓
12. I publicly compliment others when they do outstanding work.	____	✓

Scoring and Interpretation

These questions represent two related aspects of motivation theory. For the aspect of expectancy theory, sum the points for Mostly True to questions 1–6. For the aspect of reinforcement theory, sum the points for Mostly True for questions 7–12.

The scores for my approach to motivation are:

My use of expectancy theory: 6/6

My use of reinforcement theory: 6/6

These two scores represent how you see yourself applying the motivational concepts of expectancy and reinforcement in your own leadership style. Four or more points on *expectancy theory* means you motivate people by managing expectations. You understand how a person's effort leads to performance and make sure that high performance leads to valued rewards. Four or more points for *reinforcement theory* means that you try to modify people's behavior in a positive direction with frequent and prompt positive reinforcement. New managers often learn to use reinforcements first, and as they gain more experience they are able to apply expectancy theory.

Exchange information about your scores with other students to understand how your application of these two motivation theories compares to others'. Remember, leaders are expected to master the use of these two motivation theories. If you didn't receive an average score or higher, you can consciously do more with expectations and reinforcement when you are in a leadership position.

Sources: These questions are based on D. Whetten and K. Cameron, *Developing Management Skills*, 5th ed. (Upper Saddle River, NJ: Prentice Hall, 2002), pp. 302–303; and P. M. Podsakoff, S. B. Mackenzie, R. H. Moorman, and R. Fetter, "Transformational Leader Behaviors and Their Effects on Followers' Trust in Leader, Satisfaction, and Organizational Citizenship Behaviors," *Leadership Quarterly* 1, no. 2 (1990), pp. 107–142.

relation to others. **Equity theory** proposes that people are motivated to seek social equity in the rewards they receive for performance.[34] According to the theory, if people perceive their rewards as equal to what others receive for similar contributions, they will believe they are treated fairly and will be more highly motivated. When they believe they are not being treated fairly and equitably, motivation will decline. Recall the chapter-opening example of the web developer who left his job at Gravity Payments because of perceived inequity. Another example is Samantha Eckerd. Eckerd was told that she would have to move to a new job position to make more money at her financial services company, but after she changed jobs the company hired someone for her previous job at a much higher salary than Eckerd

Equity theory
a theory that proposes that people are motivated to seek social equity in the rewards they receive for performance

had made in that position. The sense of unfairness created so much anger and stress that Eckerd's performance and willingness to collaborate with others suffered, and she considered looking for a new job.[35]

People evaluate equity by a ratio of inputs to outcomes. That is, employees make comparisons of what they put into a job and the rewards they receive relative to those of other people in the organization. Inputs include such things as education, experience, effort, and ability. Outcomes include pay, recognition, promotions, and other rewards. A state of equity exists whenever the ratio of one person's outcomes to inputs equals the ratio of others' in the work group. Inequity occurs when the input/outcome ratios are out of balance, such as when an employee with a high level of experience and ability receives the same salary as a new, less-educated employee.

Some companies are sharing hiring and promotion decisions, performance appraisal data, and individual employees' pay rates with everyone in the company, saying it creates trust and keeps people from worrying about inequity. Others, though, say too much openness creates more problems. Slava Akhmechet, CEO and cofounder of database firm RethinkDB, experimented with open pay but ran into problems when he needed to hire new technical employees in a tight labor market. Akhmechet found that he needed to offer the newcomers higher salaries than current employees were making. Long-time employees began demanding more pay, and in some cases motivation, performance, and commitment declined significantly if the demands were not met because people felt treated unfairly. Akhmechet eventually shelved the open salary model.[36]

NEW LEADER
ACTION MEMO

As a leader, you can clarify which rewards a follower wants and ensure that he or she has the knowledge, skills, resources, and support to perform and obtain the desired rewards. Keep in mind that perceived equity or inequity in rewards also influences motivation.

This discussion provides only a brief overview of equity theory. The theory's practical use has been criticized because a number of key issues are unclear. However, the important point of equity theory is that, for many people, motivation is influenced significantly by relative as well as absolute rewards. The concept reminds leaders that they should be aware of the possible effects of perceived inequity on follower motivation and performance.

8-4 EMPOWERING PEOPLE TO MEET HIGHER NEEDS

Sharing everyone's salary might not always be a good idea, but many leaders have found that sharing overall company financial data and allowing people to participate in strategic decision making is a great high-level motivator. Angela Lee, a support team coordinator at Tenmast Software (which does not share salary data), says knowing where the company stands and understanding her impact on the bottom line are "empowering."[37] Other companies are also giving employees more power, information, and authority to enable them to find greater intrinsic satisfaction. **Empowerment** refers to power sharing, the delegation of power or authority to subordinates in the organization.[38]

Empowerment can enhance motivation by meeting the higher-level needs of employees. In addition, leaders greatly benefit from the expanded capabilities that employee participation brings to the organization.[39] Frontline employees often have a better understanding than do leaders of how to improve a work process, satisfy a customer, or solve a production problem. To empower followers, leaders provide them with an understanding of how their jobs are important to the organization's mission and performance, thereby giving them a direction within which to act freely.[40] At Ritz-Carlton hotels, employees have up to $1,000 to use at their discretion to create a great customer experience. When homes in the area near the Ritz in

Empowerment
power sharing; the delegation of power or authority to subordinates in the organization

Self-efficacy

Laguna Niguel, California, were evacuated due to risk of fires, the hotel made an exception to its "no-pets" rule. One employee anticipated the need for pet food and drove to the nearest grocery for dog and cat food, making life a little easier for harried guests who were temporarily homeless.[41]

NEW LEADER
ACTION MEMO

As a leader, you can give employees greater power and authority to help meet higher motivational needs. You can implement empowerment by providing the five elements of information, knowledge, discretion, significance, and rewards.

8-4a The Psychological Model of Empowerment

Empowerment provides strong motivation because individuals have a sense that they are in control of their work and success. Research indicates that most people have a need for *self-efficacy*, which is the capacity to produce results or outcomes, to feel that they are effective.[42] Most people come into an organization with the desire to do a good job, and empowerment enables leaders to release the motivation already there.

Five elements must be in place before employees can be truly empowered to perform their jobs effectively: information, knowledge, discretion, meaning, and rewards.[43]

1. *Employees receive information about company performance.* In companies where employees are fully empowered, as at Tenmast Software, described earlier, everyone is taught to think like a business owner. Employees have access to company financials and attend a financial literacy course to understand how to interpret them.[44]
2. *Employees receive knowledge and skills to contribute to company goals.* Companies use training programs and other development tools to give people the knowledge and skills they need to personally contribute to performance. For example, when DMC, which makes pet supplies, gave employee teams the authority and responsibility for assembly line shutdowns, it provided extensive training.[45]
3. *Employees have the power to make substantive decisions.* Empowered employees have the authority to directly influence work procedures and organizational direction, such as through quality circles and self-directed work teams. At a copper mine in Arizona, for example, teams of tank house workers were given the authority to identify and solve production problems and determine how best to organize themselves to get the job done.[46]
4. *Employees understand the meaning and impact of their jobs.* Empowered employees consider their jobs important and meaningful, see themselves as capable and influential, and recognize the impact their work has on customers, other stakeholders, and the organization's success.[47]
5. *Employees are rewarded based on company performance.* Reward systems play an important role in supporting empowerment. People are rewarded based on results shown in the company's bottom line. Insurer Aflac has a profit-sharing program for all employees, from call center personnel to top leaders.[48]

Job design
structuring jobs in a way to meet higher-level needs and increase motivation toward the accomplishment of goals

Job characteristics model
a model of job design that considers the core job dimensions of skill variety, task identity, task significance, autonomy, and feedback to enrich jobs and increase their motivational potential

8-4b Job Design for Empowerment

Leaders can also adjust structural aspects of jobs to enable employees to have more autonomy and feel a sense of meaningfulness and empowerment in their jobs. **Job design** refers to structuring jobs in a way to meet higher-level needs and increase motivation toward the accomplishment of goals. One model, called the **job characteristics model**, proposes that certain core job dimensions create positive psychological reactions within employees that lead to higher motivation and better performance.[49] The core job dimensions, related psychological reactions, and outcomes are illustrated in Exhibit 8.8.

EXHIBIT 8.8 The Job Characteristics Model

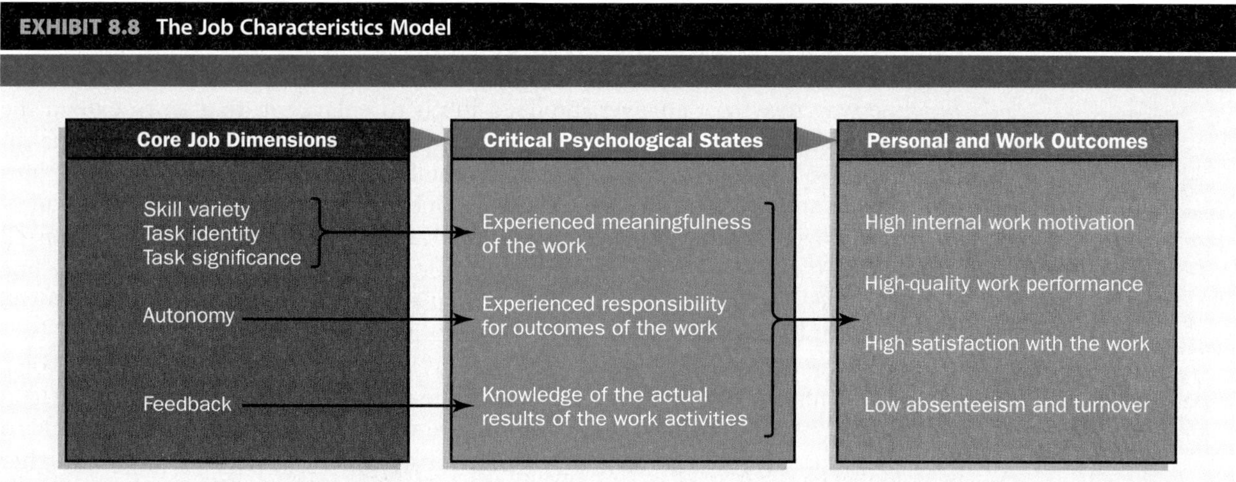

Source: Adapted from J. Richard Hackman and G. R. Oldham, "Motivation through the Design of Work: Test of a Theory," *Organizational Behavior and Human Performance* 16 (1976), p. 256.

Leaders can make alterations in five dimensions of jobs to increase the job's motivational and empowerment potential.

1. *Increase skill variety.* Jobs with a variety of activities require a diversity of skills and are thus more motivating.
2. *Structure jobs so that an employee can perform a complete task from beginning to end.* The job characteristics model refers to this as *task identity*, which means the job has a recognizable beginning and ending.
3. *Incorporate task significance into the job.* People feel an increased sense of power and self-efficacy when they are performing a job that is important and that influences customers and the company's success. At The Nerdery, a Web development firm, leaders gave all employees the job title of co-president, which increases task significance for every job because it gives everyone both the freedom and the responsibility to do what is best for customers and the company.[50]
4. *Give people autonomy for choosing how and when to perform specific tasks.* People are typically more motivated when they have freedom, discretion, and self-determination in planning and carrying out tasks.
5. *To the extent possible, design jobs to provide feedback and let employees see the outcomes of their efforts.* In cases where the job itself does not provide timely feedback, leaders have to work harder at giving people specific feedback and helping them see how the job contributes to the organization's success. For example, James Ault spends his days researching and debating issues related to state energy policy and might never see concrete results of his work. Consequently, Ault sometimes finds it difficult to get gratification from his job. "It would be nice to be an electrician," he says. "You can take pride in what you've accomplished."[51]

The more these five characteristics can be designed into the job, the higher employees' motivation will be, and the higher will be their performance. Essentially, these changes are designed to transfer authority and responsibility from leaders to employees and create job enrichment. **Job enrichment** incorporates high-level

Job enrichment
a motivational approach that incorporates high-level motivators into the work, including job responsibility, recognition, and opportunities for growth, learning, and achievement

motivators such as responsibility, recognition, and opportunities for growth and learning into the job. In an enriched job, the employee controls resources needed to perform well and makes decisions on how to do the work.

One way to enrich an oversimplified job is to enlarge it, that is, to extend the responsibility to cover several tasks instead of only one. At Ralcorp's cereal manufacturing plant in Sparks, Nevada, leaders combined several packing positions into a single job and cross-trained employees to operate all of the packing line's equipment. Employees were given both the ability and the responsibility to perform all the various functions in their department, not just a single task. In addition, line employees became responsible for all screening and interviewing of new hires as well as training and advising one another. Ralcorp invests heavily in training to be sure employees have the needed operational skills as well as the ability to make decisions, solve problems, manage quality, and contribute to continuous improvement.[52]

As illustrated in Exhibit 8.8, the five core job dimensions cause individuals to experience three positive psychological reactions. The first three dimensions—higher skill variety, task identity, and task significance—enable the employee to see the job as meaningful and significant (*experienced meaningfulness of work*), which makes the job intrinsically satisfying. Greater autonomy in a job leads to a feeling of increased responsibility for the success or failure of task outcomes (*experienced responsibility for outcomes of the work*), thus increasing commitment. The final dimension, feedback, provides the employee with *knowledge of the actual results of work activities*. Thus, the employee knows how he or she is doing and can adjust work performance to increase desired outcomes.

These positive psychological reactions in turn lead to greater intrinsic satisfaction, higher motivation, better work performance, and lower absenteeism and turnover, as illustrated in the exhibit.

8-4c Empowerment Applications

Current methods of empowering employees can be classified based on two dimensions: (1) the extent to which employees are involved in defining desired outcomes; and (2) the extent to which they participate in determining how to achieve those outcomes. Exhibit 8.9 shows that empowerment efforts range from a situation where frontline employees have no discretion (such as on a traditional assembly line) to full empowerment where workers even participate in formulating organizational strategy.[53]

When employees are fully empowered, they are involved in defining mission and goals as well as in determining how to achieve them. One organization that illustrates this high level of empowerment is Zingerman's, which started as a small sandwich shop and grew into a group of nine businesses with 650 employees and combined annual sales of $50 million.

IN THE LEAD

Zingerman's Community of Businesses

From the moment Ari Weinzweig and Paul Saginaw decided to start a business, they focused more on how they would run it than on what the business would be. Weinzweig and Saginaw "wanted to build an extraordinary organization . . . where decisions would not be based on who had the most authority but on whoever had the most relevant information." The partners opened a small delicatessen in Ann Arbor, Michigan, in 1982, and from the beginning they wanted everyone to think like an owner and help run the business.

When the deli hit a plateau in the mid-1990s, the two wrote a vision statement for what would become the Zingerman's Community of Businesses (ZCoB). ZCoB is a group of distinct, local businesses that buy and sell to one another but stand on their own. Each business, such as Zingerman's Bakehouse, Zingerman's Coffee Company, and Zingerman's Creamery, was founded and is run by a managing partner who shares the Zingerman's culture and values. ZCoB gives employees a chance to not only run the businesses but even start a new one. One employee, who is running an Asian food cart near the deli, hopes to eventually open a Korean restaurant under the ZCoB umbrella. Referring to the 50 or so internal training courses offered to employees, another says, "I feel like I have received a business degree working here."

Weinzweig and Saginaw share operating and financial data, such as sales, expenses, customer service metrics, and energy efficiency, with employees at all levels and give them responsibility for improving the metrics, which are tracked on a scoreboard. Weekly huddles and regular training courses help people understand what the numbers mean and let them offer ideas for improvement. Employees aren't required to attend, but since they are paid for their time—and also benefit from ZCoB's profit-sharing plan—most do. Krystal Walls, who works in the mail-order business, says, "I have never worked anywhere where I was trusted or respected like this."[54]

At Zingerman's employees truly do feel like owners. In addition to sharing information at the weekly huddles, employees frequently send e-mail or text messages to Weinzweig or Saginaw with tips and ideas for saving money, increasing sales, or generally doing things better.

EXHIBIT 8.9 Degrees of Empowerment

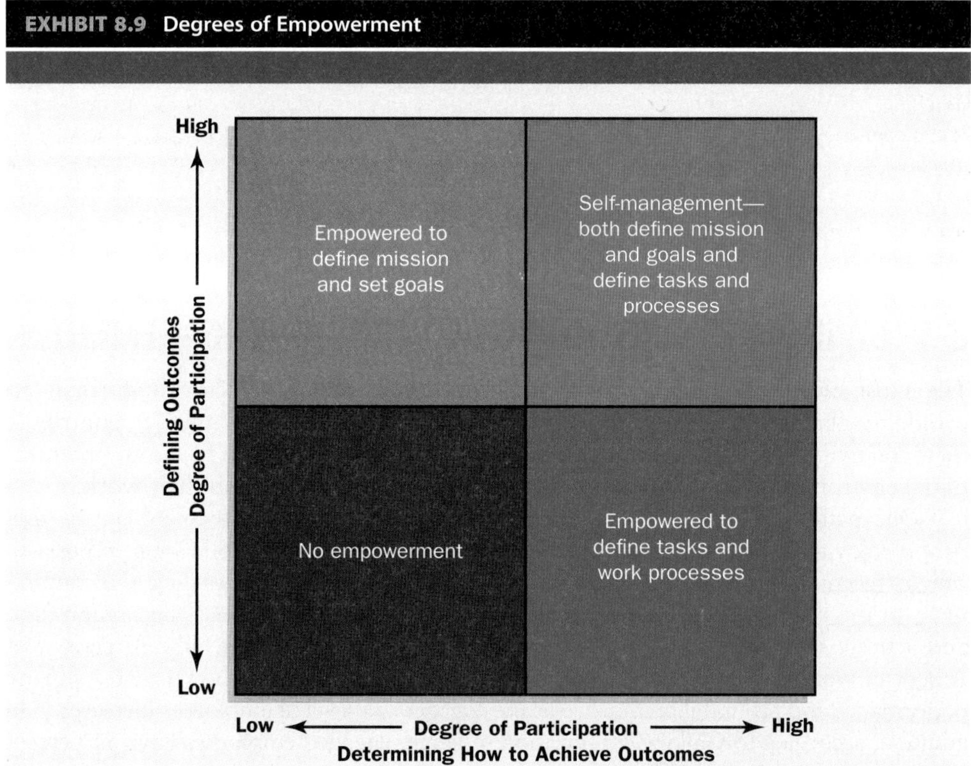

LEADER'S SELF-INSIGHT 8.3

Are You Engaged?

Instructions: Think about one of your favorite college courses that you enjoyed and in which you performed well. Answer the following questions for that favorite course. Then respond to the items in Part B for a course you did *not* enjoy and for which you probably performed poorly. Respond to the items in both Part A and Part B by indicating whether each item is Mostly True or Mostly False for you.

	Mostly False	Mostly True
Part A (for a favorite course)		
1. I made sure to study on a regular basis.	✓	
2. I put forth a lot of effort.		✓
3. I found ways to make the course material relevant to my life.		✓
4. I found ways to make the course interesting to me.		✓
5. I raised my hand in class.		✓
6. I had fun in class.		✓
7. I participated actively in small group discussions.		✓
8. I helped fellow students.		✓
Part B (for a least-favorite course)		
1. I made sure to study on a regular basis.	✓	
2. I put forth a lot of effort.		✓
3. I found ways to make the course material relevant to my life.		✓
4. I found ways to make the course interesting to me.		✓
5. I raised my hand in class.		✓
6. I had fun in class.		✓
7. I participated actively in small group discussions.		✓
8. I helped fellow students.		✓

Scoring and Interpretation

For Part A give yourself 1 point for each Mostly True answer and zero points for each Mostly False. For Part B give yourself 1 point for each Mostly True and zero points for each Mostly False. Write your scores below:

Part A score: 7/8

Part B score: 7/8

The term "employee engagement" is very popular in the corporate world. Engagement means that people are highly involved in and express themselves through their work, going well beyond the minimum effort required to do their jobs. Engagement typically has a positive relationship with both personal satisfaction and performance. If this relationship was true for your classes, your score for your favorite course should be substantially higher than the score for your least favorite course. The challenge for you as a leader is to learn to engage subordinates in the same way your instructor in your favorite class was able to engage you. Teaching is similar to leading. What techniques did your instructors use to engage students? Which techniques can you use to engage people when you become a leader?

Source: These questions are based on Mitchell M. Handelsman, William L. Briggs, Nora Sullivan, and Annette Towler, "A Measure of College Student Course Engagement," *The Journal of Educational Research* 98 (January–February 2005), pp. 184–191.

NEW LEADER
ACTION MEMO

Take the quiz in Leader's Self-Insight 8.3 to evaluate your level of engagement for a college course you enjoyed compared to one you did not enjoy.

8-5 GIVING MEANING TO WORK THROUGH ENGAGEMENT

The most recent thinking about motivation considers what factors contribute to people's willingness to be fully engaged at work and "go the extra mile" to contribute their creativity, energy, and passion on the job. One approach is to foster an organizational environment that helps people find true value and meaning in their work.

Engagement
when people enjoy their jobs and are satisfied with their work conditions, contribute enthusiastically to meeting team and organizational goals, and feel a sense of belonging and commitment to the organization

One path to meaning is through employee engagement. **Engagement** means that people enjoy their jobs and are satisfied with their work conditions, contribute enthusiastically to meeting team and organizational goals, and feel a sense of belonging and commitment to the organization. Fully engaged employees care deeply about the organization and actively seek ways to serve the mission.[55] Research shows that only 30 percent of American workers feel engaged in their jobs.[56] Research has also shown that company performance and profitability improve as the engagement level of employees increases.[57] In addition, according to Gallup Organization research, engaged employees have 51 percent lower turnover, 27 percent less absenteeism, and 18 percent more productivity.[58]

It is the behavior of leaders that makes the biggest difference in whether people feel engaged at work.[59] A leader's role is not to control others but to organize the workplace in such a way that each person can learn, contribute, and grow. Researchers at the Gallup Organization developed a metric called the Q12, a list of 12 questions that provides a way to evaluate how leaders are doing in creating an environment that provides intrinsic rewards by meeting higher-level needs. For example, one question on the Q12 concerns whether people have an opportunity at work to do what they do best. Recall from Chapter 2 the discussion of strengths and how each person has a unique set of talents and abilities. When people have an opportunity to do work that matches these natural capabilities, their satisfaction and engagement levels soar.[60] Facebook leaders believe this so strongly that they train all managers in how to put people in roles that build on their strengths.

IN THE LEAD

Facebook

When a manager asked Mike Welsh to join the team that helps train new Facebook employees, he said, "Are you crazy? I have no HR and no learning development experience and I have two accounting degrees to prove it." Welsh came to Facebook from PricewaterhouseCoopers as a risk-management accountant, but a manager noticed that he had a knack for helping people learn new concepts. Now, Welsh is a "People Engineer" for Facebook. He says it's the first place he has worked where employees are shifted into new roles or positions based on their strengths.

Facebook leaders want people to be working in areas that cater to their natural abilities and interests. Employees have an extraordinary degree of freedom to choose their assignments, even if it is something outside their area of expertise. Paddy Underwood came to Facebook as a lawyer working on the privacy team. Two years later, he decided he wanted to build products instead. Moreover, as with Mike Welsh, leaders often encourage people to shift roles based on what they do well.

The approach is based on the ideas and research of Marcus Buckingham, co-author of *Now, Discover Your Strengths*. In 2008, COO Sheryl Sandberg brought Buckingham to Facebook as a consultant. Top leaders took the StrengthsFinder 2.0 test and learned how to make the most of their strengths and work around their weaknesses. Leaders embraced the philosophy, and Buckingham's company now trains all of Facebook's managers to help put people in the jobs where they will be happiest, most motivated, and most productive.[61]

Many Internet companies, like Facebook, take engagement seriously because good technology employees are hard to find. Other characteristics evaluated by the Q12 include whether employees know what is expected of them, whether they have the resources they need to perform well, whether they feel appreciated and recognized for doing good work, whether they have a friend at work, and whether they feel that their opinions are important. The full list of questions on the Q12 survey can be found in the book *First, Break All the Rules* by researchers Marcus Buckingham and Curt Coffman.[62] When a majority of employees can answer the Q12 questions positively, the organization enjoys a highly motivated, engaged, and productive workforce.

Leaders can identify the level of engagement in their organizations and implement strategies to facilitate full engagement and improve performance. At Prudential

NEW LEADER
ACTION MEMO

As a leader, you can build an environment that unleashes employee potential and allows people to become engaged with their work and the organization. You can help people feel good about their jobs by giving them a sense of making progress toward meaningful goals.

UK and Europe, which provides life insurance and pensions for around seven million customers, leaders conducted a survey and set up an engagement board made up of senior staff from each part of the business to analyze the findings and identify areas where changes were needed to increase employee engagement. When the survey was conducted a year later, it showed that both engagement (whether people felt enough a part of the organization to "go the extra mile") and enablement (whether they felt they had the resources and autonomy to do their jobs well) had strongly increased.[63]

8-6 NEW IDEAS FOR MOTIVATION

One reason engagement and empowerment have such high motivational potential is that they address higher-level needs and provide intrinsic rewards by applying some recent ideas about what it takes to have a high-performance workplace in which people feel that they are a part of something special.

8-6a The Making Progress Principle

Recent research points to the importance of *making progress toward goals* as a key to high motivation. The **making progress principle** is the idea that the single most important factor that can boost motivation, positive emotions, and perceptions during a workday is making progress toward meaningful goals.[64] People are most motivated when they have the opportunity to experience achievement. Knowing that they are making everyday progress, even small steps, can make all the difference in how motivated people feel to continue pursuing a course of action.

Leaders can support making progress by setting clear goals, giving people autonomy, providing sufficient time and resources, and helping people see how they are contributing. In addition, leader encouragement and recognition can enable people to see their work as important and meaningful. Providing feedback on how well people are progressing and giving them a way to track their progress toward goals provides a renewable energy that fuels motivation. Sometimes managers underestimate the importance of the continuous feedback aspect of the job characteristics model, described earlier.

8-6b Building a Thriving Workforce

Taken together, many of the ideas in this chapter enable leaders to create an environment in which people can thrive. A **thriving workforce** is one in which people are not just satisfied and productive but also engaged in creating the future—their own and that of the organization.[65] Two components of thriving individuals are *vitality* and *learning*. A thriving employee is one who feels alive, energized, and passionate about what he or she is doing. The individual has a sense that his or her work has purpose and meaning. In addition, a thriving employee is one who is learning and growing, developing new knowledge, skills, and abilities that can be applied now and in the future.

Leaders promote thriving by applying many of the motivational techniques described throughout this chapter, such as meeting higher-level needs, helping people get intrinsic rewards from their work, and providing regular feedback on performance and progress. A long-term commitment to empowerment and engagement can provide the basis for a thriving workplace. The goal of empowerment and engagement is to transform the culture. Leaders talk with people one on one to understand what each person wants and needs to feel engaged and empowered, and

Making progress principle
the idea that the single most important factor that can boost motivation, positive emotions, and perceptions during a workday is making progress toward meaningful goals

Thriving workforce
A workforce in which people are not just satisfied and productive but also engaged in creating a better future for themselves and the organization; incorporates vitality and learning

then follow through with everyday action. Although there are some key drivers, there is no cookie-cutter approach because each individual and organization is different.[66] As described earlier, the immediate supervisor plays a key role in whether employees are engaged and thriving.

LEADERSHIP ESSENTIALS

- This chapter introduced a number of important ideas about motivating people in organizations. Individuals are motivated to act by various motives and to satisfy a range of needs. The leadership approach to motivation tends to focus on positive motives and meeting the higher needs of employees. The role of the leader is to create a situation in which followers' higher needs and the needs of the organization can be met simultaneously.
- Needs-based theories focus on the underlying needs that motivate how people behave. Maslow's hierarchy of needs proposes that individuals satisfy lower needs before they move on to higher needs. Herzberg's two-factor theory holds that dissatisfiers must be removed and motivators then added to cause high motivation. McClelland asserted that people are motivated differently depending on which needs they have acquired.
- Other motivation theories, including the reinforcement perspective, expectancy theory, and equity theory, focus primarily on extrinsic rewards and punishments, sometimes called *carrot-and-stick* methods of motivation. The reinforcement perspective proposes that behavior can be modified by the use of rewards and punishments. Expectancy theory is based on the idea that a person's motivation is contingent upon his or her expectations that a given behavior will result in desired rewards. Equity theory proposes that individuals' motivation is affected not only by the rewards they receive but also by their perceptions of how fairly they are treated in relation to others. People are motivated to seek equity in the rewards they receive for performance.
- A highly effective way to meet higher-level needs is to empower employees. Empowerment lets subordinates know the direction of the organization and gives them the autonomy to act as they see fit to go in that direction. Leaders provide employees with the knowledge to contribute to the organization, the power to make consequential decisions, and the necessary resources to do their jobs.
- Jobs can be designed to increase empowerment. The job characteristics model proposes that jobs are more empowering and motivating when they have greater skill variety, task identity, task importance, autonomy, and feedback.
- Employee engagement is tied to the trend toward helping employees find value and meaning in their jobs. The most motivated employees are engaged employees who enjoy their jobs and feel they are making a valuable contribution. Engaged employees contribute enthusiastically to meeting goals. Leaders create the environment that determines employee engagement.
- Two recent motivational ideas that relate to engagement are the making progress principle and creating a thriving workforce. Research suggests that the single most important factor for motivation is a sense of making progress toward meaningful goals. A thriving workforce is made up of people who are enthusiastically learning and growing as they acquire new knowledge and skills to apply in their current jobs or in the future.

DISCUSSION QUESTIONS

1. Describe the kinds of needs that people bring to an organization. How might one's personality characteristics—such as introversion/extroversion or openness to experience, as described in Chapter 4—influence the needs he or she brings to work?
2. With the economy still in a slump, some companies were freezing pay raises or even cutting pay for some employees so they could offer substantial raises to people considered star performers. As a motivational technique, does this practice seem like a good one to you? What might be some disadvantages of this technique?
3. How might empowerment provide the two conditions (vitality and learning) for a thriving workforce as described in the chapter? Consider both psychological factors and the job characteristics model in your answer.
4. Google wants employees to mingle more but not to waste a lot of time. So as part of its "people strategy," Google analyzes reams of data to determine the optimal size and shape for the cafeteria tables and the best length for the lunch line. If hygiene factors, as defined in Herzberg's two-factor theory, will not provide increased satisfaction and motivation, why do you think Google would try to increase lunchtime mingling? Discuss.
5. Why do you think *making progress in meaningful work* ranks as the most important factor contributing to motivation according to a recent study? How might leaders provide a sense of progress for employees working on long-range projects that might not show results for months or even years?
6. One small business owner says she doesn't offer her sales representatives incentives because people try to sabotage one another to get more business and stop paying attention to smaller accounts. As a leader, how would you develop a program to motivate and reward high performers without promoting the wrong type of behavior?
7. Can you think of specific motivational techniques that would motivate you in each of the four categories in Exhibit 8.3 (positive extrinsic, positive intrinsic, negative extrinsic, negative intrinsic)? Describe them.
8. Do you agree that it is the behavior of leaders that largely determines employee engagement, as defined in the text? What might be some other factors that influence engagement?
9. Discuss whether you believe it is a leader's responsibility to help people find meaning in their work. How might leaders do this for employees at a credit card call center? How about for employees who empty waste containers and clean restrooms at sports or entertainment venues?
10. As part of the federal health-care overhaul in the United States, patient satisfaction survey scores are now used to help determine how much the federal government will pay medical facilities for treating patients on Medicare. What motivation theory described in the chapter does this example illustrate? Do you think this approach will motivate employees to provide better care? What might be some potential problems with this approach?

LEADERSHIP AT WORK

Should, Need, Like, Love

Think of a school or work task that you feel an obligation or commitment to complete but that you don't really want to do. Write the task here:

____

____

____

Think of a school or work task you do because you need to, perhaps to get the benefit, such as money or credit. Write the task here:

____

____

____

Think of a school or work task you like to do because it is enjoyable or fun. Write the task here:

____

____

____

Think of a task you love to do—one in which you become completely absorbed and from which you feel a deep satisfaction when finished. Write the task here:

____

____

____

Now reflect on those four tasks and what they mean to you. How motivated (high, medium, low) are you to accomplish each of these four tasks? How much mental effort (high, medium, low) is required from you to complete each task?

Now estimate the percentage of your weekly tasks that you would rate as *should, need, like, love*. The combined estimates should total 100 percent.

Should: ____________%
Need: ____________%
Like: ____________%
Love: ____________%

If your *should* and *need* percentages are substantially higher than your *like* and *love* categories, what does that mean for you? Does it mean that you are forcing yourself to do tasks you find unpleasant? Why? Why not include more *like* and *love* tasks in your life? Might you grow weary of the *should* and *need* tasks at some point and select a new focus or job in your life? Think about this and discuss your percentages with another student in the class.

Tasks you *love* connect you with the creative spirit of life. People who do something they love have a certain charisma, and others want to follow their lead. Tasks you *like* typically are those that fit your gifts and talents and are tasks with which you can make a contribution. Tasks you do because of *need* are typically practical in the sense that they produce an outcome you want, and these tasks often do not provide as much satisfaction as the *like* and *love* tasks. Tasks you do strictly because you *should*, and which contain no *love, like*, or *need*, may be difficult and distasteful and require great effort to complete. You are unlikely to become a leader for completing *should* tasks.

What does the amount of each type of task in your life mean to you? How do these tasks relate to your passion and life satisfaction? Why don't you have more *like* and *love* tasks? As a leader, how would you increase the *like* and *love* tasks for people who report to you? Be specific.

____

____

____

In Class: The instructor can have students talk in small groups about their percentages and what the percentages mean to them. Students can be asked how the categories of *should, need, like*, and *love* relate to the theories of motivation in the chapter. Do leaders have an obligation to guide employees toward tasks they like and love, or is it sufficient at work for people to perform need and should tasks?

The instructor can write student percentages on the board so students can see where they stand compared to the class. Students can be asked to interpret the results in terms of the amount of satisfaction they receive from various tasks. Also, are the percentages related to the students' stage of life?

LEADERSHIP DEVELOPMENT: CASES FOR ANALYSIS

Commissions for Charlotte

Doris Ann Riley, the head of HR for King Conductors, was amused by the conversation drifting over the planter that separated the two booths in the employee cafeteria. She recognized the voices on the other side as those of Pete Morris, Carter Henry, and Rachael Parker. The three were involved in a heated discussion about the opening of the NFL season one week away and the continued holdout of the local team's star quarterback.

"Hey, if he can hold out for a $50 million dollar contract, I say more power to him. He's worth it," Pete announced "I say . . ."

"The guy already has millions," Rachael cut in. "He got it last year as a rookie, for heaven's sake. He's a selfish jerk. His selfishness is making everyone, the fans, the owner, probably the other players, angry."

"Yeah, and what about those other players who have been there, winning games for us for years?" Carter asked. "They get us in the playoffs year after year, and then here comes this guy who's been there one year, *one year*, Pete, and he's going to get millions or he won't play. Well, that really breaks my heart."

"Just be glad that Charlotte Forsythe knows nothing about American football or that you can make demands like that, or she'll hit up this company," Rachael remarked, breaking the tension at the table by making everyone laugh.

On the other side of the planter, Doris Ann was not laughing.

Charlotte had worked for years in the international arena as the top salesperson for rival Merrill International in the United Kingdom. A native Londoner, she followed a life-long desire to emigrate to the United States. Doris Ann was part of the team that had lured Charlotte from U.S. rival Martin Conductor to take a sales position with King Conductors (whose owners, Wylie King and James Conway, long ago hoisted the humorous nickname, *King-Con*). Capturing Charlotte was considered a real coup in the world of conductors. Long considered the big three in the industry, the companies produced in-demand conductors for electronics. King-Con's own formulation was designed for use to counter continuous flexing in data processing, rotating servo platforms, and other applications.

To capture such a high-profile salesperson, Doris Ann was the first to admit the company had given in more than usual on wage and other job perks. Charlotte had skipped the regular salary in order to receive straight commissions on sales—an arrangement that had been made by her previous employer. The arrangement was unusual but, the team thought, a necessary step in luring Charlotte away from Martin. In addition, as a native of England with the habit of driving on the left-hand side of the road, Charlotte's unfamiliarity with American driving conditions, particularly in congested metropolitan areas, resulted in the unusual arrangement of allowing her office assistant to also serve as a driver on various occasions, particularly when she was out of town. While working in the company headquarters, however, she took the train to work and made use of trains or cabs. Still, there was a rumble of discontent among employees about *Queen Charlotte* and *royal* treatment.

"Her sales are a huge percentage and she's made a tremendous difference in the year since her arrival. She really is worth the trouble," Doris Ann told company vice president Charles Owenby. "But she has come to me to suggest raising her commission—substantially—and I just don't know. But I think you and I and Wylie and Jim need to discuss this."

"I agree," Charles said. "I think they will bend within reason. . . . "

"But the problem here, I believe, will be the reaction of other employees," Doris Ann said. "I hear a lot about Queen Charlotte and royal treatment, and comparisons to how those who have put in the years here are not getting the same respect as the *rookie*, to borrow a football analogy. So the question is, do we give in or stand firm?"

"Knowing she can always move over to Martin," Charles added. "There's a risk either way, so we have to explore our options before we bring all of the parties together to hash this thing out."

QUESTIONS

1. What theories of motivation help explain Charlotte's demands and the reactions of other employees to those demands?
2. What options can you think of for handling Charlotte's demand for even higher commissions? Which option would you choose? Why?
3. How might Doris Ann Riley deal with employee morale in light of the extremely high pay demanded by a star salesperson?

Sun Spots

SunDax CEO Dax Hollandsworth turns his leather desk chair from the blinding sunlight streaming through the large office window and leans back, facing Mark Roberts, the company CFO.

"You know, Mark, on the surface this seems impossible. We look at the numbers, we look at energy trends, we look at tax breaks and the grants and loans poured into this effort, and. . ." his voice trails off as he raises his hands in a gesture of surrender.

"I dread the quarterly meeting and video feed," Mark says. "Everyone has been working really hard and they've come to expect the year-end bonus. Hell, they plan for it, their families budget for it."

"I realize this will come as a huge disappointment, but I really don't think it will come as a big shock to them. Do you want some of these?" Dax asks, taking a handful of jelly beans and extending the jar to Mark who takes a few. "They're working their tails off, but I've detected a decline in overall morale. Everyone here keeps a close eye on the industry and on the mood and efforts at the federal level. They deal every day with the competition from the Chinese, and they see this big trend toward mergers and acquisitions. They may not want to admit it any more than we want to say it, but I think they know the bonus pool is empty and they wonder what the future holds."

The question hanging over the offices throughout the U.S. solar industry echoes that of California-based SunDax, "*how could this happen?*"

To the outsider, things appear great for solar power. The numbers are staggering, with an overall increase in usage of more than 60 percent over the previous year. And American home and commercial construction shows the rising popularity of solar energy as a viable power alternative. Like the electric automobile, it is the wave of the future. But the public sees only the sun; industry insiders are looking at the sunspots.

Private investments in the early years followed by federal tax credits and Energy Department loan guarantees enabled solar companies such as SunDax to refine their products, increase inventory, and expand sales worldwide. Boom time brought U.S. Treasury grants to the industry of several hundred million dollars, and as sales increased so did employee bonuses. Many bonuses equaled up to a third of an employee's salary—money for a child's college tuition, down payments on homes, trips, and other luxuries.

Now, amid shaky global economic conditions, SunDax and others see a decline in U.S. and European solar energy incentives while Chinese competitors undercut costs, providing an inventory glut for many U.S. producers. In this climate, there is reluctance on the part of Congress to renew mini-grants or to extend tax credits. The stimulus packages upon which so many companies depended to jump-start market expansion are a thing of the past.

"I'm afraid that employees will believe we are bending to public pressure in withholding their bonuses or they will think we are holding onto financial assets in order to look stronger for a potential merger or acquisition," Dax tells Mark.

"Mergers and acquisitions are the trend right now, and some big names have given in. If we are acquired, they can share in the gains."

"We're not there yet," Dax says. "Our challenge is to shore up faith in our future among employees while dealing with the realities of the market. But if you say 'look at all of these challenges' and, 'oh, by the way, don't expect a year-end bonus,' what can we offer to shore up that faith and restore enthusiasm?"

QUESTIONS

1. What options can you think of for Dax and Mark to mitigate the damage from unfulfilled expectations for the annual bonus?
2. What specific steps would you take if you were a senior manager in this situation? Explain why for each step.
3. Do you consider it motivational and equitable when a substantial part of an employee's pay is a bonus based on company results in a highly uncertain environment? Why?

REFERENCES

1. Michael Wheeler, "Why Raising Employee Wages Sometimes Backfires," *Hospitality Business Development* (August 7, 2015), http://www.hospitalitybusinessdevelopment.com/blog/why-raising-employee-wages-sometimes-backfires (accessed October 27, 2015); and Patricia Cohen, "One Firm's Annual Pay of $70,000 Stirs Debate," *The New York Times* (April 20, 2015), p. B1.
2. Michael West and Malcolm Patterson, "Profitable Personnel," *People Management* (January 8, 1998), pp. 28–31; Richard M. Steers and Lyman W. Porter, eds. *Motivation and Work Behavior*, 3rd ed. (New York: McGraw-Hill, 1983); Don Hellriegel, John W. Slocum Jr., and Richard W. Woodman, *Organizational Behavior*, 7th ed. (St. Paul, MN: West Publishing Co., 1995), p. 170; and Jerry L. Gray and Frederick A. Starke, *Organizational Behavior: Concepts and Applications*, 4th ed. (New York: Macmillan, 1988), pp. 104–105.
3. Linda Grant, "Happy Workers, High Returns," *Fortune* (January 12, 1998), p. 81; Elizabeth J. Hawk and Garrett J. Sheridan, "The Right Staff," *Management Review* (June 1999), pp. 43–48; Anne Fisher, "Why Passion Pays," *FSB* (September 2002), p. 58; and West and Patterson, "Profitable Personnel."
4. Curt Coffman and Gabriel Gonzalez-Molina, *Follow This Path: How the World's Greatest Organizations Drive Growth by Unleashing Human Potential* (New York: Warner Books, 2002).
5. Richard M. Steers, Lyman W. Porter, and Gregory A. Bigley, *Motivation and Leadership at Work*, 6th ed. (New York: McGraw-Hill, 1996), pp. 496–498.
6. Steven Bergals, "When Money Talks, People Walk," *Inc.* (May 1996), pp. 25–26.
7. Rosabeth Moss Kanter, "How to Fire Up Employees without Cash or Prizes," *Business 2.0* (June 2002), pp. 134–152.
8. This example is from Maureen Soyars and Justin Brusino, "Essentials of Engagement: Contributions, Connections, Growth," *T + D* (March 2009), pp. 62–65.
9. This discussion is based on Bruce H. Jackson, "Influence Behavior; Become a Master Motivator," *Leadership Excellence* (April 2010), p. 14.
10. Mohana Ravindranath, "Getting a Return on Employee Rewards," On Small Business blog, *The Washington Post* (December 19, 2012), http://www.washingtonpost.com/blogs/on-small-business/post/getting-a-return-on-employee-rewards/2012/12/18/1400a9ec-4973-11e2-820e-17eefac2f939_blog.html (accessed April 16, 2013).
11. Susie Cranston and Scott Keller, "Increasing the 'Meaning Quotient' of Work," *McKinsey Quarterly* (January 2013), http://www.mckinseyquarterly.com/Increasing_the_meaning_quotient_of_work_3055 (accessed April 17, 2013).
12. Leslie Kwoh, "Shape Up or Pay Up: Firms Put in New Health Penalties," *The Wall Street Journal* (April 6, 2013), p. A1.
13. Abraham F. Maslow, "A Theory of Human Motivation," *Psychological Review* 50 (1943), pp. 370–396.
14. Kathy Chu, "China Factories Try Karaoke, Speed Dating, to Keep Workers," *The Wall Street Journal* (May 2, 2013), http://online.wsj.com/article/SB10001424127887323798104578452634075519230.html?KEYWORDS=kathy+Chu (accessed May 13, 2013).
15. Frederick Herzberg, "One More Time: How Do You Motivate Employees?" *Harvard Business Review* (January–February 1968), pp. 53–62.
16. David A. Kaplan, "Inside Mars," *Fortune* (February 4, 2013), pp. 72–82; and "Mars, Incorporated President Paul S. Michaels to Retire in December 2014; 26-YEAR Mars Veteran, Grant F. Reid to Lead Organization," Mars Press Release (March 2014), http://www.mars.com/global/press-center/press-list/news-releases.aspx?SiteId=94&Id=5590 (accessed October 26, 2015).
17. David C. McClelland, *Human Motivation* (Glenview, IL: Scott, Foresman, 1985).
18. John Brant, "What One Man Can Do," *Inc.* (September 2005), pp. 145–153.
19. David C. McClelland, "The Two Faces of Power," in D. A. Colb, I. M. Rubin, and J. M. McIntyre, eds., *Organizational Psychology* (Upper Saddle River, NJ: Prentice Hall, 1971), pp. 73–86.
20. Alfie Kohn, "Why Incentive Plans Cannot Work," *Harvard Business Review* (September–October 1993), pp. 54–63; A. J. Vogl, "Carrots, Sticks, and Self-Deception" (an interview with Alfie Kohn), *Across the Board* (January 1994), pp. 39–44; and Alfie Kohn, "Challenging Behaviorist Dogma: Myths about Money and Motivation," *Compensation & Benefits Review* (March–April 1998), pp. 27, 33–37.

21. H. Richlin, *Modern Behaviorism* (San Francisco: Freeman, 1970); B. F. Skinner, *Science and Human Behavior* (New York: Macmillan, 1953); Alexander D. Stajkovic and Fred Luthans, "A Meta-Analysis of the Effects of Organizational Behavior Modification on Task Performance 1975–1995," *Academy of Management Journal* 40 (October 1997), pp. 1122–1149; and F. Luthans and R. Kreitner, *Organizational Behavior Modification and Beyond*, 2nd ed. (Glenview, IL: Scott Foresman, 1985).
22. Alexander D. Stajkovic and Fred Luthans, "A Meta-Analysis of the Effects of Organizational Behavior Modification on Task Performance, 1975–1995," *Academy of Management Journal* (October 1997), pp. 1122–1149; and Fred Luthans and Alexander D. Stajkovic, "Reinforce for Performance: The Need to Go Beyond Pay and Even Rewards," *Academy of Management Executive* 13, no. 2 (1999), pp. 49–57.
23. Anthony DeRiso and Timothy D. Ludwig, "An Investigation of Response Generalization across Cleaning and Restocking Behaviors in the Context of Performance Feedback," *Journal of Organizational Behavior Management* 32 (2012), pp. 141–151.
24. Martin Dewhurst, Matthew Guthridge, and Elizabeth Mohr, "Motivating People: Getting Beyond Money," *McKinsey Quarterly* (November 2009), http://www.mckinseyquarterly.com/Motivating_people_Getting_beyond_money_2460 (accessed April 17, 2013).
25. Cranston and Keller, "Increasing the 'Meaning Quotient' of Work."
26. *Workforce MoodTracker Spring 2012 Report: The Growing Influence of Employee Recognition* (Southborough, MA: Globoforce, 2012).
27. Jessica Silver-Greenberg, "JPMorgan Cuts Dimon's Pay, Even as Profit Surges," *The New York Times* (January 16, 2013), http://dealbook.nytimes.com/2013/01/16/jpmorgan-4th-quarter-profit-jumps-53-to-5-7-billion/ (accessed January 16, 2013).
28. Amy Sutherland, "What Shamu Taught Me about a Happy Marriage," *The New York Times* (June 25, 2006), http://www.nytimes.com/2006/06/25/fashion/25love.html?ex=1175659200&en=4c3d257c4d16e70d&ei=5070 (accessed April 2, 2007).
29. Luthans and Kreitner, *Organizational Behavior Modification and Beyond*; L. M. Saari and G. P. Latham, "Employee Reaction to Continuous and Variable Ratio Reinforcement Schedules Involving a Monetary Incentive," *Journal of Applied Psychology* 67 (1982), pp. 506–508; and R. D. Pritchard, J. Hollenback, and P. J. DeLeo, "The Effects of Continuous and Partial Schedules of Reinforcement on Effort, Performance, and Satisfaction," *Organizational Behavior and Human Performance* 25 (1980), pp. 336–353.
30. Victor H. Vroom, *Work and Motivation* (New York: John Wiley & Sons, 1969); B. S. Gorgopoulos, G. M. Mahoney, and N. Jones, "A Path–Goal Approach to Productivity," *Journal of Applied Psychology* 41 (1957), pp. 345–353; and E. E. Lawler III, *Pay and Organizational Effectiveness: A Psychological View* (New York: McGraw-Hill, 1981).
31. Richard R. Johnson, "Explaining Patrol Officer Drug Arrest Activity through Expectancy Theory," *Policing: An International Journal of Police Strategies & Management* 32, no. 1 (2009), pp. 6–20.
32. Richard M. Daft and Richard M. Steers, *Organizations: A Micro/Macro Approach* (Glenview, IL: Scott, Foresman, 1986).
33. Jim Finkelstein and Melissa Mead, "Incentives and Rewards: What Melts Your Employees' Butter?" *Leadership Excellence* (December 2012), p. 19.
34. J. Stacy Adams, "Injustice in Social Exchange," in L. Berkowitz, ed., *Advances in Experimental Social Psychology*, 2nd ed. (New York: Academic Press, 1965); and J. Stacy Adams, "Toward an Understanding of Inequity," *Journal of Abnormal and Social Psychology* (November 1963), pp. 422–436.
35. Based on a story in Karla L. Miller, "@Work Advice: How to Deal with Pay Inequity," *The Washington Post*, October 3, 2012, http://articles.washingtonpost.com/2012-10-03/lifestyle/35502549_1_monkey-cucumber-illegal-bias (accessed April 17, 2013).
36. Ibid.
37. Quoted in Rachel Emma Silverman, "Psst . . . This Is What Your Co-Worker Is Paid," *The Wall Street Journal* (January 30, 2013), p. B6.
38. Edwin P. Hollander and Lynn R. Offerman, "Power and Leadership in Organizations," *American Psychology* 45 (February 1990), pp. 179–189.
39. David P. McCaffrey, Sue R. Faerman, and David W. Hart, "The Appeal and Difficulties of Participative Systems," *Organization Science* 6, no. 6 (November–December 1995), pp. 603–627.
40. Robert C. Ford and Myron D. Fottler, "Empowerment: A Matter of Degree," *Academy of Management Executive* 9 (1995), pp. 21–31; Golnaz Sadri, "Empowerment for the Bottom Line," *Industrial Management* (May–June 2011), pp. 8–13; and David E. Bowen and Edward E. Lawler III, "Empowering Service Employees," *Sloan Management Review* 36 (Summer 1995), pp. 73–84.
41. John Izzo, "Step-Up Initiative: Create a Culture of Initiators," *Leadership Excellence* (June 2012), p. 13.
42. Jay A. Conger and Rabindra N. Kanungo, "The Empowerment Process: Integrating Theory and Practice," *Academy of Management Review* 13 (1988), pp. 471–482; and Albert Bandura, "Self-Efficacy: Toward a Unifying Theory of Behavioral Change," *Psychological Review* 84, no. 2 (1977), pp. 191–215. See M. Travis Maynard, Lucy L. Gilson, and John E. Mathieu, "Empowerment: Fad or Fab? A Multilevel Review of the Past Two Decades of Research," *Journal of Management* 38, no. 4 (July 2012), pp. 1231–1281 for a recent review of the research on psychological empowerment.
43. These are based on Bowen and Lawler, "Empowering Service Employees"; Gretchen Spreitzer, "Social Structural Characteristics of Psychological Empowerment," *Academy of Management Journal* 39, no. 2 (April 1996), pp. 483–504; and Russ Forrester, "Empowerment: Rejuvenating a Potent Idea," *Academy of Management Executive* 14, no. 3 (2000), pp. 67–80.
44. Silverman, "Psst . . . This Is What Your Co-Worker Is Paid."
45. Forrester, "Empowerment: Rejuvenating a Potent Idea."
46. Glenn L. Dalton, "The Collective Stretch," *Management Review* 87 (December 1998), pp. 54–59.
47. Bradley L. Kirkman and Benson Rosen, "Powering Up Teams," *Organizational Dynamics* 28 (Winter 2000), pp. 48–66; and Gretchen M. Spreitzer, "Psychological Empowerment in the Workplace: Dimensions, Measurement, and Validation," *Academy of Management Journal* 38, no. 5 (October 1995), p. 1442.
48. Reported in Carol Hymowitz, "Pay Gap Fuels Worker Woes," *The Wall Street Journal* (April 28, 2008), p. B8.
49. J. R. Hackman and G. R. Oldham, *Work Redesign* (Reading, MA: Addison-Wesley, 1980); and J. R. Hackman and G. R. Oldham, "Motivation through the Design of Work: Test of a Theory," *Organizational Behavior and Human Performance* 16 (1976), pp. 250–279.
50. Issie Lapowsky, "The Motivator: The Nerdery; The One Role That Can Never Be Filled" (segment of "Hire Power Awards 2012: The Real Heroes of the American Economy"), *Inc.* (December 2012 – January 2013), pp. 84–96 (segment is on page 92).
51. Jared Sandberg, "A Modern Conundrum: When Work's Invisible, So Are Its Satisfactions," *The Wall Street Journal* (February 19, 2008), p. B1.
52. Example from Dalton, "The Collective Stretch."
53. Ford and Fottler, "Empowerment: A Matter of Degree."
54. Jennifer Conlin, "At Zingerman's, Pastrami and Partnership to Go," *The New York Times* (July 5, 2014), http://www.nytimes.com/2014/07/06/business/at-zingermans-pastrami-and-partnership-to-go.html?_r=0 (accessed October 27, 2015).
55. This definition is based on Mercer Human Resource Consulting's Employee Engagement Model, as described in Paul Sanchez and Dan McCauley, "Measuring and Managing Engagement in a Cross-Cultural Workforce: New Insights for Global Companies," *Global Business and Organizational Excellence* (November–December 2006), pp. 41–50.
56. Lillian Cunningham, "New Data Show Only 30% of American Workers Engaged in Their Jobs," On Leadership blog, *The Washington Post* (April 30, 2013), http://www.washingtonpost.com/blogs/on-leadership/wp/2013/04/30/new-data-show-only-30-of-american-workers-engaged-in-their-jobs/ (accessed May 14, 2013).

57. Richard P. Finnegan, "The Price of Employee Disengagement," *Chief Executive* (June 28, 2011), http://chiefexecutive.net/the-price-of-disengagement-and-an-exercise (accessed February 9, 2013); Curt Coffman and Gabriel Gonzalez-Molina, *Follow This Path: How the World's Greatest Organizations Drive Growth by Unleashing Human Potential* (New York: Warner Books, 2002); Rodd Wagner and James K. Harter, "The Third Element of Great Managing; Mom Was Right: You're One of a Kind," *Gallup Management Journal* (June 14, 2007); and Gerard H. Seijts and Dan Crim, "What Engages Employees the Most, or the Ten C's of Employee Engagement," *Ivey Business Journal* (March–April 2006).
58. Gallup studies reported in Pat Galagan, "Amplified and Connected," *T + D* (December 2012), pp. 34–37.
59. This discussion is based on Marcus Buckingham and Curt Coffman, *First, Break All the Rules: What the World's Greatest Managers Do Differently* (New York: Simon & Schuster, 1999); and Theresa M. Welbourne, "Employee Engagement: Beyond the Fad and into the Executive Suite," *Leader to Leader* (Spring 2007), pp. 45–51.
60. Wagner and Harter, "The Third Element of Great Managing."
61. Reed Albergotti, "At Facebook, Boss Is a Dirty Word," *The Wall Street Journal* (December 25, 2014), http://www.wsj.com/articles/facebooks-millennials-arent-entitled-they-are-empowered-1419537468 (accessed October 27, 2015).
62. Buckingham and Coffman, *First, Break All the Rules*.
63. Anna Scott, "Dear Prudence," *People Management* (January 2012), pp. 36–39.
64. This definition and discussion are based on Teresa M. Amabile and Steven J. Kramer, "The Power of Small Wins," *Harvard Business Review* (May 2011), pp. 71–80; and Teresa M. Amabile and Steven J. Kramer, "What Really Motivates Workers: Understanding the Power of Progress," *Harvard Business Review* (January–February 2010), pp. 44–45.
65. This section is based on Gretchen Spreitzer and Christine Porath, "Creating Sustainable Performance," *Harvard Business Review* (January-February 2012), pp. 92–99; and Gretchen Spreitzer, Christine L. Porath, and Cristina B. Gibson, "Toward Human Sustainability: How to Enable More Thriving at Work," *Organizational Dynamics* 41 (2012), pp. 155–162.
66. Mary Knight, "Three Strategies for Making Employee Engagement Stick," *Gallup Business Journal* (January 17, 2013), http://businessjournal.gallup.com/content/159851/three-strategies-making-employee-engagement-stick.aspx (accessed April 18, 2013); and Tracy Maylett and Julie Nielsen, "There Is No Cookie-Cutter Approach to Engagement," *T + D* (April 2012), pp. 55–59.

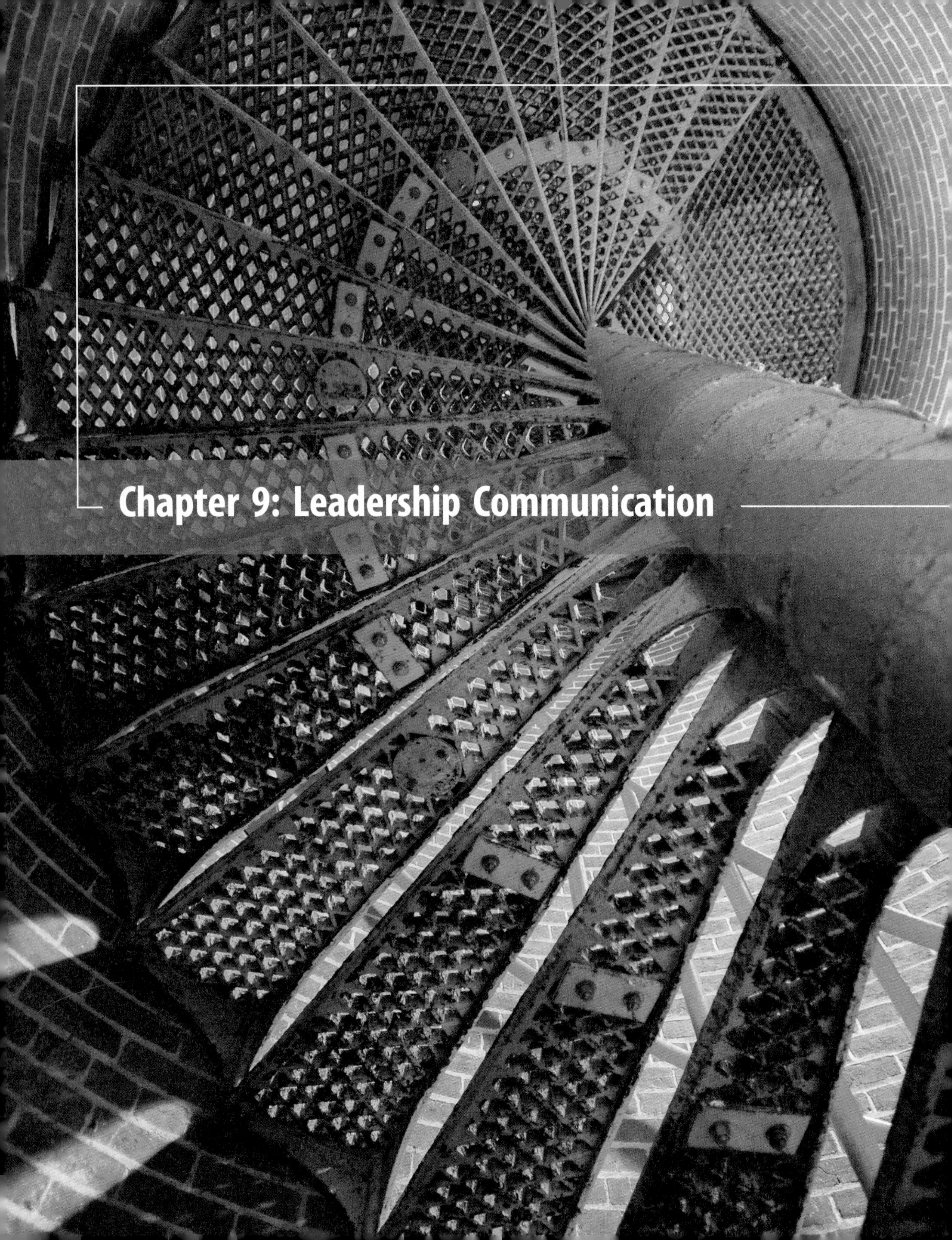

Chapter 9: Leadership Communication

YOUR **LEADERSHIP** CHALLENGE

After reading this chapter, you should be able to:

- Act as a communication champion and a "sensegiver" rather than just as an information processor.
- Use key elements of effective listening and understand why listening is important to leader communication.
- Use candor appropriately to improve your communication effectiveness, and recognize and apply the difference between dialogue and discussion.
- Incorporate metaphor and storytelling into your leadership communications.
- Select an appropriate communication channel for your message and effectively use social media and nonverbal communication.
- Communicate in a way that persuades and influences others.
- Effectively communicate during times of stress or crisis.

CHAPTER **OUTLINE**

262 **How Leaders Communicate**

266 **Leading Strategic Conversations**

275 **Communicating to Persuade and Influence**

276 **Selecting the Correct Communication Channel**

281 **Nonverbal Communication**

281 **Current Communication Challenges**

In the Lead

266 **United States Africa Command (USAFRICOM)**

273 **Seattle Seahawks**

278 **Earl's Restaurants Ltd.**

283 **Duke University**

Leader's Self-Insight

264 **Am I Networked?**

270 **Listening and Asking Questions**

273 **Do You Speak with Candor?**

Leader's Bookshelf

275 **Tell to Win: Connect, Persuade, and Triumph with the Hidden Power of Story**

Leadership at Work

285 **Listen Like a Professional**

Leadership Development: Cases for Analysis

286 **The Superintendent's Directive**

287 **Hunter-Worth**

A group of assembly line employees, factory floor managers, and quality control experts recently held a meeting in a maintenance closet. The impromptu get-together took place because workers at Honda's Anna, Ohio, engine plant were faced with having to spend more than three hours taking out, repairing, and reinstalling engines in Honda vehicles because of a previously unrecognized defect in a camshaft from a supplier. The meeting went on for several minutes with tempers flaring and petty arguments erupting. Some of the managers thought it was time to give up and just do it the obvious way, but other participants wanted to keep talking things out. When the meeting was over 20 minutes later, the group had found a way to make the camshaft repairs that would tie up only one hour per vehicle. These kinds of spontaneous meetings are called *waigaya* at Honda, and they are considered indispensable. A company story says the term *waigaya* was coined by Takeo Fujisawa, the business partner of Honda founder Soichiro Honda, because it sounded like the babble of many people talking at the same time, openly disagreeing with one another and debating ideas and opinions. Honda leaders believe involving everyone in open, candid, fearless communication is essential for finding the best, most practical way of doing things.[1]

Organizations suffer when people are afraid to speak up, don't care enough to speak up, or find that no one is listening. As a leader, you will define your team or organization's communication climate, whether things are discussed openly or suppressed, whether people know and care what is going on in the organization or do not, and whether listening is valued as a key part of the communication process.

Recall that leadership means influencing people to bring about change toward a vision, or desired future, for the organization. Leaders communicate to share the vision with others, inspire and motivate them to strive toward the vision, and build the values and trust that enable effective working relationships and goal accomplishment.

Successful leader communication also includes deceptively simple components, such as asking questions, paying attention to nonverbal communication, and actively listening to others. Unfortunately, research shows that many executives are not investing the time and energy to be effective communicators. A survey by AMA Enterprise found that nearly 40 percent of employees feel out of the loop and don't know what is going on in their companies.[2] Moreover, many leaders resist employee feedback because they don't want to hear negative information. Without feedback, leaders can miss important signals that something is going wrong, and they may make decisions that are out of alignment with employee needs or perceptions, making smooth implementation less likely.[3]

This chapter describes tools and skills that can be used to overcome the communication deficit pervading today's organizations. We examine how leaders use communication skills to make a difference in their organizations and the lives of followers.

9-1 HOW LEADERS COMMUNICATE

Have you ever had a supervisor or instructor whose communication skills were so poor that you didn't have any idea what was expected of you or how to accomplish the job you were asked to do? On the other hand, have you experienced the communication flair of a teacher, boss, or coach who "painted a picture in words" that both inspired you and clarified how to achieve an objective?

Leadership means communicating with others in such a way that they are influenced and motivated to perform actions that further common goals and lead toward desired outcomes. **Communication** is a process by which information and understanding are transferred between a sender and a receiver, such as between a leader and an employee, an instructor and a student, or a coach and a football player. Exhibit 9.1 shows the key elements of the communication process. The sender (such as a leader) initiates a communication by *encoding* a thought or idea, that is, by selecting symbols (such as words) with which to compose and transmit a message. The message is the tangible formulation of the thought or idea sent to the receiver, and the *channel* is the medium by which the message is sent. The channel could be a formal report, a blog, a telephone call, an e-mail or text message, or a face-to-face conversation. The receiver *decodes* the symbols to interpret the meaning of the message. Encoding and decoding can sometimes cause communication errors because individual differences, knowledge, values, attitudes, and background act as filters and may create "noise" when translating from symbols to meaning. People can easily misinterpret messages. *Feedback* is the element of the communication process that enables someone to determine whether the receiver correctly interpreted the message. Feedback occurs when a receiver responds to a leader's communication with a return message. Without feedback, the communication cycle is incomplete.

Communication
a process by which information and understanding are transferred between a sender and a receiver

EXHIBIT 9.1 A Circular Model of Interpersonal Communication

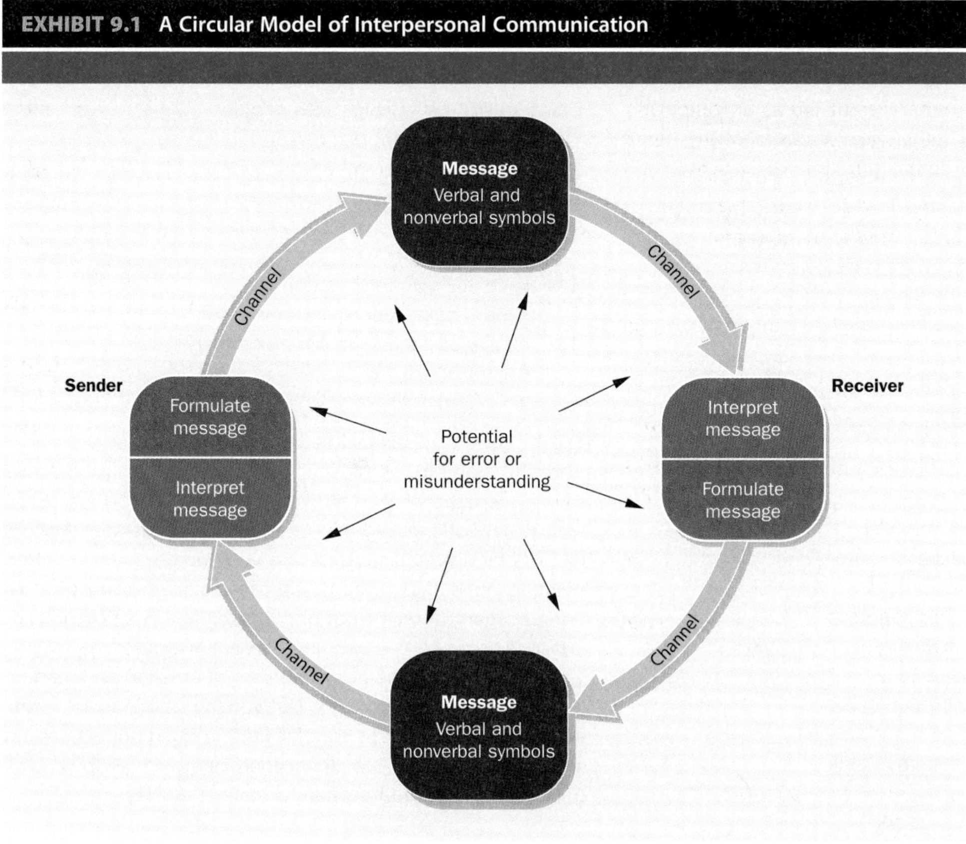

Sources: Based on Gabriela Moise, "Communication Models Used in the Online Learning Environment," *The 3rd International Conference on Virtual Learning* 2008, ICVL (http://www.icvl.edu/2008), pp 247–254; and Wilbur Schramm, *The Process and Effects of Mass Communication*, 6th ed. (Urbana, IL: University of Illinois Press, 1965).

Effective communication involves both the transference and the mutual understanding of information.[4] As illustrated in Exhibit 9.1, the nature of effective communication is cyclical, in that a sender and receiver may exchange messages several times to achieve a mutual understanding. The ongoing process of sending, receiving, and feedback to test understanding underlies both management and leadership communication.

9-1a Management Communication

The traditional role of a manager is that of an "information processor." Managers spend some 80 percent of each working day in communication with others.[5] In other words, 48 minutes of every hour are spent in meetings, on the telephone, or talking informally with others. Managers scan their environments for important written and personal information, gathering facts, data, and ideas, which in turn are sent to subordinates and others who can use them. A manager then receives subordinate messages and feedback to check understanding and determine whether to modify messages for accuracy.

Managers have a huge communication responsibility in directing and controlling an organization. They communicate facts, statistics, and decisions. Effective managers establish themselves at the center of information networks to facilitate the completion of tasks. Leadership communication, however, serves a different purpose.

NEW LEADER
ACTION MEMO

Networking is a vital part of leadership information sharing. Answer the questions in Leader's Self-Insight 9.1 to learn whether you network with other people like successful leaders do.

LEADER'S SELF-INSIGHT 9.1

Am I Networked?

Instructions: Think about your current life as an employee or as a student. Indicate whether each of the following items is Mostly False or Mostly True for you.

	Mostly False	**Mostly True**
1. I learn early on about changes going on in the organization that might affect me or my job.		✓
2. I have a clear belief about the positive value of active networking.		✓
3. I am good at staying in touch with others.		✓
4. I network as much to help other people solve problems as to help myself.		✓
5. I am fascinated by other people and what they do.		✓
6. I frequently use lunches to meet and network with new people.		✓
7. I regularly participate in charitable causes.	✓	
8. I maintain a list of friends and colleagues to whom I send holiday cards.		✓
9. I build relationships with people of different gender, race, and nationality than myself.		✓
10. I maintain contact with people from previous organizations and school groups.		✓
11. I actively give information to subordinates, peers, and my boss.		✓
12. I know and talk with peers in other organizations.		✓

Scoring and Interpretation

Add the number of Mostly True answers for your score: 11. A score of 9 or above indicates that you are excellent at networking and can be a networking leader. A score of 3 or below would suggest that you need to focus more on building networks, perhaps work in a slow-moving occupation or organization, or not put yourself in a position of leadership. A score of 4—8 would be about average.

Networking is the active process of building and managing productive relationships. Networking builds social, work, and career relationships that facilitate mutual understanding and mutual benefit. Leaders accomplish much of their work through networks rather than formal hierarchies.

Source: The ideas for this self-insight questionnaire were drawn primarily from Wayne E. Baker, *Networking Smart: How to Build Relationships for Personal and Organizational Success* (New York: McGraw-Hill, 1994).

9-1b The Leader as Communication Champion

Communication champion
a person who is philosophically grounded in the belief that communication is essential to building trust and gaining commitment to a vision

Embeddedness
when people throughout the organization are united around a common purpose based on a deep understanding and acceptance of the vision and strategy

Sensegiving
the process of influencing how others make sense of the organization, where they fit within it, and the larger purpose of their work

Although leadership communication also includes the components of sending, receiving, and feedback, it is different from management communication. Leaders often communicate the big picture—the vision, as defined in Chapter 1—rather than facts and pieces of information. A leader can be seen as a communication champion.[6]

A **communication champion** is philosophically grounded in the belief that communication is essential to building trust and gaining commitment to the vision and strategy. Leaders use communication to unite people around a common sense of purpose and identity and to ensure that the vision and strategy are deeply understood and accepted by employees. This deep understanding and acceptance of organizational direction and purpose is referred to as **embeddedness**.[7] When the vision and strategy are embedded, everyone's daily decisions and actions help move the firm in the right direction, toward achieving important goals. In many of today's organizations, command-and-control management is counterproductive. People cannot simply be told what to do. They need to understand and accept the vision and strategy so they can align their actions to support the organization's competitive intentions.

Leadership communication also shapes how people think about their work and the organization. Leaders are *sensegivers*. **Sensegiving** refers to the process of influencing how others construct meaning and make sense of the organization and their place in it.[8] Good leaders not only use communication to inspire people with a vision and instill the values that are necessary for achieving it, they also communicate to help people understand the larger purpose of their own work (find meaning) and see how they fit into the organization. Communication champions visibly and symbolically engage in communication-based activities. Whether they walk around asking questions or thoughtfully listen to a subordinate's ideas or problems, the everyday actions of communication champions convey a deep commitment to communication and sensegiving. Communication isn't just about occasional meetings, formal speeches, or presentations. Leaders actively communicate through both words and actions every day. Regular communication is essential for building personal relationships and binding people together to accomplish the vision and purpose. This chapter's *Consider This* highlights the importance of leaders taking a positive approach to communicating.

NEW LEADER
ACTION MEMO

As a leader, you can be a communication champion and a sensegiver. You can use verbal, nonverbal, and symbolic communication to unite people around a common vision, facilitate strategic conversations, and build trust.

Exhibit 9.2 shows the leader-as-communication-champion model. By establishing an open communication climate, asking questions, actively listening to others, applying the practice of dialogue, using candor, and telling stories, leaders facilitate and support *strategic conversations* that help move the organization forward. Leader communication is *purpose-directed* in that it directs everyone's attention toward the vision, values, and desired outcomes of the group or organization and persuades people to act in a way to help achieve the vision.

Consider **This!**

Communication Starts in the Mind and the Heart

The thought manifests as the word,
The word manifests as the deed,
The deed develops into habit,
And the habit hardens into character.
So watch the thought and its way with care,
And let it spring from love
Born out of concern for all things.

The words above echo what the Buddha said more than 2,500 years ago: "We are what we think. All that we are arises with our thoughts. With our thoughts we make the world." The truth of this verse is timeless: it is truth whether for the past, the present, or the future.

Source: K. Sri Dhammananda, *How to Live Without Fear and Worry* (Kuala Lumpur, Malaysia: BMS Publications, 1989), p. 192.

Leaders use many communication methods, including selecting rich channels of communication and using nonverbal communication. Leaders often use symbolic language and behavior to get their messages across and to influence others. For example, President Ronald Reagan was known as a great communicator. In communicating his message about the federal budget, Reagan spoke of a trillion dollars in terms of stacking it next to the Empire State Building. Framed this way, the message redefined the meaning of a trillion dollars and took on a new reality for the public.

EXHIBIT 9.2 The Leader as Communication Champion

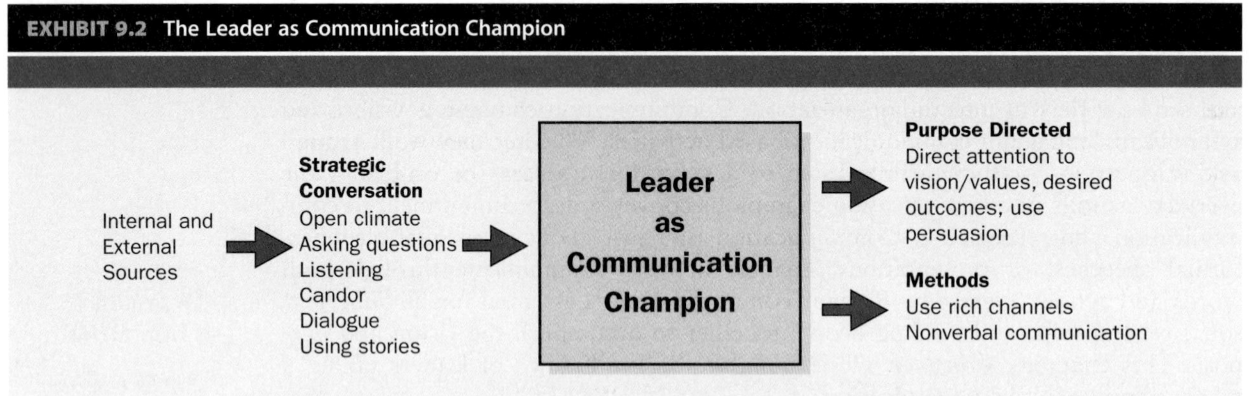

9-2 LEADING STRATEGIC CONVERSATIONS

A **strategic conversation** refers to people talking across boundaries and hierarchical levels about the group or organization's vision, critical strategic themes, and the values that can help achieve desired outcomes. Leaders facilitate strategic conversations by (1) asking questions and actively listening to others to understand their attitudes and values, needs, personal goals, and desires; (2) setting the agenda for conversation by underscoring the key strategic themes that are linked to organizational success; and (3) selecting the right communication channels and facilitating dialogue.[9] An example of strategic conversation comes from the U.S. military, which received strong criticism both at home and abroad when the Department of Defense announced the establishment of the United States Africa Command (USAFRICOM).

Strategic conversation communication that takes place across boundaries and hierarchical levels about the group or organization's vision, critical strategic themes, and values that can help achieve desired outcomes

IN THE LEAD

United States Africa Command (USAFRICOM)

When the U.S. Department of Defense announced the establishment of USAFRICOM as a Geographic Combatant Command (GCC) that would assume responsibility over Department of Defense activities on the continent of Africa, most leaders knew it could provoke suspicions and misunderstandings.

It was a seemingly simple reorganization, as these responsibilities had previously been divided among other GCCs. The first commander and other leaders of USAFRICOM were firmly committed to the reorganization as a positive step, but they needed everyone involved to see things that way as well. They implemented a comprehensive communications plan that facilitated a strategic conversation among everyone involved—a wide range of participants from across the United States, Africa, Europe, and the broader international community. Leaders deliberately developed a set of simple, consistent messages in response to a set of questions they asked themselves about the mission, purpose, and nature of USAFRICOM.

They also asked questions of stakeholders, particularly their African partners, whom they considered the most important stakeholder group. The approach "was to give them the voice that they wanted and to know that we were there to listen and understand." The goal was to support, rather than undermine, "African solutions for African problems." Rather than offering specific services or describing what they thought Africa should look like in the future, leaders sought to learn their partners' priorities and strategies. Emphasis throughout the early communications strategy was on openness, transparency, candor, and inclusivity. Leaders created a unifying theme of *building the team* and developed messages that illustrated USAFRICOM as a "listening and learning organization."[10]

Although there remain detractors and critics, USAFRICOM continues to stress openness and transparency and encourages people to check out its work at http://www.africom.mil. In other words, the strategic conversation continues. This example illustrates the six key components for facilitating strategic conversations: an open communication climate, asking questions, active listening, dialogue, candor, and using stories for communication. These six elements are described in the following sections.

9-2a Creating an Open Communication Climate

Open communication means sharing all types of information throughout the organization, especially across functional and hierarchical boundaries. Open communication runs counter to the traditional flow of selective information downward from supervisors to subordinates. Good leaders want communication to flow in all directions. Communication across traditional boundaries enables leaders to hear what followers have to say, which means the organization gains the benefit of all employees' minds. The same perspectives batted back and forth between top executives don't lead to effective change, the creation of a powerful shared vision, or the network of personal relationships that keeps organizations thriving. New voices and continuous conversation involving a broad spectrum of people revitalize and enhance communication.[11]

To build an open communication climate, leaders break down conventional hierarchical and departmental boundaries that may be barriers to communication, enabling them to convey a stronger awareness of and commitment to organizational vision, goals, and values. In an open climate, a leader's communication of the vision "cascades" through an organization, as explained in Exhibit 9.3. People throughout the organization thus have a clear direction and an understanding of how they can contribute.[12] An open communication climate helps alleviate tension and conflict between departments, builds trust, reaffirms employee commitment to a shared vision, and makes a company more competitive.

NEW LEADER
ACTION MEMO

As a leader, you can create an open communication climate by sharing both good and bad information, and you can facilitate communication across groups, departments, and hierarchical levels.

9-2b Asking Questions

Managers typically think they should be the people with the right answers. Leadership, though, is more about being the person with the right *questions*.[13] Many leaders—indeed, most people in general—are unaware of the amazing power of questions. In our society, we're conditioned to come up with answers. Very young children are

Open communication leaders sharing all types of information throughout the company and across all levels

EXHIBIT 9.3 Why Open the Communication Climate?

An open climate is essential for cascading vision, and cascading is essential because:

Natural Law 1: You Get What You Talk About

A vision must have ample "air time" in an organization. A vision must be shared and practiced by leaders at every opportunity.

Natural Law 2: The Climate of an Organization Is a Reflection of the Leader

A leader who doesn't embody the vision and values doesn't have an organization that does.

Natural Law 3: You Can't Walk Faster Than One Step at a Time

A vision is neither understood nor accepted overnight. Communicating the vision must be built into continuous, daily interaction so that over time followers will internalize it.

Source: Based on Bob Wall, Robert S. Slocum, and Mark R. Sobol, *Visionary Leader* (Rocklin, CA: Prima Publishing, 1992), pp. 87–89.

typically full of questions, but from an early age they're discouraged from asking them. Students are expected to hold up their hands in class to give the right answer, and they're often chastised for an incorrect response. Leaders often assume that if someone comes to them with a problem, their job is to solve it with the correct answer. They mistakenly fear that not having an answer means followers will lose respect for them.

What Questions Do Leaders Ask? One purpose of questioning is *leader-centered*, in that it seeks to inform the leader about what is going on in the organization; investigate specific issues, problems, or opportunities; and gather information, ideas, or insights. This type of questioning is important because it helps leaders tap into the expertise and ideas of followers. With advances in technology and communications, no one person can master all the data and information needed to meet the challenges most organizations face. Even in 1928, when Paul Galvin founded Motorola, he recognized the value of this type of questioning. His son Bob Galvin said his father learned about what was happening in the business in the company cafeteria. "He would always make a point of eating with employees at lunchtime," Galvin said. "He'd ask them lots of questions about operations, customers, and how to improve quality."[14]

Leaders also use questions for another purpose. This approach is *follower-centered*, in that it seeks to connect with followers, develop new insights, encourage critical thinking, expand people's awareness, and stimulate learning. One study found that 99 percent of top managers surveyed believe that critical thinking skills at all levels are crucial to the success of their organizations.[15]

Benefits of Asking Questions Asking the right kinds of questions benefits both leaders and followers in many ways.[16] Questions encourage people to think and empower them to find answers, helping to build positive attitudes and follower self-confidence. Asking questions rather than giving answers provokes critical thought and leads to deeper, more lasting learning. In addition, asking questions shows that leaders care about people on an individual basis, value the opinions and knowledge of others, are open to new ideas, and have faith that people want to contribute to the organization, which helps to build trusting, respectful relationships.[17] People want their leaders to recognize them as individuals and let them be part of something meaningful. Jonathan Kraft, president of the New England Patriots football team, says he and his father, team chairman Robert Kraft, have only one role: "We ask questions just as any manager would, to spur the thinking." Other than that important job, the Krafts leave the Patriots to the leadership of Coach Bill Belichick, personnel head Nick Caserio, and other team leaders.[18]

9-2c Listening

Just as important as asking questions is listening to the responses. A survey of 800 employees across a variety of industries found that about two-thirds of respondents felt that their opinion was either unwelcome or not valued at work.[19] An open communication climate is not possible if leaders aren't listening. When leaders fail to listen to employees, it sends the signal, "you don't matter," which decreases commitment and motivation. People are willing to share their ideas, suggestions, and problems when they think someone is listening and genuinely values what they have to say.

Listening
the skill of grasping and interpreting a message's genuine meaning

Hearing is easy, but really listening is hard.[20] **Listening** involves the skill of grasping and interpreting a message's genuine meaning. Remember that message reception is a vital link in the communication process. However, many leaders take listening for granted and focus their time and energy on learning how to verbalize and present their own ideas more effectively. When talking with someone, they concentrate on formulating what they're going to say next rather than on what is being said to them. Fortunately, leaders can develop their listening just as they can any other skill.[21]

What constitutes good listening? Exhibit 9.4 gives 10 keys to effective listening and illustrates a number of ways to distinguish a bad listener from a good one. A key to effective listening is focus. A good listener's total attention is focused on the message; he isn't thinking about an unrelated problem in the purchasing department, how much work is piled up on his desk, or what to have for lunch. A good listener also listens actively, keeps an open mind, works hard at listening, and uses thought speed to mentally summarize, weigh, and anticipate what the speaker says.

Effective listening is engaged listening. Good leaders get out of their offices and mingle with others, ask questions, set up listening forums where people can say whatever is on their minds, and provide feedback to let people know they have been heard.[22] Active listening is a daily, ongoing, and vital part of every leader's job. Kevin Sharer, former CEO of Amgen, admits that he was a terrible listener for much of his career. Then he realized that being a good leader is less about convincing others of your point of view and more about respecting and getting the best out of people—and that requires really listening to them. Sharer began regularly visiting

NEW LEADER
ACTION MEMO

Evaluate your skills for listening and asking questions by completing the questionnaire in Leader's Self-Insight 9.2.

NEW LEADER
ACTION MEMO

As a leader, you can learn to be a better listener. You can focus your total attention on what the other person is saying and work hard to listen—use eye contact, ask questions and paraphrase the message, and offer positive feedback.

EXHIBIT 9.4 Ten Keys to Effective Listening

	Key	Poor Listener	Good Listener
1.	Listen actively	Minimally involved, unfocused	Shows interest; nods, asks questions, paraphrases what is said
2.	Keep an open mind	Pays attention only to ideas that conform to own opinions	Looks for opportunities and new learning
3.	Resist distractions	Is easily distracted	Fights distractions; tolerates bad habits; knows how to concentrate
4.	Capitalize on the fact that thought is faster than speech	Tends to daydream with slow speakers	Challenges, anticipates, summarizes; listens between lines to tone of voice
5.	Seek understanding	Feigns agreement to bring the conversation to an end	Searches for common ground and new understanding
6.	Judge content, not delivery	Tunes out if delivery is poor	Judges content; skips over delivery errors
7.	Hold one's fire	Spouts solutions before understanding the problem or question	Does not judge or respond until comprehension is complete
8.	Listen for ideas	Listens for facts	Listens to central themes
9.	Work at listening	No energy output; passive and laid back	Works hard; exhibits active body state, eye contact
10.	Show respect	Interrupts; talks over the other person when trying to get a point across	Learns to keep quiet and let the other person do most of the talking

Sources: Based on "A Field Guide to Identifying Bad Listeners," *McKinsey Quarterly*, Issue 2 (2012), p. 112; Bernard T. Ferrari, "The Executive's Guide to Better Listening," *McKinsey Quarterly*, Issue 2 (2012), pp. 50–60; Philip Morgan and Kent Baker, "Building a Professional Image: Improving Listening Behavior," *Supervisory Management* (November 1985), pp. 34–38; and Sherman K. Okun, "How to Be a Better Listener," *Nation's Business* (August 1975), p. 62.

LEADER'S SELF-INSIGHT 9.2

Listening and Asking Questions

Instructions: Think about how you communicate during a typical day at school or work. Respond to the following statements based on whether they are Mostly False or Mostly True for you. There are no right or wrong answers, so answer honestly.

	Mostly False	Mostly True
1. I am extremely attentive to what others say.	____	✓
2. I deliberately show people that I am listening to them.	____	✓
3. I really enjoy listening very carefully to people.	____	✓
4. My mind does not wander when someone is talking.	____	✓
5. I often restate what the person said and ask if I got it right.	____	✓
6. I usually think about a response while a person is still talking.	[scribbled mark]	✓
7. I often ask people to clarify what they mean.	____	✓
8. I ask questions in every conversation.	____	✓
9. I am genuinely curious in conversations about what other people think.	____	✓
10. During a conversation, I frequently probe for deeper information.	____	✓
11. I inquire about others' points of view on topics.	____	✓
12. I don't hesitate to ask what may appear to be dumb questions.	✓	[scribbled mark]

Scoring and Interpretation

Compute two scores from your answers and insert them below. For your listening score, sum 1 point for each Mostly True answer for items 1–5 and for a Mostly False answer to item 6. For your asking questions score, sum 1 point for each Mostly True answer to items 7–11. Insert your two scores below.

Listening score __5__. Asking Questions score __5__.

Your first score reflects your listening habits. Managers face many distractions, which makes it hard to pay attention when someone is speaking. Listening attentively can prevent many communication mistakes. Your second score reflects your habit of inquiry, which means asking questions to learn more about something or to confirm your understanding. Asking questions is an important part of an effective leader's communication repertoire, as described in the text. Scores of 5–6 reflect excellent communication habits. Scores of 0–2 suggest that you may need to work on your communication practices. Scores of 3–4 imply that you are doing okay but have room for improvement.

Source: Partially based on William B. Snavely and John D. McNeill, "Communicator Style and Social Style: Testing a Theoretical Interface," *Journal of Leadership and Organizational Studies* 14, no. 1 (February 2008), pp. 219–232.

NEW LEADER
ACTION MEMO

As a leader, you can use dialogue to help people create a shared sense of meaning and purpose. You can enable people to express their hopes and fears, suspend their convictions and explore assumptions, and become motivated to search for common ground.

and genuinely listening to people throughout the company. He admits it wasn't easy. "You have to change," he says, "and you have to *want* to change.... There has to be a certain humility to listen well."[23]

9-2d Dialogue

In most organizations, there are some issues that are characterized by strong emotions and extreme uncertainty and that can't be resolved by resorting to facts and logic. With these so-called *hot topics*, the stakes for those involved are high. When hot topics involve whole groups of employees, a type of communication referred to as dialogue can help.

Dialogue
active sharing and listening in which people explore common ground and grow to understand each other and share a world view

The "roots of dialogue" are *dia* and *logos*, which can be thought of as a *stream of meaning*. In **dialogue**, people together create a stream of shared meaning that enables them to understand each other and share a view of the world.[24] People may start out as polar opposites, but by actively listening and talking authentically to one another, they discover their common ground, common issues, and common dreams on which they can build a better future. Most of us have a tendency to infuse everything we hear with our own opinions rather than being genuinely open to what others are saying. In addition, traditional business values in the United States and most other Western countries reward people for forcefully asserting their own ideas and opinions and trying to discredit or contradict others.[25] But people can engage in dialogue only when they come to a conversation free of prejudgments, personal agendas, and "right" answers. Participants in a dialogue do not presume to know the outcome, nor do they sell their convictions.

One way to understand the distinctive quality of dialogue is to contrast it with discussion.[26] Exhibit 9.5 illustrates the differences between a dialogue and a discussion. Typically, the intent of a discussion is to present one's own point of view and persuade others in the group to adopt it. A discussion is often resolved by logic or by "beating down" opposing viewpoints. Dialogue, on the other hand, requires that participants suspend their attachments to a particular point of view so that a deeper

EXHIBIT 9.5 Dialogue and Discussion: The Differences

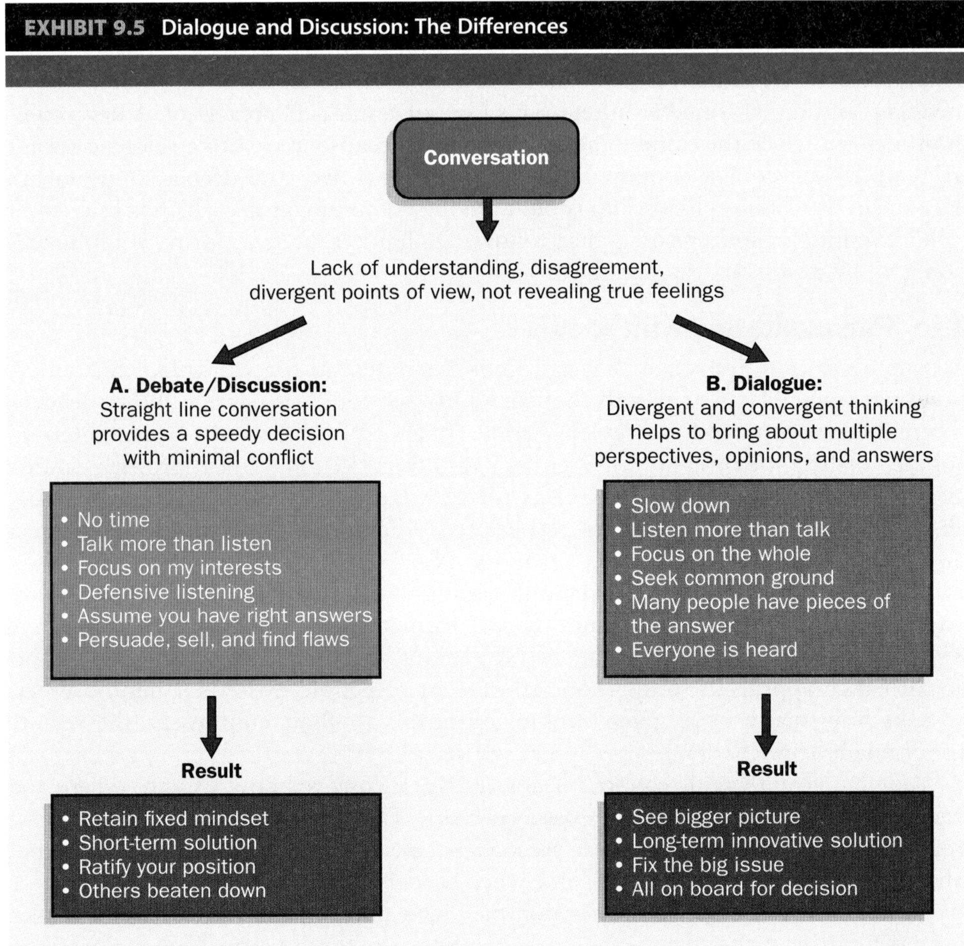

Sources: Based on Edgar Schein, "On Dialogue, Culture, and Organizational Learning," *Organizational Dynamics* 22, no. 2 (Fall 1993), pp. 40–51; Deborah L. Flick, *From Debate to Dialogue: Using the Understanding Process to Transform Our Conversations* (Boulder, CO: Orchid Publications, 1998), p. 22; and Glenna Gerard and Linda Teurfs, "Dialogue and Organizational Transformation," in *Community Building: Renewing Spirit and Learning in Business*, Kazimierz Gozdz, ed. (Pleasanton, CA: New Leaders Press, 1995).

level of listening, synthesis, and meaning can emerge from the group. A dialogue's focus is to reveal feelings and build common ground, with the emphasis on inquiry rather than advocacy.

Dialogue is particularly useful for conversations about hot topics. One example of using dialogue for hot topics occurred at NECX, an online marketplace that was acquired by Converge. Henry Bertolon, cofounder and CEO, introduced dialogue to improve communication after a period of rapid growth led to internal tensions. "We'd have meetings that just melted down," he says. "Everyone would scream at each other and then leave." Bertolon hired Wil Calmas, a psychologist with an MBA, to lead a series of programs to get people talking—and listening—to one another on a deeper, authentic level. People were encouraged to express fear, hostility, frustration, and secret wishes—whatever feelings were affecting their lives and work. The dialogue sessions created a safe environment for people to reveal their feelings, explore ideas, and build common ground. Bertolon also believed it helped employees be loose, flexible, and open to new ideas—ready to respond to the rapid changes taking place all around them.[27]

Both forms of communication, dialogue and discussion, can result in organizational change. However, the result of a discussion is limited to a specific topic being deliberated, whereas the result of dialogue is characterized by group unity, shared meaning, and transformed mindsets. This kind of result is far-reaching. A new, common mindset is not the same thing as agreement because it creates a reference point from which subsequent communication can start. As new and deeper solutions are developed, a trusting relationship is built among communicators, which is important to all communication episodes that follow. Dialogue thus transforms communication and, by extension, the organization.

9-2e Communicating with Candor

A communication approach that can limit the potential for workplace misunderstandings, incivility, and ill will that turn into hot topics is candor. When leaders communicate with candor, they encourage others to do the same. **Candor** refers to honest, forthright expression of a leader's thinking.[28] Communicating with candor means being direct, honest, and clear about what followers need to do to meet objectives, while also expressing respect for others and not making people feel slighted, controlled, or exploited. Candor is extremely important when dealing with hot topics. Unfortunately, communicating with candor is a problem for many leaders. Jack Welch, speaker, author, and former CEO of General Electric, says when he asks groups of managers how many of them have received candid performance appraisals, only about 10 percent of people raise their hands. When he asks how many have given candid appraisals to their employees, the results aren't much better.[29]

Communicating with candor means letting followers know exactly where the leader stands and what the leader expects of them. The appropriate use of candid communication acknowledges the other person's perspective and opinion, yet is very specific about what the leader wants and why. Leaders who communicate with candor keep the focus on the specific perception they have and the effect it has on the leader and organization rather than accusing or blaming the other person. They stick to facts rather than judgments and are very clear about what they want from followers.[30]

In an organization where candid communication is the norm, everything works faster and better.[31] The Seattle Seahawks football team provides a good illustration of the power of candid communication.

NEW LEADER
ACTION MEMO

Complete the questions in Leader's Self-Insight 9.3 to learn how effective you are at communicating with candor.

Candor
honest, forthright expression of a leader's thinking

LEADER'S SELF-INSIGHT 9.3

Do You Speak with Candor?

Instructions: Respond to the following statements based on how you speak to others during personal or work conversations. Answer whether each statement is Mostly True or Mostly False for you. There are no right or wrong answers, so answer honestly.

	Mostly False	Mostly True
1. I say exactly what I think to people.	_____	✓
2. I never hesitate to hurt people's feelings by telling the truth.	_____	✓
3. I like to be strictly candid about what I say.	_____	✓
4. I am very straightforward when giving feedback.	_____	✓
5. I present evidence for my opinions.	_____	✓
6. I am an extremely frank communicator.	_____	✓

Scoring and Interpretation

Give yourself one point for each Mostly True answer and write your score below.

Candor Score 6.

Your score reflects the level of candor with which you communicate. Many people have a hard time giving straightforward opinions and frank feedback because they don't want to hurt a person's feelings nor do they want people to dislike them. Hence the sharing of honest observations is limited. A score of 5–6 on this scale reflects a habit of candor, which will add to your leadership effectiveness. A score of 3–4 means that you do reasonably well at saying what you think. A score of 0–2 means you may have a hard time speaking straight, and you may want to practice to improve your candor.

IN THE LEAD

Seattle Seahawks

The Seattle Seahawks are known for having one of the best defenses in NFL football. Having talented players is only part of the formula. Another big reason the Seahawks are so good is the unusual degree of open and honest communication.

Earl Thomas, the team's star safety, says there are a lot of "hard talks," his term for candid conversations. Because of the blunt honesty players display with one another, a *Wall Street Journal* reporter said the Seahawks have "perhaps the most emotionally healthy locker room in the NFL." It's an intentional strategy by coach Pete Carroll and general manager John Schneider. With the Seahawks, whoever sees a mistake or a problem says something about it. Players admit the brutal frankness can sometimes be difficult, but in the long run they say it helps them be better on and off the field. Many also prefer not having to worry about where they stand. "It lets you be at peace," one player said. "You are never worried about what guys are thinking about."[32]

When everyone feels free to open up and speak frankly, more people get involved in organizational conversations so ideas get debated, adapted, and acted upon more quickly. "It's like being in a good marriage," said Seahawks defensive end Michael Bennett. "We're continuously learning about each other every day."

Candid communication also limits common problems such as meaningless meetings, rancorous silence, or ineffective teamwork in other types of organizations. At Taunton Press, a special-interest publishing company, the lack of candor led to endless meetings and decreased productivity. In a small, close-knit company like Taunton, people naturally don't want to offend one another. Yet over time the culture of "terminal niceness" that evolved sabotaged teamwork. Executives hired consultants from Fierce Inc. to help Taunton leaders and employees see that healthy relationships include both confrontation and appreciation. "In an honest and authentic relationship, one must communicate truthfully, and in a collaborative relationship, one must ask candid questions," says Halley Bock, former president and CEO of Fierce. Over time, Taunton transformed to a culture of candor, collaboration, and accountability.[33]

9-2f The Power of Stories

Native American tribes often made the best storytellers their tribal leaders.[34] That's because stories can have tremendous influence on people's beliefs, attitudes, and behaviors. Recall the earlier discussion of leaders as *sensegivers*. Telling stories is the foundation of sensegiving. Storytelling goes hand in hand with listening. Leaders listen to the stories of employees, customers, and others and tap into clues about how to construct their own stories to unite people with purpose and meaning. Stories can help people make sense of complex situations, bind them together in a shared purpose, inspire action, and bring about change in a way that other forms of communication cannot.

Evidence for the compatibility of stories with human thinking was demonstrated by a study at the Stanford Business School.[35] The goal was to convince MBA students that a company practiced a "no-layoffs" policy. Some students were told only a story related to the company's commitment to avoiding layoffs. A second group was given statistical data showing little turnover compared to competitors. Another group was shown the company's policy statement. A fourth group was provided with statistics and a story combined. Of all these approaches, the students presented with the story alone were most convinced that the company practiced a no-layoffs policy. This is a powerful lesson for leaders. To influence people, it is important to win their hearts, and stories are the best way to do that. Leaders who incorporate imagery and elements of story in their everyday language have a more powerful and lasting influence than those who simply marshal facts and figures to support their point.

NEW LEADER
ACTION MEMO

As a leader, use story and metaphor to help people connect emotionally with your message and the key values you want to instill.

Everyone can learn to use stories, and stories need not be long or carefully constructed to have an impact. A story can be a joke, a simple example illustrating an idea, a historical incident, something from a movie or television show, a personal experience, or something read on a blog or news page. The key point is that it should create an emotional context for getting the leader's message across.[36] One senior leader referred to Lewis and Clark's 1804–1806 expedition through 7,689 miles of uncharted territory to get people lined up in support of a new vision and strategy. Along the way, there would be "mountains," "rivers," and "friends and foes alike," he told them, but just like Lewis and Clark they could adapt to the many twists and turns of the journey. Using the image worked; the entire organization came to embrace the new vision, and people often refer back to the Lewis and Clark story to remember that they are on an adventurous journey.[37] Pulling together in the same direction is essential for change to happen, and people come together because of emotion, not logic.

"People are wired for telling and hearing stories," says Peter Guber, Hollywood film producer, CEO of Mandalay Entertainment Group, and author of *Tell to Win: Connect, Persuade, and Triumph with the Hidden Power of Story*, which is further described in this chapter's Leader's Bookshelf. "We need to plug into that and use it."[38]

LEADER'S BOOKSHELF

Tell to Win: Connect, Persuade, and Triumph with the Hidden Power of Story

by Peter Guber

Everybody in a leadership role shares the same problem, Peter Guber says in *Tell to Win*: "To succeed, you have to persuade others to support your vision, dream, or cause." Whatever the purpose of a leader communication—motivating employees, engaging customers, or organizing investors—leaders have to "get your listeners' attention, emotionalize your goal as theirs, and move them to act.... You have to reach their hearts as well as their minds." What's the best way to do that? With a story. For leaders, telling *purposeful stories* is an everyday requirement.

HOW TO TELL A PURPOSEFUL STORY

As an entrepreneur, media mogul, and producer of award-winning films including *Batman, Midnight Express, The Color Purple*, and *Rain Man*, Guber clearly knows a lot about telling a good story, but he emphasizes that you don't have to be a professional to tell a moving story. Guber gives some guidelines for what makes a successful leader story:

- ***It Has a Goal.*** Purposeful stories have a call to action. Leaders tell stories to achieve something. They are clear in their minds what they want followers to feel, think, and do because of the story. When Guber started as head of Sony Pictures Entertainment, he says the job of pulling together a disparate group of people spread across the country and overseas seemed insurmountable. He told the story from the film *Lawrence of Arabia*, where T.E. Lawrence pulls all the Arab tribal leaders together, to inspire employees to reclaim their heritage and pull together as "one tribe."
- ***It Is Authentic.*** The leader has to be motivated by the goal, or it will be impossible to motivate and inspire followers. Being personally connected to the story enables the teller to connect listeners to it. Good storytellers don't follow a script and don't always stay on point. They sometimes shift the story if needed to emotionally bond with the listener and get the point across.
- ***It Is Targeted to the Audience.*** Build your story about "what's in it for them." The leader has to know his or her "audience" (followers) to incorporate their interests into the story. By demonstrating that you are interested in what concerns followers, you change passive listeners into active participants in the story.

WHY IS STORYTELLING SO IMPORTANT?

Without stories, leaders have only "transactional elements and no relationship" with followers, says Guber. In *Tell to Win*, Guber uses not only his own experiences but those of more than 90 other leaders, including famed basketball coach and motivational speaker Pat Riley, Chad Hurley, cofounder and CEO of YouTube, and former U.S. president Bill Clinton, who have used purposeful stories to drive their success. Reading about how these leaders use stories gives a clear sense that a good story can be very simple and can come from anywhere. As Guber says, "Anyone can do it, and everyone does do it!" The key for leaders is to do it *purposefully*.

Source: *Connect to Win*, by Peter Guber, is published by Crown Business.

9-3 COMMUNICATING TO PERSUADE AND INFLUENCE

Stories are particularly useful tools for persuading and influencing people. Leaders don't communicate just to convey information. They use communication skills to sell others on the vision and influence them to behave in ways that achieve goals and help accomplish the vision.

The ability to persuade others is more critical today than ever before. The command-and-control mindset of managers telling people what to do and how to do it is gone. Employees don't just want to know *what* they should do but *why* they should do it. In addition, with new collaborative ways of working, many leaders are involved in situations where lines of authority are blurred. Companies such as Union Bank of California, Gerdau Ameristeel, and IBM are adding training programs that help people learn how to lead by influence rather than command.[39] Leaders can follow four steps to practice the art of persuasion:[40]

1. *Listen first.* A study published in the *Journal of Research in Personality* shows that when people feel that they have been listened to by someone trying to influence them, their liking of, trust in, and commitment to that person increases.[41]

Good leaders know that being attentive to others' needs and emotions is the first step toward influencing them. They realize that most people can't hear what you have to say until they have the chance to say what is on their minds. Leaders ask questions and listen actively and supportively to build rapport, find common ground, and get a grasp on how followers may react to their ideas and proposals.[42]

2. *Establish credibility*. A leader's credibility is based on the leader's knowledge and expertise as well as his or her relationships with others. When leaders have demonstrated that they make well-informed, sound decisions, followers have confidence in their expertise. Leaders also build credibility by listening to others, establishing good relationships, and showing that they have others' best interests at heart.
3. *Build goals on common ground*. To be persuasive, leaders describe how what they're requesting will benefit others as well as the leader. For example, when David Zugheri wanted to switch to a primarily paperless system at First Houston Mortgage, he emphasized to employees that storing customer records electronically meant they could now work from home when they needed to care for a sick child, or take a vacation and still keep track of critical accounts. "I could literally see their attitudes change through their body language," Zugheri says.[43] When leaders can't find common advantages, it's a good signal that they need to adjust their goals and plans.
4. *Make your position compelling to others*. Leaders appeal to others on an emotional level by using symbols, metaphors, and stories to express their messages rather than relying on facts and figures alone. By tapping into the imaginations of their followers, leaders can inspire people to accomplish amazing results. At NGM Insurance Company, leaders in the claims unit picked up on a statement made by one of the company's independent agents to appeal to people's emotions and imaginations. When discussing how the claims unit should relate to customers, the agent said, "I want my customers to feel your arm go around them when they have a claim." Leaders used this evocative image to focus employees on reengineering the claims process to provide better, faster, more caring service.[44]

NEW LEADER
ACTION MEMO

As a leader, you can increase your influence by listening first to build trust and find common ground and by establishing your credibility based on knowledge and skills. You can show how your plans will benefit followers to gain their support.

Persuasion is a valuable communication process that individuals can use to lead others to a shared solution or commitment. To be persuasive and act as communication champions, leaders must communicate frequently and easily with others in the organization. Yet for some people, communication experiences are unrewarding, so they may consciously or unconsciously avoid situations where communication is required.[45] The term *communication apprehension* describes this avoidance behavior and is defined as "an individual's level of fear or anxiety associated with either real or anticipated communication with another person or persons."[46]

9-4 SELECTING THE CORRECT COMMUNICATION CHANNEL

One key to effective communication is selecting the right channel for relaying the message. A **channel** is a medium by which a communication message is carried from sender to receiver. A leader may discuss a problem face-to-face, use the telephone, write a memo or letter, use e-mail, send a text message, post a message on a blog or Web page, or put an item in a newsletter, depending on the nature of the message.

Channel
a medium by which a communication message is carried from sender to receiver

9-4a The Continuum of Channel Richness

Research has attempted to explain how leaders select communication channels to enhance communication effectiveness.[47] Studies have found that channels differ in their capacity to convey information. **Channel richness** is the amount of information that can be transmitted during a communication episode. The channels available to leaders can be classified into a hierarchy based on information richness, as illustrated in Exhibit 9.6.

The richness of an information channel is influenced by three characteristics: (1) the ability to handle multiple cues simultaneously; (2) the ability to facilitate rapid, two-way feedback; and (3) the ability to establish a personal focus for the communication. Face-to-face discussion is the richest medium because it permits direct experience, multiple information cues, immediate feedback, and personal focus. Face-to-face discussions facilitate the assimilation of broad cues and deep, emotional understanding of the situation. Tony Burns, former CEO of Ryder Systems, always preferred handling things face-to-face. "You can look someone in the eyes," he explains. "You can tell by the look in his eyes or the inflection of his voice what the real problem or question or answer is."[48] Telephone conversations are next in the richness hierarchy. Eye contact, gaze, posture, and other body language cues are missing, but the human voice still carries a tremendous amount of emotional information.

Electronic messaging through e-mail, text messages, and social media such as Twitter is increasingly being used for communications that were once handled over the telephone. Although these channels lack both visual and verbal cues, they allow for rapid feedback and can be personalized. Blogs provide a way to get information to a wide audience and also permit rapid feedback.[49]

Print media such as notes and letters can be personalized, but they convey only the cues written on paper and are slow to provide feedback. Impersonal written media, including fliers, bulletins, and standard computer reports, are the lowest in richness.

Channel richness
the amount of information that can be transmitted during a communication episode

EXHIBIT 9.6 A Continuum of Channel Richness

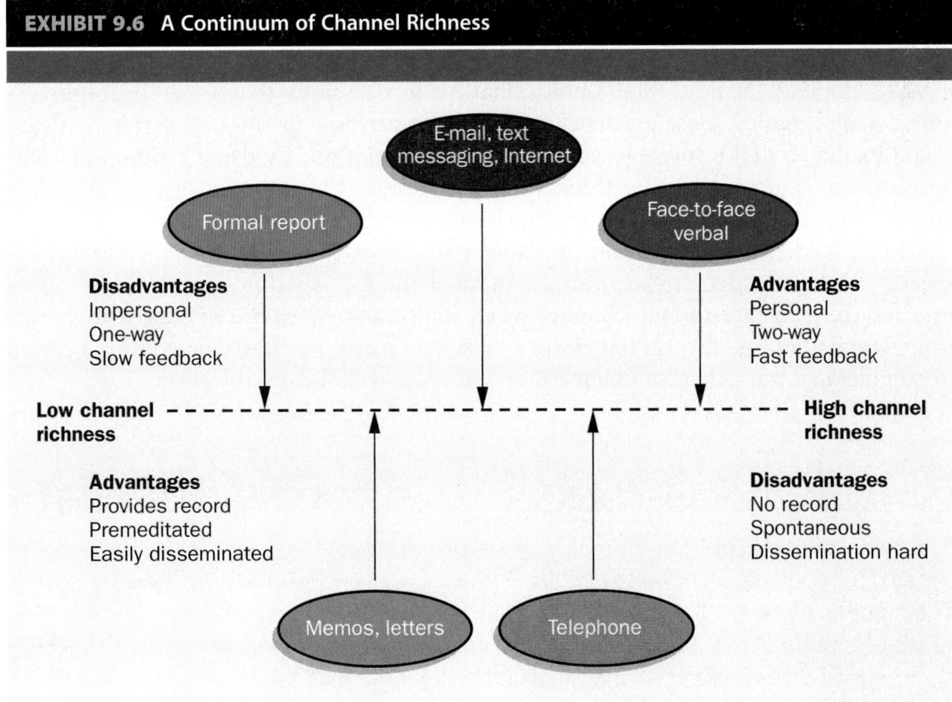

NEW LEADER
ACTION MEMO

As a leader, you can choose rich forms of communication, such as face-to-face or the telephone, when an issue is complex, emotionally charged, or especially important. For a routine, straightforward message, you can use a written or electronic form of communication.

"The more technologically advanced our society becomes, the more we need to go back to the basic fundamentals of human communication."

—Angela Ahrendts, senior vice president, retail and online stores at Apple Inc.

The channels are not focused on a single receiver, use limited information cues, and do not permit feedback.

Each communication channel has advantages and disadvantages, and each can be an effective means of communication in the appropriate circumstances.[50] Channel selection depends on whether the message is routine or nonroutine. Routine communications are simple and straightforward, such as a product price change. Routine messages convey data or statistics or simply put into words what people already understand and agree on. Routine messages can be efficiently communicated through a channel lower in richness. Written or electronic communications also are effective when the audience is widely dispersed or when the communication is "official" and a permanent record is required.[51] On the other hand, nonroutine messages typically concern issues of change, conflict, or complexity that have great potential for misunderstanding. Nonroutine messages often are characterized by time pressure and surprise. Leaders can communicate nonroutine messages effectively only by selecting a rich channel.

Leaders should select a channel to fit the message. Following layoffs, for example, people are fearful and worried about their own jobs. Many leaders, not knowing what to say, send out a written notice and hide in their offices. Good leaders, on the other hand, know face-to-face communication is the way to keep morale and productivity high. At one construction company that had to lay off employees, the CEO called employees together and told them how the mortgage crisis and downturn in the housing market was affecting their company. He acknowledged that he couldn't promise there wouldn't be more layoffs, but as he explained the situation the emotions in the room became calmer because people felt they knew what was going on.[52] Particularly in times of change, if people don't hear what's happening from leaders, they rely on rumors and will often assume the worst.[53]

When a message is highly important, leaders often use *redundant communication* by sending the same message using different channels. For example, one leader explained a request to an employee in person, then immediately composed a follow-up e-mail to the same employee that summarized the request in writing. For companywide changes, leaders might hold small group sessions to talk with employees about a new policy, post an article on the intranet and in the newsletter, and use social media to make sure everyone gets the information. By using redundant communication, saying the same thing more than once via multiple channels, leaders add weight to the message and keep the issue at the top of employees' minds.[54]

Most leader communication by its very nature is composed of nonroutine messages. Although leaders make good use of all channels, they don't let anything substitute for the rich face-to-face channel when important issues are at stake. However, some companies are also finding ways to use new forms of electronic communication to complement the richer, ongoing conversations across the organization.

IN THE LEAD

Earl's Restaurants Ltd.

Earl's, a Canadian-based chain of casual restaurants with as many as 8,000 workers at its seasonal peak, takes the engagement of its employees seriously—so seriously that it places more emphasis on that measurement than it does on sales figures. Leaders know happy and committed employees are what drive sales, after all. Earl's used to do an annual survey to make sure all employees felt that they had a chance to be heard, but new technology has given leaders an easier way to find out what people are thinking. Earl's now sends out short surveys at least every three months and people can say whatever they want, anonymously.

Using a software tool called Culture Amp, leaders can push short surveys to employees' mobile devices at any time. Being able to remain anonymous helps employees overcome their reluctance to vent about little things or to ask tough questions of leaders. The regular surveys also let people know that the company cares about what they're going through, because leaders follow up on the information they receive. Importantly, the technology seems to be spurring more face-to-face conversation too. Leaders say that since the company started using Culture Amp, employees seem to be talking more with their supervisors in person.[55]

Earl's uses electronic communication to supplement, not replace, a leader communication style that emphasizes listening to employees. Other companies are also finding anonymous electronic surveys a good way to give people a comfortable way to say what's on their minds.[56]

NEW LEADER
ACTION MEMO

As a leader, you can avoid letting electronic communications become a complete substitute for human interactions. You can resist the urge to criticize or complain in an electronic message, and never send an e-mail when you are angry or upset.

9-4b Effectively Using Electronic Communication Channels

Electronic communication has become a fact of life in today's organizations. New technologies provide highly efficient ways of communicating and can be particularly useful for routine messages. Text messaging, which allows people to share shorthand messages instantly, has rapidly grown in use and has become more common than e-mail in some organizations. Many of today's leaders also use blogs to keep in closer touch and rebuild trust among employees, customers, shareholders, and the public.

Electronic communication has many advantages, but there are disadvantages as well. The proliferation of electronic media has contributed to *poorer* communication in many organizations. Employees who work in offices down the hall from one another will often send an e-mail or text message rather than communicating face-to-face. One employee reported that he was fired via e-mail—by a manager who sat five feet away in the same office.[57] Even for less traumatic messages, electronic methods can increase the potential for communication errors. Leaders can come across as sounding cold, arrogant, or insensitive when they try to discuss delicate or complex issues via e-mail. Things that might be handled smoothly in a face-to-face conversation or over the phone turn into massive problems by fostering resentment, bitterness, and hard feelings.[58]

Another equally disturbing concern, one psychiatrist argues, is that the growing use of technology for communicating, particularly social media, has created hidden problems for both individuals and organizations by depriving people of the "human moments" that are needed to energize people, inspire creativity, and support emotional well-being.[59] People need to interact with others in physical space to build the connections that create great organizations. Electronic communication is here to stay, and the key for leaders is to benefit from the efficiencies of new technologies while preventing their unintended problems. Here are some tips for effectively using electronic communication:

- *Combine high-tech and high-touch.* Never allow electronic communication to take the place of human connections. People who work together should meet face-to-face on a regular basis, and leaders should get to know their followers in real as well as virtual space. Many companies that use virtual workers require that they come into the office at least once a month for unstructured face time.[60] A real-estate developer in Boston has a free-pizza day once a week when widely scattered workers can come by, sit around the table in his office, and just talk.[61]

- *Consider the circumstances.* People who know one another well and have worked together a long time can typically communicate about more complex issues via electronic means than can people who have a new working relationship.[62] When people have a long-term working relationship, there is less potential for misunderstandings and hard feelings. In addition, when all parties involved have a good grasp of the issues being discussed, electronic channels can be used effectively. A leader of a longstanding, well-functioning team could thus use e-mail more extensively than the leader of a team that has just been formed.
- *Think twice before you hit "Send."* Many people feel pressured to respond to electronic messages quickly, which can create unintended problems.[63] Citigroup recently sent a memo to all employees reminding them to "think before writing, read before sending."[64] Slow down and consider whether the message is something you want out there in cyberspace where anyone might read it. Never send an electronic message when you are angry or upset. Always read your messages at least twice.

Exhibit 9.7 lists some further dos and don'ts concerning subjects appropriate for electronic mail.

EXHIBIT 9.7 Dos and Don'ts of Electronic Mail

Do

- Use e-mail to set up meetings and send agenda materials, to recap spoken conversations, or to follow up on information already discussed face-to-face.
- Keep e-mail messages short and to the point. Many people read e-mail on handheld devices, which have small screens.
- Use e-mail to transmit standard reports.
- Act like a newspaper reporter. Use the subject line to grab the reader's attention and reflect what the message is about. Put the most important information in the first paragraph. Answer any questions—who, what, when, where, why, and how—that are pertinent.
- Consider making a quick phone call to clear up confusion rather than setting off a barrage of back-and-forth e-mail messages.

Don't

- Use e-mail to discuss something with a colleague who sits across the aisle or down the hall from you. Take the old-fashioned approach of speaking to each other.
- Say anything negative about a boss, friend, or colleague via e-mail. And don't forward the negative comments of others.
- Use e-mail to start or perpetuate a feud. If you get an e-mail that tempts you to respond in a scathing manner, stop yourself. You may be misinterpreting the message. Even if you're not, take the high road.
- Write anything in an e-mail you wouldn't want published in a newspaper. E-mail with sensitive or potentially embarrassing information has an uncanny way of leaking out.
- Begin responding to e-mail messages on your smartphone's tiny keyboard the minute you get out of a meeting. Get back to your office, laptop, or tablet, where you can craft a better response in less time.

Sources: Based on "15 Dos and Don'ts" box in Andrea C. Poe, "Don't Touch That 'Send' Button," *HR Magazine* (July 2001), pp. 74–80; Michael Goldberg, "The Essential Elements of E-Mail," *CIO* (June 1, 2003), p. 24; Mary Lynn Pulley and Jane Hilberry, *Get Smart! How E-Mail Can Make or Break Your Career and Your Organization* (Colorado Springs, CO: Get Smart! Publishing, 2007); and "The Management Tip: 3 Ways to Battle Email Overload," *Harvard Business Review* (January 17, 2013), http://hbr.org/tip/2013/01/17/2-ways-to-battle-email-overload (accessed April 29, 2013).

9-5 NONVERBAL COMMUNICATION

Leaders don't just communicate in words. Leaders are watched, and their appearance, behavior, actions, and attitudes are symbolic messages to others. Indeed, **nonverbal communication**, that is, messages transmitted through actions, behavior, facial expressions, and tone of voice, accounts for over one-half of the entire message received in a personal encounter.[65] Even the selection of a communication channel can convey a symbolic message. In other words, people attach meaning to the channel itself. Reports and memos typically convey formality and legitimize a message. Personal visits from a leader are interpreted as a sign of teamwork and caring.[66]

Many people don't realize that they are communicating all the time, without saying a word, by their facial expressions, body language, and actions.[67] Consider the manager who thought his new boss disliked him and didn't appreciate his hard work and commitment. "I see her talking to other managers, but she never talks to me," he told a friend, wondering if he should start looking for another job. When he finally asked his new boss what he could do to improve the relationship, the new leader was surprised. She told him that she considered him one of her most trusted managers and had been thankful to have one person she didn't have to watch over all the time. The new leader had been so busy that she didn't realize her nonverbal communication was sending an inaccurate message to a valued employee.[68]

Leaders strive to be aware of what they signal to others in addition to verbal messages. Research suggests that if there is a discrepancy between a person's verbal and nonverbal communication, the nonverbal is granted more weight by the interpreter.[69] Moreover, judgments based on nonverbal communication can occur at lightning speed. One study suggests that people form an opinion based on body language within 115 milliseconds![70] In interpreting a leader's nonverbal cues, followers determine the extent to which a leader's actions correspond with his or her verbal messages. If a leader talks about customer service but spends no time with customers, followers will likely place little value on service. If a leader talks about valuing employee feedback but stays in her office with the door closed most of the time, followers will doubt the sincerity of her words. One way leaders nonverbally communicate the value of feedback is by practicing *management by wandering around* (MBWA).[71] MBWA means that leaders leave their offices and speak directly to employees as they work. For example, Thomas Swidarski, former CEO of Diebold and current chairman and interim CEO of Bancsource Inc., is known to personally drop by employees' desks to ask about their work or see what's on their minds.[72] These impromptu encounters send symbolic positive messages to followers that leaders care about their ideas, opinions, and feelings.

NEW LEADER
ACTION MEMO

As a leader, you can symbolize important messages through your appearance, body language, facial expressions, and daily actions. You can be more effective by using management by wandering around. You can get out and mingle with followers and customers to learn about their ideas, problems, and needs through informal observation and conversation.

9-6 CURRENT COMMUNICATION CHALLENGES

Two current challenges facing leaders are using social media and developing skills for communicating in a crisis.

9-6a Leadership via Social Media

Everyone knows social media, especially Facebook and Twitter, have changed the way people carry on their social lives. Now they are changing the way people interact in the office, too. **Social media** refers to a variety of Internet-based applications, including social networking, wikis, blogs, and so forth, that allow the creation and

Nonverbal communication messages transmitted through action and behavior

Social media Internet-based applications, including social networking, wikis, blogs, and so forth, that allow the creation and sharing of user-generated content.

sharing of user-generated content. Kaiser Permanente uses an internal social media platform called IdeaBook that supports blogs, wikis, online video, and chat rooms and provides a way for people to meet and carry on conversations in virtual work spaces.[73] When leaders at Internet shoe retailer Zappos realized the economic downturn was hurting their business, CEO Tony Hsieh chose social media to communicate with people about the need to lay off employees. Wanting to get the word out quickly to alleviate stress and uncertainty, Hsieh used *redundant communication*, as defined earlier. He announced the decision and the offer of generous severance packages in an e-mail, on his blog, and with Twitter. Employees being let go were notified personally. It was a difficult time, but the response to how leaders handled the situation from both departing staffers and those remaining was generally positive.[74]

Tony Hsieh was an early adopter of Twitter, but leaders in general have been slow to embrace all forms of social media. General Electric CEO Jeffrey Immelt, for example, tweeted for the first time in September 2012, prompting this response: "@JeffImmelt how come my grandfather got on twitter before you?" Bill George, former Medtronic CEO and a professor at Harvard Business School, says leaders need to consider the use of social media to be an important part of their job description and a tool for being better leaders. "People want CEOs who are real. They want to know what you think," he says.[75]

IBM's Institute for Business Value interviewed 1,700 top executives and found that they believe "the trend toward openness" will have the greatest impact on their business and job in coming years. People are demanding closer personal relationships with leaders and more open and honest communication. Social media directly support the trend toward openness and transparency and give leaders a new way to connect and build relationships with employees all across the organization and around the world.[76] When people feel that they belong to a community with shared values, their attachment to the organization increases. Leaders should recognize that in today's world, particularly for younger employees, "community" is often built through social media.

9-6b Being Crisis-Ready

Communication is a key part of a leader's job, but at no time is it more crucial than during times of rapid change, uncertainty, or crisis. Everyone hears about the major crises that affect organizations, such as the terrorist bombing at the 2013 Boston Marathon, Volkswagen's 2015 emissions scandal, or the 2011 tsunami and nuclear disaster in Japan, but leaders encounter small crises every day, such as the loss of computer data, charges of racial discrimination, or the need for downsizing.

To be prepared for communicating in a crisis, leaders can develop four skills:[77]

1. *Stay calm.* Perhaps the most important part of a leader's job in a crisis situation is to absorb people's fears and uncertainties. "You do not pass uncertainty down to your team members," said Eugene Kranz, the NASA flight director charged with returning the crippled *Apollo 13* spacecraft safely to earth in 1970. "No matter what is going on around you, you have to be cooler than cool."[78]
2. *Be visible and supportive.* Many leaders underestimate just how important their presence and support is during a crisis.[79] Being a leader means stepping out immediately, both to reassure followers and respond to public concerns.
3. *Tell the truth.* Leaders do their best to determine the facts, and then "get the awful truth out" to employees and the public as soon as possible.[80]

Rumor control is critical. Duke University provides an example of the importance of getting the truth out.

IN THE LEAD

Duke University

Duke University was thrust into crisis when three members of its lacrosse team were charged with beating, strangling, and raping an African-American exotic dancer the team had hired for a party where team members were drinking heavily. Duke's reputation had already been tarnished by previous incidents where leaders had failed to respond quickly and appropriately, so handling this crisis could determine whether the university recovered its good name or sank further into the mud.

Duke president Richard Brodhead immediately accepted responsibility for the incident, offered an apology, and began steps for taking corrective action. He indicated that the facts of the rape case were not established and that the players were presumed innocent until proven guilty (charges against all three players were eventually dropped when the victim's story changed). However, Brodhead acknowledged that several members of the lacrosse team had clearly acted inappropriately. From the time the incident happened until the end of the case, Brodhead communicated regularly through various media with students and parents, alumni, employees, and the public. As he explained on *60 Minutes*, Brodhead realized he "had to take personal leadership of this issue from day one."[81]

NEW LEADER
ACTION MEMO

As a leader, you can learn to be an effective crisis communicator. By remaining calm and focused, you can acknowledge people's concerns and fears, provide accurate and up-to-date information, and help people see a better tomorrow.

4. *Communicate a vision for the future.* People need to feel that they have something to work for and look forward to. Moments of crisis present excellent opportunities for leaders to communicate a vision for the future that taps into people's emotions and unites them toward common goals.

LEADERSHIP ESSENTIALS

- Communicating effectively is a crucial skill for leaders. Leaders are communication champions who inspire and unite people around a common sense of purpose and identity. They lead strategic conversations that get people talking across boundaries about the vision, key strategic themes, and the values that can help the group or organization achieve desired outcomes.
- Six elements that facilitate strategic conversations are an open communication climate, asking questions, active listening, dialogue, candor, and using stories. Open communication is essential for building trust, and it paves the way for more opportunities to communicate with followers, thus enabling the organization to gain the benefits of all employees' minds. However, leaders must be active listeners to identify strategic issues and build productive relationships that help the organization succeed, and they must be straightforward and candid in communicating with followers.
- When active listening and candor spread throughout a group, a type of communication referred to as dialogue occurs. Through dialogue, people discover common ground and together create a shared meaning that enables them to understand each other and share a view of the world. Using imagery and stories

in communication helps leaders connect with people on an emotional level and be more influential.

- Leader communication is purpose-directed, and an important element is persuading others to act in ways that achieve goals and accomplish the vision. Four steps for practicing the art of persuasion are to listen first, establish credibility, build goals on common ground, and make your position compelling to others. Leaders select the appropriate communication channels, send redundant communications to reinforce important messages, and use nonverbal as well as verbal communication.
- Electronic communication channels present new challenges for leader communication. Electronic channels can be very advantageous if used appropriately, but their use increases the potential for communication errors, and these channels are not effective for complex or sensitive messages.
- Current communication challenges leaders face are using social media and communicating effectively in times of uncertainty or crisis. Leaders should consider using social media a part of their job because it can be an important aspect of an open communication climate. Four critical skills for communicating in a crisis are to remain calm, be visible, "get the awful truth out," and communicate a vision for the future.

DISCUSSION QUESTIONS

1. Why do you think storytelling is such a powerful means of communicating for a leader? How is active listening related to storytelling?
2. What does it mean to say that leaders use communication to act as "sensegivers"? How do you think this differs from conventional management communication?
3. Board members at some companies are opening the lines of communication so shareholders can voice their concerns about executive compensation and corporate governance. Do you think this is a good idea? What might be some risks associated with this type of open communication?
4. A manager in a communication class remarked, "Listening seems like minimal intrusion of oneself into the conversation, yet it also seems like more work." Do you agree or disagree? Discuss.
5. How does dialogue differ from discussion? Give an example of each from your experience.
6. Some senior executives believe they should rely on written information and computer reports because these yield more accurate data than face-to-face communications do. Do you agree? Discuss.
7. What communication channel would you choose to communicate an impending companywide layoff? News about the company picnic? New corporate quality goals that will require significant changes in how your subordinates perform their tasks? Explain your choices.
8. How do leaders use communication to influence and persuade others? Think of someone you have known who is skilled in the art of persuasion. What makes this person an effective communicator?
9. How might leaders use social media to create a sense of community among employees? What do you think are some advantages and disadvantages of a company using social media to communicate with employees?

LEADERSHIP AT WORK

Listen Like a Professional

The fastest way to become a great listener is to act like a professional listener, such as a clinical psychologist who uses listening to heal another person. Therapists drop their own point of view to concentrate on the patient's point of view. The therapist listens totally, drawing out more information rather than thinking about a response.

The next time you are in a conversation in which the other person talks about some problem or concern, practice professional listening by doing the following:

1. Hold a steady gaze on the person's left eye (not the nose or face, but the left eye)—use a soft gaze, not a hard stare.
2. Remove your thoughts and opinions from the conversation—quell your mind chatter and your desire to say something in response.
3. Suspend judgment—rather than critically analyzing what is being said, feel empathy as if you are walking in the other person's shoes.
4. Draw out the other person's thoughts with brief questions and paraphrasing. Repeat the professional listening approach at least three times with different people to get comfortable with it.

List your thoughts on how the other people responded to your listening, and what it felt like to you.

Other person responded:

1. ______________________________

____

____

2. ______________________________

____

____

3. ______________________________

____

____

What I felt:

1. ______________________________

____

____

2. ______________________________

____

____

3. ______________________________

____

____

In Class: The instructor can divide students into pairs—listener and speaker—in class to practice this exercise. The "speaking" students can be asked to talk about some small problem or annoyance they encountered in the previous day or two. The "listening" students can be given instructions to not speak during the first trial and instead just maintain a soft gaze into the speaker's left eye and respond only with body language (facial expressions and nods). The speaking students should continue until they have nothing more to say or until they feel an emotional shift and the problem seems to have disappeared. After students switch roles and play both speaker and listener, the instructor can ask the class for perceptions of what happened and what they were feeling during the conversation.

It works well to have the students choose a second pairing and redo the exercise with a new problem. The only difference the second time is that the "listener" role is given fewer restrictions, so the listener can make brief comments such as to paraphrase or ask a short question. The listeners, however, should keep spoken comments to a minimum and definitely should not offer their own ideas or point of view. After the students finish, the instructor can gather opinions about what the experience was like for both the speaker and the listener. Key questions include the following: What did it feel like to listen rather than respond verbally to what another person said? What is the value of this professional listening approach? In what situations is professional listening likely to be more or less effective? If the instructor desires, the exercise can be done a third time to help students get more comfortable with a true listening role.

Source: Adapted from Michael Ray and Rochelle Myers, *Creativity in Business* (New York: Broadway Books, 2000), pp. 82–83.

LEADERSHIP DEVELOPMENT: CASES FOR ANALYSIS

The Superintendent's Directive

Educational administrators are bombarded by requests for innovation at all levels. Programs to upgrade math, science, and social science education, state accountability plans, new approaches to administration, and other ideas are initiated by teachers, administrators, interest groups, reformers, and state regulators. In a school district, the superintendent is the key leader; in an individual school, the principal is the key leader.

In the Carville City School District, Superintendent Porter has responsibility for 11 schools—eight elementary, two junior high, and one high school. After attending a management summer course, Porter sent the following e-mail to the principal of each school:

> "Please request that teachers in your school develop a set of performance objectives for each class they teach. A consultant will be providing instructions for writing the performance objectives during the August 10 in-service day. The deadline for submitting the performance objectives to my office is September 21."

Mr. Weigand, principal of Earsworth Elementary School, forwarded Porter's e-mail to his teachers with the following message:

> "Please see the forwarded e-mail from Superintendent Porter. As he explains, you will need to write performance objectives for each course you teach. These are due one month from today. This afternoon, during the in-service meeting, you will receive training on how to write these performance objectives."

After receiving this e-mail, several teachers at the elementary school responded with a flurry of hastily written e-mail responses. One well-respected and talented teacher wrote the following e-mail, accidentally sending it to Mr. Weigand instead of her colleagues:

> "This is nonsense! I should be spending my time focused on the lesson plan for the new advanced English class the board of education approved. Porter is clueless and

has no idea the demands we are facing in the classroom. We never even hear from him until he wants us to complete some empty exercise. I am going to start looking for a school district that values my time!"

Mr. Weigand was stunned by this e-mail, wondering if he was close to losing a valuable teacher who was admired by her peers and others in the school system. He knew this e-mail had been written in haste and that this teacher would be embarrassed to know that he had received it. He was concerned that other teachers may have reacted in similar ways to his e-mail. He also wondered how to respond to the angry e-mail and how to improve morale at the start of a new school year.

QUESTIONS

1. Evaluate the e-mail communications of Mr. Porter and Mr. Weigand. To what extent are they communicating effectively about the new performance objectives? Explain. If you were a teacher, how would you have felt after receiving the e-mail? Why?
2. If you were Mr. Weigand, how would you respond to the angry teacher? Be specific about how you would communicate with her and what you would say. How could he have communicated differently about the performance objectives to influence the teachers more positively?
3. Identify the mistakes that the teacher made when composing and sending her e-mail message.

Hunter-Worth

Christmas was fast approaching. Just a short while ago, Chuck Moore, national sales manager for Hunter-Worth, a New York–based multinational toy manufacturer, was confident the coming holiday was going to be one of the company's best in years. At a recent toy expo, Hunter-Worth unveiled a new interactive plush toy that was cuddly, high-tech, and tied into a major holiday motion picture expected to be a smash hit. Chuck had thought the toy would do well, but frankly, the level of interest took him by surprise. The buyers at the toy fair raved, and the subsequent pre-order volume was extremely encouraging. It had all looked so promising, but now he couldn't shake a sense of impending doom.

The problem in a nutshell was that the Mexican subsidiary that manufactured the toy couldn't seem to meet a deadline. Not only were all the shipments late so far, but they fell well short of the quantities ordered. Chuck decided to e-mail Vicente Ruiz, the plant manager, about the situation before he found himself in the middle of the Christmas season with parents clamoring for a toy he couldn't lay his hands on.

In a thoroughly professional e-mail that started with a friendly "Dear Vicente," Chuck inquired about the status of the latest order, asked for a production schedule for pending orders, and requested a specific explanation as to why the Mexican plant seemed to be having such difficulty shipping orders out on time. The reply appeared within the hour, but to his utter astonishment, it was a short message from Vicente's secretary. She acknowledged the receipt of his e-mail and assured him the Mexican plant would be shipping the order, already a week late, in the next 10 days.

"That's it," Chuck fumed. "Time to take this to Sato." In the message to his boss, he prefaced his original e-mail and the secretary's reply with a terse note expressing his growing concern over the availability of what could well be this season's must-have toy. "Just what do I have to do to light a fire under Vicente?" he wrote. He then forwarded it all to his supervisor and friend, Michael Sato, the executive vice president for sales and marketing.

Next thing he knew, he was on the phone with Vicente—and the plant manager was furious. "Señor Moore, how dare you go over my head and say such things about me to my boss?" he sputtered, sounding both angry and slightly panicked. It seemed that Michael had forwarded Chuck's e-mail to Hunter-Worth's vice president of operations, who had sent it on to the Mexican subsidiary's president.

That turn of events was unfortunate, but Chuck wasn't feeling all that apologetic. "You could have prevented all this if you'd just answered the questions I e-mailed you last week," he pointed out. "I deserved more than a form letter—and from your secretary, no less."

"My secretary always answers my e-mails," replied Vicente. "She figures that if the problem is really urgent, you would pick up the phone and talk to me directly. Contrary to what you guys north of the border might think, we do take deadlines seriously here. There's only so much we can do with the supply problems we're having, but I doubt you're interested in hearing about those." And Vicente hung up the phone without waiting for a response.

Chuck was confused and disheartened. Things were only getting worse. How could he turn the situation around?

QUESTIONS

1. Based on Vicente Ruiz's actions and his conversation with Chuck Moore, what differences do you detect in cultural attitudes toward communications in Mexico as compared with the United States? Is understanding these differences important? Explain.
2. What was the main purpose of Chuck's communication to Vicente? To Michael Sato? What factors should he have considered when choosing a channel for his communication to Vicente? Are they the same factors he should have considered when communicating with Michael Sato?
3. If you were Chuck, what would you have done differently? What steps would you take at this point to make sure the supply of the popular new toy is sufficient to meet the anticipated demand?

Sources: Based on Harry W. Lane, *Charles Foster Sends an E-mail* (London, Ontario: Ivey Publishing, 2005); Frank Unger and Roger Frankel, *Doing Business in Mexico: A Practical Guide on How to Break into the Market* (Council on Australia Latin America Relations and the Department of Foreign Affairs and Trade, 2002), pp. 24–27; and Ignacio Hernandez, "Doing Business in Mexico—Business Etiquette," MexGrocer.com, www.mexgrocer.com/business-in-mexico.html (accessed September 18, 2006).

REFERENCES

1. Jeffrey Rothfeder, "For Honda, Waigaya Is the Way," *Strategy + Business* (Autumn 2014), http://www.strategy-business.com/article/00269?rssid=organizations_and_people&gko=48bd9 (accessed November 6, 2015).
2. AMA Enterprise, a division of American Management Association, 2012, reported in "Employees Are Clueless about What's Going On at Work," *T + D* (June 2012), p. 23.
3. Studies from the Elliot Leadership Institute, reported in Louise van der Does and Stephen J. Caldeira, "Effective Leaders Champion Communication Skills," *Nation's Restaurant News* (March 27, 2006), p. 20; and Dennis Tourish, "Critical Upward Communication: Ten Commandments for Improving Strategy and Decision Making," *Long Range Planning* 38 (2005), pp. 485–503.
4. Bernard M. Bass, *Bass & Stogdill's Handbook of Leadership*, 3rd ed. (New York: The Free Press, 1990).
5. Henry Mintzberg, *Managing* (San Francisco: Berrett-Koehler Publishers, 2009); and Henry Mintzberg, *The Nature of Managerial Work* (New York: Harper & Row, 1973).
6. Mary Young and James E. Post, "Managing to Communicate, Communicating to Manage: How Leading Companies Communicate with Employees," *Organizational Dynamics* (Summer 1993), pp. 31–43; and Warren Bennis and Burt Nanus, *Leaders: The Strategies for Taking Charge* (New York: Harper & Row, 1985).
7. This discussion is based on Charles Galunic and Immanuel Hermreck, "How to Help Employees 'Get' Strategy," *Harvard Business Review* (December 2012), p. 24.
8. This discussion is based on Dennis A. Gioia and Kumar Chittipeddi, "Sensemaking and Sensegiving in Strategic Change Initiation," *Strategic Management Journal* 12, no. 6 (September 1991), pp. 433–448; and Anne D. Smith, Donde Ashmos Plowman, and Dennis Duchon, "Everyday Sensegiving: A Closer Look at Successful Plant Managers," *The Journal of Applied Behavioral Science* 46, no. 2 (June 2010), pp. 220–244.
9. Phillip G. Clampitt, Laurey Berk, and M. Lee Williams, "Leaders as Strategic Communicators," *Ivey Business Journal* (May–June 2002), pp. 51–55.
10. General William E. "Kip" Ward, "Strategic Communication at Work," *Leader to Leader* (Winter 2011), pp. 33–38.
11. Gary Hamel, "Killer Strategies That Make Shareholders Rich," *Fortune* (June 23, 1997), pp. 70–84.
12. John Luthy, "New Keys to Employee Performance and Productivity," *Public Management* (March 1998), pp. 4–8.
13. This discussion is based on Andrew Sobel, "Leading with Questions: Ask, Don't Tell," *Leader to Leader* (Winter 2013), pp. 24–29; "The Power of Questions" (Practical Wisdom column), *Leadership: The Journal of the Leader to Leader Institute* (Spring 2005), pp. 59–60; and Quinn Spitzer and Ron Evans, "The New Business Leader: Socrates with a Baton," *Strategy & Leadership* (September–October 1997), pp. 32–38.
14. Reported in Sobel, "Leading with Questions."
15. Reported in Spitzer and Evans, "The New Business Leader: Socrates with a Baton."
16. Based on Sobel, "Leading with Questions: Ask, Don't Tell"; Steve Arneson, "People Leadership: Get to Know Your People Better," *Leadership Excellence* (November 2010), p. 18; "The Power of Questions"; and Spitzer and Evans, "The New Business Leader: Socrates with a Baton."

17. Sterling Newberry, "Difficult Communications: Going Beyond 'I' Statements," *Mediate.com* (January 2003), http://www.mediate.com/articles/redwing9.cfm (accessed July 6, 2009).
18. Kevin Clark, "Management Secrets of the NFL: The League's Best Teams Share Front-Office Habits," *The Wall Street Journal* (September 5, 2012), p. D7.
19. Fierce Inc. survey results reported in Phaedra Brotherton, "More Employee Input and Accountability Yield More Effective Practices," *T + D* (May 2012), p. 18.
20. Seth S. Horowitz, "The Science and Art of Listening," *The New York Times* (November 9, 2012), http://www.nytimes.com/2012/11/11/opinion/sunday/why-listening-is-so-much-more-than-hearing.html?_r=0 (accessed November 11, 2012).
21. Bernard T. Ferrari, "The Executive's Guide to Better Listening," *McKinsey Quarterly* no. 2 (2012), pp. 50–60; Horowitz, "The Science and Art of Listening"; and Rick Bommelje, "Listening Pays! Achieve Significance Through the Power of Listening," *Leader to Leader* (Fall 2013), pp. 18–25.
22. Tom Peters, "Learning to Listen," *Hyatt Magazine* (Spring 1988), pp. 16–21.
23. "Why I'm a Listener: Amgen CEO Kevin Sharer," (interview), *The McKinsey Quarterly* no. 2 (April 2012), pp. 61–65.
24. David Bohm, *On Dialogue* (Ojai, CA: David Bohm Seminars, 1989).
25. Bill Isaacs, *Dialogue and the Art of Thinking Together* (New York: Doubleday, 1999); and "The Art of Dialogue," column in Paul Roberts, "Live! From Your Office! It's ..." *Fast Company* (October, 1999), pp. 151–170.
26. Based on Glenna Gerard and Linda Teurfs, "Dialogue and Organizational Transformation," in Kazimierz Gozdz, ed., *Community Building: Renewing Spirit and Learning in Business* (Pleasanton, CA: New Leaders Press, 1995).
27. Scott Kirsner, "Want to Grow? Hire a Shrink!" *Fast Company* (December–January 1998), pp. 68, 70.
28. This discussion is based in part on Jack Welch with Suzy Welch, *Winning* (New York: HarperBusiness, 2005), Chapter 2.
29. Ibid.
30. E. Raudsepp, "Are You Properly Assertive?" *Supervision* (June 1992); and M. J. Smith, *When I Say No, I Feel Guilty* (New York: Bantam Books, 1975).
31. Based on Welch, *Winning*, Chapter 2.
32. Kevin Clark, "The Seattle Seahawks' Edge: Airing Their Grievances; Brutal Honesty Is the Seattle Defense's Policy," *The Wall Street Journal* (January 7, 2015), http://www.wsj.com/articles/the-seattle-seahawks-edge-airing-their-grievances-1420652292 (accessed November 4, 2015).
33. Halley Bock, "Fierce Communication," *T + D* (November 2012), p. 80.
34. This discussion is based on David M. Boje, "Learning Storytelling: Storytelling to Learn Management Skills," *Journal of Management Education* 15, no. 3 (August 1991), pp. 279–294; Peter Guber, "Telling Purposeful Stories: An Organization's Most Under-Utilized Competency," *People & Strategy* 34, no. 1 (2011), pp. 4–5; Alison Esse, "Response from The Storytellers to Peter Guber's Article," *People & Strategy* 34, no. 1 (2011), pp. 7–8; and David Fleming, "Narrative Leadership: Using the Power of Stories," *Strategy & Leadership* 29, no. 4 (July–August 2001), pp. 34–36.
35. Howard Gardner, *Leading Minds: An Anatomy of Leadership* (New York: Basic Books, 1995).
36. Art Kleiner, "The Art of the Business Narrative" (an interview with Peter Guber), *Strategy + Business* 63 (Summer 2011), http://www.strategy-business.com/article/00067?gko=3e7b3 (accessed April 29, 2013).
37. Example told in Fleming, "Narrative Leadership."
38. Kleiner, "The Art of the Business Narrative."
39. Erin White, "Theory & Practice: Art of Persuasion Becomes Key; Managers Sharpen Their Skills as Line of Authority Blurs," *The Wall Street Journal* (May 19, 2008), p. B5.
40. This section is based on Jay A. Conger, "The Necessary Art of Persuasion," *Harvard Business Review* (May–June 1998), pp. 84–95.
41. Reported in Tori Rodriguez, "How to Use Your Ears to Influence People," *Scientific American Mind* (November–December 2012), p. 20.
42. Chris Musselwhite and Tammie Plouffe, "To Have the Most Impact, Ask the Right Questions," *Harvard Business Review Blog* (March 1, 2013), http://blogs.hbr.org/cs/2012/11/to_have_the_most_impact_ask_qu.html (accessed April 26, 2013); Edward T. Reilly, "Influential Leaders," *Leadership Excellence* (January 2013), p. 10; and Stephen R. Covey, *The 7 Habits of Highly Effective People* (New York: Free Press, 2004).
43. Darren Dahl, "Trust Me: You're Gonna Love This: Getting Employees to Embrace New Technology," *Inc.* (November 2008), p. 41.
44. John Guaspari, "A Shining Example," *Across the Board* (May–June 2002), pp. 67–68.
45. J. C. McCroskey and V. P. Richmond, "The Impact of Communication Apprehension on Individuals in Organizations," *Communication Quarterly* 27 (1979), pp. 55–61.
46. J. C. McCroskey, "The Communication Apprehension Perspective," in J. C. McCroskey and J. A. Daly, eds., *Avoiding Communication: Shyness, Reticence, and Communication Apprehension* (London: Sage Publications, 1984), pp. 13–38.
47. Robert H. Lengel and Richard L. Daft, "The Selection of Communication Media as an Executive Skill," *Academy of Management Executive* 2 (August 1988), pp. 225–232; and Richard L. Daft and Robert Lengel, "Organizational Information Requirements, Media Richness and Structural Design," *Managerial Science* 32 (May 1986), pp. 554–572.
48. Ford S. Worthy, "How CEOs Manage Their Time," *Fortune* (January 18, 1988), pp. 88–97.
49. John R. Carlson and Robert W. Zmud, "Channel Expansion Theory and the Experiential Nature of Media Richness Perceptions," *Academy of Management Journal* 42, no. 2 (1999), pp. 153–170; and R. Rice and G. Love, "Electronic Emotion," *Communication Research* 14 (1987), pp. 85–108.
50. Ronald E. Rice, "Task Analyzability, Use of New Media, and Effectiveness: A Multi-Site Exploration of Media Richness," *Organizational Science* 3, no. 4 (November 1994), pp. 502–527.
51. Richard L. Daft, Robert H. Lengel, and Linda Klebe Treviño, "Message Equivocality, Media Selection and Manager Performance: Implications for Information Systems," *MIS Quarterly* 11 (1987), pp. 355–368.
52. Laura Raines, "Going Forward after Layoffs: Leaders Need to Reassure Employees, Share Vision of Company's Future," *The Atlanta Journal-Constitution* (April 26, 2009), p. G1.
53. Quint Studor, "Case for Transparency," *Leadership Excellence* (April 2010), p. 19.
54. Paul M. Leonardi, Tsedal B. Neeley, and Elizabeth M. Gerber, "How Managers Use Multiple Media: Discrepant Events, Power, and Timing in Redundant Communication," *Organization Science* 23, no. 1 (January–February 2012), pp. 98–117.
55. Christopher Mims, "Bosses Use Anonymous Networks to Learn What Workers Really Think," *The Wall Street Journal* (June 21, 2015), http://www.wsj.com/articles/bosses-use-anonymous-networks-to-learn-what-workers-really-think-1434930794 (accessed November 5, 2015).
56. Ibid.
57. Anne Fisher, "Readers Weigh In on Rudeness and Speechmaking" (Ask Annie column), *Fortune* (January 10, 2000), p. 194.
58. Edward M. Hallowell, "The Human Moment at Work," *Harvard Business Review* (January–February 1999), pp. 58–66; Andrea C. Poe, "Don't Touch That 'Send' Button!" *HR Magazine* (July 2003), pp. 74–80; and Elizabeth Bernstein, "You Can Recover From a Snippy Email, But Prepare to Grovel," *The Wall Street Journal* (October 21, 2014), http://www.wsj.com/articles/you-can-recover-from-a-snippy-email-but-prepare-to-grovel-1413829668 (accessed November 5, 2015).
59. Hallowell, "The Human Moment at Work."
60. Hallowell, "The Human Moment at Work"; Deborah L. Duarte and Nancy Tennant Snyder, *Mastering Virtual Teams: Strategies, Tools, and Techniques That Succeed* (San Francisco: Jossey-Bass, 2000).

61. Hallowell, "The Human Moment."
62. Carlson and Zmud, "Channel Expansion Theory and the Experiential Nature of Media Richness Perceptions."
63. Mary Lynn Pulley and Jane Hilberry, *Get Smart! How E-Mail Can Make or Break Your Career and Your Organization* (Colorado Springs, CO: Get Smart! Publishing, 2007).
64. Reported in Cassell Bryan-Low and Aaron Lucchetti, "George Carlin Never Would've Cut It at the New Goldman Sachs—Firms Ban Naughty Words in Emails; An 'Unlearnable Lesson' on Wall Street?" *The Wall Street Journal* (July 29, 2010).
65. Albert Mehrabian, *Silent Messages* (Belmont, CA: Wadsworth, 1971); and Albert Mehrabian, "Communicating without Words," *Psychology Today* (September 1968), pp. 53–55.
66. Jane Webster and Linda Klebe Treviño, "Rational and Social Theories as Complementary Explanations of Communication Media Choices: Two Policy Capturing Studies," *Academy of Management Journal* (December 1995), pp. 1544–1572.
67. Mac Fulfer, "Nonverbal Communication: How to Read What's Plain as the Nose ... or Eyelid ... or Chin ... on Their Faces," *Journal of Organizational Excellence* (Spring, 2001), pp. 19–27.
68. Based on a story in Christopher Hegarty, *How to Manage Your Boss* (Mill Valley, CA: Whatever Publishing, 1982), pp. 58–59.
69. I. Thomas Sheppard, "Silent Signals," *Supervisory Management* (March 1986), pp. 31–33; and Martha E. Mangelsdorf, "Business Insight (A Special Report); Executive Briefing: The Power of Nonverbal Communication" (an interview with Alex Pentland), *The Wall Street Journal* (October 20, 2008), p. R2.
70. Reported in Jane Jordan-Meier, "Appearances Do Matter: Leadership in a Crisis," *Leader to Leader* (Fall 2012), pp. 16–20.
71. Thomas H. Peters and Robert J. Waterman Jr., *In Search of Excellence* (New York: Harper & Row, 1982); and Tom Peters and Nancy Austin, *A Passion for Excellence: The Leadership Difference* (New York: Random House, 1985).
72. Carol Hymowitz, "How to Lead after Sudden Rise," *The Wall Street Journal* (May 8, 2006).
73. Vince Golla, interviewed by David Kiron, "Social Business at Kaiser Permanente: Using Social Tools to Improve Customer Service, Research and Internal Collaboration," *MIT Sloan Management Review* (March 6, 2012), http://sloanreview.mit.edu/article/social-tools-improve-service-research-collaboration/ (accessed April 30, 2013).
74. Jeffrey M. O'Brien, "Zappos Knows How to Kick It," *Fortune* (February 2, 2009), pp. 54–60.
75. Leslie Kwoh and Melissa Korn, "140 Characters of Risk: CEOs on Twitter," *The Wall Street Journal* (September 26, 2012), p. B1.
76. Peter Korsten, "Lead via Connections," *Leadership Excellence* (August 2012), p. 16.
77. This section is based on Leslie Wayne and Leslie Kaufman, "Leadership, Put to a New Test," *The New York Times* (September 16, 2001), Section 3, pp. 1, 4; Jerry Useem, "What It Takes," *Fortune* (November 12, 2001), pp. 126–132; Andy Bowen, "Crisis Procedures That Stand the Test of Time," *Public Relations Tactics* (August 2001), p. 16; Matthew Boyle, "Nothing Really Matters," *Fortune* (October 15, 2001), pp. 261–264; and Jordan-Meier, "Appearances Do Matter: Leadership in a Crisis."
78. Quoted in Useem, "What It Takes."
79. Stephen Bernhut, "Leadership, with Michael Useem" (Leader's Edge interview), *Ivey Business Journal* (January–February 2002), pp. 42–43.
80. Ian I. Mitroff, "Crisis Leadership," *Executive Excellence* (August 2001), p. 19.
81. John A. Fortunato, "Restoring a Reputation: The Duke University Lacrosse Scandal," *Public Relations Review* 34 (2008), pp. 116–123.

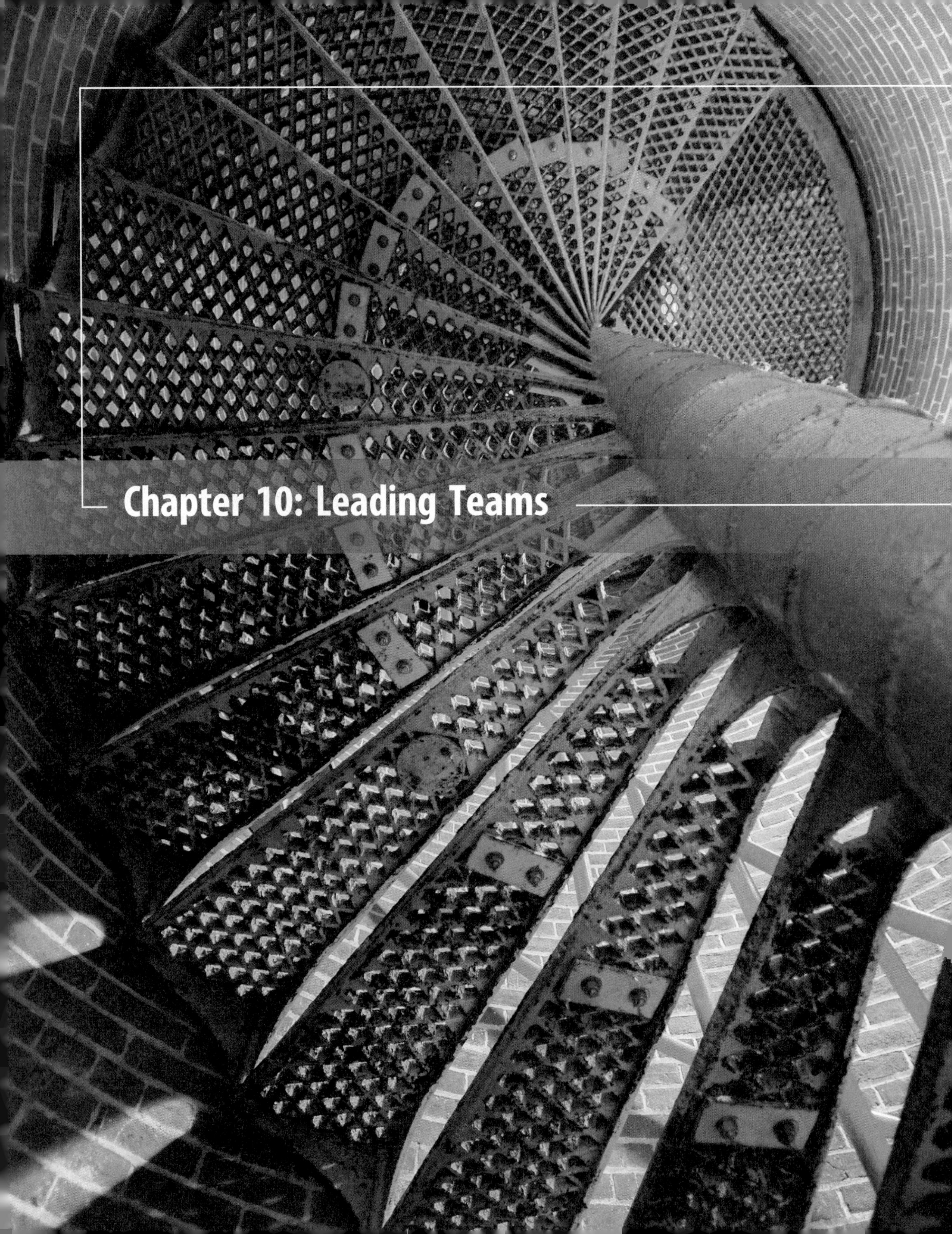

Chapter 10: Leading Teams

YOUR **LEADERSHIP** CHALLENGE

After reading this chapter, you should be able to:

- Turn a group of individuals into a collaborative team that achieves high performance through a shared mission and collective responsibility.
- Identify challenges associated with teamwork, and explain why people sometimes have negative feelings about working in a team.
- Lead a team to high performance by providing a compelling purpose and clear objectives, clarifying roles and responsibilities, designing the team in terms of size and diversity, giving team members decision authority, and providing support and coaching.
- Understand and handle the stages of team development, and know how to promote cohesiveness and shape productive team norms.
- Understand the challenges and benefits of virtual teams and the team leader behaviors that contribute to virtual team effectiveness.
- Handle conflicts that inevitably arise among members of a team.

CHAPTER **OUTLINE**

294 **The Value of Teams**

298 **The Dilemma for Team Members**

300 **Leading a Team to High Performance**

301 **Team Processes**

306 **What Team Members Must Contribute**

308 **Leading a Virtual Team**

311 **Handling Team Conflict**

In the Lead

297 **Chris Rufer, Morning Star**

304 **Golden State Warriors**

309 **Smart Balance**

Leader's Self-Insight

299 **Individual or Team?**

307 **Are You a Contributing Team Member?**

315 **How Do You Handle Team Conflict?**

Leader's Bookshelf

301 **Great Business Teams: Cracking the Code for Standout Performance**

Leadership at Work

318 **Team Feedback**

Leadership Development: Cases for Analysis

319 **Decision Time**

320 **Devereaux-Dering Group**

Mattel is the world's largest toy company, but sales have been shrinking dramatically in the rapidly changing and increasingly competitive toy industry. Mattel CEO Bryan Stockton, chief brands officer Richard Dickson, and other leaders are shaking things up to bring more creativity back to the company. "We need to push ourselves a little further, let ourselves be a little freer, a little less formulaic," said Stockton. One big part of the overhaul is creating more teamwork. Leaders restructured the company to put big brands like Barbie, Hot Wheels, Fisher Price, and so forth into their own independent divisions. Then, they put the dozens of smaller brands into the "Toy Box," a separate division where teams will have greater freedom to take risks and experiment with creative ideas. The plan is to let Toy Box teams invent new toys the way a startup company might, without being hampered by too much structure and routine.[1]

Teams are becoming the basic building blocks of organizations, but teams present greater leadership challenges than does the traditional hierarchical organization. This chapter explores teams and team leadership. We define various types of teams, look at the dilemma of teamwork, and investigate what makes a high-performing team.

The chapter then examines how teams develop, explores topics such as cohesiveness and team norms, and considers the various roles that team members must carry out for the team to function well. The new challenge of leading virtual teams is also discussed. The final part of the chapter looks at how to manage team conflict, including using negotiation.

10-1 THE VALUE OF TEAMS

Teams are not right for every situation, but much work in organizations is *interdependent*, which means that individuals and departments rely on other individuals and departments for information or resources in order to accomplish their work. When tasks are highly interdependent, a team can be the best approach for ensuring the level of coordination, information sharing, and exchange of materials necessary for successful task accomplishment. When they are effective, teams can provide benefits for both organizations and employees through higher productivity, quality improvements, greater flexibility and speed, a flatter management structure, increased employee involvement and satisfaction, and lower turnover.[2]

10-1a What Is a Team?

A **team** is a unit of two or more people who interact and coordinate their work to accomplish a shared goal or purpose to which they are committed and hold themselves mutually accountable.[3] Several key features distinguish a team. For example, a team made up of linguists, psychologists, statisticians, and software engineers at Facebook had a clear purpose (*shared goal*) of redesigning Facebook's ineffective search engine so it could better understand human (not just computer) language. Team members had to coordinate their efforts and *work interdependently* to investigate, design, test, and develop a new search engine. The development team was a *distinct unit* with membership separate from other teams. Members of the team worked together for a period of more than a year to complete the early coding and testing of a new search tool and are continuing their work to perfect the new search engine, which Facebook hopes can be competitive with search leader Google.[4]

A team is a group of people, but the two are not one and the same. People who do not interact regularly, such as those waiting in line at the company cafeteria or riding together in the elevator, do not compose a team. Even a group of employees whose work is related is not a team unless the members share a common purpose that requires them to depend on each other. In addition, the concept of teamwork implies that people sublimate their individual needs, desires, and egos and synthesize their knowledge, skills, and efforts toward accomplishing a common goal. A professor, coach, or employer can put together a *group* of people and never build a *team*. Consider the Miami Heat basketball team. In the spring of 2010, LeBron James, Dwyane Wade, and Chris Bosh were the top scorers on their respective basketball teams. The next year, they were all playing for the Miami Heat. With that kind of talent, the team should have been tough for anyone to beat, but the Heat's dream team opened with a humiliating loss and stumbled through the early weeks of the season. Star players who were used to being in charge at crunch time found themselves working at cross-purposes. Discussing the Heat's loss to the New York Knicks, former Chicago Bulls player Steve Kerr said, "It was a total meltdown. It was, 'I'm so talented, I'll take over.' They looked awful."[5]

Team
a unit of two or more people who interact and coordinate their work to accomplish a shared goal or purpose

Individual stars don't necessarily make a great team, in sports or in business. The Miami Heat struggled with issues that teams in all organizations face: How to get star performers to sublimate their egos and sacrifice their individual goals? How to bring together the right set of specialties and skills? How to define roles? How to promote cohesiveness and norms of collaboration? and How to create a team that is united in a common mission?[6] This chapter's *Consider This* illustrates the spirit and power of teamwork.

Consider **This!**

Lessons from Geese

Fact 1: As each goose flaps its wings, it creates an "uplift" for the birds that follow. By flying in a "V" formation, the whole flock adds 71 percent greater flying range than if each bird flew alone.

Lesson: People who share a common direction and sense of community can get where they are going quicker and easier because they are traveling on the thrust of one another.

Fact 2: When a goose falls out of formation, it suddenly feels the drag and resistance of flying alone. It quickly moves back into formation to take advantage of the lifting power of the bird immediately in front of it.

Lesson: If we have as much sense as a goose, we stay in formation with those headed where we want to go. We are willing to accept their help and give our help to others.

Fact 3: When the lead goose tires, it rotates back into the formation and another goose flies to the point position.

Lesson: It pays to take turns doing the hard tasks and sharing leadership. Like geese, people are interdependent on each other's skills, capabilities, and unique arrangement of gifts, talents, or resources.

Fact 4: The geese flying in formation honk to encourage those up front to keep up their speed.

Lesson: We need to make sure our honking is encouraging. In groups where there is encouragement, the production is much greater. The power of encouragement (to stand by one's heart or core values and encourage the heart and core values of others) is the quality of honking we seek.

Fact 5: When a goose gets sick, wounded, or shot down, two geese drop out of the formation and follow it down to help and protect it. They stay until it dies or is able to fly again. Then they launch out with another formation or catch up with the flock.

Lesson: If we have as much sense as a goose, we will stand by each other in difficult times as well as when we are strong.

Source: 1991 Organizational Development Network. Original author unknown.

10-1b Types of Teams

Teams are found at every level of today's organizations. At Cirque du Soleil, the CEO, chief operating officer, chief financial officer, and vice president of creation function as a top management team to develop, coordinate, and oversee acrobatic troupes that travel to approximately 100 cities on four continents a year. Google assembles teams of three or four employees to assess new ideas and recommend whether they should be implemented. IBM uses teams formed of people specializing in hardware, software, research, and sales to solve specific problems for clients such as Walmart, Charles Schwab, and the Mayo Clinic.[7] And at Tasty Catering, a family-owned business in Chicago, teams of front-line employees from across the company—chefs and accountants, clerical workers and drivers, supervisors and servers—make all strategic decisions.[8]

Organizations use various types of teams to meet internal needs or external challenges. Exhibit 10.1 illustrates three types of teams used in organizations: functional, cross-departmental, and self-directed.

Functional Teams A **functional team** is part of the traditional vertical hierarchy. This type of team is made up of a supervisor and his or her subordinates in the formal chain of command. Sometimes called a *vertical team* or a *command team*, the functional team can include three or four levels of hierarchy within a department. Typically, a functional team makes up a single department in the organization. For example, the quality control department at Blue Bell Creameries in Brenham, Texas, is a functional team that tests all incoming ingredients to make sure only the best products go into the company's ice cream. A financial analysis department, a human resources department, and a sales department are all functional or vertical teams. Each is created by the organization within the vertical hierarchy to attain specific goals through members' joint activities.

Functional team
a team made up of a supervisor and subordinates in the formal chain of command

Cross-departmental team
team made up of members from different functional departments within an organization

Cross-Departmental Teams A **cross-departmental team** is made up of members from different departments within the organization. These teams are often called *cross-functional teams*. Cross-departmental teams are typically used for projects that affect several departments and therefore require that many views be considered. Cross-departmental teams facilitate information sharing across functional boundaries, generate suggestions for coordinating the departments represented, develop new ideas and solutions for existing organizational problems, and assist in developing new practices or policies.

EXHIBIT 10.1 Evolution of Teams and Team Leadership

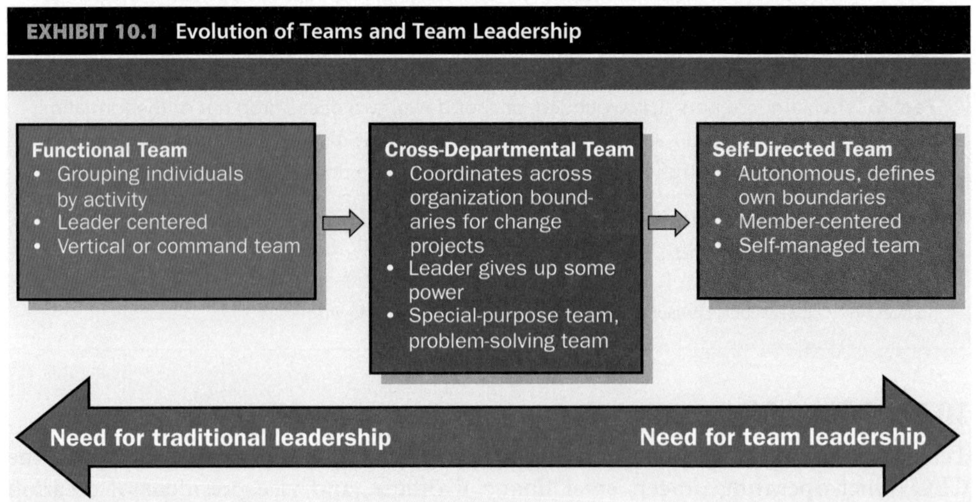

One type of cross-departmental team is the **special-purpose team**, sometimes called a *project team*. Special-purpose teams focus on a specific purpose and disband once the project is completed. They are created outside the formal organization structure to undertake a project of special importance or complexity or to develop a new product or service. The team working on a new search engine at Facebook, described earlier, is a special-purpose team.

NEW LEADER
ACTION MEMO

As a leader, you can create a cross-departmental team to handle a project that requires coordination across functional boundaries. Use a special-purpose team for a project of special importance, such as developing a new product or service.

Evolution to Self-Directed Teams Cross-departmental teams may gradually evolve into self-directed teams. **Self-directed teams** are made up of employees who work with minimum supervision and rotate jobs to produce an entire product or service, or at least one complete aspect or portion of a product or service.[9]

Exhibit 10.1 illustrates the evolution of teams and team leadership. The functional team groups individuals by common skill and activity within the traditional structure. Leadership is based on the vertical hierarchy. In cross-departmental teams, members have more freedom from the hierarchy, but the team typically is still leader-centered and leader-directed. The leader is most often assigned by the organization and is usually a supervisor or manager from one of the departments represented on the team.

In the next stage of evolution, team members work together without the ongoing direction of managers, supervisors, or assigned team leaders. One interesting example of the use of self-directed teams is tomato processor Morning Star.

IN THE LEAD

Chris Rufer, Morning Star

Chris Rufer, the founder of Morning Star, a tomato processor with three factories that produce products for companies such as Heinz and Campbell Soup Company, believes if people can manage the complexities of their own lives without a boss, there is no reason they can't manage themselves in the workplace.

Rufer founded Morning Star based on self-directed teamwork, where no one has a boss and teams of employees negotiate responsibilities with one another. However, as the company grew from the original 24 colleagues (as employees are called) to around 400, problems occurred. Some people had trouble working in an environment with no bosses and no hierarchy. Handling the inevitable conflicts that arise in any workplace was a particular challenge. Thus, Rufer created the Morning Star Self-Management Institute to provide training for people in the principles and systems of self-management.

Every colleague now goes through training, in small groups of 10 to 15 people, to learn how to work effectively as part of a team; how to handle the responsibilities that are typically carried out by managers; how to balance freedom and accountability; how to understand and effectively communicate with others; and how to manage conflicts.[10]

Empirical studies have shown that self-directed teams are associated with higher job satisfaction.[11] Job satisfaction increases partly because working in self-directed teams enables people to feel challenged, find their work meaningful, feel more control over their work lives, and develop a stronger sense of identity with the organization.[12] However, as the example of Morning Star shows, effective teamwork doesn't just happen. Leaders are responsible for shaping how teams perform, as we will

Special-purpose team team that focuses on a specific purpose of high importance and disbands once the project is completed; sometimes called a project team

Self-directed teams teams made up of members who work with minimum supervision and rotate jobs to produce a complete product or service

NEW LEADER
ACTION MEMO

As a leader, you can use a self-directed team when members are capable of working together without active supervision. Give the team access to the money, equipment, supplies, and information needed to perform its project or task, and empower the team with decision-making authority.

describe later in this chapter. In particular, ongoing training is essential for people to work effectively in self-directed teams.

Self-directed teams have access to information and resources needed to perform a complete task and are empowered with decision-making authority to take over duties such as selecting new members, scheduling work or vacations, and evaluating performance. Self-directed teams are typically not completely autonomous, in that organizational leaders set overall direction and monitor the team's work on a regular basis. However, these teams are effectively trained to work with minimum supervision, and members are jointly responsible for making decisions and solving problems. At Lockheed Martin's Missiles and Fire Control division's Pike County Operations in Troy, Alabama, all employees work in self-directed teams that set performance goals and make decisions related to assembling and testing advanced missile systems. Self-directed teams at Pike County Operations have contributed to 100 percent on-time delivery with zero customer rejects for the division.[13]

Self-directed teams typically elect one of their own to serve as team leader, and the leader may change each year. Some teams function without a designated leader, so anyone may play a leadership role depending on the situation. For example, the emergency trauma team at Massachusetts General Hospital performs so smoothly that the team switches leaders seamlessly, depending on the crisis at hand. With each new emergency, direction may come from a doctor, intern, nurse, or technician—whoever is particularly experienced with the problem at hand.[14]

10-2 THE DILEMMA FOR TEAM MEMBERS

When leaders at ICU Medical Products announced that the company was shifting to a structure based entirely on teams, the CFO quit.[15] Some people love the idea of teamwork, others hate it, and many people have both positive and negative emotions about working as part of a team. Leaders can be more effective when they understand three primary reasons teams present a dilemma for people:

- *We Have to Give Up Our Independence.* When people become part of a team, their success depends on the team's success; therefore, they are dependent on how well other people perform, not just on their own individual initiative and actions. In addition, whereas most people are comfortable with the idea of making sacrifices in order to achieve their own individual success, teamwork demands that they make sacrifices for *group* success.[16] The idea is that each person should put the team first, even if at times it hurts the individual.
- *We Have to Put Up with Free Riders.* Teams are sometimes made up of people who have different work ethics. The term **free rider** refers to a team member who attains benefits from team membership but does not actively participate in and contribute to the team's work. You might have experienced this frustration in a student project team, where one member put little effort into the project but benefited from the hard work of others when grades were handed out. Free riding is sometimes called *social loafing* because some members do not exert equal effort.[17] The potential for free riding might be one reason a survey found that 40 to 60 percent of people (depending on gender and age) like working in teams to learn from others, but no more than 36 percent report they like working in teams to complete tasks.[18]

NEW LEADER
ACTION MEMO

Do you enjoy working as part of a team, or do you prefer to do your work individually? Complete Leader's Self-Insight 10.1 to get an idea of your feelings toward teamwork and whether team leadership might present a problem for you.

Free rider
a team member who attains benefits from team membership but does not actively participate in and contribute to the team's work

LEADER'S SELF-INSIGHT 10.1

Individual or Team?

Instructions: Respond to the following statements with your preferences for working on your job or school assignments. Please answer whether each item is Mostly False or Mostly True for you.

	Mostly False	Mostly True
1. I prefer to work on a team rather than do tasks individually.		
2. Given a choice, I try to work by myself rather than face the hassles of group work.		
3. I enjoy the personal interaction when working with others.		
4. I prefer to do my own work and let others do theirs.		
5. I get more satisfaction from a group victory than an individual victory.		
6. Teamwork is not worthwhile when people do not do their share.		
7. I feel good when I work with others even when we disagree.		
8. I prefer to rely on myself rather than others to do a job or assignment.		
9. I find that working as a member of a team increases my ability to perform well.		
10. It annoys me to do work as a member of a team.		

Scoring and Interpretation

For odd-numbered items give yourself 1 point for each Mostly True answer and for even-numbered items give yourself 1 point for each Mostly False answer.

Total Score ________.

Your score indicates your preference for working as part of a team versus working as an individual. A score of 8–10 suggests a clear preference for working with others on a team. Teams can accomplish tasks far beyond what an individual can do, and working with others can be a major source of satisfaction. A score of 0–3 suggests a clear preference for working alone rather than on a team. On a team you will lose some autonomy and have to rely on others who may be less committed than you. On a team you have to work through other people and you lose some control over work procedures and outcomes. A score of 4–7 suggests you are satisfied either working on a team or alone. How do you think your preference will affect your career choices and your potential role as a leader?

- *Teams Are Sometimes Dysfunctional.* Some companies have had great success with teams, but there are also many examples of how teams in organizations fail spectacularly.[19] A civilian worker at a large U.S. Air Force base tells of an experience in which the team "streamlined" the process of handling mail by changing it from 8 steps to a ridiculous 19, meaning official mail was handled by more people and getting to its intended recipient even later than before.[20] Exhibit 10.2 lists five dysfunctions that are common in teams.[21] Over the past

EXHIBIT 10.2 Five Common Dysfunctions of Teams

Dysfunction	Attitudes and behaviors
Lack of trust	People don't feel safe to reveal mistakes, share concerns, or express ideas
Fear of conflict	People go along with others for the sake of harmony; don't express conflicting opinions
Lack of commitment	People can't truly commit to decisions because they haven't contributed their true opinions and ideas
Avoidance of accountability	People don't accept responsibility for outcomes; engage in finger-pointing when things go wrong
Inattention to results	Members put personal ambition or the needs of their individual departments ahead of collective results

Source: Based on Patrick Lencioni, *The Five Dysfunctions of a Team* (New York: John Wiley & Sons, 2002).

few decades, a great deal of research and team experience has produced significant insights into what causes teams to succeed or fail. The evidence shows that how teams are managed plays the most critical role.[22]

10-3 LEADING A TEAM TO HIGH PERFORMANCE

"High-performance teams and organizations do not arise spontaneously. They do not appear overnight. High performance is a process and a mind-set. It requires a methodology and it must be practiced—over and over."

John Foley, founder and president of John Foley, Inc.; former Marine Corps jet fighter instructor pilot and lead solo pilot of the Blue Angels jet acrobatics team

Smoothly functioning teams don't just happen. They are created and shaped by leaders. Harvard Business School professors studying surgery teams, for example, found that the attitude and actions of the team leader, and the quality of the leader's interactions with team members, are crucial to team effectiveness and the success of the surgery.[23] Teamwork is becoming common in health care, but poor coordination and communication among team members has been a real problem, leading to errors and even patient deaths. The U.S. Department of Defense and the Agency for Healthcare Research and Quality developed a team training program to teach cognitive and interpersonal skills that contribute to better health care teamwork, with significant focus on team leadership. Boston Children's Hospital reduced medical errors by 40 percent after teams began applying the tools learned from the program.[24]

To lead any team to high performance, whether in health care, manufacturing, Internet services, or NASCAR racing, leaders incorporate the following elements:[25]

1. *A Compelling Purpose, Clear Objectives, and Explicit Metrics.* To succeed, team members have to know what is expected of them and commit to accomplishing it. High-performing teams have a *specific*, clearly defined purpose and a well-defined set of goals, enabling people to come together in a shared undertaking. A team cannot succeed if people are floundering around wondering why the team exists, or if people are going in different directions rather than pulling together for a common purpose. Team members also need clear metrics so they know how well they are progressing toward meeting goals.
2. *A Diversity of Skills and Unambiguous Roles.* Effective teams contain the diverse mix of skills, knowledge, and experience needed to perform all the components of the team's project.[26] In addition, diversity in terms of race, gender, ethnic or cultural background, and other dimensions can contribute to greater innovation and better decision making because the team can draw from wider perspectives.[27] Within this diverse mix, however, individual roles and responsibilities are clearly defined. Clear roles and expectations for members lead to enhanced cooperation because people aren't butting up against one another in confusion over their duties and responsibilities.[28]
3. *Streamlined Team Size.* Although most researchers agree there is no optimal team size, teams function best when they contain just enough members to perform the job, and most experts recommend that teams should err on the side of having too few members rather than too many.[29] Much research has shown that small teams (six or fewer members) perform better than large ones.[30] Members on small teams typically ask more questions, exchange more opinions, and exhibit more cooperative behavior. In addition, people in small teams report higher motivation, more job satisfaction, and a greater sense of belonging and cohesiveness. A Gallup poll in the United States found that 82 percent of employees agree that small teams are more productive.[31]
4. *Decision Authority Over How to Achieve Goals.* Although teams need clearly defined goals spelled out by leaders, the team itself should have the authority to

LEADER'S BOOKSHELF

Great Business Teams: Cracking the Code for Standout Performance

by Howard M. Guttman

Management consultant and author Howard Guttman believes high-performance organizations begin with great teams. In his book, *Great Business Teams*, Guttman draws on research into the inner workings of several dozen high-performance teams at companies such as Johnson & Johnson, L'Oreal, Novartis, and Mars Drinks.

CHARACTERISTICS OF GREAT TEAMS

Whether it is a top leadership team, a cross-departmental project team, or a self-directed product development team, Guttman says great teams share five key characteristics:

- ***They Are Led by High-Performance Leaders***. Leaders of great teams put power and authority in the hands of the team. They see their job as making sure all members are clear about and committed to the business strategy and operational goals, understand their roles and responsibilities, and adhere to specific ground rules for decision making and interpersonal behavior.
- ***They Have Members Who Act as Leaders.*** Members of great teams act as leaders by embracing responsibility, exerting influence to accomplish tasks, and holding one another accountable for results. Everyone's performance—even the leader's—is subject to scrutiny and feedback.
- ***They Abide by Protocols***. Ambiguity kills effective teamwork, says Guttman. To achieve high performance, everyone on the team needs to be clear about what the team as a whole is going to accomplish, what each person will contribute, how the team will carry out its tasks, and how members are expected to interact with one another.
- ***They Are Never Satisfied***. On a high-performance team, self-monitoring, self-evaluation, and continually raising the performance bar are the norm.
- ***They Have a Supportive Performance Management System***. To get great teamwork, the organization's performance management and reward systems have to support the expected team behaviors.

WHY TEAMS?

Guttman believes today's organizations and the challenges they face are too complex for formal leaders to make all the decisions. He argues that companies can best succeed with distributed leadership, in which key decisions are made by layers of self-directed teams that are jointly accountable for performance.

Source: *Great Business Teams*, by Howard Guttman, is published by John Wiley & Sons.

decide how it will reach those goals. Good leaders share power, information, and responsibility and work to build consensus rather than issuing orders.[32] Members of high-performing teams determine together how they will work cooperatively to accomplish objectives and achieve the team's purpose.

5. *Support and Coaching*. Although team leaders have to keep people focused on accomplishing tasks, research shows that the soft leadership skills concerned with building positive relationships are especially important for creating a high-performance team.[33] Team effectiveness, productivity, and learning are strengthened when team leaders provide support to team members, reinforce team identity and meaning, work to maintain trusting interpersonal relationships and group cohesiveness, and offer coaching to enhance members' self-leadership skills. Periodic training that teaches skills such as communication, building relationships, developing productive norms, and resolving conflicts can have a significant impact on team collaboration and performance.

These five elements are among the most important guidelines for team leaders. The Leader's Bookshelf further discusses characteristics of teams that lead to high performance.

NEW LEADER
ACTION MEMO

As a leader, you can articulate a clear and compelling vision for the team to help members see their work as meaningful and important. You can define objectives and clarify roles but give people decision-making authority over how to achieve goals. Make room for everyone to contribute and provide people with the training, support, and coaching they need to excel.

10-4 TEAM PROCESSES

Team processes refer to the dynamics that change over time and can be influenced by leaders. In this section we discuss stages of development, cohesiveness, and norms. The fourth type of team process, conflict, will be covered later in the chapter.

10-4a How Teams Develop

It is important for leaders to understand that teams develop over time.[34] Research suggests that teams develop over several stages. Exhibit 10.3 shows one model of the stages of team development.[35] These stages typically occur in sequence, although there can be overlap.

Forming stage of team development that includes orientation and getting acquainted

Storming stage of team development in which individual personalities and conflicts emerge

Forming The **forming** stage of development is a period of orientation and getting acquainted. Team members find out what behavior is acceptable to others, explore friendship possibilities, and determine task orientation. Uncertainty is high because no one knows what the ground rules are or what is expected of them. Members will usually accept whatever power or authority is offered by either formal or informal leaders. The leader's challenge at this stage of development is to facilitate communication and interaction among team members to help them get acquainted and establish guidelines for how the team will work together. It is important at this stage for the leader to make everyone feel comfortable and like a part of the team. Leaders can draw out shy or quiet team members to help them establish relationships with others.

Storming During the **storming** stage, individual personalities emerge more clearly. People become more assertive in clarifying their roles. This stage is marked by

EXHIBIT 10.3 Five Stages of Team Development

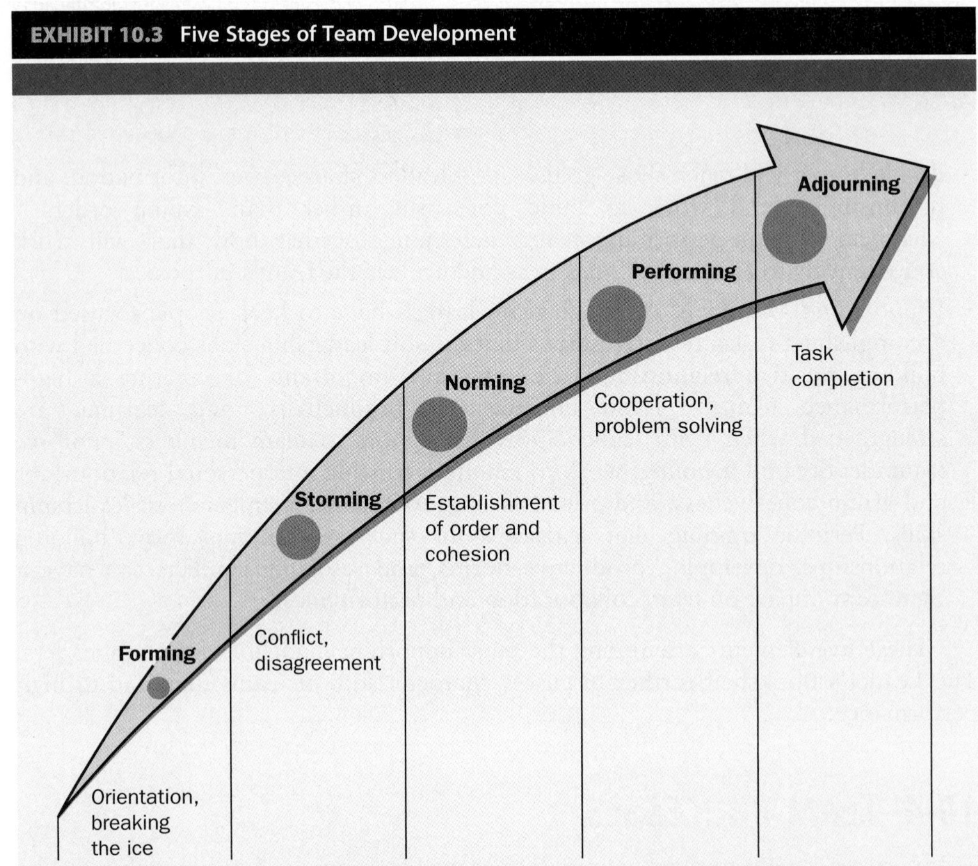

Sources: Based on the stages of small group development in Bruce W. Tuckman, "Developmental Sequence in Small Groups," *Psychological Bulletin* 63 (1965), pp. 384–399; and B. W. Tuckman and M. A. Jensen, "Stages of Small Group Development Revisited," *Group and Organizational Studies* 2 (1977), pp. 419–427.

conflict and disagreement. Team members may disagree over their perceptions of the team's mission or goals. The team is characterized by a general lack of unity and cohesiveness. It is essential that teams move beyond this stage or they will never achieve high performance. A recent experiment with student teams confirms the idea that teams that get stuck in the storming stage perform significantly less well than teams that progress to future stages of development.[36] The leader's role during the storming stage is to encourage participation by each team member and help people find their common vision and values. Members need to debate ideas, surface conflicts, disagree with one another, and work through the uncertainties and conflicting perceptions about team tasks and goals. The expression of emotions, even negative ones, helps to build camaraderie and a shared understanding of goals and tasks.[37]

Norming At the **norming** stage, conflict has been resolved and team unity and harmony emerge. Consensus develops as to who the natural team leaders are, and members' roles are clear. Team members come to understand and accept one another. Differences are resolved, and members develop a sense of cohesiveness. This stage typically is of short duration and moves quickly into the next stage. The team leader should emphasize openness within the team and continue to facilitate communication and clarify team roles, values, and expectations.

Performing During the **performing** stage, the major emphasis is on accomplishing the team's goals. Members are committed to the team's mission. They interact frequently, coordinate their actions, and handle disagreements in a mature, productive manner. Team members confront and resolve problems in the interest of task accomplishment. At this stage, the team leader should concentrate on facilitating high task performance and helping the team self-manage to reach its goals.

Adjourning The **adjourning** stage occurs in committees and teams that have a limited task to perform and are disbanded afterward. During this stage, the emphasis is on wrapping up and gearing down. Task performance is no longer a top priority, and leaders frequently focus on team members' social and emotional needs. People may feel heightened emotionality, strong cohesiveness, and depression or regret over the team's disbandment. At this point, the leader may wish to signify the team's disbanding with a ritual or ceremony, perhaps giving out certificates or awards to signify closure and completeness.

When teams are under time pressure, these stages might occur quite rapidly and even overlap. Stages may also be accelerated for virtual teams. For example, at a large consumer goods company with a virtual team of engineers working in the United States and India, leaders started the project with a couple of days of team building to help the team move rapidly through the forming and storming stages. Team members together created a shared vision, developed specific team norms and agreements, built virtual relationships, and clarified roles and responsibilities. Cultural education and exercises on virtual communication were also part of the process. The team building process not only helped people reach the performing stage quickly, it also contributed to building cohesiveness, which is generally considered an attractive feature of teams.[38]

10-4b Team Cohesiveness

Team cohesiveness is defined as the extent to which members are attracted to the team and motivated to remain in it.[39] Members of highly cohesive teams are

NEW LEADER
ACTION MEMO

As a leader, you can guide your team through its stages of development. Early on you can help members know one another, and then encourage participation and common purpose, followed by clarifying goals and expectations. Finally, you can concentrate on helping the team achieve high performance.

Norming
stage of team development in which conflicts have been resolved and team unity emerges

Performing
stage of team development in which the major emphasis is on accomplishing the team's goals

Adjourning
stage of team development that occurs in committees and teams that have a limited task to perform; the emphasis is on wrapping up, gearing down, and signifying closure

team cohesiveness
the extent to which members are attracted to the team and motivated to remain in it

committed to team activities, attend meetings, and are happy when the team succeeds. Members of less cohesive teams are less concerned about the team's welfare. Leaders typically want to encourage high cohesiveness in teams.

NEW LEADER **ACTION MEMO**

As a leader, you can facilitate team cohesiveness by providing members with opportunities to interact and know one another. You can use friendly competition with other teams to increase cohesiveness, and work with top leaders to develop high-performance norms for the team.

Determinants of Cohesiveness Leaders can use several characteristics of team structure and context to influence cohesiveness. First is *team interaction*. When team members have frequent contact, they get to know one another, consider themselves a unit, and become more committed to the team.[40] Second is the concept of *shared goals*. When team members agree on purpose and direction, they will be more cohesive. The most cohesive teams are those that feel they are involved in something immensely relevant and important. An aerospace executive, recalling his participation in an advanced design team, put it this way, "We even walked differently than anybody else. We felt we were way out there, ahead of the whole world."[41] Third is *personal attraction to the team*, meaning that members have similar attitudes and values and enjoy being together.

Two factors in the team's context also influence group cohesiveness. The first is the *presence of competition*. When a team is in moderate competition with other teams, its cohesiveness increases as it strives to win. Finally, *team success* and the favorable evaluation of the team by outsiders add to cohesiveness. When a team succeeds in its task and others in the organization recognize the success, members feel good, and their commitment to the team will be high.

Consequences of Cohesiveness The outcome of team cohesiveness can fall into two categories—morale and performance. As a general rule, morale is higher in cohesive teams because of increased communication among members, a friendly team climate, maintenance of membership because of commitment to the team, loyalty, and member participation in team decisions and activities. High cohesiveness has almost uniformly good effects on the satisfaction and morale of team members.[42]

With respect to performance, studies suggest that teams in which members share strong feelings of connectedness and generally positive interactions tend to perform better.[43] This certainly seems to be the case for the Golden State Warriors basketball team.

IN THE LEAD

Golden State Warriors

After winning the NBA Championship in June 2015, the Golden State Warriors and coach Steve Kerr kept things just as they were for the 2015–2016 season. The key parts of the team have been together for about three years. Other teams took steps to strengthen their rosters, but the continuity and cohesiveness of the Warriors had the team rated as the No. 1 defense in the league and the No.2 offense.

The success of the Warriors can be attributed not to standout individual performances (although there have been some), but to outstanding teamwork. That teamwork comes partly from having a group of people who really like one another and like being together. When the team is on the road, they go out to eat together, "bonding like Little Leaguers at a pizza party," as a *Wall Street Journal* reporter put it. Most professional basketball players go off on their own, but the Warriors make a habit of huge communal meals, deciding when and where to eat with a team-wide group text message.

The camaraderie has made the Warriors one of the best teams in the NBA. It has also made them one of the most pleasant teams to play for and one of the most enjoyable teams to watch. "Chemistry is something you can't fake," said Warriors forward David Lee. "You either have it or you don't."[44]

As with the Golden State Warriors, a friendly, positive team environment contributes to performance and productivity as well as member satisfaction in other organizations as well. Cohesive teams can sometimes unleash enormous amounts of employee energy and creativity. One explanation for this is the research finding that correlates in-person interactions among employees with higher productivity. Among call center teams at Bank of America, for example, productivity rose 10 percent when leaders scheduled more face-to-face interaction time. Simply interacting with others has an energizing effect.[45]

However, cohesiveness can also *decrease* performance in some cases. One matter of particular concern is **groupthink**, which refers to the tendency of people in cohesive groups to suppress contrary opinions. The hesitation of team members to express safety concerns that went against the group consensus has been cited as a contributing factor to the 1986 *Challenger* space shuttle disaster. People slip into groupthink when the desire for harmony outweighs concerns over decision quality.[46] Other research suggests that performance in cohesive teams may depend on the relationship between leaders and the work team. One study surveyed more than 200 work teams and correlated job performance with their cohesiveness.[47] Highly cohesive teams were more productive when team members felt top leader support and less productive when they sensed leader hostility and negativism.

10-4c Team Norms

A **team norm** is an informal standard of conduct that is shared by team members and guides their behavior.[48] Norms are valuable because they provide a frame of reference for what is expected and acceptable.

Exhibit 10.4 illustrates two common ways in which norms develop.[49] Norms begin to develop in the first interactions among members of a new team, so *first behaviors* often set a precedent for how the team will interact. At one company, a team leader began his first meeting by raising an issue and then "leading" team members until he got the solution he wanted. The pattern became ingrained so quickly into an unproductive team norm that members dubbed meetings the "Guess What I Think" game.[50]

Team leaders should use care to shape norms that will help the team be effective. For example, research shows that when leaders have high expectations for collaborative problem solving, teams develop strong collaborative norms.[51] One powerful way in which leaders influence norms is by making *explicit statements* about the desired team behaviors. When he was CEO of Ameritech, Bill Weiss established a norm of cooperation and mutual support among his top leadership team by telling them bluntly that if he caught anyone trying to undermine the others, the guilty party would be fired.[52]

Groupthink
the tendency of people in cohesive groups to suppress contrary opinions

team norm
an informal standard of conduct that is shared by team members and guides their behavior

EXHIBIT 10.4 Two Ways Team Norms Develop

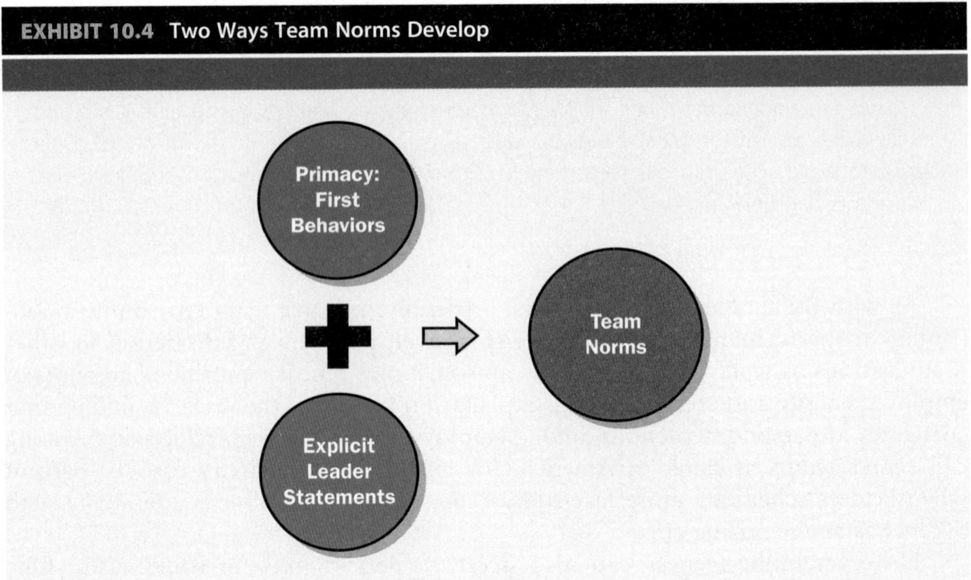

10-5 WHAT TEAM MEMBERS MUST CONTRIBUTE

Now let's turn our attention to understanding the qualities and competencies of team members that contribute to high performance. To understand the need for a variety of skills and competencies, consider the 33 miners who were trapped for months underground after a copper mine collapsed in San José, Chile, in August 2010. The miners organized into several teams in charge of critical activities such as communication with rescue workers, the transport of supplies from above ground, rationing and distribution of food, managing health concerns, and securing the mine to prevent further rock falls. Some team members were clearly focused on helping the trapped miners meet their needs for physical survival, some focused on helping people coordinate their activities, and still others focused on the group's psychological and social needs, helping people maintain hope and a sense of solidarity as the ordeal stretched to a harrowing 69 days. Experts agree that teamwork and leadership were key to the miners' survival.[53]

10-5a Essential Team Competencies

Research has identified a number of key competencies needed to make up an effective team.[54] To function well as a team, members of the team should together display each of the following five competencies:

1. *Goal Setting and Performance Management.* First and foremost, team members must have the ability to establish and execute specific, challenging team objectives, as well as ways to monitor and evaluate performance toward meeting objectives.
2. *Planning and Coordination.* The ability to plan and coordinate is an important determinant of team effectiveness.[55] Members must tightly coordinate and synchronize activities, information, and resources in order to accomplish goals.
3. *Collaborative Problem Solving.* Team members need to be able to recognize when a problem requires group participation and then appropriately involve team members in searching for alternatives and devising solutions.

LEADER'S SELF-INSIGHT 10.2

Are You a Contributing Team Member?

Instructions: Think about how you have typically behaved and contributed as a member of student or work teams. Respond to the following statements based on how you typically behaved on those teams.

	Mostly False	Mostly True
1. I proposed a clear vision of team purpose.		✓
2. I initiated up-front discussions of team goals and objectives.		✓
3. I suggested corrective actions to improve performance.		✓
4. I helped coordinate team members.	✓	
5. I came to meetings well prepared.		✓
6. I followed through on promises and commitments.		✓
7. I was a focused, active listener.		✓
8. I proactively engaged others in problem solving.		✓
9. I gave team members appreciation and support.		✓
10. I praised people for a job well done.		✓

Scoring and Interpretation

These questions pertain to your contributions as a team member as described in the chapter. These items concern various important ways for a team member to contribute to the success of a team. By comparing your scores on the following scales, you may be able to identify the ways you most contribute to a team. To calculate your scores, give yourself 1 point for each Mostly True answer for the items indicated.

A. Goal Setting: Items 1, 2: 2

B. Performance Management: Items 3, 4: 1

C. Preparation: Items 5, 6: 2

D. Communication for Problem Solving: Items 7, 8: 2

E. Social Support: Items 9, 10: 2

An effective team must have members who contribute individually. A team must have someone performing each part, but no member is expected to perform all parts. Indeed, if you scored Mostly True on all the questions, you would be playing a leader role on the team. Part A pertains to goal and direction setting, which is often a team leader role. Part B concerns performance management, which is often part of a team leader's role, but team members also contribute in this way. Part C is about your ability to be interdependent with other team members. Part D pertains to communication and problem-solving skills. Part F is about meeting the relationship needs of team members, which is also a team leader role. How do you feel about your contribution to teams? In what ways do you take the initiative to be an effective member? What might you do to be more effective?

4. *Communication.* Employees working on individual jobs can sometimes get by with poor communication skills, but the wheels of teamwork keep rolling only with good communication. Members speak their minds, ask questions, seek and provide feedback, and make skillful presentations.
5. *Conflict Resolution.* Last, but by no means least, teams need to know how to effectively manage and resolve disagreements. Even in the most cohesive of teams, conflicts will inevitably arise.

10-5b Team Member Roles

The five team competencies reflect that a team needs members who meet the important needs of the team for both accomplishing its tasks and fostering member unity, satisfaction, and well-being. Recall from Chapter 3 the discussion of situational leadership and the meta-categories of *task-oriented* and *relationship-oriented* behaviors described in that chapter (Exhibit 3.2). Task-oriented behavior places primary concern on tasks and production and is generally associated with higher productivity, whereas relationship-oriented behavior emphasizes concern for followers and relationships and is associated with higher employee satisfaction.

NEW LEADER
ACTION MEMO

What contributions do you make to a team? Complete the questionnaire in Leader's Self-Insight 10.2 to see which competencies you typically contribute to the success of a team.

NEW LEADER
ACTION MEMO

As a leader, you can make sure that both the task and socioemotional needs of team members are met so that people experience both friendly support and goal accomplishment.

For a team to be successful over the long term, both task-oriented behavior and relationship-oriented behavior are required within the team. The **task-specialist role** is associated with behaviors that help the team accomplish its goal. People who play a task-specialist role often display the following behaviors:

- *Initiate Ideas.* Propose new solutions to team problems.
- *Give Opinions.* Offer opinions on task solutions; give candid feedback on others' suggestions.
- *Seek Information.* Ask for task-relevant facts.
- *Summarize.* Relate various ideas to the problem at hand; pull ideas together into a summary perspective.
- *Energize.* Stimulate the team into action when interest drops.[56]

The **socioemotional role** includes behaviors that maintain people's emotional well-being and strengthen the social identity. People who adopt a socioemotional role display the following behaviors:

- *Encourage.* Are warm and receptive to others' ideas; praise and encourage others to draw forth their contributions.
- *Harmonize.* Reconcile group conflicts; help disagreeing parties reach agreement.
- *Reduce Tension.* Tell jokes or in other ways draw off emotions when group atmosphere is tense.
- *Follow.* Go along with the team; agree to other team members' ideas.
- *Compromise.* Will shift own opinions to maintain team harmony.[57]

Task-specialist role
team role associated with initiating new ideas, evaluating the team's effectiveness, seeking to clarify tasks and responsibilities, summarizing facts and ideas for others, and stimulating others to action

Socioemotional role
team role associated with facilitating others' participation, smoothing conflicts, showing concern for team members' needs and feelings, serving as a role model, and reminding others of standards for team interaction

Teams with mostly socioemotional roles can be satisfying, but they also can be unproductive. At the other extreme, a team made up primarily of task specialists will tend to have a singular concern for task accomplishment. This team will be effective for a short period of time but will not be satisfying for members over the long run. Effective teams have people in both task-specialist and socioemotional roles. A well-balanced team will do best over the long term because it will be personally satisfying for team members and it will accomplish its tasks.

People tend to take on different roles based on their personalities and interests. Some people naturally lean more toward behaviors that aid in accomplishing tasks, whereas others tend toward behaviors that maintain group harmony and satisfaction. People who can excel at both types of roles often emerge as team leaders. At Marriott, strengthening both task-oriented and relationship-oriented skills is a primary goal for team leader training because teams headed by leaders with both types of skills are typically more productive and innovative.[58] In any case, it is the leader's responsibility to make sure both task and socioemotional needs are met, whether through the leader's own behaviors or through the actions and behaviors of other team members.

10-6 LEADING A VIRTUAL TEAM

Virtual team
team made up of geographically or organizationally dispersed members who share a common purpose and are linked primarily through advanced information technologies

Global team
team made up of culturally diverse members who live and work in different countries and coordinate some part of their activities on a global basis

Being a team leader can be particularly challenging when people are scattered in different geographical locations and may be separated by language and cultural differences as well. Virtual teams are a reality for today's leaders. A **virtual team** is made up of geographically or organizationally dispersed members who share a common purpose and are linked primarily through advanced information and telecommunications technologies.[59] Virtual teams are sometimes also global teams. A **global team** is a cross-border work team made up of members of different nationalities whose activities span multiple countries.[60]

EXHIBIT 10.5 Differences between Conventional, Virtual, and Global Teams

Type of Team	Spatial Distance	Communications	Member Cultures	Leader Challenge
Conventional	Colocated	Face-to-face	Same	High
Virtual	Scattered	Mediated	Same	Higher
Global	Widely scattered	Mediated	Different	Very high

Exhibit 10.5 illustrates the primary differences between conventional types of teams and today's virtual teams. Conventional types of teams discussed earlier in this chapter meet and conduct their interactions face-to-face in the same physical space. Team members typically share similar cultural backgrounds and characteristics. The key characteristics of virtual teams, on the other hand, are (1) spatial distance limits face-to-face interaction and (2) the use of technological communication is the primary means of connecting team members.[61] Members of virtual teams are often scattered in different locations, whether it be different offices and business locations around the country or around the world. Team members use e-mail, telephone, text messaging, videoconferencing, Skype, other Internet technologies, and various forms of collaboration software to perform their work rather than meeting face-to-face. Although some virtual teams are made up of only organizational members, virtual teams often include contingent workers, members of partner organizations, customers, suppliers, consultants, or other outsiders. Consider the virtual teams at Smart Balance, the "heart-healthy" food company.

IN THE LEAD

Smart Balance

Smart Balance has about 67 employees, but nearly 400 people work for the company. Smart Balance started by making a buttery spread and now has a line of spreads; all-natural peanut butter; nutrient-enhanced milk, cheese, sour cream, and popcorn; and other products. Leaders decided to use virtual teams, including employees and outside contractors, to enable Smart Balance to innovate and expand rapidly.

Smart Balance keeps product development and marketing in-house but uses contractors to do just about everything else, including manufacturing, distribution, sales, information technology services, and research and testing. Each morning, virtual team members exchange a flurry of e-mails, text messages, and phone calls to update each other on what took place the day before and what needs to happen today. Leaders spend much of their time building and managing team relationships. Twice a year they hold all-company meetings that include full-time Smart Balance employees and employees of contractors participating in virtual teams. Information is exchanged widely, and leaders make a point of recognizing the contributions of virtual members to the company's success, which helps create a sense of unity and commitment.[62]

10-6a Uses of Virtual Teams

According to recent surveys, nearly half of all organizations surveyed use virtual teams, and about 80 percent of employees at multinational corporations have been part of a virtual team at some time.[63] Virtual teams may be temporary

NEW LEADER
ACTION MEMO

As a leader, you can help a virtual team perform even with limited control and supervision. You can select members who thrive in a virtual environment, arrange opportunities for periodic face-to-face meetings, and ensure that members understand goals, responsibilities, and performance standards.

cross-departmental teams that work on specific projects, or they may be long-term, self-directed teams. One of the primary advantages of virtual teams is the ability to rapidly assemble the most talented group of people to complete a complex project, solve a particular problem, or exploit a specific strategic opportunity. The diverse mix of people can fuel creativity and innovation. On a practical level, organizations can save employees time and cut travel expenses when people meet in virtual rather than physical space. IBM reported that it saved more than $50 million in travel-related expenses in one recent year by using virtual teams.[64]

10-6b Challenges of Virtual Teams

Despite their potential benefits, there is growing evidence that virtual teams are often less effective than teams whose members meet face-to-face.[65] Studies indicate that, as virtual distance grows, innovative behavior can decline by a whopping 93 percent. Trust drops 83 percent, clarity of roles and objectives falls 62 percent, and project results such as on-time delivery and customer satisfaction decline by about 50 percent.[66] The team leader can make a tremendous difference in how well a virtual team performs, but virtual teams bring significant leadership challenges.[67]

Building team relationships and trust is the biggest challenge faced by virtual team leaders. "Being authentic, connecting with others ... and all of the interpersonal skills leaders use to build relationships and trust are always important," one team leader said, but in a virtual environment, "the actions associated with these skills must be *deliberate* and *intentional*."[68] Virtual team leaders have to trust people to do their jobs without constant supervision, and they learn to focus more on results than on the process of accomplishing them. Too much control can kill a virtual team, so leaders have to give up most of their control and yet at the same time provide guidance, encouragement, support, and development. To be successful, virtual team leaders can master the following skills:[69]

- *Select the Right Team Members*. Effective virtual team leaders put a lot of thought into getting the right mix of people on the team. Team members need the right mix of technical, interpersonal, and communication skills to work effectively in a virtual environment. In addition, leaders make clear to the team why each member was chosen to participate, thus giving people a basis for trust in others' abilities and commitment. Choosing people who have open, honest, and trusting personalities is also a plus. As with other types of teams, small virtual teams tend to be more cohesive and work together more effectively. However, diversity of views and experiences is also important to the success of a virtual team. Diversity is usually built into virtual teams because when leaders can pick the right people for the job, no matter where they are located, members usually reflect diverse backgrounds and viewpoints.[70]
- *Start Off Right*. Leaders make sure people have opportunities to know one another and establish trusting relationships. Studies of virtual teams suggest that an initial face-to-face meeting is one of the best ways to get people to come together as a team and rapidly go through the *forming* and *storming* stages of development, as discussed earlier in this chapter.[71] At Mobil Corporation, leaders bring virtual team members together in one location at the beginning of a project so they can begin to build personal relationships and gain an understanding of their goals and responsibilities. LivePerson Inc., a leading cloud-based platform company, builds in ways for people from around the world to come together face-to-face whenever there seems to be a need for it. "We understand there is

a cost to this, but we see real results, so it is a price we willingly pay," said a senior vice president.[72]

- *Use Technology to Build Relationships.* Leaders also apply technology to build relationships.[73] Leaders hold team meetings using Skype, for example, to enable people to get to know one another and clarify roles and project tasks. They also encourage non-task-related communication, such as the use of online social networking where people can share photos, thoughts, and personal biographies. "Managers often assume that people are mainly interested in what their fellow team members can do, not who they are," Keith Ferrazi wrote in a *Harvard Business Review* blog. "Wrong!" Ferrazi and other virtual team experts emphasize the value of non-work-related interactions.[74] Researchers have also found that round-the-clock virtual work spaces, where team members can access the latest versions of files, keep track of deadlines and timelines, monitor one another's progress, and carry on discussions between formal meetings enhance virtual team success.[75]
- *Agree on Ground Rules.* Leaders make everyone's roles, responsibilities, and authority clear from the beginning. All team members need to explicitly understand both team and individual goals, deadlines, and expectations for participation and performance. When roles and expectations are clear, trust can develop more easily. It is also important that leaders define a clear context so that people can make decisions, monitor their own performance, and regulate their behavior to accomplish goals. For each virtual team decision, Kevan Hall, CEO of Global Integration, asks team members to summarize the decision, whether they agree with it, and the specific actions they will take as a result of the decision.[76] Another important point is shaping norms of respectful interaction. Team members need to agree on communications etiquette, rules for "verbalizing" online when members are shifting mental gears or need more feedback, whether there are time limits on responding to voice mail or e-mail, and so forth.

As the use of virtual teams grows, there is growing understanding of what makes them successful. Some experts suggest that leaders solicit volunteers as much as possible for virtual teams, and interviews with virtual team members and leaders support the idea that members who truly want to work as a virtual team are more effective.[77]

10-7 HANDLING TEAM CONFLICT

As one would expect, there is an increased potential for conflict among members of virtual teams because of the greater chances for miscommunication and misunderstandings. Studies of virtual teams indicate that how they handle internal conflicts is critical to their success, yet conflict within virtual teams tends to occur more frequently and take longer to resolve. Moreover, people in virtual teams who communicate by e-mail tend to engage in more inconsiderate behaviors such as name-calling or insults than do people who work face-to-face.[78] Some people aren't cut out for virtual teamwork and show a greater propensity for shirking their duties or giving less than their full effort when working in a virtual environment, which can lead to team conflicts.[79] Cultural value differences, little face-to-face interaction, and lack of on-site monitoring make it harder to build team identity and commitment.

Whenever people work together in teams, some conflict is inevitable. Whether leading a virtual team or a team whose members work side-by-side, bringing conflicts into the open and effectively resolving them is one of the team leader's most important jobs. **Conflict** refers to antagonistic interaction in which one party attempts to block the intentions or goals of another.[80] Effective conflict management has a positive impact on team cohesiveness and performance.[81] High-performing teams typically have lower levels of conflict, and the conflict is more often associated with tasks than with interpersonal relationships. In addition, teams that reflect healthy patterns of conflict are usually characterized by high levels of trust and mutual respect.[82]

10-7a Types of Conflict

Two basic types of conflict that occur in teams are task conflict and relationship conflict.[83] **Task conflict** refers to disagreements among people about the goals to be achieved or the content of the tasks to be performed. Two shop foremen might disagree over whether to replace a machine's valve or let it run despite the unusual noise it is making. Or two members of a top management team might disagree about whether to acquire a company or enter into a joint venture as a way to expand globally. **Relationship conflict** refers to personal incompatibility that creates tension and feelings of personal animosity among people. For example, a recurring problem for many hospitals that have implemented teams is conflict between doctors and nurses or other team members. Many physicians are accustomed to being in charge and calling all the shots, and the shift to teamwork has been difficult. A survey of hospital administrators performed for the American College of Physician Executives found that 71 percent reported that disruptive behavior, such as doctors berating nurses for "interrupting" them with questions, surgeons flinging scalpels, or physicians demeaning coworkers they considered incompetent, occurred at least monthly at their hospital.[84]

In general, research suggests that task conflict can be beneficial because it leads to better decision making and problem solving. On the other hand, relationship conflict is typically associated with negative consequences for team effectiveness.[85] One study of top management teams, for example, found that task conflict was associated with higher decision quality, greater commitment, and more decision acceptance, while the presence of relationship conflict significantly reduced those same outcomes.[86]

10-7b Balancing Conflict and Cooperation

There is evidence that mild conflict can be beneficial to teams.[87] A healthy level of conflict helps to prevent *groupthink*, as described earlier, in which people are so committed to a cohesive team that they are reluctant to express contrary opinions. When people in work teams go along simply for the sake of harmony, problems typically result. Thus, a degree of conflict leads to better decision making because multiple viewpoints are expressed.

However, conflict that is too strong, that is focused on personal rather than work issues, or that is not managed appropriately can damage productivity, tear relationships apart, and interfere with the healthy exchange of ideas and information.[88] Team leaders have to find the right balance between conflict and cooperation, as illustrated in Exhibit 10.6. Too little conflict can decrease team performance because the team doesn't benefit from a mix of opinions and ideas—even disagreements—that might lead to better solutions or prevent the team from making mistakes. At the other end of the spectrum, too much conflict outweighs the

Conflict
antagonistic interaction in which one party attempts to thwart the intentions or goals of another

Task conflict
disagreement among people about the goals to be achieved or the content of the tasks to be performed

Relationship conflict
personal incompatibility that creates tension and feelings of personal animosity among people

EXHIBIT 10.6 Balance Conflict with Cooperation

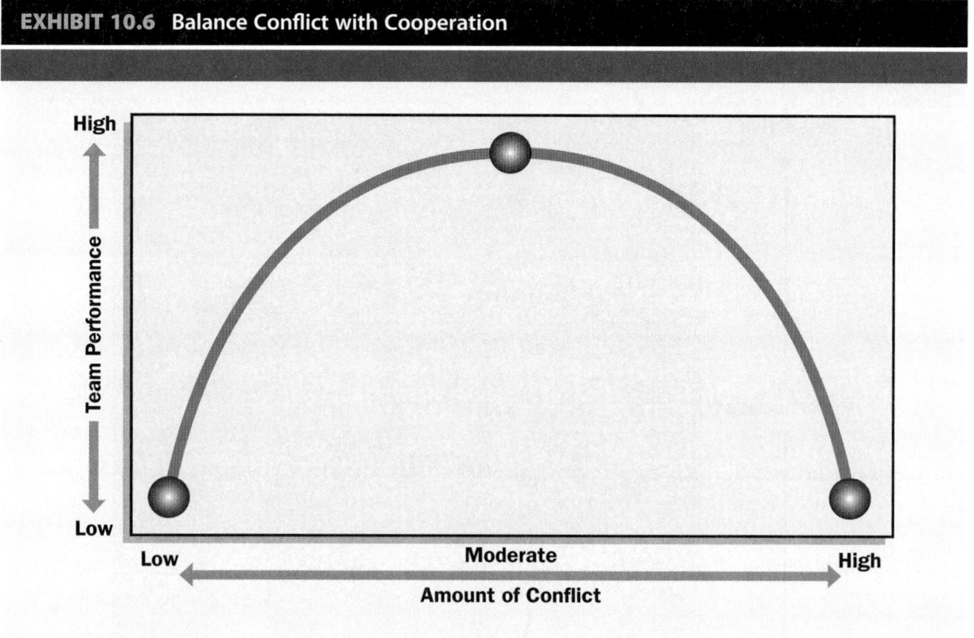

Source: From Richard L. Daft, *Management* 11th ed. (Mason, OH: Southwestern/Cengage Learning, 2014), p. 615.

team's cooperative efforts and leads to a decrease in employee satisfaction and commitment, hurting team performance. A moderate amount of conflict that is managed appropriately typically results in the highest levels of team performance.

10-7c Causes of Conflict

Several factors can lead to conflict.[89] One of the primary causes of conflict is competition over resources, such as money, information, or supplies. In similar fashion, conflict often occurs simply because people are using those resources to pursue differing goals. Goal differences are natural in organizations. For example, the sales department's goals for fast delivery on new orders might conflict with the manufacturing department's goals for high quality and efficiency.

The lack of clear roles and responsibilities can also lead to conflict. Consider the 2012 multibillion-dollar loss at JPMorgan Chase. Many people wondered how implementation of the company's careful low-risk trading strategy faltered so badly. Ina Drew, the senior banker who has been partly blamed for the problems, had won the complete trust of CEO Jamie Dimon after she steered the company through the 2008 financial crisis. However, Drew was out of the office a great deal of time due to illness beginning in 2010, and long-simmering conflicts and divisions over roles and responsibilities emerged. Drew's deputy in New York, Althea Duersten, disagreed with the risky, outsized bets being made by Achilles Macris, the deputy in London, but the London deputy used his stronger personality to shout down Duersten's objections. One trader underscored the lack of clear roles when he said he "didn't know who to listen to."[90]

10-7d Styles to Handle Conflict

Teams as well as individuals develop specific styles for dealing with conflict, based on the desire to satisfy their own concern versus the other party's concern. A model that describes five styles of handling conflict is in Exhibit 10.7. The two major

EXHIBIT 10.7 A Model of Styles to Handle Conflict

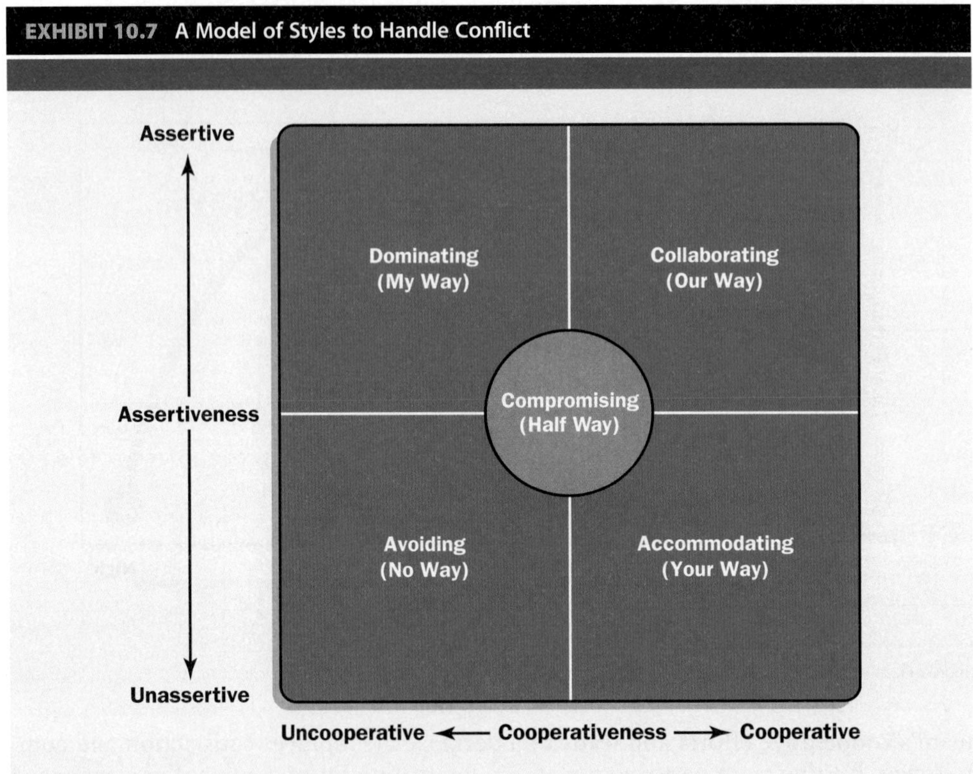

Sources: Based on Kenneth Thomas, "Conflict and Conflict Management," in *Handbook of Industrial and Organizational Behavior*, ed. M. D. Dunnette (New York: John Wiley, 1976), p 900; and Nan Peck, "Conflict 101: Styles of Fighting," *North Virginia Community College Website*, September 20, 2005, www.nvcc.edu/home/npeck/conflicthome/conflict/Conflict101/conflictstyles.htm (accessed April 13, 2011)

dimensions are the extent to which an individual is assertive versus unassertive and cooperative versus uncooperative in his or her approach to conflict.[91]

1. The *dominating style* (my way) reflects assertiveness to get one's own way and should be used when quick, decisive action is vital on important issues or unpopular actions, such as during emergencies or urgent cost cutting.
2. The *avoiding style* (no way) reflects neither assertiveness nor cooperativeness. It is appropriate when an issue is trivial, when there is no chance of winning, when a delay to gather more information is needed, or when a disruption would be costly.
3. The *compromising style* (half way) reflects a moderate amount of both assertiveness and cooperativeness. It is appropriate when the goals on both sides are equally important, when opponents have equal power and both sides want to split the difference, or when people need to arrive at temporary or expedient solutions under time pressure.
4. The *accommodating style* (your way) reflects a high degree of cooperativeness, which works best when people realize that they are wrong, when an issue is more important to others than to oneself, when building social credits for use in later discussions, and when maintaining harmony is especially important.
5. The *collaborating style* (our way) reflects a high degree of both assertiveness and cooperativeness. The collaborating style enables both parties to win, although it

NEW LEADER
ACTION MEMO

Which conflict-handling style do you tend to use most often? Answer the questions in Leader's Self-Insight 10.3 to find out. Try to think of conflict situations you've been involved in where each of the styles might be appropriate.

LEADER'S SELF-INSIGHT 10.3

How Do You Handle Team Conflict?

Instructions: Think about how you typically handle a dispute or disagreement with a team member, friend, or coworker, and then respond to the following statements based on whether they are Mostly False or Mostly True for you. There are no right or wrong answers, so answer honestly.

	Mostly False	Mostly True
1. I try hard to win my position.		✓
2. I strongly assert my opinion in a disagreement.		✓
3. I raise my voice to get other people to accept my position.		✓
4. I feel that differences are not worth arguing about.		✓
5. I would usually avoid a person who wants to discuss a disagreement.	✓	
6. I would rather keep my views to myself than argue.	✓	
7. I give in a little if other people do the same.	✓	
8. I will split the difference to reach an agreement.		✓
9. I typically give up some points in exchange for others.		✓
10. I don't want to hurt other people's feelings.		✓
11. I am quick to agree when someone I am arguing with makes a good point.		✓
12. I try to smooth over disagreements.		✓
13. I suggest a solution that includes the other person's point of view.		✓
14. I consider the merits of other viewpoints as equal to my own.		✓
15. I try to include the other person's ideas to create an acceptable solution.		✓

Scoring and Interpretation

Five categories of conflict-handling strategies are measured in this instrument: dominating, avoiding, compromising, accommodating, and collaborating. By comparing your scores on the following five scales, you can identify your preferred or natural conflict-handling strategy by the highest score.

To calculate your five scores, give yourself 1 point for each Mostly True answer for the three items indicated.

Dominating: Items 1, 2, 3: 3
Avoiding: Items 4, 5, 6: 1
Compromising: Items 7, 8, 9: 2
Accommodating: Items 10, 11, 12: 3
Collaborating: Items 13, 14, 15: 3

Briefly review the text material (pages 314, 315) about these five strategies for handling conflict. Do you agree that your highest score represents the style you use the most? Which strategy do you find the most difficult to use? How would your conflict strategy differ if the other person was a family member rather than a team member? Can you think of a situation where a conflict strategy in which you are weak might be more effective? Explain your scores to another student and listen to the explanation for his or her scores.

Source: Adapted from "How Do You Handle Conflict?" in Robert E. Quinn et al., *Becoming a Master Manager* (New York: Wiley, 1990), pp. 221–223.

may require substantial bargaining and negotiation. The collaborating style is important when both sets of concerns are too important to be compromised, when insights from different people need to be merged into an overall solution, and when the commitment of both sides is needed for a consensus.

An example of the collaborating style comes from the 2008 Beijing Olympic Games. When building the Beijing National Aquatics Center (typically called the Water Cube), two architectural firms—one Chinese and the other Australian—developed designs that were totally different. Although this created some tension, instead of fighting for their own ideas, the two sides came up with a totally new concept that excited everyone. The resulting award-winning building is spectacular.[92]

Each of the five styles is appropriate in certain cases, and effective team members and leaders vary their style to fit the specific situation and the people involved.

NEW LEADER
ACTION MEMO

As a leader, you can adopt the best approach for handling a team conflict. Choose among the dominating, avoiding, compromising, accommodating, or collaborating styles based on the degree of assertiveness and cooperativeness needed to manage the situation.

10-7e Negotiation

One distinctive type of conflict management is negotiation, whereby people engage in give-and-take discussions and consider various alternatives to reach a joint decision that is acceptable to both parties. Negotiation is typically used when a conflict is formalized, such as between a union and management.

Ways to Negotiate Conflicting parties may embark on negotiation from different perspectives and with different intentions, reflecting either an *integrative* approach or a *distributive* approach.

Integrative negotiation is based on a win–win assumption, in that all parties want to come up with a creative solution that can benefit both sides. Rather than viewing the conflict as a win–lose situation, people look at the issues from multiple angles, consider trade-offs, and try to "expand the pie" rather than divide it. With integrative negotiation, conflicts are managed through cooperation and compromise, which fosters trust and positive long-term relationships. **Distributive negotiation**, on the other hand, assumes the "size of the pie" is fixed, and each party tries to get as much of it as possible. One side wants to win, which means the other side must lose. With this win–lose approach, distributive negotiation is competitive and adversarial rather than collaborative, and it does not typically lead to positive long-term relationships.[93]

Most experts emphasize the value of integrative negotiation for today's collaborative business environment. That is, the key to effectiveness is to see negotiation not as a zero-sum game but as a process for reaching a creative solution that benefits everyone.[94]

Rules for Reaching a Win–Win Solution Achieving a win–win solution through integrative negotiation is based on four key strategies:[95]

- *Separate the People from the Problem.* For successful integrative negotiation, people stay focused on the problem and the source of conflict rather than attacking or attempting to discredit each other.
- *Focus on Underlying Interests, not Current Demands.* Demands are what each person wants from the negotiation, whereas underlying interests represent the "why" behind the demands. Consider two sisters arguing over the last orange in the fruit bowl. Each insisted she should get the orange and refused to give up (demands). If one sister had asked the other *why* she wanted the orange (interests), the sisters would have discovered that one wanted to eat it and the other wanted the peel to use for a project. By focusing on interests, the sisters would be able to arrive at a solution that gave each what she wanted.[96] *Demands* create yes-or-no obstacles to effective negotiation, whereas underlying *interests* present problems that can be solved creatively.
- *Listen and Ask Questions.* A good strategy for most negotiations is to listen and ask questions. Leaders can learn more about their opponent's position, their constraints, and their needs by being quiet or asking questions. Smart negotiators want to learn the other side's constraints so they can help overcome them. Effective negotiators don't dismiss the opposing party's limitation as unreasonable or think "that's their problem." Rather, they try to come up with a solution for the opponent so both parties can get closer to an agreement.
- *Insist that Results be Based on Objective Standards.* Each party in a negotiation has its own interests and would naturally like to maximize its outcomes. Successful negotiation requires focusing on objective criteria and maintaining standards of fairness rather than using subjective judgments about the best solution.

Integrative negotiation a cooperative approach to negotiation in which conflicting parties try to reach a win–win solution

Distributive negotiation adversarial negotiation in which conflicting parties compete to win the most resources and give up as little as possible

LEADERSHIP ESSENTIALS

- Many leaders are called upon to facilitate teams rather than manage direct-report subordinates. Teams can be effective in providing the coordination and information sharing needed to accomplish interdependent tasks. Functional teams typically are part of the traditional organization structure. Cross-departmental teams include people from different functional areas and are often formed for projects of special importance. Self-directed teams are member-centered rather than leader-centered and -directed.
- Teams present a dilemma for many people. Individuals have to give up their independence and sometimes make sacrifices for the good of the team. Other potential problems are free riders and dysfunctional teams.
- The team leader plays a big part in whether a team achieves high performance. Five things leaders provide that contribute to high performance are: compelling purpose and clear objectives, clear roles and diversity of skills, streamlined team size, decision authority over how to achieve goals, and support and coaching.
- Teams go through stages of development and change over time. Guiding a team through these stages is an important part of team leadership. In addition, leaders encourage team cohesiveness, help establish productive norms, and make sure people contribute their skills and competencies needed for the team to be effective. Every team must possess the following competencies: goal setting and performance management, planning and coordination, collaborative problem solving, communication, and conflict resolution. Team members take on various roles that meet both task needs and socioemotional needs.
- These principles apply to virtual and global teams as well. However, being a team leader is even more challenging when people are scattered in different geographic locations and may be separated by language and cultural differences. To create effective, smoothly functioning virtual teams, leaders select team members who have the skills and temperaments to work virtually, use technology to build trusting relationships, and agree on ground rules for the team.
- All teams experience some conflict because of scarce resources, goal conflicts, or power and status differences. Leaders try to balance conflict and cooperation and use varied styles to handle conflict, including the dominating style, avoiding style, compromising style, accommodating style, and collaborating style. Each style can be effective in certain circumstances.
- One type of conflict management is negotiation. Good leaders try to use integrative negotiation, which is based on a win–win assumption, rather than distributive negotiation, in which each party strives to get as much as it can at the expense of the other party.

DISCUSSION QUESTIONS

1. What is the difference between a "team" and a "group"? Describe your personal experience with each.
2. Discuss the differences between a cross-departmental team and a self-directed team. Do you believe self-directed teams could be effectively used in certain types of organizations? Explain.

3. Which of the five elements of high-performance teams do you think would be most difficult for a leader to implement in a virtual team? Explain.
4. Describe the stages of team development. How would you facilitate a team's development through each stage?
5. How might an individual's dilemma about teamwork be intensified or reduced in a virtual team? As a virtual team leader, what would you do to manage these dilemmas?
6. The chapter suggests that very small teams (say, three to six members) perform better, and most people prefer to work in small teams. However, many companies use teams of 100 or more people to perform complex tasks, such as creating and developing a new product. Do you think a unit of that size can truly function as a team? Discuss.
7. Discuss the relationship between team cohesiveness and performance. As a leader, can you think of specific ways you would encourage norms of cohesiveness and collaboration?
8. Think about a team you have participated in to do a class project or a sports team on which you participated. Can you identify members who played a task-specialist role and those who played a socioemotional role? What behaviors were associated with each?
9. What style of handling conflict do you typically use? Can you think of instances where a different style might have been more productive?
10. If you were the leader of a team developing a new computer game, how might you apply negotiation to resolve a conflict between two strong-willed members related to which features to include in the game?

LEADERSHIP AT WORK

Team Feedback

Think back to your most recent experience working in a team, either at work or school. Write down your answers to the following questions about your role in the team.

What did the team members appreciate about you?

____

____

____

What did the team members learn from you?

____

____

____

What could the team members count on you for?

____

____

____

How could you have improved your contribution to the team?

____

____

____

Evaluate your answers. What is the overall meaning of your answers? What are the implications for your role as a team member? As a team leader?

____

____

____

In Class: "Team Feedback" is an excellent exercise to use for student feedback to one another after a specific team class project or other activities done together during the class. If there were no assigned team activities but students have gotten to know each other in class, they can be divided into groups and asked to provide the information with respect to their participation in the class instead of in the student team.

The instructor can ask the student groups to sit in a circle facing one another. Then one person will volunteer to be the focal person, and each of the other team members will tell that team member the following:

- What I appreciate about you
- What I learned from you
- What I could count on you for
- My one suggestion for improvement as a team leader/member

When the team members have given feedback to the focal person, another team member volunteers to hear feedback, and the process continues until each person has heard the four elements of feedback from every other team member.

The key questions for student learning are: Are you developing the skills and behaviors to be a team leader? If not, what does that mean for you? If you are now providing team leadership, how can you continue to grow and improve as a team leader?

Source: Thanks to William Miller for suggesting the questions for this exercise.

LEADERSHIP DEVELOPMENT: CASES FOR ANALYSIS

Decision Time

Ben Dooley and Casey Stringer had agreed to stop for coffee in the atrium Starbucks before heading up to the 35th floor for a board meeting.

"You seem deep in thought," Ben said, placing the two cups of hot coffee on the table.

"Watching Johnna and Robert in previous board meetings helps me to understand why the folks in Congress can't get anything done," Casey mused. "Both sides have stated their positions and nothing, *nothing* will budge them. I dread this meeting. I'd rather have a root canal."

"Well, while the two giants battle it out, the rest of us will have to work out some sort of compromise. We outsourced manufacturing operations to China several years ago to cut costs and now things are changing rapidly and we have a major decision. Does Bishop's Engineered Plastics make the best of the situation in China ...?"

"... Or do we re-shore?" Casey added.

"Someone will have to be the voice of reason today," Ben said. "Robert Ma has overseen the outsourcing to China and, initially, it was a great move."

"I agree the cost savings were pretty amazing. The retooling and creation of a state-of-the-art factory in Wenzhou by the Chinese really propelled us to a new level within the industry."

"Well, 2012 is the Year of the Dragon, and the dragon is having a problem," Ben replied.

"Yes, Robert is going to have to face the fact that if we stay in China, we have to move from Wenzhou," Casey pointed out. "The worker shortage is bad and getting worse. The last estimates for that region were one million workers short. As wages go up and other opportunities present themselves, manufacturing jobs are losing their appeal in the cities. In our plant the managers have to come down and work on the lines. That's not good. Now, to try to stave off a mass industrial exodus, the Chinese are offering a stimulus to industries to relocate into the interior of the country. The interior offers more workers and lower wages…."

"And a factory move will delay manufacturing and make shipping even more difficult," Ben replied. "Add to that the Chinese insistence on full payment before shipping, and we're looking at some potentially serious delays."

"Johnna, on the other hand, is going to argue that the situation in China is an indication that now is the perfect time to re-shore—bring the jobs back to the good old U.S. of A.," Casey said. "She's going to dig in her heels on this one and you and I know that at least two members of that 'august' board are going to back off and let her have her way with no careful analysis of the pros and cons." I sometimes think Frank is a people pleaser, always agreeable, especially toward Johnna, because she is the chair. And Martha usually doesn't say anything, much less offer an opinion. She stares down at her hands when the going gets heavy."

"The pros for Johnna are obvious—bring jobs home when jobs are needed, shorten the supply line, reduce shipping costs, offer faster response to customers, and, I believe, offer a better quality product. It is worth a little higher labor cost."

"And what are the cons?"

"The problems are the higher wages here and the cost of retooling factories in this country that have been down for a few years."

"But," Casey asked, "Would we have to build a new factory deep in China's interior? No. And will their interior workforce be adequately trained? I would guess not. The Chinese government will help with building and relocation costs, but still…."

"So both Johnna and Robert have a strong argument and some glaring weaknesses. Is there room in here for a compromise? That's what I would like to see. They would both get something," opined Ben.

"I don't know. I'm eager to see what each one of them presents. It should be an interesting conversation."

"Or an afternoon in hell," Ben said as the two headed for the elevator. "I wonder what you and I might do to help Johnna and Robert resolve this conflict. What do you think we should do, Casey?"

QUESTIONS

1. What styles for handling conflict appear among the board members? Explain.
2. What options do Ben and Casey have for helping resolve the conflict between Johnna and Robert? What conflict styles might they adopt for this meeting?
3. What suggestions would you make to help board members arrive at a good team decision?

Devereaux-Dering Group

Dashing to catch a cab at the corner of Sixth and Vine, the account team was exhilarated. After a quick exchange of high fives, three of the four jumped into the backseat of a cab to return to the Manhattan offices of Devereaux-Dering, a global advertising agency with offices in New York, Hong Kong, and Paris. The team couldn't wait to tell their team leader, Kurt Lansing, that they had won the BMW account that morning. The fourth team member, Brad Fitzgerald, stood apart from the animated group, studying his BlackBerry and then hailing a cab for an afternoon flight out of LaGuardia.

After a two-year slump in sales, Devereaux-Dering needed a big score like the BMW account. To drive new business and land high-profile accounts like this one, the company had hired Kurt Lansing, an MBA from Wharton, with prominent status in the advertising industry. His job was to lead a new business team to study the market, develop strategies, and acquire major accounts. Lansing hand-selected four high achievers for his team that represented each area of the business: Brad Fitzgerald, creative director; Trish Roderick, account services; Adrienne Walsh, production manager; and Tyler Green, brand strategy.

"That was a shocker!" said Roderick as she scooted across the backseat of the cab to make room for her teammates. "The client didn't seem too impressed with our presentation until Fitzgerald presented the last set of slides describing the global campaign. They loved it. I think he single-handedly clinched the deal when he presented the tag line for the Asian market," she said excitedly.

"He's a real whiz, alright," muttered Green. "The eighth wonder of the world." Sighing deeply and losing his earlier exuberance, Green said, "We couldn't have bagged the deal without him, and I know we'll all get credit. But none of us knew he planned to present that last part of the global campaign. I know he was working on that tag line late last night, but there was plenty of time this morning to get team input on it. I hate surprises in front of a client. I felt like a fool, even if we did win the business."

"He's a regular white knight," chuckled Walsh, "riding in at the last minute to save the day. I suppose we should appreciate him, but he's just so irritating. He snapped at me last week for not telling him about a client who was upset about delays in their ad campaign. I reminded him that I had told him about it in our status meeting, but he wasn't listening at the time. He was glued to his precious BlackBerry, as usual. Why have team meetings if he isn't going to participate?"

Roderick was surprised by her teammates' reaction to Fitzgerald. She thought they had been working well together. She was quickly discovering, however, an undercurrent of resentment. This was the first time that she had been exposed to the conflict that was simmering below the surface. No doubt, Fitzgerald did have a strong ego and aggressive personality. A previously successful entrepreneur, Fitzgerald had a track record of success and was very ambitious. However, she did notice that he didn't show respect for differing opinions or invite collaboration on ideas. She wondered if he was placing his own success above the team's. But why complain if the team was sharing the credit and earning fat bonuses along with him? She was content to go with the status quo. "You know," she said, "we're darn lucky to be on his team."

She stared out the cab window at the passing traffic and listened to her two teammates continue to grouse. "I should have known something was up when I walked past his office last night and saw him working with the new copywriter. They must have been hashing out the new tag line," smirked Green. "We are a team, aren't we? The system is bigger than the individual, remember? He doesn't seem too concerned about the welfare of the team—only his own."

"Well, let's all have a heart-to-heart with Mr. McWhiz," said Walsh sarcastically. "I'm sure he'll see things our way. We'll give him a brief overview of Teamwork 101. That will go over great!" As the cab pulled to the curb, they tossed the driver a $20 bill and headed to their offices on the 40th floor. They would all stop to see the team leader, Kurt Lansing, first.

In the meantime, Lansing smiled broadly when he received Fitzgerald's text message that they had won the BMW account. Sinking back in his chair, he marveled at the cohesiveness and success of his team. All that time building a shared vision and building trust was starting to pay off.

QUESTIONS

1. What factors do you think are affecting this team's cohesiveness? Explain.
2. If you were the team leader, what could you do to bring Fitzgerald into the team more and foster better relationships among the team members?
3. As a team member, what would you do? Should the three members of the team confront Fitzgerald with their concerns? Should they inform Kurt Lansing? Explain your answers.

REFERENCES

1. Paul Ziobro, "Floundering Mattel Tries to Make Things Fun Again," *The Wall Street Journal* (December 22, 2014), http://www.wsj.com/articles/floundering-mattel-tries-to-make-things-fun-again-1419305830 (accessed November 6, 2015).
2. Linda I. Glassop, "The Organizational Benefit of Teams," *Human Relations* 55, no. 2 (2002), pp. 225–249; and J. D. Osburn, L. Moran, E. Musselwhite, and J. H. Zenger, *Self-Directed Work Teams: The New American Challenge* (Homewood, IL: Business One Irwin, 1990).
3. This definition is based on J. Richard Hackman, *Leading Teams: Setting the Stage for Great Performances* (Boston: Harvard Business School Press, 2002); Dawn R. Utley and Stephanie E. Brown, "Establishing Characteristic Differences between Team and Working Group Behaviors," *Institute of Industrial Engineers Annual Conference Proceedings* (2010), pp. 1–6; and Carl E. Larson and Frank M. J. LaFasto, *Team Work* (Newbury Park, CA: Sage Publications, 1989).
4. Somini Sengupta, "For Search, Facebook Had to Go beyond 'Robospeak,'" *The New York Times* (January 28, 2013), http://www.nytimes.com/2013/01/29/business/how-facebook-taught-its-search-tool-to-understand-people.html?pagewanted=all&_r=0 (accessed May 3, 2013).
5. Chuck Salter, "What LeBron James and the Miami Heat Teach Us about Teamwork," *Fast Company* (April 2011), http://www.fastcompany.com/magazine/155/the-worlds-greatest-chemistry-experiment.html (accessed April 25, 2011).
6. Ibid.
7. Telis Demos, "Cirque du Balancing Act," *Fortune* (June 12, 2006), p. 114; Erin White, "How a Company Made Everyone a Team Player," *The Wall Street Journal* (August 13, 2007); and David Kirkpatrick, "Inside Sam's $100 Billion Growth Machine," *Fortune* (June 14, 2004), pp. 80–98.
8. "A Company of 'Level 5' Leaders," *Inc.* (June 2010), pp. 87–88; and Miri McDonald, "Tasty Catering on Driving Engagement through Empowerment and Shared Decision Making," *SmartBlog on Leadership* (April 15, 2011), https://smartblogs.com/leadership/2011/04/15/tasty-catering-on-driving-engagement-through-transparency-and-shared-decision-making/ (accessed June 12, 2013).
9. This discussion of self-directed teams is based on Patricia Booth, "Embracing the Team Concept," *Canadian Business Review* (Autumn 1994), pp. 10–13; Pierre van Amelsvoort and Jos Benders, "Team Time: A Model for Developing Self-Directed Work Teams," *International Journal of Operations and Production Management* 16, no. 2 (1996), pp. 159–170; and Jeanne M. Wilson, Jill George, and Richard S. Wellins, with William C. Byham, *Leadership Trapeze: Strategies for Leadership in Team-Based Organizations* (San Francisco: Jossey-Bass, 1994).
10. Doug Kirkpatrick, "Self-Management's Success at Morning Star," *T + D* (October 2012), pp. 25–27.
11. Heleen van Mierlo, Christel G. Rutte, Michiel A. J. Kompier, and Hans A.C.M. Doorewaard, "Self-Managing Teamwork and Psychological Well-Being: Review of a Multilevel Research Domain," *Group & Organization Management* 30, no. 2 (2005), pp. 211–235.
12. Wilson et al., *Leadership Trapeze*.
13. Jill Jusko, "Engaged Teams Keep Lockheed Martin Delivering on Time, Every Time," *IndustryWeek* (January 2013), p. 26.
14. Kenneth Labich, "Elite Teams Get the Job Done," *Fortune* (February 19, 1996), pp. 90–99.
15. White, "How a Company Made Everyone a Team Player."
16. Study by G. Clotaire Rapaille, reported in Karen Bernowski, "What Makes American Teams Tick?" *Quality Progress* 28, no. 1 (January 1995), pp. 39–42.
17. Robert Albanese and David D. Van Fleet, "Rational Behavior in Groups: The Free-Riding Tendency," *Academy of Management Review* 10 (1985), pp. 244–255.
18. Reported in Matt Vella, "White Collar Workers Shoulder Together—Like It or Not" (Inside Innovation section: InData), *BusinessWeek* (April 28, 2008), p. 58.
19. See David H. Freedman, "The Idiocy of Crowds" (What's Next column), *Inc.* (September 2006), pp. 61–62; "Why Some Teams Succeed (and So Many Don't)," *Harvard Management Update* (October 2006), pp. 3–4; and Geoffrey Colvin, "Why Dream Teams Fail," *Fortune* (June 12, 2006), pp. 87–92.
20. Jared Sandberg, "Some Ideas Are So Bad That Only Team Efforts Can Account for Them" (Cubicle Culture column), *The Wall Street Journal* (September 29, 2004).
21. Patrick Lencioni, *The Five Dysfunctions of a Team* (New York: John Wiley & Sons, 2002).
22. "Why Some Teams Succeed (and So Many Don't)."
23. Studies reported in Amy Edmondson, Richard Bohmer, and Gary Pisano, "Speeding Up Team Learning," *Harvard Business Review* (October 2001), pp. 125–132; and Scott Thurm, "Teamwork Raises Everyone's Game—Having Everyone Bond Benefits Companies More Than Promoting Stars" (Theory & Practice column), *The Wall Street Journal* (November 7, 2005), p. B8.
24. Stephen H. Courtright, Greg L. Stewart, and Marcia M. Ward, "Applying Research to Save Lives: Learning from Team Training Approaches in Aviation and Health Care," *Organizational Dynamics* 41 (2012), pp. 291–301.
25. These factors are based partly on "Why Some Teams Succeed (and So Many Don't)"; Ruth Wageman, "Critical Success Factors for Creating Superb Self-Managing Teams," *Organizational Dynamics* (Summer 1997), pp. 49–61; and Richard Hackman, *Leading Teams: Setting the Stage for Great Performances* (Boston, MA: Harvard Business School Press, 2002).
26. J. Polzer, W. Swann Jr., and L. Milton, "The Benefits of Verifying Diverse Identities for Group Performance," in M. Neale, E. Mannix, and J. Polzer, eds., *Research on Managing Groups and Teams: Identity Issues in Groups*, Vol. 5 (Stamford, CT: JAI Press, 2003), pp. 91–112.
27. Warren E. Watson, Kamalesh Kumar, and Larry K. Michaelsen, "Cultural Diversity's Impact on Interaction Process and Performance: Comparing Homogeneous and Diverse Task Groups," *Academy of Management Journal* 36 (1993), pp. 590–602; and Gail Robinson and Kathleen Dechant, "Building a Business Case for Diversity," *Academy of Management Executive* 11, no. 3 (1997), pp. 21–31.
28. Lynda Gratton and Tamara J. Erickson, "Eight Ways to Build Collaborative Teams," *Harvard Business Review* (November 2007), pp. 101–109.
29. Jeffrey T. Polzer, "Leading Teams," *Harvard Business Publishing for Educators*, Background Note, Product #403094-PDF-ENG (ordered at http://cb.hbsp.harvard.edu/cb/product/403094-PDF-ENG).
30. This summary of team size research is based on Martin Hoegl, "Smaller Teams—Better Teamwork: How to Keep Project Teams Small," *Business Horizons* 48 (2005), pp. 209–214; Lillian Chaney and Julie Lyden, "Making U.S. Teams Work," *Supervision* (January 2000), p. 6; Jia Lynn Yang, "The Power of Number 4.6," part of a special series, "Secrets of Greatness: Teamwork," *Fortune* (June 12, 2006), p. 122; M. E. Shaw, *Group Dynamics*, 3rd ed. (New York: McGraw Hill, 1981); and G. Manners, "Another Look at Group Size, Group Problem Solving, and Group Consensus," *Academy of Management Journal* 18 (1975), pp. 715–724.
31. Gallup poll results reported in "Viva La Difference," box in Julie Connelly, "All Together Now," *Gallup Management Journal* (Spring 2002), pp. 13–18.
32. Stephen D. Reicher, Michael J. Platow, and S. Alexander Haslam, "The New Psychology of Leadership," *Scientific American Mind* (August–September 2007), pp. 23–29.

33. C. Shawn Burke, Kevin C. Stagl, Cameron Klein, Gerald F. Goodwin, Eduardo Salas, and Stanley M. Halpin, "What Type of Leadership Behaviors Are Functional in Teams? A Meta-Analysis," *The Leadership Quarterly* 17 (2006), pp. 288–307; Greg L. Stewart, "A Meta-Analytic Review of Relationships between Team Design Features and Team Performance," *Journal of Management* 32, no. 1 (February 2006), pp. 29–54; Abhishek Srivastava, Kathryn M. Bartol, and Edwin A. Locke, "Empowering Leadership in Management Teams: Effects on Knowledge Sharing, Efficacy, and Performance," *Academy of Management Journal* 49, no. 6 (December 2006), pp. 1239–1251; and Gratton and Erickson, "Eight Ways to Build Collaborative Teams."
34. Gervase R. Bushe and Graeme H. Coetzer, "Group Development and Team Effectiveness: Using Cognitive Representations to Measure Group Development and Predict Task Performance and Group Viability," *The Journal of Applied Behavioral Science* 43, no. 2 (June 2007), pp. 184–212; Kenneth G. Koehler, "Effective Team Management," *Small Business Report* (July 19, 1989), pp. 14–16; Connie J. G. Gersick, "Time and Transition in Work Teams: Toward a New Model of Group Development," *Academy of Management Journal* 31 (1988), pp. 9–41; and John Beck and Neil Yeager, "Moving beyond Myths," *Training & Development* (March 1996), pp. 51–55.
35. Bruce W. Tuckman, "Developmental Sequence in Small Groups," *Psychological Bulletin* 63 (1965), pp. 384–399; and B. W. Tuckman and M. A. Jensen, "Stages of Small Group Development Revisited," *Group and Organizational Studies* 2 (1977), pp. 419–427.
36. Oluremi B. Ayoko, Alison M. Konrad, and Maree V. Boyle, "Online Work: Managing Conflict and Emotions for Performance in Virtual Teams," *European Management Journal* 30 (2012), pp. 156–174.
37. Ibid.
38. This is based on a true story of an anonymous company reported in Vicki Fuller Hudson, "From Divided to Ignited to United," *Industrial Management* (May–June 2010), pp. 17–20.
39. Shaw, *Group Dynamics*.
40. Daniel C. Feldman and Hugh J. Arnold, *Managing Individual and Group Behavior in Organizations* (New York: McGraw-Hill, 1983).
41. Harold J. Leavitt and Jean Lipman-Blumen, "Hot Groups," *Harvard Business Review* (July–August 1995), pp. 109–116.
42. Amanuel G. Tekleab, Narda R. Quigley, and Paul E. Tesluk, "A Longitudinal Study of Team Conflict, Conflict Management, Cohesion, and Team Effectiveness," *Group & Organization Management* 34, no. 2 (April 2009), pp. 170–205; Dorwin Cartwright and Alvin Zander, *Group Dynamics: Research and Theory*, 3rd ed. (New York: Harper & Row, 1968); Elliot Aronson, *The Social Animal* (San Francisco: W. H. Freeman, 1976); and Thomas Li-Ping Tang and Amy Beth Crofford, "Self-Managing Work Teams," *Employment Relations Today* (Winter 1995/96), pp. 29–39.
43. Vishal K. Gupta, Rui Huang, and Suman Niranjan, "A Longitudinal Examination of the Relationship between Team Leadership and Performance," *Journal of Leadership and Organizational Studies* 17, no. 4 (2010), pp. 335–350; and Marcial Losada and Emily Heaphy, "The Role of Positivity and Connectivity in the Performance of Business Teams," *American Behavioral Scientist* 47, no. 6 (February 2004), pp. 740–765.
44. Ben Cohen, "Golden State: The Team That Eats Together," *The Wall Street Journal* (February 11, 2015), http://www.wsj.com/articles/golden-state-the-team-that-eats-together-1423682960 (accessed November 9, 2015); Jared Stearne, "Warriors' Continuity Could Prove More Valuable than Change for the Rockets, Spurs," *Golden State of Mind* (November 8, 2015), http://www.goldenstateofmind.com/2015/11/8/9692794/golden-state-warriors-continuity-san-antonio-spurs-houston-rockets (accessed November 9, 2015); and "Warriors-Pistons Preview," *NBA.com* (November 9, 2015), http://www.nba.com/warriors/gameday/20151109/preview (accessed November 9, 2015).
45. Bank of America example from Rachel Emma Silverman, "Tracking Sensors Invade the Workplace; Devices on Workers, Furniture Offer Clues for Boosting Productivity," *The Wall Street Journal* (March 7, 2013), http://online.wsj.com/article/SB10001424127887324034804578344303429080678.html (accessed May 3, 2013); and studies reported in Tang and Crofford, "Self-Managing Work Teams."
46. Shlomo Ben-Hur, Nikolas Kinley, and Karsten Jonsen, "Coaching Executive Teams to Reach Better Decisions," *Journal of Management Development* 31, no. 7 (2012), pp. 711–723; and Matt Palmquist, "The Dangers of Too Much Workplace Cohesion," *Strategy + Business* (February 10, 2015), http://www.strategy-business.com/blog/The-Dangers-of-Too-Much-Workplace-Cohesion?gko=ef547 (accessed November 6, 2015).
47. Stanley E. Seashore, *Group Cohesiveness in the Industrial Work Group* (Ann Arbor, MI: Institute for Social Research, 1954).
48. J. Richard Hackman, "Group Influences on Individuals," in M. Dunnette, ed., *Handbook of Industrial and Organizational Psychology* (Chicago: Rand McNally, 1976).
49. These are based on Daniel C. Feldman, "The Development and Enforcement of Group Norms," *Academy of Management Review* 9 (1984), pp. 47–53.
50. Wilson et al., *Leadership Trapeze*, p. 12.
51. Simon Taggar and Robert Ellis, "The Role of Leaders in Shaping Formal Team Norms," *The Leadership Quarterly* 18 (2007), pp. 105–120.
52. Colvin, "Why Dream Teams Fail."
53. Matt Moffett, "Trapped Miners Kept Focus, Shared Tuna—Foiled Escape, Bid to Organize Marked First Two Weeks Underground in Chile," *The Wall Street Journal* (August 25, 2010); and "Lessons on Leadership and Teamwork—From 700 Meters below the Earth's Surface," *Universia Knowledge @ Wharton* (September 22, 2010), http://www.wharton.universia.net/index.cfm?fa=viewArticle&id=1943&language=english (accessed September 29, 2010).
54. These are based on Michael J. Stevens and Michael A. Campion, "The Knowledge, Skill, and Ability Requirements for Teamwork: Implications for Human Resource Management," *Journal of Management* 20, no. 2 (1994), pp. 503–530.
55. R. Oser, G. A. McCallum, E. Salas, and B. B. Morgan, *Toward a Definition of Teamwork: An Analysis of Critical Team Behaviors*, Technical Report NTSC 89-004 (Arlington, VA: Office of Naval Research, 1989); and A. S. Glickman, S. Zimmer, R. C. Montero et al., *The Evolution of Team Skills: An Empirical Assessment with Implications for Training*, Technical Report NTSC 87-016 (Arlington, VA: Office of Naval Research, 1987).
56. Robert A. Baron, *Behavior in Organizations*, 2nd ed. (Boston: Allyn & Bacon, 1986).
57. Ibid.
58. Reported in Gratton and Erickson, "Ways to Build Collaborative Teams."
59. The discussion of virtual teams is based on Anthony M. Townsend, Samuel M. DeMarie, and Anthony R. Hendrickson, "Virtual Teams: Technology and the Workplace of the Future," *Academy of Management Executive* 12, no. 3 (August 1998), pp. 17–29; Deborah L. Duarte and Nancy Tennant Snyder, *Mastering Virtual Teams* (San Francisco: Jossey-Bass, 1999); and Jessica Lipnack and Jeffrey Stamps, "Virtual Teams: The New Way to Work," *Strategy & Leadership* (January–February 1999), pp. 14–18. For a recent review of virtual team research, see Lucy L. Gilson, M. Travis Maynard, Nicole C. Jones Young, et al., "Virtual Teams Research: 10 Years, 10 Themes, and 10 Opportunities," *Journal of Management* 41, no. 5 (July 2015), pp. 1313–1337.
60. Vijay Govindarajan and Anil K. Gupta, "Building an Effective Global Business Team," *MIT Sloan Management Review* 42, no. 4 (Summer 2001), pp. 63–71.
61. Bradford W. Bell and Steve W. J. Kozlowski, "A Typology of Virtual Teams: Implications for Effective Leadership," *Group & Organization Management* 27, no. 1 (March 2002), pp. 14–49.
62. Joann S. Lublin, "Smart Balance Keeps Tight Focus on Creativity" (Theory & Practice column), *The Wall Street Journal* (June 8, 2009); and Rebecca Reisner, "A Smart Balance of Staff and Contractors,"

BusinessWeek Online (June 16, 2009), http://www.businessweek.com/managing/content/jun2009/ca20090616_217232.htm (accessed April 30, 2010).

63. Surveys by Society for Human Resource Management, reported in "Team Relationships, Time Differences Are Hampering Virtual Teams," *T + D* (October 2012), p. 18 and Richard Lepsinger and Darleen DeRosa, "How to Lead an Effective Virtual Team," *Ivey Business Journal* (May-June 2015), http://iveybusinessjournal.com/how-to-lead-an-effective-virtual-team/ (accessed November 9, 2015); and Survey by RW3CultureWizard, reported in Golnaz Sadri and John Condia, "Managing the Virtual World," *Industrial Management* (January–February 2012), pp. 21–25.
64. Reported in Sadri and Condia, "Managing the Virtual World."
65. Donna J. Dennis, Deborah Meola, and M. J. Hall, "Effective Leadership in a Virtual Workforce," *T + D* (February 2013), pp. 47–51; Karen Sobel Lojeski, *Leading the Virtual Workforce: How Great Leaders Transform Organizations in the 21st Century* (Hoboken, NJ:, 2010); Stacie A. Furst, Martha Reeves, Benson Rosen, and Richard S. Blackburn, "Managing the Life Cycle of Virtual Teams," *Academy of Management Executive* 18, no. 2 (2004), pp. 6–20; R. E. Potter and P. A. Balthazard, "Understanding Human Interaction and Performance in the Virtual Team," *Journal of Information Technology Theory and Application* 4 (2002), pp. 1–23; and Kenneth W. Kerber and Anthony F. Buono, "Leadership Challenges in Global Virtual Teams: Lessons from the Field," *SAM Advanced Management Journal* (Autumn 2004), pp. 4–10.
66. Reported in Karen Sobel Lojeski, *Leading the Virtual Workforce*.
67. The discussion of these challenges is based on "Team Relationships, Time Differences Are Hampering Virtual Teams"; Dennis et al., "Effective Leadership in a Virtual Workforce"; Bradford S. Bell and Steve W. J. Kozlowski, "A Typology of Virtual Teams: Implications for Effective Leadership," *Group & Organization Management* 27, no. 1 (March 2002), pp. 14–49; Lipnack and Stamps, "Virtual Teams: The New Way to Work"; Jon R. Katzenbach and Douglas K. Smith, "The Discipline of Virtual Teams," *Leader to Leader* (Fall 2001), pp. 16–25; Lepsinger and DeRosa, "How to Lead an Effective Virtual Team"; and Gilson, et al., "Virtual Teams Research: 10 Years, 10 Themes, and 10 Opportunities."
68. Interview in Dennis et al., "Effective Leadership in a Virtual Workforce."
69. This discussion is based on Lepsinger and DeRosa, "How to Lead an Effective Virtual Team"; Arvind Malhotra, Ann Majchrzak, and Benson Rosen, "Leading Virtual Teams," *Academy of Management Perspectives* 21, no. 1 (February 2007), pp. 60–69; Benson Rosen, Stacie Furst, and Richard Blackburn, "Overcoming Barriers to Knowledge Sharing in Virtual Teams," *Organizational Dynamics* 36, no. 3 (2007), pp. 259–273; Marshall Goldsmith, "Crossing the Cultural Chasm; Keeping Communication Clear and Consistent with Team Members from Other Countries Isn't Easy, Says Author Maya Hu-Chan," *Business Week Online* (May 31, 2007), http://www.businessweek.com/careers/content/may2007/ca20070530_521679.htm (accessed August 24, 2007); Bradley L. Kirkman, Benson Rosen, Cristina B. Gibson, Paul E. Tesluk, and Simon O. McPherson, "Five Challenges to Virtual Team Success: Lessons from Sabre, Inc.," *Academy of Management Executive* 16, no. 3 (2002), pp. 67–79; Penelope Sue Greenberg, Ralph H. Greenberg, and Yvonne Lederer Antonucci, "Creating and Sustaining Trust in Virtual Teams," *Business Horizons* 50 (2007), pp. 325–333; and Elizabeth Garone, "Bonding with Remote Workers Valuable Asset," *The Wall Street Journal* (May 11, 2008), p. H1.
70. Terri L. Griffith and Margaret A. Neale, "Information Processing in Traditional, Hybrid, and Virtual Teams: From Nascent Knowledge to Transactive Memory," *Research in Organizational Behavior* 23 (2001), pp. 379–421.
71. Dennis et al., "Effective Leadership in a Virtual Workforce"; Ron Young, "The Wide-Awake Club," *People Management* (February 5, 1998), pp. 46–49; and Steve Schloss, "Listening Is the Most Powerful Connection-Building Tool," *People & Strategy* 35, no. 1 (2012), p. 9.
72. Charlene Marmer Solomon, "Building Teams across Borders," *Workforce* (November 1998), pp. 12–17; and Steve Schloss, "Listening Is the Most Powerful Connection-Building Tool."
73. Richard Lepsinger, "The Virtual Challenge: It's More than Cultural Differences," *People & Strategy* 35, no. 1 (2012), pp. 10–11; and Alanah Mitchell, "Interventions for Effectively Leading in a Virtual Setting," *Business Horizons* 55 (2012), pp. 431–439.
74. Keith Ferrazi, "How to Build Trust in a Virtual Workplace," *Harvard Business Review Blog Network* (October 8, 2012), http://blogs.hbr.org/cs/2012/10/how_to_build_trust_in_virtual.html (accessed May 6, 2013).
75. Ann Majchrzak, Arvind Malhotra, Jeffrey Stamps, and Jessica Lipnack, "Can Absence Make a Team Grow Stronger?" *Harvard Business Review* 82, no. 5 (May 2004), pp. 131–137.
76. Kevan Hall, "Culture Is Always Half about Them and Half about Us," *People & Strategy* 35, no. 1 (2012), pp. 9–10.
77. Lynda Gratton, "Working Together ... When Apart," *The Wall Street Journal* (June 18, 2007), p. R1; and Kirkman et al., "Five Challenges to Virtual Team Success."
78. S. J. Zaccaro and P. Bader, "E-Leadership and the Challenges of Leading E-Teams: Minimizing the Bad and Maximizing the Good," *Organizational Dynamics* 31, no. 4 (2002), pp. 377–387; and Yuhyung Shin, "Conflict Resolution in Virtual Teams," *Organizational Dynamics* 34, no. 4 (2005), pp. 331–345.
79. Debra L. Shapiro, Stacie A. Furst, Gretchen M. Spreitzer, and Mary Ann Von Glinow, "Transnational Teams in the Electronic Age: Are Team Identity and High Performance at Risk?" *Journal of Organizational Behavior* 23 (2002), pp. 455–467.
80. Stephen P. Robbins, *Managing Organizational Conflict: A Nontraditional Approach* (Englewood Cliffs, NJ: Prentice Hall, 1974).
81. Tekleab et al., "A Longitudinal Study of Team Conflict, Conflict Management, Cohesion, and Team Effectiveness."
82. Karen A. Jehn and Elizabeth A. Mannix, "The Dynamic Nature of Conflict: A Longitudinal Study of Intragroup Conflict and Group Performance," *Academy of Management Journal* 44, no. 2 (2001), pp. 238–251.
83. Based on K. A. Jehn, "A Multimethod Examination of the Benefits and Determinants of Intragroup Conflict," *Administrative Science Quarterly* 40 (1995), pp. 256–282; and K. A. Jehn, "A Qualitative Analysis of Conflict Types and Dimensions in Organizational Groups," *Administrative Science Quarterly* 42 (1997), pp. 530–557.
84. Sandra G. Boodman, "Anger Management Courses Are a New Tool for Dealing with Out-of-Control Doctors," *The Washington Post* (March 4, 2013), http://articles.washingtonpost.com/2013-03-04/national/37429827_1_behavior-doctors-nurses-act (accessed May 6, 2013).
85. A. Amason, "Distinguishing the Effects of Functional and Dysfunctional Conflict on Strategic Decision Making: Resolving a Paradox for Top Management Teams," *Academy of Management Journal* 39, no. 1 (1996), pp. 123–148; Jehn, "A Multimethod Examination of the Benefits and Determinants of Intragroup Conflict"; and K. A. Jehn and E. A. Mannix, "The Dynamic Nature of Conflict: A Longitudinal Study of Intragroup Conflict and Group Performance," *Academy of Management Journal* 44 (2001), pp. 238–251.
86. Amason, "Distinguishing the Effects of Functional and Dysfunctional Conflict on Strategic Decision Making."
87. Dean Tjosvold, Chun Hui, Daniel Z. Ding, and Junchen Hu, "Conflict Values and Team Relationships: Conflict's Contribution to Team Effectiveness and Citizenship in China," *Journal of Organizational Behavior* 24 (2003), pp. 69–88; C. De Dreu and E. Van de Vliert, *Using Conflict in Organizations* (Beverly Hills, CA: Sage, 1997); and Kathleen M. Eisenhardt, Jean L. Kahwajy, and L. J. Bourgeois III, "Conflict and Strategic Choice: How Top Management Teams Disagree," *California Management Review* 39, no. 2 (Winter 1997), pp. 42–62.
88. Koehler, "Effective Team Management"; and Dean Tjosvold, "Making Conflict Productive," *Personnel Administrator* 29 (June 1984), p. 121.

89. This discussion is based in part on Richard L. Daft, *Organization Theory and Design* (St. Paul, MN: West, 1992), chapter 13; and Paul M. Terry, "Conflict Management," *The Journal of Leadership Studies* 3, no. 2 (1996), pp. 3–21.
90. Jessica Silver-Greenberg and Nelson D. Schwartz, "Discord at Key JPMorgan Unit Is Blamed in Bank's Huge Loss," *The New York Times* (May 20, 2012), p. A1.
91. This discussion is based on Kenneth W. Thomas, "Towards Multidimensional Values in Teaching: The Example of Conflict Behaviors," *Academy of Management Review* 2, no. 3 (July 1977), pp. 484–490.
92. Reported in Amy C. Edmondson, "Teamwork on the Fly," *Harvard Business Review* (April 2012), pp. 72–80.
93. "Negotiation Types," *The Negotiation Experts Website* (June 9, 2010), http://www.negotiations.com/articles/negotiation-types/ (accessed September 28, 2010).
94. Rob Walker, "Take It or Leave It: The Only Guide to Negotiating You Will Ever Need," *Inc.* (August 2003), pp. 75–82.
95. Based on Roger Fisher and William Ury, *Getting to Yes: Negotiating Agreement Without Giving In* (New York: Penguin, 1983); Walker, "Take It or Leave It"; Robb Mandelbaum, "How to Negotiate Effectively," *Inc.* (November 1, 2010), http://www.inc.com/magazine/20101101/how-to-negotiate-effectively.html (accessed April 12, 2011); and Deepak Malhotra and Max H. Bazerman, "Investigative Negotiation," *Harvard Business Review* (September 2007), pp. 72–78.
96. Variations of this familiar story have been reported in many publications, including "Getting to the Point with Interest-Based Negotiations," The Negotiation Skills Company, http://www.negotiationskills.com/articleB4.php (accessed June 25, 2013); and "Negotiating Skills: Win-Win Deals," Manage Train Learn Website, http://www.managetrainlearn.com/page/win-win-deals (accessed June 25, 2013).

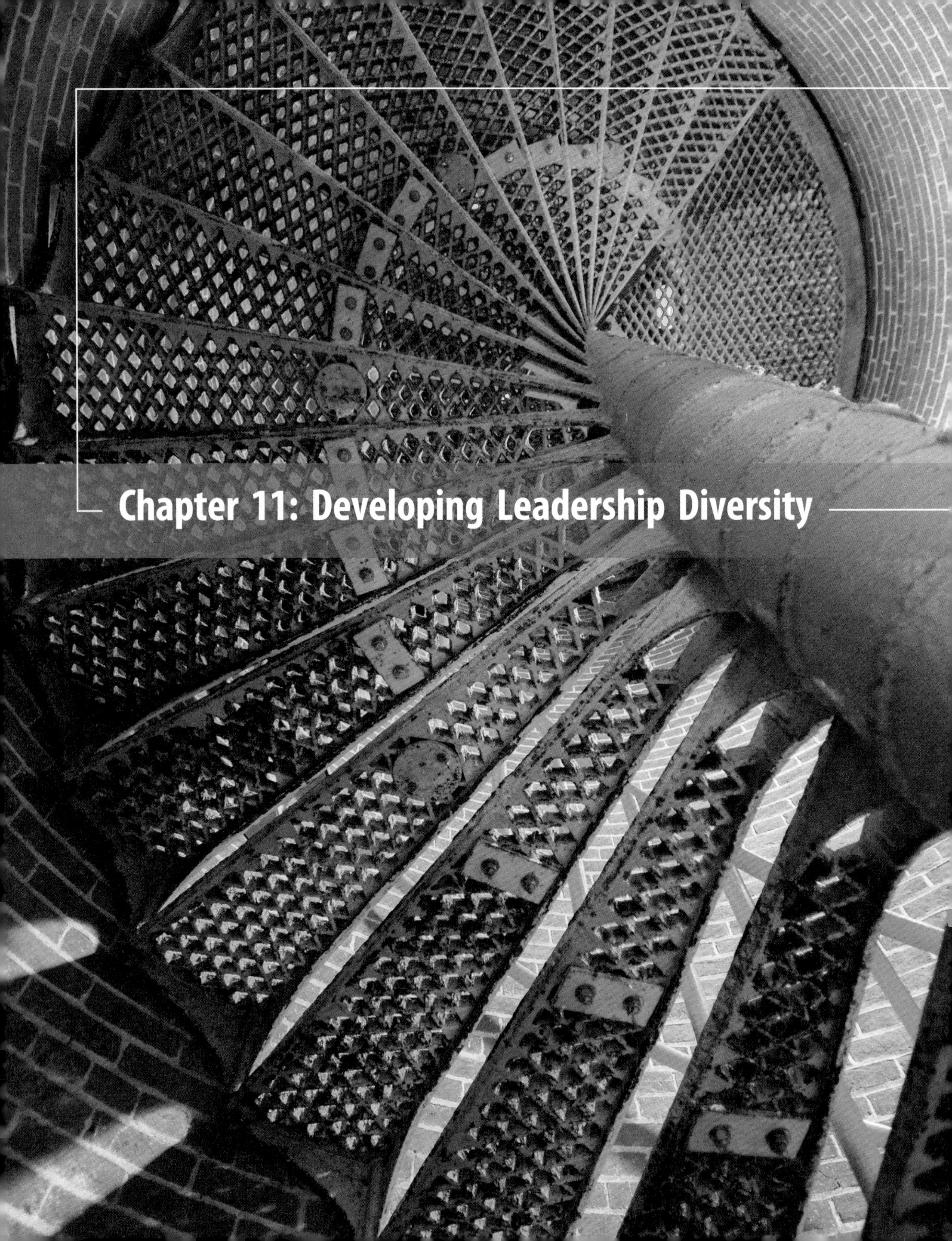

Chapter 11: Developing Leadership Diversity

YOUR **LEADERSHIP** CHALLENGE

After reading this chapter, you should be able to:

- Understand and reduce the difficulties faced by minorities in organizations.
- Apply an awareness of the dimensions of diversity and multicultural issues in your everyday life.
- Encourage and support diversity to meet organizational needs.
- Consider the role of cultural values and attitudes in determining how to deal with employees from different cultures or ethnic backgrounds.
- Break down your personal barriers that may stand in the way of becoming an inclusive leader.
- Use sponsorship and employee affinity groups to support female and minority participation and advancement.

CHAPTER **OUTLINE**

328 **Leading People Who Aren't Like You**

329 **Diversity Today**

332 **Challenges Minorities Face**

337 **Ways Women Lead**

341 **Global Diversity**

346 **Becoming an Inclusive Leader**

349 **Ways to Encourage the Advancement of Women and Minorities**

In the Lead

331 **Secret Intelligence Service (MI6) and Central Intelligence Agency (CIA)**

337 **Inga Beale, Lloyd's of London**

340 **Cindy Szadokierski, United Airlines**

347 **Google and Intel**

Leader's Self-Insight

329 **Values Balancing**

333 **Unconscious Bias**

342 **Social Values**

Leader's Bookshelf

336 **Lean In: Women, Work, and the Will to Lead**

Leadership at Work

352 **Personal Diversity**

Leadership Development: Cases for Analysis

353 **True to Myself**

355 **The Trouble with Bangles**

Early in Vivek Gupta's leadership career, a young woman fresh out of college came into his office and told him she wanted to be in sales. Gupta had spent "a tough five years" in sales, traveling all over India. How could a young woman handle the rigors of such a job, he wondered. That evening, he told his wife about the conversation and that the individual "didn't fit the role" for a sales position. On the advice of his wife, Gupta decided to give the young woman a chance. She turned out to be the best salesperson in the company. The experience changed the way Gupta, now CEO of Zensar Technologies in India, hires and leads people. He realized he was "a biased 25-year-old who grew up in a world that gave more status to men than to women." Since that day, Gupta has been a strong advocate for giving all people equal opportunities.[1]

Leaders at most companies strive to avoid discriminatory policies and practices, but a *Harvard Business Review* survey found that 93 percent of female respondents and 92 percent of non-Caucasian respondents said they had been treated unfairly at work because of someone else's bias.[2] Today's best leaders realize that diversity sparks innovation, leads to better decision making, and spurs growth. Yet subtle bias and hidden discrimination is still a significant problem in many organizations, and valuing and supporting diverse employees takes intentional effort.

Today, every leader needs to understand the complexity of diversity issues, learn to create an inclusive culture, and support the development of minorities for higher-level leadership positions. One of the most important roles for leaders in the coming years will be developing a solid base of diverse leadership talent.

This chapter explores the topic of diversity and multiculturalism. First, we look at the difficulties leaders encounter in leading people who are different from themselves. Then we define diversity, explore the value of diversity for organizations, and look at some challenges minorities face in organizations. Next, we examine a style of leadership that can support a more inclusive work environment, take a closer look at global diversity, and explore how leaders can increase their cultural intelligence quotient (CQ). Finally, we discuss the personal stages of leader diversity awareness and some ways leaders can support the career advancement of diverse people in the workplace.

11-1 LEADING PEOPLE WHO AREN'T LIKE YOU

NEW LEADER
ACTION MEMO

Complete the exercise in Leader's Self-Insight 11.1 to learn about the values you will bring to leading people who are diverse and not like you.

How does an African American, Asian, or Hispanic manager lead an all-white workforce, or a female manager lead a workforce of mostly males? How do white male top executives interact effectively and supportively with minority and female colleagues? What happens when a 29-year-old is promoted to a position of authority over a group of mostly 50- to 60-year-old middle managers? As organizations grow increasingly diverse, these questions are being asked more and more often. Consider Kenneth Frazier of Merck, one of only a handful of African American CEOs running *Fortune* 500 companies, or Cathy Lanier, the white female chief of the Washington, D.C., Metropolitan Police, who leads a mostly black and male workforce.

The benefits of diversity, which we will talk about later in this chapter, are one reason the face of America's organizations is beginning to change, with women and minorities slowly moving into upper-level leadership positions. However, there are still many challenges for creating diverse organizations with inclusive cultures. As women and minorities move up the management hierarchy, they're often finding it a lonely road to travel. Even for someone who has experienced a degree of racism or sexism at lower organizational levels, stepping into a position of higher authority can be a real eye-opener. Racism and sexism in the workplace often show up in subtle ways—the disregard by a subordinate for an assigned chore, a lack of urgency in completing an important assignment, the ignoring of comments or suggestions made at a team meeting. "I could go to a meeting and offer an opinion, and it was like I didn't even say a word," said Christine Dale. "A guy can offer the same opinion and it's like, 'Oh, that's brilliant.' "[3] Many minority leaders struggle daily with the problem of delegating authority and responsibility to employees who show them little respect.

The cultural values and organizational systems in many companies do not genuinely support and value diversity. By the end of this chapter, we hope you will better understand some of the challenges, as well as some leadership strategies that can help make organizations more inclusive and provide a better working environment for all people.

LEADER'S SELF-INSIGHT 11.1

Values Balancing

Instructions: For each of the following pairs of values, select the one that is more descriptive of you. Even if both qualities describe you, you must choose one.

1. Analytical _______ Compassionate _______
2. Collaborative _______ Decisive _______
3. Competitive _______ Sociable _______
4. Loyal _______ Ambitious _______
5. Resourceful _______ Adaptable _______
6. Sensitive to others _______ Independent _______
7. Self-reliant _______ Uniting _______
8. Helpful _______ Persistent _______
9. Risk-taker _______ Contented _______
10. Interested _______ Knowledgeable _______
11. Responsible _______ Encouraging _______
12. Tactful _______ Driven _______
13. Forceful _______ Gentle _______
14. Participating _______ Achievement oriented _______
15. Action oriented _______ Accepting _______

Scoring and Interpretation

The listed words represent two leadership values: "capacity for collaboration" and "personal initiative." Personal initiative is represented by the first word in the odd-numbered rows and the second word in the even-numbered rows. Capacity for collaboration is represented by the first word in the even-numbered rows and by the second word in the odd-numbered rows. Add the number of words circled that represent each value and record the number:

Personal Initiative: _______

Capacity for Collaboration: _______

Capacity for collaboration represents feminine values in our culture, and if you circled more of these items, you may be undervaluing your personal initiative. Personal initiative represents masculine values, and more circled words here may mean you are undervaluing your capacity for collaboration. How balanced are your values? How will you lead someone with values very different from yours?

Gender is a trait of diversity. How prevalent in organizations are feminine and masculine values? Read the rest of this chapter to learn which values are associated with successful leadership.

Sources: Based on Donald J. Minnick and R. Duane Ireland, "Inside the New Organization: A Blueprint for Surviving Restructuring, Downsizing, Acquisitions and Outsourcing." *Journal of Business Strategy* 26 (2005), pp. 18–25; and A. B. Heilbrun, "Measurement of Masculine and Feminine Sex Role Identities as Independent Dimensions." *Journal of Consulting and Clinical Psychology* 44 (1976), pp. 183–190.

11-2 DIVERSITY TODAY

The goal for today's leaders is to recognize that each person can bring value and strengths to the workplace based on his or her own combination of diverse characteristics. Organizations establish workforce diversity programs to promote the hiring, inclusion, and career advancement of diverse employees and to ensure that differences are accepted and respected in the workplace.

11-2a Definition of Diversity

Workforce diversity means a workforce made up of people with different human qualities or who belong to various cultural groups. From the perspective of individuals, **diversity** refers to all the ways in which people differ, including dimensions such as age, race, marital status, physical ability, income level, and lifestyle.[4] Decades ago, most companies defined diversity in terms of a very limited set of dimensions, but today's organizations are embracing a much more inclusive definition that recognizes a spectrum of differences that influence how people approach work, interact with each other, derive satisfaction from their work, and define who they are as people in the workplace.[5]

Workforce diversity
a workforce made up of people with different human qualities or who belong to various cultural groups

Diversity
differences among people in terms of age, ethnicity, gender, race, or other dimensions

Exhibit 11.1 illustrates the difference between the traditional model and a more inclusive model of diversity. The dimensions of diversity shown in the traditional model reflect primarily inborn differences that are immediately observable, such as race, gender, age, and physical ability. However, the inclusive model of diversity

EXHIBIT 11.1 Traditional vs. Inclusive Models of Diversity

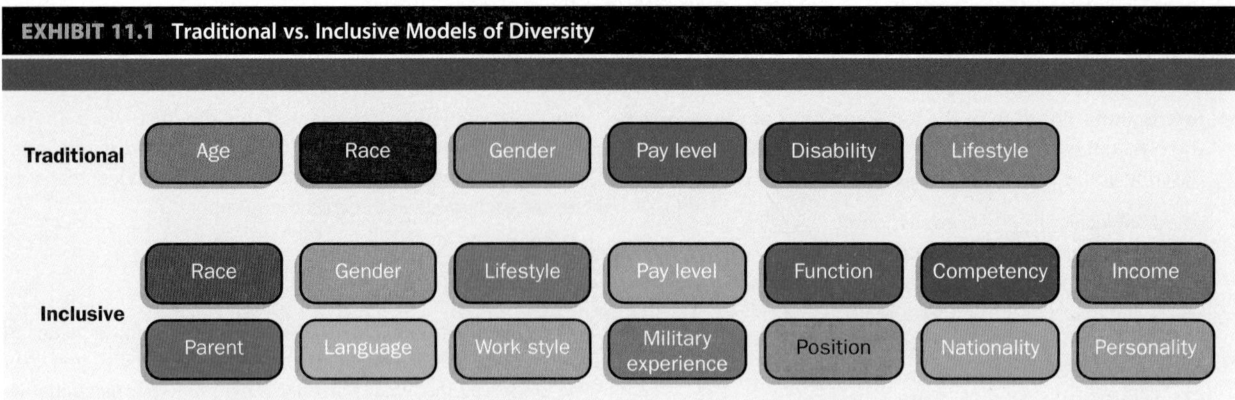

Source: Based on Anthony Oshiotse and Richard O'Leary, "Coming Creates an Inclusive Culture to Drive Technology Innovation and Performance," *Global Business and Organizational Excellence* 26, no. 3 (March/April 2007), pp. 7–21.

includes *all* of the ways in which people differ, including dimensions of diversity that can be acquired or changed throughout one's lifetime. These dimensions may have less impact than those in the traditional model but nevertheless affect a person's self-definition and worldview and influence the way the person is viewed by others.

For example, veterans of the wars in Iraq and Afghanistan may have been profoundly affected by their military experience and may be perceived differently from other people. An employee living in a public housing project will be perceived differently from one who lives in an affluent part of town. Women with children are perceived differently in the work environment than those without children. Secondary dimensions such as work style and skill level are particularly relevant in the organizational setting.[6]

11-2b Changing Attitudes toward Diversity

Attitudes toward diversity are expanding partly because they have to as leaders respond to significant changes in our society, including demographic changes, shifting social values, and globalization.[7] In the United States, minorities now make up roughly 39 percent of the total population. Around 32 million people speak Spanish at home, and nearly half of these people say they don't speak English very well.[8] Foreign-born workers make up more than 16 percent of the U.S. workforce.[9] Looking ahead, the number of Hispanic employees will grow the most, increasing 18.6 percent by 2020.[10] Women are a growing part of the workforce and are increasingly demanding more fair and equitable treatment. Polls also show that views about social mores and lifestyles are shifting. The percentage saying society should encourage greater tolerance of people with different lifestyles and backgrounds increased from 29 percent in 1999 to 44 percent in 2013. Support for gay marriage increased to 53 percent from 30 percent in 2004, and same-sex marriage became legal in the United States in June 2015.[11]

The other factor contributing to increased acceptance of diversity is globalization. Leaders are emphasizing cross-cultural understanding so that people can work smoothly across borders. "The speed of global business is accelerating diversity," says Pauline Ning Brody, a Shanghai-born diversity consultant and former director of global sales for Colgate-Palmolive.[12] An unprecedented number of foreign-born CEOs now run major companies in the United States, Britain, and several other countries.[13] Employees with global experience and cultural sensitivity are in high demand because at least some aspect of almost every business today cuts across national boundaries. As the following example shows, corporations aren't the only organizations seeking a diverse workforce to cope with the challenges of globalization.

IN THE LEAD

Secret Intelligence Service (MI6) and Central Intelligence Agency (CIA)

James Bond need not apply. Britain's secret spy agency, MI6, has embarked on an intense campaign to recruit women and minorities, not the white males who have long been the face of MI6. The agency's recruiting Web site encourages women, including mothers, to apply and assures them they won't be used as "seductresses." Applications from disabled candidates are also welcomed. But the biggest push is for ethnic minorities who speak languages such as Arabic, Persian, Mandarin, Urdu, and the Afghan languages of Dari and Pashto.

For intelligence agencies, diversity is considered *mission critical.* With terrorism being the key challenge, security agencies in the United States as well as Britain and other countries are seeking multicultural employees to act as receptionists, linguists, operational agents, technology officers, security guards, and so forth.

For Britain's MI6, the push for more minority applicants is starting to pay off. In 2010, the United Kingdom passed a new Equality Act that strengthens discrimination laws and allows organizations to give preference to minorities. As the head of human resources for MI6 put it ". . . [all] agencies have to show that they're making positive efforts [to diversify], but for us it means much more."[14]

Meanwhile, the U.S. CIA is coming under increasing attack for a homogenous culture that has contributed to intelligence failures. "For most of the agency's existence, the majority of its agents and analysts have been a relatively tight group of Caucasian, Protestant, liberal-arts-educated American males," say Philippe Silberzahn and Milo Jones, who wrote a book about strategic surprises at the CIA. Few CIA agents speak a foreign language or have foreign travel experience. Retired general David H. Petraeus, who resigned as CIA director in 2012, said "Our key challenge now is to ensure that the CIA's extraordinarily gifted and dedicated workforce is contributing to its full potential. That means we must, at every level, be as inclusive as possible in our composition and in how we make decisions. Intelligence work is teamwork. . . ."[15]

11-2c The Value of Organizational Diversity

There are clear strategic reasons why the CIA and MI6 have to be more diverse to reflect the new global reality, but all organizations need *diversity of thought* to achieve high performance.[16] People who differ in various ways, whether it be race, cultural background, gender, physical ability, educational level, lifestyle, age, marital status, or other dimensions, are more likely to have diverse opinions and perspectives. This diversity of thought means there is a broader and deeper base of ideas, opinions, and experiences for problem solving, creativity, and innovation.[17] According to the results of one study, companies that rate high on creativity and innovation have a higher percentage of women and nonwhite male employees than less innovative companies. Another recent study showed that a team's collective intelligence increases when there are more women members on the team.[18] Moreover, companies with more diverse top leadership teams outperform their peers financially. Researchers analyzed return on equity (ROE) and margins for earnings before interest and taxes (EBIT) for 180 corporations in the United States, France, Germany, and the United Kingdom and found that those with a higher percentage of women and foreign nationals performed significantly better than their peers with less diverse top teams.[19]

At Reckitt Benckiser, a U.K.-based producer of home, health, and personal care products, no nationality dominates the top leadership team. Two executives are Dutch, one is German, two are British, one is South African, two are Italian, and one is from India. Leaders believe the diversity of the company's workforce is one reason income increased 17 percent annually, on average, from 1999 to 2010. Recently retired CEO Bart Becht said, "It doesn't matter whether I have a Pakistani, a Chinese person, a Brit, or a Turk, man or woman, sitting in the same room, or whether I have people from sales or something else, so long as I have people with different experiences—because the chance for new ideas is much greater when you have people with different backgrounds."[20]

NEW LEADER
ACTION MEMO

As a leader, you can hire and promote people from diverse cultures and with diverse human characteristics. You can use organizational diversity to improve creativity and decision making, better serve customers, and enhance organizational flexibility.

Diversity can help companies meet the needs of diverse customers.[21] Culture plays an important role in determining the goods, entertainment, social services, and household products that people use, so organizations are recruiting minority employees who can understand how diverse people live and what they want and need. Fox Sports, for example, achieves a competitive advantage by segmenting its programs to target specific audience groups, such as Hispanics.[22] In addition, having a diverse workforce can build stronger connections with diverse customers. "Our country's consumer base is so varied," says Shelley Willingham-Hinton, president of the National Organization for Diversity in Sales and Marketing. "I can't think of how a company can succeed without having that kind of diversity with their employees."[23]

NEW LEADER
ACTION MEMO

Take the quiz in Leader's Self-Insight 11.2 to evaluate your personal degree of unconscious bias and think about ways you can become more diversity-aware.

11-3 CHALLENGES MINORITIES FACE

Creating an inclusive environment where all individuals feel respected, valued, and able to develop their unique talents is difficult. Most people, including leaders, have a natural tendency toward **ethnocentrism**, which refers to the belief that one's own culture and subculture are inherently superior to other cultures.[24] Recent research by Harvard psychology professor Mahzarin Banaji indicates that the human brain seems to be wired to categorize people by race in the first one-fifth of a second after seeing a face. Banaji's studies suggest that all people have an ingrained propensity to racial bias, even if they are unaware of and even disapprove of such bias. Other studies by social psychologists also suggest that there is a natural tendency among humans to identify themselves with a particular group and to feel somewhat antagonistic and discriminatory toward other groups.[25] In high school, the jocks are aligned against the geeks, for instance. In hospital cafeterias, the surgeons sit in one area and the medical residents in another. In newspaper offices, the editorial folks are antagonistic toward the advertising people. The combination of this natural force toward separation, ethnocentric viewpoints, and a standard set of cultural assumptions and practices creates a number of challenges for minority employees and leaders.

Ethnocentrism
the belief that one's own culture and subculture are inherently superior to other cultures

Prejudice
an adverse feeling or opinion formed without regard for the facts

Stereotype
a rigid, exaggerated, irrational, and typically negative belief or image associated with a particular group of people

Discrimination
treating people differently based on prejudicial attitudes and stereotypes

11-3a Prejudice, Stereotypes, and Discrimination

One significant problem in many organizations is **prejudice**, which is an adverse feeling or opinion formed without regard for the facts. Prejudiced people tend to view those who are different as deficient. An aspect of prejudice is stereotyping. A **stereotype** is a rigid, exaggerated, irrational, and typically negative belief or image associated with a particular group of people. When a leader and company act out prejudicial attitudes toward people who are the targets of their prejudice, **discrimination** occurs.[26] Paying a

LEADER'S SELF-INSIGHT 11.2

Unconscious Bias

Instructions: Think about your typical day-to-day behavior and respond to each of the following items as Mostly False or Mostly True for you.

	Mostly False	Mostly True
1. I prefer to be in work teams with people who think like me.	_____	_____
2. I have avoided talking about culture differences with people I met from different cultures because I didn't want to say the wrong thing.	_____	_____
3. My mind has jumped to a conclusion without first hearing all sides of a story.	_____	_____
4. The first thing I notice about people is the physical characteristics that make them different from the norm.	_____	_____
5. Before I hire someone, I have a picture in mind of what the person should look like.	_____	_____
6. I typically ignore movies, magazines, and TV programs that are targeted toward groups and values that are different from mine.	_____	_____
7. When someone makes a bigoted remark or joke, I don't confront them about it.	_____	_____
8. I prefer not to discuss sensitive topics such as race, age, gender, sexuality, or religion at work.	_____	_____
9. There are people I like but would feel uncomfortable inviting to be with my family or close friends.	_____	_____
10. If I were to seek a mentor, I would want someone culturally similar to myself.	_____	_____

Scoring and Interpretation

Give yourself 1 point for each Mostly True answer. Each item reflects an element of "passive bias," which can cause people different from you to feel ignored or disrespected by you. Your Score: _____. As a leader, your typical day-to-day behavior will send signals about your biases and values. Some personal biases are active and well known to yourself and others. Other biases are more subtle. Unconscious bias occurs when a person is not aware of her or his own bias and has no intent to express bias, but others may experience bias. Unconscious bias may be more insidious than active discrimination because the person would exclude diverse experiences and people from expression and interaction. The ideal score is zero, but few people reach that ideal. If you scored 3 or less, you are making a good attempt to eliminate your passive and unconscious bias. If you scored 8 or more, you should take a careful look at how you think and act toward people different from yourself. You should consider ways to become more culturally sensitive. The sooner you learn to actively include diverse views and people, the better leader you will be.

Source: Based on Lawrence Otis Graham, *Proversity: Getting Past Face Values and Finding the Soul of People* (New York: John Wiley & Sons, 1997).

woman less than a man for the same work is gender discrimination. Refusing to hire someone because he or she has a different ethnicity is ethnic discrimination. For example, some years ago, a manager at a major bank encountered resistance from senior leaders because she wanted to hire an Indian applicant who wore a turban.[27]

Such discrimination is not only unethical but also illegal in the United States. Leaders should be aware that there are a number of federal and state laws that prohibit various types of discrimination. Walmart was hit with a huge class-action lawsuit alleging that the retailer discouraged the promotion of women to management positions and paid them less than men across all job positions.[28] Many other companies, including Texaco, Coca-Cola, General Motors, Mitsubishi, FedEx, eBay, and Abercrombie & Fitch, have been troubled by suits alleging the companies broke laws that prohibit discrimination on the basis of race, gender, age, physical disability, or other diverse characteristics.

Blatant discrimination is not as widespread as in the past, but passive—and sometimes unconscious—bias is still a big problem in the workplace. Consider a report from the National Bureau of Economic Research (titled "Are Emily and Greg

More Employable than Lakisha and Jamal?"), which shows that employers sometimes unconsciously discriminate against job applicants based solely on the Afrocentric or African American–sounding names on their resumes. In interviews prior to the research, most human resource managers surveyed said they expected only a small gap, and some expected to find a pattern of reverse discrimination. The results showed instead that white-sounding names got 50 percent more callbacks than African American–sounding names, even when skills and experience were equal.[29] Similarly, recent research has found that although most men say they have good will toward women in the workplace and want them to succeed, differences in how men and women think and express emotion often lead to unconscious bias. "The male brain has the enviable ability to essentially switch off emotions when desired," writes Shaunti Feldhahn, author of *The Male Factor: The Unwritten Rules, Misperceptions, and Secret Beliefs of Men in the Workplace*. When men see someone expressing personal feelings at work, many of them view that person as less business-savvy. For many women, on the other hand, expressing emotion comes naturally and is an authentic part of work as well as personal life.[30]

NEW LEADER
ACTION MEMO

As a leader, you can appreciate differences among people but shed stereotypes and prejudicial attitudes. You can avoid discrimination and view differences among people as positive or neutral.

Sociologist William Bielby proposes that people have innate biases and, left to their own devices, they will automatically discriminate. *Unconscious bias theory* suggests that white males, for example, will inevitably slight women and minorities because people's decisions are influenced by unconscious prejudice.[31] It takes intentional leadership actions to change the status quo. Leaders can establish conditions that limit the degree of unconscious bias that goes into hiring and promotion decisions. Corporations such as BP and Becton Dickinson, for example, use tools to measure unconscious as well as conscious bias in their diversity training programs.[32]

11-3b The Glass Ceiling

These innate biases can be partially blamed for constructing the **glass ceiling**, an invisible barrier that separates women and minorities from top leadership positions. When executives are choosing a successor or someone for a top position, they tend to choose someone who is similar to them—and that has typically meant mostly male and mostly white. Women and minorities can look up through the ceiling, but prevailing attitudes are invisible obstacles to their own advancement. Research has also suggested the existence of "glass walls" that serve as invisible barriers to important lateral movement within the organization. Glass walls bar experience in areas such as line supervision or general management that would enable women and minorities to advance to senior-level positions.[33]

Although a few women and minorities have moved into highly visible top leadership positions, such as Ursula Burns at Xerox, Kenneth Chenault at American Express, Ginni Rometty at IBM, and Indra Nooyi at PepsiCo, most women and minorities are still clustered at the bottom of the organizational hierarchy. Women have made significant strides in recent years, but they still represent only a small percentage of top executives and board members in America's 500 largest companies.[34] A global study by McKinsey & Company found that in 2011 women held 15 percent of the seats on corporate boards and 14 percent of those on executive committees in the United States. Of the countries surveyed, Norway had the largest percentage of women on corporate boards and executive committees (35 percent and 15 percent, respectively), and Japan the lowest (2 percent and 1 percent).[35] In 2009, Ursula Burns made history as the first African American woman to rise to the top of a *Fortune* 500 company, but both male and female African Americans and Hispanics continue to hold only a small percentage of all management positions in the United States.[36]

Glass ceiling
an invisible barrier that separates women and minorities from top leadership positions

Leaders in other countries are struggling with similar diversity issues. A report on executive talent in the United Kingdom, for example, indicates that although employees on the front lines "reflect the rich diversity of 21st century Britain," the executive suite is overwhelmingly "white, male, able-bodied, and of a certain age."[37] Criticism of gender inequality in Germany is growing, as most European Union countries have narrowed the wage gap between men and women, but pay disparity in Germany has actually increased, according to figures from Germany's Federal Statistical Office.[38] Japanese companies face mounting criticism about the scarcity of women in management positions. In Japan, women make up 41 percent of the workforce but occupy less than 3 percent of high-level management positions.[39] In India, the situation is also dismal. India's recent economic growth has prompted a closer look at its workforce. Women represent only 24 percent of the workforce and make up about 5 percent of senior-level managers. Moreover, reports suggest that women who enter the business world in India often face intimidating and threatening work environments.[40]

In the United States, some women get off the fast track before they ever encounter the glass ceiling, which has been referred to as the *opt-out trend*.[41] In a survey of nearly 2,500 women and 653 men, 37 percent of highly qualified women reported that they had voluntarily left the workforce at some point in their careers, compared to only 24 percent of similarly qualified men.[42] Women leaders sometimes feel that the cost of climbing the corporate ladder is too high. In her controversial book *Lean In*, Facebook chief operating officer Sheryl Sandberg says many women fall behind in their careers because of their own bad choices, as described further in this chapter's Leader's Bookshelf. However, evidence shows that successful career women often have to give up personal time, outside friendships, or hobbies because they still do most of the child care and housework in addition to their business responsibilities. Exhibit 11.2 shows the discrepancy between high-achieving men and women in terms of the time they devote to domestic duties, based on one survey.

EXHIBIT 11.2 Primary Domestic Responsibilities of High-Achieving Men and Women

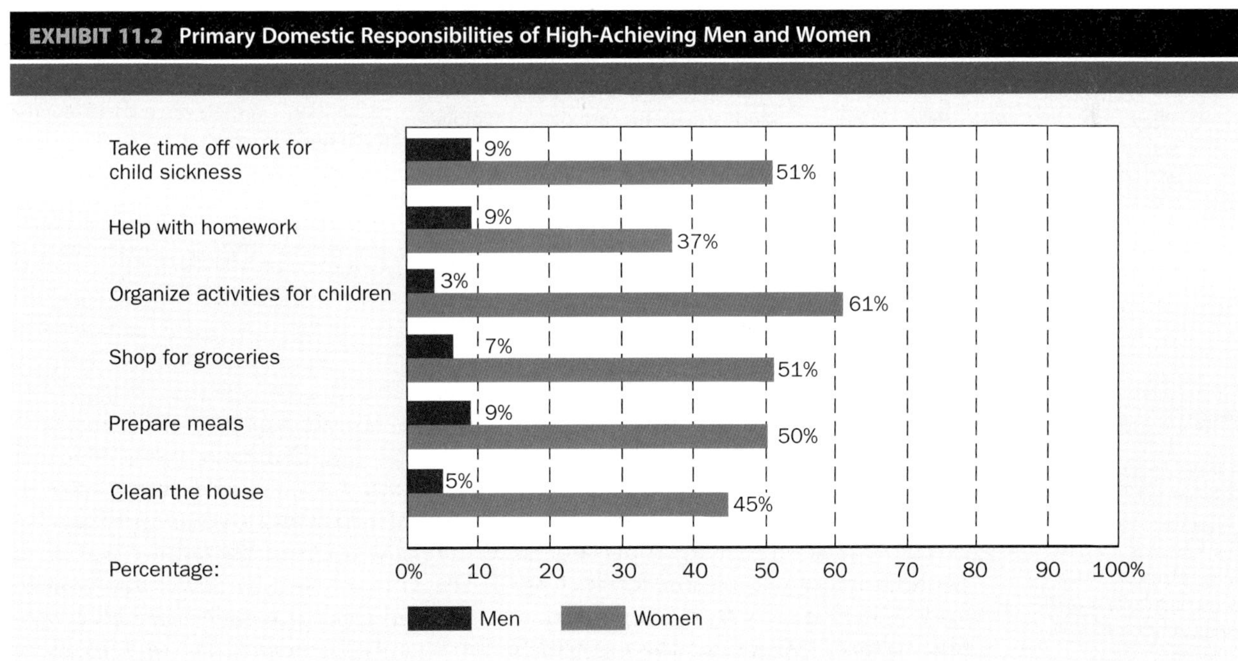

Source: National Parenting Association, as reported in Sylvia Ann Hewlett, "Executive Women and the Myth of Having It All," *Harvard Business Review* (April 2002), pp. 66–73.

LEADER'S BOOKSHELF

Lean In: Women, Work, and the Will to Lead

by Sheryl Sandberg

Lean In, by Facebook COO Sheryl Sandberg, is one of the most controversial books to come out in years. Sandberg acknowledges that women face tremendous barriers in the workplace, but she argues that women also need to break down the barriers within themselves and find their own assertiveness. She recounts workplace and social science research proving that bias and institutional barriers exist, but she also presents evidence showing that women hold themselves back. One study, for instance, found that when girls are reminded of their gender prior to taking a test, even by simply checking an "M" or an "F" at the top of the page, they don't perform as well. Gender stereotypes, Sandberg says, are so powerfully ingrained in women that they continue to perpetuate them subconsciously.

HOW WOMEN HOLD THEMSELVES BACK

"By lacking self-confidence, by not raising our hands, and by pulling back when we should be leaning in," Sandberg writes, women are largely to blame for the fact that "men still run the world." Here are a few of the career sins Sandberg says women commit:

- ***They Let Insecurity Hold Them Back***. Self-confidence is at the heart of being a leader, taking risks, and becoming powerful. It might be easier for men, Sandberg says, but women can overcome the insecurity that limits them. She describes many times in her career when she felt deeply unsure of herself but pushed through. "I still face situations that I fear are beyond my capabilities," she writes. "And I still sometimes find myself spoken over and discounted while men sitting next to me are not. But now I know how to take a deep breath and keep my hand up."
- ***They Don't Take Responsibility for Their Success***. Societal norms and stereotypes of how women "should" act in the workplace have been around for decades, but they will change only if women take responsibility for redefining expectations. Too many women, Sandberg says, get caught in the "tiara syndrome," expecting to be rewarded for good work rather than seizing opportunities and asking for what they deserve. Women have to assertively "sit at the table" rather than being observers in their own careers.
- ***They Seek Mentors***. Having a mentor can be a powerful benefit to anyone's career, but people should get mentors when they do great work and attract the attention of higher executives who *want* to help them. "Searching for a mentor has become the professional equivalent of waiting for Prince Charming," Sandberg says. Rather than expecting to get a mentor in order to excel, the logic women should use is, "excel and you will get a mentor."
- ***They Leave before They Leave***. Women tend to make incremental decisions based on future plans that chip away at their career options. "A law associate might decide not to shoot for partner because someday she hopes to have a family," she writes. "A sales representative might take a smaller territory or not apply for a management role. Often without even realizing it, the woman stops reaching for new opportunities" because of the long-term future impact. Sandberg pays tribute to women who sideline careers for children, but she emphasizes, "The time to scale back is when a break is needed or a child arrives—not before, and certainly not years in advance."

WHAT'S THE ANSWER?

"I believe that female leaders are key to the solution," writes Sandberg. She says things will get better for everyone when there are more women in high-level positions who can change organizational cultures from within. For that to happen, women have to overcome the inner barriers that are holding them back.

Source: Lean In: *Women, Work, and the Will to Lead*, by Sheryl Sandberg, is published by Alfred A. Knopf.

NEW LEADER
ACTION MEMO

As a leader, you can fight ethnocentric attitudes. You can create an environment in which people value diverse ways of thinking, dressing, or behaving, and you can help break down prejudice, stereotypes, and the glass ceiling.

Although some women voluntarily leave the fast track, there are many who genuinely want to move up the corporate ladder but find their paths blocked. Fifty-five percent of executive women surveyed by Catalyst said they aspire to senior leadership levels.[43] In addition, a survey of 103 women voluntarily leaving executive jobs in *Fortune* 1000 companies found that corporate culture was cited as the number-one reason for leaving.[44] The greatest disadvantages for women leaders stem largely from prejudicial attitudes and a heavily male-oriented corporate culture.[45] Consider the experiences of Inga Beale, now CEO of Lloyd's of London.

IN THE LEAD

Inga Beale, Lloyd's of London

When Inga Beale began her career in the insurance industry in the early 1980s, she was the only woman in a group of 30 insurance underwriters. "[You] had to be quite male in your behavior," Beale says. When Beale complained about posters of half-naked women that had been put up around the office, her male colleagues responded by plastering them across her chair and computer.

In 2013, Beale was appointed as the first female CEO of Lloyd's of London, where women weren't allowed in the underwriting room until 1972 and even in the early 1980s, she says, "you couldn't get inside the Lloyd's building as a woman wearing trousers." Beale's experiences as a female leader in a heavily male-dominated industry have made her very aware of the challenges women and minorities face, as well as the unconscious bias that can go into hiring and promotion decisions. "You only have to look at the stats around the hiring of musicians in orchestras; as soon as they do it anonymously behind a screen, they hire double the amount of women," she says. Beale is working with a new human resources director at Lloyd's to find ways to minimize unconscious bias.

Beale says she turned down the first management position offered to her partly because, like many women, a male-oriented culture made her feel that she didn't have the skills. It was only after a female leader took her out to dinner and asked why she had turned down the job that she began developing the self-confidence and assertiveness to move into a leadership position. Beale believes diversity is essential throughout an organization. Lloyd's cannot be successful in today's global world, she says, "if we keep hiring the same people from the same backgrounds." In addition, she considers conversations about how to make people feel included an important part of her leadership responsibility.[46]

Other organizations are also looking for ways to help women and minorities succeed in leadership positions. MetLife uses a leadership development program called Leadership Circles specifically to advance and support women with high potential. "Companies need to support these women, or they may go somewhere else," said one program participant.[47] Many organizations have found that high-performing women leave the company when they fail to receive opportunities for growth and advancement. Companies need women leaders more than ever in today's environment because of the strengths they bring to leadership, as we will discuss in the following section. Organizations such as McKinsey & Company, Bain & Company, and Boston Consulting Group have implemented initiatives including mentoring, professional development programs, and flexible work options to lure back women who left as part of the opt-out trend.[48]

11-4 WAYS WOMEN LEAD

Studies show that organizations with more women leaders have up to 65 percent higher financial results than those without female representation. There is increasing evidence that companies where women make up a significant percentage of board members and senior management perform better than those with only a few women in high-level positions.[49] There has been growing interest in what leadership approach women use that contributes to these positive outcomes. Women often use a style of leadership that is different from men's and that is highly effective in today's turbulent, culturally diverse environment.[50]

There is some evidence that men may become less influential in the U.S. workforce, with women becoming dominant players, because women's approach is more attuned to the needs and values of a multicultural environment. For example, there's a stunning gender reversal in U.S. education, with girls taking over almost every leadership role from kindergarten to graduate school.[51] Hanna Rosin, journalist and author of *The End of Men*, suggests that women are more adaptable and easier to educate.[52] Empirical studies do show that women students are more achievement oriented, less likely to skip classes, spend more time studying, and typically earn higher grades.[53] This chapter's *Consider This* box takes a closer look at various ways in which women appear to be outpacing men in the United States.

Consider **This!**

Are Men Failing?

Here are some recent observations in the United States that suggest men are falling behind in today's world:

- In 1954, 96 percent of men between the ages 25 and 54 worked. In 2012, that number was down to 80 percent.
- Men still dominate the top of organizational hierarchies, but women are gaining in other areas.
- Of the 15 fastest-growing professions, 12 of them are dominated by women.
- Although men still earn more, men's incomes have generally declined in the past decade while women's have grown. Women in their 20s earn more money than men in the same age group.
- In 2011, 57 percent of bachelor's degrees, 60 percent of master's degrees, 51 percent of Ph.D. degrees, 48 percent of law degrees, and 45 percent of MBAs went to women. Among 25- to 29-year-olds, 32 percent of women have college degrees, compared to 27 percent of men.
- Both Republican and Democratic political consultants say that, all else being equal, women candidates are now more desirable than men.

Overall, women's participation in both the labor force and civic affairs has steadily increased since the mid-1950s, whereas men's participation has slowly but steadily declined.

When there is a major upheaval in society, the people who were at the top of the old order of things (men) tend to cling to the old ways, whereas the people who were on the bottom (women) experience a burst of energy and take advantage of new opportunities. Are men failing? Or is this just a course correction that will have men and women making equal contributions to society?

Sources: Based on Hanna Rosin, *The End of Men—and the Rise of Women* (New York: Riverhead/Penguin 2012); David Brooks, "Why Men Fail," *The New York Times* (September 10, 2012), http://www.nytimes.com/2012/09/11/opinion/brooks-why-men-fail.html?_r=0 (accessed May 10, 2013); U.S Department of Education statistics reported in David Wessel, "The Positive Economics of 'Leaning In,' " *The Wall Street Journal* (April 4, 2013), p. A4; Michelle Conlin, "The New Gender Gap," *BusinessWeek* (May 26, 2003), pp. 74–82; and Molly Ball, "A Woman's Edge: Why Both Political Parties Now Think That Voters Prefer Female Candidates," *The Atlantic* (May 2013), pp. 15–17.

11-4a Women as Leaders

According to James Gabarino, an author and professor of human development at Cornell University, women are "better able to deliver in terms of what modern society requires of people—paying attention, abiding by rules, being verbally competent, and dealing with interpersonal relationships in offices."[54] His observation is supported by the fact that female leaders are typically rated higher by subordinates on interpersonal skills as well as on factors such as task behavior, communication, ability to motivate others, and goal accomplishment.[55]

As illustrated in Exhibit 11.3, one survey of followers rated women leaders significantly higher than men on several characteristics that are crucial for developing fast, flexible, adaptive organizations. Female leaders were rated as having more idealized influence, providing more inspirational motivation, being more individually considerate, and offering more intellectual stimulation.[56] *Idealized influence* means that followers identify with and want to emulate the leader; the leader is trusted and respected, maintains high standards, and is considered to have power because of who she is rather than what position she holds. *Inspirational motivation* is derived from the leader who appeals emotionally and symbolically to employees' desire to do a good job and help achieve organizational goals. *Individual consideration* means each follower is treated as an individual but all are treated equitably; individual needs are recognized, and assignments are delegated to followers to provide learning opportunities. For example, one of the strengths of Cynthia Carroll, who from 2007 to 2013 was the first female CEO of global mining company Anglo American, is "getting the most out of each individual." Carroll also brought a new mindset to Anglo American to help the company become more global in its approach, reflecting intellectual stimulation.[57] *Intellectual stimulation* means questioning current methods and challenging employees to think in new ways. In addition to these qualities, women leaders were judged by subordinates in the survey as

EXHIBIT 11.3 Comparison of Male and Female Leaders by Their Subordinates

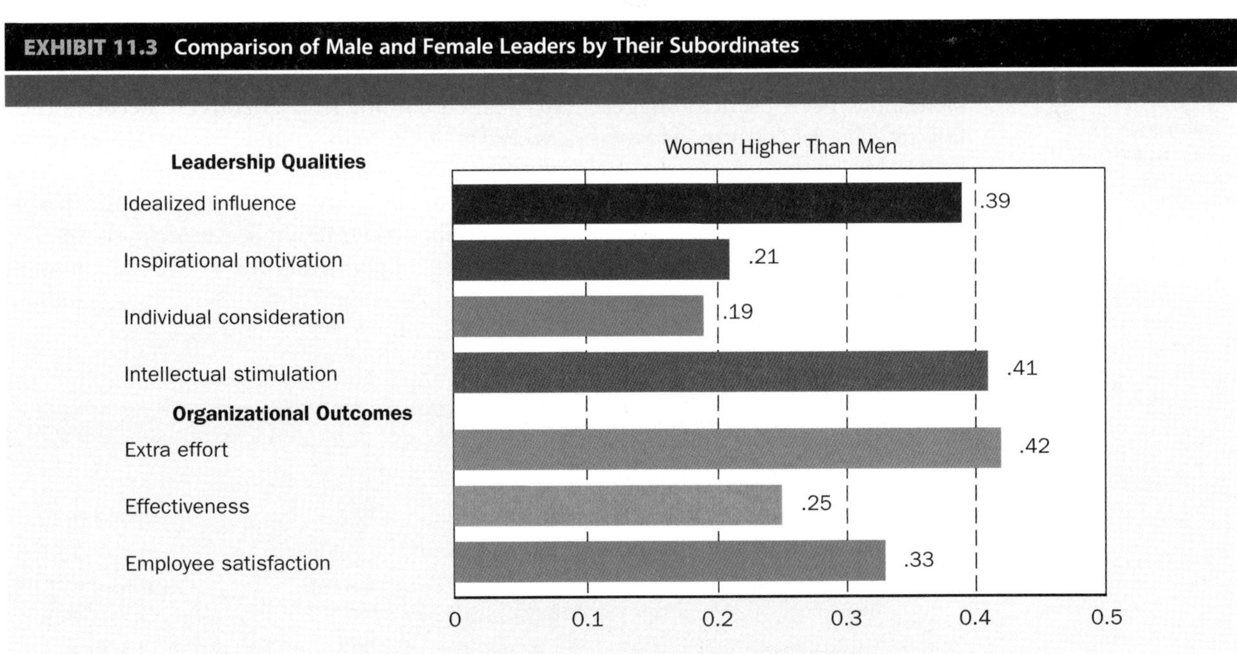

Source: Based on Bernard M. Bass and Bruce J. Avolio, "Shatter the Glass Ceiling: Women May Make Better Managers," *Human Resource Management* 33, no. 4 (Winter 1994), pp. 549–560.

"*Diversity: the art of thinking independently together.*"

Malcolm Forbes (1919–1990), American businessman and publisher of *Forbes* magazine

more effective and satisfying to work for and were considered able to generate extra levels of effort from employees.

11-4b Is Leader Style Gender-Driven?

Several researchers have examined the question of whether women lead differently than men. Although they are broad generalizations, social science research suggests that predominantly *communal* qualities, such as compassion and kindness, are more associated with women in general and predominantly *agentic* qualities, such as assertiveness and competitiveness, are more associated with men.[58] Refer to Leader's Self-Insight 11.1 earlier in the chapter to see if your values are more communal or agentic.

Leadership traits traditionally associated with white, American-born males include aggressiveness or assertiveness, rational analysis, and a "take charge" attitude. Male leaders tend to be competitive and individualistic and prefer working in vertical hierarchies. They rely on formal authority and position in their dealings with subordinates.

NEW LEADER
ACTION MEMO

As a leader, you can choose to employ an interactive, collaborative leadership style. You can develop personal relationships with your followers and make everyone feel like an important part of things.

Some women also reflect these characteristics, of course, but research has found that, in general, women prefer less competitive environments than men, tend to be more collaborative, and are more concerned with relationship building, inclusiveness, participation, and caring.[59] Female leaders such as Deborah Kent, the first woman to head a vehicle assembly plant for Ford Motor, or Terry Kelly, CEO of W. L. Gore & Associates, are often more willing to share power and information, to encourage employee development, and to strive to enhance others' feelings of self-worth. "It does no good have a diverse workforce if you don't listen to their opinions and thoughts," says Kent. "I treat people the way I want to be treated."[60]

Interactive leadership a leadership style in which people develop personal relationships with followers, share power and information, empower employees, and strive to enhance others' feelings of self-worth

Professor and author Judy B. Rosener has called women's approach to leadership **interactive leadership.**[61] The leader favors a consensual and collaborative process, and influence derives from relationships rather than position power and authority. Some psychologists have suggested that women may be more relationship oriented than men because of different psychological needs stemming from early experiences. This difference between the relationship orientations of men and women has sometimes been used to suggest that women cannot lead effectively because they fail to exercise power. However, whereas male leaders may associate effective leadership with a top-down command-and-control process, women's interactive leadership seems appropriate for the future of diversity, globalization, and learning organizations. Cindy Szadokierski applies interactive leadership to handle the complex and demanding job of managing operations for United Airlines in Chicago.

IN THE LEAD

Cindy Szadokierski, United Airlines

Twenty-five years ago, Cindy Szadokierski quit her job teaching high school French and went to work as a reservations agent for United Airlines. Today, she is vice president in charge of operations for United's largest hub at O'Hare International Airport.

After joining the company, Szadokierski served in positions of increasing responsibility, including being general manager of United's hub at Washington's Dulles International Airport.

From the beginning of her career with United, Szadokierski wanted to be in operations because she liked the idea of bridging the gap between what goes on in the field and what happens at headquarters. At O'Hare, where she oversees 4,000 employees and 600 flights a day, her favorite times are the weekly afternoon walkabouts on the O'Hare ramp and the weekly morning strolls through the terminal. Why? Because they give her a chance to connect with employees and customers. Pete McDonald, chief operating officer of United's parent, UAL Corporation, says there were serious operations problems at O'Hare, so they put "the most communicative person" in the job. "She's everywhere. She talks to everybody," said Don Wolfel, president of United's mechanics union at O'Hare.

Szadokierski's approach to leadership is more collaborative than command-and-control. In addition to learning from employees and customers, Szadokierski emphasizes regular meetings with her leadership team to talk about what's going right, what's going wrong, and how to collaboratively fix any problems.[62]

Although the values associated with interactive leadership, such as inclusion, relationship building, and caring, are generally considered "feminine" values, interactive leadership is not gender-specific. These values are becoming increasingly valuable for both male and female leaders.[63] Any leader can learn to adopt a more inclusive style by paying attention to nonverbal behavior and developing skills such as listening, empathy, cooperation, and collaboration.

11-5 GLOBAL DIVERSITY

One of the most rapidly increasing sources of diversity is globalization, which means that leaders are confronting diversity issues across a broader stage than ever before. For leaders interacting with people from other cultures, even something as seemingly simple as a handshake can be confusing, as illustrated in Exhibit 11.4. If the proper way to shake hands can vary so widely, no wonder managers have trouble knowing how to act when doing business with people from or in other countries.

Leaders can get a handle on the challenges of global diversity by understanding the sociocultural environment and by developing a higher cultural intelligence quotient (CQ) to know how to behave appropriately.

NEW LEADER
ACTION MEMO

Social value differences can significantly affect leadership, working relationships, and organizational functioning. Answer the questions in Leader's Self-Insight 11.3 to better understand the social values of your classmates or coworkers.

11-5a The Sociocultural Environment

Social and cultural differences may provide more potential for difficulties and conflicts than any other source. For instance, after hundreds of mostly Somali Muslim employees walked out to protest not being allowed extra break times to pray during Ramadan, leaders at a JBS Swift & Company meatpacking plant in Omaha, Nebraska, altered their policies so the workers could pray at the appropriate times. That, however, led to protests by non-Muslim workers, who alleged "preferential treatment," causing leaders to reconsider allowing extra breaks for prayer. The tensions and conflicts led to a near-riot, and Swift's leaders were working overtime to resolve the issues between the different groups.[64]

Cultural factors have also created problems for leaders in some U.S. corporations trying to transfer their diversity policies and practices to European divisions. Policies designed to address diversity issues in the United States don't take into consideration the complex social and cultural systems in Europe. In Britain, for example, class

LEADER'S SELF-INSIGHT 11.3

Social Values

Instructions: Different social groups (work colleagues, family, professional groups, and national, religious, and cultural groups) are all around us. Focus on the group of individuals whom you consider to be your colleagues (e.g., team members, coworkers, classmates). Respond to each of the following statements and indicate its level of importance to your colleague group on the scale of (1) Not at all important to (5) Very important.

How Important Is It:	**Not at All Important**				**Very Important**
1. To compromise one's wishes to act together with your colleagues?	1	2	3	4	5
2. To be loyal to your colleagues?	1	2	3	4	5
3. To follow norms established by your colleagues?	1	2	3	4	5
4. To maintain a stable environment rather than "rock the boat"?	1	2	3	4	5
5. To not break the rules?	1	2	3	4	5
6. To be a specialist or professional rather than a manager?	1	2	3	4	5
7. To have an opportunity for high earnings?	1	2	3	4	5
8. To have an opportunity for advancement to higher-level jobs?	1	2	3	4	5
9. To work with people who cooperate well with one another?	1	2	3	4	5
10. To have a good working relationship with your leader?	1	2	3	4	5
11. To have a leader who gives detailed instructions?	1	2	3	4	5
12. To avoid disagreement with a leader?	1	2	3	4	5

Scoring and Interpretation

There are four subscale scores that measure the four social values described by Hofstede. For the dimension of individualism–collectivism, compute your average score based on responses to questions 1, 2, and 3. For the dimension of uncertainty avoidance, compute your average score based on responses to questions 4, 5, and 6. For the dimension of masculinity–femininity, reverse score your responses to questions 9 and 10 (5 = 1, 4 = 2, 2 = 4, and 1 = 5) and then compute your average score for questions 7, 8, 9, and 10. For the dimension of power distance, compute the average score for questions 11 and 12.

My average social value scores are:
Individualism–collectivism (I–C) ________.
Uncertainty avoidance (UA) ________.
Masculinity–femininity (M–F) ________.
Power distance (PD) ________.

An average score of 4 or above on the I–C scale means that *collectivism* is a social value in your colleague group, and a score of 2 or below means that the value of *individualism* dominates. A score of 4 or above on the UA scale means that your group values the absence of ambiguity and uncertainty (*high uncertainty avoidance*), and a score of 2 or below means that uncertainty and unpredictability are preferred. A score of 4 or above on the M–F scale means that *masculinity* is a social value in your colleague group, and a score of 2 or below means that the value of *femininity* dominates. A score of 4 or above on the PD scale means that *high power distance*, or hierarchical differences, is a social value in your colleague group, and a score of 2 or below means that the value of *low power distance*, or equality, dominates.

Compare your four scores to one another to understand your perception of the different values. On which of the four values would you like to score higher? Lower? Analyze the specific questions on which you scored higher or lower to analyze the pattern of your group's social values. Show your scores to a student from another country and explain what they mean. How do your social values differ from the social values of the international student? How do these social values differ across the nationalities represented in your class?

Sources: Adapted from Geert Hofstede, *Culture's Consequences* (London: Sage Publications, 1984); and D. Matsumoto, M. D. Weissman, K. Preston, B. R. Brown, and C. Kupperbausch, "Context-Specific Measurement of Individualism–Collectivism on the Individual Level: The Individualism–Collectivism Interpersonal Assessment Inventory," *Journal of Cross-Cultural Psychology* 28, no. 6 (1997), pp. 743–767.

distinctions are as big an aspect of diversity as race, gender, or disability.[65] Even the meaning of the term *diversity* can present problems. In many European languages, the closest word implies separation rather than the inclusion sought by U.S. diversity

EXHIBIT 11.4 How Do You Shake Hands?

Culture	Preferred Style of Handshake
Asian	Gentle (shaking hands is unfamiliar and uncomfortable for some Asians; the exception is the Korean, who usually prefers a firm handshake)
British	Soft
French	Light and quick; repeated on arrival and departure; not offered to superiors
German	Brusque and firm; repeated on arrival and departure
Latin American	Moderate grasp; repeated frequently
Middle Eastern	Gentle; repeated frequently
North American	Firm

Source: From *Bridging Cultural Barriers for Corporate Success* by Sondra Thiederman. Copyright © 1991. Lexington Books. Reprinted by permission of the author.

programs.[66] Foreign firms doing business in the United States face similar challenges understanding and dealing with diversity issues. C. R. "Dick" Shoemate, chairman and CEO of Best Foods, says, "It takes a special kind of leadership to deal with the differences in a multicountry, multicultural organization. . . ." Best Foods uses cross-border assignments and extensive individual coaching to train people to lead a multicultural workforce.[67]

11-5b Social Value Systems

Research done by Geert Hofstede on IBM employees in 40 countries discovered that mindset and cultural values on issues such as individualism versus collectivism strongly influence organizational and employee relationships and vary widely among cultures.[68] Exhibit 11.5 shows examples of how countries rate on four significant dimensions.

EXHIBIT 11.5 Rank Orderings of 10 Countries along Four Dimensions of National Value System

Country	Power[a]	Uncertainty[b]	Individualism[c]	Masculinity[d]
Australia	7	7	2	5
Costa Rica	8	2 (tie)	10	9
France	3	2 (tie)	4	7
India	2	9	6	6
Japan	5	1	7	1
Mexico	1	4	8	2
Sweden	10	10	3	10
Thailand	4	6	9	8
United States	6	8	1	4

[a]1= highest power distance; 10 = lowest power distance
[b]1 = highest uncertainty avoidance; 10 = lowest uncertainty avoidance
[c]1 = highest individualism; 10 = highest collectivism
[d]1 = highest masculinity; 10 = highest femininity

Sources: From Dorothy Marcic, *Organizational Behavior and Cases*, 4th ed. (St. Paul, MN: West, 1995). Based on Geert Hofstede, *Culture's Consequences* (London: Sage Publications, 1984); and *Cultures and Organizations: Software of the Mind* (New York: McGraw-Hill, 1991).

- *Power distance.* High **power distance** means people accept inequality in power among institutions, organizations, and individuals. Low power distance means people expect equality in power. Countries that value high power distance are Malaysia, the Philippines, and Panama. Countries that value low power distance include Denmark, Austria, and Israel.
- *Uncertainty avoidance.* High **uncertainty avoidance** means that members of a society feel uncomfortable with uncertainty and ambiguity and thus support beliefs and behaviors that promise certainty and conformity. Low uncertainty avoidance means that people have a high tolerance for the unstructured, the unclear, and the unpredictable. High uncertainty avoidance cultures include Greece, Portugal, and Uruguay. Singapore and Jamaica are two countries with low uncertainty avoidance values.
- *Individualism and collectivism.* **Individualism** reflects a value for a loosely knit social framework in which individuals are expected to take care of themselves. **Collectivism** is a preference for a tightly knit social framework in which people look out for one another and organizations protect their members' interests. Countries with individualist values include the United States, Great Britain, and Canada. Countries with collectivist values are Guatemala, Ecuador, and Panama.
- *Masculinity and femininity.* **Masculinity** reflects a preference for achievement, heroism, assertiveness, work centrality, and material success. **Femininity** reflects the values of relationships, cooperation, group decision making, and quality of life. Japan, Austria, and Mexico are countries with strong masculine values. Countries with strong feminine values include Sweden, Norway, Denmark, and the former Yugoslavia. Both men and women subscribe to the dominant value in masculine or feminine cultures.

Power distance
how much people accept equality in power; high power distance reflects an acceptance of power inequality among institutions, organizations, and individuals; low power distance means people expect equality in power

Uncertainty avoidance
the degree to which members of a society feel uncomfortable with uncertainty and ambiguity and thus support beliefs and behaviors that promise certainty and conformity

Individualism
a value for a loosely knit social framework in which individuals are expected to take care of themselves

Collectivism
a preference for a tightly knit social framework in which people look out for one another and organizations protect their members' interests

Masculinity
a preference for achievement, heroism, assertiveness, work centrality, and material success

Femininity
a preference for relationships, cooperation, group decision making, and quality of life

Cultural intelligence
the ability to use reasoning and observation to interpret unfamiliar situations and devise appropriate behavioral responses

Terry Neill, a managing partner at a London-based change management practice, uses Hofstede's findings in his work with companies. Based on his experiences with global companies such as Unilever PLC, Royal Dutch Shell, and BP, Neill points out that the Dutch, Irish, Americans, and British are generally quite comfortable with open argument. However, Japanese and other Asian employees often feel uneasy or even threatened by such directness.[69] In many Asian countries, leaders perceive the organization as a large family and emphasize cooperation through networks of personal relationships. In contrast, leaders in Germany and other central European countries typically strive to run their organizations as impersonal, well-oiled machines.[70] How leaders handle these and other cultural differences can have tremendous impact on the satisfaction and effectiveness of diverse employees.

11-5c Developing Cultural Intelligence

Although understanding the sociocultural environment and social value differences is crucial, a person cannot expect to know everything necessary to be prepared for every conceivable situation. Thus, in a multicultural environment, leaders will be most successful if they are culturally flexible and able to easily adapt to new situations and ways of doing things. In other words, they need a high CQ. **Cultural intelligence** refers to a person's ability to use reasoning and observation skills to interpret unfamiliar gestures and situations and devise appropriate behavioral responses.[71] Developing a high CQ enables a person to interpret unfamiliar situations and adapt quickly. Rather than a list of global "dos and don'ts," CQ enables a person to ferret out clues to a culture's shared understandings and respond to new situations in culturally appropriate ways.

Cultural intelligence includes three components that work together: cognitive, emotional, and physical.[72] The cognitive component involves a person's observational and learning skills and the ability to pick up on clues to understanding. The emotional aspect concerns one's self-confidence and self-motivation. A leader has to believe in his or her ability to understand and assimilate into a different culture. Difficulties and setbacks are triggers to work harder, not a cause to give up. The third component, the physical, refers to a person's ability to shift his or her speech patterns, expressions, and body language to be in tune with people from a different culture. Most people aren't equally strong in all three areas, but maximizing CQ requires that they draw upon all three facets.

Developing a high CQ requires that a leader be open and receptive to new ideas and approaches. Working in a different country is one of the best ways people can stretch beyond their comfort zones and develop a broader, more global perspective. One study found that people who adapt to global management most easily are those who have grown up learning how to understand, empathize, and work with others who are different from themselves. For example, Singaporeans consistently hear English and Chinese spoken side by side. The Dutch have to learn English, German, and French, as well as Dutch, to interact and trade with their economically dominant neighbors. English Canadians must not only be well versed in American culture and politics, but they also have to consider the views and ideas of French Canadians, who, in turn, must learn to think like North Americans, members of a global French community, Canadians, and Quebecois.[73] People who have grown up without this kind of language and cultural diversity, which includes most leaders in the United States, typically have more difficulties with foreign assignments, but willing managers from any country can learn to open their minds and appreciate other viewpoints.

11-5d Leadership Implications

A study of executives in five countries found that although the globalization of business seems to be leading to a convergence of managerial values and attitudes, executives in different countries differ significantly in some areas, which can create problems for leadership.[74] To lead effectively in a diverse global environment, leaders should be aware of cultural and subcultural differences. Chapter 3 examined contingency theories of leadership that explain the relationship between leader style and a given situation. It is important for leaders to recognize that culture affects both style and the leadership situation. For example, in cultures with high uncertainty avoidance, a leadership situation with high task structure as described in Chapter 3 is favorable, but those in low uncertainty avoidance cultures prefer less-structured work situations. Research into how the contingency models apply to cross-cultural situations is sparse. However, all leaders need to be aware of the impact that culture may have and consider cultural values in their dealings with employees and colleagues.

NEW LEADER
ACTION MEMO

As a leader, you can develop cultural intelligence. You can study other languages and cultures and form relationships with people from different countries. You can learn to be sensitive to differences in social value systems and find creative ways to address delicate diversity issues.

How leader behavior is perceived differs from culture to culture. For example, there is tremendous variation across countries in what people expect leaders to do and be. For example, should leaders be experts who provide precise answers to their employees' questions or should they instead be facilitators who help employees discover solutions rather than providing them with direct answers? The answer varies from country to country, and problems can occur when unaware leaders from one culture interact with employees from another. For example, most leaders in the

EXHIBIT 11.6 Are Leaders Expected to Be Experts?

Source: André Laurent, "The Cultural Diversity of Western Conceptions of Management," *International Studies of Management and Organization* 13, no. 1–2 (Spring–Summer, 1983), pp. 75–96. Adapted from ADLER, International *Dimensions of Organizational Behavior*, 5E.

United States think merely providing answers limits subordinates' initiative and creativity. In France, though, leaders believe they should give exact answers in order to maintain their credibility as experts.[75] If a leader from the United States working in France tells an employee she doesn't know the answer and suggests the employee consult with someone else about the problem, the employee might conclude that the U.S. leader is incompetent. Similarly, employees in the United States working for a French boss might consider the boss egotistical when he continually provides specific answers rather than offering suggestions for how to find solutions to a problem. Exhibit 11.6 gives some examples of how the leader's role varies across countries based on whether leaders are expected to provide answers to employee questions.

Other behavioral misunderstanding can also trip up leaders. An American manager nearly blew a deal with a Korean company because he complained directly to higher-level executives when he had difficulty getting the information he needed from his Korean counterparts. In the United States, such an approach would be acceptable, but in Korea, it was seen as a sign of disrespect. The lower-level Korean managers were horrified and embarrassed, the upper-level managers were offended, and the crisis was resolved only when top executives from the United States made a trip to Korea to apologize and show respect.[76]

11-6 BECOMING AN INCLUSIVE LEADER

One goal for today's global organizations is to ensure that *all* people—women, ethnic minorities, younger people, gays and lesbians, the disabled, older people, racial minorities, as well as white males—are given equal opportunities and treated with fairness and respect.[77] The following example describes how big technology companies such as Google and Intel are beginning to respond to growing criticism about the lack of diversity in their organizations.

IN THE LEAD

Google and Intel

Laszlo Bock, Google's head of human resources, says "you don't usually see outright manifestations of bias," at the company. "Occasionally you'll have some idiot do something stupid and hurtful, and I like to fire those people." But Bock and other Google leaders know it's the hidden and often unconscious biases that can be the real problem. Google began diversity training workshops for all employees in 2013 to help people confront and overcome the bias hidden within themselves, with particular focus on how unconscious biases affect hiring and promotion decisions. Although there are few explicit results yet, Google leaders say just acknowledging the problem is starting to shift Google to a more inclusive culture

At Intel, leaders are taking even more concrete steps. In early 2015, the company announced a goal of increasing the number of women, African Americans, Hispanics, and other minority groups by at least 14 percent within five years. "This is the right time to make a bold statement," said Intel CEO Brian M. Krzanich. Intel also set up a $300 million fund to be used to improve diversity in Intel's workforce, attract more women and minorities to the technology field, and make the industry more open to minorities. The Rev. Jesse L. Jackson, Sr., who led a campaign to pressure technology companies on diversity, welcomed Intel's bold move and believes it will compel other companies to follow their lead.[78]

Google and Intel are certainly not alone in needing to address the lack of diversity in their organizations. The workforce and leadership at most large technology companies are overwhelmingly male and primarily white and Asian. Leaders hope bringing the problem into the open is a start toward a more diverse technology industry. Leaders in other industries are also struggling to increase diversity and inclusiveness.

Leaders vary in their sensitivity and openness to other cultures, attitudes, values, and ways of doing things. Exhibit 11.7 shows a model of five stages of individual diversity awareness and actions.[79] The continuum ranges from a defensive, ethnocentric attitude, in which leaders meet the minimum legal requirements regarding affirmative action and sexual harassment, to a complete understanding and acceptance of people's differences, in which leaders value diversity as an inherent part of the organizational culture.

People at stage 1 see differences as a threat against their own comfortable worldview and frequently use negative stereotyping or express prejudicial attitudes. Leaders at this stage of diversity awareness consider themselves successful if their legal record is good. They may view women and minorities as a "problem" that must be dealt with. Typically, these leaders promote a few minorities to executive-level jobs to meet legal requirements. At stage 2, people try to minimize differences and focus on the similarities among all people. This is the stage where unconscious and subtle bias is most evident because people have moved beyond openly

EXHIBIT 11.7 Stages of Personal Diversity Awareness

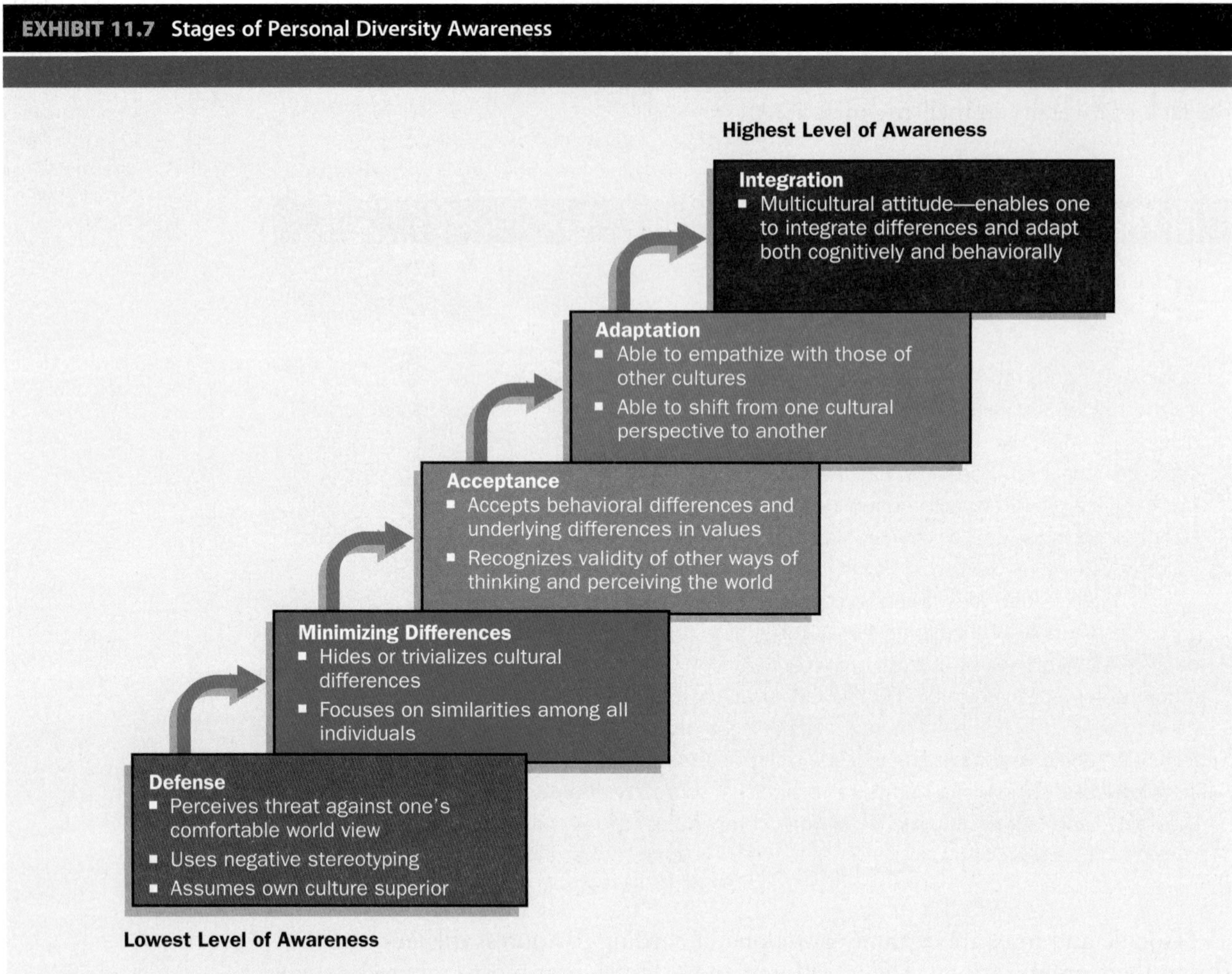

Source: Based on M. Bennett, "A Developmental Approach to Training for Intercultural Sensitivity," *International Journal of Intercultural Relations* 10 (1986), pp. 179–196.

prejudicial attitudes. Leaders don't adequately recognize or respond to the challenges minorities and women face in the organization. When an individual moves to stage 3 of diversity awareness, he or she accepts cultural differences and recognizes the validity of other ways of thinking and doing things. Here, leaders become proactive and acknowledge that addressing issues of gender, race, disability, and so forth is important not just for the minority employees but also for the health of the organization. They recognize that women and minorities can bring needed insight into developing and marketing products for new customers, so they look for ways to attract and retain high-quality minority employees. In stage 3 organizations, more women and minorities make it to high-level positions, and leaders begin providing diversity training to all employees.

When people reach stage 4, they are able to empathize with people who are different from themselves and can comfortably shift from one cultural perspective to another. Leaders at this stage make a strong commitment to broad equality and community and rectify the undervaluation and underutilization of women and minorities. Leaders make a genuine attempt to develop policies and practices that are inclusive rather than exclusive. For example, a series of highly publicized incidents of racial discrimination at Denny's Restaurants in the early 1990s spurred leaders to implement diversity programs and provide serious diversity awareness training at every level of the company. Today, Denny's is a model for diversity. By 2014, 46 percent of Denny's franchises were minority-owned, and minorities made up 44 percent of overall management. Since 1993, the company has spent over $1.6 billion with minority- and women-owned suppliers.[80] The results of Denny's diversity initiatives have far exceeded expectations and have moved Denny's leaders toward stage 5 of the diversity awareness scale in Exhibit 11.7.

NEW LEADER
ACTION MEMO

As a leader, you can advance to higher stages of diversity awareness and action. You can commit to valuing diversity and providing equal opportunities for everyone.

At stage 5 of diversity awareness, people are capable of integrating differences and adapting both cognitively and behaviorally. It is at this stage where leaders can create organizations that are gender- and color-blind. All employees are judged on their competence, and stereotypes and prejudices are completely erased. No group of employees feels different or disadvantaged. Stage 5 represents the ideal leader and organization. Although it may seem unreachable, many of today's best leaders are striving to achieve this stage of diversity awareness and acceptance. The commitment of top leaders is critical to building organizations that embrace diversity in all aspects of the business.

11-7 WAYS TO ENCOURAGE THE ADVANCEMENT OF WOMEN AND MINORITIES

Personal diversity awareness is the first step to creating a culture that embraces inclusion and enables all people to reach their potential, thereby enabling the organization to perform at its best. Leaders have tried a variety of approaches to encourage an inclusive culture. Two effective options for getting more minority representation at higher levels are employee affinity groups and minority sponsorship.

11-7a Employee Affinity Groups

Employee affinity groups are based on social identity, such as gender or race, and are organized to focus on the concerns of employees from specific groups.[81] These groups are sometimes called *diversity networks* or *employee resource groups*. Employee affinity groups let persons of similar background share common experiences and success strategies, enabling them to make greater contributions to the organization and advance their careers. Affinity groups first emerged in the 1970s, primarily to focus on the recruitment and retention of African Americans. Today, they have evolved to incorporate employees from a wide variety of backgrounds. Cisco Systems has groups that provide leadership and growth opportunities for Asians, African Americans, women, Middle Eastern employees, veterans, Latinos, gays and lesbians, the disabled, and others. The company's 11 affinity groups represent more than 18 percent of 72,000 Cisco employees worldwide.[82]

Affinity groups pursue a variety of activities, such as meetings to educate top leaders, mentoring programs, networking events, training sessions and skills seminars, minority intern programs, and community volunteer activities. These activities give people a chance to meet, interact with, and develop social and professional ties to others throughout the organization, which often includes influential executives and key decision makers. Affinity groups are a powerful way to reduce social isolation for women and minorities, help these employees be more effective, and

Employee affinity groups
Groups based on social identity that focus on concerns of employees from specific groups and enable them to make greater contributions to the organization

NEW LEADER
ACTION MEMO

As a leader, you can support the personal development and career advancement of women and minorities by creating and encouraging employee affinity groups. Use sponsorship to help high-potential minority employees reach higher levels.

enable members to achieve greater career advancement. Studies confirm that these groups can be important tools for helping organizations retain managerial-level minority employees.[83]

Important characteristics of effective affinity groups are that they involve senior leaders in group events and that they find ways to directly contribute to organizational effectiveness. As president of Cisco's Latino group, Conexión, Guillermo Diaz Jr. transformed it from a "social club with a happy hour" into a business resource, influencing Spanish-speaking customers and organizing conferences for Latino IT leaders. Three years later, Diaz was promoted to a vice president position.[84] At BT (formerly called British Telecom), members of the disability network, Able2, trained installation engineers to let visually impaired customers feel the box before it was installed. "Rather than developing slightly artificial programmes that give the networks visibility, they get noticed for all the right reasons because they are helping the business," Caroline Walters, BT's director of people and policy, says of the new approach to affinity groups.[85]

When employee affinity groups raise their sights from providing personal support to enabling people to bring value to the business, it helps both the organizations and the individuals involved.[86] Anne F. Ackerley earned a promotion to chief marketing officer of BlackRock, the world's largest money manager by assets, largely because of the role she played in the company's affinity group for women and the exposure it gave her to senior leaders.[87] Ackerley continued to advance in her career, and in 2015 she was a managing director and head of BlackRock's US & Canada Defined Contribution (USDC) Group. When people feel that they are making genuine contributions and have a chance to advance in their careers because of it, engagement soars. "At some of our events, the buzz in the room is magnificent," said Shakrat Alli, chairwoman of Britain's Crown Prosecution Service's affinity group for African Americans (the National Black Crown Prosecution Association). "People return to the workplace with the sense that everything is possible."[88]

11-7b Minority Sponsorship

Another benefit of employee affinity groups is that people often obtain sponsors through their affiliation with the groups. Ken Wilson, a vice chairman and member of BlackRock's powerful global advisory committee, for example, became a sponsor for Anne Ackerley after seeing her in action with the company's women's group, and he supported her career and eventually helped her get the promotion to chief marketing officer. Ackerley's work with the women's network, says Wilson, "gave her a firm-wide profile. She wasn't that well known [before]."[89]

Sponsorship refers to strong support from a powerfully positioned executive who is willing to put his or her reputation on the line to promote an individual's advancement to higher organizational levels.[90] Sponsorship is mentorship on steroids. Mentors are important because they offer advice and guidance, but a sponsor actually advocates on behalf of the protégé and connects the individual to important people and assignments. Because they go out on a limb, sponsors expect outstanding performance and unwavering commitment.[91]

Sponsorship
strong support from a powerfully positioned executive who is willing to put his or her reputation on the line to promote an individual's career advancement

Sylvia Hewlett, author of *Forget a Mentor, Find a Sponsor*, led a two-year study that shows that sponsorship makes a measurable difference in career advancement.[92] Sponsors make sure their protégés get considered for important projects and have opportunities to show what they can do. In addition, people with sponsors are more likely to ask for stretch assignments, request salary increases, and seek opportunities. Yet only 5 percent of minorities have sponsors compared to 21 percent of white employees. Just as with job promotions, when senior leaders pick someone to sponsor, they almost automatically turn to people like themselves. Companies such as American Express, AT&T, Citigroup, Credit Suisse, Deloitte, Genentech, and Morgan Stanley have made sponsorship more accessible for minorities by making sure senior executives know of high-potential female and minority candidates.[93]

LEADERSHIP ESSENTIALS

- One main point of this chapter is that diversity is a fact of life in today's world, and leaders can create change in organizations to keep pace with the changing environment. The U.S. population, the workforce, and the customer base are changing. In addition, organizations are operating in an increasingly global world, which means dealing with diversity on a broader stage than ever before.
- Diversity is defined as all the ways in which people differ. This definition has been broadened in recent years to be more inclusive and to recognize a broad spectrum of characteristics. The inclusive definition of diversity embraces not only dimensions such as gender and race but also characteristics such as work style, nationality, and income level.
- There are several reasons why organizations are recognizing the need to value and support diversity. Diversity of thought provides a broader and deeper base of experience for problem solving and is essential to keep organizations thriving in today's rapidly changing environment. A diverse workforce helps organizations build better relationships with diverse customers and helps develop employee potential. One aspect of diversity of recent interest is women's style of leadership, referred to as interactive leadership. The values associated with interactive leadership, such as inclusion and relationship building, are emerging as valuable qualities for both male and female leaders in the twenty-first century.
- Today's leaders face significant challenges leading people who are different from themselves. The first step for leading diverse people is understanding the hardships that people who do not fit the mainstream white, U.S.-born, male culture often endure. These include prejudice, stereotypes, discrimination, and the glass ceiling.
- Another important issue is global diversity. Leaders can be aware of the impact culture may have, understand social and cultural value differences, and develop cultural intelligence.
- People differ in their level of diversity awareness and their sensitivity to other cultures, values, and ways of doing things. Leaders evolve through stages of personal diversity awareness and action ranging from minimum efforts to meet affirmative action guidelines to valuing diversity as an integral part of organizational culture. Strong, culturally sensitive leadership is the only way organizations can become inclusive.
- The ultimate goal for leaders in the twenty-first century is to build organizations as integrated communities in which all people feel encouraged, respected, and committed to common purposes and goals. Employee affinity groups and sponsorship are two important ways leaders can support the participation and advancement of women and minority employees.

DISCUSSION QUESTIONS

1. Do you agree with sociologist William Bielby that people have innate biases and will automatically discriminate if left to their own devices? Discuss.
2. Why is diversity of thought important for today's organizations? Do you think an organization can have diversity of thought if all employees are of the same race and approximately the same age and background?
3. What is interactive leadership, and why might this approach be increasingly important for all leaders in the twenty-first century?
4. Discuss ways in which low power distance as a social value among followers could affect their interaction with a leader who displays high power distance.
5. Why do you think many women *opt out* from seeking higher levels of corporate leadership? Discuss why you think this either is or is not a trend that might hurt organizations over the next decade.
6. Take another look at this chapter's *Consider This* box. What might be some reasons men seem to be falling behind in today's world? If this is true, why is it that women are still so poorly represented at higher organizational levels?
7. Why is it important for today's leaders to develop cultural intelligence? Do you think a leader who has never had experience with people different from himself or herself can develop the ability to smoothly adapt to culturally different ways of thinking and behaving? Discuss.
8. Recall a leader you worked for. At what stage of personal diversity awareness (refer to Exhibit 11.7) was this leader? Explain. At what stage of diversity awareness are you?
9. Do you think people and organizations can ever become gender- and color-blind? Discuss.
10. The chapter described a conflict at a meatpacking plant over providing break times for Muslims to pray. How might leaders accommodate the needs of diverse groups without offending other groups or appearing to show favoritism?

LEADERSHIP AT WORK

Personal Diversity

Each of us feels different in many ways from the average behavior or expectations that other people seem to value. This reflects our own feelings of diversity. The differences you feel compared to others could be about your physical characteristics (height, age, skin color) but also could reflect a difference in your thinking style, feelings, personality, or behavior, especially when you feel different from what other people expect or what you perceive are the social norms. Write in the following list six ways you feel different from others:

1. ______________________ 4. ______________________

2. ______________________ 5. ______________________

3. ______________________ 6. ______________________

Now answer the following questions with respect to your perceived diversity.
What are your feelings about being different?

____

____

____

Which elements of diversity are you proud of? Why?

____

____

____

What element would you like to change to be less diverse? Why?

____

____

____

How do your differences contribute to a student team or work organization?

____

____

____

In Class: This exercise can be adapted for group discussion in class about underlying diversity. The instructor can ask students to sit in teams of three to five members in a circle facing each other. A student (focal person) then volunteers to describe the ways he or she feels different from others based on the previous list. Other students take turns providing feedback to the focal person on what the perceived differences mean to them with respect to team or class contributions. Each student takes a turn as the focal person, describing their feelings of being different and hearing feedback from others on the perception and impact of those differences.

Here are the key questions for this exercise: What did you learn about perceived diversity and interpersonal relations? What does it mean when our differences appear larger to ourselves than they appear to others? How does personal diversity affect team or organizational performance? (A list can be written on the board.)

LEADERSHIP DEVELOPMENT: CASES FOR ANALYSIS

True to Myself

Ethney Gentry was thrilled to have infiltrated the ultimate good old boy network, landing a job with a mid-size Tulsa-based oil company. Armed with solid credentials and what she considered the strengths of female leadership—listening, collaboration, consensus building, and organization—she looked forward to her first meeting with the company's retiring first female manager, Alexis Bale.

Alexis offered a firm, almost painful handshake and a cup of coffee.

"I've been looking forward to meeting you, Alexis," Ethney said.

"It's Alex."

"Oh, I didn't know." Ethney took a sip of piping hot coffee with a sudden vague feeling of discomfort. The first moments of this much-anticipated meeting seemed awkward and somewhat strained.

"I'll be honest with you," Alex said as she walked around and sat in the oversized chair behind her desk. "You're here for the same reason I was here. When our founder, Champ Luman, died twelve years ago, his three middle-aged daughters, referred to throughout the company as *the girls*, became major shareholders. They pushed hard for the inclusion of a woman in management. That *was* me. Now it's you."

Ethney tried to show no reaction as she set her cup on the desk. "Are you implying that I was selected over more qualified male candidates?"

"No. I was not on the selection team. I've seen your resume and you are an excellent addition to the organization. But qualifications aside, you and I fulfill, shall we say—the 'diversity' requirements for an otherwise all-male club."

Ethney could not believe the undisguised cynicism of the woman across the desk. She was torn between a desire to get up and march out of the office and a desire to stay and hear the entire lecture. She decided to take the high road. "My understanding was that you have been very successful here," she said.

"I suppose so." Alex gazed up at the numerous photographs showing oil rigs scattered across the Oklahoma plains. "I learned to play the game," she said somewhat wistfully and then suddenly turned and looked at Ethney. "I'm not trying to intimidate you. But I think that coming in, you should understand some things."

"Such as?"

"Such as . . . don't be too eager with your ideas or opinions. When I started, I intended to jump right in and contribute. The men resented it. I was considered a 'pushy broad' as one *gentleman* told me to my face. The reaction to me was harsh. They may have been stuck with me, but these guys could marginalize me, make sure I didn't count, and make sure I knew it."

"What did you do?"

"I stewed awhile and finally tried the opposite tactic. I jumped up to get coffee for everyone. I sought the *wise counsel* of their opinions before daring to make a suggestion in meetings. I played the female image that was in their minds. I felt like an idiot. I kowtowed till I thought I would throw up."

"How did they react?"

"I was no longer marginalized. But I wasn't respected either. I had quietly stepped back and accepted *my place*."

"Why didn't you just quit?"

"Because I knew that's exactly what they wanted me to do. And I'm just stubborn enough not to give them what they wanted."

Ethney took a deep breath and shook her head. "This sounds like the 1950s. I can't believe men in management act like this."

"Uh-huh. It may be a little better now, but they are still throwbacks to *Mad Men*."

"So how did you develop this reputation for success if you went from being ignored to being a doormat?"

"Have you met Bill Ledson?" Ethney nodded, took a sip of coffee, and leaned forward, waiting to hear the secret of success.

"At an industry meeting in Houston, his wife, Margaret, got tipsy, cornered me, and drawled, 'Listen, Honey. I've been around oil men all my life. My daddy and his daddy were oil men. You're going to have to wise up and take the plunge—become one of the boys. It's the only way you'll ever be accepted.' She reminded me that I'm on *their* turf. Margaret told me, 'Honey, as a wife and hostess for this crowd, I've talked more football than you can imagine. I hate football. I hang on for the commercials. But they don't know that. Bill doesn't know that. Me and God—we're the only ones who know that. Trust me,' she said. 'These guys do get down to some serious business, but not until they grouse about how Oklahoma State was robbed of its chance to play LSU for the national championship.' "

"Isn't that trivializing the men in this company?" Ethney asked.

Alex shrugged. "It worked. I became Alex and I became one of the guys. And, over time, I came to be treated with grudging respect, and promotions followed. I held the room spellbound for fifteen minutes at the last board meeting with my theory that Texas A&M joined the Southeastern Conference in order to up their chances for better bowls because the BCS favors the SEC. Later, when I submitted my ideas for improving coordination of teams in the oil fields, they thought it was *brilliant*! I'm one of them!"

Ethney nodded, somewhat impressed.

"Take my advice. Change your name. Ethney is too girlie. What's your middle name?"

"Madison."

"Be Madison." Alex walked Ethney to the door and shook her hand. The meeting was over.

As the door closed behind her, Ethney's feelings about what she had just heard ranged from bewilderment to anger to depression. *She sold out. All of these women sold out. They can't even be who they are. I am an experienced, educated, qualified, capable woman. I don't want to be Madison*, Ethney thought confidently and pushed the elevator button.

The elevator opened and she stepped inside. *What have I gotten myself into*?

QUESTIONS

1. If you were Ethney, how would you try to conduct yourself at the oil company? Why do you think your approach would be successful?
2. Do you think male-dominated cultures like this one still exist? Do you think women have to plot a strategy to be accepted? Would you adopt a strategy in which you acted different from your normal personality? Why?
3. What does it mean to be "True to yourself"? Is being true to yourself more important than achieving personal career success in a male-dominated company? Is it okay to *enable* the continuation of an "unhealthy" work environment for women? Why?

The Trouble with Bangles

Leela Patel was standing by her machine, as she had for eight hours of each working day for the past six years. Leela was happy; she had many friends among the 400 or so women at the food processing plant. Most of them were of Indian origin like herself, although Asian women formed less than a fifth of the female workforce. Leela was a member of a five-woman team that reported to supervisor Bill Evans.

Leela saw Evans approaching now, accompanied by Jamie Watkins, the shop steward. "Hello, Leela; we've come to explain something to you," Evans began. "You must have heard about the accident last month when one of the girls caught a bangle in the machine and cut her wrist. Well, the Safety Committee has decided that no one will be allowed to wear any bangles, engagement rings, earrings, or necklaces at work—only wedding rings, sleepers for pierced ears, and wristwatches will be allowed. So I'm afraid you'll have to remove your bangles." Leela, as was her custom, was wearing three bangles—one steel, one plastic, and one gold. All the married Asian women wore bangles, and many of the English girls had also begun wearing them. Leela explained that she was a Hindu wife and the bangles were important to her religion.

"Don't make a fuss, Leela," Evans said between clenched teeth. "I've already had to shout at Hansa Patel and Mira Desai. Why can't you all be like Meena Shah? She didn't mind taking her bangles off; neither did the English girls." Leela could see that Evans was very angry, so, almost in tears, she removed the bangles. When the two had moved off, however, she replaced the gold bangle and carried on with her work.

Within two or three days, the plant manager, Sam Jones, noticed that all the Asian women were wearing their bangles again—some, in fact, were wearing more than ever before. "I'm staggered by the response that this simple, common-sense restriction on the wearing of jewelry has brought," Jones remarked to the regional race relations employment advisor. "I have had several deputations from the Asian women protesting the ban, not to mention visits by individuals on the instruction of their husbands. In addition, I've just had a letter from something called the Asian Advisory Committee, asking that the ban be lifted until we meet with their representatives. The strength of this discontent has prompted me to talk to you. Jewelry constitutes both a safety and a hygiene hazard on this site, so it must be removed. And I'm afraid if I talk to this Asian Committee, they'll turn out to be a bunch of militants who'll cause all sorts of trouble. At the same time, we can't afford any work stoppages. What do you suggest?"

Several days later, the advisor had arranged for Mr. Singh from the local Council for Community Relations to talk to Jones and other managers. Singh explained that in his opinion there were no obstacles arising from *religious* observance that prevented implementation of the ban on bangles. However, he pointed out, the bangles do have a custom base that is stronger than the English tradition base for wedding rings. "The bangles are a mark not only of marriage but of the esteem in which a wife is held by her husband. The more bangles and the greater their value, the higher her esteem and the greater her social standing. The tradition also has religious overtones, since the wearing of bangles by the wife demonstrates that each recognizes the other as 'worthy' in terms of the fulfillment of their religious obligations. This position is further complicated in that women remove their bangles if they are widowed, and some fear that the removal of the bangles may lead to their husbands' deaths."

QUESTIONS

1. What is your initial reaction to this story? Why do you think you had this reaction?
2. Based on this limited information, how would you rate this organization in terms of developing leadership diversity? Discuss.
3. If you were a top executive at this company, how would you handle this problem?

Source: Adapted from "Bangles," in Allan R. Cohen, Stephen L. Fink, Herman Gadon, and Robin D. Willits, *Effective Behavior in Organizations: Cases, Concepts, and Student Experiences*, 7th ed. (Burr Ridge, IL: McGraw-Hill Irwin, 2001), pp. 413–414.

REFERENCES

1. Adam Bryant, "Vivek Gupta of Zensar Technologies: Beware of Hiring People Just Like You," *The New York Times* (March 7, 2015), http://www.nytimes.com/2015/03/08/business/vivek-gupta-of-zensar-technologies-beware-of-hiring-people-just-like-you.html?_r=0 (accessed November 13, 2015).
2. Harvard Business Review Staff, "HBR Survey: Were You Ever Treated Unfairly at Work Because of Someone Else's Bias?" *Harvard Business Review* (May 2015), p. 19.
3. Quoted in Colleen McCain Nelson, "Poll: Most Women See Bias in the Workplace," *The Wall Street Journal* (April 12, 2013), p. A4.
4. Marilyn Loden and Judy B. Rosener, *Workforce America*! (Homewood, IL: Business One Irwin, 1991); and Marilyn Loden, *Implementing Diversity* (Homewood, IL: Irwin, 1996).
5. Anthony Oshiotse and Richard O'Leary, "Corning Creates an Inclusive Culture to Drive Technology Innovation and Performance," *Global Business and Organizational Excellence* 26, no. 3 (March–April 2007), pp. 7–21.
6. Frances J. Milliken and Luis I. Martins, "Searching for Common Threads: Understanding the Multiple Effects of Diversity in Organizational Groups," *Academy of Management Review* 21, no. 2 (1996), pp. 402–433.
7. C. Keen, "Human Resource Management Issues in the '90s," *Vital Speeches* 56, no. 24 (1990), pp. 752–754.
8. U.S. Census Bureau figures reported in Population Distribution by Race/Ethnicity," The Henry J. Kaiser Family Foundation, http://kff.org/other/state-indicator/distribution-by-raceethnicity/ (accessed November 13, 2015); and Russ Wiles, "Businesses Encourage Employees to Learn Spanish," *USA Today* (December 7, 2008), http://www.usatoday.com/money/workplace/2007-12-08-spanish_n.htm?loc=interstitialskip (accessed March 17, 2008).
9. Bureau of Labor Statistics, U.S. Department of Labor, *The Economics Daily*, "Foreign Born Represented 16.5 Percent of the U.S. Labor Force in 2014, Up from 14.8 Percent in 2005," http://www.bls.gov/opub/ted/2015/foreign-born-represented-17-percent-of-the-labor-force-in-2014-up-from-15-percent-in-2005.htm (accessed November 13, 2015).
10. Occupational Outlook Handbook, *Bureau of Labor Statistics*, http://www.bls.gov/ooh/about/projections-overview.htm#laborforce (accessed June 29, 2012).
11. *Wall Street Journal* poll, reported in Colleen McCain Nelson, "Poll: Most Women See Bias in the Workplace," *The Wall Street Journal* (April 12, 2013), p. A4.
12. Edward Iwata, "Companies Find Gold Inside Melting Pot; Diverse Staff Helps Business Run Smoothly across Borders," *USA Today* (July 9, 2007), p. B1.
13. Louise Story, "Seeking Leaders, U.S. Companies Think Globally," *The New York Times* (December 12, 2007), p. A1; Justin Martin, "The Global CEO: Overseas Experience Is Becoming a Must on Top Executives' Resumes," *Chief Executive* (January–February 2004), p. 24; and G. Pascal Zachary, "Mighty Is the Mongrel," *Fast Company* (July 2000), pp. 270–284.
14. "Britain Recruiters Seek Female Spies," *USA Today* (July 12, 2008), http://www.usatoday.com/news/world/2008-07-12-spy_N.htm (accessed June 5, 2009).
15. "Lack of Diversity Paralyzed the CIA. It Can Cripple Your Organization, Too," Guest post by Philippe Silberzahn and Milo Jones, Frederick E. Allen Leadership Blog, *Forbes*, http://www.forbes.com/sites/frederickallen/2012/04/26/lack-of-diversity-paralyzed-the-cia-it-can-cripple-your-organization-too/ (accessed May 8, 2013); and Petraeus quote from the CIA Web site, https://www.cia.gov/careers/diversity/directors-diversity-commitment.html (accessed July 19, 2012).
16. Thomas E. Poulin, "The Other Diversity," *PA Times*, American Society for Public Administration (March 2009), p. 8; and Clayton H. Osborne and Vincent M. Cramer, "Fueling High Performance through Diversity," *Chief Learning Officer* (November 2005), p. 22.
17. Yair Holtzman and Johan Anderberg, "Diversify Your Teams and Collaborate: Because Great Minds Don't Think Alike," *Journal of Management Development* 30, no. 1 (2011), pp. 75–92.
18. Taylor H. Cox, *Cultural Diversity in Organizations* (San Francisco: Berrett-Koehler, 1994); Anita Woolley and Thomas Malone, "What Makes a Team Smarter? More Women," *Harvard Business Review* (June 2011), pp. 32–33
19. Thomas Barta, Markus Kleiner, and Tilo Neumann, "Is There a Payoff from Top-Team Diversity?" *McKinsey Quarterly*, Issue 2 (April 2012), pp. 13–15.
20. Quoted in Herminia Ibarra and Morten T. Hansen, "Are You a Collaborative Leader?" *Harvard Business Review* (July–August 2011), pp. 69–74.

21. Vanessa Lau and Brian Kleiner, "A Diverse Workforce for Diverse Markets," *Industrial Management* (July–August 2012), pp. 28–30; Tanzina Vega, "With Diversity Still Lacking, Industry Focuses on Retention," *The New York Times* (September 3, 2012); and Orlando C. Richard, "Racial Diversity, Business Strategy, and Firm Performance: A Resource-Based View," *Academy of Management Journal* 43, no. 2 (2000), pp. 164–177.
22. Lau and Kleiner, "A Diverse Workforce for Diverse Markets."
23. Quoted in Susan Caminiti, "The Diversity Factor," *Fortune* (October 19, 2007), pp. 95–105.
24. G. Haight, "Managing Diversity," *Across the Board* 27, no. 3 (1990), pp. 22–29.
25. Mahzarin Banaji's research as discussed in Nicholas Kristof, "Our Biased Brains," *The New York Times* (May 7, 2015), p. A29; and Atul Gawande, " Manning the Hospital Barricades: Why Do Groups— Even Groups of Doctors—Hate Each Other?" *Slate* (June 26, 1998), http://www.slate.com/articles/health_and_science/medical_examiner/1998/06/manning_the_hospital_barricades.html (accessed July 10, 2013).
26. Norma Carr-Ruffino, *Managing Diversity: People Skills for a Multicultural Workplace* (Tucson, AZ: Thomson Executive Press, 1996), p. 92; and Judy Rosener, *America's Competitive Secret: Women Managers* (New York: Oxford University Press, 1995), pp. 33–34.
27. Susan Webber, "Fit vs. Fitness," *The Conference Board Review* (July–August 2007), pp. 19–25.
28. Reported in Roger Parloff, "The War over Unconscious Bias," *Fortune* (October 15, 2007), pp. 90–102.
29. Marianne Bertrand, "Racial Bias in Hiring: Are Emily and Brendan More Employable than Lakisha and Jamal?" *Capital Ideas* (February 2005), pp. 7–9; and Marianne Bertrand and Sendhil Mullainathan, *Are Emily and Greg More Employable than Lakisha and Jamal?* (National Bureau of Economic Research Report), as reported in L. A. Johnson, "What's in a Name: When Emily Gets the Job over Lakisha," *The Tennessean* (January 4, 2004), p. 14A.
30. Shaunti Feldhahn, "Cracking the Male Code of Office Behavior," *The New York Times* (February 5, 2011), http://www.nytimes.com/2011/02/06/jobs/06pre.html?_r=0 (accessed May 9, 2013).
31. Reported in Michael Orey, "White Men Can't Help It," *BusinessWeek* (May 15, 2006), pp. 54, 57.
32. Johnson, "What's in a Name: When Emily Gets the Job over Lakisha."
33. Debra E. Meyerson and Joyce K. Fletcher, "A Modest Manifesto for Shattering the Glass Ceiling," *Harvard Business Review* (January–February 2000), pp. 127–136; Julie Amparano Lopez, "Study Says Women Face Glass Walls as Well as Glass Ceiling," *The Wall Street Journal* (March 3, 1992), pp. B1, B2; and Joann S. Lublin, "Women at Top Still Are Distant from CEO Jobs," *The Wall Street Journal* (February 28, 1996), pp. B1, B8.
34. John Beeson and Anne Marie Valerio, "The Executive Leadership Imperative: A New Perspective on How Companies and Executives Can Accelerate the Development of Women Leaders," *Business Horizons* 55 (2012), pp. 417–425.
35. Joanna Barsh, Sandrine Devillard, and Jin Wang, "The Global Gender Agenda," *McKinsey Quarterly* (November 2012), http://www.mckinsey.com/insights/organization/the_global_gender_agenda (accessed May 10, 2013).
36. "African American CEOs of *Fortune* 500 Companies," *BlackEntrepreneurProfile.com*, http://www.blackentrepreneurprofile.com/fortune-500-ceos (accessed June 3, 2009); Heidi Evans, "Ursula Burns to Head Xerox, Will Be First Black Woman to Be CEO of *Fortune* 500 Company," *NY Daily News* (May 22, 2009), http://www.nydailynews.com/news/money/ursula-burns-head-xerox-black-woman-ceo-fortune-500-company-article-1.412330 (accessed July 11, 2013); and Barbara Reinhold, "Smashing Glass Ceilings: Why Women *Still* Find It Tough to Advance to the Executive Suite," *Journal of Organizational Excellence* (Summer 2005), pp. 43–55; Jory Des Jardins, "I Am Woman (I Think)," *Fast Company* (May 2005), pp. 25–26; and Meyerson and Fletcher, "A Modest Manifesto for Shattering the Glass Ceiling."
37. Anat Arkin, "Hidden Talents," *People Management* (July 14, 2006).
38. "Salary Gap Widens between German Men and Women," *Spiegel Online* (March 5, 2010), http://www.spiegel.de/international/europe/gender-inequality-salary-gap-widens-between-german-men-and-women-a-682026.html (accessed May 9, 2013); and Sarah Plass, "Wage Gaps for Women Frustrating Germany," *The New York Times* (September 3, 2008), p. C1.
39. Ginny Parker Woods, "Japan's Diversity Problem," *The Wall Street Journal* (October 24, 2005), pp. B1, B4.
40. Sheelah Kolhatkar, "Arrested Development," *Bloomberg Businessweek* (February 4–10, 2013), pp. 6–7.
41. Lisa Belkin, "The Opt-Out Revolution," *The New York Times Magazine* (October 26, 2003), pp. 43–47, 58.
42. Sylvia Ann Hewlett and Carolyn Buck Luce, "Off-Ramps and On-Ramps: Keeping Talented Women on the Road to Success," *Harvard Business Review* (March 2005), pp. 43–54.
43. Sheila Wellington, Marcia Brumit Kropf, and Paulette R. Gerkovich, "What's Holding Women Back?" *Harvard Business Review* (June 2003), pp. 18–19.
44. The Leader's Edge/Executive Women Research 2002 survey, reported in "Why Women Leave," *Executive Female* (Summer 2003), p. 4.
45. Reinhold, "Smashing Glass Ceilings"; Des Jardins, "I Am Woman (I Think)"; and Alice H. Eagly and Linda L. Carli, "The Female Leadership Advantage: An Evaluation of the Evidence," *The Leadership Quarterly* 14 (2003), pp. 807–834.
46. Sonia Kolesnikov-Jessop, "Developing the Confidence to Move Up," *The New York Times* (June 21, 2015), http://www.nytimes.com/2015/06/22/business/international/developing-the-confidence-to-move-up.html?_r=0 (accessed November 16, 2015); Alistair Gray, "Inga Beale, Lloyd's of London CEO: In Search of New Risks," *Financial Times* (November 15, 2015), http://www.ft.com/intl/cms/s/0/6a588e60-8af5-11e5-8be4-3506bf20cc2b.html#axzz3rfmuAX8w (accessed November 16, 2015); and Alistair Gray, "Inga Beale, The Steely Trailblazer Shaking Up a Masculine Bastion," *Financial Times* (December 20, 2013), http://www.ft.com/cms/s/0/7b2265d0-68ac-11e3-bb3e-00144feabdc0.html#ixzz3rfnC6jxV (accessed November 16, 2015).
47. Joelle K. Jay and Amber Barnes, "Rising Above the Glass Ceiling," *T + D* (January 2013), pp. 52–55.
48. Beeson and Valerio, "The Executive Leadership Imperative"; Leslie Kwoh, "McKinsey Tries to Recruit Mothers Who Left the Fold," *The Wall Street Journal* (February 19, 2013), http://online.wsj.com/article/SB10001424127887323764804578314450063914388.html (accessed May 10, 2013).
49. Reported in Sharon Hadary and Laura Henderson, "Lead Boldly!" *Leadership Excellence* (January 2013), pp. 16–17; and studies reported in Avivah Wittenberg-Cox and Alison Maitland, "Financial Diversity: Why Women in Business Became the Solution, Not the Problem; Numbers of Top Female Executives Are Falling Yet Evidence Suggests They May Hold the Key to Corporate Success," *The Guardian* (February 5, 2008), p. 23; and Dwight D. Frink, Robert K. Robinson, Brian Reithel, Michelle M. Arthur, Anthony P. Ammeter, Gerald R. Ferris, David M. Kaplan, and Hubert S. Morrisette, "Gender Demography and Organization Performance: A Two-Study Investigation with Convergence," *Group & Organization Management* 28, no. 1 (March 2003), pp. 127–147.
50. Sharon Hadary and Laura Henderson, *How Women Lead* (McGraw-Hill 2013); Carol Kinsey Goman, "What Men Can Learn from Women about Leadership in the 21st Century," *The Washington Post* (August 10, 2011), http://articles.washingtonpost.com/2011-08-10/national/35271442_1_female-leaders-leadership-women (accessed May 10, 2013); Judy B. Rosener, *America's Competitive Secret: Women Managers* (New York: Oxford University Press, 1995); Judy B. Rosener, "Ways Women Lead," *Harvard Business Review* (November–December 1990), pp. 119–125; Sally Helgesen, *The Female Advantage: Women's Ways of Leadership* (New York: Currency/Doubleday, 1990); Joline Godfrey, "Been There, Doing That," *Inc.* (March 1996), pp. 21–22;

Chris Lee, "The Feminization of Management," *Training* (November 1994), pp. 25–31; and Bernard M. Bass and Bruce J. Avolio, "Shatter the Glass Ceiling: Women May Make Better Managers," *Human Resource Management* 33, no. 4 (Winter 1994), pp. 549–560.

51. Reported in Tamar Lewin, "The New Gender Divide: At Colleges, Women Are Leaving Men in the Dust," *The New York Times* (July 9, 2006), Section 1, p. 1; and Mary Beth Marklein, "College Gender Gap Widens: 57% Are Women," *USA Today* (October 20, 2005), p. A1.
52. Hanna Rosin, *The End of Men—and the Rise of Women* (New York: Riverhead/Penguin 2012); Hanna Rosin, "The End of Men," *The Atlantic* (July–August 2010), http://www.theatlantic.com/magazine/archive/2010/07/the-end-of-men/308135/ (accessed May 10, 2013).
53. Lewin, "At Colleges, Women Are Leaving Men in the Dust"; and Jon Swartz, "Women Break to Front of Tech," *USA Today* (July 10, 2008), http://www.usatoday.com/money/companies/management/2008-07-10-women-ceos_N.htm (accessed July 11, 2008).
54. Quoted in Michelle Conlin, "The New Gender Gap," *BusinessWeek* (May 26, 2003), pp. 74–82.
55. Kathryn M. Bartol, David C. Martin, and Julie A. Kromkowski, "Leadership and the Glass Ceiling: Gender and Ethnic Group Influences on Leader Behaviors at Middle and Executive Managerial Levels," *The Journal of Leadership and Organizational Studies* 9, no. 3 (2003), pp. 8–19; Bass and Avolio, "Shatter the Glass Ceiling"; and Rochelle Sharpe, "As Leaders, Women Rule," *BusinessWeek* (November 20, 2002), pp. 75–84.
56. Bass and Avolio, "Shatter the Glass Ceiling."
57. Cynthia Carroll, "Why Different Is Better," *Newsweek* (January 29, 2007), p. E4.
58. Reported in Carol Kinsey Goman, "What Men Can Learn from Women."
59. The study on competitiveness was reported in Hal R. Varian, "The Difference between Men and Women, Revisited: It's about Competition," *The New York Times* (March 9, 2006), p. C3. For reviews and analyses of the research on gender differences in leadership, see Hadary and Henderson, "Lead Boldly!"; Nicole Z. Stelter, "Gender Differences in Leadership: Current Social Issues and Future Organizational Implications," *The Journal of Leadership Studies* 8, no. 4 (2002), pp. 88–99; and Alice H. Eagly, Mary C. Johannesen-Schmidt, and Marloes L. van Engen, "Transformational, Transactional, and Laissez-Faire Leadership Styles: A Meta-Analysis Comparing Women and Men," *Psychological Bulletin* 129, no. 4 (July 2003), p. 569ff.
60. Quoted in Lena Williams, "A Silk Blouse on the Assembly Line? (Yes, the Boss's)," *The New York Times* (February 5, 1995), Business Section, p. 7.
61. Based on Rosener, *America's Competitive Secret*, pp. 129–135.
62. Susan Carey, "More Women Take Flight in Airline Operations," *The Wall Street Journal* (August 14, 2007), p. B1; Ann Therese Palmer, "Teacher Learns All About Airline; United VP Began as Reservations Clerk, Rose through Ranks," *Chicago Tribune* (December 24, 2006), p. 3; Paul Merrion, "Cindy Szadokierski," *Crain's Chicago Business* (May 5, 2007), http://www.chicagobusiness.com/article/20070505/ISSUE02/100027750/cindy-szadokierski (accessed May 10, 2013).
63. Susan J. Wells, "A Female Executive Is Hard to Find," *HR Magazine* (June 2001), pp. 40–49; Hadary and Henderson, "Lead Boldly!"; Goman, "What Men Can Learn from Women"; and Helgesen, *The Female Advantage*.
64. "Muslim Leader: 150 Workers Fired over Prayer Dispute in Nebraska," *USA Today* (September 19, 2009), http://www.usatoday.com/news/religion/2008-09-19-muslim-prayer-business_N.htm (accessed September 20, 2008).
65. Kevin Maguire, "Harriet Harman's Equality Bill Signposts the Route to a Better Britain," *Mirror.co.uk* (April 29, 2009), http://www.mirror.co.uk/news/columnists/maguire/2009/04/29/harriet-harman-s-equality-bill-points-to-the-route-for-a-better-britain-115875-21316506 (accessed June 5, 2009).
66. Helen Bloom, "Can the United States Export Diversity?" *Across the Board* (March/April 2002), pp. 47–51.
67. Reported in "Molding Global Leaders," *Fortune* (October 11, 1999), p. 270.
68. Geert Hofstede, "The Interaction between National and Organizational Value Systems," *Journal of Management Studies* 22 (1985), pp. 347–357; and G. Hofstede, "The Cultural Relativity of the Quality of Life Concept," *Academy of Management Review* 9 (1984), pp. 389–398.
69. Debby Young, "Team Heat," *CIO* (September 1, 1998), Section 1, pp. 43–51.
70. Geert Hofstede, "Cultural Constraints in Management Theories," excerpted in Dorothy Marcic and Sheila M. Puffer, *Management International: Cases, Exercises, and Readings* (St. Paul, MN: West Publishing, 1994), p. 24.
71. The discussion of cultural intelligence is based on P. Christopher Earley and Elaine Mosakowski, "Cultural Intelligence," *Harvard Business Review* (October 2004), p. 139ff; Ilan Alon and James M. Higgins, "Global Leadership Success through Emotional and Cultural Intelligence," *Business Horizons* 48 (2005), pp. 501–512; P. C. Earley and Soon Ang, *Cultural Intelligence: Individual Actions across Cultures* (Stanford, CA: Stanford Business Books, 2003); and David C. Thomas and Kerr Inkson, *Cultural Intelligence: People Skills for Global Business* (San Francisco: Berrett-Koehler, 2004).
72. These components are from Earley and Mosakowski, "Cultural Intelligence."
73. Karl Moore, "Great Global Managers," *Across the Board* (May–June 2003), pp. 40–43.
74. Alison M. Konrad, Roger Kashlak, Izumi Yoshioka, Robert Waryszak, and Nina Toren, "What Do Managers *Like* to Do?" *Group & Organization Management* 26, no. 4 (December 2001), pp. 401–433.
75. Based on Nancy Adler, *International Dimensions of Organizational Behavior*, 5th ed. (Mason, OH: South-Western, 2008), pp. 49–52.
76. Reported in Jeanne Brett, Kristin Behfar, and Mary C. Kern, "Managing Multicultural Teams," *Harvard Business Review* (November 2006), pp. 84–91.
77. Renee Blank and Sandra Slipp, "The White Male: An Endangered Species?" *Management Review* (September 1994), pp. 27–32; and Sharon Nelton, "Nurturing Diversity," *Nation's Business* (June 1995), pp. 25–27.
78. Farhad Manjoosept, "Exposing Hidden Bias at Google," *The New York Times* (September 25, 2014), p. B1; Nick Wingfield, "Intel Budgets $300 Million for Diversity," *The New York Times* (January 6, 2015), p. B1; and Jena McGregor, "Google Admits It Has a Diversity Problem," *The Washington Post* (May 29, 2014), https://www.washingtonpost.com/news/on-leadership/wp/2014/05/29/google-admits-it-has-a-diversity-problem/ (accessed November 17, 2015).
79. Based on M. Bennett, "A Developmental Approach to Training for Intercultural Sensitivity," *International Journal of Intercultural Relations* 10 (1986), pp. 179–196.
80. "Diversity Speaks," Denny's Web site, http://dennysdiversity.com/about.asp (accessed November 17, 2015); Irwin Speizer, "Diversity on the Menu," *Workforce Management* (November 2004), p. 41; and Jim Adamson, "How Denny's Went from Icon of Racism to Diversity Award Winner," *Journal of Organizational Excellence* (Winter 2000), pp. 55–68.
81. This definition and discussion is based on Raymond A. Friedman, "Employee Network Groups: Self-Help Strategy for Women and Minorities," *Performance Improvement Quarterly* 12, no. 1 (1999), pp. 148–163; and Joann S. Lublin, "To Climb the Ladder, Try Joining a Group," *The Wall Street Journal* (December 26, 2012), p. B6.
82. Lublin, "To Climb the Ladder, Try Joining a Group"; and "Employee Resource Groups," Cisco Systems, http://www.cisco.com/web/about/ac49/ac55/diversity_inclusion_employee.html (accessed May 13, 2013).
83. Raymond A. Friedman and Brooks Holtom, "The Effects of Network Groups on Minority Employee Turnover Intentions," *Human Resource Management* 41, no. 4 (Winter 2002), pp. 405–421; and

Raymond A. Friedman, Melinda Kane, and Daniel B. Cornfield, "Social Support and Career Optimism: Examining the Effectiveness of Network Groups among Black Managers," *Human Relations* 51, no. 9 (1998), pp. 1155–1177.
84. Lublin, "To Climb the Ladder, Try Joining a Group."
85. Hashi Syedain, "Premium Bonds," *People Management* (September 2012), pp. 23–26.
86. Elizabeth Wasserman, "A Race for Profits," *MBA Jungle* (March–April 2003), pp. 40–41.
87. Lublin, "To Climb the Ladder, Try Joining a Group."
88. Syedain, "Premium Bonds."
89. Lublin, "To Climb the Ladder, Try Joining a Group."
90. Sylvia Ann Hewlett, "Mentors Are Good. Sponsors Are Better," *The New York Times* (April 13, 2013), http://www.nytimes.com/2013/04/14/jobs/sponsors-seen-as-crucial-for-womens-career-advancement.html?_r=0 (accessed May 13, 2013); and Stephanie Castellano, "Sponsoring Career Success for Minority Workers," *T + D* (November 2012), p. 18.
91. Hewlett, "Mentors Are Good. Sponsors Are Better."
92. Sylvia Hewlett, *Forget a Mentor, Find a Sponsor: The New Way to Fast-Track Your Career* (Boston: Harvard Business Review Press, 2013).
93. Hewlett, "Mentors Are Good. Sponsors Are Better."

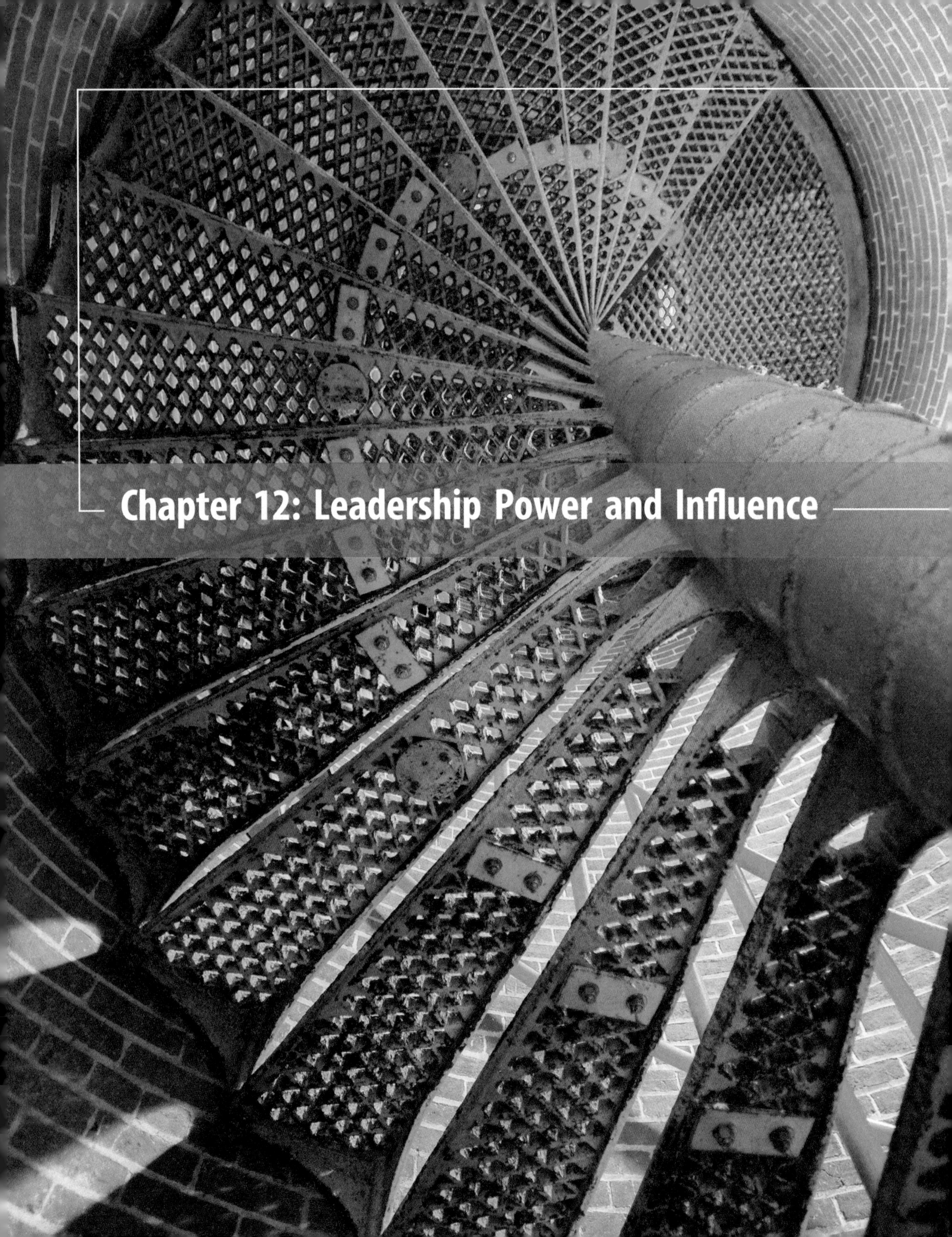

Chapter 12: Leadership Power and Influence

YOUR **LEADERSHIP** CHALLENGE

After reading this chapter, you should be able to:

- Use power and politics to help accomplish important organizational goals.
- Practice aspects of charismatic leadership by pursuing a vision or idea that you care deeply about and want to share with others.
- Apply the concepts that distinguish transformational from transactional leadership.
- Use coalitional leadership to build alliances that can help you achieve important goals for the organization.
- Call upon characteristics of Machiavellian-style leadership when tough actions are needed to benefit the organization in difficult times.
- Explain the difference between soft power and hard power and identify specific types of power in organizations.
- Describe structural, human resource, political, and symbolic frames of reference and identify your dominant leadership frame.
- Know how to increase power through political activity and use the influence tactics of appealing to a higher vision, rational persuasion, friendliness, reciprocity, developing allies, and direct persuasion.

CHAPTER **OUTLINE**

362 **Four Kinds of Influential Leadership**

371 **Using Hard versus Soft Power**

376 **Increasing Power through Political Activity**

382 **Don't Take Power Personally**

In the Lead

366 **Norman Seabrook, Riker's Island**

371 **The Evans Family**

374 **Patricia Sellers, *Fortune* Magazine**

382 **Paul Wolfowitz, World Bank**

Leader's Self-Insight

364 **Transformational Leadership**

370 **What's Your Mach?**

379 **Your Leadership Orientation**

Leader's Bookshelf

369 **Power: Why Some People Have It and Others Don't**

Leadership at Work

386 **Circle of Influence**

Leadership Development: Cases for Analysis

387 **The Suarez Effect**

388 **Waite Pharmaceuticals**

When top executives at Minneapolis-based HealthFitness needed to quickly implement a new technology platform, they turned to some of the company's most powerful people to help ease the transition. HealthFitness, which provides corporate health services, had a lot riding on the $30 million project, so they needed everything to go smoothly. The top leaders knew they did not have the clout to quickly get everyone on board with the new initiative. So, they depended on a group of staff members identified as "influencers," or employees who are well-connected, well-liked, and trusted throughout the organization. The company brought 30 influencers together and provided them with training and detailed information about the project so they could help build positive buzz. It's a strategy that many companies are using to spread information, help with difficult transitions such as mergers, or get employees on board with new projects.

The rise of social media has brought attention to the importance of connections that can't be seen on an organization chart. "There's this whole underground world," said Kristin Kassis, a managing partner at Work Wise LLC, a consulting firm that has helped companies identify influencers.[1] In organizations, people who are friendly to others, willing to listen and collaborate, like to help others, and enjoy interacting with people from across the organization typically have strong influence. All leaders use power and influence to get their jobs done, but power often depends on much more than a job title.

This chapter explores the topic of leadership power and influence in detail. The chapter opens with a consideration of four types of influential leadership. We next examine what we mean by the terms *power* and *influence*, consider different leader frames of reference that affect how leaders think about and use power, look at the differences in using soft power versus hard power, and outline ways leaders exercise power and influence through political activity. Finally, we briefly consider some ethical aspects of using power and influence.

12-1 FOUR KINDS OF INFLUENTIAL LEADERSHIP

New leaders often think of leadership power as something granted by an organization through the leader's position. However, leaders also have power that doesn't depend on job authority, and they influence people through a variety of means. Four types of influential leadership that rely on a leader's personal style and relationships are transformational, charismatic, coalitional, and Machiavellian-style leadership.

12-1a Transformational Leadership

Transformational leadership is characterized by the ability to bring about significant change in both followers and the organization. Transformational leaders have the ability to lead changes in an organization's vision, strategy, and culture as well as promote innovation in products and technologies.

One way to understand transformational leadership is to compare it to transactional leadership.[2] The basis of **transactional leadership** is a transaction or exchange process between leaders and followers. The transactional leader recognizes followers' needs and desires and then clarifies how those needs and desires will be satisfied in exchange for meeting specified objectives or performing certain duties. Thus, followers receive rewards for job performance, whereas leaders benefit from the completion of tasks. Transactional leaders focus on the present and excel at keeping the organization running smoothly and efficiently. They are good at traditional management functions such as planning and budgeting and generally focus on the impersonal aspects of job performance. Transactional leadership can be quite effective. However, because it involves a commitment to "follow the rules," transactional leadership maintains stability within the organization rather than promoting change.

Transactional skills are important for all leaders. However, in a world in which success often depends on continuous change, organizations also need transformational leadership.[3] Rather than analyzing and controlling specific transactions with followers using rules, directions, and incentives, transformational leadership focuses on intangible qualities such as vision, shared values, and ideas in order to build relationships, give larger meaning to separate activities, and inspire people to participate in the change process. Transformational leadership is based on the personal values, beliefs, and qualities of the leader rather than on an exchange process between leaders and followers.

Transformational leadership
leadership characterized by the ability to bring about significant change in followers and the organization

Transactional leadership
a transaction or exchange process between leaders and followers

Studies support the idea that transformational leadership has a positive impact on follower development, performance, and even organizational profitability.[4] Moreover, transformational leadership skills can be learned as they are not ingrained personality characteristics. Transformational leadership differs from transactional leadership in four significant areas.[5]

1. *Transformational leadership paints a grand vision of a desired future and communicates it in a way that makes the pain of change worth the effort.*[6] The most significant role of the transformational leader may be to articulate a vision that is significantly better than the old one and to enlist others in sharing the dream. It is the vision that launches people into action and provides the basis for the other aspects of transformational leadership. Without vision, there can be no transformation.
2. *Transformational leadership inspires followers to go beyond their own self-interests for the good of the group.* Transformational leaders motivate people to do more than originally expected. They make followers aware of the importance of change goals and outcomes and, in turn, enable them to transcend their own immediate interests for the sake of the whole organization.
3. *Transformational leadership elevates the concerns of followers from lower-level physical needs (such as for safety and security) to higher-level psychological needs (such as for self-esteem and self-actualization).* Lower-level needs are met through adequate wages, safe working conditions, and other considerations, but the transformational leader also pays attention to each person's need for growth and development. Therefore, the leader sets examples and assigns tasks not only to meet immediate needs but also to elevate followers' needs and abilities to a higher level and link them to the organization's mission.
4. *Transformational leadership develops followers into leaders.* Instead of strictly controlling people, transformational leaders strive to bring out the best in followers. They rally people around the mission and vision and define the boundaries within which followers can operate with greater freedom to accomplish goals. They enlist followers in identifying problems and help them look at things in new ways so they can bring about productive change to reach the vision.

Effective leaders exhibit both transactional and transformational leadership patterns. They accentuate not only their abilities to build a vision and empower and energize others, but also the transactional skills of designing structures, control systems, and reward systems that can help people achieve the vision.[7]

NEW LEADER
ACTION MEMO

As a leader, you can act like a transformational leader by rallying people around an inspiring vision, expressing optimism about the future, helping followers develop their potential, and empowering people to make change happen.

NEW LEADER
ACTION MEMO

Complete the questions in Leader's Self-Insight 12.1 to learn how a supervisor of yours rates on transformational leadership. Then, answer the questions for how you would behave in a leadership situation.

12-1b Charismatic Leadership

Charisma has been called "a fire that ignites followers' energy and commitment, producing results above and beyond the call of duty."[8] **Charismatic leaders** have an emotional impact on people and inspire them to do more than they would normally do, despite obstacles and personal sacrifice. Their passion for a mission inspires people to follow them and motivates people to transcend their own interests for the sake of achieving the goal. Whereas transformational leadership seeks to increase follower engagement and empowerment, charismatic leadership typically instills both awe and submission in followers.[9] Transformational leadership motivates people not just to follow the leader personally but also to believe in the need for change and be willing to make sacrifices for the sake of the vision rather than just out of admiration for the leader.

Charismatic leaders
Leaders who have the ability to inspire and motivate people to do more than they would normally do, despite obstacles and personal sacrifice

LEADER'S SELF-INSIGHT 12.1

Transformational Leadership

Instructions: Think of a situation in which someone (boss, coach, teacher, group leader) was in a leadership position over you. Indicate whether each of the following items is Mostly False or Mostly True for you.

In general, the leader over me:

	Mostly False	Mostly True
1. Listened carefully to my concerns	____	✓
2. Showed conviction in his/her values	____	✓
3. Helped me focus on developing my strengths	____	✓
4. Was enthusiastic about our mission	____	✓
5. Provided coaching advice for my development	____	✓
6. Talked optimistically about the future	____	✓
7. Encouraged my self-development	____	✓
8. Fostered a clear understanding of important values and beliefs	____	✓
9. Provided feedback on how I was doing	____	✓
10. Inspired us with his/her plans for the future	____	✓
11. Taught me how to develop my abilities	____	✓
12. Gained others' commitment to his/her dream	____	✓

Scoring and Interpretation

These questions represent two dimensions of transformational leadership. For the dimension of *develops followers into leaders*, sum your Mostly True responses to questions 1, 3, 5, 7, 9, and 11. For the dimension of *inspires followers to go beyond their own self-interest*, sum your Mostly True responses for questions 2, 4, 6, 8, 10, and 12.

The scores for my leader are:

Develops followers into leaders: 6
Inspires followers to go beyond their own self-interest: 6

These two scores represent how you saw your leader on two important aspects of transformational leadership. A score of 5 or above on either dimension is considered high because many leaders do not practice transformational skills in their leadership or group work. A score of 2 or below would be below average. Compare your scores with those of other students to understand your leader's practice of transformational leadership. How do you explain your leader's score?

Remember, the important learning from this exercise is about yourself, not your leader. Analyzing your leader is simply a way to understand the transformational leadership concepts. How would you rate on the dimensions of *developing followers into leaders* or *inspiring followers to go beyond their own self-interest*? These are difficult skills to master. Answer the 12 questions for yourself as a leader. Analyze your pattern of transformational leadership as revealed in your 12 answers.

Sources: These questions are based on B. Bass and B. Avolio, *Multifactor Leadership Questionnaire*, 2nd ed. (Mind Garden Inc.) and P. M. Podsakoff, B. MacKenzie, R. H. Moorman, and R. Fetter, "Transformational Leader Behaviors and Their Effects on Followers, Trust in Leader Satisfaction, and Organizational Citizenship Behaviors," *Leadership Quarterly* 1, no. 2 (1990), pp. 107–142.

NEW LEADER
ACTION MEMO

As a leader, you can use aspects of charismatic leadership by articulating a vision, making personal sacrifices to help achieve it, and appealing to people's emotions more than to their minds. Expand your charismatic potential by pursuing activities that you genuinely love.

Charisma can be used for good or ill, but applied wisely and ethically, it can lift the entire organization's level of energy and performance. Although charisma itself cannot be learned, there are aspects of charismatic leadership that anyone can use. For one thing, charisma comes from pursuing activities that you have a true passion for.[10] Charismatic leaders are engaging their emotions in everyday work life, which makes them energetic, enthusiastic, and attractive to others. For example, Sir Richard Branson, founder and chairman of Virgin Group, which includes about 400 companies, never gets involved in a new business unless it is something he has fun doing. His enthusiasm rubs off on everyone around him.[11] The late Steve Jobs, former CEO of Apple, who commanded a rock-star-like following and was more than once called "the model of a charismatic leader," was intensely passionate about Apple and its products.[12]

A number of studies have identified the unique qualities of charismatic leaders, documented the impact they have on followers, and described the behaviors that help them achieve remarkable results.[13] Exhibit 12.1 compares distinguishing characteristics of charismatic and noncharismatic leaders.[14]

Charismatic leaders articulate an idealized vision of a better future. They have an ability to communicate complex ideas and goals in clear, compelling ways, so that people understand and identify with their message. Charismatic leaders also act in unconventional ways and use unconventional means to transcend the status quo and create change. The final quality shared by charismatic leaders is that their source of influence comes from personal characteristics rather than a formal position of authority. People admire, respect, and identify with the leader and want to be like him or her. Although charismatic leaders may be in formal positions of authority, charismatic leadership transcends formal organizational position because the leader's influence is based on personal qualities rather than the power and authority granted by the organization.

12-1c Coalitional Leadership

Transformational and charismatic leadership both suggest it is the individual leader who acts as a catalyst for bringing about valuable change toward achieving a goal or vision. Yet in most cases, successful change results from the efforts of a *coalition* of people rather than those of a single leader. **Coalitional leadership** involves building a coalition of people who support the leader's goals and can help influence others to implement the leader's decisions and achieve the goals.[15] Coalitional leaders observe and understand patterns of interaction and influence in the organization. They are skilled at developing connections with a broad network of people and can adapt their behavior and approach to diverse people and situations.

Coalitional leadership leadership that involves developing allies and building a coalition of people who support the leader's goals and can help influence others to implement the leader's decisions and achieve the goals

EXHIBIT 12.1 Distinguishing Characteristics of Charismatic and Noncharismatic Leaders

	Noncharismatic Leaders	Charismatic Leaders
Likability:	Shared perspective makes leader likable	Shared perspective and idealized vision make leader likable and an honorable hero worthy of identification and imitation
Relation to status quo:	Tries to maintain status quo	Creates atmosphere of change
Future goals:	Limited goals not too discrepant from status quo	Idealized vision that is highly discrepant from status quo
Articulation:	Weak articulation of goals and motivation to lead	Strong and inspirational articulation of vision and motivation to lead
Behavior:	Uses available means to achieve goals within framework of the existing order	Uses unconventional means to transcend the existing order
Influence:	Primarily authority of position and rewards	Transcends position; personal power based on expertise and respect and admiration for the leader

Source: Adapted from Jay Conger and Rabindra N. Kanungo and Associates, *Charismatic Leadership: The Elusive Factor in Organizational Effectiveness* (San Francisco: Jossey-Bass, 1988), p. 91.

Coalitional leaders develop positive relationships both within and outside the organization, and they spend time learning others' views and building mutually beneficial alliances. Coalition building seems to be especially important in the political arena. For example, Abraham Lincoln is considered by historians to be one of America's greatest presidents partly because he listened carefully to a broad range of people both inside and outside of his immediate circle when the nation was so bitterly divided over the Civil War. He included people who didn't agree with him and were critical of his goals and plans. On the other hand, some scholars have suggested that George W. Bush squandered his chance to be a great president when he failed to listen to a broad range of other people and involve them in decisions related to the Iraq War. The failure to reach out and build a coalition left the country deeply divided when Iraq became a quagmire, and Bush left office with the lowest poll ratings since opinion surveys of outgoing presidents began in the 1930s.[16] As for President Barack Obama, the jury is still out on how his presidency will be evaluated. However, Obama was criticized for failing to develop relationships with even his biggest donors and leaving the coalition building with Democrats on Capitol Hill and others to Vice President Joe Biden. Obama was widely viewed as a loner who preferred policy to people and consulted primarily with a close circle of advisors, although some reports indicated that he liked to listen to a wide range of people when considering important decisions.[17]

Failing to build a coalition can allow conflict and disagreements to derail a leader's decision, particularly if the opposition builds a powerful coalition of its own. An investigative report by *The New York Times*, for example, suggests that the strong coalitional power of a union leader prevented New York City government officials from implementing their plans to solve problems at the Rikers Island jail complex.

IN THE LEAD

Norman Seabrook, Riker's Island

"I came to think that my wardens believed Norman was more important to their career than I was," said a former commissioner for the New York City Department of Correction. He was referring to Norman Seabrook, the president of the Correction Officers' Benevolent Association, who wields tremendous power using coalitional smarts combined, some say, with intimidation.

Leaving aside the matter of what have been called Seabrook's bullying tactics, there is no doubt that he is a skilled coalitional leader. He invests tremendous time and energy building loyalty among the union membership, and he spends just as much time forging alliances with high-ranking uniformed officers and commission officials, as well as with powerful city and state leaders. Recently, Seabrook has begun speaking regularly with New York City Mayor Bill de Blasio about department policy.

Seabrook has achieved positive results for New York City correction officers, who have seen large gains in pay and benefits, as well as promotions to higher levels in the department. Yet some current and former city officials say Seabrook's power is also the biggest obstacle to curbing the excessive violence and corruption at the Riker's Island jail complex. After Florence Finkle, the chief investigator for the Department of Correction, announced plans before a roomful of senior officials and union leaders to crack down on the abuse at Riker's, Seabrook began a campaign that eventually led to Finkle being forced out.

She was replaced by a former police department official, who was also a childhood friend of Seabrook's. Some say one of Finkle's problems was a failure to pay attention to negotiating the department's politics and building a coalition.

Mayor de Blasio and his handpicked correction commissioner, Joseph Ponte, have vowed to overhaul the corrections department and end the abuse at Riker's. One of the biggest challenges, however, will be working effectively with Seabrook, who "has outmaneuvered a long line of mayors and commissioners over the years."[18]

The issues with the New York City Department of Correction and Riker's Island are complicated and beyond the scope of this text. However, the example of Norman Seabrook illustrates how coalitional leadership increases power and helps leaders accomplish their goals. Leaders always have to anticipate resistance, talk with people all across the organization, and make sure their decisions will benefit the overall organization.

Leaders can be more successful if they follow four steps for effective coalitional leadership:[19]

1. *Coalitional leaders do lots of interviews.* Leaders conduct informal interviews with people from all across the organization to gather information and get a clear sense of the challenges and opportunities they face. In addition to interviews, leaders talk informally with people whenever they get a chance.
2. *Coalitional leaders visit customers and other stakeholders.* Coalitional leaders also solicit the views and input of customers as well as other potentially influential stakeholders, such as board members, government agencies, creditors, or others. Jan Frank found that this was a big part of her job bringing change to California's State Compensation Insurance Fund. When Frank took over, the agency was reeling from financial scandal, ethical violations, and a criminal investigation. In addition to talking with managers, employees, and board members, Frank also met regularly with lawmakers and regulators to solicit their input regarding how to repair the agency's credibility. She knew their support was crucial to achieving what she wanted for the agency.[20]
3. *Coalitional leaders develop a map of stakeholder buy-in.* Leaders typically find that there are some people who strongly support their goals and plans, some who adamantly oppose them, and a large percentage who could swing either way. As illustrated in Exhibit 12.2, in mapping the level of buy-in for any significant change, about 10 percent of people can typically be classified as *advocates*, those stakeholders inside and outside the organization who are strong supporters and will help lead the change effort. Another 10 percent might be *partners*, who support and encourage the change but will not actively lead it. Twenty percent are typically strongly opposed to the change. These *resisters* might even disrupt or sabotage change efforts. The remaining 60 percent are classified as *observers* because they have a neutral attitude toward the proposed ideas and changes.[21]
4. *Coalitional leaders break down barriers and promote cross-silo cooperation.* The final critical step in coalitional leadership is continually breaking down barriers and promoting cooperation and collaboration across departments, divisions, and levels. For example, when Colin Powell was U.S. chairman of the Joint Chiefs of Staff, he regularly brought together the heads of the Army, Air Force, Navy, and Marines so they could understand one another's viewpoints.[22]

EXHIBIT 12.2 Mapping Stakeholder Buy-In

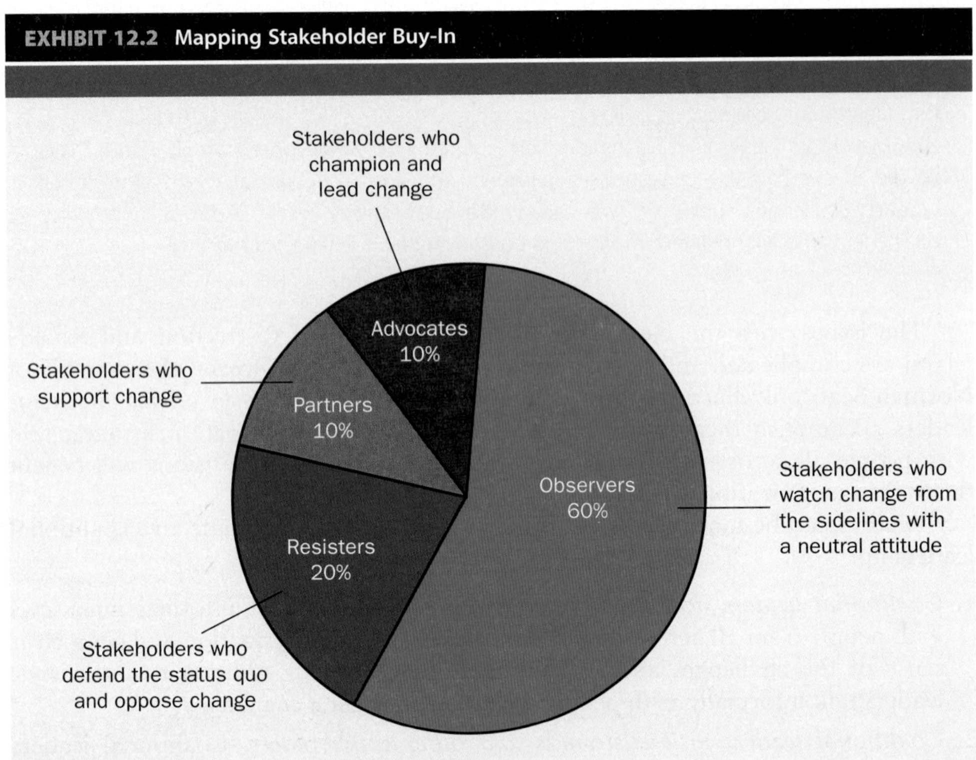

Source: Data are adapted from materials supplied by ExperiencePoint, Inc., in conjunction with the GlobalTech simulation, 2007.

12-1d Machiavellian-Style Leadership

Niccolò Machiavelli was an Italian philosopher, historian, and political strategist who wrote *The Prince* in 1513 as a guide for political leaders of the day on how to acquire and use power.[23] The term *Machiavellian* is often associated with unscrupulous, even diabolical behavior aimed at increasing one's power for personal gain, but in reality Machiavelli's essential argument in *The Prince* is that the welfare of the state must come first and foremost and that leaders must often do tough, even ruthless things in the spirit of the ends justifying the means. In other words, power is a tool used for securing the safety and stability of the organization. Despite the emphasis today on agreeableness and collaboration, many organizational leaders, scholars, and politicians agree with Machiavelli that it isn't possible in an imperfect world to lead with "perfectly clean hands."[24]

Jeffrey Pfeffer, Stanford University professor and an expert on organizational power and politics, refers to the need for leaders to use *bare-knuckle strategies* to attain the clout they need to accomplish great things.[25] As further described in the Leader's Bookshelf selection for this chapter, Pfeffer believes that despite laudable personal achievements, power and politics almost always trump performance as a source of impact, so leaders had better be comfortable acquiring and using these tools. In today's less-hierarchical organizations, leaders actually need more power than before to influence people. When Zia Yusuf, president and CEO of Streetline Inc., was an executive vice president at SAP, he advised and taught the people who worked for him how to court favor with the top 50 people in the company. Yusuf knew that having people in high places increases power and helps accomplish goals.

LEADER'S BOOKSHELF

Power: Why Some People Have It and Others Don't

by Jeffrey Pfeffer

Managers may be granted positions of authority, but real power doesn't just fall into a person's hands. It takes ambition, resolve, energy, and skill to accumulate the power a leader needs to be effective and successful, Jeffrey Pfeffer says in *Power: Why Some People Have It and Others Don't*. Think doing a good job gets you power? Think again. As Pfeffer puts it, "welcome to the real world—not necessarily the world we want, but the world that exists."

POWER IN THE REAL WORLD

To accumulate power, you need to get noticed. Here are some of Pfeffer's tips for doing so.

- ***Play Up to the Boss.*** Pfeffer advises regularly asking people who have power what aspects of your job they think are most crucial and how they think you should be doing them. This is one tactic for making your boss and other people with power feel good about themselves. "The surest way to keep your position and to build a power base is to help those with more power enhance their positive feelings about themselves." In Pfeffer's view, flattery really can get you everywhere.
- ***Master the Art of Networking.*** Try to forge a link between different parts of the company or between the company and important outsiders so that you become the center of a network. Build relationships with people that you can help and who can help you with information and resources. Playing the political game is necessary for acquiring power and getting things done.
- ***Be Forceful but Pick Your Battles Carefully.*** People who appear forceful and self-confident gain power, whereas those who seem uncertain fade away. Something as simple as interrupting others in a meeting expresses confidence. Pfeffer says Andy Grove of Intel used to insist that his brilliant but shy managers attend *wolf school* where they "learned how to lean into a superior's face and shout out an idea or proposal."
- ***Judiciously Break Some Rules.*** "The practice of flouting rules and violating norms actually *creates* power, as long as the culprit gets away with the behavior," says Pfeffer. The rules favor the people who make the rules—those who already have power, and they don't always benefit those who want to acquire it.

IS THIS THE RIGHT WAY FOR A LEADER TO ACT?

Pfeffer's book has been criticized for failing to acknowledge that too much focus on obtaining power—and power itself—can be corrupting. Yet, as Pfeffer points out, without power leaders and organizations cannot hope to succeed. In addition, Pfeffer cites research showing that powerful people are wealthier, have more friends, enjoy a better quality of life, and even live longer, healthier lives. He offers this book as a how-to manual for getting and keeping power.

Source: *Power: Why Some People Have It and Others Don't*, by Jeffrey Pfeffer, is published by HarperCollins.

Yusuf was in charge of an initiative that linked suppliers, users, and developers and had to influence many people that he had no formal authority over, not only from across SAP but from many different organizations. He says he succeeded because he was skilled at what he called "organizational dynamics"—the ability to influence people to get them to do what needed to be done.[26]

As discussed in the previous sections, many types of leadership are used to influence people. Each style—transformational, charismatic, coalitional, and Machiavellian—relies on different assumptions and behaviors. With Machiavellian-style leadership, the leader is willing to use any means necessary to preserve and protect the well-being of the organization. The characteristics of Machiavellian-style leaders include the following:[27]

1. *They are always on guard for risks and threats to their power.* Machiavellian-style leaders assume that people are basically fickle, greedy, and deceitful, so the leader is always alert to shifting loyalties and is not above using manipulation or pitting people against one another to retain or acquire more power to achieve goals.
2. *They don't mind being feared.* Machiavelli warned that striving to be the most-liked leader can backfire when difficult times call for tough actions. By being too merciful and generous, leaders can ultimately allow disorder to destroy the organization.

LEADER'S SELF-INSIGHT 12.2

What's Your Mach?

Instructions: Leaders differ in how they view human nature and the tactics they use to get things done through others. Answer the following questions based on how you view others. Think carefully about each question and be honest about what you feel inside. Please answer whether each item is Mostly False or Mostly True for you.

	Mostly False	Mostly True
1. Overall, it is better to be humble and honest than to be successful and dishonest.		
2. If you trust someone completely, you are asking for trouble.		
3. A leader should take action only when it is morally right.		
4. A good way to handle people is to tell them what they like to hear.		
5. There is no excuse for telling a white lie to someone.		
6. It makes sense to flatter important people.		
7. Most people who get ahead as leaders have led very moral lives.		
8. It is better to not tell people the real reason you did something unless it benefits you to do so.		
9. The vast majority of people are brave, good, and kind.		
10. It is hard to get to the top without sometimes cutting corners.		

Scoring and Interpretation

To compute your Mach score, give yourself one point for each Mostly False answer to items 1, 3, 5, 7, and 9, and one point for each Mostly True answer to items 2, 4, 6, 8, and 10. These items were drawn from the works of Niccolò Machiavelli, an Italian political philosopher who wrote *The Prince* in 1513 to describe how a prince can gain the power to protect and control his kingdom. From 8 to 10 points suggests a high Machiavellian score. From 4 to 7 points indicates a moderate score, and 0 to 3 points would indicate a low "Mach" score. Successful political intrigue at the time of Machiavelli was believed to require behaviors that today might be considered manipulative. A high Mach score today does not mean a sinister or vicious person but probably means the person has a cool detachment, sees life as a game, and is not personally engaged with people. Discuss your results with other students, and talk about whether politicians in local or federal government, or top executives in a company like Bear Stearns, discussed in Chapter 6, would likely have a high or a low Mach score.

Source: Adapted from R. Christie and F. L. Geis, *Studies in Machiavellianism* (New York: Academic Press, 1970).

NEW LEADER
ACTION MEMO

Do you have characteristics associated with Machiavellian-style leadership? Complete the questionnaire in Leader's Self-Insight 12.2 to find out.

3. *They will use deception if necessary*. The Machiavellian-style leader has no problem maintaining or using power by deceptive means to ensure the safety of the organization.
4. *They use rewards and punishments to shape behavior*. Machiavellian-style leaders don't mind exploiting the fears and desires of people to get them to follow the rules and do what is necessary for the overall good.

Like coalitional leaders, Machiavellian-style leaders are highly political, but whereas coalitional leaders focus on reaching out and working with others, Machiavellian-style leaders typically focus on gaining and using individual power. They may strive to gain control over information and resources such as jobs, rewards, financial support, and materials so that people depend on them for what they need, which increases their power.[28] These leaders may also use any means necessary to preserve their power, but they do so because they believe the organization can be secure only if it has powerful leaders. There are times in every organization when tough, even bare-knuckle leadership is needed. The following example describes how one woman says she used Machiavellian-style leadership to save her family.

IN THE LEAD

The Evans Family

Suzanne Evans was newly married, finishing a dissertation for her Ph.D. in history, and caring for four children under the age of 8. It was total chaos, but like many mothers dealing with blended families, Evans was trying to be kind and generous to the children. "Yet as I read *The Prince*," she says, "I realized that the more things I gave them, the more they expected and the less grateful they became."

Evans decided that a tough Machiavellian-style approach might be just what was needed to control the chaos that was threatening to tear her family apart. Here are some of the actions she took based directly on maxims she read in *The Prince*.

- *Guard against a reputation for being too generous*: On previous shopping trips, if she didn't buy the children whatever they wanted, they would pitch temper tantrums. The next time they went to Target, she gave each one $10 and told them they could spend it on whatever they wanted but to use it wisely because it was all they were getting.
- *Divide and conquer*: To get her son Daniel to do better in school, Evans pitted him and her daughter Teddy in a not-so-friendly competition. When Teddy brought home a nearly perfect report card, she was rewarded with a celebratory dinner at her favorite restaurant. Daniel, whose report card wasn't so good, got nothing except a reminder that he lost to his younger sister.
- *Use punishment*: Having children obey certain rules that ensure their safety is always important but even more so with a special needs child. When 5-year-old Katie, who has Down syndrome, kept trying to escape from the house unless she was watched constantly, Evans took action. She led her straight to her room and announced that whenever she broke the rule, she would have to stay in her room for half an hour. "Every. Single. Time."
- *Be deceptive*: Evans desperately needed a break, and she and her husband needed some time alone. To avoid the whining and crying that would ensue if the children weren't allowed to go along, Evans told them "that their dad and I were going away for the weekend on a business trip. And I didn't feel a bit guilty about it."

The strategies worked. Shopping trips went much more smoothly, and the children learned the value of money. By the end of the school year, both Daniel and Teddy brought home excellent report cards. The tough approach with Katie kept her from trying to sneak out of the house and kept her safe. And Evans and her husband had a great weekend away while the children wore out their grandparents. "When I returned home, I was well-rested and relaxed . . . and having a happy, relaxed mom always benefits a child," Evans says.[29]

Although Machiavellian-style leadership appears to be the approach most motivated to gain and use power, all leaders rely on the use of power to influence others and get things done.[30] In the following sections, we examine various types of power and how leaders apply power through influence tactics.

12-2 USING HARD VERSUS SOFT POWER

Power is often defined as the potential ability of one person to influence others to carry out orders[31] or to do something they otherwise would not have done.[32]

Other definitions stress that power is the ability to achieve goals or outcomes that power holders desire.[33] "Simply put, [power is] the ability to have things your way."[34] The achievement of desired outcomes is the basis of the definition used here. **Power** is the potential ability of one person in an organization to influence other people to bring about desired outcomes. It is the potential to influence others within the organization with the goal of attaining desired outcomes for power holders.

Power can be categorized as either *hard power* or *soft power*. Hard power is power that stems largely from a person's position of authority. This is the kind of power that enables a supervisor to influence subordinates with the use of rewards and punishments, allows a manager to issue orders and expect them to be obeyed, or lets a domineering CEO force through his or her own decisions without regard for what anyone else thinks. This is the approach to power typically taken by Machiavellian-style leaders. Transformational, charismatic, and coalitional leaders also use hard power, but they rely more often on soft power, which is based on personal characteristics and interpersonal relationships. Similarly, Machiavellian-style leaders also sometimes use soft power.

Power is realized through the processes of politics and influence.[35] **Influence** refers to the effect a person's actions have on the attitudes, values, beliefs, or actions of others. Whereas power is the capacity to cause a change in a person, influence may be thought of as the degree of actual change. For example, as a child you may have had the experience of playing a game you didn't really want to play because one person in the group influenced others to do what he or she wanted. Or you may have changed your college major because of the influence of someone important in your life, or shifted your beliefs about some social issue based on the influence of political or religious leaders.

12-2a Specific Types of Power

Most discussions of power include five types that are available to leaders.[36] Exhibit 12.3 illustrates the five types of leader power, categorized as either hard power or soft power. Hard power includes legitimate, reward, and coercive power, which are defined largely by the organization's policies and procedures. However, it is important to remember that position power and leadership are not the same thing. As we discussed in Chapter 1, a person might hold a formal position of authority and yet not be a leader.

Effective leaders don't rely solely on the hard power of their formal position to influence others. Soft power includes expert power and referent power, as shown in the exhibit. In today's world, soft power is, more than ever, the tool of the leader. Consider that Jeffrey Immelt, CEO of General Electric, considers himself a failure if he exercises his formal authority more than seven or eight times a year. The rest of the time, Immelt is using softer means to persuade and influence others and to resolve conflicting ideas and opinions.[37] Even the United States military is talking about the importance of building relationships rather than using brute force. Former Defense Secretary Robert Gates, for instance, says that in the battle for hearts and minds abroad, the United States has to be "good at listening to others" rather than just good at kicking down doors, and the Army's new stability operations field manual openly talks about the value of soft power.[38] Wesley Clark, former supreme commander of NATO who led the mission against Serb president Slobodan Milosevic, suggests that, for leaders in businesses as well as nations, building a community of shared interests should be the first choice rather than using threats, intimidation, and raw power.[39]

Power
the potential ability of one person to influence other people to bring about desired outcomes

Influence
the effect a person's actions have on the attitudes, values, beliefs, or actions of others

EXHIBIT 12.3 Five Types of Leader Power

Hard Power	Soft Power
Legitimate: Based on leader holding a formal position or title. People accept leader's right to issue orders or direct activities.	**Expert**: Based on leader's special knowledge or skills. People trust and respect decisions because of leader's expertise.
Reward: Based on leader having the ability to provide or withhold rewards. People comply in order to obtain desired rewards.	**Referent**: Based on leader's personal characteristics. People admire and respect leader, like to be around him or her, and adopt the leader's viewpoint.
Coercive: Based on leader's ability to punish or to recommend punishment. People follow orders to avoid punishments.	

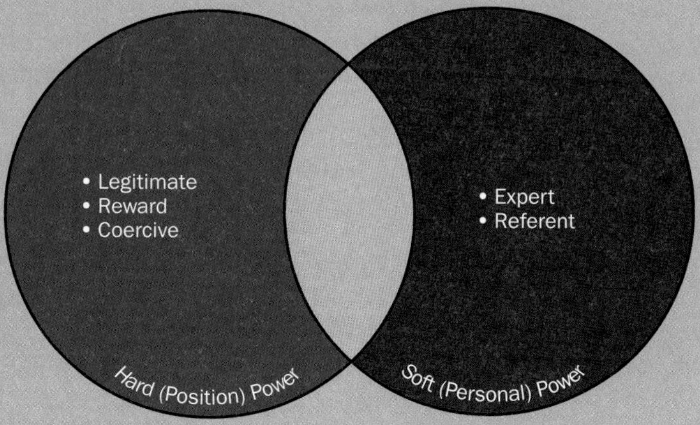

Each of the five types of leader power illustrated in Exhibit 12.3 is discussed in detail in the following paragraphs.

Legitimate Power **Legitimate power** is the authority granted from a formal position in an organization. For example, once a person has been selected as a supervisor, most employees accept that they are obligated to follow his or her direction with respect to work activities. Certain rights, responsibilities, and prerogatives accrue to anyone holding a formal leadership position. Followers accept the legitimate rights of formal leaders to set goals, make decisions, and direct activities.

Reward Power Power that stems from the authority to bestow rewards on other people is called **reward power**. For example, appointed leaders may have access to formal rewards, such as pay increases or promotions. Moreover, organizations allocate huge amounts of resources downward from top leaders. Leaders control resources and their distribution. Lower-level followers depend on leaders for the financial and physical resources to perform their tasks. Leaders with reward power can use rewards to influence subordinates' behavior.

NEW LEADER
ACTION MEMO

As a leader, you can expand your personal power by developing good relationships and acquiring advanced knowledge and experience. You can use power to gain the commitment of others to achieve the vision. Use position power when appropriate, but don't overdo it.

Legitimate power
authority granted from a formal position

Reward power
authority to bestow rewards on other people

Coercive Power The opposite of reward power is **coercive power**. It refers to the power to punish or recommend punishment. Supervisors have coercive power when they have the right to fire or demote subordinates, criticize, or withhold pay increases. For example, if a salesman does not perform as well as expected, the sales manager has the coercive power to criticize him, reprimand him, put a negative letter in his file, and hurt his chance for a raise. Coercive power is the negative side of legitimate and reward power.

Expert Power Power resulting from a leader's special knowledge or skill regarding tasks performed by followers is referred to as **expert power**. When a leader is a true expert, subordinates go along with recommendations because of his or her superior knowledge. Based on one scholar's research, leaders who are high in expert power are three times more influential than those without this type of power.[40] Leaders at supervisory levels often have experience in the production process that gains them promotion. At top management levels, however, leaders may lack expert power because subordinates know more about technical details than they do. People throughout the organization with expertise and knowledge can use it to influence or place limits on decisions made by people above them in the organization.[41]

Coercive power
authority to punish or recommend punishment

Expert power
authority resulting from a leader's special knowledge or skill

Referent power
authority based on personality characteristics that command followers' attention, respect, and admiration so that they want to emulate the leader

Referent Power This kind of power comes from leader personality characteristics that command followers' identification, respect, and admiration so they want to emulate the leader. When workers admire a supervisor because of the way he or she deals with them, the influence is based on referent power. **Referent power** depends on the leader's personal characteristics rather than on a formal title or position and is especially visible in the area of charismatic leadership. Consider the power of Patricia (Pattie) Sellers, who is the brains—and the brawn—behind *Fortune* magazine's 50 Most Powerful Women rankings.

IN THE LEAD

Patricia Sellers, *Fortune* Magazine

She rubs elbows with Sheryl Sandberg, Indra Nooyi, and Warren Buffett. Never heard of her? Maybe that's because she's the one sometimes writing the splashy articles that are featured on the cover of *Fortune* magazine, rather than being the subject of them. Patricia Sellers, who is known as Pattie to friends, joined *Fortune* in 1984, two years out of college, and has been exploring power in her stories ever since. Over those years, she has also consistently expanded her own power based on expertise, relationships, and personal style.

"She is just unabashed in her hunt, her quest, for the perfect story," said Sue Callaway, Sellers's former editor. Sellers came up with the idea of ranking the most powerful women in 1998 and sold it to the higher-ups at *Fortune*, and to high-ranking women themselves, based on her enthusiasm and the credibility she had built with her journalism. A year later, a passionate desire to connect women and give them a chance to talk about the big business issues of the day led her to start *Fortune*'s annual Most Powerful Women Summit.

Known for being somewhat shy early in her career, Sellers now charms conference attendees as easily as if they are old friends (and by now, many of them are). "I get invited to a lot of things," Warren Buffett said, "but this is the one I clear the calendar for." At the 2011 event, Buffett sat patiently waiting because a photographer wanted a shot of him with Sellers. Many people would have dropped everything to do the photo shoot, but part of

Sellers's power comes from treating everyone the same. She was busy with other guests. The "Oracle of Omaha" had to wait, just like anyone else would. He didn't mind. "She gets together women that no one else has ever gotten together before," he says. "And she makes you feel good about it."[42]

Charismatic leadership, described earlier, is intensely based on the relationship between leader and followers and relies heavily on either referent or expert power. However, all good leaders make use of these types of power rather than using position power alone. The *Consider This* box talks about the far-reaching impact of referent power.

12-2b Follower Responses to the Use of Power

Leaders use the various types of power to influence others to do what is necessary to accomplish organizational goals. The success of any attempt to influence is a matter of degree, but there are three distinct outcomes that may result from the use of power: compliance, resistance, and commitment, as illustrated in Exhibit 12.4.[43]

When people successfully use hard, position power (legitimate, reward, coercive), the response is compliance. **Compliance** means that people follow the directions of the person with power, whether or not they agree with those directions. They will obey orders and carry out instructions even though they may not like it. The problem is that in many cases, followers do just enough work to satisfy the leader and may not contribute their full potential. Recall our earlier definition of *observers* in the discussion of coalitional leadership. These people don't actively resist or sabotage the leader's efforts, but they don't fully participate in achieving the vision. However, if the use of hard power, especially the use of coercion, exceeds a level people consider legitimate, some followers will actively resist the attempt to influence. **Resistance** means that employees will deliberately try to avoid carrying out instructions or will try to disobey orders. Thus, the effectiveness of leaders who rely solely on position power is limited.

Compliance
following the directions of the person with power, regardless of how much agreement there is with that person's directions

Resistance
the act of disobeying orders or deliberately avoiding carrying out instructions

EXHIBIT 12.4 Responses to the Use of Power

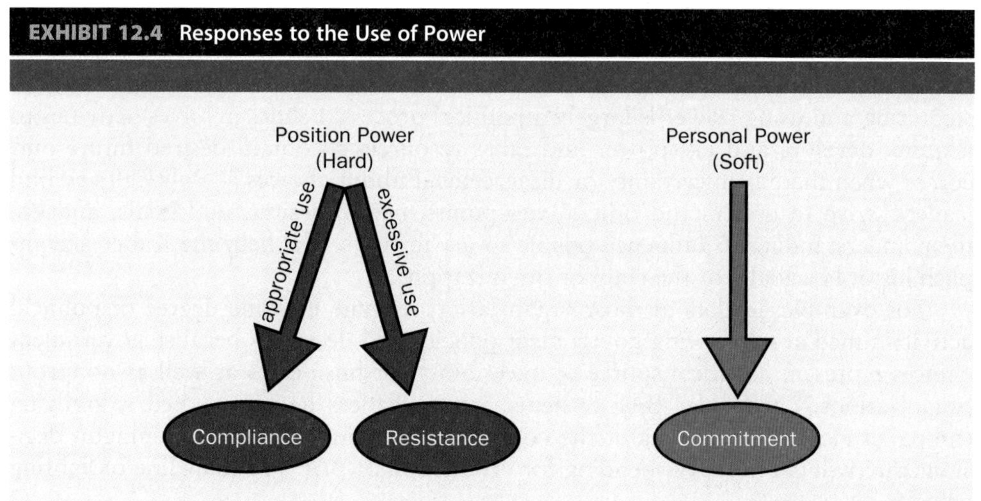

Consider**This!**

The Ripple Effect

Do you want to be a positive influence in the world? First, get your own life in order. Ground yourself in this single principle so that your behavior is wholesome and effective. If you do that, you will earn respect and be a powerful influence.

Your behavior influences others through a ripple effect. A ripple effect works because everyone influences everyone else. Powerful people are powerful influences.

If your life works, you influence your family.
If your family works, your family influences the community.
If your community works, your community influences the nation.
If your nation works, your nation influences the world.
If your world works, the ripple effect spreads throughout the cosmos.

Source: John Heider, *The Tao of Leadership: Leadership Strategies for a New Age* (New York: Bantam Books, 1985), p. 107. Copyright 1985 Humanic Ltd., Atlanta, GA. Used with permission.

"Power is of two kinds. One is obtained by the fear of punishment and the other by acts of love. Power based on love is a thousand times more effective and permanent than the one derived from fear of punishment."
Mahatma Gandhi

The follower response most often generated by soft, personal, and interpersonal power (expert, referent) is commitment. People become *partners* or *advocates*, rather than resisters or observers, as defined earlier. **Commitment** means that followers adopt the leader's viewpoint and enthusiastically carry out instructions. Needless to say, commitment is preferred to compliance or resistance. Although compliance alone may be enough for routine matters, commitment is particularly important when the leader is promoting change. Change carries risk or uncertainty, and follower commitment helps to overcome fear and resistance associated with change efforts. Successful leaders exercise both personal and position power to influence others.

Commitment
adopting the leader's viewpoint and enthusiastically carrying out instructions

Politics
activities to acquire, develop, and use power and other resources to obtain desired future outcomes when there is uncertainty or disagreement about choices

12-3 INCREASING POWER THROUGH POLITICAL ACTIVITY

Acquiring and using power is largely a political process. **Politics** involves activities to acquire, develop, and use power and other resources to obtain desired future outcomes when there is uncertainty or disagreement about choices.[44] Politically skillful leaders strive to understand others' viewpoints, needs, desires, and goals, and use their understanding to influence people to act in ways that help the leader accomplish his or her goals for the team or organization.[45]

For example, leaders at most organizations engage in some degree of political activity aimed at influencing government policies and decisions because government choices represent a critical source of uncertainty for businesses as well as nonprofit organizations.[46] Consider BAE Systems, where leaders have launched a lobbying campaign along with dozens of the company's suppliers to reverse Pentagon decisions that will cut military spending for production of BAE's Bradley line of fighting vehicles.[47]

Individuals also engage in political activity within organizations. Although some people have a negative view of politics, the appropriate use of political behavior serves organizational goals. Politics is a natural process for resolving differences among organizational interest groups.[48] Political behavior can be either a positive or a negative force. Uncertainty and conflict are natural in organizations, and politics is the mechanism for accomplishing things that can't be handled purely through formal policies or position power.

12-3a Leader Frames of Reference

The appropriate use of power and politics to get things done is an important aspect of leadership. Before exploring political tactics, let's consider leadership frames of reference and how a political approach combines with other leadership philosophies.

A **frame** is a perspective from which a leader views the world, and it influences how the leader interacts with followers, makes decisions, and exercises power. Four leader frames of reference illustrated in Exhibit 12.5 are structural, human resource, political, and symbolic.[49] Leaders often begin with a limited structural perspective and develop the other frames as they mature and climb higher in their leadership development, thus achieving a more balanced mindset and approach.

Frame
a perspective from which a leader views the world; influences how the leader interacts with followers, makes decisions, and exercises power

The Structural Frame The organization as a machine is the dominant image in the structural frame of reference. Leaders strive for machine-like efficiency and value hard data and analysis for decision making. The **structural frame** places emphasis on plans, goal setting, and clarifying expectations as a way to provide order, efficiency, and stability. Leaders rely heavily on the power and authority granted through their organizational position to influence others (position power), and they emphasize clear job descriptions, rules and procedures, and administrative systems. This frame

Structural frame
a leader frame of reference that places emphasis on planning, setting goals, and clarifying expectations as a way to provide order, efficiency, and stability

EXHIBIT 12.5 Four Leader Frames of Reference

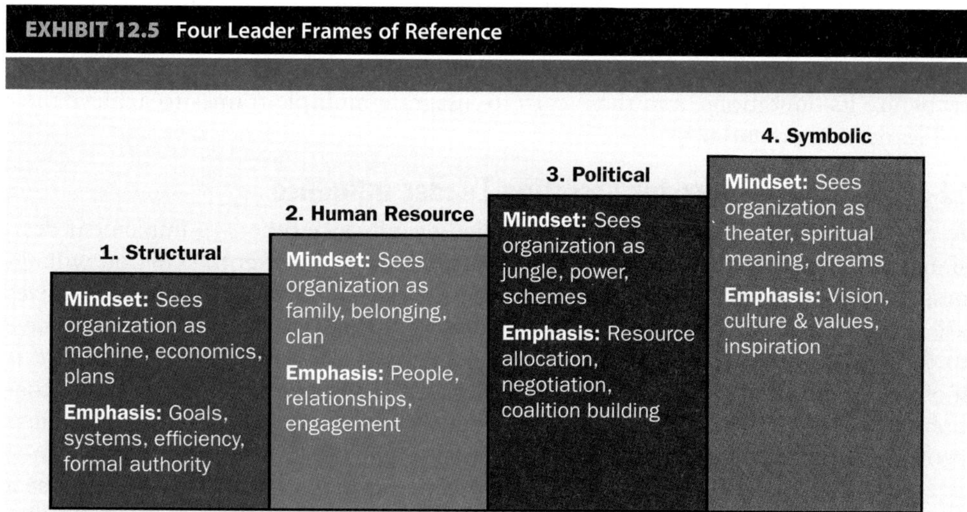

Sources: Based on Lee G. Bolman and Terrence E. Deal, *Reframing Organizations* (San Francisco: Jossey-Bass, 1991); and L. G. Bolman and T. E. Deal, "Leadership and Management Effectiveness: A Multi-Frame, Multi-Sector Analysis," *Human Resource Management* 30, no. 4 (Winter 1991), pp. 509–534. Thanks to Roy Williams for suggesting the stair sequence.

views the organization as a rational system and strives for clarity of direction and control of results.

The Human Resource Frame According to the **human resource frame**, people are the organization's most valuable resource. This frame defines problems and issues in interpersonal terms and looks for ways to adjust the organization to meet human needs. Leaders do not rely solely on their position power to exert influence. Instead, they focus on relationships and often lead through empowerment and engagement. Leaders use the human resource perspective to involve followers and give them opportunities for personal and professional development. The images in this view are a sense of family, belonging, and the organization as a clan.

The Political Frame The **political frame** views organizations as arenas of ongoing conflict or tension over the allocation of scarce resources. Leaders spend their time networking and building coalitions to influence decisions and actions. As with the coalitional leadership style we discussed earlier in this chapter, leaders with this frame of reference strive to build a power base, and they use both position and personal power to achieve desired results. The mindset in the political frame is to be aware of the organization as a jungle. Power and politics are considered a natural and healthy part of organizational life.

The Symbolic Frame To use full leadership potential requires that leaders also develop a fourth frame of reference—the **symbolic frame**—in which leaders perceive the organization as a system of shared meaning and values. Rather than relying only on the use of formal power or the use of political tactics, leaders focus on shared vision, culture, and values to influence others. The dominant image is to see the organization as theater. Leaders are concerned with spirit and meaning, and they focus on harnessing followers' dreams and emotions for the benefit of the organization and all of its people.

NEW LEADER
ACTION MEMO

Use each of the structural, human resource, political, and symbolic frames of reference to maximize your leadership effectiveness. Complete the questionnaire in Leader's Self-Insight 12.3 to understand your dominant frame.

Each of the four frames of reference provides significant possibilities for enhancing leadership effectiveness, but each is incomplete. Many new leaders have not yet developed a political frame. Leaders can first understand their own natural frame, recognize its limitations, and then learn to integrate multiple frames to achieve their full leadership potential.

Human resource frame
a leader frame of reference that defines problems and issues in interpersonal terms and looks for ways to adjust the organization to meet human needs

Political frame
a leader frame of reference that views the organization as an arena of conflict or tension over the allocation of scarce resources

Symbolic frame
a leader frame of reference that perceives the organization as a system of shared meaning and focuses on shared vision, culture, and values to influence others

12-3b Political Tactics for Asserting Leader Influence

A leader's power is useless unless it is applied to influence others to implement decisions, facilitate change, and accomplish goals, which requires both skill and willingness. Not all attempts to use power result in actual influence. Some power moves are rejected by followers, particularly if they are seen to be self-serving. Leaders have to determine the best approach for using their power—that is, the approach that is most likely to influence others—by considering the individuals, groups, and situations involved.[50] In addition, they understand the basic principles that can cause people to change their behavior or attitudes.

Leaders often use a combination of influence strategies, and people who use a wider variety of tactics are typically perceived as having greater power and influence. One survey of a few hundred leaders identified more than 4,000 different techniques by which these people were able to influence others to do what the leader wanted.[51] However, the myriad successful influence tactics used by leaders

LEADER'S SELF-INSIGHT 12.3

Your Leadership Orientation

Instructions: This questionnaire asks you to describe yourself as a leader. For each of the following items, give the number 4 to the phrase that best describes you, 3 to the item that is next best, and on down to 1 for the item that is least like you.

1. My strongest skills are:
   - __3__ a. Analytical skills
   - __4__ b. Interpersonal skills
   - __2__ c. Political skills
   - __1__ d. Flair for drama
2. The best way to describe me is:
   - __1__ a. Technical expert
   - __4__ b. Good listener
   - __2__ c. Skilled negotiator
   - __3__ d. Inspirational leader
3. What has helped me the most to be successful is my ability to:
   - __4__ a. Make good decisions
   - __1__ b. Coach and develop people
   - __2__ c. Build strong alliances and a power base
   - __3__ d. Inspire and excite others
4. What people are most likely to notice about me is my:
   - __3__ a. Attention to detail
   - __4__ b. Concern for people
   - __2__ c. Ability to succeed in the face of conflict and opposition
   - __1__ d. Charisma
5. My most important leadership trait is:
   - __2__ a. Clear, logical thinking
   - __3__ b. Caring and support for others
   - __4__ c. Toughness and aggressiveness
   - __1__ d. Imagination and creativity
6. I am best described as:
   - __2__ a. An analyst
   - __3__ b. A humanist
   - __1__ c. A politician
   - __4__ d. A visionary

Scoring and Interpretation

Compute your scores as follows:

Structural = 1a + 2a + 3a + 4a + 5a + 6a = __15__

Human Resource = 1b + 2b + 3b + 4b + 5b + 6b = __19__

Political = 1c + 2c + 3c + 4c + 5c + 6c = __13__

Symbolic = 1d + 2d + 3d + 4d + 5d + 6d = __13__

Your answers reveal your preference for four distinct leader orientations or frames of reference. The higher your score, the greater your preference. A low score may mean a blind spot. "Structural" means to view the organization as a machine that operates with efficiency to be successful. "Human Resource" means to view the organization primarily as people and to treat the family well to succeed. "Political" means to view the organization as a competition for resources and the need to build alliances to succeed. "Symbolic" means to view the organization as a system of shared meaning and values and to succeed by shaping the culture.

Do you view politics in a positive or negative light? Most new leaders succeed first by using either or both of the structural or people orientations. New leaders often have a blind spot about politics. As managers move up the hierarchy, they learn to be more political or they miss out on key decisions. The symbolic view usually comes last in a leader's development. Compare your scores to those of other students and see which orientations are more widely held.

Source: *Reframing Organizations: Artistry, Choice, and Leadership*, 5e, Bolman. Copyright © 2013 Lee G. Bolman. Reproduced with permission of John Wiley & Sons, Inc.

fall into basic categories of influence actions. Exhibit 12.6 lists six principles for asserting leader influence. Notice that most of these involve the use of soft, personal power rather than relying solely on hard, position power or the use of rewards and punishments.

1. *Appeal to a vision or higher purpose*. One effective way to attract people to new behaviors or to make significant changes is to frame the request in a way that emphasizes the vision or higher purpose of the change.[52] Providing people with *meaning* can help them see that the effort of doing what you ask is worthwhile. For example, Matt Van Vranken, president of Spectrum Health Hospital

EXHIBIT 12.6 Six Principles for Asserting Leader Influence

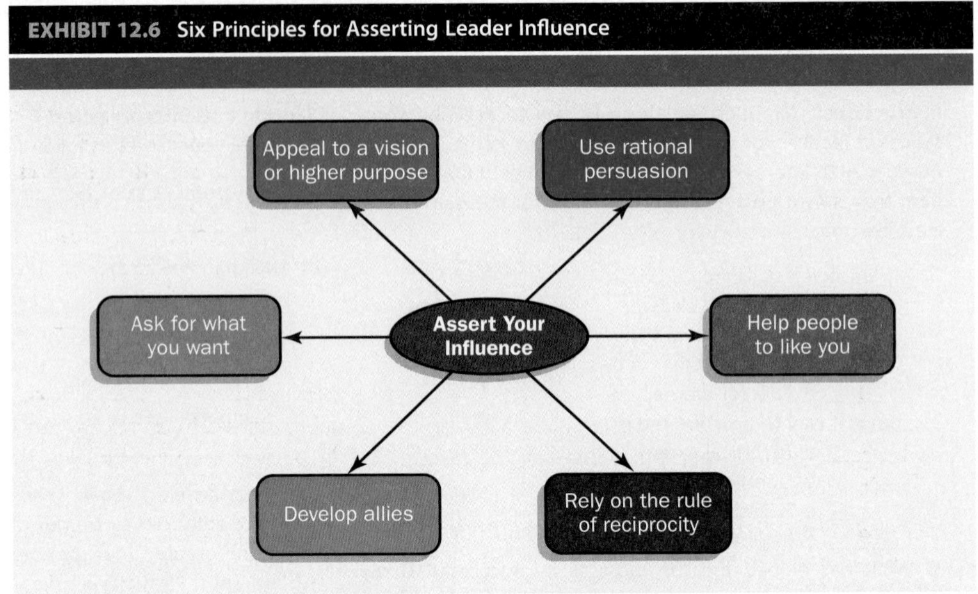

Group, needed a way to influence 10,000 overworked, stressed-out health-care professionals to go beyond their job descriptions and provide exceptional patient service. One key approach he uses to influence people to make the right decision is to connect what they do to the welfare of individual patients. Every so often, Van Vranken brings groups of employees together to hear former patients talk about their experiences and how the actions of individual workers affected their health and well-being.[53]

NEW LEADER
ACTION MEMO

As a leader, you can use political activity to achieve important organizational goals when there is uncertainty or disagreement about choices. You can develop connections with powerful people by volunteering for difficult projects and serving on committees.

2. *Use rational persuasion.* Perhaps the most frequently used influence tactic is rational persuasion, which means using facts, data, and logical arguments to persuade others that a proposed idea or request is the best way to complete a task or accomplish a desired goal. It can be effective whether the influence attempt is directed upward toward superiors, downward toward subordinates, or horizontally, because most people have faith in facts and analysis.[54] Rational persuasion is most effective when a leader has technical knowledge and expertise related to the issue (expert power), although referent power is also used. Frequently, some parts of a rational argument cannot be backed up with facts and figures, so people have to believe in the leader's credibility to accept his or her argument.
3. *Help people to like you.* We all know it's easier to say yes to someone we like than to someone we don't like.[55] One author of a book on influence tells a story about an American working in Saudi Arabia, who learned that getting information or action from government offices was easy when he'd drop by, drink tea, and chat for a while.[56] Cultural values in Saudi Arabia put great emphasis on personal relationships, but people in all cultures respond to friendliness and consideration. When a leader listens, shows concern for what others want and need, finds common ground, demonstrates respect, and treats people fairly, people are more likely to want to help and support the leader by doing what he or she asks. In addition, most people will like a leader who makes them feel good about themselves. Leaders never underestimate the importance of praise.

4. *Rely on the rule of reciprocity.* A primary way to turn power into influence is to share what you have—whether it be time, resources, services, or emotional support. There is much research indicating that most people feel a sense of obligation to give something back in return for favors others do for them.[57] This is one reason that organizations like Northrup Grumman, Kraft Foods, and Pfizer make donations to the favorite charities of House and Senate members. Leaders attempt to curry favor with lawmakers whose decisions can significantly affect their business.[58] The "unwritten law of reciprocity" means that leaders who do favors for others can expect others to do favors for them in return. Leaders also elicit the cooperative and sharing behavior they want from others by first demonstrating it with their own actions.[59] Some researchers argue that the concept of exchange—trading something of value for what you want—is the basis of all other influence tactics. For example, rational persuasion works because the other person sees a benefit from going along with the plan, and making people like you is successful because the other person receives liking and attention in return.[60]
5. *Develop allies.* Reciprocity also plays an important role in developing networks of allies, people who can help the leader accomplish his or her goals. Leaders can influence others by taking the time to talk with followers and other leaders outside of formal meetings to understand their needs and concerns, as well as to explain problems and describe the leader's point of view.[61] Leaders consult with one another and reach a meeting of minds about a proposed decision, change, or strategy.[62] A leader can expand his or her network of allies by reaching out to establish contact with additional people. Some leaders expand their networks through the hiring, transfer, and promotion process. For example, when Michael Corbat became CEO of Citigroup in 2012, he asked some of the former CEO's top allies to resign and reduced the responsibilities of others so he could put his own trusted advisors in key roles.[63] Identifying and placing in key positions people who are sympathetic to the desired outcomes of the leader can help achieve the leader's goals.

   One study found that political skill, particularly network building, has a positive impact both on followers' perceptions of a leader's abilities and performance and on the actual, objective performance of the work unit.[64] Sheila Bair, former chairman of the Federal Deposit Insurance Corporation (FDIC), enhanced her reputation and power base by courting allies to support her views on how to fix the troubled U.S. financial system. Her efforts also expanded the agency's power. Under her leadership, the FDIC gained broad new powers to police large financial institutions, including installing examiners at financial firms to monitor managers' activities.[65]
6. *Ask for what you want.* Sheila Bair, now president of Washington College, also employs another technique for influencing people, which is to be clear about what you want and openly ask for it. Leaders have to be willing to sometimes argue forcefully to persuade others to their point of view. Even opponents praise Bair's knack for being forceful at the right times in order to achieve her goals. If leaders are not willing to ask and persuade, they seldom get the results they want. Political activity is effective only when the leader's vision, goals, and desired changes are made explicit so the organization can respond. Leaders can use their courage to be assertive, saying what they believe to persuade others. In addition, leaders can use techniques of persuasion such as listening, building

NEW LEADER
ACTION MEMO

As a leader, you can influence others by using rational persuasion, developing allies, and expanding your expertise and credibility. Remember that people respond to friendliness and consideration, and they typically feel obligated to return favors.

goals on common ground, and appealing to people's emotions, as described in Chapter 9, to get what they want. Machiavellian-style leaders may even manipulate people's emotions, such as activating peer pressure or phrasing a request in a way that emphasizes the potential loss rather than the potential gain. People will often go along with the request because people respond more strongly to a potential loss (loss aversion) than to a gain, as described in Chapter 8.[66]

Leaders can use an understanding of these tactics to assert influence and get things done. When leaders ignore political tactics, they may find themselves failing without understanding why. For example, at the World Bank, Paul Wolfowitz tried to wield power without building the necessary relationships he needed to assert influence.

IN THE LEAD

Paul Wolfowitz, World Bank

After former Deputy Secretary of Defense Paul Wolfowitz lost his bids to become defense secretary or national security advisor in the Bush administration, he jumped at the chance to be the new president of World Bank. But Wolfowitz doomed his career at World Bank from the start by failing to develop relationships and build alliances.

Most World Bank leaders had been in their positions for many years when Wolfowitz arrived, and they were accustomed to "promoting each other's interests and scratching each other's backs," as one board member put it. Wolfowitz came in and tried to assert his own ideas, goals, and formal authority without considering the interests, ideas, and goals of others. He quickly alienated much of the World Bank leadership team and board by adopting a single-minded position on key issues and refusing to consider alternative views. Rather than attempting to persuade others to his way of thinking, Wolfowitz issued directives to senior bank officers, either personally or through his handpicked managers. Several high-level officers resigned following disputes with the new president.

Eventually, the board asked for Wolfowitz's resignation. "What Paul didn't understand is that the World Bank presidency is not inherently a powerful job," said one former colleague. "A bank president is successful only if he can form alliances with the bank's many fiefdoms. Wolfowitz didn't ally with those fiefdoms. He alienated them."[67]

Wolfowitz realized too late that he needed to use a political approach rather than trying to force his own agenda. Even when a leader has a great deal of power, political tactics are more effective than force for turning power into influence.

NEW LEADER
ACTION MEMO

As a leader, you can be ethical in your use of power and politics. You can build long-term productive relationships to achieve important goals and benefit the entire team or organization.

12-4 DON'T TAKE POWER PERSONALLY

Harry Truman once said that leadership is the ability to get people to do what they don't want to do and like it.[68] His statement raises an important issue: Leadership is an opportunity to use power and influence to accomplish important organizational goals, but power can also be abused. People and organizations get hurt when leaders fall into the temptation to use power for their own benefit rather than for the good of the whole.

One consideration is the difference between *personalized* leaders and *socialized* leaders.[69] This distinction refers primarily to the leader's approach to the use of power.[70] Personalized leaders are typically selfish, impulsive, and exercise power for their own self-centered needs and interests rather than for the good of the organization. Socialized leaders exercise power in the service of higher goals that will benefit others and the organization as a whole. Personalized leaders are characterized as self-aggrandizing, nonegalitarian, and exploitative, whereas socialized leaders are empowering, egalitarian, and supportive. Personalized behavior is based on caring about self; socialized behavior is based on valuing others.

A specific area in which the unethical use of power is of increasing concern for organizations is sexual harassment. People in organizations depend on one another—and especially on leaders—for many resources, including information, cooperation, and even their jobs. When access to resources seems to depend on granting sexual favors or putting up with sexually intimidating or threatening comments, the person in a dependent position is being personally violated, whether or not the leader actually withholds the resources. Consider the U.S. military, which is embroiled in a nasty sexual harassment and abuse scandal. In May 2013, the Pentagon released an embarrassing and shameful report detailing pervasive sexual abuse in the military, estimating a rate of about 500 men and women assaulted each week during 2012. Although many of these were assaults by fellow soldiers, some were also by officers. For example, an Army officer in charge of sexual abuse prevention at Fort Hood, Texas, was under investigation for allegedly assaulting two soldiers and forcing another into prostitution. Moreover, statistics showed that the system of military justice perpetuated the crime. Commanding officers often decided to dismiss charges or decrease penalties. Two Air Force three-star generals tossed out jury convictions for sexual assault, in one instance saying the defendant couldn't possibly be guilty because he was "a doting father and husband."[71] Sexual harassment and sexual abuse are not just unethical; they are illegal and represent a clear abuse of power.

However, there are many other situations in organizations that are not so clear-cut, and leaders may sometimes have difficulty differentiating ethical from unethical uses of power and politics. Exhibit 12.7 summarizes some criteria that can guide ethical actions. First and foremost is the question of whether the action is motivated by self-interest or whether it is consistent with the organization's goals. One Internet company has a rule that any employee can be terminated for a political act that is in the individual's own self-interest rather than in the interest of the company or that

EXHIBIT 12.7 Guidelines for Ethical Action

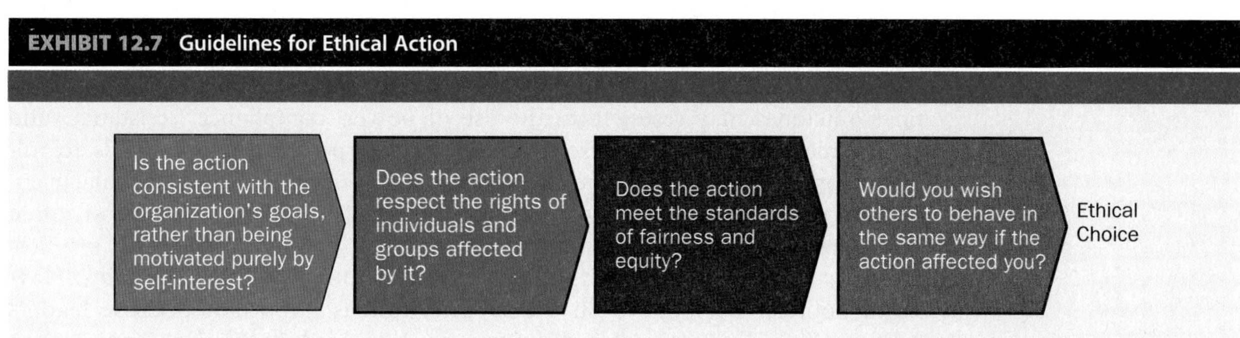

Sources: Based on G. F. Cavanaugh, D. J. Mobert, and M. Valasques, "The Ethics of Organizational Politics," *Academy of Management Journal* (June 1981), pp. 363–374; and Stephen P. Robbins, *Organizational Behavior*, 8th ed. (Upper Saddle River, NJ: Prentice Hall, 1998), p. 422.

harms another person in the organization.[72] Once a leader answers this primary question, there are several other questions that can help determine whether a potential influence action is ethical, including whether it respects the rights of individuals and groups affected by it, whether it meets the standards of fairness, and whether the leader would want others to behave in the same way. If a leader answers these questions honestly, they can serve as a guide to whether an intended act is ethical.

In the complex world of organizations, there will always be situations that are difficult to interpret. The most important point is for leaders to be aware of the ethical responsibilities of having power and take care to use their power to help rather than harm others. Leaders should think not in terms of getting their own way but rather in terms of building long-term productive relationships that can achieve goals and benefit the entire organization.

LEADERSHIP ESSENTIALS

- This chapter looked at how leaders use power and political processes to influence others and get things done. Four types of influential leadership that rely strongly on a leader's personal characteristics and relationships are transformational, charismatic, coalitional, and Machiavellian-style leadership. Charismatic leaders have an emotional impact on people. They create an atmosphere of change, articulate an idealized vision of the future, inspire faith and hope, and frequently incur personal risks to influence followers. Transformational leaders also create an atmosphere of change, and they inspire followers not just to follow them personally but also to believe in the vision. Transformational leaders inspire followers to go beyond their own self-interest for the good of the whole. Coalitional leadership involves developing a coalition of people who can help influence others to implement the leader's decisions and achieve the leader's desired goals. To have broad influence, leaders develop relationships with others, listen to others' needs and goals, and promote cooperation. Machiavellian-style leadership is based on the belief that leaders must often do tough, even ruthless, things in the spirit of protecting the organization. Machiavellian leaders focus on acquiring individual power more than on collaborating with others.
- All leaders use power and politics to influence people and accomplish goals. Power is the ability to influence others to reach desired outcomes. Power can be characterized as either *hard power* or *soft power*. Hard power includes legitimate, reward, and coercive power, which are associated with a leader's formal position of authority. Soft power includes expert and referent power, which are based on the leader's knowledge, expertise, and personal qualities. Three distinct outcomes may result from the use of power: compliance, resistance, and commitment. The effective use of hard, position power generally leads to follower compliance, whereas the excessive use of position power—particularly coercive power—may result in resistance. The follower response most often generated by personal power is commitment.
- Power is acquired, developed, and exercised through political activities. Having a political perspective on the organization is important because leaders need to use politics to accomplish important goals. A political perspective can be combined with other leader frames of reference. Frames of reference

influence how the leader interacts with followers, makes decisions, and exercises power. Four leader frames of reference are structural, human resource, political, and symbolic. Leaders typically begin with a structural frame and develop other frames of reference as they mature in their leadership responsibilities and understanding.

- Leaders use a wide variety of influence tactics, but they fall within some broad categories based on general principles for asserting influence. Six principles for asserting leader influence are appeal to a higher vision, rational persuasion, liking and friendliness, reciprocity, developing allies, and direct appeal. One important consideration for leaders is how to use power and politics ethically and responsibly. Ethical leaders use power to serve the organization's goals, respect the rights of individuals and groups, and strive to be fair in their dealings with others.

DISCUSSION QUESTIONS

1. Lord Acton, a British historian of the late nineteenth century, said that "power tends to corrupt; absolute power corrupts absolutely," suggesting that a person's sense of morality lessens as his or her power increases. Do you agree? Considering this idea, is it ethical for leaders to try to increase their power? Discuss.
2. How do you feel about personally using Machiavellian-style leadership? What do you see as some positive and negative aspects of Machiavellian-style leadership?
3. What do you consider the most important difference between transformational leadership and transactional leadership? Between transformational and charismatic leadership? How is transformational leadership similar to charismatic leadership?
4. Assume you are on a search committee to replace the CEO of a large financial services firm that is recovering from problems related to the mortgage crisis. Which do you think would be most valuable for a new top leader trying to solve the problems within the organization—charismatic, transformational, coalitional, or Machiavellian-style leadership? What about for a new top leader of a small private university? Discuss.
5. Which of the four organizational frames of reference do you most admire? How do you think this frame of reference could be beneficial or detrimental to your leadership capability?
6. A recent magazine article suggested that young college graduates just entering the workforce are refusing to "play the political game." Why might this be the case? If politics is important for getting things done, can these people succeed as leaders? Discuss.
7. Which types of power would you rely on to implement an important decision quickly? Which types would you consider most valuable for sustaining power over the long term?
8. Describe ways in which you might increase your personal power.
9. Which of the six influence tactics would you be most comfortable with as leader of a study group? Of a work team? Discuss.
10. A leadership observer said in an interview that most women leaders view power differently than men do and prefer a collaborative, relationship-oriented use of power. If this is the case, what does it suggest about women leaders' ability to accomplish goals? What does it suggest about women's ability to rise to higher organizational levels? Discuss.

LEADERSHIP AT WORK

Circle of Influence

How do you personally try to influence others? Think carefully about how you get others to agree with you or do something you want. Watch the way you influence others in a team, at home, or during your work. Make a list of your influence tactics:

1. ____________________ 4. ____________________

2. ____________________ 5. ____________________

3. ____________________ 6. ____________________

Of the influence and political tactics discussed in the chapter, which ones do you typically not use?

____

____

____

During the next two days, your assignment is to (1) monitor the influence tactics you typically use and (2) try one new tactic that you don't normally use. The new influence tactic you will try is:

____

____

____

Another important concept is called the *circle of influence*. Think carefully about the people who have influence *over you*. These people are your circle of influence. You may have one circle of influence at work, another at home, and others for your social life or career. Write down the people who would have some influence over you at work or school:

____

____

____

This is your circle of influence.

A person's circle of influence can be important when you really want to influence that person. If someone doesn't respond to your normal influence attempts, think about identifying the individual's circle of influence—the people who have influence over him or her. You can then influence people in the "circle" as an indirect way to influence the person you want to change.

Pick an individual at work or school, or even your instructor, and plot out that person's circle of influence. List the key people you believe are in the person's circle of influence:

____

____

____

How would you get more information on the person's true circle of influence?

____

____

____

How can you use your knowledge of the person's circle to have influence over him or her? What are the possible disadvantages of using this approach to influence someone?

In Class: The instructor can ask students to sit in small groups of three to five people and share the circles of influence they identified for themselves. After listing the circle of influence at work or school, students can also talk about the circles of people who might influence them in their professional, social, or family activities. Key questions for this discussion are, What are the common themes in the students' circles of influence? When and how could the circle idea be applied to influence someone? How might it be misapplied and backfire on your effort to influence another?

LEADERSHIP DEVELOPMENT: CASES FOR ANALYSIS

The Suarez Effect

Pat Talley stood and watched, with grudging admiration, as Carmelita Suarez worked the room. Sharp, charming, and armed with a personality that left an indelible memory, Carmelita at one moment had the ear of CEO Chris Blount and the next could be observed smiling and studying something on her electronic notebook with the executive assistant of a major board member.

"She's amazing," Kent Schlain whispered to Pat as he gave him a cocktail. "I like to observe and learn. She's a real education in office politics."

"We're not in politics," Pat answered somewhat defensively. "We're in IT."

"Come on, Pat." Kent teased. "Tell me she doesn't worry you. Everyone knows she's your main competition for the CIO job."

Pat smirked, took a sip from his scotch and water, and said sarcastically, "I'm *worried.* Satisfied?"

Walking away from Kent's mischievous goading, Pat's usual confidence suffered a fleeting twinge of fear. *No. I'm OK. I'm OK,* he thought. *I have more expertise than anyone, including Carmelita, and I'm not afraid to lay down the law to get projects completed.*

After weeks of speculation, interviews, on-site visits by top execs, and endless waiting, a decision on the new CIO was to be made and announced by CEO Blount this week during the annual meeting. Although Mansfield, Inc. boasted an extraordinarily talented IT group, company insiders and industry watchers agreed that the decision would come down to a choice between Carmelita Suarez and Pat Talley.

To this point, Pat carried the confidence of a sterling 20-year record with Mansfield. Technically gifted, he was one of the team members that designed and implemented the company's original IT system and had been a major player throughout the years in guiding its growth and expansion. Task oriented almost to a fault, Pat built a reputation as a guy who relentlessly analyzed needs and then charged ahead until the job was completed—usually under budget. His special strength lay in the twin areas of electronic security and risk management.

Pat considered technical expertise and competence to be *the* qualifications for the position as CIO, as he explained during a recent interview with executives and board members. "Our work and reputation should be the *only* considerations," Pat emphasized. "My job is not to schmooze and glad hand. I'm not running for public office. I'm running an IT division."

Over the years, Pat maintained strictly defined areas of work and friendship and, in fact, could count on one hand the number of casual, work-related friendships he had developed over 20 years. He was proud of his ability to compartmentalize these areas so that personal relationships had no bearing on management decisions. He considered this an important part of his reputation as a fair but tough leader. He demanded excellence and could be unforgiving in his attitude toward those with less technology interest or expertise.

The word *politics* was odious to Pat Talley, and he considered office politics a waste of time. However, at company gatherings such as this, he also carried a slight chip on his shoulder, aware that, despite his importance to the company, he was only on the periphery of this group—not *excluded*, but not really *included* either. The significance of this particular meeting—and now watching Suarez put on a clinic in office politics—only increased those feelings for Pat, making him defensive and uncharacteristically concerned about his future.

Could office politics really be the deciding factor, he suddenly wondered. *Carmelita knows her stuff. She does her research and stays on top of the latest trends and products in IT. She can handle any situation, particularly those sticky people problems that arise within teams or with suppliers.* Pat smiled ruefully. *Heck, I've even brought her in a time or two.*

Now, as he stood and observed the activity in the room, he watched as his rival moved effortlessly among individuals and various groups. *I feel like I'm watching "Survivor." Does the guy who trusts his own abilities win, or is it the one who builds coalitions and alliances?* He shook his head as if to shake off the imagery. *That was stupid. This is not a reality television show. This is corporate America. Do your job. I've built my reputation on that, and I'll stand by that.*

His attention snapped back as Carmelita handed him a fresh scotch and water. "You could use a fresh one," she said, smiling and pointing to his empty glass. "I guess tomorrow's the big day and I wanted to come by and wish you well. These are exciting days for the company and for IT, and whichever way it goes tomorrow I look forward to working together. Cheers."

"Same here," he answered. Their glasses clinked together in a toast. *Dang, she's good*, Pat thought.

QUESTIONS

1. Who do you think the CEO should appoint as CIO? Why?
2. Is Pat sabotaging his career by thinking of relationship building as "office politics" that takes the focus away from day-to-day work? What advice would you give Pat, who is not a natural relationship builder?
3. What sources of power do Pat and Carmelita seem to use in the company? Which person do you believe will be more influential as CIO? Explain.

Waite Pharmaceuticals

Amelia Lassiter is chief information officer at Waite Pharmaceuticals, a large California-based company. In an industry where it generally takes $500 million and 10 to 12 years to bring a new drug to market, companies such as Waite are always looking for ways to increase productivity and speed things up. After about eight months on the job, Lassiter suggested to company president James Hsu that Waite implement a new global knowledge-sharing application that promises to cut development time and costs in half. She has done extensive research on knowledge-sharing systems and has talked closely with an IT director at global powerhouse Novartis, a company on the cutting edge in pharmaceuticals and animal health care, as well as other diverse products. The Novartis director believes the knowledge-sharing system plays an important role in that company's competitiveness.

Hsu presented the idea to the board of directors, and everyone agreed to pursue the project. He has asked Lassiter to investigate firms that could assist Waite's IT department in developing and implementing a global knowledge-sharing application that would be compatible with Waite's existing systems. Hsu explained that he wants to present the information to the board of directors for a decision next month.

Lassiter identified three major firms that she believed could handle the work and took a summary of her findings to Hsu's office, where she was greeted by Lucy Lee, a young, petite, attractive woman who served as a sort of executive assistant to Hsu. Word was that the relationship between Lee and Hsu was totally proper, but besides the value of her good looks, no one in the company could understand why she was working there. Her lack of talent and experience made her a liability more than a help. She was very deferential to Hsu but condescending to everyone else. Lee was a constant source of irritation and ill will among managers throughout the company, but there was no doubt that the only way to get to Hsu was through Lucy Lee. Lee took the information from Lassiter and promised the president would review it within two days.

The next afternoon, Hsu called Lassiter to his office and asked why Standard Systems, a small local consulting firm, was not being considered as a potential provider. Lassiter was surprised—Standard was known primarily for helping small companies computerize their accounting systems. She was not aware that they had done any work related to knowledge-sharing applications, particularly on a global basis. Upon further investigation into the company, she learned that Standard was owned by an uncle of Lucy Lee's, and things began to fall into place. Fortunately, she also learned that the firm did have some limited experience in more complex applications. She tried to talk privately with Hsu about his reasons for wanting to consider Standard, but Hsu insisted that Lee participate in all his internal meetings. At their most recent meeting, Hsu insisted that Standard be included for possible consideration by the board.

During the next two weeks, representatives from each company met with Hsu, his two top executives, and the IT staff to explain their services and give demonstrations. Lassiter had suggested that the board of directors attend these presentations, but Hsu said they wouldn't have the time and he would need to evaluate everything and make a recommendation to the board. At the end of these meetings, Lassiter prepared a final report evaluating the pros and cons of going with each firm and making her first- and second-choice recommendations. Standard was dead last on her list. Although the firm had some excellent people and a good reputation, it was simply not capable of handling such a large and complex project.

Lassiter offered to present her findings to the board, but again, Hsu declined her offer in the interest of time. "It's best if I present them with a final recommendation; that way, we can move on to other matters without getting bogged down with a lot of questions and discussion. These are busy people." The board meeting was held the following week. Lassiter was shocked when the president returned from the meeting and informed her that the board had decided to go with Standard Systems as the consulting firm for the knowledge-sharing application.

QUESTIONS

1. How would you explain the board's selection of Standard Systems?
2. Discuss the types, sources, and relative amount of power for the three main characters in this story.
3. How might Lassiter have increased her power and influence over this decision? If you were in her position, what would you do now?

Sources: Based on "Restview Hospital," in Gary Yukl, *Leadership*, 4th ed. (Upper Saddle River, NJ: Prentice Hall, 1998), pp. 203–204; "Did Somebody Say Infrastructure?" in Polly Schneider, "Another Trip to Hell," *CIO* (February 15, 2000), pp. 71–78; and Joe Kay, "Digital Diary," Part I, http://www.forbes.com/asap/2000 (accessed November 19, 2000).

REFERENCES

1. Rachel Feintzeig, "Office 'Influencers' Are in High Demand," *The Wall Street Journal* (February 12, 2014), http://www.wsj.com/articles/SB10001424052702303874504579375313680290 81 (accessed November 17, 2015).
2. The terms *transactional* and *transformational leadership* are from James MacGregor Burns, *Leadership* (New York: Harper & Row, 1978); and Bernard M. Bass, "Leadership: Good, Better, Best," *Organizational Dynamics* 13 (Winter 1985), pp. 26–40.
3. This discussion is based on Bernard M. Bass, "Theory of Transformational Leadership Redux," *Leadership Quarterly* 6, no. 4 (1995), pp. 463–478; Noel M. Tichy and Mary Anne Devanna, *The Transformational Leader* (New York: John Wiley & Sons, 1986); Lloyd Moman Basham, "Transformational and Transactional Leaders in Higher Education," *SAM Advanced Management Journal* (Spring 2012), pp. 15–23; and Badrinarayan Shankar Pawar and Kenneth K. Eastman, "The Nature and Implications of Contextual Influences on Transformational Leadership: A Conceptual Examination," *Academy of Management Review* 22, no. 1 (1997), pp. 80–109.
4. See Taly Dvir, Dov Eden, Bruce J. Avolio, and Boas Shamir, "Impact of Transformational Leadership on Follower Development and Performance: A Field Experiment," *Academy of Management Journal* 45, no. 4 (2002), pp. 735–744; Ronald F. Piccola and Jason A. Colquitt, "Transformational Leadership and Job Behaviors: The Mediating Role of Core Job Characteristics," *Academy of Management Journal* 49, no. 2 (2006), pp. 327–340; and Jens Rowold and Kathrin Heinitz, "Transformational and Charismatic Leadership: Assessing the Convergent, Divergent, and Criterion Validity of the MLQ and CKS," *Leadership Quarterly* 18 (2007), pp. 121–133.
5. Based on Bass, "Theory of Transformational Leadership Redux"; Bernard M. Bass, "From Transactional to Transformational Leadership: Learning to Share the Vision," *Organizational Dynamics* 18, no. 3 (Winter 1990), pp. 19–31; Francis J. Yammarino, William D. Spangler, and Bernard M. Bass, "Transformational Leadership and Performance: A Longitudinal Investigation," *Leadership Quarterly* 4, no. 1 (Spring 1993), pp. 81–102; and B. M. Bass, "Current Developments in Transformational Leadership," *The Psychologist-Manager Journal* 3, no. 1 (1999), pp. 5–21.
6. Noel M. Tichy and Mary Anne Devanna, *The Transformational Leader* (New York: John Wiley & Sons, 1986), pp. 265–266.
7. Manfred F. R. Kets De Vries, "Charisma in Action: The Transformational Abilities of Virgin's Richard Branson and ABB's Percy Barnevik," *Organizational Dynamics* (Winter 1998), pp. 7–21; and Basham, "Transformational and Transactional Leaders in Higher Education."
8. Katherine J. Klein and Robert J. House, "On Fire: Charismatic Leadership and Levels of Analysis," *Leadership Quarterly* 6, no. 2 (1995), pp. 183–198.
9. Rakesh Khurana, "The Curse of the Superstar CEO," *Harvard Business Review* (September 2002), pp. 60–66.
10. Jerry Porras, Steward Emery, and Mark Thompson, "The Cause Has Charisma," *Leader to Leader* (Winter 2007), pp. 26–31.
11. Carmine Gallo, "7 Tips from Charismatic Leaders," *AskMen.com*, http://www.askmen.com/money/successful_100/142b_success.html (accessed May 17, 2013).
12. Steve Moore, "Not Bad for a Hippie Dropout," *Management Today* (March 2009), p. 27; Connie Guglielmo, "What Makes Steve Jobs Run?" *National Post* (May 17, 2008), p. FW–8; and "Editorial: Apple—and U.S.—Need Steve Jobs," *McClatchy-Tribune Business News* (January 18, 2009).
13. Jay A. Conger, Rabindra N. Kanungo, and associates, *Charismatic Leadership: The Elusive Factor in Organizational Effectiveness* (San Francisco: Jossey-Bass, 1988); Robert J. House and Jane M. Howell, "Personality and Charismatic Leadership," *Leadership Quarterly* 3, no. 2 (1992), pp. 81–108; Klein and House, "On Fire: Charismatic Leadership and Levels of Analysis"; Harold B. Jones, "Magic, Meaning, and Leadership: Weber's Model and the Empirical Literature," *Human Relations* 54, no. 6 (June 2001), pp. 753–771; and Boas Shamir, Michael B. Arthur, and Robert J. House, "The Rhetoric of Charismatic Leadership: A Theoretical Extension, A Case Study, and Implications for Future Research," *Leadership Quarterly* 5, no. 1 (1994), pp. 25–42.
14. The following discussion is based primarily on Conger et al., *Charismatic Leadership*.
15. This discussion is based on Stephen Friedman and James K. Sebenius, "Organizational Transformation: The Quiet Role of Coalitional Leadership," *Ivey Business Journal* (January–February 2009), p. 1; Gerald R. Ferris, Darren C. Treadway, Pamela L. Perrewé, Robyn L. Brouer, Ceasar Douglas, and Sean Lux, "Political Skill in Organizations," *Journal of Management* (June 2007), pp. 290–320; Vadim Liberman, "Mario Moussa Wants You to Win Your Next Argument," Questioning Authority column, *Conference Board Review* (November–December 2007), pp. 25–26; Samuel B. Bacharach, "Politically Proactive," *Fast Company* (May 2005), p. 93; and Lauren Keller Johnson, "Debriefing Jay Conger: Exerting Influence without Authority," *Harvard Management Update* (December 2003), pp. 3–4.
16. Nancy F. Koehn, "Lincoln's School of Management," *The New York Times* (January 26, 2013); Hitendra Wadhwa, "Lessons in Leadership: How Lincoln Became America's Greatest President," *Inc.com* (February 12, 2012), http://www.inc.com/hitendra-wadhwa/lessons-in-leadership-how-abraham-lincoln-became-americas-greatest-president.html (accessed March 4, 2013); and Gil Troy and Karl Moore, "Leading from the Centre: What CEOs Can Learn from U.S. Presidents," *Ivey Business Journal* (September–October, 2010), http://www.iveybusinessjournal.com/topics/leadership/leading-from-the-centre-what-ceos-can-learn-from-u-s-presidents (accessed May 21, 2013).
17. Scott Wilson, "Obama, the Loner President," *The Washington Post* (October 7, 2011), http://articles.washingtonpost.com/2011-10-07/opinions/35280751_1_president-obama-politics-obama-administration (accessed October 8, 2011); and Peter Nicholas, "Obama's Insular White House Worries His Allies," *The Los Angeles Times* (December 24, 2010), http://articles.latimes.com/2010/dec/24/nation/la-na-obama-insular-presidency-20101225 (accessed December 25, 2010).
18. Michael Schwirtz and Michael Wineripdec, "At Riker's, a Roadblock to Reform," *The New York Times* (December 15, 2014), p. A1.
19. Friedman and Sebenius, "Organizational Transformation: The Quiet Role of Coalitional Leadership."
20. Cari Tuna, "Repairing an Agency's Credibility," *The Wall Street Journal* (March 23, 2009), p. B6.
21. These data are adapted from materials supplied by ExperiencePoint Inc. in conjunction with the Global Tech simulation, 2007.
22. Friedman and Sebenius, "Organizational Transformation."
23. This discussion is based on Howard Hill, "Machiavellian-Style Leadership," *The Times and Democrat* (August 8, 2009), http://thetandd.com/news/opinion/machiavellian-style-leadership/article_c8ea4911-839a-5c48-b1d9-c7e80ed3734f.html (accessed May 18, 2013); David Brooks, "Florence and the Drones," *The New York Times* (February 7, 2013), http://www.nytimes.com/2013/02/08/opinion/brooks-florence-and-the-drones.html?_r=0 (accessed May 20, 2013); and Tamara L. Gillis, "Machiavelli for Modern Times: An Interpretation of Machiavelli's *The Prince* for the College President and the Public Relations Officer," Elizabethtown College, 1997, http://users.etown.edu/g/gillistl/nickmach.html (accessed May 9, 2013).
24. Brooks, "Florence and the Drones."
25. Jeffrey Pfeffer, "Power Play," *Harvard Business Review* (July–August, 2010), pp. 84–92.
26. Pfeffer, "Power Play"; and Jeffrey Pfeffer, "Don't Dismiss Office Politics—Teach It," *The Wall Street Journal* (October 24, 2011),

http://online.wsj.com/article/SB10001424053111904060604576570574190457198.html (accessed May 21, 2013).

27. These are based on Gillis, "Machiavelli for Modern Times"; Hill, "Machiavellian-Style Leadership"; Ozan Örmeci, "Machiavelli's Ideal Leadership," *Caspian Weekly* (February 18, 2011), http://en.caspianweekly.org/main-subjects/turkish-foreign-policy/3731-machiavellis-ideal-leadership-.html (accessed May 20, 2013); and Suzanne Evans, "How Machiavelli Saved My Family," *The Wall Street Journal* (April 6, 2013), p. C1.
28. R. E. Emerson, "Power-Dependence Relations," *American Sociological Review* 27 (1962), pp. 31–41.
29. Evans, "How Machiavelli Saved My Family."
30. James MacGregor Burns, *Leadership* (New York: Harper & Row, 1978).
31. Robert A. Dahl, "The Concept of Power," *Behavioral Science* 2 (1957), pp. 201–215.
32. W. Graham Astley and Paramijit S. Pachdeva, "Structural Sources of Intraorganizational Power: A Theoretical Synthesis," *Academy of Management Review* 9 (1984), pp. 104–113; and Abraham Kaplan, "Power in Perspective," in Robert L. Kahn and Elise Boulding, eds., *Power and Conflict in Organizations* (London: Tavistock, 1964), pp. 11–32.
33. Gerald R. Salancik and Jeffrey Pfeffer, "The Bases and Use of Power in Organizational Decision Making: The Case of the University," *Administrative Science Quarterly* 19 (1974), pp. 453–473.
34. Pfeffer, "Power Play."
35. Earle Hitchner, "The Power to Get Things Done," *National Productivity Review* 12 (Winter 1992/93), pp. 117–122.
36. John R. P. French Jr., and Bertram Raven, "The Bases of Social Power," in D. Cartwright and A. F. Zander, eds., *Group Dynamics* (Evanston, IL: Row Peterson, 1960), pp. 607–623.
37. Reported in Liberman, "Mario Moussa Wants You to Win Your Next Argument."
38. Anna Mulrine, "Harnessing the Brute Force of Soft Power," *US News & World Report* (December 1–8, 2008), p. 47.
39. Wesley Clark, "The Potency of Persuasion," *Fortune* (November 12, 2007), p. 48.
40. Terry R. Bacon, "Power at Work," *Leadership Excellence* (July 2011), p. 6. Bacon's *The Elements of Power: Lessons on Leadership and Influence* (New York: AMACOM, 2011), discusses various types of leadership power that derive from personal and organizational sources.
41. Jeffrey Pfeffer, *Power in Organizations* (Marshfield, MA: Pitman Publishing, 1981).
42. Lillian Cunningham, "The Rolodex That Redefined Power," *The Washington Post* (December 23, 2011), http://articles.washingtonpost.com/2011-12-23/national/35287278_1_fortune-indra-nooyi-sheryl-sandberg (accessed May 21, 2013).
43. The following discussion is based on Gary A. Yukl and T. Taber, "The Effective Use of Managerial Power," *Personnel* (March–April 1983), pp. 37–44.
44. Pfeffer, *Power in Organizations*, p. 70.
45. Gerald R. Ferris, Darren C. Treadway, Robert W. Kolodinsky, Wayne A. Hochwarter, Charles J. Kacmar, Ceasar Douglas, and Dwight D. Frink, "Development and Validation of the Political Skill Inventory," *Journal of Management* 31, no. 1 (February 2005), pp. 126–152.
46. See Amy J. Hillman and Michael A. Hitt, "Corporate Political Strategy Formulation: A Model of Approach, Participation, and Strategy Decisions," *Academy of Management Review* 24, no. 4 (1999), pp. 825–842, for an examination of organizational approaches to political action.
47. Dion Nissenbaum, "Cut Defense? A Fight Begins," *The Wall Street Journal* (April 23, 2013), p. B1.
48. Jeffrey Pfeffer, *Managing with Power: Politics and Influence in Organizations* (Boston, MA: Harvard Business School Press, 1992); Amos Drory and Tsilia Romm, "The Definition of Organizational Politics: A Review," *Human Relations* 43 (1990), pp. 1133–1154; Donald J. Vredenburgh and John G. Maurer, "A Process Framework of Organizational Politics," *Human Relations* 37 (1984), pp. 47–66; and Lafe Low, "It's Politics, as Usual," *CIO* (April 1, 2004), pp. 87–90.
49. This section is based on Lee G. Bolman and Terrence E. Deal, *Reframing Organizations: Artistry, Choice, and Leadership* (San Francisco: Jossey-Bass, 1991); and L. G. Bolman and T. E. Deal, "Leadership and Management Effectiveness: A Multi-Frame, Multi-Sector Analysis," *Human Resource Management* 30, no. 4 (Winter 1991), pp. 509–534.
50. Tony Manning, "The Art of Successful Influence: Matching Influence Strategies and Styles to the Context," *Industrial and Commercial Training* 44, no. 1 (2012), pp. 26–34; and John R. Carlson, Dawn S. Carlson, and Lori L. Wadsworth, "The Relationship between Individual Power Moves and Group Agreement Type: An Examination and Model," *SAM Advanced Management Journal* 65, no. 4 (Autumn 2000), pp. 44–51.
51. D. Kipnis, S. M. Schmidt, C. Swaffin-Smith, and I. Wilkinson, "Patterns of Managerial Influence: Shotgun Managers, Tacticians, and Bystanders," *Organizational Dynamics* 12, no. 3 (Winter 1984), pp. 58–67.
52. Based on Joseph Grenny, David Maxfield, and Andrew Shimberg, "How to Have Influence," *MIT Sloan Management Review* 50, no. 1 (Fall 2008), pp. 47–52.
53. Ibid.
54. Kipnis et al., "Patterns of Managerial Influence"; Manning, "The Art of Successful Influence: Matching Influence Strategies and Styles to the Context"; and Pfeffer, *Managing with Power*, Chapter 13.
55. This discussion is based partly on Robert B. Cialdini, "Harnessing the Science of Persuasion," *Harvard Business Review* (October 2001), pp. 72–79; and Edward T. Reilly, "Influential Leaders: They Follow Five Proven Steps," *Leadership Excellence* (January 2013), p. 10.
56. Judith Tingley, *The Power of Indirect Influence* (New York: AMACOM, 2001), as reported by Martha Craumer, "When the Direct Approach Backfires, Try Indirect Influence," *Harvard Management Communication Letter* (June 2001), pp. 3–4.
57. Robert B. Cialdini, *Influence: Science and Practice*, 4th ed. (Boston, MA: Allyn & Bacon, 2001); Cialdini, "Harnessing the Science of Persuasion"; Allan R. Cohen and David L. Bradford, "The Influence Model: Using Reciprocity and Exchange to Get What You Need," *Journal of Organizational Excellence* (Winter 2005), pp. 57–80; and Jared Sandberg, "People Can't Resist Doing a Big Favor—Or Asking for One" (Cubicle Culture column), *The Wall Street Journal* (December 18, 2007), p. B1.
58. Raymond Hernandez and David W. Chen, "Keeping Lawmakers Happy through Gifts to Pet Charities," *The New York Times* (October 19, 2008), p. A1.
59. Cialdini, "Harnessing the Science of Persuasion."
60. Cohen and Bradford, "The Influence Model."
61. Pfeffer, *Power in Organizations*, p. 70.
62. V. Dallas Merrell, *Huddling: The Informal Way to Management Success* (New York: AMACOM, 1979).
63. Suzanne Kapner, "New CEO Shuffles the Deck at Citi," *The Wall Street Journal* (January 8, 2013), p. C1.
64. Ceasar Douglas and Anthony P. Ammeter, "An Examination of Leader Political Skill and Its Effect on Ratings of Leader Effectiveness," *Leadership Quarterly* 15 (2004), pp. 537–550.
65. Mark DeCambre, "Bair Breaks Rank—FDIC Chief Challenges Geithner, Treasury Plan," *The New York Post* (March 20, 2009), p. 39; Joanna Chung, "Bair Lobbies for Stronger Position," *Financial Times* (June 12, 2009), p. 6; and Deborah Solomon, "Bair's Legacy: An FDIC with Teeth," *The Wall Street Journal* (July 7, 2011), p. C1.
66. Based on ideas in Heidi Grant Halvorson, "How to Be a Better Boss in 2013," *The Wall Street Journal* (January 2, 2013), http://online.wsj.com/article/SB10001424127887323635504578215391693878364.html (accessed May 21, 2013).

67. Steven R. Weisman, "How Battles at Bank Ended 'Second Chance' at a Career," *The New York Times* (May 18, 2007), p. A14.
68. Quoted in Allan R. Cohen, Stephen L. Fink, Herman Gadon, and Robin D. Willits, *Effective Behavior in Organizations*, 7th ed. (New York: McGraw-Hill Irwin, 2001), p. 254.
69. This section is based on Robert J. House and Jane M. Howell, "Personality and Charismatic Leadership," *Leadership Quarterly* 3, no. 2 (1992), pp. 81–108; Jennifer O'Connor, Michael D. Mumford, Timothy C. Clifton, Theodore L. Gessner, and Mary Shane Connelly, "Charismatic Leaders and Destructiveness: An Historiometric Study," *Leadership Quarterly* 6, no. 4 (1995), pp. 529–555; and Rob Nielsen, Jennifer A. Marrone, and Holly S. Slay, "A New Look at Humility: Exploring the Humility Concept and Its Role in Socialized Charismatic Leadership," *Journal of Leadership & Organizational Studies* 17, no. 1 (February 2010), pp. 33–43.
70. For a discussion of personalized and socialized power, see David C. McClelland, *Power: The Inner Experience* (New York: Irvington, 1975). A recent review of McClelland's research related to the use of power is in D. Keith Denton, "Enhancing Power," *Industrial Management* (July–August 2011), pp. 12–17.
71. Tom Vanden Brook and Gregg Zoroya, "Why the Military Hasn't Stopped Sexual Abuse," *USA Today* (May 15, 2013), http://www.usatoday.com/story/news/2013/05/15/why-the-military-hasnt-stopped-sexual-abuse-/2162399/ (accessed May 21, 2013).
72. Rodes Fishburne, "Stop the Politics," *Forbes ASAP* (April 3, 2000), p. 126.

Part 5: The Leader as Social Architect

Chapter 13: Creating Vision and Strategic Direction
Chapter 14: Shaping Culture and Values
Chapter 15: Leading Change

Chapter 13: Creating Vision and Strategic Direction

YOUR **LEADERSHIP** CHALLENGE

After reading this chapter, you should be able to:

- Explain the relationship among vision, mission, strategy, and mechanisms for execution.
- Create your personal leadership vision.
- Use the common themes of powerful visions in your life and work.
- Describe four basic approaches for framing a noble purpose that followers can believe in.
- Understand how leaders formulate and implement strategy.
- Apply the elements of effective strategy.

CHAPTER **OUTLINE**

396 **The Leader's Job: Looking Forward**

400 **Leadership Vision**

407 **Mission**

413 **The Leader as Strategist-in-Chief**

In the Lead

399 **John Riccitiello, Electronic Arts**

406 **Satya Nadella, Microsoft**

412 **TeamBank, Volksbanken Raiffeisenbanken Group**

415 **BNSF Railway**

Leader's Self-Insight

402 **My Personal Vision**

404 **Visionary Leadership**

416 **Your Strategy Style**

Leader's Bookshelf

408 **Do the KIND Thing: Think Boundlessly, Work Purposefully, Live Passionately**

Leadership at Work

420 **Future Thinking**

Leadership Development: Cases for Analysis

422 **The New Museum**

423 **The Visionary Leader**

At a recent managers' meeting focusing on vision and strategy, Twitter CEO Dick Costolo drew three circles on a whiteboard to illustrate "how the company should be described going forward." One circle, he said, represented core users of Twitter; another represented those who visited the site but didn't log in; and the third circle represented people who saw Twitter content embedded on other sites. Managers, hearing about the so-called "geometrically eccentric circles" idea for the first time, were confused. Nothing new there. Confusion and frustration has been mounting at Twitter as Costolo struggles to define a coherent mission, vision, and strategy for the company. Twitter has become a household word and is a popular social media tool used by millions. Yet growth has slowed and the company continues to lose money. Pressure from investors is mounting. Costolo's tendency to easily bounce from one idea to the next worked great during Twitter's formative years, but it has hampered his ability to establish a clear identity and direction for the company. "It's like this tension within the company in terms of what they want to be and how they want to do things," said Walter Price, a senior portfolio manager of Allianz Global's Technology Fund. After weeks of management meetings debating how to sum up the three circles idea to investors, Costolo articulated the vision as "to build the world's largest audience." He continues working with other top leaders to define a clear strategic plan that managers can follow.[1]

Can Dick Costolo and his leadership team formulate a solid vision and strategic plan that will ease the confusion and frustration and move Twitter forward? One of the most important functions of a leader is to articulate and communicate a powerful vision that will motivate and energize people toward the future and then help them implement the plans that will achieve that future. In this chapter, we first provide an overview of the leader's role in creating the organization's future by stimulating both vision and action. Then, we examine what vision is, the underlying themes that are common to effective visions, and the steps to creating a powerful vision. The distinction between vision and the organization's mission is also explained. Finally, we discuss how leaders formulate and execute a strategy to achieve the vision.

13-1 THE LEADER'S JOB: LOOKING FORWARD

Many cars and mobile phones have built-in GPS systems that will guide you to the restaurant, business, or residence you're trying to get to. If you take a wrong turn, the unit will reset and report something like "recalculating route." That's similar to what leaders do. They look forward and recalculate the route when it is necessary to keep the organization thriving.[2] Superior organizational performance is not a matter of luck. It is determined largely by the choices leaders make. Top leaders are responsible for knowing the organization's environment, considering what it might be like in 5 or 10 years, and setting a direction for the future that everyone can believe in. Lorraine Monroe, former principal of the renowned Frederick Douglass Academy in Harlem and founder of the Lorraine Monroe Leadership Institute, refers to a leader as "the drum major, the person who keeps a vision in front of people and reminds them of what they're about."[3]

13-1a Stimulating Vision and Action

In the waiting lounge of a fine lakeside restaurant, a sign reads, "Where there is no hope in the future, there is no power in the present." The owner explains its presence there by telling the story of how his small, picturesque village with its homes and businesses was sacrificed to make way for a flood-control project. After losing their fight to reverse the decision, most business leaders simply let their businesses decline and die. Soon, the only people who came to the village did so to eat at the cheery little diner, whose owner became the butt of jokes because he continued to work so hard. Everyone laughed when he chose to open a larger and fancier restaurant on the hill behind the village. Yet, when the flood-control project was finally completed, he had the only attractive restaurant on the edge of a beautiful, newly constructed lake that drew many tourists. Anyone could have found out, as he did, where the edge of the lake would be, yet most of the business owners had no vision for the future. The restaurant owner had a vision, and he took action on it.

NEW LEADER
ACTION MEMO

As a leader, you can combine vision with action. You can make a difference for your team or organization by both having big dreams and transforming them into significant strategic action.

Hopes and dreams for the future are what keep people moving forward. Read the story in the *Consider This* box for some insight into the importance of vision as a window to the world that followers may not see. Leaders not only tap into dreams for the future; to make a real difference, they link those dreams with *strategic actions*. Vision has to be translated into specific goals, objectives, and plans so that employees know how to move toward the desired future. An old English churchyard saying applies to organizations as it does to life:

Life without vision is drudgery.
Vision without action is but an empty dream.
Action guided by vision is joy and the hope of the earth.[4]

Consider This!

Opening a Window to a Brighter World

A blind man was brought to the hospital. He was both depressed and seriously ill. He shared a room with another man, and one day asked, "What is going on outside?" The man in the other bed explained in some detail about the sunshine, the gusty winds, and the people walking along the sidewalk. The next day, the blind man again asked, "Please tell me what is going on outside today." The roommate responded with a story about the activities in a park across the way, the ducks on the pond, and the people feeding them. The third day and each day thereafter for two weeks, the blind man asked about the world outside and the other man answered, describing a different scene. The blind man enjoyed these talks, and he grew happier learning about the world seen through the window.

Then the blind man's roommate was discharged from the hospital. A new roommate was wheeled in—a tough-minded businessman who felt terrible, but wanted to get work done. The next morning, the blind man said, "Will you please tell me what is going on outside?" The businessman didn't feel well, and he didn't want to be bothered to tell stories to a blind man. So he responded assertively, "What do you mean? I can't see outside. There is no window here. It's only a wall."

The blind man again became depressed, and a few days later he took a turn for the worse and was moved to intensive care.

Source: Based on a story the author heard at a spiritual service in Santa Fe, New Mexico.

Exhibit 13.1 illustrates four possibilities of leadership in providing direction. Four types of leaders are described based on their attention to vision and attention to action. The person who is low both on providing vision and stimulating action is *uninvolved*, not really a leader at all. The leader who is all action and little vision is a *doer*. He or she may be a hard worker and dedicated to the job and the organization, but the doer is working blind. Without a sense of purpose and direction, activities have no real meaning and do not truly serve the organization, the employees,

EXHIBIT 13.1 Linking Strategic Vision and Strategic Action

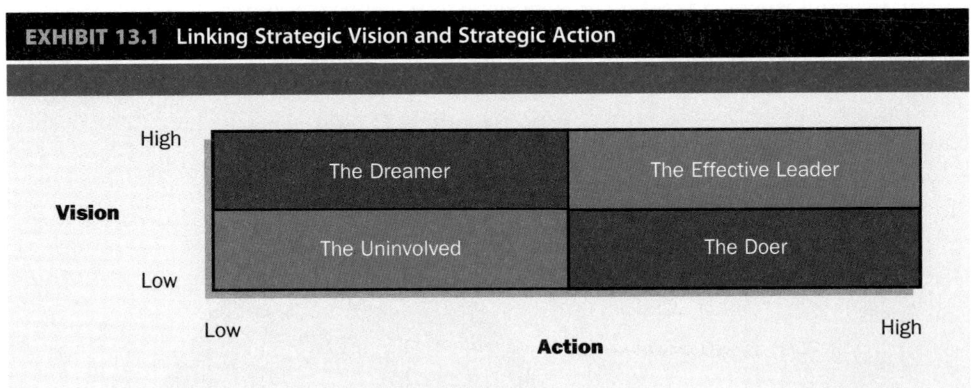

Source: Based on William D. Hitt, *The Leader–Manager: Guidelines for Action* (Columbus, OH: Battelle Press, 1988), p. 7.

or the community. The *dreamer*, on the other hand, is good at providing a big idea with meaning for self and others. This leader may effectively inspire others with a vision, yet he or she is weak on executing strategic action. The vision in this case is only a dream, a fantasy, because it has little chance of ever becoming reality. To be an *effective leader*, one both dreams big *and* transforms those dreams into significant strategic action, either through one's own activities or by hiring other leaders who can effectively execute the vision and strategy.

13-1b Strategic Leadership

Strategic leadership is one of the most critical issues facing organizations.[5] **Strategic leadership** means the ability to anticipate and envision the future, maintain flexibility, think strategically, and work with others to initiate changes that will create a competitive advantage for the organization in the future.[6] In a fast-changing world, leaders are faced with a bewildering array of complex and ambiguous information, and no two leaders will see things the same way or make the same choices.

The complexity of the environment and the uncertainty of the future can overwhelm a leader. In addition, many leaders are inundated with information and overwhelmed by minutiae. They may have difficulty finding the quiet time needed for "big-picture thinking." One study looked at the time executives in various departments spend on long-term, strategic activities and found discouraging results. In the companies studied, 84 percent of finance executives' time, 70 percent of information technology (IT) executives' time, and 76 percent of operational managers' time is focused on routine, day-to-day activities.[7] Another study found that, on average, senior executives spend less than 3 percent of their energy on building a corporate perspective for the future.[8] Yet no organization can thrive for the long term without a clear viewpoint and framework for the future.

NEW LEADER
ACTION MEMO

As a leader, you can learn to think strategically. You can anticipate and envision the future, and you can initiate changes that can help the group or organization thrive over the long term.

Exhibit 13.2 illustrates the levels that make up the domain of strategic leadership. Strategic leadership is responsible for the relationship of the external environment to choices about vision, mission, strategy, and their execution.[9] At the top of Exhibit 13.2 is a clear, compelling vision of where the organization wants to be in 5 to 10 years. A vision is an aspiration for the future and answers the question "Where are we headed?"[10] The vision works in concert with the company's mission—its core values, purpose, and reason for existence. Mission answers the question, "Who are we as an organization?" The next level in Exhibit 13.2, strategy, responds to the question, "How do we achieve the vision?" Strategy provides

Strategic leadership the ability to anticipate and envision the future, maintain flexibility, think strategically, and initiate changes that will create a competitive advantage for the organization in the future

EXHIBIT 13.2 The Domain of Strategic Leadership

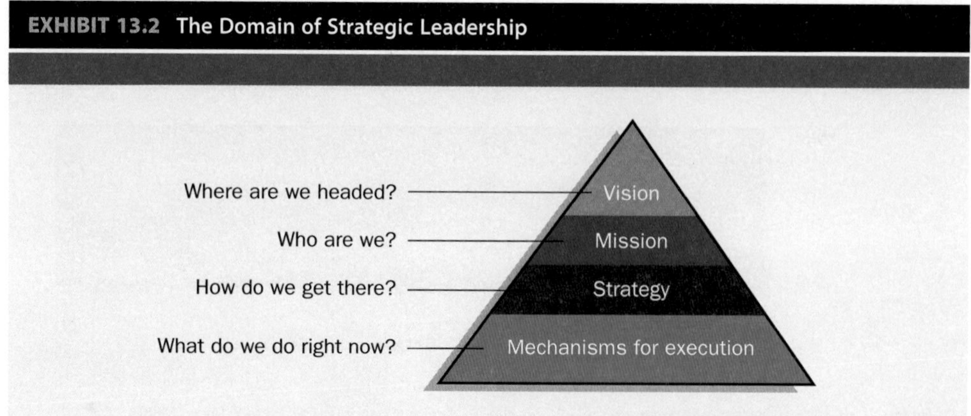

direction for translating the vision into action and is the basis for the development of specific mechanisms to help the organization achieve goals. Execution specifies "What do we do right now?" Strategies are intentions, whereas execution is through the basic organizational architecture (structure, incentives) that makes things happen. Each level of the hierarchy in Exhibit 13.2 supports the level above it. Each part of this framework will be discussed in the remainder of this chapter.

Strategic leadership doesn't come naturally, but leaders can develop the necessary skills for thinking strategically and navigating uncertainty:[11]

- *Anticipate threats and opportunities*. Effective leaders are continuously scanning the environment—talking to customers and other outsiders, researching the industry and markets, and so forth—so they don't miss important signs of change that could help or hurt the organization.
- *Challenge the status quo*. Strategic thinkers question their own and others' assumptions and mental models, as we discussed in Chapter 5. They examine problems or opportunities from many perspectives.
- *Interpret trends*. Leaders look for patterns in what they see and hear and seek new insights rather than accepting the easy answer. One food company executive was developing a marketing plan for the company's low-carb cake line, but she noticed that most of the customers she talked to kept mentioning problems with eating too much sugar. She worked with other leaders and came up with a highly profitable change in the product mix from low-carb to sugar-free cakes.
- *Achieve alignment*. Leaders have to get buy-in among employees and other stakeholders who may have different, even conflicting views and interests. To achieve the vision, everyone must be aligned in the same direction.

To improve strategic leadership, leaders can identify weak points in these skills and work toward correcting them. John Riccitiello, former CEO of Electronic Arts (EA), talks about the importance of these leader skills.

IN THE LEAD

John Riccitiello, Electronic Arts

Several years ago, John Riccitiello saw that EA was in trouble. Social networks and smartphones were threatening the traditional video game business, and people in the company were scared. Riccitiello had a realization that as a leader, "you need to paint a picture that everyone can buy into, even though you're not sure yourself it's going to work because you're trying to see the other side of a technology transition."

Riccitiello listens to people both inside and outside the organization to try to make sure he's not heading left when he should be heading right, but he understands that being a leader in a fast-changing industry requires continual adjustment. He is honest with people and tells them that charting a new direction means that sometimes it may be only 70 percent certain because of the uncertainty of the industry, but he emphasizes that everyone has to be 100 percent committed to the direction and know that leaders will pull back and make adjustments when they learn something isn't working. Riccitiello successfully steered EA through a major transformation from console games to the world of smartphones and tablets by aligning everyone in the same direction. In a large organization, he says, "you're mostly painting a picture for a lot of people for whom you're just a concept.... So you've got to find a way to be incredibly consistent, so when other people repeat the same thing it conjures up the same image for everyone else." Without a vision that everyone understands and buys into, people can find themselves pulling in opposite directions—that makes it tough for the company to get where it needs to go.[12]

Riccitiello resigned in 2013, saying he felt it was time for a new top leader to take EA to the next phase of growth. During his time with EA, Riccitiello took some bold and risky moves. Some paid off and some didn't, but his approach to strategic leadership was generally positive for the company. One person who worked closely with Riccitiello on shaping strategy says, "The truth is that the game industry continues to pivot very rapidly. EA is in a good place but it requires a lot of energy and laser focus.... He's been pivoting the company hard for many years, but the industry keeps pivoting faster."[13]

Firm strategic leadership is essential for organizations to be effective. Consider that the Conference Board reported that 40 percent of all IT development projects are canceled before they are completed, at a significant cost to organizations, and the primary factor explaining their failure is ineffective strategic leadership.[14]

13-2 LEADERSHIP VISION

A **vision** is an attractive, ideal future that is credible yet not readily attainable. It is an ambitious view of the future that everyone involved can believe in, one that can realistically be achieved, yet one that offers a future that is better in important ways than what now exists.[15] Strong, inspiring visions have been associated with higher organizational performance and greater employee motivation and satisfaction.[16] After the financial crisis, leaders at Standard Chartered Bank, which had been a regular takeover target for some years, came out with a brief vision statement, "Here for good," that reflected a dual aspiration: staying around for the long term, and doing good in the world.[17] The vision fired people's imaginations and renewed their sense of pride. Other examples of this type of brief, compelling, and slogan-like vision include Coca-Cola's "A Coke within arm's reach of everyone on the planet," Canon's "Beat Xerox," and Komatsu's "Encircle Caterpillar." These visions can be easily communicated and understood by everyone in the organization and serve to motivate all employees.

Exhibit 13.3 lists a few more brief vision statements that let people know where the organization wants to go in the future. Not all successful organizations have such short, easily communicated slogans, but their visions are powerful because leaders paint a compelling picture of where the organization wants to go. The vision expressed by civil rights leader Martin Luther King, Jr., in his "I Have a Dream" speech is a good example of how leaders paint a vision in words. King articulated a vision of racial harmony, where discrimination was nonexistent, and he conveyed the confidence and conviction that his vision would someday be achieved. Courage and conviction are characteristics of successful visionary leaders. Vision isn't magic; it relies on skills and qualities that leaders can develop.

Vision
an attractive, ideal future that is credible yet not readily attainable

Leaders in nonprofit organizations also create visions so people know where the organization wants to go. For example, leaders at the Greater Chicago Food Depository have a vision of transforming the nonprofit agency from an organization that just feeds the hungry to one that helps end hunger. The agency sponsors an intense

EXHIBIT 13.3 Examples of Brief Vision Statements

- **Apple**: To make a contribution to the world by making tools for the mind that advance humankind.
- **Four Seasons**: Achieve first-choice ranking among guests.
- **BAE Systems (defense company)**: To protect those who protect us.
- **Virginia Department of Transportation**: Keep Virginia moving.
- **Deloitte Touche Tohmatsu**: To be recognized as the best professional services firm in the world.
- **Ukrop's Food Group**: To be a world-class provider of food and services.
- **United Way**: Improve lives by mobilizing the caring power of communities.

Sources: These examples are from Pieter Klass Jagersma, "Aspiration and Leadership," *Journal of Business Strategy* 28, no. 1 (2007), pp. 45–52; Douglas A. Ready and Emily Truelove, "The Power of Collective Ambition," *Harvard Business Review* (December 2011), pp. 95–102; "We Protect Those Who Protect Us," *York Daily Record*, May 12, 2010, http://www.ydr.com/ci_15067292 (accessed May 16, 2013); James G. Clawson, *Level Three Leadership: Getting Below the Surface*, 4th ed. (Upper Saddle River, NJ.: Pearson/Prentice Hall, 2009), pp. 120–124; Sooksan Kantabutra and Gayle C. Avery, "The Power of Vision: Statements That Resonate," *Journal of Business Strategy* 31, no. 1 (2010), pp. 37–45; and Nancy Lublin, "Wordplay," *Fast Company* (November 2009), p. 86.

12-week program aimed at teaching low-income, low-skilled workers the basics of cooking, along with life skills such as punctuality, teamwork, commitment, and personal responsibility, with the goal of landing each person a good job. The vision of helping people change their lives has energized employees in a way that simply providing food to low-income clients never did.[18] Vision is just as important for nonprofit agencies like the Greater Chicago Food Depository, the United Way, and the Salvation Army as it is for businesses such as Coca-Cola, Google, or General Electric. Indeed, nonprofits sometimes need vision even more than do businesses, since they operate without the regular feedback provided by profit and loss.[19]

In Exhibit 13.4, vision is shown as a guiding star, drawing everyone along the same path toward the future. Vision is based in the current reality but is concerned

EXHIBIT 13.4 The Nature of the Vision

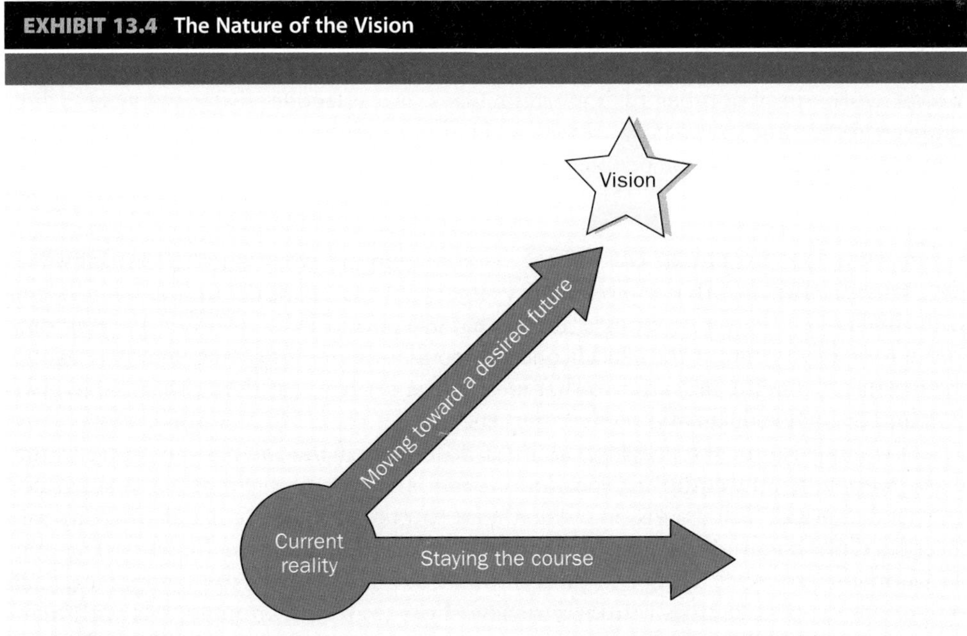

Source: Based on William D. Hitt, *The Leader–Manager: Guidelines for Action* (Columbus, OH: Battelle Press, 1988).

LEADER'S SELF-INSIGHT 13.1

My Personal Vision

Instructions: How much do you think about the positive outcomes you want in your future? Do you have a personal vision for your life? Indicate whether each of the following items is Mostly False or Mostly True for you.

	Mostly False	Mostly True
1. I can describe a compelling image of my future.		✓
2. Life to me seems more exciting than routine.		✓
3. I have created very clear life goals and aims.		✓
4. I feel that my personal existence is very meaningful.		✓
5. In my life, I see a reason for being here.		✓
6. I have discovered a satisfying "calling" in life.		✓
7. I feel that I have a unique life purpose to fulfill.		✓
8. I will know when I have achieved my purpose.		✓
9. I talk to people about my personal vision.		✓
10. I know how to harness my creativity and use my talents.		✓

Scoring and Interpretation

Add the number of Mostly True answers for your score: 10. A score of 7 or above indicates that you are in great shape with respect to a personal vision. A score of 3 or below would suggest that you have not given much thought to a vision for your life. A score of 4–6 would be about average.

Creating a personal vision is difficult work for most people. It doesn't happen easily or naturally. A personal vision is just like an organizational vision in that it requires focused thought and effort. Spend some time thinking about a vision for yourself and write it down.

Sources: The ideas for this questionnaire were drawn primarily from Chris Rogers, "Are You Deciding on Purpose?" *Fast Company* (February/March 1998), pp. 114–117; and J. Crumbaugh, "Cross-Validation of a Purpose-in-Life Test Based on Frankl's Concepts," *Journal of Individual Psychology* 24 (1968), pp. 74–81.

with a future that is substantially different from the status quo.[20] Taking the group or organization along this path requires leadership. Compare this to rational management (as described in Chapter 1), which leads to the status quo.

13-2a What Vision Does

Vision works in a number of important ways. An effective vision provides a link between today and tomorrow, serves to energize employees and focus their attention, provides meaning for people's work, and sets a standard of excellence and integrity in the organization.[21]

NEW LEADER
ACTION MEMO

Go to Leader's Self-Insight 13.1 and answer the questions to learn where you stand with respect to a personal vision.

Vision Links the Present to the Future Vision connects what is going on right now with what the organization aspires to. A vision is always about the future, but it begins with the here and now. At Google, employees are guided by a vision of unifying data and information around the world, one day totally obliterating language barriers via the Internet.[22] They create services that meet current needs, but they also strive to envision and create products and services that encourage other, broader applications.

In organizations, the pressures to meet deadlines, make the big sale, solve immediate problems, and complete specific projects are very real. Some have suggested that leaders need "bifocal vision," the ability to take care of the needs of today and meet current obligations while also aiming toward dreams for the future.[23] The ability to operate on both levels can be seen in a number of successful companies, such as DuPont. Top executives routinely review short-term operational goals with managers throughout the company, reflecting a focus on the present. However, DuPont has succeeded over the long haul because of its leaders' ability to keep an eye on the future and shift gears quickly to take advantage of new opportunities. Since its beginning, DuPont's business portfolio has shifted from gunpowder to specialty chemicals, and today, the company has moved into biotechnology and life sciences.[24]

Vision Energizes People and Focuses Attention When people have a clear picture of where the organization wants to be in the future, they can help take it there.[25] Many people commit their time and energy voluntarily to projects they believe in—a political campaign, community events, or environmental causes, for example. These same people often leave their energy and enthusiasm at home when they go to work because they don't have anything to inspire them. A clear vision lets people know what they should be doing and, just as importantly, what they *should not* be doing. Sometimes, what is left out or "not done" is just as valuable as what is done for building the desired future.[26] Consider TeamBank, a rapidly growing and profitable subsidiary of the German Volksbanken Raiffeisenbanken Group. The innovative financial services company has a vision to "be a responsible partner for fair consumer financing." Based on the vision, managers have chosen to stay out of point-of-sale financing, often used for purchases of cars or expensive consumer electronics, because they know people often sign loans on impulse that they later cannot repay. Similarly, employees know not to consider socioeconomic scores of residential areas when offering loans because this goes against the company's vision.[27]

Vision Gives Meaning to Work Vision needs to transcend the bottom line to provide employees with a sense of meaning and purpose. People are generally not willing to make emotional commitments just for the sake of increasing profits, but they are often eager to commit to something truly worthwhile, something that makes life better for others or improves their communities.[28] Consider Henry Ford's original vision for Ford Motor Company:

> *I will build a motor car for the great multitude.... It will be so low in price that no man making a good salary will be unable to own one and enjoy with his family the blessings of hours of pleasure in God's open spaces.... When I'm through, everybody will be able to afford one, and everyone will have one. The horse will have disappeared from our highways, the automobile will be taken for granted [and we will give many people] employment at good wages.*[29]

Employees were motivated by Ford's vision because they saw an opportunity to make life better for themselves and others.

People want to find significance and dignity in their work. Even employees performing routine tasks can find pride in their work when they have a larger purpose for what they do. For example, an insurance clerk who thinks of her job as helping victims of fire or burglary put their lives back in order will feel very differently than one who thinks of his job as "processing insurance claims."[30] "People want to accomplish great things," advises former UPS CEO Michael L. Eskew. "They want to make a difference."[31]

Vision Establishes a Standard of Excellence and Integrity A powerful vision frees people from the mundane by providing them with a challenge that requires them to give their best. A quote from Antoine Saint-Exupery illustrates this aspect of leader vision: "A rock pile ceases to be a rock pile the moment a single man contemplates it, bearing within him the image of a cathedral."[32] Vision also provides a measure by which employees can gauge their contributions to the organization. Most workers welcome the chance to see how their work fits into the whole. Think of how

LEADER'S SELF-INSIGHT 13.2

Visionary Leadership

Instructions: Think about a situation in which you either assumed or were given a leadership role in a group. Imagine your own behavior as a leader. To what extent do the following statements characterize your leadership? Indicate whether each of the following items is Mostly False or Mostly True for you.

	Mostly False	Mostly True
1. I have a clear understanding of where we are going.	______	✓
2. I work to get others committed to our desired future.	______	✓
3. I initiate discussion with others about the kind of future I would like us to create together.	______	✓
4. I show others how their interests can be realized by working toward a common vision.	______	✓
5. I look ahead and forecast what I expect in the future.	______	✓
6. I make certain that the activities I manage are broken down into manageable chunks.	______	✓
7. I seek future challenges for the group.	______	✓
8. I spend time and effort making certain that people adhere to the values and outcomes that have been agreed on.	______	✓
9. I inspire others with my ideas for the future.	______	✓
10. I give special recognition when others' work is consistent with the vision.	______	✓

Scoring and Interpretation

The odd-numbered questions pertain to creating a vision for the group. The even-numbered questions pertain to implementing the vision. Calculate your score for each set of questions. Which score is higher? Compare your scores with those of other students.

This questionnaire pertains to two dimensions of visionary leadership. Creating the vision has to do with whether you think about the future, whether you are excited about the future, and whether you engage others in the future. Implementing the vision is about the extent to which you communicate, allocate the work, and provide rewards for activities that achieve the vision. Which of the two dimensions is easier for you? Are your scores consistent with your understanding of your own strengths and weaknesses? What might you do to improve your scores?

NEW LEADER
ACTION MEMO

As a leader, you can articulate an optimistic vision for the future that will inspire and challenge people to give their best, set a standard of excellence and integrity, and help people find meaning in their work. Evaluate your potential for visionary leadership by completing the questionnaire in Leader's Self-Insight 13.2.

frustrating it is to watch a movie when the projector is out of focus. Today's complex, fast-changing business environment often seems just like that—out of focus.[33] A vision is the focus button. It clarifies an image of the future and lets people see how they can contribute. A vision presents a challenge—asking people to go where they haven't gone before.

Good visions clarify and connect to the core values and ideals of the organization and thus set a standard of integrity for employees. A good vision brings out the best in people by illuminating important values, speaking to people's hearts, and letting them be part of something bigger than themselves.

13-2b Common Themes of Vision

Four themes are common to powerful, effective visions: they have broad, widely shared appeal; they help organizations deal with change; they reflect high ideals; and they define both the organization's destination and the basic rules to get there.

Vision Has Broad Appeal Although it may seem obvious that a vision can be achieved only through people, many visions fail to adequately involve employees. Isolated top leaders may come up with a grand idea that other employees find ridiculous, or they might forget that achieving the vision requires understanding and commitment throughout the organization. The vision cannot be the property of the leader alone.[34] The ideal vision is identified with the team or organization as a whole. It "grabs people in the gut" and motivates them to work toward a common end.[35] Admiral Vernon Clark, the former chief of naval operations we described in Chapter 4, involved sailors in the vision of creating a twenty-first-century U.S. Navy that is "strategically and operationally agile, technologically and organizationally innovative, networked at every level, highly joint [with the other services], and effectively integrated with allies" by emphasizing each individual's personal role. "What we do matters," he told them. "We do it because it's important and we are people of service. We are committed to something larger than ourselves: the protection of America's interests around the world and democracy."[36]

Vision Deals with Change Effective visions help the organization achieve bold change. Online retailer Amazon.com's early vision was to be "Earth's largest bookstore." That aspiration achieved, the company expanded into all types of merchandise. However, by 2004, Jeff Bezos was exploring a radical idea for a retailer: he wanted Amazon to make the hardware people could use to buy Amazon's stuff. A few years later, the Kindle and Kindle Fire were born. Jateen Parekh, who joined Amazon to help develop the Kindle, recalls Bezos asking him *What should Amazon be doing in 20 years?* "The fact that the CEO was thinking that far out was huge," Parekh says.[37] Change can be frightening, but a clear sense of direction helps people face the difficulties and uncertainties involved in the change process. When employees have a clear and consistent guiding vision, everyday decisions and actions throughout the organization respond to current problems and challenges in ways that move the organization toward the future.[38]

Vision Reflects High Ideals Good visions are idealistic. Vision is an emotional appeal to our fundamental human needs and desires—to feel important and useful, to believe we can make a real difference in the world.[39] Visions that portray an uplifting future have the power to inspire and energize people. For example, when John F. Kennedy announced a vision for NASA to send a man to the moon by the end of the 1960s, NASA had only a small amount of the knowledge it would need to accomplish the feat. Yet in July 1969, the vision became a reality.[40] A business example comes from Qualcomm, where former CEO Paul Jacobs articulated an idealistic vision to improve the capacity of wireless networks by 1,000 times, as well as provide tiny home equivalents of cellular broadcast towers. Since there is growing demand for wireless data transmission, leaders believe some of that traffic can be moved to home bases that are about the size of a deck of cards and would plug into a home computer or Wi-Fi connection.[41]

People at Qualcomm have been developing the technology to make the vision a reality. When every person understands and embraces a vision, the organization becomes self-adapting. Although each person acts independently, everyone is working in the same direction. In the new sciences, this is called the principle of self-reference. **Self-reference** means that each element in a system will serve the goals of the whole system when the elements are imprinted with an understanding of the whole. Thus, the vision serves to direct and control people for the good of themselves and the organization.

Self-reference
a principle stating that each element in a system will serve the goals of the whole system when the elements are imprinted with an understanding of the whole

Vision Defines the Destination and the Journey A good vision for the future includes specific outcomes that the organization wants to achieve. It also incorporates the underlying values that will help the organization get there. For example, a private business school might specify certain outcomes such as a top-20 ranking, placing 90 percent of students in summer internships, and getting 80 percent of students into jobs by June of their graduating year. Yet in the process of reaching those specific outcomes, the school wants to increase students' knowledge of business, ethical values, and teamwork, as well as prepare them for lifelong learning.

Additionally, the vision may espouse underlying values such as no separation between fields of study or between professors and students, a genuine concern for students' welfare, and adding to the body of business knowledge. A good vision includes both the desired future outcomes and the underlying values that set the rules for achieving them.

Consider how the vision for Microsoft under new CEO Satya Nadella reflects many of these common themes.

IN THE LEAD

Satya Nadella, Microsoft

Bill Gates started Microsoft with a grand vision for software, and for much of its history Microsoft remained primarily a software company. Windows and Microsoft Office dominated the PC era. But times have changed, and Microsoft has a bold, expansive vision that leaders hope will make the company as dominant in the new environment as was its software in the PC world.

Microsoft will continue to make Windows and software for Windows, but now it also makes hardware, including its own smartphones and Surface devices, as well as applications for iOS, Apple's mobile operating system. Moreover, Microsoft is working on numerous innovative hardware products that don't serve current customers but could create entirely new market niches. CEO Satya Nadella and other leaders believe the future of computing will be fragmented, even chaotic. Under Nadella, Microsoft is willing to make big bets on new technologies and try new products even if they might fail. Rather than killing new ideas because of cost or time concerns, leaders are embracing forward-looking, risky projects. When the team working on the HoloLens, the first fully un-tethered holographic computer, introduced the then-secret project to Nadella, they were worried he would kill it, but Nadella said right away, "We are going to create a new product category, and this is the type of thing that Microsoft should be working on."

People at Microsoft have been reenergized by a vision of being a leader in future-defining technologies. Achieving the vision requires that people collaborate extensively both within the company and with outsiders, even with main rivals Apple and Google. Researchers and engineers are working closely together so that experimental technologies get developed into new products rather than languishing in the lab.[42]

NEW LEADER
ACTION MEMO

As a leader, you can co-create a shared vision so that every individual, team, and department is moving in the same direction. You can help people see the values, activities, and objectives that will attain the vision.

13-2c Leader Steps to Creating a Vision

In innovative companies, leaders co-create the vision with followers so that everyone is intimately involved in building the desired future. With co-creation, everyone can identify with the vision and have a deeper understanding and commitment to achieving it. In addition, co-creation demonstrates that leaders value the thoughts, ideas, dreams, and power of others.[43]

To co-create a vision, leaders share their personal visions with others and encourage others to express their dreams for the future. This requires openness, good listening skills, and the courage to connect with people on an emotional level. A leader's ultimate responsibility is to be in touch with the hopes and dreams that drive employees and find the common ground that binds personal dreams into a shared vision for the organization. The vision becomes the common thread connecting people, involving them personally and emotionally in the organization.[44] Leaders use the following steps to co-create a vision:[45]

1. *Target a vision for a desired future.* Vision typically begins with the leader, who has a vivid and compelling idea of where the team or organization should go. The leader has to be excited by the idea before anyone else will be. To target a vision, spend time imagining where you want the organization to be and what it will look and feel like when it gets there.
2. *Co-create the vision.* Even though leaders get the ball rolling, they don't present a fully formed vision to followers. People want visions of the future that reflect their own dreams and hopes. Consult as many people from different areas as possible to learn what frustrates them, what energizes them, and what they want the future to be like. Use focus groups or other mechanisms to get people talking about the future and what they want it to be.
3. *Identify strengths.* Put together a list of what the organization does well and the things people are proud of. Based on talks with people across the organization or what comes out of focus groups, list past achievements, skills, resources, and so forth that might be assets in achieving the desired future. Create a vision that builds on and extends the current strengths of the organization.
4. *Write a first draft.* It's important to get something down in writing, but make sure people know it is a draft that needs feedback. Write from the heart, remembering that it is emotion that drives people. Aim for something great and put yourself into the future you are envisioning.
5. *Solicit feedback and create the final vision statement.* The vision statement may go through several drafts before it is final. The important thing is that everyone has a chance to provide feedback.
6. *Share the vision widely.* Communicate broadly and often, using multiple channels. During the Civil War, Abraham Lincoln was a master at preaching the vision of an America that offered equality, freedom, and a fair chance for all. Through speeches, writings, and conversations, at every conceivable opportunity, he reminded people of the basic principles on which the nation was founded.[46]

13-3 MISSION

Mission is not the same thing as a company's vision, although the two work together. The **mission** is the organization's core broad purpose and reason for existence. It defines the company's core values and reason for being, and it provides a basis for creating the vision. Whereas vision is an ambitious desire for the future, mission is what the organization "stands for" in a larger sense.

13-3a What Mission Does

Whereas visions grow and change, the mission persists in the face of changing technologies, economic conditions, or other environmental shifts. It serves as the glue that holds the organization together in times of change and guides strategic choices and decisions about the future. The mission defines the enduring character—the spiritual DNA—of the organization.[47] The mission that John D. Rockefeller

Mission
the organization's core broad purpose and reason for existence

LEADER'S BOOKSHELF

Do the KIND Thing: Think Boundlessly, Work Purposefully, Live Passionately

By Daniel Lubetzky

When he launched KIND Healthy Snacks in 2004, Daniel Lubetzky's main product was fruit-and-nut bars, but making snacks wasn't the main purpose of the organization. Lubetzky founded and built the company with a mission of promoting a kinder world. As the son of a Holocaust survivor, Lubetzky grew up hearing stories from his father about life in a concentration camp. He says his father "made sure to remind me about the occasions of kindness when in the worst and darkest moments, people were being kind to him." One story recalled a German soldier who gave him a potato. "He could have gotten in trouble for throwing that potato at the floor to my father. But he threw that potato at him. It was one of those moments where my dad felt—as he told us when we were kids—that that potato gave him the sustenance maybe to live."

Lubetzky decided early on that he wanted to create a company that, as its core purpose, inspired people to live a kind life and spread kindness. In his book, *Do the KIND Thing*, Lubetzky points out that all leaders can incorporate kindness into their organizations.

LESSONS FOR BEING KIND

Lubetzky organizes his book around the principles used to build the company—purpose, grit, truth and discipline, keeping it simple, originality, transparency and authenticity, empathy, trust, and ownership and resourcefulness. Here are a few of Lubetzky's lessons for leaders:

- ***Use the Power of Thinking with AND.*** The fundamental tenet of KIND Snacks is that you can have a snack that tastes good AND is good for you. The notion of thinking with AND rather than OR is the heart of Lubetzky's philosophy. He says leaders should remember that they can be successful professionally AND show empathy and kindness to those around them. "You don't have to accept the way things are," he says. "All you need to do is ask: Why does it have to be that way? When your default thinking is 'AND' instead of 'or,' you start to break down the roadblocks that prevent you from getting more out of life."
- ***Think of Empathy as a Business Skill.*** Lubetzky points out that simply acknowledging how someone else feels and sees things can help that person see your side of things, thus enabling people to reach a fair outcome to a dispute. Leader empathy is also necessary for building a loyal culture because it shows that leaders care about employees as people. KIND builds in ways to show care, such as the KINDOs program (their version of "kudos"). Each month team members celebrate a colleague for doing things the KIND way. Sometimes the recognition is based on job performance, but other celebrations focus on how a team member handled a situation with kindness and respect or demonstrated a key company value.
- ***Set a Precedent for Openness and Honesty.*** At KIND, leaders are open and honest with employees and they expect the same in return. Transparency builds a culture of healthy discussion, in which people are expected to provide honest feedback to leaders and colleagues and feel comfortable challenging anyone else's ideas, even the CEO's. At KIND, candid feedback is seen as a way to help people develop to their fullest potential.

CONCLUSION

Lubetzky's company motto is: "Do the kind thing for your body, your taste buds and your world." In *Do the KIND Thing* he outlines key principles for how leaders can build a sustainable business and a thriving social enterprise.

Source: *Do the Kind Thing*, by Daniel Lubetzky, is published by Ballantine Books.

established for the Rockefeller Foundation—to promote the well-being of mankind throughout the world—still stands 100 years after the organization was founded.[48] For Johnson Development Corporation, founded by former basketball star Earvin "Magic" Johnson in 1993 as part of Magic Johnson Enterprises, the mission has always been to be the nation's foremost development company through enrichment of underserved markets. Some retailers see urban communities as economic wastelands, but Johnson sees them as lands of opportunity.[49]

Particularly in today's environment, people are drawn to companies that have a compelling purpose. Companies with strong missions that give people purpose, such as Medtronic's "To restore people to full life and health" or Liberty Mutual Company's "Helping people live safer, more secure lives" typically attract better employees, have better relationships with external parties, and perform better in the marketplace over the long term.[50] This chapter's Leader's Bookshelf describes an interesting snack food company with a mission of spreading kindness as well as fruit and nut bars.

Recall the discussion of intrinsic rewards from Chapter 8. When people connect their jobs to a higher cause or purpose, the work itself becomes a great motivator. The Gallup organization's Q12 study, also discussed in Chapter 8, has found that when employees believe the company's mission makes their job important, they are typically more engaged with their work, feel a greater sense of pride and loyalty, and are more productive. Exhibit 13.5 compares the Gallup results for those who agree that the mission makes their job important to those who do not feel that the mission of the company makes their job important. The differences are quite striking. For example, 60 percent of respondents who agreed that the mission makes their job important reported feeling engaged with their work, whereas none of the respondents who disagreed felt engaged with their work. Sixty-six percent would recommend their company's products or services, compared to only 20 percent of those who did not believe the mission made their job important.[51]

Typically, the mission is made up of two critical parts: the core values and the core purpose. The *core values* guide the organization "no matter what." The mission also includes the company's *core purpose*. Leaders take care when defining a core purpose so that the organization can grow and change. Consider Zenith and Motorola. Both were once successful makers of televisions, but while Zenith stayed there, Motorola continued to move forward to microprocessors, integrated circuits, and other products and became one of the most highly regarded companies in the world. The difference is that Zenith defined its purpose as "making television sets" whereas Motorola defined its purpose as "applying technology to benefit the public."[52]

EXHIBIT 13.5 The Power of a Strong Mission

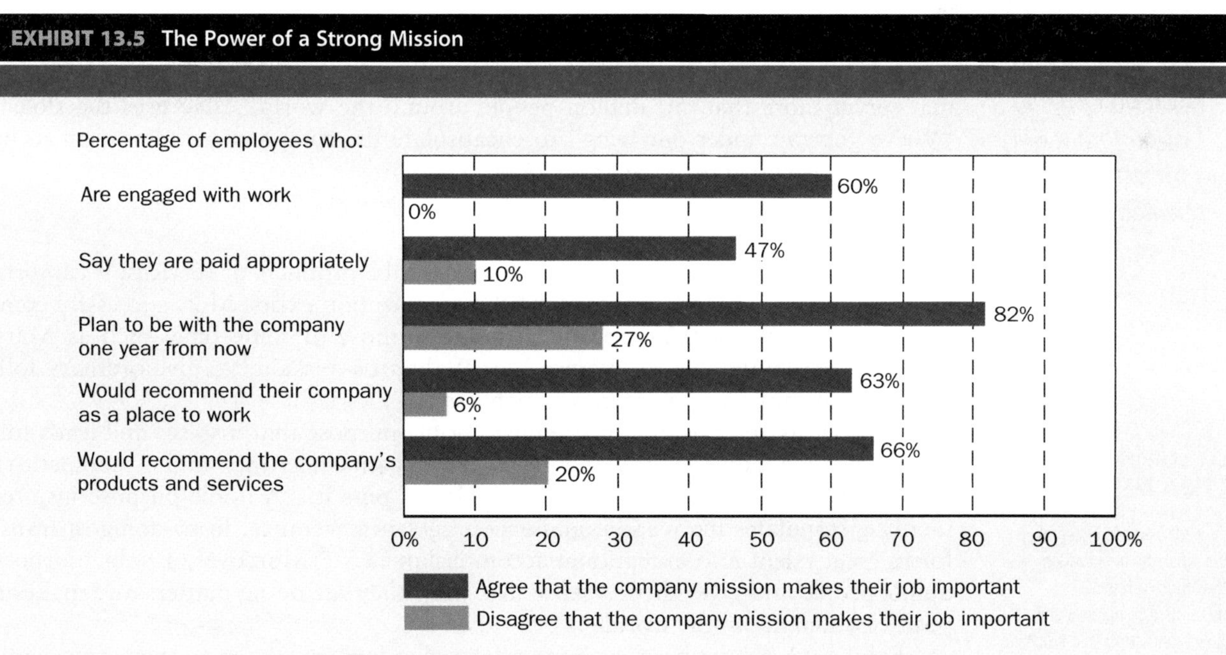

Source: Susan Ellingwood, "On a Mission," *Gallup Management Journal* (Winter 2001), pp. 6–7.

EXHIBIT 13.6 Aflac's Mission and Values

Mission and Values

We pledge to be there for our policyholders in their time of need.

Aflac's philosophy is to combine innovative strategic marketing with quality products and services at competitive prices to provide the best insurance value for consumers.

* Building better value for our shareholders.
* Supplying quality service for our agents.
* Providing an enriching and rewarding workplace for our employees.

Source: http://www.aflac.com/aboutaflac/corporateoverview/ourphilosophy.aspx

"Great companies must have a noble cause. Then it's the leader's job to transform that noble cause into such an inspiring vision that it will attract the most talented people in the world to want to join it."

Steve Jobs (1955–2011), cofounder and former CEO of Apple

The core values and core purpose are frequently expressed in a *mission statement*. Exhibit 13.6 shows the mission and values for Aflac, an insurance company that serves more than 50 million people around the world. Aflac uses the slogan "We've got you under our wing" to encapsulate the company's commitment to be there for policyholders in their time of need.

13-3b A Framework for Noble Purpose

An effective mission statement doesn't just describe products or services; it captures people's idealistic motivations for why the organization exists. Most successful companies have missions that proclaim a noble purpose of some type, such as Mary Kay's "to enrich the lives of women," or Walmart's mission "to give ordinary folk the chance to buy the same things as rich people."[53]

NEW LEADER
ACTION MEMO

As a leader, you can keep in mind what the organization stands for in a broader sense—its core purpose and values—and create the vision around that central mission.

Leaders are responsible for framing a noble purpose that inspires and leads followers to high performance and helps the organization maintain a competitive advantage. As management expert Gary Hamel puts it: "A noble purpose inspires sacrifice, stimulates innovation, and encourages perseverance. In so doing, it transforms great talent into exceptional accomplishment."[54] Moreover, a noble purpose uplifts people and gives them a sense that what they are doing matters and makes a positive difference in the world.

Exhibit 13.7 describes four basic approaches leaders take in framing an organizational purpose that can tap into people's desire to contribute and feel that their

EXHIBIT 13.7 A Leader's Framework for Noble Purpose

Purpose	Description	Basis for Action	Examples
Discovery	Finding the new	Pioneer, entrepreneur	Google, 3M, Samsung
Excellence	Being the best	Fulfillment	Berkshire Hathaway, AlliedSignal, Apple
Altruism	Providing service	Happiness	Dollar General, Dannon Milk Products
Heroism	Being effective	Achievement	Microsoft, Southwest Airlines, ExxonMobil

Source: Based on Nikos Mourkogiannis, *Purpose: The Starting Point of Great Companies* (New York: Palgrave Macmillan, 2006); and Nikos Mourkogiannis, "The Realist's Guide to Moral Purpose," *strategy + business Issue* 41 (Winter 2005), pp. 42–53.

work is worthwhile.[55] Each of these approaches is described in more detail in the following paragraphs.

Discovery Many people are inspired by the opportunity to find or create something new. Discovery for its own sake can serve as a noble purpose, as it does for employees at Google, where people are energized by the psychic rewards they get from working on intellectually stimulating and challenging technical problems.[56] As another example, leaders at Samsung Electronics reenergized the company by focusing employees on discovery rather than imitation, transforming Samsung into a world-class innovator rather than a manufacturer known for cheap, low-quality knockoffs. Samsung invests heavily in research and development and even began threatening Apple's dominance in smartphones with the innovative features in its Galaxy phones. The shift in purpose has led to amazing results at Samsung.[57] This type of purpose inspires people to see the adventure in their work and experience the joy of a pioneering or entrepreneurial spirit.

Excellence With this approach, rather than emphasizing discovery, leaders focus people on being the best, both on an individual and an organizational level. AlliedSignal's mission, for example, is to "be one of the world's premier companies: distinctive and successful in everything we do."[58] For these companies, excellence is defined by the work itself rather than by customers. Indeed, organizations that pursue excellence would rather turn customers away than compromise their quality. Consider Apple, another company with excellence as a purpose.[59] The company has always built high-quality, cleverly designed computers, yet it holds less than 10 percent of the personal computer market. Leaders would like to increase their share of the market, but they aren't willing to sacrifice their commitment to high quality and what they consider superior technology.[60] In companies with excellence as a guiding purpose, managers and employees are treated as valuable resources and provided with support to perform at their peak. People are motivated by the opportunity to experience intrinsic rewards and personal fulfillment.

Altruism Many nonprofit organizations are based on a noble purpose of altruism because they emphasize serving others, but businesses can use this approach as well. For example, leaders at Dollar General stress the purpose of giving low-income people a good deal, not just making sales and profits. The U.S. division of the giant global food company Danone, Dannon Milk Products, has a mission of "bringing health to the greatest number of people across America through our products' benefits."[61]

Even financial services companies, frequently perceived as being exploitative, can operate based on a noble purpose of altruism, as illustrated by Germany's TeamBank, introduced earlier in the chapter.

IN THE LEAD

TeamBank, Volksbanken Raiffeisenbanken Group

The vision for TeamBank, "to be a responsible partner for fair consumer financing," grows out of its mission to serve the country as an honorable financial services company. Leaders at TeamBank, a subsidiary of the German Volksbanken Raiffeisenbanken Group, rejected the assumption that it is impossible for a bank to make money by being fair, and even generous, to its customers.

They overhauled the consumer credit product, called easyCredit, to compete on the concept of fairness rather than price. It offers a 30-day customer retraction period, eliminates the penalty on partial repayments, and offers protection packages that allow for short repayment extensions. There are no hidden fees, and terms can be adjusted to reflect unexpected changes in the borrower's circumstances. Many credit processes are handled personally so that if people fall behind in making payments, customer advisers can work with them to find a solution rather than threatening them with legal action. When loans become delinquent, TeamBank offers customers the opportunity to make minimal payments that will get them back on the road to financial stability and avoid damaging their credit ratings. "We try to help as long as we see goodwill on the customer's side," a manager said. A customer council, made up of 14 volunteer customers and one representative from a consumer protection nongovernmental organization (NGO), provides ongoing feedback to TeamBank leaders about how well the company is living up to its mission and values.

TeamBank rejects profitable products and features that are inconsistent with its values of transparency, honesty, and fairness. Now the number-three consumer finance provider in the German market, TeamBank is both profitable and growing. Moreover, the delinquency rate is much lower than the industry average.[62]

TeamBank's mission and values clearly place it in the category of altruism as a guiding purpose. In addition to its business practices, the company provides financial literacy education to high school students all across Germany and sponsors a lecture series on finance and economics for a local university. Any company that puts a high premium on customer service can be considered to fall in this category as well. Marriott, for instance, encapsulates its purpose in the slogan, "The Spirit to Serve."[63] The basis of action for this type of purpose is to increase personal happiness. Most people feel good when they are doing something to help others or make their communities or the world a better place.

Heroism The final category, heroism, means the company's purpose is based on being strong, aggressive, and effective. Companies with this basis of noble purpose often reflect almost an obsession with winning. Bill Gates imbued Microsoft with a goal of putting the Windows operating system into every personal computer, for example.[64] At General Electric, former CEO Jack Welch wanted the company to strive to be number one or number two in each industry in which it did business.

As another example, Southwest Airlines was founded with a heroic goal of winning against much larger competitors such as American and Delta. With this approach, the basis of action is people's desire to achieve and to experience *self-efficacy*, as described in Chapter 8. People want to feel capable of being effective and producing results.

Companies that remain successful over the long term have leaders who lead with a noble purpose. A well-chosen noble purpose taps into the emotions and instincts of employees and customers and can contribute to better morale, greater innovativeness, and higher employee and organizational performance.

13-4 THE LEADER AS STRATEGIST-IN-CHIEF

Strong missions that reflect a noble purpose and guiding visions are both important, but they are not enough alone to make strong, powerful organizations. For organizations to succeed, leaders have to translate vision, values, and purpose into action, which is the role of leader as strategist-in-chief. **Strategic management** refers to the set of decisions and actions used to formulate and implement specific strategies that will achieve a competitively superior fit between the organization and its environment so as to achieve organizational goals.[65]

When leaders link vision and strategic action, they can make a real difference for their organization's future. Research has shown that strategic thinking and planning for the future can positively affect a company's performance and financial success.[66] One study found that as much as 44 percent of the variance in profitability of major firms can be attributed to strategic leadership.[67]

13-4a How to Achieve the Vision

To formulate a strategy, leaders ask questions such as "Where is the organization now? Where does the organization want to be? What changes and trends are occurring in the competitive environment? What courses of action can help us achieve our vision?" **Strategy** can be defined as the general plan of action that describes resource allocation and other activities for dealing with the environment and helping the organization attain its goals and achieve the vision. Leaders have to be clear on the organization's purpose and vision before they can adopt an effective strategy. Strategy involves making decisions every day based on what the organization wants to do and be.[68]

Strategic management
the set of decisions and actions used to formulate and implement specific strategies that will achieve a competitively superior fit between the organization and its environment so as to achieve organizational goals

Strategy
the general plan of action that describes resource allocation and other activities for dealing with the environment and helping the organization attain its goals

Developing Effective Strategy To develop strategy, leaders actively listen to people both inside and outside the organization, and they examine trends and discontinuities in the environment that can be used to gain an edge. Rather than reacting to environmental changes, strategic leaders study the events that have already taken place and act based on their anticipation of what the future might be like.[69] When leaders rely solely on formal strategic planning, competitor analysis, or market research, they miss new opportunities. Consider that when Ted Turner first talked about launching a 24-hour news and information channel in the 1970s, many dismissed him as delusional. Every source of conventional wisdom, from market research to broadcast professionals, said the idea was crazy and bound to fail. Yet Turner looked at emerging social and demographic trends, listened to his intuition, and launched a global network that generates 35 percent gross margins. Other media leaders had the same information, but they didn't interpret it the same way or

NEW LEADER
ACTION MEMO

As a leader, you can prepare for the future based on trends in the environment today. Don't be afraid to think radically. You can shift your strategies to fit changing conditions.

formulate the same strategy to tap into emerging trends.[70] Good leaders anticipate, look ahead, and prepare for the future based on trends they see in the environment today, which often requires radical thinking.

Of course, leaders should also use hard analysis to help set a course for the future. They strive to develop industry foresight based on trends in technology, demographics, government regulation, values, and lifestyles that will help them identify new competitive advantages. Situation analysis, for example, includes a search for SWOT—strengths, weaknesses, opportunities, and threats—that affect organizational performance. Leaders using situation analysis obtain external information from a variety of sources, such as customers, government reports, suppliers, consultants, or association meetings. They gather information about internal strengths and weaknesses from sources such as budgets, financial ratios, profit-and-loss statements, and employee surveys.

Sometimes leaders have to shift their strategy several times before they get it right.[71] In addition, strategy necessarily changes over time to fit shifting environmental conditions.

Elements of Strategy To improve the chances for success, leaders develop strategies that focus on three qualities: core competence, developing synergy, and creating value for customers.

An organization's **core competence** is something the organization does extremely well in comparison to competitors. Leaders identify the organization's unique strengths—what makes their organization different from others in the industry. L.L. Bean succeeds with a core competence of excellent customer service and a quality guarantee. Leaders at Family Dollar focus on a core competence of operational efficiency that enables them to keep costs low.

Synergy occurs when organizational parts interact to produce a joint effect that is greater than the sum of the parts acting alone. As a result the organization may attain a special advantage with respect to cost, market power, technology, or employee skills. Synergy was the motivation for Yahoo to buy mobile app startups, for example, to obtain both the products and the engineering talent. Another way companies gain synergy is through alliances and partnerships. Leaders at Coinstar, the company behind Redbox movie rentals, take this approach. As rentals of physical videos declined, the Redbox division partnered with Verizon Communications on a service that combines DVD rental and streaming video, benefiting both companies.[72]

Focusing on core competencies and attaining synergy help companies create value for their customers. **Value** can be defined as the combination of benefits received and costs paid by the customer.[73] For example, Panera Bread doesn't have the lowest costs for sandwiches and other food and drink products, but it works hard to create an environment where people want to spend time. "If you give people food they want, in an environment that they want, they will spend a dollar or two more, they will go out of their way for it," says CEO Ron Shaich.[74] Delivering value to the customer is at the heart of strategy.

Strategy formulation integrates knowledge of the environment, vision, and mission with the company's core competence in such a way as to attain synergy and create value for customers. When these elements are brought together, the company has an excellent chance to succeed in a competitive environment. But to do so, leaders have to ensure that strategies are executed—that actual behavior within the organization reflects the desired direction.

Core competence
something the organization does extremely well in comparison to competitors

Synergy
the interaction of organizational parts to produce a joint effect that is greater than the sum of the parts

Value
the combination of benefits received and costs paid by the customer

Strategy formulation
integrating knowledge of the environment, vision, and mission with the core competence in such a way as to attain synergy and create customer value

13-4b How to Execute

Strategy execution means that leaders use specific mechanisms, techniques, or tools for directing organizational resources to accomplish strategic goals. This is the basic architecture for how things get done in the organization. Strategy execution, sometimes called *implementation*, is the most important as well as the most difficult part of strategic management, and leaders must carefully and consistently manage the execution process to achieve results.[75] One survey found that only 57 percent of responding firms reported that managers successfully implemented the new strategies they had devised over the past three years.[76] Other research has estimated that as much as 70 percent of all business strategies never get implemented, reflecting the complexity of strategy execution.[77] Following the merger of Burlington Northern Railroad and the Atchison, Topeka, and Santa Fe Railway, leaders worked hard to create a vision and strategy to guide the new BNSF Railway, along with a system to ensure strategy execution.

Strategy execution putting strategy into action by adjusting various parts of the organization and directing resources to accomplish strategic goals

IN THE LEAD

BNSF Railway

BNSF Railway is one of the largest railroads in North America, covering more than 32,000 miles spread out over 28 states and two Canadian provinces. When the company was formed from the merger of two railroads, leaders faced tremendous complexity as they struggled to integrate two different cultures as well as various transportation systems, accounting processes, maintenance practices, and other processes and systems. They started with setting the direction for change—a guiding vision—and then developed a set of practices to make sure everyone was aligned with the vision and strategy.

The BNSF *Vision* is "to realize the tremendous potential of BNSF Railway by providing transportation services that consistently meet the customer's expectations." The vision reminds all employees that the customer comes first. Next, leaders developed a list called *Evidences of Success*, so everyone could measure how well the company was achieving the vision. The list measures progress in four key groups—customers, employees, owners, and communities—and keeps people moving forward in a positive way. Leaders also developed a set of *Shared Values* to articulate the types of behaviors expected of everyone in the company.

BNSF leaders systematically communicated the Vision, Evidences of Success, and Shared Values in varied ways and provided training at all levels so people could incorporate the expected behaviors and values into their processes, decisions, and activities. They also created a Pyramid of Success that tied the company's short- and long-term strategic goals to team and individual goals. By helping people understand their role in achieving the vision and strategic goals, BNSF makes sure everyone in the organization is focused in the right direction.[78]

NEW LEADER
ACTION MEMO

Strategic management is one of the most critical jobs of a leader, but leaders may exhibit different strategy styles that can be effective. Leader's Self-Insight 13.3 lets you determine your strengths based on two important ways leaders can bring creativity to strategic management.

The Vision, Shared Values, and Evidences of Success continue to be the principal guiding statements for BNSF. The company continues an annual training process for all employees. It also holds people accountable for the behaviors through its performance management processes, considering both "what needs to be done" and "how things are done."[79]

LEADER'S SELF-INSIGHT 13.3

Your Strategy Style

Instructions: Think about *how you handle challenges and issues* in your current or a recent job. Then circle A or B for each of the following items, depending on which is generally more descriptive of your behavior. There are no right or wrong answers. Respond to each item as it best describes how you respond to work situations.

1. When keeping records, I tend to
   A. be very careful about documentation.
   B. be more haphazard about documentation.
2. If I run a group or a project, I
   A. have the general idea and let others figure out how to do the tasks.
   B. try to figure out specific goals, timelines, and expected outcomes.
3. My thinking style could be more accurately described as
   A. linear thinker, going from A to B to C.
   B. thinking like a grasshopper, hopping from one idea to another.
4. In my office or home, things are
   A. here and there in various piles.
   B. laid out neatly or at least in reasonable order.
5. I take pride in developing
   A. ways to overcome a barrier to a solution.
   B. new hypotheses about the underlying cause of a problem.
6. I can best help strategy by making sure there is
   A. openness to a wide range of assumptions and ideas.
   B. thoroughness when implementing new ideas.
7. One of my strengths is
   A. commitment to making things work.
   B. commitment to a dream for the future.
8. For me to work at my best, it is more important to have
   A. autonomy.
   B. certainty.
9. I work best when
   A. I plan my work ahead of time.
   B. I am free to respond to unplanned situations.
10. I am most effective when I emphasize
    A. inventing original solutions.
    B. making practical improvements.

Scoring and Interpretation

For Strategic Innovator style, score one point for each A answer circled for questions 2, 4, 6, 8, and 10 and for each B answer circled for questions 1, 3, 5, 7, and 9. For Strategic Adaptor style, score one point for each B answer circled for questions 2, 4, 6, 8, and 10, and for each A answer circled for questions 1, 3, 5, 7, and 9. Which of your two scores is higher and by how much? The higher score indicates your strategy style.

Strategic Innovator and Strategic Adaptor are two important ways leaders bring creativity to strategic management. Leaders with an adaptor style tend to work within the situation as it is given and improve it by making it more efficient and reliable. They succeed by building on what they know is true and proven. Leaders with the innovator style push toward a new paradigm and want to find a new way to do something. Innovators like to explore uncharted territory, seek dramatic breakthroughs, and may have difficulty accepting an ongoing strategy. Both innovator and adaptor styles are essential to strategic management, but with different approaches. The Strategic Adaptor asks, "How can I make this better?" The Strategic Innovator asks, "How can I make this different?" Strategic Innovators often use their skills in the formulation of whole new strategies, and Strategic Adaptors are often associated with strategic improvements and strategy execution.

If the difference between the two scores is 2 or less, you have a mid-adaptor/innovator style, and work well in both areas. If the difference is 4–6, you have a moderately strong style and probably work best in the area of your strength. And if the difference is 8–10, you have a strong style and almost certainly would want to work in the area of your strength rather than in the opposite domain.

Innovator style: 5
Adaptor style: 5

Sources: Adapted from Dorothy Marcic and Joe Seltzer, *Organizational Behavior: Experiences and Cases* (Cincinnati: South-Western, 1998), pp. 284–287; and William Miller, *Innovation Styles* (Dallas, TX: Global Creativity Corporation, 1997). The adaptor/innovator concepts are from Michael J. Kirton, "Adaptors and Innovators: A Description and Measure," *Journal of Applied Psychology* 61, no. 5 (1976), p. 623.

Leader Tools for Strategy Execution By making sure everyone understands the Vision, Values, and Strategic Pyramid, and applies them in day-to-day operations, BNSF leaders provide followers with *line of sight* to the organization's strategic objectives, which means followers see and understand the goals and how their actions will contribute to achieving them.[80] Leaders create the environment that determines whether people understand and feel committed to achieving strategic objectives. The following techniques can help leaders effectively implement strategy:[81]

1. *Create ongoing communication.* Leaders must communicate about the strategy continuously so that people throughout the organization can understand and internalize it. One strategy thinker says effective strategy execution requires that you "communicate 21 times." When you are "mind-numbingly bored with talking about your strategy," people will take it seriously and feel confident acting on it.[82]
2. *Teach the "why."* Leaders explain why they decided to do what they are doing. Followers are busy doing the everyday work of the organization and often don't think about the big picture. Leaders have to persuade people of the business reasons for the new vision and strategy.
3. *Explain what this new thing means to each person.* People are often fearful of change, and that includes fear of a new strategic direction. Leaders can anticipate people's fears and questions—what will be expected of me? will I lose my job? will my job duties and responsibilities change?—and address them head on. In addition, good leaders ask people what they are thinking and feeling.
4. *Tell what is not changing.* It is often a good idea to remind employees about company strengths, what is currently working, and what will not change. People have a hard time taking in new information when they feel that everything around them is shifting. Leaders give people a "place to stand" by telling them what is not changing.

By following these guidelines, leaders can ensure smoother strategy execution. In addition, a new strategy is implemented through organizational elements such as structural design, pay or reward systems, budget allocations, and organizational rules, policies, or procedures. Leaders make decisions about changes in structure, systems, policies, and so forth, to support the company's strategic direction. For example, when he was CEO at Home Depot, Frank Blake loosened rules, revised procedures, and shifted reward systems to emphasize quality customer service in support of a strategy to take Home Depot back to its roots as a source of not only products but also help and information. Blake sold off the wholesale housing supply unit to invest in an "army of orange aprons" and improve customer service at the retail stores.[83] John Legere, CEO of T-Mobile, implemented a cost-cutting strategy to improve efficiency and free up cash for investing in new services that can help the wireless carrier gain more customers and be more competitive. Legere eliminated free sodas in the corporate office and installed vending machines, cut merit-based pay increases, and ended the program that gave long-term employees free phones.[84]

The Leader as Strategic Decision Maker Leaders make decisions every day—some large and some small—that support company strategy. Exhibit 13.8 provides a simplified model for how leaders make strategic decisions. The two dimensions considered are whether a particular choice will have a high or low strategic impact on the business and whether execution of the decision will be easy or difficult. A change that both produces a high strategic impact and is easy to execute would be a leader's first choice for putting strategy into action. For example, when CEO Shigetaka Komori and other leaders at Fujifilm saw the digital age surging toward them, they knew the company had to transform to survive. An easy decision was to begin

EXHIBIT 13.8 Making Strategic Decisions

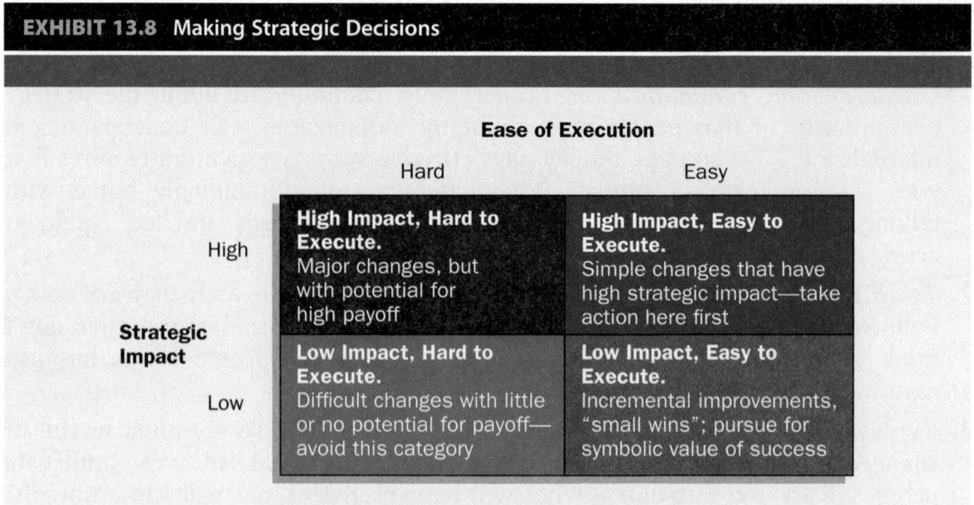

Source: Adapted from Amir Hartman and John Sifonis, with John Kador, *Net Ready: Strategies for the New E-conomy* (New York: McGraw-Hill, 2000), p. 95.

cutting resources going toward the film business and shift them into digital photography.[85] This had a big strategic impact and was relatively easy to implement.

Some strategic decisions, however, are much more difficult to execute. For example, maintaining revenue and pursuing growth meant Fujifilm needed to find new areas of business or grow through mergers and acquisitions. The latter approach can present difficulties of blending production processes, accounting procedures, corporate cultures, and other aspects of the organizations into an effectively functioning whole. Komori and other leaders pumped resources into R&D to begin developing existing technologies into new businesses, including films used for LCD panels and television sets, chemicals for cosmetics, and even drugs and health care. This last endeavor eventually led them to begin acquiring health-care companies, such as drug maker Toyama Chemical Company and U.S. medical-equipment manufacturer SonoSite Inc. Although these decisions were high-risk, the potential impact was tremendous. Leaders often initiate major changes despite the risks and difficulties because the potential strategic payoff is very high. For example, at Fuji, the health-care operation is a growing part of the overall business.[86]

Leaders also sometimes pursue activities that have a low strategic impact but are relatively easy to execute. Incremental improvements in products, work processes, or techniques are examples. Over time, incremental improvements can have an important effect on the organization. In addition, small changes can symbolize improvement and success to people within the organization. It may be important for leaders to produce quick, highly visible improvements to boost morale, keep people committed to larger changes, or keep followers focused on the vision. For example, the manager of a purchasing department wanted to reengineer the purchasing process to increase efficiency and improve relationships with suppliers. He wanted requisitions and invoices to be processed within days rather than the several weeks it had been taking. Employees were skeptical that the department could ever meet the new standards and pointed out that some invoices currently awaiting processing were almost two months old. The manager decided to make some simple revisions in the flow of paperwork and employee duties, which enabled the department to process all the old invoices so that no remaining invoice was more than a week old.

This "small win" energized employees and helped keep them focused on the larger goal.[87] The positive attitude made execution of the larger change much smoother.

The final category shown in Exhibit 13.8 relates to changes that are both difficult to execute and have low strategic impact. An illustration of a decision in this category was the attempt by new management at a highly successful mail-order clothing company to implement teams. In this case, the decision was not made to support a new strategic direction but simply to try out a new management trend—and it was a miserable failure that cost the organization much time, money, and employee goodwill before the teams were finally disbanded.[88] Effective leaders try to avoid making decisions that fall within this category.

Although good leadership calls for actively involving everyone, leaders are still ultimately responsible for establishing direction through vision and strategy. When leadership fails to provide direction, organizations flounder. To keep organizations competitive, leaders consciously adopt a focused vision and strategy and make sure everyone's activities move the organization in the right direction.

LEADERSHIP ESSENTIALS

- Leaders establish organizational direction through vision and strategy. They are responsible for studying the organization's environment, considering how it may be different in the future, and setting a direction everyone can believe in. The shared vision is an attractive, ideal future for the organization that is credible yet not readily attainable. Leaders make a real difference for their organizations when they link vision to strategic action, so that vision is more than just a dream. Superior organizational performance is not a matter of luck. It is determined by the decisions leaders make.
- A clear, powerful vision links the present and the future, energizes employees and focuses attention, and gives people an inspiring picture of the future to which they are eager to commit themselves. The vision can also give meaning to work and establish a standard of excellence by presenting a challenge that asks all workers to give their best.
- The mission includes the company's core values and its core purpose or reason for existence. Visions for the future change, whereas the mission should persist, as a reflection of the enduring character of the organization. Effective leaders frame a noble purpose that inspires followers and helps the organization maintain a competitive advantage. To frame an organizational purpose that helps people find their work meaningful, leaders can choose among four basic concepts as the basis of purpose: discovery, excellence, altruism, and heroism.
- Strategic management is the serious work of figuring out how to translate vision and mission into action. Strategy is a general plan of action that describes resource allocation and other activities for dealing with the environment and helping the organization reach its goals. Like vision, strategy changes, but successful companies develop strategies that focus on core competence, develop synergy, and create value for customers. Strategy is executed through the systems and structures that are the basic architecture for how things get done in the organization.

DISCUSSION QUESTIONS

1. A management consultant said strategic leaders are concerned with vision and mission, while strategic managers are concerned with strategy. Do you agree? Discuss.
2. A vision can apply to an individual, a family, a college course, a career, or decorating an apartment. Think of something you care about for which you want the future to be different from the present and write a vision statement for it.
3. If you worked for a company like Amazon or Google that has a strong vision for the future, how would that affect you compared to working for a company that did not have a vision?
4. Do you agree with the principle of self-reference? In other words, do you believe if people know where the organization is trying to go, they will make decisions that support the desired organizational outcome?
5. What does it mean to say that the vision can include a description of both the journey and the destination?
6. Many visions are written and hung on a wall. Do you think this type of vision has value? What would be required to imprint the vision within each person?
7. Do you think most employees know what the mission of their company is? Suggest some ways leaders can effectively communicate the mission to people both inside and outside the organization.
8. Do you think every organization needs a noble purpose in order to be successful over the long term? Discuss. Name one company that seems to reflect each category of noble purpose as defined in the chapter.
9. Strategic vision and strategic action are both needed for a leader to be effective. Which do you think you are better at doing? Why?
10. If vision is so important, why do analysts and commentators sometimes criticize a new CEO's emphasis on formulating a vision for a company that is struggling to survive? Discuss.

LEADERSHIP AT WORK

Future Thinking

Think of some problem you have in your life right now. It could be any problem you are having at school, home, or work that you would like to solve. Write a few words that summarize the problem:

____

____

____

Now write brief answers to the following questions for that specific problem. (Do not look ahead to the next set of four questions. This exercise is more effective if the questions are seen in sequence.)

1. Why do I have this problem?

____

____

____

2. Who/what caused this problem?

___

___

___

3. What stands in the way of a solution?

___

___

___

4. How likely is it that I'll solve this problem?

___

___

___

5. After you have answered these four questions, write down what are you feeling about the problem.

___

___

___

Now, for the same problem, write brief answers to the following four questions.

1. What do I really want instead of this problem? (Your answer equals your desired future outcome.)

___

___

___

2. How will I know I've achieved this future outcome? (What will I see, hear, and feel?)

___

___

___

3. What resources do I need to pursue this future outcome?

___

___

___

4. What is the first step I can take to achieve this outcome?

___

___

___

5. After you have answered these four questions, what are you feeling about the problem?

___

___

___

The human mind is effective at focusing on problems to diagnose what is wrong and who is to blame. The first four questions reflect that approach, which is called *problem-focused thinking*.

The second set of four questions reflects a different approach, called *outcome-directed thinking*. It focuses the mind on future outcomes and possibilities rather than on the causes of the problem. Most people feel more positive emotion, more creative ideas, and more optimism about solving the problem after answering the second four questions compared to the first four questions. Shifting the mind to the future harnesses the same power that a vision has to awaken creativity and inspire people to move forward. Future thinking is using the idea of future vision on a small, day-to-day scale.

In Class: This exercise is very effective when each student selects a problem, and then students interview each other about their problems. Students should work in pairs—one acting the role of leader and the other acting as a subordinate. The subordinate describes his or her problem (one minute), and then the leader simply asks the first four questions (*changing each "I" to "you"*) and listens to the answers (four minutes). Then the two students can switch leader/subordinate roles and repeat the process for the same four questions. The instructor can then gather students' observations about what they felt when answering the four questions.

Then, students can be instructed to find a new partner, and the pairs can again adopt the role of leader and subordinate. The subordinate will relate the same problem as before to the leader, but this time the leader will ask the second four questions (outcome-directed thinking, *again changing each "I" to "you"*). After the subordinate answers the four questions, the pair switches leader/subordinate roles and repeats the process. Then the instructor can ask for student observations about how they felt answering these four questions compared to the first four questions. Generally the reaction is quite positive. The key questions for students to consider are: How did the questions about future outcomes affect your creative thoughts for solving the problem compared to the first four questions that were problem-oriented? As a leader, can you use future-oriented questions in your daily life to shape your thinking and the thinking of others toward more creative problem solving? Future-oriented thinking is a powerful leadership tool.

Sources: This approach to problem solving was developed by Robert P. Bostrom and Victoria K. Clawson of Bostrom and Associates, Columbia, Missouri, and this exercise is based on a write-up appearing in *Inside USAA*, the company newsletter of USAA (September 11, 1996), pp. 8–10; and Victoria K. Clawson and Robert P. Bostrom, "Research-Driven Facilitation Training for Computer-Supported Environments," *Group Decision and Negotiation* 5 (1996), pp. 7–29.

LEADERSHIP DEVELOPMENT: CASES FOR ANALYSIS

The New Museum

The recently completed new building to house the exhibits and staff of the Central City Museum was located adjacent to the campus of a private university. The new building was financed by the generosity of local donors. The university provided the land and would cover annual operating expenses with the understanding that the museum would provide a resource for student education. The new governing board would be made up of key donors as well as selected university administrators and faculty members.

The planning committee of the governing board hired two business students to interview various stakeholders about the future direction of the museum in its new relationship with the university. These interviews were conducted in person, and the interviewees seemed uniformly interested and eager to help. The major questions pertained to the future mission and goals for the museum. Some excerpts from the interviews are listed below.

A major donor: *I think the museum should be a major community resource. My wife and I gave money for the new building with the expectation that the museum would promote visits from the public schools in the area, and particularly serve the inner-city children who don't have access to art exhibits. We don't want the museum to be snobbish or elitist. The focus should definitely be local.*

A university administrator: *The important thing is to have lively contemporary exhibits that will attract both university students and community adults and provide new insight and dialogue about current events. We can bring attention to the museum by having an occasional controversial exhibit, such as on Islamic art, and exhibits that appeal to Hispanics and African Americans. This approach would entail bringing in traveling exhibitions from major museums, which would save the administrative costs and overhead of producing our own exhibits.*

Head of the art history department: *The key thing is that the museum will not have the artistic resources or the financial resources to serve the community at large. We have a wonderful opportunity to integrate the museum with the academic faculty and make it a teaching institution. It can be a major resource for both undergraduate and graduate students in art education and art history. We can also work with engineering students, architecture students, and liberal arts students. This is a unique opportunity that will distinguish our art history department's teaching mission from others in the country.*

A faculty member in the art history department: *The best use of the museum's relationship with the university is to concentrate on training Ph.D.-level students in art history and to support scholarly research. I strongly urge the museum to focus on graduate education, which would increase the stature of the university nationally. Graduate students would be involved in the design of exhibits that would fit their research. Trying to make the museum popular on campus or in the community will waste our limited resources. Our Ph.D. graduates will be sought after by art history departments throughout the country.*

The reason you have been given this information from the interviews is that you have been invited to interview for the position of museum director. The previous director retired with the understanding that a new director would be hired upon the completion of fundraising and construction of the new building. You are thinking about what you would do if you took the job.

QUESTIONS

1. What mission for the Central City Museum do you personally prefer? As director, would you try to implement your preferred mission? Explain.
2. How would you try to resolve the underlying conflicts among key stakeholders about the museum's purpose and direction?
3. What actions would you take to implement the mission you decide to adopt? Be specific.

The Visionary Leader

When Frank Coleman first began his job as president of Hi-Tech Aerostructures, most managers and employees felt a surge of hope and excitement. Hi-Tech Aerostructures is a 50-year-old, family-owned manufacturing company that produces parts for the aircraft industry. The founder and owner had served as president until his health began to decline, and he felt the need to bring in someone from outside the company to get a fresh perspective. It was certainly needed. Over the past several years, Hi-Tech had just been stumbling along.

Coleman came to the company from a smaller business, but one with excellent credentials as a leader in advanced aircraft technology. He had a vision for transforming Hi-Tech into a world-class manufacturing facility. In addition to implementing cutting-edge technology, the vision included transforming the sleepy, paternalistic culture to a more dynamic, adaptive one and empowering employees to take a more active, responsible role in the organization. After years of just doing the same old thing day after day, vice president David Deacon was delighted with the new president and thrilled when Coleman asked him to head up the transformation project.

Deacon and his colleagues spent hours talking with Coleman, listening to him weave his ideas about the kind of company Hi-Tech could become. He assured the team that the transformation was his highest priority, and he inspired them with stories about the significant impact they were going to have on the company as well as the entire aircraft industry. Together, the group crafted a vision statement that was distributed to all employees and posted all over the building. At lunchtime, the company cafeteria was abuzz with talk about the new vision. And when the young, nattily dressed president himself appeared in the cafeteria, as he did once every few weeks, it was almost as if a rock star had walked in.

At the team's first meeting with Coleman, Deacon presented several different ideas and concepts they had come up with, explaining the advantages of each for ripping Hi-Tech out of the past and slamming it jubilantly into the twenty-first century. Nothing, however, seemed to live up to Coleman's ambitions for the project—he thought all the suggestions were either too conventional or too confusing. After three hours the team left Coleman's office and went back to the drawing board. Everyone was even more fired up after Coleman's closing remarks about the potential to remake the industry and maybe even change the world.

Early the next day, Coleman called Deacon to his office and laid out his own broad ideas for how the project should proceed. "Not bad," thought Deacon, as he took the notes and drawings back to the team. "We can take this broad concept and really put some plans for action into place." The team's work over the next few months was for the most part lively and encouraging. Whenever Coleman would attend the meetings, he would suggest changes in many of their specific plans and goals, but miraculously, the transformation plan began to take shape. The team sent out a final draft to colleagues and outside consultants, and the feedback was almost entirely positive.

The plan was delivered to Coleman on a Wednesday morning. When Deacon had still not heard anything by Friday afternoon, he began to worry. He knew Coleman had been busy with a major customer, but the president had indicated his intention to review the plan immediately. Finally, at 6 P.M., Coleman called Deacon to his office. "I'm afraid we just can't run with this," he said, tossing the team's months of hard work on the desk. "It's just ... well, just not right for this company."

Deacon was stunned. And so was the rest of the team when he reported Coleman's reaction. In addition, word was beginning to get out around the company that all was not smooth with the transformation project. The cafeteria conversations were now more likely to be gripes that nothing was being done to help the company improve. Coleman assured the team, however, that his commitment was still strong; they just needed to take a different approach. Deacon asked that Coleman attend as many meetings as he could to help keep the team on the right track. Nearly a year later, the team waited in anticipation for Coleman's response to the revised proposal.

Coleman called Deacon at home on Friday night. "Let's meet on this project first thing Monday morning," he began. "I think we need to make a few adjustments. Looks like we're more or less headed in the right direction, though." Deacon felt like crying as he hung up the phone. All that time and work. He knew what he could expect on Monday morning. Coleman would lay out his vision and ask the team to start over.

QUESTIONS

1. How effective would you rate Coleman as a visionary leader? Discuss.
2. Where would you place Coleman on the chart of types of leaders in Exhibit 13.1? Where would you place Deacon?
3. If you were Deacon, what would you do?

Sources: Based on "The Vision Failed," Case 8.1 in Peter G. Northouse, *Leadership—Theory and Practice*, 2nd ed. (Thousand Oaks, CA: Sage Publications, 2001), pp. 150–151; Joe Kay, "My Year at a Big High Tech Company," *Forbes ASAP* (May 29, 2000), pp. 195–198; "Digital Diary (My Year at a Big High Tech Company)," http://www.forbes.com/asap/2000 (accessed November 19, 2000); and "Digital Diary, Part Two: The Miracle," *Forbes ASAP* (August 21, 2000), pp. 187–190.

REFERENCES

1. Yoree Koh and Kirsten Grind, "Twitter CEO Dick Costolo Struggles to Define Vision," *The Wall Street Journal* (November 6, 2014), http://www.wsj.com/articles/twitter-ceo-dick-costolo-struggles-to-define-vision-1415323289 (accessed November 23, 2015).
2. This image comes from Lisa Haneburg, "Recalculating the Route," *The Conference Board Review* (March–April 2009), p. 13.
3. Keith H. Hammonds, "The Monroe Doctrine," *Fast Company* (October 1999), pp. 230–236.
4. Quoted in Pat McHenry Sullivan, "Finding Visions for Work and Life," *Spirit at Work* (April 1997), p. 3.
5. R. Duane Ireland and Michael A. Hitt, "Achieving and Maintaining Strategic Competitiveness in the 21st Century: The Role of Strategic Leadership," *Academy of Management Executive* 13, no. 1 (1999), pp. 43–57; M. Davids, "Where Style Meets Substance," *Journal of Business Strategy* 16, no. 1 (1995), pp. 48–60; and R. P. White, P. Hodgson, and S. Crainer, *The Future of Leadership* (London: Pitman Publishing, 1997).
6. Ireland and Hitt, "Achieving and Maintaining Strategic Competitiveness."
7. Louisa Wah, "The Dear Cost of 'Scut Work,'" *Management Review* (June 1999), pp. 27–31.
8. Gary Hamel and C. K. Prahalad, "Seeing the Future First," *Fortune* (September 5, 1994), pp. 64–70.
9. Ray Maghroori and Eric Rolland, "Strategic Leadership: The Art of Balancing Organizational Mission with Policy, Procedures, and External Environment," *The Journal of Leadership Studies* 4, no. 2 (1997), pp. 62–81.
10. Pieter Klaas Jagersma, "Aspiration and Leadership," *Journal of Business Strategy* 28, no. 1 (2007), pp. 45–52.
11. This discussion is based heavily on Paul J. H. Schoemaker, Steve Krupp, and Samantha Howland, "Strategic Leadership: The Essential Skills," *Harvard Business Review* (January–February, 2013), pp. 131–134.
12. Adam Bryant, "The Importance of Painting a Clear Picture" (an interview with John Riccitiello), *The New York Times* (November 26, 2011), http://www.nytimes.com/2011/11/27/business/electronic-arts-chief-on-painting-a-consistent-picture.html?pagewanted=all&_r=0 (accessed June 4, 2013).
13. Daniel Nye Griffiths, "John Riccitiello Steps Down as EA CEO—Why, and What Now?" *Forbes* (March 18, 2013), http://www.forbes.com/sites/danielnyegriffiths/2013/03/18/john-riccitiello-steps-down-as-ea-ceo/ (accessed June 4, 2013); and Kim-Mai Cutler, "EA CEO John Riccitiello Steps Down over 'Shortcomings' in Financial Performance," *TechCrunch* (March 18, 2013), http://techcrunch.com/2013/03/18/ea-ceo-john-riccitiello-steps-down-larry-probst-becomes-executive-chairman/ (accessed June 4, 2013).
14. Conference Board study, reported in John J. Sosik, Don I. Jung, Yair Berson, Shelley D. Dionne, and Kimberly S. Jaussi, "Making All the Right Connections: The Strategic Leadership of Top Executives in High-Tech Organizations," *Organizational Dynamics* 34, no. 1 (2005), pp. 47–61.
15. Burt Nanus, "Leading the Vision Team," *The Futurist* (May–June 1996), pp. 20–22; Warren Bennis and Burt Nanus, *Leaders: The Strategies for Taking Charge* (New York: Harper & Row, 1985); and Burt Nanus and Stephen M. Dobbs, *Leaders Who Make a Difference: Essential Strategies for Meeting the Non-Profit Challenge* (San Francisco: Jossey-Bass, 1999).
16. R. J. Baum, E. A. Locke, and S. Kirkpatrick, "A Longitudinal Study of the Relations of Vision and Vision Communication to Venture Growth in Entrepreneurial Firms," *Journal of Applied Psychology* 83 (1998), pp. 43–54; studies reported in Anthony Bell, "Using Vision to Shape the Future," *Leader to Leader* (Summer 2007), pp. 17–21; and Sharda Prashad, "The Value Chain," *Canadian Business* (February 17–March 2, 2009), pp. 65–69.
17. Nathaniel Foote, Russell Eisenstat, and Tobias Fredberg, "The Higher Ambition Leader," *Harvard Business Review* (September 2011), pp. 94–101.
18. Roger Thurow, "Different Recipe; To Tackle Hunger, a Food Bank Tries Training Chefs," *The Wall Street Journal* (November 28, 2006), pp. A1, A13; and Joseph Weber, "Waging War on Hunger," *BusinessWeek* (May 16, 2005), pp. 94, 96.
19. Andrea Kilpatrick and Les Silverman, "The Power of Vision," *Strategy & Leadership* 33, no. 2 (2005), pp. 24–26.
20. Andrew Douglas, John O. Burtis, and L. Kristine Pond-Burtis, "Myth and Leadership Vision: Rhetorical Manifestation of Cultural Force," *The Journal of Leadership Studies* 7, no. 4 (2001), pp. 55–69.
21. This section is based on Burt Nanus, *Visionary Leadership* (San Francisco: Jossey-Bass, 1992), pp. 16–18; and Richard L. Daft and Robert H. Lengel, *Fusion Leadership: Unlocking the Subtle Forces That Change People and Organizations* (San Francisco: Berrett-Koehler, 1998).
22. Alan Deutschman, "Can Google Stay Google?" *Fast Company* (August 2005), pp. 62–68.
23. Oren Harari, "Looking Beyond the Vision Thing," *Management Review* (June 1997), pp. 26–29; and William D. Hitt, *The Leader-Manager: Guidelines for Action* (Columbus, OH: Battelle Press, 1988), p. 54.
24. Nancy Chambers, "The Really Long View," *Management Review* (January 1998), pp. 11–15; and Arie de Geus, "The Living Company," *Harvard Business Review* (March–April 1997), pp. 51–59.
25. Robert S. Kaplan, "What to Ask the Person in the Mirror," *Harvard Business Review* (January 2007), pp. 86–95.
26. Matthew E. May, "The Art of Adding by Taking Away," *The New York Times* (January 19, 2013), http://www.nytimes.com/2013/01/20/jobs/matthew-may-on-the-art-of-adding-by-taking-away.html?_r=0 (accessed January 20, 2013).
27. Christoph H. Loch, Fabian J. Sting, Arnd Huchzermeier, and Christiane Decker, "Finding the Profit in Fairness," *Harvard Business Review* (September 2012), pp. 111–115.
28. Nanus, *Visionary Leadership*, p. 16; and Gregory Gull, "Gravity of Vision: It Brings Unity or Wholeness," *Leadership Excellence* (February 2012), p. 16.
29. James C. Collins and Jerry I. Porras, "Building Your Company's Vision," *Harvard Business Review* (September–October 1996), pp. 65–77 (quote on p. 74).
30. Roger E. Herman and Joyce L. Gioia, "Making Work Meaningful: Secrets of the Future-Focused Corporation," *The Futurist* (December 1998), pp. 24–26.
31. "What I Know Now," an interview with Michael L. Eskew by Paul B. Brown, *Fast Company* (November 2008), p. 108.
32. Antoine Saint-Exupery, *Pilote de Guerre* (1942); as quoted in Michael M. Reuter and John H. Shannon, "Leadership Think: Imagine the Unimaginable," *Leadership Excellence* (November 2012), p. 8.
33. James M. Kouzes and Barry Z. Posner, *The Leadership Challenge: How to Get Extraordinary Things Done in Organizations* (San Francisco: Jossey-Bass, 1988), p. 98.
34. Marshall Sashkin, "The Visionary Leader," in Jay Conger and Rabindra N. Kanungo, eds., *Charismatic Leadership: The Elusive Factor in Organizational Effectiveness* (San Francisco: Jossey-Bass, 1988), pp. 122–160.
35. James C. Collins and Jerry I. Porras, "Organizational Vision and Visionary Organizations," *California Management Review* (Fall 1991), pp. 30–52.

36. Vernon Clark quoted in Michael Lee Stallard and Jason Pankau, "To Boost Performance, Connect with the Core," *Leader to Leader* (Summer 2010), pp. 51–57.
37. Brad Stone, "The Omnivore," *Bloomberg BusinessWeek* (October 3–9, 2011), pp. 58–65.
38. Neville Pritchard, "Commitment to Purpose—The Catalyst for Organisation Change and Performance," *Industrial and Commercial Training* 42, no. 7 (2010), pp. 360–365.
39. Nanus, *Visionary Leadership*, p. 26; John W. Gardner, "Leadership and the Future," *The Futurist* (May–June 1990), pp. 9–12; and Bennis and Nanus, *Leaders: The Strategies for Taking Charge*, p. 93.
40. Gardner, "Leadership and the Future."
41. Don Clark, "Boss Talk: Qualcomm CEO Envisions Cell Base Stations in Your Home," *The Wall Street Journal* (December 11, 2012), http://online.wsj.com/article/SB10001424127887324339204578173332194107300.html (accessed June 3, 2013).
42. Farhad Manjoo, "Microsoft's Rule-Breaking Vision of Myriad Devices," *The New York Times* (October 22, 2015), p. B1; and Nick Wingfield, "Microsoft (Yes, Microsoft) Has a Far-Out Vision," *The New York Times* (April 30, 2015), http://www.nytimes.com/2015/05/03/technology/microsoft-yes-microsoft-has-a-far-out-vision.html?_r=0 (accessed November 25, 2015).
43. Gregory Gull, "Lead with Vision: Develop Your Thinking Skills," *Leadership Excellence* (November 2011), p. 9; and Dave O'Connell, Karl Hickerson, and Arun Pillutla, "Organizational Visioning: An Integrative Review," *Group & Organization Management* 36, no. 1 (2011), pp. 103–125.
44. Peter M. Senge, *The Fifth Discipline: The Art and Practice of the Learning Organization* (New York: Doubleday/Currency, 1990), pp. 205–225.
45. This is based on Tara Jones, "What's Your Vision?" *Leadership Excellence* (March 2010), pp. 6–7; James M. Kouzes and Barry Z. Posner, "To Lead, Create a Shared Vision," *Harvard Business Review* (January 2009), pp. 20–21; Robert P. Hewes, "Power of Visioning," *Leadership Excellence* (October 2012), p. 14; and Ari Weinzweig, "Step into the Future," *Inc.* (February 2011), http://www.inc.com/magazine/20110201/creating-a-company-vision.html (accessed June 4, 2013).
46. Donald T. Phillips, *Lincoln on Leadership: Executive Strategies for Tough Times* (New York: Warner Books, 1992), pp. 162–165.
47. Susan Ellingwood, "On a Mission," *Gallup Management Journal* (Winter 2001), pp. 6–7; and Jim Collins, "What Do You Stand For? It's Not Just about What You Make," *Leadership Excellence* (October 2011), p. 5.
48. Judith Rodin, "Anniversaries Are Not to Be Wasted," *Harvard Business Review* (November 2012), p. 36.
49. Stephen Xavier, "Great Leaders," *Leadership Excellence* (December 2010), p. 13.
50. Bill George, "The Company's Mission Is the Message," *strategy + business* 33 (Winter 2003), pp. 13–14; and Jim Collins and Jerry Porras, *Built to Last: Successful Habits of Visionary Companies* (New York: HarperBusiness, 1994).
51. Ellingwood, "On a Mission."
52. Collins "What Do You Stand For?"
53. Art Kleiner, George Roth, and Nina Kruschwitz, "Should a Company Have a Noble Purpose?" *The Conference Board Review* (January–February 2001).
54. Gary Hamel, "Hole in the Soul: Leaders Either Cause It or Fix It," *Leadership Excellence* (October 2011), p. 3.
55. This discussion is based on Nikos Mourkogiannis, "The Realist's Guide to Moral Purpose," *strategy + business* 41 (Winter 2005), pp. 42–53; and Nikos Mourkogiannis, "Purpose: The Starting Point of Great Leadership," *Leader to Leader* (Spring 2007), pp. 26–32.
56. Deutschman, "Can Google Stay Google?"
57. Brian X. Chen, "Samsung Emerges as a Potent Rival to Apple's Cool," *The New York Times* (February 10, 2013), http://www.nytimes.com/2013/02/11/technology/samsung-challenges-apples-cool-factor.html?pagewanted=all (accessed February 11, 2013); Bill Breen, "The Seoul of Design," *Fast Company* (December 2005), pp. 90–99; and Peter Lewis, "A Perpetual Crisis Machine," *Fortune* (September 19, 2005), pp. 58–76.
58. Cited in David K. Carr, Kelvin J. Hard, and William J. Trahant, *Managing the Change Process: A Field Book for Change Agents, Consultants, Team Leaders, and Reengineering Managers*, Exhibit 6.2 (New York: McGraw Hill, 1996).
59. Mourkogiannis, "Purpose: The Starting Point of Great Leadership."
60. Steve Lohr, "Apple, a Success at Stores, Bets Big on Fifth Avenue," *The New York Times* (May 19, 2006), p. C1; and Michael V. Copeland, "The Apple Ecosystem," *Fortune* (November 23, 2009), pp. 102–109.
61. Reported in Douglas A. Ready and Emily Truelove, "The Power of Collective Ambition," *Harvard Business Review* (December 2011), pp. 94–102.
62. Loch et al., "Finding the Profit in Fairness."
63. Mourkogiannis, "The Realist's Guide to Moral Purpose."
64. Ibid.
65. John E. Prescott, "Environments as Moderators of the Relationship between Strategy and Performance," *Academy of Management Journal* 29 (1986), pp. 329–346.
66. C. Chet Miller and Laura B. Cardinal, "Strategic Planning and Firm Performance: A Synthesis of More Than Two Decades of Research," *Academy of Management Journal* 37, no. 6 (1994), pp. 1649–1665.
67. Sydney Finkelstein and Donald C. Hambrick, *Strategic Leadership: Top Executives and Their Effect on Organizations* (St. Paul, MN: West Publishing, 1996), p. 23.
68. Cynthia A. Montgomery, "Strategist-in-Chief," *Leadership Excellence* (July 2012), p. 12.
69. Ireland and Hitt, "Achieving and Maintaining Strategic Competitiveness."
70. Oren Harari, "Catapult Your Strategy over Conventional Wisdom," *Management Review* (October 1997), pp. 21–24.
71. Christopher Hoenig, "True Grit," *CIO* (May 1, 2002), pp. 50–52.
72. Nick Wingfield, "Thinking Outside the Redbox," *The New York Times* (February 18, 2012), p. B1.
73. Gregory M. Bounds, Gregory H. Dobbins, and Oscar S. Fowler, *Management: A Total Quality Perspective* (Cincinnati, OH: South-Western, 1995), p. 244; and Michael Treacy, "You Need a Value Discipline—But Which One?" *Fortune* (April 17, 1995), p. 195.
74. "Not by Bread Alone" (an interview with Ron Shaich by Corey Hajim), *Fortune* (July 10, 2006), p. 126.
75. L. J. Bourgeois III and David R. Brodwin, "Strategic Implementation: Five Approaches to an Elusive Phenomenon," *Strategic Management Journal* 5 (1984), pp. 241–264; Anil K. Gupta and V. Govindarajan, "Business Unit Strategy, Managerial Characteristics, and Business Unit Effectiveness at Strategy Implementation," *Academy of Management Journal* 27, no. 1 (1984), pp. 25–41; and Michael K. Allio, "A Short Practical Guide to Implementing Strategy," *Journal of Business Strategy* 26, no. 4 (2005), pp. 12–21.
76. 2004 *Economist* survey, reported in Allio, "A Short, Practical Guide to Implementing Strategy."
77. M. Corboy and D. O'Corrbui, "The Seven Deadly Sins of Strategy," *Management Accounting* 77, no. 10 (1999), pp. 29–33.
78. Jeanne Michalski, "BNSF's Leadership Engine," *Organizational Dynamics* 42 (2013), pp. 35–45.
79. Ibid.
80. Wendy R. Boswell, John B. Bingham, and Alexander J. S. Colvin, "Aligning Employees through 'Line of Sight,'" *Business Horizons* 49 (2006), pp. 499–509.
81. These are based largely on Patty Azzarello, "New Strategy? How Can You Execute It," *Leadership Excellence* (May 2012), p. 17.
82. Azzarello, "New Strategy?"
83. Jennifer Reingold, "Home Depot's Total Rehab," *Fortune* (September 29, 2008), pp. 159–166.

84. Thomas Gryta, "T-Mobile's CEO Looks for Pennies to Pinch," *The Wall Street Journal* (May 7, 2013), http://online.wsj.com/article/SB10001424127887324582004578461340841270144.html (accessed June 4, 2013).
85. Kana Inagaki and Juro Osawa, "Fujifilm Thrived by Changing Focus; CEO Says Firm, Kodak Saw Digital Age Coming, 'The Question Was, What to Do about It,'" *The Wall Street Journal* (January 20, 2012), http://online.wsj.com/article/SB10001424052970203750404577170481473958516.html (accessed June 4, 2013).
86. Ibid.
87. Thanks to Russell Guinn for the story on which this example is based.
88. Based on Gregory A. Patterson, "Land's End Kicks Out Modern New Managers, Rejecting a Makeover," *The Wall Street Journal* (April 3, 1995), pp. A1, A6.

Chapter 14: Shaping Culture and Values

YOUR **LEADERSHIP** CHALLENGE

After reading this chapter, you should be able to:

- Understand why shaping culture is a vital function of leadership.
- Recognize the characteristics of a responsive, as opposed to a resistant, culture.
- Know how to establish a high-performance culture by paying attention to both values and results.
- Understand and apply how leaders shape culture and values through ceremonies, stories, symbols, language, selection and socialization, and daily actions.
- Identify the cultural values associated with adaptability, achievement, involvement, and consistency cultures and the environmental conditions associated with each.
- Act as a values-based leader and instill healthy values in the organizational culture.
- Apply the principles of spiritual leadership to help people find deeper life meaning and a sense of membership through work.

CHAPTER **OUTLINE**

430 **Organizational Culture**

435 **Culture Strength, Responsiveness, and Performance**

440 **Cultural Leadership**

443 **The Competing Values Approach to Shaping Culture**

448 **Ethical Values in Organizations**

449 **Values-Based Leadership**

In the Lead

433 **Natarajan Chandrasekaran, Tata Consultancy Services**

439 **Menlo Innovations**

446 **Brett Wilson, TubeMogul**

448 **Harvard Business School, Columbia Business School, Yale School of Management, Wharton School of the University of Pennsylvania**

449 **Jim Sinegal and Craig Jelinek, Costco**

Leader's Self-Insight

436 **Working in a Responsive Culture**

445 **Culture Preference Inventory**

451 **How Spiritual Are You?**

Leader's Bookshelf

431 **How Google Works**

Leadership at Work

454 **Walk the Talk**

Leadership Development: Cases for Analysis

456 **Culture Clash**

457 **5 Star and Amtech**

Rui Sousa of Providence, Rhode Island, recently attended a ceremony during which his jersey was retired to the rafters of his building, where it dangles as an inspiration to others. No, Sousa isn't a basketball or football star. He's a UPS driver who was recently inducted into an elite circle—the 7 percent of the company's 102,000 drivers who manage to drive their big brown trucks without having an "avoidable" traffic accident for 25 years. Sousa now wears a new shirt with a small patch with the number 25 on it. He also got his choice of a camel hair blazer or a leather bomber jacket (he chose the jacket) and gets to park his truck in a reserved space in front of the building. Each year, UPS honors drivers who reach the 25 year safe driving mark with a small ceremony to induct them into the Circle of Honor. Reaching the mark isn't easy. New drivers at UPS attend intensive weeklong training courses on safety and ethics and have to memorize the company's more than 600 mandatory "methods," which include guidelines such as checking the mirrors every five to eight seconds and leaving precisely one full car length in front when stopping.

UPS thrives on a culture of safety and efficiency, and the jersey ceremony is one way leaders illustrate and reinforce important cultural values. The most impressive safety record belongs to Ronnie McKnight, who has driven safely for 46 years in the tough streets of New York City. But McKnight isn't the record-holder. That honor belongs to 73-year-old Tom Camp, who has 51 years of safe driving in Michigan, where roads are snow- and ice-covered for several months of the year. Camp says he has no plans to retire. "Every day is a challenge out there," he says. "It takes your full concentration, all the time."[1]

In the previous chapter, we talked about creating an inspiring vision and defining the strategies to help achieve it. Successful leaders recognize that culture is a core element in helping the organization meet strategic goals and attain the vision. Like UPS, most companies with strong cultures use various symbols, ceremonies, and other activities to shape the culture the company needs to be successful. Leaders align people with the vision by influencing organizational culture and shaping the environment that determines morale and performance.

This chapter explores the role of leaders in shaping organizational culture and values. Most leaders recognize that culture is an important mechanism for attracting, motivating, and retaining talented employees, a capability that may be the single best predictor of overall organizational excellence.[2] In a survey of Canada's top 500 companies, 82 percent of leaders said culture has a strong impact on their company's performance.[3] One long-term study discovered that organizations with strong cultures outperform those with weak cultures two to one on several primary measures of financial performance.[4] In another Canadian study, the three-year average revenue growth for the top 10 companies ranked as having positive cultures was 63 percent higher than that of the 60 largest public companies in Canada.[5] The first section of this chapter describes the nature of corporate culture and its importance to organizations. Then we turn to a consideration of how shared values can help the organization stay competitive and how leaders influence cultural values for high performance. The final section of the chapter briefly discusses ethical and spiritual values and how values-based leadership shapes an organization's cultural atmosphere.

14-1 ORGANIZATIONAL CULTURE

Corporate culture is powerful because it affects a company's performance for better or worse. Thriving companies such as Google, Southwest Airlines, and Apple have often attributed their success to the cultures their leaders helped create. This chapter's Leader's Bookshelf provides a glimpse into the culture at Google. On the other hand, dysfunctional cultures or the wrong cultural values have been blamed for many of the problems at companies like Bear Stearns, Research in Motion (maker of the once-ubiquitous Blackberry), and Kodak, the company whose little yellow packages of film once dominated photography. A shifting environment often calls for new values and fresh approaches to doing business. Most leaders now understand that when a company's culture fits the needs of its external environment and company strategy, employees can create an organization that is tough to beat.[6]

14-1a What Is Culture?

Some people think of culture as the character or personality of an organization. How an organization looks and "feels" when you enter it is a manifestation of the organizational culture. For example, if you visit headquarters at ExxonMobil, you

LEADER'S BOOKSHELF

How Google Works

by Eric Schmidt and Jonathan Rosenberg

Google is arguably the world's most influential company and one of the most sought-after workplaces ever. *How Google Works*, written by Eric Schmidt, Google's executive chairman and former CEO, and Jonathan Rosenberg, a former senior Google leader, provides a glimpse into the leadership ideas that made it so. Schmidt and Rosenberg both arrived at Google as seasoned executives during the company's chaotic early years of growth and found that they had to shift their ways of thinking and acting.

NO CONVENTIONAL COMPANY

"The only thing we could say for sure back then was that much of what the two of us had learned in the 20th century was wrong, and that it was time to start over," the authors write. They assert that leaders in all types of organizations have to think about the culture they want the company to have and unite people around a direct and inspiring mission (Google's is *Don't be evil*). Here are some additional insights into the Google culture:

- ***Think Really Big and Fail Fast***. They call it the "moonshot" in Silicon Valley. Leaders at Google frequently pull people away from seeking a 10 percent improvement toward a goal of one that is "10X," or ten times better. People are encouraged to think and do things in entirely new ways. That means a lot of attempts will fail, but mistakes and failure are accepted. The Google approach is to fail fast and learn from the experience, perhaps turning some aspect of it into a new success.
- ***Make Sure All Ideas Get Heard***. The core of Google's culture is to empower employees. Leaders use a variety of systems to enable ideas from anywhere in the company to get heard and acted upon. In addition, people have the chance to spend 20 percent of their time on projects of their own choosing. This approach led to many of Google's biggest products and features, such as Gmail.
- ***Remember That Hiring Is Your Most Vital Task***. Leaders should be constantly on the lookout for talent, and they should "pay outrageously good people outrageously well, regardless of their title or tenure." In addition, the authors say good interviewing is "the most important skill any business person can develop." At Google, leaders make sure everyone has good interviewing skills because teams of employees, not managers, make all hiring and promotion decisions.

A BASIC RULE FOR LEADERS

Schmidt and Rosenberg had to learn a different approach to leadership to get the best out of what they call "smart creatives," a term referring to highly intelligent, creative, self-motivated employees who can come up with the next big thing. To lead this new type of worker, they say, leaders have to start with self-evaluation: "Make sure you would work for yourself," they advise.

Source: *How Google Works*, by Eric Schmidt and Jonathan Rosenberg with Alan Eagle, is published by Grand Central Publishing.

will likely get a sense of formality the minute you walk in the door. Most employees are in conventional business attire, desks are neat and orderly, and the atmosphere is tinged with competitiveness and a rigorous, analytical approach to taking care of business. "They're not in the fun business," said one oil industry analyst. "They're in the profit business."[7] At a company such as Zappos, though, where fun is a core value, employees may be wearing jeans and sneakers, sport pierced lips or noses, and have empty pizza boxes, coffee cups, and drink bottles on their desks. Both of these companies are highly successful, but the underlying cultures are very different.

Culture can be defined as the set of key values, assumptions, understandings, and norms that is shared by members of an organization and taught to new members as correct.[8] *Norms* are shared standards that define what behaviors are acceptable and desirable within a group of people. At its most basic, culture is a pattern of shared assumptions and beliefs about how things are done in an organization. As organizational members cope with internal and external problems, they develop shared assumptions and norms of behavior that are taught to new members as the correct way to think, feel, and act in relation to those problems.[9]

Culture
the set of key values, assumptions, understandings, and norms that is shared by members of an organization and taught to new members as correct

Culture can be thought of as consisting of three levels, as illustrated in Exhibit 14.1, with each level becoming less obvious.[10] At the surface level are visible artifacts, such as manner of dress, patterns of behavior, physical symbols, organizational

EXHIBIT 14.1 Levels of Corporate Culture

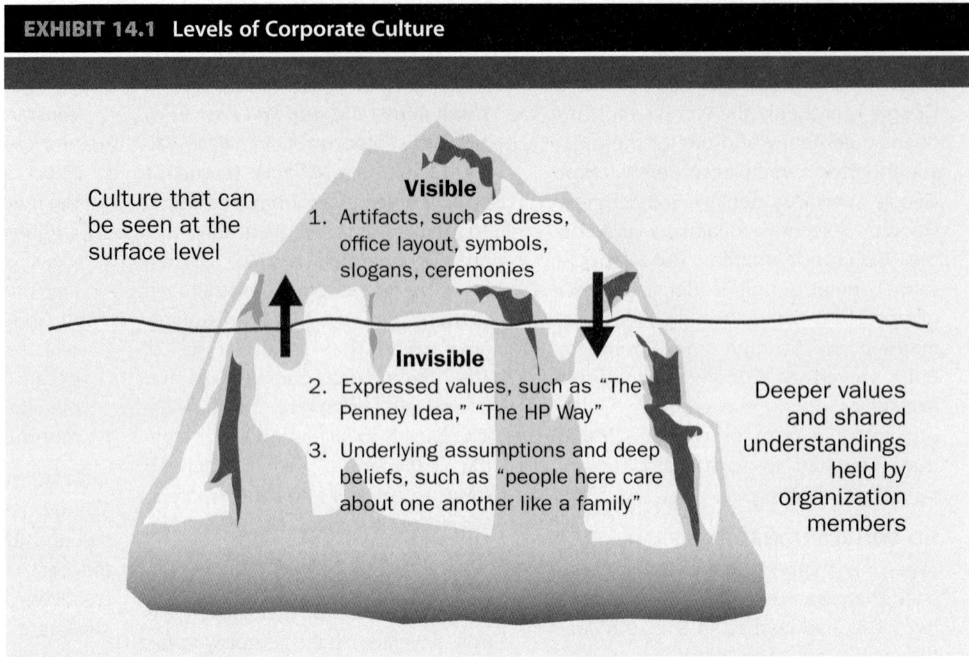

ceremonies, and office layout—all the things one can see, hear, and observe by watching members of the organization. Consider some observable aspects of culture at John Lewis, a successful retailer in Great Britain. People working in John Lewis stores are typically older than staff members at other retailers and are called partners, not employees. Everyone shares in company profits and has a say in how the business is run. The entrance to leaders' offices is small and functional rather than ostentatious, and stores exude an air of simplicity, calmness, and order.[11] At a deeper level of culture are the expressed values and beliefs, which are not observable but can be discerned from how people explain and justify what they do. These are values that members of the organization hold at a conscious level. For example, John Lewis partners consciously know that dependability, service, and quality are highly valued and rewarded in the company culture.

Some values become so deeply embedded in a culture that organizational members may not be consciously aware of them. These basic, underlying assumptions are the essence of the culture. At John Lewis, these assumptions might include (1) that the company cares about its employees as much as it expects them to care about customers, (2) that individual employees should think for themselves and do what they believe is right to provide exceptional customer service, and (3) that trust and honesty are an essential part of successful business relationships. Assumptions generally start out as expressed values, but over time they become more deeply embedded and less open to question—organization members take them for granted and often are not even aware of the assumptions that guide their behavior, language, and patterns of social interaction.

14-1b Importance of Culture

When people are successful at what they undertake, the ideas and values that led to that success become institutionalized as part of the organization's culture.[12] Culture gives employees a sense of organizational identity and generates a commitment to particular values and ways of doing things. Culture serves two important functions in organizations: (1) it integrates members so that they know how to relate to one another, and (2) it helps the organization adapt to the external environment.

NEW LEADER
ACTION MEMO

As a leader, you can pay attention to organizational culture and develop an awareness of how cultural values, norms, and beliefs influence people's behavior in the organization.

Internal Integration Culture helps employees develop a collective identity and know how to work together effectively. It is culture that guides day-to-day working relationships and determines how people communicate in the organization, what behavior is acceptable or not acceptable, and how power and status are allocated. Culture can imprint a set of unwritten rules inside employees' minds, which can be very powerful in determining behavior, thus affecting organizational performance.[13] At Tata Consultancy Services, CEO Natarajan Chandrasekaran has shaped a culture in which people are expected to help and care for one another.

IN THE LEAD

Natarajan Chandrasekaran, Tata Consultancy Services

Natarajan Chandrasekaran grew up on a farm in a small village in Southern India. He returned to take over the farm after college but was so miserable after five months that he and his father agreed that he would return to school for a master's degree in computing. His first job was at Tata Consultancy Services (TCS), which at the time (1987) had about 500 employees. Today, Chandrasekaran is CEO of TCS, which now has around 315,000 employees and operates in 46 countries.

He leads the organization with many of the values his parents instilled in him, including honesty, determination, and accountability. Chandrasekaran says his father always wanted him and his five siblings "to be accountable for what we did." Chandrasekaran has built accountability into the culture of TCS, but part of the culture is also being accountable for others. "Everybody has to take some accountability for other people, and look for ways to make small contributions to help others," Chandrasekaran says. At TCS, each individual is expected to find ways to help someone else achieve just a little more. This can apply to work activities, but it might also apply to some other aspect of a colleague's life. Looking after others is an important part of the culture, so people are open to both giving and receiving help and advice.

When hiring, TCS leaders look for people who fit the culture of accountability and caring. The culture supports an environment in which people learn from and collaborate with others. In executive team meetings, leaders share stories of both successes and failures, and larger meetings often start with having people describe examples of their collaborations. "Learning cannot be achieved by mandate" Chandrasekaran points out. "It has to be achieved by culture."[14]

Many organizations, like Tata Consultancy Services, want strong cultures that encourage teamwork, collaboration, and mutual trust.[15] In an environment of trust, people are more likely to share ideas, be creative, and be generous with their knowledge and talents.

External Adaptation Culture also determines how the organization meets goals and deals with outsiders. The right cultural values can help the organization respond rapidly to customer needs or the moves of a competitor. Culture can encourage employee commitment to the core purpose of the organization, its specific goals, and the basic means used to accomplish goals.

The "right" culture is determined partly by what the organization needs to meet external challenges. The culture should embody the values and assumptions needed by the organization to succeed in its environment.[16] If the competitive environment requires speed and flexibility, for example, the culture should embody values that support adaptability, collaboration across departments, and a fast response to customer needs or environmental changes. When Lou Gerstner took over as CEO of IBM in 1993, it was on the brink of collapse partly because of an "inbred and ingrown" culture that slowed decision making and prevented adaptation to the rapidly changing environment. One step Gerstner took early on was to change the way meetings were handled. To put more value on dialogue and shared decision making rather than presentations, he limited the number of slides that could accompany a report to five.[17] By the time Gerstner had left nearly 10 years later, IBM had a new culture in which everyone knew they were rewarded for collaborating and getting things done fast, not for hoarding information and making impressive presentations.[18]

All effective cultures encourage adaptation to the environment in order to keep the organization healthy and profitable. This chapter's *Consider This* highlights the importance of individual learning and adaptability. Just like people, organizational cultures have to grow and change to meet new challenges.

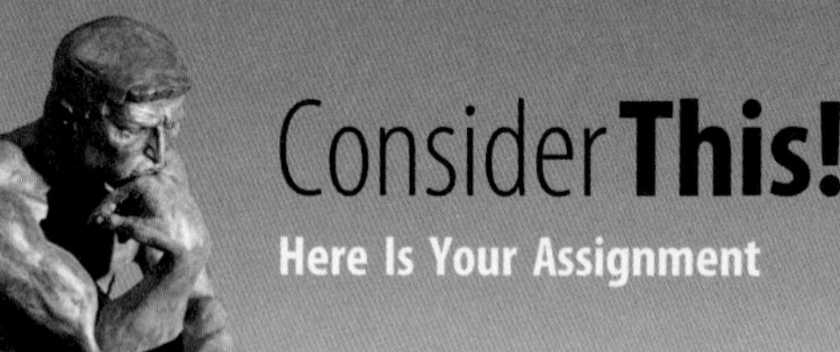

Consider **This!**

Here Is Your Assignment

1. You will receive a body. You may like it or not, but it will be yours for the entire period this time around.
2. You will learn lessons. You are enrolled in a full-time, informal school called life. Each day in this school you will have the opportunity to learn lessons. You may like the lessons or think them irrelevant and stupid.
3. There are no mistakes, only lessons. Growth is a process of trial and error, experimentation. The "failed" experiments are as much a part of the process as the experiment that ultimately "works."
4. A lesson is repeated until it is learned. A lesson will be presented to you in various forms until you have learned it; then you can go on to the next lesson.
5. Learning lessons does not end. There is no part of life that does not contain its lessons. If you are alive, there are lessons to be learned.
6. "There" is no better than "here." When your "there" has become a "here," you will simply obtain another "there" that will, again, look better than "here."
7. Others are merely mirrors of you. You cannot love or hate something about another person unless it reflects to you something you love or hate about yourself.
8. What you make of your life is up to you. You have all the tools and resources you need; what you do with them is up to you. The choice is yours.
9. All you need to do is look, listen, and trust.
10. Whether you think you can or can't, in either case you'll be right. Think about it.

14-2 CULTURE STRENGTH, RESPONSIVENESS, AND PERFORMANCE

Culture strength refers to the degree of agreement among employees about the importance of specific values and ways of doing things. If widespread consensus exists, the culture is strong and cohesive; if little agreement exists, the culture is weak.[19] The effect of a strong culture is not always a positive one. Sometimes a strong culture can encourage the wrong values and cause harm to the organization and its members. Think of the now-defunct Bear Stearns, which had a strong, highly competitive corporate culture that supported pushing everything to the limits in the pursuit of wealth. As long as an employee was making money for the firm, leaders took a hands-off approach, which allowed increasingly risky and sometimes unethical behavior.[20]

Culture strength
the degree of agreement among employees about the importance of specific values and ways of doing things

A strong culture increases employee cohesion and commitment to the values, goals, and strategies of the organization, but companies can sometimes have unethical values or values that are unhealthy for the organization because they don't fit the needs of the environment. Research at Harvard into some 200 corporate cultures found that a strong culture does not ensure success unless it also encourages a healthy response and adaptation to the external environment.[21] A strong culture that does not encourage adaptation can be more damaging to an organization than a weak culture.

NEW LEADER
ACTION MEMO

As a leader, you can build a responsive culture by showing concern for customers and other stakeholders and by supporting people and projects that bring about useful change. To improve your understanding of responsive versus resistant cultures, go to Leader's Leader's Self-Insight 14.1.

14-2a Responsive Cultures

Cultures can be thought of as either responsive or resistant. As illustrated in Exhibit 14.2, responsive corporate cultures have different values and behavior from resistant cultures.[22] In responsive cultures, leaders are concerned with customers and with people, processes, and procedures within the organization that bring about useful change. In resistant cultures, leaders are concerned with

EXHIBIT 14.2 Responsive versus Resistant Cultures

Visible behavior	Leaders pay attention to all stakeholders and initiate change when needed to serve the legitimate interests of customers, employees, partners, or others, even if it entails taking some risks.	Managers tend to be inward-looking and politically motivated. As a result, they do not change their goals and strategies quickly to adjust to changes in the environment.
Expressed values	Leaders genuinely care about customers, employees, partners, and shareholders. They value all the people, processes, and mechanisms up and down the hierarchy that can create useful change.	Managers care mainly about their own interests and the products or technologies of their immediate team or department. They value the orderly and risk-reducing management system more highly than change initiatives.
Underlying assumption	Serve whole organization, trust others.	Meet own needs, distrust others.

Source: Based on John P. Kotter and James L. Heskett, *Corporate Culture and Performance* (New York: The Free Press, 1992), p. 51.

LEADER'S SELF-INSIGHT 14.1

Working in a Responsive Culture

Instructions: Think of a specific full-time job you have held. Indicate whether each of the following items is Mostly False or Mostly True according to your perception of the managers above you when you held that job.

	Mostly False	Mostly True
1. Good ideas got serious consideration from management above me		✓
2. Management above me was interested in ideas and suggestions from people at my level in the organization.		✓
3. When suggestions were made to management above me, they received fair evaluation.		✓
4. Management did not expect me to challenge or change the status quo.	✓	
5. Management specifically encouraged me to bring about improvements in my workplace.		✓
6. Management above me took action on recommendations made from people at my level.		✓
7. Management rewarded me for correcting problems.		✓
8. Management clearly expected me to improve work unit procedures and practices.		✓
9. I felt free to make recommendations to management above me to change existing practices.		✓
10. Good ideas did not get communicated upward because management above me was not very approachable.	✓	

Scoring and Interpretation

To compute your score: Give yourself one point for each Mostly True answer to questions 1, 2, 3, 5, 6, 7, 8, and 9 and for each Mostly False answer to questions 4 and 10. Total points: 10.

A responsive culture is shaped by the values and actions of top and middle executives. When managers actively encourage and welcome change initiatives from below, the organization will be infused with values for responsiveness and change. These 10 questions measure your management's openness to change. A typical average score for management openness to change is about 4. If your average score was 5 or higher, you worked in an organization that expressed cultural values of responsiveness. If your average score was 3 or below, the culture was probably a resistant one.

Thinking back to your job, was the level of management openness to change correct for that organization? Why? Compare your score to that of another student, and take turns describing what it was like working for the *managers above you*. Do you sense that there is a relationship between job satisfaction and management's openness to change? What specific manager characteristics and corporate values accounted for the openness (or lack of) in the two jobs?

Source: Based on S. J. Ashford, N. P. Rothbard, S. K. Piderit, and J. E. Dutton, "Out on a Limb: The Role of Context and Impression Management in Issue Selling," *Administrative Science Quarterly* 43 (1998), pp. 23–57; and E. W. Morrison and C. C. Phelps, "Taking Charge at Work: Extrarole Efforts to Initiate Workplace Change," *Academy of Management Journal* 42 (1999), pp. 403–419.

themselves or their own special projects, and their values tend to discourage risk taking and change. Thus, a strong culture is not enough because an unhealthy culture may encourage the organization to march resolutely in the wrong direction. Healthy cultures help companies respond to changes in the external environment.

An organization's culture may not always be in alignment with the needs of the external environment. The values and ways of doing things may reflect what worked in the past. The difference between desired and actual values and behaviors is called the **culture gap**.[23] Many organizations have some degree of culture gap, though leaders often fail to realize it. An important step toward shifting the culture toward more adaptive values is to recognize when people are adhering to the wrong values or when important values are not held strongly enough.[24]

Culture gap
the difference between desired and actual values and behaviors

Culture gaps can be immense, particularly in the case of mergers. Leaders at Alpha Natural Resources Inc. struggled to merge two distinct cultures after acquiring Massey Energy Company. Massey was in control of the mine in West Virginia at which an explosion killed 29 workers in 2010. Alpha CEO Kevin Crutchfield makes safety a core value, and he scheduled 400 training sessions to train every Massey employee in the management system called Running Right. "There is no ton of coal worth an injury, an accident, or, God forbid, a life," he says. "It's just a ton of coal. So, if we can't get it out the right way, we're not going to bother. I think that is a little different from what the Massey folks were used to."[25]

Despite the popularity of mergers and acquisitions as a corporate strategy, many fail. Studies by consulting firms such as McKinsey & Company, the Hay Group, and others suggest that performance declines in almost 20 percent of acquired companies after acquisition. Some experts claim that 90 percent of mergers never live up to expectations.[26] One reason for this is the difficulty of integrating cultures. Organizational leaders should remember that the human systems—in particular, the norms and values of corporate culture—are what make or break any change initiative. The problem of integrating cultures increases in scope and complexity with global companies and cross-cultural mergers or acquisitions.

14-2b The High-Performance Culture

Creating and sustaining a responsive, high-performance culture is one of the most important jobs for organizational leaders.[27] A number of studies have found a positive relationship between culture and performance.[28] In *Corporate Culture and Performance*, Kotter and Heskett provided evidence that companies in which leaders intentionally managed cultural values outperformed similar companies whose leaders did not.[29] Even the U.S. government is recognizing the link between culture and effectiveness. The U.S. Office of Personnel Management created its Organizational Assessment Survey as a way for federal agencies to measure aspects of culture and shift values toward high performance.[30]

Companies that succeed have leaders who pay careful attention to both cultural values *and* business performance. Exhibit 14.3 illustrates four organizational outcomes based on the relative attention leaders pay to cultural values and business performance.[31] For example, leaders in Quadrant C of Exhibit 14.3 pay little attention to either cultural values or business results, and the company is unlikely to survive for long. Leaders in Quadrant D are highly focused on creating a strong culture, but they don't tie the values directly to goals and desired results.

When leaders don't connect cultural values to business performance, the values aren't likely to benefit the organization during hard times. For example, the corporate culture at The LEGO Group headquarters in Billund, Denmark, nearly doomed the toymaker when sales plummeted as children turned away from traditional toys to video games. At that time, LEGO leaders reflected the characteristics found in Quadrant D of Exhibit 14.3. Imagination and creativity, not business performance, were what guided Lego. The attitude was, "We're doing great stuff for kids—don't bother us with financial goals." A new CEO, Jørgen Vig Knudstorp, transformed the culture with a new employee motto: "I am here to make money for the company." Shifting leader attitudes to incorporate bottom-line results as well as values had a profound effect, and Lego has become one of the most successful companies in the toy industry.[32]

Quadrant A in Exhibit 14.3 represents organizations in which leaders focus primarily on bottom-line results and pay little attention to values. This approach may

EXHIBIT 14.3 Combining Culture and Performance

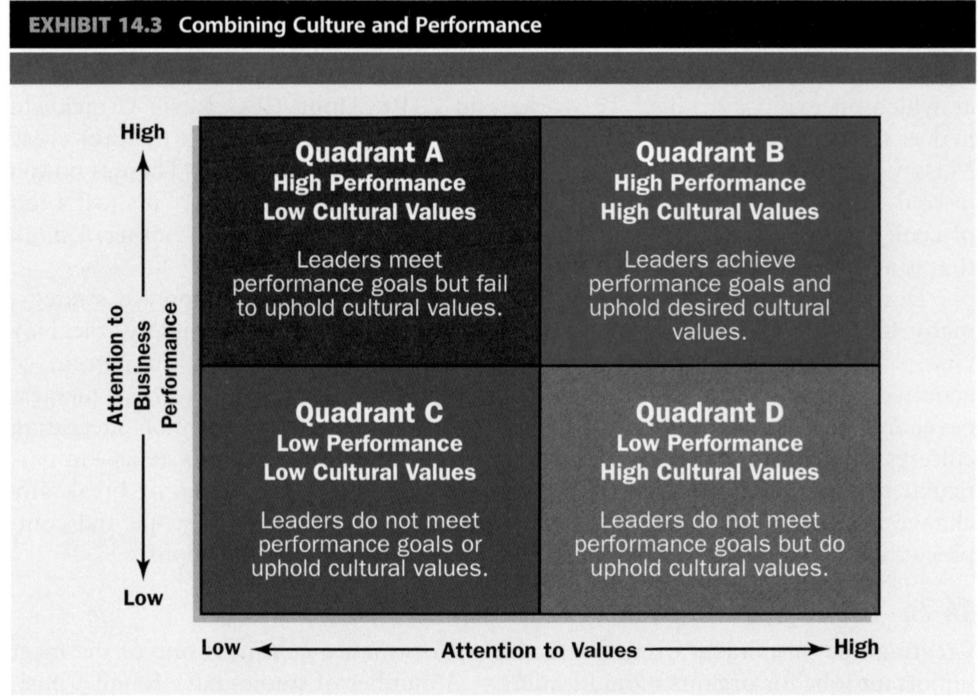

Source: Adapted from Jeff Rosenthal and Mary Ann Masarech, "High-Performance Cultures: How Values Can Drive Business Results," *Journal of Organizational Exellence* (Spring 2003), pp. 3–18; and Dave Ulrich, Steve Kerr, and Ron Ashkenas, Figure 11–2, GE Leadership Decision Matrix, *The GE Work-Out: How to Implement GE's Revolutionary Method for Busting Bureaucracy and Attacking Organizational Problems—Fast!* (New York: McGraw-Hill, 2002), p. 230.

be profitable in the short run, but the success is difficult to sustain over the long term because the "glue" that holds the organization together—that is, shared cultural values—is missing. Consider how a bottom-line focus at social games company Zynga damaged the organization. Zynga, led by founder and CEO Mark Pincus, recorded a phenomenal $828 million in revenue in the first nine months of 2011, more than double the period a year earlier. Zynga also met ambitious profitability goals, rare among Internet start-ups. With this type of financial performance, one might assume working for Zynga would be enjoyable and gratifying. However, teams for each game, like FarmVille and CityVille, worked under aggressive deadlines and were continuously challenged to meet lofty performance goals. Leaders emphasized performance reports, relentlessly aggregating data, and using the data to demote or fire weak employees. Little attention was paid to cultural values that bind people into a unified whole. The relentless focus on financial performance began to take a toll when people started voicing their frustration, complaining about long hours and aggressive deadlines that left little room for creativity. Former employees describe emotionally charged encounters, including loud outbursts from Pincus, threats from senior leaders, and moments when colleagues broke down into tears. The company's success could not be sustained without some attention to building a positive and responsive culture. Zynga's stock price dropped 80 percent between March 2012 and July 2013. At that time, Pincus turned the CEO job over to Don Mattrick but remained as chair of the board and retained majority voting power. In 2015, Mattrick was fired and Pincus returned as CEO. It remains to be seen if he will bring a greater focus on building a positive culture that can help to renew the company.[33]

Companies that maintain success over the long term have leaders who fit into Quadrant B. They put high emphasis on both culture and solid business performance as drivers of organizational success. Quadrant B organizations represent the **high-performance culture**, a culture that (1) is based on a solid organizational mission or purpose, (2) embodies shared responsive values that guide decisions and business practices, and (3) encourages individual employee ownership of both bottom-line results and the organization's cultural backbone.[34]

In Quadrant B companies, leaders align values with the company's day-to-day operations—hiring practices, performance management, budgeting, criteria for promotions and rewards, and so forth. For example, when he was CEO of General Electric, Jack Welch helped GE become one of the world's most successful and admired companies. He achieved this by evaluating and rewarding leaders throughout the company based on whether they honored important cultural values in addition to "making their numbers."[35] Another example of an organization where leaders tie values to business performance is Menlo Innovations, which was described in the Chapter 8 Leader's Bookshelf.

High-performance culture
a culture that is based on a solid mission, embodies shared responsive values that guide decisions, and encourages individual ownership of both bottom-line results and cultural values

IN THE LEAD

Menlo Innovations

Richard Sheridan, James Goebel, Robert Simms, and Thomas Meloche founded Menlo Innovations to create custom software for organizations, but one of their primary goals was to create a unique culture that embraces the values of equality, teamwork, learning, and fun. The founders say they were inspired by the collaborative and creative work environment demonstrated at Thomas Edison's Menlo Park, New Jersey, "Invention Factory" more than 120 years ago.

At many software companies developers work alone and are driven to meet rigorous performance goals, but at Menlo, collaboration is valued above anything else. Everyone works in a large, open room with no barriers of any kind to limit communication and information sharing. Employees work in pairs, sharing a single computer and passing the mouse back and forth as they brainstorm ideas and troubleshoot problems. The pairs stay together for a week and then all switch around to new partners. The variety of partners and tasks helps keep energy high as well as bringing fresh perspectives to ever-evolving projects.

Curiosity, willingness to learn, and the ability to "play well with others" are the qualities Menlo wants in its employees. The goal for each person is not to get the right answer, make the right connection, be the smartest, or know the most, but rather to bring out the best in one's partner. Consider Menlo leaders' approach to hiring. People who apply for jobs are divided into pairs and assigned an exercise, then evaluated on how effective they are at making the other applicant look good. It's tough for some people to handle—trying to make sure a competitor looks good enough to get the job you want. However, at Menlo, if you can't do that, you won't fit the culture—and fitting the culture is essential. Anyone who says, "I'm right, so let's do it this way" won't last long. "Constant collaboration means we are constantly transferring knowledge to one another," says Sheridan. "I grow my team an inch every day." Menlo's culture has been a competitive advantage for the company, enabling it to adapt quickly to an ever-shifting environment and meet the changing technology needs of varied clients, including Domino's, Thomson Reuters, Pfizer, Nationwide Financial, and the University of Michigan.[36]

At companies with high-performance cultures, such as GE and Menlo Innovations, leaders care about both values and performance. A study of corporate values by Booz Allen Hamilton and the Aspen Institute found that leaders in companies that report superior financial results typically put a high emphasis on values and link them directly to the way they run the organization.[37]

14-3 CULTURAL LEADERSHIP

An organization exists only because of the people who are a part of it, and those people both shape and interpret the character and culture of the organization. That is, an organization is not a slice of objective reality; different people may perceive the organization in different ways and relate to it in different ways. Leaders in particular formulate a viewpoint about the organization and the values that can help people achieve the organization's mission, vision, and strategic goals. Therefore, leaders enact a viewpoint and a set of values that they think are best for helping the organization succeed. A primary way in which leaders influence norms and values to build a high-performance culture is through *cultural leadership*.

A **cultural leader** defines and uses signals and symbols to influence corporate culture. Cultural leaders influence culture in two key areas:

1. *The cultural leader articulates a vision for the organizational culture that employees can believe in.* This means the leader defines and communicates central values that employees believe in and will rally around. Values are tied to a clear and compelling mission, or core purpose.
2. *The cultural leader heeds the day-to-day activities that reinforce the cultural vision.* The leader makes sure that work procedures and reward systems match and reinforce the values. Actions speak louder than words, so cultural leaders "walk their talk."[38]

For values to guide the organization, leaders model them every day. WestJet Airlines, which is consistently ranked as having one of Canada's most admired corporate cultures, provides an illustration. Employees (called simply "people" at WestJet) regularly see top leaders putting the values of equality, teamwork, participation, and customer service into action. At the end of a flight, for example, everyone on hand pitches in to pick up garbage—sometimes even the CEO. Customer-facing employees have "guidelines" rather than rules in terms of what they can do for customers, and no one is ever punished for well-intended errors of judgment. A new gate agent who gave free tickets to an entire flight for a minor inconvenience, for instance, was hailed as a hero for her effort, even though leaders coached her through understanding the impact of her action on the company so she might make a less costly decision the next time.[39]

Creating and maintaining a high-performance culture is not easy in today's turbulent environment and changing workplace, but through their words—and particularly their actions—cultural leaders let everyone in the organization know what really counts. Some of the mechanisms leaders use to enact cultural values are organizational rites and ceremonies, stories, symbols, and specialized language. In addition, they emphasize careful selection and socialization of new employees to keep cultures strong. Perhaps most importantly, leaders signal the cultural values they want to instill in the organization through their day-to-day behavior.

Cultural leader
a leader who actively uses signals and symbols to influence corporate culture

14-3a Ceremonies

A **ceremony** is a planned activity that makes up a special event and is generally conducted for the benefit of an audience. Leaders can schedule ceremonies to provide dramatic examples of what the company values. Ceremonies reinforce specific values, create a bond among employees by allowing them to share an important event, and anoint and celebrate employees who symbolize important achievements.[40]

A ceremony often includes the presentation of an award. At Mary Kay Cosmetics, one of the most effective companies in the world at using ceremonies, leaders hold elaborate award ceremonies at an annual event called "Seminar," presenting jewelry, furs, and luxury cars to high-achieving sales consultants. The most successful consultants are introduced by film clips like the ones used to present award nominees in the entertainment industry.[41] These ceremonies recognize and celebrate high-performing employees and help bind sales consultants together. Even when they know they will not personally be receiving awards, consultants look forward to Seminar all year because of the emotional bond it creates with others.

14-3b Stories

A **story** is a narrative based on true events that is repeated frequently and shared among employees. Leaders can use stories to illustrate the company's primary values.[42] Employees at IBM often hear a story about the female security guard who challenged IBM's chairman. Although she knew who he was, the guard insisted that the chairman could not enter a particular area because he wasn't carrying the appropriate security clearance. Rather than getting reprimanded or fired, the guard was praised for her diligence and commitment to maintaining the security of IBM's buildings.[43] By telling this story, employees emphasize both the importance of following the rules and the critical contributions of every employee from the bottom to the top of the organization. Russell Goldsmith, chairman and CEO of City National Bank in Los Angeles, believes in the force of storytelling so much that he brought in consultants to teach people how to share their stories about teamwork or customer service, which reinforces the company culture.[44]

In some cases, stories may not be supported by facts, but they are consistent with the values and beliefs of the organization. A widely told story at Nordstrom, for example, is about the associate who, in order to satisfy a customer who was unhappy with the performance of his automobile tires, gave the customer his money back. The only thing is, Nordstrom does not sell tires. The story reinforces the company's no-questions-asked return policy.[45]

14-3c Symbols

Another tool for conveying cultural values is the **symbol**. A symbol is an object, act, or event that conveys meaning to others. For example, top leaders at Germany's TeamBank, described in the previous chapter, made the informal *Du* the mandatory form of address rather than the formal *Sie* commonly used in German workplaces. The change is a symbol of top management's respect for every employee. At tomato processor Morning Star, described in Chapter 10, administrative offices are located near the factory floor to symbolize that everyone is on the same team with the same purpose.[46]

Leaders can also use physical artifacts to symbolize important values. After the national hotel chain Extended Stay America emerged from bankruptcy, employees remained fearful of losing their jobs if they made any decision that might cost the

Ceremony
a planned activity that makes up a special event and is generally conducted for the benefit of an audience

Story
a narrative based on true events that is repeated frequently and shared among employees

Symbol
an object, act, or event that conveys meaning to others

company money. To implement a new culture where people aren't afraid to take risks to serve customers, CEO Jim Donald began handing out lime-green "Get Out of Jail, Free" cards. All people had to do, he told them, was call in the card when they took a big risk on behalf of the company—no questions asked. Donald successfully led the company for several years, resigning in 2015.[47]

14-3d Specialized Language

Language can shape and influence organizational values and beliefs. Leaders sometimes use slogans or sayings to express key corporate values. Slogans can easily be picked up and repeated by employees. For example, at Averitt Express, the slogan "Our driving force is people" applies to customers and employees alike. The culture emphasizes that drivers and customers, not top executives, are the power that fuels the company's success.

Leaders also express and reinforce cultural values through written public statements, such as corporate mission statements or other formal statements that express the core values of the organization. When Sidney Taurel, former chairman and CEO of Eli Lilly and Company, wanted to create a more adaptive culture able to respond to the demands of the global marketplace, he worked with other leaders to develop a formal statement of how to put Lilly's core values (respect for all people, honesty and integrity, and striving for excellence) into action. The statement includes descriptions and mottos such as "Model the values: Show us what you're made of," "Implement with integrity, energy, and speed: Provide the powder and supply the spark," and "Get results through people: Set people up to succeed."[48]

14-3e Selection and Socialization

To maintain cultural values over time, leaders emphasize careful selection and socialization of new employees. Companies with strong, healthy cultures, such as Nordstrom, Southwest Airlines, Google, and Zappos, often have rigorous hiring practices.

> NEW LEADER
> **ACTION MEMO**
>
> As a leader, you can shape cultural values through rites and ceremonies, stories, symbols, and language. You can keep the culture strong by carefully selecting and socializing people and by making sure your actions match the espoused values.

Once the right people are hired, the next step is socializing them into the culture. **Socialization** is the process by which a person learns the values, norms, perspectives, and expected behaviors that enable him or her to successfully participate in the group or organization.[49] When people are effectively socialized, they "fit in" because they understand and adopt the norms and values of the group. Socialization is a key leadership tool for transmitting the culture and enabling it to survive over time. Leaders act as role models for the values they want new employees to adopt, and they implement formal training programs, which may include pairing the newcomer with a key employee who embodies the desired values.

Rituals can also be used for socialization. At Gentle Giant, a Somerville, Massachusetts, moving company that has won nine Best of Boston awards from *Boston* magazine, new hires participate in the "stadium run." CEO Larry O'Toole decided to have new hires run the tiers of Harvard University stadium as a way to emphasize that people at the company work hard, challenge themselves, and go the distance rather than letting up if things get tough. After the run, O'Toole provides a hearty breakfast and gives an orientation speech. "You're not a Gentle Giant until you've done the run," said employee Kyle Green.[50]

Socialization
the process by which a person learns the cultural values, norms, and behaviors that enable him or her to "fit in" with a group or organization

Good leaders don't leave employee socialization to chance. Formal socialization programs can be highly effective. One study of recruits into the British Army surveyed newcomers on their first day and then again eight weeks later.

Researchers compared the findings to a sample of experienced "insider" soldiers and found that after eight weeks of training, the new recruits' norms and values had generally shifted toward those of the insiders.[51] Another field study of around 300 people from a variety of organizations found that formal socialization was associated with less stress for newcomers, less ambiguity about expected roles and behaviors, and greater job satisfaction, commitment, and identification with the organization.[52]

14-3f Daily Actions

One of the most important ways leaders build and maintain the cultures they want is by signaling and supporting important cultural values through their daily actions. Employees learn what is valued most in a company by watching what attitudes and behaviors leaders pay attention to and reward, how leaders react to organizational crises, and whether the leader's own behavior matches the espoused values.[53] Former AmerisourceBergen CEO Dave Yost supported values of frugality and egalitarianism by answering his own phone, flying coach, and doing without fancy perks and stylish office furniture.[54] Leaders can also change negative or unproductive cultures by their actions. At Dynergy, a Houston-based power producer, new CEO Bob Flexon's office is a 64-square-foot cubicle identical to those of the 235 or so headquarters employees surrounding him. People often stop by just to chat. Flexon is instilling values of openness, egalitarianism, and collaboration to try to get Dynergy back in growth mode after the company went through bankruptcy.[55]

Good leaders understand how carefully they are watched by employees. As former GE CEO Jack Welch says, "Look, it's Management 101 to say that the best competitive weapon a company can possess is a strong culture. But the devil is in the details of execution." Welch says one sure route to destroying the culture is to let strong performers get away with not honoring the cultural values. People notice, and they conclude that the cultural values aren't important. Leaders make sure people are evaluated for both making their numbers and demonstrating the values, as described earlier in Exhibit 14.3, and they don't hesitate to fire people who refuse to uphold important values.[56]

14-4 THE COMPETING VALUES APPROACH TO SHAPING CULTURE

Organizational values are the enduring beliefs that have worth, merit, and importance for the organization. The economic crisis, the breakdown of corporate ethics and responsibility that contributed to it, and the crash of once-thriving companies have brought values to the forefront. Unhealthy cultural values played a crucial role in many of the mistakes these companies made.[57] Ethical values will be discussed later in the chapter. Changes in the nature of work, globalization, increasing diversity in the workforce, and other shifts in the larger society have also made the topic of values one of considerable concern to leaders. They are faced with such questions as, "How can I determine what cultural values are important? Are some values 'better' than others? How can the organization's culture help us be more competitive?"

In considering what values are important for the organization, leaders consider the external environment and the company's vision and strategy. Cultures can vary widely across organizations; however, organizations within the same industry often share similar values because they are operating in similar environments.[58] Key values

Organizational values the enduring beliefs that have worth, merit, and importance for the organization

should embody what the organization needs to be effective. Rather than looking at values as either "good" or "bad," leaders look for the right combination. The correct relationship among cultural values, organizational strategy, and the external environment can enhance organizational performance.

Organizational cultures can be assessed along many dimensions, such as the extent of collaboration versus isolation among people and departments, the importance of control and where control is concentrated, or whether the organization's time orientation is short-range or long-range.[59] Here, we will focus on two specific dimensions: (1) the extent to which the competitive environment requires flexibility or stability, and (2) the extent to which the organization's strategic focus and strength is internal or external. Four categories of culture associated with these differences, as illustrated in Exhibit 14.4, are adaptability, achievement, involvement, and consistency.[60] These four categories relate to the fit among cultural values, strategy, structure, and the environment, with each emphasizing specific values, as shown in the exhibit.

NEW LEADER
ACTION MEMO

Determine your own cultural preferences by completing the exercise in Leader's Leader's Self-Insight 14.2.

An organization may have cultural values that fall into more than one category, or even into all categories. However, successful organizations with strong cultures will lean more toward one particular culture category.

EXHIBIT 14.4 Four Corporate Cultures

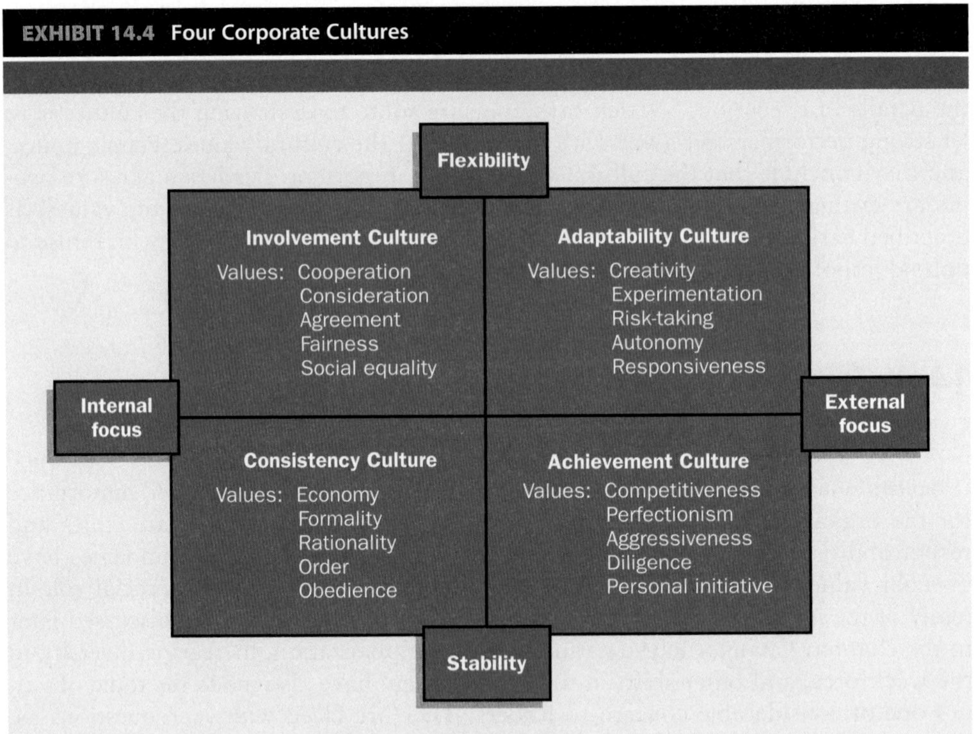

Source: Based on Paul McDonald and Jeffrey Gandz, "Getting Value from Shared Values," *Organizational Dynamics* 21, no. 3 (Winter 1992), pp. 64–76; Deanne N. Den Hartog, Jaap J. VanMuijen, and Paul L. Koopman, "Linking Transformational Leadership and Organizational Culture," *The Journal of Leadership Studies* 3, no. 4 (1996), pp. 68–83; Daniel R. Denison and Aneil K. Mishra, "Toward a Theory of Organizational Culture and Effectiveness," *Organizational Studies* 6, no. 2 (March–April 1995), pp. 204–223; Robert Hooijberg and Frank Petrock, "On Cultural Change: Using the Competing Values Framework to Help Leaders Execute a Transformational Strategy," *Human Resource Management* 32, no. 1 (1993), pp. 29–50; and R. E. Quinn, *Beyond Rational Management: Mastering the Paradoxes and Competing Demands of High Performance* (San Francisco: Jossey-Bass, 1998).

LEADER'S SELF-INSIGHT 14.2

Culture Preference Inventory

The following inventory consists of 14 sets of four responses that relate to typical values or situations facing leaders in organizations. Although each response to a question may appear equally desirable or undesirable, your assignment is to rank the four responses in each row according to your preference. Think of yourself as being in charge of a major department or division in an organization. Rank the responses in each row according to how much you would like each one to be a part of your department. There are no correct or incorrect answers; the scores simply reflect your preferences for different responses.

Rank each of the four in each row using the following scale. You must use all four numbers for each set of four responses.

1. Would not prefer at all
2. Would prefer on occasion
4. Would prefer often
8. Would prefer most of all

	I	II	III	IV
1.	1 Aggressiveness	8 Cost efficiency	2 Experimentation	4 Fairness
2.	1 Perfection	8 Obedience	2 Risk taking	4 Agreement
3.	1 Pursue goals	4 Solve problems	2 Be flexible	8 Develop people's careers
4.	4 Apply careful analysis	8 Rely on proven approaches	2 Look for creative approaches	1 Build consensus
5.	1 Initiative	4 Rationality	2 Responsiveness	8 Collaboration
6.	2 Highly capable	4 Productive and accurate	1 Receptive to brainstorming	8 Committed to the team
7.	1 Be the best in our field	2 Have secure jobs	4 Recognition for innovations	8 Equal status
8.	2 Decide and act quickly	4 Follow plans and priorities	1 Refuse to be pressured	8 Provide guidance and support
9.	4 Realistic	2 Systematic	1 Broad and flexible	8 Sensitive to the needs of others
10.	1 Energetic and ambitious	2 Polite and formal	4 Open-minded	8 Agreeable and self-confident
11.	4 Use key facts	8 Use accurate and complete data	2 Use broad coverage of many options	1 Use limited data and personal opinion
12.	1 Competitive	2 Disciplined	4 Imaginative	8 Supportive
13.	1 Challenging assignments	8 Influence over others	4 Achieving creativity	2 Acceptance by the group
14.	2 Best solution	4 Good working environment	1 New approaches or ideas	8 Personal fulfillment
	26	68	32	84 =210

Scoring and Interpretation

Add the points in each of the four columns—I, II, III, IV. The sum of the point columns should be 210 points. If your sum does not equal 210 points, check your answers and your addition.

The scores represent your preference for I, achievement culture; II, consistency culture; III, adaptability culture; and IV, involvement culture. Your personal values are consistent with the culture for which you achieved the highest score, although all four sets of values exist within you just as they exist within an organization. The specific values you exert as a leader may depend on the group situation, particularly the needs of the external environment. Compare your scores with those of other students and discuss their meaning. Are you pleased with your preferences? Do you think your scores accurately describe your values?

Source: Adapted from Alan J. Rowe and Richard O. Mason, *Managing with Style: A Guide to Understanding, Assessing, and Improving Decision Making* (San Francisco: Jossey-Bass, 1987).

14-4a Adaptability Culture

The **adaptability culture** is characterized by strategic leaders encouraging values that support the organization's ability to interpret and translate signals from the environment into new behavioral responses. Employees have autonomy to make decisions and act freely to meet new needs, and responsiveness to customers is highly valued. Leaders also actively create change by encouraging and rewarding creativity, experimentation, and risk taking. Leaders at TubeMogul have emphasized selection and socialization of employees to build an adaptability culture at the successful digital advertising software company.

IN THE LEAD

Brett Wilson, TubeMogul

Brett Wilson and John Hughes founded TubeMogul while they were MBA students at the UC Berkeley Haas School of Business. The partners won the Haas Business Plan Competition in 2007, which gave them the seed money they needed to get the company started. From the beginning, leaders wanted values of being fast and flexible to guide the company.

"Culture and people are everything," says Wilson, who serves as CEO of TubeMogul. "We were determined to build a company that had a certain culture, and that was just as important to us . . . as the software we were building." The first cultural value at TubeMogul is that people shouldn't be afraid to make mistakes. If people aren't making mistakes, leaders know they're not moving fast enough to keep pace with a fast-changing industry. They encourage people to take risks, be creative, make mistakes, and figure things out. The company also values people who have a high "do-to-say ratio," meaning they have a bias for action and follow through on what they commit to doing. Everyone from the CEO on down is expected to acknowledge mistakes and make quick course corrections as needed.

As the company grew (it now has around 500 employees), leaders wanted to make sure the culture stayed strong. Every person who interviews applicants at TubeMogul goes through an interviewing class where they learn how to screen for culture fit. All new employees attend a class led by Wilson called "Culture and Values," where they learn about the principles that guide the organization. The values, says Wilson, are "the reasons we hire, fire and promote people."[61]

To remain competitive, leaders at TubeMogul know that everyone throughout the organization needs to be innovating and responding quickly to shifting needs in a rapidly growing industry. Many technology and Internet-based companies, like TubeMogul, use the adaptability type of culture, as do many companies in the marketing, electronics, and cosmetics industries, because they must move quickly to satisfy customers.

Adaptability culture culture characterized by values that support the organization's ability to interpret and translate signals from the environment into new behavior responses

Achievement culture culture characterized by a clear vision of the organization's goals and leaders' focus on the achievement of specific targets

14-4b Achievement Culture

The **achievement culture** is characterized by a clear vision of the organization's goals, and leaders focus on the achievement of specific targets such as sales growth, profitability, or market share. An organization concerned with serving specific customers in the external environment but without the need for flexibility and rapid change is suited to the achievement culture. This is a results-oriented culture that values competitiveness, aggressiveness, personal initiative, and the willingness to work long and hard to achieve results. An emphasis on winning is the glue that holds the organization together.[62]

Anheuser-Busch InBev reflects an achievement culture. Professionalism, ambition, competitiveness, and aggressiveness are key values. Managers keep employees focused on achieving high sales and profit levels, and those who meet the demanding goals are handsomely rewarded. Bonuses and promotions are based on performance, not seniority, and top executives are unapologetic about giving special treatment to high achievers. Distribution center managers frequently start the day with a sort of pep rally reviewing the day's sales targets and motivating people to get out and sell more beer.[63]

NEW LEADER
ACTION MEMO

As a leader, you can align the organization's culture to its strategy and the needs of the external environment. You can choose to implement the appropriate culture (adaptability, achievement, involvement, or consistency) depending on environmental requirements and the organization's strategic focus.

14-4c Involvement Culture

The **involvement culture** has an internal focus on the involvement and participation of employees to meet changing expectations from the external environment. More than any other, this culture places value on meeting the needs of organization members. Companies with involvement cultures are generally friendly places to work, and employees may seem almost like a family. Leaders emphasize cooperation, consideration of both employees and customers, and avoiding status differences. Leaders put a premium on fairness and reaching agreement with others.

Consider the approach to culture taken by William Rogers, CEO of UKRD, which owns a number of commercial radio stations in the United Kingdom: "If your people are the key to great performance, then facilitating their enjoyment, engagement, and commitment are fundamental to ultimate success.... Our values are intended to change people's lives for the better." When UKRD leaders visit one of the 17 stations around the country for a meeting, they build in plenty of time to talk to people and say good-byes around the station. Every year, all of the company's teams take a day out to talk together about the values, behaviors, and working environment they want. UKRD has a "cast-iron commitment" to a *people first* culture, and any manager who doesn't live up to that is asked to leave.[64]

14-4d Consistency Culture

The **consistency culture** has an internal focus and a dependability orientation for a stable environment. The culture supports a methodical, rational, orderly way of doing business. Following the rules and being thrifty are valued. The organization succeeds by being highly integrated and efficient.

Safeco Insurance has functioned well with a consistency culture. Employees take their coffee breaks at an assigned time, and a dress code specifies white shirts and suits for men and no beards. However, employees like this culture—reliability is highly valued and extra work isn't required. The consistency culture works for the insurance company, and Safeco succeeds because it can be trusted to deliver on insurance policies as agreed.[65]In today's fast-changing world, very few organizations operate in a stable environment, and most leaders are shifting away from this type of culture because of a need for greater flexibility. However, even some software companies, such as SAS Institute and Pacific Edge Software (now part of Serena Software), have used some elements of the consistency culture to keep projects on time and on budget and to ensure saner lives for employees. Emphasis on order and discipline means the formal workweek at SAS can be 35 hours, for instance.[66]

Involvement culture culture with an internal focus on the involvement and participation of employees to meet changing expectations from the external environment

Consistency culture culture with an internal focus and consistency orientation for a stable environment

Each of the four cultures can be successful. The relative emphasis on various cultural values depends on the organization's strategic focus and the needs of the external environment. Leaders might have preferences for the values associated with one type of culture, but they learn to adjust the values they emulate and encourage, depending on the needs of the organization. It is the responsibility of leaders to ensure that organizations don't get stuck relying on cultural values that worked in the past but are no longer effective. As environmental conditions and strategy change, leaders work to instill new cultural values to help the organization meet new needs.

14-5 ETHICAL VALUES IN ORGANIZATIONS

Organizations incorporate many types of values into their cultures. Taunton Press, for example, lists its cultural values as "integrity, teamwork, excellence, independent thinking, and creativity." Zappos, the online retailer, has a slightly offbeat list of core values that includes: "create fun and a little weirdness," "deliver WOW through service," and "be adventurous, creative, and open-minded."[67] Some values that seem to be important to many companies today, whatever the industry or type of culture, include open communication, teamwork, and quality.

In addition, of the values that make up an organization's culture, ethical values have gained renewed emphasis in today's era of financial scandals and moral lapses. **Ethics** is the code of principles and values that governs the behavior of a person or group with respect to what is right or wrong. Ethics sets standards as to what is good or bad in conduct and decision making.[68] Chapter 6 discussed ethics and moral leadership in detail.

Most organizations that remain successful over the long term have leaders who include ethical values as part of the formal policies and informal cultures of their companies. Commentators on the crisis a few years ago in the mortgage system, for instance, point out that a big part of the problem was a lack of ethical values that guided employee behavior. "Technical economics is crucial to understanding the crisis, but only goes so far," one wrote. "There was a hint that more than technical factors were involved when subprime loans were referred to as 'liar's loans.'"[69] In response to the recent crisis, some business schools and students are taking a fresh look at how future business leaders are trained.

Ethics
the code of moral principles and values that governs the behavior of a person or group with respect to what is right and wrong

IN THE LEAD

Harvard Business School, Columbia Business School, Yale School of Management, Wharton School of the University of Pennsylvania

Some members of a recent graduating class of Harvard Business School did something unusual. They signed a voluntary student-led pledge saying that the goal of a business leader is to "serve the greater good" and promising that they would act responsibly and ethically and refrain from advancing their "own narrow ambitions" at the expense of others.

At Harvard and other business schools, there has been an explosion of interest in ethics classes and activities that focus on personal and corporate responsibility. Many students, as well as educators, are recognizing a need to give future leaders a deeper understanding of how to practice ethical leadership rather than just how to make money. At Columbia

Business School, which requires an ethics course, students formed a popular "Leadership and Ethics Board" that sponsors lectures and other activities. Yale School of Management has developed sessions in its core curriculum related to the recent crisis and worked with the Aspen Institute to create a curriculum aimed at teaching business students how to act on their values at work. About 55 business schools are using all or part of the curriculum in pilot programs.

Professor Diana C. Robertson at the Wharton School of the University of Pennsylvania says she sees a generational shift, with today's students expressing a greater concern for how organizations affect the community, the lives of employees, and the natural environment. "There is a feeling that we want our lives to mean something more and to run organizations for the greater good," said Max Anderson, one of the organizers of Harvard's pledge. "No one wants to have their future criticized as a place filled with unethical behaviors."[70]

Changing how future leaders are trained could be one key to solving the ethics deficit pervading organizations. In a survey about unethical conduct in the workplace, more than half of the respondents cited poor leadership as a factor.[71] Leaders can create and sustain a climate that emphasizes ethical behavior for all employees.

14-6 VALUES-BASED LEADERSHIP

Values in organizations are developed and strengthened primarily through **values-based leadership**, an influence relationship between leaders and followers that is based on shared, strongly internalized values that emphasize the common good and are consistently advocated and acted upon by the leader. Values-based leaders give meaning to activities and goals by connecting them to deeply held values.[72]

Leaders influence organizational culture by demonstrating their personal values and by practicing spiritual leadership.

14-6a Personal Values

Employees learn about values from watching leaders. Values-based leaders generate a high level of trust and respect from employees based not just on stated values but on the courage, determination, and self-sacrifice they demonstrate in upholding those values. Leaders have to discover their own personal values and the values they want to guide the team or organization, and actively communicate the values to others through both words and actions.[73] When faced with difficult decisions, values-based leaders know what they stand for, and they have the courage to act on their principles.

Values-based leadership
an influence relationship between leaders and followers that is based on shared, strongly internalized values that emphasize the common good and are consistently advocated and acted upon by the leader

Consider the example of Costco, where cofounder and former CEO Jim Sinegal and new CEO Craig Jelinek believe treating people right matters.

IN THE LEAD

Jim Sinegal and Craig Jelinek, Costco

In 2009, as the recession deepened and many employers were slashing jobs and cutting salaries, Costco CEO Jim Sinegal was handing out raises. Costco is the second-largest retailer in the United States, behind Walmart, and while Walmart leaders are seeing growing troubles, Costco leaders seem to be seeing nothing but growing sales and profits. Costco was one of the top performers during the recession and sales and memberships continue to increase, proving that paying employees above-average wages and treating them well in other ways can pay off.

Minimum wage in the United States is still a paltry $7.25 per hour, but Costco's starting hourly wage is around $12.00. Because people stay around so long, the average hourly wage paid to Costco workers is $20.89, and the company offers good health-care benefits even to part-time employees. Current CEO Craig Jelinek wrote a public letter urging Congress to increase the minimum wage. The letter sparked an interest in Costco's culture and business philosophy. Wall Street has repeatedly been critical of Costco leaders, asking them to reduce wages and health benefits. Instead, leaders have increased them every three years since the company began. In 2009, according to CFO Richard Galanti, "the first thing out of Jim [Sinegal's] mouth was, 'This economy is bad. We should be figuring out how to give them more, not less.' " Galanti admits Costco could make more money if the average wage was two or three dollars lower. "But we're not going to do it."

Jelinek, who took over as CEO in 2012, has vowed to continue Sinegal's values-based legacy. For instance, Jelinek is paid well, but the CEO earns only about 28 times more than the average employee, whereas CEOs in many companies earn a whopping 380 times more than the average employee. Costco doesn't hire business school graduates as managers. It cultivates employees who work the floor and sponsors them through graduate school. Seventy percent of Costco's warehouse managers started by ringing cash registers and pushing carts. Turnover is around 5 percent, extremely low for the retail industry. "If you treat consumers with respect and treat employees with respect, good things are going to happen to you," Jelinek says.[74]

Leaders at Costco believe values of taking a long-term view and treating people humanely are just good business. Other conscientious companies known for treating people well, such as Nordstrom, Whole Foods Market, and the Container Store, are supporting that idea. All have prospered and outpaced their rivals in recent years. "A lot of people working [in retail] go home and live below the poverty line. You expect that person to come in and develop a rapport with customers who may be spending more than the person is making in a week?" says Doug Stephens, founder of the consulting firm Retail Prophet.[75]

NEW LEADER
ACTION MEMO

As a leader, you can be ethical and act on high moral principles in your daily behavior. You can help people find deeper fulfillment in their jobs. Complete Leader's Self-Insight 14.3 to see if you might be a leader who incorporates spiritual values as part of the corporate culture.

The values at Costco are based largely on the personal values of founders Jim Sinegal and Jeffrey Brotman. Several factors contribute to an individual leader's values. Every individual brings a set of personal beliefs, personality characteristics, and behavior traits to the job. The family backgrounds and spiritual beliefs of leaders often provide principles and values by which they conduct business, and these are sometimes incorporated into the organizational culture. In terms of ethical values, personality characteristics such as ego strength, self-confidence, and a strong sense of independence may enable leaders to make the right decisions even if those decisions might be unpopular.

14-6b Spiritual Values

Costco is an example of a company where leaders incorporate values that might be considered spiritual into their workplace practices and policies.[76] Managers who

LEADER'S SELF-INSIGHT 14.3

How Spiritual Are You?

Instructions: Think about your current life. Indicate whether each of the following items is Mostly False or Mostly True for you.

	Mostly False	Mostly True
1. I often reflect on the meaning of life.	______	______
2. I want to find a community where I can grow spiritually.	______	______
3. I have made real personal sacrifices in order to make the world a better place.	______	______
4. Sometimes when I look at an ordinary thing I feel that I am seeing it fresh for the first time.	______	______
5. I sometimes have unexpected flashes of insight or understanding while relaxing.	______	______
6. It is important to me to find meaning and mission in the world.	______	______
7. I often feel a strong sense of unity or connection with all the people around me.	______	______
8. I have had experiences that made my role in life clear to me.	______	______
9. After reflecting on something for a long time, I have learned to trust my feelings rather than logical reasons.	______	______
10. I am often transfixed by loveliness in nature.	______	______

Scoring and Interpretation

Spiritual leadership engages people in higher values and missions and tries to create a corporate culture based on love and community rather than fear and separation. Spiritual leadership is not for everyone, but when spiritual ideals guide a leader's behavior, an excellent culture can be created.

Add the number of Mostly True answers for your score: ______________. A score of 7 or above indicates that you are highly spiritual and will likely become a values-based or spiritual leader. A score of 4–6 would suggest that you are spiritually average. A score of 0–3 means that you may be skeptical about developing spiritual awareness.

Source: Based on Kirsi Tirri, Petri Nokelainen, and Martin Ubani, "Conceptual Definition and Empirical Validation of the Spiritual Sensitivity Scale," *Journal of Empirical Theology* 19, no. 1 (2006), pp. 37–62; and Jeffrey Kluger, "Is God in Our Genes?" *Time* (October 25, 2004), pp. 62–72.

incorporate spiritual values in addition to the traditional mental and behavioral aspects of leadership tend to be successful as leaders. Values and practices considered as spiritual ideals include integrity, humility, respect, appreciation for the contributions of others, fair treatment, and personal reflection. This approach to leadership can be effective because many people are struggling with how to combine their spiritual journey and their work life.[77]

Polls indicate that American managers as well as workers would like deeper fulfillment on the job, and evidence suggests that workplace spirituality programs provide people with better mental and physical health, an enhanced sense of self-worth, and greater personal growth, while organizations benefit from increased productivity along with reduced absenteeism and turnover.[78] Some companies have put chaplains on the payroll to help people as they struggle with problems that might or might not relate to the business. "You're at work 8 to 10 hours a day," says Tim Embry, owner of American LubeFast, a chain of oil change companies. "Work is where people are at and where they need to be cared for."[79]

However, even leaders who don't provide formal spirituality programs can lead with spiritual values. Consider India-born Sanjiv Das, currently serving as chief of staff for First Data Corporation. Das was CEO of CitiMortgage from 2008 to 2013, taking over the job in the midst of the U.S. mortgage crisis. Das approached the job with goals of keeping people in their homes and keeping employees focused on the help they could offer to alleviate the financial pressure of those caught in economic turmoil. By doing so, he helped demoralized employees find purpose, meaning, and self-respect again. CitiMortgage went further than many banks to help people keep their homes. Das pioneered a first-of-its-kind program to temporarily lower payments and waive interest and penalties for borrowers who had lost their jobs. Das says his leadership approach is based in the spiritual values he learned growing up in Delhi—such as maintaining purpose and integrity during difficult times and helping others rather than trying to acquire more materials goods for oneself.[80]

Spiritual leadership is the display of values, attitudes, and behaviors necessary to intrinsically motivate oneself and others toward a sense of spiritual expression through calling and membership.[81] As illustrated in Exhibit 14.5, spiritual leaders start by creating a vision through which organization participants experience a sense of calling that gives meaning to their work. An appropriate vision would have broad appeal, reflect high ideals, and establish a standard of excellence. Second, spiritual leaders establish a corporate culture based on altruistic love. Altruistic love includes forgiveness, genuine caring, compassion, kindness, honesty, patience, courage, and appreciation, which enables people to experience a sense of membership and feel understood. Spiritual leaders also engage hope and faith to help the organization achieve desired outcomes. Faith is demonstrated through action. Faith means believing in the ability to excel, exercising self-control, and striving for excellence to achieve a personal best. A leader's hope/faith includes perseverance, endurance, stretch goals, and a clear expectation of victory through effort.[82] As illustrated in Exhibit 14.5, spiritual leadership behaviors enable employees to have a sense of calling that provides deeper life meaning through work. Spiritual leadership also provides a sense of membership through a work community in which one feels understood and appreciated. The outcome for the organization is improved commitment and productivity.

Spiritual leadership
the display of values, attitudes, and behaviors necessary to intrinsically motivate oneself and others toward a sense of spiritual expression through calling and membership

Spiritual leadership can decrease or eliminate negative emotions and conflicts in the workplace and provide a stronger foundation for personal well-being.[83] The four main types of destructive emotions are (1) fear, including anxiety and worry;

EXHIBIT 14.5 Model of Spiritual Leadership

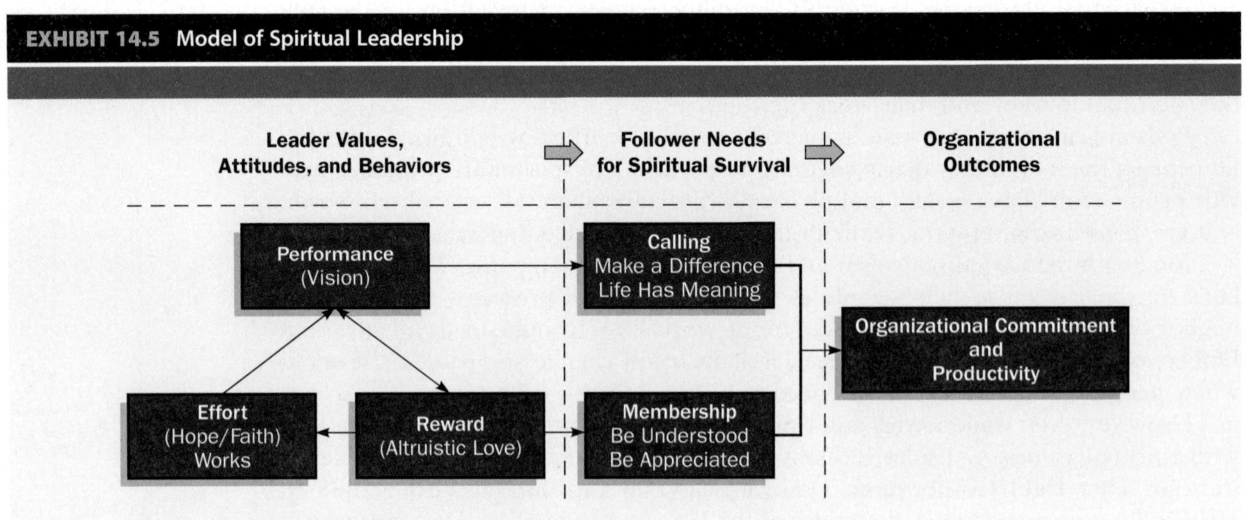

Source: Based on Louis W. Fry, Sean T. Hannah, Michael Noel, and Fred O. Walumbwa, "Impact of Spiritual Leadership on Unit Performance," *The Leadership Quarterly* 22 (2011), pp. 259–270; and Louis W. Fry, "Toward a Theory of Spiritual Leadership," *The Leadership Quarterly* 14 (2003), pp. 693–727. Used with permission.

(2) anger, including hostility, resentment, and jealousy; (3) sense of failure, including discouragement and depressed mood; and (4) pride, including prejudice, selfishness, and conceit. These destructive emotions typically arise from fear of losing something important or not getting something one desires.

Spiritual leadership is related to ideas discussed in Chapter 8 on motivation and Chapter 6 on moral leadership. The spiritual leader addresses followers' higher-order needs for membership and self-actualization. This is intrinsic motivation at its best because work provides interest and enjoyment for its own sake. People are actively engaged in tasks they find meaningful, interesting, or fun. Intrinsic motivation is typically associated with better learning, higher performance, and enhanced well-being. Spiritual leadership often provides substantial autonomy and self-management, for example, through participation in empowered teams that direct activities and do work that is significant and meaningful. An employee's task involvement is under the control of the individual or team, thereby providing feedback and satisfaction through achievement, performance, and problem solving. The spiritual leader, like the servant leader described in Chapter 6, engages people in work that provides both service and meaning and creates a positive impact on employees and the community.

LEADERSHIP ESSENTIALS

- Creating the right culture is one of the most important jobs of the leader. Culture is the set of key values, norms, and assumptions that is shared by members of an organization and taught to new members as correct. Culture serves two critically important functions—to integrate organizational members so they know how to relate to one another and to help the organization adapt to the environment.
- Strong, responsive cultures have a positive impact on organizational outcomes. Creating and influencing a responsive culture is important because the right culture can drive high performance. Leaders build high-performance cultures by emphasizing both values and solid business operations as the drivers of organizational success.
- A culture gap exists when an organization's culture is not in alignment with the needs of the external environment or company strategy. Leaders use ceremonies, stories, symbols, specialized language, selection, and socialization to instill and strengthen the needed cultural values. In addition, leaders influence cultural values most strongly through their daily actions.
- Leaders consider the external environment and the company's vision and strategy in determining which values are important for the organization. Four types of culture may exist in organizations: adaptability, achievement, involvement, and consistency. Each type emphasizes different values, although organizations may have values that fall into more than one category.
- Many types of values make up an organization's culture; ethical values are considered among the most important. Ethics is the code of moral principles and values that governs the behavior of a person or group with respect to what is right or wrong. Leaders shape cultural values through values-based leadership. They know their personal values and beliefs and the values they want the organization to honor. Many good leaders practice spiritual leadership, which

means displaying values, attitudes, and behaviors that motivate people toward a sense of spiritual expression through calling and membership. The principles of spiritual leadership can improve both organizational performance and employee well-being.

DISCUSSION QUESTIONS

1. How difficult would it be for you as a leader to fire someone who is bringing in big sales and profits for the company but not living up to the cultural values? Explain.
2. How might leaders use symbolic acts to strengthen a cultural value of teamwork and collaboration? How about a value of customer care and responsiveness?
3. Describe the culture for an organization you are familiar with. Identify some physical artifacts—such as logo, mascot, building, advertising images—associated with the company and discuss what underlying values these suggest. What did you learn?
4. Name one or two companies in the news that seem to have strong corporate cultures, and describe whether the results have been positive or negative. Discuss how a strong culture could have either positive or negative consequences for an organization.
5. As a leader, how might you recognize a culture gap? What techniques might you use to influence and change cultural values when necessary?
6. Compare and contrast the achievement culture with the involvement culture. What are some possible *disadvantages* of having a strong involvement culture? A strong achievement culture?
7. If you were the leader of a small technology firm, how might you imprint in people's minds the values shown in Exhibit 14.2 for responsive cultures in order to create a high-performance culture? Be specific with your ideas.
8. Discuss the meaning of *calling* and *membership*, as related to spiritual leadership. Identify an organization or leader that uses these concepts. To what extent were these concepts present where you have worked?
9. If a leader directs her health-care company to reward hospital managers strictly on hospital profits, what kind of values is she encouraging within the company culture? Discuss.
10. Some mortgage company leaders have said that providing subprime mortgages (earn a commission by making loans to people at high interest rates who may have difficulty making the payments) was based on the noble purpose of giving poor people a chance to participate in the American dream of home ownership. Discuss your opinion of this explanation.
11. Some people believe that all good leadership is spiritual in nature. Others think spiritual values have no place at work. Discuss these two opposing viewpoints.

LEADERSHIP AT WORK

Walk the Talk

Often in an organization the culture is characterized both by what people say (talk) and by what people actually do (walk). When this happens, there is a gap between organizational leaders' espoused values and the values in action within the company. One example would be an espoused value of "a balanced life for employees," whereas managers and employees are actually expected to work nights and weekends to meet demanding performance goals. This is the difference between the "walk" and the "talk" in an organization.

Your assignment for this exercise is to think of one example in your own student or work experience where the walk and talk in a corporate culture did not align. Why do you think the gap occurred? Then interview four other people for examples of when an organization's espoused values did not align with the values in action. Also ask them why they think the walk and talk differed. Summarize the findings from your interviews:

My example (and why):

Second person's examples (and why):

Third person's examples (and why):

Fourth person's examples (and why):

Fifth person's examples (and why):

What patterns and themes do you see in the responses? Is there a common type of walk/talk gap? What is the most common reason why these gaps occur? Which is the real culture—the leader's espoused values or the values in action?

In Class: Students can be organized into small groups in class and do this exercise all at once. Each person in the circle can give examples from student or work experiences of an organization's walk not fitting its talk and explain why he or she thinks the gaps occurred. Then students can identify the common themes from their discussion. The instructor can help students probe into this issue by writing good examples from students on the board and asking students to help identify key themes. Students can be engaged to discuss the walk versus talk phenomenon via key questions, such as: What does it mean to you when you discover a walk/talk gap in your organization? Are espoused values or values in action more indicative of a company's culture (or are both the culture)? Are walk/talk gaps likely to be associated with a responsive culture? A strong culture? Do symbols, stories, ceremonies, and other signals of corporate culture mean what they imply?

LEADERSHIP DEVELOPMENT: CASES FOR ANALYSIS

Culture Clash

CEO Jane Lionel has some hard decisions to make with regard to some of the company's older hands, and even on the eve of that decision, I believe she is wavering about what she should do. I will be in that meeting, assisting with that decision, and I'm not certain which way to go, either. And so here I am, sorting through and writing down my thoughts.

When Jim Lionel started manufacturing heavy-duty construction equipment here in Alaska 40 years ago, his personal management style reflected the ruggedness of Alaska and the construction business. He understood that he was producing tough equipment for tough men working in an unforgiving environment. At 6′ 5″ and over 300 pounds, Lionel personified the bigger-than-life image of Alaskan workers. He had a no-nonsense management style. He coddled no one. Jim Lionel expected and got results. He chewed—not smoked—a cigar. I swear that in the 30 years I worked for him, I never saw that thing lit up as he barked—yes, *barked*—orders.

I'd have to say that Jim Lionel gained respect because he always delivered and his word was his bond. But he never achieved admiration. There was no finesse. A new HR director once mentioned to me that Jim should create bonds with his workers through techniques such as management by walking around. I said, "Believe me, you do *not* want him walking around—that simply means he's stressed and he's mad." You could actually *feel* him and hear him before you saw him, and as one employee said, "When he barked your name, your heart stopped, because until that moment you were certain that he did not *know* your name." We all figured that his temper would explode one day and he would die on the shop floor from a heart attack. Then suddenly, he did.

Following his death, we were certain that the company would have to be sold in order to continue operations. However, Jim's one true friend and confidante was his wife Jane, and with unanimous board approval, she moved in to take his place as the head of the company. The initial concerns and fears of employees were soon calmed. Jane knew the company to a degree that surprised employees. But her management style, developed over 20 years as head of marketing for a regional health-care organization, was in stark contrast to that of her husband.

While Jane shared her husband's goals and high standards for quality and on-time delivery, she also believed in the importance of demonstrating to employees their value to the company. She not only communicated her vision, but she took the time to listen to the employees, to give them opportunities to voice opinions, express concerns, and submit ideas. She met regularly with individual departments and assisted line workers in the movement toward self-managed teams. The reaction from workers was positive. And a year later we can see a huge change. Production is up slightly, but the real change can be seen in people's attitudes and pride in their jobs. Communication and the overall level of civility among employees have improved dramatically. But while these cultural changes have been embraced by the majority of workers and supervisors, there are two glaring exceptions.

Supervisors Curtis Willett and Morgan Elder were among the first people hired by Jim Lionel. Their long service to the organization and their consistency in meeting all production goals and deadlines is impressive. They take pride in their ability to push themselves and their crews relentlessly. However, their management styles are a throw-back to the old culture. They succeed by intimidation. The civility and cooperation that characterizes other parts of the plant is shoved aside or drowned out in a barrage of yelling. "Shock and Awe," the joint nickname briefly given to the two men by employees following the 2003 U.S. aerial assault on Iraq, has been revived. If these men are aware of the label, they are probably proud.

So here's our dilemma: They are too old to change. Curtis and Morgan not only do not fit the new culture, but through tactics of control and intimidation they also encourage workers to ignore the new cultural initiatives. Everyone is on board except the employees in these two adjoining areas of the plant. So we cannot reach the full potential of the new culture while the old culture pulls us back. Fire them? Demote them? I don't think so. They've done nothing wrong. Their crews are meeting their production and quality targets. Furthermore, these two guys have been with the company for 40 years. A move on our part that appears unjustified opens us to an age discrimination suit. But I also don't see how we can change the culture unless they leave.

So, we meet tomorrow to determine what we can do. Writing about a problem usually helps me to sort things out. When I finish, I generally have an answer or at least an idea about how to proceed. I've finished writing. And I haven't got a clue.

QUESTIONS

1. What options do you think Jane and her management team should consider with regard to these two long-time supervisors? Discuss the positives and negatives of each option.
2. Do you think it is appropriate for Jane to remove two long-time, high-performing managers in order to create a new culture for everyone else? Why? Consider the material in Exhibit 14.3 in your answer.
3. What do you recommend that Jane do? Explain why.

5 Star and Amtech

5 Star Electronics and Amtech Electronics both manufacture integrated circuits and other electronic parts as subcontractors for large manufacturers. Both 5 Star and Amtech are located in Ohio and often bid on contracts as competitors. As subcontractors, both firms benefited from the electronics boom of the 1990s, and both looked forward to growth and expansion. 5 Star has annual sales of about $100 million and employs 950 people. Amtech has annual sales of $80 million and employs about 800 people. 5 Star typically reports greater net profits than Amtech.

The president of 5 Star, John Tyler, believed that 5 Star was the far superior company. Tyler credited his firm's greater effectiveness to his managers' ability to run a "tight ship." 5 Star had detailed organization charts and job descriptions. Tyler believed that everyone should have clear responsibilities and narrowly defined jobs, which generates efficient performance and high company profits. Employees were generally satisfied with their jobs at 5 Star, although some managers wished for more empowerment opportunities.

Amtech's president, Jim Rawls, did not believe in organization charts. He believed organization charts just put artificial barriers between specialists who should be working together. He encouraged people to communicate face to face rather than with written memos. The head of mechanical engineering said, "Jim spends too much time making sure everyone understands what we're doing and listening to suggestions." Rawls was concerned with employee satisfaction and wanted everyone to feel part of the organization. Employees were often rotated among departments so they would be familiar with activities throughout the company. Although Amtech wasn't as profitable as 5 Star, they were able to bring new products on line more quickly, work bugs out of new designs more accurately, and achieve higher quality because of superb employee commitment and collaboration.

It is the end of May, and John Tyler, president of 5 Star, has just announced the acquisition of Amtech Electronics. Both management teams are proud of their cultures and have unflattering opinions of the other's. Each company's customers are rather loyal, and their technologies are compatible, so Tyler believes a combined company will be even more effective, particularly in a time of rapid change in both technology and products.

The Amtech managers resisted the idea of an acquisition, but the 5 Star president is determined to unify the two companies quickly, increase the new firm's marketing position, and revitalize product lines—all by year end.

QUESTIONS

1. Using the competing values model in Exhibit 14.4, what type of culture (adaptability, achievement, involvement, consistency) would you say is dominant at 5 Star? At Amtech? What is your evidence?
2. Is there a culture gap? Which type of culture do you think is most appropriate for the newly merged company? Why?
3. If you were John Tyler, what techniques would you use to integrate and shape the culture to overcome the culture gap?

Source: Adapted from John F. Veiga, "The Paradoxical Twins: Acme and Omega Electronics," in John F. Veiga and John N. Yanouzas, *The Dynamics of Organization Theory* (St. Paul: West Publishing, 1984), pp. 132–138; and "Alpha and Amtech," Harvard Business School Case 9–488-003, published by the President and Fellows of Harvard College, 1988.

REFERENCES

1. Laura Stevens, "UPS Drivers Who Avoid Accidents for 25 Years Get Arm Patch and Bomber Jacket; Those in the Coveted Circle of Honor Have Dodged Taxis, Traffic and Bears," *The Wall Street Journal* (June 4, 2014), http://www.wsj.com/articles/ups-drivers-who-avoid-accidents-for-25-years-get-arm-patch-and-bomber-jacket-1401933961 (accessed November 27, 2015).
2. Sanam Islam, "Execs See Link to Bottom Line; Gap Is Closing; More Firms Keen to Be Seen as Best Corporate Culture," *National Post* (November 19, 2008), p. FP.16; Jeremy Kahn, "What Makes a Company Great?" *Fortune* (October 26, 1998), p. 218; James C. Collins and Jerry I. Porras, *Built to Last: Successful Habits of Visionary Companies* (New York: HarperBusiness, 1994); and James C. Collins, "Change Is Good—But First Know What Should Never Change," *Fortune* (May 29, 1995), p. 141.
3. Islam, "Execs See Link to Bottom Line."
4. T. E. Deal and A. A. Kennedy, *The New Corporate Cultures: Revitalizing the Workforce after Downsizing, Mergers, and Reengineering* (New York: Basic Books, 2000).
5. Islam, "Execs See Link to Bottom Line."
6. Andrew Klein, "Corporate Culture: Its Value as a Resource for Competitive Advantage," *Journal of Business Strategy* 32, no. 2 (2011), pp. 21–28; Yoash Wiener, "Forms of Value Systems: A Focus on Organizational Effectiveness and Culture Change and Maintenance," *Academy of Management Review* 13 (1988), pp. 534–545; V. Lynne Meek, "Organizational Culture: Origins and Weaknesses," *Organization Studies* 9 (1988), pp. 453–473; and John J. Sherwood, "Creating Work Cultures with Competitive Advantage," *Organizational Dynamics* (Winter 1988), pp. 5–27.
7. Geoff Colvin, "The Defiant One," *Fortune* (April 30, 2007), pp. 86–92.
8. W. Jack Duncan, "Organizational Culture: Getting a 'Fix' on an Elusive Concept," *Academy of Management Executive* 3 (1989), pp. 229–236; Linda Smircich, "Concepts of Culture and Organizational Analysis," *Administrative Science Quarterly* 28 (1983), pp. 339–358; and Andrew D. Brown and Ken Starkey, "The Effect of Organizational Culture on Communication and Information," *Journal of Management Studies* 31, no. 6 (November 1994), pp. 807–828.
9. Edgar H. Schein, "Organizational Culture," *American Psychologist* 45, no. 2 (February 1990), pp. 109–119.
10. This discussion of the levels of culture is based on Edgar H. Schein, *Organizational Culture and Leadership*, 2nd ed. (San Francisco: Jossey-Bass, 1992), pp. 3–27.
11. Chris Blackhurst, "Sir Stuart Hampson," *Management Today* (July 2005), pp. 48–53.
12. John P. Kotter and James L. Heskett, *Corporate Culture and Performance* (New York: The Free Press, 1992), p. 6.
13. Peter B. Scott-Morgan, "Barriers to a High-Performance Business," *Management Review* (July 1993), pp. 37–41.
14. Adam Bryant, "Natarajan Chandrasekaran of Tata Consultancy Services: Making a Habit of Accountability," *The New York Times* (February 10, 2015), http://www.nytimes.com/2015/02/15/business/natarajan-chandrasekaran-of-tata-consultancy-services-making-a-habit-of-accountability.html?_r=0 (accessed November 27, 2015).

15. Arthur Ciancutti and Thomas Steding, "Trust Fund," *Business 2.0* (June 13, 2000), pp. 105–117.
16. Robert Bruce Shaw and Mark Ronald, "Changing Culture—Patience Is Not a Virtue," *Leader to Leader* (Fall 2012), pp. 50–55.
17. Example described in Shaw and Ronald, "Changing Culture—Patience Is Not a Virtue."
18. Lisa DiCarlo, "How Lou Gerstner Got IBM to Dance," *Forbes.com* (November 11, 2002), http://www.forbes.com/2002/11/11/cx_ld_1112gerstner.html (accessed June 5, 2013).
19. Bernard Arogyaswamy and Charles M. Byles, "Organizational Culture: Internal and External Fits," *Journal of Management* 13 (1987), pp. 647–659.
20. William D. Cohan, *House of Cards: A Tale of Hubris and Wretched Excess on Wall Street* (New York: Doubleday 2009); Chuck Leddy, "When Wall Street Bet the House," *Boston Globe* (March 28, 2009), p. G8; and Robin Sidel and Kate Kelly, "Bear Stearns a Year Later: From Fabled to Forgotten—Bear's Name, and Culture, Fade Away after J.P. Morgan's Fire-Sale Deal," *The Wall Street Journal* (March 14, 2009), p. B1.
21. Kotter and Heskett, *Corporate Culture and Performance.*
22. This discussion and the exhibit are based on Kotter and Heskett, *Corporate Culture and Performance*, p. 51
23. Ralph H. Kilmann, Mary J. Saxton, Roy Serpa, and Associates, *Gaining Control of the Corporate Culture* (San Francisco: Jossey-Bass, 1985).
24. Larry Mallak, "Understanding and Changing Your Organization's Culture," *Industrial Management* (March–April 2001), pp. 18–24.
25. Kris Maher, "Post Massey Merger, Alpha CEO Makes Safety Priority No. 1" (Boss Talk), *The Wall Street Journal* (August 8, 2011), http://online.wsj.com/article/SB10001424053111903885604576490391464803316.html (accessed June 5, 2013).
26. Reported in Chip Jarnagan and John W. Slocum, Jr., "Creating Corporate Cultures Through Mythopoetic Leadership," *Organizational Dynamics* 36, no. 3 (2007), pp. 288–302.
27. Jennifer A. Chatman and Sandra Eunyoung Cha, "Leading by Leveraging Culture," *California Management Review* 45, no. 4 (Summer 2003), pp. 20–34; and Jeff Rosenthal and Mary Ann Masarech, "High-Performance Cultures: How Values Can Drive Business Results," *Journal of Organizational Excellence* 22, no. 2 (Spring 2003), pp. 3–18.
28. Abby Ghobadian and Nicholas O'Regan, "The Link between Culture, Strategy and Performance in Manufacturing SMEs," *Journal of General Management* 28, no. 1 (Autumn, 2002), pp. 16–34; G. G. Gordon and N. DiTomaso, "Predicting Corporate Performance from Organisational Culture," *Journal of Management Studies* 29, no. 6 (1992), pp. 783–798; G. A. Marcoulides and R. H. Heck, "Organizational Culture and Performance: Proposing and Testing a Model," *Organization Science* 4 (1993), pp. 209–225; Micah R. Kee, "Corporate Culture Makes a Fiscal Difference," *Industrial Management* (November–December 2003), pp. 16–20; and Rosenthal and Masarech, "High-Performance Cultures: How Values Can Drive Business Results."
29. Kotter and Heskett, *Corporate Culture and Performance.*
30. Tressie Wright Muldrow, Timothy Buckley, and Brigitte W. Schay, "Creating High-Performance Organizations in the Public Sector," *Human Resource Management* 41, no. 3 (Fall 2002), pp. 341–354.
31. This section is based on Rosenthal and Masarech, "High-Performance Cultures: How Values Can Drive Business Results."
32. Nelson D. Schwartz, "One Brick at a Time," *Fortune* (June 12, 2006), pp. 45–46; and Nelson D. Schwartz, "Lego's Rebuilds Legacy," *International Herald Tribune* (September 5, 2009).
33. Evelyn M. Ruslie, "Zynga's Tough Culture Risks a Talent Drain," *The New York Times Online* (November 27, 2011), http://dealbook.nytimes.com/2011/11/27/zyngas-tough-culture-risks-a-talent-drain/ (accessed June 18, 2012); Thomas Lee, "Mark Pincus Is Back as CEO, Because No One Could Stop Him," *SFGate* (April 14, 2015), http://www.sfgate.com/business/article/Mark-Pincus-is-back-as-CEO-because-no-one-could-6197313.php (accessed November 30, 2015); and Matthew Lynley, "Mark Pincus Is Back — And His Vintage Management Style Might Be, Too," *TechCrunch* (May 16, 2015), http://techcrunch.com/2015/05/06/mark-pincus-is-back-and-his-vintage-management-style-might-be-too/ (accessed November 30, 2015).
34. Rosenthal and Masarech, "High-Performance Cultures."
35. Dave Ulrich, Steve Kerr, and Ron Ashkenas, *The GE Work-Out* (New York: McGraw-Hill, 2002), pp. 238–230.
36. "Core Value: Teamwork," segment in Leigh Buchanan, "2011 Top Small Company Workplaces: Core Values," *Inc.* (June 2011), pp. 60–74; and "Our Story," Menlo Innovations Web site, http://www.menloinnovations.com/our-story/history and http://www.menloinnovations.com/our-story/culture (accessed September 12, 2011).
37. Reggie Van Lee, Lisa Fabish, and Nancy McGaw, "The Value of Corporate Values: A Booz Allen Hamilton/Aspen Institute Survey," *strategy+ business* 39 (Summer 2005), pp. 52–65.
38. Rosenthal and Masarech, "High-Performance Cultures"; Patrick M. Lencioni, "Make Your Values Mean Something," *Harvard Business Review* (July 2002), pp. 113–117; and Thomas J. Peters and Robert H. Waterman, Jr., *In Search of Excellence* (New York: Warner, 1988).
39. "About Canada's 10: Canada's 10 Most Admired Corporate Cultures, 2005–2012," Waterstone Human Capital Web site, http://www.waterstonehc.com/cmac/about-canadas-10/10-most-admired-corporate-cultures-2005–2011 (accessed June 6, 2013); Andrew Wahl, "Culture Shock," *Canadian Business* (October 10–23, 2005), pp. 115–116; Calvin Leung, Michelle Magnan, and Andrew Wahl, "People Power," *Canadian Business* (October 10–23, 2005), pp. 125–126; and John Izzo, "Step-Up Initiative: Create a Culture of Initiators," *Leadership Excellence* (June 2012), p. 13.
40. Harrison M. Trice and Janice M. Beyer, "Studying Organizational Culture through Rites and Ceremonials," *Academy of Management Review* 9 (1984), pp. 653–669.
41. Alan Farnham, "Mary Kay's Lessons in Leadership," *Fortune* (September 20, 1993), pp. 68–77.
42. John Marshall and Matthew Adamic, "The Story Is the Message: Shaping Corporate Culture," *Journal of Business Strategy* 31, no. 2 (2010), pp. 18–23.
43. Joanne Martin, *Organizational Culture: Mapping the Terrain* (Thousand Oaks, CA: Sage Publications, 2002), pp. 71–72.
44. Adam Bryant, "What's Your Story? Tell It, and You May Win a Prize" (Corner Office column, an interview with Russell Goldsmith), *The New York Times* (April 21, 2012), http://www.nytimes.com/2012/04/22/business/russell-goldsmith-of-city-national-on-storytellings-power.html?_r=0 (accessed April 29, 2013).
45. Sam Silverstein, "Sustainable Culture: Create One of Your Own," *Leadership Excellence* (December 2012), pp. 17–18; and Joan O'C. Hamilton, "Why Rivals Are Quaking as Nordstrom Heads East," *BusinessWeek* (June 15, 1987), pp. 99–100.
46. Christoph H. Loch, Fabian J. Sting, Arnd Huchzermeier, and Christiane Decker, "Finding the Profit in Fairness," *Harvard Business Review* (September 2012), pp. 111–115; and Doug Kirkpatrick, "Self-Management's Success at Morning Star," *T+ D* (October 2012), pp. 25–27.
47. Leslie Kwoh, "Memo to Staff: Take More Risks; CEOs Urge Employees to Embrace Failure and Keep Trying" (Theory & Practice column), *The Wall Street Journal* (March 20, 2013), p. B8.
48. Ian D. Colville and Anthony J. Murphy, "Leadership as the Enabler of Strategizing and Organizing," *Long Range Planning* 39 (2006), pp. 663–677.
49. D. C. Feldman, "The Multiple Socialization of Organization Members," *Academy of Management Review* 6 (1981), pp. 309–318; J. Van Maanen, "Breaking In: Socialization to Work," in R. Dubin, ed., *Handbook of Work, Organization, and Society* (Chicago: Rand-McNally,

1976), p. 67; and Blake E. Ashforth and Alan M. Saks, "Socialization Tactics: Longitudinal Effects on Newcomer Adjustment," *Academy of Management Journal* 39, no. 1 (February 1996), pp. 149–178.

50. Leigh Buchanan, "Managing: Welcome Aboard. Now, Run!" *Inc.* (March 2010), pp. 95–96.
51. Helena D. C. Thomas and Neil Anderson, "Changes in Newcomers' Psychological Contracts during Organizational Socialization: A Study of Recruits Entering the British Army," *Journal of Organizational Behavior* 19, no. 1 (1998), pp. 745–767.
52. Ashforth and Saks, "Socialization Tactics."
53. Deanne N. Den Hartog, Jaap J. Van Muijen, and Paul L. Koopman, "Linking Transformational Leadership and Organizational Culture," *The Journal of Leadership Studies* 3, no. 4 (1996), pp. 68–83; and Schein, "Organizational Culture."
54. Aili McConnon, "Lessons from a Skinflint CEO," *BusinessWeek* (October 6, 2008), pp. 54–55.
55. Joann S. Lublin, "Can a New Culture Fix Troubled Companies?" *The Wall Street Journal* (March 13, 2013), p. B1.
56. Jack and Suzy Welch, "Opinion: Goldman, Wall Street, and the Culture-Killing Lesson Being Ignored," *Fortune* (April 30, 2012), p. 56.
57. Ram Charan and Jerry Useem, "Why Companies Fail," *Fortune* (May 27, 2002), pp. 50–62.
58. Jennifer A. Chatman and Karen A. Jehn, "Assessing the Relationship between Industry Characteristics and Organizational Culture: How Different Can You Be?" *Academy of Management Journal* 37, no. 3 (1994), pp. 522–553.
59. James R. Detert, Roger G. Schroeder, and John J. Mauriel, "A Framework for Linking Culture and Improvement Initiatives in Organizations," *Academy of Management Review* 25, no. 4 (2000), pp. 850–863.
60. Paul McDonald and Jeffrey Gandz, "Getting Value from Shared Values," *Organizational Dynamics* 21, no. 3 (Winter 1992), pp. 64–76; and Daniel R. Denison and Aneil K. Mishra, "Toward a Theory of Organizational Culture and Effectiveness," *Organization Science* 6, no. 2 (March–April 1995), pp. 204–223.
61. Adam Bryant, "For Brett Wilson of TubeMogul, It's All in the Follow-Through," *The New York Times* (May 24, 2014), http://www.nytimes.com/2014/05/25/business/corner-office-for-brett-wilson-of-tubemogul-its-all-in-the-follow-through.html?ref=business (accessed November 30, 2015); and "Guiding Principles," *TubeMogul.com*, https://www.tubemogul.com/guiding-principles/ (accessed November 30, 2015).
62. Robert Hooijberg and Frank Petrock, "On Cultural Change: Using the Competing Values Framework to Help Leaders Execute a Transformational Strategy," *Human Resource Management* 32, no. 1 (1993), pp. 29–50.
63. Matt Moffett, "At InBev, a Gung-Ho Culture Rules; American Icon Anheuser, A Potential Target, Faces Prospect of Big Changes," *The Wall Street Journal* (May 28, 2008), p. B1; and Matt Moffett, "InBev's Chief Built Competitive Culture," *The Wall Street Journal* (June 13, 2008), p. B6.
64. William Rogers, "Sound Advice," *People Management* (August 2012), pp. 40–43.
65. Carey Quan Jelernter, "Safeco: Success Depends Partly on Fitting the Mold," *Seattle Times* (June 5, 1986), p. D8.
66. Gerald D. Klein, "Creating Cultures That Lead to Success: Lincoln Electric, Southwest Airlines, and SAS Institute," *Organizational Dynamics* 41 (2012), pp. 32–43; and Rekha Balu, "Pacific Edge Projects Itself," *Fast Company* (October 2000), pp. 371–381.
67. "Our Culture," Taunton Press Web site, http://www.taunton.com/thetauntonpress/our_culture.asp (accessed April 28, 2013); and Tony Hsieh, *Delivering Happiness: A Path to Profits, Passion, and Purpose* (New York: Business Plus, 2012).
68. Gordon F. Shea, *Practical Ethics* (New York: American Management Association, 1988); and Linda Klebe Treviño, "Ethical Decision Making in Organizations: A Person–Situation Interactionist Model," *Academy of Management Review* 11 (1986), pp. 601–617.
69. Brian Griffiths, "Markets Can't Be Improved by Rules, Only by Personal Example," *The Times* (April 9, 2009), p. 30.
70. Leslie Wayne, "A Promise to Be Ethical in an Era of Temptation," *The New York Times* (May 30, 2009), p. B1; and Kelley Holland, "Is It Time to Retrain B-Schools?" *The New York Times* (March 15, 2009), p. BU1.
71. Alison Boyd, "Employee Traps—Corruption in the Workplace," *Management Review* 86, no. 8 (September 1997), p. 9.
72. Based on "What Is Values-Based Leadership?" Values-Based Leadership Institute, Royal Roads University, http://values-based-leadership.institute.royalroads.ca/content/what-values-based-leadership (accessed July 12, 2013); K. Dean, "Values-Based Leadership: How Our Personal Values Impact the Workplace," *The Journal of Values-Based Leadership* 1, no. 1 (2008), pp. 60–67; and Robert J. House, "Path-Goal Theory of Leadership: Lessons, Legacy, and a Reformulated Theory," *Leadership Quarterly* 7, no. 3 (1996), pp. 323–352.
73. Alan Lewis, "Values Compass: Align around True North Values," *Leadership Excellence* (February 2012), p. 13; Krista Jaakson, "Management by Values: Are Some Values Better than Others?" *Journal of Management Development* 29, no. 9 (2010), pp. 795–806; and Kathy Whitmire, "Leading through Shared Values," *Leader to Leader* (Summer 2005), pp. 48–54.
74. Brad Stone, "Costco CEO Craig Jelinek Leads the Cheapest, Happiest Company in the World," *Bloomberg Businessweek* (June 6, 2013), http://www.businessweek.com/articles/2013-06-06/costco-ceo-craig-jelinek-leads-the-cheapest-happiest-company-in-the-world (accessed June 7, 2013); "Costco's Profit Soars to $537 Million Just Days after CEO Endorses Minimum Wage Increase," *The Huffington Post* (March 13, 2013), http://www.huffingtonpost.com/2013/03/12/costco-profit_n_2859250.html (accessed June 7, 2013); Bud Meyers, "Hail to the Chief (Executive Officer) Craig Jelinek of Costco!," *The Daily Kos* (March 8, 2013), http://www.dailykos.com/story/2013/03/08/1192632/-Hail-to-the-Chief-Executive-Officer-Craig-Jelinek-of-Costco (accessed June 8, 2013); and Satinder Dhiman and Joan Marques, "The Role and Need of Offering Workshops and Courses on Workplace Spirituality," *Journal of Management Development* 30, no. 9 (2011), pp. 816–835.
75. Stone, "Costco CEO Craig Jelinek Leads the Cheapest, Happiest Company in the World."
76. Dhiman and Marques, "The Role and Need of Offering Workshops and Courses on Workplace Spirituality."
77. Laura Reave, "Spiritual Values and Practices Related to Leadership Effectiveness," *The Leadership Quarterly* 16 (2005), pp. 655–687; and Louis W. Fry, Sean T. Hannah, Michael Noel, and Fred O. Walumbwa, "Impact of Spiritual Leadership on Unit Performance," *The Leadership Quarterly* 22 (2011), pp. 259–270.
78. Fry et al., "Impact of Spiritual Leadership on Unit Performance; R. A. Giacalone and C. L. Jurkiewicz, "Toward a Science of Workplace Spirituality," in R. A. Giacalone and C. L. Jurkiewicz, eds., *Handbook of Workplace Spirituality and Organizational Performance* (New York: M. E. Sharp, 2003), pp. 3–28; K. Krahnke, R. A. Giacalone, and C. L. Jurkiewicz, "Point-Counterpoint: Measuring Workplace Spirituality," *Journal of Organizational Change Management* 16, no. 4 (2003), pp. 396–405; Louis W. Fry, "Toward a Theory of Ethical and Spiritual Well-Being, and Corporate Social Responsibility through Spiritual Leadership," in R. A. Giacalone, ed., *Positive Psychology in Business Ethics and Corporate Responsibility* (Greenwich, CT: Information Age Publishing, 2005), pp. 47–83; and I. I. Mitroff and E. A. Denton, *A Spiritual Audit of Corporate America* (San Francisco: Jossey-Bass, 1999).

79. Neela Banerjee, "At Bosses' Invitation, Chaplains Come into Workplace and onto Payroll," *The New York Times* (December 4, 2006), p. A16.
80. Stephanie Armour, "CEO Helps People Keep Their Homes; That's CitiMortgage Chief's Personal Goal," *USA Today* (April 27, 2009), p. B4; Ruth Simon, "Citi to Allow Jobless to Pay Less on Mortgages for a Time," *The Wall Street Journal Europe* (March 4, 2009), p. 17; and Sanjiv Das, "Viewpoint: Early Intervention Can Stem Foreclosures," *American Banker* (December 10, 2008), p. 11.
81. Louis W. Fry, "Toward a Theory of Spiritual Leadership," *The Leadership Quarterly* 14 (2003), pp. 693–727; and Fry et al., "Impact of Spiritual Leadership on Unit Performance."
82. Ibid.
83. Fry, "Toward a Theory of Spiritual Leadership."

Chapter 15: Leading Change

YOUR **LEADERSHIP** CHALLENGE

After reading this chapter, you should be able to:

- Recognize the environmental forces creating a need for change in today's organizations.
- Describe the qualities of a change leader and how leaders can serve as role models for change.
- Implement the eight-stage model of planned change.
- Use appreciative inquiry to engage people in creating change by focusing on the positive and learning from success.
- Apply techniques of enabling immersion, facilitating brainstorming, promoting lateral thinking, allowing pauses, and nurturing creative intuition to expand your own and others' creativity and facilitate organizational innovation.
- Provide a positive emotional attractor, supportive relationships, repetition of new behaviors, participation and involvement, and after-action reviews to overcome resistance and help people change.

CHAPTER **OUTLINE**

464 **Leadership Means Leading Change**

467 **A Framework for Change**

469 **Using Appreciative Inquiry**

473 **Leading Creativity for Change**

481 **Implementing Change**

In the Lead

466 **Michelle Rhee, Washington, D.C., Public School System**

472 **The Red Team**

484 **Jon Fairest, Sanofi Canada**

Leader's Self-Insight

466 **Resistance to Change**

470 **Are You a Change Leader?**

477 **Do You Have a Creative Personality?**

Leader's Bookshelf

473 **Switch: How to Change Things When Change Is Hard**

Leadership at Work

487 **Organizational Change Role Play**

Leadership Development: Cases for Analysis

488 **"From This Point On ..."**

489 **Riverside Pediatric Associates**

Marvin Ellison, the current CEO of J.C. Penney, recently told a group of executives attending the Women's Wear Daily Apparel and Retail CEO Summit that Penney has moved past the stage of "patching holes" and is in solid rebuilding mode. Leaders have been working for several years to undo the damage that resulted from a turnaround strategy that almost killed the company. It's a cautionary tale of just how difficult change can be. When Ron Johnson, a former Apple executive known for his creativity, was hired as CEO of Penney in the fall of 2011, hopes were high that he could breathe new life into the struggling retailer. Penney needed radical change, but Johnson's approach to implementing changes doomed them almost from the start. Early in his tenure, Johnson threw a party to celebrate his plans for the company, a move that irked both employees and customers. He also began poking fun at the company's traditional way of doing business almost from the moment he took the job. Employees felt that the new managers Johnson brought in ridiculed them and made them feel dumb and uninteresting. Johnson refused to listen to long-established leaders, customers, or employees and even shunned suggestions made by board members. He got rid of many of Penney's long-standing processes and systems, radically redesigned many stores, and eliminated hundreds of brands, even running an Oscars ad telling customers they "deserved to look better." Customers decided they deserved to shop at a store where they were respected instead. Some analysts say rolling out changes too soon and with little input from others drove old customers away without giving new ones any reason to try the retailer, in essence, offering pain but no gain. Johnson was fired after only 17 months, and the damage repair began. Penney has brought back many of its popular brands, updated stores, and improved e-commerce operations. Customers are back, but the company still has a long climb to get back to the $20 billion in sales it enjoyed a decade ago.[1]

As the example of J.C. Penney illustrates, change—especially radical change—is tough to accomplish. Johnson made mistakes, but major turnarounds are exceedingly difficult for any leader, especially in retail. One study indicates that leader efforts at just getting a money-losing retailer back to profitability succeed only 30 percent of the time.[2] This chapter explores how leaders in companies such as J.C. Penney can facilitate change, creativity, and innovation. We first look briefly at the role of leader as change agent and examine a step-by-step framework for leading change. We explore the appreciative inquiry (AI) technique and how it can be used to lead both major changes and ongoing, everyday change. Next, the chapter examines how leaders instill the conditions that nurture creativity within people and organizations. The final sections of the chapter consider why people resist change and how leaders can overcome resistance and help people successfully make needed changes.

15-1 LEADERSHIP MEANS LEADING CHANGE

It is the job of the leader to make sure organizations change as needed to respond to threats, opportunities, or shifts in the environment. Recall from our definition used throughout this book that leadership is about change rather than stability. Leaders have to help people see the need for change and buy into a new way of doing things.

Change is necessary if organizations are to survive and thrive, and the sharp downturn in the economy a few years ago, combined with other environmental shifts, forced leaders in all industries to take a fresh look at how they do business. The turmoil not only pressured leaders to rethink the economics of their business but also brought changes in social attitudes that require new leadership responses.[3] Exhibit 15.1 shows some of the environmental forces, such as rapidly changing technologies, shifting social attitudes, globalization, increasing government regulation, changing markets, the growth of e-business, and the swift spread of information via the Internet, that are creating a greater need for change leadership within organizations.[4]

15-1a Resistance Is Real

Leaders initiate many changes, but most of these don't meet expectations. Consider that among leaders in 166 U.S. and European companies making major changes, only about one-third reported success in most types of their changes. Some studies have estimated that 90 percent of strategies fail to achieve intended objectives and that 70 percent of all change initiatives in organizations fail.[5]

There are many reasons why change programs don't produce the intended results. One significant problem is that most people have a natural tendency to resist change—even when the changes are ones that could make their lives better. At Rio Tinto Aluminium (formerly called Comalco), based in New South Wales, Australia, for example, leaders wanted to make changes to create a more egalitarian workplace

EXHIBIT 15.1 Forces Driving the Need for Change Leadership

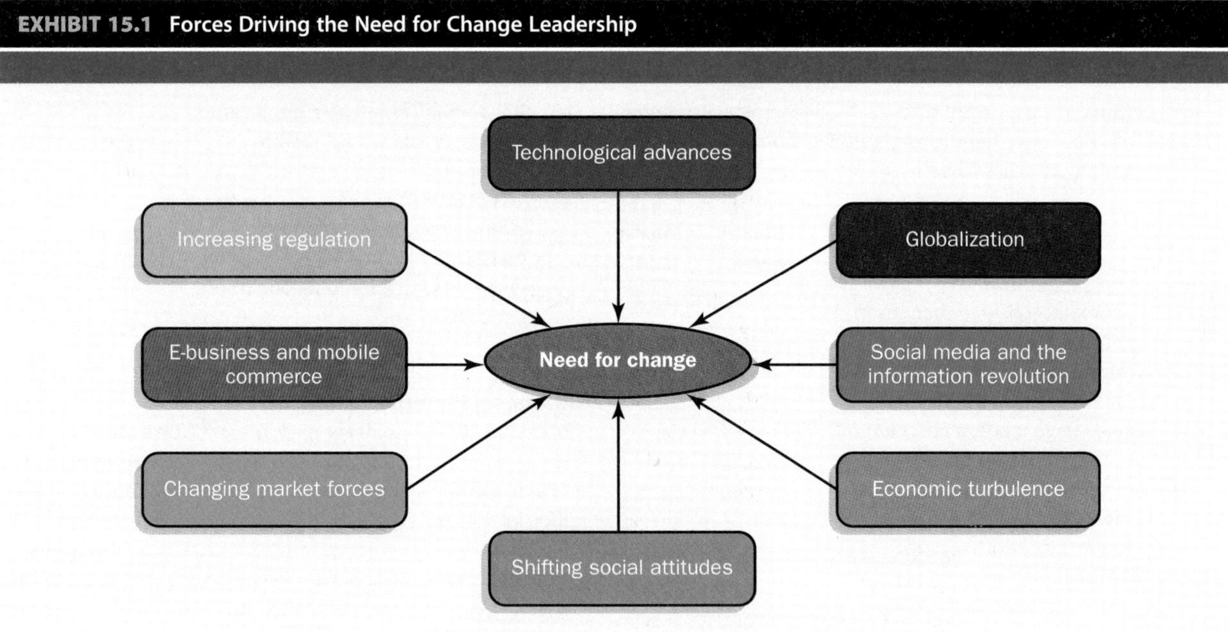

with less separation between management and workers. They did away with all the separate uniforms for electricians, fitters, operators, foremen, and so forth; eliminated the time clock for hourly workers; and got rid of the separate parking lot for managers. Each change was resisted. Employees said they liked the uniforms because they were less costly and identified who they were compared to wearing different clothes every day. Workers were strongly opposed to elimination of the time clock because, they said, "We won't be able to prove we've been to work, so they'll be able to cheat us on our pay." They were suspicious that doing away with the managers' car parking was so employees couldn't see that managers could afford a new car every year.[6] If people resist changes designed to add value to their lives, imagine what it is like trying to implement changes that significantly shift their job responsibilities, task procedures, or work interactions!

Leaders should be prepared for resistance and should find ways to enable people to see the value in changes that are needed for the organization to succeed. Later in this chapter, we will talk about how leaders can overcome resistance and help people successfully change.

NEW LEADER
ACTION MEMO

Complete the questions in Leader's Leader's Self-Insight 15.1 to see if you have a natural tendency to resist change.

15-1b The Leader as Change Agent

Change does not happen easily, but good leaders can facilitate needed changes to help the organization adapt to external threats and new opportunities. For people throughout the organization to view change as positive and natural, they need leaders who serve as role models for change and provide the motivation and communication to keep change efforts moving forward. Research has identified some key characteristics of leaders who can accomplish successful change projects:[7]

- They define themselves as change leaders rather than as people who want to maintain the status quo.
- They demonstrate courage.

LEADER'S SELF-INSIGHT 15.1

Resistance to Change

Instructions: Please respond to each of the following items based on how you handle day-to-day issues in your life. Think carefully in order to be as accurate as possible.

	Mostly False	Mostly True
1. I generally consider changes in my life to be a negative thing.		
2. When I am told of a change of plans, I may tense up a bit.		
3. Once I have made plans, I am not likely to change them.		
4. I often change my mind.		
5. Whenever my life fits a stable routine, I look for ways to change it.		
6. I feel less stress when things go according to plan.		
7. I sometimes avoid making personal changes even when the change would be good for me.		
8. My views are very consistent over time.		
9. I prefer a routine day to a day full of unexpected surprises.		
10. If I were informed of a significant change in my work, I would tighten up.		
11. When someone pressures me to change something, I tend to resist it.		
12. Once I have come to a conclusion, I stick to it.		

Scoring and Interpretation

Give yourself one point for each Mostly True answer to items 1 to 3 and 6 to 12 and for each Mostly False to items 4 and 5. Everyone feels some resistance to change, but people do differ in their tolerance for frequent change. A higher score of 8 or above on this scale means you probably prefer a predictable and routine life. Frequent or dramatic changes at work may be difficult for you, probably creating feelings of resistance, stress, and tension. If you received a score of 5 or lower, your resistance to change may be low, so you probably find surprises and changes to be somewhat stimulating.

Source: Based on Shaul Oreg, "Resistance to Change: Developing an Individual Differences Measure," *Journal of Applied Psychology* 88, no. 4 (2003), pp. 680–693. Used with permission.

- They believe in employees' capacity to assume responsibility.
- They can assimilate and articulate values that promote adaptability.
- They recognize and learn from their own mistakes.
- They are capable of managing complexity, uncertainty, and ambiguity.
- They have vision and can describe their vision for the future in vivid terms.

Michelle Rhee, former chancellor of the Washington, D.C., public school system, provides a good example of the characteristics of a change leader.

IN THE LEAD

Michelle Rhee, Washington, D.C., Public School System

Michelle Rhee, former chancellor of Washington, D.C., public schools and founder of StudentsFirst, is one of the most controversial figures in U.S. education, but love her or hate her you can't say she's afraid of change. A daughter of Korean immigrants, Rhee wanted to quit halfway through her first year in Teach for America, the organization we described in Chapter 1 that sends new college graduates into some of America's toughest schools, but her father made her go back and finish the job. That's where she first embarked on a personal mission to change the system for America's poorest students. Rhee noticed that students responded to teachers who pushed them hard and kept them interested.

A couple of decades later, Rhee had the chance to put some of her change ideas into action on a large scale as she tried to revamp one of the most expensive, worst performing school systems in the country. As chancellor of the D.C. public schools, Rhee attacked the dysfunctional culture that rewarded teachers for seniority rather than performance, revised systems and structures to slash bureaucracy, held school principals accountable for improving student performance, and focused people on a mission of putting the best interests of students first.

Her vision of making D.C. schools "the highest-performing urban school district in the nation" brought new energy and movement to a long-stagnant system. "We have a system that does wrong by poor kids of color," Rhee said. "If we're going to live up to our promise as a country . . . that has got to stop." Rhee becomes angry when people say "teachers cannot make up for what parents and students will not do," emphasizing that each teacher can make a difference. She didn't hesitate to cut administrative positions that weren't contributing value, fire teachers and principals who didn't meet performance standards, and close underperforming schools. She instituted new procedures to handsomely reward high-performing teachers and give principals more control over hiring, promoting, and firing. New evaluation procedures put people on alert that low performance and complacency would not be tolerated.[8]

Rhee stepped down as CEO of StudentsFirst in 2014 but continues to drive change in the educational system. "Some people think she is a transformative leader, and some people think she is a controversial figure, but everyone agrees she gets people talking," said one organizer of a recent conference in Michigan.[9]

15-2 A FRAMEWORK FOR CHANGE

When leading a major change project, it is important for leaders to recognize that the change process goes through stages, each stage is important, and each may require a significant amount of time. Exhibit 15.2 shows a model developed by John Kotter that can help leaders navigate the change process.[10]

1. *Light a fire for change.* People have to believe that change is really needed. Leaders communicate the urgency for change in a way that touches people's emotions—in other words, they help people *feel* the need for change rather than just giving them facts and figures. Consider Peter Löscher, the first outsider ever hired as CEO of Siemens, who says "never miss the opportunities that come from a good crisis." Löscher, who has now left Siemens, stepped in at a very difficult time, with the company facing bribery charges, and he needed to make massive changes in structure and culture. He spent his first 100 days traveling around the world talking with employees about how the bribery scandal had tarnished Siemens's proud heritage.[11]
2. *Get the right people on board.* Considering the complexities of change, no single person can implement a change, especially a major one, alone. For successful change, leaders build a strong coalition of people with a shared commitment to the need for and possibility of change. They include people with enough power to make sure the change happens, as well as people who can make the change more acceptable to end users.

EXHIBIT 15.2 The Eight-Stage Model of Planned Organizational Change

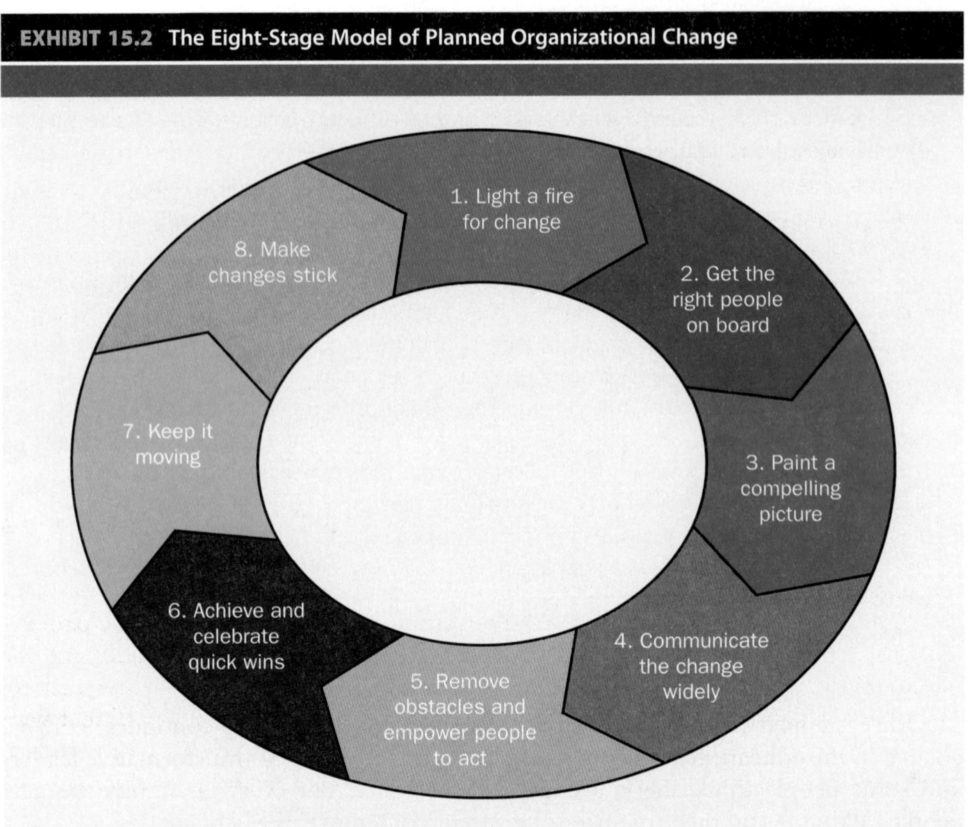

Sources: Based on John P. Kotter , *Leading Change* (Boston: Harvard Business School Press, 1996), p. 21.

3. *Paint a compelling picture*. People need a clear vision and strategy to inspire them to believe that a better future is possible and they can achieve it through their actions. The energy for true change comes from seeing how the change can be positive for individuals and the organization. Leaders create a picture that helps people understand why the organization is undertaking the effort and how the change will help it to achieve long-term goals. It's also important to develop a strategy for achieving the vision and let people know how they fit into the big picture.
4. *Communicate, communicate, communicate*. Leaders tell the message not just once but over and over again. Change throws everyone into doubt and uncertainty, and people don't listen well when they feel anxious. Another point to remember is that actions speak louder than words. Change leaders model the new behaviors needed from employees. At Siemens, Peter Löscher mapped the amount of time the company's top executives spent with customers and presented it at the annual leadership conference. Löscher was number 1, having spent 50 percent of his time with customers. He told people that had to change and that the rankings would be presented each year to see if people running the businesses were honoring the new focus on customer contact.[12]
5. *Get rid of obstacles and empower people to act*. Leaders give people the time, knowledge, resources, and discretion to take steps and make the change happen. This might mean revising structures, systems, or procedures that hinder or

undermine the change effort. After setting a vision and broad outline for change, Bill Glavin, former CEO of OppenheimerFunds, Inc., gave his team members leeway to move forward with their own ideas for implementing desired changes. Glavin said his approach was to meet with direct reports regularly and to "try to keep a light hand on the tiller."[13]

6. *Achieve and celebrate quick wins.* Unless people see positive results of their efforts, energy and motivation can wane during a major change project. To keep the momentum going, leaders identify some short-term accomplishments that people can recognize and celebrate. A highly visible and successful short-term accomplishment boosts the credibility of the change process and renews everyone's enthusiasm and commitment.
7. *Keep it moving.* Don't get stuck on short-term wins. One study suggests that nearly 50 percent of all change initiatives crumble simply from lack of attention.[14] It's important for leaders to build on the credibility of early accomplishments and keep the change process moving forward. At this stage, they confront and change any remaining issues, structures, or systems that are getting in the way of achieving the vision.
8. *Find ways to make the changes stick.* At this stage, leaders look for ways to institutionalize the new approach, striving to integrate the new values and patterns into everyone's work habits. At Del-Air, a Florida heating, ventilation, and air conditioning contractor, managers linked a new GPS-enabled time-tracking system with the company's bonus system. Employees who are more efficient with their time get rewarded for it. By integrating the change with the incentive system, managers made the new time-tracking system an accepted, integral part of everyone's daily work.[15]

NEW LEADER
ACTION MEMO

As a leader, you can develop the personal characteristics to be a change leader. To improve the success of a major change, you can follow the eight-stage model for leading change, remembering to devote the necessary time, energy, and resources to each stage.

NEW LEADER
ACTION MEMO

Answer the questions in Leader's Leader's Self-Insight 15.2 to see if you have what it takes to initiate changes and follow the eight-stage model of change.

Stages in the change process generally overlap, but each of these stages is important for successful change to occur. When dealing with a major change effort, leaders can use the eight-stage change process to provide a strong foundation for success.

15-3 USING APPRECIATIVE INQUIRY

One of the most exciting approaches to leading change is a process known as appreciative inquiry. **Appreciative inquiry (AI)** engages individuals, teams, or the entire organization in creating change by reinforcing positive messages and focusing on learning from success.[16] Rather than looking at a situation from the viewpoint of what is wrong and who is to blame for it, AI takes a positive, affirming approach by asking, "What is possible? What do we want to achieve?" For example, rather than looking at a problem such as decreasing sales, AI would investigate what makes sales increase. Appropriately framing a topic—to investigate what is right rather than what is wrong—is critical to the success of AI because it gets people away from blame, defensiveness, and denial and sets a positive framework for change. As David Cooperrider, cocreator of the AI methodology, puts it, "the more you study the true, the good, the better, the possible within living human systems, the more the capacity for positive transformation."[17] AI can be applied on either a large or a small scale.

Appreciative inquiry
a technique for leading change that engages individuals, teams, or the entire organization by reinforcing positive messages and focusing on learning from success

15-3a Applying Appreciative Inquiry on a Large Scale

AI can accelerate large-scale organizational change by positively engaging a large group of people in the change process, including leaders and employees, as well as

LEADER'S SELF-INSIGHT 15.2

Are You a Change Leader?

Instructions: Think specifically of your current or a recent full-time job. Please answer the following 10 questions according to *your perspective and behaviors in that job*. Indicate whether each item is Mostly False or Mostly True for you.

	Mostly False	Mostly True
1. I often tried to adopt improved procedures for doing my job.		✓
2. I often tried to change how my job was executed in order to be more effective.		✓
3. I often tried to bring about improved procedures for the work unit or department.		✓
4. I often tried to institute new work methods that were more effective for the company.		✓
5. I often tried to change organizational rules or policies that were nonproductive or counterproductive.	✓	
6. I often made constructive suggestions for improving how things operate within the organization.		✓
7. I often tried to correct a faulty procedure or practice.		✓
8. I often tried to eliminate redundant or unnecessary procedures.	✓	
9. I often tried to implement solutions to pressing organizational problems.	✓	
10. I often tried to introduce new structures, technologies, or approaches to improve efficiency.		✓

Scoring and Interpretation

Please add the number of items for which you marked Mostly True, which is your score: __7__. This instrument measures the extent to which people take charge of change in the workplace. Change leaders are seen as change initiators. A score of 7 or above indicates a strong take-charge attitude toward change. A score of 3 or below indicates an attitude of letting someone else worry about change.

Before change leaders can champion large planned change projects via the model in Exhibit 15.2, they often begin by taking charge of change in their workplace area of responsibility. To what extent do you take charge of change in your work or personal life? Compare your score with other students' scores. How do you compare? Do you see yourself being a change leader?

people from outside the organization, such as customers or clients, partners, and other stakeholders.

Once a topic has been identified for exploration, the group follows a four-stage AI process, as illustrated in Exhibit 15.3.[18]

1. **Discovery**. In the discovery stage, people identify "the best of what exists"—the organization's key strengths and best practices. This stage is about discovering the unique qualities of the group that have contributed to success. Leaders interview people, asking them to tell stories that identify the best of their experiences with the organization. During an AI session focused on building a winning culture at American Express, for example, leaders asked people to describe an instance when they felt the most proud working for the company. Based on these stories, people together identify common themes.
2. **Dream.** Next, people reflect on what they learned during the discovery stage and imagine what it would be like if these extraordinary experiences were the norm—what if people at American Express, for instance, experienced the kind of environment every day that made them feel proud of working for American Express? The dream stage is about imagining "what could be" and creating a shared vision of the best possible future, grounded in the reality of what

EXHIBIT 15.3 Four Stages of Appreciative Inquiry

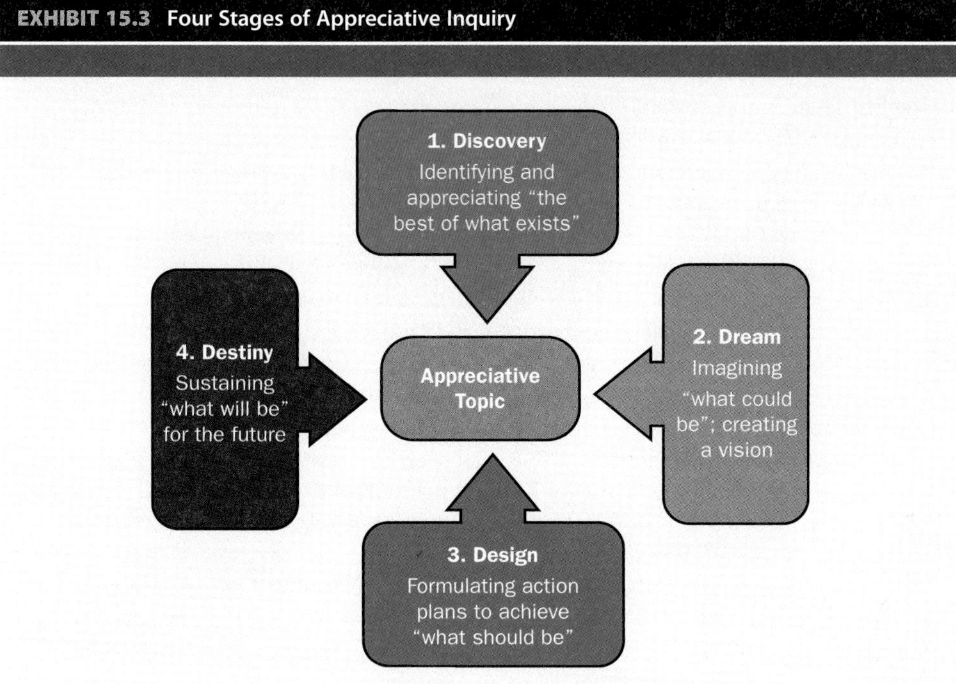

Source: Based on Gabriella Giglio, Silvia Michalcova, and Chris Yates, "Instilling a Culture of Winning at American Express," *Organization Development Journal* 25, no. 4 (Winter 2002), pp. 33–37

already exists. By allowing people to express their dreams for the future, AI inspires hope and energy for change.

3. **Design.** The design stage formulates action plans for transforming dreams into reality. This involves people making decisions about what the organization needs to do in order to be what it wants to be. At American Express, people identified the values that would support the kind of culture they wanted, the leadership behaviors that would instill and support the values, and the structures, systems, and processes that would keep the new cultural values alive.
4. **Destiny.** The final stage of AI is creating a destiny by translating the ideas identified in the previous stages into concrete action steps. This involves both celebrating the best of what exists and pushing forward to realize the dream by creating specific programs, activities, and other tangible forces that will implement the design and ensure the continuation of change begun during the AI process. For example, specific changes in training programs, performance evaluation, and reward systems were part of the destiny stage at American Express.

Using the AI methodology for a large-scale change may involve hundreds of people over a period of several days and may be conducted off-site to enable people to immerse themselves in the process of creating the future. A wide variety of organizations, including businesses, school systems, churches and religious organizations, communities, government agencies, and social service organizations, have used AI for large-scale change.[19] A team at a large oil refinery in the Middle East used AI to help achieve a vision of making the refinery "the best place in the company to work."

IN THE LEAD

The Red Team

When the general manager (GM) of the oil refinery where they worked asked them to "re-imagine the organization," the group of young engineers known as the Red Team naturally wondered what he meant.

The GM said he wanted the refinery to be the best place to work in the huge Middle East oil and gas organization. Success, he added, would be measured by the level of happiness among the 1,600 workers at the refinery. Happiness among the workers, the GM believed, would improve safety, performance, and productivity. The Red Team immediately began talking among themselves and identifying issues and potential recommendations for making the refinery a happier place to work. Then they decided it was a good idea to get input from the other employees.

They came up with a simple theme, based on the word "Smile," around which to connect people and get their ideas for how to improve morale, motivation, and happiness. Using the AI model, the team asked people to share their best experiences of working at the refinery (Discover), which created an energized and fun atmosphere. Next, people contributed ideas for what they thought the refinery *could* be if these experiences were the norm (Dream). In the third (Design) stage, ideas included seeing managers more often in the plant, strengthening worker–supervisor relationships, improving the cafeteria menu, providing shade canopies over employee parking areas, and holding regular employee-family appreciation events. Volunteer teams were asked to champion each initiative for follow-up action to turn them into reality (Destiny).

The process has already improved morale by giving people a chance to participate in shaping their own future. People have a stronger sense of belonging and commitment, and the vision of being "the best place in the company to work" is well on its way to becoming a reality.[20]

15-3b Applying Appreciative Inquiry Every Day

AI can also be applied by individual leaders on a smaller scale. The nature of leadership means influencing people in many small ways on an ongoing basis. This chapter's Leader's Bookshelf describes a three-stage change model that incorporates elements of AI and can be used for everyday change efforts. Good leaders work daily to gradually shift attitudes, assumptions, and behavior toward a desired future. When individual leaders in an organization are involved in daily change efforts, they have a powerful cumulative effect.[21]

Leaders can use the tools of AI for a variety of everyday change initiatives, such as developing followers, strengthening teamwork, solving a particular work issue, or resolving conflicts.[22] Again, the key is to frame the issue in a positive way and keep people focused on improvement rather than looking at what went wrong. Jim (Gus) Gustafson, chief transformation officer and chief ministry officer for the Lutheran Church of Hope in West Des Moines, Iowa, provides an example of the everyday use of AI. Gustafson loves using AI to develop followers. One example comes from the time he took over as director of sales and marketing for a major electrical manufacturer. While sitting in on several employees' performance reviews with the outgoing executive, Gustafson noticed that two employees in particular were treated by the outgoing manager with disrespect and disinterest as they were

LEADER'S BOOKSHELF

Switch: How to Change Things When Change Is Hard

by Chip Heath and Dan Heath

"Big changes can start with very small steps. Small changes tend to snowball," write authors Chip Heath, a professor at the Graduate School of Business at Stanford University, and Dan Heath, a senior fellow at Duke University's Center for Advancement of Social Entrepreneurship. "But this is not the same as saying that change is easy." Indeed, the stories told in *Switch: How to Change Things When Change Is Hard* illustrate just how difficult change can be, whether it is a personal change such as losing 40 pounds or an organizational change such as improving how employees treat customers.

A THREE-PART FRAMEWORK FOR CHANGE

Switch offers some solid advice that can be applied to both individuals and organizations that need to change. Here is a quick summary of their three-step plan for change:

- ***Provide Direction: Look for the Bright Spots***. The first step involves setting a clear direction and scripting the moves that can help people get there. A key point here is to focus on the positive. Many people facing a need for change are demoralized and depressed. To bring about change, leaders shift people to thinking about things they have done in the past that were positive and how to do those kinds of things more often. To help solve the chronic malnutrition problem in Vietnam, for example, the Save the Children organization stopped looking at what was wrong and instead looked for the children who were well-nourished, learned what their parents were doing, and taught the parents of undernourished children to follow the same steps.
- ***Get Emotional: Motivate People to Change***. Why do charitable organizations use photos of needy children to attract donations? Because they appeal to people's emotions. The lesson is that people don't "think" their way into a new behavior. Change depends on changing emotions. Microsoft leaders kept telling a group of programmers that customers couldn't figure out how to use a new feature, but the stubborn programmers thought their software was brilliant. Only when the programmers actually watched customers struggling with using the feature and becoming frustrated and unhappy did they start looking for ways to make it more user friendly.
- ***Shape the Path: Make Change More Comfortable.*** Old habits die hard, but the opportunity for change to take hold is enhanced when the new habits are more comfortable. One of the best illustrations of this step comes from Bart Millar, a teacher in Portland, Oregon, who transformed his classroom by getting the most disruptive students to come to class early and sit in the front row. How did he do it? He put a comfortable sofa at the front of his history classroom. It didn't take long for the students who used to be back-seat wisecrackers to start showing up early enough to get the cool seats.

TEST YOUR CHANGE LEADERSHIP

One of the most interesting features of *Switch* is the use of "Clinics," which are sidebars describing real-life situations needing change. Readers are invited to apply what they've learned from a particular section of the book to craft a change strategy. Then, the authors describe what actually happened and what they would advise based on their change research. The numerous rich examples, combined with research pulled from the fields of psychology, sociology, and other fields, make *Switch* a fun, inspiring read.

Source: *Switch: How to Change Things When Change Is Hard*, by Chip Heath and Dan Heath, is published by Broadway Books.

given poor evaluations of their performance. Gustafson used AI by asking the two employees questions such as, "What have you done in the last six months that you are most proud of?" "What is your greatest source of job satisfaction?" and "What motivates you to excel?" He worked with the two to identify how they could be satisfied and productive, carrying forward the best from their past but moving toward a better future. Thanks to Gustafson's coaching and the use of AI, both employees were eventually promoted to management positions in the organization.[23]

15-4 LEADING CREATIVITY FOR CHANGE

The American Management Association asked 500 CEOs the question: "What must one do to survive in the twenty-first century?" The top answer? "Practice creativity and innovation."[24] Effective leaders find ways to promote creativity and innovation, particularly in the departments where it is most needed. For example, some organizations, such as hospitals, government agencies, and nonprofit organizations, may need frequent changes in policies and procedures, and leaders can promote creativity among administrative workers. For companies that rely on new products, leaders promote the generation and sharing of ideas across departments and, increasingly, with outsiders.

Creativity is the generation of ideas that are both novel and useful for improving the efficiency or effectiveness of an organization.[25] Creative people come up with ideas that may meet perceived needs, solve problems, or respond to opportunities and are therefore adopted by the organization. However, creativity itself is a process rather than an outcome, a journey rather than a destination. One of the most important tasks of leaders today is to harness the creative energy of all employees.

15-4a Instilling Creative Values

Leaders can build an environment that encourages creativity and helps the organization be more innovative. Fostering a creative culture and promoting collaboration will spread values for creativity throughout the organization.

Foster a Creative Culture For creative acts that benefit the organization to occur consistently, the interests and actions of everyone should be aligned with the organization's purpose, vision, and goals, and leaders should make a commitment of time, energy, and resources to support creativity.[26] One popular approach is to provide an **idea incubator**. An idea incubator provides a safe harbor where ideas from people throughout the organization can be developed without interference from company bureaucracy or politics.[27] Companies as diverse as Yahoo, Boeing, Adobe Systems, and UPS have used idea incubators to make sure good ideas don't get lost in the day-to-day organizational system.

To build a culture that encourages **corporate entrepreneurship**, leaders encourage the creative spirit of all employees by promoting cultural values of curiosity, openness, exploration, and informed risk-taking. At W. L. Gore, best known for Gore-Tex fabrics, leaders basically did away with the rules so that people feel free to explore and experiment. There are no bosses at Gore; people explore ideas on their own and recruit others who believe in and want to work on the idea. That's how Gore got into businesses as diverse as Glide dental floss, Ride-On bike cables, and Elixir guitar strings.[28] One important outcome of entrepreneurship is to facilitate idea champions. **Idea champions** are people who passionately believe in an idea and fight to overcome natural resistance and convince others of its value. Change does not happen by itself. Personal energy and effort are needed to successfully promote a new idea.

A creative culture is an *open culture* that encourages people to look everywhere for new ideas. Leaders promote openness by rotating people into different jobs, allowing them time off to participate in volunteer activities, and giving them opportunities to mix with people different from themselves. One aerospace company uses the phrase *Get out of Kansas*! to stress the importance of looking for novel ideas in the world outside company walls.[29] Leaders can also give people opportunities to work with customers, suppliers, and people outside the industry, which contributes to a flow of fresh ideas. Executives at Productos Cementos Mexicanos (known as Cemex) ride in cement trucks to get ideas about customer needs, for instance.[30]

Promote Collaboration Although many individuals have creative ideas, creativity soars when people work together. Rather than leaving people stuck in their departmental

Creativity
the generation of ideas that are both novel and useful for improving the efficiency and effectiveness of the organization

Idea incubator
a safe harbor where ideas from employees throughout the organization can be developed without interference from company bureaucracy or politics

Corporate entrepreneurship
internal entrepreneurial spirit that includes values of exploration, experimentation, and risk taking

Idea champions
people who passionately believe in a new idea and actively work to overcome obstacles and resistance

silos, smart leaders find ways to get them communicating and collaborating across boundaries. Creative collaboration is one of the most important activities leaders can support for a creative culture.[31] That's one reason companies use cross-functional teams and self-managed teams, as described in Chapter 10. Some remodel their physical spaces so that people from different areas work side by side on a daily basis. Many companies use internal Web sites that encourage cross-organizational collaboration. For example, Arup Group, a British engineering services company, developed an online "knowledge map" that shows the company's different areas of expertise and how departments and employees are connected to one another in terms of important information flows.[32]

NEW LEADER
ACTION MEMO

As a leader, you can help the organization be more innovative. You can encourage values of curiosity, openness, and exploration, and give employees time to work with people outside their normal areas. You can build in mechanisms for cross-functional collaboration and information sharing.

A recent approach to promoting one-on-one collaboration is speedstorming. **Speedstorming**, as the name suggests, was inspired by the phenomenon of speed-dating. It uses a round-robin format to get people from different areas talking together, generating creative ideas, and identifying areas for potential collaboration. People are divided into pairs, with each person from a different department, and given a specific topic with a goal of generating ideas to pursue collaboratively by the end of each three- to five-minute round. By the end of the session, the goal is for each participant to have formed ideas for creative collaboration with several others. Speedstorming can be a fun experience that enriches existing approaches to collaboration.[33]

15-4b Leading Creative People

Many organizations that want to encourage change and innovation strive to hire people who display creative characteristics. However, recent research on creativity suggests that anyone can learn to be creative and can get better at it with practice.[34] That is, everyone has roughly equal creative potential. The problem is that many people don't use that potential. Leaders can help individuals be more creative by facilitating brainstorming, promoting lateral thinking, enabling immersion, allowing pauses, and nurturing creative intuition, as illustrated in Exhibit 15.4.

NEW LEADER
ACTION MEMO

Complete the exercise in Leader's Leader's Self-Insight 15.3 to see if you have a creative personality.

Facilitate Brainstorming One common way to encourage creativity is to set up brainstorming sessions focused on a specific problem or topic. Assume your organization faces a problem such as how to reduce losses from shoplifting, speed up checkout, reduce food waste, or lessen noise from a machine room. **Brainstorming** uses a face-to-face interactive group to spontaneously suggest a wide range of creative ideas to solve the problem. The keys to effective brainstorming are:[35]

1. *No criticism*. Group members should not criticize or evaluate ideas in any way during the spontaneous generation of ideas. All ideas are considered valuable.
2. *Freewheeling is welcome*. People should express any idea that comes to mind, no matter how weird or fanciful. Brainstormers should not be timid about expressing creative thinking. As a full-time developer of ideas at Intuit said, "It's more important to get the stupidest idea out there and build on it than not to have it in the first place."[36]
3. *Quantity desired*. The goal is to generate as many ideas as possible. The more ideas the better. A large quantity of ideas increases the likelihood of finding excellent solutions. Combining ideas is also encouraged. All ideas belong to the group, and members should modify and extend ideas whenever possible.

Brainstorming has both ardent supporters and intense critics, but it remains the most common way leaders use groups to generate new ideas.[37] Leaders are

Speedstorming
using a round-robin format to get people from different areas talking together, generating creative ideas, and identifying areas for potential collaboration

Brainstorming
a technique that uses a face-to-face group to spontaneously suggest a broad range of ideas to solve a problem

EXHIBIT 15.4 Tools for Helping People Be More Creative

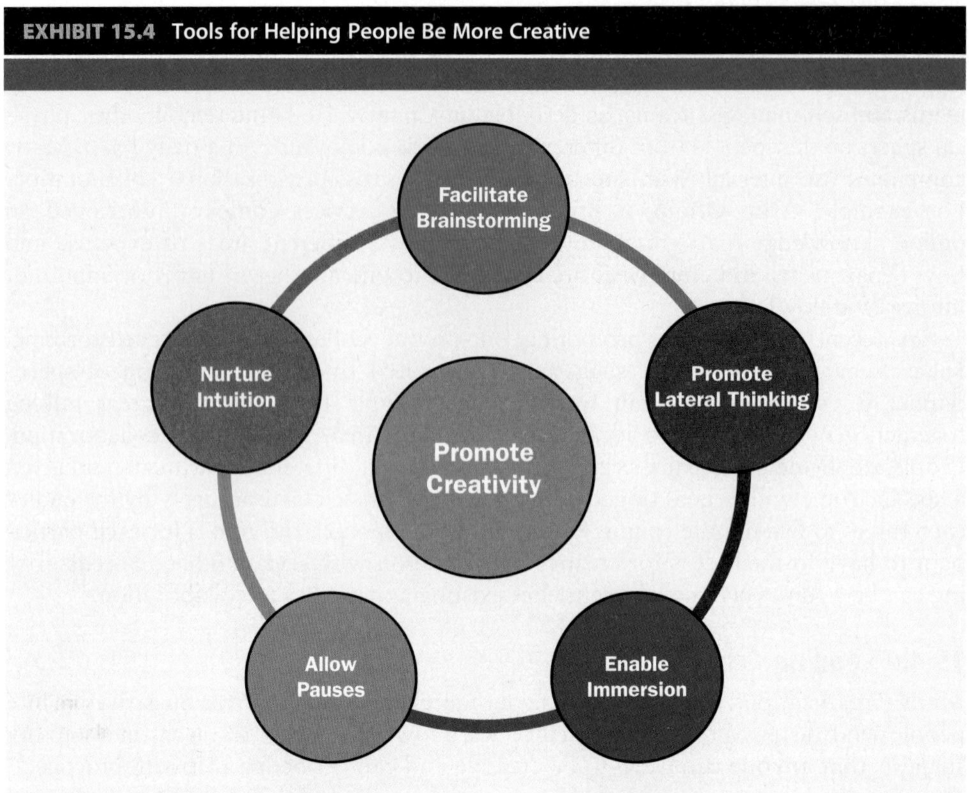

continually searching for ways to improve the brainstorming process. Some companies are practicing an extreme type of brainstorming, based on the popularity of television reality shows, that puts people together for an extended time period to come up with ideas. Under a program called Real Whirled, for example, Whirlpool sends teams of eight people to live together for seven weeks—and to use Whirlpool appliances for cooking and cleaning, of course. Best Buy has used a similar program, with teams of people who previously didn't know one another living together for 10 weeks in a Los Angeles apartment complex. A new service, Best Buy Studio, which provides Web-design consulting for small businesses, came directly out of ideas hatched at one of the sessions.[38]

Another recent approach, called **electronic brainstorming**, or *brainwriting*, brings people together in an interactive group over a computer network.[39] People can submit ideas and can also read and extend others' ideas. Austin, Texas–based ad agency GSD&M uses electronic brainstorming sessions that include outsiders as well as employees to quickly come up with ideas for ad campaigns. Leaders say the sessions generate thousands of ideas, and keeping things anonymous "keeps the boss and the new hire on the same level."[40] Studies show that electronic brainstorming generates about 40 percent more ideas than individuals brainstorming alone, and 25 percent to 200 percent more ideas than regular brainstorming groups, depending on group size.[41] Why? Primarily because people participate anonymously, the sky's the limit in terms of what they feel free to say. Creativity also increases because people can write down their ideas immediately, avoiding the possibility that a good idea might slip away while the person is waiting for a chance to speak in a face-to-face group.

Electronic brainstorming bringing people together in an interactive group over a computer network; sometimes called *brainwriting*

LEADER'S SELF-INSIGHT 15.3

Do You Have a Creative Personality?

Instructions: In the following list, check each adjective that you believe accurately describes your personality. Be very honest and check all the words that fit your personality.

1. affected ______
2. capable ______
3. cautious ______
4. clever ______
5. commonplace ______
6. confident ______
7. conservative ______
8. conventional ______
9. egotistical ______
10. dissatisfied ______
11. honest ______
12. humorous ______
13. individualistic ______
14. informal ______
15. insightful ______
16. intelligent ______
17. narrow interests ______
18. wide interests ______
19. inventive ______
20. mannerly ______
21. original ______
22. reflective ______
23. resourceful ______
24. self-confident ______
25. sexy ______
26. snobbish ______
27. sincere ______
28. submissive ______
29. suspicious ______
30. unconventional ______

Scoring and Interpretation

Add one point for checking each of the following words: 2, 4, 6, 9, 12, 13, 14, 15, 16, 18, 19, 21, 22, 23, 24, 25, 26, and 30. Subtract one point for checking each of the following words: 1, 3, 5, 7, 8, 10, 11, 17, 20, 27, 28, and 29. The highest possible score is +18 and the lowest possible score is −12.

The average score for a set of 256 assessed males on this creativity scale was 3.57, and for 126 females was 4.4. A group of 45 male research scientists and a group of 530 male psychology graduate students both had average scores of 6.0, and 124 male architects received an average score of 5.3. A group of 335 female psychology students had an average score of 3.34. If you received a score above 6.0, your personality would be considered above average in creativity.

This adjective checklist was validated by comparing the respondents' scores to scores on other creativity tests and to creativity assessments of respondents provided by expert judges of creativity. This scale does not provide perfect prediction of creativity, but it is reliable and has moderate validity. Your score probably indicates something about your creative personality compared to other people.

To what extent do you think your score reflects your true creativity? Compare your score to those of others in your class. What is the range of scores among other students? Which adjectives were most important for your score compared to other students? Can you think of types of creativity this test might not measure? How about situations where the creativity reflected on this test might not be very important?

Source: Harrison G. Gough, "A Creative Personality Scale for the Adjective Check List," *Journal of Personality and Social Psychology* 37, no. 8 (1979), pp. 1398–1405.

Promote Lateral Thinking Most of a person's thinking follows a regular groove and somewhat linear pattern from one thought to the next. But linear thinking does not often provide a creative breakthrough. Linear thinking is when people take a problem or idea and then build sequentially from that point. A more creative approach is to use lateral thinking. **Lateral thinking** can be defined as a set of systematic techniques used for changing mental concepts and perceptions and generating new ones.[42] With lateral thinking, people move "sideways" to try different perceptions, different concepts, and different points of entry to gain a novel solution. Lateral thinking appears to solve a problem by an unorthodox or apparently illogical method. Lateral thinking makes an unusual mental connection that is concerned with possibilities and "what might be."

Companies such as Boeing, Nokia, IBM, and Nestlé have trained people to use lateral thinking as a way to help the organization meet the demands of a rapidly changing global environment.[43] To stimulate lateral thinking, leaders provide people with opportunities to use different parts of their brains and thus to make novel, creative connections. If the answer isn't in the part of the brain being used, it might be in another that can be stimulated by a new experience. Consider the NASA scientist who was taking a shower in a German hotel while pondering how to fix the distorted lenses in the Hubble telescope in 1990. Nobody could figure out how to fit a corrective mirror into the hard-to-reach space inside the orbiting telescope. The engineer noticed the European-style showerhead mounted on adjustable rods.

Lateral thinking
a set of systematic techniques for breaking away from customary mental concepts and generating new ones

NEW LEADER
ACTION MEMO

As a leader, you can expand the creative potential of people in the organization by facilitating brainstorming, promoting lateral thinking, enabling immersion, allowing for pauses, and fostering creative intuition.

NEW LEADER
ACTION MEMO

Right now, see if you can think of three additional opposites in each of the categories of physical, biological, management, and business. Look at opposites to stretch your thinking for a problem you face.

Immersion
to go deeply into a single area or topic to spark personal creativity

This perception connected with the Hubble problem as he realized that corrective mirrors could be extended into the telescope on similar folding arms. Lateral thinking came to the rescue.[44] Another example comes from Atlanta pediatrician Amy Baxter, who had been trying for years to find a way to use cold to relieve the pain children felt when getting vaccinations. Driving home tired after an all-night shift at the emergency room, Baxter noticed that the steering wheel was vibrating because she hadn't had time to get her tires aligned. As she pulled into the driveway, she realized the vibration had made her hands numb. Baxter had a flash of insight—combining vibration and cold might be enough to ease the pain of a shot. Buzzy, a toylike vibrating bee with a tiny ice pack, is now used in around 500 hospitals to ease injection pain for children.[45]

Alex Osborn, the originator of brainstorming, developed many creative techniques. One effective technique that is widely used to stimulate lateral thinking is the checklist in Exhibit 15.5. The checklist seems to work best when there is a current product or service that needs to be improved. If the problem is to modify a cell phone design to increase its sales, for example, the checklist verbs in Exhibit 15.5 can stimulate an array of different perceptions about the item being analyzed.

An exercise of *considering opposites* will also stretch the mind in a lateral direction. Physical opposites include back/front, big/small, hard/soft, and slow/fast. Biological opposites include young/old, sick/healthy, male/female, and tortoise/hare. Management opposites would be bureaucratic/entrepreneurial, or top-down/bottom-up. Business opposites are buy/sell, profit/loss, and hire/fire.[46]

Enable Immersion Lateral thinking might be considered thinking outside the box. **Immersion** means to go deeply into a single area or topic to spark personal creativity,

EXHIBIT 15.5 Lateral Thinking Checklist

Verb	Description
Put to other uses?	New ways to use as is? Other uses if modified?
Adapt?	What else is like this? What other ideas does this suggest?
Modify?	Change meaning, color, motion, sound, odor, form, shape? Other changes?
Magnify?	What to add: Greater frequency? Stronger? Larger? Plus ingredient? Exaggerate?
Minify?	What to subtract: Eliminate? Smaller? Slower? Lower? Shorter? Lighter? Split up? Less frequent?
Substitute?	Who else instead? What else instead? Other place? Other time?
Rearrange?	Other layout? Other sequence? Change pace?
Reverse?	Transpose positive and negative? How about opposites? Turn it backward? Turn it upside down? Reverse role?
Combine?	How about a blend, an alloy, an assortment, an ensemble? Combine units? Combine purposes? Combine appeals? Combine ideas?

Source: Based on Alex Osborn, *Applied Imagination* (New York: Charles Scribner's Sons, 1963).

which has been called thinking "inside the box."[47] One approach to immersion is to focus on the internal aspects of a situation or problem. People can take a product, situation, or process and break it down into component parts. Manipulating the components in unusual ways can create a valuable new idea. For example, contact lenses arose by removing one component—the eyeglass frame. Phillips Electronics revolutionized the DVD player by shifting functions from the player to a hand-held device. This manipulation created a slimmer and cheaper DVD player.

Another way to get people to break out of habitual thinking patterns and ingrained perceptions is to immerse them in *new* experiences that give them a different perspective on a familiar topic. Top leaders at a bank wanting to get managers thinking in new ways sent them not only to visit competing banks but also to an Apple retail store. One executive says it made him see familiar banking in a whole new light. "Many of us in the industry are trying to put lipstick on a pig—making old banking look new and innovative with decorations but not really changing what's underneath it all, the things that matter most to consumers."[48] Some leaders reorganize often to immerse people in different jobs and responsibilities. Frequent change can be unsettling, but it keeps people's minds fresh and innovative.[49]

Allow Pauses Some of the best ideas often occur when people take time off from working on a problem and change what they are doing. Allowing pauses activates different parts of the brain. Recent research in creativity suggests that having an "aha moment" often requires that a person stop trying to solve a problem and allow the mind to wander.[50] "When you are trying too hard to focus your attention, you are going to miss new ideas," says Jennifer Wiley, a psychology professor at the University of Illinois at Chicago.[51]

Where or when do you get your best ideas? The most popular response is "in the shower." One man got good ideas so consistently in the shower that he regularly experienced a 20-minute mental core dump of ideas. He purchased a piece of clear plastic and a grease pencil to write down the creative ideas while in his "think tank." Creativity often occurs during a mental pause, a period of mixed tension and relaxation. In the shower, or while exercising, driving, walking, or meditating, the mind reverts to a neutral, somewhat unfocused state in which it is receptive to issues or themes that have not been resolved. If the analytical part of the mind is too focused and active, it shuts down the spontaneous part. The semi-relaxed mental "pause" is like putting the analytical left brain on hold and giving room for the intuitive right brain to find the solution in the subconscious mind.[52] C. S. Lewis, author of *The Chronicles of Narnia*, was fond of long, contemplative walks to facilitate his creative juices. Similarly, Jerry Kathman, president and CEO of brand design agency LPK, says he gets many of his ideas during his morning jog.[53] Exercise is often considered a good way to give the mind a chance to work freely.[54]

"After you plant a seed in the ground, you don't dig it up every week to see how it is doing."

William Coyne, former head of R&D at 3M

Leaders can apply this idea by allowing people to have quiet spaces when they need them. Simply breaking up a group session and telling people to go take a walk or work on something simple and repetitive for a while can kick-start the creative process. David Rock, cofounder of the NeuroLeadership Institute, has worked with leaders in many organizations and says leaders have generated a 100 percent to 500 percent improvement in the ability to solve complex problems by using techniques and models that allow pauses so that people have mental space to reflect.[55]

Nurture Creative Intuition The creative flash of insight leaders want to awaken is actually the second stage of creativity. The first stage is data gathering. The mind is gathering data constantly, especially when you are studying background material on a problem to be solved. Then the creative insight bubbles up as an intuition from the deeper subconscious. It may be hard to trust that intuitive process because it seems "soft" to many business executives. The subconscious mind remembers all experiences that the conscious mind has forgotten. Creative intuition has a broader reach than any analytical process focused solely on the problem at hand.

To understand your own creative intuition, consider the following question:[56]

> *A man has married 20 women in a small town. All the women are still alive, and none of them is divorced. The man has broken no laws. Who is the man?*

If you solved this problem the answer came in a sudden flash: the man is a preacher, priest, or justice of the peace. That flash of insight arose from your creative intuition.

Here are some additional problems that might be a little tougher. Each of the following sets of three words has something in common.[57] Do not overanalyze. Instead just relax and see if the common element pops up from your intuition.

1. rat	blue	cottage
2. pine	crab	sauce
3. curtain	fisherman	nuclear reactor
4. envy	golf	beans
5. bowling alley	tailor	wrestling match

Don't rush to find the answers. Give your intuitive subconscious time to work. After it's finished working on these problems, consider the following question you might be asked if you interview for a job at Microsoft: *How would you weigh a large jet aircraft without a scale?* This question combines logical thinking and intuition. Before reading on, how might you compute the airplane's weight doing something that is technologically feasible even if not realistic?[58]

The next challenge may appear to have no solution until your intuition shows you the obvious answer. In the following illustration, remove three matches to leave four.[59]

Here is another problem that may force your mind to respond from a different place to get the answer. The matches are an equation of Roman numerals made from 10 matches. The equation is incorrect. Can you correct the equation without touching the matches, adding new matches, or taking away any matches?

Have you given adequate time to your creative intuition? The answers to these creative challenges follow:

For the word sets, the correct answers are (1) cheese, (2) apple, (3) rods, (4) green, and (5) pins.

One answer to weighing the jet aircraft would be to taxi the jet onto a ship big enough to hold it. You could put a mark on the hull at the water line and then remove the jet and reload the ship with items of known weight until it sinks to the same mark on the hull. The weight of the items will equal the weight of the jet.

The answer to the first match puzzle depends on how you interpret the word "four." Rather than counting four matches, remove the matches at the top, bottom, and right and the answer is obvious—the Roman numeral IV. For the second match puzzle, you can solve this problem by looking at it from a different perspective—turn the page upside down. Did your creative intuition come up with good answers?

15-5 IMPLEMENTING CHANGE

Leaders often see innovation, change, and creativity as a way to strengthen the organization, but many people view change only as painful and disruptive. A critical aspect of leading people through change is understanding that resistance to change is natural—and that there are often legitimate reasons for it. This chapter's *Consider This* box takes a lighthearted look at why employees may resist changes in some overly bureaucratic organizations.

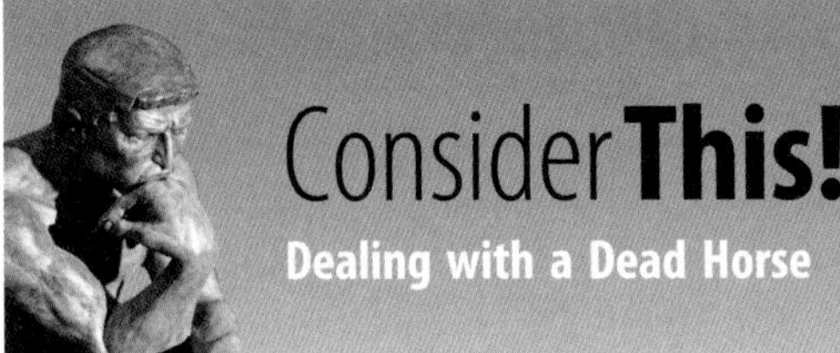

Consider **This!**

Dealing with a Dead Horse

Ancient wisdom says that when you discover you are astride a dead horse, the best strategy is to dismount. In government and other overly bureaucratic organizations, many different approaches are tried. Here are some of our favorite strategies for dealing with the "dead horse" scenario:

1. Change the rider.
2. Buy a stronger whip.
3. Beat the horse harder.
4. Shout at and threaten the horse.
5. Appoint a committee to study the horse.
6. Arrange a visit to other sites to see how they ride dead horses.
7. Increase the standards for riding dead horses.
8. Appoint a committee to revive the dead horse.
9. Create a training session to improve riding skills.
10. Explore the state of dead horses in today's environment.
11. Change the requirements so that the horse no longer meets the standards of death.
12. Hire an external consultant to show how a dead horse can be ridden.
13. Harness several dead horses together to increase speed.
14. Increase funding to improve the horse's performance.
15. Declare that no horse is too dead to ride.
16. Fund a study to determine if outsourcing will reduce the cost of riding a dead horse.
17. Buy a computer program to enhance the dead horse's performance.
18. Declare a dead horse less costly to maintain than a live one.
19. Form a work group to find uses for dead horses. And … if all else fails …
20. Promote the dead horse to a supervisory position. Or, in a large corporation, make it a vice president.

Source: Author unknown. Another version of this story may be found at http://www.abcsmallbiz.com/funny/deadhorse.html.

The underlying reason why employees resist change is that it violates the **personal compact** between workers and the organization.[60] Personal compacts are the reciprocal obligations and commitments that define the relationship between employees and organizations. They include such things as job tasks, performance requirements, evaluation procedures, and compensation packages. These aspects of the compact are generally clearly defined and may be in written form. Other aspects are less clear-cut. The personal compact incorporates elements such as mutual trust and dependence as well as shared values. When employees perceive that change violates the personal compact, they are likely to resist. For example, a new GM at the Dallas–Fort Worth Marriott wanted to change the incentive system to offer bonuses tied to the hotel's financial performance, but employees balked. "They were thinking, 'Here comes the Wicked Witch of the West taking my stuff away,' " the manager said. There are tools available to help leaders implement change.

15-5a Helping People Change

Many leaders don't understand why change is so difficult for many people. But for something new to begin, something old has to end, and most of us have a hard time letting go of something we value, even if we want something new. For example, we want to lose weight, but giving up the chocolate cake seems too much to ask. Rather than focusing on a new beginning and what we might gain from a change, our emotions are stuck on the ending of our current situation and what we might lose.

Changing behavior always depends on changing people's emotions about the situation. People have to psychologically and emotionally let go of the old before they can embrace the new.[61] Exhibit 15.6 illustrates the transition people have to go through to make a successful change. To help someone change means first dealing with the emotions associated with endings and losses rather than denying those emotions or trying to talk people out of feeling them. Then, people move into a neutral zone, where they've let go of the old but the new hasn't yet gelled into an accepted pattern. Finally, they transition into a new beginning. No one gets to a new beginning without first dealing with an ending.

Personal compact
the reciprocal obligations and commitments that define the relationship between employees and the organization

Leaders who want to implement change always have to ask, "who's going to lose what?"[62] In organizations, changes in job design, technology, or structure may mean that some people will no longer have the same type of power or prestige they

EXHIBIT 15.6 Endings Precede Beginnings for Successful Change

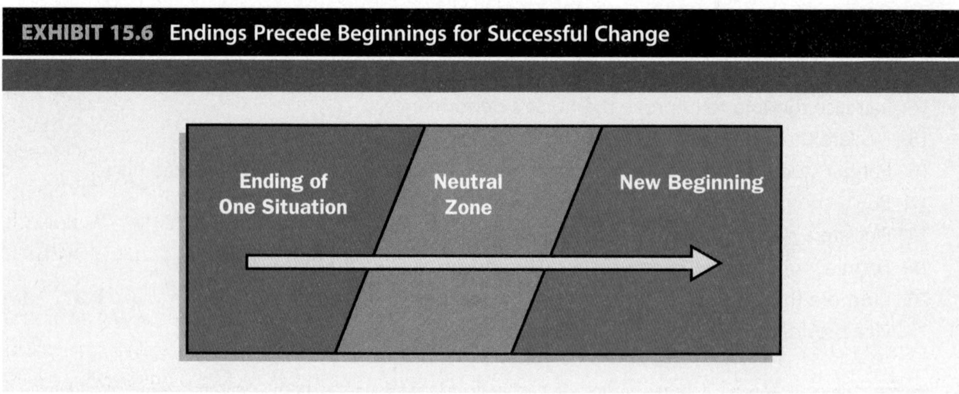

Source: Based on ideas in William Bridges, *Managing Transitions: Making the Most of Change* (Cambridge, MA: Da Capo Lifelong Books, 2009).

once had, for example. Recall from Chapter 14 how a new CEO at Dynergy did away with private offices. Many managers initially resisted the change because they viewed their offices as symbols of their power and prestige in the organization.[63] In addition, when changes are imposed from outside the individual, many people feel a loss of control over their own lives and circumstances, which provokes a strong emotional reaction. Sometimes a change conflicts with the goals of some individuals or departments. At pharmaceuticals company Pfizer, top executives wanted to implement a computerized system for collecting and processing research trial data, which could cut 40 percent off the cost of new drug development. Research and development managers fought the change, citing their concern that the automation and standardization of case report forms would hamper their flexibility and creativity.[64]

Change also means that people have to give up their stable routines. Hospitals that have spent millions of dollars adopting electronic medical records are having a hard time getting doctors to use them. One reason is that electronic records require doctors to change how they go about their daily work, and many are having trouble giving up their standard routines.[65] Most people have at least some fear of the unknown and are more comfortable dealing with the tried-and-true. Particularly when people don't understand how a change will affect them, they find it more reassuring to stick with what they know, even if it is unpleasant, than to jump into the unknown.[66] Utility companies installing wireless smart meters in states from Maine to California have faced a strong backlash from customers who say the meters invade privacy, increase costs, and threaten health.[67] Getting people to switch to new CFL bulbs has been as tough as pulling hens' teeth, and when the U.S. Energy Independence and Security Act was passed to phase out the manufacture and sale of certain wattages of incandescent bulbs, consumers began stockpiling them rather than switching to the CFL versions.[68]

At work, employees might worry that a needed change in work procedures will mean an end to the camaraderie among their work group or fear that a new technology might cause them to lose autonomy or status. At SuperShuttle, a national transportation provider, for example, drivers were opposed to using GPS-enabled phones. The drivers felt that the new technology meant an end to their freedom, since managers could track their movements. SuperShuttle learned that, "if you don't tell employees what to expect, they'll invent something, and inevitably, it will be bad."[69]

15-5b The Keys That Help People Change

Most of us think if we were given a clear choice—change or die—we'd change in a hurry. But in fact, scientific studies demonstrate that most people have a hard time changing even when told that *not* changing will lead them to an early grave.[70] For example, Dr. Dean Ornish, a professor of medicine at the University of California at San Francisco and founder of the Preventive Medicine Research Institute, found that an astonishing nine of ten critically ill patients couldn't change their poor diet and exercise habits even though it meant they would die.[71] But change is possible. When Jon Fairest took over as CEO of pharmaceutical company Sanofi Canada, he led a successful change effort by using a model based on the stages of major change described earlier in this chapter and by incorporating some elements that have been shown to increase the chances of successful personal change.

IN THE LEAD

Jon Fairest, Sanofi Canada

Jon Fairest became CEO of Sanofi Canada just as the organization was about to move employees to a new corporate headquarters, a move that would also shift hundreds of employees to an open-plan workplace. Many employees had spent decades working in a closed environment, and anxiety was high.

Leaders made employees active participants in the change process from the beginning. Three groups of 10 employees each were selected to serve as "Change Ambassadors." People were selected from across the organization based on their credibility, networks, influence, and ability to communicate. Leaders were also careful to include people who might be most resistant to the proposed culture changes. The Change Ambassadors shared information with employees and also shared employee concerns and ideas with leaders so that everyone had a chance to be heard. The groups visited the new headquarters ahead of the move, which helped turn apprehension into excitement. Sample workstations were set up for everyone to view, and employees were polled on their preferences for things such as workstation modules, chairs, carpets, and lighting.

Because the change would significantly alter work habits, leaders also implemented a variety of initiatives to transition people to the new behaviors needed in an open, collaborative environment. For example, an "Open Door" challenge encouraged employees with closed offices to commit to keeping their doors open for a full month. People began preparing weekly job reports to allow issues to be discussed openly. Two months prior to the move, quick "Getting to Know You" sessions were held during morning and lunch breaks to let employees who would be seated together in the new office interact and get acquainted. A set of guidelines for the open-plan workplace was developed, addressing issues such as noise, distracting behavior, clutter, eating, and so forth, along with the proper use of community areas.

The transition to the new headquarters went smoothly, and collaboration and transparency became second nature at Sanofi Canada. In a follow-up survey, 88 percent of employees reported being "satisfied" with the new environment, and 61 percent reported seeing "a positive impact on engagement." Furthermore, the company succeeded in retaining 100 percent of employees during the relocation.[72]

NEW LEADER
ACTION MEMO

As a leader, you can understand the reasons for resistance to change and use tools such as a positive emotional attractor, supportive relationships, repetition, involvement, and after-action reviews to help people change.

Fairest says the change at Sanofi Canada "turned out to be the challenge of my career, perhaps even a bigger challenge than I'd bargained for when signing on." Yet by implementing smart change leadership strategies, leaders helped people shift to a new way of working that put Sanofi in a stronger competitive position.

Changing people's thinking and behavior is possible, and the keys to doing so incorporate five elements: a positive emotional attractor, supportive relationships, repetition of new behaviors, participation and involvement, and after-action reviews.[73]

- *Provide a positive emotional attractor.* A positive emotional attractor (PEA) is something that awakens a person's hopes and dreams about the future, about possibilities of what could be, rather than focusing on trying to "fix" weaknesses or shortcomings. For example, studies by Dr. Dean Ornish, introduced earlier, show that when people feel convinced that they can enjoy life more, they are much more likely to make significant changes in their lifestyle and stick with the changes over the long term. Instead of motivating with the "fear of dying," Dr. Ornish began inspiring people with a clear vision of the "joy of living." People learn and change because they *want to*, not because they *ought to*, which means they need an inspiring vision of what the future can be.[74]

- *Make sure people have a support system.* Leaders help people establish new, emotional relationships that provide hope, make people believe they have the power to change, and inspire people with the expectation that change will happen. Effective leaders of social movements, for example, are highly skilled at giving people hope and faith that change is possible. This emotional relationship with a leader, a mentor, or a community helps people learn and practice the new skills and habits needed to change. This is what Alcoholics Anonymous or Weight Watchers meetings are all about, for example.
- *Use repetition.* People need the opportunity to experiment and practice the new skills and habits over and over until the new pattern of behavior becomes automatic. At Cedars-Sinai Medical Center, an epidemiologist used an experiment that showed doctors that their hands were covered with gobs of harmful bacteria. By showing one of the filthiest images as a screen saver on the hospital's computer network, everyone on the staff was continually reminded of the importance of frequent hand washing. With repeated practice, hand-hygiene compliance eventually spiked to nearly 100 percent and stayed there.[75]
- *Involve people early.* When people are involved in helping to design the change, they will be more committed to it. Although this approach is time-consuming, it pays off by giving people a sense of control over the change activity. They come to understand the change better and become committed to its successful implementation. Leaders at contracting and research firm Noblis wanted to do away with traditional job titles and replace the system with "career bands" that would enable people to move sideways, not just up the hierarchy. The new system was part of a broader redefinition of jobs and responsibilities as Noblis shifted its strategy to a greater emphasis on competitive bid work. Leaders knew it could be a tough sell, so they had a group of employees spend six months studying the new plans and seeking feedback from people all around the company. "It was a fine-tooth comb with all our stakeholders, because we wanted to have a model that was built by Noblis for Noblis," said Amy Rivera, a member of the HR team.[76]
- *Apply after-action reviews.* An excellent mechanism for evaluation and feedback on a change is the after-action review. After-action reviews are quick sessions during which leaders review the outcome of change activities to see what worked, what didn't, and what can be learned from it. The concept of after-action reviews comes from the United States Army. After every identifiable activity—whether in field operations or training simulations—people take 15 minutes to ask four simple questions: What was supposed to happen? What actually happened? What accounts for the difference? What can we learn? Many businesses, including consulting firm Jump Associates, oil giant BP, and Steelcase, Inc., which makes office furniture, use after-action reviews for feedback and learning.[77]

Effectively and humanely leading change is one of the greatest challenges for leaders. The nature and pace of change in today's environment can be exhilarating, but it can also be inconvenient, painful, and downright scary. Savvy leaders can help people navigate the change process and make it successful.

LEADERSHIP ESSENTIALS

- The important point of this chapter is that tools and approaches are available to help leaders facilitate creativity and change. The increased pace of change in today's global environment has led to even greater problems for leaders struggling to help their organizations adapt. Many people have a natural resistance to change, but leaders can serve as role models to facilitate change. Leaders who can successfully accomplish change typically define themselves as change leaders, describe a vision for the future in vivid terms, and articulate values that promote change and adaptability. Change leaders are courageous, are capable of managing complexity and uncertainty, believe in followers' capacity to assume responsibility for change, and learn from their own mistakes.
- Major changes can be particularly difficult to implement, but leaders can help to ensure a successful change effort by following the eight-stage model of planned change—light a fire for change; get the right people on board; develop a compelling vision and strategy; go overboard on communication; empower employees to act; generate short-term wins; keep up the energy and commitment to tackle bigger problems; and institutionalize the change in the organizational culture.
- An exciting approach to change management known as appreciative inquiry engages individuals, teams, or the entire organization in creating change by reinforcing positive messages and focusing on learning from success. Rather than looking at a situation from the viewpoint of what is wrong and who is to blame, AI takes a positive, affirming approach and follows the stages of discovery, dream, design, and destiny. AI is powerful for leading both major changes and smaller, everyday changes.
- Leading creativity for change and innovation is a significant challenge for today's leaders. Leaders instill creative values in particular departments or the entire organization by fostering a creative culture and promoting collaboration. Although some people demonstrate more creativity than others, research suggests that everyone has roughly equal creative potential. Leaders can increase individual creativity by facilitating brainstorming, promoting lateral thinking, enabling immersion, allowing pauses, and fostering creative intuition.
- Implementation is a critical aspect of any change initiative. Leaders should strive to understand why people resist a change. For something new to begin, something old has to end, and most people have a hard time letting go of something they value. Leaders can help people change by changing emotions so that people can let go of the old and embrace the new. They can provide a positive emotional attractor, supportive relationships, repetition of new behaviors, participation and involvement, and after-action reviews.

DISCUSSION QUESTIONS

1. As a leader, how might you overcome your own felt resistance to a change from above and act as a role model for implementing the change?
2. How are Kotter's eight-stage framework for change and the AI method similar? How are they different? Explain.

3. Think of a problem situation you would like to change at work, school, or home and describe how you would provide a positive emotional attractor for this change.
4. How could you increase the number of novel and useful solutions you can come up with to solve a problem?
5. Of the five elements that help people change (positive emotional attractor, supportive relationships, repetition of new behaviors, participation and involvement, and after-action reviews), which do you think leaders are most likely to overlook? Why?
6. How would you suggest a leader overcome resistance to a change that is going to cause some people to lose their jobs?
7. Why are idea champions important for a creative culture? Do you think these people would be more important in a large organization or a small one?Discuss.
8. Planned change is often considered ideal. Do you think unplanned change could be effective? Discuss. Can you think of an example?
9. Is the world really changing faster today, or do people just assume so?
10. Do you believe the Wall Street meltdown of 2008 will lead to any lasting changes in U.S. financial services institutions? What kinds of lasting changes do you envision? What about companies in other industries?

LEADERSHIP AT WORK

Organizational Change Role Play

You are the new director of the Harpeth Gardens not-for-profit nursing home. Harpeth Gardens is one of 20 elder-care centers managed by Franklin Resident Care Centers. Harpeth Gardens has 56 patients and is completely responsible for their proper hygiene, nutrition, and daily recreation. Many of the patients can move about by themselves, but several require physical assistance for eating, dressing, and moving about the nursing home. During daytime hours, the head of nursing is in charge of the four certified nursing assistants (CNAs) who work on the floors. During the night shift, a registered nurse is on duty, along with three CNAs. The same number of CNAs are on duty over the weekend, and either the head of nursing or the registered nurse is on call.

Several other staff also report to you, including the heads of maintenance, bookkeeping/MIS, and the cafeteria. The on-call physician stops by Harpeth Gardens once a week to check on the residents. You have 26 full- and part-time employees who cover the different tasks and shifts.

During your interviews for the director's job, you became aware that the previous director ran a very tight ship, insisting that the best way to care for nursing home patients was by following strict rules and procedures. He personally approved almost every decision, including decisions for patient care, despite not having a medical degree. Turnover has been rather high, and several beds are empty because of the time required to hire and train new staff. Other elder-care facilities in the area have a waiting list of people wanting to be admitted.

At Harpeth Gardens, the nonnursing offices have little interaction with nurses or each other. Back-office staff people seem to do their work and go home. Overall, Harpeth Gardens seems to you like a dreary place to work. People seem to have forgotten the compassion for patients and for each other that is essential to working in a health-care environment. You believe that a new strategy and culture are needed to give more responsibility to employees, improve morale, reduce turnover, and fill the empty beds. You have read about concepts for leading organizational change and would like to implement some new ideas to make the culture at Harpeth Gardens more creative, decentralized, and participative. You decide to start with the idea of engaging employees in decision making and encouraging more direct collaboration between departments. If those two ideas work, then you will implement other changes.

During your first week as the director, you have met all the employees, and you have confirmed your understanding of the previous director's rigid approach. You call a meeting of all employees for next Friday afternoon.

Your assignment for this exercise is to decide how you will implement the desired changes and what you will tell employees at the employee meeting. Start by deciding how you will accomplish each of the first three steps in the model in Exhibit 15.2. Write your answers to these three questions:

How will you get employees to feel a sense of urgency?

____

____

____

How will you form a guiding coalition, and who will be in it?

____

____

____

What is your compelling vision?

____

____

____

Your next task is to prepare a *vision speech* to employees for the changes you are about to implement. In this speech, explain your dream for Harpeth Gardens and the urgency of this change. Explain exactly what you believe the changes will involve and why the employees should agree to the changes and help implement them. Sketch out the points you will include in your speech:

____

____

____

In Class: The instructor can divide the class into small groups to discuss the answers to the preceding three questions and to brainstorm the key points to cover in the vision speech to employees. After student groups have decided what the director will say, the instructor can ask for volunteers from a few groups to actually give the speech to employees that will start the Harpeth Gardens transition toward a more adaptive organization. The key questions are: Did the speech touch on the key points that inspire employees to help implement changes? Did the speech convey a high purpose and a sense of urgency? Did the speech connect with employees in a personal way, and did it lay out the reality facing Harpeth Gardens?

LEADERSHIP DEVELOPMENT: CASES FOR ANALYSIS

"From This Point On..."

Bernini Foods is one of several companies offering healthy, frozen-packaged meals in the once-laughable and nutritionally challenged frozen dinner industry. Meeting the changing needs of modern, on-the-go, budget-conscious consumers, the new meals offered by Bernini face unprecedented competition from long-time industry leaders including Bertolli, Marie Callendar, Healthy Choice, Lean Cuisine, and others.

Cutthroat competition within the industry means every corporation must hustle for quality ingredients, improved packaging, efficiency in delivery systems, and decreased cooking times. Like its competitors, Bernini looks to increased market share through a combination of price cuts and the introduction of new products.

To meet these challenges, CEO Roberto Bernini created a new management position to monitor pricing and purchasing. VP for Finance Ted McCann hired Lucian Wilkes, a retired army colonel, for the new position, giving him wide latitude for setting up new rules and procedures. With an announcement from CEO Bernini, Wilkes was introduced to the company. Following an intense period of in-house research and information gathering, Wilkes zeroed in on what he saw as the major problems—the fragmentation of pricing and purchasing decisions, with managers in various regions devising their own standards and making their own contracts.

The process sent up red flags for Wilkes. He made an across-the-board e-mail announcement for new sustainability procedures, basically informing each regional office that "from this point on . . ." regional managers must inform his office of any price change above 3 percent. In addition, all local purchase contracts above $10,000 must also be approved by Wilkes's office prior to implementation.

Directives for these new standardization procedures were issued to regional managers for their policy manuals. These managers, according to their immediate feedback, were all in agreement with the changes. But as one month followed another, Wilkes's concern and level of frustration grew, and a culture of business as usual appeared to continue. Managers did not resist. Frequent correspondence across the various regions including e-mails, faxes, and conference calls brought repeated assurances that change was coming.

"We just need time to make the changes," one manager said.

But weeks dragged on and the situation remained unaltered. Complicating the situation, Wilkes appeared to have no vocal support from company executives, who were busy with their own concerns. While both Bernini and McCann offered lukewarm comments about the need for new initiatives to spur efficiency, neither demonstrated wholehearted support for the changes. The new plan was going nowhere, and Wilkes was aware that the failure of the company to increase profits could result in the loss of his own position.

"If nothing changes," Wilkes complained to his wife, "the regional managers will remain on the job. My job will be cut."

Wilkes wondered what his next move should be. In how many ways could he inform the managers to implement the new procedures? What pressures could he apply? How could he impress upon Bernini and McCann the importance of their support for the changes? He felt at a loss for what he should do. Did Bernini Foods want these new standards implemented or not?

QUESTIONS

1. Why do you think the regions are not responding to Wilkes's initiative for change? What did Wilkes do wrong with respect to implementing the change?
2. Should Wilkes solicit more active support from Bernini and McCann for the change he is trying to implement? How might he do that?
3. Develop a plan that Wilkes can use to successfully restart the implementation of this change.

Riverside Pediatric Associates

Five years ago, doctors Alvero Sanchez and Josh Hudson opened a small pediatrics office in Riverside, California. These longtime friends, who had graduated from medical school together, had finally achieved the dream of starting a pediatrics practice with the vision of providing excellent care to children in their community. The five doctors, six nurses, and accountant who staffed the office quickly developed a reputation for being caring and conscientious.

The staff also partnered with local organizations to serve the underprivileged in the community, providing free flu shots and health clinics at the local YMCA. Sanchez and Hudson were energized and ecstatic that they were living out their dream, managing their small practice in the midst of a community that respected them.

Their dream started to unravel, however, as the practice began growing at an unwieldy pace. The population of nearby Hispanic communities was burgeoning, and so was the number of patients coming to Riverside. Although Sanchez and Hudson had always dreamed of a large, profitable practice, they realized they were not prepared for such unprecedented growth. The number of new patients was skyrocketing, and the staff at Riverside was unprepared to handle the influx. Waiting rooms were packed, the staff was becoming short-tempered, and communication among staff was breaking down. Internal systems—like the electronic medical records systems—were overloaded, and patient health records were getting lost. Patient scheduling was chaotic, causing long waits for many people. The systems and procedures that once provided a firm underpinning for the small practice could no longer sustain the rapid patient growth.

Frustration mounted as the founding doctors spent more of their time managing the growing business and less time on patient care. They realized their original vision of providing excellent pediatric care in a comforting environment was fading fast. Most importantly, they were growing dissatisfied with their work. Instead of diagnosing illnesses and building relationships with patients, they were spending more time overseeing the expansion and growth of their practice: interviewing and hiring additional doctors and nurses, supervising construction of the office expansion, and training new staff on office procedures. Their primary reason for opening a practice seemed like a long-forgotten memory.

Under the growing pressure, staff morale began to buckle. Heated arguments and short tempers among the staff were becoming commonplace. One stellar nurse had resigned, feeling powerless and disenfranchised by the conditions in the office. Another had been fired after arguing with a frazzled parent. Even Sanchez and Hudson were growing frustrated and unhappy in their work. Secluded for a quick lunch in the break room, Hudson confided in Sanchez. "There was a time," he said, "when we found meaning in our work. I felt most alive and fulfilled when we were just starting out. Now, we're just scrambling to keep pace with the change, but we're falling behind and drifting away from what's important—excellent care for our patients."

Their lunch was interrupted by a knock at the door and some unexpected news from their accountant. The quarterly financial reports painted a grim picture, she told them. The recent pattern of decreasing revenue and escalating costs was continuing in this quarter. A financial crisis was beginning to brew, affecting both cash flow and profitability. The accountant explained that quick action would need to be taken to improve the practice's financial health. "We have three problems," she explained, "and those are declining reimbursement from insurance companies, delinquent payments from patients, and rising costs of medical supplies and lab work." She paused and then added, "It doesn't help that our billing software is archaic. It simply can't manage the size of this practice."

Sanchez tore a page from his prescription pad, flipped it over, and scratched out the following: *To survive, Riverside Pediatric Associates must (1) improve service to patients and family; (2) improve respect and collaborative communication among the staff; (3) save money; (4) collect fees from patients in a timely manner; and (5) encourage innovation and creativity from our staff to solve routine problems.* He slid this list across the table to Hudson, asking, "How do we make this happen?"

QUESTIONS

1. Assume you are Sanchez or Hudson and plan to implement immediate organizational change within the practice. Where would you start? What steps would you take?
2. The accountant recommended that Sanchez and Hudson consider using AI to facilitate positive change within the practice. How would you implement the four steps of AI? Be specific.

What kinds of things would you expect to arise during the Discover and Dream steps of AI?

3. Sanchez and Hudson are caught between being physicians and being leaders of their practice. How do you suggest they resolve this dilemma? What leadership qualities will Sanchez and Hudson need to display in order to lead positive change in their practice?

Source: Based on Caroline Carter et al., "An Appreciative Inquiry Approach to Practice Improvement and Transformative Change in Health Care Settings," *Q Manage Health Care* 16, no. 3 (© 2007 Wolters Kluwer Health; Lippincott Williams and Wilkins), pp. 194–204.

REFERENCES

1. Phil Wahba, "J.C. Penney Tapping Tech to Claw Back Billions in Lost Sales," *Fortune* (October 28, 2015), http://fortune.com/2015/10/28/jcpenney-tech/ (accessed December 1, 2015); Emily Glazer, Joann Lublin, and Dana Mattioli, "Penney Backfires on Ackman," *The Wall Street Journal* (April 10, 2013), http://online.wsj.com/article/SB100014241278873245047045784124402 93890624.html (accessed June 11, 2013); Jena McGregor, "J.C. Penney's Ron Johnson Shows the Perils of a Star CEO," *Washington Post* (April 9, 2013), http://articles.washingtonpost.com/2013-04-09/national/38392404_1_ron-johnson-ceo-bob-nardelli (accessed June 11, 2013); Stephanie Clifford, "Chief's Silicon Valley Stardom Quickly Clashed at J. C. Penney," *The New York Times* (April 9, 2013), http://www.nytimes.com/2013/04/10/business/how-an-apple-star-lost-his-luster-at- penneys.html?pagewanted=all&_r=0 (accessed June 11, 2013); and James Surowiecki, "The Turnaround Trap," *The New Yorker* (March 25, 2013), p. 44.
2. Reported in Surowiecki, "The Turnaround Trap."
3. Steve Lohr, "How Crisis Shapes the Corporate Model," *The New York Times* (March 29, 2009), p. BU4.
4. Based on John P. Kotter, *The New Rules: How to Succeed in Today's Post-Corporate World* (New York: The Free Press, 1995); and David K. Carr, Kelvin J. Hard, and William J. Trahant, *Managing the Change Process: A Field Book for Change Agents, Consultants, Team Leaders, and Reengineering Managers* (New York: McGraw-Hill, 1996).
5. The Conference Board, *Change Management: An Overview of Current Initiatives* (New York: The Conference Board, 1994); and studies reported in Rodrigue Fontaine, Gapur Oziev, and Hussein Hassan-Hussein, "Evaluating Chris Argyris's Ideas: An Islamic Perspective," *Journal of Management Development* 31, no. 10 (2012), pp. 1046–1057.
6. This is based on an interview with Justin O'Connell of Comalco, Exhibit 4.1, "Uniforms and Parking Space at Comalco," in David K. Carr, Kelvin J. Hard, and William J. Trahant, *Managing the Change Process* (New York: McGraw-Hill, 1996), pp. 70–71.
7. Alain Vas, "Top Management Skills in a Context of Endemic Organizational Change: The Case of Belgacom," *Journal of General Management* 27, no. 1 (Autumn 2001), pp. 71–89.
8. Naomi Schaefer Riley, "Seeing through the School Daze; Michelle Rhee Fired 241 Teachers, 36 Principals, and 22 Assistant Principals after Taking Over the District's Schools," *The Wall Street Journal* (February 19, 2013), p. A13; Michelle Rhee and Adrian Fenty, "Review—The Education Manifesto—Michelle Rhee and Adrian Fenty on What They Learned While Pushing to Reform D.C.'s Failing Public Schools," *The Wall Street Journal* (October 30, 2010), p. C1; Jeff Chu, "The Iron Chancellor," *Fast Company* (September 2008), pp. 112–143; Amanda Ripley, "Can She Save Our Schools?" *Time* (December 8, 2008), pp. 36–44; and William McGurn, "Giving Lousy Teachers the Boot; Michelle Rhee Does the Once Unthinkable in Washington," *The Wall Street Journal* (July 27, 2010).
9. Jonathan Oosting, "StudentsFirst's Michelle Rhee Returns to Michigan as Education Reform Group Makes Mark," *MLive* (May 26, 2013), http://www.mlive.com/politics/index.ssf/2013/05/studentsfirst_spotlight_michel.html (accessed June 11, 2013).
10. The following discussion is based on John P. Kotter, *Leading Change* (Boston: Harvard Business School Press, 1996), pp. 20–25; John P. Kotter, "Leading Change: Why Transformation Efforts Fail," *Harvard Business Review* (March–April 1995), pp. 59–67; John P. Kotter, "Accelerate!," *Harvard Business Review* (November 2012), pp. 44–58; and Steven H. Appelbaum, Sally Habashy, Jean-Luc Malo, and Hisham Shafiq, "Back to the Future: Revisiting Kotter's 1996 Change Model," *Journal of Management Development* 31, no. 8 (2012), pp. 764–782.
11. Peter Löscher, "How I Did It ... The CEO of Siemens on Using a Scandal to Drive Change," *Harvard Business Review* (November 2012), pp. 39–42.
12. Ibid.
13. John Beeson, "On Leading Change: A Conversation with Bill Glavin of OppenheimerFunds, Inc.," *Business Horizons* (2013), pp. 23–25.
14. Larry Hirschhorn, "Campaigning for Change," *Harvard Business Review* (July 2002), pp. 98–104.
15. Christopher Lindquist, "Watch Carefully," *CIO* (June 8, 2005), http://www.cio.com.au/article/181417/watch_carefully/ (accessed May 19, 2011).
16. David L. Cooperrider and Shuresh Srivastva, "Appreciative Inquiry in Organizational Life," in R. Woodman and W. Pasmore, eds., *Research in Organizational Change and Development*, vol. 1 (Greenwich, CT: JAI Press, 1987); and D. Cooperrider and D. Whitney, *Appreciative Inquiry: A Positive Revolution in Change* (San Francisco, CA: Berrett-Koehler, 2005).
17. Quoted in Dave Kovaleski, "Appreciating Appreciative Inquiry," *Corporate Meetings & Incentives* (August 2008), pp. 10–11.
18. This discussion draws from Sarah Lewis, Jonathan Passmore, and Stefan Cantore, "Using Appreciative Inquiry in Sales Team Development," *Industrial and Commercial Training* 40, no. 4 (2008), pp. 175–180; Steven J. Skinner and Scott W. Kelley, "Transforming Sales Organizations through Appreciative Inquiry," *Psychology & Marketing* 23, no 2 (February 2006), pp. 77–93; and Gabriella Giglio, Silvia Michalcova, and Chris Yates, "Instilling a Culture of Winning at American Express," *Organization Development Journal* 25, no. 4 (Winter 2007), pp. 33–37.
19. See http://appreciativeinquiry.case.edu/practice/bibAiStories.cfm (accessed July 16, 2009) for examples of the uses of appreciative inquiry.
20. Example described in Mark Bechtold, "Improving Worker Morale through the Use of Appreciative Inquiry," *Industrial and Commercial Training* 43, no. 1 (2011), pp. 25–30.
21. Debra Meyerson, *Tempered Radicals: How People Use Difference to Inspire Change at Work* (Boston: Harvard Business School Press, 2001).
22. William B. Locander and David L. Luechauer, "Leader as Inquirer: Change Your Approach to Inquiry," *Marketing Management* (September–October

2007), pp. 46–49; Skinner and Kelley, "Transforming Sales Organizations through Appreciative Inquiry."

23. Thomas J. Griffin, "In the Eye of the Beholder: Interview with Jim 'Gus' Gustafson," *Appreciative Leadership Interviews* (The Taos Institute), http://www.taosinstitute.com/resources/gustafson.html (accessed July 16, 2009); and "Getting to Know … Gus Gustafson, CCL Donor and Alumnus," *Making a Difference: A Report on Activities and Impact from the Center for Creative Leadership* (Greensboro, NC: Center for Creative Leadership, January 2009), http://www.ccl.org/leadership/pdf/news/newsletters/mad0109.pdf (accessed July 16, 2009).
24. Stanley S. Gryskiewicz, "Cashing In on Creativity at Work," *Psychology Today* (September–October 2000), pp. 63–66.
25. Dorothy A. Leonard and Walter C. Swap, *When Sparks Fly: Igniting Creativity in Groups* (Boston: Harvard Business School Press, 1999), pp. 6–8.
26. Alan G. Robinson and Sam Stern, *Corporate Creativity: How Innovation and Improvement Actually Happen* (San Francisco: Berrett-Koehler, 1997).
27. Sherry Eng, "Hatching Schemes," *The Industry Standard* (November 27–December 4, 2000), pp. 174–175.
28. Alan Deutschman, "The Fabric of Creativity," *Fast Company* (December 2004), p. 54.
29. Robert D. Austin, Lee Devin, and Erin Sullivan, "Oops! Accidents Lead to Innovations. So, How Do You Create More Accidents?" *The Wall Street Journal* (July 7, 2008), p. R6.
30. Example cited in Phred Dvorak, "Businesses Take a Page from Design Firms; Sloan-Kettering Taps Industry for Innovative Ideas on Management," *The Wall Street Journal* (November 10, 2008), p. B4.
31. Caneel K. Joyce, Kyle E. Jennings, Jonathan Hey, Jeffrey C. Grossman, and Thomas Kalil, "Getting Down to Business: Using Speedstorming to Initiate Creative Cross-Disciplinary Collaboration," *Creativity and Innovation Management* 19, no. 1 (2010), pp. 57–67.
32. John Bessant, Kathrin Möslein, and Bettina Von Stamm, "Business Insight (A Special Report): In Search of Innovation," *The Wall Street Journal* (June 22, 2009), p. R4.
33. Joyce et al., "Getting Down to Business: Using Speedstorming to Initiate Creative Cross-Disciplinary Collaboration."
34. Jonah Lehrer, "How to Be Creative," *The Wall Street Journal* (March 10, 2010), p. C1.
35. These tips are based on Leigh Thompson, "Improving the Creativity of Organizational Work Groups," *Academy of Management Executive* 17 (2003), pp. 96–109; Bruce Nussbaum, "The Power of Design," *BusinessWeek* (May 17, 2004), pp. 86–94; and the ideas of Alex Osborn as described in Anya Kamenetz, "Building a Better Brainstorm," *Fast Company* (February 2013), pp. 32–35.
36. David Kirkpatrick, "Throw It at the Wall and See if It Sticks," *Fortune* (December 12, 2005), pp. 142–150.
37. Anya Kamenetz, "Building a Better Brainstorm," *Fast Company* (February 2013), pp. 32–35; Kevin P. Coyne and Shawn T. Coyne, "Seven Steps to Better Brainstorming," *McKinsey Quarterly* (March 2011).
38. Reena Jana, "Real Life Imitates Real World," *BusinessWeek* (March 23–30, 2009), p. 42.
39. R. B. Gallupe, W. H. Cooper, M. L. Grise, and L. M. Bastianutti, "Blocking Electronic Brainstorms," *Journal of Applied Psychology* 79 (1994), pp. 77–86; R. B. Gallupe and W. H. Cooper, "Brainstorming Electronically," *Sloan Management Review* (Fall 1993), pp. 27–36; and Alison Stein Wellner, "A Perfect Brainstorm," *Inc.* (October 2003), pp. 31–35.
40. Example described in Burt Helm, "Wal-Mart, Please Don't Leave Me," *BusinessWeek* (October 9, 2006), pp. 84–89.
41. Wellner, "A Perfect Brainstorm"; Gallupe and Cooper, "Brainstorming Electronically."
42. Edward DeBono, *Serious Creativity: Using the Power of Lateral Thinking to Create New Ideas* (New York: HarperBusiness, 1992).
43. Dave Waller, "The Gospel According to Edward DeBono," *Management Today* (August 2007), http://www.managementtoday.co.uk (accessed July 27, 2009).
44. Francine Russo, "The Hidden Secrets of the Creative Mind," *Time* (January 16, 2006), pp. 89–90.
45. Reported in Sue Shellenbarger, "Tactics to Spark Creativity," *The Wall Street Journal* (April 2, 2013), http://online.wsj.com/article/SB10001424127887323611604578398342398991844.html (accessed June 13, 2013).
46. Derm Barrett, *The Paradox Process: Creative Business Solutions … Where You Least Expect to Find Them* (New York: American Management Association, 1997).
47. This discussion is based on Drew Boyd and Jacob Goldenberg, "Think Inside the Box," *The Wall Street Journal* (June 15–16, 2013), pp. C1, C2.
48. Quoted in Marla Capozzi, Renée Dye, and Amy Howe, "Sparking Creativity in Teams: An Executive's Guide," *McKinsey Quarterly* (April 2011).
49. Ronald T. Kadish, "Mix People Up," *Harvard Business Review* (August 2002), pp. 39–49.
50. Shellenbarger, "Tactics to Spark Creativity"; David Rock, "Neuroscience Provides Fresh Insight into the 'Aha' Moment," *T +D* (February 2011), pp. 45–49; and Evangelina G. Chrysikou, "Your Creative Brain at Work," *Scientific American Mind* (July–August 2012), pp. 24–31.
51. Quoted in Shellenbarger, "Tactics to Spark Creativity."
52. R. Donald Gamache and Robert Lawrence Kuhn, *The Creativity Infusion: How Managers Can Start and Sustain Creativity and Innovation* (New York: Harper & Row, 1989); Alison Stein Wellner, "Cleaning Up," *Inc.* (October 2003), p. 35; and Roger von Oech, *A Kick in the Seat of the Pants* (New York: Harper & Row, 1986).
53. Alison Stein Wellner, "Creative Control: Even Bosses Need Time to Dream," *Inc.* (July 2007), pp. 40–42.
54. Richard A. Lovett, "Jog Your Brain," *Psychology Today* (May/June 2006), pp. 55–56; and Mary Carmichael, "Stronger, Faster, Smarter," *Newsweek* (March 26, 2007), pp. 38–46.
55. Rock, "Neuroscience Provides Fresh Insight into the 'Aha' Moment."
56. This question comes from Lehrer, "How to Be Creative."
57. This word challenge and the answers given for it later in the chapter are from Will Shortz, "RD Challenge," *Readers Digest* (March 2004), p. 204; Lehrer, "How to Be Creative"; and Sarnoff A. Mednick, "The Associative Basis of the Creative Process," *Psychological Review* 69, no. 3 (1962), pp. 220–232.
58. This question and the answer given later are from Tahl Raz, "How Would You Design Bill Gates' Bathroom?" *Inc.* (May 2003), p. 35.
59. These match puzzles are from Michael Michalko, *Thinkertoys*, 2nd ed. (Berkeley, CA: Ten Speed Press, 2006).
60. Based on Paul Stebel, "Why Do Employees Resist Change?" *Harvard Business Review* (May–June 1996), pp. 86–92.
61. William Bridges, *Transitions: Making Sense of Life's Changes* (Reading, MA: Addison-Wesley, 1980); and William Bridges, "Three Questions," *Leadership Excellence* (February 2010), p. 11.
62. Bridges, "Three Questions."
63. Joann S. Lublin, "Can a New Culture Fix Troubled Companies?" *The Wall Street Journal* (March 13, 2013), p. B1.
64. Todd Datz, "No Small Change," *CIO* (February 15, 2004), pp. 66–72.
65. Katherine Hobson, "Getting Docs to Use PCs," *The New York Times* (March 15, 2011).
66. Brian J. Hurn, "Management of Change in a Multinational Company," *Industrial and Commercial Training* 44, no. 2 (2012), pp. 41–46.
67. Mark Chediak, "Utilities Try to Tame the Backlash against Smart Meters," *Bloomberg BusinessWeek* (May 10, 2012), http://www.businessweek.com/articles/2012–05-10/utilities-try-to-tame-the-backlash-against-smart-meters (accessed June 13, 2013).
68. Michelle Manetti, "Incandescent Lightbulb Phase-Out Has People Hoarding High Watts," *The Huffington Post* (October 18, 2012), http://www.huffingtonpost.com/2012/10/18/incandescent-lightbulb-phase-out-hoarders_n_1981215.html (accessed June 13, 2013).
69. Lindquist, "Watch Carefully."

70. See studies reported in Alan Deutschman, "Change or Die," *Fast Company* (May 1, 2005), http://www.fastcompany.com/magazine/94/open_change-or-die.html (accessed July 23, 2008); and Alan Deutschman, "The Three Keys to Change," *Fast Company* (January 2, 2007), http://www.fastcompany.com/articles/2007/01/change-or-die.html (accessed July 23, 2008).
71. Dr. Ornish's story is told in Deutschman, "Change or Die."
72. Jon Fairest, "Leading Employees Through Major Organizational Change," *Ivey Business Journal* (July-August 2014), http://iveybusinessjournal.com/publication/leading-employees-through-major-organizational-change/ (accessed December 2, 2015).
73. The following is based in part on Richard E. Boyatzis, "How People Change: Create Positive Attractors," *Leadership Excellence* (October 2010), p. 17; and Deutschman, "The Three Keys to Change."
74. Deutschman, "Change or Die"; and Boyatzis, "How People Change."
75. Dan Heath and Chip Heath, "Passion Provokes Action," *Fast Company* (February 2011), pp. 28, 30.
76. Sarah Halzack, "Noblis Does Away with Traditional Job Titles to Improve Career Development," *The Washington Post* (March 10, 2013), http://articles.washingtonpost.com/2013–03-10/business/37605632_1_band-project-manager-staffer (accessed March 11, 2013).
77. Thomas E. Ricks, "Army Devises System to Decide What Does, Does Not, Work," *The Wall Street Journal* (May 23, 1997); John O'Shea, "Army: The Leader as Learner-in-Chief," *The Officer* (June 2003), p. 31; and Dan Heath and Chip Heath, "Made to Stick: Watch the Game Film," *Fast Company* (June 1, 2010), http://www.fastcompany.com/1646990/made-stick-watch-game-film (accessed June 13, 2013).

NAME INDEX

A

Ackerley, Anne F., 350
Acton (Lord), 385
Adams, John Quincy, 105
Addams, Jane, 105
Ahrendts, Angela, 119, 120, 278
Akbar, Noorjahan, 186
Akhmechet, Slava, 243
Alfonso, Michael (case), 162, 163
Alli, Shakrat, 350
Allio, Robert J., 25
Anderson, Max, 449
Andrews, Bill (case), 189–191
Armstrong, Lance, 169
Arrington, Michael, 50
Ashford, S. J., 436
Ashkenas, Ron, 438
Augustine, Norman, R., 112
Ault, James, 245
Autry, Gene, 12
Avery, Gayle C., 401
Avolio, Bruce J., 143, 339, 364

B

Bair, Sheila, 381
Bale, Alexis (case), 353
Ball, Molly, 338
Ballmer, Steve, 65
Banaji, Mahzarin, 332
Barnes, Brenda, 103
Barsoux, Jean-Louis, 53, 107
Bartz, Carol, 4
Bass, Bernard M., 39, 78, 142, 143, 339, 364
Batiste, John, 213
Battley, Susan, 217
Baxter, Amy, 478
Beale, Inga, 336, 337
Becht, Bart, 332
Beers, Charlotte, 100, 101
Belichick, Bill, 268
Benfari, Robert C., 110
Bennett, M., 348
Bennett, Michael, 273
Bennis, Warren, 136, 210
Bernini, Roberto (case), 489
Bertolon, Henry, 272
Bettinger, Walt, 158
Bezos, Jeff, 405
Biden, Joe, 366
Bielby, William, 334, 352
Blake, Frank, 417
Blake, Robert R., 49
Blanchard, Kenneth H., 68–72, 79, 91
Block, Allen (case), 94, 95
Blount, Chris (case), 387
Bock, Halley, 274
Bock, Laszlo, 347
Bogart, Humphrey, 162
Bogenrief, Margaret, 138
Bolman, Lee G., 377, 379
Bond, Zane, 151
Bosh, Chris, 294
Bossidy, Larry, 200
Bostrom, Robert P., 422
Boyatzis, Richard E., 150
Branson, Richard, 106, 364
Braverman, Lois, 102
Brevig, Eric, 71
Briggs, William L., 248
Broderick, Ryan, 216
Brodhead, Richard, 283
Brody, Pauline Ning, 330
Brookhiser, Richard, 30
Brooks, David, 338
Brotman, Jeffrey, 450
Brown, Aaron, 72
Brown, B. R., 342
Brown, Michael, 173
Buckingham, Marcus, 249
Buddha, 265
Buffett, Warren, 42, 45, 103, 106, 169, 374
Burger, J. M., 108
Burns, James McGregor, 4
Burns, Tony, 277
Burns, Ursula, 334
Bush, George W., 206, 366
Bussard, Tony (case), 220, 221

C

Cain, Susan, 106
Callaway, Sue, 374
Calmas, Wil, 272
Cameron, K., 242
Camp, Tom, 430
Capparell, Stephanie, 67
Carmody, Aaron (Case), 162
Carr, Tom (case), 161
Carroll, Cynthia, 339
Carroll, Pete, 273
Carter, Caroline, 491
Carter, Jimmy, 152
Carver, Barry (case), 130, 131
Caserio, Nick, 268
Cashman, Kevin, 15
Cavanaugh, G. F., 383
Chambers, Robert, 6
Chandrasekaran, Natarajan, 433
Chenault, Kenneth, 334
Chislett, David, 212
Chisum, Marcus (case), 129, 130
Christie, R., 370
Clark, Vernon E., 111, 112, 405
Clark, Wesley, 372
Clark, William, 274
Clawson, James, G., 131, 401
Clawson, Victoria K., 422
Clinton, Bill, 275
Coffman, Curt, 249
Cohen, Allen R., 356
Coleman, Frank, 423, 424
Collins, Jim, 13
Collins, Michael (case), 60–61
Conant, Douglas, 50
Conger, Jay, 365
Conlin, Michelle, 338
Conway, James (case), 254, 255
Cook, Tim, 51, 103, 120
Cooperrider, David, 469
Copeland, Kenneth, 4
Corbat, Michael, 381
Costolo, Dick, 395
Covey, Stephen, 156
Coyne, William, 479
Craddock, John (case), 30
Creighton, Harry (case), 129, 130
Crumbaugh, J., 402
Crutchfield, Kevin, 437
Cue, Eddy, 51
Curley, Tim, 172

D

Daft, Richard L., 143, 161, 239, 313
Dalai Lama, 152
Dale, Christine, 328
Dalgaard, Lars, 101
Danereau, Fred, 52
Das, Sanjiv, 451, 452
Deacon, David (case), 423, 424
Deal, Terrence E., 377
de Blasio, Bill, 366
De la Vega, Juan Carlos (case), 220, 221
Den Hartog, Dean N., 444
Denison, Daniel R., 444
Desai, Mira (case), 355
Dhammananda, K. Sri, 265

Diaz, Guillermo, Jr., 350
Dickson, Richard, 293
Dimon, Jamie, 240, 313
Dollar, Creflo, 4
Donald, Jim, 442
Dooley, Ben (case), 319, 320
Dorfman, H. A., 145
Douglass, Frederick, 105
Dowdy, Joe D., 47, 48
Drew, Ina, 313
Drexler, Millard S., 35, 36
Drucker, Peter, 7
Duersten, Althea, 313
Dumaine, Brian, 17
Dunn, Brian, 168
Dunn, Christopher (case), 190, 191
Dunnette, M. D., 314
Dutton, J. E., 436

E

Ebmeyer, Mary Beth, 121
Eckerd, Samantha, 242, 243
Edison, Thomas, 439
Efraty, David, 237
Elder, Morgan (case), 457
Ellingwood, Susan, 409
Ellison, Marvin, 138, 463
Embry, Tim, 451
Eskew, Michael L., 403
Evans, Bill (case), 355
Evans, Suzanne, 371

F

Fairest, Jon, 483, 484
Farley, Frank, 157
Farmer, Bill, 111
Feldhahn, Shaunti, 334
Ferrazi, Keith, 311
Fetter, R., 143, 364
Fiedler, Fred E., 68, 69, 73, 75–77, 80, 91, 92
Filak, Vincent F., 238
Fink, Stephen L., 356
Finkle, Florence, 366, 367
Finley, Bob (case), 94, 95
Fitzgerald, Brad (case), 321
Fleishman, Edwin A., 47
Flexon, Bob, 443
Foley, John, 300
Forbes, Malcolm, 340
Ford, Henry, 173
Forsythe, Charlotte (case), 254, 255
Frank, Jan, 367
Frankel, Roger, 288
Franklin, Benjamin, 41
Franklin, Samuel S., 238
Frazier, Kenneth, 328
Fry, Louis W., 452
Fujisawa, Takeo, 261

G

Gabarino, James, 339
Gadon, Herman, 356
Galanti, Richard, 450
Galvin, Bob, 268
Galvin, Paul, 268
Gandz, Jeffrey, 444
Garcia, J. E., 93, 220
Gardner, Howard, 175
Gates, Bill, 55, 56, 106, 406, 412
Gates, Robert, 372
Gee, Rich, 197, 198
Geis, F. L., 370
Gentry, Ethney (case), 353–355
George, Bill, 169, 282
Gerrit, Adam (case), 221, 222
Gerstner, Lou, 434
Ghosn, Carlos, 12
Gibson, Jane Whitney, 111
Giglio, Gabriella, 471
Gilson, Richard L., 203
Glavin, Bill, 469
Godin, Seth, 182
Goebel, James, 439
Goldberg, Michael, 280
Goldsmith, Marshall, 141
Goldsmith, Russell, 441
Goleman, Daniel, 150
Goltz, Jay, 77
Gordon, Angela, 68, 70
Gordon, Marshall (case), 29, 30
Gough, Harrison G., 477
Graen, George B., 52
Graham, Jill W., 175
Graham, Lawrence Otis, 333
Grant, Adam, 38, 179, 180, 182
Grassley, Chuck, 4
Gray, Nicholas, 131
Green, Kyle, 442
Green, Tyler (case), 321
Greenleaf, Robert, 179
Greenwood, Regina A., 111
Griffin, Jack, 151, 152
Groopman, Jerome, 143
Grove, Andy, 369
Guber, Peter, 274, 275
Gupta, Ankit, 155
Gupta, Vivek, 327
Gustavson, Jim (Gus), 472, 473
Guttman, Howard M., 301

H

Hagans, Phil, 71
Hall, Kevan, 311
Hamel, Gary, 410
Handelsman, Mitchell M., 248
Hannah, Sean T., 452
Hannum, Kelly M., 22
Harris, Sue (case), 219
Hart, Russell (case), 189–191
Harter, Lynn M., 203
Hartman, Amir, 418
Hartman, Laura Pincus, 173
Hartnett, Jack, 45
Harvey, Jerry, 183
Hatala, Lewis J., 51, 157
Heath, Chip, 473
Heath, Dan, 473
Heider, John, 80, 376
Heilbrun, A. B., 329
Henrnandez, Ignacio, 288
Henry, Carter (case), 254
Hermann, Ned, 117, 119
Hersey, Paul, 68–72, 79, 91
Herzberg, Frederick, 234, 237
Heskett, James L., 435, 437
Hesselbein, Frances, 7
Hevesi, Alan, 171
Hewlett, Sylvia Ann, 335, 350
Hewson, Marillyn A., 104, 105
Hilberry, Jane, 280
Hildebrand, Carol, 161
Hitt, William D., 230, 397, 401
Hoenig, Christopher, 173
Hofstede, Geert, 342–344
Holden, Daniel, 156
Hollandsworth, Dax (case), 255, 256
Honda, Soichiro, 261
Hoojberg, Robert, 444
Hsieh, Tony, 282
Hsu, James (case), 388, 389
Hudson, Josh (case), 489–491
Hughes, Chris, 107, 108
Hughes, John, 446
Hughes, Wayne (case), 129
Huntsman, Jon, 38, 169
Hurd, Mark, 168
Hurley, Chad, 275
Hurwitz, Marc, 209
Hurwitz, Samantha, 209

I

Iger, Robert, 37
Immelt, Jeffrey, 282, 372
Ireland, Duane, 329
Ivey, Mitch (case), 129
Ivey, Sandra (case), 161

J

Jackson, Jesse L., Jr., 347
Jacobs, Paul, 405
Jacobson, Karl (case), 129
Jagersma, Pieter Klass, 401
Jago, Arthur G., 81
James, Erika H., 131
James, LeBron, 294
Jefferson, Thomas, 105
Jelinek, Craig, 449, 450
Jensen, M. A., 302
Jobs, Steve, 106, 139, 155, 364, 410
Johnson, Dewey, 70
Johnson, Earvin "Magic," 408
Johnson, Robert Wood, 178
Johnson, Ron, 138, 463, 464
Johnston, Lynne (case), 94, 95
Jones, Milo, 331
Jones, Phil (case), 59
Jones, Sam (case), 355
Jordan, Phillip (case), 221, 222
Jung, Carl, 120, 123, 125

K

Kador, John, 418
Kane, Robert, 47
Kantabutra, Sooksan, 401
Kanungo, Rabindra N., 365
Kassis, Kristin, 362
Kathman, Jerry, 479
Kay, Joe, 389, 424
Kearns Goodwin, Doris, 149
Keiko, Lee (case), 130
Keleman, K. J., 93, 220
Keller, Fred, 178
Kelley, Robert E., 201–203
Kelly, Kevin, 116
Kelly, Terry, 340
Kennedy, Barbara (case), 129
Kennedy, John F., 405
Kent, Deborah, 340
Kerr, Steve, 294, 304
Khemka, Ashok, 184
Kiel, Fred, 172
King, Martin Luther, Jr., 58, 400
King, Wylie (case), 254, 255
Kinicki, Angelo, 13
Kirkpatrick, S. A., 37, 39
Kirton, Michael J., 416
Kluger, Jeffrey, 451
Knauss, Donald, 213
Knudstorp, Jørgen Vig, 437
Koehn, Nancy F., 30
Kohlberg, Lawrence, 175

Kohn, Alfie, 238
Komori, Shigetaka, 417, 418
Koopman, Paul L., 444
Kopp, Wendy, 6
Kothari, Akshay, 155
Kotter, John P., 15, 17, 435, 437, 467, 468
Kouzes, James M., 39, 214
Kraft, Jonathan, 268
Kraft, Robert, 268
Kranz, Eugene, 282
Krzanich, Brian M., 347
Kullman, Ellen, 9
Kupperbausch, C., 342

L

Lane, Harry W., 288
Lanier, Cathy, 328
Lansing, Kurt (case), 320, 321
Lash, Alex, 207
Lashinsky, Adam, 137
Lassiter, Amelia (case), 388, 389
Laurent, André, 346
Lawrence, T. E., 275
Lazear, David, 11
Leahy, Terry, 13
Ledson, Bill (case), 354
Ledson, Margaret (case), 354
Lee, Angela, 243
Lee, David, 305
Lee, Dong-Jin, 237
Legere, John, 417
Lencioni, Patrick, 299
Lengel, R. M., 143
Lennick, Doug, 172
Leno, Jay, 35
Leslie, Jean Brittain, 22
Lesser, Marc, 152
Lewin, Kurt, 43
Lewis, C. S., 479
Lewis, Meriwether, 274
Liden, Robert C., 55
Likona, Thomas, 175
Lincoln, Abraham, 3, 12, 58, 105, 149, 366, 407
Lionel, Jane (case), 456
Lionel, Jim (case), 456, 457
Livingston, Barry (case), 94
Locke, E. A., 37, 39
Loizos, Constance, 207
Löscher, Peter, 467, 468
Lovelace, K. J., 93, 220
Lubetzky, Daniel, 408
Lublin, Joann S., 107
Lublin, Nancy, 401
Luman, Champ (case), 353

M

Ma, Robert (case), 319
MacArthur, Donald (case), 162
Machiavelli, Niccolò, 368–370
MacKenzie, S.B., 143, 242, 364
Macris, Achilles, 313
Maddock, Mike, 15
Madoff, Bernard, 38, 39
Mansell, Zequine (case), 94, 95
Manzoni, Jean François, 53
Marchionne, Sergio, 75–77
Marcic, Dorothy, 125, 343, 416
Marshall, Dawn, 204
Marshall, George, 30
Masarech, Mary Ann, 438
Maslow, Abraham, 233, 234, 237, 251
Maslyn, John M., 55
Mason, Richard O., 445
Matheny, Sam (case), 95
Matsumoto, D., 342
Mattis, James, 47, 48
Mattrick, Don, 438
May, Douglas R., 203
Mayer, Marissa, 4, 40, 41
McCamus, David, 144
McCann, Ted (case), 489
McCanse, Anne Adams, 49
McCarthy, Kevin (case), 93, 94
McChrystal, Stanley A., 186
McClelland, David, 236, 251
McDonald, Paul, 444
McDonald, Pete, 341
McDonnell, Stephen, 46
McGinnis, Ross, 157
McGregor, Douglas, 113
McIntyre, Glenn, 187
McKnight, Melvin R., 28
McKnight, Ronnie, 430
McQueary, Mike, 171, 172, 188
Meloche, Thomas, 439
Michaelson, Adam, 202
Michalcova, Silvia, 471
Milgram, Stanley, 183
Millar, Bart, 473
Miller, William, 319, 416
Milosevic, Slobodan, 372
Minnick, Donald J., 329
Mintzberg, Henry, 15
Mishra, Aneil K., 444
Mitchell, S., 44
Mobert, D. J., 383
Moise, Gabriela, 263
Monroe, Lorraine, 396
Moore, Chuck (case), 287, 288
Moore, Ethel (case), 161
Moorman, R. H., 143, 242, 364
Moreton, Catherine, L., 30
Morrell, Margot, 67
Morris, Hank, 171
Morris, Pete (case), 254
Morrison, Denise, 50
Morrison, E. W., 470
Moskovitz, Dustin, 107
Mother Teresa, 58
Mourkogiannis, Nikos, 411
Mouton, Jane S., 49
Mulcahy, Anne, 104
Murphy, Edward F., Jr., 111
Murray, Sue, 101
Myers, Rochelle, 286

N

Nadella, Satya, 65, 406
Nayar, Vineet, 10
Neill, Terry, 344
Newland, Ian, 157
Newstrom, John W., 47
Newton, Elizabeth, 142
Nixon, Richard, 169
Noel, Michael, 452
Nokelainen, Petri, 11, 451
Nolan, Sam (case), 160, 161
Nooyi, Indra, 239, 334, 374
Northouse, Peter G., 424

O

Obama, Barack, 5, 35, 107, 183, 206, 366
Obama, Michelle, 35
O'Connell, Mark, 51, 53
O'Leary, Richard, 330
Olson, Howard, 135
Opsvik, Peter (case), 30
Oreg, Shaul, 466
Ornish, Dean, 483–485
Ornstein, Jonathan, 148
Osborn, Alex, 478
Oshiotse, Anthony, 330
O'Toole, Larry, 442
Owenby, Charles (case), 255

P

Page, Larry, 103
Parekh, Jateen, 405
Paris, Barry, 201, 202
Parker, Rachael (case), 254
Patel, Hansa (case), 355
Patel, Leela (case), 355
Paterno, Joe, 171
Paulhus, D. L., 108
Payne, Peggy, 187
Peace, William, 185
Peck, Nan, 314
Peres, Shimon, 10
Petraeus, David H., 4, 331
Petrock, Frank, 444
Pfeffer, Jeffrey, 368, 369
Phelps, C. C., 436, 470
Phillips, Sally (case), 94
Piderit, S. K., 436
Pierce, Jon L., 47
Pincus, Mark, 438
Podsakoff, P.M., 143, 242, 364
Poe, Andrea C., 280
Pope Francis, 13, 14
Porter (Superintendant) (case), 286, 287
Posner, Barry Z., 39, 214
Pottruck, David, 169
Powell. Colin, 367
Powell, Ken, 140
Preston, K., 342
Price, Dan, 227, 228
Price, Jim, 236
Price, Walter, 395
Pritchard, Robert S., 238
Pulley, Mary Lynn, 280

Q

Quinn, R. E., 444

R

Rauch, Doug, 101
Rawls, Jim (case), 457, 458
Ray, Michael, 286
Raymond, Lee, 104
Ready, Douglas A., 401
Reagan, Ronald, 112, 265
Reeves, Paul, 91
Reid, Grant, 235
Reid, Paula, 182, 183
Reiter, Mark, 141
Reynolds, Marcia, 199, 200
Rhee, Michelle, 466, 467
Riccitiello, John, 399, 400
Ricks, Thomas F., 163
Riley, Doris Ann (case), 254, 255
Riley, Pat, 275

Rivera, Amy, 485
Rivera, Ron, 138, 139
Robbins, Alan, 78, 79
Robbins, Stephen P., 383
Roberts, Mark (case), 255, 256
Robertson, Diana C., 449
Rock, David, 479
Rockefeller, John D., 407
Roderick, Trish (case), 321
Rogers, Chris, 402
Rogers, William, 447
Rohn, Jim, 101
Rokeach, Milton, 109, 110
Rometty, Ginni, 334
Rosenberg, Jonathan, 431
Rosener, Judy B., 340
Rosenthal, Jeff, 438
Rosin, Hanna, 338
Rost, Joseph C., 17
Rothbard, N. P., 436
Rothkopf, David, 3
Rowe, Alan J., 445
Rowe, John W., 182
Rufer, Chris, 297
Ruiz, Vicente (case), 287, 288

S

Saginaw, Paul, 246, 247
Said, Youssef (case), 190, 191
Saint-Exupery, Antoine, 403
Samuels, Ben (case), 58, 59
Sanchez, Alvero (case), 489–491
Sandberg, Sheryl, 56, 71, 249, 335, 336, 374
Sandusky, Jerry, 171, 172
Santosus, Megan, 161
Sato, Michael (case), 287, 288
Schlain, Kent (case), 387
Schmidt, Eric, 431
Schmidt, Warren, 44, 45, 86
Schneider, John, 273
Schneider, Polly, 389
Schramm, Wilbur, 263
Schultz, Howard, 3
Seabrook, Norman, 366, 367
Selfridge, H. Gordon, 78
Seligman, Martin, 151
Sellers, Patricia (Pattie), 374, 375
Seltzer, Joe, 416
Senge, Peter, 144, 145
Shackleton, Ernest, 67
Shah, Meena (case), 355
Shaich, Ron, 414
Sharer, Kevin, 269, 270
Sheridan, Rich, 232, 439
Shih, Clara, 56
Siegel, Laurie, 212
Siegel, Phillip, 237
Sifonis, Joohn, 418
Silberzahn, Phillipe, 331
Silverstein, Craig, 40
Simms, Robert, 439
Sims, Peter, 169
Sinegal, Jim, 449, 450
Sirgy, M. Joseph, 237
Slocum, Robert S., 267
Smith, Beverly, 151
Smith, Charles M., 185, 186
Smith, Laura, 72
Snyder, Daniel, 89
Sobol, Mark R., 267
Sousa, Rui, 429
Spielberg, Steven, 3
St. Francis of Assisi, 13
Steers, Richard M., 239
Stein, Laura, 212, 213
Stephens, Doug, 450
Stewart, Potter, 4
Stockton, Bryan, 293
Stogdill, R. M., 36, 37, 39
Strauss-Kahn, Dominique, 104
Strickland, Bill, 236
Stringer, Casey (case), 319, 320
Stroup, John, 208–210
Suarez, Carmelita (case), 387, 388
Sullivan, Mark, 183
Sullivan, Nora, 248
Sullivan, Paul (case), 162
Sutton, Robert, 101
Swidarski, Thomas, 281
Szadokierski, Cindy, 340, 341

T

Taber, Thomas, 51, 53, 68, 70
Talley, Pat (case), 387, 388
Tan, Chade-Meng, 152
Tannenbaum, Robert, 44, 45, 86
Taurel, Sidney, 442
Tedlow, Richard, 169
Terrill, John (case), 29
Thiederman, Sondra, 341
Thomas, Earl, 273
Thomas, Kenneth, 314
Thompson, Loren, 105
Thompson, Scott, 168
Tillerson, Rex, 104
Tindell, Kip, 170
Tirri, Kirsi, 11, 451
Tiwari, Kuldip, 184
Toegel, Ginka, 107
Torres, Alfredo, 241
Towler, Annette, 248
Townsend, Robert, 137
Treviño, Linda Klebe, 173
Truelove, Emily, 401
Truman, Harry, 382
Tuchman, Bruce W., 302
Turner, Ted, 413
Twillman, Brian, 121
Tyler, John (case), 457, 458

U

Ubani, Martin, 11, 451
Uhl-Bien, Mary, 52
Ulrich, Dave, 438
Underwood, Paddy, 249
Unger, Frank, 288

V

Valasques, M., 383
Van Dahlen, Barbara, 6
VanMuijen, Jaap J., 444
Van Vranken, Matt, 379, 380
Vines, John, 186
Voyer, Peter, 181
Vroom, Victor H., 81, 82, 85, 86, 240

W

Wade, Dwyane, 294
Wadhwa, Hitendra, 30
Wall, Bob, 267
Wallington, Patricia, 107, 173
Walsh, Adrienne (case), 321
Walters, Caroline, 350
Walton, Sam, 239
Walumbwa, Fred O., 452
Warren, Leslie (case), 30
Watkins, Jamie (case), 355
Weed, William Speed, 207
Weigand (Principal) (case), 286, 287
Weinstein, Art, 87, 88
Weinzweig, Ari, 246, 247
Weisinger, Hendrie, 153
Weiss, Bill, 305
Weissman, M. D., 342
Welch, Jack, 101, 272, 412, 439, 443
Welsh, Mike, 249
Wessel, David, 338
Whetten, D., 242
Whitall, Jan (case), 221, 222
Wiley, Jennifer, 479
Wilkes, Lucian (case), 489
Willett, Curtis (case), 457
Williams, Roy, 377
Williamson, Marianne, 205
Willingham-Hinton, Shelley, 332
Willits, Robin D., 356
Wilson, Brett, 446
Wilson, Ken, 350
Wojohowski, Max (case), 94
Wolfel, Don, 341
Wolfowitz, Paul, 382
Woodford, Michael, 185
Wozniak, Steven, 106
Wright, Will, 217

Y

Yalom, Irvin D., 199
Yates, Chris, 471
Yemen, Gerry, 131
Yost, Dave, 443
Yousafzai, Malala, 167, 168, 182
Yukl, Gary, 51, 53, 68, 70, 389
Yusuf, Zia, 368

Z

Zauderer, Donald, G., 171
Zhang, Yi, 22
Zoroya, Gregg, 157
Zuckerberg, Mark, 107
Zuckerman, Marilyn R., 51, 157
Zugheri, David, 276

INDEX OF ORGANIZATIONS

A

Abercrombie & Fitch, 333
Able2, 350
Access Designs, 187
Ackerman Institute for the Family, 102
ACM Partners, 138
Adobe Systems, 474
A&E Networks, 99
Aetna, 182
Aflac, 244
Agency for Healthcare Research and Quality, 300
AIG, 168
Air Force, U. S., 146, 299, 367
Air Force Academy, U. S., 175
Alcoholics Anonymous, 485
Allianz Global's Technology Fund, 395
AlliedSignal, 200, 411
Alpha Natural Resources, 437
Alvis Corporation (case), 93
Alvon Biometrics (case), 220
AMA Enterprise, 262
Amazon, 405, 420
American Airlines, 413
American College of Physician Executives, 312
American Express, 334, 351, 470, 471
American LubeFast, 451
American Management Association, 473
AmerisourceBergen, 443
Ameritech, 305
Amgen, 269
Amtech Electronics (case), 457, 458
Anglo American mining, 339
Anheuser-Busch InBev, 447
Apple, 51, 103, 106, 119, 120, 138, 139, 278, 364, 401, 406, 410, 411, 430, 463, 479
Applegate Farms, 46
Arizona State University, 13
Army, U. S., 135, 185, 186, 212, 367, 485
Arup Group, 475
Aspen Institute, 440, 449
Atchison, Topeka, and Santa Fe Railway, 415
AT&T, 236, 351
Autodesk, 4
Averitt Express, 442
Avis Rent-a-Car, 137

B

BAE Systems, 376, 401
Bain & Company, 337
Bancsource Inc., 281
Bank of America, 305
Bare the Burden, 6
BBC, 4
Bear Stearns, 168, 170, 171, 430, 435
Becton Dickinson, 334
Belden Inc., 208, 209
Berkeley Haas School of Business, UC, 446
Berkshire Hathaway, 42, 45, 103, 411
Bernini Foods (case), 488
Bertolli (case), 489
Best Buy, 168, 476
Best Foods, 343
Bishop's Engineered Plastics (case), 319
Bi-Tech (case), 220
BlackBerry, 139
BlackRock, 350
Blockbuster, 188
Blue Bell Creameries, 296
BMW, 9, 320–321 (case)
BNSF Railway, 415, 416
Boeing, 474, 477
Booz Allen Hamilton, 440
Boston Children's Hospital, 300
Boston Consulting Group, 337
BP (British Petroleum), 142, 334, 344, 485
Britain's Crown Prosecution Association, 350
British Broadcasting Corporation (BBC), 4
British Petroleum (BP), 142, 334, 344, 485
BT (British Telecom), 350
Burberry, 119, 120
Burlington Northern Railroad, 415

C

Campbell Soup Company, 50, 297
Canon, 400
Carolina Panthers, 138, 139
Carville City School District (case), 286
Cascade Engineering, 178
Catalyst, 336
Caterpillar, 400
Cedars-Sinai Medical Center, 485
Cemex, 474
Center for Creative Leadership, 8, 21
Central Intelligence Agency (CIA), 4, 121, 331
Century Medical (case), 161
Charles Schwab, 158, 169, 296
Chicago Bulls, 294
Chisum Industries (case), 128
Chrysler, 75–77
Cirque du Soleil, 295
Cisco, 350
Citigroup, 280, 351, 381
CitiMortgage, 451, 452
City National Bank, Los Angeles, 441
Clorox Company, 212, 213
Coca-Cola, 333, 400, 401
Coinstar, 414
Colgate-Palmolive, 330
College of Business Administration, Northern Arizona University, 28
Columbia Business School, 448, 449
Conexiòn, 350
Consolidated Products (case), 58
Container Store, 170, 450
Converge, 272
Correction Officer's Benevolent Association, 366
Costco, 449
Council of Cardinal Advisers, 14
Countrywide, 168, 202
Credit Suisse, 351
Creighton Auto Parts (case), 60
Culture Amp, 279

D

D. L. Rogers Corporation, 45
Danaher Corporation, 208
Dannon Milk Products, 411
Danone, 411
Del-Air, 469
Deloitte Touche Tohmatsu Limited, 351, 401
Delta Airlines, 413
Denny's Restaurant, 349

Department of Defense, U. S., 266, 300
Department of Veterans Affairs, 121
Devereaux-Dering Group (case), 320
DGL International (case), 29
Diamond Gift Shop, 241
Diebold, 281
Dollar General, 411
Domino's, 439
Duke University, 283, 473
DuPont, 9, 402, 403
Dynergy, 443, 483

E

Earl's Restaurants Ltd., 278, 279
eBay, 333
Electronic Arts, 399
Eli Lilly and Company, 442
Elixir, 474
Emerald Packaging, 116
Environmental Designs International (case), 130
Environmental Protection Agency (EPA), 121
European Union (EU), 9
Eveready, 140
Exert (case), 94
Extended Stay America, 441
ExxonMobil, 104, 411, 430–431

F

Facebook, 56, 71, 107, 187, 249, 281, 294, 335, 336
Family Dollar, 414
Fannie Mae, 202
Fast Company magazine, 107
FAVI, 200
FBI, 4
Federal Deposit Insurance Corporation, 381
FedEx, 333
FedEx Office, 89
Fiat Chrysler Automobiles, 75
Fierce Inc., 274
First Data Corporation, 451
First Houston Mortgage, 276
5 Star Electronics (case), 457, 458
Ford Motor Company, 340, 403
Fortune, 7, 17, 23, 120, 374
Four Seasons, 401
Fox Sports, 332
Frances Hesselbein Leadership Institute, 7
Franklin Resident Care Centers (case), 487
Frederick Douglass Academy, 396
Freedom Riders, 236
French Grains Bakery (case), 92
Fujifilm, 417, 418

G

Gallup Management Journal, 149
Gallup Organization, 229, 248, 249, 300, 409
Gap, 35
Genentech, 351
General Electric (GE), 101, 117, 272, 282, 372, 401, 412, 439, 440
General Mills, 140
General Motors, 76, 333
Gentle Giant, 442
Geographic Combatant Command (GCC), 266
George Foundation, 101
Gerdau Ameristeel, 275
Girl Scouts of the USA, 7
Give an Hour, 6
Glide, 474
Global Integration, 311
Globoforce MoodTracker Survey, 239
Gogobot, 231
Golden State Warriors, 304, 305
Google, 4, 13, 23, 40, 41, 103, 137, 138, 152, 252, 294, 296, 347, 401, 402, 406, 411, 420, 430, 431, 442
Governance Metrics International, 174
Governor's School of North Carolina, 187
Gravity Payments, 227, 228, 242
Greater Chicago Food Depository, 400, 401
GSD&M, 476

H

Hallmark Cards, 121, 127
Harmon Auto Parts, 91
Harpeth Gardens (case), 487, 488
Harvard Business Review, 53
Harvard Business School, 169, 282, 300, 435, 448, 449
Harvard Medical School, 143
Harvard University, 107, 138, 175
Hasso Plattner Institute of Design, 155
Hay Group, 41–43, 437
HCL Technologies, 10
HealthFitness, 361
Healthy Choice (case), 489
Hearsay Social, 56
Heinz, 297
Hewlett-Packard, 168
Hi-Tech Aerostructures (case), 423, 424
Home Depot, 417
Honda, 261
Honeywell, 200
Hostess Brands, 188
Huffington Post, 50
Hunter-Worth (case), 287–288
Huntsman Chemical, 38
Hyperlink Systems, 219

I

IBM, 72, 219, 275, 296, 310, 334, 343, 434, 441, 477
IBM Institute for Business Value, 282
iCloud Service, 51
ICU Medical Products, 298
IdeaBook, 282
IKEA, 15
Imperial Oil, 212
Industrial Light and Magic, 71
IndyMac Bank, 202
Intel, 347, 369
International Monetary Fund, 104

J

J. C. Penney, 138, 463, 464
J. Crew, 35
Jake's Pet Land (case), 221
JBS Swift & Company, 343
John Lewis stores, 432
Johnson Development Corporation, 408
Johnson & Johnson, 178, 301
Joint Chiefs of Staff, 367
Journal of Empirical Theology, 11
JPMorgan Chase, 240, 313
Julia's House, 178
Jump Associates, 485
Justice Department, U. S., 168

K

Kahn Academy, 40
Kaiser Permanente, 282
KBR, 185, 186
King Conductors (case), 254
Kinko's, 89
Kodak, 430
Komatsu, 400
Kraft Foods, 381
Kresk International (case), 189

L

Leadership Circles, 337
Leader to Leader Institute, 7
Lean Cuisine (case), 489
LEGO Group, 437
Lehman Brothers, 168
Liberty Mutual Company, 408
LivePerson Inc., 310
L.L. Bean, 414
Lloyd's of London, 336, 337
Lockheed Martin, 104, 105
Lockheed Martin Missile and Fire Control Pike County Operations, 298
L'Oreal, 301
Lorraine Monroe Leadership Institute, 396
LPK, 479
Lutheran Church of Hope, 472

M

Macy's, 138
Magic Johnson Enterprises, 408
Manchester Bidwell, 236
Mandalay Entertainment Group, 274
Mansfield, Inc. (case), 387
Marie Callendar (case), 489
Marine Corps, U.S., 47, 48, 367
Marriott, 308, 412, 482
Mars Drinks, 301
Marshall Plan (Marshall Gordon) (case), 29–30
Mars Incorporated, 234–236
Martin Conductor (case), 254
Mary Kay Cosmetics, 410, 441

Massachusetts General Hospital, 298
Massey Energy Company, 437
Mattel, 293
Mayo Clinic, 296
McDonald's, 71
McKinsey & Company, 239, 334, 337, 437
Medtronic, 169, 282, 408
Menlo Innovations, 231, 439, 440
Mercedes, 9
Merck, 89, 328
Merrill International (case), 254
Mesa Airlines, 148
MetLife, 151, 337
Miami Heat, 294
Microsoft, 56, 65, 406, 411, 412
Mississippi Freedom Summer Project, 186
Mitsubishi, 333
Mobil Corporation, 310
Mohawk Industries, 231
Monsanto, 89
More Than Wheels, 7, 173, 174
Morgan Stanley, 351
Morning Star, 297, 441
Morning Star Self-Management Institute, 297
Morrison Management Specialists, 229
Motorola, 14, 268, 409
MyBarackObama.com, 107

N

Nabisco, 50
NASA, 405
NASCAR, 300
National Bureau of Economic Research, 333
National Organization for Diversity in Sales and Marketing, 332
Nationwide Financial, 439
NATO, 372
Naval Education and Training Command, 112
Navy, U. S., 111, 112, 162, 367, 405
NECX, 272
The Nerdery, 245
Nestlé, 477
NeuroLeadership Institute, 479
New England Patriots, 268
New York City Department of Correction, 366, 367
New York City Economic Development Corporation, 117
New York Knicks, 294
New York Times, The, 366
NGM Insurance Company, 276
Nissan, 12
Noblis, 485
Nokia, 219, 477
Nordstrom, 138, 441, 442, 450
Northern Arizona University, 28
Northrup Grumman, 381
Novartis, 301, 388 (case)

O

Ogilvy & Mather Worldwide, 100
Ohio State University, 46, 48, 50, 51
Olympic Games, 315
Olympus, 185
OPEC, 20
OppenheimerFunds, Inc., 469

P

Pacific Edge Software, 447
Panera Bread, 414
Pathmark, 204
Pennsylvania State University, 171–173, 188
PepsiCo, 239, 334
Pfizer, 381, 439, 483
Phillips Academy, 107
Phillips Electronics, 479
Pittsburgh Post Gazette, 201
Plastic Lumber Company, 79
Preventive Medicine Research Institute, 483
PricewaterhouseCoopers, 249
Princeton University, 6
Productos Cementos Mexicanos (Cemex), 474
Prudential UK and Europe, 249–250
Pulse News, 155

Q

Qualcomm, 405
Quality Suites, 187

R

Ralcorp, 246
Ralston Purina, 140
Reckitt Benckiser, 332
Red Team, The, 472
Renaissance Ramada, 187
Rensselaer Polytechnic Institute, 147, 148
Research in Motion, 139, 430
Retail Prophet, 450
RethinkDB, 243
Rich Gee Group, 197
Ride-On, 474
Riker's Island, 366, 367
Rio Tinto Aluminum, 464
Ritz-Carlton Hotel, 243
Riverside Pediatric Associates (case), 489, 490
Rockefeller Foundation, 408
Rolls Royce, 4
Roman Catholic Church, 13
Royal Dutch Shell, 344
Royal Navy, Britain, 37
Ryder Systems, 277

S

Safeco Insurance, 447
Salvation Army, 401
Samsung Electronics, 139, 411
Sanofi Canada, 483, 484
SAP, 368, 369
Sara Lee, 103
SAS Institute, 447
Save the Children, 473
Sbarro, 188
Search Inside Yourself, 152
Seattle Seahawks, 272, 273
Secret Intelligence Service (MI6), 331
Secret Service, U. S., 182, 183
Selfridges, 78
Serena Software, 447
ServiceMaster, 180
Siemens, 467, 468
60 Minutes, 282
Skype, 309, 311
Smart Balance, 309
SonoSite Inc., 418
Sony Pictures Entertainment, 275
Southwest Airlines, 217, 411, 413, 430, 442
Spectrum Health Hospital, 379
Standard Chartered Bank, 400
Standard & Poor's, 168
Standard Systems (case), 389
Stanford Graduate School of Business, 100, 104, 274
Stanford University, 155, 199, 473
Starbucks, 3, 319 (case)
State Compensation Insurance Fund, California, 367
Steelcase, Inc., 485
Streetline Inc., 368
StudentsFirst, 467
Stuyvesant High School, 175
SuccessFactors, 101
SunDax (case), 255
SuperShuttle, 483
Synod of Bishops, 14

T

Target, 138, 371
Tasty Catering, 296
Tata Consultancy Services (TCS), 433
Taunton Press, 273, 274, 448
Teach for America, 6, 466
TeamBank, 403, 412, 441
TechCrunch, 50
Tenmast Software, 243
Tesco, 13
Texaco, 333
Thomson Reuters, 439
3M, 411, 479
Time, 13
Time Inc., 151
Time Warner, 111
T-Mobile, 417
Tokyo Electric Power Company (Tepco), 9
Toyama Chemical Company, 418
Toy Box, 293
Trader Joe's, 101
TubeMogul, 446
Twitter, 187, 277, 281, 282, 395
Tyco International, 212

U

U. S. Air Force, 146, 299, 367
U. S. Air Force Academy, 175
U. S. Army, 135, 185, 186, 212, 367, 485
U. S. Department of Defense, 266, 300
U. S. Justice Department, 168
U. S. Marine Corps, 47, 48, 367
U. S. military, 266, 372, 383

U. S. Navy, 111, 112, 162, 367, 405
U. S. Office of Personnel Management, 437
U. S. Secret Service, 182, 183
UAL Corporation, 341
UKRD, 447
Ukrop's Food Group, 401
Unilever PLC, 344
Union Bank of California, 275
United Airlines, 340, 341
United States Africa Command (USAFRICOM), 266
United Way, 401
United Way of the Bluegrass, 111
University of California at San Francisco, 483
University of California Berkeley Haas School of Business, 446
University of Chicago, 76
University of Illinois at Chicago, 479
University of Iowa, 43, 46
University of Michigan, 48, 50, 51, 439
University of Pennsylvania, 38, 151, 179
University of Texas, 49, 50
UPS, 403, 429, 430, 474
USAFRICOM (United States Africa Command), 266, 267
US & Canada Defined Contribution (USDC) Group (Black Rock), 350
USS *Florida* (case), 162

V

Verizon Communications, 414
Virgin Group, 106, 364
Virginia Department of Transportation, 401
Volksbanken Raiffeisenbanken Group, 403, 412
Volkswagen, 9, 282

W

W. L. Gore & Associates, 340, 474
Waite Pharmaceuticals (case), 388
Walmart, 296, 333, 410, 450
Washington, D. C. Metropolitan Police, 328
Washington, D.C. Public School System, 466, 467
Washington College, 381
Washington Post, 4
Washington Redskins, 89
Weight Watchers, 485
Westinghouse, 185
WestJet Airlines, 440
Wharton School of the University of Pennsylvania, 24, 38, 179, 448, 449
Whirlpool, 476
Whitlock Manufacturing, 87
Whole Foods Market, 450
Women's Wear Daily Apparel and Retail, 463
Work Wise LLC, 362
World Bank, 382
W.P. Carey School of Business at Arizona State University, 13
Wyckoff Heights Medical Center, 168

X

Xerox, 104, 334, 400
Xerox Canada, 144

Y

Yahoo, 4, 40, 41, 168, 414, 474
Yale School of Management, 448, 449
Yola, 72
Young Women for Change, 186
YouTube, 275

Z

Zappos, 282, 431, 442, 448
Zenith, 409
Zensar Technologies, 327
Zingerman's Coffee Company, 247
Zingerman's Community of Businesses, 246, 247
Zingerman's Creamery, 247
Zynga, 438

SUBJECT INDEX

A

Abilene Paradox, 183–184
abuse of power, 382–383
accommodating style (conflict management), 314
achievement culture, 444, 446–447
achievement needs, 236
achievement-oriented leadership, 78
acquired needs theory, 236–237
active vs. passive behavior, 201
adaptability, 151
adaptability culture, 444, 446
adaptation, as entrepreneurial trait, 56
adjourning stage (team development), 303
advisory role, 43
advocates, 367, 376
affiliation needs, 236
affinity groups, 349–350
African-Americans, discrimination and, 334
after-action reviews, 485
agentic qualities, 340
agile leadership, 20–21
agility, culture of, 16
agreeableness, 104
alienated follower, 201
alignment, 399
allies, 381
altruism, 411–412
anger, 146, 147, 187
appreciative inquiry, 464, 469–473
asking for what you want, 381
assumptions, 101, 113, 114, 138
attitudes, 112–113
  diversity, 330–331
  make-it-happen, 200
  social perception and, 114
attributions, 115–116
authoritarianism, 109
authoritarian management, 176–177
authority, 16, 20, 39, 43–45. *See also* power
authority-compliance management, 49
autocratic behavior, 43–46
autonomy, 245
avoidance behavior, 155
avoidance learning, 239
avoiding style (conflict management), 314

B

bare-knuckle strategies, 368, 370
barriers, 334, 336
beginner's mind, 142, 143
behavior
  active vs. passive, 201
  changing, 482–483
  personality traits and, 106–109
behavior approaches, 43–52, 56
  autocratic vs. democratic, 43–46
  in-group vs. out-group members, 53
  Leadership Grid, 49
  Ohio State studies, 46–48
  research themes, 50–52
  University of Michigan studies, 48
behavior modification, 238
behavior theories, 18
beliefs
  fighting for, 184
  in higher purpose, 186
belongingness, need for, 233
biases, 327, 333
  racial, 332
  self-serving, 116
  unconscious, 333, 334
Big Five personality dimensions, 102–105, 126
blind spots, 101
brain dominance, 117–120
brainstorming, 475
brainwriting, 476
bureaucracies, 474, 478, 481

C

calmness, 282
candor, 272–274, 283
carrot-and-stick approach, 237
cases for analysis. *See* leadership development cases
causality, circles of, 144–145
CEOs, foreign-born, 330
ceremonies, 441
Challenger space shuttle disaster, 305
change, 9, 463–464
  appreciative inquiry, 469–473
  creativity for, 473–481
  followership and, 212
  framework for, 467–469
  implementing, 481–491
  leaders and, 464–467
  leadership development cases, 488–491
  leadership essentials, 486
  model for, 468
  resistance to, 464–466
  role play, 487–488
  vision and, 405
change agent, 464, 465–467
change leaders, 464–467, 470. *See also* change
channels (communication), 276–280
charismatic leaders, 363–365, 375
charismatic leadership, 18, 363–365
Chilean miners' survival and rescue, 306
circles of causality, 144–145
clarity of direction, 214
clarity of mind, 145
clarity of objectives, 145
coaching, 214–215, 301
coaching style, 70–72
coalitional leadership, 365–368
coercive power, 374
cognitive differences, 116–122
  Jungian types, 120–122
  patterns of thinking and brain dominance, 117–120
cognitive style, 115–116, 126
collaborating style (conflict management), 314–315
collaboration, 10, 200, 474–475
collaborative role, 43
collectivism, 344
comfort zone, 183
command team, 296
commitment, 376
communal qualities, 340
communication. *See also* feedback; strategic conversation
  candid, 272–274
  change and, 468
  channels, 276–280
  circular model of, 263
  compelling, 276
  crisis readiness, 282–283
  current challenges in, 281–283

definition of, 262
electronic, 277, 279–280, 284
fear and, 155
leaders and, 262–266
leadership development cases, 286–287
management, 263–264
nonroutine, 278
nonverbal, 281
persuasion and influence, 275–276
purpose-directed, 265, 284
social media, 281–282
strategy implementation and, 417
team, 307
communication apprehension, 276
communication champion, 264–266
communication channels, 262
channel richness, 277–279
effective use of, 279–280
competing values approach, 443–448
competition, between teams, 304
compliance, 375
compromising style (conflict management), 314
conflict management, 311–321
balancing conflict and cooperation, 312–313
causes of conflict, 313
conflict handling styles, 313–316
negotiation, 316
types of conflict, 312
conflict resolution, 307
conformist, 202
Connect to Win (Guber), 275
conscientiousness, 104, 151
conscious capitalism, 170
consideration, 46
considering opposites exercise, 478
consistency culture, 444, 447–448
contextual intelligence, 138
contingency, 66
contingency approaches, 65–95
Fiedler's model, 73–77, 91
leadership development cases, 93–95
path-goal theory, 77–81
situational theory (Hersey and Blanchard), 69–73, 91
substitutes, 88–95
task vs. relationship role play, 92–93
vs. universalistic approach, 66–67
Vroom-Jago model, 81–88, 91
contingency theories, 18
continuous reinforcement, 240
conventional level, 175
core competence, 414
core purpose, 409
core values, 409
corporate culture. *See* organizational culture
Corporate Culture and Performance (Kotter and Heskett), 437
corporate entrepreneurship, 474
corporate mission statements, 410, 442
corruption, 171
country club management, 49
courage, 180–192
defined, 181–184
followership, 211–213
harnessing frustration/anger, 187
moral leadership and, 184–185
personal, 185–187
small steps toward, 187
Cowboy Code, 12
creativity
allowing pauses for, 479
brainstorming, 475–476
for change, 473–481
definition of, 474
diversity and, 331
fostering a creative culture, 474
immersion, 478–479
lateral thinking, 477–478
nurturing creative intuition, 479–481
promoting collaboration, 474–475
tools, 476
credibility, 276
crisis readiness, 282–283
critical thinking, 201
cross-departmental teams, 296–297
cross-functional teams, 296
cross-silo cooperation, 367
cultural intelligence, 344–345
cultural intelligence quotient (CQ), 341
cultural leader, 440
cultural leadership, 440–443
culture, definition of, 431. *See also* organizational culture
culture gap, 436, 453
culture preference inventory, 445
culture strength, 435
customer service representatives, 151

D

daily actions, 443
data gathering, 479–480
decision making, 417–418
decoding, 262
deficiency needs, 234
delegating style, 70–72
democratic behavior, 43–46
derailment, 21, 22
design stage, 471
destiny stage, 471
development-based decision model, 84, 86–88
dialogue, 270–272. *See also* communication; strategic conversation
directing style, 70–72
directive leadership, 78
discovery (organizational purpose), 411
Discover Your True North (George and Sims), 169
discovery stage, 470
discrimination, 332
discussion, 271. *See also* dialogue
disgust, 147
distributive negotiation, 316
diversity, 11–12, 327–356
benefits of, 328
changing attitudes toward, 330–331
definition of, 329–330
employee affinity groups, 349–350
glass ceiling, 334–337
global, 341–346
inclusive leadership, 346–349
individual diversity and awareness, 347–349
leadership development cases, 353–356
leadership essentials, 351
minority challenges, 332–337
organizational diversity, value of, 331–332
teams and, 300
of thought, 331
traditional vs. inclusive models of, 329–330
women, 337–341
diversity networks, 349
dominance, 103
dominating style (conflict management), 314
Do the Kind Thing (Lubetzky), 408
dreamers, 398
dream stage, 470–471
drive, 40–41
dyads, 52. *See also* vertical dyad linkage model

E

earning power, and emotional intelligence, 147–148
earnings before interest and taxes (EBIT), 331–332
effective follower, 204, 218
efficiency, culture of, 16
electronic brainstorming, 476
electronic communication, 277, 284
e-mail, 277, 279, 280
embeddedness, 264
emotional contagion, 148
emotional intelligence, 105, 149–153, 159
components of, 149–153
relationship management, 151–153
self-awareness, 150
self-management and, 150–151
social awareness, 151
emotional stability, 104–105
emotions, 146–149, 159
contagious nature of, 148
defined, 146–147
destructive, 452–453
earning power and, 147–148
importance of, 147–149
influence of, on performance, 148–149
negative and positive, 147
empathy, 151

employee affinity groups, 349–350
employee-centered leaders, 48
employee selection and socialization, 442–443
Employees First, Customers Second: Turning Conventional Management Upside Down (Nayar), 10
empowerment, 243–248, 251
  applications of, 246–248
  change and, 468–469
  definition of, 243
  degrees of, 246, 247
  job design for, 244–246
  psychological model of, 244
encoding, 262
The End of Men (Rosin), 338
end values, 109–111
engagement, 248–251
enjoyment, 147
entrepreneurial leadership, 55–57
entrepreneurship, 55, 474
envy, 147
Equality Act (United Kingdom), 331
equity theory, 241–243
esteem, need for, 233, 234
ethics, 39, 188, 453
  abuse of power, 382–383
  business climate and, 168–169
  definition of, 448
  ethical maturity, 172
  ethical values in organizations, 448–449
  leaders and tone of, 169–172
  opposing unethical conduct, 185
ethnic discrimination, 333–334
ethnocentrism, 332
excellence (organizational purpose), 411
excellence standards, 403–404
execution, 56
executive coaching, 23
expectancy theory, 240–241
experience, openness to, 105
expert power, 374
external adaptation, 433–434
external attribution, 115
extinction, 240
extrinsic rewards, 229–230, 238
extroversion, 103–104

F

facilitation, 9–10
False Evidence Appearing Real (F.E.A.R.), 182
fear, 147
  consequences of, 155–156
  motivation and, 158
  in organizations, 155–156
feedback, 56, 218, 245
  in communication cycle, 262–263
  follower need for, 216
  on visions, 407
femininity, 344
Fiedler's contingency model, 73–77, 91
  contingency theory, 75–77
  leadership style, 73–74
  situation, 74–75
The Fifth Discipline (Senge), 144
First, Break All the Rules (Buckingham and Coffman), 249
first behaviors, 305
flexibility, 56
flow of information, 211
follower-centered questions, 268
follower development contingency, 71–73
followers, 6
  alienated, 201
  aligning, 15–16
  effective, 204, 218
  love-based motivation and, 158
  need for feedback, 216
  requirements wanted of leaders, 213–217
followership, 197–222. *See also* managing up
  art of, 198–200
  courage, 211–213
  leadership development cases, 220–222
  management of leaders by, 205–210
  power of, 203, 210–213
  qualities and behaviors needed, 200–201
  resources for the leader, 206–207
  role play, 219–220
  styles of, 201–205
The Foreclosure of America (Michaelson), 202
foreign-born executives and employees, 330. *See also* diversity
Forget a Mentor, Find a Sponsor (Hewlett), 350
forming stage (team development), 302
frame, 377
frames of reference, 377–378, 384–385
France, 346
free rider, 298
frustration, harnessing, 187
functional teams, 296
fundamental attribution error, 115–116

G

gender. *See also* women
  discrimination, 333
  leadership style and, 340–341
Germany, 335
Give and Take: A Revolutionary Approach to Success (Grant), 38
global diversity, 341–346
  cultural intelligence, 344–345
  leadership implications, 345–346
  sociocultural environment, 342–343
global mindset, 140
global team, 308
goals. *See also* path-goal theory
  building on common ground, 276
  diagnostic questions for determining, 83
  making progress principle and, 250, 251
  shared, 304
  teams and, 294, 300–301, 306
Google's Eight Rules for Good Leader Behavior, 23
Great Business Teams (Guttman), 301
Great Man theories, 18, 35–36
Greek recession, 9
groupthink, 305, 312
growth needs, 234
growth opportunities, 201, 214–215
guilt, 147

H

halo effect, 114–115
handshakes, cultural differences, 341
heroism, 412–413
Herrmann Brain Dominance Instrument (HBDI), 117
Hersey and Blanchard's situational theory, 69–73, 91
  follower development contingency, 71–73
  leader style, 70–71
Herzberg's two-factor theory, 234–236
hierarchy of needs theory, 233–234, 251
"high-high" leader theories, 50–52
high-responsive culture, 437–440
honesty, 38–40
hot topics, 270, 272
How Doctors Think (Groopman), 143
How Google Works (Schmidt and Rosenberg), 431
human nature assumptions, 101, 113, 138
human resource frame, 378
humility, 12–14
hygiene factors, 234

I

idea champions, 474
idea incubator, 474
idealistic visions, 405
idealized influence, 339
"I Have a Dream" (King), 400
immersion, 478–479
implementation of strategy, 415–419
impoverished management, 49
inclusive diversity model, 329–330. *See also* diversity
independent thinking, 140–142
India, 335
individual consideration, 339
individualism, 344
individualized leadership, 52–55
  leader-member exchange (LMX), 54, 55
  partnership building, 54–55

vertical dyad linkage (VDL) model, 52, 53–54, 56–57
individual leadership, 99–131
attitudes, 112–113
blind spots in, 101
cognitive differences, 116–122
leadership development cases, 160–163
personality and, 102–109
personality types, working with, 122–127
self-awareness and, 100–101
social perceptions and attributions, 114–116
values, 109–112
influence, 5, 385
communication and, 275–276
definition of, 372
political tactics for asserting, 378–383
influence theories, 18
influential leadership, 362–371
charismatic leadership, 363–365
coalitional leadership, 365–368
transformational leadership, 362–364
information economy, 10
information flow, 211
in-group relationship, 53
initiating structure, 46
innovation, 331
inspirational motivation, 339
instrumental values, 109–111
integrative negotiation, 316
integrity, 16, 38–40, 403–404
intellectual stimulation, 142, 339
intelligence agencies, 331
interactive leadership, 340
interdependence, 41
internal attribution, 115
internal integration, 433
intrinsic rewards, 229–230, 236
introverts, 105–106
involvement culture, 444, 447

J

Japan, 335
Japanese earthquake and tsunami, 9
job-centered leaders, 48
job characteristics model, 244–245
job design, 244
job enrichment, 245–246
job satisfaction, 297
joy, 232
Joy: How We Built a Workplace People Love (Sheridan), 232
Jungian typology, 120–125

L

language, specialized, 442
language diversity, 345
lateral thinking, 477–478
leader-centered questions, 268
leader-member exchange (LMX), 54, 55
leader-member relations, 74
leaders. *See also* moral leadership; servant leadership
charismatic, 363, 375
coalitional, 365–368
comparison of male and female, 339
ethics and, 169–172
fear and, 156
frame of reference, 377–378
Machiavellian-style, 368–371
new reality for, 8–14
understanding of, by followers, 205–206
unrealistic follower expectations of, 210
leadership, 3–30. *See also* behavior approaches; influential leadership; individual leadership
art and science of, 24, 25
change and, 464–467 (*See also* change)
characteristics, 36–41
defining, 5–6
derailment, 21, 22
developing personal qualities of, 16
development cases, 29–30
entrepreneurial, 55–57
everyday leadership, 6–7
evolution of, 19–21
good behaviors, 23
individualized, 52–55
learning new paradigms of, 21–23
vs. management, 14–17
maximizing effectiveness, 107
need for, 4–7
orientation, determining, 379
paradigm shift, 8–14, 26–27
strategic, 398–400
theories of, 17–21
women's leadership styles, 337–341
leadership coaching, 214–215
leadership continuum, 44, 45
leadership development cases
communication, 286–288
contingency approaches, 93–95
diversity, 353–356
followership, 220–222
individual leadership, 128–131
leadership mind and heart, 160–163
moral leadership and courage, 189–192
motivation and empowerment, 254–256
organizational change, 488–491
organizational culture, 456–458
power and influence, 387–389
strategic direction, 422–424
team leadership, 319–321
transition to leadership, 58–61
USS *Florida,* 162–163
leadership diversity. *See* diversity
Leadership Eras 1 through 4, 19–20
leadership essentials
change, 486
communication, 283–284
contingency approaches, 91
diversity, 351
followership, 218
individual leadership, 126–127
leadership, 26–27
leadership mind and emotion, 158–159
moral leadership and courage, 187–188
motivation and empowerment, 251
organizational culture and values, 453–454
power and influence, 384–385
strategic direction, 419
teams, 317
traits, behaviors, and relationships, 56–57
Leadership Grid, 49–50
Leadership is Half the Story (Hurwitz and Hurwitz), 209
leadership mind, 135–146. *See also* emotional intelligence; emotions
independent thinking, 140–152
love vs. fear, 153–159
mental models, 136–140, 159
open-mindedness, 142–144
personal mastery, 145–146
systems thinking, 144–145
"whole leader," 136, 159
leadership skills development, 21, 24
leadership theories, 18
leadership traits, 36–41
development cases, 58–61
drive, 40–41
honesty and integrity, 38–40
optimism and self-confidence, 37–38
leadership vision, 18
Lean In: Women, Work, and the Will to Lead (Sandberg), 336
least preferred coworker (LPC) scale, 74
legitimate power, 373
Level 5 leaders, 13
listening, 268–270, 275–276, 283, 316
locus of control, 107–109
loss aversion, 231
love, 147
motivation and, 158
practical aspects and outcomes of, 156–157

M

Machiavellian-style leadership, 368–371
Mach score, 370
make-it-happen attitude, 200
making progress principle, 250, 251

The Male Factor: The Unwritten Rules, Misperceptions, and Secret Beliefs of Men in the Workplace (Feldhahn), 334
management
  communication, 263–264
  defined, 14
  vs. leadership, 14–17
management by walking around (MBWA), 281
managing up
  definition of, 199
  power and courage for, 210–213
  strategies for, 205–210, 218
margins for earnings before interest and taxes (EBIT), 331–332
Marshall Plan, 29–30
marshmallow experiment, 150
masculinity, 344
Maslow's hierarchy of needs theory, 233–234, 251
McClelland's acquired needs theory, 236–237
mental models, 136–140, 159
  assumptions, 138
  changing or expanding, 138–140
mentors, 336
middle-of-the-road management, 49
mindfulness, 140–143
mindlessness, 141, 142
minorities. *See also* diversity
  encouraging advancement of, 349–356
  glass ceiling, 334–337
  prejudice, stereotypes, and discrimination, 332–334
minority sponsorship, 350–351
mission, 407–413, 419
  definition of, 407
  power of, 409
  values and, 409–410
mission statement, 410, 442
money, motivation and, 227–228, 239
morale, 413
moral leadership, 168–76, 188. *See also* courage
  acting like a moral leader, 173–174
  assessing moral courage, 184
  becoming a moral leader, 174–176
  ethics, 168–169
  leadership development cases, 189–192
motivation
  carrot-and-stick approach, 237
  categories of, 231
  definition of, 228
  empowerment, 243–248
  engagement, 248–251
  equity theory, 241–243
  expectancy theory, 240–241
  inspirational, 339
  intrinsic and extrinsic rewards, 229–230
  leadership and, 228–232
  leadership development cases, 254–256
  love- and fear-based, 158
  model of, 228–229
  money and, 227–228, 239
  needs and, 229, 230
  needs-based theories of, 232–237, 251
  new ideas for, 250–251
  positive and negative, 230–232
  reinforcement perspective on, 238–240
  to stay up-to-date, 200–201
motivators, 234
motives, 231
multiculturalism, 328. *See also* diversity
multiple-intelligence theory, 11
Myers-Briggs Type Indicator (MBTI), 120–121
My Life in Leadership (Hesselbein), 7

N

needs
  acquired needs theory, 236–237
  empowerment and, 243–248
  hierarchy of, 233–234
  motivation and, 232–237
  two-factor theory, 234–236
negative reinforcement, 239–240
negotiation (conflict management), 316
network building, 381
networking, 369
network of relationships, 211
neutralizer, 88, 89
nonconformity, 182–183
nonroutine messages, 278
nonverbal communication, 281
norming stage (team development), 303
norms, 431
Now, Discover Your Strengths (Buckingham), 249

O

objectives
  clarity of, 145
  organizing to achieve, 146
observers, 367
Ohio State studies, 46–48
open communication, 267
open culture, 474
open-mindedness, 142–144
openness to experience, 105
operational role, 42
opportunities for growth, 214–215, 399
optimism, 37
opt-out trend, 335
organizational awareness, 151
organizational culture, 18, 430–434
  combining culture and performance, 437, 438
  competing values approach to shaping, 443–448
  cultural leadership, 440–443
  ethical values in, 448–449
  high-responsive culture, 437–440
  importance of, 432–434
  leadership essentials, 453–454
  levels of, 431–432
  responsive cultures, 435–437
  strength, 435
organizational diversity. *See* diversity
organizational environment
  emotional contagion and, 148–149
  ethical climate, 168–170
organizational values, 443
organizations
  fear in, 154–156
  love in, 156–158
outcomes, creating, 16
out-group relationship, 53

P

paradigm shift, 8–14
partial reinforcement, 240
participative leadership, 78
participative management, 177
partners, 367, 376
partnership building, 54–55
passive follower, 202
passive vs. active behavior, 201
path-goal theory, 77–81
  leader behavior, 77–79, 81
  rewards, 80–81
  situational contingencies, 79–81
people-oriented behaviors, 50–51
perception, 114
  diversity and, 330
perceptual defense, 115
perceptual distortions, 114–115, 126
performing stage (team development), 303
peripheral vision, 144
persistence, 56
personal compact, 482
personality, 102–109
  creative, 477
  model of, 102–106
  traits and leader behavior, 106–109
  working with different types of, 122–127
personality assessment, 120–125
personality types, 121–127
  assessment of, 123–125
  classifications, 121
  working with various, 122, 126–127
personalized leaders, 383
personal mastery, 145–146
personal moral development, 174–176
personal power sources, 210–211
personal values, 449–450
personal vision, 402
persuasion, 275–276
physiological needs, 233, 234
Pike Syndrome, 142
political frame, 378
politics, 376, 384
position power, 74, 211
positive emotional attractor (PEA), 484–485
positive reinforcement, 238, 240

postconventional level, 175, 176
power, 361–362
  coercive power, 374
  definition of, 372
  expert power, 374
  follower responses to use of, 375–376
  hard vs. soft, 371–376, 384
  leadership development cases, 387–389
  leadership essentials, 384–385
  legitimate power, 373
  Machiavellian-style leadership and, 368–371
  need for, 236
  personal sources of, 210–211
  political activity and, 376–378
  position sources of, 211
  preventing abuse of, 382–383
  referent power, 374
  reward power, 373
  sources of, 210–211
  specific types of, 372–375
Power: Why Some People Have It and Others Don't (Pfeffer), 369
power distance, 344
The Power of Introverts in a World That Can't Stop Talking (Cain), 106
pragmatic survivor, 202
preconventional level, 175
prejudice, 332
pride, 147
The Prince (Machiavelli), 368
principled level, 176
print media, 277
problem-solving
  collaborative, in teams, 306
  styles (Jungian typology), 120–125
projection, 115
project team, 297
psychological model of empowerment, 244
punishment, 240
purpose-directed communication, 265

Q

Quadrants A-D (whole brain model), 117–119
questions
  benefits of asking, 268
  diagnostic, 83
  leader- and follower-centered, 268
  in negotiations, 316
  in strategic conversation, 267–268, 270

R

racial biases, 332
rational persuasion, 380
redundant communication, 278, 282
referent power, 374
reinforcement, 238
reinforcement perspective on motivation, 238–240
reinforcement theory, 238
relational theories, 19
relationship behavior, 68, 156
relationship conflict, 312. *See also* conflict management
relationship management, 151–153
relationship-oriented behaviors, 307
relationship-oriented leader, 73, 75–76
relationships
  building, 16, 208, 210
  network of, 211
relief, 146, 147
resistance, to power, 375
resistant vs. responsive cultures, 435
resisters, 367
resources, followers as, 206–207
respect, 154
responsibility, accepting, 182, 212
responsive cultures, 435–437
return on equity (ROE), 331–332
reward power, 373
rewards
  intrinsic and extrinsic, 229–230, 238
  use of, 80–81
risk, 184. *See also* courage
rituals, 442
role play, 219–220, 487–488
roles
  advisory, 43
  collaborative, 43
  matching strengths with, 42–43
  operational, 42–43
rule-breaking, 369
rule of reciprocity, 381

S

sadness, 146, 147
safety, need for, 233, 234
Search Inside Yourself courses, 152
self-actualization, 234
self-awareness, 100–101, 150
self-confidence, 37–38, 336
self-directed teams, 297–298
self-efficacy, 38, 244, 413
self-management, 150–151
self-reference, 405
self-serving bias, 116
sensegiving, 264, 274
servant leadership, 19, 176–180
Servant Leadership (Greenleaf), 179
service orientation, 151
Shackleton's Way: Leadership Lessons from the Great Antarctic Explorer (Morrell and Capparell, 67
situational theories, 18
  follower development contingency, 71–73
  Hersey and Blanchard's, 69–73
  leader style, 70–71
situation analysis, 414
situations, Fiedler's contingency model, 74–75
skill variety, 245
slogans, 442
social awareness, 151
socialization, 442
socialized leaders, 383
social loafing, 298
social media
  as communication venue, 277
  connectivity and, 10
  leadership via, 281–282
social values, 342, 343–344
sociocultural environment, 342–343
socioemotional role, 308
specialized language, 442
special-purpose team, 297
speedstorming, 475
spiritual leadership, 452–453
spiritual values, 450–453
sponsorship, 350–351
stakeholder buy-in, mapping, 367, 368
status quo challenges, 399
stereotyping, 114, 332, 336
stewardship, 177–178
stories, 274–275, 441
storming stage (team development), 302–303
strategic conversation, 265, 266–275, 283
  asking questions, 267–268
  candor and, 272–274
  definition of, 266
  dialogue, 270–272
  listening, 268–270
  open communication climate, 267
  power of stories, 274–275
strategic direction
  decision-making, 417–418
  leadership essentials, 419
  looking forward, 396–400
  mission and, 407–413
  strategic leadership, 398–400, 413–424
  vision and, 400–407
strategic leadership, 398–400
strategy and strategic management, 413–424
  definitions of, 413
  effective, 413–414
  elements of, 414
  execution of strategy, 415–419
  style of, 416
strategy formulation, 414
strengths, 41–43, 407
  drawing strength from others, 186–187
structural frame, 377
subprime mortgages, 202
substitutes, 88–95
supporting style, 70–72
supportive leadership, 77
support systems, 485
Switch: How to Change Things When Change is Hard (Heath and Heath), 473
SWOT, 414
symbolic frame, 378
symbolic language, 265
symbols, 441–442
synergy, 414
systems thinking, 144–145

T

task behavior, 68
task conflict, 312

task identity, 245
task-oriented behaviors, 50–51, 307
task-oriented leader, 74, 75
task significance, 245
task-specialist role, 308
task structure, 74
team cohesiveness, 303–305
team members
- competencies of, 306–307
- contributions of, 306–308
- roles of, 307–308

team norms, 305–306
teams, 49, 293–321
- conflict management, 311–321
- definition of, 294–295
- development stages, 302–303
- dilemma of, 298–300
- dysfunctions of, 299–300
- high performance, 300–301
- leadership development cases, 319–321
- processes, 301–306
- types of, 295–298
- value of, 294–298
- virtual, 308–311
- women and, 331

Tell to Win: Connect, Persuade, and Triumph with the Hidden Power of Story (Guber), 274
terminal values, 109
terrorism, 331
text messages, 277, 279
Theory X, 113, 126, 138
Theory Y, 113, 126, 138
thinking patterns and styles, 117–120
thriving workforce, 250, 251
time-based decision model, 84, 85–88
trait approach, 36–41
traits, 36
trait theories, 18
transactional leadership, 362
transformational leadership, 19, 362–364
trends, 399
trust, 154
trustworthiness, 151
Twitter, 277
two-factor theory, 234–236

U

uncertainty avoidance, 344
unconscious bias theory, 334
uncritical thinking, 201
United Kingdom, 335
United States diversity issues, 335, 342–343, 346. *See also* diversity
University of Michigan studies, 48

V

valence, 241
value, 414
values, 109–112, 126, 329, 453. *See also* social values
- core values, 409
- end values, 109–111
- ethical, 448–449
- influences on, 110–111
- instrumental, 109–111
- mission and, 409–410
- moral leaders and, 173
- organizational, 443–448
- personal, 449–450
- spiritual, 450–453

values-based leadership, 449–458
vertical dyad linkage model, 52, 53–54, 56–57
vertical team, 296
virtual teams, 308–311
- challenges of, 310–311
- uses of, 309–310

vision, 14–15, 400–407
- achieving, 413–414
- change and, 405
- common themes of, 404–406
- defining destination and journey, 405–406
- energizing and focusing, 403
- as entrepreneurial trait, 55
- excellence and integrity standards, 403–404
- idealistic, 405
- leadership vision, 400–407
- linking present to future, 402–403
- nature of, 401–402
- personal, 402
- spiritual leadership and, 452
- steps to creating, 406–407
- stimulating vision and action, 396–398

Vroom-Jago contingency model, 81–88, 91
- decision style selection, 83–88
- diagnostic questions, 83
- leader participation styles, 82–83

W

waigaya, 261
walk the talk, 454–456
What Got You Here Won't Get You There (Goldsmith and Reiter), 141
whistleblowing, 185
whole brain concept, 117–119
"whole leaders," 136, 159
win-win solutions, 316
women
- domestic responsibilities of, 335
- encouraging advancement of, 349–356
- glass ceiling and, 334–337
- internal barriers, 335–336
- leadership approaches, 337–341
- opt-out trend, 335
- on teams, 331

work environment. *See* organizational environment
workforce diversity, 329. *See also* diversity